NAVAL OPERATIONS

FROM FEBRUARY 1797 TO OCTOBER 1798

QUASI-WAR WITH FRANCE

U. S. SHIP OF WAR DELAWARE CAPTURING THE FRENCH PRIVATEER LA CROYABLE OFF EGG HARBOR, NEW JERSEY, 7 JULY 1798.

[MOST SOURCES RATE LA CROYABLE AS A SCHOONER.]

NAVAL DOCUMENTS

RELATED TO THE

QUASI-WAR BETWEEN THE UNITED STATES AND FRANCE

NAVAL OPERATIONS

FROM FEBRUARY 1797 TO OCTOBER 1798

PUBLISHED UNDER DIRECTION OF

The Honorable CLAUDE A. SWANSON
Secretary of the Navy

PREPARED BY THE OFFICE OF NAVAL RECORDS AND LIBRARY
NAVY DEPARTMENT, UNDER THE SUPERVISION OF
CAPTAIN DUDLEY W. KNOX, U. S. NAVY (RET.)

By Authority of an Act of Congress
Approved March 15, 1934

UNITED STATES
GOVERNMENT PRINTING OFFICE
WASHINGTON : 1935

FOREWORD

The many-sided lessons locked up in old naval manuscripts are well worthy of public attention. Our early naval and maritime history is closely associated with the country's pioneer settlement and expansion, with the winning of its independence and with its subsequent security in very precarious times.

From the beginning also the sea was a direct source of sustenance, the greatest means of domestic transportation, and a prime agency of economic welfare through profitable overseas commerce. The integrity of all this throughout our earlier history rested upon naval protection.

In addition the early Navy played a notable part in the development of the national spirit. Nonpartisan and nonsectional in sympathy, it devoted itself exclusively to the promotion and defense of broad national interests. Its faithful and arduous service together with brilliant victories served constantly to stimulate national pride, patriotism and unity.

It may therefore be said that in many senses our naval forces, including both the regular and irregular armed ships, were among the important makers of the Nation.

For these reasons I have been glad to initiate the publication of naval manuscript source material in order that their contents may become generally accessible for research, and also to insure against loss of their substance through possible destruction of the originals.

I have an especial interest in the publication of manuscript records heretofore practically inaccessible to the public because of my own long time research into all forms of American Naval records.

In 1913, soon after I went to the Navy Department, I discovered a large number of old wooden cupboards under the eaves of the State, War and Navy Building—shelves lined with the "Captain's letters" from the Commanding Officers of our earliest ships.

Since those days the Office of Naval Records has been adequately housed and the records themselves have been properly safeguarded and catalogued.

The establishment, at my request, of a special fund by the Seventy-third Congress will, I hope, make possible the printing of the more important manuscript material relating to the Navy, now in the possession of the Government.

Franklin D Roosevelt

THE WHITE HOUSE,
13 June 1934.

PREFACE

The present volume is the first of a projected series of early documentary material on American naval history. Its preparation and publication is in accordance with Congressional authorization, obtained at the instance of President Franklin D. Roosevelt.

It is expected that ultimately the set will comprise a large number of volumes authoritatively recording from colonial times, many aspects of our early naval experiences, which have heretofore been but imperfectly known because of widely scattered and largely inaccessible source material.

The Navy Department's archives, together with other conveniently available naval collections, are at present very incomplete prior to the year 1798, which marks the beginning of the first extensive naval operations after the adoption of the Constitution. It was therefore decided to start the series with that period, in which began the Quasi-War with France, and to work forward chronologically as practicable in subsequent volumes; but also with the intention of proceeding with the collection of material in earlier dates and of publishing the same later on. Single volumes will bear no serial number so that the title, together with the dates of the events covered, will conveniently place any one of them in the series regardless of the time of its publication.

The Quasi-Naval War with France, which extended over a period of nearly three years (1798–1801), had its origins in extensive and long continued depredations upon American shipping. After the sale in 1785 of the Frigate *Alliance,* the last survivor of the Revolutionary Navy, our seaborne commerce had no naval protection whatever and was frequently interfered with by the armed ships of the Barbary Powers, Spain, England and France.

The hostile actions of the former were kept within partial bounds for a number of years through diplomacy and tribute, while reliance upon diplomatic effort alone had to serve with the others. Early in 1794, upon the recommendation of President Washington, Congress passed an act for the construction of six frigates with a view to providing protection for American seaborne commerce, especially in the Mediterranean where at the moment the depredations upon it were most severe.

When a treaty of peace was concluded with Algiers in 1795 the shipbuilding program came to a halt under the terms of the law, but the completion of three of the ships was authorized by Congress in the following year (April 1796). Construction continued at a slow rate and no other naval preparations were made until the Spring of 1798 when growing French spoliations rendered it imperative that some active defensive measures be taken afloat.

Following a report from the Secretary of State summarizing the condition of affairs Congress on 27 March 1798 provided for the early fitting out of the three frigates approaching completion (*United*

States, Constitution, and *Constellation*), and on 27 April the President was empowered to build, purchase or hire twelve additional ships of not more than 22 guns each. On 4 May the acquisition of ten more smaller vessels was authorized.

While hostilities had thus virtually been decided upon no ship could be gotten ready until 24 May when the recently purchased armed merchantman *Ganges* sailed from Philadelphia under Captain Dale. Upon the passage of the Act of 28 May the President directed ships of the Navy to "seize, take and bring into any port of the United States" French armed vessels.

It was not until 24 June that the next ship sailed—the Frigate *Constellation* from Baltimore under Captain Truxtun. She was followed on 6 July by the *Delaware*, another purchased merchantman sailing from Philadelphia under Captain Decatur, and by the Frigate *United States*, Captain Barry, from the same port early in July. Gradually this small force grew to a total of fifty-four government vessels, including eight Revenue Cutters, which operated off our Atlantic coast and in the West Indies, with occasional cruises to Europe.

To supplement these naval efforts on 25 June 1798 Congress authorized armed merchant vessels to repel attack from armed French ships; and by the Act of 9 July authorized the issue of Commissions to our armed merchantmen. These ships were not privateers in the strict sense since they were permitted to attack only armed ships of the French and were forbidden to prey upon enemy commerce in general.

During the first nine months of hostilities such commissions were issued to 365 armed merchant ships while others carried guns for defense without obtaining formal authorization. In the entire three years of war probably upwards of a thousand armed merchantmen supplemented the naval efforts against the very numerous French privateers which continued actively to harass American commerce on the ocean.

Meantime our Navy also sought out ships of the regular French Navy and succeeded on several occasions in bringing them to action, with a view to affording further protection to American shipping. The most notable among the engagements between regular naval ships were two fought by the American Frigate *Constellation*. Her opponent on the first occasion was the Frigate *L'Insurgente* and on the second the Frigate *La Vengeance*. Both actions were fought in the West Indies and will be covered in subsequent volumes.

The creation and mobilization of naval forces for this war was rendered especially difficult because at the start there were neither completed ships, nor any adequate personnel, or machinery of organization and administration. At a later time it is expected to publish volumes dealing with the design and construction of the early frigates, and with matters of naval administration.

This first volume aims to present data related to the operations of ships and other naval units, and to exclude questions of logistics (material, personnel, supply, etc.) except in so far as they may affect the readiness and operations of Naval forces with a reasonable degree of immediacy.

The documents as far as practicable, are arranged chronologically, and the dates of the communications generally determine their chronological arrangement. The exceptions are documents which bear dates later than the dates of the events which they describe. In such cases the dates of the events have been used to determine their chronology. It has been the endeavor to make the text of the printed document identical with that given in the archives; i. e., communications coming into the Navy Department being from the originals and those going out from the Navy Department from copies. Spellings, punctuations, abbreviations, etc., are reproduced as they are found in the originals and copies now in the archives. It may be well to note, however, that the spelling of proper names is in no way consistent, and that the capitalizations and punctuations found in the copies on file are not always identical with those appearing on the originals, the errors having been made at the time they were copied into the records.

Many organizations and individuals have generously cooperated in the preparation of this work. Besides proposing and sponsoring it in the first instance President Roosevelt has contributed his valuable time and advice towards its success, and has made his large personal collection of old naval manuscript available for copying.

Governmental agencies, whose archives have been made freely accessible and to whose heads and subordinate personnel thanks are due for very helpful cooperation, include:—the Library of Congress, and especially its Manuscript Division and Rare Book Room; the State Department, Archives Division; the Treasury Department, with the Coast Guard and the Bureau of Customs; the War Department, Old Records Division; General Accounting Office; Court of Claims; Marine Corps Historical Section; Veterans' Administration; Senate Library; U. S. Naval Academy; U. S. Naval War College; Navy Hydrographic Office; Connecticut State Library; Rhode Island State Library; New York Public Library; Boston Public Library, and Newburyport Public Library.

Among many private organizations where collections have been made available and generous assistance rendered are:—New York Historical Society; Naval History Society; Pennsylvania Historical Society; Massachusetts Historical Society; Essex Institute; Newport Historical Society; Rhode Island Historical Society; Boston Atheneaum; Harvard College Library; Historical Society of Old Newbury; Baker Library, Harvard University; Peabody Museum; Maryland Historical Society; American Philisophical Society, Philadelphia; Haverford College Library; Maine Historical Society; Massachusetts Institute of Technology; Naval Historical Foundation; Connecticut Historical Society; New Haven Colony Historical Society; Bostonian Society; Pierpont Morgan Library, and University of Pennsylvania Library.

Numerous individuals have been most helpful in the work. Mr. Edward C. Dale has kindly permitted extensive copying from the papers of his distinguished ancestor Commodore Dale. Other persons to whom especial thanks are due include Colonel E. N. McClellan, U. S. M. C.; Captain Byron McCandless, U. S. N.; Dr. Gardner W. Allen; Mr. Jonathan Sawyer; Mr. Charles H. Taylor; Mr. Stephen Decatur; Captain Thomas G. Frothingham, O. R. C.; the Hon. Charles Francis Adams; Mr. Henry Adams; Mr. Charles Bittinger; Mr. Gershom Bradford; Professor C. S. Alden, U. S. N.; Mr. G. A. Moriarty; Commander L. S. Stewart, U. S. N.; Rear Admiral W. C.

Watts, U. S. N.; Mrs. D. W. Knox; Mr. Allan Forbes; Mr. A. J. Wessen; Colonel Seth Williams, U. S. M. C., and Mr. Moses Brown.

The printing of these naval records was authorized by an act of Congress approved March 15, 1934, which contained the following provisions:

> "*Provided*, That, in addition to the appropriation herein made for the Office of Naval Records and Library, there is hereby appropriated $10,000 to begin printing historical and naval documents, including composition, clerical copying in the Navy Department, and other preparatory work, except that the 'usual number' for congressional distribution, depository libraries, and international exchanges shall not be printed, and no copies shall be available for free issue: *Provided further*, That the Superintendent of Documents is hereby authorized to sell copies at the prorated cost, including composition, clerical work of copying in the Navy Department and other work preparatory to printing without reference to the provisions of section 307 of the Act approved June 30, 1932 (U. S. C., Supp. VI, title 44, sec. 72a)."

DUDLEY W. KNOX,
Captain, U. S. Navy (Retired),
Officer in Charge of Office of Naval Records and Library,
Navy Department.

ILLUSTRATIONS

Facing page

U. S. Ship of War *Delaware* capturing the French Privateer *La Croyable* off Egg Harbor, New Jersey, 7 July 1798 . Frontispiece

From decoration on a punch bowl made to order for Captain Stephen Decatur (senior). Photographed by courtesy of Mr. Stephen Decatur. The punch bowl also carries an accurate reproduction of the St. Memin miniature of Captain Decatur as well as a handsome monograph of his initials. [Most sources rate the *Croyable* as a schooner.]

Old Map of Western North Atlantic and Caribbean Areas . . 34

From Raynal's Atlas, published about 1783.

Benjamin Stoddert, First Secretary of the Navy 78

From original painting by E. F. Andrews, in Navy Department, Washington.

Captain John Barry, U. S. Navy 114

From an engraving in the Navy Department by Edwin, after the painting by Gilbert Stuart.

U. S. Frigate *United States* 162

Engraving by T. Clarke, Philadelphia. From the American Universal Magazine, 24th July 1797. Reproduced by courtesy of the New York Historical Society.

Order issued by the San Domingo Agents of the French Executive Directory, relative to neutral vessels bound for Santo Domingo, dated 18 July 1798 218

From Massachusetts Historical Society, Pickering Papers.

Captain Samuel Nicholson, U. S. Navy 270

From photograph at the Navy Yard, Boston, believed to have been taken from an old portrait in the former museum at that place.

U. S. Revenue Cutter *Pickering* 328

From original in the collection of Mr. Charles H. Taylor.

Captain Richard Dale, U. S. Navy 368

From engraving by R. W. Dodson, after a drawing by J. B. Longacre, from a portrait by J. Wood, in Peale's Museum, New York, by courtesy of Mr. Edward C. Dale, a descendant of Captain Dale.

Captain Stephen Decatur (Senior) U. S. Navy 458

From the St. Memin miniature as reproduced on the Decatur punch bowl. Photographed by courtesy of Mr. Stephen Decatur.

Map of West Indies Area 546

[illegible]

[illegible]

[illegible] 1776

[illegible]

[illegible]

[illegible]

U. S. Frigate Alliance [illegible]

[illegible]

[illegible]

[illegible]

[illegible]

[illegible]

[illegible]

[illegible]

Map of [illegible]

ABBREVIATIONS INDEX TO SOURCES

Am. State Papers..	American State Papers.
Appts	Appointments.
Bk.	Book.
CL.	Consular Letters, State Department.
Col. or Coll.	Collector of Port of ————; or Collection.
Conn. HS.	Connecticut Historical Society.
Dip. Cor.	Diplomatic Correspondence, State Department.
Disp	Dispatches, State Department.
Dom. L.	Domestic Letters, State Department.
Emmet	Emmet Papers.
GAO	General Accounting Office.
GLB	General Letter Book, Navy Department Archives.
HS of Pa.	Historical Society of Pennsylvania.
Inst. to Min.	Instructions to U. S. Ministers, State Department.
J. McH. P.	James McHenry Papers, Mss, Library of Congress.
J. R. P.	John Rodgers Papers, Mss, Library of Congress.
LB.	Letter Book.
LC.	Library of Congress.
LR	Letters received, U. S. Marine Corps.
LS.	Letters sent, U. S. Marine Corps.
Mass. HS.	Massachusetts Historical Society, Boston, Mass.
MC	Either Major Commandant or Marine Corps.
MCA	United States Marine Corps Archives.
Misc. L.	Miscellaneous Letters, State Department.
NA	United States Naval Academy.
NDA.	Navy Department Archives.
NHSC	Naval Historical Society Collection, New York, N. Y.
Newport HS.	Newport Historical Society.
Nom.	Nominations.
NR&L	Office of Naval Records and Library, Navy Department.
N. War C.	Naval War College, Newport, R. I.
NYHS	The New York Historical Society, New York, N. Y.
NYPL	New York Public Library, New York, N. Y.
OSW.	Letters from Secretary of Navy to Officers of Ships of War.
Req.	Requisitions.
Rhode Island HS...	Rhode Island Historical Society.
SDA	State Department Archives.
Sec Files, TDA.	Secretary's Files, Annex No. 1, Treasury Department. Secretary's Files, Coast Guard, Treasury Department.
Sec War.	Secretary of War.
Statute I, II etc.	United States Statutes at Large, Volumes I, II, etc.
TDA.	Treasury Department Archives.
Tingey LB.	Captain Thomas Tingey's Letter Book.
Truxtun LB.	Captain Thomas Truxtun's Letter Book.
USN	United States Navy.
US T.	United States Treasury.
WO.	United States War Office.

NAVAL OPERATIONS

FROM FEBRUARY 1797 TO OCTOBER 1798

QUASI-WAR WITH FRANCE

NAVAL OPERATIONS

FROM FEBRUARY 1797 TO OCTOBER 1798

QUASI-WAR WITH FRANCE

Extract from Secretary of State Timothy Pickering's report communicated to the Fourth Congress, second session, 28 February 1797

The Secretary of State, in pursuance of an order of the Senate of the eighteenth of May, 1796, on the memorial and petition of sundry citizens of the United States, residing in the city of Philadelphia, relative to the losses they had sustained by the capture of their property by French armed vessels on the high seas, or in consequence of the forced or voluntary sales of their provisions and merchandise, to the officers of the colonial administration of the French republic, having examined the same, together with accounts of similar losses sustained by American citizens from the French, in the European seas, or in the ports of France, which, in the details, were necessarily connected with the former, respectfully reports:

That, since the commencement of the present war, various and continual complaints have been made by citizens of the United States to the Department of State, and to the ministers of the United States in France, of injuries done to their commerce under the authority of the French republic, and by its agents. These injuries were

1st. Spoliations and maltreatment of their vessels at sea by French ships of war and privateers.

2d. A distressing and long continued embargo laid upon their vessels at Bordeaux, in the years 1793 and 1794.

3d. The non-payment of bills, and other evidences of debts due, drawn by the colonial administrations in the West Indies.

4th. The seizure or forced sales of the cargoes of their vessels, and the appropriating of them to public use, without paying for them, or paying inadequately, or delaying payment for a great length of time.

5th. The non-performance of contracts made by the agents of the Government for supplies.

6th. The condemnation of their vessels and cargoes under such of the marine ordinances of France, as are incompatible with the treaties subsisting between the two countries. And

7th. The captures sanctioned by a decree of the National Convention of the 9th of May, 1793, (hereto annexed, and marked A.) which, in violation of the treaty of amity and commerce, declared enemy's goods on board of their vessels lawful prize, and directed the French ships of war and privateers, to bring into port neutral vessels laden with provisions and bound to an enemy's port. It may be proper to remark here, that this decree of the Convention, directing the capture of neutral vessels laden with provisions and destined for enemy ports, preceded, by one month, the order of the British Government for capturing "all vessels loaded with corn, flour, or meal, bound to any port in France, or any port occupied by the armies of France."

Such was the general nature of the claims of the citizens of the United States upon the French republic, previous to the departure of Mr. Monroe, as minister plenipotentiary to France, in the summer of 1794, and since his residence there. To him were intrusted the documents which had been collected to substantiate particular complaints: and he was instructed to press the French Government to ascertain and pay what might be found justly due. From time to time, as additional cases rose, they were transmitted to him, with the like view. In September of that year, he assigned to his secretary, Mr. Skipwith, (with the provisional appointment of consul for Paris) the charge of stating the cases, and placing them in the proper train of settlement, reserving to himself the duty of fixing general principles with the Government, and of patronizing and superintending his proceedings.

In conformity with the direction of the minister, Mr. Skipwith, shortly afterwards, made a general report on the injuries, and difficulties and vexations to which the commerce of the United States was subjected by the regulations and restraints of the French Government, or by the abuses practised by its agents; to which he added a number of particular cases. A copy of the whole, marked B, is hereto annexed. This report was laid before the French Government; and, added to the various representations of Mr. Monroe, and his predecessor, it produced a decree of the joint committees of public safety, finance, commerce, and supplies, dated the 15th November, 1794, a copy of which, marked C, is annexed. This decree, apparently calculated to remedy many of the evils complained of, afforded but a very partial, in respect to compensations a comparatively small, relief, while it continued in force the principle of the decree of the 9th of May, 1793, which rendered liable to seizure and confiscation the goods of enemies found on board neutral vessels. American vessels had been declared exempt from that part of the decree of the 9th of May, which authorised the seizing of vessels going to an enemy's port with provisions, by the decree of the National Convention of the 27th of July, 1793.

On the appearance of the decree of the 9th of May, the American minister at Paris remonstrated against it, as a violation of the treaty of commerce between France and the United States. In consequence hereof, the Convention, by a decree of the 23d of the same month, declare, "That the vessels of the United States are not comprised in the regulations of the decree of the 9th of May." M. le Brun, the minister for foreign affairs, on the 26th of May, communicated this second decree to our minister, accompanying it with these words: "you will there find a new confirmation of the principles *from which the French people will never depart*, with regard to their good friends and allies, the United States of America." Yet, two days only had elapsed before those principles were departed from: on the 28th of May, the Convention repealed their decree of the 23d. The owners of a French privateer that had captured a very rich American ship, (the *Laurens*) found means to effect the repeal, to enable them to keep hold on their prize. They had even the apparent hardiness to say, beforehand, that the decree of the 23d would be repealed.

The American minister again complained. So, on the first of July, the Convention passed a fourth decree, again declaring "That the vessels of the United States are not comprised in the regulations of the decree of the 9th of May, comformably to the sixteenth [it should be the twenty-third] article of the treaty concluded the 6th of February, 1778." The new minister for foreign affairs, M. Desforgues, accompanies this new decree of July 1st, with the following expression: "I am very happy in being able to give you this new proof of the fraternal sentiments of the French people for their allies, and of their determination to maintain to the utmost of their power, the treaties subsisting between the two republics." Yet this decree proved as unstable as the former—on the 27th of July it was repealed.

The next decree on this subject was, that of the joint committees, of the 15th of November, 1794, already mentioned. Then followed the decree of the committee of public safety, of the 4th of January, 1795, (14th Nivose, 3d year) repealing the 5th article in the decree of the 15th of November preceding, and, in effect, the articles in the original decree of the 9th of May, 1793, by which the treaty with the United States had been infringed. It is not necessary for the secretary to add, that the decree of the 4th of January, 1795, has been repealed by the decree of the executive directory of the 2d of July, 1796, under color of which are committed the shocking depredations on the commerce of the United States which are daily exhibited in the newspapers. The agents of the executive directory to the Leeward Islands, (Leblanc, Santhonax, and Raimond) on the 27th of November, 1796, passed a decree (marked C. C.) for capturing all *American* vessels bound to or from British ports. The Secretary presumes this is not an arbitrary, unauthorised act of their own, but that it is conformable to the intentions of the executive directory, the privateers of the French republic in Europe having captured some American vessels on the same pretence, and the consul of the republic, at Cadiz, having explicitly avowed his determination to condemn American vessels on that ground, pleading the decree of the directory for his authority.

The Secretary has already intimated that the decree of the 15th of November, 1794, was not followed by the extensively good effects expected from it. By a communication from Mr. Skipwith, of the 10th of last September, (the latest communication from him in answer to the Secretary's request for information) it appears that the claims for detention of one hundred and three American vessels, by the embargo, at Bordeaux, remained undetermined, no funds having been appropriated by the legislature for payment of them, and that none of the bills drawn by the colonial administrations in the West Indies had been paid to him, the treasury having tendered payment in assignats at their nominal value, and, afterwards, in another species of paper called mandats, which had suffered a great depreciation, even before they were put into circulation; both which modes of payment were refused to be accepted. The progress made by

Mr. Skipwith in the adjustment of other claims, so far as known to the Secretary, will appear in the annexed printed statement, marked D, copies of which were transmitted, ten months ago, to the offices of the principal collectors of the customs, from the Department of State, for the information of our mercantile citizens.

That nothing might be left undone which could be accomplished by the Executive, the attention of General Pinckney, the present minister of the United States to France, was particularly directed to the subject of these claims: but the interval which has elapsed since his departure has not admitted of any interesting communication from him, on this business.

In connexion with other spoliations by French armed vessels, the Secretary intended to mention those committed under a decree dated the 1st of August, 1796, issued by Victor Hugues and Lebas, the special agents of the Executive directory, to the Windward Islands, declaring all vessels loaded with contraband articles of any kind, liable to seizure and confiscation, with their entire cargoes; without making any discrimination in favor of those which might be bound to neutral, or even to French ports. This decree has been enforced against the American trade, without any regard to the established forms of legal proceedings, as will appear from the annexed deposition, marked E, of Josiah Hempstead, master of the brigantine *Patty* of Weathersfield. A copy of the decree, marked F, is also annexed.

The Secretary has received a printed copy of another decree, of the same special agents to the Windward Islands, dated the 13th of Pluviose, fifth year, answering to February 1st, 1797, authorizing the capture of all neutral vessels destined to any of the Windward or Leeward Islands in America, which have been delivered up to the English, and occupied or defended by emigrants, naming Martinique, Saint Lucia, Tobago, Demarara, Berbice, and Essequibo: and to Leeward, Port-au-Prince, Saint Marc, L'Archaye, and Jeremie; declaring such vessels and their cargoes to be good prize; as well as all vessels cleared out *vaguely* for the *West Indies*. A copy of this last decree will be added to this report, as soon as it shall be translated.

All which is respectfully submitted.

TIMOTHY PICKERING.

DEPARTMENT OF STATE, *February 27, 1797*.

[NOTE.—The enclosures, including summaries of more than 200 individual cases of depredations upon American Ships, may be found in "American State Papers, Foreign Relations", volume I, pages 749–759.]

[American State Papers, Foreign Rel., Vol. I, pages 748, 749.]

Circular from Secretary of Treasury to Collectors of the Customs

TREASURY DEPARTMENT,
April 8th 1797

Circular to the Collector of the Customs

SIR The depredations, to which the commerce of the United States is at present exposed, have given rise to a question which being of general concern, is therefore made the subject of a circular communication.

The question is, *whether it be lawful to arm the Merchant Vessels of the United States for their protection and defence, while engaged in regular commerce?*

It is answered—that no doubt is entertained, that defence, by means of Military force, against mere Pirates and Sea Rovers, is lawful;—the arming of Vessels *bona fide* engaged in trade to the East Indies, is therefore on account of the danger from Pirates to be permitted as heretofore; but as the arming of Vessels destined for European or West India commerce raises a presumption, that it is done with hostile intentions against some one of the belligerent Nations, and may cover collusive practices inconsistent with the Act of Congress of June 1794, unless guarded by provisions more effectual than have been hitherto established; it is directed that the sailing of armed Vessels, not *bona fide* destined to the East Indies, be restrained, until otherwise ordained by Congress.

Information has been received that some Vessels are arming by Strangers for the purpose of capturing the Vessels of the United States. The utmost vigilance on the part of the Collectors to prevent the progress of this evil, is enjoined; — Where there is reasonable ground to believe that Vessels are quipped for the purpose of being employed against the commerce of this Country, they are to be arrested, and the circumstances stated to this Department.

I am very respectfully,

&c &c.

Examined.

[NDA, Area 11, April 8, 1797.]

[10 May 1797]

Memorandum of Secretary of War

The Frigate *United States*. of 44 Guns was launched from Mr Joshua Humphreys. Yard (Southwark) Philadelphia Wednesday May 10th 1797 at 15 Minutes past One OClock PM

[NDA, LB. Correspondence when Navy was under War Department, 1790–1798.]

[21 June 1797]

Letter to House of Representatives from President Adams, enclosing report of Secretary Pickering respecting depredations committed on our commerce. Fifth Congress, first session, No. 125

UNITED STATES, *June 22, 1797.*

Gentlemen of the House of Representatives:

Immediately after I had received your resolution of the 10th of June, requesting a report respecting the depredations committed on the commerce of the United States, since the 1st of October, 1796, specifying the name of the vessel taken, where bound to or from, species of lading, the value (when it can be ascertained) of the vessel and cargo taken, and by what Power captured, particularizing those which have been actually condemned, together with the proper documents to ascertain the same, I directed a collection to be made of all such information as should be found in the possession of the Government. In consequence of which, the Secretary of State has made the report and the collection of documents which accompany this message, and are now laid before the House of Representatives, in compliance with their desire.

JOHN ADAMS.

[Enclosure]

DEPARTMENT OF STATE, *June 21, 1797.*

SIR: I have the honor to lay before you a report respecting the depredations committed on the commerce of the United States since the 1st of October, 1796, as far conformable to the resolve of the House of Representatives of the 10th instant as the materials in my possession would admit. The number of captures will give a tolerably correct idea of the extent of our losses, and the documents will show the nature of the depredations, and the causes or pretences for which they have been committed.

I am with the greatest respect, &c.

TIMOTHY PICKERING, *Secretary of State.*

The PRESIDENT OF THE UNITED STATES.

[NOTE.—The report of the Secretary of State, with enclosures summarizing more than 316 individual cases of depredations upon American Ships, may be found in "American States Papers, Foreign Relations", Volume II, pp. 28–63.]

[Am. State Papers, Vol. II.]

To Captain Thomas Truxtun, U. S. Navy, from Secretary of War

[PHILADELPHIA,]
War Office June 29 1797

Captn T. TRUXTUN,
Baltimore,

SIR Congress have just passed the Bill for completing and Manning the Frigates, as therefore the appointment of the Officers will be entered upon early in the ensuing week. I shall be glad if you would as soon as possible come to Philadelphia that I may consult with you on the Merit of some of the Candidates.

[NDA, LB. Correspondence when Navy was under War Department, 1790–1798.]

[29 June 1797]

Launching of the Frigate *Crescent* for Algiers

The Frigate *Crescent* of 36 Guns built by Mr James Hackett at Portsmouth (N H) for the Dey of Algiers, was Launched from the "U. S." Navy Yard the 29th of June 1797, at 4 OClock PM.

	ft.	in.
Draught of Water Forward	9	2
D° ---------- aft	12	–

JOSIAH FOX.

[NDA, LB. Correspondence when Navy was under War Department, 1790–1798.]

[1 July 1797]

Act Providing for Naval Armament

SECTION 1. *Be it enacted by the Senate and House of Representatives of the United States of America in Congress assembled,* That the President of the United States be and he is hereby empowered, should he deem it expedient, to cause the frigates *United States, Constitution,* and *Constellation,* to be manned and employed.

SEC. 2. *And be it further enacted,* That there shall be employed on board each of the ships of forty-four guns, one captain, four lieutenants, two lieutenants of marines, one chaplain, one surgeon, and two surgeon's mates; and in the ship of thirty-six guns, one captain, three lieutenants, one lieutenant of marines, one surgeon, and one surgeon's mate.

SEC. 3. *And be it further enacted,* That there shall be employed in each of the said ships, the following warrant officers, who shall be appointed by the President of the United States, to wit: one sailing master, one purser, one boatswain, one gunner, one sail-maker, one carpenter, and eight midshipmen; and the following petty officers, who shall be appointed by the captains of the ships respectively, in which they are to be employed, viz: two master's mates, one captain's clerk, two boatswain's mates, one cockswain, one sail-maker's mate, two gunner's mates, one yeoman of the gun-room, nine quarter gunners, (and for the two larger ships two additional quarter gunners) two carpenter's mates, one armourer, one steward, one cooper, one master at arms, and one cook.

SEC. 4. *And be it further enacted,* That the crews of each of the ships of forty-four guns, shall consist of one hundred and fifty seamen, one hundred and three midshipmen and ordinary seamen, three sergeants, three corporals, one drum, one fife, and fifty marines: and that the crew of the ship of thirty-six guns shall consist of one hundred and thirty able seamen and midshipmen, ninety ordinary seamen, two sergeants, two corporals, one drum, one fife, and forty marines, over and above the officers herein before mentioned.

SEC. 5. *And be it further enacted,* That the pay and subsistence of the respective commissioned and warrant officers, be as follows: A captain, seventy-five dollars per month, and six rations per day, a lieutenant, forty dollars per month, and three rations per day; a lieutenant of marines, thirty dollars per month, and two rations per day; a chaplain, forty dollars per month, and two rations per day; a sailing master, forty dollars per month, and two rations per day; a surgeon, fifty dollars per month, and two rations per day; a surgeon's mate, thirty dollars per month, and two rations per day; a purser, forty dollars per month, and two rations per day; a boatswain, twenty dollars per month, and two rations per day; a gunner, twenty dollars per month, and two rations per day; a sail-maker, twenty dollars per month, and two rations per day; a carpenter, twenty dollars per month, and two rations per day.

SEC. 6. *And be it further enacted,* That the pay to be allowed to the petty officers, midshipmen, seamen, ordinary seamen and marines, shall be fixed by the President of the United States: *Provided,* that the whole sum to be given for the whole pay aforesaid shall not exceed fifteen thousand dollars per month, and that each of the said persons shall be entitled to one ration per day.

SEC. 7. *And be it further enacted*, That the ration shall consist of as follows: Sunday, one pound of bread, one pound and a half of beef, and half a pint of rice; Monday, one pound of bread, one pound of pork, half a pint of peas or beans, and four ounces of cheese; Tuesday, one pound of bread, one pound and a half of beef, and one pound of potatoes, or turnips and pudding; Wednesday, one pound of bread, two ounces of butter, or in lieu thereof six ounces of molasses, four ounces of cheese, and half a pint of rice; Thursday, one pound of bread, one pound of pork, and half a pint of peas or beans; Friday, one pound of bread, one pound of salt fish, two ounces of butter, or one gill of oil, and one pound of potatoes; Saturday, one pound of bread, one pound of pork, half a pint of peas or beans, and four ounces of cheese; and there shall also be allowed one half pint of distilled spirits per day, or in lieu thereof one quart of beer per day, to each ration.

SEC. 8. *And be it further enacted*, That the officers, non-commissioned officers, seamen, and marines, belonging to the navy of the United States, shall be governed by the rules for the regulations of the navy heretofore established by the resolution of Congress of the twenty-eighth of November, one thousand seven hundred and seventy-five, as far as the same may be applicable to the constitution and laws of the United States, or by such rules and articles as may hereafter be established.

SEC. 9. *And be it further enacted*, That the appointment of the officers to the frigates may be made by the President alone in the recess of the Senate; and their commissions, if so appointed, shall continue in force till the advice and consent of the Senate can be had thereupon at their next meeting which may happen thereafter.

SEC. 10. *And be it further enacted*, That the seamen and marines shall not be engaged to serve on board the frigates, for a period exceeding one year; but the President may discharge the same sooner if in his judgment their services may be dispensed with.

SEC. 11. *And be it further enacted*, That if any officer, non-commissioned officer, marine or seamen belonging to the navy of the United States, shall be wounded or disabled, while in the line of his duty in public service, he shall be placed on the list of the invalids of the United States, at such rate of pay and under such regulations as shall be directed by the President of the United States: *Provided always*, that the rate of compensation to be allowed for such wounds or disabilities to a commissioned or warrant officer shall never exceed for the highest disability half the monthly pay of such officer at the time of his being so disabled or wounded; and that the rate of compensation to non-commissioned officers, marines and seamen, shall never exceed five dollars per month: *And provided also*, that all inferior disabilities shall entitle the person so disabled to receive an allowance proportionate to the highest disability.

SEC. 12. *And be it further enacted*, That the President of the United States be, and he is hereby authorized, if circumstances should hereafter arise, which in his opinion may render it expedient, to increase the strength of the several revenue cutters, so that the number of men employed do not exceed thirty marines and seamen to each cutter; and cause the said revenue cutters to be employed to defend the sea coast, and to repel any hostility to their vessels and commerce, within their jurisdiction, having due regard to the duty of the said cutters, in the protection of the revenue.

SEC. 13. *And be it further enacted,* That the compensations established by the first section of the act passed on the sixth day of May, one thousand seven hundred and ninety-six, entitled "An act making further provision relative to the revenue cutters," be, and the same is hereby continued and confirmed, on the terms and conditions of the said act, to the mariners and marines, who are or may be employed as aforesaid.

SEC. 14. *And be it further enacted,* That this act shall continue in force for the term of one year, and from thence to the end of the then next session of Congress and no longer.

Approved, July 1, 1797.

[Statute I, page 523.]

To Joshua Humphreys, Naval Constructor, from Secretary of War

[PHILADELPHIA,]
W. O. July 25th 1797

JOSHUA HUMPHREYS
Naval Constructor

SIR You will be pleased to proceed forthwith to the Navy Yard at Baltimore in Maryland, and in conjunction with Captn Truxtun, and Mr David Stodder the Constructor, consult on the best Method to be pursued in Launching the Frigate *Constellation* into the Water (so as to float) without Sustaining injury by the Operation. It may be proper for you to survey the State of the Ship as she stands on the Stocks. observe with what descent the Keel is laid, and also sound the water at several distances from the wharf: You will also examine the depth of Mud where she may come in contact with it, and ascertain whether its consistance be such as to endanger, or injure the Ship in her progress thro it.

I have also to request that you will be pleased to State to this Office as soon as possible whether it will be proper to completely copper the Bottom of said Frigate on the stocks, or to heave her] down after she is launched to perform that work.

[NDA, LB. Correspondence when Navy was under War Department, 1790–1798.

To Captain Staats Morris, Baltimore, from Secretary of War

[PHILADELPHIA,]
W. O. July 26th 1797.

Captn STAATS MORRIS
Baltimore

SIR Captn Truxtun reports that there are several Guns, Twelve pounders at Whetstone Point that are suitable and much wanted for the Frigate *Constellation* at Baltimore.

You will therefore be pleased to deliver to Capt. Truxtun or his order, Twelve Guns of that Calibre, and such as he may point out proper for that Ship, for which you will take duplicate receipts, one of which you will be pleased to transmit to this Office —

[NDA, LB. Correspondence when Navy was under War Department, 1790–1798.]

To General Henry Jackson, Navy Agent, Boston, from Secretary of War

[PHILADELPHIA,]
W. O. August 1st 1797.

Genl HENRY JACKSON,
Boston.

SIR Mr Francis having been greatly disappointed in his indeavours to have the two Fire Engines for the Frigate *Constitution*, made in this City: and relying on the report of Captn Nicholson who informs me that a Mr Thayer at Boston makes the best Fire Engines in America, and on the simplest principles.

It is therefore my wish, that the two Fire Engines for that Ship may be made by him under the inspection of Captn Nicholson, who will be pleased to give such necessary directions for their sizes as he may judge proper.

[NDA, LB. Correspondence when Navy was under War Department, 1790–1798.]

To Captain Thomas Truxtun, U. S. Navy, from Josiah Fox

[PHILADELPHIA,]
War Office August 7th 1797

Capt THOMAS TRUXTUN.

SIR I am directed by the Secretary of War to request that you will make enquiry whether it may be possible to procure at Baltimore by purchase 26 nine pounders and 12 six pounders suitable for the Algerine Frigate, if such guns are procureable you will be pleased to State the price demanded for them, and if of one Mould it will be preferable.

Mr Hughes having failed in his Contract with the Secretary of the Treasury for nine and six pounders for that Ship has greatly disapointed the Secretary of War; as that Ship is completly rigged, Ballasted, and in other respects ready for Sea, it is a great pity she should be Detained on that account.

The Secretary of War by last post received a letter from Captain Nicholson in which he requests the Anchor lying at Portsmouth for his Ship, I could have wished it had been ordered for Baltimore as its size is much more suitable for the *Constellation* vizt 44ct 2bt 14lb.

I am &c,

JOSIAH FOX.

[NDA, LB. Correspondence when Navy was under War Department, 1790–1798.

Uniform Regulations, 24 August 1797

UNIFORM FOR THE NAVY OF THE UNITED STATES OF AMERICA

Captains Uniform

Full dress Coat. Blue Cloth, with long buff lappels, and standing collar and lining of buff to be made and trimmed full with a gold Epaulet on each shoulder. the cuffs, Buff, with four Buttons, and four Buttons to the pockets. Lappels to have nine buttons and one to the Standing Collar, Buttons Yellow metal, and to have the foul Anchor and American Eagle on the same.

Vest and Breeches. Buff. with flaps and four Buttons to the pockets of the Vests, so as to correspond and be in uniform with the Coat. Buttons the same kind as the Coat, only proportionably smaller.

Lieutenants

Coat Long; Blue: with half lappels standing collar and lining of buff. the lappels to have six buttons and one to the collar; below the lappel, right side three buttons, left side, three close worked button holes: three buttons to the pocket flaps, and three to a slash sleeve with a buff cuff. one gold Epaulet on the right shoulder Trimmings, plain twist.

Vest and Breeches. Buff — The former to be made with skirts, and pocket flaps but to have no buttons to the pockets. The buttons for the Vest and Breeches, and Coat, the same as for the Captains Uniform.

Lieutenants of Marines

Coat Long: blue; with long lappels of red; standing collar and lining red; The lappels to have nine buttons, and one to the standing collar. Three buttons to the pocket flaps and three to a slash sleve with a red cuff. one gold Epaulet on the right shoulder for the Senior Lieutenant, where there are two Lieutenants for the same ship, and one on the left shoulder for the second officer. Where there is only one Lieutenant he is also to wear the Epaulet on the right shoulder. Trimmings plain.

Vest and Breeches. The former, red with skirts & pocket flaps, but to have no buttons to the pockets — The latter blue — buttons for the suit the same as the Captains and Lieutenants.

Surgeons

Coat — long. Dark Green, with black velvet lappels, and standing collar, Lappels to have nine buttons and one to the standing collar — no lining other than being faced with the same cloth as the coat. Slash Sleeves. the cuff the same as the facings, with three buttons. Pocket flaps, plain.

Vest and Breeches. The former red, double Breasted — the latter, Green, same as the coat. Buttons, the same as the Officers.

Surgeon's Mates

The same as the Surgeons, with only this difference in the Coat, to wit — half Lappels, with six buttons and one to the collar; below the lappel, right side three buttons; left side three close worked button holes.

Sailing Master

Coat. Long. Blue; with facings and standing collar of the same, edged with buff Nine buttons to the lappells, and one to the standing collar. Lining blue or faced with the same as the coat — slash sleeve, with three buttons. pockets plain.

Vest and Breeches. Plain Buff Vest — and blue Breeches. Buttons (for the suit) the same as for the Officers.

Purser

Coat. Plain frock Blue Coat, with the proper naval buttons: No lappels.
Vest and Breeches. Buff and plain.

Midshipmen

Coat. Plain frock coat of blue, lined and edged with buff: without lappels. a standing collar of Buff, and plain buff cuffs, open underneath with three buttons.
Vest and Breeches. Buff — former to be made round and plain, buttons (for the suit) the same as before described.

Marines

Plain Short coats of blue, with red belt, edged with red, and turned up with the same, with common small naval buttons, with blue pantaloons edged with red & red Vests. — Captains, Lieutenants, and Marine Officers to wear when full dressed cocked hats with black cockades, and small swords (Yellow Mounted) — & when undressed such swords as may be hereafter fixed on, or ordered, which said swords are to be worn at all times by the Midshipmen, who are to wear cocked hats, &c when full dressed *only* — Surgeons; Mates; Sailing Masters; & Pursers — cocked hats and black cockades.

N. B.—Summer dress — Vests and breeches (excepting for Marine Soldiers) to be White, or Nankeen, as may correspond with the Uniform &c &c Marines White linen overalls.

(Coppy) signed James McHenry, *Sec^y of War.*

Dated War Office, 24 Augt 1797.

[NDA. Area 11, 24 Aug. 1797.]

To Lieutenant Simon Gross from Captain Thomas Truxtun, U. S. Navy

Baltimore *30th Augt 1797*

Dear Sir As you are the first Lieutenant of the United States Frigate *Constellation*, under my Command, you will be pleased to repair at your post, on the first day of September next, and do your duty as such it being understood, that your pay and rations are to commence from that time, Agreeable to an Act of Congress passed the last Session, Copy of which I delivered you, with your appointment received from the Secretary of War.

Whether I continue any Length of time in the Navy or not, depends on Circumstances, but whether I do or do not, I wish you prosperity and honour, the Source of which is attention to duty, fondness for the Ship and the general and particular Interest of the Service.

Numerous are the Officers in every Country, that from a want of fidelity, sobriety and attention to duty, put it out of the power of their respective Governments, and friends to promote and serve them, and this fact shou'd be known and engraven on the mind of every one who wishes to become an Officer. Permit me then to offer you such advice, as flows from the heart of a man, much disposed at all times to interest himself in your behalf. Naval business in its various branches, I am sorry to say is not as generally understood in the United States as could be wish'd, and it is by time only, that many of the Officers can be thoroughly initiated, so as to comprehend properly what they undertake to perform, this every day experience Convinces me more and more, hence I have found much trouble, in having executed many things, that you now see completely arranged, and which I trust will not only serve as example and benefit the service, but at the same time when our Frigate is Completed, will be gratifying to every seamans eye: but of what avail are the best arrangements, if unattended to by Officers, who individually & collectively ought to consider themselves as a part of the sinues and vital parts of the Ship.

The new order of things have led me Sir, to observations in this letter (which I present to you before you enter on the duties of your Office) that cannot well be introduced in the rules and regulations that I shall form and establish for the ship, all of which must be minutely attended to, and while I mention to you the necessity of a discreet manlike Conduct and proper subordination to be observed, by every Officer belonging to the Ship it must not be understood, that I shall ever countenance tyranny, any more than I shall pass over impotency and a Sluggardly demeanour in any person.

You will therefore be pleased to receive the following; as the Out lines and Basis of that Conduct, which I expect will be observed by all who wish to merit my esteem while I have any thing to do with their Service and I am the more particular on this Subject, as I ardently desire to see that harmony prevail on board the Frigate, which with good Subordination must insure a happy result, Should it be necessary to bring forward our United efforts against an enemy.

In the first place, it is the duty of every one and more particularly Officers, to Support Studily the Constitution and Government under which we derive our Commissions, and in a regular Service Such as we are engaged in, no Officer must attempt to offer an opinion to me on the duty to be performed, without its being previously asked, but on the Contrary, Carry all orders into execution without hesitation or demur. Such example will act as a Stimulus to Officers of an inferior grade, as well as others, and introduce that sort of Subordination, which can only insure a happy and well govern'd Ship. Secondly an Officer in Carrying on duty agreeable to his Station or otherwise, Shou'd be Civil and polite to every one, and particularly so to Strangers for Civility does not interfer with discipline; So that the detestable and ruinous practice to Subordination in being too familiar with Petty Officers &c is not practised. — Thirdly — While an Officer is diligent in doing his duty and Causing Others to do theirs, and in preventing Sculking and Loitering about, he is at the same time never to lose sight of that humanity and Care that is due to those who may be really Sick, or otherwise Stand in need of his assistance and attention.

Fourthly, No Officer must ever Sleep out of the Ship or absent himself, or grant that permission to others without leave from me or my representative for the time being — Fifthly I must always be informd by the Officer on duty of any impropriety Committed or

Attempted to be Committed particularly where it has a Mutinous tendency — Sixthly every Officer is to be particularly attentive to the rules and regulations of the Ship; the Quarter Bill and the Articles of war; for to obey without Hesitation, is a maxim always practised by me to my Superiors, in every point of duty, and the same sort of Conduct I expect in return by all Officers under my orders. — Seventhly, the Ettequete to be observ'd by Officers on duty, going out or Coming on board the Ship, Stepping on the Quarter Deck, addressing each other on duty, and of every inferior discription of persons in Service, to Officers passing each other on or off duty, is to simply lift their hat, and on delivering a Message or bringing an answer &c Petty Officers, Seamen, Ordinary Seamen or Marines Speak holding their hats in hand.

The State rooms & Cabbins of all the Various officers, will be lettered So, as each on going on board can emediatily repair to his birth, without disputes or altercations respecting a Choice. the Order of hanging the Hammocks and Marking them will be such as to prevent any difficulty or Confusion among the different grades of people, or from their being improperly intermixed, and no Officer or man whatever is to Change the place allotted for him, but by a Special order from me — As the regulations of the Ship, which I shall frame in due time, will explain all the Minute points of duty necessary to be observed by the whole Crew; you must consider the present as a Communication merely for your own Government in the mean time, and that of the Gentlemen of the Gun room, and but little more than preparatory to such regulations; tho always to be attended to notwithstanding. — Before I conclude this epistle I must once more remind you; that from thirty two Long Years experience and Constant Practice at Sea, on board Various Ships from a 64 down, that I have remark'd that no sort of Conduct in any officer on board, have a tendency to lessen his Authority and the respect due to himself So much as an improper familiarity with the petty Officers &c and on the Contrary, the effect a free open polite Conduct among those, who are of his Mess is always the reverse. — When I invite any of the Gentlemen of the Quarter deck to my Table, I shall expect all that reserve when on duty Set aside, except what a just decorum and becomeing deference may warrant among Gentlemen, for by throwing off restraint on Such Occasions all will be at their ease, and I Shall be better able to judge of the Capacities of each, as to men and things and employ them on Certain Occasions accordingly; for in Naval Service different abilities are often Necessary, and altho' each may be Equally a good Seamen and brave Officer Yet each may not have talents alike in other respects. — too great a disposition to punish where we have power is not necessary either to facilitate business, or to keep alive good Subordination (Tho punishment among refractory Men Cannot be dispenced with) provided the deportment of an Officer is Correct, and where his temper is unhappily inclined, he Should Strive to Check it, as much as is Consistent with the Character of a Gentleman, for that Character Shoud never be Separated from the Officer. Altho' it is expected that every dangerous procedure will be communicated to me from time to time, as soon as it is Known or discovered; it is not expected or required that I Should be troubled with such trifling circumstances as are of no Consequence, and may be adjusted without any interference on my part, particularly when they are of a private Nature —The United States of America must have a Navy or Cease to be a Commercial Nation, it is therefore highly necessary that a proper System of Subordination attention to duty and respect be introduced in its first out set, otherwise the Consequences are easy to be foreseen (by Men of discernment) especially when at this day, there is Scarcely Officers of tollerable abilities to be found (who have had any experience) for the few heavy Ships we have built, and among these few Scattered from one end of the United States to the other, we find them frequently given up to that detestable vice drunkeness, which must always render every officer unworthy and unfit for Service particularly for any important Service; in fact every drunkard is a Nuisance and no drunkard ought to be employ'd and if employ'd Shall ever remain an Officer with me; I do not mean to insinuate that a Convivial fellow is a drunkard, who may become Chearful in Company, the distinction is too great to make it necessary for me to draw any line on that Subject. — The sentiments Contain'd in this letter, you will be pleased to make Known, to every one who may be appointed to the Ship, in order that we set out fair, and a Steady adherence to the same will be expected by me.

I shall open a book the day you enter on duty in which I shall place from time to time, all essential Orders.

I am Sir with great respect Your

Very Ob[t],

THOMAS TRUXTUN.

Lieutenant SIMON GROSS.

STOWAGE OF THE *Constellation's* HOLD

Every Sea Officer ought to know, that a Ships tendency to pitch and Roll, may be diminished in a great measure, by a Judicious distribution of her Stowage, the heaviest parts therefore, should be placed as near the Center of Gravity as possible; this all experienc'd men who have talked and wrote on the Subject are agreed in—The Center of Gravity is that point by which a body may be suspended, and the parts remain in perfect equilibrum, but to come at the Center of Gravity Minutely, requires judgment as well as to ascertain exactly the Center of Cavity[Gravity], Center of Motions and Metacentre, all of which must be determined, otherwise a Ship Cannot be loaded, so as to be easy on riging and Spars or to Sail fast.

Altho' our Frigates are the best built Ships, that was ever known to be Composed of wood and Metal, they are not without their faults; the principle one is the extreme breadth, being placed so Very far for head that it causes both an uncommon great draught of water & great difference of draught; hence their ballast must be placed and hold stowed, different to almost any other sort of Ships; the Center of Gravity being so very different; this being the Case I have Considered, Calculated and determind as follows to Wit,

The Iron Kentledge to be Stowed from the fore part of the Step of the Main mast in two tier to the Cole room Bulk head, which is [space] feet abaft the Step of the fore mast, placing the greatest part of it in the Center of this space and as high as the floor heads on each side agreeable to the annex'd plan. The Iron Kentledge which I calculated for this Frigate and made requisitions for before She was half built is 75 Tons which I find will be fully Sufficient, after receiving 100 pieces of it to be kept at hand to trim the Ship Occasionally, and to ballast boats — over the Iron ballast is to be levelled a Quantity of Shingle ballast, So as the ground tier of water may be Stowed on an even Surface, and the diameter of the Casks Sunk down about ¼ in it, In Stowing the Water Casks, they are placed Chine and Chine and bouze[?] & Chine according to the different Size Casks, beginning at the Coal room bulk head and leaveing any breakage that there may be in the after hold — the different Teirs are Carried up to the beams, and Clean Shingle ballast is to be laid between every rise, so that the whole quantity of Shingle ballast does not exceed for this ship 150 Tons. — Over the ground rise of Water under the fore Orlope Wet provitions wood and other unperishable Stores are to be Stowed as also abrest and under the fore hatchway, and abrest the Main Mast and after pump Wells but abaft the after pump wells, dry provisions are to be Stowed.

All Ships after being properly ballasted: Shou'd have their Stowage Arranged, as to enable the trim to be preserved Notwithstanding the daily Consumption of provisions and Water and if this precaution is not taken, no Ship Can be kept in trim any length of time at Sea.

The Stores of the different Officers, will be placed in the Store rooms, prepared for that purpose, and the Spirits in the room of that name the Powder in the Magazine, the key of which ought always to be kept by the Commander of every Ship of War.

BALTIMORE, *18th September 1797.*

To Mr SIMON GROSS,
1st Lieutenant of Frigate Constellation.

[LC. J. R. P., Vol. 1, Second Series, 1775–1805.]

To Captain John Barry, U. S. Navy, from Secretary of War

Near DOWNINGSTOWN, *30th August. 1797*

Captn JOHN BARRY.

SIR: I have your letter of the 28th instant. and am very happy to learn that the Careening business is finished and the damage which the Frigate had received in launching completely repaired. As soon as you get your ballast &c replaced, I think it will be proper to Moor the Ship in the Stream, at a safe distance from the wharves. You will then take on board your Guns and such Articles to fit her for sea as the Purveyor has had orders to provide: and should there be any yet to be procured you will address Mr Francis on the subject.

Lieut McRea with the Men he has enlisted ought to go on board as soon as possible, and the present guard sent to their company at Fort Mifflin. With respect to Seamen to assist in fitting the Ship for Sea, I have no Objection to your engaging for a Month at such wages as will Obtain good seamen, as many as may be wanted. If possible you will not give more than 14 dollars, but I leave the Wages to be determined by circumstances and your own judgment.

You may order Dr Gillaspy on board whenever you may think proper.

[NDA, LB. Correspondence when Navy was under War Department, 1790–1798.]

To Joshua Humphreys from Captain Thomas Truxtun, U. S. Navy

BALTIMORE 7th *September 1797*

DEAR SIR — At 9 A M, the Frigate *Constellation* was Safely launched — A Better Launch I never Saw; the Ship Cleared the ways, without touching or Meeting with the Smallest Accident — in fact every precaution to Guard Against Accident, Stodder tooke, and for the Manner he Secured, and laid the Ways, I cannot but give him, the highest Credit as a Master Builder &c. — Tomorrow I shall erect the Sheers, and on Saturday take in the Mizzen Mast.

I hope Soon to hear more favorable Accounts from Philadelphia, with Respect to the fever. —

Health and Happiness
in great haste

THOMAS TRUXTUN

N. B. The Ship did not Strain in the least, or Straiten her Sheer —

Mr JOSHUA HUMPHREYS.

[HS of Pa. NDA photostat.]

To George Claghorne from Secretary of War

[PHILADELPHIA,]
W O. *Septr 10th 1797 —*

GEO. CLAGHORNE

SIR I received your letter of the 4th instant — yesterday, informing me of the present State of the Frigate *Constitution*, and submitting the propriety of Launching her during the high tides of the present month, noticing at the same time that the work which must be done after getting her into the Water could be cheapest performed while on the Stocks —

If in your opinion it would be unsafe to trust to tihe tdes in October — I very readily agree to her being launched in this Month; but if we may venture the delay till October and it would be a saving in point of expence I should prefer it, especially as it does not appear to me that any thing could be gained by a premature launch to counterballance the expence —

[NDA, LB. Correspondence when Navy was under War Department, 1790–1798.]

To Tench Francis, Purveyor, from Secretary of War

Near DOWNINGSTOWN *18th Septr 1797*

TENCH FRANCIS

SIR The Frigate *Constellation* requiring a heavy Anchor to keep her from accidents during heavy Squalls or Spurts of wind, I beg you will be pleased to inform me whether the one of this description that I requested you to have brought round from Portsmouth or the eastward has yet arrived or if not what measures have been taken for its transfer to Baltimore. I am getting better.

[NDA, LB. Correspondence when Navy was under War Department, 1790–1798.]

To David Stodder, a naval constructor, from Secretary of War

Near Downings Town *6th Octr 1797*

Mr David Stodder —

Sir The necessity there is for completing the Ship *Constellation* in the shortest possible time, makes it proper that I should request that you will use your utmost diligence to put her in a situation to leave Baltimore by the most prompt, full and undivided exertion of your whole time, talents and force —

Should she suffer by any want of Industry or exertion upon your part, it will necessarily and justly be ascribed to you. I wish this to be avoided, and am with great regard &c —

[NDA, LB. Correspondence when Navy was under War Department, 1790–1798.]

To Jacob Sheafe, Navy Agent, Portsmouth, N. H., from Secretary of War

[Philadelphia]
War Office November 10th 1797 —

Jacob Sheafe Esqre

Sir The Anchor which is in the Navy Yard at Portsmouth of 44ct 2bt 14lb being suitable and much wanted for the Frigate *Constellation* lying in the Chesapeak below Baltimore I have to request that you will be pleased to get it conveyed to the Said Ship in the cheapest and most expeditious manner possible

If no opportunity should offer at Portsmouth for any port in the Chesapeak, you are in that case to send it thro' the medium of Boston or New York and by no means to be landed at either of those places, but to be taken along side of the Frigate which will be by that time at Anchor in some part of the Chesapeak Bay or Potapsco

I am &c

J. McH[enry]

[NDA, LB. Correspondence when Navy was under War Department, 1790–1798.]

To J. Wilkens from Secretary of War

[PHILADELPHIA,]
War Office 1st December 1797 —

J. WILKENS Esquire

SIR I inclose you a Draught of a Gally & an Estimate of the probable cost (if built here) and particular definition of the prices of Timber &c to be employed in its construction.

Two of these will be wanted for the better protection of our Ports, on the Ohio and Missisipi; and it is expected can be built at or near Pittsburgh and completed in time to fall down to Massac with the first rise of the waters in the Spring.

You will be pleased to inform me as soon as possible whether you can procure qualified Workmen who will undertake to build them, the terms on which they can be procured, the price of the Timber and Materials within your reach, and what Articles it will be Necessary should be sent from this quarter.

I can send a Superintendant to direct the Constructn and forward the Work by his Knowledge and exertion —

In the mean while you will commence to engage the timber and have it brought to the place where it will be proper to build the Galleys.

I am &c

It is probable that a departure from the plan may be ordered vizt the upper part of the side to flaire off about one foot — particulars will be sent you in time for the Construction. This alteration however need not prevent the procuring the timber &c

[NDA, LB. Correspondence when Navy was under War Department, 1790–1798.]

To S. & J. Sterretts from Secretary of War

[PHILADELPHIA,]
War Office 4th December 1797

Messrs S & J. STERRETTS

GENTLEMEN The Chairman of the Committee of the House of Representatives on the Subject of the protection of Commerce have requested the Secretary of War to inform the Committee what further provissions appear to be necessary to complete and Man the Three Frigates for Sea —

It may therefore be proper to request that you will be pleased to furnish the Estimate and necessary information called for in my letter of the 6 ultimo as early as convenient —

I am &c

[NDA, LB. Correspondence when Navy was under War Department, 1790–1798.]

[27 Dec. 1797]

To Samuel Sewall from Secretary Timothy Pickering

Department of State, *Decr 27th 1797.*

Honble. Samuel Sewall, Esqr

One of the Committee of Commerce & Manufactures.

Sir In consequence of your request to be furnished with the information received by this department of Captures by the Belligerent powers, not noticed in former reports, I have received the communications which have been made to me, I have distributed the information they contain under three heads, 1st as it respects the Spaniards: 2^{ndly} as it respects the British: & 3^{rdly} as it respects the French.

The present present in connection with former communications suggest the following Observations.

Besides the capturing, detaining & plundering of American vessels, of which the Spanish privateers are guilty, the Government of Spain has not afforded to our citizens the protection to which they are entitled by treaty & the law of Nations.

American vessels trading to Spain have been captured within its territorial limits. Others have been brought into the ports of Spain & condemned upon unjustifiable pretences in the Chanceries of the French Consuls, which hitherto have assumed & exercised the powers of Courts of Admiralty within the Spanish Territory, examining witnesses, hearing causes & pronouncing formal Sentences of confiscation & sale of American property. With a view probably of restraining some irregularities, his Catholic Majesty issued a Royal Cedula or declaration, dated at Aranjuez on the 14th of last June, of which a translation is enclosed. But this declaration, by limiting the immunity of the coasts to about half the distance, to which the usual jurisdiction of country has been deemed to extend, cannot fail to increase the depredations of armed vessels upon the commerce of Neutrals, more especially as they are permitted to lie in wait in the ports of Spain for the Sailing of American vessels, & immediately on their departure to Sally forth, capture & bring them back as prize. To so great an excess has this violation of our rights as neutrals been extended in Spain, that in March last there were lying in the port of Malaga, at one time, 14 American vessels, which were prevented from sailing, by the open & public threats of the crews of two French, privateers, then at Malaga, that it was their intention to capture them, as they departed. They were relieved from this embarrasment only by applying to Admiral Nelson at Gibralter, who sent a frigate up the Bay to protect them. The *Polacre* independent (Mentioned in the last report) laden with Stores for Algiers, in pursuance of the treaty, having been Captured by a Spanish cruiser, on the 16th February last, & carried into Cadiz, was detained there until the 13th Augt nor could She be permitted to depart for some time after her acquittal, as the French consul openly declared, She was liable to capture & *would be captured*, on account of her not having a rôle d'équipage & other documents, which he pretended were necessary: it was therefore feared, that he would send out a privateer to capture her: finally, however he gave her a passport.

Few complaints have been made of American vessels being captured by the British; except such as have been conducted within the jurisdiction of a Court of Vice Admiralty lately organized at the Mole of St. Nickolas. It having been alledged upon oath, that the Judge of that Court has in two instances refused (in one of them with circumstances of indency) to furnish American Claimants with copies of his proceedings & sentences in their cases, & there being some reason to suppose, that in other respects his official conduct was not unexceptionable, the minister of the United States at London has been instructed to make a representation of his conduct to the British Government, in order to obtain an investigation of the improprieties imputed to him.

Little remains to be added to the former report concerning French depredations, beside a reference to the details contained in the extracts from the consular & other letters & the cases abstracted from the documents furnished by individuals; whence it may be concluded, that those depredations have at least suffered no dimunition either in extent or atrocity. With the aid of the old Marine Ordinances of France, the various decrees of it legislative bodies before & of the Executive Directory & their Agents since the formation of their new Government, at once in operation, & with the arbitrary constructions, which have been placed upon their treaty with us, few of our vessels are so fortunate as to escape condemnation, when they fall within the power of a French tribunal. We have heard of two of those tribunals, influenced by more liberal views, who have acquitted two American vessels, not provided with the rôle d'équipage in the form usually demanded; but the judgement of one, founded on those principles of justice & good faith for which we contend, has been reversed by the superior tribunal; & the same fate no doubt awaits the other.

The numerous captures of our Vessels in the West Indies by the French, & the forlorn & miserable situation in which their crews are turned on Shore, without subsistence or Cloathing, claimed at once the commiseration & aid of the Government. Their sufferings are fully detailed in the extracts from Mr Mayer's letters, & in the letter from the Master of American vessels at St Jago in Cuba. The United States Brigantine *Sophia* was therefore dispatched in August last to the various French & Spanish ports in the West Indies, where it was probable they might be found, to collect & bring home the Sufferers: — She has not yet returned.

On the 25th instant I received from our Consul, Mr Mayer, at Cape Francois, an extract from the Register of the deliberations of the Commission delegated by the French Government to the Leeward Islands of which I have caused a translation to be sent to the Printer of the Gazette of the United States for Publication this day, & to which I beg leave to refer you for information of the alteration of their rules, relative to the capture of Neutral Vessels, going to or coming from *Old British Ports*.

I have the Honour &cc..

TIMOTHY PICKERING.

[SDA. Dom. L, Vol. 10.]

[NOTE.—Enclosures 1, 2, 3 & 4, not included herewith, are as follows:—
1. Extracts from the consular letters respecting Captures by the Spanish, etc.
2. Royal Cedula of 14 June, 1797.
3. Extracts from the Consular letters, respecting Captures by the British.
4. Abstract of cases of capture of American Vessels by British cruizers, wherein documents have been received at the Department of State from the individuals aggrieved.
These documents are in the Archives of the State Department, Washington, D. C., in volume 10, of Domestic Letters.]

[Enclosure No. 5]

EXTRACTS FROM THE CONSULAR LETTERS RESPECTING CAPTURES BY THE FRENCH

The ship *Providence*, Wm Furnace, Master, belonging to Colo. Hamilton & others, of Portsmouth, was carried into Curracoa, on the 18th July 1797 by the French Privateer *Voltaguere*, Captain Lombard, fitted out & owned at Curracoa. She had been bound from Trinidada to Portsmouth. The papers relative to the Ship & cargo were secretly dispatched to St Domingo, where a condemnation was obtained. They were worth together 50,000 dollars.

B. H. PHILLIPS, *3^{d} Augt 1797.*

The Ship *Nancy*, Wm Perry, master, of Philadelphia was condemned at St Domingo on the frivolous pretext, "that there was found on board a letter in Hieroglyphicks or other Characters, & to which a key was found." I think it is very probably both were manufactured, in Curracao. ibid. This vessel was bound to London, & captured, the day after she left the land, by the French privateer *Pandor*, Capt Garriscan, who placed a prize Master on board of her & sent her to Curacao. On the passage the prize-master treated the Captain & crew in a very cruel manner; & even whilst at Curacao threats were permitted to be used against the Captain's life, by means of which he was induced to abandon the vessel & return. B. H. Phillips, 21 June 1797.

Since my last the following vessels & their cargoes have been condemned & Sold. Some of them indeed were Sold previous to Condemnation, & the *Ann & Susan* adjusted without Sale. Ship *Fame*, Schooner *Gideon*, Ship *Ann & Susan*, Sloop *Sally*, Brig *Orange*, Schooner *Act*, Schooners *Richmond*, *Esther & Eliza*, & *Isabella*. B. H. Phillips 15 June 1797.

The following is a list of the vessels brought into this port.

1. The *Rainbow*, Capt. Smith, bound from Charleston to London with rice, cotton & Coffee. The vessel was owned by Mr John Geyer of Charleston & the Cargo loaded by Messrs Banks & Co. Bold & Rhodes & George Lockey.

2. The *Charlotte*, Capt. Lindsay from Charleston to Bremen with Rice, Cotton, Sugar, Coffee & Skins. The vessel was owned by Messrs J. H. Large & Co Charleston; & the cargo was loaded by them, Mr Peter Graaft, George Forrest, Macbeth & Ross & John Cockle.

3. The *Juna*, Capt Walter, from Charleston to Hamburg with Rice, Coffee &c. The vessel owned by Mr James Sheafe, & the cargo loaded by Messrs Tunno & Cox of Charleston.

4. The *Hebe*, Capt. Lindegreen, bound from Savannah to Lancaster, with cotton, rice & lumber — The vessel owned by Mr E. Swarbuck of Savannah & Loaded by himself.

5. The *Catherine* Capt. Carneau, bound from Virginia to Rotterdam, with Tobacco — the vessel owned by Messrs Anthony & Moses Davenport of Newbury Port, Massachusetts, & the Cargo loaded by Alexander Henderson & John Gibson of Dumfries

6. The *Oneida*, Capt Sherry, bound from New York to London, with Sugar, Coffee &c. The vessel owned by Mr James J. Burkley of New York; & the cargo loaded by different Merchants & consigned to divers people.

7. The *Briseis*, Capt James Breath, bound from New York to Amsterdam with Sugar & Coffee — the Vessel owned by Messrs Rutgers, Seaman & Ogdin of New York — the cargo chiefly loaded by Messrs Pearsoll & Pell.

All these vessels have been brought in on the plea, that they had not the *Rôle d'équipage* or list of Seamen, required to be signed by a public officer, as expressed in the Sea letter. P. F. Dobree, Consul at Nantes, 7 June 1797.

List of American vessels brought into Nantes, subsequently to the 7 June 1797, by privateers.

1. The *Confederacy*, Capt. Scott Jenks, bound from Canton to Hamburg & a Market, loaded with teas, China, Cassia sugar &c. owned by Messrs Leffingwell & Pierpont of New York.

2. The *Mary*, Capt Thomas Curtis, bound from Marblehead to Lisbon with fish, owned by Mr John Brown of Norfolk.

3. The *American Hero*, Capt Alexander Mc Dougall, bound from New York to Cadiz with Rice & flour, loaded by Messrs Douglass & Lawrence & Brothers Coster of New York — the vessel owned by him.

4. The *Mercury*, Capt Thomas Vicoun bound from Norfolk to Breman, owned by himself & W. Hector Calbraith of Philadelphia, loaded with Tobacco.

5. The *Mary*, Capt. Robert Holmes, bound from Boston to Naples, with Sugar, Coffee, Nankeens &c owned by Mr James B. Marshall of Boston.

6. The *Light Horse*, Capt. John Hoff, bound from Bristol to New York, with Sundry articles, owned by Messrs Nathaniel Ingraham & Comfort Sands of New York.

7. The *Sally*, Capt Benjamin Russell of Salem, Chartered by W. W. Gray of Said Port & Bound to Bilbao with a cargo of fish.

8. The *Bacchus*, Capt Richard George bound from Philadelphia to London with Molasses, peltry, rice &c. owned by Messrs J. Campbell & John Brown of Said Phiiladelphia. P. F. Dobree, 11 July 1797.

The Brig *Carolina*, of Boston, Capt Morton, & her cargo were condemned in the Court of Commerce at Bayonne. There remains at that port for trial the *Molly*, Capt. Stumper, carried into Bilbao by a privateer of this Place; & the [space] Capt. Ross of Marblehead, taken by a privateer of Bayonne, bound from Massachusetts to Spain, with fish &cc under the pretext of the want of a rôle d'équipage. At this port there have been brought in the Brigantine *Washington*, Capt Graham of New York bound from Cork to New York with passengers & some few goods, & the Ship *Venus*, Capt Berril, of Wiscasset, from Wales bound to New York, loaded with earthen ware & Slates, both taken by National Vessels, under the same pretext. J. Fenwicke Bordeaux 25 Augt 1797.

The Brig *Venus*, Capt. John Harmon, from Port au Prince to Massachusetts, with Molasses, the proceeds of her outward cargo, was captured & carried into Gonaives. She was condemned at Cape Francois for want of a Sea letter. Jacob Mayer Sepr 30 1796.

I have lately had much trouble & vexation about 52 of our Vessels which have been carried into the french port of St Domingo & Condemned by the delegate residing in that port. Seven of the Captains thus carried in & Condemned, arrived here, Viz.

Thomas Boyle, Brig *Mary*, from Baltimore
Daniel Stay[?], Schooner *Catherine*, Philadelphia
Augustus Peck, Brig *Franklin* — Philadelphia
[space] Lillibridge, Brig *Kerumhappuch*, do.
John May, Brig *Nancy*, New York
John Wier, Brig *Free Mason*, New York
John Howland, Schooner *Rainbow*, Massachusetts.

I am certain they mean to condemn all our vessels bound to British Ports, particularly to those ports possessed by the English in this Island. With respect to the Captains already mentioned, I have not yet been able to obtain the decision of the delegates, save that a Condemnation was pronounced upon one, viz, Brig *Mary*, Thomas Boyle, on the principle of his owner being a Frenchman born, & that another was acquitted, Viz. Schooner *Rainbow*, Joseph Howland, because previous to his Capture, he had cleared out from a French Port. I have no expectation of recovering the other five vessels, altho' they are owned by American Citizens. Same 10th Novr 1796.

The Schooner *Zephir*, owned in Norfolk, & Commanded by Edward Hansford, last from the Mole was brought into this port yesterday afternoon. Same 26 Novr 1796.

Our commerce is in a most deplorable State. Not a day passes, but one or more American Masters arrive in this City in quest of their Vessels. The captors generally take these masters on board of their privateers, send the prize into one port & run themselves into another. Indeed Sometimes they cruize about with them for one Month & when the number increases, so as to endanger the privateer, they throw some on Shore without a Shilling in their pockets or a second Shirt to some of their *Beaten Backs*. It would swell a volume, Sir, were I to give you particular details of the ill treatment we receive. Some time since the French privateer Brigg called the *Triumphant*, commanded by one Anthony Lobo, captured the Brigg *Friendship* of Salem, and forcibly took from on board of her the following Seamen, not giving them time to Carry their little trunks with them:

James Darby, *Mate*
John Allen
William Dawson
William Low
Robert Osborn
John Jefferson
} Born in Salem in the United States & having protections.

Archibald McLean, with a Protection
One black man commonly called Sip Salem

Altho' the Brigantine hath been condemned these two weeks, nobody knows what has become of the Privateer. Perhaps in two weeks more, I have Some of the poor men, She forced on board, lying at my door half dead, it would wring your heart to see the distresses of our Seamen. Congress have not make sufficient provision for them. As a favor I got some into the Hospital; but they begin to be tired of me & will receive no more; & when I offer them to American Masters, they make a thousand excuses — I cannot force them. Same AUGT. 5th 1797.

I had the honor to write to you on the 5th instant, via Rhode Island. Since this Short period the commission have condemned about *twenty* of our vessels. Not a day passes, but one or two, & Sometimes three or four are adjudicated. The captors never bring them to this port: they carry them into other ports & send their papers hither; that is, such papers as Suit them. Hence before the masters have time or even permission to come here their vessels are condemned. The Commission will not listen to me on this subject.

I informed you in my last letter of the miserable State of our Seamen, & that I could not get any more into the Hospital. After much entreaty I have prevailed on the Director to receive them at half a dollar a day. Poetic language with all its glowing colours cannot convey to you even a faint idea of their distresses. Same AUGt 13, 1797.

The civil Tribunal of St Omer, on the arretté of the Directory of the 12th Frémaire taken on the arreté of the Directory of the 12th Frémaire taken on the report of the Minister of Justice, has confirmed the judgement of the tribunal of commerce of Bologne, Condemning the *Royal Captain*, John Bryant, Master & owner, & her cargo.

The Tribunal of Commerce of LaRochelle has cleared the American Ship, *Roxana*, Capt. Pollard captured on her passage from Surinam to London, but the owners of the privateer have appealed.

The *Charlotte*, Capt. John Vincent is brought into Dunkirk, where it is supposed she will be condemmed, having no sea — letter.

The *Hare*, Capt. Halley, belonging to Mr Clazen of New York, bound from London to New York, is brought into Dieppe, & libelled before the Tribunal of Commerce. Fulwar Skipwith, Paris, 17 March 1797.

The tribunal of commerce of Dieppe decided on the capture of the *Hare*, Capt. Halley, & condemned the vessel & Cargo to the profit of the Republic, it appearing on trial, that the Master of the *Hare* was the Captain of the privateer, the war commission being in his own name. That of Calais has condemned the American Cutter *Dark*, Captain Davison, under the pretence, that her papers were not in Order — that vessel was seized in port. That of Dunkirk has condemned the *Charlotte*, Captain Vincent.

The *Sally;* Capt. Timothy Davis is capture & carried into Dieppe — no decision as yet. The Brig *Leonard* of Newbury port is in the same predicament. The tribunal of Commerce has condemned vessels & cargoes of the *John* of Boston, Capt Js Scott Jr & the D. of N. York, Capt. Andrew Foster. All the ships papers were in perfect order but they had no rôles d'équipage. Same 17 Apr 1797. The Brig *Leonard*, Cap. Willm Hackett has been condemned by the Commercial tribunal of Brest The *John* of Boston. Capt. James Scott, &

the D. of New York Cap. Andrew Foster have been condemned by the Commercial tribunal of Morlaix. Appeals are made from these three condemnations grounded on the want of a *rôle d'equipage.* The Captains of the *Hope & Antelope,* whose vessels have been condemned on appeal from the Commercial tribunal of L'orient are coming up here, where I will advise them to try the tribunal of Cassation. The *Juliana* from Norfolk, Capt. Hayward is captured & sent into Havre.

The consular Agent at L'orient advises me, that they are arming & manning every little craft to cruize for our vessels along Shore, as every one they will meet is sure to be condemned for want of a rôle d'équipage in the form required by the antiquated private regulations of France. Same. 10th May 1797.

The *Sally* of Alexandria, Capt. Js Crawdhill, owned by M. Hodgson bound for Rotterdam to Norden, was carried into Morlaix and condemned by the Commercial Tribunal. The *Cincinnatus* of Baltimore, Capt. Martin, from London to Baltimore, was sent into L'orient. Same 28th June 1797.

The *Virginia Packet,* Capt. Robert Wells was sent into Teneriffe on the 11th June 1797 by the *Buonoparte* privateer, Capt. Michel. The *Virginia Packet* was bound from Norfolk to Cadiz with flour &cc — but being turned off from the latter port on account of its Blockade, she proceeded from Madeira, to enquire the State of the Markets, and when off that place she was captured. The french Consul at Teneriffe condemned both vessel and Cargo. John Culnam, Teneriffe 4 July 1797. —

On the 12th Sept. was sent in here (by the same privateer *Buonoparte,* that Captured the *Virginia Packet*) the Schooner *Sophia,* Capt. O'Meara, bound from Madeira to Alexandria, & released because they could not find out the least flaw to lay hold of, otherwise the absolute power of the French Consul would have condemned her. Please to observe, that during the process of the *Virginia Packet* this government received preemptory orders not to interfere in Neutral prizes brought in here by French Cruizers. Same 25th Sepr 1797.

The *Governor Mifflin,* Capt. John Dove, was condemned at Carthagena by the French Consul, as prize to the French privateer *Zenadore,* Capt. Poule, because She had no rôle d'équipage, on the 8th Floreal, 5 year, = 27 April 1797. — Robert Montgomery, Alicante, 13 May 1797.

The following vessels, *Pomona,* John Craft; *Telemachus,* Wm S. Plummer; *Abigail,* James Atwood; & *Eliza,* Wm. Mugford, sailed from hence on the 18th ult. for Salem & Boston, were captured within this Bay, carried into Carthagena & Condemned there by the French Consul, under the usual pretext of a defect in the Ship's roll. Same 10 June 1797.

Since my last of the 10th June, three more of our Vessels have been captured by French Cruizers, Viz. the *Brothers,* Capt. James Sumner, of Boston, & Captain Samuel Hill of the [Space] are carried into Carthagena & Capt John Proud of the Brig *Friendship,* of Providence Rhode Island, brought in here & condemned under the usual pretext of the Rôle d'équipage. Same 1 July, 1797.

Since I had the pleasure to hand you my last respects of the 16th March, the French have been committing the most vile depredations on our Flag along this Continent. They are now publickly robbing us of our property, capturing & bringing our vessels into the Spanish ports, where their Consuls in the course of five days condemn Vessels & Cargoes as good & lawful prize to France from no other cause, which they give to the public, than our Ships not carrying rolls of their crew properly authorized by a public Officer of the port she belongs to. There is at this present moment five American prizes that have been brought in here within this month, which I shall note at foot. Three of them are already condemned, & the remainder must Suffer the same fate as well as all others that may fall into their Clutches. Michael Morphy 3 May 1797. —

The list referred, viz. 1797 April 1st Ship *Three Brothers* of Portland, Lendal Smith, From Portland, laden with lumber & provisions, bound to Alicante.

April 2, Brig *Dispatch* of Philadelphia, Philip Brum, from Gibralter, with provisions, for Malaga.

April 29. Ship *Polly* of Salem, William Bradshaw, from Salem, with flour & other provisions, coming to Malaga.

May 1, Schooner *Orrington* of Penobscot, Ambrose Atkins, from Edenton, with Staves coming to Malaga.

Thirteen American vessels, which lay at Malaga, a considerable time blockaded by french privateers, sailed on the 27th of May with a favourable wind, of which they availed themselves to get under the protection of two English frigates, & I have now the pleasure to inform you, that only one of the fourteen fell a prey to the Cruizers that night, on account of her being a dull Sailor, & She was brought back the following day. She is called the *Betsy* of Boston, Gideon Snow master, laden with Brandy & Wine for Said Port, Same 3D June 1797.

The Brig *George* of Salem, Cap. Rust, from Bourdeaux with wines, bound to Salem, but having to touch here, is just this moment brought in by a French cruizer, on the Supposition, that She was going to Gibralter, because she was found four leagues off Here — However unquestionable everything may be concerning this Vessel and on the face of the business there appears not the least suspicion against her, I am afraid it will be a very unpleasant affair. Joseph Yznardi, Cadiz, 28 March 1797. She was afterward released. Same 7th April 1797.

The ship *Alfred* Capt Asquith, was taken by a french privateer, &c retaken by an English, liberated & sent for Cadiz; but the Frenchmen who remained on board of her run her ashore, which has been Clearly proved; but the French Consul of this City in consequence of his absolute power, has condemned her as a prize. Same 15th May 1797.

I must inform you, that the French consul here told me that he had given instructions to all french privateers to detain indiscriminately & carry into the next Spanish Port every American vessel they can meet with, & that any one which may come under his jurisdiction Shall be instantly condemned. Same 15 May 1797.

The tribunals continue condemning for want of the *Rôle d'équipage* demanded & we must expect to see every one of the vessels without it declared valid prizes. I am now occupied in making a proper Statement of those brought in here to send to the commissioners in Paris & will likewise transmit it to you. Hurried at this moment to make use of the present opportunity of Addressing you, I will only add, that I have now 19 prizes or Captured Americans to defend, besides 4 more condemned in the first instance in Spain, & who appeal before the Civil Court of this department, one of which has been condemned on Sunday last. Viz. the *John & James*, Capt. Johnson. I am forced to make all these Captains the necessary advances to carry on their Suits & to Support themselves & their Crews. This begins to be very heavy & Embarrassing. P. F. Dobree, Nantz, 20th Sepr 1797.

[Enclosure No. 6]

Abstract of the Cases of Capture of American Vessels by the French, Wherein Documents Have Been Received at the Department of State from the Individuals Aggrieved

The Ship *Hope*, John Rogers, master, belonging to Buchanan & Young of Baltimore, loaded with 99 Hhds, of Tobacco on their account & bound for Falmouth & a market, was captured in Feby 1797. by the French privateer *O'Hardy* & carried into L'Orient, where on the 6th March following her cargo was condemned (with payment of freight) by the tribunal of commerce at L'Orient, because a certificate containing the detail of the cargo sworn to by the master of the *Hope* before a Justice of the peace at Baltimore, & another containing evidence of the neutrality of the cargo, granted by a Notary Public, were not accompanied by a certificate recognizing the Justice & the Notary as such: 2nd because the clearance & manifest were certified by the collector & naval officer "with two oval circles, without the impression of a Seal," & 3d because three of the bills of lading expressed the vessels destination to be "for a Market," whilst the remaining one alone expressed it to be for "Falmouth in England." On an appeal, on behalf of the owners, to the tribunal of the Department, the vessel, cargo & freight were all condemned. The vessel & cargo were worth 23,000 dolls

The Snow *Isabella*, Capt. James Helm, belonging to Buchanan & Young of Baltimore, bound from Trinite in Martinique to Baltimore, was captured on the 19th March 1797, by a French privateer & carried to Point a Petre in Guadeloupe. The master was taken on board of the privateer & carried to Mariegalante & from thence to Basseterre, where he was turned on Shore without the means of Subsistence & threatened to be put in prison. The vessel & cargo were condemned.

The Schooner *Orrington*, Ambrose Atkins, master, belonging to Thatcher Avery of Penobscot & Richard Flunewell of Castine in the State of Massachusetts, was captured on the 30th April 1797. near Malaga in Spain by the French privateers *Le Neuf Thermidor* & *Le Chasseur*, carried into Malaga & condemned there by the French Consul. The loss is Stated to be 20,020 dollars.

The Brigantine *Friendship*, George Hodges, Master, belonging to Ichabod Nicholls & Benjamin Hodges of Salem in the State of Massachussets, was captured on the 27th June 1797, on a Voyage from Calcutta in Bengal to Salem, by a French privateer, called *Le Triumphant*, Capt Anthony Sobo, & carried to Port Liberty. She was condemned as well as her cargo; at Cape Francois, because She was coming from a British port, & because (it was pretended) She had "no certificate respecting her cargo."

The Schooner *Active*, Nathaniel Atkins, master, belonging to James Crawford of Castine in the State of Massachusetts, sailed from Barbadoes on the 10th January 1797 with a cargo of Sugar & rum, &

was captured on the next day by the French privateer *Flying Fish* & carried into Guadeloupe, where the Cargo was Condemned. The loss is Stated to be 2381 16/100 dolls.

The Brigantine *Philanthropist*, Capt. Hodgdon of Portsmouth, New Hampshire, Sailed from Demarary bound to Altona, with a Cargo of coffee, cotton, & rum, on the 9th May 1797; and on the 5th day afterwards she was captured by the French Privateer *Decius*, Capt. Gabot, & carried to Guadeloupe, where both vessel & Cargo were condemned on the 9th June following.

The Brigantine *Nabby*, John Lawrence, master, belong to Ralph Pomeroy & Thomas Sandford junr of Hartford in the State of Connecticut, bound from Antigua for New York, with a cargo of Sugar rum & hides, belonging partly to the owners of the vessel & partly to Isaac Deforest, a passenger, was captured on the 25th March 1797 by a French privateer called *L'Espiegle*, Capt Debon, who carried her to St Juan in the Island of Puerto Rico. She was condemned at Cape Francois on the 25th April 1797 together with her cargo, in virtue of the decree of the Commission of the French Government at Windward Islands of the 1st February 1797. inasmuch as Demerary (the port of her original destination) had been given up to the English, & in virtue of another decree of the 7th January 1797 (made in consequence of the decree of the Executive Directory of the 2nd July 1796) declaring good prize all neutral vessels bound to or from a British port.

The Danish Brige *Uricke Kock* was chartered in Leghorn in July 1797, by J Brush of New York, for a voyage to be performed by months, to the Island of St Thomas & to New York, with liberty to touch, Stay & trade at any other Islands or places not blockaded. She was accordingly loaded with a valuable cargo, in which Joseph Donaldson of Philadelphia took an interest & embarked with the Same to transact the business. He was instructed to call at Cayenne & Surinam, & sell or depart at his own discretion. He accordingly arrived at Cayenne on the 4th Octr but not finding the market agreeable to his expectation, he determined to depart. Having received permission to do so, and the vessel being cleared & upon the point of Sailing, he was arrested & the Brigantine taken possession of by an armed force; & the officers were Sent on board of a corvette. The papers that appertained to the cargo were then demanded, the officers and crew of the vessel underwent an examination, & a report was made by the Governor to the Agent Jeanet, that the vessel was Danish & the cargo American property, & Mr. Donaldson a citizen of the United States. On the 17th the Cargo was Condemned on the ground that the Charter party was open to proceed to any port or ports, also on account of her touching at Cayenne, when She had taken her departure for St Thomas. It is estimated that the cargo thus condemned would have produced 50,000 dollars.

The Brige *Six Brothers* belonging to Isaac Needham & John Needham of Salem, Massachusetts, bound from Martinique to Salem in Ballast, was captured on the 29th April 1797. by the French Privateer *Leoradie* & carried to Guadeloupe, where, she was condemned on the 19th May, in pursuance of the decree of the Agents of the Directory there, dated on the 22d January 1797.

The Brige *Nathaniel*, David Young, master belonging to said Young & to Moses Gale of Haverhill, & bound to Jamaica from Norfolk, with a cargo of Staves, heading, Shingles, Indian-meal & flour, was captured on the 1st August 1797 by a French privateer called *Lacassas*, carried into Port de Paix, & on the 12th the Captain received the condemnation of the vessel & Cargo without any trial or hearing.

The Brig^{e} *Maria*, John Morgan, Master belonging to Richard Dennis of Savannah, was captured on her passage from Jamaica to Savannah by a French privateer, called *La Pearl*, Commanded by Michale Williams & carried into Havannah, where the vessel was Stripped & Sold, & the Cargo also disposed of without the semblance of a trial.

The Ship *Commerce*, Godfrey Wood Master, belonging to Murray & Mumford of New York, bound from Liverpool to Baltimore, was captured on the 27th June 1797. by the French privateer *L'Espeigle*, Capt Barre, & Sent to Puerto Rico. She had on board a quantity of Salt belonging to the owners of the Vessel, & Some Crockery & other goods on freight. She was condemned together with her cargo at Cape Francois principally because She was coming from a British port on the Ground of the decree of the Agents at the Cape of the 7th Jany 1797. The Condemnation is dated 6 Sepr 1797.

The Sloop *Olinda*, William Darnel, Master, from Savannah bound to Jeremie; with lumber, tobacco & live-stock, was captured on the 17th June 1797 by a French privateer, called *L'Espiegle*, Cap^{n} Barre who ordered her for St Juan in Puerto Rico. They robbed Capt. Darnel of all his sea-cloaths, bedding, books, quadrant, &c. He entreated them to let him remain with his vessel, that he might see her condemned, which they preremptorily refused. On the next day they fell in with an American sloop, on board of which they put Capt Darnel & three of his men, keeping the Mate & two more in the *Olinda*.

The Brig^{e} *Harmony*, Samuel Clapp, master, belonging to Francis Becker of New York, from thence to Port au Prince, with a cargo of pipe Staves, hoops & Shingles, was captured on the 21st June 1797 by the French privateers *La'Vengence* & *L'Amiable Louise*, & carried to Jean Rabel. She was condemned as well as her cargo, at Cape Francois on the 30th June, as being bound to Rebel port of Port au Prince, declared to be in a State of Permanent Siege by the decree of the Commission of the 26th Decr 1796. The loss is Stated to be 2864 96/100 dollars.

The Schooner *Industry*, Rufus Low, Master, from St Thomas to St Domingo, was captured on the 7th April 1797 by the British frigate *Ceres*, James Newman Esqr Commander, who manned her & ordered her for Cape Nickola Mole: but on the next day She was recaptured by a French privateer called the "*Foundling*," Capt. Bras, who sent her to Port de Paix. Being at Cape Francois engaged about the defence of his vessel & cargo, Capt Low received a message from the Commissaries of the place, informing him, that if he did not deliver up to them so much of the cargo as amounted to near 15,000 dollars, & take bills of Exchange for the same on the national Treasury at Paris, they would immediately condemn the Schooner & her cargo; to prevent which he was constrained to take Such bills; but during his absence, the administrator at Port de paix ordered her hatchways to be broken open & her cargo landed, by which means the privateer's people & others were enabled to plunder many things from on board, there being no officer there to prevent it. The loss is stated to be 20,538 72/100 dollars.

The Brig^{e} *Electa*, Pardon Almy, master, being bound to Jacmel, was met with by a French privateer of 12 guns on the 22^{d} Sepr 1797 at night, which ordered Capt Almy to hoist out his boat, which he did & went on board the privateer. His people on going on board were immediately put in Irons & lashed to the foremast; & he was taken into the Cabin, where his papers were overhauled & being found perfectly clear, he was ordered to be put into irons until day-light & then hanged to the fore-yard. A pair of Pistols was also laid before him; but the privateersmen finding their threats of no Effect, they hoisted out his boat on the following morning plundered from the *Electa* various articles of the Cargo & Stores, & also kept the boat.

The Schooner *John* having been carried to the mole of St Nickola^{s} for Adjudication was acquitted as well as her cargo on payment of costs. She sailed thence for Leogane to dispose of her Cargo under protection of an armed vessel, but becoming leaky, She was under the necessity of leaving her convoy & bearing away for the mole. Having freed the vessel & discovered the leaks the Captain tacked again & Stood for Leogane. On the 18th Octr She was boarded by two brigand barges, which declared her good prize; but an English Ship coming up, they thought fit to abandon her, after they had plundered every thing they could lay their hands upon, such as all the peoples cloaths, the cabin furniture, a trunk of Handkerchiefs &cc. The *John* then proceeded for Leogane, & whilst Standing in for the port, She was boarded by a lugger Republican barge, the commander of which took the helm of the *John* & Steered her for Gonaives; but another British vessel coming up, the French began to plunder a second time with tenfold the rage of the first. They burst the Hatches open & plundered linen, handkerchiefs, bags, beef, bread, wine cast &cc &cc ransacking the Schooner from Stem to Stern, knocking down the Sailors & cutting & Stealing the rigging. In the mean time the British vessel (*The Roman Emperer*) came up & carried the *John* to [illegible]. The Owners of the *Roman Emperor* demanded a Salvage of 1/8 for releasing the *John* from the French, which the Captain consented to. Capt Kearney of the *Roman Emperor* generously refused to receive any part of the Salvage for his Services.

The *Lovely Lass*, William Moore, Master, belonging to John & Joseph Coster, & Chartered to John Brown, Henry Dixen & Warren Ashly, all of Norfolk in Virginia, bound from Port au Prince to Norfolk, was captured on the 6th of June by two barges, which robbed the Captain of all his cloaths & money, beat him most barbarously with a cutlass, & carried him to Gonaives.

The Schooner *Rebecca*, John Hall, master, belonging to Valck & Company of Baltimore, bound to St Thomas's & a market, with an assorted cargo, was captured on the 5th Octr 1796 by two French privateers, which sent her to St Martins. The Supercargo was kicked, beat & put in irons by the privateer — men. On the arrival of the Schooner at St Martins, the Supercargo, mate & people were sent on board a prison Ship & all put in Irons: the people were kept at hard labor all day upon Short allowance & at night were kept in irons. From St Martins the Captain & Supercargo were carried to Guadeloupe in a privateer, & during the whole passage exposed on deck to the sun, rain & the sea, which (it being tempestuous weather) constantly covered the vessel. On the 14th they arrived at Guadeloupe, where the supercargo was committed to prison. On the 6th November Capt. Hall was informed of the condemnation of his vessel

& Cargo. The following is the principle of the condemnation. The Supercargo (formerly a French Citizen) had become a naturalized Citizen of the United States on the 29th Augt 1796, & in his certificate of naturalization it was recited, that he had renounced all allegiance & fidelity to all nations to whom he might before that time owe it, & *particularly to the French Republic:* now by the 12th art. of the French ordinance of 21st Octr 1744, it is declared that every foreign vessel, on board of which there Shall be found a Supercargo factor &cc. of an enemy Country, shall be prize. From the Certificate of naturalization it was inferred that the Supercargo was an emigrant & an enemy of the Republic, & therefore that the vessel & cargo were liable to confiscation: nevertheless he was released from prison about the 12th Novr following, & permitted to depart. Valck & Co. State their loss to be 36,160 88/100 dollars.

The Sloop *George*, John Grant, master, belonging to Wise & Grant & John Grant of Kennebunk in the State of Massachusetts, from Demarary bound to Kennebunk with a cargo of West Indian produce, was captured on the 19th Feby 1797 by the French privateer *L'Hirondelle*, commanded by Capt. Seber, who carried her to Cabo Roxa in the Island of Puerto Rico, where the privateersmen plundered the cargo, took possession of the sloop's paper, for the purpose (as they said) of sending them to St Domingo & turned the master & people from on board, after robbing them of their cloaths. Capt. Grant having nothing whereon himself & his people might subsist, availed himself of the opportunity of the Sailing of an American vessel, & returned home. The loss is Stated to be 9559 58/100 dollars.

The Ship *Fame*, Joseph Brown, master, belonging to Elijah Hall & John McClintock of Portsmouth N. Hampshire, from Grenada for Portsmouth, was captured on the 12th March 1797 by the French privateer *Le Pandour* Capt. Garrison, who sent her Curacao, where she was condemned as well as her cargo by the maritime Agent of the French Republic residing there; 1st because she was cleared out originally under "*the vague terms of the West Indies,*" which by the decree of the French Agents to the Windward Islands of the 1st Feby 1797. is a cause of confiscation: & 2ndly in virtue of another decree of the same Agents, dated 7 Jany 1797, subjecting to confiscation all neutral vessels going to or coming from British Ports. The loss is stated to be 15,468 64/100 dolls.

The Ship *Louisa*, Holder Fullman, master, belonging to John Clark of Bath in the State of Massachusetts, from Savannah to the West Indies, with provisions & Lumber, was captured on the 13th February 1797 by a French privateer called the "*Foundling*" Cap. Bras, who carried her to Jean Rabel & from thence to Port de Paix. The vessel & Cargo were condemned on the 23d of the same month at Cape Francois. The loss is Stated to be 18,216 54/100 dollars.

The Ship *Polly*, William Bradshaw, master, belonging to John Norris of Salem in Massachusetts, with flour, beef, fish & pepper, sailed on the 23d Feby 1797 for Vigo in Spain: but the markets being dull there, she proceeded to Lisbon & departed thence for Cadiz. On attempting to enter the last mentioned place, She was turned back by Admiral Jarvis's Fleet, who were then Blockading it.

She now proceeded for Malaga, but on the 16th of April she was captured by a Spanish privateer & carried into Ceuta, whence after ten days detention She was dismissed, & continued her voyage for

Malaga. On the 28th April, however, in sight of that City & within two & a half leagues from the land, she was captured by two french privateers, Called *Le Chasseur* & *Le Neuf Thermidor*, & carried into Malaga, where she was Condemned on the 14th May by the French Consul, because she was without a Rôle d'équipage. The loss is Stated to be upwards of 27,0000 [sic] dollars.

[Enclosure No. 7]

COPY OF A LETTER FROM THE MASTERS OF CAPTURED AMERICAN VESSELS AT ST JAGO OF CUBA, DATED 21st JUNE 1797

TIMOTHY PICKERING Esquire,
Secretary of State of the United States.

SIR The Subscribers, Masters of American Vessels captured & brought into this port by the armed Vessels of the French Republic think it their duty to lay before you, a Statement of the Situation of the Americans & their Vessels brought in as aforesaid. —

The cruisers of the French Republic bring in all vessels bound to & coming from any port, belonging to their Enemies, & in many instances, Vessels going to or coming from their own or neutral ports. As soon as the vessels arrive in port a general Scene of plunder & depredation takes place, & if it is supposed the vessel will not be condemned the greater exertions are made to rob both vessels & cargoes. No person belonging to the vessels is suffered to do any thing for the preservation of the property, nor is there either person or law to gaurd it from distruction. The Captains, Masters & people in many instances are put on Shore, deprived of their money & every means of getting their bread, by reason of which, Some have been forced by necessity to enter on board the cruizers of the French Republic, others to go on board Spanish vessels for subsistance — & those that remain are supported by the Charity of the few Vessels here that are not prizes.

This is a tax to heavy for Masters of vessels to bear, & the owners are not always here to give their assent.

The Schooner *Little John*, of Philadelphia, Capt. Pease & the *Polly* of Baltimore Cap. Kirby, have supported more than 20 for many weeks. We beg leave to suggest to the Government of the United States the necessity of appointing some person to reside here, as Agent for the following purposes. Viz.

1st To take charge of Such American Seamen as have no means of subsistence, & send them home to the United States.

2nd To take charge of such Vessels & their cargoes as may be sent in to Port, where the legality of the capture is doubtful.

3rd To prevent persons having Certificates of Citizenship of the United States from entering on board armed Vessels of the Bellegerent Powers.

4th To prevent American Registers, Sea Letters & papers being used where the property is not Bona fide American, And lastly to assist the Masters, Mates or such as are permitted to come in, in prizes, to take such steps as the nature of the case may require, for claiming the property ascertaining the Value, & defending the same if practicable.

We have reason to believe that Such an appointment would be agreeable to the Governor here, that it is necessary & would be very useful. The Brig *Commerce* of Charleston bound from Aux Cayes to Charleston was brought into this Port libelled & tried as a prize — & would have been condemned had there not been Some American Gentlemen here who undertook to defend her & Saved her from Condemnation. The Schooner *Dorchester* of Baltimore was in the same predicament & was also acquitted — both vessels stripped & cargoes plundered, & a loss of five or six hundred Dollars accrued to each vessel, which might in part have been Saved had there been any person here authorized by the United States to take charge of the vessels & Cargoes.

Herewith we transmit a list of American Vessels brought in & now lying here — Some of which might doubtless have been saved had there been a Judicious Person authorized to apply for them. Urged by a desire to promote the happiness of the Citizens of the United States, & to relieve them from a perplexed state in which we are now involved, Should any be so unfortunate as to suffer as ourselves we have been induced to make this a representation to you & beg you to accept it with our warmest Wishes for the happiness & prosperity of our beloved Country.

We are very respectfully, your Excellency's Most Obedient & very humble Servants.

St Jago de Cuba
June 12th 1797

DANIEL GREEN
JOSEPH WHITE Junr
JOHN FRANKFORD
MARSHAL PEASE
Wm H. NICHOLS.
Wm CLARK
MICHl JOSE
TOBIAS E. STANSBURY.
NICHOLAS KIRBY.
CONSTANT BOOTH
MITCHELL CUTTER
Wm DEANE WILSON
JAMES WOODEND
JACOB SINGLETON
THOMAS SMITH
GARDNER LILLIBRIDGE

[Jan'y to June, 1797]

[Enclosure to Enclosure 7]

[Extracts from — "1797 Marine Lists of American Vessels captured by French Cruizers and brought into St Jago de Cuba"]

Mo.	Day	Reg.	Ves. Name	Where Reg.	Commanded by	Taken by
		Brig	TWO SISTERS	Boston	Wm Worth	
Jany		do	JOHN	N. York	John Tucker	FOGUES
		do	WOOLWICH	Philada	T. McCutchin	CANONEIR
		Sch	WILMINGTON	Charleston		
		do	LIVELY	Portland		
		Sloop	POLLY	N. York		
Feby	18	Brig	AMELIA	Sea Brook	Sam Williams	
		Schr	MERCURY	Charleston		
		Brig	VALERIA	Newbury Port		
		Schr	POLLY & MARIA	Philada		
		do	BETSY	do		REVENGE
April	1	do	NEEDHAM	Charleston	Wm Grant	TROIS SOEURS
	4	do	DORCHESTER	Baltimore	Constant Booth	FRANCIS ZERBY
	6	do	INDUSTRY	Charleston	Misroon	FAVOURITE
	9	Brig	NEUTRALITY	Bath	Clark	PAULINE
	6	do	COMMERCE	Charleston	Danl Green	SERPAUSONET
	14	do	SEA NYMPH	Philada	Geo. Hastin	GENl TOUSAINT
	20	do	HONEY or ALONEY	N. York	Michel Cutter	PAULINE
	26	do	BELL	Norfolk	J. Woodent	FAVOURITE
	26	do	CAROLINE	Middletown	Elihu Cotton	TRIUMPHANT
May	4	do	JUNO	N. York	W. H. Nickols	RESERVE
April	26	Sloop	POLLY	Baltimore	W. D. Wilson	TROIS SOEURS
May	13	Schr	SALLY	Norfolk	Robt Churn	FAVOURITE
	28	do	KITTY	PHILAD.	J. Singleton	TROIS SOEURS
	28	Brig	AURORA	do	J. Frankfort	PAULINE
May	29	Sloop	REBECCA	do	Wm Clark	SANS PAREIL
June	9	Ship	ATLANTIC	Boston	Michel Jose	MISSICIPIAN

[Enclosure No. 8]

Extracts from the Letters of General Charles C. Pinckney

M[r] Montgomery, our Consul at Alicant, advises, that the Brig *Telemachus*, Capt. W. S. Plummer, the Ship *Pomona*, Capt. John Craft, the Schooner *Abigail*, Capt James Atwood, all three belonging to Boston, & the Brig[e] *Eliza* Cap[t] Mugford, belonging to Salem took in at Alicant, Cargoes of Wine & Brandies on account of their owners, for Boston, & sailed from Alicant the 18th of May; that they had been but a very Short time under way, *& were not yet out of reach of the Cannon of the Castle*, when they were boarded by two launches under Spanish Colours, who immediately took possession of the Vessels & carried then round to Carthagena. M[r] Montgomery seeing this immediately went to Carthogena to know why the Vessels were seized, & to his astonishment he found that the launches belonged to two French privateers, at anchor in that port, & that the launches were sent for the express purpose of taking our Vessels. The launches had not commissions for cruizing. M[r] Montgomery says that all the Ships papers were in order except that the role d'equipage was not in the form required by the French. The French Consul has condemned the four vessels with their Cargoes & has inhumanly turned on Shore, without any support, the crews, amounting to 36 persons, to you it is not necessary to make a Single remark on this Transaction. 22[d] June 1797.

The rapacious Activity of the French privateers seems to encrease, & Since my last I have received accounts, that the Ship *Ohio* from New York to Greenock has been captured & carried into Morlaix; & that the Ship *Raven* of Philadelphia, bound to Bourdeaux with 17 french passengers on board, has been taken & sent into l'Orient by the French privateer *Eagle* belonging to Benjamin Callender of Boston — July 21st 1797.

Since my last I am informed, that the Ship *Ceres*, Capt. Roswell Roath, of Norwich in Connecticut, was captured on her passage from New London to Liverpool, by the French privateer *Hydra*, Capt. Desmoliers & sent into Rochelle. The Same privateer has also captured, & sent into the Isle of Rhee, the Brig *Sally*, Capt. Eden Wadsworth, belonging to Mess[rs] Adams & Loring of Boston on her passage, from Boston to Hamburg; likewise the American Ship *Bacchus*, of 300 tons, bound to London. — 26 July 1797.

A privateer of Boulogne has sent into Calais an American Vessel, the *William*, Capt. Colin Campbell, of Portland, taken on her passage from Zante to Danzric. The Commercial tribunal of l'Orient has released both the vessel & cargo of the *Raven*, Capt. Reilly. The Same tribunal likewise released the *Ohio*, but condemned her cargo July 30th 1797.

The Brig *Charleston* of Charleston, Capt. Reed, bound to Bilbas is taken by a french privateer, & carried into L'Orient. The *Mary* of Boston, Capt. Choates from New York to Havre, is taken & carried into Nantz — Aug[t] 27th 1797

The Brig[e] *Mary* of Boston, Capt. Jedediah Southworth, with a Supercargo on board, Son of the owner, Mr. Tilden, sold her cargo at Bourdeaux & took in return some brandies & sailed for Boston, but meeting with head winds as soon as they got out of the Garronne, &

the master being confined to his bed by Sickness, they made the island of Rhé in distress, where the Ship's papers being examined by the Commissary of the marine, who finding She had no rôle D'équipage, agreeably to the French form, but the Seaman's Articles attested by Mr Fenwick, detained the vessel & sent the papers to the Minister of Marine, to decide whether She is to be considered lawful prize, or to be returned to the Captain. Application has been made to the Minister of Foreign Affairs for his interference with the Minister of Marine. Septr 14th 1797.

NOTE.—Other cases of capture are mentioned by Genl Pinckney beside the above; but they were not added because they have been noticed by the Consuls & are contained in the extracts from their Letters, No. 5.

[SDA. Dom. L., Vol. 10.]

[January, 1798]

Communication by Robert Burns, late of the Ship *Ann and Mary*, captured by the Privateer *Vulture*

I was captured on my voyage to London in the above ship about the middle of January last, in lat 49, 25, long. 11, by the privateer ship *Vulture*, captain Penchen, of Bordeaux, in the early part of a six months cruise, and detained on board, with many more, till the cruise was ended, when I was turned ashore at Corunna in Spain, without one single stitch of cloathing, except what I had on. We were suffered to write by neutral vessels to Hamburg, or any other place, but not suffered to go in them.

The following vessels were captured during my stay on board said ship:

One brig, from Cork, laden with salt for the Banks of Newfoundland — burnt.

One brig, from Liverpool, laden with pork and porter, for the Banks of Newfoundland.

One brig, from Jersey, with an assorted cargo — burnt.

One large snow, from Charleston, bound to Hamburgh, laden with rice and coffee, recaptured and sent into Lisbon.

One large coppered brig, laden with whale oil and bone, and sea-cow teeth, recaptured and sent into Falmouth.

One brig laden with sugar — was very leaky, and it is supposed, has gone down.

Also the ship *Peggy*, of New-York, with an assorted cargo, and was condemned on account of having naval stores on board.

This ship had a great number of letters on board, that ought to have been destroyed; they have given fatal information for many merchants and underwriters in New-York, as they contained information of goods shipped on account and risk of many merchants in London, Liverpool, Bristol, Cork, Dublin, &c. &c. and some shipowners, writing for insurance. All vessels so insured in any part of Great Britain, is bona fide British property with the French. In consequence of this information there are three privateers cruizing for the ships so loaded, and to sail from New-York to the different ports in Britain. Their cruise is from 16 degrees West of Paris to 35, and lat. 48, N.

☞I came passenger in the brig *Charlotte*, Captain John Mellory, and am happy that I have it in my power, thus publicly to return my humble and sincere acknowledgments of gratitude to this gentleman for the many favors that I have received at his hands since my first arrival, in distress, at Lisbon, to the present moment.

ROBERT BURNS.

[LC, "Claypoole's American Daily Advertiser" (Phila.), 10 Sept. 1798.]

To Captain John Barry, U. S. Navy, from Secretary of War

[PHILADELPHIA,]
War Office 4th January 1798 —

Capt JOHN BARRY

SIR 'Till such time as permanent regulations can be matured and adopted by the President respecting the Government of the Navy, you will be pleased to have the Marines and Seamen mustered monthly while in Port and regular muster rolls made out Alphabetically and signed by the persons appointed to muster them, as well as by the Lieutenant of Marines for the Marines, and the acting Lieutenant and yourself for the Seamen —

Colonel Mentges is to muster the Marines and an experienced Sea Capt the Seamen —

You are requested to direct the first Muster to be made as soon as possible, and mention to me a proper person to Muster the Seamen that orders may be taken accordingly —

All requisition for provissions while in port are to be founded on these Musters, Certified by the Lieutenant of Marines the acting Lieut and your own signiture —

The Contractor is to furnish rations conformably to the 7 Section of the act providing a Naval Armament. He will also when an Equivalent in Beef or any other articles for the rations of any day is required grant the same. Regulations of this nature are to be Signed by the Captain who is to Certify that the equivalent is agreeable to the parties.

I am &c

[NDA, LB. Correspondence when Navy was under War Department, 1790–1798.]

To John Harris from Secretary of War

[PHILADELPHIA,]
War Office January 10th 1798.

Mr JOHN HARRIS

SIR Be pleased to deliver to Lieut McRea for the Marines on board the Frigate *United States*, John Barry Esquire Commander eighteen Marines Muskets with accoutrements &c complete, one suit of Serjeant's Cloathing and three dozen of flints. —

The Muskets he now has on hand to be returned by him to the store. —

JAMES MCHENRY

[NDA, LB. Correspondence when Navy was under War Department, 1795–1798.]

To John Harris from Secretary of War

[PHILADELPHIA,]
War Office January 12th 1798

JOHN HARRIS

SIR Please to deliver to Lieut. John Mullowney Twenty five short Cartridges of two pounds each for 24 pounders, for the use of scaling the Guns for the Frigate *United States* — also three sticks of Port fire.

JAMES McHENRY

[NDA, LB. Correspondence when Navy was under War Department, 1795–1798.]

To John Harris from Secretary of War

[PHILADELPHIA,]
War Office January 18th 1798

Mr JOHN HARRIS

SIR Be pleased to deliver to Lieut John Mullowny for the Frigate *United States* Twenty five paper Cartridges, one powder-horn, bit and priming wire, one Rammer and spunge, also one worm and Ladle — proper for 24 pounders. — and in addition to the above you will be pleased to supply him with Fifty five pounds of Cannon powder, and Twenty sticks of Port fires. —

JAMES McHENRY. —

[NDA, LB. Correspondence when Navy was under War Department, 1795–1798.]

To General Jackson from Secretary of War

[PHILADELPHIA,]
War Office 20th of Jany 1798

General JACKSON

SIR I have received your letter of the 17th inst enclosing a Statement of Articles purchased in Decemr last, and also one other containing a great number of Articles required by Captain Nicholson as Cabbin furniture for his Ship

I beg leave to observe that no other furniture can be allowed by the Public to the Commissioned officers on board of Ships of War, than what is absolutely necessary to their immediate accommodation on Board; and whatever articles they may want for their own use and convenience must be provided at their own expence

I have therefore to request that you will provid[e] the following only for their accommodation

Dining Tables
Windsor Chairs
1 accommodation Chair
1 Globe Lamp
2 Copper Stoves. Should any other arrangements be made you will have notice given you of it

I am &c

[NDA, LB. Correspondence when Navy was under War Department, 1790–1798.]

[February 1798]

Extract from letter to Thomas Appleton from Timothy Pickering

Standing Instructions to Consuls and Vice-Consuls of the United States

"The Consuls and Vice-Consuls of the United States are free to wear the Uniform of their Navy, if they chuse to do so. This is a deep blue coat with buff facings, linen and cuffs, the cuffs slashed and a standing collar, a buff waistcoat (laced or not at the election of the wearer) and buff breeches; yellow buttons with a foul anchor and black cockades and small swords."

[SDA. Dip. Cor., Inst. to Min., Vol. 4, Feb. 1, 1797–Nov. 30, 1798.]

[6 February 1798]

Statement of Secretary Timothy Pickering

In a conversation last June between the Governor General of Louisiana, the Baron de Carondelet, and Mr. Benoist, the former said — That he had no orders from the Spanish Government to retain the posts from the Americans: but that considering the critical situation of affairs in this country and in Europe, he had no doubt that he should be justified in thus delaying the evacuation of the posts.

Received the above information from Asher Miller Esq. the 6th of February 1798, to whom it was communicated by Mr Benoist at the Natchez.

T. PICKERING.

[Mass. HS. Pickering Papers, Misc. 1799–1812, p. 21.]

To General H. Jackson, Navy Agent, Boston, from Secretary of War

[PHILADELPHIA,]
War Office 1st Mar 1798 —

Genl H. JACKSON

SIR: There being more Howertzers in the Navy Yard at Boston than is probable, will be wanted for the *Constitution*, you will be pleased to enquire of Captain Nicholson the number he may wish to have for his Ship and the remainder I wish to have transported immediately to Philadelphia to the address of Tench Francis Esquire

I beg the favour of Capt Nicholson's determination by post

I am &c

[NDA, LB. Correspondence when Navy was under War Department, 1790–1798.]

[1 March, 1798]

Data furnished by Richard O'Brien, United States Consul, Algiers

Marine force of Algiers March the 1st 1798 —

	Guns
One Ship of	36
One do. of	24
One do. of	22
Xebeck of	24
Xebeck of	24
Xebeck of	22
Xebeck of	12
Xebeck of	12
Cutter of	18
Schooner of	12
Xebeck building of	20
Xebeck do. of	12
Marine force guns	238

60 Gun boats.

Yrs

OB [O'BRIEN]

[SDA. Algiers, Vol. 3, 1798.]

To Captain Samuel Nicholson, U. S. Navy, from Secretary of War

[PHILADELPHIA,]

Capt S. NICHOLSON *War Office 14 March 1798* —

SIR I have the honour to transmit herewith the Letters of notification to the Commissioned Officers for the *Constitution* which I beg you will be so obliging as to transmit to those Gent[lemen] for whom they are directed. I am in daily expectation that the Warrant Officers will be appointed, every preparation is going forward here to get the Naval business in a train of actual Service the regulation for the genl discipline of the Navy is ready to be printed and I expect the commissions will be shortly issued to the Officers appointed at which time their rank in the Navy will be established. Congress past the app yesy

[NDA, LB. Correspondence when Navy was under War Department, 1790–1798.]

To Lieutenant of Marines, Frigate *Constellation*, from Secretary of War, 16 March 1798

To Lieut. Marines Frig. Constellation

[PHILADELPHIA,]

LIEUTENANT OF MARINES,
Frigate Constellation

To

SIR, The President of the United States, by & with the Advice & Consent of the Senate, having appointed you a Lieutenant of Marines in the Frigate *Constellation*, you will be pleased to commence the Recruit the Complement of Marines allowed by Law to the sd Ship, to wit, Three Serjeants, three corporals, One Drum & Fife, & fifty Privates. — In the Performance of this duty, you will pay particular Attention to the rules and Regulations herein after mentioned.

1st. It being essential that those who enlist, should feel an Inclination for that kind of Life, no indirect Methods are allowable to inveigle Men into the Service of the United States; it is forbidden therefore to inlist any Individual while in a State of Intoxication, or to have him sworn untill twenty four hours after he shall have signed the Inlistment. —

2. No Individual is to be inlisted (Musicians excepted) who is not five feet and six Inches high without Shoes, and above Eighteen and under Forty Years of Age. He must be healthy robust and sound in his Limbs and Body, and of a Make to support the Fatigues and acquire the honors of a Soldier. —

3. No Negro, Mulatto or Indian to be enlisted nor any Description of Men except Natives of fair Conduct or Foreigners of unequivocal Characters for Sobriety & Fidelity. (Any recruiting Officer inlisting a vagrant transient Person, who shall desert, shall reimburse out of his Pay the Loss sustained by such Desertion. —

4. The Recruits are to be inlisted to serve the Term of one Year, unless sooner discharged. The Monthly Pay allowed them will be as follows vizt — Serjeants, Nine Dollars, Corporals, eight Dollars; Musicians Seven Dollars; Privates, six Dollars, two Dollars whereof, may be advanced them, at the Time of their being sworn. To reimburse the Cost of attesting the Recruits, and other necessary Expences, One Dollar will be allowed for every Recruit duly enlisted. —

5. Each Recruits before he is sworn, is to have distinctly read to him the Rules and Articles of the Navy against Mutiny and Desertion and such Acts of Congress as concern his Pay, Duties and the public Engagement. —

The Oath shall be as follows. to wit. —

I ——— do solemnly swear to bear true Allegiance to the United States of America, and to serve them faithfully against all their Enemies or Opposers whomsoever, and to obey the orders of the President of the United States of America, and the orders of the officers appointed over me according to the Articles of the Navy. —

6. No Recruit is to be permitted to keep in his possession after being sworn any of his Clothing, except that which he may receive from the Public. The Officer is therefore to oblidge him to dispose of his private Clothing immediately, or to take the Keeping of it upon himself till an opportunity offer to sell it for account of the Recruit. —

7. No Recruit is to be allowed to absent himself from his Quarters, till such Time as he has proved himself faithful without a Corporal or trusty Private to attend him. —

8. Each Recruit after being sworn, is to be attached to a Squad to consist of a Number sufficient to form a Mess, who must live together and be under the Inspection and Command of a Serjeant or Corporal. —

9. The Commanding Officer of a recruiting Party, shall make out on every Saturday, a Return of the Number of Recruits under his Command and of the Number joined, and of the Incidents that have taken place and the Arms, Accoutrements and Clothing, delivered them during the Course of the Week and transmit the same to the Secretary for the Department of War, and a Duplicate to the Commander of the Ship, to which he belongs. —

10. He shall keep a recruiting Book, in which He shall record. —

The Name, Trade and Description of each Recruit.

A Copy of the Oath taken before the Magistrate signed by the Magistrate and Recruit. —

The Money paid to every Recruit. —

The Articles of Clothing Arms & Accoutrements delivered each Recruit. —

11. The Commanding Officer at each Rendezvous will sign Returns for the Issues of all Rations and other necessary Supplies for the Recruits, and on the Saturday of each Week, the Returns made in the Week are to be taken up, and one general Return made out and signed for the Rations received in the course of the Week noticing the daily Issues. —

12. On the Desertion of a Recruit, besides the usual Exertions and Means to be employed on such Occasions, the recruiting Officer will transmit as soon as possible a description of the Deserter to the Secretary of War, and will cause all Descriptions of Deserters that may be sent to him to be entered in a Book kept for that Purpose, and will use his Endeavours to discover and apprehend all Deserters. —

Given at the War Office of the United States the sixteenth day of March 1798, and in the twenty second Year of the Independence of the said States. —

[NDA. OSW, Vol. 1.]

To Captain Thomas Truxtun, U. S. Navy, from Secretary of War

[PHILADELPHIA,]
War Office 16th March, 1798

Capt Thos TRUXTON

SIR, I have it in command from the President of the United States, to direct you to repair with all due Speed on board the Ship *Constellation* lying at Baltimore. —

It is required that no Time be lost in carrying the Ship into deep Water, taking on board her Cannon, Amunition, Water Provisions & Stores of every kind — completing what Work is yet to be done, shipping her Complement of Seaman & Marines, and preparing her in every Respect for Sea.

The Lieutenant of Marines will immediately proceed to inlist the Marines, agreeably to the "Act for providing a Naval Armament" passed the first of July 1797. You will be pleased to transmit to him the annexed Regulations for that Purpose. —

You will herewith receive Commissns and Warrants for the following Officers. Vizt —

John Rogers, of Maryland, Second Lieutenant.
William Cooper, of Virginia, Third ditto
Philip Edwards, of Maryland, Lieutenant of Marines.
George Balfour, of Virginia, Surgeon.
Isaac Henry, of Pennsylvania, Surgeon's Mate.
Edward Hansford, of Virginia, Sailing Master.
Isaac Garretson, of Maryland, Purser.
Philemon Charles Wederstranett, Maryland, Midshipman
Jabez Bowen, Junior, Rhode Island, ditto
Henry Van Dyke Delaware do
John Dent Maryland do
John Marshal Clajett do do

You will be pleased to signify to the Warrant Officers, that their being appointed at this Time, is not to affect the Question of relative Rank as it respects Midshipmen, for the other Vessels not yet appointed. —

You will cause such of the Sea Officers as may appear best calculated for the Business, to open Houses of Rendezvous in proper Places & to exert Themselves to engage One hundred & thirty able Seamen at the following Terms of Service and Rules of Wages — The Seamen to engage for twelve Months unless sooner discharged. The pay of the able Seamen to be fifteen Dollars per Month and Three Dollars Bounty — The Ordinary Seamen, Ten Dollars per Month and two Dollars, Bounty. —

You will instruct the Officers at each Rendezvous to engage none other than healthy robust and well organized Men, and to reject those who may be scorbutic or consumptively affected.

You will direct the Surgeon, or a Mate to attend at those Places to examine each Sailor and Marine, and to certify to the recruiting Officer, that they are well organized, healthy, robust, and free from scorbutic and consumptive Affections, before he engages Them or pays them any Bounty. If Bounty or Wages is paid to any without such a Certificate, it will be at the risk of the Officer paying it.

The Officer of each Rendzvous shall make out on every Saturday, a Return of the Number of Seamen recruited within the Week, stating therein the Number delivered over to the Ship, and transmit the same to the Captain, and a Duplicate to the Secretary for the Department of War. —

You will also transmit to the Secretary for the Department of War, a weekly return, exhibiting the Number of Marines, able and ordinary Seamen on board the Ship, and the Incidents that have taken place respecting Them or any of them, as also the Progress that has been made for preparing her for sea. —

The commanding Officer at each Rendezvous, on the desertion of a Seaman, besides the usual Exertions and Means to be employed on such Occasions to recover and apprehend him will transmit as soon as possible, a Description of him to the Secretary of War. —

Having selected proper Characters for the remaining Midshipman, Gunner, Carpenter and Sailmaker, you will return their Names that they may be laid before the President. —

With respect to the Pay of the Marines and Seamen. The Purser, 'till ordered otherwise, will act as Paymaster to the Officers and Crew, and will receive from Time to time, Money for that purpose. —

Marines are to be advanced Two Dollars out of their first Month's Pay. The Advance to Seamen if they can not be obtained without it, may be One Month's Pay, besides the Bounty.

As soon as you give Notice of the Places of Rendezvous and the Arrival of the Officers who will have Charge of them, a sufficient Sum will be remitted to each, to commence the recruiting Service. The Officers receiving this Money will be held accountable for it's faithful Application, & must produce at the Accountant's Office, proper vouchers for it's Expenditure. —

The Names of the Marines and Seamen, are to be entered alphabetically, in the Muster and Pay Rolls, and the Men to be mustered while in Port by a qualified Person, whose Certificate as well as your's is to be attached to the Muster roll.

It is the President's express Orders, that you employ the most vigorous Exertions, to accomplish these several Objects and to put your Ship as speedily as possible in a situation to sail at the shortest Notice. —

I shall make a Requisition on the Secretary of the Treasury, for provisioning the Crew while in port, independent of the Provisions destined for the Voyage or Cruize. —

Monthly Pay of the Petty Officers, Seamen, Ordinary Seamen and Marines. —

Frigate Constellation

Altered since—See page 10.

			Drs
8 Midshipmen at	19	Drs Each	152
2 Master's Mates at	20	Drs each	40
1 Captain's Clerk at	25	d°	25
2 Boatswain's Mates	18	d°	36
1 Cockswain	17	d°	17
2 Gunner's Mates	18	d°	36
1 Yeoman of the Gunroom	18	d°	18
9 Quarter Gunners	17	d°	153
2 Carpenter's Mates	18	d°	36
1 Armourer	18	d°	18
1 Steward	18	d°	18
1 Cooper	18	d°	18
1 Master at Arms	18	d°	18
1 Sail Maker's Mate	17	d°	17
4 Quarter Masters	17	d°	68
1 Cook	18	d°	18
126 Seamen & Midshipmen @	15	d°	1890
90 Ordinary Seamen	10	d°	900
2 Serjeants	9	d°	18
2 Corporals	8	each	16
1 Drum	7	d°	7
1 Fife	7	d°	7
40 Privates	6	d°	240
		Dollars	3666 p. Month

WAR OFFICE, *17th March, 1798*

[NOTE.—Page 10 contains the list coming in the letter book between 7 May 1798 and 18 April 1798, headed, "Monthly Pay of Petty Officers, Seamen, Ordinary Seamen, and Marines on board the Frigates of the United States."]

[NDA. OSW, Vol. 1.]

To Governor John Jay from Secretary of War

[PHILADELPHIA,]
War Office 19 March 1798 —

His Excellency JOHN JAY

SIR The Iron 24 pound Cannon intended for the Frigate *United States* being unfit for service in their present State, and it being disirable to have their place Supplied as early as possible, I am instructed by the Presidt to submit to your Excellency a request for the loan of thirty of the Iron 24 pound Cannon which it is understood the State of New York have procured from a Foundery in Connecticut and further to engage to return in a short time, should this request be complied with, an equal number of new Cannon of the same Caliber and goodness.

Permit me to expect an answer to this Letter as early as it may suit with your convenience, that measures may be taken to have the Cannon if obtained inspected and Carriages prepared for them

With great respect I have the honour to be your Excellency &c

[NDA, LB. Correspondence when Navy was under War Department, 1790–1798.]

To John Harris, storekeeper, from Secretary of War

[PHILADELPHIA,]
War Office 22d March 1798

Mr JOHN HARRIS

SIR Be pleased to deliver to Saml Hodgdon Esquire to be immediately transported to the Frigate *Constellation*, Ninety Barrels of Cannon, Eight Barrels of Musket, and two Barrels of Pistol Powder. —

[NDA, LB. Correspondence when Navy was under War Department, 1795–1798.]

To Joshua Humphreys, Naval Constructor, from Secretary of War

[PHILADELPHIA,]
War Office 23 Mar. 1798

Mr J. HUMPHREYS

SIR Captain John Barry of the Frigate *United States*, reports that the seams in the Decks topsides and other parts of that ship are much opened & the oakum loosened, and those parts will require caulking previously to her leaving the Delaware

I request therefore that you would be pleased to proceed on board said ship and take a careful survey of the Defects complained of, and endeavour to form an Estimate of the probable expence attending such repairs, which I beg you will transmit to this office without loss of time

I am &c

[NDA, LB. Correspondence when Navy was under War Department, 1790–1798.]

To Joshua Humphreys from Secretary of War

[PHILADELPHIA,]
War Office 26th March 1798

Mr JOSHUA HUMPHREYS

SIR Your Letter of the 24th has been received. You will be pleas'd to take order to have the defects on board the Frigate *United States*, put into complete repair, in as short a time, and with as little expense as possible —

I am Sir

Yr &c —

[NDA, LB. Correspondence when Navy was under War Department, 1790–1798.]

[27 March 1798]

An act for an additional appropriation to provide and support a naval armament

SECTION 1. *Be it enacted by the Senate and House of Representatives of the United States of America in Congress assembled,* That there be and there hereby are appropriated a further sum, not exceeding one hundred and fifteen thousand eight hundred and thirty-three dollars, to complete and equip for sea, with all convenient speed, the frigates, the *United States*, the *Constitution* and the *Constellation;* and a further sum, not exceeding two hundred and sixteen thousand six hundred and seventy-nine dollars for the pay and subsistence, for the term of one year, of the officers and crews which are, or shall be engaged in the service of the United States on board the said frigates, in addition to the sums heretofore appropriated for those purposes, respectively, remaining unexpended; also, a sum, not exceeding sixty thousand dollars, to defray the wear, losses, expenditures of ammunition, and other current and contingent expenses of the naval armament; also a sum not exceeding two thousand two hundred dollars, to defray the salaries of persons having charge of the navy yards at Norfolk, New York, and Portsmouth; and for the rents of the same.

SEC. 2. *And be it further enacted,* That the sums hereby appropriated, shall be paid and discharged out of the surplus revenue and income of the current year, not before appropriated.

Approved, March 27, 1798.

[Statute II, page 547.]

To Captain Henry Geddes from Secretary of State

[PHILADELPHIA,]
29 March 1798

Instructions to Capt. Henry Geddes, Master of the Brigantine *Sophia* belonging to the United States of America.

The President of the United States, desirous of conveying, in the most direct and speedy manner, a letter of instructions to M[r] Pinckney, M[r] Marshall and M[r] Gerry, the Envoys Extraordinary and Ministors Plenepotenitary from the United States to the French Republic, has directed the Brigantine *Sophia* to be prepared for that purpose. You are therefore to proceed with the said Brigantine directly to Havre de Grace in France, there land M[r] Clement Humphreys, who is charged with the said letter, that he may proceed to Paris and deliver it to our Envoys: and wait his return.

If the wind should be adverse, and you apprehend any considerable delay by beating up the channel to Havre, then you are to put into any convenient port in France, and proceed as before directed. If the Envoys or either of them be there, you will obey the orders which they or he shall send you: or, in want of their orders, proceed as M[r] Humphreys shall direct.

If on your arrival at any port in France you shall find that all our Envoys shall have left France, then also you will observe the orders of M[r] Humphreys about your further proceeding.

In case of any accident to Mr Humphreys, you are to execute the orders with which he is charged, relative to the delivery of the letter to our envoys or either of them, and to the collecting of American Seaman, at the port or ports in France, at which you shall touch with the *Sophia*.

Given under my hand and the Seal of the Department of State of the United States of America, the 29th day of March 1798.

TIMOTHY PICKERING
Secretary of State —

[SDA. Dom. L., Vol. 10.]

To Mr Clement Humphreys, bearer of dispatches to France, from Secretary of State

INSTRUCTIONS TO M. CLEMENT HUMPHREYS—OF PHILADELPHIA

SIR, The President of the United States having directed that a special messinger should be engaged to carry a letter to the Envoys from the United States to the French Republic, you have been selected for that service.

You are to embark forthwith in the United States brigantine *Sophia*, whereof Captain Henry Geddes is master. The *Sophia* is to sail directly to Havre De Grace, whenced you will proceed immediately to Paris, with the letter to our Envoys: and take their orders for your further proceedings and return.

But it may happen that all our Envoys will have left France before you arrive in any of its ports: In this case, having well ascertained the fact, you are immediately to return to the United States. If, however, either of the Envoys should remain in France you will proceed and deliver the letter to him, and receive his orders relative to your further proceeding and your return.

Into whatever French port you shall fall, if there be an American consul there, request his Assistance in procuring a passport for Paris, and any information which circumstances may require.

Given under my hand, and the seal of the department of State, at Philadelphia, the 29th day of March, 1798. —

TIMOTHY PICKERING,
Secretary of State.

[SDA. Dom. L., Vol. 10.]

[29 March 1798]

Instructions to Mr Clement Humphreys of Philadelphia

SIR The direct object of your voyage to France is to carry a letter to the Envoys from the United States of America to the French Republic, agreeably to the orders herewith delivered to you. If their answer should not require your immediate return, the President directs me to call your attention to another object interesting to humanity and to your country: I mean the relief of American Seamen in the ports of France. With this view, you will show these instructions to our Envoys, or either of them whom you shall find in France. If it shall be practicable to execute them, then procure a passport to visit the several ports of France for that purpose. The Consul

General, Skipwith, or his Chancellor Major Mountflorence, can aid you in this and in whatever relates to the execution of these instructions. In this case you will first return to the port where you shall leave the *Sophia,* and commit your dispatches to Captain Geddes, to bring to America. And altho' these dispatches may require his immediate return, yet he may take on board all the American Seamen whom he may find in such port: and he should seek for them as soon as he arrives. If your orders from the Envoys should not require the immediate return of the *Sophia,* she may proceed from port to port, receiving as many American seamen on board as she can conveniently bring; and then return home.

We have received repeated information of many of our seamen being turned ashore from our vessels captured and carried into the ports of France, and there suffering for want of the means of Subsistence, or as an alternative, to save themselves from starving entering on board French privateers. So many of these citizens as you shall find destitute of the means of returning home, are to be received on board the *Sophia;* and for want of room in her (should that happen) you will otherwise afford all the relief in your power to such distressed fellow-citizens, providing passages for them in any vessels bound to the United States, or elsewhere from whence you judge their return to their Country will be effected with more ease than from France: or chartering or purchasing one or more vessel for the purpose of bringing them home. — In this business you will address yourself to the consuls of the United States and their agents in the ports of France: of their names and places of residence a list is herewith delivered you. We have advice from Some of the consuls, by which it appears that they have very humanely afforded their friendly aid and pecuniary assistance to numbers of American Seamen, and to the masters and supercargoes of captured American vessels, in the prosecution of their claims. You will inform these and other Consuls who have thus kindly advanced their monies, that they will be reimbursed by the United States; and that a bill is now under consideration in Congress to make an appropriation of money for that purpose. Such of them as shall have the opportunity of furnishing you with their accounts for such disbursements had better do it, as it may facilitate their reimbursement. If they think proper, they may deliver you their vouchers (for which you will give them receipts) for their expenditures for the object here referred to, and advise you in what way they choose to receive repayments. It is probable, however, that in many cases the American owners of captured vessels and cargoes, or their agents in France will have made due provision for refunding to the Consuls the sums they have advanced in the prosecution of their claims; and these, of course, will not require the aid of the provision now making by the United States.

In expectation that you will collect a considerable number of American Seamen in French ports, I have directed an extra quantity of provisions to be put on board the *Sophia:* and if these should be insufficient, you will procure what shall be found requisite in France.

Given under my hand and the Seal of the Department of State, at Philadelphia, the 29th day of March 1798

TIMOTHY PICKERING
Secretary of State

[SDA. Dom. L., Vol. 10.]

To Captain John Barry, U. S. Navy, from the Secretary of War

[PHILADELPHIA,]
War Office 31 March, 1798.

Capt. BARRY Commander of the Frigate, *United States.*

SIR It is represented, that the Frigate *U[nited] S[tates]* incommodes in her present Station the Merchant Vessels in coming in and going out and that One equally good at the Bight opposite the Rope Walks where the Channel is wider, would occasion less risk and Embarrassment. —

If on Examination, that or any other Station can be found commodious and proper for the Frigate to lay in, I have to request that She be removed to such Place as early as convenient, but should her Removal from her present Station, be attended with Risk or Inconvenience, you will be pleased to report the same without delay. —

[NDA. OSW, Vol. 1.]

To Lieutenant John Rodgers, U. S. Navy, from Captain Thomas Truxtun, U. S. Navy

UNITED STATES SHIP *Constellation,*
April — 1798.

SIR You are hereby directed to open a Rendezvous at the house of Mr Cloney, at Fells Point in the City of Baltimore, For the purpose of entering One hundred and thirty able Seamen, and Ninety ordinary Seamen, to Serve in the Navy of the United States, and for the present, on board the Ship under my command.

These men must be engaged for the term of Twelve calendar months, unless sooner discharged by order of the President of the United States.

The pay of the able Seamen, is to be Fifteen Dollars per month, and the ordinary Seamen ten dollars, and each class may have two months pay in advance on giving good and Sufficient Security, for their repairing on board, when order'd with their Clothes and bedding — or on their repairing on board and their names being returned to you that they are actually on board with their effects —

None but able bodied, robust healthy men are to be entered, and the Surgeon or his Mate, must Certify that they are So: as well as of their being free from Scorbutic or Consumptive affections if any are entered and paid their advance without the Officer So entering them, producing Certificates as aforesaid, it will be at his risk & Charge — A return must be made to me without fail every Saturday evening of the number of men you have enter'd, and Such as have been delivered over to the Ship, and a duplicate return sent by post to the Secretary of War.

Shou'd any of these Seamen or others attempt to run away after having Signed the Articles received the advance & taken the Oath, you must immediately give information to the Secy of War, describe the man minutely, using at the Same time all your endeavours to apprehend and lodge in jail Such runaway untill Further orders from me — Mr Garretson the Purser is to act as Pay Master to the Ship. he will consequently make a requisition and provide money Sufficient to accomplish all the business with which you are charged, and you must produce to him the Vouchers he shall require for the Settlement of his accounts.

The Agents Mess[rs] Sam[l] & Ja[s] Sterett will provide Victuals on board the Pilot Boat for the men you enter (say 1½ lbs. of beef & 1 lb. of Bread with ½ a pint of Rum for each man untill he joins the Ship) and whenever you can collect ten or more men with their clothes, you are to Dispatch the boat under the Charge of a Midshipman or Some other trusty Person. —

Every expence attending the rendezvous for fire, candle, Liquor, house rent, &c &c, must not exceed one dollar for every man actually entered & received on board — you must come to a clear understanding with M[r] Cloney on this subject, before you open the rendezvous, a reasonable allowance will be made you for music to indulge and humour the Johns in a farewell frolic;

In order to encourage the entering of Seamen, you may agree to pay to M[r] Cloney, one dollar for every Seaman he procures that is healthy and able to do his duty like a man, which Sum is to be paid him, when our Complement is complete, and the Ship ready to Sail from the Chesapeake Bay — it is absolutely necessary notwithstanding the Certificate required of the Surgeon and his Mates, that you pay particular attention in examining the men you enter, So that none but hale hearty men compose the Crew of this Ship, and the more real natives you can procure the better.

I understand that Cap[t] Moore is well acquainted with the attending of Rendezvous. You must Call on M[r] Sterett, and let him make some agreement with him, to aid you in this business. the Compensation must in all cases be so much p man, but you must take care, that it is not paid to two people, for procuring one man.

The form which you and every officer & man must take is as follows to wit —

I, AB. ——— do Solemnly Swear to bear true allegiance to the United States of America and to Serve them faithfully and honestly against all their enemies or opposers Whomsoever, and to observe and obey the orders of the President of the United States of America and the orders of all the officers appointed over me according to the Articles of War, and that I will Support the Constitution of the United States So help me God. —

Sworn before me this day of — —

You must be very particular and Oblige every man that offers, of the description I have mentioned to take the Oath as well as to sign the articles; before he receives a Single Cent, or that you attempt to Send him on board. —

You must be very civil and good humour'd with every body, and endeavour to attach them to the Service, by pointing out the rations &c &c allowed.

You will make every exertion in your power to complete the number of men required, in as short a time as possible. —

This service, will require your devoting your whole time & attention to it, in fact you must be at the rendezvous night and day, untill the object of your mission is completed. —

I am Sir with the greatest respect —

Your ob[t] Serv[t]

THOMAS TRUXTUN.

N. B. You must not Suffer any of our marines, to visit the rendezvous, except When they are Collecting to go on board; for various good reasons. —

The more men you Can enter and Send down, without the aid of Messrs Moore & Cloney, the better as it will be a Saveing of So much to the United States.

T. T.

Lieu^t JOHN RODGERS.

[HS of Pa. NDA photostat. Truxtun's LB, 1798–9.]

To Captain Richard Dale, U. S. Navy, from Secretary of War

[PHILADELPHIA,]
War Departm^t 3^d Ap^l 1798.

Capt DALE.

SIR, I have to inform you, that the Purchase of the Ship *Ganges* is now effected, & that she will be manned & destined for the Purposes intended by the Law, providing the additional Naval Armament as speedily as possible — The President continues to give you a Preference for the Command of this Ship — & I cannot, but permit my self to believe, you will not decline it.

[NDA. OSW, Vol. 1]

To Samuel and Joseph Sterrett, Navy Agents, Baltimore, from Secretary of War

[PHILADELPHIA,]
War Office 4th April 1798

Messrs SAM^l & JOSEPH STERRETT

GENT^n Captain Staats Morris commanding the Fort at Whetstone point near Baltimore, has been directed to deliver to you, Twelve — 12 pounders — I request that you will be pleas'd to have them Shipp'd immediately to Philadelphia, addressed to Captain John Barry, commanding the Frigate *United States.* —

I am Gent^n, w^h great respect

[NDA, LB. Correspondence when Navy was under War Department, 1790–1798.]

[9 April, 1798]

To Hon. Samuel Sewall from Secretary of War James McHenry

WAR DEPARTMENT, *April 9th, 1798.*

SIR,

I DO myself the honor to inclose you a detailed view of the provisional measures, it appears to me proper, should, in the present conjuncture of the affairs of this country, be immediately taken, to protect our commerce, and secure and defend our territory and sovereignty.

I have the honor to be,
With great respect,
Your most obedient servant,

JAMES M'HENRY.

Hon. SAMUEL SEWALL,
Chairman, &c. &c.

[Enclosure]

WAR DEPARTMENT, *9th April, 1798.*

What measures are necessary and proper to be adopted by Congress, in the present conjuncture, to preserve character abroad, esteem for the government at home, safety to our sea-property, and protection to our territory and sovereignty?

France derives several important advantages from the system she is pursuing towards the United States. Besides the sweets of plunder, obtained by her privateers, she keeps in them, a nursery of seamen, to be drawn upon, in all conjunctures, by her navy. She unfits, by the same means, the United States for energetic measures, and thereby prepares us, for the last degree of humiliation and subjection.

To forbear under such circumstances, from taking naval and military measures, to secure our trade, defend our territory in case of invasion, and prevent or suppress domestic insurrection, would be, to offer up the United States a certain prey to France, and exhibit to the world a sad spectacle of national degradation and imbecility.

The United States possess an extensive trade, heavy expences must be submitted to for its protection. The United States border upon the provinces of great and powerful kingdoms, heavy expences must be incurred, that we may be at all times in a situation to assert our rights to our own territory. The measures which appear indispensably necessary for Congress to take, are as follows, viz.

1st. An increase of the naval force, to serve as convoys, protect our fisheries, coast and harbours. 2d. An augmentation of the present military establishment. 3d. Arrangements which in case of emergency, will give to the President, the prompt command of a further and efficacious military force. 4th. The more complete defence of our principal ports by fortifications. 5th. A supply of ordnance, small arms, powder, salt-petre, copper and military stores. 6th. Additional revenue.

To answer the 1st. Congress ought to provide for the building or purchasing, equipping, &c. of 2 vessels of 22 guns, 8 of 20 guns, and ten of 16 guns, in addition to the three frigates.

Congress ought also to vest the President with authority, in case of open rupture, to provide, equip, and by such means as he may judge best, a number of ships of the line, not exceeding six, or an equivalent force in frigates.

The first may be either built or purchased in the United States. The latter may, perhaps, be obtained in Europe; for which purpose the law should use general expressions, admitting this mode of procuring them.

To build the twenty vessels, equip, man, and provision them for twelve months, will require, as per estimate, dolls. 1,941,131

It may, under this head, be also advisable, to make a provision for six gallies, carrying each one or two 24 pounders. This will require for gallies carrying one 24 pounder each, as per estimate, dolls. 68,826

2d. An augmentation of the present military establishment. This ought to consist of one regiment of infantry—1 regiment of artillery, and 1 regiment of cavalry. The artillery is considered as indispensable, and the cavalry may be highly useful in the southern states. These will require, agreeably to the estimate, dolls. 517,998

3. An arrangement which in case of emergency, will give to the President, the prompt command of a further and efficacious military force.

This ought to be, a provisional army of 20,000 men, and may be organized agreeable to the principles of a bill proposed in the Senate during the late extraordinary session, to which I beg leave to refer.

4. The more complete defence of our principal ports by fortifications.

This may require, 100,0000 of dollars, but should the naval force be rendered respectable, much of this sum may be saved.

5. A supply of cannon, small arms, salt petre, copper, &c. which, severally, will require—

For cannon, as per estimate, dolls. 308,900

For small arms, say 50,000 stands, at 12 dolls. 600,000

For powder, salt petre, copper for sheathing, &c. 200,000

In framing the law, to furnish our magazines with ordnance, it will be proper to employ such expressions, as will enable the President to procure brass cannon, mortars, &c. with the necessary quantities of ball, shells, &c. These have not been specified in the estimate; but the sum may, perhaps, be sufficient to comprehend them.

To render the regiment of infantry as useful as possible, it is proposed, that the men should be enlisted to act in the double capacity of marines and infantry. By an arrangement of this kind, and having the men stationed at the principal sea ports, they will be always ready to be put on board such vessels as want them, and when not so wanted, will serve to defend the coast, work upon the fortifications, or in dock yards, and guard the public property from thefts or embezzlement.

All which is respectfully submitted.

JAMES MCHENRY.

HON. SAM. SEWALL, *chairman of the committee for the protection of commerce, and the defence of the country.*

[LC, "Claypoole's American Daily Advertiser" (Phila.), 20 April, 1798.]

To Samuel Hodgdon, indendant of military stores, from Secretary of War

[PHILADELPHIA,]
War Office, April 9th 1798

SAMl HODGDON Esquire.

SIR I have to request that you will be pleased to have the Military Stores contained in the list herewith enclosed, transported to the Frigate *Constitution* at Boston in the safest and most expeditious manner.—

I beg the favor of you to report what part are deposited in the public stores.—

A List of Articles to be transported to Boston for the Frigate *Constitution*.—Vizt.

100 pairs of Pistols.
200 Cutlasses
750 Stools of grape and Cannister shot ---------- 24 pounders
300-- Do----Do----------do---------- 12 pounders

450	Double Headed & chain Shot	24 pounders
210	Double Headed Chain shot	12 pounders
1750	Round Shot	12 pounders
60	Muskets with accoutrements & Complete for Marines	
8	Brass Hilted Hangers with Belts for Serjeants &c	
3	Suits of Serjeants Cloathing — including Blankets	
55	— d. Privates (including 2 Musicians & 3 Corporals)	d°
60	Knapsacks.	
2	Drums Complete with spare heads	
2	Fifes with slings complete.	
360	Musket Flints.	
80	Flints for Blunderbusses	
720	__ d°____assorted.	
3000	Flannel Cartridges	for 24 pounders
1400	__ d°	for 12 pounders
20	Dozen Portfires	
180	Priming Tubes —	
60	__ ditto___d°	
12	Dressed Sheep Skins	
4	Cwt of Match Stuff	
50	Quire Cannon Cartridge paper	
20	__ d°__of Musket __ d°	
10	__ d°__of Pistol ____d°	
12	Pouch Barrels	
1	Box Spermacita or Wax Candles	
30	Lynch Stocks.—	

[NDA, LB. Correspondence when Navy was under War Department, 1795–1798.]

To Samuel Hodgdon from Secretary of War

[PHILADELPHIA,]
War Office 12th April 1798.

SAML HODGDON Esquire. —

SIR I have inclosed an Order on Tench Francis Esquire to deliver you the Provisions intended for the Frigate *Constellation*, which I request you will be pleased to take order to have transported to that Ship as soon as may be. —

By the last account from Captain Truxtun it appears that the *Constellation* was at anchor at the mouth of the Patapsco in his way to the Patuxent, whither he intended to proceed with the first favorable wind. —

I am &c

[NDA, LB. Correspondence when Navy was under War Department, 1795–1798.]

[14 April, 1798]

Information furnished by Captain John B. Thurston, of the Brig *Commerce*, concerning the French Privateer *La Revenge*, et cetera

Sailed from Gibraltar, March 30, '98 — April 14, in lat. 36 degrees N. long. 26 W. saw a vessel at break of day, and soon perceived she was in chase of us. We made all the sail we could, but about 9 o'clock

a. m. she came up and gave us a gun. I then hove our main-topsail to the mast, and showed our colors. The captain ordered me to hoist out my boat and come on board, with my papers, which I did. She proved to be the French ship *La Revenge*, capt. Grallet, of 16 guns from Bourdeaux. He immediately hoisted out his boat and sent on board the *Commerce*, but they returned with only plundering a few boxes of raisins, fruit, &c. The captain then ordered a research by different officers, who, after digging in the salt about two hours, discovered 22 jars, in which were 11,000 dollars, the property of Mess. Murray and Mumford, and John and R. B. Forbes, of New-York, which was taken on board the privateer. I was then stripped in the privateer's cabin, even to my shirt and robbed of money to the amount of 160 dollars in gold, belonging to Mr. Benj B. Mumford. They threatened to burn or sink my vessel, if I withheld any money, which on search they should afterwards discover. Capt. Grallet ordered 5 Americans on board of my vessel, belonging to the brig *Farmer*, capt. Jacob Whittimore, of New-York, from Liverpool and Milford-Haven, bound to St. Michaels which they captured on the 11th April, in lat. 38, 40, N. long. 26, 16. W. and sent into Bourdeaux. After refusing to give up my letters, we were ordered to make off, when we soon lost sight of the privateer.

[LC, "Claypoole's American Daily Advertiser" (Phila.), 2 June 1798.]

To Captain John Barry, U. S. Navy, from Secretary of War

[PHILADELPHIA,]
War Department 18th April 1798

Capt JOHN BARRY

SIR, I enclose you a Copy of the Letter which you are to deliver to the Governor of the State of New York. You will wait upon Mr Jay if at New York and receive such orders as he may be pleased to give, and make such Examination of the Cannon as will enable you to ascertain their effectiveness and fitness for the service. Should you approve of them, you will put Things in a Train to have them shipped for Philada as soon as I can send the Governor the Assurance from the President required by the Resolution of the Legislature of the State of N. York. —

[NDA. OSW, Vol. 1.]

To Captain John Barry, U. S. Navy, from David Porter

BALTIMORE *April 18th 1798*

SIR After Saluteing You. Beg leave once more to trouble you. As Ships of War is to be provided, and to every appearance a War is inevitable, (*in consequence I offer to Serve,*) I wish to be on the Stage of Action once more, Be pleased to take the Necessary Steps, that I may if possible Obtain a Command, let me request of you to inform me of the channel through which the applications are made, and if further Steps is necessary to be taken by me." " " "

Wishing you health and prosperity,
And Remain Dear Sir,
Yours with the Greatest Respect

My Best respects to Mrs Barry } DAVID PORTER

Captain BARRY

P. S. I have put my Son David on board the frigate *Constellation.* (A Midshipman) he is Just Entered his 19th year, he is active, and promising, and understands navigation Well, a tolerable good Scholer other ways; has been Several voyages to Sea, And flatter myself he will use exertions to merit Something in our Young Navy.

[HS. of Pa. NDA photostat.]

To John Harris, Storekeeper, from Secretary of War

[PHILADELPHIA,]
War Office, 19th April 1798.

Mr JOHN HARRIS

SIR Be pleased to deliver to the Purveyor a sufficient quantity of Iron and Lead Grape shot for filling the Cannisters for the Frigates, *United States*, *Constitution*, and *Constellation.* —

[NDA, LB. Correspondence when Navy was under War Department, 1795–1798.]

To Benjamin Lincoln, Collector, Boston, from Secretary of the Treasury Oliver Wolcott

TREASURY DEPARTMENT,
April 20 1798.

BENJAMIN LINCOLN Esq.
Collector of Boston Massachusetts

SIR, I have received your letter of April 13th with the letter to you from sundry merchants of Boston, These Gentlemen must be better judges of what would be the most suitable construction of an armed vessell than I can pretend to be, and I authorize you to follow their opinion so far as it consists with your judgment, It ought however to be recollected that Congress are providing a naval force for the defence of Commerce and that a principal — though not a sole object of the Cutter establishment is the *protection of the Revenue.*

It is my wish that the work may be completed as soon as possible, and to avoid delay I have to request you to take measures for providing the Gun Carriages and whatever else may be necessary to a speedy and effectual equipment without waiting for further advices from this department.

I am with Consideration Sir
Your Mo. Obedt. Servt.

OLIVER WOLCOTT.

[TD. Coast Guard Out. Letters, No. 0, 1790–1833.]

To Captain Samuel Nicholson, U.S. Navy, from Secretary of War

[PHILADELPHIA,]
War Office, 21st April 1798

Capt Saml NICHOLSON

SIR, Your Letters of the 15th Current, have been received. —

I have no Objection to the Canonades being cast for your Ship on the Plan proposed. Mr Revere will accordingly prepare them with all convenient Dispatch. —

It should be understood that the Canonades must undergo the usual Proofs and Examinations, and will not be received if their Defects should be greater than usually tolerated.

You will be pleased to select proper Characters for Boatswain, Gunner, Carpenter, Sailmaker and Midshipmen, and report their Names, that I may be enabled to lay them before the President. —

The Medicine Chest for your Ship, and a complete Sett of Instruments are preparing and will be sent on as soon as possible.

[NDA, OSW, Vol. 1.]

To Henry Philips, merchant, from Secretary of War

[PHILADELPHIA,]
War Office 23rd April 1798.

Mr HENRY PHILIPS
Merchant

SIR, I am informed that a vessel of yours, called the *America* which arrived this morning in the Port of Philadelphia is calculated for an armed Ship and capable of being moulded with 16 nine or Six pounders — Should you be inclined to dispose of the vessel alluded to — I beg the favor of you to inform me of the lowest Price you would require, and also a fair description of the vessel & Stores —

I am with great respect &c:

[NDA, LB. Correspondence when Navy was under War Department, 1790–1798.]

To Joshua Humphreys and Captain Thomas Thompson from Secretary of War

[PHILADELPHIA,]
War Office 25th Apl 1798.

JOSHUA HUMPHREYS Esq
THOS THOMPSON Capt.

GENTn You will be pleased to examine the Ship *Two Friends*, and report her age, the exact State of her Hull, Masts & Yards, rigging, Sails, and every other particular by which a Judgement can be formed of her Value, also the number of Guns she can carry, and your opinion as to her fitness for a vessel of War — You will also State the alterations, repairs & articles, which she will require to fit her for Sea — The Time in which she can be so fitted, and an estimate of the expense. —

[NDA, LB. Correspondence when Navy was under War Department, 1790–1798.]

[27 April 1798]

An act to provide an additional armament for the further protection of the trade of the United States; and for other purposes

SECTION 1. *Be it enacted by the Senate and House of Representatives of the United States of America in Congress assembled,* That the President of the United States shall be, and he is hereby authorized and empowered, to cause to be built, purchased or hired, a number of vessels, not exceeding twelve, nor carrying more than twenty-two guns each, to be armed, fitted out and manned under his direction.

SEC. 2. *And be it further enacted,* That the number and grade of the officers to be appointed for the service of the said vessels, shall be fixed by the President of the United States, as well as the number of men of which the respective crews shall be composed, who, as well officers as seamen and marines, shall receive the same pay and subsistence, be entitled to the same advantages and compensations, be governed by the same rules and regulations, and be engaged for the same time, and on the same conditions, as by an act of the United States, passed the first of July, one thousand seven hundred and ninety-seven, entitled "An act providing a naval armament," is ascertained and established, as fully, as if the particular provisions of that act, having reference thereto, were herein inserted at large. *Provided always, and be it further enacted,* That the President of the United States be, and he is hereby authorized to cause the term of enlistment of the seamen and marines, to be employed in any vessel of the United States, to be extended beyond one year, if the vessel should then be at sea, and until ten days after such vessel shall arrive in some convenient port of the United States, thereafter; any thing contained in this act, or in the act entitled "An act providing a naval armament," to the contrary notwithstanding.

SEC. 3. *And be it further enacted,* That the officers of the aforesaid vessels may, during the recess of the Senate, be appointed and commissioned by the President alone.

SEC. 4. *And be it further enacted,* That the sum of nine hundred and fifty thousand dollars, be and are hereby appropriated out of any monies in the treasury of the United States, beyond the appropriations that may heretofore have been charged thereon, for the purpose of carrying the objects of this act into effect.

Approved, April 27, 1798.

[Statute II.—Page 552.]

To James Craufurd and John Donaldson from Secretary of War

[PHILADELPHIA,]
War Department 28th April 1879

Messrs JAMES CRAUFURD }
& JN^o DONALDSON }

GENT^n Should your convenience admit, you are requested to examine the Ship *Ganges* — and report her age, the exact State of her Hull, Masts & Yards, Rigging, Sails, and every other particular by which a Judgment can be formed of her value, also the Number of Guns she can carry, and your opinion as to here fitness for a vessel of War — You will also State the alterations, repairs, and articles, which She will require to fit her for Sea — The Time in which She can be so fitted, and an Estimate of the Expense —

I am Gentⁿ &cª

[NDA, LB. Correspondence when Navy was under War Department, 1790–1798.]

[28 April, 1798]

Purchase of Revenue Cutter *Active*

Sale at Auction of The Revenue Cutter *Active*, Captain David Porter, & order of Robert Purviance Esqr — for Account of The United States on 90 Days Credit —

BALTIMORE *April 28th 1798*

The Revenue Cutter *Active* with all her Tackle &c	Doll 750.0	Davd Porter		$750.0
Charges				
Duties & Commission 2 p Cent			$15. 0	
Pd Advertising in The Several news papers			1. 50	
				16.50
Net Proceeds —				$733.50

Errors Excepted —

YATES & CAMPBELL
Auctioneers

Received from Robt. Purviance Esqr Sixteen Dolls & fifty cents in full for the above charges

YATES & CAMPBELL
27 June '98

$16.50

Robert Purviance Agent for the Sale of the Cutter *Active*
To the United States .... Dr
For Net proceeds of the Sale of said Cutter per the within acct .. Dollars 733.50

Auditors office
February 26th 1800

FERRALL

[GAO, #11,271.]

[30 April 1798]

An act to establish an executive department, to be denominated the Department of the Navy

SECTION 1. *Be it enacted by the Senate and House of Representatives of the United States of America in Congress assembled*, That there shall be an executive department under the denomination of the Department of the Navy, the chief officer of which shall be called the Secretary of the Navy, whose duty it shall be to execute such orders as he shall receive from the President of the United States, relative to the procurement of naval stores and materials and the construction, armament, equipment and employment of vessels of war, as well as all other matters connected with the naval establishment of the United States.

SEC. 2. *And be it further enacted*, That a principal clerk and such other clerks as he shall think necessary, shall be appointed by the Secretary of the Navy, who shall be employed in such manner as he shall deem most expedient. In case of vacancy in the office of the secretary, by removal or otherwise, it shall be the duty of the principal clerk to take the charge and custody of all the books, records and documents of the said office.

SEC. 3. *And be it further enacted*, That the Secretary of the Navy be and he is hereby authorized and empowered, immediately after he shall be appointed and shall enter upon the duties of his office, to take possession of all the records, books and documents and all other matters and things appertaining to this department, which are now deposited in the office of the Secretary at War.

SEC. 4. *And be it further enacted*, That there shall be allowed to the Secretary of the Navy an annual salary of three thousand dollars, payable quarter yearly at the treasury of the United States, and the respective clerks in the office of the said department shall receive the same compensations and be subject to the same regulations, as are provided by an act, supplemental to the act, establishing the treasury department, and for a further compensation to certain officers, in the office of the other executive departments.

SEC. 5. *And be it further enacted*, That so much of an act, entitled "An act to establish an executive department, to be denominated the department of war," as vests any of the powers contemplated by the provisions of this act, in the Secretary for the department of War, shall be repealed, from and after the period when the Secretary of the Navy shall enter on the duties of his office.

Approved, April 30, 1798.

[Statute II., page 553.]

[May, 1798.]

Extract of letter from Captain John Pitman, concerning Captain Very's ship being boarded by a French Privateer

SALEM, *May 29.*

[Extract of a letter from Capt. John Pitman, dated at Baltimore, May 28]

"Last Monday, being in the Bay, beating up, with the wind from the northward, fell in with Capt. Very, of Salem, off New Point Comfort. He informed of his being boarded by a French privateer sloop of 16 guns, on his passage, which put on board of him the masters and crews of five American vessels which they had taken on our coast belonging to Boston and New-York, who were then all on board, 48 in number, as I understood. Having a fresh breeze, and passing by him quick, could not get particulars, but understood they were all outward bound. Expect the particulars by to-morrows post from Alexandria, as I think Capt. V. must have arrived there on Friday or Saturday last."

[LC, "Columbian Centinel" (Boston, Mass.), 30 May 1798.]

To James Yeomans, master carpenter, from Captain Thomas Truxtun, U. S. Navy

UNITED STATE'S SHIP, *Constellation*
Patuxent May 1st 1798—

SIR, You will in your Capacity as Master Carpenter of this Ship in the Navy of the United States, be particularly careful of all the Spars, Boats Oars, Pump Gear, Tools, Pitch, Rosin, Turpentine, Varnish, Paints, Oil, and all other Stores in your Department, and have the same at Hand, and ready for Use at all Times. You will see, that every Matter appertaining to your Business, is kept in repair, and report any Defects, that may appear, as soon as it is seen. You are particularly charged with having the Ship well wet Night and Morning, *inside and out*, and to enable you to do all and every Part of your Business with Convenience, you may partially employ such of the Crew to aid you, as the Officer of the Deck may deem necessary, independent of your Mates; and Yeoman. You will be very particular in keeping an Account of all Expenditures. I am Sir,

Your Obedient &c.

THOMAS TRUXTUN.

Mr JAMES YEOMANS.

[HS of Pa. NDA Photostat. Truxtun's LB, 1798–9.]

To Colonel Thomas Thompson from Secretary Timothy Pickering

DEPARTMENT OF STATE *Philadelphia*
May 2, 1798

Colo THOMAS THOMPSON

SIR, As the officers and crew of the *Cresent* frigate were engaged chiefly at Portsmouth in New Hampshire, it is probably that the vessel which Captain O'Brian shall procure to bring them home, may steer for that place; or for some port in Massachusetts; in which case it will be convenient to have them paid off by you — at least all those who shall return to Portsmouth and Newbury-Port, and probably the others, few in number, belonging to the neighbouring ports.

I have therefore to request you to settle the accounts of Officers and men of the *Crescent*, and pay them the balances due to them; which you will be enabled to do satisfactorily from your acquaintance with every matter concerning them previous to their sailing.

Should any money, cloathing or other articles have been furnished to them by Captain O'Brien, or others, Captain Newman or other officer of the ship will doubtless furnish you with the documents requisite for an exact adjustment of their accounts.

If any stores procured on public account for the use of the officers and crew of the *Crescent* should remain, on their return, you will receive and dispose of them for the best advantage of the U. States.

You may draw on me for the monies necessary to execute these Orders. I am respectfully &c

TIMOTHY PICKERING

[SDA. Dom. L., Vol. 10.]

[3 May 1798]

Purchase of Ship *Adriana*

KNOW ALL MEN by these presents, That I Seth Barton of the City of Baltimore Merchant Sole Owner of the Ship *Adriana* for and in consideration of the Sum of twenty Seven thousand Dollars current Money of the U. S. to Me in hand paid by the United States of America, the receipt whereof is hereby acknowledged, HAVE, and by these Presents Do, Grant, Bargain, Sell, Assign, Transfer, and set over unto the said United States, all that the Ship *Adriana* together with all her Masts, Yards, Sails, Rigging, Anchors, Cables, Boats, Tackle, Apparel and Appurtenances, Which said Vessel is Registered in the Port of Baltimore in the words following, to wit:

Permanent.

[SEAL OF THE TREASURY OF THE UNITED STATES]

"No. 69, Sixty nine In pursuance of an Act of Congress "of the United States of America, entitled, "An Act "concerning the Registering and recording of Ships or "Vessels — Seth Barton of Baltimore Town Merchant "having taken or subscribed the Oath required by the "said Act, and having Sworn that he is the only Owner "of the Ship or Vessel, called the *Adriana* of Baltimore, "whereof Philemon Dawson is at present Master, and is "a Citizen of the United States, as he has Sworn and that "the said Ship or Vessel was built at this place this "present Year; as also appears by the Certificate of "Joseph Caverly of this place, Master Builder, and "Daniel DeLozier, Surveyor of this District, having "certified that the said Ship or Vessel has two Decks and "three Masts, that her Length is one hundred and three "feet-nine inches,
"her Breadth thirty feet and eight inches, her Depth "____________________ and that she measures Four "hundred and twenty two & 32/95 Tons, that she is a "square sterned Ship, has quarter Galleries and a Woman "figure head and the said Seth Barton having agreed to "the Description and ad Measurement above specified "and sufficient security having been given according to "the said Act, the said Ship has been duly registered at "the Port of Baltimore

"Given under our Hands and Seals At the Port of "Baltimore Maryland this second Day of May in the "Year One Thousand Seven Hundred and Ninety-five."

TO HAVE AND TO HOLD the said Ship *Adriana* with the appurtenances as aforesaid unto the said United States of America, their Executors, Administrators and Assigns, for ever. And I the said Seth Barton for me, my Heirs, Executors and Administrators, Do hereby Covenant and Agree to and with the said United States, their Executors, Administrators and Assigns, that at the Execution of these Presents, I the said Seth Barton have full right and authority to Sell and Dispose of the same, freed from and cleared of all Claims, Incumbrances or Demands whatsoever.

IN WITNESS WHEREOF, I have hereunto set my Hand and Seal the Twenty third Day of May, in the Year of our Lord One Thousand Seven Hundred and Ninety eight.

Signed, Sealed, and Delivered
In Presence of } SETH BARTON
THOMAS FISHER
R WEDERSTRANDT.

[GAO, No. 9, 803.]

[3 May 1798]

Purchase of Ship *Ganges*

KNOW ALL MEN by these Presents, that I Thomas Willing Francis, together with Thomas Willing, and Thomas Mayne Willing, of the City of Philadelphia and State of Pennsylvania, Merchants, Owners of the Ship called the *Ganges* of Philadelphia, on the one part, for and in consideration of the Sum of Fifty eight thousand Dollars, to us in Hand paid by the United States of America, of the other part, the receipt whereof, is hereby acknowledged, Have, and by these Presents, do grant, Bargain, Sell, Assign, transfer, and Set over, unto the said United States of America, the whole of the said Ship, called the *Ganges* of Philadelphia, together with all and every her Masts, Yards, Sails, Rigging, Anchors, Cables, Boats, Tackle, Guns, Stores, Provisions, Apparel and Appurtenances, as She now lays in this Port— which said Vessel is Registered in the Port of Philadelphia, in the Words following to. Wit: Nº 7. Seven. —

Permanent.

Seal of the Treasury of the United States Joseph Nourse Register—

In Pursuance of An Act of the Congress of the United States of America, entitled, An Act concerning the registering and recording of Ships or Vessels, Thomas Willing Francis, of the City of Philadelphia, Merchant, having taken or subscribed the Oath required by the said Act, and having Sworn that he said Thomas Willing Francis together with Thomas Willing and Thomas Mayne Willing both of said City, Merchants, are the true and only owners of the Ship or Vessel called the *Ganges* of Philadelphia, whereof Richard Dale is at present Master, and is a Citizen of the United States as he hath Sworn, and that the said Ship or Vessel was built at Philadelphia, in the State of Pennsylvania in the Year One thousand Seven hundred and ninety five, Per former Register Nº 221, issued from this office, and dated 6th July 1796. now delivered up to be Cancelled — And Walter Stewart late Surveyor of this District, having Certified that the said Ship or Vessel, has two Decks, and three Masts, and that her length is One hundred sixteen feet four inches — her breadth Thirty one feet four inches — her depth Fifteen feet eight inches — and that She measures Five hundred and four Tons — that She is a carved square Sterned Ship, has double quarter Galleries, and Stern Gallery,

Seal of the Custom House of Philada

Sharp Delany Collr

Wm Tilton Dynoff

round house, and a [space]head; and the Said Thomas William Francis having agreed to the description, and admeasurement above Specified, and Sufficient Security having been given according to the said Act, the Said Ship, has been duly Registered at the Port of Philadelphia — Given under My Hand and Seal, at the Port of Philadelphia, this Seventeenth Day of January, in the Year, One thousand seven hundred and ninety eight.

To have and to hold the Said Ship, called the *Ganges* of Philadelphia, together with all and every her appurtenances as aforesaid, unto the said United States of America, for ever. And I the Said Thomas Willing Francis together with Thomas Willing and Thomas Mayne Willing, for ourselves, our Heirs, Executors, and Administrators, do hereby Covenant, and Agree, to and with the Said United States of America, that the the Execution of these presents, We the Said Thomas Willing Francis, Thomas Willing, and Thomas Mayne Willing, are the true and lawfull Owners of the said Ship, called the *Ganges* of Philadelphia, and appurtenances, and We now have full right and Authority, to Sell and dispose of the Same, freed from and Cleared of all Claims, Incumbrances, or Demands, whatsoever —

In Witness whereof, We have hereunto Set our Hands, and Seals, the third Day of May, in the Year of our Lord One Thousand seven hundred and ninety eight —

Sign'd and Seal'd in the presence of
Wm Govett.
Sam Smith.

Thos Willing.
Thos M. Willing
Thos W. Francis.

[GAO, No. 9749.]

[4 May 1798]

An act to authorize the President of the United States to cause to be purchased, or built, a number of small vessels to be equipped as gallies, or otherwise.

Section 1. *Be it enacted by the Senate and House of Representatives of the United States of America in Congress assembled,* That the President of the United States be, and he is hereby authorized if the same shall appear to him necessary for the protection of the United States, to cause a number of small vessels, not exceeding ten to be built, or purchased, and to be fitted out, manned, armed and equipped as gallies, or otherwise, in the service of the United States, the officers and men to be on the same pay, and to receive the same subsistence, as officers of the same rank and men are entitled to, in the navy of the United States.

Sec. 2. *And be it further enacted,* That the said officers shall be appointed and commissioned by the President of the United States alone during the recess of the Senate; and the said gallies or vessels shall be stationed in such parts of the United States, as he may direct.

Sec. 3. *And be it further enacted,* That there be appropriated for the purpose aforesaid, the sum of eighty thousand dollars, out of any monies in the treasury not otherwise appropriated.

Approved, May 4, 1798.

[Statute II, page 556.]

To Messrs. Willings & Francis, agents, from Secretary of War

[PHILADELPHIA,]
War Department 4th May 1798

Messrs WILLINGS & FRANCIS

GENTn Captain Dale has accepted the Command of the *Ganges*, and received Instructions to direct the Naval Constructor to cause such alterations and improvements to be promptly made, as may be necessary to prepare the Ship in every respect for Sea, and as effective as possible for the purposes she is destined — You are requested to accept the Agency of paying the Workmen employed and procuring such additional Stores and other Articles as being indispensible and proper, may be directed — In all these cases you will procure and preserve such vouchers as may be proper to be produced to the accounting officers —

[NDA, LB. Correspondence when Navy was under War Department 1790–1798.]

To Midshipman James McDonough from Secretary of War

[PHILADELPHIA,]
War Department 4th May, 1798.

JAs McDONOUGH

SIR, You will forthwith and without Loss of Time repair on Board the Frigate *Constitution* commanded by Capt Samuel Nicholson laying at Boston, and put yourself under his Orders, any thing contained in my letter of the 26th April ultimo notwithstanding, to which vessel you will consider Yourself appointed a Midshipman.

[NDA. OSW, Vol. 1]

To Captain Samuel Nicholson, U. S. Navy, from Secretary of War

[PHILADELPHIA,]
War Department, 5th May, 1798.

Capt NICHOLSON Boston

SIR, I have it in command from the President, to direct you to repair on board the Ship *Constitution* laying at Boston, and to lose no Time in completing, equipping and manning her for Sea. —

The Lieutenant of Marines will immediately proceed to inlist, agreeably to the inclosed Instructions, and the Act intitled an "Act providing a Naval Armament" passed the first of July 1797. —

You will forthwith cause such of the Sea Officers, as may appear best calculated for the Business, to open houses of Rendezvous in proper Places, and to exert Themselves to engage One hundred and Fifty able Seamen, and One hundred and Three Midshipmen and ordinary Seamen, at the following Terms of Service and Rates of Wages. The Seamen to engage for twelve Months unless sooner discharged. The Pay of the Able Seamen to be seventeen dollars per Month the ordinary Seamen Ten Dollars. —

You will instruct the Officers at each Rendezvous, to engage none other than healthy robust and well organized Men, and to reject those who may be scorbutic or consumptively affected. You will direct the Surgeon or a Mate to attend at these Places to examine each Sailor and Marine, and to certify to the recruiting Officer, that they are well organized, healthy and robust, and free from scorbutic and consumptive Affections, before he engages them or pays them any Money. If Money is advanced or paid to any without such a Certificate, it will be at the risk of the Officer paying it. —

The Officer of each Rendezvous shall make out on every Saturday a Return of the Number of Seamen recruited within the Week, Stating therein the Number delivered over to the Ship, and transmit the same to the Captain, and a Duplicate to be forwarded to the Sec^y^ for the department of War. —

You will also transmit to the Sec^y^ of the Department of War — a weekly Return exhibiting the Number of Marines, able and ordinary Seamen on board the Ship, and the Incidents that have taken place respecting Them or any of Them; as also the Progress that has been made in preparing her for Sea. —

The commanding officer at each Rendezvous, on the desetion of a Seaman or Marine, besides the usual Exertions and Means to be employed on such occasions to recover and apprehend them, will transmit as soon as possible a Description of Them to the Secretary of War. —

With respect to the Pay of the Marines and Seamen. The Purser, 'till order'd otherwise, will act as Pay-Master to the officers and Crew, and will receive from time to time Money for that Purpose.

Marines may be advanced Two Dollars, out of their first Month's Pay — and Seamen Two Month's Pay, if they cannot be obtained without such Advance. —

The recruit^g^ Officers will be held accountable for all Monies paid in their hands for the recruiting service — for the Expenditure of which, proper vouchers must be produced at the Accountant's Office.

The Names of the Marines and Seamen are to be entered alphabetically in the Muster and Pay Rolls, and the Men to be mustered while in Port by a qualified Person, whose Certificate as well as your's is to be attached to the Muster Roll. —

It is the President's express orders, that you employ the most vigorous Exertions, to accomplish these several Objects and to put your Ship, as speedily as possible, in a Situation to sail at the shortest Notice. —

Should any Articles for this Purpose, be yet wanting, you will specify them without delay, in order to their being procured. —

[NDA. OSW, Vol. 1.]

[5 May 1798]

To Daniel Carmick, lieutenant of Marines, from Secretary of War

[PHILADELPHIA,]

DAN^l^ CARMICK Lieu^t^ Marines on board the *Ganges*.

Sir, The President of the United States, by and with the Advice and Consent of the Senate, having appointed you a Lieutenant of Marines on board the Ship *Ganges*,

You will be pleased to commence the recruiting the Complement of Marines allowed by Law to the said Ship. — to wit — One Searjeant, One Corporal, One Drum and Fife, and Twenty one Privates. In performance of this Duty, you will pay particular Attention to the Rules and Regulations hereinafter mentioned.

Here follows the Rules and Regulations, similar to those given to the Lieutenant on Board the *Constellation*, for which refer to Pages 5, 6, & 7. —

Given at the War Office of the United States, this fifth day of May A. D. 1798 and in the Twenty second year of the Independence of said States. —

[NOTE.—Pages 5, 6 and 7 above referred to contain enlistment instructions dated 16 March 1798, addressed to the Lieutenant of Marines on board the Frigate *Constellation.*]

[NDA. OSW, Vol. 1.]

[5 May 1798]

To Lemuel Clerk, lieutenant of Marines, from Secretary of War

[PHILADELPHIA,]
War Department,

LEMUEL CLERK Lieutenant of Marines. Boston.

Sir, The President of the United States, by and with the Advice and Consent of the Senate, having appointed you a Lieutenant of Marines on board the *Constitution*, You will be be pleased to commence the recruiting the Complement of Marines allowed by Law to the said Ship — to wit — Three Serjeant — Three Corporals — One Drum, and Fife, and Fifty Privates. In the Performance of these Rules and Regulations you will pay particular Attention to the Rules and Regulations herein after mentioned. —

Here follows the Rules and Regulations, similar to Those given to the Lieutenant on board the *Constellation* for which, See Pages 5, 6. & 7. —

Given at the War Office of the United States, this 5th day of May — A. D. 1798. and in the twenty second Year of the Independence of said States. —

[NOTE.—Pages 5, 6 and 7 above referred to contain recruiting instructions dated 16 March 1798, addressed to the Lieutenant of Marines on board the Frigate *Constellation.*]

[NDA. OSW, Vol. 1.]

[5 May 1798]

Purchase of Ship *Hamburgh Packet*

KNOW ALL MEN by these presents, that I Philip Nicklin, together with Robert E. Griffith, of the City of Philadelphia, and State of Pennsylvania, Merchants, Owners of the Ship called the *Hamburgh Packet* of Philadelphia, on the one part, for and in Consideration of the Sum of Forty five thousand Dollars, to us in Hand paid by the United States of America, of the other part, the receipt whereof is hereby acknowledged, Have, and by these Presents do Grant, Bargain, Sell, Assign, transfer and Set over, unto the Said United States of America, the whole of the Said Ship, called the *Hamburgh Packet* of Philadelphia, together with all and every her Masts, Yards, Sails, rigging, Anchors, Cables, Boats, Tackle, Guns, Stores, Provisions, Apparel, and Appurtenances, as She now lays in this

Port. — Which Said Vessel is Registered in the Port of Philadelphia, in the Words following to Wit: Nº 269. Two hundred and Sixty nine. —

Permanent

Seal of the Treasury of the United States

Joseph Nourse Register

Seal of the Custom House of Phiadª

Sharp Delany Collº

W Macpherson N. Off —

In Pursuance of an Act of the Congress of the United States of America, entitled, An Act concerning the registering and recording of Ships or Vessels, Philip Nicklin of the City of Philadelphia, Merchant, having taken or Subscribed the Oath required by the Said Act, and having Sworn, that he said Philip Nicklin, together with Robert E Griffith of said City Merchant, are the true and only Owners of the Ship or Vessel, called the *Hamburgh Packet* of Philadelphia, whereof Silas Swain is at present Master, and is a Citizen of the United States as he hath Sworn, and that the said Ship or Vessel was built at Philadelphia, in the State of Pennsylvania, in the Year One thousand Seven hundred and Ninety four, per former Register Nº 351. Issued from this Office, and dated 31st October 1795. now delivered up to be Cancelled. And Walter Stewart Surveyor of this District, having Certified that the said Ship or Vessel has two decks, and three Masts, and that her length is Ninety four feet nine inches, her Breadth Twenty eight feet, — her depth Fourteen feet, — and that She Measures Three hundred twenty one & 64/95 Tons that She is a carved square Sterned Ship, has quarter Galleries, Ten Carriage Guns, and a Man Indian head, and the Said Philip Nicklin having agreed to the description and admeasurement above specified, and sufficient Security having been given according to the said Act, the said Ship has been duly registered at the port of Philadelphia. —

Given under my Hand and Seal at the Port of Philadelphia, this Eighth Day of December, in the Year One Thousand seven hundred and ninety seven.

To have and to hold the said Ship called the *Hamburgh Packet* of Philadelphia, together with all and every her Appurtenances as aforesaid, unto the said United States of America forever. — and I the said Philip Nicklin together with Robert E Griffith, for ourselves, our Heirs, Executors, and Administrators, do hereby Covenant and Agree, to and with the said United States of America, that at the Execution of these Presents, we the Said Philip Nicklin and Robert E Griffith, are the true and lawful Owners of the said Ship, called the *Hamburgh Packet* of Philadelphia, and Appurtenances, and We now have full right and Authority to Sell and dispose of the same, freed from and Cleared of all Claims, Incumbrances or Demands whatsoever. —

In Witness whereof, We have hereunto Set Our Hands and Seals, the fifth Day of May, in the Year of our Lord, One Thousand Seven hundred and Ninety eight.

Sign'd and Seal'd
in the presence of
SAM SMITH. .
PHILIP YONGE.

PHILIP NICKLIN
ROBt E. GRIFFITH

[GAO, No. 9,800.]

To Captain John Barry, U. S. Navy, from Secretary of War

[PHILADELPHIA,]
Navy Department, 5th *May. 1798.*

Capt BARRY.

SIR, I have it in command from the President of the United States, to direct you to repair with all due Speed on board the Frigate *United States* laying at Philadelphia

It is requested that no Time be lost in compleating what Work is yet to be done and preparing her in every respect for Sea.

The Lieutenant of Marines will immediately proceed. &c &c. Refer to pages 21. 22. 23 & 24. [Note. These pages contain letter of 5 May, 1798 to Captain Samuel Nicholson.]

Having selected proper Characters for Boatswain, Gunner, Carpenter and Sail Maker — you will return their Names, that they may be laid before the President. —

[NDA. OSW, Vol. 1.]

To John Harris, storekeeper, from Secretary of War

[PHILADELPHIA,]
War Department May 5th *1798*

Mr JOHN HARRIS

SIR Be pleased to deliver to the order of Captain Richard Dale for the use of the *Ganges* Forty Tons Iron Kentledge. —

[NDA, LB. Correspondence when Navy was under War Department, 1795–1798.]

The following list bears no date, but its place in Letter Book is between May 7, 1798 and April 18, 1798, on page 10

Monthly Pay of Petty Officers, Seamen, Ordinary Seamen, and Marines on board the Frigates of the United States.

Midshipmen	19	Dollars	Each	per	Month
Masters Mates	20	do	–"–		do
Captain's Clerks	25	do	–"–		do
Boatswain's Mates	19	do	–"–		do
Cockswain	18	do	–"–		do
Sail Maker's Mates	19	do	–"–		do
Gunner's Mates	19	do	–"–		do
Yeomen of the Gun Room	18	do	–"–		do
Quarter Gunners	18	do	–"–		do
Carpenter's Mates	19	do	–"–		do
Armourers	18	do	–"–		do
Steward's	18	do	–"–		do
Coopers	18	do	–"–		do
Master's at Arms	18	do	–"–		do
Quarter Masters	18	do	–"–		do
Cooks	18	do	–"–		do
Seamen	17	do	–"–		do
Ordinary Seamen	10	do	–"–		do
Marines—					
Serjeants	9	do	–"–		do
Corporals	8	do	–"–		do
Drums & Fifes	7	do	–"–		do
Privates	6	do	–"–		do

[NDA. OSW, Vol. 1.]

To Governor John Jay from Secretary of War

[PHILADELPHIA,]
War Department 7th *May 1798*

His Excellency JOHN JAY

SIR I had the honour to receive your excellency's letters dated the 7th of April Ulto and am now authorized to communicate to you the assurance of the President of the United States, that he will cause an equal number of Cannon of the like dimensions, and cast at the same Foundery to be delivered to the State of New York, in return for such cannon as may be received from the said State for the use of the United States, under a resulution of the legislature of the said State dated the 27th of April Ulto —

Capt Barry commander of the *United States* Frigate, was sent some time since to examine and prove the cannon in question. He has reported favorably of a part, being all he had an opportunity of determining the suitableness of, and left instructions, respecting the remainder necessary to complete the number, which I have no doubt will be observed when they are sent down the River

Those approved of, are at Governors Island, and as the exigency requires no time shou'd be lost in forwarding them to the vessel they are destined for. I have taken the Liberty to send orders to Capt Fry to deliver them to such person as may be ordered to receive them for transportation to this Port — To these orders I pray you to add, those necessary upon your part —

I wish you to believe that it would give me great pleasure to see the Harbour & City of New York put in a respectable State of defence

I am sorry however to inform you that from the best Judgment I am able to form, this cannot be accomplished without aid from the State, or by the means at present in the power of the Executive, without an abandonment of other ports in the Union, which it wou'd be inexpedient and improper to neglect — Colo Stevens has favored me with some very judicious observations on the subject of the necessary fortifications, and an estimate of their probable cost amounting to about 150,000 Dollars — Colo Burr has not called upon me, but as he is in Town I expect he will — I shall not fail to avail myself of whatever information he may be pleas'd to impart, and to determine, as soon as possible upon the sum that may be applied of the appropriations to the defence of the Harbour, as well as the points upon which to expend it —

With great respect &ca

[NDA, LB. Correspondence when Navy was under War Department, 1790–1798.]

To Mr. Bankson, armorer, from Captain Thomas Truxtun, U. S. Navy

UNITED STATES SHIP *Constellation*
Patuxent May 7th *1798.*

SIR Your general duty as Armourer consists in obeying the orders you may receive from time to time from the Commanding Officer on deck Your particular duty is to take Charge of all tools and apparatus belonging to the department of Armourer and Gun Smith and to assist the gunner in the Survey of all Small Arms and to keep them Clean an in good order. You are further to Consider Yourself Under the gunner's direction and to be of his Crew.

You will also in performing your duty obey the directions of the Lieutenant of Marines and Master of Arms and make Yourself as Useful as possible in Makeing & Repairing all sorts of tools in every department on Board.

I hope by a Steady attention to duty you will be enabled to give all who you are to Coopperate with Sattisfaction and thereby Make Yourself comfortable on Board.

I am Sir Your obt St —

THOMAS TRUXTUN

To Mr BANKSON.

[HS of Pa. NDA photostat. Truxtun's LB, 1798-9.]

To Lieutenant John Rodgers, U. S. Navy, from Secretary of War

[PHILADELPHIA,]
War Department 7th May 1798.

Lieutt JOHN ROGERS Baltº

SIR, To facilitate the manning the Frigates as much as possible it is judged proper, that the Pay of the able Seamen should be increased to seventeen Dollars per Month. You will therefore be pleased to proceed to enter the able Seamen accordingly, at that rate of Pay and endeavour to procure the Number of able and ordinary Seamen required for the *Constellation* with as much Expedition as possible. —

It may be proper to inform those able Seamen that have already entered at 15 Dollars per Month, that they will have the Benefit of this Advance, and that Orders will be given to pay them the additional sum therefor. —

This Alteration of Pay is not to be considered to extend to any other than able Seamen. —

[NDA. OSW, Vol. 1.]

To John Harris, storekeeper, from Secretary of War

[PHILADELPHIA,]
War Department 8th May. 1798.

Mr JOHN HARRIS

SIR Be pleased to deliver to Captain Richard Dale of the Ship of War *Ganges*, the following Military Stores, which are to be charged to that Ship. — Vizt

2600 lbs Powder for Cannon and Muskets in Barrels and half Barrels. —
800 Round Shot of 9 pounders.
200 Double headed --- ditto
6000 lb of Grape fixt. in cannisters, and put in boxes. — 9 pounders. —
3000 Musket Cartridges
300 Pistol --- ditto
4 Muskets — with accoutrements Complete
10 Cutlasses with scabbards.
6 Boarding Pikes.
20 Scabbards for Cutlasses. (the Cutlasses are on board). —

[NDA, LB. Correspondence when Navy was under War Department 1795-1798.]

To Captain Richard Dale, U. S. Navy, from Secretary of War

[PHILADELPHIA,]
War Department 11th May. 1798.

Capt DALE.

SIR, The Ship *Ganges* now in the Port of Philada being purchased on account of the United States, and intended to be equipped and employed as a Vessel of War. —

I am directed by the President of the United States, to order you as a Captain in the Navy of the United States, to repair forthwith on Board, and take the Command of the said Ship. —

You will use your Exertions, to get the Ship if possible to Sea, in the course of a Week, and direct only such Improvements, and Alterations to be made in her, as will not occasion a Detention. In the Time mentioned, it is expected She will be completely fitted and manned for a cruise of three Months. —

You will furnish the Names of such Persons, as you may think qualified for the following Appointments respectively vizt

1st Lieutenant
2nd Lieutenant
Lieutenant of Marines
Surgeon
Surgeon's Mate
Purser
Sailing Master
2 Masters' Mates — 2 Midshipmen
Boatswain
Gunner. — and Carpenter. —

The Lieutenant of Marines when appointed, will immediately proceed to enlist twenty one Privates — 1 Serjeant — 1 Corporal and 2 Musicians, to serve as Marines, in the Navy of the United States, for a Term not exceeding Twelve Months, unless sooner discharged — You will transmit to him the annexed Regulations for his Government. —

You will cause such of your Officers as may appear best calculated for the Business, to open houses of Rendezvous, in proper Places and exert themselves to engage 64 able Seamen, and 32 ordinary Seamen, for a Term of Service of three Months (in Case the Serjeant be engaged for twelve months) unless sooner discharged. — The Pay of the able Seamen to be seventeen Dollars per Month, and that of the ordinary Seamen, Ten dollars per Month. —

It is directed that none other, than healthy robust and well organized Men, be enlisted or engaged. To this End, you will cause the Surgeon to attend at the Place or Places of Rendezvous, to examine each Sailor and Marine, and to certify to the recruiting Officer, that they are well organized, healthy and free from scorbutic or consumptive Affections, before he engages them. If Wages are paid to any without such Certificate — it will be at the Risk of the Officer paying it.

The Officer at each Rendezvous, shall make out a Return of the Number of Seamen and Marines recruited or engaged each day, stating therein the Number delivered over to the Ship, and transmit the same to the Captain and a Duplicate to the Secretary of War.—

The Officer at each rendezvous on the desertion of a Seaman or Marine, besides the usual Exertions and Means to be employed on such Occasions to recover and apprehend him, will transmit as soon as possible a description of him, to the Secretary of War. —

The Purser until further Orders, will act as Paymaster to the Officers and Crew, and will receive from time to time, Money to make Payments. —

Marines are to be advanced, Two dollars each, out of their first Month's Pay. The Advance to Seaman, if they cannot be obtained without it, may be two Months Pay.

As soon as you give Notice of the Places of Rendezvous, and the Names of the Officers who will have Charge of Them, a sufficient sum will be remitted to the Purser, to be paid over occasionally to them to promote the recruiting service — The Officers receiving this Money will be held accountable for it's faithful Application, and must produce at the Accountant's Office, proper Voucher's for it's Expenditure.

The Names of the Marines and Seamen are to be entered Alphabetically, in the Muster and Pay Rolls, and the Men to be mustered while in Port, by a qualified Person, whose Certificate as well as your's, is to be attached to the Muster Roll. —

You will be pleased to make out an Inventory of and Receipt for, on behalf of the United States, all military Stores, and Ammunitions, including Arms & Cannon, Tackle Apparel, all other Stores and Articles of Equipment, provisions &c. comprized in the purchase of the Ship, and delivered to you — A Duplicate of which Inventory and Receipts, you will transmit to the Secretary of the Department of War. —

You will make out and return as aforesaid, a List of all Warlike Articles, Equipments Stores &c. that may be wanted, in addition to what shall be delivered to you; in order that the same may be procured as speedily as possible. —

[NDA. OSW, Vol. 1.]

[12 May, 1798]

Captain Samuel Nicholson's recruiting advertisement for the U. S. Frigate *Constitution*

FRIGATE *Constitution*

To all *able-bodied* and *patriotic Seamen*, who are willing to serve their Country, and Support its Cause:

The President of the United States, having ordered the Captain and Commander of the good Frigate *Constitution*, of 44 guns, now riding in the harbor of *Boston*, to employ the most *vigorous exertions* to put said ship, as speedily as possible, in a situation to sail at the shortest command.

Notice is hereby given, That a HOUSE OF RENDEZVOUS is opened at the sign of the *Federal Eagle*, kept by Mrs. BROADERS, in Fore-street; — where ONE HUNDRED and FIFTY able Seamen, and NINETY-FIVE ordinary Seamen, will have an opportunity of entering into the service of their country for One Year, unless sooner discharged by the President of the United States. — To all able bodied

Seamen, the sum of SEVENTEEN DOLLARS; and to all ORDINARY SEAMEN the sum of TEN DOLLARS per month, will be given; and two months advance will be paid by the Recruiting Officer, if necessary.

None will be allowed to enter this honorable service, but such as are well organized, healthy and robust; and free from scorbutic and consumptive affections.

A glorious opportunity now presents to the brave and hardy Seamen of New-England, to enter the service of their country—to avenge its wrongs—and to protect its rights on the ocean. Those brave Lads, are now invited to repair to the FLAGG of the *Constitution* now flying at the above rendezvous; where they shall be kindly received, handsomely entertained, and may enter into immediate pay.

SAMUEL NICHOLSON,
Commander, United States Frigate Constitution.

At the above rendezvous Lt. Clark of the Marines, will enlist three Sargeants, three Corporals, one Armourer, one Drummer, one Fifer, and fifty privates to compose a company for the Ship *Constitution*. None can be inlisted who are not five feet, six inches high.

BOSTON, MASSACHUSETTS, *May 12.*

[LC, "Columbian Centinel" (Boston, Mass.), 19 May 1798.]

To Doctor Gillaspy from Secretary of War

[PHILADELPHIA,]
War Department, 12th May 1798

Dr GILLASPY

SIR, I have to request that you will be pleased to inspect the Medicine Chests and Instruments, belonging to the Ships *Ganges* and *Hamburgh Packet*, and report their State.

You will obtain from the Surgeon of the *Ganges* an Estimate of Medicine, Instruments and Hospital Stores for that Ship for three Months.—

[NDA. OSW, Vol. 1.]

To Alexander Hamilton from Secretary James McHenry

PHILAD. *12 May 1798*

MY DEAR HAMILTON. I shall in a short time be able to get to sea, one or two of our frigates, and perhaps in less than six or seven days, Capn Dale, in the *Ganges*, a lately purchased vessel. Can you spare an hour or two to help me to the instructions that it will be proper to give to their Captains. Our ships of war it is probable will meet with French privateers who may be in possession of our merchantment; or with our merchant vessels having French Prize Masters on board; or with French Privateers cruising upon our coast to capture American vessels: They may also when acting as convoys be obliged to employ force to protect their convoy and may even be obliged to board a French ship of war to terminate a contest and insure its safety. What instructions ought to be given to meet such cases, or enable them to afford competent protection to our merchantmen, and preserve the

Executive from any future accusation of having by its orders involved the Country in a war. I foresee these instructions will fall to my lot, there being no chance that we shall have a [word illegible] or relieve me from the responsibility. The President has not mentioned this subject to me, nor any other Gentleman. You will easily conceive how necessary it is I should be assisted with your ideas and a sketch of such instructions as in your opinion will comport with the existing state of things and the profound reserve of Congress.

Your sincere & affectionate friend

JAMES M[c]HENRY

[LC, J. M[c]H. P., Vol. 4, 1797–1798.]

To Francis DaCosta from Secretary of War

[PHILADELPHIA,]
War Department 16th May 1798

M[r] FRANCIS DACOSTA

SIR I have to request that you will be pleased as soon as convenient to examine and prove in the usual manner, the Six eight inch Howitzers lately received from Boston —

I am with respect &c[a]

[NDA, LB. Correspondence when Navy was under War Department, 1790–1798.]

[17 May 1798]

To Secretary James McHenry from Alexander Hamilton

MY DEAR SIR I have received your letter of the [space] instant. Not having seen the law which provides the *Naval Armament*, I cannot tell whether it gives any new power to the President that is any power whatever with regard to the employment of the Ships. If not, and he is left at the foot of the Constitution, as I understand to be the case, I am not ready to say that he has any other power than merely to employ the Ships as Convoys with authority to *repel* force by *force*, (but not to capture), and to repress hostilities within our waters including a marine league from our coasts —

Any thing beyond this must fall under the idea of *reprisals* & requires the sanction of that Department which is to declare or make war.

In so delicate a case, in one which involves so important a consequence as that of War — my opinion is that no doubtful authority ought to be exercised by the President — but that as different opinions about his power have been expressed in the house of Representatives, and no special power has been given by the law, it will be expedient for him, and his duty, and the true policy of the Conjuncture to come forward by a Message to the two houses of Congress declaring that "*so far* and *no farther*" he feels himself *confident* of his authority to go in the employment of the naval force; — that as in his opinion the depredations on our trade demand a more extensive protection he has thought it his duty to bring the subject under the review of Congress by a communication of his opinion of his own powers — having no desire to exceed the constitutional limits.

This course will remove all clouds as to what the President will do — will gain him credit for frankness and an unwillingness to shecane the Constitution — and will return upon Congress the Question in a shape which cannot be eluded.

I presume you will have heard before this reaches you that a French Privateer has made captures at the mouth of our harbour. This is too much humiliation after all that has passed — Our Merchants are very indignant — Our Government very prostrate is the view of every man of energy

Y^rs^ *truly*

A Hamilton

May 17 — 1798
James M^c^Henry Esq

[LC, J. M^c^H. P., 1778–1799.]

To John Harris, storekeeper, from Secretary of War

[Philadelphia,]
War Department 17th May 1798

Mr John Harris.

Sir It having been represented that the Iron grape delivered to Mr Francis for the *Ganges* are of too large a size. I have therefore to request that you would be pleased forthwith to deliver to him an equal quantity in weight of 4 oz: Grape, or as near it as possible, on his returning into Store those already delivered. — Mr Francis will attend to this business, and afford such assistance as may be necessary. —

[NDA, LB. Correspondence when Navy was under War Department, 1795–1798.]

To John Harris, storekeeper, from Secretary of War

[Philadelphia,]
War Department 21st May. 1798

Mr John Harris

Sir Be pleased to deliver to Lieu^t^ Carmick for the Marines on board the Ship of War *Ganges* the following Articles. Viz^t^

1	Serjeants' Coat,	1 Waistcoat.	1 Pantaloon.
2	Music---- d^o^-	2 ---d^o^----	2 --ditto
21	privates-- d^o^	21 ---d^o^----	21 --ditto
48	Shirts —		
26	pairs of shoes		
1	Musket complete.		
1	Bayonet.		
1	Fife and case		
2400	Musket Cartridges.		

And for the Ship's use 5 reams of Musket Cartridge Paper, and 10 quire of Cannon d^o^

[NDA, LB. Correspondence when Navy was under War Department, 1795–1798.]

To Captain Richard Dale, U. S. Navy, from Secretary of War

[PHILADELPHIA,]
War Department. 22 May. 1798.

Capt Dale.

SIR, Although Congress have authorized the arming, equipping and employing a Number of Ships, an evident object of which is the Protection of the Commerce of the United States, yet as Congress possess exclusively the Power to declare War, grant Letters of Marque & Reprisal, and make Rules concerning Captures on Land and Water, and as neither has yet been done, your Operations must accordingly be partial & limited. For the present, you will be governed by the following Instructions, which relate to the Prevention of Violations of our jurisdictional Rights and to Self-defence. —

1. The Jurisdiction of the United States, on our Coast, has been determined to extend One Marine League from our Shores, and to comprehend all our Rivers and Inlets and all the Bays and Sounds, land-locked by the Territory of the United States. If within these Limits, you find any armed Vessel whatever, committing Depredations on our Coast or attacking or having taken, or in the act of pursuing to attack or take any Vessel of the United States, or the Vessel of any Nation whatever, you are to make every Exertion to prevent the Execution of such unlawful Proceedings, and to defend or liberate or retake the Vessel pursued, attacked or captured, and send in the offending Vessel, to some port of the United States, to be delt with according to Law, in such cases. —

2. If on the high Seas, you are attacked by any armed Vessel whatever, you are to defend Yourself to the Utmost. If the Assailant strikes, examine her Papers, and if She has not a regular Commission, and then in force, bring her into some Port of the United States, to be tried as a Pirate. —

3. You will consider your Cruising Ground, till further Orders, to be, between the Capes of Virginia and Long-Island, and will change your Course, from time to Time, so as to afford the best Protection in your power to our jurisdictional Rights, and especially to all Vessels of the United States, in coming in or going off the Coast. —

4. On the twelth of June, you are if possible to be at the Capes of Delaware, between Cape Henlopen & Cape James — and there to wait for additional Orders from the President.

5. You will engage a Pilot if you think it necessary to remain with you during the Cruise, or 'till the 12th of June.

6. You will as often as Opportunities present, transmit a Journal of your Proceedings and such Events as it may be proper to communicate. —

[NDA. OSW, Vol. 1.]

[22 May 1798]

To Lieutenant James Triplett from Captain Thomas Truxtun, U. S. Navy

Lieut James Triplett will be pleas'd to repair to Alexandria, with all the expedition that is possible, and engage as many Seamen and Marines as he can find disposed to enter on board the Frigate *Constellation* under my Command, and to hire a boat and repair to the Ship with them without loss of time — Lieut Triplett will take Capt

Moor an experienced Seaman with him, to assist in this business, the greatest frugality must be observed in all matters of expence, expected to be allowed by the Government, as the Secretary of War will only admit Such charges as he will consider reasonable or proper. A copy of the Articles and blank Oaths of Allegiance &c will be furnished by Lieut. Rodgers, who I have desired to send up a sufficient number from the rendezvous for this purpose a number of men having been put on board a Vessel bound to Alexandria by a french Privateer has induced me, to order you to make this expedition, which I hope and Trust will be attended with Success.

[T. TRUXTUN]

BALTIMORE *22d May 1798.*

[HS of Pa. NDA photostat. Truxtun's LB, 1798–9.]

To Secretary Benjamin Stoddert from Secretary Pickering

[PHILADELPHIA,]
Department of State, 22 May 1798

BENJAMIN STODDERT Esqr

SIR The President of the United States being desirous of availing the public of your Services as Secretary of the Navy, I have now the honor of enclosing the commission and of expressing the Sentiments of respect with which I am, Sir, &c.

TIMOTHY PICKERING

[SDA. Dom. L., Vol. 10.]

To Captain John Barry, U. S. Navy, from Secretary of War

[PHILADELPHIA,]
War Department, May 23d 1798

Capt JOHN BARRY

SIR, I request that you would be pleased to have one of your Boats and a Crew in Readiness tomorrow Morning at Ten — oClock to go on Board the *Ganges.* —

[NDA. OSW, Vol. 1.]

To Secretary Timothy Pickering from Stephen Cathalan, Jr., United States Commercial Agent

MARSEILLES *the 24th May 1798 —*

SIR here Inclosed I have the honour of Remitting you a Copy of my Respects of the 1st January Last;

Capt Js Freeman of the Brig *Betsey* of Boston, being on his Departure, for Boston, I Embrace this opportunity to advise you — That the Brig of the United States *Sophia*, with Clement Humphreys in her, is arived the 11th Inst at the Port of Havre;

M. Humphreys has wrote me on the 13th Inst from Paris, Requesting to Send to havre the distressed Seamen who might be in my District; one only was in this harbour (Wam hermon) who had voluntary Left the american Brig *Independt* at Alicante, & being Destitute, I have shipped him on the Brig *Betsey* Capt

BENJAMIN STODDERT, FIRST SECRETARY OF THE NAVY

Freeman, in virtue of my order, & to be paid of the Expences & vittles supplied to him during the passage, on his arival, by our Govern^{t} according to the law; I have found this, more convenient & less expensive than to send him to havre by Land; I have answered to M. Humphreys yesterday at Paris, & Promised to him, all the Informations he is desiring from me;

Just now I received a Letter from J. C. Mountflorence Esqr dated Paris the 17th Ins^{t} mentionning me — M. Humphreys Letter of To Day to Go to Genl Pinckney at Lyons where he is still detained by his Daughters health on his Journey to Montpellier; — nothing as yet transpired of the contents of the Dispatches, Tho' it continues to be believed that M. Gerry will Return to america by the above vessel —

I Remit you here Inclosed a list of the american vessels condemned by appeal at the Tribunal of Aix, in Conformity of the arrete of the Directoire executive of the 12th Ventose, for want of Proper Rolles of equipage;

Three american vessels are in the harbour, not any others in my District; [2 words illegible] They have Proper Rolles of Equipage & Shipm^{t} Paper in the best order.

1^{t} The Brig *Betsey* Bearer of this Letter was visited by french Privateer, on his way to this Port; but not Captured, & has always been Free, I hope she will return safe —

2^{d} The Ship *Flora* of Gloucester Capt Sil. Calder, from Gloucester, Massachuse^{t} bound for Leghorn, was captured on the 21st January after being Signalized, by a Corsican Privateer and against the order of the French Consul at Leghorn, not to mollest this Ship; she arived here; The Consul having advised the Minister of Marine & forcing Relations of this violation, The Minister of Marine has ordered to the Tribunal^{s} to Judge this affair in the shortest delay; The Tribunal of Commerce in this Place Judged this Prize to be Illegal, & Restuated [sic] to Cap^{n} Calder, under bound in case of appeal, The Privateer appealed at Aix. I have been accepted as bound, and Sold almost all the Cargo, Cap^{n} Calder has also appealed to obtain Damages, which were not Granted to him by the first Judgment; This affair which cannot be Lost for us, (Tho' the owner is a Brother of Gal BuonaP^{t}) has been postponed from one Day to another; — however I hope it will be Judged in our favour on the 28th Ins^{t} which is the day appointed by the Judges.

3^{d} The Ship *Eagle* of Marblehead Cap^{n} Stephen Sweet, bound for Marseilles was taken and carried into this Port; The Consigners, Capt Sweet of one Side, & the Privateer of the other, after having Pleaded before this Tribunal of Commerce, have compromised, together, & I was called by the Captain to Sign the Transaction, by which Cap^{n} Sweet has been Restored in his Ship & Cargo on his Paying to the Privateer the Sum of £ 50 Thousand livres, & the charges & fees of the law suit was 14,000.. —

I cannot Blame this agreement, — considering that not only the Americans, but the Danes, Sweeds, Russians, Genoese &^{c} &^{c} are almost all condemned, under various motives; and on more than 100 Prizes not Six till now, have been Returned to their owners;

I am not yet Reimbursed for my advances to Cap^{n} Smith & crew of the Ship *Fortune*; — I am Deprived of your favours since your Letter of the 27th October last; —

Making ardent Wishes that in this Crisis, Peace & harmony may be now restored between U. S. & France;

I have the honour to be with Sincere Respect

Sir

Your Most obedient humble & Devoted Servant

STEPHEN CATHALAN Jun[r]

T[thy] PICKERING

Secretary of State

Philadelphia —

24th May

at Three o clock afternoon, The Sloop *Prudence* of Nantukett Cap[n] Eliha Russel, Loaded with Whale Bones & Staves, is Just arived in this Port. She was bound from Nantuckett, for Genoa & Taken by a Corsican Privateer, was of Genoa & carried to that Port; but by Judg[nt] of Consul, C. Belleville, of the french Republic released & Free; She is come here to sell her Cargo, the Price being not answerable at Genoa.

[Enclosure]

[Enclosure]

[24 May 1798]

A LIST of the American Vessels Captured by french Privateers & Condemned by the Tribunal of Appeal at Aix

Ship's Names	Captains	Privateer's Names	Port they have been Carried to,	Condemnation's date, in Aix.
The Brig DISPATCH of Philadelphia	Philip Brown	LA ZENODORE, Capt Poule	Malaga	The 28th of Nivose 6th year 17th of January 1798,
The Ship THREE BROTHERS of Portland	Lindal Smith	LA ZIZA, Clemt Roux	do	23d Nivose 6th year 12 of January 1798.
The Brig ATALANTA	Elnathan Minor	LA ZIZA, Clemt Roux	Carthagenes	23d of Nivose 6th year 12th January 1798.
The Ship POLLY, of Salem	William Bradshaw	LES THERMIDOR	Malaga	28. Nivose 6th year 17th of January 1798,
The Ship POMONA	John Grafts	LA REVANCHE & LA ZENODORE, Gibouin & Poule.	Carthagenes	21. Nivose 6th year 10th January 1798,
The Brig TWO FRIENDS	Gilbert Howland	LES THERMIDOR	Malaga	27th Nivose 6th year 16th January 1798,
The Brig THELEMACHUS	William Plummer	LA REVANCHE & LA ZENODORE, Gibouin & Poule.	Carthagenes	21 Nivose 6th year 10. Jany 1798,
The Ship FRIENDSHIP	John Proud	LA FORTUNE		21 Pluviose 6th year 9th January 1798,
The Ship OUTRAM	Saml Clarkhill	LA COURAGEUSE, Capt Alaise	Carthagenes	
The Skooner ABIGAIL	James Atwood	LA REVANCHE & LA ZENODORE, Gibouin & Poule.	do	23 Nivose 6th year 12th January 1798,
The Sloop PEGGY of Bristol	Henry Leader	LES THERMIDOR, Capt	Malaga	1st Pluviose 6th year 20th January 1798,
The Skooner ORRINGTON	Ambrose Atkins	LES THERMIDOR & LE CHAUFFEUR, Capt	do	4 Pluviose 6th year 23d January 1798,
The Ship GOVERNOR MIFFLIN	John Dove	LA ZENODORE, Capt Poule	Cathagenes	27. Nivose 6th year 16. January 1798,
The Ship PLATO	Andrew Lawrence	LA FURET, Capt	Almeria	24. Ventose 6th yr 14 March 1798.

Two other Vessels, appealed by other houses have been Condemned — also

These Vessels where Condemned on the want of Proper Rolles of equipage, in Conformity of the arrete of the Directoire executif, & on other sundry motives stated in their respective Judgments —

Chancery of the Consulate of Marseilles the 24th May 1798 —

STEPHEN CATHALAN Junr

[SDA. Marseilles, Vol. 1, 1790–1802.]

To Francis DaCosta from Secretary of War

[PHILADELPHIA,]
War Department 24th May 1798

Mr FRANCIS DACOSTA

SIR I have to request that you will be pleased to examine the nine pound cannon belonging to the Ship of War, the *Delaware*, Commanded by Stephen Ducatur Esquire, and prove such of them as you may find suitable for service — The result of the examination and proof you will report to me as soon as possible —

[NDA, LB. Correspondence when Navy was under War Department, 1790-1798.]

To Captain Thomas Truxtun, U. S. Navy, from Secretary of War

Confidential

[PHILADELPHIA,]
War Department. 25th May 1798. —

Capt TRUXTUN Balto

SIR, The depredations committed upon the Southern Coast, within our jurisdictional Limits, by armed Vessels; and the exposed and almost defenceless situation of that Part of the Union, render It extremely necessary that it should be succoured, with such naval Force as We have in our Power, and that this should be applied, with as little delay as possible. —

The President has observed with Pleasure, the Exertions, which you have made, and are making, to prepare your Ship for Sea. —

Thinking it likely that you will be disposed, to venture out with the Men, you have engaged, and can pick up, before reaching the Capes; you will put every Thing, in as good order as Circumstances will admit of for sailing immediately after receiving your Orders, which it is possible may be sent you, in a few days. — I send you inclosed an Appointment for a Sailg Master, of the *Constellation*; You will select a proper and qualified Character for this Station — and direct the appointment in his Name.

Send me a few copies of your printed Orders. —

[NDA. OSW, Vol. 1.]

To John Harris, storekeeper, from Secretary of War

[PHILADELPHIA,]
War Department 25th May 1798

Mr JOHN HARRIS

SIR Be pleased to deliver to Captain Decatur for proving the nine pounders for the Ship of War the *Delaware*, the Articles following, which are to be sent down to Mr Humphrey's Office. Southwark — Vizt—

1 Barrel of Powder
36 Wads.
3 sticks Port fire
Rammer, Sponge, Ladle & Worm.
18 Nine pound shot
A Searcher with its ring.
A priming Wire.

[NDA, LB. Correspondence when Navy was under War Department, 1795-1798.]

[25 May, 1798]

Extract of letter, from the supercargo of the Ship *Nonpareil*, dated at Wilmington, N. C., 7th June

"Mail just closing, have only time to advise of my safe arrival here, and state briefly, that we sailed from Tortola on the 20th ult. under convoy, and on the 24th parted from the fleet, they too far to the eastward, on the next day in lat. 26, 10, long. 65, 30, was captured by a French privateer out of Guadaloupe, and ordered for Porto Rico, they took out both mates and all the people, the cook, two hands, Capt. Fanning and myself excepted, and put on board two prize masters and fourteen men, finding them very ignorant, except one of the prize masters, (who was an American) I adopted a method to alter their course, on the following plan, first bribing the American prize master, who alone was acquainted with navigation. We privately started some of our water, and made them believe that they would not be able to reach any of the islands for want of water, and persuaded them to bear away for St. Augustine, telling them I was perfectly acquainted with that coast, and that the French frequently carried their prizes there. My intention was to have went into Savannah, but falling to the northward I brought my ship in here, still making the wise believe it was St. Augustine, till I had got them snug into the river. I shall give you further accounts per next post, and ship new crew and proceed on to New York along shore. Yours, &c.

SILAS S. WEBB."

[LC, "Boston Gazette" (Mass.), July 9, 1798.]

To Garrett Holsteincamp, pilot, from Secretary of War

[PHILADELPHIA,]
War Department 26th May 1798.

Mr GARRETT HOLSTEINCAMP Pilot

SIR You will proceed with your Pilot-Boat immediately to New Castle where you will wait for further orders from the Secretary of War, and hold yourself in readiness to sail, at a moments warning.—

[NDA, LB. Correspondence when Navy was under War Department, 1790–1798.]

To John Harris, storekeeper, from Secretary of War

[PHILADELPHIA,]
War Department 26th May. 1798

Mr JOHN HARRIS

SIR You will deliver to Captain John Barry or his order when called for from time to time, the Articles deposited in the Public Store for the Frigate *United States* agreeably to the annexed Statement.—

I am &c.

Military and other Stores to be delivered to Captain Barry for the Frigate *United States.* —

3000	Round Shot for 24 pounders
600	Double Headed shot for ditto
600	Grape with Iron Stools for ditto
2400	Flannel Cartridge's for ditto
300	-- Paper ----ditto for d°
300	----d°-- to make--d°--for d°
48	Cartridge Boxes--- for ----d°
48	Large Powder Horns for---d°
100	Priming Wires for 24 pounders
80	Boring Bitts ---- for -- ditto
60	Rammer Heads--------ditto
60	Sponge Heads---------ditto
60	Wooden Staffes--------ditto
30	Ropes for Rammers & Sponges ditto
30	Ladles for ---- 24 pounders
60	Worms------------ ditto
60	Cork and wood Tompions ditto
30	Linch stocks-------------- d°
	Lead for Aprons. —
1400	Round Shot for 12 pounders
280	Double Headed shot for ditto
280	Grape with Iron Stools for d°
1120	Flannel Cartridges for---- d°
300	-- Paper -- ditto -- for-- d°
300	----d° to make -- d° for-- d°
28	Rammer Heads for------- d°
28	Sponge Heads for-------- d°
28	Staves for the above for-- d°
14	Ladles---------------- d°
24	Cartridge Boxes -- for --- d°
34	Powder Horns-----for --- d°
28	Worms--------------------for---------- 12 pounders
48	Priming Wires---------------for------------ d°
30	Boring Bitts----------------for------------ d°
14	Ropes for Rammers & Sponges for------------ d°
32	Cork and wood Tompions for---------------- d°
2	Tons Lead for Aprons &c
140	Paper Cartridges for 8 Inch Howitzers
8	Tompions for------------------------------ ditto
100	Cutlasses
76	Boarding Pikes
100	-- ditto----Axes
98	pairs of Pistols
150	Ships Muskets (complete)
500	lbs Match Rope.
8	Copper Measures for filling Powder.
2	Cooper's Copper Adzes.
2	Copper screws.
2	Copper Funnels.
	Cartouch Boxes for Muskets.
1000	Flints — assorted.—
48	Sheep skins for sponges.
12	Pouch Barrels
6000	lb. Cannon Powder.
800	lbs Powder for priming Muskets.
100	8 inch Shells for Howitzers.
60	Cannister grape, 8 Inch, ditto
800	Shot for 6 pound Howitzers
800	Cannisters of Shot-----------for------------ d°
1000	Paper Cartridges-------------for------------ d°

Ship Chandlery

1 Azimuth Compass.
4 Brass............ditto
2 ..Wooden........ditto
1 Hanging.........ditto
3 spy Glasses.
1 Night............ditto
2 Glasses of 2 hours each.
6 ..ditto of half d°....d°
6 Half Minuite Glasses.
6 Quarter..ditto..ditto
6 Tinder Boxes with Steels.
28 lbs Brimstone.
3½ Dozen best Pad Locks.
6 Ship and 6 Boat skids.
4 Copper Pumps.
2 Candle Boxes & 14 lb. Cotton wicks.
25 Cord Fire wood.
600 lb. Tallow Candles.
50 lb. Spermaciti ..ditto
7 Dozen Fish Hooks (assorted)
6 pair Grains.
6 Harpoons &c
2 Dozen Clamps for scrubing the Deck.
10 Dozen Brooms.
5 Dozen Common Canns.
20 Hooks and Thimbles (assorted)
20 Thimbles.
20 Dozen Staples.
20 Rigging Hides.
6 Speaking Trumpets.
6 Rat Traps.
6 Dozen Paint & Hair Brushes.
6 Dozen log & Fish lines (assorted)
6 Hambro' Lines.
6 Quire Log Book Paper.
4 Cwt Oakam for Stores.
10 Barrels of Tar.
10 ....ditto....Pitch.
10 ....ditto....Turpentine.
6 Dipsy Lines. —

Paints

Red } Black & } Paints. Yellow }

Charts

A complete set for America
Europe
Asia and
Africa

Cabin Furniture

6 Decanters (common)
2 Copper Tea Kettles (or Patent)
4 Dozen Wine Glasses (common)
2 Jappaned Servers
3 Dozen Tumblers. (common)
2 Wash Hand Basons (Pewter)
2 Plate Baskets.
4 Tim Funnels.
6 Salts.
6 Butter Boats.
1 Black Jack.
2 Tin Pudding Pans for Baking.
2 Looking Glasses, sconces &c
2 Dozen Diaper Table Cloths.

Cabin Furniture—Continued

2 Dozen Table spoons
2 Dozen Silver Tea ditto
1 Soup Ladle.
2 Large Turenes
2 Small—ditto
1 Set of Castors
1 Set of China Tea Equipage complete
4 Tin Boxes for Pepper Flour &c
1 Culinder
4 Candlesticks Snuffers &c
2 Candle Boxes.
1 set Curtains
1 Coffee Pott
1 Chocolate — d°
2 Ladles. (Iron)
2 pair Tormenters
1 Cabin Bell. —
4 Patent Lamps
4 Hair Brushes
6 Mops.
6 Scrubing Brushes.
12 Stew and Sauce pans.
2 Iron Potts.
2 Frying Pans
1 Chaffing Dish
1 Grid Iron.
2 Carving Knives and forkes —
2 Dozen Table Knives
2 Dozen — D° Forkes
2 Dozen Dishes different sizes
10 Dozen Flat & Soup Plates
3 Dozen Mugs. Quart, pint & half pint Queensware —
1 Cheese Toaster.
2 Chamber Potts. (Pewter). —

Hospital Stores, Utensils &c

56 Gallons Molasses
256 — ditto — Vinegar
4½ — ditto Lemon Juice.
20 d° French Brandy
90 — ditto — Sherry Wine
45 — ditto — Port Wine
90 — ditto — Low White Wine
55 — ditto Porter
24 lbs Raisins
9 d° Tamarinds
15 d° Tea.
36 d° Chocolate.
112 bls Brown Sugar
12 d° Sago.
110 d° Rice
9 d° Julap
45 d° Portable Soap
12 d° Essence of Spruce
4½ d° Alspice
1 d° Ginger
1 d° Mustard
3½ d° Pepper.
182 d° Barley.
18 d° Oatmeal.
90 d° Linsead Meal
2½ Gallons of Oil.
24 dozen of Eggs. —

Utensils

2 Dozen Quart Mugs (of Tin)
2 — d° pint — d° —
3 Large Sauce Pans
3 Small —— d°
4 Camp Kettles
2 — Tea — Ditto
4 Tea Potts. (of Tin)
2 Dozen Table spoons
1 Doz: Tea spoons
1 two pound Cannister.
1 four pound Sugar Box.
6 two Gallon Jugs.
2 Bed Pans.
2 Urinals. —

Stationary

1 Slate and Pencils
1 Ink Stand
1 Day Book
1 Book of Memoirs
1 Ditto to keep an Account of Hospital stores
½ Ream Writing paper
200 Quills
2 Boxes Wafers
3 Papers Ink Powder
1 pound of Sand. 1 Small hand Bell.
2 Quires of blotting paper
Candlesticks or Lamp for Cock pit
6 Potts or Grates for making fire in y° Well &c
3 Marine Ventilators
A Set of Signals and other Colours. —

Provisions

66248 Pounds of Bread.
28392 — ditto Beef
28392 —ditto Pork
14196 Pints of Peas or Beans
9464 — ditto of Rice.
7089 pounds of Cheese.
18928 — ditto of Potatoes or Turnips
9464 — ditto of Salt Fish. —
4732 — ditto — Flour
3549 — ditto — Molasses
33124 pints Rum
1183 pounds Butter. —

[NDA, LB. Correspondence when Navy was under War Department, 1795–1798.

[28 May, 1798]

Act pertaining to the Navy

[United States Statutes at Large. Fifth Congress. Sess. II]

AN ACT MORE EFFECTUALLY TO PROTECT THE COMMERCE AND COASTS OF THE UNITED STATES

WHEREAS armed vessels sailing under authority or pretence of authority from the Repuplic of France, have committed depredations on the commerce of the United States, and have recently captured the vessels and property of citizens thereof, on and near the coasts, in violation of the law of nations, and treaties between the United States and the French nation. THEREFORE:

Be it enacted by the Senate and House of Representatives of the United States of American in Congress assembled, That it shall be lawful for the President of the United States, and he is hereby authorized to instruct and direct the commanders of the armed vessels belonging to the United States to seize, take and bring into any port of the United States, to be proceeded against according to the laws of nations, any such armed vessel which shall have committed or which shall be found hovering on the coasts of the United States, for the purpose of committing depredations on the vessels belonging to citizens thereof; — and also to retake any ship or vessel, of any citizen or citizens of the United States which may have been captured by any such armed vessel.

Approved, May 28, 1798.

[Statute 1, page 561.]

Instructions to commanders of armed vessels, 28 May 1798

JOHN ADAMS

President of the United States —

Instructions to the Commanders of armed Vessels, belonging to the United States, given at Philadelphia, this Twenty Eighth day of May in the Year of our Lord, One thousand seven hundred and Ninety Eight, and in the Twenty second Year of the Independence of the said States: —

WHEREAS, it is declared by an Act of Congress, passed the twenty Eighth day of May, 1798, that armed Vessels, sailing under authority or Pretence of Authority from the French Republic, have committed Depredations on the Commerce of the United States, and have recently captured the Vessels and Property of Citizens thereof; on and near the Coasts, in violation of the Law of Nations, and Treaties between the United States, and the French Nation:

THEREFORE, & in Pursuance of the said Act, you are instructed and directed, to seize take and bring into any Port of the United States, to be proceeded against according to the Laws of Nations, any armed Vessel sailing under Authority or Pretence of Authority from the Republic of France, which shall have committed, or which shall be found hovering on the Coasts of the United States, for the purpose of committing Depredations on the Vessels belonging to Citizens thereof; and also to retake any Ship or Vessel of any Citizen or Citizens of the United States, which may have been captured by any such armed Vessel. —

By Command

[NDA. OSW, Vol. I.]

To Captain Richard Dale, U. S. Navy, from Secretary of War

[PHILADELPHIA,]
War Department. 28th May 1798.

Capt RICHd DALE.

SIR, I have dispatched two Pilot Boats, with the inclosed Instructions, one to the Southward of the Capes of Delaware, the other to the Eastward, to cruise for you on your Station, should you have left the Bay.

I have only to add, that your Zeal, Courage and Prudence, is relied upon, for the most prompt vigorous and effectual Execution of these Instructions, and to wish you, your Officers and Crew, in all of whom I have the utmost Confidence every Thing honorable and fortunate. —

[NDA. OSW, Vol. 1.]

From Secretary of War

[PHILADELPHIA,]
War Department 28th May 1798

To Messrs DANL RODNEY Esqr HENRY NEALE & Mr THOMPSON,
Deputy Collector Lewis Town

GENTn I have to request you to be so obliging as to engage on the Account of the United States, a fast sailing Pilot Boat, with a trusty & experienced Commander, to convey the enclosed Instructions to Captain Richard Dale, Commander of the Ship of War, The *Ganges*— Shou'd the *Ganges* not have passed Lewis Town, The Pilot will remain in readiness to convey the dispatch on board, as she passes — You will assure the Pilot you may engage, of a Liberal compensation for the service, his Instructions which are herein enclosed may call upon him to perform —

[NDA, LB. Correspondence when Navy was under War Department, 1790–1798.]

Pilot's order from Secretary of War

[PHILADELPHIA,]
War Department May 28th 1798

To the Pilot engaged to convey dispatches from Lewis Town to Capt Rd DALE on board the Ship *Ganges*

SIR You will immediately proceed in your Pilot Boat from Lewis Town in quest of the Ship of War the *Ganges* commanded by Capt Richard Dale — Should you not find the *Ganges* in the Mouth of Delaware Bay, you will proceed to look for her at Sea, and may expect to find her somewhere within a few leagues of the Shore, between the Bay of Delaware and the Capes of Virginia —

When you have come up with the *Ganges*, you will deliver to Capt Dale, or in case an accident shou'd have happened to him, the Officer then Commanding the Ship, the dispatches herewith delivered to you —

You will charge yourself with such dispatches, as the Commander of the *Ganges* may deliver to you, for the Secretary of War. — The utmost diligence is required of you to find out the *Ganges*, and deliver the dispatches, wherewith you are charged — You will also lose no time, in returning with such, as her Commander may charge you with for the Secretary of War —

[NDA, LB. Correspondence when Navy was under War Department, 1790–1798.]

To Garrett Holsteincamp, Pilot, from Secretary of War

[PHILADELPHIA,]
War department 28th May 1798

Mr GARRETT HOLSTEINCAMP Pilot

SIR You will immediately proceed in your Pilot Boat down the River & Bay of Delaware in quest of the Ship of War, the *Ganges* commanded by Capt Richard Dale

Should you not come up with the *Ganges* in the River, or find her in the Bay — you will proceed to look for her at sea, and may expect to find her somewhere within a few leagues of the Shore, between the Bay of Delaware and long Island — When you have come up with the *Ganges*, you will deliver to Captain Dale, or in case any Accident should have happened to him, to the Officer then commanding the Ship the dispatches herewith delivered to you — You will charge yourself with such dispatches, as the Commander of the *Ganges* may deliver to you for the Secretary of War — The utmost diligence is required of you to find out the *Ganges*, and deliver the dispatches, wherewith you are charged — You will also lose no time in returning with such dipatches as her Commander may charge you with — for the Secretary of War —

[NDA, LB. Correspondence when Navy was under War Department, 1790–1798.]

To Samuel Fisher, express rider, from Secretary of War

[PHILADELPHIA,]
War Department 28th May 1798

Mr SAML FISHER Express Rider

You will proceed with all expedition to Newcastle upon Delaware, where you will enquire for Garrett Holsteincamp a Pilot, who commands a Boat called the *Flying Fish* of Philadelphia.

Should Mr Holsteincamp not be in New-Castle, he will be found on board his boat, at the Diamond Pier — She will be known by the Danish Flag at Mast head, red with a white cross —

When you have found him you will deliver to him the dispatch you are charged with, directed in his name — You will then without loss of time proceed with expedition to Lewis Town with, and there deliver as directed the other dispatch you are charged with — You will receive Instructions for Mr Hodgden agent for the Quarter Master General respecting reliefs of Horses —

P. S. If Capt Dale is at New Castle, or near it so that the dispatches can be delivered to him, You not proceed to Lewis Town —

[NDA, LB. Correspondence when Navy was under WarDepartment, 1790–1798.]

To Secretary of State Pickering from Secretary of Navy Stoddert

GEO TOWN *28 May 1798.*

SIR I am honored with your letter of the 22nd inst — Notifying to me, my appointment to the Office of Secretary of the Navy.

No circumstance would be more grateful to my feelings, than, that the President of the United States, whose Character I have always revered, & which has grown upon me, & his Country, in proportion as it has been developed; should have been induced (no doubt by the partial representation of the virtuous men around him, to some of whom I have been long known) to think so favorably of mine, as to deem me worthy of an appointment so honorable, and at this crises, so important.

I accept the appointment with more sensibility than I can express, but with the determination to discharge to the best of my power, the Duties of it — Tho' not without (I fear) well founded apprehensions, that it will be found, my qualifications have been greatly over-rated.

I have consolation however in the reflexion, that those great & comprehensive minds which stand least in need of indulgence for themselves, are ever most disposed to accord it to others, if the will to act right, be not wanting.

I have the honor to be with great respect & esteem

Sir Yr most obed. servt

BEN STODDERT.

TIMOTHY PICKERING Esq. — *Department of State.*

[SDA. Misc. L, Jan-Aug. 1798.]

To Captain Richard Dale, U. S. Navy, from Secretary of War

[PHILADELPHIA,]
War Department. 29. May. 1798

RICHd DALE

SIR, It is stated that the Barque *Adriana*, belonging to Phila a has lately put into New York, and remains there, waiting a Convoy which has been earnestly solicited from the Government of the United States.

The President, therefore, directs you to repair with the Ship of War, the *Ganges*, under your Command, to Sandy Hook, near the Port of New York, and take under Protection and conduct in Safety, to the utmost of your Power the said Barque *Adriana*, from the Port aforesaid to the Bay of Delaware, after which Service you will proceed according to your former Orders. —

The Concerned in the *Adriana*, will have a Pilot Boat stationed off the Hook to give immediate Notice of your Arrival. —

Inclosed is a Triplicate of your Instructions of the 28th Instant. —

[NDA. OSW, Vol. 1.]

To John Harris, storekeeper, from Secretary of War

[PHILADELPHIA,]
War Department 29th May 1798

MR JOHN HARRIS

SIR You will be pleased to have sent down to Mr Humphrey's Office, fourteen Nine pound Ball for the use of proving Captain Decatur's Guns. — please to send them this afternoon. —

[NDA, LB. Correspondence when Navy was under War Department, 1795–1798.]

To the Governor of Massachusetts from the Secretary of War

[PHILADELPHIA,]
War Department 30th May 1798

His Excellency The GOVERNOR of MASSACHUSETTS

SIR It is extremely desireable, that all the Naval forces the United States can command, should be put into a State of Activity as speedily as possible —

Hitherto and particularly by the failure of a Contract, the Government has found it impracticable, to procure the Cannon requisite for the upper Battery for the Frigate *Constitution* at Boston — It has however lately been stated that there were at Castle-Island, in the Harbour at Boston, nineteen Iron cannon of Caliber to carry Eighteen pound Shot, which from their Length and Weight appear to have been designed for Ships use, and to be improper for the embrazures of Fortifications — That Captain Nicholson has seen and examined these Cannon, and is very desirous to obtain them for his Ship —

By the direction of the President, I have therefore to request of your Excellency a loan of fourteen or Sixteen of the Cannon mentioned, and to offer on the part of the United States, an engagement, either to return the same Guns as soon as others can be provided for the Frigate, or to replace them, with Guns equally good, and in the mean time, if desired, to order the same Number of thirty two pound Cannon from Providence to, and for the defence of, Boston Harbour —

It is presumed that the State of Massachusetts have had balls purposely cast for these 18 pounders, if so, and your Excellency will furnish with the Cannon a suitable Quantity of Shott, the United States will punctually & promptly return an equal quantity. —

[NDA, LB. Correspondence when Navy was under War Department, 1790–1798]

To Captain Thomas Truxtun, U. S. Navy, from Secretary of War

[PHILADELPHIA,]
War Department. 30 May, 1798

THOS TRUXTUN

SIR, The Number of French Privateers, we have daily Accounts of, upon our Coasts, and the Depredations they are constantly committing, or attempting upon our Trade, renders it extremely desireable, that We should have at sea, as soon as possible, all the Force, which the United States can command. —

I flatter Myself that by the Time this Letter will reach you, you have completed, or so nearly completed your Complement of Men, as to be in a Condition, to enter upon a Cruise; and that the Articles you may still want, or which may not yet have arrived, are not so essentially necessary, as to prove a cause for your detention. If however essential Articles are wanted, and they can be procured where you are, or at Norfolk, without Delay, you are permitted to purchase them, using a sound Discretion, and to draw upon Me for the Amount. — With the same View of avoiding delay, I enclose a Letter to Lieu^t^ Triplett, directing him to repair on board, and to put himself under your Orders, until releived by the Lieutenant of Marines appointed to your Ship, who writes Me, he has arrived at Charleston, and is on his way to join you; and also a Letter to join you; and also a Letter to Lieutenant Dyson, to furnish you with as many of his Recruits, as you may want to complete your Establishment of Marines. —

Enclosed are your Instructions, the Result of a late Act of Congress. The President desires Me, to mention to you, his entire Confidence, that you will lose no Opportunity, to distinguish Yourself, and maintain the Rights and honor of your Country. —

You will consider your Cruising Ground, until further Orders, to extend from Cape Henry, to the Extremity of our Southern Limits. You will protect this Extent of Coast, to the utmost of your Power, and in so doing will pay particular Attention to it's exposed Parts, and the principal harbour of South Carolina and of Georgia; and you will also afford all possible Protection, to the Vessels of the United States, coming on or going off the Coast.

Captain Dale's cruising Ground, is between Long-Island, and Cape Henry. —

You will as often as Opportunities present, transmit a Journal of your Proceedings, and such Events or Occurrences, as may be proper to communicate.

All the military and other Stores ordered by you, have been sent forward, except those enumerated in the enclosed List — These with your Cabin Furniture are preparing; but I suppose if they do not soon arrive, you will not think it necessary to wait for Them. I can send them to Charleston, where you may have occasion to call, and will find them. —

For instructions, see Page 69 & 70.—

[NOTE.—Pages 69 and 70 contain Instructions to armed Vessels, dated 28 May 1798.]

Hospital Stores Utensils &c for the Frigate *Constellation*, for three Months — *Requisition* made the 24th May. 1798. —

56 Gallons of Molasses.
256 ditto " Vinegar
4½ ditto " Lemon Juice
20 ditto " French Brandy
90 ditto " Sherry Wine
45 ditto " Port Wine
90 ditto " low White Wine
55 ditto " Porter
24 lb. of Raisins.
9 lb. of Tamarinds
15 lb. of Tea
35 lb. of Chocolate
112 lb. of brown Sugar
11 lb. of Sago

110 lb. of Rice
9 lb. of Salep
45 lb. of Portable Soup
18 lb. of Essence of Spruce
4½ lb. of Alspice
1 d° Ginger
7 d° Mustard
3½ d° Pepper
182 d° Barley
18 d° of Oatmeal
90 lb of Linseed Meel
2½ Gallons Oil
24 doz. of Eggs

Utensils

2 doz. Quart Mugs — of Tin —
2 d° Pint d° d°
3 large Sauce Pans
4 Camp Kettles
2 Tea Kettles
4 Tea Potts of tin
2 doz. Table Spoons
1 ditto Tea ditto
1 two Pound Tea Canister
1 four ditto Sugar Box
6 two Gallin Jugs
2 Bed Pans
2 Urinals

Stationary

1 Slate & Pencils
1 Ink Stand
1 day Book
2 Books for Memoirs
1 d° to keep an acc^t^ of Hospital Stores.
1/2 ream of writing paper
200 Quils
2 Boxes of Wafers
3 Papers of Ink Powder
1 Pound of Sand
2 Quires Blotting Paper
Candlestick or Lamp for Cock-Pit
1 small Hand Bill.
6 Pots or Grates for making Fires, in the Well &c
3 Marine Ventilators
12th May 1798 — (13 Iron bound kegs of 20 Gallons Each)

Cabin Furniture. Requisition made the 26th of May. 1798. —

6 Decanturs (common)
2 Copper Tea Kettles or patent.
4 dozn Wine Glasses.
2 Japaned Servers
3 doz. Tumblers, common
2 Wash Hand Basons (pewter)
2 Plate Baskets
4 Tin Funnels
6 Salts
6 Butter Boats
1 Black Jack
2 Tin pudding Pans for Baking.—
1 Looking Glass Sconces &c.
2 Dozn Diaper Table Cloths
2 d° Table Spoons

2 d° Silver Tea Spoons
1 Soup Ladle
2 large Tureens
2 small ditto
1 Set of Castors
1 Set China Tea Equipage complete.
4 Tin boxes for Pepper Flour &c
1 Cullender
6 Candlesticks Snuffers &c.
2 Candle Boxes.
1 Set of Curtains
1 Coffee Pot
1 Chocolate Pot
2 Iron Ladles
2 pair Tormentors
1 Cabin Bell
4 Patent Lamps
4 Hair Brushes
6 Mops
6 Scrubing Brushes.
12 Stew & Sauce Pans of different sizes.
2 Iron Pots
2 Frying Pans
1 Chaffing Dish
1 Grid Iron
2 Carving Knives & Forks
2 doz. Table Knives
2 doz. Dishes of different sizes.
2 doz. Forkes
10 doz. Flat & Soup Plates. —
3 doz. Mugs — Q^t P^t & ½ Pint (Queen's Ware).
1 Cheese Toaster. —
2 Chamber Pots. —

WANTED, agreeably to the Order from the Secretary of War, issued the 15. Novem^r 1797. and 15 March 1798 — Viz^t —

19 June. 1797 700 Grape & Cannister Shot, for 24 Pounders.
" 300 ditto ________________ 12 Pounders
" 247 Bar Shot ________________ 24 ditto
13. Mar. 1798 200 Cannister Shot for 3 pound Howitzers.
19 June 1797 386 round Shot — 12 Pounders

Of the above, the following are ready in Store, and under order to be immediately forwarded. Viz^t

210 Cannisters of Shot for 24 Pounders
140 d° " " 12 d°
152 d° " " 3 pound Howitzers
and 12 Boxes of Candles. —
19. May. 1798 — Complete Set of Signal Flags & Pendants —

[NDA. OSW, Vol. 1.]

To Samuel Hodgdon, indendant of military stores, from Secretary of War

[PHILADELPHIA,]
War Department 30th May 1798.

SAM^l HODGDON Esqr

SIR: I have to request that you will be pleased to take order to have two hundred and Sixty Barrels of Cannon and eight Barrels of Musket powder transported from Springfield to the Frigate *Constitution* lying at Boston. —

I have ordered Mr Harris to deliver to you for transportation to the Frigate *Constellation* laying in the Chesapeak twelve Boxes of Candles, two hundred & ten 24 pound cannister shot, One hundred & forty 12 pound D° and One hundred & fifty two d° for small Howitzers. —

[NDA, LB. Correspondence when Navy was under War Department, 1795–1798.]

To Lieutenant Dyson from Secretary of War

[PHILADELPHIA,]
War Department, 30th May 1798

Lieut^t DYSON

SIR, Should you be called on by Capt Truxtun, for a few of your Recruits, to complete his Complement of Marines, for the Frigate *Constellation*; you will furnish them from the Men, who offer voluntarily to enter into that Service, for the intended Cruise; making it known to the Men, that they are to return to the Infantry, when the Cruise shall terminate, agreeably to their Engagements, with the United States, and that while borne as Marines on the Pay Rolls of the Ship, they will be entitled to the Pay of Marines. —

[NDA. OSW, Vol. 1.]

To Captain Samuel Nicholson, U. S. Navy, from Secretary of War

[PHILADELPHIA,]
War Departm^t 30. May. 1798

Capt NICHOLSON

SIR In consequence of a Letter from Genl Jackson, and the Impossibility of procuring the 12 Pounders for the Frigate in due Time, I have written to the Governor of the State of Massachusetts, to obtain on Loan, as many of the 12 or 18 Pounders, with a suitable Quantity of Ball, from Castle Island, as you may require for the upper Battery. As soon as you are apprized that these Guns will be loaned, you will select as many of Them as you want, and use all possible Expedition, in getting them mounted and in their proper Places. —

[NDA. OSW, Vol. 1.]

To Secretary Timothy Pickering from T. Williams

BOSTON *May 31st 1798.*

RESPECTED SIR, A new Cutter is building at Newbury Port for Government, to carry 14 four pounders, to be named the *Pickering*.— She may be ready for Sea in 50 Days. As she will be an excellent vessel, sufficient in some measure to protect our coast, many people are anxious that a Captain of some reputation and Spirit should have the command of her. To give her to I. [or J] F. W., would be to render her useless. He is old, without enterprize, & has been not a little *tainted* in his politics.—

This Brig, will not be wanted as a mere Revenue Cutter; she will be efficient for more important purposes. Some one ought to have the command of her who can render Some Service towards the protection of our trade, and the annoyance of our enemy. I have not heard any one named more eligible, than a Capt Jonathan Chapman, of this town. He is a respectable, well informed man; a thorough Seaman &

disciplinarian. — As you have been made acquainted with this business, I need not enlarge. —

The manning of our Frigate, I am sorry to observe, has made little progress; owing considerably to the *unpopularity* of the Commander; tho' no one alleges any thing against him that partakes of misconduct in any respect. He is poor — it is his only living. What can be done, I know not. It is to be regretted, that So fine a Ship should lie uselessly at her anchors. —

It is nearly 4 months since I purchased the wet provisions for her — they still remain in a store! In a few days, all her Bread will be ready. No one has orders to receive or deliver. —

Till there is some system — a Department, and proper agents under & dependent on it, I despair of our receiving any benefit, at least, from *this* Frigate. I believe there has been a Scandalous waste of property in building her; owing, I conceive, to the *entire ignorance* in the Agent of all *naval* affairs.

Economy of the public money at any time is almost a phenomenon; but where *inattention* was combined with *unskillfulness*, we could not expect a particle of it.

I have heard from my Brother Saml, that he has accepted the Consulship & Agency in London. I calculate that he was there by the middle of March.

Respectfully, I am

Your Neph.

T. Williams.

[Mass. H. S. Pickering Papers, Vol. 22.]

To Secretary Timothy Pickering from Stephen Cathalan, commercial agent, Marseilles

Marseilles *the 31st May 1798.*

Sir, I am, just now, returned from Aix, with Captn Saml Calder & have the pleasure of informing you, That yesterday morning by a Judg^t^ of Tribunal of appeal of the department of the Bourges [?] du Rhone.

The appeal interjected by the privateer, The *Patroit* Captn Felix Potestat (a Corsican) has been rejected, the first Judgment of the Tribunal of Commerce returning The Captured Ship, by her, *Flora* of Gloucester to Captn Saml Calder, & cargo, Confirmed The Contra-Appeal of Captn Calder from That Judgment to obtain the heavy damages & Interests, which had not been granted to him, by that Judgment in the first instance — admitted & these damages & Interests, Since the 1st Pluviose 20th January last That she was taken near of Leghorn, where She was bound to, granted, as well as the *depends*, (law Suits Expenses) & my Guarrantee or bound as the depositary of the proceeds of the Cargo, Concealed in Short, We have Succeeded and obtained all our demands, in spite of all the Evasive reasons of our adverse Lawyer, who at Length despairing of the success of his Cause, desired it to be referred to the Minister of Justice before a judgment Could be rendered.

It is my duty to acknowledge that this Tribunal in issuing this just judgment, has paid a due respect & regard to the principles to the

True Spirit of the french laws, Their Treaties with Tuscany in short to the rights of Nations & neutral Property, without any Kind of Consideration Whatever, moreso, as the owner of the privateer is Cit^{en} Lucien Buonaparte, now legislator at the five Hundred, who was doing Every Thing in his power at Paris, to have the Ships & Cargo Condemned or Causing it to be done at aix, he is a brother of the great General Buonaparte.

It is also my duty To Inform you That in this affair of Captain Calder, my Colleague Philip Felichy our Consul at Leghorn did not loose a moment, in Concert with the Governor of Leghorn to apply to the french Consul Kerry and obtain from him his interference, near the privateer & near the french Government for the Violation of the Tuscanish Territory & it is to this interference on the 20th last January The moment The *Flora* was Captured & on the proofs of that Violation That This Cause has obtained the full success to our Wishes & to the positive order of the Minister of Marine

I mention you in a peculiar manner the good behaviour of our Consul felichy on this occasion

I Confirm you my last of the 24th May 1798, by Captn James freeman — bound for Boston — by which I advised you that Captn Stephen Swett of the american Ship *Eagle* of Marblehead taken and carried here, by a french privateer, Tho' with proper papers & roll' d' Equipage, has Compromised with his privateer, he paying £50000 & the charges, fees, &ca of the law-suit amounting to £14000 Thereabouts — A Judgment has been rendered in Conformity, Sina, & this Ship & Cargo is, now, free. I hope she will Sail in 2 or 3 Weeks.

The american Sloop *Prudence* of Nantuckett Captn Elisha Russell, loaded with Whalebones & Staves, is just arrived in this port. She was bound from Nantuckett to Genoa & taken by a Corsican privateer near of Genoa & carried to that port, but by a Judgmt from Consul Belleville of the french Republik, released and free; She is come here, to sell his Cargo, the price being not answerable at Genoa.

I have the honour to be with respect

Sir

Your most obdt humb. Servt

STEPHEN CATHALAN Junr

TIMOTHY PICKERING Esqr
Secretary of State
Philadelphia.

[SDA. Marseilles, Vol. 1, 1790–1802.]

[31 May 1798]

To Abraham Long, boatswain, from Captain Thomas Truxtun, U. S. Navy

SIR, All Such Articles as have been put under your charge or may hereafter be put under your charge, Such [as] Rigging, Anchors, Cables, blocks and other Boatswains Stores — you will be particularly attentive and keep in repair; and receive Such orders from the Sea Lieutenants and Master, as may be communicated to you by them in person or through a Subordinate Officer by their order. For Such directions as I do not give in writing or in person, is to [illegible] by one of those Gentlemen by my order from time to time.

It is your duty under Such orders as may be issued to direct whatever relates to the Rigging. to observe [illegible] the Masts are properly supported by their Shrouds, Stays[ail] backe stays. So that each may sustain a proportional effort when the Masts are strained by the violence of the wind, or the agitation of the Ship.

You are to take care that the blocks and running ropes are regularly placed, So as to answer the purpose intended, & you are also to take care that the sails are properly fitted, kept in repair handsomely and Securely bent, well furled and reefed when orders are issued for the latter purpose.

It is your duty to Summon the Crew to theirs. to assist in the necessary business of the Ship. and to relieve the watch when it expires, to examine the Condition of the Masts Sails and Rigging; remove what is unfit for Service and Supply what is deficient, and to perform this duty with as little noise as possible.

Your Mates are to assist you, in all the functions of your office; they are to be vigilant in turning up the Watch or all hands as occasion may require; they as well as yourself are to carry and wind a call. Compel a manly exertion in the Crew on all occasions, and to punish (as orders may be given) where it is deemed Necessary — You will keep a regular account of all articles received and expended. Attend Minutely to the rules and regulations issued by the President of the United States, through the Department of the Navy and with those of your Crew, have every article in your department kept in good order and at hand and to direct your Yeoman, not to suffer any of the store apparatus under your Charge to be left lying about the decks or otherwise kept out of place but to keep An Account of all Stores received and expended.—

I am Sir with Respect
Your ob^t humble Servant

THOMAS TRUXTUN

United States Ship *Constellation*
Patuxent River 31 May 1798
To ABRAHAM LONG
Boatswain.

[HS of Pa. NDA Photostat.]

[31 May 1798]

To James Morgan, gunner, from Captain Truxtun, U. S. Navy

SIR As Gunner of the Frigate *Constellation* under my Command you are now considered in Charge of the Artillery and Ammunition rec^d on board, and such as may hereafter be received you are to observe that the Cannon are always kept in order, and properly fitted with tackles and other furniture, and to instruct the Seamen &^c in the use and management of them. You are to keep the Cannon well tompioned and putty'd and have every thing prepared agreeable to the instructions I have, and may hereafter issue, so that in a few minutes warning the ship may be ready at any time to go into an Engagement by night or day — The Gunner's Mate and his Yoeman, are to assist you in every part of your duties; they should (particularly his mate's) be as well acquainted with Gunnery and every thing respecting the ordinance and Military Stores as the Gunner himself, their particular business under the Gunner, is to have everything ready for action in a moment's warning, they should never be at a loss [illegible] where to lay their hands upon any article belonging to the Gunners department; they should be expert in preparing to [illegible] Match Stuff, Grenadoes, and every sort of Combustible [illegible] and in a word, in doing every part of a Gunner's duty [on board] a Ship of War — The Quarter Gunners are to assist in every part of this duty, as keeping the Guns and their Carriages in [illegible] order and duly furnished with whatever is necessary, filling powder into Cartriges, Scaling the Guns, and keeping them always in a condition for Service — You will henceforward be particular in attending to your duty and causing all under you to do the same — The Stowage of the Magazine, Store Room, [illegible] Care and distribution of all the Stores of your department [should] be Minutely attended to In fact Sir the Manner in which Every thing was prepared, when you entred on the functions of your Office, Makes the duty under these and the regulations issued by order of the President (which must also be minutely [adhered] to) very easy for you & those acting with you —

In hopes of seeing great attention and regularity in all your Conduct and a lively expertness on all occasions

I remain Sir with great respect

Your Humble Servant

THOMAS TRUXTUN

United States Ship *Constellation*
Patuxent River 31st May, 1798.

To Mr JAMES MORGAN
Gunner.

[HS of Pa. NDA photostat.]

[1 June, 1798]

Affidavit of Secretary Timothy Pickering, regarding Flag of Truce Ship *Benjamin Franklin*

I Timothy Pickering, Secretary for the Department of State of the United States of America, hereby certify and make known, that the Ship *Benjamin Franklin,* whereof Lloyd Jones, a citizen of the said States, is master, and Francis Breuil, also a citizen thereof, is owner, is employed as a flag of truce by the consul General of the French Republic to the said United States, to transport a number of the citizens of his nation to France: wherefore I request all armed vessels, sailing under the flag of the Said States, and whomsoever else it may concern, to permit the said Ship *Benjamin Franklin,* freely to pursue her intended voyage without giving or suffering to be given to her any let or molestation but on the contrary to afford her every aid and protection of which she may Stand in need: In Faith whereof I have signed these presents and caused my Official Seal to be hereto affixed, at Philadelphia, this first day of June. A. D. 1798, and in the twenty second year of the Independence of the Said States.

TIMOTHY PICKERING.

[L. S.]

[SDA. Dom. L., Vol. 10.]

To Willings & Francis, agents, Philadelphia, from Captain Richard Dale, U. S. Navy

June 1. 1798 —

Messrs WILLINGS & FRANCIS
At Sea Off Sandy Hook

GENTLEMEN, I got to sea on Wednesday morning the wind was blowing fresh from the N. E. with rain and thick weather, at any other time, I should not thought of going to sea, but I was anxious to git a sight of the French Privateer, I thought if I could git out before he heard of me, he would not hisitate in comeing long side, when I got out to sea, I was told by a Pilot he went out of Cape May Road the morning I got to sea, the weather was very thick could not sea far, Thursday was a fine day and a good breeze, I fully expected to have had the pleasure of sending up to you, but to my mortification, I could not git sight of him, I was told by a Pilot in the afternoon, that he was a longside of him the day before. The Capt of the Privateer told him that he understood that I was out, if so, it was time for him to be off — Some *Dam rascal* has been giveing him information of my giting out. I am in hopes of finding him yet. the ship sails well from the wind, but not so well by the wind as I expected — I left the Capes of Delaware yesterday at 6 P. M. I expect to be back in a few days — I am a little disapointed in my Seamen. a number that shipt for seamen, is not much better Landsmen — I must make the best of them.

I am Gentlemen,
With much Esteem
Your Obt Servant,

RId DALE

9 A. M. Sandy Hook. N. N. W. 3 or 4 leagues.

[HS of Pa. NDA photostat.]

To John Harris, storekeeper, from Secretary of War

[PHILADELPHIA,]
War Department 1st June 1798.

Mr JOHN HARRIS.

SIR Be pleased to deliver to the Order of Captain Decatur for the Ship of War *Delaware* the following Articles.
Vizt:

3000	pounds of Gunpowder
667	Round Shot for 9 pounders
138	Double headed Do for Do
164	--Do-- --Do-- 6 pounders
26	Double Headed Do for ditto
5000	lbs of Grape for 9 pounders in Cannisters
420	lbs of do ------ 6 pounders -----ditto
16	Cartridge Boxes & Belts for Marines
800	Blank Cartridges for 9 pounders
200	-Do-- ---Do------- 6 do
100	lbs of Slow Match. —

[NDA, LB. Correspondence when Navy was under War Department, 1795–1978.]

To Secretary of War James McHenry from Alexander Hamilton

MY DEAR SIR Our citizens are extremely anxious that some further measures for their defence should take place. Do me the favour to inform me confidentially what means are *actually* in the disposition of your department for this purpose when & how they will be applied.

Yrs truly

A HAMILTON

June 1, 1798

A Capt *Hacker* formerly of our Navy is desirous of being employed. One or two good men have recommended him to me. It seems however — that he has been heretofore rather Democratic — I barely wish that his pretensions may be fairly but carefully considered & that he may have just chance as he merits

The sooner I hear from you the better

J MCHENRY Esq

[LC, J. McH. P., 1778–1799.]

To the Purser's Steward from Captain Thomas Truxtun, U. S. Navy

[2nd JUNE 1798.]

I again do desire that you attend minutely to the Act of Congress in Serving the Provisions to the Ship's Company, with this exception only, you are untill further orders to deliver each Man One pound of beef on Wednesdays — No other deviations to be made —

THOMAS TRUXTUN

United States Ship *Constellation*
Patuxent River 2d June 1798

To the Purser's Steward

Order of 4th June 1798

To Mr MORGAN Gunner

Musket Cartriges to be made & filled	11. 000
Pistol ditto	3. 600
Blunderbuss ditto	1. 000
Howitzers ditto	300
24 pd Cannon Cartriges (8 lb.) of Flannel	280
12 pd ditto ditto (3 lb.) of ditto	100

Cartriges for the Muskets, Pistols, Blunderbuss's and Howitzers must be put in Budge barrels, Seperately, which barrels are to have marked the number of dozn Contained therein.—

28 Cannon Cartriges of 24 lbs. and 10 Cartriges of 12 lbs. are to be filled for Scaling the Guns.— the remainder of the Paper Cartriges must be well dried and put up in dozens, ready to fill in case of Salute's — we shall Salute with only 4 lbs. of powder, fired from the 24 pdrs but the Cartriges are to Contain 6 lbs. for Scaling the 24 pdrs and 3 lbs. for Scaling the 12 pdrs—

[HS of Pa. NDA photostat. Truxtun's LB, 1798–9.]

To Captain Thomas Cole from Secretary of War

[PHILADELPHIA,]
War Department 2d June 1798.

Capt THOMAS COLE
Superintd of Navy Yard. Baltimore

SIR You will be pleased to deliver to the Order of Oliver Wolcott Esquire Secretary of the Treasury, such parts of the materials &c which are deposited in the Navy Yard at Baltimore, as may be by him required for the equipment of the Ship *Adrianna.* — You will be careful to keep a particular account of all articles you may deliver in conformity to this order, and take duplicate receipt, for the same, one of which you are requested to transmit to this Office with the account, when that ship shall be compleated. —

I am &c

[NDA, LB. Correspondence when Navy was under War Department, 1790–1798.]

[4 June 1798.]

To John Marshall from Captain Thomas Truxtun, U. S. Navy

SIR Your duty as Master at Arms is to exercise the Crew and teach them the use of Small Armes — To Confine and plant Centinels over the prisoners, and Superintend whatever relates to them during their Confinement-You are to see all lights and fire extinguished according to the regulations except Such as shall be permitted by proper Authority, or under the inspection of Centinels.

It is likewise your duty to attend the Gangway, when any boates arrive along Side, and Search them Carefully, together with their rowers, that no Spirituous liquors may be conveyed into the Ship, Unless by permission of the Commanding Officer — You are to See that the Small Arms be kept in proper order, to visit all vessels comeing to, or going from the ship without leave — You are to Acquaint the Officer of the watch with all irregularities in the Ship, which Shall come to your Knowledge — In these Several duties You are to be assisted by the Corporals, who relieve one Another at proper periods —

I expect you will attend Minutely to this duty while on board of the *Constellation* under my Command, by which means You will make your own Situation agreeable and Comfortable to Yourself. —

I am Yours &c

THOMAS TRUXTUN

UNITED STATES SHIP *Constellation*
4th June 1798.

To Mr JOHN MARSHALL.

[HS of Pa. NDA photostat.]

To Mr. William Pennock, Navy Agent, Norfolk, from Captain Thomas Truxtun

[4 JUNE, 1798.]

WILLIAM PENNOCK Esqr.

DEAR SIR Mr Francis has wrote me that you were to supply certain articles but whether it is expected that you are to furnish the remainder of the Stores or not, I cannot conjecture from his mode of doing business — The articles yet wanting on board, besides such refreshments as are necessary to lay in for the sick are as follows to vizt

Bread
Butter
Cheese
Molasses
Rice
Pease
Potatoes
Flour
Rum

You will be pleased to inform me whether you have instructions, to furnish the whole of the above articles, and what quantity of each — If you are ordered to furnish the quantity estimated for six months I think it will be best to take one half the bread on board immediately and one third of the other articles, as it will be easy to run into the Roads, every two months to fill up the Water, and to receive this proportion of Stores — Otherwise we shall be too much lumbered for the warm Season, and home station-particularly as we have Six months Beef & Pork on board You will also inform me, whether you are directed to furnish any supplies for those that may be sick or wounded — The Secy of War wrote me a few days ago intimating a desire that I should proceed to sea, as soon as I received my Instructions, but I am totally in the dark as to the above Supplies — The Grape Shot demanded, pursers Cloathing and a variety of other articles are still wanting from Philadelphia —

I have about 260 Men shipt including Officers, and 240 are on board — If Lieutenants Rogers Cowper & Triplett have been fortunate this last Week in getting Seamen. I shall proceed to Sea as Soon as I have the above articles, and receive my Instructions — I expect to get underway from here in a few days, and will receive my Stores as soon as they are sent along side — A Copy of this letter I forward to the Secy of War this day that he may see exactly how I am situated.

I am with respect Yours &C.

United States Ship *Constellation* THOMAS TRUXTUN
Patuxent 4 June, 1798 —.

[HS of Pa. NDA photostat. Truxtun's LB, 1798–9.]

To Captain Thomas Truxtun, U. S. Navy, from Secretary of War

[PHILADELPHIA,]
War Department. 4 June. 1798.

THOS TRUXTUN

SIR, I have the honor to transmit you a List of Articles, shipped on board the Sloop *May-Flower*, for the Frigate *Constellation*, which

I hope may arrive in Safety. They are ordered to Hampton Roads. —

List of Articles on Board the Sloop *May-Flower*, addressed to Captain Truxtun — vizt —

10 Boxes of Tallow & Wax Candles. —
2 ditto ditto –"– Mould. —
1 Slate and Pencil.
1 Pewter Ink Stand.
1 Day Book.
1 Memorandum Book.
1 Book to keep the Acc^{t} of Hospital Stores. —
5 Quires of Foolscap Paper. —
5 ditto " Letter ditto
200 Quills.
2 Boxes Wafers.
3 Paper Inkstands
1 Pound of Black Sand
2 Quires Blotting Paper
100 Yards of Table Linen
½ lb. Scotch Thread
18 d^{o} Sago
4 lb Jalip
6 lb Tapioca
12 lb Essence of Spruce
252 Cannister Shot — 24 Pd'rs
156 ditto 12 d^{o}
200 ditto 3 pd Howitzers
24 Sailor's
24 Pint Cups riveted
6 Sauce Pans
4 Camp Kettles
2 Copper Tea Kettles
4 tin Tea Pots
24 Iron Spoons
12 Tea Spoons
2 Tea Canisters
2 Pewter Bed Pans
2 d^{o} Chamber Pots
2 Candlesticks
4 Sconces
24 Silver Tea Spoons and
all the Hospital Stores ordered. —

[NDA. OSW, Vol. 1.]

To Robert G. Harper from Captain George Cross

New York *June 4th 1798.*

Sir I have taken the liberty to request my Friends Messrs Gustavus & H Colhoun of Phi^{a} to wait on you for information respecting some papers I have sent them, relative to the Capture & condemnation of the Brig *Fox* & Cargo of Charleston, by the French Pirates. I conceived it necessary the whole of these papers should be lodged in the Secretary's Office to establish the Claim, at a future day. should esteem it a favor of you on their application to put them in the right path, I also Sir from the knowledge you have of me, offer myself as a Candidate for the Command of an Armed Vessell. should any be fitted out by Government for the State of South Carolina. if on enquiry you find me capable & worthy of the Trust, will be thankfull for your Interest.

I am Sir with Respect
Yours &c

GEO. CROSS.

ROBERT GOODLOE HARPER Esqr

[NDA. Area 7, June 4, 1798.]

[5 June, 1798]

Extract of a letter from St. Martin's, regarding capture of the Brig *Active*, Captain Simkins

"This will inform you of our being captured and brought into this place. The fate of the brig * is yet undetermined, but expect the condemnation from Guadaloupe every day. I have not the most distant idea of her being cleared, as there have been nearly 20 condemnations since my arrival here (4 weeks) and not one solitary instance of a vessel cleared (except a Hamburgher and a brig owned by Frenchmen and bound from Guadaloupe to St. Bartholomews). Danes and Swedes share the same fate as Americans.

*Brig. *Active*, Simkins.

[LC, "Claypoole's American Daily Advertiser" (Phila.), 25 June 1798.]

Presumably to Secretary of War from Stephen Higginson, Navy Agent

BOSTON, *June 6, 1798.*

D^r SIR I received yours of 31 ult^o & note the contents. it is both unpleasant & injurious to have popular clamours at the appointments & other measures of Government, especially when it is the general opinion that the complaints are well founded; but it is impossible for the Executive to know characters sufficiently to avoid the Evil in many instances. Men readily or easily are drawn in to sign recommendations which they do not approve; but few will venture to join in a representation which goes to criminate or reprove the conduct of those who are already in Office. even those who will join in the clamor, & say severe things at the Corners, will start at the Idea of affixing their names to their own Sentiments openly avowed in their own way. it will not be easy therefore to obtain, perhaps, such a representation as you suggest respecting the Officers of the Frigate; nor shou'd I probably have communicated to you as I did, had not the business I have engaged in given me a natural opening to observe to you somewhat upon the Subject. But having gone so far, I can not hesitate to explain to you farther my own Sentiments. — Capt N: is in my estimation a rough blustering Tar merely, he is a good Seaman probably & is no doubt acquainted with many or most parts of his duty, So far as relates to practical seamanship; but he wants points much more important as a Commander in my view, prudence, judgement & reflection are no traits in his character, nor will he ever improve. his noise & vanity is disgusting to the Sailors; but a belief that he wants courage goes much farther to render him unpopular with them, for Sailors love to have brave Commanders. This opinion or belief however may not be well founded, I suspect it is not, it may have arisen from another opinion which is indeed often true, that blusterers are not apt to fight. M[r] Cordis the second L[t] is a young man, who possesses none of the requisites, he is deficient in every point, essential to a good Officer, he is said to be intemperate, & he looks like it. — the Surgeon, Read, is the opposite of what he ought to be in Morals, in politics & in his profession. there is not a man in this Town who would trust the life of a dog in his hands. his second, Blake, is of the same cast of character as Read, but not so highly finished. I believe that 19 in 20 of our steady Citizens, who know them would say these characters are correct. if you state the description to M[r] Otis he will probably confirm it. — M[r] Prebble the first L[t] is not here, he is a smart active popular man, judicious & qualified well for his station, or for the first command; but I do not believe he will go in the Ship when he sees his Associates.

I think we can prevail on Men to go in the *Herald* & Cutter that every one will not only approve but respond for. — Chapman I before recommended for the Cutter; & I will in a few days send you a list for both Vessels. — we shall want the general arrangements as well as Officers by the time they can be appointed & sent on. What are to be the Emoluments &c. it is presumed they will be equal in all the Vessels. —

I am glad M[r] Stoddert accepts, if he is a good man for the office he will soon put our Naval Affairs in train to become more respectable. —

In haste I remain respectfully yours &c.

STEPHEN HIGGINSON.

[Mass. HS. Pickering Papers, Vol. 22.]

To James S. Deblois, purser, from Secretary of War

[PHILADELPHIA,]
War Department. 6 June. 1798.

JAMES S. DEBLOIS

SIR In answer to the several Enquiries contained in your Letter of the 24 Ultimo. I have to observe. 1st. It is determined that the Contract Price, at which the Rations of the Crews of the Ships of War of the United States are furnished at the Ports where the Ships are fitted out, shall be the data to fix the Payment of the Rations to the officers, till such Time, as more regular Rules can be matured and established. —

2nd. The Pursers will act till further Orders as Pay Masters to the Officers, Seamen and Marines. Money will be furnished them from time to time for that Purpose. —

3rd. The military and other Stores, will be placed in the keeping of the proper Officers agreeably to the printed Regulations. —

4th. The Officer of Marines will be charged with the keeping of the Marine Arms Accoutrements and Clothing. If it any Time, Slops are required of the Purser for the Marines, the Persons requiring Them, will be charged with the Amount, and the same deducted from their Pay in the succeeding Pay Roll. —

5th. The Captain will designate to each Officer his proper Cabin. —

6th. The Stationary for the Ships Use, will be furnished by the Purser under order from the Captain, as directed in other Cases. —

[NDA. OSW, Vol. 1.]

To Secretary of State from Captain Timothy Newman

BOSTON *June 7th 1798.*

SIR, I can inform you of my safe Arrival at this place, with my Crew, I have but this moment got up to town from Nantaskett Roads, where I left the Ship in which I came Passenger. (The *Sarah* Capt Hopkins) in order to forward your Dispatches by this Mornings Post, The *Crescent* was very Joyfully Recieved and a very fine Ship. The Post going out in a few minutes will not admit of my being so Particular as I could wish. Nothing very Particular turn'd up on our very long passage of 90 days from Algiers, Except our falling in and Exchangeing a few Shott with a French Privateer Cutter near the Island of Madeira, She fired several Shott at us under English Colours, which our being very certain she was French, we Returnd & proved to our Satisfaction, it being calm and her Companion, (in sight) not being able to come to her assistance proved favourable to us. The English Consul at Madeira sent off Three Boats to our Assistance, and to inform us they were Two French Privateers, In your dispatches from Algeirs and Gibralter you will be informed of the disagreable State of our Commerce in the Medeteranian, and the Necessity of some force to protect it

Not knowing wheither any Provision is made here for paying the *Crescents* Porterage Bill, I am to se General Jackson (in one Hour) on that subject, and shall give you Information.

As soon as the People are paid off shall proceed to Newbury, and shall then send you on the Porterage Bill Receipts &ce

Haveing an ardent desire of Serveing my Country which at great Expence has Releived me from Slavery, and heareing their is a Number of Sloops of War, prepairing to protect our Commerce, I would willingly devout the Remainder of my life in its Service, your Informing me wheither those Vessells Commanders is appointed, and your Intrest in pointing out to me the most proper method to make Application will be Acknowledgd with Gratitude, Should esteem it a favour if you will write me a line. —

I am Sir with the Greatest Respect

Your Obedt Servt

TIMOTHY NEWMAN

[SDA. Algiers, Vol. 3, 1798.]

[7 June 1798.]

Order issued by Captain Truxtun, U. S. Frigate *Constellation*

In the River Patuxent Single Anchor
There are to be four Watches for the present
to Viz

1st	2 Midshipmen 1 Masters Mate 1 Quarter Master 1 Boatswain Mate	thirty Seamen & ordinary &c
2nd	2 Midshipmen 1 Masters Mate 1 Boatswain " 1 Quarter Master	Ditto — do.
3rd	2 Midshipmen 1 Masters Mate 1 Quarter Master 1 Carpenters Mate	Ditto ditto
4th	2 Midshipmen 1 Coxswain 1 Quarter Master 1 Carpenters Mate	ditto ditto

The Marines with a Corporal to Stand Guard as usual The Quarter Master's will attend Glass on Quarter Deck &c — Pilot to be Called on any Change & I am to be informed of any particular occurrence — — —

THOMAS TRUXTUN

UNITED STATES SHIP *Constellation*
7th June 1798 —

[HS of Pa. NDA photostat. Truxtun's LB, 1798–9.]

Presumably to Secretary of War from Stephen Higginson, Navy Agent

BOSTON *June 11, 1798.*

D. SIR There is now a better prospect of the Frigate being manned, Several parties of Sailors having been obtained in the out posts, it is said She has near 200 Men on board. — Mr Beals who is appointed 3d Lt is a smart young man, & will be a good Officer, he & Prebble, if he goes, will animate the rest, and give some efficiency. I have as yet heard nothing from Mr Wolcott respecting Capt Chapman & the other Officers for the Cutter, nor whether the mode of appointing for her & the *Herald* will be adopted; but in my view it is the only safe way, at least it is the surest to have men who will harmonize, & it will tend in the outset to facilitate the dispatch of the Vessels. it will also relieve the President from teasing applications, & will give more influence & respectability to the Captains. — we want also the general Arrangements for the Service as to Men, Marines, rations, regulations, &c &c, we shall wait I fear for Commissions &c — by a late arrival from Nantes we learn that Mr Marshal was there and Mr Pinckney was daily expected when they were to sail for Alexandria in a Ship taken up for them. Mr Gerry was to remain in Paris longer & will have a trying time of it. it will appear that our fears of embarrassment from the peculiar habits &c of this last were not without foundation.—
With much Sincerity, I am yours &c

STEPHEN HIGGINSON.

[Mass. HS. Pickering Papers, Vol. 22.]

To Captain Edward Miller from Secretary of War

[PHILADELPHIA,]
War Department 11th June 1798

Capt EDWd MILLER

SIR The Ship of War the *Delaware* (late *Hamburg Packet*) is nearly completed, her quantity of Men except only Marines are Stated to be engaged

It is indispensible that this Ship should proceed to sea immediately for the protection of the Commerce and Coasts of the United States — You will propose to the recruits under your command to offer themselves to serve on board the *Delaware*, as Marines for a short cruise, and may assure them, that if the number wanted, will voluntarily offer, they shall have their pay during this service, made equal to, Vizt — Sergeant 9, Corporal 8, Musician 7, and private 6 Ds per Month

You will make this proposition forthwith, to your men, and report the issue to the Secretary for the Department of War —

It is to be understood that the men, when no longer wanted on board the *Delaware*, are to return to the Infantry service under their former engagement —

I am Sir respectfully &ca

[NDA, LB. Correspondence when Navy was under War Department, 1790–1798.]

To Captain Richard Dale, U. S. Navy, from Secretary of War

[PHILADELPHIA,]
War Department. 11 June. 1798.

RICHd DALE.

SIR, The Intention of requiring you by your Instructions of the 22d May ultimo with the Ship *Ganges* under your command, to repair to a Station between Cape Henlopen and Cape James by the 12th instant, was, that you might receive additional Instructions, in case any Law which might be enacted by Congress should make it necessary. —

Instructions of the 28th May additional to Them of the 22d have been forwarded, and received by you — and as no new Law, or Change of Circumstances known to the President, make it necessary to add to these — You will not, if arrived at the Station mentioned, delay there but proceed (as I confidently flatter Myself) under your former Instructions, to act successfully and honorably. —

The last Letter I had the Pleasure to receive from you, as under the date of the 2d instant off Sandy-Hook. — It is thought adviseable to send this by a Pilot-boat. —

It is confidently stated, in a Letter from the Eastward, that there is a Twenty Gun Ship of War directly from France on the Coast — that She had made some Prizes, and that She said there were Five others of the same size to follow her, destined for our Coast. —

Captain Truxtun has received his orders, & I flatter Myself will soon be on his Cruising Ground, which is from Cape Henry, as far as the Southern Limits of our Coast. —

I expect the Secretary of the Navy here today or Tomorrow & am &c.

[NDA. OSW, Vol. 1.]

To Tench Francis, Purveyor, from Secretary of State

[PHILADELPHIA,]
Department of State 12 June 1798.

TENCH FRANCIS Esq[r]

SIR, I request you to inform me, whether a vessel can be loaded with stores for Algiers, in season to avail of the convoy of the armed Schooners about to depart for that place. Capt Tew's vessel is at Boston and may, if necessary, be employed for that object. Perhaps you have others in view. The convoy should not be lost if practicable to avoid it. I am, sir, &c

TIMOTHY PICKERING.

[SDA. Dom. L., Vol. 10.]

Presumably to Secretary of War from Stephen Higginson

BOSTON *June 12. 1798*

D SIR Your letter of the 7th instant I this day received, & note what you say as to Cap[t] Nicholson & his Ship &c. my last will have informed you that he is making much more progress in manning his Ship than was expected, he has now near 200 on board, & more are expected from the out posts, but the Ship has not Officers to give her a fair chance if She can be got to Sea, which I begin to think may take place. Cap[t] N: is not intemperate that I have either seen or heard of, he has exerted himself all he could to man & get out the Ship. his defects are more natural than acquired, they consist in want of natural talents rather than vicious habits; he is neither a Gentleman, nor a popular man with the Sailors, as some rough men are; but I know of no criminal conduct or neglect, nor such a gross incapacity as would justify perhaps a dismissal from Office in the public opinion. But I really wish he & some others of our old Naval Officers had never been appointed. it was natural for M[r] Washingtons Eye to be upon them at first; but our Navy in the revolutionary war was a bad school to educate good Officers in. — I believe that the characters I sketched to you in a former Letter will give a correct view of the Officers of the Frigate here. Prebble & Beals are the only men belonging to her, who appear to have any talents for the Navy; & I should tremble for the issue should She meet a french Cruiser of equal force, though I am sure we have a great national superiority over them for naval operations.

As to the Cutter & the *Herald*, I have this day written freely to M[r] Wolcott about the appointments for them; and I am confirmed in the belief that the Service cannot be promoted by them, unless they are officered in the way & by the men which I have mentioned. it is a wrong & a dangerous Idea, that Ships are to be provided for Men, to keep them in pay & give them a living. on the contrary Men are to be sought for & appointed to the Ships who will render them useful & efficacious. — I hope however that appointments will soon be made for those Vessels, or the Captains allowed to select their Officers for appointment, as we shall soon want all the Arrangements for dispatching them on a Cruise, every day lost is or may be important to our Commerce. —

No Letters have been received from Mr Wolcott requesting the Opinions of certain men as to Capt Nicholson, they may not perhaps be necessary; but if they do come you must not expect explicit answers from all the names mentioned, decission does not mark every mans character, still less such kind of responsibility as the appeal will appear to involve. it is invidious; it is inconvenient, & sometimes it will incur difficulty to give explicit opinions upon such questions, which few men will care to hazard. —

Capt Sever has not had much experience in a naval war, he has seen very little actual Service; but he is supposed to possess all the requisites to form a very good Officer, such as Spirit, Judgement, prudence, firmness &c^a^ sense of character which urges to great & brilliant actions; & with these points a man soon becomes very eminent even in naval Combat, of which our late War gave us many proofs. — Sever has a man ready to go as his first L^t^ who has seen Service in our late War, & is considered as eminent in every respect; indeed the *Herald* will be as well appointed as any Vessel need be, if the list prepared will be accepted. —

Chapman has been two years in the british Navy, is well versed in the practical parts of Naval operations, & has all the requisites to make an excellent Officer. —

I am glad to find that Congress continue rising, they must keep on & adopt Mr Fosters motion for open War, it is the path of safety & honour, & notning short of it will save our Country from being revolutionized. —

Wishing your labours may produce the good intended to our Country, I remain respectfully your hum. Serv.

STEPHEN HIGGINSON.

[Mass. HS. Pickering Papers, Vol. 22.]

To Messrs. Willings & Francis, agents, Philadelphia, from Secretary of War

War Department 12th June 1798

Messrs WILLINGS & FRANCIS

GENT^n^ Capt Dale with the *Ganges* Ship of War has been ordered to be on the 12th Instant at a Station between Cape Henlopen, and Cape James — Will you be so obliging as to employ a pilot Boat, with a prudent Master to convey to him the enclosed letter, and instruct the Master accordingly —

I have the honor to be

Gent^n^ with great respect &c^a^.

[NDA, LB. Correspondence when Navy was under War Department, 1790–1798.

To Captain Timothy Newman from Secretary Timothy Pickering

DEPARTMENT OF STATE *June 13, 1798.*

Captain TIMOTHY NEWMAN *Boston*

SIR, I rec^d^ yesterday your letter advising of the return of yourself and the crew of the *Crescent* to Boston. Captain Thompson who lately left Philadelphia for Portsmouth, carried with him my orders to pay your portage bill. I hope he has left notice of it at Boston, that you may all be promptly paid.

I am, Sir, &c.

TIMOTHY PICKERING

[SDA. Dom. L., Vol. 10.]

To Josiah Parker from Secretary Timothy Pickering

DEPARTMENT OF STATE, *June 13th 1798.*

JOSIAH PARKER Esqr

SIR, Agreeably to your request, I have the honor to inform you, that in August 1797, the United States Brigantine *Sophia* was sent to the West Indies, to collect and bring home such American Seamen, as should be found destitute of the means of returning. She visited Guadeloupe, Porto Rico, St Domingo and Cuba: but found such destitute seamen only at Porto Rico, from which she brought upwards of ninety to St Domingo, where many American vessels wanting hands, they were distributed among them; four only being brought home in the *Sophia*. A severe and dangerous Sickness of the Captain of the *Sophia* caused some detention, so that she did not get home until the latter end of December: and this mode of relieving our Seamen proved very expensive.

Lately two vessels arrived at Philadelphia from Porto Rico, and each brought as many American Seamen (about Sixty in all) as were willing to return: for many declined the invitation; *chusing rather to enter on board French privateers.* A son of Colo Talbot returned in one of those vessels from Porto Rico, having gone thither from Guadeloupe, I enquired into the situation of American Seamen, at that Island; and found that all had frequent opportunities of returning home.

Upon the whole, I do not think any further provisions are necessary to be made by Law to enable the President to afford relief to American seamen left in foreign countries, upon the principles of the act for the aid and protection of American Seamen. I have thought it my duty to offer some pecuniary aid to the Seamen, who are lately brought to Philadelphia from Porto Rico, as above mentioned to enable them to travel to their respective homes in other States. Perhaps it may be expedient to encourage all American vessels to receive on board any American seamen, destitute of the means of returning by advertising a compensation of a certain sum per man. This is a thought, which has just occurred, but which I will submit to the President. Another suggestion I beg leave to make, that an Act Should be made limiting the times within which all American Seamen on board of any privateers of the belligerent powers should abandon them and return into the Service of their country, or be subjected to proper and adequate penalties: this act to operate as an amnesty for past offences. I am very respectfully &c.

TIMOTHY PICKERING

[SDA. Dom. L., Vol. 10.]

Building of Revenue Cutter *Eagle* by William and Abra Brown

JUNE 13. 1798.

SIR Please to pay William & Abra Brown One thousand dollars, and charge to their a/c for Building the Revenue Cutter *Eagle* for the Georgia Station

JOSHUA HUMPHREYS

Sharp Delany Esquire Collector of the Port of Philadelphia —

Received June 13, 1798 from Sharp Delany Collector One thousand Dollars being on acc[t] of building the Revenue Cutter *Eagle* for the Georgia Station.

W[m] & ABRA BROWN

[GAO, No. 11381.]

To Captain John Barry, U. S. Navy, from Lieutenant David Ross

CHESTER *June 13th* 1798.

SIR The sloop with the Powder and Stores arrived on Evening of the 12th ins[t] this Morning discharged her. you will be pleased to excuse me not sending a list of the Crew, as [torn space mutilating one word] have been Employ[d] — the water is all filled — the ship draws 20 feet 11 Inches abft and 18 feet 8 Inches froward. the Pilot request you not to send aney more Stores on board untill we get as low as New Castle — the officer is all well we have 12 of the Ship Companey in the doctor list

I Remain Sir your
Humb[e] S[t] at Command

D[AVID] ROSS

Commodore BARRY
Philadelphia

[NYPL.]

To John Fitzgerald from Secretary T. Pickering

PHILAD[a] *June 14th 1798*

Col[o] JOHN FITZGERALD
Collector of the Port of Alex[a]

SIR The Secretary of War being absent, I am charged by the President of the United States with the Business of that department, which occasions this address to you — Yesterday were laid before me Two Letters from Leiut[t] James Triplett of the Corps of Artillery with an estimate of 682 Dollars, on account of the advanced wages, bounties and expences for enlisting a number of Seamen & Marines for the *Constitution* [*Constellation*] Frigate, Cap[t] Truxton — It was too late to go thro' the ordinary process of remitting money, and as Lieutenant Triplett is waiting only for that, to discharge a variety of demands at Alexandria — and as I apprehend Cap[t] Truxton will be waiting for him at Hampton Roads, and incur some delay even with the utmost dispatch that Lieut[t] Triplett can make — I have to request that you will advance to him seven hundred Dollars for the purpose above mentioned, taking duplicate Receipt — By tomorrow's Post, I will reimburse to you that sum —

CAPTAIN JOHN BARRY, U. S. NAVY.

Capt Truxton wrote on the 10th Instant, that he should go down the Bay, and be ready to put to Sea by next Sunday or Monday, and I was extremely unwilling that the Frigate should be delayed for want of this small sum, or that she should go to sea without an officer to command her marines —

I am with great respect &ca

T. Pickering

[NDA, LB. Correspondence when Navy was under War Department, 1790–1798.]

To Captain Thomas Truxtun, U. S. Navy, from Secretary Timothy Pickering in absence of Secretary of War

Phila. *June 14th 1798.*

Thos Truxtun

Dr Sir, The Secretary of War being absent. the President has charged me [T. Pickering] with the Business of that Department for a few days. Yesterday I saw two Letters from Lieut Triplett, calling for Money to discharge various Demands, incurred by him at Alexandria, for inlisting Seamen & Marines, for your Frigate, & sending them on board: but it was now too late to remit the money in the ordinary Way by this day's Mail: I have therefore written to my friend Colo Fitzgerald, Collector of the Port, to advance to Lieut Triplett, seven hundred dollars: his estimate was 682. I hope there will be no difficulty in the Way of this Advance, as I have engaged to remit by tomorrow's Mail the 700$ to Colo Fitzgerald. I have also written to Lieut Triplett to pay or make Arrangements to pay the above Demands, and to hasten to join you in Hampton Roads, agreeably to your Orders, informing him that I had seen your Letter of the 10th in which you say, that you should proceed to Hampton Roads, & be ready to put to Sea by Sunday or Munday; & therefore, if he made any delay, you would go to Sea without him.—

[NDA. OSW, Vol. 1.]

To Lieutenant of Marines James Triplett from Secretary Timothy Pickering in absence of Secretary of War

Philada. *June 14th 1798*

Lieut Jas Triplett

Sir, Yesterday were shewn to me [T. Pickering] your Letters, of the 3rd & 10th Instant, but too late to go through the ordinary Process of remitting Money. In the former, you inclosed an Estimate of Demands incumbent on you to discharge, amounting to 682 dollars, besides some Expences for Captain Moore. I have also seen Captain Truxtun's Letter of the 10th informing that he should proceed down the Bay, and be ready to go out to Sea by Sunday or Monday next, the 17th or 18th Inst Hence it follows, that he will be detained on your Account, or proceed — to Sea without you. To prevent, as far as possible, the former, I have concluded to desire Colo Fitzgerald, Collector of the Port of Alexandria, to advance to you seven hundred Dollars, which I will replace in his hands by Tomorrow's Post — You will therefore, call on him immediately for the Purpose. — pay, or make an adequate Arrangement for paying the demands, above referred to — and hasten to Hampton to embark, agreeably to Captain Truxtun's orders. —. — The Secretary of War, being absent, I am charged by the President with the business of his Office. —

[NDA. OSW, Vol. 1.]

To Joshua Humphreys, naval constructor, and Captain Thomas Thompson from Secretary of War

[After 14 June 1798]

To Mr Joshua Humphreys and Captn Thos Thompson

You will be pleased, with all convenent speed to repair to Baltimore in the State of Maryland and there examine such vessels, as can be furnished, and appear calculated to carry from 16 to 22 Guns — Six nines & 12 pounders

The ——— ——— belonging to Mr Barton has been offered for the public — I have also been informed that there is one belonging to Mr Lorman just from the West Indies, which may be obtained

You will ascertain and report the age of each vessel, The exact state of her Hull, Timbers, Masts Rigging, Sails, and every other particular by which a Judgment can be formed of her value, as well as her qualities, and fitness for the purposes for which they are wanted — You will state the alterations, repairs, and articles which she will require to fit her for Sea, the time in which she can be so fitted, and an estimate of the Expense —

You will also obtain from the owner of each vessel the lowest price at which they will part with them to the Government. —

It will be proper to keep an account of Your Expences, that the same may be settled for in the usual manner —

[NDA, LB. Correspondence when Navy was under War Department, 1790–1798.]

To Captain Stephen Decatur (senior), U. S. Navy, from Secretary of War

[Philadelphia,]
War Department. 15 June, 1798.

Capt S. Decatur

Sir The Ship *Delaware*, heretofore called the "*Hamburgh Packet*" now in the Port of Philadelphia, being purchased on account of the United States, and intended to be equipped and employed as a Vessel of War. —

I am directed by the President to order you, as a Captain in the Navy of the United States, to repair forthwith on board and take the Command of said Ship. —

You will use your Exertions to get the Ship as soon as possible, ready for Sea; and direct only such Improvements and Alterations to be made in her, as will not incur great Expence, or occasion a long detention.

She is to be completely equipped for a Cruise of three Months.—

You will furnish the Names of such Persons, as you may think qualified for the following Appointments respectively.—

1 Lieutenant.
1 Surgeon
1 Purser
1 Sailing Master
2 Mid Shipmen
1 Boatswain
1 Gunner.
1 Carpenter
1 Sailmaker.

The Lieutenant when appointed will act as Lieutenant of Marines, and will immediately proceed to enlist Eleven Privates, One Serjeant, one Corporal and Two Musicians, to serve as Marines in the Navy of the United States, for the term of Twelve Months, unless sooner discharged. You will transmit to him the annexed Regulations for the Government of his Proceedings. —

You will cause such of your Officers, as may appear best calculated for the Business, to open houses of Rendezvous in proper Places, and exert Themselves to engage Seventy able Seamen and Thirty five ordinary Seamen for the aforesaid term of Service. —

The pay of the able Seamen to be seventeen dollars; and that of ordinary Seamen, Ten dollars per Month. —

It is directed that none other than healthy robust and well organized Men, be enlisted or entered. To this End, you will cause the Surgeon to attend at the place or Places of Rendezvous to examine each Sailor and Marine, and certify to the recruiting officer, that they are well organized, healthy and free from scorbutic or consumptive affections, before he engages Them. If Wages are paid to any without such Certificate, it will (be) at the Risk of the Officer paying It. —

The officer at each Rendezvous will make a Return of the Number of Seamen and Marines recruited or engaged each day, stating therein the Number delivered over to the Ship, and transmit the same to the Captain, and a Duplicate to the Secretary of War. —

The Officer of each Rendezvous, on the Desertion of a Seaman or Marine, besides the usual Exertions and Means to be employed on such occasions to recover and apprehend Them, will transmit as soon as possible, a description of Them to the Secretary of War. —

The Purser, until further orders, will act as Paymaster to the Officers and Crew and will receive from Time to Time Money to make Payments. —

Marines are to be advanced Two dollars each out of their first Month's Pay. —

As soon as you give Notice of the Places of Rendezvous and the Names of the Officers who will have Charge of them, a sufficient sum will be remitted to the Purser, to be paid over occasionally to Them to promote the recruiting Service. The officers receiving the Money will be held accountable for it's faithful Application, and must produce at the Accountant's Office, proper Vouchers for it's Expenditure.

The Names of the Marines, and Seamen are to be entered Alphabetically in the Muster & Pay Rolls, and the Men to be mustered while in Port, by a qualified Person, whose Certificate as well as your's, is to be attached to the Muster Roll.

You will be pleased to make out an Inventory of and Receipt for, on behalf of the United States all military Stores and Ammunition, including Arms and Cannon, Tackle, Apparel, all other Stores and Articles of Equipment Provisions &c. comprized in the Purchase of the Ship and delivered to you; a duplicate of which Inventory and Receipts you will transmit to the Secretary for the department of War.

You will make out, and return as aforesaid, a List of all Warlike Stores, Articles of Equipment &c that may be wanted in addition to what shall be delivered to you; in order that the same may be procured as speedily as possible.—

[NDA. OSW, Vol. 1.]

To Charles Biddle from Captain Thomas Truxtun, U. S. Navy

United States Ship *Constellation*
Off Rappahanock 15th June 1798

Dear Sir I am now on my way down the Chesapeak, having 300 men on board, the remaining thirteen which will complete my Crew, by Act of Congress, I shall receive, as soon as I arrive in the Roads. (Point Comfort) —

Altho' my Compliment will be Complete as to Numbers, we shall have too few Seamen, and too many ordinary among them.—

War is Certain, and perhaps with you the business is conclusive, I only hear from Philadelpa about once a fortnight, of course every thing is stale with you when it is new to me. —

I am directed to send in all French Cruizers Only, but should I meet a fat Merchantman, or a Neutral Covering French property, it will seem hard to let such pass. —

Before this reaches you, I shall be on the Coast, and I hope soon to pay my respects to some of the piratical Junto Should a French Man Commanding one of those fall in my way I must consider him simply as a prisoner of War, but an *American* or *Englishman* otherwise.

I find by some papers sent me from Baltimore, that the British have Actually left Port au Prince, and the Post's they held in that Neighbourhood — If this be True and it seems pretty strait — they should employ that Army in taking possession of the Florida's — I would secure to them an uninterrupted passage up the Mississippi, and to us they would be better Neighbours than the French, who will otherwise oblige the Spaniards to put them in possession of those two Provinces. —

Altho' the British failed in their attack on Portorica, it was owing to bad arrangements and worse management — Should Louisiana & the Florida's not be their Object, It would be a great Conquest for them, the Island of Porto Rica, on Account of the excellence of the harbour, as well as the fertility of the Soil; and a Good harbour for Men of War is much wanted to windward — We should only be interested by having a Nest of pirates distroyed, that have and will continue to do us much mischeif. —

I shall be glad to hear from you as often as convenient, and should any accident happen at Amboy (life is uncertain) I shall thank you for your attention, to my (in that Case) Unfortunate little ones, untill I Return. —

You will oblige me by good advice to Harry, he is Young and has much of My property in hand, His obligations are among My Papers at Amboy — Should he by any misapplication of money leave me to begin the world again, at this time of day, with a large family, it would be hard indeed. —

It was my wish to provide for My Child; I have did it in the best manner I could. Without injustice to My family Generally — that is by a loan to Harry and by giving him Good Advice — Whether he now pays any attention to it or not, I cannot say, tho' I hope he does. —

My Best Respects to all friends and with sincere good wishes for your health & happiness and that of M[rs] Biddle & Family — I remain

Dear Sir

Your very obt

THOMAS TRUXTUN

CHARLES BIDDLE Esq[r]

[NHSC, NYHS.]

[15 June 1798.]

To Lieutenant of Marines James McKnight from Secretary of War

[PHILADELPHIA.]

Lieut[t] JAMES MCKNIGHT

SIR, The President of the United States by and with the Advice and Consent of the Senate, having appointed you a Lieutenant of Marines, in the Ship of War *Delaware*, you will be pleased to commence the recruiting the Complement of Marines allowed to said Ship — to wit — one Serjeant — one Corporal, one Drum — one Fife and twenty one Privates. —

In the Performance of this Duty, you will pay particular Attention to the Rules and Regulations herein after mentioned. —

For Rules & Regulations. refer to pages 5, 6 & 7.

Given at the War Office of the United States, this fifteenth day of June A. D. 1798, and in the twenty second year of the Independence of said States. —

[NOTE.—Pages 5, 6, and 7 above referred to contain recruiting instructions dated 16 March 1798, and addressed to the Lieutenant of Marines on board the Frigate *Constellation*.]

[NDA. OSW, Vol. 1.]

To John Harris, storekeeper, from Secretary of War

[PHILADELPHIA,]
War Department 15th June 1798

Mr JOHN HARRIS

SIR Be pleased to deliver to Lieutenant M^c^Knight for the Marines on board the Ship of War the *Delaware*. —

1 Serjeants Suit of Cloathing complete.
2 ________ ditto Musicians d^o^
21 Privates, ditto and 1 Corporal d^o^
3 Hangers for non commissioned Officers
25 Knapsacks.
6 Dozen Musket Flints
15 Prickers and Brushes
50 Blankets
10 Cutlasses.

In case any of the above articles are not in Store you will be pleased to state the same immediately that they may be procured without delay. —

[NDA, LB. Correspondence when Navy was under War Department, 1795–1798.]

Concerning purchase of Ship *Herald*

[15 JUNE 1798.]

TO ALL PEOPLE to whom this present Bill of Sale shall come, I Edward Davis of Boston in the County of Suffolk & State of Massachusetts Mariner Send Greeting.

KNOW YE, That I the said Edward Davis for and in Consideration of the Sum of Twenty one thousand Dollars to me in Hand, well and truly paid, at or before the Ensealing and Delivery of these Presents, by Stephen Higginson Esquire of Boston aforesaid Merchant for and in behalf of the United States of America the Receipt whereof I do hereby acknowledge, and am therewith fully and entirely satisfied and contented, have granted, bargained and sold, & by these Presents do grant, bargain and sell, unto the said Stephen Higginson as aforesaid — all the Hull or Body of the good Ship *Herald* — together with all and singular her masts, yards, spars, sails, rigging, cables, anchors, Boats & appurtenances &c stores as per Inventory delivered — now lying at Boston — and registered at the Port of Boston & Charleston, the Certificate of whose Registry is as follows, viz.

"In Pursuance of an Act of Congress of the United States of America, entitled 'An Act concerning the registering and recording of Ships or Vessels,' Edward Davis of Boston in the State of Massachusetts Mariner having taken or Subscribed the oath required by the said Act; and having sworn that he is the only Owner of the Ship or Vessel called the *Herald* of Boston, whereof the said Edward Davis is at present Master, and is a Citizen of the United States as he hath sworn; and that the said Ship or Vessel was built at Newbury in the State aforesaid this present year as appears by a Register No. 57, granted

Permanent N° 218— Two hundred eighteen

S S Joseph Nourse Register

at the port of Newbury port on the twenty first day of October, 1797, now given up and cancelled — And Michael Hodge, Surveyor of that District having certified that the Said Ship or Vessel has two Decks and three Masts; and that her Length is Ninety two feet eight inches, her Breadth Twenty six feet, three inches one half, her Depth Thirteen feet, one inch and three quarters and that she measures Two hundred seventy nine tons; & 75/95; that She is a square sterned Ship, has Quarter Galleries, and a man figure Head; And the said Edward Davis having agreed to the description and Admeasurements above Specified, and sufficient security having been given according to the said Act, the said Ship has been duly registered at the Port of Boston & Charleston

SS Benjn Welde D^y Cours

James Lovell New Off—

Given under my Hand and Seal at the Port of Boston and Charleston this twenty seventh Day of October, in the Year One thousand seven hundred and nine seven."

TO HAVE and to HOLD the said granted and bargained Ship and Premises, with the Appurtenances, unto the said Stephen Higginson as aforesaid his Heirs, Executors, Administrators, or Assigns to his & their only proper Use, Benefit and Behoof forever. And I the said Edward Davis do avouch myself to be the true and lawful Owner of the said Ship and her Appurtenances, and have in me full Power, good Right, and lawful Authority to dispose of the said Ship and her Appurtenances, in Manner as aforesaid. And furthermore I the said Edward Davis do hereby covenant and agree to warrant and defend the said Ship and Appurtenances, against the lawful Claims and Demands of all Persons whatsoever, unto him the said Stephen Higginson as aforesaid.

IN WITNESS WHEREOF, I the said Edward Davis have hereunto set my Hand and Seal the twelfth Day of June —, in the Year of our Lord One Thousand seven hundred and ninety eight.

ED^d DAVIS.

Signed, Sealed and delivered in Presence of us,
J. WATERS, J^r
THOS. SMITH

BOSTON *June 15 1798*

This certifies that I have received of Capt Edward Davis in virtue of the written Bill of Sale possession & delivery of the Ship *Herald* for & on account of the United States, with all the articles belonging to her as stated in the enclosed Inventory.

JAMES SEVER.

[GAO, No. 9847.]

To Rufus King, United States Minister, London, from Rob W. Fox

FALMOUTH, *15th June 1798.*

R. W. Fox —
RUFUS KING Esqr

ESTEEMED FRIEND In consequence of the information contained in thy esteemed of the 12th Ins^t, I have wrote to Plymouth, Scilly, Dartmouth, Penzance & Ilfracombe of the risk American Ships run in attempting to enter the Port of the Texel, We have no Vessel here bound for the U. S. so I have not an opportunity of communicating it to my Friends there —

The Bremen Vessel *See Blhum* loaden at Charleston for Amsterdam with Tobacco Rice &c the property of a Citizen of the U S of America was Captured by the *Triton* Frigate & sent in here — I have caused the Cargo to be claimed & its restored by Decree of the Court — Now the Captain says he'l proceed to the Texel notwithstanding he has been told of the great risk — I presume if he perseveres & the Cargo is Captured it will be condemned, do favor me with thy opinion hereon, & if I am justified in insisting on the Vessells not proceeding

I am with great respect

Thy assured Friend —

ROB W. FOX

LONDON —

[SDA. Falmouth, CL, Vol. 1, 1790–1802.]

To Secretary of War from Captain Thomas Truxtun, U. S. Navy

[17 JUNE 1798.]

SIR After long Calms and adverse Winds, I have at length reached these Roads, having Three Hundred and five Men on Board, a particular List of which I shall send you as soon as possuble.

Being all ready for Sea, I only wait the arrival of the *May Flower* from Philadelphia with the Shot, and when I receive that indispensible Article, I shall be out in a few Hours after.

Lieutenant Triplett did not come down with Mr Rogers as I expected. Rogers supposes his Want of Money to defray the recruiting Business, is the Cause; be that as it may, I shall not wait here a Moment on his Account.

I have the Honour to be with great Respect &c.

THOMAS TRUXTUN

HAMPTON ROADS —

17th June 1798 —

UNITED STATES SHIP *Constellation*

Mr McHENRY

Secretary of War.

[HS of Pa. NDA photostat. Truxtun's LB, 1798–99.]

To Jeremiah Yellott, Navy Agent, Baltimore, from Secretary of Navy

[PHILADELPHIA,]

Navy Department June 18. 1798

JEREMIAH YELLOTT

Baltimore

I had not before this day entered upon the Duties of my Office, or you would have sooner heard from me. —

Mr John Donaldson of this City, has sold to the Public 18 twelve pound Cannon, and engaged I believe to deliver 12 of them to the Ship *United States* at New Castle; he it seems first wrote to Mr Stewart who did not send the Guns, afterwards to Mess William

M^c^Donald & Co to forward them to Mr Zebulon Hollingsworth at Elkton, they make difficulties, and there is no certainty, that the Guns will be sent on, although the Ship waits for nothing else. — In this state of things, will you permit me to request, that you will immediately enquire into the state of this Business, and if the Guns should not be sent on, to forward them, either by a fast sailing Vessel hired for the purpose, or by way of the head of Elk, as you shall judge most expeditious.

I trouble you on this subject because the Guns are wanted without delay.

[NDA. GLB, Vol. 1.

To Jeremiah Yellott, Navy Agent, Baltimore, from Secretary of Navy

[PHILADELPHIA,]
Navy Department June 18. 1798

JEREMIAH YELLOTT
Baltimore

I mentioned to you in a Letter of to Day that I had not before entered upon the duties of my Office, in fact I have not yet taken the Oath of Office, this I shall do Tomorrow, & by the next Post shall write you officially; — my opinion is that the *Montezuma* ought to be purchased, I shall Tomorrow consult the President on the subject, in the mean time I wish Mr Taylor would suspend her loading.

M^r^ McHenry has been absent ever since my arrival here, — now Mr Wolcot is gone to New York, these circumstances have kept back the Business of my Department, I hope it will be better attended to in future, and while the assistance of Gentlemen of your knowledge & worth can be obtained, I shall not despair of discharging the duties of my Office with promptness, and economy, two things highly essential to be observed in the present crisis of our Affairs

[NDA. GLB, Vol. 1.]

To Mr. Jones, Treasury Department, from Secretary of Navy

[PHILADELPHIA]
Navy Department June 18. 1798

Mr JONES.
Treasury Depart.

Mr Wolcot informed me, you would be so good as to afford me any information in your power in relation to the Department of the Navy. —

Will you be so obliging as to inform me how many of the twelve Ships, authorised by Congress, have been procured, and what steps have been taken to procure others? —

Be so good as to add, when the *Adriana* at Baltimore will be ready to receive her Guns. —

[NDA. GLB, Vol. 1.]

To Jeremiah Yellott, Navy Agent, Baltimore, from Secretary of Navy

[PHILADELPHIA,]
Navy Department June 19, 1798

JEREMIAH YELLOTT
Baltimore

Being satisfied from the information contained in your Letter to Mr Wolcot, that the *Montezuma* is a proper Ship for the Public service, I have to request the favor of you to purchase her on account of the United States, as to the price, I know you will get her on the best terms in your power. —

I have also to solicit, calculating on your Skill, and Patriotism, that you will with as much expedition as possible have this Ship fitted and prepared for war, I think you mentioned in one of your Letters to Mr Wolcot that you would undertake the superintendence of this Vessel, and it is this consideration, as much as the fast sailing of the Ship which determines me to buy her, in preference to any others that are offerred.

I hope it will be in your power to procure Guns, and all the Military and other Stores she may want in Baltimore which will save the expence, and the delay of transportation, Will you be so good as to let me know as soon as you can determine, what cannot be procured with you, that I may make arrangements in season for providing them elsewhere. — Mr Wolcot is now at New York, and I am at a loss for the correspondence between you and him, but I can see generally, that it is expected, that every Article of every kind, which can be procured by you for the two Ships, will be so obtained, and that no measures will be taken to procure any article which you can have supplied, I have requested the Treasury Department to forward on to you, One thousand Dollars.

P. S. I have just seen your Letter of the 12th Ins^t^ to Mr Wolcot, the information requested shall be given Tomorrow

[NDA. GLB, Vol. 1.]

To Mr. Morgan of the *Constellation* from Captain Thomas Truxtun, U. S. Navy

JUNE 19th 1798.

Mr MORGAN, Two Boxes, containing seventy two Cannisters of Shot for the Howitzers, have been placed in the Three Tops by my Order to Viz —

Thirty in the Fore, and Thirty in the Main Top, and twelve in the Mizzen Top, two Lynch Stocks with Matches (besides one to be sent up lighted when the Orders to Quarters are given) must always be in each of the Chests, as also the Sponges, and about ten Dozen of Wads; the Cartridges in the Budge Barrels, must be kept handy and ready for sending up in each Top at a Moments Warning, as also a Powder Horn, and Pricker.

As I directed the Hole at the End of the Sponge Staff to be made, for the Purpose of putting the Cartridge in the Howitzers, you must explain that Part of the Business to the Top Men, in Order that they comprehend the Intention.

Three Muskets and three Cartouch Boxes, filled with Cartridges, are to be sent to each Top, whenever the Order for Quarters is given. — At the same Time fourteen Boxes of Cannister Shot for the 24 Pounders, and five for the 12 Pounders are to be got up, and placed conveniently, to the Guns, as well as the Bar Shot,—the Boxes containing the Cannister Shot will serve, when [they] are expended, to pass up round Shot in &c. I do again require of you to be attentive to the Duty assigned you by your Station, and that every Article at any Time Night or Day, be ready for Action in a Moment's Warning. You will therefore have at least half a Dozen spare Breechings ready, and as many Spare Tackle Falls &c. —

I am Sir

Your Obed[t] humble Serv[t]

THOMAS TRUXTUN.

[HS of Pa. NDA photostat. Truxtun's LB, 1798–9.]

To Isaac Garretson, purser, from Captain Thomas Truxtun, U. S. Navy

HAMPTON ROADS — *19th June 1798.*

M[r] ISAAC GARRETSON

Purser of the Frigate *Constellation*

SIR The Hospital Stores per List on other Side, you will cause to be delivered from Time to Time to Doctor Balfour (as he may direct) in the original Package or Cask, as the Case may be. — The Doctor will direct the Issue of each Article, and keep a regular Account of the same, to be transmitted to the Government, or made to me. —

Such Kettles and Pots as are in your List of Stores, and may be wanted for the Surgeon's Use, you will be pleased to deliver to his Order, keeping a regular Register or Account of the same. —

I am Sir

With Respect Your Obed[t] Serv[t]

THOMAS TRUXTUN.

Hospital Stores

1 Box Containing		9 lbs. Tamarinds
" "		4 " Salep
" "		6 " Tapioca
" "		12 Essence of Spruce
1 Keg "		18 Lags
1 Barrel "		32½ Gallons Brandy
3 Quarter Casks		98 " Sherry Wine
3 " "		99 " Lisbon ditto
1½ " "		47¾ " Port — "
8 Kegs "		66 " Porter
3 Hogsheads "		400 " Vinegar
1 Barrel "		214 lbs. Barley
2 " "		62 Gall[s] Molasses
1 " "		Linseed Meal
1 " "		156 lbs. Sugar
1 Box "		50 " Chocolate
1 Barrel "		213 " Rice
1 Keg "		25 " Oatmeal
1 Box "		Raisons
1 Keg "		5 Gallons Lime Juice
1 Barrel "		15 lbs. Bohea Tea
"		6½ lbs. Hyson Skin Tea
"		9 " Allspice
"		7 " Mustard
"		3½ " Pepper
"		1½ " Ginger
1 Keg "		2½ " Linseed Oil

[HS of Pa. NDA photostat. Truxtun's LB, 1798–9.]

To Secretary of the Treasury from Secretary of Navy

[PHILADELPHIA,]
Navy Department June 19. 1798

SECRETARY OF THE TREASURY

Capt Yellott of Baltimore who has the direction of the Public Ship *Adriana* [renamed *Baltimore*], mentions in his Letter of the 12th Inst to the Secretary of the Treasury, that he is in want of money to pay laborers and other contingencies.

If no money has been sent him in consequence of his requisition, be pleased to direct that One thousand Dollars be remitted him by the Mail of Tomorrow

[NDA. GLB, Vol. 1.]

To Daniel Eldridge and Ambrose Shirley from Captain Thomas Truxtun, U. S. Navy

[JUNE 20, 1798.]

SIR, As you have repaired on Board this Frigate to take on the Functions of a Master you will please to consider the following as the general Duty assigned to you.

The Keeping of the Ship, in order and having a Watchful Eye, that Part of the Rigging, Sails, Materials, or other Furniture remain unrepaired, with a due Attention to the Navigation of the Ship under my particular Orders, and to the keeping & Account of all Articles received & expended in Every department: You are to see that the Stores of every Description are preserved, and that none are wasted; to see that the Log, and Log Book be regularly, and correctly kept, by noting all Occurrences, and making proper Remarks at the Time. It is your Business to attend to the Ship's Movements in every Situation at Sea, or in Port, to keep the Hawse clear when at Anchor, preserve the Cables, and have constantly the Tiers clear, and kept clean; proper mathematical Instruments, and Books for your own Use, and the Purpose of navigating must be provided by you, Charts are furnished by Government.

It is your particular Duty to attend the Stowage of the Hold, for which and other Purposes in the Line of your Station, you have your Mates, and Quarter Masters to aid, and be subservient to your Orders.

You are to examine all Provisions and report the State of such as may be injured, or unfit for Use, to cause Justice to be done in the Issue of every Article, as well to the United States, as the Ship's Crew, at the End of each Expedition, or when the Ship is laid up, you are to deposit with the Secretary of the Navy a Copy of the Log Book, as well as of your Journal.

I Shall only add that it will be expected a proper Attention to all these points of Duty so essential to the Welfare of the Ship, and her Stores will be minutely attended to. The printed, and other Orders will be a further Guide.

I am, Sir, with great Respect
Your Obedt humble Servt

THOMAS TRUXTUN.

UNITED STATES SHIP *Constellation*
20th June 1798.

Mr DANIEL ELDRIDGE
Mr AMBROSE SHIRLEY

[HS of Pa. NDA photostat. Truxtun's LB, 1798–9.]

To Captain Stephen Decatur (senior), U. S. Navy, from Secretary of Navy

[PHILADELPHIA,]
Navy Dep^t June 21. 1798.

Capt DECATUR

SIR, The Acts of Congress make no Provision for the employment of Boys on board the Ships of War, — I presume a Regulation admitting of their Employment, will be made in a few days, but not in time for you, as you are so nearly ready for a Cruise —

As your opinion of the Propriety of employing some Boys, corresponds so entirely with my own, I will venture to permit, that you take as many boys as you think proper, not exceeding one for every Gun — You will get them on the best Terms in your power, not exceeding for a Boy half the Pay of an able Seaman, but it must be understood that you are to reduce the Number of able Seamen, allowed your Ship, at the rate of one Seaman for every two Boys — This Regulation, I understand from you, would still leave you a sufficient Number of able Seamen. —

[NDA. OSW, Vol. 1.]

Act providing a naval armament

[22 June 1798]

AN ACT TO AMEND THE ACT, INTITULED "AN ACT PROVIDING A NAVAL ARMAMENT," AND THE ACT, INTITULED—"AN ACT TO AUTHORIZE THE PRESIDENT OF THE UNITED STATES TO CAUSE TO BE PURCHASED OR BUILT, A NUMBER OF SMALL VESSELS, TO BE EQUIPPED AS GALLIES OR OTHERWISE."

SECTION 1. *Be it enacted by the Senate and House of Representatives of the United States of America in Congress assembled,* That the President of the United States shall be, and he is hereby authorized, when he shall think fit to increase the strength of any revenue cutter, for the purposes of defence, against hostilities near the sea coast, to employ on board the same, at his discretion, not exceeding seventy marines and seamen: any thing in the act, intituled "An act providing a naval armament," to the contrary hereof, notwithstanding.

SEC. 2. *And be it further enacted,* That the President of the United States shall be, and he is hereby authorized to fix the degree of rank, and the rate of pay and subsistence, not exceeding what is allowed upon the naval establishment, which shall be granted and allowed to the officers who shall be duly commissioned in the service of the United States on board of any small vessel or galley, which shall be fitted out under his orders, pursuant to the act, intituled "An act to authorize the President of the United States to cause to be purchased, or built, a number of small vessels, to be equipped as gallies, or otherwise," anything therein to the contrary hereof, notwithstanding.

Approved, June 22, 1798.

[Statute II, page 569.]

To Captain Stephen Decatur (senior), U. S. Navy, from Secretary of Navy

[PHILADELPHIA,]
Navy Department — 22 June 1798

Capt. DECATUR

SIR, In answer to your Letter of Yesterday, there is no Coasting Pilot, allowed by Law — yet as you think such a Character necessary, & as the Expence will be but little more than Pilotage up & down the River, I hereby authorize you to employ Mr Mariner, to act as your Coasting Pilot, on the Terms expressed in your Letter. — Thirty five Dollars per month— & Two Rations per day. —

[NDA. OSW, Vol. 1.]

To Jeremiah Yellott, Navy Agent, Baltimore, from Secretary of Navy

[PHILADELPHIA,]
Navy Department June 22d 1798

JEREMIAH YELLOTT *Baltimore*

I have your Favor of the 20th Inst. — I hope you have purchased the *Montezuma*. — I will take immediate steps to have procured & forwarded on the Copper for the *Adriana* & for the *Montezuma* should you have purchased her; — if possible procure Kentledge, it is not to be had here.

I answered in my Letter of the 20th, some of your enquiries of Mr Wolcot, I now enclose the number of men allowed to Ships of different sizes, — I wait with impatience for your recommendation of Officers for the *Adriana*, it is likely before I receive it, I may recommend to the President, the appointment of a Capt Speake to be Lieutenant, in order that an Officer with a sufficient number of men may be engaged at once for the guard of the Ship; Please to keep in mind, that you are to procure every thing for the compleat equipment of the Ship, or Ships for Sea & War if in your power, — those things which you cannot procure, & those only be pleased to apply for here — an able Seaman is allowed 17 Dols an ordinary Seaman 10 Dols p. Month, a Midshipman, such men as promise to make good Officers after a little experience 19 Dollars per Month, if you deem a guard immediately necessary, please to appoint a proper person Midshipman, his appointment will be confirmed, & let him engage as many Seamen, or ordinary Seamen as you shall judge sufficient for a guard; The Men here have received two Months pay in advance as the bounty for enlisting, they must be engaged for twelve months, unless sooner discharged.

[NDA. GLB, Vol. 1.]

To Joshua Humphreys, naval constructor, from Secretary of Navy

[PHILADELPHIA,]
Navy Department June 22. 1798

JOSHUA HUMPHREYS

The enclosed is the dimentions of a Ship at one of the Wharves, there are suspicions that she was built for a French Privateer, it is said she is constructed for a swift sailing, & that she will carry 18 Guns, I presume 6 pounders, Mr Steel informs me that from particular circumstances, the person who has the disposition of her here, will take 10,000 Dollars, though the Collector of the Customs who can give all the necessary information about her, thinks her worth 20,000 Ds Will you be so good as to examine the Ship, & if you judge her to be a swift sailer, & fit for a Cruiser purchase her for the Public at 10,000 Dollars

Ship *Superior*
her length is 81 feet. 8 Inches
her breadth is 22 feet 8 Inches
her depth — 10 feet 7 Inches
she measures 171–83/95 Tons

[NDA. GLB, Vol. 1.]

To Robert Liston, British Ambassador to Washington, from Secretary Pickering

DEPARTMENT OF STATE, PHILADELPHIA,
June 22. 1798.

ROBERT LISTON Esquire,
Envoy Extraordinary &c.

SIR, I take the liberty to inform you, that Mr Adam Babcock, a merchant of reputation in Boston, has entered into a contract with the Secretary of the treasury, to import from the East Indies five hundred tons of Salt petre, to be delivered at Philadelphia, for the use of the United States. I have understood that he had obtained permission from the British Government to purchase the Salt petre in the British Settlements. Be this as it may, by the 13th article of the commercial treaty: the British Government in the East-Indies may permit the exportation of that article: and Mr Babcock supposes it may be of some consequence to have, in addition to the certificate of the Secretary of the Treasury (to whom he has given bond for the purpose) some evidence that the Salt petre above mentioned is destined solely for the use of the United States.

I have therefore to request of you the favour of a letter to the Governor General of Bengal in Council, desiring his permission to lade, at the port of Calcutta, the five hundred tons of Salt petre; which is intended to be put on board Mr Babcock's ship called the *Martha* of Boston, Captain Banjamin Moore master.

I should hope that every facility would be granted in this case; and the rather because the salt petre will be so important to us in the prosecution of the war in which we are actually, and very soon must formally be engaged, against the inveterate and inexorable enemy of Great Britain.

The readiness with which the British Government furnished a convoy to the American trade coming from Great Britain the past

Spring, leaves no room to doubt a like disposition in those who administer that Government in the East Indies: Still it may ensure to Mr Babcock's vessel the benefit of a convoy at least as far as the Cape of Good-Hope, if you suggest your wishes that She may be allowed the protection of any British Armed vessel or vessels coming on the same course. I have the honour to be &c.

TIMOTHY PICKERING

[SDA. Dom. L., Vol. 10.]

To Secretary Oliver Wolcot from Secretary of Navy

[PHILADELPHIA,]
Navy Department June 22, 1798

OLIVER WOLCOT

I have your Favor, [Space] I have no doubt of the propriety of getting a ship at New York, Mr Higginson has engaged Mr Hackett to build one at Portsmouth at 30 D^s p Ton; I know of no means to pursue, to obtain a Ship at New York, so proper as to get the favor of you to contract for one there, or to employ a proper person to make such contract, you are at least, as well acquainted with the whole of the Subject as I am, and I shall with the utmost pleasure subscribe to whatever you may do; — remember your own sistem, — leave nothing to be done here.

I wish sincerely Mr^s Wolcot was so much recovered as to permit your return.

[NDA. Req. on US T, 1798–1803.]

To Lieutenant of Marines James Triplett from Captain Thomas Truxtun, U. S. Navy

UNITED STATES SHIP *Constellation*
Hampton Roads 22^d June 1798.

SIR, Your particular Duty as Lieutenant of Marines on Board this Ship, is to train, or cause to be trained, the Marines to the Use of small Arms, to discipline and exercise them Morning and Evening, according to the Orders Issued, and at such other Times, as I may direct according to Circumstances. — It is your Duty to direct them on all Occasions, agreeable to my Orders, and to have a due Regard to the Preservation of the Arms, and Accoutrements, and that they be kept clean, and always fit for Service — It is your Duty to cause the Centinels to be placed according to the Regulations of the Ship, and to call on the Master at Arms, to aid your Sergeants and Corporals in doing this duty — The Armourer being occasionally under your Orders, you will call on him as often as may be necessary to clean the small Arms &c and the Drummer and Fifer [obliterated several words] is to perform the Duties annexed to those Stations [obliterated 3 words] in Conformity to the Regulations aforesaid. —

As it often happens, that Marines are sent on Shore on certain Enterprizes during an Expedition or Cruize, as well as to coopperate with the Army on particular Occasions at Home, you should pay particular Attention to every Part of the Duty of a Soldier in all

Situations, so as not to be outdone by any other Officer of your Rank, whenever it may be necessary to try your Skill &c with them —

The putting the Fire, and Lights out agreeable to the Regulation of the Ship, you will be pleased to have done by the Master at Arms and Corporals, in order that the Officer of the Watch may not be compelled to leave the Deck on all occasions, to see this Order executed —

The Marine Cloathing, and the Arms, Accoutrements &c. will be received by you agreeable to the Invoice [obliterated] —

I have the Honor to be, Sir, with great Respect

Your Obed Servt

THOMAS TRUXTUN.

Lieutenant JAMES TRIPLETT.

[HS of Pa. NDA photostat. Truxtun's LB, 1798-9.]

To Charles Wadsworth, purser, from Secretary of Navy

[PHILADELPHIA,]
Navy Department — 22 June. 1798.

CHAS WADSWORTH
Purser of Frigate U. S.

SIR, In answer to your Letter of this day, the Price of a ration in the Navy, must be estimated at twenty eight Cents. —

[NDA. OSW, Vol. 1.]

To Samuel Sewall from Secretary of Navy

[PHILADELPHIA],
Navy Department June 23d 1798

SAMUEL SEWALL Esquire in Congress

SIR Capt Barry represents to me that his Ship the Frigate *United States*, requires more men than the Acts of Congress authorize, she is allowed in all including the Captain, & every man on board 364 Officers Seamen & Marines, four hundred the Captain thinks are absolutely necessary to govern & fight the Ship to the greatest advantage. I am so new to this Business, that I cannot form such a judgment on the subject, as to authorize a formal representation to Congress, I observe that the Act provided an additional Armament & to permit the President to regulate the number & grade of Officers & the number of men of which the Crews of the twelve Ships contemplated by that Act, shall be employed, perhaps it might be proper & useful, to extend this provision to the Crews of the Frigates; hereafter the subject will be better understood, & Congress may Act on surer ground, in determining the exact number of Officers & men to be allowed to Ships of all sizes. — By the present regulations of Congress no provision is made for Boys on board of the Ships of War, beside the good policy of teaching Boys to become Seamen, experienced men inform me that one Boy for each Gun is highly necessary

[NDA. GLB, Vol. 1.]

To Rufus King, United States Minister, London, from James Maury, United States Consul, Liverpool

LIVERPOOL, *23^d June 1798*

D^r SIR In addition to the vessels mentioned in my former I have just been informed that the arm'd ship *Planter* Captain Driver is to sail about the middle of next week for Virginia

I have the Honor to be with
Much Respect
Your Excellency's
Most Obet Ser^t

JAMES MAURY

His Excellency
RUFUS KING
Minis^r Plen^y to the U. S. of America
London

[SDA. Liverpool, Vol. 1, C. L., 1790–1800.]

To Secretary James McHenry from Captain Thomas Truxtun, U. S. Navy

UNITED STATES SHIP *Constellation*
Hampton Roads 23^d June 1798.

SIR In order that the Ship should not be detained, I gave directions to Mr Garretson to advise with the Naval Agent at Norfolk, and to purchase a small Quantity of Slops (per List delivered him) on the best Terms he could, and to draw on you for the Am^t this he has done, but the Day after the Purchase was made, the Transport from Philadelphia arrived. —

I have directed those Slops to be placed in the publick Magazine under Care of Mr Pennock, — subject to your Order; they will be ready and convenient for the Ships under Equipment at Baltimore, or any other of the publick Ships in Want of Such Articles, when calling into these Roads for Refreshments. — I have also landed, and left in Charge as aforesaid:

44 horn Lantherns, eight of which are Signal. They are of the best Sort; our Supply of this Article was greater than I directed, in Consequence of Mr Christie of London, sending them out with the Poop, and Top Lanthern, contrary to the Directions of L. and J. Sterett, but as they were very good and cheap, it was thought best to make no Difficulty about the Receipt of them, they will also suit one of the Ships at Baltimore, but this Frigate ought to have credit for such Articles, as have been purchased for her Use, but not applied to it.

The Ventilators have not arrived, if they were forwarded to Norfolk, they would be very serviceable, particularly at this Season of the Year.

I before informed you, that this Ship's Draught of Water exceeded Twenty two Feet, which renders it impossible for her to go into any Port in the United States southward of the Chesapeake, without taking out her Guns. Yesterday about 3 P. M. the Ring of the small Bower Anchor gave Way, we afterwards endeavoured to weigh the Anchor by the Buoy Rope, which was new, and as stout as a 64 Gun Ship's: but it parted, and we lost that Anchor. Much has been said on the Subject of these Anchors, it is therefore unnecessary for me to say any Thing further at this Time, except that I should not have received them, even after their Arrival at Baltimore, had there been any Alternative. —

Suitable Anchors should be provided for all sorts of Ships, but particularly for heavy Vessels, I have never seen any made in this Country fit for a Frigate. —

[HS of Pa. NDA photostat. Truxtun's LB, 1798–9.]

To Secretary James McHenry from Captain Thomas Truxtun, U. S. Navy

Constellation OFF CAPE HENRY *June 23* [?] *1798—*

SIR, After every Exertion being made, that was possible for me to get the Ship to Sea, I have at length arrived at the Door of the Ocean with 313 Men of every Description on Board; the precise Number allowed by Act of Congress, and whoe's Names and Stations you will see fixt by the enclosed Copy of the Quarter Bill.

The Merchants of Norfolk having applied to me to convoy a Fleet of their Ships, which they assured me, was worth at least One Million of Dollars; I considered it proper, and within the Power given to me in my Instructions, to grant their Request, as far as the Distance mentioned in the accompanying papers, which I forward for your Information. —

As soon as I have performed my Promise to the Merchants aforesaid, I shall take the Range you have (by Order of the President) directed, and I hope most sincerely, that the Time is at Hand, when I shall have it in my Power, to give you a good Account of some of those French Pirates, who very properly are at this Moment hovering within the Tract of Sea, allotted for my cruizing Ground.

The Frigate goes through the Water with great Swiftness indeed, I hope we shall soon have Oppertunities to try her Sailing by and large. — It has been impossible as yet to furnish you a Muster Roll as complete as I wished, for I have not had Time to examine Day and Dates from the Recruiting Officer's Documents. The first lesiure Moment I have, the Roll shall be completed, and the first good Oppertunity after it shall be transmitted, to you. — As a unanimous Spirit, and vigorous Measures, will always insure us Justice, the United States have my most ardent Wishes for the Adoption complete of those Objects, and that we may be soon restored triumphantly to Peace, and the Enjoyment of a free and uninterrupted Commerce. —

* * * * * * *

I have the Honor to be, Sir, with great Respect,
Your very Obedient — humble Servant —

THOMAS TRUXTUN.

(P. S.) Since I returned you the Copy of a Quarter Bill, made out the 19th Current, I have received several Seamen from Norfolk, and have discharged several inanimate Animals, that could never have been of any Use to the Service, the present Quarter Bill stands correct.— To prevent Scorbutic Appearances, an Order should be lodged with the Naval Agent to furnish certain Articles of Refreshment,

& a plenty of Vegetables, whenever the Ship comes into the Roads.— People, who are not accustomed to the Sea, particularly requires these Things, and they come as cheap as Salt Provision.— Had Pennock not been acquainted with me for many years, in Fact sailed with me as an Officer, he would not have furnished the necessary Supplies, having no Order for that Purpose, from the regular Departments.

Honble JAMES McHENRY,
Secretary of War.

[HS of Pa. NDA photostat. Truxtun's LB, 1798–9.]

Convoy signals, U. S. Frigate *Constellation*

Signals by Day.	Signals by Night.
To get under Way, Ensign at Ensign Staff, and fore top Sail loose	Eight lights in a Range.
To make Sail, US. Jack at Mizen peek	Seven lights in..Ditto
To shorten Sail, " " at Mizen top Gallant Mast head	Six Ditto in..Ditto
On seeing a Sail to Windward, US. Jack, at Fore Top Mast head	Five Ditto in..Ditto
On seeing a Sail to Seaward, a Pendant at Fore Top Gallant mast head.	Four Ditto in..Ditto
To tack, or ware a Pendant, under Jack at Mizen Peek	Three Ditto in..Ditto
To make best of your Way, One Gun, & Ensign at Ensign Staff	One Gun, and two Lights in After.

SIR, As you are only to expect any Convoy about twenty or thirty Leagues at most from Cape Henry, I have only made out a few Signals, such as I have deemed sufficient for your Government in keeping with the Frigate so short a Distance.— Your Attention to them will however be necessary.— Wishing you safe to your consigned Port, I am, Sir,—

Your Obedient Servant—

United States ship *Constellation*
Lynn Haven Bay 24 June 1798
(Copy of Order to each Master of a Vessel under Convoy)

T T

[HS of Pa. NDA photostat. Truxtun's LB, 1798–9.]

Extract from Captain Thomas Truxtun's journal, U. S. Frigate *Constellation*, 24 June 1798, Sunday

Had my Business on Board this Frigate been confined simply to that of a Commander; My Journal should have commenced, when the Ship went out of the Builder's Hands, and my Functions as a Superintendant in the Yard ceased; but it has been very much otherwise, and I have been so occupied, that I could only find Leisure to commence it this Day.

The Guns having been scaled, Men quartered, Watch Lists, and Order of Boarding made out, with various Stores allowed, being received; I delivered the Signals for the Fleet under my Convoy (which I agreed to protect to the Distance of Twenty or Thirty Leagues from Cape Henry, agreeable to the Request of the Merchants of Norfolk) to the Masters of the different Ships, and Vessels, bound to Europe, and the West Indies per Register; and at 11 AM got under Way and sailed down towards Cape Henry, having previously lost our small Bower Anchor, owing to the Ring giving Way in a Common Gale and the Buoy Rope parting after, in our Efforts to weigh the Anchor, which was buried very deep in the Mud.

Altho' we have too few Seamen on Board our Compliment as far as respects Numbers is complete, after discharging a Number of Rotten and inanimate Animals that found their Way into the Ship, by imposing on the recruiting Officers and Surgeon's Vigilance.

Throughout the whole of these Twenty four Hours, the Weather has been cloudy, and warm, with a fresh South West Breeze of Wind. The present Cruize ordered by the President of the United States being Coastwise, I shall omit stating any Thing more of the Result of our Sailing in the Column of Day's Works, than the Latitude and Longitude, except on particular Occasions, the Rest being unnecessary, and the more so, as we shall often be in the Gulph Stream, and in the Way of Currents, when great allowance must be made from the Distance run by log, in Order to fix the true situation of the Ship at Noon of each Day. But whenever I am ordered to cruize off the Coast, any Distance from Land, all the Blanks in said Column shall be filled up.

THOMAS TRUXTUN.

[HS of Pa. NDA photostat.]

[24 June 1798]

List of vessels convoyed by *Constellation*

Vessels under Convoy per Order of the 24th June.

Vessels Names	Owners	Masters	where bound	Burthen in Tons
Ship LITTLE WILLIAM	Wm Pennock of Norfolk.	James Wilkerson	Liverpool	162.
Ship CHARLES	Brown & Tracey of Newberry.	Jos. Perkins	Dublin	225.
Ship ANN	Robt Hambleton of Alexandria.	David Black	Rotterdam	224.
Brig ELIZA	Conway Whittle	Alex. McConnel	Belfast	280.
Schoonr ANTHOy WALLIS	Davd of Patterson	Isaac Luke	Barbadoes	85.
" HAZARD	Thos Willick	Wm Montgomery	Nevis	96.
" HOPE	Wm Jet	Wm Baldwin	Barbadoes	73.
Ship FAIR AMERICAN	M. Myers	O. P. Finley	London	317.

N. B. About as many more Vessels sail with us. It blowing fresh, they did not receive Signals, which in Fact is of no Consequence for so short a distance, as I shall keep with them.

[HS of Pa. NDA photostat. Truxtun's LB., 1798–1799.]

Act authorizing defence of merchant vessels

[25 June 1798]

AN ACT TO AUTHORIZE THE DEFENCE OF THE MERCHANT VESSELS OF THE UNITED STATES AGAINST FRENCH DEPREDATIONS

SECTION 1. *Be it enacted by the Senate and House of Representatives of the United States of America in Congress Assembled,* That the commander and crew of any merchant vessel of the United States, owned wholly by a citizen or citizens thereof, may oppose and defend against any search, restraint or seizure, which shall be attempted upon such vessel, or upon any other vessel, owned, as aforesaid, by the commander or crew of any armed vessel sailing under French colours, or acting, or pretending to act, by, or under the authority of the French republic; and may repel by force any assault or hostility which shall be made or committed, on the part of such French, or pretended French vessel, pursuing such attempt, and may subdue and capture the same; and may also retake any vessel owned, as aforesaid, which may have been captured by any vessel sailing under French colours, or acting, or pretending to act, by or under authority from the French republic.

SEC. 2. *And be it further enacted,* That whenever the commander and crew of any merchant vessel of the United States shall subdue and capture any French, or pretended French armed vessel, from which an assault or other hostility shall be first made, as aforesaid, such armed vessel with her tackle, appurtenances, ammunition and lading, shall accrue, the one half to the owner or owners of such merchant vessel of the United States, and the other half to the captors: And being brought into any port of the United States, shall and may be adjudged and condemned to their use, after due process and trial, in any court of the United States, having admiralty jurisdiction, and which shall be holden for the district into which such captured vessel shall be brought; and the same court shall thereupon order a sale and distribution thereof, accordingly, and at their discretion; saving any agreement, which shall be between the owner or owners, and the commander and crew of such merchant vessel. In all cases of recapture of vessels belonging to citizens of the United States, by any armed merchant vessel, aforesaid, the said vessels, with their cargoes, shall be adjudged to be restored, and shall, by decree of such courts as have jurisdiction, in the premises, be restored to the former owner or owners, he or they paying for salvage, not less than one eighth, nor more than one half of the true value of the said vessels and cargoes, at the discretion of the court; which payments shall be made without any deduction whatsoever.

SEC. 3. *And be it further enacted,* That after notice of this act, at the several custom-houses, no armed merchant vessel of the United States shall receive a clearance or permit, or shall be suffered to depart therefrom, unless the owner or owners, and the master or commander of such vessel for the intended voyage, shall give bond, to the use of the United States, in a sum equal to double the value of such vessel, with condition, that such vessel shall not make or commit any depredation, outrage, unlawful assault, or unprovoked violence upon the high seas, against the vessel of any nation in amity with the United States; and that the guns, arms and ammunition of such vessel shall be returned within the United States, or otherwise accounted for, and shall not be sold or disposed of in any foreign port or place; and that such owner or owners, and the commander and crew of such merchant vessel, shall, in all things, observe and perform such further instructions in the premises, as the President of the United States shall establish and order, for the better government of the armed merchant vessels of the United States.

SEC. 4. *And be it further enacted,* That the President of the United States shall be, and he is hereby authorized to establish and order suitable instructions to, and for, the armed merchant vessels of the United States, for the better governing and restraining the commanders and crews who shall be employed therein, and to prevent any outrage, cruelty or injury which they may be disposed to commit; a copy of which instructions shall be delivered by the collector of the customs to the commander of such vessel, when he shall give bond as aforesaid. And it shall be the duty of the owner or owners, and commander and crew, for the time being, of such armed merchant vessel of the United States, at each return to any port of the United States, to make report to the collector thereof of any rencounter which shall have happened with any foreign vessel, and of the state of the company and crew of any vessel which they shall have subdued or captured; and the persons of such crew or company shall be delivered to the care of such collector, who, with the aid of the marshal of the same district, or the nearest military officer of the United States, or of the civil or military officers of any state, shall take suitable care for the restraint, preservation and comfort of such persons, at the expense of the United States, until the pleasure of the President of the United States shall be known concerning them.

SEC. 5. *And be it further enacted,* That this act shall continue and be in force for the term of one year, and until the end of the next session of Congress thereafter.

SEC. 6. *Provided, and be it further enacted,* That whenever the government of France, and all persons acting by, or under their authority, shall disavow, and shall cause the commanders and crews of all armed French vessels to refrain from the lawless depredations and outrages hitherto encouraged and authorized by that government against the merchant vessel[s] of the United States, and shall cause the laws of nations to be observed by the said armed French vessels, the President of the United States shall be, and he is hereby authorized to instruct the commanders and crews of the merchant vessels of the United States to submit to any regular search by the commanders or crews of French vessels, and to refrain from any force or capture to be exercised by virtue hereof.

Approved, June 25, 1798.

[Statute II, page 572.]

To Isaac Pollock, Washington, from Secretary of Navy

PHILA^a NAVY DEPARTMENT
25th June, 1798

ISAAC POLLOCK Esqr
City Washington,

SIR, Your favor of the 14th June, has been neglected like many other Things, in my new Line of Life. I will have the Subject of a purchase of your Island considered, & let you know before long the Result. In the mean Time, let me know if you please, at what rate you will contract to deliver live oak Timber, proper for Frigates, by the Post and how soon you will undertake to deliver enough for one two or three Frigates at Norfolk, Balt^e Phila^a Boston, Portsmouth in New Hampshire — If it be wanted it will probably be at One or more of these places I presume the Public will advance some money — But ample sec^y[security] will be required for a strict compliance as to Time & every thing else, for live oak Timber. —

[NDA. GLB, Vol. 1.]

To Rufus King, United States Minister, London, from James Maury, United States Consul, Liverpool

LIVERPOOL, *25th June 1798.*

DEAR SIR, I have the Honor of your Letter of 22nd instant & shall pay especial attention to it's contents — The letter for Mr Pickering is in the *Caroline*, Motley for Philadelphia to sail to-morrow —

There are five or six Vessells expected to sail in Company about the 5th next month, several of them to be armed & it is proposed that they continue together all the way out.

I have the Honor to be with perfect respect.

Your Excellency's

Most obedient Servant

JAMES MAURY

His Excellency RUFUS KING

Minister Plenipotentiary to the U. S. A.

London —

[SDA. Liverpool, Vol. 1, C. L., 1790–1800]

[25 June 1798.]

Concerning marines on board the *Constellation*

To The Lieutenants, and Master of the Frigate Constellation

GENTLEMEN, The Marines on Board this Frigate have been directed to pull, hawl, and heave at the Capstern, in Addition to the Duty assigned them under the Lieutenant of Marines. No other Duty is expected from them, which you will please to attend, particularly as I have discovered a Carelessness in those People, and Neglect in taking Care of their Cloathes, and of keeping them clean.

I have given Mr Triplett a Copy of this Order for his Government, and another Copy I forwarded to the Secretary of War with Copies of all general Instructions, which I issue, and request minute Attention to.

I have the Honor to be, Gentlemen, with great Respect,

Your Obedient humble Servant

JUNE 25th 1798. THOMAS TRUXTUN.

T. T. The Lieutenant of Marines is always to parade and exercise the Marines, when in Port, at Sun Rise, and Sun Setting, and to exercise them agreeable to Order, when all Hands are called to Quarters, and the Cannon are exercised. The Lieutenant of Marines will attend to the same Rule at Sea, with this Difference only, that instead of Sun Rise, and Sunset, the Men will parade &c at half past 7 AM. and at Sun Setting. —

T. T.

[HS of Pa. NDA photostat. Truxtun's LB, 1798–9.]

Extract from Captain Thomas Truxtun's journal, U. S. Frigate *Constellation*, 25 June 1798, Monday

At about 5 PM, anchored in Lynn Haven Bay with the Larboard Bower Anchor in six Fathoms Water, a stick'y Bottom; the Light House when at Anchor bore E.S.E. about five Miles Distance. —

The Fleet anchored at the same Time a little above us. Just as we anchored a very heavy Squall came on from the S.W. accompanied with Whirl Winds, and very sharp Flashes of Lightning and Thunder, which continued most of the Night with constant, and heavy Rains.

Wind from S.S.W. to W.S.W. all these 24 Hours, — most of the Time blowing fresh.

Had all Hands to Quarters agreeable to the Order of Battle & exercised great Guns, and Marines.

The two Schooners sent from Hampton Roads to Norfolk for Water, not having arrived; we were compelled to anchor or leave behind a large Quantity of that precious Article.

I must remark however, that these Boats ought to have returned from the Time they have been absent, before the End of this Day.

The one belonged to the Pilot Mr Barry, and had his People on Board, the other was hired promiscuously.

[HS of Pa. NDA photostat.]

To The President of the United States from H. Knox

Private

BOSTON *26th June 1798.*

MY DEAR SIR, I have often intended, in the ardor of my unqualified admiration of the measures of the Supreme executive, to express the Same respectfully to you. But hitherto I have been restrained from an apprehension of intruding upon your important duties. A crisis however is rapidly approaching which renders it indispensible that the mind of the meanest citizen be known as to the part he intends to act.

The other nations of the world, if they are not too much occupied by the means of their own safety, and if they are, posterity will be astonished, at the constant perseverance of the different succession of French Rulers rising upon the ruins of each other, and yet holding steadily the same unjust conduct towards us, and urging irresistably, that we either submit to be a dependent portion of that nation, and assist in their crimes, or that we assert our own rights, and repel their disgraceful claims by force. This now is the only alternative. The conflict will be arduous. Our existence as a nation will depend upon our Success.

We ought therefore in its commencement to take every possible precaution, and make every possible establishment, not only to limit the duration of the war to a short period, but to give it a bias towards a successful issue, from its beginning. The people will rest with confidence upon the wisdom of their government (which has managed its political concerns with France in so dignified a manner, as completely to establish its own unoffending purity and truth) that it will take all the measures & money by which the legislature will authorize to secure the United States from external injury. But whether the authority will in the first instance be adequate; or whether the Legislature are solemnly impressed with the importance of such energetic laws, as shall effectually prevent internally, either opposition to our own government, or assistance to an invading enemy, are highly questionable. Timely precautions on this head may prevent much confusion, distress and bloodshed among ourselves. Every intelligent principle requires, that we should not, like another Switzerland, afford the means of our own subjugation. It may be too late when the enemy makes his appearance, to prevent effectually our own bad people from joining him. And it will be folly in the extreme to suppose that we have not desperadoes desirous of such a step.

Indeed we are vulnerable in the Southern States to an alarming degree. The British navy is the only preventative against an invasion of those States from the West India Islands. But that navy may be prevented by several causes from opposing at the moment the French. A few Ships of war, and the French have a few, would in a few days convoy an army of ten thousand blacks and people of colour in vessels seized from our own citizens. They might land on the defenceless parts of South Carolina or Virginia. Under such circumstances, the slaves would instantly join them, & greatly encrease their force. I do not believe this picture is too highly coloured. The event is possible, and whatever is possible the enemy will have the enterprise to attempt.

New York & its vicinity is of peculiar importance, & at the same time weakness, and too much precaution cannot be taken to prevent a lodgement there. It appears necessary that a body of troops should be in that neighbourhood and another in Virginia for the double purpose of internal & external defence.

New England may be left to its militia, excepting the defenceless and important point of Rhode Island, which ought to be guarded by one thousand good troops to prevent surprize.

If the events here stated be possible only, and I believe they may be deemed probable, if not certain, it would then result that the means afforded the government should be instantly put into effect.

The expence of raising and disciplining the army would be abundantly compensated by its utility. And if anything could prevent an actual war, it would be the prompt preparation to meet it. The enemy are audacious in the highest degree and their success is in a great degree owing to the exercise of this principle.

We have no just cause to fear our ultimate success, because it may be relied upon that our citizens are equal in perseverance, in active courage and in enterprize & Stratagem to the French or any other people on the globe. But instant organization is essential.

Whoever you should please to appoint as the immediate commanding officer of the provisional army you will I am persuaded contemplate General Washington as the efficient commander in chief. His name would be an host, and the occasion would be worthy of his name. He alone would be able to combine and draw into activity, and harmonize all that remains of the late army that could be useful. My diffidence in uttering these sentiments is inexpressible, and only to be equalled by my respect and attachment to you.

After having said so much, I should lose all self respect were I not to say, that if there be any sort of service to which my humble abilities should be judged equal, that I should faithfully and ardently endeavour to execute it, believing as I do, that the occasion will demand the labours of all the friends of their country to defend its rights and liberties against the all devouring rapacity of the French rulers.

I have the honor to be, my dear Sir,
with sincere respect & attachment
your devoted servant,

H. KNOX.

The PRESIDENT OF THE UNITED STATES.

[Mass. HS. Pickering Papers, Vol. 8.]

[26 June 1798.]

To Joseph Sterett, Navy Agent, Baltimore, from Captain Thomas Truxton, U S. Navy.

Mr JOSEPH STERETT
Naval Agent

SIR, Mr Berry's account settled this Day for Boat Hire, Pilotage, and Attendance on the Ship, amounts to the Sum of Nine Hundred, Sixty three Dollars, and Eighty Cents, which you will pay him, the Statement is made below, to viz:

Boat Hire from 6th April, to 26th June inclusive at 8$	656.
60 Lay Days at $2.50	150.
To Pilotage to Patuxent $27.50 to Cape Henry $53.33	80. 83
To ditto in and out of Hampton Roads	32. 00
To 1 Seine	45. 00
	$963. 83

United States Ship *Constellation*
off Cape Henry 26th June 1798.

THOMAS TRUXTUN.

[HS of Pa. NDA photostat. Truxtun's LB, 1798–9.]

To Captain Stephen Decatur (senior), U. S. Navy, from Secretary of Navy

[PHILADELPHIA,]
Navy Departmt 26. June. 1798.

Capt S. DECATUR

SIR, The Ship *Delaware*, under your Command, being equipped, manned and armed, you will proceed to Sea, with the first fair wind. —

Capt Dale of the *Ganges*, whose cruising Ground extends from Cape Henry to Long Island, being but badly prepared to meet an Enemy, you will endeavour to fall in with him as early as possible and will cruise in Company with him, until the 10th of July, unless you should be sooner joined by Capt Barry of the Frigate *United States* — Whenever you are joined by Capt Barry, or on the 10th day of July, whether Capt Barry should have fallen in with you, or otherwise — You will proceed to the Southward, and endeavour to fall in with the Frigate *Constellation*, Capt Truxtun. — When you have joined Capt Truxtun, he being your superior Officer, you will of course consider Yourself under his Command. His cruising Ground extends from Cape

Henry, to the Extremity of our Southern Limits: You will consider your's to be the same, until further orders. —

The President expects that in Conjunction with Capt Truxtun, you will protect this Extent of Coast, to the utmost of your Power — that you will pay particular attention to the principal Harbour of South Carolina & of Georgia: and that you will so act as to afford all possible Protection to the Vessels of the United States, coming on, or going off the Coast against the Depredations of the French Cruisers. —

You will as often as opportunities offer, transmit to Me, a Journal of your Proceedings, & such Events as may be proper to communicate. —

I am instructed by the President, to mention to you, his entire Confidence in your Activity, skill and Bravery — and that the Rights and honor of your Country will not suffer in your hands. —

Inclosed you will receive your Instructions; founded on the present Acts of Congress, & by which you are for the present to be governed. —

Wishing you a pleasant, successful & honorable Cruise, I am &c.

[NDA. OSW, Vol. 1.]

To Captain Thomas Truxtun, U. S. Navy, from Secretary of Navy

[PHILADELPHIA,]
Navy Departmt 26th June. 1798.

Capt Th. TRUXTUN.

SIR, Captain Decatur, in the armed Ship, the *Delaware*, now ready to proceed to Sea, will cruise until about the 10th of July, between Cape Henry and Long-Island — and at that Time he will endeavour to join you. —

The Southern Coast of the United States, being most exposed to the depredations of the French Cruisers — It affords me great satisfaction, that it is to be protected by Officers of Activity, Enterprize and Bravery, who will not suffer the rights of their Country to be violated, nor it's honor to be insulted, with Impunity, by Vessels, sailing under authority, or the Pretence of Authority, from the French Republic. —

It is the desire of the President, that you will in concert with Capt Decatur's Force, take the best means in your power of fulfilling the objects of your Cruise, as contained in the Letter to you, from the Secretary of War of the 30th ultimo. — You will judge from the Information you will be able to obtain of the Force you will be likely to encounter, whether it be necessary that you should cruise in Company with each other — or whether you may not safely separate for several days, taking different Directions. —

Capt Decatur, you will find to be an Officer, ardent to distinguish himself in fulfilling the Expectations of his Country; and from your well known Character, it is not doubted, that every opportunity which Prudence does not forbid, will be afforded him to do so. —

The Congress have not, since the Date of your Instructions, passed any Act, to authorize a Departure from them. —

[NDA. OSW, Vol. 1.]

To Thomas Fitzsimmons, Philadelphia, from Secretary of Navy

[PHILADELPHIA,]
Navy Department, 26th June 1798

Thos FITZSIMMONS *Phila*

SIR, A Bill is now before Congress, which it is presumed will pass into a Law, authorizing the President to receive from the Merchants, Four Frigates, carrying not less than thirty Two Guns — It is supposed that one such Vessel may be furnished by each of the large commercial Cities of Phila Baltimore — New York & Boston. — The Bill also contemplates smaller Vessels — but these it is imagined the small Towns will supply. —

It appears to me, to be highly desireable, that the Patriotic Merchants and Citizens of Phila should furnish one Ship as large as the Contribution will afford, & not less than 32 Guns, even if to build so large a Vessel, some public Money should be required in Aid of the private Contributions. — I say not less than 32 Guns — But if a Frigate capable of carrying 36 or 44 Guns, could be obtained from Phila it would be more agreeable, and more useful to the Public. —

Our Three Frigates, already built, are of a Size, one third at least larger than Frigates of the same number of Guns in Europe — An English Frigate of 38 Guns will not measure so much as 900 Tons. — Our 36 Guns Frigate measures near 1200 — I doubt whether a Ship of 900 Tons could not be found equal to 44 Guns. —

[NDA. GLB, Vol. 1.]

Extract from Captain Thomas Truxtun's journal, U. S. Frigate *Constellation*, 26 June, 1798, Tuesday.

All these 24 Hours we have had squally and uncertain Weather, with the Wind blowing from the Southward, and S. W. Quarter, accompanied with much Rain.

Loaded the Great Guns, and got every Thing as clear as possible, received the Water, for which we have been detained, since we anchored in these Roads, and at 11 AM made the Signal for the Fleet to get under Way, — hove up immediately, and at Noon abreast the Light House, standing out to Sea, East by Compass; the whole Fleet being under Sail, and in Order.

[HS of Pa. NDA photostat.]

[26 June 1798.]

Purchase of the Ship *Montezuma*

To UNITED STATES OF AMERICA.
To WILLIAM TAYLOR *Dr*

For the Ship *Montezuma* with all her materials agreeable to Inventory sold and delivered Jeremiah Yellott Esqr	Dollars 28,000

Baltimore June 26, 1798.

Wm TAYLOR.

[GAO, No. 9884.]

To the Sea Lieutenants and Master, Ship *Constellation*, from Captain Thomas Truxtun, U. S. Navy

June 27th 1798.

Gentlemen, The Watch Lists being subdivided, in the Mode I prescribed, You are to observe, that when all Hands are employed, otherwise than at Quarters; the Division of Work should be made under the various Officers of each Watch, according to the Nature of the Work; as for Instance, when at the Rigging the Master will direct the Boatswain, to employ his first Mate in performing what is to be done at the Foremast, and Bowsprit, and his second Mate, the Main, and Mizen Mast, and these take in every Thing, that is wanting to be done, or repaired, from the Top Gallant Mast's heads down, as well as the Jib Boom, Gaff and what relates to the Cables, Sails, Anchors, Boats &c. &c. &c. &c. —

In cleaning the Ships, and performing the various Work below, the Boatswain's Mates, under Direction of the Midshipmen, and Master's Mates, are to have that Business performed; the Carpenter, and his Crew, is to have every Thing in Order respecting the Pumps, and what relates to his Duty in stopping Leaks, and preserving the Hull &c. &c. &c.

The Gunner, and his Crew are to see the Guns kept dry, well putty'd, and every Thing belonging to the Cannon, or connected with the Cannon, in good Order, and in Readiness at a Moments Warning.

The Purser, Steward, and Cooper's Duty has been so clearly defined, as well as the other Officers, that it is unnecessary to mention it here.

Whenever a Sail is in Sight, I must be immediately informed Night, or Day, a good Look out must always be kept, and in Day Light a Man at each Mast head. The printed, and other Instructions, if attended to, must make every Thing appear plain, and clear.

The general Superintendance of the Duty is by the Commissioned Officers; The Lieutenants are particularly answereable for what relates to the Guns, in their respective Divisions.

The Master and Boatswain the Riggin &c. — The People as well as Officers must repair to their Stations, whenever all Hands, or the Watch is called, and they are not to leave their Post under any Pretence whatever, without Leave.

We have an Infant Navy to foster, and to organize, and it must be done.

I am, Gentlemen,
Your Obedient Servant

Thomas Truxtun.

To the Sea Lieutenants and Master Ship Constellation

[HS of Pa. NDA photostat. Truxtun's LB, 1798–9.]

To Secretary of State from United States Consul Elias VanderHorst, Bristol, England

Bristol *June 27th 1798.*

Dear Sir. I have been Honored with your Circular of the 22d Inst. together with the Copies of Letters and form of a Certificate that accompanied it, and you may depend I shall pay every attention to your Instructions on the subject to which they relate.

The American ship *Roba & Betsey*, Capt Vimmo arrived here last Friday in 29 Days, from Virginia. On the 18th Inst. she was Boarded by the Master of a French Privateer Brig of 14 Guns who after examining the Ships Papers & Letters, with so much care as to detain him four Hours, suffered the Ship to proceed on her Voyage for Hamburgh, where, *by her Papers* it *appeared* she was bound * & that the Cargo was American Property consisting of between 5 & 600 Hogs of Tobacco. the Capt says he was treated with great civility & Politeness by the French Officers of the Privateer on board of which he was upwards of three Hours.—

I have the Honor to with the greatest esteem & respects.

Dear Sir,

Your most Obt & Most hbl Servt

ELIAS VANDERHORST

* "tho" in Fact she was bound here.

[SDA. Bristol, Vol. 1, 1791–1799.]

To Captain Richard Dale, U. S. Navy, from Secretary of Navy

[PHILADELPHIA,]
Navy Department. 27. June. 1798.

RICHARD DALE.

SIR, I have just time to say, that your Letters to the Secretary at War, to the 24th Instant, have been received, and that due attention will be paid to their Contents, that your Services heretofore, tho' not so brilliant as your Wishes, have not been the less meritorious or useful — You have frightened the French Cruisers from our Coasts, and have releived in a considerable degree our Commerce from Depredations on our own Shores — Before long, you will be permitted to return into Port, to prepare Yourself better — Capt Decatur will join you for a few days in the Ship *Delaware*, If you see an Advantage by going for a day out of your cruising Ground, your Conduct will be approved. — About the 10th of July, Capt Decatur will go South, but before that Time Captain Barry I expect, will join you. —

[NDA. OSW, Vol. 1.]

To Jeremiah Yellott, Navy Agent, Baltimore, from Secretary of Navy

[PHILADELPHIA,]
Navy Department, 27th June, 1798.

Capt JEREMIAH YELLOTT *Baltimore*

SIR, Your Letter of the 24 Inst is just received — 6000 feet of Copper, will be forwarded to you this day, with the proper Quantity of Sheathing Nails. — The Copper will not all be such as you desired, about ad Ozs to the Foot, but will come as near to your Directions as possible. — The Captain and other Officers recommended by you, shall be attended to and without Delay. I will direct the Cambouses for both Ships to be forwarded to you from New York. —

There is a Bill before Congress which will pass into a Law, authorizing the President to receive from the Merchants, Ships of 32 Guns & upwards, as well as small Ships. It is hoped that the Merchants of Baltimore Phila New York & Boston, will each furnish a Ship of the largest size, instead of two smaller Ones. — The smaller Towns will furnish the smaller Ships. The Money expended by the Merchants will be paid in 6 p. C[t] Stock — The Merchants here are about to begin a Ship of 1000 Tons, to carry 44 Guns — I hope one at least as large can be built at Baltimore, where the Spirit of the Merchants and Citizens has been so patriotically displayed, in the size of their subscription. Will you be so good as to communicate with M[r] Oliver and other Gentilemen, on this subject.—

[NDA. GLB, Vol. 1.]

To George Champlin, Newport, R. I., from Secretary of Navy

[PHILADELPHIA,]
Navy Department, *27th June 1798* —

GEORGE CHAMPLIN
New Port R. Island

SIR, Your Letter to M[r] Wolcott of the 19th Ins[t], is now before me, — It gives me pain, that the situation of your health, will not permit you to render those services to the public, to which you are so competent. —

The Ship building at Warren by Mess[rs] Gibbs & Channing, appears from her Dimensions & their Description, to be such a one as will suit the Public, and their Terms, except their Commission of 5 p. C[t] reasonable. — But it is right that some Gentleman of competent knowledge on the subject, & of Character to be relied on, should first examine her, before She be purchased for the Public. — Your relation in Congress, encourages me to expect, that you will take this Trouble — and if upon a View of her, She meets your Approbation, then the Letter inclosed with Mess[rs] Gibbs & Channing, closing with their offer, except in the single Instance of 5 p. C[t] Commission, may be delivered to Them.

Cap[t] Christopher Raymond Perry, will command this Ship. It is desireable, that the Captain should like his Ship — if he also approved of her, it would be an agreeable circumstance. —

I must solicit the favor of you to drop a Line to Cap[t] Perry on this Subject. You know where to direct to him. I do not. No answer having been rec[d] to a Letter written him the 9th Instant. —

[NDA. GLB, Vol. 1.]

From Secretary of Navy

[PHILADELPHIA,]
Navy Department. *27th June*. *1798*

JOHN MURRAY GEO. BARNEWALL W[m] BAYARD J. P. MUMFORD & J. C. CLASON. *New York*

GENTLEMEN, I am honored with your Letter of the 26th Ins[t] — There is a Bill before Congress, which there is no Doubt, will be passed into a Law, authorizing the President to receive from the Merchants &[c] Four Ships, to carry not less than 32 Guns — It is hoped that New York, Boston, Phila[a] & Baltimore will each furnish one such Vessels, instead of more of smaller size, as it is expected, that the latter can be obtained from the Towns of less commercial Importance.

The Money advanced by the Merchants is to be returned in six p. cent Stock of the United States. —

The Merchants of this place are about determining to set up a Ship of about 1000 Tons, to carry 44 Guns. — If those of New York can undertake one of similar Size — or one not less than 36 Guns, it would better answer the Views of Government, than to obtain from them two twenty Gun Ships. —

Presuming that the Merchants of New York, will undertake a Ship of 36 or 44 Guns, I will in a day or two forward on the Dimensions for each size — and in about Ten Days will send on the Model for the size adopted. In the mean Time, if it be thought proper, Preparations for Beginning can be making — as with all the Efforts of Patriotic Citizens like Yourselves. The Vessel may be wanted before She can be finished. —

[NDA. GLB, Vol. 1.]

To Gibbs & Channing, agents, Newport, R. I., from Secretary of Navy

[PHILADELPHIA,]
Navy Department, 27th June, 1798.

GIBBS & CHANNING, *New Port*

GENTLEMEN, Your Letter to G. Champlin Esqr is now before Me. —

Altho' from the respectability of your Character, I should not in my private Concerns hesitate a Moment to purchase your Ship, upon your own Representation of her — yet, acting for the Public it may be incumbent on me to make use of a Precaution, which I should not think of in my own Case. —

I have, therefore, requested the favor of Mr Champlin, to view the Ship, and if he approves of her for a Public Ship of War; I agree to take her for the public Service on the Terms of your Letter to him, except in the single Article of 5 p. Ct Commission, which is more than the Public has paid — and which I flatter Myself, Gentlemen of your Patriotism, will not in the present crisis of our Affairs, requiring the Aid of every heart and every hand, exact. —

The Dimensions of the Ship are very pleasing, and the Character of the Builder stands high — I shall therefore have but few Directions to give. — It is of the first Importance, that She be a swift Sailor.

The hold must be 11 feet (Beam to spring four Inches) — height between Decks, 5 feet 10 Inches — Waiste 6 feet. — This I understand can be easily done & without additional Expence — And this being done, the Ship will carry 24 — 12 Pounders on her main Deck, if found expedient — & six 6 pounders on her Quarter Deck and Forecastle. —

Capt Christr R. Perry who will command this Ship, will pay Attention to her Building & fitting for a Ship of War. —

She may be sheathed and coppered in the manner you propose in your Letter to Mr Champlin — tho' in other Instances the Iron Bolts have been rejected. —

It will be desireable, to get her to Sea as early as possible — sooner than 90 days if practicable, by setting a greater Number of hands to Work. —

It is not doubted that you will build & equip her with the same Regard to the purchase, & contract for Materials, as if intended for your own Service. I must rely on you to procure the best of Cordage — Sails — Cannon, & every Article, to complete her for a Cruise. Any Article which you can not obtain, shall be furnished, if you will let me know in Season what you can not procure.

For your Expenditures on the Hull of the Ship, I will agree that you be allowed at the rate of 5 p. C^t^ Commission, as you have already made Advances — But for all your other Expenditures, You must be content with a Commission of 2 p. C^t^, which is the Commission paid by the Public in all similar Cases. and with which I hope you will be satisfied. You must consider, that a part of your Compensation will be received in the satisfaction of rendering a public service, at a Time when the Public stand in need of the services of all the Friends of the Government. —

Money shall be advanced from Time to Time, on your Requisition, and as you may want It.

[NDA. GLB, Vol. 1.]

Extract from Captain Thomas Truxtun's journal, U. S. Frigate *Constellation*, 27 June 1798, Wednesday

At 4 PM I discharged the Pilot, having previously delivered him my Dispatches for the Secretary of War, under Cover to Mr Joseph Sterett, Naval Agent, at Baltimore, with Instructions to forward the same to Philadelphia, as soon as he received them.

At 6 spoke a stout Ship from Hamburgh bound to Baltimore. As she had taken a Pilot on Board, and was standing in, I did not send a Boat on Board her, they informed of having had Fifty three Days Passage, and meeting no Cruizers, and that there was no News at Hamburgh.

Throughout the whole of these Twenty four Hours, — stood off to the Eastward, the Weather very uncertain with large Quantities of Rain, and the Wind variable. At Noon all the Fleet in Company, but one Brigg, which bore away to the S.E. about 7 AM. This Vessel, I understand, is owned by a Mr Kennedy of Baltimore. No observation of the Sun to Day, but the Depth of Water at Meridian — was Sixteen Fathoms, brown Sand, and Shells, with green Moss on the Shells. The Latitude by Account 36.43′ N^o^ and the computed Bearing, and Distance of Cape Henry from the Ship was W.N.W. sixteen Leagues.

It is well to remark in this Place, that it is high Water at Cape Henry full and Change at ¼ past 11 o'clock, and at Cape Charles two Hours earlier. In coming from the Southward, and bound into the Bay of Chesapeake, keep in six Fathoms Water, and do not go off beyond nine Fathoms.

In Doubling the Cape, the Water deepens so, that you get into 10 or 11 Fathoms, and when the Cape bears South borrow into 6 Fathoms, and then run up West, untill the Cape bears East South East, then steer West North West, and keep in from Seven to Five Fathoms. On the Horse Shoe the Bottom is hard, and on the South Shore into Four, and half Fathoms, it is soft. Coming from the Northward, do not attempt entering the Chesapeake Bay, untill the Cape bears from West, to West North West, on Account of the Middle Ground, that is, if your Vessel is of a great Draught of Water, for only four Fathoms is to be found in that Bank, with the Cape bearing West.

[HS of Pa. NDA photostat.]

[27 June, 1798.]

Extract of a letter from Major Lewis Toussard to the Secretary of War, dated Fort Mifflin, June 28, 1798, regarding a sloop-of-war manned by Negroes

SIR,

"I have the honor of informing you, that yesterday, ten o'clock in the evening, the Resident Doctor of the Hospital of Pennsylvania came on purpose to give me the alarming information, that there existed a mutiny among the vessels in quarantine, now lying above the Fort; that he thought, in consequence of the report of four of the captains, it was proper to postpone till the morning, the order of the Governor of Pennsylvania, to be made known to the convoy. The boat of the sloop of war manned only with negroes, has been seen the whole day plying round all the other vessels which have negroes on board; they seem to have adopted between them the most desperate measures to the execution of which they are incited by their owners. There is now in those vessels between 250 and 300 negroes, well armed, trained to war, and saying they will land. They know no laws and count their lives for nothing.— Two of the pilots have left the vessels, one of them was so alarmed that he is sick at the hospital.

"On this information, I immediately sent an officer to captain Stephen Decatur, whose armed ship was at anchor below the Fort, with a request of coming up with the tide, and cast anchor on the north east side of the island, where I had no guns to direct upon the insurgents. During that time, with the assistance of the laborers, whose exertion, I cannot but highly commend, I had two heavy pieces transported and mounted on that side, when the *Delaware* passed up, and went to anchor in the middle of the convoy; she is now under weigh and proceeds down.

"As to oppose the landing of these negroes, and their proceeding thro' Jerseys with their owners to Philadelphia, it is not in my power, in the situation they lay above the fort. I have agreed with the Doctor, that he would order them this morning below and abreast of my battery — then I may watch their motions."

[LC, "Argus, or Greenleaf's Daily Advertiser" (New York), 2 July 1798.]

To Captain Stephen Decatur (senior), U. S. Navy, from Secretary of Navy

[PHILADELPHIA,]
Navy Departmt 28. June. 1798.

Capt S. DECATUR

SIR, I have your Letter of this day. You will receive a Letter from me, by a Pilot, dispatched for the Purpose, requesting you to remain near the Vessels with the French Passengers and Negroes, until Congress determine what is to be done with them. — You have acted with great Propriety and Prudence. —

[NDA. OSW, Vol. 1.]

To Captain Stephen Decatur (senior), U. S. Navy, from Secretary of Navy

[PHILADELPHIA,]
Navy office, 28. June. 1798

Capt. STEPHEN DECATUR

SIR, The Vessels under Quarantine, near Fort Mifflin, have a Number of Passengers on board, French Men and Negroes. — The Negroes it seems are impatient to land & have discovered a Disposition to outrage.—

Congress have the subject of these People before them, but until they determine what shall be done with them, it is expedient that they should be prevented from landing, if they should attempt it, without Permission or by Force. —

Under these Circumstances, you will immediately move your ship up to Fort Mifflin & take a Position between the Vessels and the Jersey Shore, so as to give the most effectual Aid in your power to the commanding Officer of the Fort, with whom you will communicate, in keeping these People in Subordination and order, & in preventing their landing on either shore — or moving down the river to land at any other Place. —

You will use every degree of Prudence, to avoid coming to Extremities, but at all Events the Negroes are not to be suffered to land, until Congress shall have come to a Decision respecting Them. —

[NDA. OSW, Vol. 1.]

To James Watson, Navy Agent, New York, from Secretary of Navy

[PHILADELPHIA,]
Navy Department, 28th June 1798.

Jas. WATTSON, *New York*

SIR, The Secy. of the Treasury having commenced a Correspondence with you, on the subject of procuring a Ship for the United States, & informing me that you will take upon Yourself the Trouble of contracting for one to be built in New York, I take the Liberty of requesting that you will as early as possible contract for the Building of one to carry twenty four Guns, having regard to the following principles. —

1st. that the Materials be of the best live Oak or red Cedar, except the Floor Timbers & Floor Futtocks — or of the best seasoned white Oak, to be determined by Inspection. No Timber inferior to seasoned white Oak to be used. —

2nd. The Public to furnish the Copper Sheathing, Copper Bolts and Spikes — The Iron Work to be contracted for separately by the Pound, and delivered under the Check of an Agent. — the whole of the Materials however to be placed in the Ship, at the Expence of the Contractor. —

3rd. The Dimensions to be 93 feet keel, 31 Feet Beam, & 13½ feet hold — to be pierced for 20 Guns, exclusive of the Bridle Ports on the main Gun Deck, and two on the Quarter Deck — to have an Orlope Deck, and to be of sufficient Strength, and in all Respects completed for a Ship of War. Permission to be reserved to vary the Dimensions but without injury or Expence to the Contractor. —

4th. The Contract must be made per Ton of Carpenter's Measurement, according to the rule in Phila[a] — the shortest Time possible must be given for launching & completing the Ship — It is hoped the Time will not exceed 90 days.

5th. A Bond with Sureties to be required to secure the Execution of the Contract, and a due Settlement for all Advances. —

6th. No after Bills to be admitted. —

It will be important to dispose of the Business in such a Manner, that it will proceed with Dispatch and order — of course the Contract should be made with none but a man of Skill and responsible Character. — And I must depend on you to procure the Sails — the Rigging, Guns, Copper and every Article wanted for the Ship, to fit her for a complete sloop of War — & so to make your Arrangements, as to let nothing be waited for.—

The Compensation heretofore given by the Public for such Services, has been 2 p. Cent. on all Expenditures — The Public furnishing the Money as wanted. — It is expected you will be content with the same, in addition to the Satisfaction of rendering important Service to your Country. —

This Ship is for Captain Morris, who will give some Attention to her Building. —

[NDA. GLB, Vol. 1.]

To Nicklin & Griffith, Phliadelphia, from Secretary of Navy

[PHILADELPHIA,]
Navy Office, 28th June 1798.

Mess[rs] NICKLIN & GRIFFITH

The Secretary of the Navy having some communications to transmit to Captain Decatur of the *Delaware*, requests Mess[rs] Nicklin & Griffiths will be so good as to procure a careful Pilot with the greatest Dispatch possible — it will be necessary that he should call at the Navy Office, by which Time the Dispatches will be ready — If M[r] Gerret Hulsacamp is up, he is a trusty Person and has been employed to carry Orders to Captain Dale — He resides at N[o] 16 South Street. —

[NDA. GLB, Vol. 1.]

Extract from Captain Thomas Truxtun's journal, U. S. Frigate *Constellation*, 28 June 1798, Thursday

At 4 PM brought to the Schooner *Andrew* from Philadelphia, bound to Charleston, South Carolina, the Master informed me, that the Frigate, *United States* was between Philadelphia, and Marcus Hook, when he sailed; and that he spoke the *Ganges* off the Delaware.

At 5 Ditto fired a Gun to Leeward, and hoisted the Ensign at the Ensign Staff, as a Signal for parting with the Fleet, there being no strange Sail in Sight, and my Promise being performed of convoying those Vessels about Twenty or Thirty Leagues at most from Cape Henry.

Being in Twenty Fathoms Water, and at the Distance of Twenty one Leagues from Cape Henry, when I left the Fleet, with the Wind at East, I bore away to the Southward, in Order to pass Cape Hatteras as soon as possible, and so proceed on as far as the Southern Limites of my Station.

At 7 AM spoke a Brigg, belonging to Mr Marcus M^c^Causlin of Baltimore; from the Havannah, bound to Baltimore, out nine Days, and had seen no Cruizers.

Throughout the whole of these Twenty four Hours, we have had light variable Winds, but mostly from the Eastward. No observation of the Sun. — Latitude Account 36°5′ North Longitude Account 74°35′, West from Greenwich in GB

[HS of Pa. NDA photostat.]

[29. June 1798.]

Order to the Sea Lieutenants and Master, etc., from Captain Thomas Truxtun, U. S. Navy

ON BOARD THE *Constellation*

Order for the Preservation of Health, and Care of Water, to commence on the 29th of June 1798 —

At seven Bells, or at half past seven o'clock every Morning, the Crew is to be served one Pint of Water. at half an Hour before Noon, one Pint of Grog. — At half past 3 in the Afternoon, another Pint of Grog; at half an Hour before Sun Set every Evening they are to have served them a Pint and half a Pint of Water, making in the whole four Pints, and half a Pint of Water, and half a Pint of Rum, which is mixed as aforesaid. —

This is the Allowance of Rum and Water, — (Exclusive of that for boiling Pease) for Twenty four Hours, under existing Circumstances, and is to continue, untill further Orders from me in Writing.

In serving out the Water, each Man may be allowed, to take his Allowance with him, provided he has Anything to put it in, those who have not, must have it put in the Scuttle Cask, under a Centinel who is to guard the same with a Cutlass; as no Muskets are suffered on Deck at Sea, but when at Quarters. —

N. B. No more Water is to be allowed for my use, than for any other Man — without a Special Order, two Quarts per Day excepted for the Use of Officers at my Table. —

THOMAS TRUXTUN.

To The Sea Leiutenants and Master &C.

[HS of Pa. NDA photostat. Truxtun's LB, 1798–9.]

To Jeremiah Yellott, Navy Agent, Baltimore, from Secretary of Navy

[PHILADELPHIA,]
Navy Department June 29. 1798

JEREMIAH YELLOTT

SIR The President has this day nominated to the Senate, the following Officers

I[saac] Phillips to be Captain
Josias M. Speake, John West } to be Lieutenants
George Calder, Arthur Sinclair } to be Midshipmen

and there is no doubt they will be appointed; — Should you have appointed a Midshipman, one of these may be turned over to the *Montezuma.* The President desires the name of the *Adriana* to be changed into that of the *Baltimore,* & wishes — the Ship may prove herself worthy of the name; — there have been heretofore sent to you, two Statements shewing the number & grades of Officers allowed to Ships of the size of the two under your direction; — please to forward on the names of proper persons to fill the different Stations, still vacant for the Ship *Baltimore;* a Doc^r Wells has been recommend[ed] for Surgeons Mate, is he proper?

[NDA. GLB, Vol. 1.]

Extract from Captain Thomas Truxtun's journal, U. S. Frigate *Constellation,* 29 June 1798, Friday

The Wind blowing fresh from the South East, and every Appearance of a Gale, at 2 PM took in the Jib, and Stay Sails, and hawled the Main Sail up. At 5 PM exercised Great Guns, and Marines, and at 6 Ditto tacked to the Eastward, and handed the Main Sail, Not thinking it prudent to approach the Land at Night with such Appearances.

At 10 in double Reefs, the Gale encreasing at South South West; at 2 AM, it blowing harder, took in the Top Sails; the Rigging having got very slack, I sat up the Lee Shrouds, and the Stays.

At 9 AM the Wind being at West, and clear, made all Sail. Several Merchant Vessels in Sight, bound in. Employed in repairing Sundries, Latitude observed 35°20′ N° Longitude Account 74°00 Minutes. Put the People to an Allowance of four, and half Pints a Man, exclusive of Water for cooking and ordered their Allowance of Provisions &c strictly to be served out, agreeable to Act of Congress.

[HS of Pa. NDA photostat.]

To John Murray, George Barnewall, and others of New York from Secretary of Navy

[PHILADELPHIA,]
Navy Department June 30th 1798

JOHN MURRAY GEORGE BARNEWALL & others
Comittee Merch^ts New York

I have the honor to transmit herewith the principal dimensions of Ships of War, calculated to carry 44. 38. & 36 Guns of 18 pound Calibre on the Gun deck.

As soon as the Committee have informed me of the Force & dimentions of the Ship to be built by the Citizens of New York, I will direct a Draft to be prepared without delay.

I have this moment received your Favor of the 29th Inst although the Bill mentioned in my Letter of the 27th has passed both Houses, I am not yet in possession of it, I hope on Monday to be able to be very particular, in the meantime I can only say, it will be infinitely most desireable to have a large Ship if the Public contribute to the building of it.

[NDA. GLB, Vol. 1.]

[Enclosure]

Dimensions of Ships of War calculated for carrying 18 pounders

	Ships of 44 Guns	Ditto of 38 d°	Ditto of 36 d°
Number of Guns on Main Deck	30	28	26
Weight of Metal	18 Pounders	18 Pounders	18 Pounders
Length of Gun deck between the perpendiculars	167. 6	155. 7	144. 2
Length of Keel for Tonnage	140–"	130–"	120–
Moulded breadth of Beams	40—	$38\frac{1}{2}$	37
Depth of Hold	13—	12—	11. 3
Height between decks	6—	$5.\ 10\frac{1}{2}$	5. 9
Height from Gun to Upper Deck	6. 9	6. 6	6. 3
Carpenters Tonnage by the Old Mode	$1178\frac{99}{95}$	$1014\frac{16}{95}$	$864\frac{69}{95}$

(Signed) JOSHUA HUMPHREYS —

JUNE 28. 1798

Extract from Captain Thomas Truxtun's journal, U. S. Frigate *Constellation*, 30 June 1798, Saturday

At 5 PM came on a Squall from the Westward, which shifted the Wind round to the N. West, and brought us clear, pleasant Weather, the Gulph Stream this Twenty four Hours sat us to the Northward 45; consequently it must have run with very great Velocity indeed.

At 6 PM brought to with a Shot, a Brig from New York, bound to Savannah in Georgia (belonging to Major Saunders) out 13 Days; the Master had seen no Cruizers; at 7 Ditto spoke a Sloop from Baltimore, bound to Charleston, South Carolina; at 10 AM brought to after a short Chace, a Schooner from Georgetown called the *Nancy*, Benjamin West Master bound to Philadelphia, this Man informed me, he had been chaced by a Schooner yesterday afternoon; I inquired of him how he had steered since, and he told me N. E. B. E., I accordingly directed the Course to be steered S. W. B. W., in Hopes of falling in with this Vessel.

Latitude observed 34°38′ N° Longitude Acct 75°11′ W

[HS of Pa. NDA photostat.]

[1 July 1798.]

To Lieutenants Rogers, Cowper, and Sterett, Doctor Balfour, Lieutenant Triplett of the Marines, and Messrs. Shirley and Garrettson from Captain Thomas Truxtun, U. S. Navy

Captain Truxtun presents his Compliments to the Gentlemen of the Gun Room to viz: Lieutenants Rogers, Cowper, and Sterett. Doctor Balfour, Lieutenant Triplett (of the Marines) and Messrs. Shirley & Garretson, and requests the Favour of their Company, to dine with him in Rotation, on the following Days, without further Invitation. Some Neglect of his Steward has induced Captain Truxtun to have Recourse to this Mode of inviting, and entertaining his Officers, which he hopes will be equally as agreeable, as a particular Invitation.

On Sunday the Officer of the Watch bringing 12 o'clock on that Day, as also Doctor Balfour.
On Monday ditto, with Lieutenant Clinch of the Marines —
On Tuesday ditto, and first Lieutenant
On Wednesday, Mr Shirley the Master, and Mr Garretson, Purser
On Thursday, Officer of Watch with Dr Balfour
On Friday, Lieutenant Clinch and Mr Shirley
On Saturday, Officer of the Watch, & Mr Garretson

The Hour of dining is ¼ past two o'Clock. —
UNITED STATES SHIP, *Constellation* 1st July 1798

Mr VanDyke	✓	Van Dyke
Mr Dent	✓	Dent
Mr Clagett	✓	Clagett
~~Mr Porter~~		Porter
~~Mr McDonnough~~		McDonnough
~~Mr Talbott~~ Mr Robinson	✓	Wederstrant
Mr Wederstrant		Harvey
~~Doctor Harvey~~		Davis
~~Mr Davis~~	✓	✓Robinson
~~xxxxxxxxx~~Mr Herbert	✓	✓~~T~~ Herbert
	✓	✓Sinclair

Captain Truxtun presents his Compliments to the above Gentlemen & requests the Favour of their Company to Dinner in Rotation, every Day at one Quarter past Two o'clock.

United States Ship *Constellation* 1st July 1798 —

THOMAS TRUXTUN.

[HS of Pa. NDA photostat. Truxtun's LB, 1798–9.]

Extract from Captain Thomas Truxtun's Journal, U. S. Frigate *Constellation*, 1 July 1798, Sunday

Light Airs from the Westward throughout the whole of this Day, and clear. The Gulph Stream I find to have sat us 45′ to the Northward, of Course that much to the Eastward, as it runs N. E. the latter Part, wore Ship, and stood to the Southward. Exercised Great Guns, and Marines, &c. &c. Nothing further remarkable — Latitude observed 35°23′ No Longitude 74°16′ W.

[HS of Pa. NDA photostat.]

[2 July 1798.]

Captain Truxtun concerning mutinous assemblies on board U. S. Frigate *Constellation*

WHEREAS it has been represented to me by unquestionable Authority in various Ways, that there has been several mutinous Assemblies on Board of the United States Frigate, *Constellation*, under my Command, and that the same has been made, with a View to excite, cause, and effect a Mutiny, to the great Injury of the Naval Service, and of the People, and Government of the said States: And whereas the Promoters thereof are well known to me, I have thought proper to give this public Warning (after first causing the Articles of War to be read, as a second Proof of the Mildness with which I commenced, and hoped to have been enabled to succeed in the Government of the Ship) to viz:— That in Case I ever hear of a Murmur in the Ship, or any Expressions, that have a Tendency to disorganize, or cause Disorder, or Discontent in any Way whatever, or of any Threats, I am determined to put the following Article of War in Execution, and comply strictly with the Orders of the President of the United States.

The Article is in these Words

"Any Officer, Seaman, or Marine, who shall begin, excite, cause, or join in any Mutiny, or Sedition in the Ship to which he belongs, on any Pretence whatsoever, shall suffer Death, or such other Punishment, as a Court Martial shall direct. Any Person in or belonging to the Ship, who shall utter any Words of Sedition, and Mutiny, or endeavour to make any mutinous Assemblies on any Pretence whatsoever Shall suffer such Punishment, as a Court Martial shall inflict.

The Order of the President of the United States under the Head of Regulations respecting the Duties of Officers at Sea in the 23^{d} Article, runs thus.

He will (speaking of the Captain) be ready on the first Appearance of Mutiny to use the most vigorous Means to suppress it, and to bring the Ring leaders to Punishment.

In the 48th Article it is thus

He will pay Attention to, and maintain the strictest Subordination among the Officers, and among the People of the Crew, he will not suffer any Boat to leave the Vessel, unless there be a trusty Person, or Officer on Board who will be responsible for it's Crew, and their Behaviour on Shore.

In the 68th Article it is thus

As soon as a Vessel of the United States shall have set Sail, the Commander will see, that his Officers discharge their respective Duties with the greatest Vigilance, and Exactness.

In the 85th Article it is thus

He will conduct himself during his Voyage, or Campaign according to his Instructions; if his Mission has for it's Object to cruize to cover the Trade of the Citizens of the United States, he will perform it so, that there will remain to him on his Return to Port, but fifteen Days Provisions for his Crew, unless he receives contrary Instructions from the President, or is forced to return sooner by some unforeseen Cause, which cannot admit of Delay.

Under Regulation respecting the Watch Article 6th it is thus

The President strictly enjoins the Captain of every Vessel, to keep, during the whole of the Watch an under Lieutenant, or where Circumstances will not admit of employing an Officer of this Grade, a Midshipman upon the Fore-Castle to maintain Order and Viligance.

Under Regulation respecting Provisions Article 5th it is thus

One half Gallon of Water at least shall be allowed every Man in foreign Voyages, and such further Quantity, as shall be thought necessary on the Home Station, but on particular Occasions the Captain may shorten this Allowance.

Having thus quoted that Part of the Articles of War in Question, and the public Instructions of the President (to say Nothing of my private Instructions from Government which can never be communicated) no Person whatever can commit any Misdemeanor, and plead Ignorance after. Altho' like other Nations we make a System for ourselves, the Government is just, and mild in every Respect, and my Conduct has uniformly corresponded with it. If I have at any Time erred, it has been in not observing that Rigor, — which the infamous Conduct of some On Board have deserved, and which I should have been warranted in inflicting by the Orders of the President, and the Articles of War just read in toto. It is well known, that since the first Man was entered for this Frigate to the present Moment, only one (a worthless Marine) among the Numbers that have deserved it, has been seized up, and flogged, and that Man, I afterwards turned on Shore, as a Disgrace to the Ship, finding he was too abandoned to give me any Hope of a Reform. Notwithstanding this Fact, such has been the Conduct of some on Board, that various Things have been represented otherwise, and that too with Circumstances of Aggravation. —

You have the Law before you, and, I repeat, you know the Consequence, if, in future, you transgress. I must and will do my duty, and every Governor, and Officer, Civil and military in every State in the Union, as well as all those Nations, with whom we have Treaties, is obliged to aid and assist me, wherever, I go, in bringing to Justice any Offenders. The Seamen of Great Britain have sat such an Example of Infamy, that the Marine Laws of the United States, England, France, Spain, and Holland, as well as the Rest of the Maritime Powers of Europe, have been, and will still be made more severe in Consequence thereof. It is the Interest of all Parties at War, to pass Laws, and check such Proceedings, and it has been wise in them to do it. Having the best Disposition towards my People, I hope after this Statement, and this Warning, I shall behold a contrary Behaviour in those, who have been misled, and that the Corrupt, and evil minded will be watched, and guarded against, as so many Serpents.

Should Injustice be done you, or any of you at any Time, make your Complaints with Decency, and in an orderly and becoming Manner, and I will always hear, and remedy them.

United States Frigate, *Constellation* at Sea, 2d July 1798.

THOMAS TRUXTUN.

[HS of Pa. NDA photostat. Truxtun's LB, 1798–9.]

To Captain Thomas Truxtun, U. S. Navy, from Secretary of Navy

[PHILADELPHIA,]
Navy Departmt 2 July. 1798

THOS TRUXTUN

SIR, The enclosed Letter, given to me by the Speaker of the house of Representatives, has created a little Alarm among some of the Members of Congress, I hope without Reason, but it shews that there is a spirit of Mutiny in some part of your Crew, which should be suppressed by every prudent Means.

I send you the original Letter, that you may discover the Writer — I should presume, that your safest Line of Conduct would be, to take no Notice of having received such a Letter — to examine well, whether the Sailors have any just Cause of Dissatisfaction on the score of ill Treatment from any of the Officers, which I cannot suppose, — to reform silently any abuse of Authority: — and to suffer to exist no just cause of Complaint, against oppression by the Officers, — nor on the score of Provisions — By causing full Justice to be done to the Sailors, you will be more justified in treating as they merit, at a proper Time, those turbulent and ungovernable Men (and such there is too much reason to dread will find their way into the American Navy) who can only be restrained by Severity. —

I would beg leave to suggest, the propriety of your discharging with disgrace, at the first Port you put into, if you should discover them, the Writer of the Letter & his Confederates, sending their Names, Country and Description of their Persons to me; that measures may be taken, to prevent their being received hereafter into our Navy.

Capt Barry, in the *United States* Frigate, will be out in a day or two — Capt Decatur has already sailed — I have no doubt, you will have your Ship & Men in such order, as to be ready to undertake in a Moment, any Enterprize — You may expect to hear from Me again, in a few days. — I have desired Mr Pennock to send a Pilot Boat after you with this. —

I have the honor &c

[NDA. OSW, Vol. 1.]

To Benjamin Lincoln, Collector, Boston, from Secretary Oliver Wolcott

[PHILADELPHIA,]
Treasury Department, July 2, 1798.

BENJAMIN LINCOLN Esq.
Collector of Boston

SIR, I enclose a Commission for Jonathan Chapman to be Commander of the new Revenue Cutter building at Newburyport also an act of Congress passed on the 22d June 1798 authorizing an increase of the complement of the Cutters to a number not exceeding Seventy Marines and Seamen.

You will inform Captain Chapman that his pretensions to an appointment with rank in the Navy will be hereafter considered; the same observations may be made to Captain Williams — the old Cutter is to be continued in service the present season and exclusively devoted to the service of the Revenue. The new Cutter is to cruize in concert with the *Herald.*

Captain Chapman is to look out for a sett of officers for whom he will be responsible they must be men who can be recommended also by yourself and Mr. Higginson — If the vessell can be got ready for sea before Commissions for the subordinate officers can be made out and transmitted you will make out Certificates to be signed by yourself as Collector denoting the stations in which they are to serve the vessell will proceed to sea and the Commissions hereafter transmitted. It may be expedient for you to concert with Mr. Higginson suitable arrangements for the new Cutter. I shall be satisfied if the direction of the equipments is assigned to him the expense must however be distinctly stated and must be paid out of the proceeds of Revenue collected in your office.

I am very respectfully Sir,

Your Obedt. Servt.

OLIVER WOLCOTT.

P. S. The enclosed instructions and marine regulations you will be pleased to deliver to Mr. Chapman.

[TDA. Coast Guard, Out. Letters, No. 0, 1790–1833.]

To William Pennock, Navy Agent, Norfolk, from Secretary of Navy

[PHILADELPHIA,]
Navy Department July 2d 1798

WILLIAM PENNOCK *Norfolk*

SIR, Presuming that Capt Truxtun has left Hampton Roads — I have to request that you will immediately employ a Pilot Boat to carry the enclosed Letter to him —

His present Cruising Ground, is between Cape Henry & our Southern Extremity. This if not before known, please to keep to yourself. —

[NDA. GLB, Vol. 1.]

Extract from Captain Thomas Truxtun's journal, U. S. Frigate *Constellation*, 2 July 1798, Monday

Alternately fresh and light Breezes from the Southward with pleasant Weather all these Twenty four Hours.

At 7 PM spoke a Schooner from Boston bound to Savannah, she was called the *Republican,* and informed us, that the Frigate, *Constitution* had some Difficulty in manning, but would be at Sea in two Weeks.

Called all Hands, and had the Articles of War read to the People, with a Paper I prepared for the Occasion, having had some Information of Discontents appearing among some of the men.

Was flogged at the Gang Way (by my Order) John Dianen, a Marine, with one Dozen of Stripes on his bare Back, with a Cat of nine Tails, for Insolence to the Sergeant of Marines, and endeavouring to arest a Pistol out of his Hands.

Latitude observed 34°45′ N° Longitude Acc^t 72°36′ [W].

[HS of Pa. NDA photostat.]

To Samuel Sewall from Secretary of Navy

[PHILADELPHIA,]
Navy department, 2 July 1798. —

Saml SEWALL

SIR, The Letter of which the above is the Copy, was I believe sent to you several days ago without the Estimates. Presuming, that the Estimates may still be useful I have now the honor of forwarding them.

I will take the Liberty to add, that the Frigates carrying 38 Guns in the British Service, the largest sized Frigates they employ, measure not exceeding 940 Tons. The Frigates heretofore built the *Constellation* to carry 36 Guns, but actually carrying 38, measures upwards of 1300 Tons. It is still to be determined whether, a Ship carrying the same Number of Guns, is better for being so much larger, than the size adopted by the British Nation.

[NDA. GLB, Vol. 1.]

To Samuel Anderson from Secretary of Navy

[PHILADELPHIA,]
Doc^r SAM^l ANDERSON *Navy Department 2 July 1798*
Present

SIR, The Ship *Delaware*, now on her way out on a Cruise, will be past your reach if you wait to get a regular Appointment of Surgeon's Mate — which will require Two days, perhaps three —

If you will immediately proceed after the Ship, & enter upon the duties of Surgeon's Mate, I will present your Name to the President for that Appointment, and there can be no doubt of your receiving it. —

[NDA. GLB, Vol. 1.]

To Captain James Sever, U. S. Navy, from Secretary of Navy

[PHILADELPHIA,]
Navy Deparm^t 2 July. 1798.

JA^s SEVER

SIR, The Officers and Men, engaging in the Navy Service who leave Wives or Children behind, may have any Proportion of their Monthly Pay, not exceeding one half, advanced Quarterly to their Families — But the Person who avails himself of this Privilege, must leave a Power of Attorney witnessed by the commanding Officer, and the Purser of the Ship to which he belongs, in favor of the Person who is to receive the Money.— The commanding Officer, will just before sailing on a Cruise, transmit to Me a List of the Names, Rank & monthly Pay of the Persons executing such Powers of Attorney, & I will make Arrangements for paying the money at the Port, from whence the Vessel takes her Departure.

Inclosed is the Form of the Power of Attorney to be used. The Men must be settled with at the Time the Power is executed, & it must be particularly ascertained in the Power of Attorney, when the Pay is to commence — It is customary to advance to the Seaman 2 Month's Pay — Where Advances have been made, the Pay, one half of which may be received under the Power of Attorney, can only commence from the Time, when the Sailors shall have served the Time for which they received the Advance.—

The Purser should be particular in keeping the Accounts of the Men who leave Powers of Attorney, & should be careful to avoid paying them in Slops or Money, more than the balance of their Monthly Pay, after deducting the sums to be received under their Letters of Attorney. —

For Copy of Power of Attorney—See Page 64.

[NOTE.—Page 64 contains enclosure to letter of 30 June 1798 to Captain Samuel Nicholson.]

[NDA. OSW, Vol. 1.]

To Captain John Barry, U. S. Navy, from Secretary of Navy

[PHILADELPHIA,]
Navy Departm^t 3^d July. 1798.

Capt JOHN BARRY

SIR, The Frigate, *United States*, under your Command, being equipped manned & armed, you will proceed to Sea, with the first fair Wind. —

Enclosed, you will receive your Instructions, founded on the existing Acts of Congress, and by which you are to be governed, until further Orders. These Instructions confine you within narrow Limits, and you can do little more under them, than exercise your Men along the Coast — It is scarcely to be expected that the French Cruisers will have the Temerity to throw Themselves in your Way. But it is not improbable, that a very few days, & before your Men are sufficiently disciplined, you may be ordered on more important Service with greater Latitude; under this Idea, I am directed by the President, to call your Attention to the Necessity of losing no Time in putting your Ship & Men into a State to be prepared for any Enterprize — and to express his entire Conviction, that Nothing on your Part will be wanting to justify the high Confidence reposed by him, and your Country, in your Activity, skill & Bravery. —

After stretching off & on the Capes of Delaware for four days, if in that Time you should receive Nothing from Me, You will consider your Cruising Ground to extend from Cape Henry to Nantucket, and will use all the Means in your power to defend this Extent of Coast, against the Depredations of the Vessels sailing under Authority or Pretence of Authority from the French Republic — and it is particularly enjoined by the President, that you will in Conjunction with the Force of Capt Dale, whose Cruising Ground has heretofore been between Cape Henry & long Island, & with whom you will doubtless fall in, afford all possible Protection to the Vessels of the United States, coming on or going off the Coast. —

It will be proper for you, as you pass the Capes of Delaware from Time to Time, to stand in, hoisting a Danish Flag, on the main top Mast head, that you may be known to any express Boat, that may be dispatched after You. —

Capt Decatur had orders to cruise with Capt Dale, until the 10th Instant — If you should fall in with Decatur sooner than the 10th you will direct him to proceed to join Capt Truxtun on the Southern Station. —

[NDA. OSW, Vol. 1.]

To Robert Liston, British Ambassador to United States, from Secretary of State

DEPARTMENT OF STATE
Philadelphia July 3, 1798.

SIR, Your note of the 29th of June, received the 30th, & that of the 1st of July received the same day, I laid before the President of the United States, by whose direction I this morning send to the Governor of Pennsylvania, copies of the declaration of the captain, officers & passengers of the armed Ship *Melpomene*, and of the certificate of the masters and pilots of the other vessels which brought passengers from the *Mole*, confirming all the essential facts stated in the former. By these notes and documents, and the verbal information of others, it satisfactorily appears that the charges brought against those French passengers are destitute of foundation: and in consequence thereof, I have informed the Governor, "that it will be entirely agreeable to the President, that those passengers and their servants be permitted to land, and with as little delay as will comport with the health laws of the State of Pennsylvania."

While the unfounded suspicions and reproaches against these people, and the inconveniences to which they have consequently been subjected, are subjects of real regret, no terms will now be required on the part of the General Government, which may cause additional inconvenience. At the same time, it seems proper to remark (what must have occurred to the passengers themselves since their arrival) that the actual state of things between the United States and France, induced by the violence, intrigues and real hostilities of the latter, may render their residence here less eligible than at any former period; and that the further progress of the differences between the two countries, may hereafter, and possibly very soon, render it a duty in the Government of the U. States, to prescribe regulations and measures, in regard to French citizens, not before contemplated, but which the public security may require. These, however, will certainly be

U. S. FRIGATE UNITED STATES.

formed and executed with that humanity which has ever distinguished the U. States, while their safety must be considered as the supreme law.

I have the honor to be, with great respect,

Sir, your obedt Servant

TIMOTHY PICKERING.

ROBERT LISTON Esqr
Envoy Extraordinary &c. &c.

[Conn. HS. Mss. no. 22.]

To Tench Francis, Purveyor, from Secretary of Navy

[PHILADELPHIA,]
Navy Department July 3. 1798

TENCH FRANCIS

Cap Barry informs me that he is waiting only for two Coil of Rope, one Coil 7½ Inch rope, the other Coil 5½ Inch rope & 50 lb. of marline; His Gunner calls on you with this to get the rope, the Boat is waiting for it & I want to get Capt Barry off this day; pray therefore furnish these articles without the least delay.

[NDA. Req. on US T., 1798–1803.]

Extract from Captain Thomas Truxtun's journal, U. S. Frigate *Constellation*, 3 July 1798, Tuesday

A pleasant Breeze from the South West, the first of this Day, with smooth Water. Saw two Sail to the North West, gave Chace, and at seven PM spoke the armed Ship *Sterling* of Boston from Edenton, North Carolina, bound to Surinam, with a Schooner in Company from the same Place, these Vessels had been out 36 Hours, and seen no Cruizers.

The middle light Airs, and the latter, a fresh Breeze from the South South East.

All Hands employed at the various Duties of the Ship

Latitude observed 34°19′ N°. Longitude Account 72°54′ W.

[HS of Pa. NDA photostat.]

Extract from the Journal of Lieutenant John Mullowny, U. S. Frigate *United States*, Wednesday, 4 July 1798

Newcastle River Delaware. Winds light & variable. Loosed all the sails to dry, exercised the crew at their proper Quarters.

At 4 P. M. Capt. Barry came on board.

[NA.]

Extract from Captain Thomas Truxtun's journal, U. S. Frigate *Constellation*, 4 July 1798, Wednesday

The breeze encreasing, and from the East South East, in Jib, and Stay Sails, top Gallant Sails, Main Sail, and the second Reefs in the

Top Sails. At 4 PM it blows harder, in Mizen top Sail, at 7 Ditto, the Gale encreasing in Foresail, and at 11 Ditto, down top Gallant Yards. At 8 AM the Wind having backed round to the Northward, blowing a violent Hurricane, with much Rain, took in the Main and Fore Top Sails, and scudded under bare Poles. At 9 Ditto the Wind backed still further round, and into the West North West, and West, where it continues to blow as before, with a high and cross Sea running.

The Ship has made much Water, since the Commencement of the Gale, tho' the Guns were housed, and all was made as snug as possible. This Circum. is owing to the Upper Works being caulked during the Winter Season.

No observation of the Sun.

Latitude Account 32°.18′ N.
Longitude ditto 73°.42′ W.

[HS of Pa. NDA photostat.]

[July 5, 1798.]

Deposition of Neil Mac Neal reference the Ship *Eliza*

Before me, Moses Young, Consul of the United States of America for the city of Madrid, (and for such parts of the kingdom of Spain as are nearer to the said city than to the residence of any other Consul or Vice Consul of the United States) personally appeared Neil Mac Neal, a citizen of the said States, late Master and Commander of the American Ship *Eliza*, who being duly sworn, deposeth and sayeth,

That on the twelvth day of June last he sailed over the [Bar of] Charleston in South Carolina in the above mentioned Ship *Eliza* [words obliterated] command, mounting twelve guns, and manned with thirty men, bound to London. On the fifth of July instant at day break, a sail was discovered astern, giving chase, and gaining upon the *Eliza* very fast, in latitude 48.35 N. and longitude 13 W. from London. When the chasing ship came within a mile, she fired with shot at the *Eliza*, and hoisted french colours; upon which, the said Neil Mac Neil prepared to defend himself and the property entrusted to his care. The french ship then coming close up under the *Eliza's* quarter, fired a nine pound shot into the American, together with a volley of musketry: then, and not until then, did the American fire upon the frenchman; the consequence was a close action within pistol shot, for one hour and an half, when the American was obliged to haul down his colours to *L'Heureux Decidé*, privateer, of Bordeaux, mounting eighteen nine pounders, and one hundred and eighty five men. The *Eliza* had one man killed and three wounded, her sails and rigging very much cut, her braces all shot away, her mainmast wounded, and there was no command of the ship when she struck. That the said Captain Neil Mac Neal was afterwards put on board of the privateer with twenty three of his people, where, at the end of two days the frenchman by threats obliged him to sign an untruth, to wit; that the United States were at war with France, and that he, the American, fired the first shot. On the eleventh day of the month they arrived at the port of Los Pasages near Saint Sebastian: the Mate of the *Eliza* and the crew (except such as were wounded) were sent as prisoners into France. Against all which illegal and piratical conduct, I the said Neil Mac Neal make this immediate formal Protest at the first practicable place to do it, having been a prisoner at St Sebastian, where there is no American Consul, and in custody of a french soldier there, from whom I have just made my escape, and arrived here yesterday the 19th of July.

NEIL MAC NEAL

In testimony whereof I have hereunto set my hand and affixed my Seal of Office at Madrid this twentieth day of July one thousand seven hundred and ninety eight, and in the twenty third year of the Independence of the United States.

M. YOUNG

Recd in Colo Humphreys No 155

[SDA. Disp. Spain. Bk. 4, Humphreys.]

To James Watson, Navy Agent, New York, from Secretary of Navy

[PHILADELPHIA,]
Navy Departmt 5. July 1798. —

JAMES WATTSON
New York

SIR, Mr Sileas Webb, has a Vessel building at New York, which he represents as fit for a Cruiser — The Acts of Congress authorize 6 Vessels of 18 Guns — 12 not less than 20, nor more than 24 Guns & 6 of 32 or upwards — It is meant that they shall be as follows —

6 of 18 Guns
12 of 24 "
3 of 36 "
3 of 44 "

You will judge whether the Vessel building by Mr Webb will answer for 18 Guns — & whether She will possess the essential Qualities of Swift Sailing & considerable Strength. No Vessel ought to be purchased for the Public without these Qualities.

You will also determine, whether the Vessels expected to be built at New York — one of 36 or 44 Guns — by the Merchants — one Frigate, the keel of which has been sometime laid — & the 24 Gun Ship, which you will contract for, will not be enough to employ all your Carpenters — and whether, undertaking to fit out another Vessel at that Port, will not interfere with the Progress of the larger and more Material Ships.

If New York is fully equal to the Four, and you find the Ship of Mr Webb well calculated for the Public service; you may if you please, purchase her on the best Terms in your Power, provided You think the Terms reasonable, and provided too you will undertake to fit her for a Cruiser. —

If you purchase the Ship, you must procure the Copper, as well as every Thing else. —

[NDA. GLB, Vol. 1.]

To Stephen Higginson, Navy Agent, Boston, from Secretary of Navy

[PHILADELPHIA,]
Navy Department 5th July 1798

STEPHEN HIGGINSON Esqr.

I have requested Mr Wolcott to answer that part of your Letter of the 28th Ulto which relates to the Cutter — The Cutters are considered as belonging to the Treasury department; they will be fitted out under the directions of the Secretary of the Treasury, and when they are prepared for a cruise, they will, in some instances, be turned over to me; — this will be the case with the Cutter at Newbury. —

I shall with this, send on to Capt Sever, the Commissions for the Officers recommended in a late letter from you, receiving Instructions & money for that Service — As to the other Officers not yet appointed, please to have reference to my Letter of the 30th June. —

It is right not to overlade the Ships with Stores, but if they shou'd be ordered to the West Indies, three months provisions will be too Small an allowance — If Six months provisions could be taken in, without inconvenience, it wou'd be better — but if provision for 4 months seems highly expedient — This quantity then, you'll be so good as to provide, & put on board, If it can be received without inconvenience. —

I wish I knew the exact situation of the Frigate *Constitution* — You have Judged right in procuring, every thing for the Ship, building at Portsmouth, which cou'd be got with you; instead of depending on Philaa — This line of Conduct will be right in all future instances — The freight, delay &ca will always make up for more than any difference in price, even if the Articles could be procured cheaper here, which is doubted — The Copper has been ordered on, and the Ballast Shall be sent in time. — Your suggestions as to an understanding with the British Shall be attended to. —

Presuming that men can be immediately had for the *Herald*, I will in two or three days send on Captn Sever's instructions for a cruise; Our Coast, at least from New York to Cape Henry, has been for some time past, clear of French Privateers — From Cape Henry to the Southern Extremity will be sufficiently guarded for the present — Capt Sever & the Cutter I presume will be equal to the protection of the Eastern Coasts, and the fisheries — and the three Frigates, two of which are out, might do Something in the West Indies; I wish I had your full advice and opinion on this Subject — I shall always receive with satisfaction your Ideas as to the proper employment of our Vessels — The force we Shall be able to command in one month will be as follows —

Frigate *U[nited] States*	48 Guns
Constellation	38 —
Constitution	44
Two Ships from Balto	20 Guns each
Two, from this Port, now out the Same force	
Two or three Cutters	
The *Herald*	

Your Letter does not state the sum Wanted for fitting out the *Herald* — Expecting to hear shortly from you on this Subject, I have requested the Secretary of the Treasury to remit you by this days Mail 8000 Dolls on that acct — And a further sum of 4000 Dolls to be paid over by you to Capt Sever, for the purpose of recruiting the Men — If there was a purser appointed, he would be the proper person to receive & distribute it to the recruiting officers, under the direction of the Captain — Be so good as to have a proper person fixed on for this office, and let him act as if he had received his appointment, — sending his name to me, and if more money be necessary be pleas'd to have it furnished. —

[NDA. GLB, Vol. 1.]

To Secretary of Treasury from Secretary of Navy

[PHILADELPHIA,]
Navy Department 5. July 1798

SECY OF TREASURY

SIR Mr. Higginson, in a Letter of the 28th Ulto mentions that the Brigt Cutter, building at New Bury, will be ready for a cruise very quickly, if the officers for the Cutter be appointed, a List of which he says will be sent on, if desired — but he adds, it is deemed improper to suggest a List of Officers for her 'till it Shall have been determined by Government whether She is to be used as a Naval Cruiser or to be considered as attached to the Revenue.

It is his opinion that this Vessel ought to cruise in Concert with Capt Sever in the *Herald*. I think it is understood that you direct every Thing relating to the Cutters and when They are ready for a cruise that you then turn Them over to my Department.

This Idea being correct you will be so good as to reply to that part of Mr. Higginson's Letter, the Substance of which I have given you above. —

[NDA. Req. on US T, 1798–1803.]

To Rufus King, United States Minister, London, from James Maury, United States Consul, Liverpool

LIVERPOOL 5th *July 1798*

DEAR SIR The two inclosures in your letter of the 2d Instant are in the armed American Ship *Diana*, Williams, ready to sail for Philadelphia.

Inclosed is a note of my postages amount £2. 19. 11 for which I draw on you in favor of Mr Bickerton.

Scarcely any of the American Vessels mentioned in my last are sailed, possibly some of them may be here in time for any farther Dispatches.

I have the Honor to be with perfect respect
Your Excellency's
Most obedient Servant

JAMES MAURY

His Excellency RUFUS KING
Minister Plenipov of the U. S. of America London

[SDA. Liverpool, Vol. 1, C. L., 1790–1800.]

General Order of Captain Thomas Truxtun, U. S. Navy

[5 July 1798.]

GENERAL ORDER

The Bread is to be delivered out daily, half-weekly, or weekly, as is most agreeable, and convenient, to the different Messes at Sea to receive and preserve it.

THOMAS TRUXTUN.

UNITED STATES SHIP *Constellation*
5th July 1798.

[HS of Pa. NDA photostat. Truxtun's LB, 1798–1799.]

[5 July, 1798.]

Regarding subscription for building vessel in Boston

[From the Gazette of the United States]

Mr. FENNO,

I will thank you to publish the following extract of a letter from a gentleman in Boston,

I. PARKER.

"I now with pleasure inform you of the spirited and honorable conduct of the citizens of Boston.

"Yesterday we had a meeting for the purpose of opening a subscription for a sum of money to be appropriated to the building of a vessel for the United States. Thirty-three persons attended — In half an hour Seventy-two thousand five hundred dollars were [s]ubscribed by the citizens present.

Wm. Philips, esq. With a promise to double the sum if it should become necessary.	10,000 dollars
Samuel Parkman	4, 000
Samuel Eliot	4, 000
David Sears	3, 000
Theodore Lyman	3, 000
Samuel Salisbury	3, 000
J. Coolidge & Sons	3, 000
N. Frazier	2, 000
A. Wells, senior	2, 000
Jeffrey & Russell	2, 000
Wm. Parsons	2, 000
James & T. H. Perkins	3, 000
Eben Parsons	3, 000
Thomas Dickason, jr	3, 000
Stephen Higginson	3, 000
Stephen Higginson, jr	2, 000
Samuel G. Perkins	1, 500

Others subscribed 1,500 and none less than 1,000 dollars. I know thirty gentlemen who will subscribe from one to three thousand dollars and sixty more who will give 500—you may fairly calculate on 120,000, reasonably hope for 150,000 dollars. The Legislature have voted 50,000 dollars for purchase of arms &c. and given the governor authority to draw 50,000 more if nesessary in the recess."

[LC, "Claypoole's American Daily Advertiser" (Phila.), 5 July 1798.]

Extract from the journal of Lieutenant John Mullowny, U. S. Frigate *United States*, Thursday, 5 July 1798

Newcastle River Delaware. Winds S. E. Fine weather, exercised the crew at their proper quarters. At 2 P. M. the ship *Fame* of Philadelphia Saluted, returned her salute with three Guns. The Ship of war *Delaware* sailed on a Cruise at 8 A. M.

[NA.]

Extract from Captain Thomas Truxtun's journal, U. S. Frigate *Constellation*, 5 July 1798, Thursday

Hard Gales from the West South West, and an Abundance of Rain. Under bare Poles, Ship making much Water, and the Sea running very Cross. At about 6 PM set the Mizen Stay Sail, and Mizen; and shortly after the Close reefed fore top Sail, the Gale abating, and there being some appearance of the Weather breaking.

At 5 AM wore, and stood to the West North West, with the Wind at South West, and then made Sail. Got up all the wet cloathes of the People, with their hammocks &c. to day as well as some Bread that got damaged.

Overhawlled and repaired various little Matters, in the Boatswain, Gunner, Carpenter, and Sail-Makers' Departments, overhawlled the Hold &c. &c. &c.

Latitude observed 32°.24′ N°
Longitude Account 73°.00′ W.

[HS of Pa. NDA photostat.]

To Mr. Malcolm from the Secretary of Navy

[PHILADELPHIA,]
Navy Office 6th July 1798.

Mr MALCOLM.

Sir, I have the honor to enclose the Commissions and Warrants for the following officers on board the *Constitution*, which I beg you would lay before the President for his Signature —

— Commissions. —

John Blake Cordis	Lieutenants
Isaac Hull	
Richd C. Blake	
Lemuel Clerk	Lieut of Marines
William Read	Surgeon
Chs Blake	Surgs Mate
James L. DeBlois	Purser
Henry J. Knox	Midshipman
Sl Nicholson jr	ditto

These Commissions are wanted to send by the Mail at 12 oClock. —

[NDA. Nom. Appts. LB, 1798–1820.]

To David Sears and others, Boston, from Secretary of Navy

[PHILADELPHIA,]
Navy Department 6th July 1798

DAVID SEARS Esqr & others
Committee of Merchts Boston

I am honored with your favor of the 2nd Instant — Inclosed you will receive an Act of Congress, lately passed on the Subject of your letter; by this Act you will perceive, that Six Frigates of 32 Guns or upwards, as well as a number of Smaller Ships are expected to be obtained through the Patriotism of our Citizens — It has been hoped, and it is still hoped, that Boston, New York, Philadelphia and Baltimore, would each furnish one of the largest sized Ships — Philaa has undertaken to build one of 44 Guns, New York will build one of 36 or 44. and it is very desireable that Boston, which has taken the lead in public-Spirit, as evidenced by their liberal Subscriptions, Should not be outdone in the Size of their Ship —

Inclosed you will receive the dimensions of Ships to carry 44, — 38 & 36 Guns, as soon as I am informed of the Size of the one you fix upon, a model Shall be sent to you — Any Timber or other materials in the Navy Yard at Boston may be taken by you, on the Terms of your Letter — Inclosed you have an order on Mr Gibbs for the purpose. —

[NDA. GLB, Vol. 1.]

To David Stewart, Baltimore, from Secretary of Navy

[PHILADELPHIA,]
Navy Department July 6th 1798

DAVID STEWART Esqr
Baltimore

I am honored with your Letter of the 4th Instant — I wrote this morning to Capt Yellott on the subject of the Ship or Ships to be built at Baltº by the Merchts Be pleased to be referred to that Letter — If you still think it would be better to build small Ships in Baltimore, I must acquiesce — Tho I fear we shall have ample occasion for the largest size Ships — and tho' I believe that if Baltº will not, or rather cannot, afford one such Ship, the number of Ships of 32 Guns & upwards contemplated by the Law, which you will find enclosed, cannot be obtained. — You will observe that Ships carrying less than 18 may be received — Yet it is desireable to have them of 18 Guns — I mean the Smallest Sized Ships permitted by the Law. —

[NDA. GLB, Vol. 1.]

To Captain James Sever, U. S. Navy, from Secretary of Navy

[PHILADELPHIA,]
Navy Departmt 6. July. 1798.

Capt JAMES SEVER

SIR, I have it in Command from the President, to direct that you loose no Time in completing equipping & Manning the *Herald* for sea. —

The Lieut^t^ of Marines &c. &c. to engage sixty four able Seamen & Thirty two Midshipmen and ordinary Seamen. —

See Pages 21, "2 "3 & 24. Letter to Capt Nicholson — with the following Addition —

The Number of Seamen is estimated upon the Presumption, that the *Herald* carries but Twenty Guns — Should She carry Twenty Two Guns, you will be allowed Six more able & Three more ordinary Seamen. Strange as it may seem, I can find no Documents to ascertain the Force of this Ship. —

Four Thousand Dollars, will be remitted to S. Higginson Esqr to be paid over to you, or to the Purser — to be distributed by him under your Directions to the Recruiting Officers.

Presuming that it will require but little Time to prepare your Crew, I shall send on in two or three days, your Cruising Orders. —

Inclosed you will receive the Commissions for the Officers recommended by you — As to the Stations, not yet filled, you must in Concert with Mr Higginson find proper Characters for them — and as there will not be Time for the Formality of a regular Appointment, before you are ready for a Cruise, they must for the present be under your Warrant — The Names you will take the first opportunity to transmit to me.

[NOTE.—Pages 21 to 24 contain letter to Captain Samuel Nicholson from the Secretary of War, dated May 5, 1798.]

[NDA. OSW, Vol. 1.]

From Captain Samuel Nicholson, U. S. Navy, aboard the U. S. Frigate *Constitution*

KING ROAD *July 6th 1798*

D^r^ SIR, I rec^d^ Yours of the 5th last evening inclosing one from Mr Humphreys under the authority of the Secretary of the Navy, requesting I would Transmit to him the true State of the Ship after being at Sea. &c. &c. Morton will bring me down a load of water next, we regularly make 2 load a day in the long boat from the Island, are obliged to unstow the hold in order to come at the ground Tier. Our Carpenters are mount^g^ the Carronades in the Tops, and slinging the lower yds with Chains &c. they shall not be taken off from that business till completed, the Gunner with 5 of his Crew are gone to the Castle, filling carteridges &c. Coll^o^ Perkins was ordered to deliver us 18 lb. shot for proving *only*. I should be glad to have a few on board imediately, pray sent him an order. we are now covering the lead in the bread room with thin boards, after which I will take the bread and Sails, likewise the powder, on b^d^ — We are very busey, every Man constantly employd, and still a great deal to do. I dont know when I can come to Town, Lieut^t^ Cordis, sends me word today, he is so much better as to be able to come on board again tomorrow, or next day I shall attend to the Boatswains matters myself today and tomorrow. I am respectfully Sir

Yr Hble Servt

SAM^l^ NICHOLSON

p. s.

I wish you or Mr Wells could send me down a clever fellow as my Clerk, imediately. Pay 25 doll^rs^ per m^th^. You can send the young French lad (as Act^g^ Midshipman) when ever you please — I have got the Men quarter'd to the Cannon on the 2 decks, and will exercise them tomorrow. great dispatch with Morton and the Water is absolutely necessary. or we shall be along time watering the Ship, all we can possibly do in the long boat is but little.

[Emmet 7093, NYPL.]

[NOTE.—There is no indication as to whom the above letter was addressed.]

Extract from Captain Thomas Truxtun's journal, U. S. Frigate *Constellation*, 6 July 1798, Friday

For two Days past, we have not seen a Vessel of any Sort, which is something remarkable in this Latitude and Longitude, and at this Season of the Year.

I have continued to employ all Hands as before in repairing sundry small Matters, that got rubbed, chafed, and out of Order in the Gale, and in doing such other Jobs, as I conceived necessary and proper.

The Weather very unsettled indeed, made and took in Sail according to appearances.

Latitude 32° .43′ North

Longitude obs[d] ⊙ East of η } 74.45 West

[HS of Pa. NDA photostat.]

To Captain Samuel Nicholson, U. S. Navy, from Secretary of Navy

[PHILADELPHIA,]
Navy Departm[t] 6. July. 1798.

Cap[t] SAM[l] NICHOLSON

SIR, It is highly probable, that by the next Mail, you may receive orders, for a Cruise of two or Three Months — You will use every Means to be prepared at a Moment's Warning. The Commissions for the Petty Officers you have recommended, shall be sent on, as soon as the Appointm[ts] are made — Don't however suffer any Delay on this Acc[t] — If the Commissions should not arrive in Time, sail without Them, & let the Officers act under your Appointment — You will receive enclosed the only Rules and Regulations yet established for the Navy.

Six thousand Dollars have lately been sent on to M[r] DeBlois & I will direct Three Thousand Dollars more to be sent this day to him — Let me repeat again my wish, & I may add, that the Presidents also, that you make such arrangements, & without a Moment's Delay, as will enable you to sail on the Receipt of your Instructions — Both Barry & Truxtun are out. —

[NDA. OSW, Vol. 1.]

To Captain James Sever, U. S. Navy, from Secretary of Navy

[PHILADELPHIA,]
Navy Departm[t] 6. July. 1798. —

Cap[t] JA[s] SEVER

SIR, The Regulations heretofore established for the Navy, do not admit of Boys on board of the Ships of War — This is certainly a defect. Perhaps the Proportion required of able Seamen, is too large — You may take as many Boys as you shall judge proper, not exceeding the Number of Guns in the *Herald* & Provided, for every Two Boys you take, you leave out one able Seaman. But altho' it is permitted you, to give as much to two Boys as to one able Seaman, yet it is expected that you will get them on the best Terms in your power. —

[NDA. OSW, Vol. 1.]

To Lieutenant of Marines of *Herald* from Secretary of Navy

[PHILADELPHIA,]
Navy Department 6. July. 1798

Lieut[t] of Marines of the *Herald*

SIR, You will immediately commence recruiting the Complement of Marines, allowed to the Ship *Herald* — Viz[t] Twenty five Marines, including Serjeant Corporal &[c]

In the Performance of this duty, you will pay particular Attention to the following Rules and Regulations.

For Rules and Regulations Refer to Pages 5–6 & 7.

[NOTE.—Pages 5, 6 and 7 contain letter to the Lieutenant of Marines, Frigate *Constellation*, from Secretary of War, dated 16 March 1798.]

[NDA. OSW, Vol. 1.]

To Jeremiah Yellott, Navy Agent, Baltimore, from Secretary of Navy

[PHILADELPHIA,]
Navy Department July 6. 1798

JEREMIAH YELLOTT

The duties of my Office have pressed upon me so much, that I have not been able to attend to your last Letter, The Copper &c for both the Ships under your direction I hope you have received, it was forwarded by way of the head of Elk, a Week ago or nearly.

The Commissions for Cap[t] Phillips & Officers, as well as recruiting Instructions shall go by Tomorrows Mail.

I am sorry you prefer small Vessels to be built at Baltimore, to one Ship of larger size; enclosed you have the late Law upon that subject, —

You will perceive that six Ships of 32 Guns at least, are to be procured, — it has been calculated that Baltimore would afford one of these, The smaller Ships can be obtained in the smaller places, but the larger ones can only be expected from Baltimore, Philadelphia, New York, & Boston and I cannot relinguish the hope that my Native State, not less Federal, & not less in earnest to defend the rights of the Country, than any in the Union, will afford one of these, I know that this will greatly depend on you, & I hope for your acquiescence in the views of Government

The Frigates heretofore built have been on a scale too large, a ship of 800 Tons will be equal to 36 Guns, — 900 Tons will be equal to 44 Guns, — Here they mean to build one of 1000 Tons, the same in New York with less means.

Please to consider this subject well & let me know your final opinion, I shall dispair of getting the Ship & soon if you do not concur, The Public Timber at Baltimore might be taken for the Ships.

[NDA. GLB, Vol. 1.]

To Mr. Malcolm from Secretary of the Navy

[PHILADELPHIA,]
Navy Office, 7, *July*, *1798*

Mr MALCOLM

SIR, I have the honor to inclose Commissions and Warrants for the following Officers on board the ship of War *Herald* at Boston, which I beg you would lay before the President for his Signature. —

These Commissions and Warrants are wanted to send by the Mail at 12 OClock. —

Commissions:
- James Sever, Capt
- Wm V. Huchings } Lieutenants
- Jos. Strout } Lieutenants
- Larkin Thorndike Surgeon

Warrants:
- Samuel Carnes Sailing Master.
- John Marshall Gunner.
- Isaac Steel Sail Maker
- John S. K. Cox Midship Man

[NDA. Nom. Appts. LB, 1798–1820.]

Extract from the Journal of Lieutenant John Mullowny, U. S. Frigate *United States*, Saturday, 7 July 1798

Newcastle River Delaware. Winds S. by W. Fresh breezes (cloudy) at 6 A. M. unmoored, at 9 weighed Anchor and got under way, at M Tacked Ship, missed Stays, and took the ground, run out the Stream anchor to the S. W. brought to and hove taught, at ½ 3 P. M. the ship tended[?] to her anchor, gave her a broad sheer in the Channel and let go the anchor, and moored with the two [remainder of page mutilated]

[NA.]

To Captain John Barry, U. S. Navy, from Secretary of Navy

[PHILADELPHIA,]
Navy Departm^t^. *7 July 1798*

JOHN BARRY

SIR, You will please keep on & off the Capes, of Delaware — and always in reach of a Pilot Boat, 'till further orders — Some late Acts of Congress make a variation in your Instructions necessary. —

[NDA. OSW, Vol. 1.]

To Captain Stephen Decatur (senior), U. S. Navy, from Secretary of Navy

[PHILADELPHIA,]
Navy Department. *7 July. 1798*

STEPHEN DECATUR

SIR, The Intention of this is to request, that you, instead of proceeding to the Southward to join Capt Truxtun on the 16th Ins^t^ as directed in your Instructions, you will continue on & off the Capes of Delaware, so that a Pilot Boat may be sure to find you, until further orders. —

[NDA. OSW, Vol. 1.]

To Garrett Hulsecamp, pilot, from Secretary of Navy

[PHILADELPHIA,]
Navy Department 7th *July 1798*

GARRETT HULSECAMP, Pilot

You will please to proceed with your Pilot Boat forthwith to the Capes of Delaware, and exert yourself to find the Frigate *United States*, Capt Barry, and the *Delaware*, Capt Decatur. You have three Letters for each of these Captains — If you fall in with the *Ganges* Capt Dale, deliver one of each to him — and if you fall in with either Capt Barry or Capt Decatur, give to the Captain you so fall in with, one of the Letters for the other, — It is most probable you will find them off the Capes of Delaware — You will sail off and on the Capes four or five days, till you fall in with them both

[NDA. GLB, Vol. 1.]

[July 7, 1798.]

Extract from letter to Rufus King, London, from Secretary of State, July 9, 1798

"Last week, Captain Decatur in a public twenty gun ship [the *Delaware*] sailed from the Delaware, on a cruize, and yesterday returned with a prize, a French privateer of ten guns [*La Croyable*] and 53 men; pierced for 14 guns, and manned with 70 men. She had been but two or three days on our coast, yet had taken a British Brigantine, and the ship *Liberty* belonging to Philadelphia, and destined for Liverpool, on board of which ship I had put some letters for you * * *"

[SDA. Dip. Cor. Inst. to Min., Vol. 4, 1797–1798.]

[7 July, 1798.]

Newspaper accounts relative to capture of *La Croyable*

[From "Columbian Centinel (Boston)", July 14, 1798]

"A FRENCH PIRATE CAPTURED.

"PHILADELPHIA, [*Monday*] *July 9.* [*1798*]

"Yesterday Capt. Decatur, of the United States Sloop *Delaware* arrived at the *Navy Office*. He informs, that the *Delaware* sailed on Friday, last, and on Saturday evening [7 July 1798] captured a French privateer schooner of 12 guns and 70 men, close in with *Egg Harbour*, and last evening the prize was brought to *Fort Mifflin*. Capt. Decatur left his ship at *New-Castle* and brought this intelligence to town. Capt. Decatur after he had got to sea on Saturday morning, met with the ship *Alexander Hamilton* from New York to Baltimore, the Captain of which informed him, that he had been plundered by a *French* privateer, and gave him directions what course he had steered. Capt. Decatur immediately went in search of her, and soon got in sight of four schooners; but not knowing which was the armed schooner that he had received information of, he thought it best to stand off as if he were a merchantman, and alarmed at what might be armed vessels.

The maneuvre had the intended effect, for the armed schooner gave her chace, until she discovered the *Delaware* to be a vessel of force, when she attempted to sheer off and get in land (where she supposed she could be safe, taking the *Delaware* for an *English* vessel of war) but she was obliged to surrender after a pretty long chace to the *Delaware*, and several shots being fired at her. This privateer is a new vessel, said to have been built at Baltimore. She sailed from *Cape Francois* on the 19th June, and has been on our Coast only two days, during which time she has captured the ship *Liberty*, Capt. Verdenberg, which sailed a few days since from this port [Philadelphia] for Liverpool; the vessel was sent to the West Indies, and the Capt. and crew of the *Liberty* were put on board a vessel bound for Boston, the privateer had also taken an *English* brig."

[From "Columbian Centinel (Boston)", Aug. 8, 1798]

"PHILADELPHIA,

The Captain of the French privateer, taken a few days ago, seemed astonished when he went on board of Capt. Decatur's sloop of war, at his being taken by an American vessel, and said he knew of no war between the two republics. Decatur observed that the French had been making war upon us for a long time, and it was now necessary for us to take care of ourselves. The Frenchman seemed to be vastly mortified at seeing his Colours hauled down, and wished he had been sunk. Decatur told him he should have been gratified if he had stood on board his vessel and fought her!"

[LC. Newspapers, Columbian Centinel (Boston), July 14 and Aug. 8, 1798.]

To Secretary of State Timothy Pickering from Captain Stephen Decatur (senior) U. S. Navy

S. DECATUR — Capture of Several Vessels

[*U. S. S.*] *Delaware*, July 12 — 1798

SIR I enclose you a paper handed me by Mr Kitchin, (the person who collects, maritime intelligence for the Merchants of Philad^a^,) the list of vessels captured &c was furnished by one of the crew who lately arrived at Philad^a^ from, their privateer having been put on board a Schr. bound to Philad^a^ by the master of the privateer —

I am Sir with great respect
Your M^o^ Obed^t^ Servt

STEPHEN DECATUR

TIM^Y^ PICKERING Esqr

[SDA. French Spol.]

[Enclosure]

The Sch^{r} [space] from Penobscot on the Evening of the 6th was brought too off C May by the privateer, & detained until near 12 oClk, threatining to scuttle her, & abusing the crew, telling them they would hang them &^{c} — plundered the people of their cloaths & then dismissed her — after putting on board a person, belonging to the Ship *Alex^{r} Brown,* of Newburyport which vessel they had captured on the 13th ult^{o}, out 15 days from Charleston to Oporto, on the 15th they fell in with & captured the Sch^{r} *Leander,* from NYork to the Havanna, — soon afterwards boarded two Schooners, from St Croix, bound to Salem & Newbury port plundered & dismissed them, boarded several others particularly a Sch^{r} from Phila^{a} out 2 days for Surinam which she plundered & let pass, she boarded a number of Vessels previous to her falling in with the *Liberty,* which vessel she sent for Monte Christe as well as her other prizes, The Crew of the *Liberty* were put on board of a Brig from Newburn bound to Boston, leaving Capt Vredenbury in the Ship to condemn her, — taking out what Money they could find — the Capt is a Spaniard the person who acted a first Lieutenant, is an Englishman — formerly belonging to the *Queen* of 98 guns, who after committing murder made his escape to the Cape with the Tender of that Ship —

[SDA. French Spol.]

To the Secretary of State from John Hollins, owner of the Ship *Alexander Hamilton*

Ship *Alexander Hamilton*

BALTIMORE *17th July 1798*

SIR I consider'd it proper to forward you the inclosed protest of Cap^{n} Wyse &c &c of my Ship *Alex^{r} Hamilton,* who was boarded by the French Privateer [*La Croyable*] lately captured & carried into Philad^{a}

The value of the property stole out of the Ship I presume does not exceed One hundred & forty or fifty Dollars; if not too much trouble I will thank you to give me your advice what plan to adopt to get satisfaction, if it can be done thro' you, or if it is worth while taking legal steps against the Freebooters

Your reply, will greatly oblige me who has the honor to be very respectfully

Sir

Y: Mo: obd^{t} S^{t}

JOHN HOLLINS

The Honorable SECRETARY of STATE —

Philad^{a}

[SDA. French Spol.]

[Enclosure]

STATE OF MARYLAND }
Baltimore County Sst }

By this Public Instrument of Protest, be it made known and manifest unto all persons before whom the same shall come — that on the twelfth day of July in the Year of our Lord one thousand seven hundred and ninety eight before me Thomas Donaldson Notary public by lawful authority commissioned and sworn residing in the City of Baltimore in the County and State aforesaid personally appeared Captain William Wise Master of the Ship *Alexander Hamilton* of the burthen of two hundred and seventy Tons and laden with Wine and Brandy now laying in this Port of Baltimore who noted and entered his Protest with me the said Notary against the French armed Privateer [space] her Officers Mariners and Owners for forcibly capturing the said Ship on a Voyage from New York to the port of Baltimore and plundering her of a number of Articles on board. And on this day the fourteenth of July in the year of our Lord one thousand seven hundred and ninety eight, aforesaid, again appeared the said Captain together with Henry Hale Mate and William Hayman Seaman belonging to the said Ship who upon their solemn Oaths which they then took before me on the holy Evangelists of Almighty God did depose and declare that on the fourth day of the present month of July they these Deponents in their said several Capacities sailed and departed in and with said Ship laden with Wine Brandy and Sundries from the port of New York bound on a Voyage to this port of Baltimore and being in the due prosecution of the said Voyage off Little Egg Harbour, on the Sixth following about the hour of ten oClock A. M. they met the aforesaid French armed Privateer which forcibly captured the said Ship *Alexander Hamilton* and detained these Deponents and said Ship until the hour of two oClock of said Sixth of July, during which time the Men belonging to the said Privateer plundered these Deponents and the said Ship *Alexander Hamilton* of the following Articles to wit: Seven Cases of Wine each case containing twelve bottles; about, thirty Dollars in Cash; one large Bayonne Ham; a case of razors the property of the Deponent Captn Wise; one Box of Sweetmeats belonging to the British Consul at Baltimore; one elegant embroidered Fan made in Paris. These Deponents are not certain whether the said Privateersmen took any Ladies Shoes out of a Box which contained three hundred pair which they opened: or what was taken out of some trunks belonging to this Deponent Captain Wise; and out of a trunk belonging to a certain Mr Abernethy; all of which trunks were also opened by the men belonging to the said Privateers: also several pounds of prunes and a number of other small articles. That at the aforesaid hour of two oClock P. M. the said Privateer permitted these Deponents to proceed on their Voyage — on the Evening of same day they these Deponents fell in with the United States Ship of War *Delaware* commanded by Captain Decatur and gave him information concerning the said French Privateer, who steered for the same by which she was afterwards captured, and they these Deponents arrived in and with said Ship *Alexander Hamilton* at this port of Baltimore the end of their said Voyage on the eleventh following of the said Month of July — Whereupon the said Master does in due form Note and enter protest with me the said Notary against the Owners Officers & Crew of the said French Privateer [space] for the unjust Capture and Detention of the said Ship *Alexander Hamilton;* and for the Robbery and plunder committed as aforesaid: to the end that all Losses and Damages, suffered in the premises, may be submitted unto, and borne by those to whom of right the same may appertain to be adjusted and recovered in time and place convenient

Thus done and protested at Baltimore aforesaid —

In Testimony whereof the said Deponents have hereto subscribed their names aad I the said Notary have granted the said Master this Public Instrument under my hand and Notarial Seal, to serve and avail him and all whom it may concern as need and occasion shall require —

THO^s DONALDSON
Not^y Pub. for Balt^o Coun^y

Wm WYSE
HENRY HALE
WILLIAM HAYMAN

[SDA. French Spol.]

To General Henry Jackson, Navy Agent, Boston, from Secretary of Navy

[PHILADELPHIA,]
7 July 1798

Genl HENRY JACKSON *Boston*

SIR, Congress have passed an Act, to admit more general Captures of French Vessels — Pray suffer Nothing to prevent Capt Nicholson's being ready for Sea, at a Moments Warning.

In two Days it is likely he may be ordered on a Cruise.

[NDA. GLB, Vol. 1.]

To Captain Isaac Phillips, U. S. Navy, from Secretary of Navy

[PHILADELPHIA,]
Navy Departm^t 7 July. 1798

I. PHILLIPS *Balt^o*

SIR, With this you will receive recruiting Instructions. As the Ship *Baltimore* will be entirely ready by the last of the Month, it is of Importance, that the Men should be ready as early — and you have no Time to loose. Lieut^t Speake lives on Patomak, I think in Alex^a — Lieut^t West on the Eastern Shore of Virginia. Some Merch^{ts} in Baltimore, for whom he has sailed, can tell you the place — You should order Them immediately to the Ship, to be employed in the recruiting — You should if possible get your Men in Bal^t — If you can not get them there, Lieut^t Speake might be a proper Person to recruit some at Alexandria — The recruiting Officers for the Seamen, will be allowed Two Dollars a day for the Time they are employed in that service, and their reasonable & actual Expences for the Men, where they are recruited at a distance & the Expence of getting the Men to the Ship, provided Vouchers are produced, but not otherwise. —

The Lieut^t of Marines is to be allowed one D^r for each Recruit — In two or three days, I shall be more particular. —

For Instructions see Pages 5, 6, & 7. —

[NOTE. — Pages 5, 6 and 7 contain letter to the Lieutenant of Marines, Frigate *Constellation*, from Secretary of War, dated 16 March 1798.]

[NDA. OSW, Vol. 1.]

To Lieutenant Josias M. Speake, U. S. Navy, from Secretary of Navy

[PHILADELPHIA]
Navy Departmt July. 7. 1798.

JOSIAS M. SPEAKE *Alexandria*

SIR, You being appointed the first Lieutenant of the Ship *Baltimore* lying at Baltimore, you will please to repair to that Place, without delay — It is necessary that you should be there immediately to raise Recruits — On your Arrival at Baltimore, you will apply to Capt Phillips the commanding Officer of the *Baltimore* for Instructions. —

Lieut JOSIAS M SPEAKE *Alexandria*

[NDA. OSW, Vol. 1.]

Extract from Captain Thomas Truxtun's journal, U. S. Frigate *Constellation*, 7 July 1798, Saturday

Squally Wether with much Rain, and a cross Sea running. At 8 PM it threatened a violent Tornado, took in all Sail, except the close reefed fore Top Sail. At 4 AM it cleared away a little, set all Sail, and out Æ. At 11 Ditto appearances as before, took in all the light Sails, and double reefed the Top Sails, no Vessels in Sight, at Noon in Main Sail &c.

Employed drying and airing the Sails, and Gunner's Stores, &c. &c. &c. all the latter Part of this Day, untill it commenced raining, and looked likely to blow heavy.

observed
Latitude/32°. 59′ No
Longitude account 74.55 W.

[HS of Pa. NDA photostat.]

Extract from Captain Thomas Truxtun's journal, U. S. Frigate *Constellation*, 8 July 1798, Sunday

Very squally disagreeable Weather, throughout the whole of these Twenty four Hours with much Rain, and at Times blowing very heavy from South South West to West South West; made and took in Sail according to the Weather, and stretched to the Southward, and Northward, as I considered it most probable that we should be enabled to hold our own, or gain to the Westward, and withal lower our Latitude, which we have made many fruitless Efforts to do, for several Days past, owing to the Perversness of the Winds.

Employed the People in repairing the little Chafings and Rubbings, occasioned by this uncommon, and unseasonable Weather, — and doing such other necessary Matters, as have deemed expedient.

Latitude 33°.46′ N°.
Longitude 75.45 W

[HS of Pa. NDA photostat.]

[9 July, 1798.]

Congress authorizes special commissions for private armed vessels

[United States Statutes at Large. Fifth Congress. Sess. II]

An Act Further to Protect the Commerce of the United States. (a)

Section 1. *Be it enacted by the Senate and House of Representatives of the United States of America in Congress assembled,* That the President of the United States shall be, and he is hereby authorized to instruct the commanders of the public armed vessels which are, or which shall be employed in the service of the United States, to subdue, seize and take any armed French vessel, which shall be found within the jurisdictional limits of the United States, or elsewhere, on the high seas, and such captured vessel, with her apparel, guns and appurtenances, and the goods or effects which shall be found on board the same, being French property, shall be brought within some port of the United States, and shall be duly proceeded against and condemned as forfeited; and shall accrue and be distributed, as by law is or shall be provided respecting the captures which shall be made by the public armed vessels of the United States.

Sec. 2. *And be it further enacted,* That the President of the United States shall be, and he is hereby authorized to grant to the owners of private armed ships and vessels of the United States, who shall make application therefor, special commissions in the form which he shall direct, and under the seal of the United States; and such private armed vessels, when duly commissioned, as aforesaid, shall have the same license and authority for the subduing, seizing and capturing any armed French vessel, and for the recapture of the vessels, goods and effects of the people of the United States, as the public armed vessels of the United States may by law have; and shall be, in like manner, subject to such instructions as shall be ordered by the President of the United States, for the regulation of their conduct. and the commissions which shall be granted, as aforesaid, shall be revocable at the pleasure of the President of the United States.

Sec. 3. *Provided, and be it further enacted,* That every person intending to set forth and employ an armed vessel, and applying for a commission, as aforesaid, shall produce in writing the name, and a suitable description of the tonnage and force of the vessel, and the name and place of residence of each owner concerned therein, the number of the crew and the name of the commander, and the two officers next in rank, appointed for such vessel; which writing shall be signed by the person or persons making such application, and filed with the Secretary of State, or shall be delivered to any other officer or person who shall be employed to deliver out such commissions, to be by him transmitted to the Secretary of State.

Sec. 4. *And provided, and be it further enacted,* That before any commission, as aforesaid, shall be issued, the owner or owners of the ship or vessel for which the same shall be requested, and the commander thereof, for the time being, shall give bond to the United States, with at least two responsible sureties, not interested in such vessel, in the penal sum of seven thousand dollars; or if such vessel be provided with more than one hundred and fifty men, then in the penal sum of fourteen thousand dollars; with condition that the owners, and officers, and crews who shall be employed on board of such commissioned vessel, shall and will observe the treaties and laws of the United States, and the instructions which shall be given them for the regulation of their conduct: And will satisfy all damages and injuries which shall be done or committed contrary to the tenor thereof, by such vessel, during her commission, and to deliver up the same when revoked by the President of the United States.

SEC. 5. *And be it further enacted,* That all armed French vessels, together with their apparel, guns and appurtenances, and any goods or effects which shall be found on board the same, being French property, and which shall be captured by any private armed vessel or vessels of the United States, duly commissioned, as aforesaid, shall be forfeited, and shall accrue to the owners thereof, and the officers and crews by whom such captures shall be made; and on due condemnation had, shall be distributed according to any agreement which shall be between them; or in failure of such agreement, then by the discretion of the court before whom such condemnation shall be.

SEC. 6. *And be it further enacted,* That all vessels, goods and effects, the property of any citizen of the United States, or person resident therein, which shall be recaptured, as aforesaid, shall be restored to the lawful owners, upon payment by them, respectively, of a just and reasonable salvage, to be determined by the mutual agreement of the parties concerned, or by the decree of any court of the United States having maritime jurisdiction according to the nature of each case: *Provided,* that such allowance shall not be less than one eighth, or exceeding one half of the full value of such recapture, without any deduction. And such salvage shall be distributed to and among the owners, officers and crews of the private armed vessel or vessels entitled thereto, according to any agreement which shall be between them; or in case of no agreement, then by the decree of the court who shall determine upon such salvage.

SEC. 7. *And be it further enacted,* That before breaking bulk of any vessel which shall be captured, as aforesaid, or other disposal or conversion thereof, or of any articles which shall be found on board the same, such capture shall be brought into some port of the United States, and shall be libelled and proceeded against before the district court of the same district; and if after a due course of proceedings, such capture shall be decreed as forfeited in the district court, or in the circuit court of the same district, in the case of any appeal duly allowed, the same shall be delivered to the owners and captors concerned therein, or shall be publicly sold by the marshal of the same court, as shall be finally decreed and ordered by the court. And the same court, who shall have final jurisdiction of any libel or complaint of any capture, as aforesaid, shall and may decree restitution, in whole or in part, when the capture and restraint shall have been made without just cause, as aforesaid; and if made without probable cause, or otherwise unreasonably, may order and decree damages and costs to the party injured, and for which the owners, officers and crews of the private armed vessel or vessels by which such unjust capture shall have been made, and also such vessel or vessels shall be answerable and liable.

SEC. 8. *And be it further enacted,* That all French persons and others, who shall be found acting on board any French armed vessel, which shall be captured, or on board of any vessel of the United States, which shall be recaptured, as aforesaid, shall be reported to the collector of the port in which they shall first arrive, and shall be delivered to the custody of the marshal, or of some civil or military officer of the United States, or of any state in or near such port; who shall take charge for their safe keeping and support, at the expense of the United States.

Approved, July 9, 1798.

[Statute 1, pages 578–580.]

To Secretary of War from Secretary of Navy

[PHILADELPHIA,]
Navy Department. 9. July. 1798.

SEC^{y} at WAR

SIR, The French Prize Schooner, taken by Capt Decatur, is now at Fort Mifflin, with 53 Men, her crew on Board. —

The Laws of Penns^{a} will not it seems, permit her to pass up to Phila^{a} — nor the Crew who are Prisoners, to be landed on either of the Shores of the Delaware. They may, I understand, be landed in the Fort. —

The Schooner is represented to be a fine Sailor, well fitted for a cruise, & I am anxious to make immediate use of her. — I have therefore the honor to request, if you see no Impropriety in It, that you will give orders which Capt Decatur will take down, to the commanding Officer at the Fort to receive the Prisoners and to have them safely kept, until the Quarantine Laws of the State, will permit Their Removal. —

[NDA. Sec War LB, 1798–1824.]

To Rufus King, United States Minister, London, from James Maury, United States Consul, Liverpool

LIVERPOOL, *9th July 1798*

DEAR SIR, The packet for Mr Low is in the *Henrietta*, Stevenson, an unarmed Vessell, for Philadelphia this week — That for Mr Pickering with one for Mr Morris in the armed Ship *Sally*, Morgan, for New-York to morrow —

On the 10th January last I drew on you for £2. 8. 5 amount of my postages to 31st December, which appears to have been duly paid — These Vessells are going in the course of the Week —

I have the Honor to be with perfect respect
Your Excellency's
Most obedient Servant

JAMES MAURY

His Excellency RUFUS KING
Minister Plenipotentiary to the U. S. A.
London —

[SDA. Liverpool, Vol. 1, C. L., 1790–1800.]

[Enclosure]

Henrietta —	Stevenson for	Philadelphia —	unarmed
Sally	Morgan	New-York	armed
Sally	Campbell	Boston	unarmed
Trio	Congas	New-York	unarmed
Eliza	Benson	Baltimore	armed

[SDA. Liverpool, Vol. 1, C. L., 1790–1800.]

Extract from Captain Thomas Truxtun's journal, U. S. Frigate *Constellation*, 9 July 1798, Monday

Fresh Breezes from the South West, the first Part. At 4 PM saw a Sail in the North North West, gave Chace. About 5 Ditto brought her to with two Shot, and afterwards spoke the Ship *Rachel* from Charleston South Carolina bound to New York, out three Days; discharged her, and gave Chace to a Sail bearing North B. W. of us, at 6 Ditto spoke the Brig *Beaver* from Philadelphia bound to Savannah in Georgia, at 7 Ditto sounded in 60 Fathoms Water, dark Mud and Sand, Cape Hatteras at that Time bearing North, Twenty Leagues Distance. — The Wind being to the West South West, and blowing a violent Gale wore and stood to the Southward, under the double reefed main, and fore Top Sails only.

At Day Light saw a Schooner in the North East, which tacked, and stood in Shore, at 6 AM the Wind came to the Westward, and soon after hawlled to the Northward, when I directed the Course to be steered West to get out of the Gulph Stream, which runs very strong, made Sail, and set up the Rigging. Employed as before.

Latitude observed 34°.58′ N°
Longitude Account 75.20 W

[HS of Pa. NDA photostat.]

To Secretary of War from Secretary of Navy

[PHILADELPHIA,]
Navy Departmt 10 July. 1798

SECy of WAR.

SIR, The French Prize at the Fort having got clear of her Crew, & the Marshall being about to take possession of her, There will be no Difficulty in preparing her for a Cruise, if the Goods on Board can be landed. This too can be done, if they can be stored in any House at the Fort.

Will you be so good as to give orders to the commanding officer at the Fort — to furnish Room if he can for the reception of the Goods — In this Case, Mr. Humphreys will take immediate Steps to prepare the Schooner for a Cruise, & She may be ready to receive her men by the Time She is condemned. —

[NDA. Sec War LB, 1798–1824.]

To Jeremiah Hubbard, agent, Middleton, Conn., from Secretary of Navy

[PHILADELPHIA,]
Navy Department July 10th 1798

JEREMIAH HUBBARD Esqr
Middleton Connecticut

SIR Altho I have not the pleasure of a personal acquaintance with you, yet your character is sufficiently known to me to induce the present application, which will call for an attention and exertion on your part for the service of the United States, & which I flatter myself from my Idea of your public Spirit & Patriotism, you will be willing to bestow on the object in question —

This being premised, I beg leave to inform you, that there is Wanting for the United States, a Ship, capable of carrying 24 Guns, which you will please to contract for the building of, with as little delay as possible, keeping in view the following principles. —

1st That the materials be of the best live Oak or red Cedar, except the floor Timbers and the Floor futtocks, or of the best seasoned White Oak, to be determined by Inspection — No Timber inferior to seasoned White Oak to be used. —

2nd The public to furnish the Copper Sheathing, Copper Bolts, and Spikes, the Iron Work to be contracted for Seperately by the pound, and delivered under the Check of an Agent — The whole of the materials however, to be placed in the Ship, at the Expence of the Contractor. —

3rd The Dimensions to be 93 feet Keel, 31 feet Beam and 13½ feet Hold — to be pierced for 20 Guns, exclusive of the bridle Ports on the main Gun Deck and two on the Quarter Deck — to have an Orlope deck, and to be of sufficient strength, and in all respects compleated for a Ship of War, Permission to be reserved to vary the dimensions, but without Injury or expense to the Contractor. —

4th The Contract must be made per Ton of Carpenters Measurement, according to the Rules of Philadelphia — The shortest time possible, must be given for launching and compleating the Ship. It is hoped the time will not exceed 90 days —

5th A Bond with Sureties to be required to secure the Execution of the Contract, and a due Settlement for all Advances —

6th No after Bills to be admitted —

It will be important to dispose of the business in such a manner, that it will proceed with dispatch and order, of course the contract should be made with none but a man of Skill, and responsible Character, and I must depend on you to procure the Sails, the Rigging, Guns, Copper and every Article wanted for the Ship, to fit her for a compleat Sloop of War, and so to make your arrangements that nothing may be waited for —

The Compensation heretofore given by the public for such services, has been 2 p. Cent on all expenditures — The public furnishing the money as wanted — It is expected you will be content with the same, in Addition to the Satisfaction of rendering important service to Your Country —

You will please to advise me regularly of your proceedings in this Business —

A Captain in due time will be appointed, — who will superintend the Building — Seth Overton of Chatham & Arthur Magill of Middleton, are persons who I am inform'd have now on hand a quantity of Excellent and Well seasoned Timber — which I mention for your government. —

[NDA. GLB, Vol. 1.]

To General Lincoln, Collector, Boston, from Secretary of State

Gen[l] LINCOLN, *Collector Boston.*

[PHILADELPHIA,]
Department of State July 10th 1798

SIR The haste with which the law for capturing armed French vessels on the high Seas, and recapturing American vessels and property, was carried thro' Congress, occasioned some errors which there is now not time to correct, as well as some omissions. We must execute the law as we find it.

To accomodate the citizens who fit out armed vessels, the commissions, bonds and instructions must be transmitted to all our ports; and the Collectors and other officers of the Customs are the persons obviously most proper to receive applications and deliver out the commissions and instructions, and take the requisite bonds. I therefore transmit herewith [space] commissions, and a like number of bonds and instructions, to be used accordingly in your district. More will be forwarded as soon as possible for yours and the neighbouring ports, either from my office or that of the Treasury; that no time may be lost I send these few setts.

I am respectfully, your ob[t] Serv[t]

TIMOTHY PICKERING.

[SDA. Dom. L., Vol. 11.]

To Mr. Malcolm from Secretary of the Navy

[PHILADELPHIA,]
Navy Office 10, July 1798

M[r] MALCOLM.

SIR, I have the honor to inclose, a Commission for a Lieutenant on board the Frigate *Constitution;* a Warrant for a Sailing Master, and another for a Midshipman, intended to serve on board the Ship to be built for Cap[t] Rich[d] V. Morris, at N. York, which I beg you will lay before the President, for his Signature. —

Commission —
Patrick Fletcher — Lieutenant
Warrants —
Stephen Lee Sailing Master.
Benjamin Carpender Midshipman. —

[NDA. Nom. Appts. LB, 1798–1820.]

Instructions of Secretary Stoddert, 10 July 1798, to commanders of United States armed vessels

[PHILADELPHIA,]

— JOHN ADAMS —

— *President of the United States* —

Instructions to the Commanders of armed Vessels, belonging to the United States, given at Philadelphia, the Tenth day of July, in the Year of our Lord, One thousand seven hundred and Ninety Eight, and in the Twenty third Year of our Independence.

In Pursuance of the Acts of Congress, passed the 28th day of May, the Twenty Eighth day of June, and the Ninth day of July: —

You are, hereby, authorized, instructed and directed to subdue seize and take any armed French Vessel, or Vessels sailing under Authority or Pretence of Authority from the French Republic, which shall be found within the Jurisdictional Limits of the United States, or elsewhere on the high Seas: and such captured Vessel with her Apparel, Guns and Appurtenances, and the Goods and Effects which shall be found on board the same, together with all French persons and others, who shall be found acting on board, to bring within some Port of the United States; and also to retake any Vessels, Goods, and Effects of the Citizens of the United States, or Persons resident therein which may have been captured by any French Vessel — in Order that Proceedings may be had concerning such Capture or Recapture in due Form of Law, and as to right shall appertain. —

By Command &c

Signed BEN STODDERT

[NDA. OSW, Vol. 1.]

[10 July, 1798.]

Copy of a letter from Captain Hall of the H. M. S. *Lynx*, regarding the capture of the *Liberty*, Vredenburgh

"Your ship the *Liberty*, from Philadelphia bound to Liverpool, had not reached the edge of soundings, when she was captured by a French privateer and sent for C. Francois, six days afterwards (the 10th inst.) I had the good fortune in his majesty's ship, under my command to retake her — the capt. is on board and well, the ship is gone to Halifax where, before you receive this, I hope she will have arrived."

[LC, Phila. "Claypoole's American Daily Advertiser", 31 July, 1798.]

Extract from Captain Thomas Truxtun's journal, U. S. Frigate *Constellation*, 10 July 1798, Tuesday

[10 JULY, 1798. TUESDAY.]

All these Twenty four Hours, moderate Breezes from the Northward, and Eastward, and Summerlike Weather; what we have not experienced before, since leaving the Chesapeake Bay.

At 4 PM made the Land of Cape Hatteras from the Masthead bearing West B. North, Distance about 9 Leagues, sounded at the same Time, and found Thirty five Fathoms Depth of Water over a small Shelly, and muddy Bottom. Steered from South West B. South to South West B. West according as we deepened, or shoaled the Water, untill 11 PM when we were in Twenty three Fathoms Water fine Grey Sand, I then judged myself to be as far to the Southward as 34°. 40′ N. entirely clear of all the Shoals of Hatteras, when I shaped the Course South West B. West along the Coast, many small Coasting Vessels in Company.

At 8 AM sounded in Eleven Fathoms Water, dark fine Sand, and at 9 Ditto made from the Mast head the Shoals of Cape Lookout on the Starboard Beam.

At Noon the Depth of Water was seventeen Fathoms, over a Bottom of Coarse black Sand. Untill we struck Soundings for Several Days past have found the Gulph Stream run North East at the Rate of three knots per Hour.

Latitude observed 34° .10′ N°
Longitude Account 77.00 W.

[HS of Pa. NDA photostat.]

[11 July 1798.]

Congress authorizes the establishment of U. S. Marine Corps

AN ACT FOR THE ESTABLISHING AND ORGANIZING A MARINE CORPS

SEC. 1. *Be it enacted by the Senate and House of Representatives of the United States in Congress assembled,* That in addition to the present military establishment, there shall be raised and organized a corps of marines, which shall consist of one major, four captains, sixteen first lieutenants, twelve second lieutenants, forty-eight sergeants, forty-eight corporals, thirty-two drums and fifes, and seven hundred and twenty privates, including the marines who have been enlisted, or are authorized to be raised for the naval armament; and the said corps may be formed into as many companies or detachments, as the President of the United States shall direct, with a proper distribution of the commissioned and non-commissioned officers and musicians to each company or detachment.

SEC. 2. *And be it further enacted,* That the pay and subsistence of the said officers, privates and musicians, shall be as follows, to wit: To a major, fifty dollars per month, and four rations per day; to a captain, forty dollars per month, and three rations per day; to a first lieutenant, thirty dollars per month, and three rations per day; to a second lieutenant, twenty-five dollars per month, and two rations per day; and to the non-commissioned officers, privates and musicians, conformably to the act, intituled "An act providing a naval armament," as shall be fixed by the President of the United States: And the President of the United States shall be, and is hereby authorized to continue the enlistment of marines, until the said corps shall be complete; and of himself, to appoint the commissioned officers, whenever, in the recess of the Senate, an appointment shall be necessary. And the enlistments, which shall be made by virtue hereof, may be for the term of three years, subject to be discharged by the President of the United States, or by the ceasing or repeal of the laws providing for the naval armament. And if the marine corps, or any part of it, shall be ordered by the President to do duty on shore, and it shall become necessary to appoint an adjutant, paymaster, quartermaster, sergeant-major, quartermaster-sergeant, and drum and fife-major, or any of them, the major or commandant of the corps, is hereby authorized to appoint such staff officer or officers, from the line of subalterns, sergeants and music, respectively, who shall be entitled, during the time they shall do such duty, to the same extra pay and emoluments, which are allowed by law, to officers acting in the same capacities in the infantry.

SEC. 3. *And be it further enacted,* That the detachments of the corps of marines hereby authorized, shall be made in lieu of the respective quotas of marines, which have been established or authorized for the frigates, and other armed vessels and gallies, which shall be employed in the service of the United States; And the President of the United States may detach and appoint such of the officers of the marine corps, to act on board the frigates, and any of the armed vessels of the United States, respectively, as he shall, from time to time, judge necessary; any thing in the act "providing a naval armament" to the contrary hereof notwithstanding.

SEC. 4. *And be it further enacted,* That the officers, non-commissioned officers, privates, and musicians aforesaid, shall take the same oath, and shall be governed by the same rules and articles of war, as are prescribed for the military establishment of the United States, and by the rules for the regulation of the navy, heretofore, or which shall be established by law, according to the nature of the service in which they shall be employed, and shall be entitled to the same allowance, in case of wounds or disabilities, according to their respective ranks, as are granted by the act "to ascertain and fix the military establishment of the United States."

SEC. 5. *And be it further enacted,* That the non-commissioned officers, musicians, seamen and marines, who are or shall be enlisted into the service of the United States; and the non-commissioned officers and musicians, who are or shall be enlisted into the army of the United States, shall be, and they are hereby exempted, during their term of service, from all personal arrests for any debt or contract.

SEC. 6. *And be it further enacted,* That the marine corps, established by this act, shall, at any time, be liable to do duty in the forts and garrisons of the United States, on the sea-coast, or any other duty on shore, as the President, at his discretion, shall direct.

Approved, July 11, 1798.

[Statute II, page 594.]

To Captain John Barry, U. S. Navy, from Secretary of Navy

[PHILADELPHIA,]
Navy Departmt 11. July. 1798

JOHN BARRY

SIR, The Congress have lately passed an Act, which you will find enclosed, as well as your Instructions, founded upon that Act, authorizing the Capture of French armed Vessels, wherever found on the high Seas.

From the best Information, to be obtained here, it does not appear that the French have any considerable Force, in the West-Indies; three light Frigates, blocked up by the English, at Cape Francois, comprise, as I understand, the whole of their Public Force. and these, it is beleived, only wait a safe Opportunity to leave the Island and return to France. Their Cruisers of smaller size, are numerous, &

find Shelter in the Spanish, Danish & Dutch Islands, as well as their own. —

Under such Circumstances, it is thought probable, that a small Squadron, under the Command of an Officer of your Intelligence, Experience & Bravery might render essential service, & animate your Country to Enterprize, by picking up a Number of Prizes in the short Cruise to the Islands. —

I am, Therefore, instructed by the President to direct, that taking the *Delaware*, Capt Decatur, under your Command, you proceed without Delay to Cape Cod (& not finding Capt Sever there to Nantasket road) where you will be joined by the *Herald* Capt Sever of 20 Guns, and a Revenue Cutter of 14 Guns, from Boston, with this Force you will proceed with all practicable Expedition to the West Indies, endeavouring to fall in with the Islands, three or four degrees to the Windward of Barbados. & thence, keeping to the Windward of Martinico, Guadaloupe, & Antigua, & so disposing of the Vessels under your Command, as to afford the greatest chance of falling in with the French-armed Vessels — and yet keeping each within protecting distance of the whole — You will look into St Johns, the principal Harbour of Porto-Rico, & after two or three days cruising on the South Side of that Island, you will return again to the Continent, making for Delaware, New York, or Rhode Island, according to Circumstances. —

Altho' I have pointed out your course, yet it is to be understood, that you are not rigidly to adhere to It, if Circumstances should intervene to render in your Judgment, a Departure therefrom, expedient or necessary. The object of the Enterprize is, to do as much Injury to the armed Vessels sailing under the Authority of France, & to make as many Captures as possible, consistently with a due Regard (& more than a due Regard you will not suffer to be paid) to the Security of our own — and you will use your best Means to accomplish this Object. —

The Ship *New Jersey*, Capt Clay, from the East Indies, the Property of Messrs Nicklin & Griffith has been captured by the French and carried into St Johns in Porto Rico. These Gentlemen expect that the Ship & Cargo will soon be in the Power of their own Agent, Doct Edward Stevens at St Johns. The duties this Vessel will pay to Government, if she arrives safe, make her an Object meriting Public Protection, to say Nothing about the duty of Government to protect the Property of all it's Citizens.

You will, therefore, give every Aid to this Vessel in your power, & if She can be got out of the harbour of St John's, take her under your Convoy — When you arrive in the Neighbourhood of the Island, you will judge whether you can prudently detach Capt Decatur to hover about the harbour, & to communicate with the Agent or Capt of the Ship, before your own Arrival. —

Porto Rico is the Place it seems, where the greater Part of our captured Seamen collect to return to their own Country — It is said, they are exposed to great Sufferings there — to releive their distresses and to restore so valuable a Body of Men to their Country, ought to be Objects with Government & it's Officers — When you get off the harbour of St John's, there will be no Impropriety in your writing a civil Letter to the Governor, requesting that the American Seamen in that Port, may be restored to you — I have drafted a Letter which it appears to Me proper that you should address to the Governor — Being at Peace with Spain, you must take no hostile Measures to obtain them, if the civil Demand contained in the Letter, should not produce Them — This Letter may be sent into the harbour by one of the Ships under your Command, or the Cutter — & the Vessel so sent, may immediately take the *New Jersey* under her Protection, if She be permitted to sail for America. — The Act of Congress enclosed, will direct the Measures to be pursued with respect to your Prizes. I need not add on that Subject. —

In your Treatment of the Vessels, Citizens & Subjects of all Nations, except the French armed Vessels, & the Persons found on board of Them — You will bear in mind, that We are at Peace, and wish to continue in Peace with all Nations who will suffer us, to be at Peace with them, and that the Commander of an American Squadron, ought to be as much distinguished for his Attention and Adherence to all the rights of Humanity & Hospitality, as by his firmness in the support of the honor of his Country. —

Should you even see an American Vessel captured by the armed Ship of any Nation at War, with whom WE are at Peace, you cannot lawfully interfere to prevent such Capture — It must be presumed until the Contrary be proved, that the Courts of that Nation will render Justice. — Nor must you recapture any American Vessel taken by any such Nation — The Law of Nations, forbids It, and We must respect that Law. —

To the Dishonor of the American Name, some Officers of the United States, I wish I could not with Truth add many, in the Civil Line as well at home as abroad, Officers whose Conduct proved them unworthy of the Distinction they had received; too frequently have indulged Themselves in the disgraceful Licentiousness of villifying our Government & those Characters in It best entitled to the Esteem & Gratitude of the Country. If We do not respect Ourselves, how can it be expected that We are to command Respect from others — It is scarcely necessary, for Me in writing to a brave Man, who values his own Country, it's Government & it's Laws, to suggest the Usefulness of inculcating upon those under his Command, the Propriety of preserving in their Language and Conduct, the same Respect which he himself feels for those Constitutions and those Characters, which deserve the Respect of all — It is Time We should establish an American Character — Let that Character be a Love of Country and Jealousy of it's honor — This Idea comprehends every Thing that ought to be impressed upon the Minds of all our Citizens, but more especially of those Citizens who are also Seamen & Soldiers. —

The Length of Time to be consumed in your Expedition, will depend upon such a Variety of Circumstances, that no accurate Judgement can be formed of the Time of your Return. Yet it is hoped, that you may be on our Coasts in two Months, from the Time you depart from Boston Bay. —

Wishing you all possible Success & honor in this Enterprize, & adding the Assurances of the President's Confidence, that Nothing will be left undone on your Part, to insure both honor & Success I remain &c

[Enclosure]

DRAFT OF A LETTER, PROPOSED TO BE WRITTEN BY CAP^T BARRY, TO THE GOV^R OF PORTO RICO — VIZ^T

At sea, off PORTO RICO —
1798

SIR, The Government of the United States, have received repeated Information that many American Seamen belonging to Vessels which have been captured by French Cruizers and carried into Porto Rico, have some times been confined as Prisoners, and if not so confined, have been exposed to much Inconvenience and real Suffering for want of adequate Supplies of Provisions, and the Means of returning to their Country. — The President of the United States has therefore directed Me, when on this Station, to address your Excellency on this subject; and particularly to request that any American Citizens under Confinement in the Island of Porto Rico (if such there be) may be released, and with others of their Countrymen, permitted to come on board the Ships under my Command, that they may return to the United States. —

This Request, I make to your Excellency in the Confidence due from one friendly Nation to another, and especially in the Case of two Nations like our's reciprocally entitled by a Treaty of Friendship to all the Offices of Humanity, & to Favor, Protection and Assistance.

Captain   will have the honor to deliver to your Excellency this Letter, and if convenient to receive your Answer.

I have the honor to be
Sir, your Excellency's
most obed^t & most hble Servt

His Excellency, The GOVERNOR OF PORTO RICO.

For Instructions to Capt Barry, See Page 98.

[NOTE.—Page 98 contains instructions to commanders of armed vessels, given at Philadelphia, 10 July 1798, included in this volume.]
[NDA. OSW, Vol. 1.]

To Captain Stephen Decatur (senior), U. S. Navy, from Secretary of Navy

[PHILADELPHIA,]
Navy Departm^t 11. July. 1798.

Capt STEPHEN DECATUR

SIR, Enclosed, you will receive new Instructions, founded on a late Act of Congress, which is also enclosed. —

You will immediately proceed with your Ship at the Capes of Delaware, where you will fall in with the Frigate *United States* Captn Barry, under whose Command you will place Yourself, on an Enterprize, about which he has particular Orders, which he will communicate to you — on that subject, I need not be more explicit. —

You are now at Liberty by the present Instructions to capture French armed-Vessels wherever to be found on the high Seas, but you will remember that We are at War only with the armed Vessels of France — The Vessels, Citizens & Subjects of Nations, with whom We are at Peace, are entitled to the same Civility Respect & Friendship from Us, which We wish to receive from Them. — American

Officers must not be outdone in the Offices of Humanity & Politeness, any more than in Bravery & Enterprize. —

You are not even authorized by the Law of Nations nor by our own Laws, to recapture an American Vessel taken by the armed Vessels of any Nation but France — We are to presume until the Contrary be proven, that their Courts will do us Justice. —

To the disgrace &c see Page 92 Paragraph beginning with To the Dishonor &c —

Wishing you all Manner of Success & honor, & not doubting but that you merit both. —

I remain &c

See Instructions on following Page. —

[NOTE.—Page 92 contains part of letter to Captain John Barry dated 11 July 1798. The "following page" represents page 98 which contains instructions to commanders of armed vessels, at Philadelphia, 10 July 1798, included in this volume.]

[NDA. OSW, Vol. 1.]

To Lieutenant Harwood, U. S. M. C., from Secretary of Navy

[PHILADELPHIA,]
Navy Department 11. July. 1798

Lieut[t] HARWOOD

SIR, Being appointed Lieutenant of Marines for the Ship *Baltimore* at Balt[o] Cap[t] Isaac Philips Commander, you will without delay proceed to Balt[o] and take Instructions for Cap[t] Phillips, respecting your Conduct in recruiting the Marines — I would suggest the Propriety of getting as large a Proportion as possible of your Men Americans, — they can be depended upon to defend the rights & honor of their Country. —

Cap[t] Phillips will supply you with Money for the recruiting Service — Wishing you success in getting Men & a successful & honorable Cruise, I am &c

[NDA. OSW, Vol. 1.]

To Captain James Sever, U. S. Navy, from Secretary of Navy

[PHILADELPHIA,]
Navy Departm[t] 11 July 1798

Captain JAMES SEVER

SIR, Presuming that your Ship the *Herald* will be ready by the Time this Letter gets to your hands, for a Cruise. — I have it in Command from the President, to direct that you will without delay, repair to Nantasket Road, where it is expected you will fall in with the Frigate *United States*, Cap[t] Barry — & the *Delaware*, Cap[t] Decatur — The Revenue Cutter at New Bury will join you there, or at Cape Cod, whither you will proceed if you should not find Cap[t] Barry at Nantasket — Cap[t] Barry will sail from the Capes of Delaware tomorrow, & will make the best of his way to Cape Cod, from whence, if he should not find you there, he will proceed to Nantasket Road; it is very desireable that you should early fall in with each other. —

When you join Capt Barry, You will put Yourself under his Command, on a Cruise, which will probably not be ended sooner than Two Months, if so soon — As you will receive your Orders from him, I need not add on that Subject — You will find enclosed your authority for making Prize of all armed French Vessels wherever found — & the Act of Congress on which this Authority is founded — You will recollect that We are at War only with the armed Vessels of France, and that the Vessels Citizens and Subjects of all other Nations, have a right to expect from Us, all those Offices of Friendship humanity and Politeness, which We are desirous of receiving from Them.

To the dishonor of the American Name &c &c &c &c. See Page 92. Paragraph of Letter to Capt Barry beginning with To the dishonor &^c [Note. This letter to Captain Barry on page 92 is dated 11 July, 1798.]

For Instructions — See Page 98 & 99. —

Wishing you Success & honor, & adding the President's Assurances of his Confidence that you will merit both — I have the honor &^c

[NOTE.—Pages 98 and 99 contain instructions to commanders of armed vessels, at Philadelphia, 10 July 1798, included in this volume.]

[NDA. OSW, Vol. 1.]

To Stephen Higginson, Navy Agent, from Secretary of Navy

[PHILADELPHIA,]
Navy Department 11th July 1798

STEPHEN HIGGINSON Esqr *Boston*

SIR I have only time to say, that Captn Sever and the Cutter will receive orders by the Mail of to morrow, for a three months cruise — pray so order, that they may be ready — They will join Capt Barry, and a 20 Gun Ship at Cape Cod, or Nantucket road — The Secretary of the Treasury will give directions for the Cutter to attend to my orders — As to the cloathing for the Marines, Slops, and pursers acc^ts no arrangements have been made, except for the clothes which are here, but which cannot be sent on, and I hope, are provided at Boston— The powder & Muskets, will certainly be in time from Springfield, if not, they must be procured, at whatever expence— The pursers Acc^ts must be kept in the best way to avoid confusion, untill permanent arrangements can be made — The Slops must be delivered to the purser, to be by him charged to the men, as they receive them — These and all other things you will be so good as to regulate, as you think best, and let nothing intervene to delay Capt Sever, and the Cutter, after they receive Instructions — Whatever you do, will be Judicious, & will be approved of — —

[NDA. GLB, Vol. 1.]

To James Watson, Navy Agent, New York, from Secretary of Navy

[PHILADELPHIA,]
Navy Department July 11th 1798

JAs WATSON Esqr *New York*

SIR I have received your favours of the 7th & 9th Instant — Being desirous to alter the dimensions of the Ship intended for Capt Morris, I will thank you to conform to the following Vizt

108 feet Keel
34 feet Beam
10 feet 9 Ins Hold
5 feet 6 Ins Between decks
5½ to 6 feet Waist

She must be calculated to carry 24 *Twelve* pounders on the main deck, and you will contract for Cannon of that size, and as there has yet been no rules established in this respect, Capt Morris can choose one that he approves of, — which may be given as a Model — You will please to inform yourself if a contract can be made, and on what Terms, for finishing the Frigate, the Keel of which has been so long ago laid —

[NDA. GLB, Vol. 1.]

To Jeremiah Yellott, Navy Agent, Baltimore, from Secretary of Navy

[PHILADELPHIA,]
Navy Department July 11th 1798

JERh YELLOTT Esqr *Balto*

SIR Your Letter of the 9th Instant is before me — I hope you will be able to procure the Guns for the *Montezuma*, but should this not be the case I will ascertain, whether those in possession of Mr Hughes can be spared for that purpose — and advise you accordingly — I thank you for your hints, respecting the disgraceful and pernicious practice prevailing, in the Sale of American Vessels for Foreign privateers — which shall be attended to. —

[NDA. GLB, Vol. 1.]

Extract from Captain Thomas Truxtun's journal, U. S. Frigate *Constellation*, 11 July 1798, Wednesday

Moderate Breezes all these Twenty four Hours, and smooth Water. I perceive a strong Current setting in the Bight, between the Shoals of Cape Lookout, and those of the frying Pan, near Cape Fear. I therefore recommend great Caution to such as navigate hereabouts.

At 10 PM the Wind, that had been from East South East to South East, shifted to South; sounded in 9½ Fathoms Water off the Frying Pan, dark Sand, at 11 Ditto tacked, and stood to the Eastward untill 6 AM, when we tacked again, and stood to the Westward, and at 8 Ditto sounded, and had Twenty two Fathoms Water. Bottom as before

At 9 ditto saw a Ship to Leeward in the North North West, got to Quarters, and bore down upon her; at 10 Ditto spoke the Ship *South*

Carolina, John German, Master, from Charleston, bound to Philadelphia, out two Days, had seen no Cruizers.

At noon the depth of Water was Twenty one Fathoms, dark Sand, like Pepper and Salt mixed.

Latitude observed 33°.35′ N°
Longitude Account 77.30 W.

[HS of Pa. NDA photostat.]

To the Comptroller of the Treasury from Secretary Pickering

[PHILADELPHIA,]
Department of State, 12 July 1798.

The COMPTROLLER OF THE TREASURY.

SIR, The President having granted a permission to the Collector of Baltimore to clear the Brigantine *Liberty*, belonging to Jesse Fearson, for Cape Francois, to aid the departure of French persons, I have thought it necessary to write the enclosed letter to the Collector, in order to caution him against the abuse that is practicable under such permissions. As the subject is novel, I shall be obliged by your considering it and suggesting any other expedient that may occur to you of a nature to guard against the possibility of carrying on an intercourse with the French possessions, not allowed by law, As permissions of this kind will generally pass through my office, I propose to write a similar letter to the Collectors to whom they may be addressed from time to time as they are issued. I enclose you a copy of the permission granted in the case of the *Liberty* which with the letter to the Collector, be pleased to return.

I am, Sir, very respectfully &c

TIMOTHY PICKERING.

[Enclosure]

DEPARTMENT OF STATE *July 12. 1798.*

ROBERT PURVIANCE Esqr *Collector of Baltimore*

SIR, I have just delivered to Captain Jesse Fearson of Baltimore the President's permission for you to clear his brigantine called the *Liberty*, to carry French passengers to Cape Francois. Under the terms "goods and effects" of French persons, if great care be not taken, a traffic will still be carried on with the French ports, and the object of the law referred to, be frustrated. If an American vessel, fairly designed to deport French persons, according to the act, as many passengers will ordinarily be engaged as she can conveniently carry: and this circumstance may be considered as a good criterion of the real object of the voyage. On the other hand, if few passengers embark, with many "goods and effects," they may justly be suspected of collusion.

I have taken the liberty to suggest these remarks as they occurred, in a measure which in this country is novel, and from the singularity of our political situation, perhaps unexampled.

I am very respectfully, Sir, Your Ob^t^ Servt

TIMOTHY PICKERING

[SDA. Dom. L., Vol. 11.]

To Captain Jonathan Chapman, Revenue Cutter *Pickering*, from Secretary of Navy

[PHILADELPHIA,]
Navy Department 12. July. 1798.

Capt JONATHAN CHAPMAN *Boston*

SIR, By an Arrangement with the Secretary of the Treasury, your Cutter is to be put under my direction as soon as she is fitted for sea — I presume you have received Letters from the Secy of the Treasury to this Effect — and I hope this will find you prepared for Sea — with at least 3 months Provisions on board. —

This being the Case, you will without delay proceed with your Cutter, to Nantasket Road, & endeavour to fall in with the Frigate *United States* Capt Barry, under whose Command you will place Yourself. Not finding Capt Barry at Nantasket Road, you will proceed to Cape Cod, at one or other of these places you will certainly fall in with him.

He will leave the Capes of Delaware, I take for granted this day — & will make the best of his way to Cape Cod — & not finding you & Captain Sever there, to Nantasket Road. —

Enclosed you will receive a late Act of Congress, & your Authority founded thereon, to capture French armed Vessels, whenever found. —

Wishing you success & honor, I have the honor to be &c. &c.

[NDA. OSW, Vol. 1.]

To Captain Samuel Nicholson, U. S. Navy, from Secretary of Navy

[PHILADELPHIA,]
Navy Departmt 12 July. 1798

Capt SAMl NICHOLSON

SIR, Presuming that the Frigate *Constitution* under your Command, will be ready for a Cruise, by the Time this gets to your hands, I have enclosed your Instructions founded upon the late Acts of Congress, and by which you are to be governed.— You will observe, that you are permitted to capture, French armed Vessels, wherever found on the high Seas, as well as within our Jurisdictional Limits. —

There will be Employment found for our other Vessels of War, and you will be relied on solely for the Protection of the Eastern Coast, at least for the Present — With so fine a Ship — a good Crew & a Commander of your Activity & Bravery, It will want no other Protection. —

Your Object must be to secure from the Depredations of the French Cruisers, the principal Ports of New Hampshire, Massts & Rhode Island, & to pay some Attention to that of New York — This can be best done, by considering your cruising Ground, & so you will consider It until further Orders, to extend from about 10 or 15 Leagues, Eastward of the East End of George's Bank, to the West End of Long-Island. — and I am directed by the President to express to you his entire Confidence, that you will do every Thing that can be expected from a brave intelligent and active Officer, to afford to this Extent of Coast the most effectual Protection. —

The Cruising Ground of Capt Dale in the *Ganges* extends from Cape Henry to Long Island. —

It will be desireable, that there should be frequent Opportunities of communicating with you, & to afford this, you will in every 10 or 12 Days, endeavour to appear off New Port, Rhode Island, & at such a distance as to be seen from the Town, with the Swedish Flagg hoisted on your Main Topmast Head — when any Thing occurs, to be communicated to you, it will be done from New Port, by means of a Pilot Boat. —

You will consider, that We are at War, with the Public & Private armed Ships of the French Republic, only, — To the Vessels, Citizens, & Subjects of other Nations, you will conduct Yourself as the Citizen of a Nation, desirous of maintaining Harmony with all the World & wishing to be distinguished by a scrupulous Adherence to all the duties of Hospitality.

Any Prizes you may take, you will send into the nearest Port of the U:S: to be proceeded against according to Law: The Persons, found on board of them, must be reported to the Collector of the Port, at which they first arrive — and be delivered over to the Marshall, or some other civil or military Officer of the United States — Prizes of Force inferior to your own will be divided between the Captors and the United States — those of equal or superior Force, go entirely to the Captor. —

There is one Point which I wish strongly to impress on your Mind, that should you even see an American Vessel captured by the armed Ship of any Nation at War, with whom WE are at Peace, you cannot lawfully interfere to prevent such Capture — It must be presumed until the Contrary be proved, that the Courts of that Nation will render Justice; nor must you recapture any American Vessel taken by any such Nation — The Law of Nations, forbids It, & WE must respect that Law. —

To the Dishonor &c. &c. See Page 92. —

For Instructions see Page 98.

[NOTE.—Page 92 contains a letter to Captain John Barry dated 11 July 1798, giving instructions regarding cruise to West Indies. Page 98 contains instructions to commanders of armed vessels, at Philadelphia, 10 July 1798, included in this volume.]

[NDA. OSW, Vol. 1.]

To Stephen Higginson, Navy Agent, Boston, from Secretary of Navy

[PHILADELPHIA,]
Navy Department July 12th 1798

STEPHEN HIGGINSON Esqr *Boston.*

SIR I have this day sent on orders to Captain Nicholson, & Capt Sever, to proceed to Sea —

The Cutter at Newbury is to be under my direction when equipp'd for sea — I enclose orders for the Captain, which I presume the Secretary of the Treasury has ordered him to obey — I can say to you in confidence, that Barry, in the Frigate *United States* 48 Guns, that Decatur in the *Delaware*, a strong ship of 22 Guns, have orders to proceed immediately from the Capes of Delaware and to fall in with Capt Sever, and the Cutter, at Cape Cod — Or not finding them there, to Nantasket Roads, from whence the four vessels, are to proceed under the command of Barry to the West Indies, to fall in with the Islands 3 or 4 degrees to the Windward of Barbadoes, and thence keeping to the Windward of Martinico, Antigua & ca to Porto Rico, from whence after a short cruise, and attempting to get our Seamen from that Island, where it is said, there are a great many, they are to return — Captain Nicholson meantime, is to protect the Eastern Coast — his cruising ground from about fifteen leagues East, of the East end of George's Island, to the West of Long Island —

I wish you would give me your candid opinion of this Arrangement, and add such Observations as shall direct me better in future — It was unfortunate, that in conferring the Appointment of Secretary of the Navy upon me, the President, cou'd not also confer the knowledge necessary for the Secretary of the Navy to possess, to make him most useful to his Country — No person could have a greater desire to acquire this knowledge, or could be more grateful to those enlightened men who will assist him in obtaining it than myself — I fear many things have been neglected from this quarter respecting Capt Sever — I have been obliged to Act — & under great disadvantages — without having a moment to think, — I shall soon have time to make better arrangements — Meantime I have no doubt you will cause all difficulties to be removed and suffer nothing to prevent Capt Sever's sailing with the Cutter to join Barry, The Cutter I hear to day, for the first time, has not her Guns, but that they were expected, & I hope they will be recd in time — If not the other Ships must sail without her — She ought to have at least three mo provisions — four mo for both the Cutter & the *Herald*, wou'd do better —

[NDA. GLB, Vol. 1.]

To The Governor of Porto Rico from Secretary Timothy Pickering

DEPARTMENT OF STATE
Philadelphia July 12th 1798.

The GOVERNOR OF PORTO RICO.

SIR, Doctor Thomas Henry Junr Surgeon of the American Ship *New-Jersey*, will have the honor to present to your Excellency this letter. Doctor Henry is charged with some business by the original owners of that Ship, in consequence of her being captured by a French cruizer and carried into Porto-Rico. I have to request your Excellency that Doctor Henry may be hospitably received in the Island, and enjoy your protection while he remains there. Such hospitality and protection the officers of the United States will ever be ready to reciprocate in their ports towards the subjects of His Catholic Majesty. I have the honor &c.

TIMOTHY PICKERING

[SDA. Dip. Cor. Inst. to Min., Vol. 4, 1797–1798.]

To Captain John Barry, U. S. Navy, from Secretary of Navy

[PHILADELPHIA,]
Navy Departmt 12. July. 1798 —

JOHN BARRY

SIR, It is possible, tho' I hope not probable, that the Revenue Cutter (*Pickering*) Capt Chapman may not be ready to join you; in this case, & you will receive the information from Mr Higginson, Boston, — you will proceed on your Expedition without her. —

Enclosed is a letter from Mr Nicklin, which I forgot to send you by Capt Decatur.

[NDA. OSW, Vol. 1.]

To Stephen Higginson, Navy Agent, Boston, from Secretary of Navy

[PHILADELPHIA,]
Navy Department. 12 July [1798]

STEPHEN HIGGINSON

SIR, If the Revenue Cutter, cannot be ready to sail with Barry, he must go without her. I have desired him to take his Information on this subject from you. —

[NDA. GLB, Vol. 1]

[12 July, 1798]

Extract of a letter from a gentleman in New York, 2 Sept., 1798, regarding capture by French Privateer *Flower of the Sea*, Captain Dupayn, of ship which ultimately was recaptured, by H. M. S. *Aquilon*

"Since writing my last, informing you that I was going to New-Orleans shortly — On the 27th of June I set sail at ten o'clock, wind N. N. W. — could not stand our course. On the 12th of July, was so unfortunate as to be captured by the French privateer *Flower of the Sea,* Captain Dupayn, in lat. 31, 52, who informed us that he had taken three days before, two ships belonging to Baltimore, and one belonging to New-York — would not tell their names. As soon as he fired to bring us to, we drew up our foresail and bore down upon him: because we did not please the rascal, he fired a musket ball in out boom, when all the passengers were on deck. We remained in his possession fifteen days, and were intended for St. Domingo, but luckily the prize master knew very little of navigation, and our captain instructed wrong; in consequence, we had nearly been shipwrecked, for we ran a very great risque. In making the land it was very dark, and we were within half a mile of it before we discovered it; instead of St. Domingo it happened to be near Port a Plate. When they found their mistake they stood for Fort Dauphin, being within four hours sail of it — we met with his Majesty's ship *Aquilon,* who captured and sent us into St. Nichola Mole. In passing Cape Francois, I saw Barney's squadron, afraid to come out, there being three English 74's and several other ships off there. As soon as the Frenchmen saw the frigate they cut away our boat, and they all got in her excepting the prize master and one hand; they took away with them a number of articles — but as soon as the frigate saw them she gave chace and caught them, we then bore down to her, and they were all made prisoners. — For recapture the English claim one half, and the court expences to be paid out of the other half, belonging to the underwriters — There are a great number of Baltimore vessels there, waiting for trial."

[LC, "Claypoole's American Daily Advertiser"(Phila.), 11 Sept. 1798.]

To Acting Lieutenant William Davis from Captain Thomas Truxtun, U. S. Navy,

UNITED STATES SHIP *Constellation*
12th July 1798.

SIR I have thought proper to Appoint you an Acting Lieutenant at Arms, on board this Ship; you will by your Zeal, activity and attention, discharge the duties of that Office, as becomes, a vigilant Officer.

The General duty expected from you, will be the Exercise of the Cannon &c. The co-opperating with the Gunner, and seeing that the

Arms and accoutrements, powder & Shot, and every Article appertaining to or belonging to the Cannon or Small Arms, and in fact all and every of the Military Stores and Apparatus be kept at hand, in good order, and fit for Service at a moments warning and to report to me what is otherwise or wanting of Repair.

Your Appointment to this Office, is not to take off from any Officer of the Ship, the duties enjoin'd him to perform by the Articles of War, the Orders of the President, or my Private orders, it is done to accellerate the business without any relaxation on the part of any Officer.

I am Sir Your Ob^t Servt

THOMAS TRUXTUN.

Lieu^t Wm Davis.

[HS of Pa. NDA photostat. Truxtun's LB, 1798–9.]

Extract from Captain Thomas Truxtun's journal, U. S. Frigate *Constellation*, 12 July 1798, Thursday

Throughout the whole of this Day, the Weather has been pleasant, and the Water smooth, the Wind blowing generally from the Southward, tho' at Times, it was variable. A number of Coasters beating along Shore in Company with us. Stretched in to 12 Fathoms Water, and off to 20 Fathoms, the Bottom a Grey Sand. At Noon the Breakers of the Frying Pan, were seen from the Mast Head, bearing about North North West, five Leagues Distance, find a North East Current these Twenty four Hours within the Stream, a little uncommon. Depth of Water 14½ Fathoms, Breakers bearing as before mentioned

Latitude observed 33°.26′ North
Longitude Account 78.10 West

[HS of Pa. NDA photostat.]

Extract from the journal of Lieutenant John Mullowny U. S. Frigate *United States*, Thursday, 12 July 1798

Bay of Delaware. Winds N. N. W. Fine moderate and clear weather, at 10 A. M. all hands to Quarters, exercised the crew at their proper stations, at 11 A. M. fired Twenty-seven shot at a wreck (ship *John*), at 3 P. M. anchored below the Cross Ledge, in the Bay, six fathoms.

[NA.]

[July 12, 1798]

Report of the state of the cruisers now fitting out by the Government of the United States for His Excellency the Dey of Algiers

	Hull	Hold	Boats, &ca	Masts & Spars	Rigging	Sails	Artillery	Provisions	When ready for Sea	Men wanted for immediate Service	Full Compt
Brig HASSAN BASHAW	Compleat ready for taking on board Stores & Cargo	Wanted 50 Tons of Shot or other heavy articles for Ballast	Compleat, Ship chandlers coopers Block Makers Stores &ca ready to take on board	Compleat & in their places	Standing compt running ready for receiving —	Compleat	13 pieces mounted 9 do. not proved	Ready to take on board	In twenty Days	Twenty	52 —
Schooner SKJOLDEBRAND	do. do. do.	40 Tons. do.	do. do. do.	do. do. do.	do. do. do.	do.	Compleat.	do.	Fifteen days	Fifteen	40
Schooner LELLA AISHA	do. do. do.	30 Tons. do	do. do. do.	do. do. do	do. do. do.	do.	do.	do.	Ten days	Twelve	35 —

PHILADELPHIA *July 12th 1798*
JAMES LEAR CATHCART

[SDA, Tripoli. Vol. 1, 1796–1799.]

To the Governor of New Jersey from Secretary Pickering

[PHILADELPHIA,]
Department of State July 13th 1798.

His Excellency GOVERNOR HOWELL,

Dr SIR, You have noticed the capture of a French privateer by the American armed Ship *Delaware*. The persons found on board the privateer, who by law are to be detained as prisoners, amount to Fifty three. They are at present at Mud-Island, guarded by the troops at Fort Mifflin: but they must in a few days be removed. The prison of Philadelphia being entirely occupied, some other place of confinement must be procured. The new and spacious prison lately erected at Lamberton, by the State of New-Jersey, presents itself as the most safe and suitable, as well as the most easy of access. Shall I beg of you the information, whether it is now or soon will be in a state to receive such prisoners, and whether they can be admitted? I shall be obliged by an early answer. I am with great respect

TIMOTHY PICKERING

P. S. The President highly approves of the plan here suggested and will be gratified if it succeeds.

[SDA. Dom. L., Vol. 11.]

To Garrett Hulsecamp, Pilot, from Secretary of Navy

[PHILADELPHIA,]
Navy Department July 13. 1798

GARRETT HULSECAMP *Pilot*

You will receive herewith a Letter, directed for Capt Richard Dale, of the Ship *Ganges*, with which you will proceed immediately in your Pilot Boat to the Capes of Delaware, sailing off, & on, until you meet with that Ship, when you will deliver the said Letter, & receive from Capt Dale, any dispatches he may give you, for this Department.

[NDA. GLB, Vol. 1.]

To Stephen Higginson, Navy Agent, Boston, from Secretary of Navy

[PHILADELPHIA,]
Navy Department 13th July 1798

STEPHEN HIGGINSON Esqr *Boston*

SIR, The enclos'd Letter to Capt Barry contains a Letter from the Secretary of State, to the Governor of Port To Rico — be pleas'd to give it a conveyance.

[NDA. GLB, Vol. 1.]

Extract from the journal of Lieutenant John Mullowny, U. S. Frigate *United States*, Friday, 13 July 1798

Bay of Delaware. Winds N. by W. Pleasant breezes and clear weather, at 8 A. M. hove short, at 10 weighed anchor, and stood down the Bay, at 11 observed the *Delaware* Capt Decatur astern, hove to, till she came up, Capt Decatur came on board. when he left the ship made sail, at M Cape Henlopen bore W. N. W. dist 3 leagues.

[NA.]

To Captain Richard Dale, U. S. Navy, from Secretary of Navy

[PHILADELPHIA,]
Navy departmt 13. July. 1798.

Capt RICHd DALE

SIR, Enclosed you will receive an Act of Congress, which passed the 9 Inst and new Instructions, founded upon that Act, authorizing you to capture French armed Vessels wherever found. You may therefore allow Yourself a wider Range, & keep further from the shores — The French Cruisers have too good Information of your Cruising Ground to come within your reach. You will try whether you can not fall in with them, two or three degrees further from the Coast — indeed, if you have sufficient Confidence in your Crew, and your Ship, which I wish was better prepared, you may have a better Chance of falling in with the French Cruisers, coming on the Coast, & going off with their Prizes, by standing as far to the Southward as Latitude 34 — and as far Eastward as Longitude 65 — which will be about one degree Westward of Bermudas & in the Track of the Enemy Vessels. —

The Cutter of New York, of 14 Guns, will be prepared for Sea by the 20th Inst — The Capt will be ordered to join you, & I hope will be ready to do It on that day. You will judge whether it will be most prudent to wait until you are joined by this Vessel, before you venture so far as I have suggested, & will act accordingly. —

Capt Decatur in a better appointed Ship than your's has been more fortunate, than you have yet been — but let not that Circumstance make you uneasy — Your services have been highly advantageous in protecting the Merchant's Vessels — & in keeping in a great degree, the Cruisers from our Coasts — and the Confidence of the President, and your Country, in your Vigilance, Enterprize & Bravery is undiminished — The Coast from Cape Henry to Long Island, is still to be the Object of your Protection — It is not unlikely you may in stretching further South, fall in with Capt Truxtun.

Congress it is expected will adjourn in two or three days without a positive declaration of War; yet, We shall not on that Account be the less at War, with the armed Vessels of France. But it is the Policy of this Country, & Justice requires, that We should not forget, that We are at Peace, with all the rest of the World — You will, therefore, treat the Vessels, Citizens & Subjects of all other Nations, as you would wish to be treated by them — American Commanders will not suffer Themselves to be outdone in Zeal & Bravery in the service of their Country, nor should they in their Attention to the duties of Hospitality & humanity, if you should even fall in with an American Vessel captured by an armed Vessel of any Nation but the French, you must not retake her. The Law of Nations forbids It, & We must respect that Law — It must be presumed that their Courts will render Justice. —

It is hardly necessary in writing to a brave Man, who loves his Country, to suggest the Propriety of inculcating upon the minds of those under his Command, the same respect which he himself feels for our Government — Chief Magistrate — & our Laws — It has been too much the Fashion with too many of our Civil Officers both at home and abroad, to indulge Themselves in the Licentiousness of villifying the Government — those Institutions & those Virtuous Characters, which it has been the honor and the happiness of our Country, to have produced — I hope this disgraceful Licentiousness, will never be tolerated in our Navy — How can We expect to command respect to our Government from other Nations, if We ourselves do not set the Example. It is time We should establish a National Character. Let that Character be a Love of Country & Jealousy of it's honor & in Seamen also veneration for our Flag — This Idea comprises every thing that ought to be impressed & no more than ought to be impressed upon the Minds of all our Citizens; but more especially Those who are also Seamen & Citizens. —

You will still call at the Capes of Delaware, every 10 or 12 days to receive any Communications necessary to send you. —

For Instructions See Page 98.

[NOTE.—Page 98 contains instructions to commanders of armed vessels, at Philadelphia, 10 July 1798, included in this volume.]

[NDA. OSW, Vol. 1.]

To Captain Samuel Nicholson, U. S. Navy, from Secretary of Navy

[PHILADELPHIA,]
Navy Departm^t 13 July. 1798.

SAM^l NICHOLSON

SIR, I have to acknowledge the Receipt of your letter of the 8th Instant — In my last of 6th the existing Regulations for the Navy were enclosed, and upon Enquiry I find that Commissions for such of the Officers as are appointed, have been transmitted; and where Appointments are not made it is proposed, that in such Case the Officers were not to act under your Authority 'till Appointments take Place. I hope Lieut^t Cordis has recovered and proceeded successfully in the Business of recruiting — and that upon Inspection you'll find the Powder of better Quality than you apprehend.

By the Time this Letter reaches you, I hope you will be ready to pursue the destination given in my late Instructions — The Letter from Mr P. Jarvis which you enclose, is very satisfactory. —

[NDA. OSW, Vol. 1.]

Extract from Captain Thomas Truxtun's journal, U. S. Frigate *Constellation*, 13 July 1798, Friday

Light Southerly, and Westerly Breezes, intermixed with Calms, and some squally Appearances, accompanied with Lightning, and Thunder, stood off and on, having from 13 to 18 Fathoms Water, white Sand, with black Specks, and Shells. Several Coasters in Company, beating to the Southward, People employed at Sundries, and setting up the Rigging. Find no Current.

Latitude observed 33°.14′ N^o
Longitude Account 78.17 W

[HS of Pa. NDA photostat.]

[14 July 1798.]

From Secretary of State

TIMOTHY PICKERING,
Secretary of State of the United States of America,
To all whom it may concern.

The President of the United States having given permission to the brigantine called the *Liberty*, owned by Stephen Girard of the city of Philadelphia merchant, to clear out and depart with French passengers and their effects for Bourdeaux; all armed vessels, public and private belonging to the United States, are desired not only to let the said brigantine pass unmolested on her voyage, but to afford her any assistance that circumstances may require and admit. And the armed vessels of other friendly powers are in like manner requested to suffer the said brigantine to proceed on her voyage, without molestation.

Given under my hand and the Seal of my office, at Philadelphia, the fourteenth day of July 1798.

TIMOTHY PICKERING

[SDA. Dom. L., Vol. 11.]

To George Latimer, Collector, Philadelphia, from Secretary Pickering

DEPARTMENT OF STATE *July 14th 1798.*

GEORGE LATIMER ESQr
Collector of the Customs Philadelphia

SIR, I have just delivered to David Summis of this City the Presidents permission for you to clear out his Schooner called the *Harriet* and another to Messrs. Smith & Ridgway on behalf of Edward Burrowes to clear out the Sloop *Lark*, both vessels being destined to carry French passengers to Cape Francois. Under the terms "goods and effects" of French persons, if great care be not taken a traffic will still be carried on with the French ports, and the object of the law referred to be frustrated. If an American vessel is fairly designed to deport French persons according to the act, as many passengers will ordinarily be engaged as she can conveniently carry: and this circumstance may be considered as a good criterion of the real object of the voyage. On the other hand, if few passengers embark, with many "goods and effects," they may justly be suspected of collusion.

I have taken the liberty to suggest these remarks as they occurred, in a measure which in this country is novel and from the singularity of our political situation, perhaps unexampled. I am very respectfully, Sir, &c.

TIMOTHY PICKERING

[SDA. Dom. L., Vol. 11.]

To Captain Thomas Truxtun, U. S. Navy, from Secretary of Navy

[PHILADELPHIA,]
Navy Departmt, July 14. 1798

Capt TRUXTUN

SIR, I flatter Myself you have received my last Letter, which was sent under cover to Mr Pennock at Norfolk, and dispatched by a Pilot Boat from that Port. You will find enclosed an Act of Congress of 9 Inst with Instructions founded, thereon, which will admit of greater Latitude for your Operation, & probably lead to more certain Success — You are therefore authorized to extend your Limits by stretching further out to Sea occasionally so as to take a greater Range, in doing which I am confident your Prudence and Discretion may confidently be relied on, and you will please to bear in mind the former Limits as to distance Coastwise: before closing this Letter I can not avoid mentioning that many of our Civil Officers both at home & abroad, have been too frequently in the habit of indulging Themselves in the Licentiousness of villifying the Government, those Institutions and those virtuous Characters which it has been the Honor and Happiness of our Country to have produced — I hope this disgraceful Licentiousness will never be tolerated in our Navy, for We can not expect to command Respect to our Government from other Nations, if we ourselves do not set the Example — It is time We should establish a National Character — Let that Character be a love of Country & Jealousy of it's honor, and in Seamen also veneration for our Flag — You will I doubt not impress these Sentiments strongly on the Minds of your Officers and Crew — because a Man of your acknowledged Bravery & Understanding must feel, & can not fail to have his own Mind impressed with their Propriety. —

Congress it is expected will adjourn in two days without a positive declaration of War, yet We shall not on that Account be the less at War with the armed Vessels of France — But [it] is the Policy of this Country and Justice requires, that We should not forget that We are at Peace with the rest of the World — You will therefore treat the Vessels Citizens and Subjects of all other Nations, as you would wish to be treated by them.

In order to facilitate any Communication, I think it proper that you should appear off the Light House once in every Ten or Fifteen days, with a Swedish Flag hoisted at the Main top Mast Head, of which arrangements will be taken to give Information at Norfolk, where dispatches for you will be occasionally lodged & forwarded to you. —

I had nearly omitted to observe that should you meet with any American Vessel that has been captured by the Cruisers of any other Nation but the French, you must not interfere or attempt to recapture, because we must presume that the Courts of such Nation will do Justice in Cases of Captures improperly made. —

For Instructions — see Page 98 —

[NOTE.—Page 98 contains instructions to commanders of armed vessels, at Philadelphia, 10 July 1798, included in this volume.]

[NDA. OSW, Vol. 1.]

To William Pennock, Navy Agent, Norfolk, from Secretary of Navy

[PHILADELPHIA,]
Navy Departm^t 14. July. 1798

Wm PENNOCK

Sir, The Vessel building or built at Gossport, by N. Harbut, is described by Capt McNeill, & Capt Williams as a Vessel so proper for the public service, that I have to request you will purchase her, & fit her out as quickly as possible, for Capt Williams, who will assist in superintending the Alterations necessary to be made, which he represents as not considerable, & thinks the Vessel can be bought for 20 Drs if not less per Ton. —

Presuming that you can procure on proper Terms, Sails, Rigging and every Article necessary to equip the Vessel for Sea & War, except a Cambouse Guns, Shot, Powder & indeed all military Stores & Copper, I shall immediately make Arrangements for furnishing these Articles, leaving every Thing else to be obtained by you. — I wish it was possible for you to obtain Copper, but I fear it is not — The price here for the Patent kind is 50 Cents p. ' lb. — If you can get the proper kind at once; do it — What I send, will be wanted for another Vessel. —

The Carpenter, from whom you will purchase, must deliver the Vessel afloat & must in the 20 Drs per Ton, furnish Masts & Spars — You can probably agree with him for putting on the Copper. I understand this Vessel may be at Sea in Six Weeks — Shew, that you can prepare Vessels as well as quickly, & as frugally, as these things can be done at other Places — & Norfolk will have it's full share of this Kind of Business. —

Capt Williams will suggest the Alterations necessary for the Vessel — I hope they will not be considerable or expensive — As he is to command her, he should be indulged in all reasonable Things — She must be made into a Brig — & pierced to carry 18 six Pounders on one Deck. —

Expecting to hear quickly from you. I am &c.

It is likely I shall in a few days, write you on the subject of the Frigate — If the Merchants attempt a Vessel for the Public at Norfolk. I hope She will carry 24. 12 pounders on one Deck, if the Public furnish part of the money. —

[NDA. GLB, Vol. 1.]

To William Pennock, Navy Agent, Norfolk, from Secretary of Navy

[PHILADELPHIA,]
Navy Departmt 14. July. 1798

Wm PENNOCK

SIR, I must request you will take the Trouble to forward the enclosed Letter to Capt Truxtun, by a Pilot Boat.

It being proper, that a better mode of communicating with Capt Truxtun should be adopted, I have desired him to appear off the light House at Cape Henry, every 10 or 15 days — & hoist on his Maintopmast Head. — the Swedish Flag, to be known. — You will attend to give the proper Instructions at the light House, & make the proper Arrangements, so that when he does appear, any Letter for him, may be immediately sent to him. —

[NDA. GLB, Vol. 1.]

To Secretary of the Navy from Joshua Humphreys, Naval Constructor

JULY 14, 1798

SIR I went on board the French ship of War now laying at Lattimers wharf in this port in order to examine her, I find she was in the first Instance built for a Guineyman, but now converted into a Ship of War carrying eighteen Cannon on One Deck, she is fitted with a light temporary waist amidships, her decks in a very bad State, upon the whole, I conceive her to be an old slight built ship, and in my opinion not suitable for a Ship of War for the U States, altho I am of opinion she will sail fast —

I am very Respect[y]

J. HUMPHREYS [signature not plain]

The Hon SECRETARY OF THE NAVY

[HS of Pa. NDA photostat.]

Extract from the journal of Lieutenant John Mullowny, U. S. Frigate *United States*, 14 July 1798

At M. Cape Henlopen Light bore W by N dist 3 Leagues, at 1 P. M. took in 2 reefs in each Topsail.

At 3 P. M., out one reef, each Topsail The ship *Delaware* in C[o]

At M Tacked to the N[d]

Latt[de] Obs[d] 38.5 N.

[NA.]

[14 July 1798.]

To Isaac Garretson, Purser, from Captain Thomas Truxtun, U. S. Navy

Whereas the Purser of the United States Ship *Constellation* under my Command haveing this day represented to me that the Potatoes furnished agreeable to an Act of Congress and put on board of the Said Ship, is rotten and unfit for men to eat, and has requested a Survey thereon —

I do hereby in conformity with Said request direct any one of the Sea Lieutenants, with the Master, Boatswain, & Carpenter to Survey the Said potatoes, and Issue Certificate as Shall be just & honorable; and in case the Said Potatoes are in the State represented; I do hereby direct that they be immediately thrown overboard & into the Sea, but in case they Shou'd be found otherwise, that then and in that case they are to be served out agreeable to Law.

Given from under my hand on board the *Constellation* the 14th July 1798. —

THOMAS TRUXTUN.

To M[r] ISAAC GARRETSON

Purser of the U. S. Ship Constellation. —

We the Subscribers do Certify that the above Potatoes contain'd in Twenty & ¾ Bbl[s] are rotten and Unfit for men to eat, and that the Same was thrown into the Sea Conformable to the above order.

Signed —

JN[o] RODGERS, Lieu[t]
AMBROSE SHIRLEY, Master
JA[s] YEOMANS, Carp[r]
THO[s] GREEN, Boats[n]

[HS of Pa. NDA photostat. Truxtun's LB, 1798–9.]

To Secretary of Treasury from Secretary of Navy

[PHILADELPHIA,]
Navy Departm^t, 14. July, 1798.

SEC^y OF TREASURY

SIR Capt Price of the Revenue Cutter of ten Guns of this Place, informs Me that He is ready for Sea in all respects but the Want of Men. — He has 30 Men and 5 Boys. —

If you will be pleased to direct the proper Number of Men to be obtained; and will then turn her over to Me. I will endeavor to employ him usefully.

[NDA. Req. on US T, 1798–1803.]

Extract from Captain Thomas Truxtun's journal, U. S. Frigate *Constellation*, 14 July 1798, Saturday

Light Airs of Wind Southerly the first of this Sea Day; the Middle moderate and Northerly, and the latter, light, Easterly, with smooth Water, several Coasters in Company standing to the Westward.

People employed washing and cleaning the Ship; condemned a Number of Potatoes, that proved unfit for Men to eat, and hove the same into the Sea.

Cape Roman at Noon bore N. N. W. ½ West, 8 Leagues Distance, Depth of Water Thirteen Fathoms, fine grey Sand, Charleston Light House at same Time W. B. S. 19 Leagues.

Latitude observed 32°49′ N^o
Longitude Account 79.42 W.

[HS of Pa. NDA photostat.]

To Secretary of the Navy from Stephen Higginson, Navy Agent, Boston

BOSTON *July 15. 1798*

D^r SIR Capt Sever this moment mentions that you had intimated to him that you could no where find the force of the *Herald* stated. This I wonder at as I had mentioned in more than one Letter that she was to carry 16 six pounders, & six four pounders on quarter Deck & fore Castle; & Capt Sever has arranged to take 54 able Seamen, 26 ordinary, Sergeant Corporal two Musicians & 14 Marines, which with the commissioned & warrant Officers will make 128 in all. I seize the moment of the post going off to state this to you —

& remain respectfully your hum S^t

STEPHEN HIGGINSON

[NDA. Area 7, July 15, 1798.]

Extract from Captain Thomas Truxtun's journal, U. S. Frigate *Constellation*, 15 July 1798, Sunday

Light Winds Easterly all these Twenty four Hours, and sultry squally Weather. At 5 P M made Bulls Island from the Mast head bearing North West, Eight Leagues Distance. Gave chace to a Brig in the South South West, and fired several Shot to bring her to, but it coming on dark, and threatening to blow a Gale from the Eastward on Shore, add to our being in ten Fathoms Water, induced me to hawl the Wind to the South South East, particularly as the Brig was deep loaded, and standing in for the Bar of Charleston.

At Noon the Depth of Water was Twenty five Fathoms, Coarse Sand with black Specks, when Charleston Bar bore North West, Thirteen Leagues Distance.

Latitude was observed 32°.12′ N°
Longitude Account 80.06 W.

[HS of Pa. NDA photostat.]

Extract from the journal of Lieutenant James Mullowny, U. S. Frigate *United States*, 15 July 1798

Light wind, weather clear —
At 3 P. M. shorten'd sail for the ship *Delaware*
Set up Fore & Top mast rigging
At 5 A. M. set jib and Royals a sail in sight bearing N. E. at 6 A. M. set Main sail

Latt^de^ 38.34 N°

[NA.]

[16 July 1798.]

An act to make a further appropriation for the additional naval armament

SECTION 1. *Be it enacted by the Senate and House of Representatives of the United States of America in Congress assembled,* That the sum of six hundred thousand dollars shall be, and hereby is appropriated, to enable the President of the United States to cause to be built, and equipped, three ships or vessels, to be of a force not less than thirty-two guns each, and of the dimensions and model which he shall deem most advantageous for the public service, as part of the additional naval armament authorized by law.

SEC. 2. *And be it further enacted,* That the timber and other materials belonging to the United States proper for building and equipping the ships or vessels aforesaid, remaining in their several dock-yards, and elsewhere, may be employed under the direction of the President of the United States, in effecting the purposes of this act; or may be otherwise disposed of, as he shall think best. And the sum hereby appropriated, shall be paid out of any unappropriated money in the treasury.

Approved, July 16, 1798.

[Statute II, page 608.]

To Honorable James McHenry, Secretary of War, from Captain Thomas Truxtun, U. S. Navy

UNITED STATES SHIP, *Constellation,*
at Sea off Charleston Bar, July 16th 1798.

SIR, I have the Honor of transmitting to you by Post from Charleston, South Carolina, a Muster Roll, and Register, of the Officers, Seamen, and Others, composing the Crew of the Frigate, I command.

The Wages per Month, Money advanced, Time of Entry, and every Matter, and Thing, relating to that Business, that I considered necessary, to put on Record in the War Office, (or Marine Office, if such there be) is here mentioned, and stands correct.

The Returns made to you by the various Recruiting Officers, must from the Documents exhibited to me, have been very erroneous, owing to the Nature of the Business on the one Hand, and the Haste, in which it was done on the other, added to their Inexperience in such Employment.

I left the Capes of Chesapeake Bay on the 26th Ultimo (as before advised) with the Convoy, and parted with them, upwards of Twenty Leagues from Cape Henry, in an eastern Direction. The Wind soon after coming unfavourable to pass along the Southern Coast, near it's Shores, I stretched just without the Gulph Stream, as far as the Latitude of Bermudas, and then back again to the Northward, untill I crossed within the Stream, and made Cape Hatteras: Since which I have been cruizing along the Coast of North, and South Carolina, standing in to seven Fathoms Water, and off to Forty, without having been fortunate enough to meet any of the Enemy; I am therefore induced to believe, they keep off the Coast a considerable Distance. The Number of Coasters I have accompanied, along the Shores of the Carolinas, and the Merchantmen I have spoken, my Journal will show; having received no Intelligence of any Moment, it would be a Waste of Time to enumerate them here: I Shall pay Attention to the Coast of Georgia, and as far as our Southern Limits, and advise you, when Oppertunities offer, of whatever may occur of any Sort of Consequence.

I have a clean, healthy Ship, and have no Doubt, but in Case of Need, my Men will freely do their Duty. I have endeavoured to attach them to the naval Service, by mild Treatment, and rigid Justice.

The Ship behaves well in all Sorts of Weather, and sails fast, but from being caulked in the Winter, her upper Works are open.

I have the Honor to be, Sir, with great Respect and Esteem —

Your very Obedient, humble Servant —

THOMAS TRUXTUN.

Honble JAMES McHENRY
Secretary of War

N B. The papers that Accompany the above letter & Register of Seamen are Lieutenants recruiting Instructions and their Accounts Relating to that business. —

T. T.

[HS of Pa. NDA photostat. Truxtun's LB, 1798–9.]

To Chief Clerk Caldwell, War Deparment, from Secretary of State Pickering

[PHILADELPHIA,]
Department of State July 16th 1798.

Mr JOHN CALDWELL
Chief Clerk in the Department of War

SIR, There being an immediate call for cannon shot to be laden on board the armed vessels destined for Algiers, I have to request that an order may be made out to be signed by me in behalf of the Secretary of War, for the following, viz,

9 pound round shot	1804.
18 d° d°	635
6 pound bar Shot	663
9 pound d°	306
12 d° d°	854
18 d° d°	538

Which I will cause to be replaced or paid for out of the funds for the affairs of Barbary. I am, Sir, &c.

TIMOTHY PICKERING

[SDA. Dom. L., Vol. 11.]

To Joshua Sands, Collector, New York, from Secretary Pickering

DEPARTMENT OF STATE *July 16th 1798.*

JOSHUA SANDS Esq.
Collector of the Customs, New York

SIR, On the 14th I received from M. Rozier late vice-Consul of the French Republic at New-York, a letter mentioning "a difficulty that had arisen at the Custom House there from the law prohibiting all *commercial* intercourse with France and its dependencies." It was a question, whether this prohibition "should extend to the part of St Domingo ceded to France by her treaty of peace with Spain, but of which the possession is yet in the hands of the Spanish Government?" And if the answer to this question were in the affirmative, he requested the permission to clear out a flag of truce (ún parlementairé) for the port of santo Domingo, with French passengers. Such a permission I now inclose to you. The blanks for the owners name, and the first name of the master you will fill up; and be pleased to transmit those names to me, that the copy of the permit may also be rendered compleat. This was the Shortest way of answering M. Rozier. But the question he has stated is important. I shall confer with the Treasury department on the subject. It appears indispensably necessary to stop the commercial intercourse with the Spanish as well as with the French part of St Domingo, or the latter will not answer the views of Congress in the general prohibition. It will also I believe be literally correct. Fortunately in reading this morning a French newspaper ("Bulletin Officielle de Saint-Domingue") printed at Cape Francois the 17th of June last, I met with an arret of Hedouville, particular agent of the Executive Directory, to abolish the duty or tax imposed on the beasts drawn from the part *heretofore* Spanish, on their entry into the French part of St Domingo: — "droit sur les animaux tirés de la partie *ci-devant Espagnole*, á lour entrée dans la partie Française de l'isle de Saint-Domingue." This expression of the agent seems to me sufficient to settle the question. I have the honor, &c

TIMOTHY PICKERING

[SDA. Dom. L., Vol. 11.]

To William Bartlett, Newbury Port, from Secretary of Navy

[PHILADELPHIA,]
Navy Department 16th. July 1798

Wm BARTLETT Esqr
Newbury Port

SIR I am honored with the receipt of your favor of the 9th Instant, with its enclosures, and am happy to perceive the celerity contemplated in the Equipment of the Ship, undertaken to be built at your Port — The very honorable Testimony you are pleas'd to give in favour of the character & abilities of Capt Moses Brown, naturally induces an acquiescence with the wishes of the Committee in this respect, and that Gent^{n} will of course be mentioned to the President with a view to his being commissioned for the purpose — You will please to inform me, how soon the Copper will be wanted, in order that it may be got in readiness, as I observe you intend to prepare for a copper Bottom; no doubt you will direct that the Bolts be of that Metal —

The President wishes the Inhabitants of Newbury Port to be convinced of the high Sense he entertains of their Patriotic exertions on this Occasion — Altho' from their long established character for Patriotism, less coud not be expected —

[NDA. GLB, Vol. 1.]

To Jacob Sheafe, Navy Agent, Portsmouth, N. H., from Secretary of Navy

[PHILADELPHIA,]
Navy Department 16th July 1798

JACOB SHEAFE Esqr
Portsmouth (N. H.)

SIR, Congress have just passed an Act, appropriating money for finishing the Frigate at Portsmouth, as well as the two others at New York & Norfolk — My own opinion is, that while the practice continues, of building our Ships at a number of places, the public Interest will be best promoted, by putting the entire direction into the hands of inteligent Merchants of great respectability of character; — under this impression, and wishing that the whole power, and of course the whole responsibility, respecting the Frigate begun at Portsmouth, should be with you, I have the honor to request, that you will without delay take such measures as you shall judge best to compleat this vessel, with the greatest dispatch and the greatest Occonomy — attending no further to former arrangements than you think, for the public Interest — Knowing that Col^{o} Hackett, the former constructor has contracted to build a Ship for the Public in a short time, I presume you will not be able to get him so soon as the Public exigencies may require, and may therefore be under the necessity of engaging a constructor of less established character —

The live-Oak & other Timber landed at Portsmouth, particularly the other Timber, I fear has been so much pillaged that but little remains — The White Oak Timber I presume can be easily replaced, not so the Live Oak — and it will be very unfortunate if much of it has been pillaged —

It will be necessary that you should as quickly as possible, have it ascertained, what live oak Timber will be wanted — What Boston can supply, and that you make immediate arrangements to procure the plank & White Oak Timber — There is some Live Oak Timber here — perhaps at Portsmouth, Boston & this place there may be enough to supply all the Timber essential to be of the Live Oak — Good White Oak will do for the Floor Timbers; and also the lower Futtocks, if Live Oak cannot be got — The sooner you can inform me what live oak Timber you want, which Boston cannot supply, the sooner Measures can be taken to provide it from here or elsewhere —

I have written to Mr Caleb Gibbs at Boston, who has the care of the Timber there, to furnish you with an account of what remains on hand — Money shall be remitted on your requisitions — You must take care to make them in time —

[NDA. GLB, Vol. 1.]

Extract from the journal of Lieutenant John Mullowny, U. S. Frigate *United States*, 16 July 1798

Light winds, weather clear

Spoke the *Delaware*, spoke a schooner from New providence to Boston

Reefed Topsails, 2 Reefs in each
up courses.

Three sail in sight, bore away for the Largest & found her to be the British 50 Gun Ship *Asistance* Capt Hardy

Cloudy weather, Rain.

[Lat^de^ p^r^ Acc^t^ 39.58]

[NA.]

Extract from Captain Thomas Truxtun's journal, U. S. Frigate *Constellation*, 16 July 1798, Monday

Light Airs, and variable the first and Middle; the latter a moderate Breeze from South South West, to West South West.

At 2 P M saw a Sail to the Northward, Gave Chace, and at 6 ditto spoke the Schooner *Peggy* from Martinica, bound to Charleston; this Vessel parted with a British Convoy bound Home from the Windward Islands in Latitude 23 North, and Longitude 65 W. since which has seen no Vessel of War of any Sort.

At 9 A M made the Southern Part of the Land, on which the Light House of Charleston stands, having at the same Time 10 & ¼ Fathoms Water, fine white Sand. Tacked and stood to the Southward.

Latitude observed 32°.20′ N^o^
Longitude Account 80.30 W.

[HS of Pa. NDA photostat.]

[17 July 1798.]

Agreement between John T. Morgan and Thomas FitzSimons re timber for Frigate *Philadelphia*

The agreement made at Philadelphia on the 17th day of July one thousand seven hundred and Ninety eight between Thomas Fitz-Simons chairman of the Frigate Committee on the one part an John T. Morgan on the other part —

WITNESSETH that the said John T. Morgan for the consideration herein after mentioned doth agree to deliver to the order of the aforesaid Committee at this port of Philadelphia on or before the 1st day of November next the Quantity of live Oak timber specified in the list A annex'd hereto, and on or before the 1st day of December next at the port of New York the live Oak timber specified in the list B likewise annexed, which said timber shall be sound & good agreeable to the dimensions therein mentioned and as near to the shape according to the Moulds as such Timber is usually obtained, all which timber shall be so delivered at the proper cost and charge of the said John T. Morgan — In consideration whereof the said Thomas FitzSimons in behalf of the Committee doth agree to pay the said John T. Morgan or his Assigns the rate of Seventy five cents for every Cubic foot of timber so delivered agreeably to the measurements which shall be made at the time of delivery — AND it is further agreed between the said parties that in case any part of the timber shipped in pursuance of this agreement shall be lost in the transportation by danger of the Sea or by capture — that the said John T. Morgan shall be allowed the further term of three Months from the time herein before mentioned to replace such loss — AND for the due performance of this agreement the parties bind themselves that is to say Thomas FitzSimons doth bind the Frigate Committee and the said John T. Morgan doth bind himself his Heirs, Executors, Administrators and Assigns in the penal sum of Two thousand Dollars to be paid by the party defaulting to the party complying —

Signed

JOHN T. MORGAN.
THOS FITZSIMONS
C. F. C.

JULY 17th 1798
Copy—John T. Morgan Contract.

[Enclosure]

List A to be delivered at Philadelphia

45 lower Futtocks 18 feet long sided to 11½ Inches
86 middle do 14½ do 11 inches
50 upper do 14 feet long to side 11 do
20 Top timbers 14 feet long " " 11 do
2 Corner counter timbers
2 common -----do------
2 Knights heads —
1 Stern post 25 feet long 18 square at the head and as large fore and aft at the heel as can be got —
1 Main transom 25½ feet long to square when worked 18 inches

List B to be delivered at New York

103 first Futtocks
63 second do
98 third do
129 top timbers
8 fore lower Cants
8 fore upper ditto
8 Diagonal riders
6 Mast partners
4 Counter timbers
6 Hawse pieces
4 half timbers
22 Staunchins
1 Stem piece
1 Apron do

NB Top timbers moulded at the Gunwale 7 inches, at the port cill 9 inches, all the other timbers sized by a diminishing line from the port cill to the Hoorsumark which is 14½ inches —

14 floor raising timbers for breast hooks Step for Masts &c
24 Cant timbers aft that is 1st Futtocks 2d Foothooks 3d Foothooks & top timbers — 145 Knees.

[NDA. AC, 1798–1808, various statements, frigate *Philadelphia.*]

To Messrs. Gibbs & Channing, agents, Newport, R. I., from Secretary of Navy

[PHILADELPHIA,]
Navy Department July 17th 1798

Messrs GIBBS & CHANNING
Newport (R. I.)

GENTn Your esteemed favour of the 10th Instant is received, and I am well pleased to find, that you agree to accept the Agency for the public, and will attend to the compleat equipment of the Ship in question — It is of importance that the Bolts to be used shoud be of Copper, for it is found that a vessel bolted with Iron & then coppered will not last more than three years, as the copper corrodes, and soon destroys the Iron — I shall therefore take measures for sending on the copper, the nails and the Bolts, and should Iron Bolts be made use of before these arrive, they must be extracted and the others substituted — I had Intended to consent to the mode of Sheathing and coppering pointed out by you, but have now decided that it will be better to adopt the usual method, and use flannel soaked in Tar, on which the Copper will be placed. —

As you will be likely soon to want Spikes & Bolts, I intend in the course of two or three days to send you about 150 lbs — and if no better conveyance offers they shall be sent by one of the Land Stages — The residue will be sent you very speedily —

With regard to the several enquiries contained in your Letter, you shall receive a full reply in a few days —

[NDA. GLB, Vol. 1.]

To James Watson, Navy Agent, New York, from Secretary of Navy

[PHILADELPHIA,]
Navy Department July 17th 1798

JAMES WATTSON Esqr.
New York

SIR Believing that so long as the present system continues of procuring our Ships of War at different places, and not more than one or two at a place, the Public Interest will be promoted by giving the entire direction of the Business to Merchants of Intelligence & great respectability of Character I have the honor to request that you will take under your management the Frigate, the Keel of which was laid so long ago in New York — attending no more to former arrangements, than you shall Judge proper, and employing such men to complete her, as you shall think best qualified — I mean that the whole direction & the whole responsibility shall be with you, requiring only your attention to three things — That the Frigate be well built, that She be finished with the greatest possible dispatch — and with the greatest practicable Occonomy —

I will in a day or two, have an acct furnished of what live Oak Timber wanted for the Frigate at New York, can be supply'd from this place — The rest must be got from Georgia — No Time should be lost in engaging the plank, & White Oak Timber, wanted — and every proper means shou'd be used to give it every chance of durability — Money shall be furnished to your requisitions — you must take care to make them in season —

[NDA. GLB, Vol. 1.]

Extract from Captain Thomas Truxtun's journal, U. S. Frigate *Constellation*, 17 July 1798, Tuesday

The Beginning light Winds from the South West, stood in towards the Bar of Charleston, untill half past 4 PM when we were in one quarter less Eight Fathoms, and near to it's Latitude, but the Weather was so hazy, could not see the Land, tho' our Distance from it could not have been more than four Leagues; at 5 Ditto saw a Pilot Boat with her Colours flying, and standing towards us, but a Brig being in Sight, to which I gave Chace, did not bring to for the Boat; at half past six, it came on to blow hard from South South West, I thought it prudent, as we were still in the above Depth of Water to hawl off to the South East by the Wind, particularly as the Brig we were in Chace of, had just come over the Bar, and must of Course be a Friend. At 7 in double Reefs in the Top Sails, and in Main Sail. At 2 AM it became more moderate, and the Depth of Water being 40 Fathoms, tacked and stood in towards the Land, untill 11 Ditto, when we got twelve Fathoms, then stood off, untill Noon, when I laid her Head in Shore again, there being little Wind, since we tacked, and the Depth the same, white and black Sand. Charleston Bar at Noon bore West B. North 3/4 North, Distance 7 Leagues.

Latitude observed 32°. 35′ Nº
Longitude Account 80.17 W.

[HS of Pa. NDA photostat.]

To Mr. Létombe, late French Consul-General, from Secretary Pickering

DEPARTMENT OF STATE *July 18, 1798.*

Mr LÉTOMBE,
late Consul General of the French Republic

SIR, I have received your letter of the 15th and have the honor to inform you, that the President of the United States, assents to your request, of being permitted to continue the performance of the business stated in your letter, of giving certificates to your fellow citizens, and removing them in flags of truce from the U. States to the dominions of France. The same permission is extended to your colleagues. But no definite time can be fixed when these permissions shall cease; it must be governed by circumstances. It will be expedient to use all reasonable expedition in your operations.

I am, Sir, Your Most Obdt Servant.

TIMOTHY PICKERING

[SDA. Dom. L., Vol. 11.]

To N. Hubbard, Middleton, Conn., from Secretary of Navy

[PHILADELPHIA,]
Navy Department July 18th 1798

Mr N. HUBBARD
Middleton, Connt

SIR Mr Seth Overton arrived this morning and handed me your letter of the 14th in reply to mine of the 10th Inst — We have had much conversation on the subject, the result of which is, that I now authorize you to contract with him for the Ship in question, at any

ARRÊTÉ

Contenant des Dispositions relatives aux Bâtimens neutres destinés pour les Ports français de Saint-Domingue.

Extrait du Registre des Délibérations de l'Agence du Directoire exécutif à Saint-Domingue.

L'AGENCE du Directoire exécutif, arrête :

ARTICLE PREMIER.

Les Bâtimens neutres et par conséquent Américains, chargés de comestibles ou de marchandises sèches, continueront à être admis dans les Ports français de Saint-Domingue.

II.

Il ne sera pris au compte de l'Administration qu'une partie des comestibles, laquelle sera payée de suite en denrées coloniales, au cours, et en compensation des droits d'importation et d'exportation.

Les Armateurs auront le libre débit des marchandises sèches.

III.

Ces Bâtimens ne pourront être saisis par les vaisseaux de guerre et corsaires de la République, lorsque leur destination sera évidemment pour un des Ports français de Saint-Domingue restés fidelles à la République, même en cas d'hostilités entre la République et une des puissances actuellement Neutre.

Le présent arrêté sera imprimé, lu, publié, affiché, adressé aux Juges de Paix et Commissaires du Directoire exécutif, près les Administrations municipales des cantons maritimes, à tous les Consuls et Agens de la République, près les puissances Neutres ou Alliées, lesquels sont invités à lui donner la plus grande publicité ; il sera en outre inséré dans le Bulletin Officiel de Saint-Domingue.

Fait au Cap, le 30 Messidor, l'an sixième de la République française, une et indivisible.

Signé, au registre des procès-verbaux, l'Agent particulier du Directoire exécutif, T. HEDOUVILLE ; le Secrétaire général de l'Agence, GAUTHIER.

Pour copie conforme,

Le Secrétaire général de l'Agence.

Signé GAUTHIER.

ORDER ISSUED BY THE SAN DOMINGO AGENTS OF THE FRENCH EXECUTIVE DIRECTORY, RELATIVE TO NEUTRAL VESSELS BOUND FOR SANTO DOMINGO, DATED 18 JULY 1798.

price, not exceeding 30½ Dollars per Ton, and deliverable at any time previous to the 15th of November next —

He promises that she shall be built of the best materials, and finished, at or before that period — You will have a regular contract drawn & executed, as soon after his return as possible — wherein you will keep in view, the above limits & the several particulars mentioned in my Letter of the 10th Instant, and add any others that you may consider for the Interest of the United States — This Ship must have an orlope, by which is meant a compleat Spar, Deck

You will have to make a seperate contract for the Iron Work, with whoever will execute it on the best Terms — Mr Overton has some Idea of engaging for this also, and I see no objection, provided you are of opinion that he will have the work performed as good & as cheap as another

Care must be taken in drawing the contract to guard against, the United States being exposed to any chance of having the Ship delivered at any place, from whence, it may be impracticable or even difficult to get her out to sea when compleated — You will please to recollect that dispatch is essential — She must be got into Operation, early this Winter, if possible, and you will lend your attention to this point, in doing which, you will have the satisfaction of rendering a Service to the United States — The limits to which you are authorized to extend this Contract, are liberal, and I hope the consequence will be, that they will produce a capital Ship to the Government —

The rule for measurement here is, To take the length from one foot afore the Rabbit of Stem at the upper Edge of the second strake of Wale, to the after part of the Wing Transam, and deduct from it the ⅗ of the moulded breadth of Beam for Rake of Stem and 2–½ Inches for every foot the Wing Transam is above the Rabbit of Keel for the Rake of Post — The remainder is the length of Keel — for Tonnage — multiply the Keel for Tonnage by the moulded breadth of Beam — and divide the sum by 95 gives the Tonnage —

[NDA. GLB, Vol. 1.]

Extract from Captain Thomas Truxtun's journal, U. S. Frigate *Constellation*, 18 July 1798, Wednesday

Light Winds from the South South West, and hazy Weather. At 3 PM saw the Land, and Light House of Charleston, bearing West B. North, four Leagues Distance, Depth of Water Eight Fathoms, coarse black and white Sand; Tacked and stood to the South East, the Evening squally, the Morning fine Weather; stood off to Twenty Eight Fathoms Water, and in again to seven, when we made the Land, a little to the Northward of the Bar of Charleston. Several Sail in Sight, two of which we chaced to Windward. Charleston Bar at Noon bore West B. South, half South, 5 Leagues Distance.

Latitude observed 32°. 46′ N°
Longitude Account 80.23 W.

[HS of Pa. NDA photostat.]

Extract from the journal of Lieutenant John Mullowny, U. S. Frigate *United States*, 18 July 1798

Light winds, Top Gallant sails down waiting for the *Delaware*
Spoke the *Delaware* and made sail
Sounded, 35 fathm, red sand.
At 1 again 32 D° D°
At 4 again 32 D° D°
At ½ 6 spoke the *Delaware*. Foggy
More clear Spoke a brig of & bound to Kennebunk.
[Lattd Obsd 41.7]

[NA.]

To Archibald Campbell, Baltimore, from Secretary of Navy

[PHILADELPHIA,]
Navy Department July 19th 1798

ARCHd CAMPBELL Esqr *Baltimore*

SIR, You must pardon me, for not attending to your last Letter — You can form no Idea how much I have been engaged. —

The purport of this, is to request, that the two vessels building by the Merchants for the public, may be constructed for 18 Guns — The number of the Ships 20 to 24 Guns is engaged, or within one — & that one will probably be furnish'd at Norfolk — As to a draft, and every thing relating to these Vessels, the subject is as well understood at Baltimore as here — It is desirable, that they should be fine Sailors, so as to suffer nothing to escape them, & to be taken by nothing — This can be done at Baltimore, if any where — You know the Genls Hamilton, Pinckney & Knox. Majr Generals–Lee & Hand, ditto in the Provincial Army — Some demur in the Senate about the Brigadiers. —

[NDA. GLB, Vol. 1.]

To Joseph Anthony from Secretary of Navy

[PHILADELPHIA,]
Navy Department 19th July 1798

Mr JOSEPH ANTHONY

SIR I am much obliged to you for the perusal of the Letter from Providence — I am sorry the Gentlemen of that place should think the Town neglected by the officers of Government — When I entered upon the duties of my office, the business having before commence, I really thought all the offers of Ships handed over to me, had been acted upon — I found too an opinion prevailing, that New Ships had better be built; — and that the public had made bad bargains in their purchases — Hence my attention has been directed entirely to New Ships — for the few of those which the appropriations would enable me to contract. I have endeavoured to get them, where they could be supply'd most speedily — I was not well acquainted with Providence, — The Ships so far as I can venture, are all, I beleive contracted for, at least as far as the appropriations will go — Three Ships of 18 Guns still remain to be procured, and these it is hoped will be furnished by the contributions of the Merchants, in different places — If Providence should build part of one of those Ships, I wou'd try to save at least 10,000 Doll[s] of the appropriated money, towards assisting in the Business — I wish you could bring this about, through your correspondents. —

[NDA. GLB, Vol. 1.]

To Captain George Price, Revenue Cutter *General Greene*, from Secretary of Navy

[PHILADELPHIA,]
Navy Departm[t] 19 July 1798

Cap[t] GEORGE PRICE
Cutter *Gen[l] Green.*

SIR, The Cutter, *General Green*, of Ten four Pound Guns, under your Command, being now equipped for a Cruise — I have enclosed your Authority to capture French armed Vessels wherever to be found — You will immediately proceed to Sea, and endeavour to fall in with the *Ganges* Cap[t] Dale, and the Cutter, *Governor Jay*, Cap[t] Leonard — This latter Vessel I expect will leave New York Tomorrow, & will fall in with Cap[t] Dale, somewhere off Sandy Hook — but it is possible, that Cap[t] Dale may not have received my Instructions to this Effect — in which Case, You and the Cutter *Gov. Jay*, will cruise together until you fall in with Cap[t] Dale, which you will do somewhere between Cape Henry & Long Island, being his Cruising Ground — and when You fall in with him, you will consider Yourself under his Command — Wishing you a great deal of Success & honor, I am &c.

For Instructions See Page 98.

[NOTE.—Page 98 contains instructions to commanders of armed vessels, at Philadelphia, 10 July 1798, included in this volume.]
[NDA. OSW, Vol. 1.]

To Captain Richard Dale, U. S. Navy, from Secretary of Navy

[PHILADELPHIA,]
Navy department 19 July. 1798.

RICH[d] DALE.

SIR, In my last of 13th Ins[t] I enclosed your Authority to capture French armed Vessels, whereever found — and the Act of Congress upon which that Authority was founded. I also informed you that the Cutter *Gov[r] Jay*, Cap[t] Leonard would be ready to sail from New York the 20th Ins[t] — an requested you would be about Sandy Hook at that Time and take her under your Command. — Cap[t] Price of the Cutter *Gen[l] Green*, 10 four Pounders, has orders to join you as quickly as possible — With this Vessel & the Cutter of 14 Guns from New York, your force will be formidable to any Thing likely to come from the West Indies — You will therefore allow Yourself a larger Field & go further to Sea — & pay some Attention to the Neighbourhood of Bermudas; still however, keeping in View, that the Protection of the Coast from Long Island to Cape Henry is your principal Object. & must not be lost sight of — It will still be desireable to communicate with you as often as Occasion may require from

Delaware — When you come in the Coast in that direction, you will hover about for a day, that Pilot Boats, which may be dispatched from hence, may fall in with you. — We have no News, The Appointments of Generals in our Army, are now taking Place — & preparations making to strengthen Ourselves at Sea. —

[NDA. OSW. Vol. 1.]

To Captain John Leonard, Revenue Cutter *Governor Jay,* from Secretary of Navy

[PHILADELPHIA,]
Navy Departmt 19. July. 1798

Capt Jno LEONARD
Rev. Cutter Governor Jay. New York.

SIR, By an arrangement with the Secretary of the Treasury, the Cutters as soon as prepared for Sea, are to be put under the direction of the Navy Department. I am informed, that the *Govr Jay,* under your Command, of 14 Guns, will be prepared for Sea, tomorrow. In consequence of which I now enclose you Authority for capturing armed Vessels sailing under Authority or pretence of Authority from the French Republic, wherever found. — Capt Dale in the Ship *Ganges,* has orders to be near the Hook, about the 20th Inst with whom you will endevaour to fall in, as early as possible, & under whose Command you will cruise. —

His Cruising Ground extends from Long Island to Cape Henry — You will if he should not be at the Hook, endeavour to find him — Wishing you great Success & honor I am &c.

[NDA. OSW, Vol. 1.]

Extract from the journal of Lieutenant John Mullowny, U. S. Frigate *United States,* 19 July 1798

Light wind clear weather.
Fresh breeze
Rain, hoisted a light for the ship *Delaware*
Sounded every hour in the night 80 fathoms no bottom.
At 10 A. M. made the land W dist 5 or 6 Leagues
Spoke a fishing schooner, who told us the Land in Sight was Cape Cod.
Clear weather beating up the Bay.
[Latde Obsd 42.7]

[NA.]

Extract from Captain Thomas Truxtun's journal, U. S. Frigate *Constellation,* 19 July 1798, Thursday

Fresh Gales all these 24 Hours, the first Part from South South West, to South West; the latter from North, to North North East, and throughout, the Weather has been very squally, and uncertain with an Abundance of Rain, Lightning and Thunder. At 2 PM spoke a Ship, that had left the Bar of Charleston two Hours before, bound to Malaga, and a Schooner that came out at half past 10 AM bound to Cadiz. I wished them well, and stood to the South East, double reefed the Top Sails, took in the Main Sail, Jib, and Mizen Top Sail, and at 8 PM hawled up the Fore Sail.

At 4 AM wore and stood to the Westward, at 10 Ditto saw a Sail in the North North West, gave Chace, and at 11 Ditto brought her to with a Shot, she proved to be the Brig *Eliza* from Boston bound to Savannah; this Vessel had seen no Cruizer, except the British Ship *Resolution* of 74 Guns off Cape Henry. Charleston Bar at Noon bore W. B. N. eleven Leagues Distance, Depth of Water twenty Fathoms, Stones with coarse Sand, and Shells; the Bottom having a greenish Appearance.

Latitude observed 32°.35′ N°
Longitude Account 80.00 W.

[HS of Pa. NDA photostat.]

Men recruited for Frigate *Constitution*, 1798

[July 19, 1798.]

The United States
Dr to John B. Cordis.

For cash advanced sundry seamen recruited for the U. S. Frigate Constitution, viz.

Dates 1798	Men's Names		Money Advanced
May 31	James Hoyt,	Seaman	$36. "
June 4	William Salisbury	Seaman	26. 50
	James Carter	d°	36. "
	James Wall	d°	34. "
	William Botsford	d°	34. "
	Richard Walter	d°	34. "
	Andrew Mellings	d°	34. "
	John Lewis	d°	26. "
	William Osborn	Ordinary Seaman	24. "
5	John Hunt	d°	20. "
6	Sam! Oakes	Carpenters mate	36. "
July 19	Henry Dillaway	Steward	36. "
	Isaac Hooton [or Hoston]	Ordinary Seaman	20. "
	Nathan Crooker	Seaman	34. "
	William Jones	d°	34. "
	Roger Bainard	Ordinary Seaman	20. "
	John Robinson	Seaman	34. "
	Dennis Carney	d°	21. "
	William Smith	Ordinary Seaman	20. "
	William Brooks	Seaman	34. "
8	Joseph Baker	quartermaster	36. "
9	John Sawyer	d°	26. "
	Anthony Josephus	Ordinary Seaman	20. "
11	William Armstrong	d°	5. "
	John Holston	Seaman	34. "
	Henry Kirk	d°	34. "
	Thomas Evens	Ordinary Seaman	20. "
12	Peter Pero	d°	10. "
	Ezekiel Davis	d°	20. "
	Edward Sidons	d°	20. "
	James Patersons	Seaman	" "
	Daniel Davis	Ordinary Seaman	20. "
13	Robert Kemble	d°	34. "
	David Knitmyer	Seaman	34. "
	John P. Mack	Midshipman	40. "

For cash advanced sundry seamen recruited for the U. S. Frigate Constitution, viz—
Continued

Dates 1798	Men's Names		Money Advanced
July 13	John Copeland	Boatswains Mate	$36. "
	John Caruth	Seaman	34. "
	Daniel Spriggs	Ordinary Seaman	12. "
	Henry Collins	Seaman	34. "
	George Jenkins	Seaman	38. "
	Levi Dodge	d°	39. "
	John Smith	Seaman	34. "
	Peter Swan	d°	34. "
	John Marshall	Ordinary Seaman	34. "
July 13	John Gay	Seaman	34. "
	Samuel Cavilier	d°	34. "
	Henry Burnett	d°	36. "
	William McCullock	d°	34. "
19	William Morris	d°	26. "
	John Gendall	Ordinary Seaman	20. "
	John Hancock	Seaman	22. "
	Matthew Wake	Ordinary Seaman	20. "
	Richard Williams	Seaman	34. "
	Edward West	d°	30. "
	Thomas Bumford	d°	34. "
	Andrew Robb	Ordinary Seaman	20. "
	Thomas Cole	Seaman	36. "
	Cornelius Howard	Ordinary Seaman	4. "
	James Norris	Seaman	20. "
	Archibald Thompson	d°	36. "
	Jacob Libby	Carpenter	50. "
	John Robson	Seaman	30. "
	John Pearce	Ordinary Seaman	25. "
	William Ray	Seaman	28. 25
	William Taylor	d°	34. "
	Thomas Hall	Ordinary Seaman	20. "
	Richard Blaw	Seaman	34. "
	John Shepherd	d°	25. "
	William Grant	Ordinary Seaman	10. "
	Joseph Fort	Seaman	21. "
	John Hardy	d°	34. "
	Samuel Harvey	Ordinary Seaman	32. "
	James Moore	Seaman	38. "
	Charles Major	d°	6. "
	William Felt	Sail Maker	42. "
	Josh Poland [or Voland]	Armourers Mate	28. "
	Philemon Noble	Ordinary Seaman	5. "
	Richard Nickells	Seaman	34. "
	John Essenburgh	d°	36. "
	John Doyle	d°	34. "
	Joseph Torrey	Gunner	40. "
	William Grimes	Seaman	34. "
	John Hendrickin	Ordinary Seaman	18. "
	Thomas Williams	Seaman	34. "
	Adam Nutt	d°	38. "
	Josiah Chase	d°	34. "
	William Coolidge	Ordinary Seaman	11. "
	William Fulkes	Seaman	36. "
	Moses Burchard	d°	36. "
	John Smith	Ordinary Seaman	10. "
	Simeon Wyman.	Steward	30. "
	John Swins	Seaman	18. "
	Isaac Wendale	Ordinary Seaman	20. "
	Richard Collins	d°	20. "

For cash advanced sundry seamen recruited for the U. S. Frigate Constitution, viz—Continued

Dates	Men's Names		Money Advanced
1798			
July 19	Peter Crosby	Master's mate	$40. "
	Benjamin Davis	Seaman	34. "
	Isaac Stevens	Ordinary Seaman	20. "
	Michael Cosgrave	d°	20. "
July	Gideon Hunt	Seaman	23. 50
	John Landen	d°	34. "
	Arch^d McDougale	quarter master	36. "
	Jacob Phelps	Ordinary Seaman	20. "
	Benjamin Butler	d°	20. "
	David Fry	d°	20. "
	William Pearce	d°	20. "
	James Hincks	d°	20. "
	John Lewis	d°	20. "
	James Neale	Seaman	38. 30
	George Murrey	d°	34. "
	Francis Vassure	Ordinary Seaman	20. "
	Edmund Flinn	Ordinary Seaman	20. "
	Johiel Earle	d°	10. "
	Charles Hodge	d°	12. "
	James Connell	Boatswain	45. "
	John Abbott	Ordinary Seaman	20. "
	Alex^r McCabe	d°	10. "
	Job Foster	Seaman	23. "
	George Brown	d°	35. "
	William Cox	Ordinary Seaman	20. "
	Charles Sand	Seaman	37. 50
	Henry Phelps	Ordinary Seaman	10. "
	Thomas Pitts	d°	20. "
	James McLaughlin	d°	10. "
Twice	Ezekiel Davis	d°	20. "
	Rufus Norton	d°	20. "
	John Wilson	Seaman	34. "
	William Mahany	d°	36. "
	Fra^s McKinsey	Ordinary Seaman	14. "
	William Schofield	Seaman	34. "
	Thomas Smith	d°	34. "
	Oliver Algers	d°	34. "
	Henry Barns	d°	34. "
	Robert Corbett	d°	28. "
	Christopher Kerling	d°	29. "
	Joseph Hemmingway	Ordinary Seaman	20. "
	John Philbrook	Carpenters mate	36. "
	Thomas Webb		6. "
	James Cary	Seaman	36. "
	John Haley	d°	34. "
	Hugh Burns	Ordinary Seaman	9. 10
	Beth Hamilton		5. "
	John Swain	Seaman	34. "
	Masquerade, John	d°	34. "
	William Hamilton	d°	23. 30
	John Green	Ordinary Seaman	20. "
	Joseph Cutts	Seaman	19. 50
	Patrick Reed	Ordinary Seaman	10. "
July	John Donolly	Ordinary Seaman	17. "
	George Horn	Seaman	17. "
	Hugh Birch	Ordinary Seaman	7. "
	Clark Cushman	d°	16. "
	Joseph Jeffries	Seaman	34. "
	Benjamin Hazer	d°	34. "
	John Thompson	d°	17. "
	John Willing	d°	34. "

For cash advanced sundry seamen recruited for the U. S. Frigate Constitution, viz—Continued

Dates	Men's Names		Money Advanced
1798			
July	Ja[s] Featherstone	Master's mate	$17. "
	Philip Solomon	Ordinary Seaman	20. "
	William Hall	d°	10. "
	John Maisden	Seaman	26. "
	Ja[s] Perkins	Sail Maker's mate	36. "
	Sam[l] Bailey	Cook	16. "
	John Brown	Ordinary Seaman	20. "
	William Hutchins	Seaman	34. "
	James Dronne	Ordinary Seaman	11. "
	John Osmant	d°	20. "
	Edward Durnant	Master's mate	40. "
	John Dade	d°	41. "
	Robert Hilman	Ordinary Seaman	31. 25
	William Collins	Seaman	31. "
	John N. Smith	d°	33. 50
	Thomas Welsh	d°	34. "
	David Armstrong	d°	17. "
	John McDonald	d°	34. "
	Thomas Nelson	d°	20. "
	Caleb Hogg	Acting Midshipman	20. "
	Tom Woodman	Seaman	34. "
	Rufus Blanden	Ordinary Seaman	11. "
	James Bates	d°	8. 50
	Charles Caton	Seaman	10. "
	William Shaw		9. 50
	John Swinney	Quartermaster	36. "
	James Watson	Seaman	34. "
	James Walter	d°	34. "
	John Aldbro	Ordinary Seaman	13. 25
	Philip Sutton	Seaman	3. 50
	Sharp Gardiner	Cook	6. 50
	Henry Brown	Seaman	30. "
	Amos Larcom	Ordinary Seaman	8. 75
	William Holland	Seaman	40. 50
	Anthonio Francisco	d°	18. 67
	Robert Sharkey	Ordinary Seaman	5. "
	Will Coffin	Quarter Master	. . . . .
	Peter Sancree	Ordinary Seaman	20. "
	Thomas April	d°	20. "
	James Jackson	d°	10. "
	John Lamson	Capt[s] Clerk	25. "
	Joseph Copeland	Seaman	30. "
July	Artemas Harrington	Seaman	10. "
	Valentine Hickey	Ordinary Seaman	20. "
	Will[m] McMacklin	Cooper	36. 50
	Thomas Moody	Ordinary Seaman	20. "
	John Mahany	Seaman	34. "
	Joseph Norris	Ordinary Seaman	20. "
	Samuel Phillips	Seaman	40. 50
	Thomas Spells	Seaman	25. "
	Barnard Truman		36. "
	Samuel Wilson		20. "
	Henry Johnson		20. "
			$5, 300. 87

Errors Excepted

J. B. Cordis.

Account of J. B. Cordis Recruiting Officer 1798.

N B. There will be observed in the above account a very considerable difference between that & the one formerly forwarded to the Accountants Office which arises in consequence of my having lost a part of the original account — but I presume the Accountant will be so good as to correct the former by the present & vis a vis by which it will stand right.

J. B. CORDIS.

[NDA. NR, Men recruited by J. B. Cordis, for *Constitution*, 1798.]

To James Watson, Navy Agent, New York, from Secretary of Navy

[PHILADELPHIA,]
Navy Department July 20th 1798

JAS WATSON Esqr *New York*

SIR I fear you will find me a very troublesome correspondent — Two Ships are building for the public, — one at Newport, R. I., under the direction of Messrs Gibbs & Channing, One at Middleton, Connecticut River under the direction of Nehemiah Hubbard for which Copper Bolts are immediately wanted. Indeed I am apprehensive the Ship at Newport is now waiting for them — I understand these kind of Bolts — can be immediately obtained in New York — Will you be so good then, as to have procured and sent off without delay to each place, copper bolts agreeably to the list enclosed — I have requested the Secretary of the Treasury to remit you 2000 Ds

Capth McNeil who goes to New York by this days mail, & thence to Newport will take any trouble to get on the bolts to their destination — He is in the Navy. —

A good deal of sheathing Copper, Nails, and Spikes will be wanted, and soon for the Ships in preparation — Can these articles be furnished in any quantity at New York? The price for Patent Copper at this place is 50 Cents but it is difficult to be had — If you can buy Twenty or 25 Thousand feet, not exceeding this price, I wish you would at once do it — The money shall be remitted to your order — You have contracted for Guns, for the Ship building under your direction — could further contracts be made for Guns of different sizes, from Six, to Twenty four pounders?

P. S. What can Powder be procured for with you?

[NDA. GLB, Vol. 1.]

To Secretary of State from Secretary of Navy

[PHILADELPHIA,]
Navy Departmt 20th July 1798

SECY of STATE

DR SIR The Signals put into your hands by Mr Liston, as received from Admiral Vandeport to be used between the British and American Ships of War, Shall be communicated by the first Opportunity to our Commanders of Ships, with Orders to observe them.

[NDA. Sec. State LB, 1798–1824.]

Extract from Captain Thomas Truxtun's journal, U. S. Frigate *Constellation*, 20 July 1798, Friday

Fresh Breezes from the North East, and pleasant Weather, but the Water a little rough. At 2 PM spoke the Brig *Hellen* from Charleston, bound to Bristol; came out at 6 AM and had seen no Cruizers. Shortly after several Sail hove in Sight, to which I gave Chace, and at half past 2 PM saw the Land a little to the Southward of the Bar of Charleston; at 3 Ditto spoke a Dutch Brig bound to Amsterdam; at ¼ past 3 spoke a Danish Ship bound to the same Place; and at 4 Ditto an English Ship, bound to London, these Vessels all left Charleston in Company with two American Brigs that were ahead early in the Morning.

At half past 6 Ditto brought to with a Shot the English Schooner *Concord*, Peter Buchard Master, from Jamaica bound to Charleston, loaded with Rum; this Vessel had been out 15 Days, and seen no Cruizers, except an English Sloop of War off the Hole in the Rock (Bahamas). I examined his Papers and permitted him to proceed.

At 9 AM spoke a small Schooner from Wilmington, North Carolina, bound to Saint Mary's; came out Yesterday, and had seen no Vessel, except this Frigate. I desired the Master to present my Compliments to Mr Seagrove, for whom he said, he had Letters; at 11 Ditto spoke a Schooner from Boston bound to Savannah, out 30 Days, had experienced violent South West Gales, saw no Sort of Cruizers.

At Noon the Light House of Charleston bore North B. West, 10 Leagues Distance, and that of Savannah West South West, Eighteen Leagues the Depth of Water Eleven Fathoms, black and white Sand.

Latitude observed 32°.14′ N°
Longitude Account 80.33 W.

[HS of Pa. NDA photostat.]

To John Gavino, United States Consul, Gibraltar, from Secretary Timothy Pickering

DEPARTMENT OF STATE,
Philadelphia July 21. 1798.

JOHN GAVINO Esqr

SIR, Herewith you will receive two Commissions and two bonds, the former for the two armed ships *Washington* and *Mercury* of Boston, and the bonds to be signed by the respective captains in the presence of yourself or chancellor or clerk, and two of the inferior officers of each ship. This trouble is given to you in consequence of those ships having sailed before the Commissions authorized by an Act of Congress reached Boston. If the ships should increase their force in guns or men or either, I should think it advisable for you to endorse the same on the commissions respectively, and certify the same under your Consular seal.

Duplicates of these papers will be forwarded to you, by Mr Jones, the sole or chief owner of the ships; and the duplicate bonds when executed by the respective captains, I must request you to return to me by the best conveyances that shall occur. I inclose a copy of the Act and of the instructions founded thereon. I am, Sir, &c.

TIMOTHY PICKERING

[SDA. Dip. Cor., Inst. to Min., Vol. 4, 1797–1798.]

To John Coffin Jones, Boston, from Secretary Pickering

[PHILADELPHIA]
Department of State July 21. 1798

JOHN COFFIN JONES Esqr *Boston.* —

SIR, Captain Anthony has just sent me your letter of the 15th and one from Mr Hays of the same date, relative to your ships *Washington* and *Mercury,* which Sailed a day or two before the arrival of commissions at the collectors office in Boston. Such cases were not anticipated, or instructions would have been sent to the Collector how to provide for them. I shall as soon as I have time write to Genl Lincoln on the subject. To prevent any possible delay I address the Commissions immediately to you, accompanied with a letter to John Gavino Esqr Consul of the United States at Gibraltar, to ask his aid in putting the affair in the best form the State of things will now admit.

I inclose the forms of applications for commissions for both Ships, which you (and your partners, if you have any) will sign, after you have filled up the blanks. The items specified in the applications, you will introduce in the proper blanks in the commissions — particularly the names of the other owners, if any, the numbers of carriage guns and men and the names of the lieutenants, that is the two officers next in command to the captain. — In the bonds insert also the names of the other owners, and the names of the two sureties required by law. You will put as many seals to the bonds as there are persons to sign them; and then with your sureties execute them in the presence of witnesses. One of the bonds thus executed, for each ship, you will be pleased to transmit to me, with your applications for commissions. The other bonds, to be filled up with the same names for the respective ships, and executed by the owners and sureties, you will inclose in the letter to Mr Gavino, who will obtain the Signatures of the Captains to their respective bonds, and then transmit them to me. Inclosed are duplicate bonds thus to be executed by you and your sureties and forwarded to Mr Gavino, together with duplicate commissions, and a duplicate of my letter to Mr Gavino.

These expedients which at this instant have occurred I hope will answer the wishes of yourself and all concerned.

I am respectfully, Sir, your Ob^t Servant,

TIMOTHY PICKERING

[SDA. Dom. L., Vol. 11.]

To Joshua Sands, Collector, New York, from Secretary Pickering

[PHILADELPHIA,]
Department of State July 21st 1798.

JOSHUA SANDS Esqr
Collector of the Customs New York.

SIR, Having lately transmitted to you a permit to clear the Schooner *William,* Capt Burr, for the Port of Santo Domingo, I beg leave to remark, that under the terms "goods and effects" of French persons, if great care be not taken, a traffic will still be carried on with the French Ports, and the object of the law referred to be frustrated. If an American vessel is fairly designed to deport French persons according to the act, as many passengers will ordinarily be engaged as she can conveniently carry: and this circumstance may be considered as a good criterion of the real object of the voyage. On the other hand, if few passengers embark with many "goods and effects," they may justly be suspected of collusion.

I have taken the liberty to suggest these remarks as they occurred, in a measure which in this Country is novel, and from the singularity of our political situation, perhaps unexampled. I am very respectfully, Sir, &cc

TIMOTHY PICKERING

[SDA. Dom. L., Vol. 11.]

To James Simons, Charleston, from Secretary of Navy

[PHILADELPHIA,]
Navy Department July 21. 1798

JA[s] SIMONS Esq[r]
Charleston

SIR I have *this day* received from the Treasury Department, your Letters to the Secretary of the Treasury, from May to the 8th July — M[r] Wolcott has unfortunately been absent, almost the whole time I have been in office — You will perceive by the Act of Congress enclosed, the number of Vessels to be procured, & the Funds. And you may Judge how much is expected from the Patriotism of our Citizens. —

Of those, Vessels, arrangements have been made through the public appropriations & patriotic subscriptions for all but 3 Vessels not exceeding 18 Guns — one not exceeding 24 — & one not less than 32 — As from the Letter of Cap[t] Cochran — the *Unanimity* cannot be made a proper cruizer — She must be given up to the Owner, at the stipulated time — There is now a fine Frigate on your Coast — There will shortly be at least one 20 Gun Ship, perhaps more, & several Cutters — still it would be very desirable, that the Public Spirit of Charleston, should furnish one, or assist in furnishing one Vessel to the public.

The Vessel of W[m] Pritchard, so strongly recommended by Cap[t] Cochran, could soon be got ready with the aid of the public materials on board the *Unanimity* — Pray try to have this effected through the Patriotism of the Citizens — Should further public aid, than the Articles on board the *Unanimity* be necessary, it will not be withheld, altho I believe the Engagements I have already made, will exhaust the appropriations — If this Vessel should be offered by the Citizens to the public it will be necessary that she should be coppered — You have Copper, — I presume She is Iron bolted — In this case it wou'd be well to give her a Coat of well tarred Sheathing paper, then a sheath of half-Inch Cedar boards — then another coat of thin paper, and over the whole, Copper — She cannot I presume mount more than 18 — 6 pound[s] and it wou'd be better to mount 16, than to have 18 — & be too much crowded — The distance between this place & Charleston is so great, that if the Citizens purchase this, or any other Vessel, it will be best that they should appoint some person, to fit her without waiting for advice or information from hence — It will be enough to say in season, the articles wanted from hence — which shall be furnished —

[NDA. GLB, Vol. 1.]

Extract from Captain Thomas Truxtun's journal, U. S. Frigate *Constellation*, 21 July 1798, Saturday

The first Part of this Day, the Weather was clear and pleasant, and we were favoured with a charming Breeze from the North East, and smooth Water. At AM it became squally, and rained incessantly untill about 6 AM, when the Clouds began to seperate, and it cleared away.

Steered along the Coast in from 11 to 23 Fathoms Water, various Courses as per Column, in Order to visit our most Southern Limits (which is the Middle of the River Saint Mary's) as settled by the Definitive Treaty of Peace with Great Britain, Signed at Paris on the 3d Day of September 1783. At Noon found ourselves beyond our Southern Limits a few Miles, and no Vessels being in Sight, bore away towards the Entrance of Tybee, on the South Shore of which stands a Light House, to facilitate the Arrival of Vessels bound to Savannah &c. The Current these 24 Hours has set us to the Southward at the Rate of one half Knot per Hour. Our Southern Extremes, the Middle of Saint Mary's River, at Noon bore West half North, 15 Leagues Distance; Depth of Water 19 Fathoms, round black Sand, with some white mixed.

Latitude observed 30°.22′ No
Longitude Account 80.48 W.

[HS of Pa. NDA photostat.]

French Privateer *La Croyable* advertised for sale

[21 July 1798]

United States, }
Pennsylvania District. } SS

In pursuance to a writ directed from the Hon. Richard Peters, Esq., Judge of the District Court of the United States for the Pennsylvania District, will be exposed to PUBLIC SALE, at the Merchant's Coffee House, in the City of Philadelphia, on Monday, the 30th day of July instant, at 12 o'clock at noon —

The Schooner called

La Croyable

with all and singular, her apparel, guns, and appurtenances, lately captured by the armed vessel belonging to the United States, called the *Delaware*, Stephen Decatur, Esq. commander, the same being in my custody and possession, by virtue of a writ of attachment, lately issued out of the court aforesaid, at the suit of the United States, and condemned as forfeited.

William Nichols, Marshal

Marshal's Office }
21 July, 1798 } dts

N. B. The inventory may be seen at my office.

[LC, "Claypoole's American Daily Advertiser" (Phila.), Monday, July 23, 1798.]

To Joshua Humphreys, Naval Constructor, from Captain John Barry, U. S. Navy

FRIGATE *U. States* IN NANTASKET ROAD
July 22^d 1798

DEAR SIR It is not in my power at present to reply fully to your letter, but so much I can say, that in sailing out of the Delaware the ship drew twenty two feet 6 Inches water abaft, and twenty feet forward — no ship ever went to Sea answers her helm better, and in all probability will surpass every thing afloat — Captn Decatur thought he could sail with any thing, for he never saw a vessel he could not come up with or leave with ease, untill he got along side of the *United States* he with me is of opinion that she will sail with any thing that floats; she is rather tender, but when I get clear of the Firewood between decks, and some of the lumber on Deck I hope she will be stiffer. — The day I left the Capes I discovered your favourite foretop Mast sprung, but nursed it untill I got here, I have got it down, and am now getting another up, that I hope will do better I beg you will make my best respects to Mrs Humphreys & family and believe me long

Dear Sir

Your Obed^t hum^ble Servt

JOHN BARRY.

[TO JOSHUA HUMPHREYS]

[HS of Pa. NDA photostat.]

[22 July 1798.]

Water rations, U. S. Frigate *Constellation*

An Encrease of

Water to be added to the Order of the 29th June; so that each Man have five Pints per Day, instead of *four* and one half Pints; exclusive of that allowed for Cooking as aforesaid.

At Seven Bells every Morning	three Half Pints
At half past 11 AM	two Ditto —
At half past 3 PM	two Ditto —
At half past 6 Ditto	three Ditto —
	Ten half Pints per Man

JULY 22^d 1798. THOMAS TRUXTUN.

[HS of Pa. NDA photostat. Truxtun's LB, 1798–9.]

Extract from Captain Thomas Truxtun's journal, U. S. Frigate *Constellation*, 22 July 1798, Sunday

Throughout these Twenty four Hours, the Winds have been baffling and light, with a Southerly Current, and squally disagreeable Weather, which induced me after One PM to endeavour to get off Shore a little, in Hopes of finding less Current, and better Weather; no Vessels in Sight these two Days past. Set up the Rigging, and repaired various little Matters, that had got out of Order. Depth of

Water at Noon 19½ Fathoms, grey Sand with black Specks. At the same Time, we were near the Line of our Southern Limits.

Increased the Allowance of Water to five Pints per Man each Day.

Latitude observed 30°.35′ N.º
Longitude Account 80.48 W.

[HS of Pa. NDA photostat.]

To Joshua Humphreys, Naval Constructor, from James Morris

NANTUCKET ROAD *July 23d 1798.*

SIR I have sent this to inform you as I think it will be a satisfaction to you hear of the *United States* how she behaves at sea I believe she will be a little wet but for sailing and steering I believe there is but few will match her one spoak and a half of the wheel is all she wants we have been going 12 knots at the same time we could have carried a good deal of more sail I saw Mr Barron carry a lighted candle for & aft when she was going 9 knots by the Wind. She is a little crank but very little and we have a great deal of top weight upon deck which is a good deal the occasion of it we shifted our fore top mast as it complain'd greatly at sea: So with my duty to you and all the family, I remain — Sir

Your very humble Servant

JAS MORRIS.

[To JOSHUA HUMPHREYS]

[HS of Pa. NDA photostat.]

To Captain Patrick Fletcher, Boston, from Secretary of Navy

[PHILADELPHIA,]
Navy Department, 23rd July 1798

Capt PATRICK FLETCHER, *Boston*

SIR, Upon Examination I find Mr Fox, who keeps the Register of Commissions, forwarded your's to Capt Nicholson, with an observation, that your Commission being of a later date, you were to act as youngest Lieutenant on board the Frigate — The Fact is — It was intended by the President that you should supply the Place of Mr Preeble, as first Lieutenant on board the Ship. — Your Commission ought to have been Nº 1 — to this Effect I have written Capt Nicholson, and in this Character, I hope you will go on board, for I should lament, that by a Mistake at this Office — The Public should be deprived of the Services of an Officer so well qualified as you are known to be for the Present, or a higher Command.

[NDA. OSW, Vol. 1.]

To Jeremiah Yellott, Navy Agent, Baltimore, from Secretary of Navy

[PHILADELPHIA,]
Navy Department 23rd July, 1798

JERh YELLOTT Esqr

SIR Your favor of the 20th Instant is at hand The usual mode of proving cannon is by two successive discharges, the weight of Powder for the first to be equal to two thirds of the Weight of the Ball and for the second, equal to half the Weight of the Ball — The allowance for windage, 1⅒ Inches —

You will be pleased to purchase the Quantity of Slops that may be deemed necessary, as the United States are to supply them & not the Purser — In consequence of the favorable recommendation you enclosed of Mr Thos Rowland, I shall mention his name to the President, and have no doubt he will receive the appointment solicited for him, of which you shall be advised —

P. S. Since writing the foregoing, I have refered to a copy of the Contract made by the Secretary of the Treasury with Mr Hughes in October 1796 — and the following is an extract so far as relates to the proving of the cannon —

9th That the proof by Powder shall be as follows Vizt — Each "cannon shall be proved by two successive discharges — The "Weight of the powder for the first discharge, shall be equal to "⅔rd of the Weight of the Ball, and for the second, equal to half the "Weight of the Ball — The Cartridge to be well rammed down "with a rod over it — Two Balls to be placed over the Cartridge "with a wad between them, and a wad above, which also shall be "well rammed down — The Balls to be measured, so as to allow "a sufficient Windage to be approved of by the Officers who shall "make the Experiments and the said Samuel Hughes, on behalf of "the Cecil Company, or any person he may appoint for that purpose."

10th That to ascertain the Strength of the Trunnions, The cannon "shall be placed on two pieces of Wood, having Indentions large "enough to receive two thirds of the Trunnions, and with the "hinder part at a sufficient distance from where the Trunnions "lodge, so that the Breach of the Cannon, may be inclined in any "direction, but never so as to rest on the Ground — The Proof "by Powder to be made on the said pieces of Wood. —

11th — That the Cannon which shall have stood the Proof by "Powder shall be raised from off the Temporary carriage, and placed "upon a supporter, and filled with Water, and should the Water "on being compress'd filter through any part of the Cannon, the "same shall not be received by the United States, altho' they have "stood proof by Powder.

12th — That the Cannon which shall have stood the aforesaid "examination & Proofs, shall be subject nevertheless to be reex-"amined — and if new holes are detected, or the ones tolerated "found to have been enlarged by the firing, all such cannon shall "undergo a second Proof, but of one discharge only with two thirds "powder, and two Balls, as before specified when if the Holes "exhibit no further enlargement, the said cannon shall be admitted "& receipted for, after being weighed — "

NDA. GLB, Vol. 1.]

To Secretary of War from Secretary of Navy

[PHILADELPHIA,]
Navy Depart. 23 July. 1798

SECY AT WAR,

SIR The Ship *Montezuma* and the Ship *Baltimore* are nearly ready for Sea, and want before I can have them procured by other means, one hundred Muskets & Fifty pair of Pistols.

Will you be pleased to lend me these Articles & have them delivered to Capt Gill. —

[NDA. Sec. War LB, 1798–1824.]

To Secretary of Navy from Secretary of State

[PHILADELPHIA,]
Department of State July 23, 1798.

BENJAMIN STODDERT. Esqr
Secretary of the Navy.

Dr SIR, Mr Liston to-day handed me the inclosed list of Signals which he has received from Admiral Vandeput, in anticipation of your wishes of a mutual understanding on this subject. If you approve of them, be pleased to let me know it, and that you will by the earliest opportunities give them in orders to the armed vessels of the U. States.

I am very respectfully your & cc.

TIMOTHY PICKERING

[SDA. Dom. L., Vol. 11.]

[23 July, 1798.]

Extract of a letter from the owner of the Ship *Hetty Jane* regarding capture of said ship

Another French Hug

ST. PIERRE, MARTINICO, *Oct. 14.*

MY DEAR SIR, I have the concern to inform you of the capture and condemnatioon of my ship the *Hetty Jane* and cargo, at Basseterre, in the island of Guadaloupe. We were taken on 23d July, about 500 miles from Charleston, and arrived at Basseterre the 6th or 7th Sept. and immediately, I may say, thrown into prison, crouded with all sorts, colours, and conditions of people. In this we were left on a course of living greatly below the most ordinary expectations of humanity, being simply bread, water, and sometimes hardly two ounces of beef or fish, generally in a very offensive, not to say, putrid state. We were released the 30th Sept. on our parole of honour, to the number of forty or upwards, and put on board an English cartel and sent to Port Royal in this island, and from thence to this place. We here have dispersed our selves on board the different vessels of our countrymen, who have humanely received us, and continue to shew us those marks of kindness so peculiarly grateful to the feeling and the unfortunate.

[LC, "Claypoole's American Daily Advertiser" (Phila.), 28 November 1798.]

Extract from Captain Thomas Truxtun's journal, U. S. Frigate *Constellation*, 23 July 1798, Monday

Light Easterly Winds, and variable all these 24 Hours, with smooth Water; and some Squalls of Rain. Employed setting up the Rigging, no Vessels in Sight. Died at 11 AM Patrick Leonard, an

Ordinary Seaman; this Man had an old sore Leg, and a Complication of Disorders. I directed the first Lieutenant to attend to his Effects, agreeable to the President's Orders, and soon after his Demise, his Body was committed to the Deep, with the usual Ceremonies.

Tybee Light House at Noon bore North North West, Twenty Leagues Distance.

Latitude observed 31°.02′ N.°
Longitude Account 81.00 W.

[HS of Pa. NDA photostat.]

Extract from journal of James Pity, U. S. Frigate *Constitution*, 23 July 1798, Monday

Steady Breezes fine & Pleasant Weather.

At 8 P. M. Took my departure from Boston Light House bearing W. ½ N. 3½ Leagues dist[t] Middle part fresh Breezes and clear Weather at 4 A. M. call[d] all Hands sent down T. Gall[t] Yards Small Sails & booms out of the Tops. Sett up the Stays and Rigging fore and aft. at Eight Spoke Brig[t] from Boston bound to Barbadoes, Tho[s] Emery Gates Com[r] at 9. Wore Ship to Eastw[d] and let one Reef out of Top Sails. Set the fore Sail at 10 D[o] Sett y[d] Gibb & M[n] Top Mast Stay Sail

[Latitude observed 42.04 N[o]]

117 miles 6 fath[s] per log from Boston Light House.

Bearing & Dist. from Cape Cod at Noon N[o] 8.5 miles W.

[NDA.]

To Benjamin Lincoln, Collector, Boston, from Secretary Pickering

[PHILADELPHIA,]
Department of State July 24, 1798.

BENJAMIN LINCOLN Esq[r]
Collector of the Port of Boston —

SIR, Last Saturday Captain Anthony wrote me a letter enclosing two others, one from John Coffin Jones Esq[r] the other from M[r] Hays. He entreated an answer by that days post. To prevent any delay, I immediately made out duplicate commissions for two private armed vessels of M[r] Jones's which had sailed from Boston on the 12th instant, two or three days before the arrival of the commissions which I had transmitted to you; in expectation that the commissions might meet with the vessels at Gibralter And that there might be, as far as practicable a literal conformity with the law, I sent duplicate bonds also, to be executed by the owner or owners and their Sureties at Boston, and then transmitted to John Gavino Esq[r] American Consul at Gibraltar, before whom the captains were to sign and seal the bonds, which were then to be returned to me. And lest these duplicate bonds might miscarry, I sent a third for each vessel to M[r] Jones, to be executed by him (and the other owners if there were any) and the sureties, and then returned to me.— This, I trusted, would effect the object of the law respecting the giving of bond — viz. to ensure an observance of the conditions set forth in the law, in the exercise of the powers granted by the commission to private armed Ships. I the less hesitated to adopt this course, as a case had before occurred where the *owner* of the private armed ship was in London, and his ship in Philadelphia; and consequently a *literal* compliance with the law was impossible; nevertheless, with the President's express approbation, a commission was issued, the *agent* of the owner giving bond with sureties in his behalf.

On this same principle, that the security of commerce may not fail thro' a *formality* and a *literal* compliance with the terms of the law, when its *true object* could otherwise be effectually attained, I have transmitted to Mr King, our Minister in London, blank commissions, bonds and instructions, to be issued to any American vessels who should arm in the British ports in Europe. This was important in two points of view — that there would be a considerable number of our vessels there, which sailed before the Act authorizing such commissions was passed — and that many would have afterwards sailed un-armed from our ports, from the impossibility of procuring cannon, at present, in the United States. — I shall continue to send commissions &c. to Mr King, a few by each conveyance, until I think the supply sufficient for every probably call.

I shall probably send a few sets of commissions, bonds and instructions to Mr Smith at Lisbon. These provisions however should not prevent the arming of any of our vessels at home, where the means are attainable.

Upon the whole — where the owners and captains of private armed vessels are on the Spot, the bonds should be signed by them and their Sureties: but if either or both be absent, and their agent or agents, in their stead, with compleat sureties, will execute the bonds. — I should not hesitate to issue the commissions. I am &c.

TIMOTHY PICKERING.

P. S. This detail is what, as mentioned in my letter to J. C. Jones, I intended to give you. Your letter to the Secretary of the Treasury of July 17th on this subject has been sent to me; and the foregoing you will have the goodness to consider as an answer.

[SDA. Dom. L., Vol. 11.]

To Mr. Létombe, late Consul General of French Republic, from Secretary Pickering

[PHILADELPHIA,]
Department of State July 24. 1798.

Mr LÉTOMBE

SIR, Your letter of this date is before me. Mr Byrd, the Collector of Norfolk, has not stopped the two flags of truce at that Port, destined for St Domingo, under *pretext* of the *intercourse bill*; but in conformity with his *duty*, under the express injunctions of the act of congress for suspending all commercial intercourse between the United States and the French Dominions.

Upon Mr Byrd's own application, which was sent me yesterday from the Department of the Treasury, two permits were made out, and are to go in tomorrow's mail, authorizing him to clear out the two flags of truce in question.

I inclose a passport for M. Mozard late consul of the French Republic at Boston, to go to France, with his books, papers and effects — agreeably to your request of the 21st which I received yesterday.

I had not before heard of any insult having been offered to Mr Mozard at Boston, or to any persons pertaining to his office. I shall be very sorry if an unprovoked insult or injury has been offered to him or any other French citizen. I am &

TIMOTHY PICKERING.

[SDA. Dom. L., Vol. 11.]

To James Watson, Navy Agent, New York, from Secretary of Navy

[PHILADELPHIA,]
Navy Department, 24th July 1798

JAS. WATTSON Esqr *New York*

SIR, Capt. Dale, in the Ship *Ganges* will be off Sandy Hook, on the 26th — Will you be so good as to hire a Pilot to put the enclosed Letter on board of him? —

In answer to your favor of the 23rd please to purchase all the Copper of the Patent kind Just arrived at New York, and the nails — also all the Six pound Cannon, if they can be had without the fours, the price of the Patent Copper here, is 50 Cents but it is scarce As to Copper Nails & Spikes, I must get those wanted immediately for distant places, at this place — If you can procure every Article of this kind for the Ships at N York It will be desireable — What you cannot procure shall be furnished from hence if you will let me know in season, and the sooner you let me know, the better, as I am about contracting for the quantity — On the 20th I directed 2000 Ds to be remitted you, & on the 21st 10,000 Ds —

I have the honor to be &c.

[NDA. GLB, Vol. 1.]

[Enclosure]

To Captain Richard Dale, U. S. Navy, from Secretary of Navy

NAVY DEPARTMENT,
July 24th 1798

Capt RICHd DALE

SIR, I have received your favours of the 17th & 22nd Instant. The Ship *Baltimore* Capt Philips from Baltimore will I expect be ready for Sea by the 1st August. — It is intended that She should take your Station, and it is desirable that you should not leave it, untill relieved by the *Baltimore* — This I calculate will be about the 10th of August — at all events you may come into Port on the 15th—should you not sooner fall in with the *Baltimore*, or receive certain Accounts that she is out. — Whenever either of these events happen you will please to return into Port — As to getting a Supply of Water, you will Judge what step will be best for you to pursue on that subject — If your Water will not last 'till the 15th August, you should get a Supply. —

I have the honor to be &c.

[NDA. OSW, Vol. 1.]

To Captain John W. Leonard, Revenue Cutter *Governor Jay*, from Secretary of Navy

[PHILADELPHIA,]
Navy Department 24th July 1798

Capt JOHN W. LEONARD
of the Cutter Gov. Jay New York

SIR I have your Letter of the 23rd Instant. By an Arrangement of the Treasury department the Cutters are to be fitted under his direction for Sea, and then turned over to my department.

He informed me that your Cutter would be ready the 20th Instant — and on the 19th I wrote to you, and enclosed your Instructions for a Cruise. — It does not appear by your Letter now before me, that you had received mine — I am sorry to find that the information I received from the Secretary of the Treasury respecting the time you would be ready was not correct — and that you do not expect ~~that~~ your Guns before the 1st of August — Pray keep me advised of your progress, that I may certainly know when to send you other Instructions for your Cruise. —

Enclosed you will receive the Uniform adopted in the Navy.

I have the honor to be &c.

[NDA. OSW, Vol. 1.]

To Jeremiah Yellott, Navy Agent, Baltimore, from Secretary of Navy

Navy Department 24th July 1798

JERh YELLOTT Esqr *Balta*

SIR The Slops are furnished by the Public to the Purser, who ought to receive with them, an Invoice of the prices at which he is to sell them to the men — The Prices ought to be enough to cover the whole actual expense of procuring them — I am sorry this part of your Letter was not instantly attended to, I fear you will be perplexed to provide them in time for the *Baltimore*

You will be so good as to make arrangements for preparing them for the *Montezuma* also — They could be furnished from hence, but I think it no more than Justice, that each Town where Ships are fitted, should supply as much as it can —

Enclosed you have a List of Articles — deemed necessary for each Ship —

Estimate of Slops for a Ship of 20 Guns —

70 Wool Hatts
100 Single Blanketts
70 Outside Jackets (of Blue Cloth lined)
100 Inside Ditto (of Swanskin)
70 pairs of Woolen Trousers
70 pr Ravens Duck do
100 Check Shirts
70 Raven's Duck Frocks
70 pr Worsted Stockings
100 pr Strong Shoes.—
70 Bandana Handkfs.
70 pr. Drawers (Flannel)
100 Woolen Caps
50 Beds or Mattrasses
150 lbs. of Tobacco

[NDA. GLB, Vol. 1.]

Extract from journal of James Pity, U. S. Frigate *Constitution*, 24 July 1798, Tuesday

First Part this 24 Hours Fresh Breezes and Fair Weather. at 8 P.M. Reef^t Top Sails Handed Jibb and Stay Sails. a 8. hauld up S. East and ⩞ Ship to the West^d

Considerable Swell f^m W. N. W.

Latter part this 24 hours Squally with Rain

[Latitude observed 41° 17′ N°]

Ship Sails remarkably, & Well and Works Easy

Bearing & Dis^t fm Georges Banks, N° 81.W. 147^m

[NDA.]

Extract from Captain Thomas Truxtun's journal, U. S. Frigate *Constellation*, 24 July 1798, Tuesday

The Wind and Weather very much the same as Yesterday, but accompanied with more Rain. Stood towards Tybee Light House, into Twelve Fathoms Water, and off again to seventeen Fathoms, which we had at Noon, over a Bottom of coarse reddish Sand. — I gave Directions for six Fires at least to be made in Pots on the Birth Deck, to purify the Air, and dry the Apartments of the People. No Vessels in Sight, some thing remarkable for so many Days, but a convincing Proof, that the foreign Trade of Georgia, is by no Means equal to that of the Atlantic States to the Northward of it. Tybee Light House at Noon bore West B. North half North, 15 Leagues Distance, and that of Charleston, North 21 Leagues Distance.

Latitude observed 31°.37′ N°

Longitude Account 80.40 W.

[HS of PA., NDA photostat.]

To Secretary of Treasury from Secretary of Navy

[PHILADELPHIA,]
Navy Departm^t 25 July 1798. —

SEC^Y of TREASURY

SIR Be pleased to direct, that one hundred & Eleven Dollars, be paid to Joseph Brussells, for Pilotage of the *United States* Frigate, down to the Capes of Delaware, & Twenty six days demurrage — as p.acc^t & cer^t of Capt Barry enclosed. —

[NDA. Req. on US T, 1798–1803.]

To Tench Francis, Purveyor, from Secretary of Navy

[PHILADELPHIA,]
Navy Departm^t 25 July. 1798

TENCH FRANCIS

SIR, The following Articles are required for the Ship *Baltimore*. You will please to procure Them of the *best Quality* as speedily as possible, and deliver them to Capt Robert Gill, that they may be forwarded.

2 Long Spy Glasses
1 Short D° for the Mast head.
1 Good Night Glass

I am Sir &c

[NDA. Req. on US T, 1798–1803.]

[25 July, 1798.]

Declaration of Thomas Smith, master of Schooner *Lemmon*

June 18th, 1798, sailed from Beverly, in the State of Massachusetts, in the schooner *Lemmon*, whereof Thomas Smith was master, for the West Indies, — That on the 25th day of July following we were short of water, by our watercasks proving leaky; in consequence of which we made the best of our way to the main to get a supply of water; that at 10 o'clock the same day we saw two armed boats coming towards us, and as they came within gun-shot began to fire on the schooner *Lemmon* unceasingly, and obliged us to surrender, not having ammunition or fire-arms on board said schooner to defend ourselves; that they then asked captain Smith where he was bound, his reply was to Curracoa. Capt. Loran, of the privateer *La Raquir National* told him that he was a damned liar, and with other threats, struck him several times in the face, and pointed a loaded pistol to destroy him, with opprobious language, at the same time, beating him and his people with unfriendly treatment, which they conceived should be observed in the line of neutrality.

They then took charge of the said schooner *Lemmon*, taking out all his people, except himself and cabbin-boy. They then ordered her, with a prize-master and a part of the said privateers crew, for Curracoa, where they arrived on the 29th of July last, where he now remains for trial or acquittance.

The said capture was made by a privateer as before mentioned; of *Curracoa*, and fitted out and owned by *Burghers of Curracoa*, in violation of existing treaties between America, France, and Holland.

The said schooner *Lemmon's* papers were equipped for the island of Curracoa, and, that her cargo consisted of nothing but provisions, manufactured in America, to which I declare this to be the truth, as witness my hand, Curracoa, this 29th August, 1798.

THOMAS SMITH.

☞ I have omitted mentioning the manner in which they boarded us. They came on board of us like savages, driving captain, mate, and people below, making use of their cutlasses and handspikes in such a manner that we were were obliged to ask for quarters.

THOMAS SMITH.

[LC, "Claypoole's American Daily Advertiser" (Phila.), 24 Sept. 1798.]

Extract from journal of James Pity, U. S. Frigate *Constitution*, 25 July 1798, Wednesday

First part this 24 Hours. Hazy. W^{m} with light Showers Rain all hands employ'd Stow^{g} Booms Anchors. &c at 2 P. M. Sett the Main Sail at 4 D^{o} beat to Quarters Station'd the Men and Exercized them at the Guns. $\overline{AK}$ Ship to Westw^{d} handed the Main Stay Sail and haul'd the Mizen up. handed Mizen Stay Sail & Clew^{d} up the Mizen Top Sail at 12 $\overline{AK}$ Ship to East^{d} at 2 Sett mizen Top Sail at 5. A.M. Sett Main Top Mast Stay Sail and Jibb a 6. Sett Mizen Top

Mast Stay Sail a 8 Lett out all Reefs of T. Sails and sett all Stay Sails at Meridn hand Sprit Sail & Sprit sail Top Sails very large.

Shark close along side of us. NO. OB.

Bearing & Dist fm Georges Banks 73 West. 198 M.

[NDA.]

Extract from Captain Thomas Truxtun's journal, U. S. Frigate *Constellation*, 25 July 1798, Wednesday

The first of these Twenty four Hours very uncertain Weather with Squalls of Wind from the Southward, and Rain, brought the Ship under the Main, and Fore top Sails close reefed.

At 4 AM the Weather appeared more settled, made Sail, and at 11 AM, saw the Land, and Light House of Charleston bearing West ¾ North between five and six Leagues Distance, Depth of Water eight Fathoms. Brought to with two Shot the Brig *Commerce*, bound to Cadiz, which had left the Bar at half past 9 AM, and informed us, the other Vessels, that were in Sight, came out in Company with her, and that they belonged to Charleston. Exercised Great Guns, and small Arms. Saw a small Vessel coming down, which I take for, a Pilot Boat.

Latitude observed 32°.40′ No

Longitude Account 80.20 W.

[HS of Pa. NDA photostat.]

To Captain Robert Wharton from Secretary of Navy

[PHILADELPHIA,]
Navy Department 26 July 1798

Captt Robt WHARTON
Commanding the Volunteer Cavalry

SIR Being informed that the French Prisoners on their way to Lancaster, under a Small Guard, have exhibited proofs of an unruly & mutinous Spirit, & being apprehensive they may overpower the guard, I have the honor to request the favor of a detachment from your Troop of Horse, to follow the Prisoners, and see them safe in Lancaster Goal — I presume that 10 or 12 Troopers under the command of an officer or noncommissioned officer will be sufficient for this duty —

I have the honor to be &ca

[NDA. GLB, Vol. 1.]

To Robert Oliver, Baltimore, from Secretary of Navy

[PHILADELPHIA,]
Navy Department 26 July. 1798

ROBERT OLIVER *Baltimore*

SIR, I am honored with your Letter of 24th and enclose you an order for all or any part of the Timber in the Navy Yard at Balt — except the live oak Timber, which I presume you will not want — and which will be wanted immediately at Norfolk, for the Frigate to be finished there. Please to appoint one or two Men of Character to value the

Timber, & send the Valuation to me. I hope you will sweep the Yard. —

Copper Bolts shall be prepared here, & forwarded to you, as soon as they can be prepared, for both your Ships. I fear it may be ten days before they can be sent off. —

All the Ships authorized by Acts of Congress between 20 & 24 Guns are engaged. To comply with the Law, those you are building must not exceed 18 Guns — They may be, and had better be on the main Deck — Hereafter a few more Guns may be mounted — The Ships I presume will be strong enough for 9 or 12 pounders — If you want Copper Spikes & Nails — that is, if you can not get them in Bal^t let me know early and I will have them furnished — but what can be furnished by Balt^o, for many reasons ought not to be got elsewhere — Is it intended that the Merchants furnish Guns? If so, let me know, that I may send a Model — We are endeavouring to adopt in the Navy, the Guns most useful by Nations of more Experience —

I should be glad you would continue to recommend such Men as you think will do honor to the Navy — There are a Number of Applicants, but the greater the Choice the better —

Altho' I have mentioned an Exception of live Oak in my order — yet if you can not do without It, you must have that also. —

[NDA. GLB, Vol. 1.]

Extract from journal of James Pity, U. S. Frigate *Constitution*, 26 July 1798, Thursday

First part this 24 hours Cloudy Weather at 4 P. M. Exercized ye Men at the Guns, & Sett the Main Sail a 7 P. M. Hauld up the Main Sail handed M. Top & Mizen Top mast Stay Sail Reef'd top Sails and furld Main Sail Middle part Calm. Swell from the S. W. at 8 A. M. call^d all Hands & Made Sail D^o Saw Strange Sail to the East^d gave her Chase. Latter part Light Airs Inclinable to a Calm.

[Latitude observed 40°. 29′ N^o]

[NDA.]

Extract from Captain Thomas Truxtun's journal, U. S. Frigate *Constellation*, 26 July 1798, Thursday

Moderate Breezes from South Westward, and warm Weather. At 1 PM spoke the Ship *Polly*, from Charleston bound to Cadiz, as also the Brig *Harriot* from same Place bound to Jamaica. At 3 PM Mr Delany a Pilot, came from Charleston along Side in his Boat; I invited him on Board, and delivered him the Muster Roll, and Register of the Crew, recruiting Officer's Instructions, and their Accounts, forming with a Letter to the Secretary of War, a Packet for that Officer, which I put under Cover to the Collector of Customs at Charleston, and requested he would forward them on by first Post. Mr Delany informed me, that there was a Dispatch Boat at Charleston with Letters from Government for me, I shall consequently keep as near to the Bar, as it is prudent, or as Circumstances will admit, in Order to get them as early as possible. I desired Delany to inform the Master of the Dispatch Boat, that I would hoist a United States Jack at the Fore Top Mast Head, whenever I stretched in Shore, and to request of the Master of the Boat to hoist his Colours, when he saw the Frigate. At 5 PM saw a Sail to the Eastward, gave Chace, at 7 Ditto, it being dark, and the Schooner being evidently an American from all Appearances, I hawled my Wind to the Southward. At 6 AM Gave Chace to a Schooner, at half past 7 Ditto brought her to, she proved to be the *Republican* from Savannah bound to Boston, left the Tybee yesterday at Noon, and had neither seen or heard of any Cruizers. Exercised Pettee Officers, and Seamen at small Arms. Charleston Bar at Noon bore North West, seven Leagues Distance, Depth of Water 13 Fathoms over a Bottom of black and white Sand, that was pretty fine.

Latitude observed 32°.28′ N°.
Longitude Account 80.23 W.

[HS of Pa. NDA photostat.]

To Secretary of Treasury from Secretary of Navy

[PHILADELPHIA,]
*Navy Departm*t *27. July 1798*

SEC^y OF TREASURY

SIR, It appears to Me, that the Revenue Cutters which are to be employed in the Navy Service, should be allowed Men in proportion to the Number of their Guns — and that five Men for each Gun — exclusive of officers would be the proper Allowance.

In the Navy Service, there are three descriptions of Men — Able Seamen at 17 dollars per Month — Ordinary Seamen who are in Fact Landsmen, at ten dollars per Month — and Marines at six dollars per month. I think the Laws relative to the Revenue Cutter, permit you to give twenty dollars, for all the Men employed on board of them. If Landsmen or ordinary Seamen are employed on the same Terms as able Seamen, the latter will be discontented and the former will be paid too much — If you employ None but able Seamen, the Merchant Service or the Navy Service will suffer. permit Me then, without presuming to dictate, to suggest the propriety of adopting something like the Navy System, in manning the Cutters. I am under the strongest Conviction, that if you direct that one half of the Men in each Cutter be able Seamen — one quarter ordinary Seamen, & the remaining quarter to be Landsmen & Boys, these Vessels will be sufficiently manned and there will, besides other Advantages, be a great Saving to the Public by such a Regulation. In the Navy, I intend to have four descriptions of Men — Able Seamen at 17 dollars p. month. Ordinary Seamen — such Men as have made a few voyages but are not Seamen, and better than Landsmen at 14 dollars per Month — Landsmen, who are nearly Seamen at 10 Dollars per Month — Marines, at 6 doll's per Month — But you can have none of the latter description in the Cutters. —

Capt Leonard in the 14 Gun Cutter at New York, wants Nothing but Men, to enable him to proceed on a Cruise. He writes to Me, for Instructions on the subject of his Men, but these I have informed him, he is to receive from you. Will you be pleased to attend as early as convenient to this business. He will probably want a Gunner, a Carpenter & a Boatswain — and might probably obtain Them at 20 dollars per Month.

I am &c

[NDA. Req. on US T, 1798–1803.]

Extract from journal of James Pity, U. S. Frigate *Constitution*, 27 July 1798, Friday

First part this 24 hours, Light Winds Inclinable to Calms. Could not come up with the Vessell in chace on Acc^t^ of Small Winds at 3 P. M. exercized the men at the Guns. They come on Bravely. At 8 A. M. ⩘ Ship at 9 Wore Ship to the Westward Sett T. Gall^t^ Sails. Sent up Royal Yards & Sails. Latter Part clear and Pleasant People employ'd at Sundry Jobbs.

[Latitude observed 40.19 N°]

[NDA.]

Extract from Captain Thomas Truxtun's journal, U. S. Frigate *Constellation*, 27 July 1798, Friday

Pleasant Breezes, and charming Weather, at 2 PM made the Land, at 5 Ditto Mr Barnes, a Pilot dispatched as Express to me, by William Pennock, Esquire, Naval Agent, Norfolk, arrived along Side, and delivered me Letters from Government, to which I immediately paid Attention.

At half past 5 Ditto Mr Delany in a Pilot Boat from Norfolk, brought a Number of Gentlemen along Side from Charleston to visit the Ship (and various Presents of Fruit, &c.) which I showed them throughout with Pleasure.

At half past 6 the Gentlemen left us giving three Cheers, which we returned, and stood to the Southward under easy Sail, and at 3 AM wore and stood to the Northward, employed making up my Dispatches for the Secretary of the Navy, which I delivered about Noon, and dispatched Mr Barnes for Norfolk in his Pilot Boat. Depth of Water 12 Fathoms, the Light House bearing North and lee West, seven Leagues Distance. Spoke the Revenue armed Brig on a Cruize, belonging to Charleston, Captn Cochran.

Latitude observed 32°.25′N°

Longitude Account 80.23 W.

[HS of Pa. NDA photostat]

Letter to the first Minister of State

MADRID *July 28th 1798.*

To the first MINISTER OF STATE.

SIR, I find it expedient to repeat in this paper the representation which I had the honour to make to your Excellency in my conference this day; that the crew of the American Ship *Eliza*, captain Neal Mac Neal late master, captured by a French Privateer and carried into Port Passage, have been marched as prisoners of war into France; to reclaim the liberation of those persons as citizens of the United States of America; and to request that the most peremptory orders may be expedited to prevent a repetition of similar subjects of complaint for the future. On this occasion I owe it as a tribute to truth and justice to declare, that by the reports made to me in several late instances, the Governors and Commanders for his catholic Majesty in many of the Ports of Spain, have manifested a sincere desire to protect as far as they were able the Citizens of the United States of America and their property against the atrocious proceedings of some French Consuls and French Privateers.

I am

[NOTE.—It is believed that this letter was written by David Humphreys, although the manuscript does not contain his signature.]

[SDA. Disp. Spain, Bk 4, Humphreys.]

To John Chaplin, Jr., and others, Beaufort, South Carolina, from Secretary of Navy

[PHILADELPHIA,]
Navy Department 28th July 1798

JNº CHAPLIN Jr. Esqr & others, *Beaufort South Carolina*

GENTn The Secretary of War has communicated to me, your Letter to him of the 7th Instant

So much of it, as relates to the General defence of your part of the Country, he will doubtless attend to — That part of it, which relates to Gallies falls within the Business of my Department. —

The President is authorized to procure to be built — Ten Gallies — Six of these are preparing — 2 at Charleston, 2 in North Carolina, and two in Georgia, — One will be got here, and probably, two at Newport, Rhode Island — Under such circumstances, I can only authorize the Building of one in your place, — And I have the honor to request, that you, Gentlemen, or any one of you who may be appointed by the others — will immediately contract for this one on the part of the Public to be furnished as early as possible, — She ought to be coppered, & I shall rely that Copper can be had with you, and shall take no measures to furnish it — I enclose the dimensions of the Galleys already contracted for — You may, if you please vary these dimensions, so as to make the Beam 15 instead of 13½ feet — The estimated expense you will observe is 2279 Dollars, exclusive of Copper & Military Stores — The Military Stores shall be forwarded to you in full time for the Galley —

I have requested the Secretary of the Treasury to remit to you, directed to John Chaplin Jr. Esqr 1500 Dollars to begin with, and the moment I have your estimate of the cost of the Galley the residue shall be remitted —

You will observe that I rely on you for every thing relating to the Galley, to her completion — It is too far to furnish from hence, any articles you may want, in time, unless I now knew what these articles were —

As to your liberal and public spirited offer to build Galleys, and loan them to the public &c on the condition, that they shall be manned and armed at public expense, and employed solely in the district; I am very sorry that the Laws will not authorize the President to accede to all the conditions — I have enclosed the Law on that subject, by which you will perceive that he is authorized to accept of any number of vessels as a free Gift to the Public, — Your offer is to loan them during the War —

If the Citizens of Beaufort will build, any Number of Galleys not exceeding three, and will make a free Gift of them to the public, they will be manned, armed, and maintained by the public — And it is highly probable, they will be employed entirely in your district, but I am not authorized by the Law to condition that they shall be employed no where else — When I am informed of the Number of Galleys you furnish on the Terms authorized by the Law, and the time they will be ready, I will take measures to send you by that time, all the arms and military stores necessary, and to provide the officers & Men — Please to recommend proper officers for the Galley to be built for the Public, as well as those you may undertake at the expense of the Citizens —

I wish very sincerely it was in my power to deal on the part of the public, more liberally with you —

I have the honor to be Gent^n^ &c^a^

[NDA. GLB, Vol. 1.]

To Thomas Pinckney, Charleston, South Carolina, from Secretary of the Navy

[PHILADELPHIA,]
Navy Department 28th July 1798*

THO^s^ PINCKNEY Esqr *Cha^ston^ So. Carolina*

SIR The Secretary at War, has this day sent me an extract of your Letter to him of the 3rd Instant — In answer to which, I take the Liberty to observe, that young Gentlemen of good principles, and reputable connexions, with or without nautical skill, will be received in the Navy as Midshipmen, at 19 D^s^ per month. By the regulations heretofore established, two Midshipmen only were allowed to a Ship of 20 Guns — The number was not sufficient; and the President having authority, the number is doubled.

There is a Brig preparing at Charleston for public service, under the direction of Mr Simons. — There ought to be two Midshipmen appointed for this Vessel; and I presume, Six for the ship which the Citizens of Charleston are about building for the public — It would be very agreeable to receive from you, the names of Young Gentlemen for these appointments; who may hereafter render service to their Country in more important Stations.

Midshipmen rank as officers & Gentlemen. Their first promotion will be to the rank of Lieutenant; and on the qualifications & Bravery of the Young Gentlemen, who may now enter the service, will doubtless depend the future usefulness & honor of our Navy. —

I have the honor to be &c^a^

[*Among letters dated 28 August, in Letter Book.]
[NDA. GLB, Vol. 1.]

[28 July 1798.]

Master Abraham Outten's account of the capture of Brig *Planter* by French cruiser

Abraham Outten of Newbern Craven County and State of North Carolina Master and Commander of the Brig *Planter* of said Newbern deposeth and saith That on the 23rd of July 1798, he set sail in said Brig from the port of Green Island in the Island of Jamaica bound for Newbern aforesaid. — That on the 28th early in the morning he saw Cape Antonia on the West end of Cuba and about 9 o'clock A. M.

the said Cape bearing S. E. distant 4 or 5 leagues was brought to by a french cruizer which made prize of him and put on board a prize Master and Six hands — That the prize Master & hands took charge of his Vessel put her about & stood in for the land. The breeze being light off shore the Brig continued to ply to windward and about 6 o'clock p. m. Cape Antonia then bearing about E by N. 2½ leagues distant and the Cruizer which had also continued to ply to Windward being about 1½ leagues distant from the Brig three sails were discovered to the Southward. That on sight of these Sail, the prize Master Supposing them to be British appeared to be much alarmed and gave orders to put the Brig about — That while the prize Master and hands were engaged in putting the Vessel about this deponent with the assistance of some of his Crew seized their Arms and after a short struggle two of them threw themselves overboard, the rest submitted and this deponent retook his vessel, — This deponent then ordered out the boat to save the two who were in the Water, but a heavy Squall striking them sank the boat and put it out of his power to save them. This deponent then made the best of his way to Newbern his destined port where he arrived the 16th August following bringing with him the prize Master and four hands who were by order of a Majistrate Committed to Newbern Jail where they now remain — The prize Master is a white man, one of the hands is a Mulatto, the rest are black — The prize Master says that two of the blacks are Spanish Slaves. — They have no Commission or any other paper to shew by what authority they acted — The prisoners call themselves and are committed by the following names — The prize Master Pon Fricon, the Mulatto Sigue Antonio, the blacks John Nicholas, Jean Francois. & Charley Lewis. — The two last are those said to be Slaves.

ABRAHAM OUTTEN

[SDA. Misc. L., Jan.–Aug. 1798.]

To Henry William Desaussure, Charleston, agent for galleys, from Secretary of Navy

[PHILADELPHIA,]
Navy Department July 28th 1798

Hy Wm DESAUSSURE Esqr *Charleston*

SIR I have this day received from the Department of the Treasury (the Secretary of the Treasury having been some time absent) your favours to him of the 29 & 30th June & 13th July —

As you have proceeded so far in the business of the Galleys, I hope you will continue your agency till their completion. — If this should not be agreeable to you, you will please in that case to turn over the Business, to Mr Crafts, the Gentleman you so strongly recommend — I have requested the Treasury to remit you two thousand five hundred Dollars, and further remittance shall be made you when I am informed that it is necessary — Be pleased to accompany your requisition, with an estimate of the whole sum wanted to complete the Galleys —

It appears by Humphreys' Estimate that 2279 Dollars would be about the Cost of each Galley and that 1300 Dollars would be necessary to provide Military Stores &c^a It is unfortunate that I cannot judge what Military Stores can be supplyed at Charleston — In this state of things, and that delay may be avoided, — I shall leave the Article, powder, to be procured by you, and shall send on every other article from hence, — included in the estimate — I observ by the Correspondence between you, and the Secretary of the Treasury, that 24 pound cannon have been sent on by the Secretary at War — The Secretary at War confirms this, & altho their arrival is not announced I shall presume they will arrive, and only send the other articles as follows —

Brass Howitzers
Musketts complete
Pikes
Rammers, Spunges, Ladles, & Worms
Cannon, Ball, & Grape Shott—

The President is absent at Massachusetts, or I have no doubt, I should now be able to announce to you, the appointments as Captains of the Galleys, the two Gentlemen so respectably recommended — I shall immediately transmit their Names to the President, and in Ten days I take for granted I shall be authorized to send on their appointments. —

The Acts of Congress, authorize the procurement of 24 vessels, carrying from 18 to 32 Guns & upwards — The funds are, an insufficient sum appropriated of public money, and the public Spirit of the Citizens, who are to be paid in 6 p.C^t Stock for their advances. — I have already contracted to the full amount of the public money and with the aid of Private subscriptions all the vessels are preparing, but three of 18 Guns and one of 32 — for one of the three, I have relyed partly on the public spirit of Charleston — I have before written to Mr Simmonds, the Collector, on this subject — I have proposed that a vessel said to be well calculated, for a cruiser, building by Wm Pritchard, should be purchased by the Citizens — and if their subscriptions did not amount to enough, with the aid of Sails, Rigging, Guns &c^a belonging to the public, and used on board a vessel of Paul Pritchard's, & Copper which has been sent for sheathing that vessel, I mentioned that if wanted, public money should be supplyed towards the object — I hope this matter has been taken up and that the vessel is in forwardness — If the Merchants engage in it, they should appoint one or more persons, to transact the whole Business, to completing the Ship for receiving her men, Guns, & Military, & other Stores which, upon hearing from them, I will take immediate arrangements for supplying in due time.

I have the honor to be &c^a

P. S. I am glad you increased the size of one of the Galleys I wish you had done so with both —

[NDA. GLB, Vol. 1.]

To Secretary Pickering from Messrs. William and Thomas Walter, Boston

[July 28, 1798.]

The Hon'ble TIMOTHY PICKERING Esqr

SIR Three weeks since the Ship *Merchant* John Traill commander belonging to us, sailed for London, where we have order'd her to be armed, and have asked Genl Lincoln, the Collector for this District, in what way we can furnish Cap. Traill with a Commission agreeable to the late Act of Congress, authorising the arming of Merchant Vessels, or whether one can be obtained in London, but as the General cannot give us the Information, we have taken this liberty, respectfully to beg you will have the goodness to acquaint us, as, if we have to send on one, we shall have but little time to do it, that it may reach him in Season.

With very great consideration we are

Sir

Your most obedt Servants.

WM. & THO. WALTER.

BOSTON *28th July 1798.*
Philadelphia.

[SDA. Misc. L., Jan.-Aug. 1798.]

Extract from the journal of Lieutenant John Mullowny, U. S. Frigate *United States*, 28 July 1798

Foggy weather
Fired a signal gun for the *Delaware*
A 3 P. M. Fog cleared. See the *Delaware*, N. W. distance 1 mile
Shortened sail for the *Delaware*
At 10 P. M. sounded, no bottom
Fired a gun every hour which was ansd by the *Delaware*
Frequently sounded, no ground.
[Latde Pr acct 41.8]

[NA.]

Extract from journal of James Pity, U. S. Frigate *Constitution*, 28 July 1798, Saturday

First part this 24 hours light Airs & Clear Wr a 4. Beat to Quarters and Exercized the Guns.

Middle Part Thick and foggy Weather.
Latter Hazy and then clear at Intervals.
At 10 Clock sounded in 47. fathoms Water.
a 12 sounded in 40 fathms
No Observation.

[NDA.]

Extract from Captain Thomas Truxtun's journal, U. S. Frigate *Constellation*, 28 July 1798, Saturday

Moderate Breezes from the Southward, and a small Swell from the South East; stood in to 6 Fathoms Water, in fair Sight of the City of Charleston, the Shipping at the Wharfs, and within two Miles of the Bar. A Pilot Boat soon after came along Side, and by her I forwarded a Letter to the Collector of the Port, and another to Messrs Robert Hazlehurst and Company, &c. &c. &c. in Reply to an Application made by a Number of Merchants of Charleston to me for a Convoy for their Vessels from Havannah; I referred them to Government, as by my Instructions I had no Power to leave the Coast on such Business. At half past 6 saw a Sail to the Eastward; gave Chace, and at half past 7 Ditto, brought to with a Shot a Brig in Ballast from Hallifax, bound to Charleston, called the *South Carolina*. This Vessel had been taken by the *Thetis* (an English Frigate) on her Passage Home from the Havannah, and her cargo landed at Hallifax. At 5 AM saw a Sail, gave Chace and at 6 Ditto spoke a Ship from Charleston bound to Martinica. At 8 Ditto discovered another Sail, gave Chance, and at 10 spoke the Brig *Melony* of New York from Savannah, bound Home; the Master informed, that he had neither seen, or heard of any French Cruizers on the Coast. Made six large Fires below, after the Appartments of the Crew were washed &c. &c. At half past 11 AM saw a Sail in the Southern Board, to which I gave Chace, and at Noon Charleston Bar bore West North West, fifteen Leagues Distance, Depth of Water Thirty two Fathoms, over a Botton of dark fine Sand.

Latitude observed 32°.27′ North
Longitude Account 79.50 W.

[HS of Pa. NDA photostat.]

[28 or 29 July, 1798.]

Sworn statement of John Pearsall relative to capture of Ship *Friendship* by French Privateer

LAST MAIL

City of New-York, ss.

Personally appeared before me, GABRIEL FURMAN, Esq.; one of the Aldermen of the city of New-York, John Pearsall, of the state of New-York, Mariner, son of William Pearsall, Queen's County, Long Island, who being duly sworn on the Evangelists of Almighty God, doth depose and say, that on the 7th of July, 1798, he sailed from New-York, in the ship *Friendship*, of Boston, Capt. Brown, that on the 28th or 29th of the same month the said vessel was captured by a French privateer, in lat. 29, to the best of his knowledge and belief; that about four days after he the said John Pearsall with others, were put on board the American sloop *Lark*, belonging to Philadelphia, commanded by capt. Adams: that on the 17th of August, the said deponent and the above eight persons were forcibly taken out of the said sloop *Lark*, by a boat's crew of the British ship *Hannibal*, carrying 74 guns, commanded by capt. Smith, who, notwithstanding, that the said Deponent and five others had American protections, in due form, paid not the least attention to them, nor would even condescend to look at them: that on the 12th November, while the above mentioned ship the *Hannibal*, was lying on the vicinity of Kingston (Jamaica,) the said deponent about 10 o'clock in the evening swam on shore at the iminent danger of his life, and that at that time, the following American citizens all of whom had protections, were detained on board, viz. Earl Stephens of Massachusetts, John Lewis of New-Haven and Thomas Williams of New-York, that your deponent the day after his escape from the *Hannibal*, shiped on board the brig *Lively* of Philadelphia, capt. Stewart; and that he arrived at the port of Philadelphia about the 14th of February last; from whence he soon after proceeded to this city, and farther this deponent saith not.

JOHN PEARSALL.

Sworn before me, this 9th March, 1799.
GABRIEL FURMAN, *Alderman.*

[LC, "Independent Chronicle" (Mass.), March 14–18, 1799, p. 42.]

[29 July, 1798.]

Extract from H. M. Sloop *Musketo's* log book—encounter with American Brig *Unanimity*, Captain Cochran

Nassau (N. P.) Aug. 28.

On Saturday arrived here from convoying two homeward bound vessels to the latitude of 32, and a cruise, his majesty's sloop *Musketo*, capt. Whyte.

Off the coast of South-Carolina, the *Musketo* had a rencontre with the American revenue brig *Unanimity*, capt. Cochran; respecting which our readers will find ample details in the following extracts.

EXTRACT FROM THE *Musketo's* LOG-BOOK

"Nothing remarkable occurred till the 29th July, at 1 P. M. discovered a brig bearing down on us under her topsails. Supposing her to be a cruiser, cleared for action. At 2h. 30m. the brig hauled her wind on the starboard tack, hoisted American colours, and made all sail on the wind. The *Musketo* instantly tacked, fired a gun, and hoisted English colours. At 3, the brig tacked and stood in for the land, bearing W. by S. On passing us, fired a shot a head to bring her to; they paying no attention to this, but making off as fast as possible, capt. Whyte ordered four shot to be fired at them. Tacked and chased the brig. At 5, P. M. the brig was close in with the breakers, off Dewees's Inlet, 22 miles N. of Charleston bar. She then tacked; we did the same; finding that the *Musketo* could completely cut him off from superiority in sailing, tacked again, and wore round for the breakers; instantly followed her, and fired as our guns would bear. The brig returned a broadside, put his helm hard a weather, and run on shore. The *Musketo* being then close on the breakers, and in quarter less three fathoms water, capt. White not having any person on board who had ever been on that part of the coast before, judged it most prudent to hawl the ship off into deeper water. At 5h. 30m. tacked, with intention to stand in, destroy the brig, and if possible save the prisoners, which would have been difficult as the sea was then making a fair roll over her. The man on the mast head called out, a strange sail on the starboard bow, bearing down on us. Supposing it to be a pilot boat, hove to, and made the signal for a pilot. At 6h. 30m. the pilot came alongside, and to capt. Whyte's utter astonishment, informed him, the brig he had driven ashore, was the *Unanimity* of 14 six pounders and 65 men, belonging to the State of South-Carolina, and had sailed that morning from Charleston on a cruise. On board the pilot boat were several gentlemen of respectability who had witnessed the greater part of this day's proceedings."

[LC, "Independent Chronicle" (Mass.), Oct. 1 to 4, 1798, p. 110.]

Extract from the journal of Lieutenant John Mullowny, U. S. Frigate *United States*, 29 July 1798

Foggy. A 1 P. M. the *Delaware* on the Quarter (lee) dist about 4 Miles.

Reefed Topsails 2 reefs

Stiff breeses

Shortened sail, At M the *Delaware* made signal for a Strange sail being in sight, we answ^d & made signal to speak her. Clear Ship for action.

[Lat^de Obs^d 39.56.]

[NA.]

Extract from journal of James Pity, U. S. Frigate *Constitution*, 29 July 1798, Sunday

First part this 24 Hours clear and Moderate a 4 P. M. furld Main Sail at 5 Beat all hands to Quarters At 12. Tack'd Ship to the Northward.

Middle part fresh Breezes & Clear —

At 7 A. M. sounded ground in Twenty five fath^ms with grey sand intermixd with Shells —

At 8. hove in Stays and Stood Southw^d & Saw a Ship bear^g down upon clear'd Ship for Action prov'd to be Ship *Industry* bound to Boston from Turks Island. Thos Lewis & Son owners — at 10 Double Reef Top Sails. Latter part Clear.

[Latitude Observed 40.24]

[NDA.]

Extract from Captain Thomas Truxtun's journal, U. S. Frigate *Constellation*, 29 July 1798, Sunday

Moderate Breezes from the Southward, and pleasant Westher, at 2 PM spoke the Sail to which I gave Chace the preceding Day at 11 AM as mentioned in the Transactions of that 24 Hours. She proved to be the Ship, *Swift Packet* from Savannah bound to Philadelphia, out twelve Hours. At 6 PM saw a Sail to the Northward at a great Distance, made Sail, and gave Chace; she appeared to be bound to North Carolina from her Course, at half past 7 it being dark, lost Sight of her. Shortened Sail, and hawled up to the Westward, and directed the Course after, according to Depth of Water, standing in to 11 Fathoms, and off to 24 Fathoms; Charleston Bar at Noon bore North North West 8 Leagues Distance, saw a Sail to the Northward, to which I gave Chace.

Latitude observed 32°22′ N^o

Longitude Account 80.30 W.

[HS of Pa. NDA photostat.]

To Lieutenant Triplett of Marines from Captain Thomas Truxtun, U. S. Navy

United States Ship *Constellation*
30th July 1798.

Sir, Had I excercised my Authority as the Commander of this Ship, and arrested in all Cases, where many in my Situation would not have hesitated a Moment, The *Constellation* must 'ere now, have exhibited for the Out set of a Navy, a sad Spectacle indeed, to the People of the United States. But Sir, I have cast a Veil, or Curtain over so many Improprieties, and Neglects from Tenderness, and Delicacy to Gentlemen's Characters, and in Hopes daily of more Attention, and Regularity; that Patience, and temper in me is now nearly exhausted. — As I know full well, that it is much easier to make a deep Wound, than to heal a small one, I have been actuated in my Conduct to you by Principles mild and inherent in my Nature, believing at the same Time, that a little Reflection would induce you to appreciate the Measures I have taken, to make your Duty plain, and easy, and excite you to a more minute Attention thereto. I have hitherto been disappointed, I can no longer continue disobeyed, If I am, Recourse must be had to an Alternative, by no Means pleasant to me, or honorable to you.

I hope therefore, the present will have the desired effect, and in that Hope I remain

Your most Obed^t humble Servt

THOMAS TRUXTUN.

N. B. Two Vessels were brought to, and spoke last Night, when you was not on Deck. — Under the Orders I gave you, it was as much your Duty, to leave Directions for the Sergeant of the Watch, to call you, as I consider it mine to be called on certain Occasions, by the Officer of the Watch, and not to wait for all Hands to be called, when I deem it unnecessary, in speaking trifling Merchantmen.

T. T.

Lieutenant TRIPLETT of Marines.

[HS of Pa. NDA photostat. Truxtun's LB, 1798–9.]

To Captain James Sever, U. S. Navy, from Secretary of Navy

[PHILADELPHIA,]
Navy departm^t July 30. 1798

Capt JOHN [JAMES] SEVER *Boston*

SIR, As it has been impracticable for you to join the Frigate *United States* & Sloop of War *Delaware* on their intended Cruise, I have now to direct that as soon as your Ship and Cutter are ready for Sea, you will in company with her immediately set Sail, and cruise agreeably to the following Instructions. Your Object must be to secure from the depredations of the French Cruisers, the principal Ports of New Hampshire, Massachusetts, and Rhode Island, and pay some Attention to New York, for which Purpose you will consider your Cruising Ground, to extend from about ten or fifteen Leagues Eastward of the East End of Georgia Bank to the West end of Long Island. —

It may not be necessary, that the Cutter and the *Herald* should be constantly close in with each other — the object is to make your small force as useful as possible by affording the greatest Extent of Protection it is capable of — it will be proper however, that you are never at such a distance, as to prevent your affording Protection to each other in case of need. It will be desireable that there should be frequent opportunities of communicating with you, to facilitate which you will every Ten or 12 days endeavour to appear off New Port, Rhode Island & at such a distance from the town as to be seen, with the Swedish Flag hoisted at your Main top Mast — When any Thing occurs to be communicated to you, it will be done by means of a Pilot Boat from New Port.

Any Prize that you may take you will send into the nearest port of the United States to be proceeded against according to Law — The persons found on board of them must be reported to the Collector of the Port at which they first arrive and be delivered over to the Marshall or some other Civil or Military Officer of the United States — Prizes of force inferior to your own will be divided between the Captors & the United States, those of equal or Superior force go entirely to the Captor. —

Wishing you great Success

I remain &c

The enclosed Letter for Captn Nicholson is to be delivered only by yourself. —

[NDA. OSW, Vol. 1.]

To President John Adams from Secretary of Navy

[PHILADELPHIA,]
Navy Department 30th July 1798.

JOHN ADAMS Esqr
President of the United States

SIR. By Letters previously received from Stephen Higginson Esqr of Boston, I had been taught to expect, that both the *Herald* of 20 Guns, and the Boston Cutter of 14 Guns, would have been prepared to join Capt Barry, at Cape Cod, or Nantasket road, about the 20th Instant. —

Barry arrived at the place of destination, about the time appointed, but found the Boston Vessels in an unprepared state, and I have reason to conclude from his Letters to me, that he has proceeded with Decatur only, on the expedition to the Islands — This, I believe, is a circumstance, not to be regretted, for from all the information, I can get, there is no probability, that Barry will meet in the West Indies, a force superior to his own. —

At this season of the Year, and during the Months of August & September, & part of October, the British armed-Ships are less alert in the West Indies, than at other times, in consequence of Apprehensions of danger from the Hurricanes.

Some of their Frigates are now in our Ports, as being more secure from the Elements, than the Islands. — Our own force, on our own Coasts, it is not to be doubted, is well known to the French — And having no force in the Islands equal to ours, (except three light Frigates, blocked up by the British at Cape Francois) it is not to be apprehended, that our Coasts will be much molested by their Cruisers — at least for some months to come, unless indeed, they could send a Force from Europe, which is far from being probable — The French Islands having no authorized intercourse with the United States, must depend in a great degree upon Captures for supplies of Bread & Salt meat — Not having much to fear from the British about the Islands, during the Hurricane season, and not daring to send their

Cruisers on our Coasts, it is likely that a greater number of them than usual, will be employed during that season in the Neighbourhood of the Islands. —

The Hurricanes I understand are not so very dangerous, as they are generally believed to be. — It is not oftener than once, in four or five years, that much Injury is done by them, and at such times the danger is partial, and extends not beyond one or two Islands —

Under such circumstances, and impressed with the Opinion, that the American Navy should be taught to disregard problematical dangers; And that our Force should be employed, while the French have but little force, in destroying what they have, and in producing a scarcity of Provisions, and the consequent discontent, flowing from such a source, in their Islands, I have the honor Sir, to submit for your consideration, the following proposed Arrangement. —

To leave the Coast, from the East end of Georges Bank, to Long Island, to be guarded by the *Herald*, Capt Sever of 20 Guns & the Boston Cutter of 14 Guns; From Long Island to Cape Henry by the *Baltimore* of 20 Guns and two Cutters, one of which (of 10 Guns) is now out, and another of 14 Guns will be ready by the end of this Week, to sail from New York; — From Cape Henry to our Southern extremity, by one of the Frigates, and two Cutters, which will proceed from hence to the Southward in a short time. —

This destination, will leave one Frigate, and the Ship *Montezuma* of 20 Guns, as soon as she can be prepared for Sea, which I hope will be by the 20th or 25th of August, to be employed in any enterprize and these, if you Sir, approve, I would propose to send on a cruise among the Islands, as soon as the latter can be prepared. —

It is likely that Barry & Decatur, will leave the Islands on their return, about the time this second expedition would leave our Coasts — and by the time Barry returns, it is to be presumed, that the *Ganges*, Capt Dale, who must shortly return into Port, to refit, may be prepared to join the other Frigate, which 'till then, will be kept on the Southern Station, in a third expedition to the Islands. —

By keeping up incessant attacks upon the French Cruisers on their own ground, they will in a degree at least be prevented from coming on ours. In about three months our force will be so increased as to admit of more frequent attacks, or attacks with stronger force. —

I have the honor to be
With the Highest respect & esteem
Sir, &c.

[NDA. OSW, Vol. 1.]

To Captain Samuel Nicholson, U. S. Navy, from Secretary of Navy

PHILADELPHIA,
[*Navy Departmen*t *30 July. 1798*]

Capt SAMl NICHOLSON

SIR, Capt Sever & Capt Chapman, in the *Herald* and Boston Cutter, being ready for a Cruise, is directed to occupy the cruising Ground pointed out for you, in your Instructions of the 12th Instant.

You will therefore proceed more Southward, & consider your Cruising Ground, for the present, to extend from the Eastward of long Island, to Cape Henry — but soon after your arriving on this Station, you will appear off the Capes of Delaware, & stand off and on for two days, in the Expectation of receiving from Me, by that time, some additional Instructions. In the Event of your not receiving such Instructions, you will pursue the best Means in your power, for protecting from French Depredations, the Commerce of our Country—but you must appear off the Capes of Delaware every ten or 12 days, & hover off and on for two days, to afford an opportunity of communicating with you. You will at such Times, hoist the same Signal, you were directed to hoist off New Port. —

Should you fall in with Capt Dale, in the Ship *Ganges*, you will direct him to return to this Port, to be refitted. There will be two Revenue Cutters (*Governor Jay*) Capt Leonard of 14 Guns, & (*General Greene*) Capt Price of 10 Guns to cruise under your Command, while you remain between Long Island & Cape Henry. —

[NDA. OSW, Vol. 1.]

To Captain Jonathan Chapman, Revenue Cutter *Pickering*, from Secretary of Navy

[PHILADELPHIA,]
Navy departmen^t July 30, 1798.

Capt JONA. CHAPMAN
Cutter "Pickering" Boston.

SIR, As your Cutter was not ready to join Capt Barry and Capt Decatur agreeably to my former Instructions, I have now to direct that you will immediately join the Ship *Herald*, and cruising in Company with that Ship follow such Instructions as you shall from Time to Time receive from her Commander Capt John [James] Sever, whose orders are sent by this Conveyance

I have the honor &c.

[NDA. OSW, Vol. 1.]

To Jeremiah Yellott, Navy Agent, Baltimore, from Secretary of Navy

[PHILADELPHIA,]
Navy Department July 30th 1798

JERh YELLOTT Esqr. *Baltimore*

SIR Your Letter of the 27th Instant is received and I am pleased with the progress, you are making in the dispatch of the *Baltimore* — The cambouse has or will soon arrive — Common Rum of good Proof is what is allowed for our Ships of War; which you will of course provide — You are perfectly right in not purchasing on credit, and to relieve the advance you may have been under, I have directed a remittance of Ten Thousand Dollars, to be forwarded to you immediately —

I have the honor to be &c.

P. S. The Guns & Pistols have been delayed too long, but I hope will go off tomorrow or next day — The cambouse has been sent from New York for Baltimore.

[NDA. GLB, Vol. 1.]

To Stephen Higginson, Navy Agent, Boston, from Secretary of Navy

[PHILADELPHIA,]
Navy Department 30th July 1798

STEPn HIGGINSON Esqr *Boston*

SIR, I am honoured with your favour of the 22nd Instant — Also several days ago, your confidential Letter, for which I am much obliged —

I am rather pleased that Capt Sever, and the Cutter were, not ready, as I am confident the Force of Barry & Decatur will be quite sufficient for that enterprize, and the other Vessels can take Nicholson's station, who can be employed to advantage farther south —

The Hurricanes I understand are not dangerous, oftener than once in three or four years — and then the danger is very partial, and by no means extends over all the West India Islands, nor even many of them

It is the custom of the British Cruisers to lie still and to come into our Harbours during the Hurricane season, — at least in a great degree — Knowing this, the French cruise with less caution during that season — knowing too, that our force on our own Coasts, is superior to any they can send, — they will employ their cruisers more about the Islands — Under such circumstances, tell me if you please freely your opinion, whether in making arrangements for the employment of our Ships, I ought at all to consider that there are Hurricanes in the West Indies? It is only from the lights I can receive from intelligent men, that I shall be able to conduct the Business of my Department, with tolerable advantage — The remains of the 40,000 Dollars I requested the Secretary of the Treasury to have remitted several days ago — Your wants early in August, shall be immediately attended to —

I have enclosed Instructions for Capt Sever, which be pleased to have delivered — I hope the Ship & Cutter will be ready to proceed on their cruise

I have the honor to be &c.

[NDA. GLB, Vol. 1.]

To Joshua Humphreys, Naval Constructor, from Secretary of Navy

[PHILADELPHIA,]
Navy Department July 30th 1798

Mr JOSHUA HUMPHREYS

SIR The Prize Schooner, *La Croyable*, will be sold this day at 12 o'clock, at the Merchants Coffee House, with her apparel & Guns. —

I request the favor of you to attend the sale and bid for her, the first bid, what you Judge to be a fair price, taking into consideration the value of the kind of Guns she has, her present condition, & what it will take to fit her completely for a cruiser — The money arising from the sale, will be divided between the public, and the Crew of Capt Decatur, — my wish is, that the Crew, should get the value of their half the prize — but not more than the value. —

I am sir, &ca

[NDA. GLB, Vol. 1.]

[30 July, 1798.]

Extract from a letter dated Baltimore, July 30, from Captain John Cruft, late master of Brig *Sally*, captured by French

"I have again experienced a fate similar to that of my last voyage, being captured by the French frigate *La Decade*, and sent into Cayenne, there condemned both vessel and cargo, in the most unjustifiable manner, and myself and crew turned ashore without a farthing. In this situation I made application to both the commander of the frigate, and the commissary of the port, for a small part of my adventure to support me, or even part of my cabin stores, that were left, but was by them treated with an eye of contempt, and refused even to a biscuit. This treatment might only be expected from the most uncivilized, and savage nation, but at present, I compute the French to be no better, as they certainly are possessed with neither the principles of men, nor the feelings of humanity. *Liberty*, which they first contended for, is now changed into greater slavery than in the reign of any of their Kings, as never was their a monarch yet ever reigned, that was invested with so much power, *as the Directory's agent in Cayenne*, he has both the military and civil power in his hands, and can put to death whom he pleases, without any trial; several instances, which had happened just before my arrival, by his ordering several black soldiers shot for only complaining of their allowance of provisions not being sufficient to support them. — *Americans* were treated with disdain, and those of the inhabitants that were any ways disposed well towards them, were forbidden connecting themselves with them.

"Reasons assigned for condemnation: — 1st, Being bound to Surrinam and a market, as expressed by the clearance. — 2d, Role d'Equipage not in order, as by being expressed on the back of it, being given by request of merchants and captains, and not acknowledged by Congress. — 3d, It not being witnessed (as they say) of the Notary's signing it when he did."

[LC, "Columbian Centinel" (Boston, Mass.), 8 August 1798.]

Extract from journal of James Pity, U. S. Frigate *Constitution*, 30 July 1798, Monday

First part this 24 hours fresh Breezes and Clear.

at 4 P. M. TK Ship to the West[d] at 5 bent down T. Gall[t] Yards at 8 A.M. Saw a Sail Stand[g] to the Eastw[d] wore Ship and gave chace She prov'd to be the *Louisa* Daniel Lewis Com[r] from New York bound to hamburgh 3 days out Tack'd Ship and Stood to the West[d] all Hands Setting up Rigging. Latter part Light Wind and Clear Weather.

[Latitude observed 40.17]

[NDA.]

Extract from Captain Thomas Truxtun's journal, U. S. Frigate *Constellation*, 30 July 1798, Monday

At 2 PM spoke the Chace mentioned at the End of the preceding Day, she was a Schooner called the *Sally* from Charleston, bound to Saint Augustine out 24 Hours, and informed me that the other

Vessel to Leeward was a Schooner from same Place bound to Virginia. At 4 Ditto saw two Sail, gave Chace, and at 6 Ditto brought to with a Shot the Ship *Maria* of New York, Conchlin, Master, from Charleston, bound Home, left the Bar at 9 o'Clock this Morning, he informed me, he had seen a large Ship to Leeward, but no Cruizers, I wished him safe in, and bore down on the other Sail, which proved to be the *Essabella** of and from Saint Thomas bound to Savannah lading Sugar, and out 15 Days; at Midnight having fell in with this Schooner a second Time, being in Pursuit of the Ship to the Westward, as I was informed of by the *Maria*, I ordered him to hoist out his Boat, and come on Board with his Papers, which he did, finding them all clear and regular, dismissed him. At 3 AM saw a Sail, gave Chace, and at 4 Ditto, brought to with a Shot the Sloop, *Driver*, Alexander McGivan, Master, from Jamaica, bound to Nixington, North Carolina, out 10 Days, and had seen no Cruizers, her Cargo consisted of Rum. Stood off to 26 Fathoms Water, and in to 18½ which was the Depth at Noon, when Charleston Bar bore West B. North, twelve Leagues Distance.

Latitude observed 32°.36′ No

Longitude Account 80.00 W.

[* Also spelled *Issabella*; see entry of 1 August 1798.]
[HS of Pa. NDA photostat.]

Extract from the journal of Lieutenant John Mullowny, U. S. Frigate *United States*, 30 July 1798

Stiff gales at ½ P. M. wore ship and made sail after the strange sail in sight, found her to be danish Ship from New York bound to Altona

A 4 P. M. made signal for a sail in sight, at 5 spoke the sail which was the *Old Tom* of & bound to Philada from Liverpoole

Reefed Top sails 2 reefs.

A heavy squall with rain settled Top sails at 9 hoisted them Up.

Clear weather

[Latde Obsd 38.15]

[NA.]

To Captain Isaac Phillips, U. S. Navy, from Secretary of Navy

[PHILADELPHIA,]

Navy Departmt July 21 [31]. 1798

Capt ISAAC PHILLIPS

SIR, I have received your Letter of the 28th Instant. I thought all the necessary Papers had been sent on to you in my last, and I still beleive they are. There are no printed Regulations denominated "Articles of War" The only ones of that Nature are entitled "Rules for the Regulation of the Navy" — a few copies of which I now send, and by which you will govern yourself — I shall nominate Mr Stanton Hazard, who will be appointed a Midshipman as you request, but the Number cannot be extended beyond four — If however, you can turn one of these already mentioned as appointed for your Ship to the *Montezuma*, you can then introduce in his place Capt Cox the Gentleman you mention, in which case inform me his Christian name that it may be recorded. The arrangement you propose as to the Number of Seamen Landsmen &c I agree to and you may ship them accordingly. I hope the Camboose has arrived as it has been shipped some time from New York.

Your Instructions shall soon be transmitted to you. —

[NDA. OSW, Vol. 1.]

To Messrs. Rabainne and P. T. Baudot, Boston, from Secretary Pickering

DEPARTMENT OF STATE, *Philadelphia July 31, 1798*

Messrs RABAINNE, and P. T. BAUDOT — *Boston.*

GENTLEMEN, I duly received your letter of the 20th inst. requesting the President's permission for the Schooner *Ranger* of Boston to carry French Passengers to Guadaloupe, St Thomas, and Gonaives in Hispaniola. To-day I have received the permit, signed by the President, from New York, and now forward it to the Collector of the Customs at Boston, to whom you will be pleased to make your Application. I am, &c.

TIMOTHY PICKERING

[SDA. Dom. L., Vol. 11.]

To James Campbell, Petersburg, Va., from Secretary of Navy

[PHILADELPHIA,]
Navy Department 31st July 1798

JAMES CAMPBELL Esqr *Petersburg*

SIR I received with pleasure, your esteemed favour of the 15th Instant, and it is an agreeable circumstance to observe the zeal, with which the Inhabitants in the vicinity of Richmond and Petersburg, are animated — Only one of the Ships of 24 Guns, authorized by Law, remains to be provided; and she could readily have been furnished from the Northward, but I am rather inclined to the acceptance of the one in your Quarter, and shall be happy to find that she is speedily compleated — Copper is very scarce, and difficult to be obtained here — Copper Bolts may be had, and if they cannot be had in Virginia, I will send them from hence, altho it would be more agreeable that they should be provided on the spot, to prevent delay— I hope this Ship will be compleated in the time you mention, and that she will do honor to the promoters of the laudable spirit, which has been shewn on this occasion. —

[NDA. GLB, Vol. 1.]

To Secretary of Treasury from Secretary of Navy

[PHILADELPHIA,]
Navy Department. 31. July. 1798.

SEC^y of TREASURY

SIR, The Prize Schooner, *La Croyable*, having been purchased for the Public, with her Guns &^c for seven Thousand Dollars, I have the honor to request that you will be pleased to direct, that that sum be paid to Wm. Nicholls Esquire Marshall, in full payment for the said Schooner and Appurtenances.

I have the honor &c

[NDA. Req. on US T, 1798–1803.]

To President John Adams from Secretary of Navy

[PHILADELPHIA,]
Navy Department July 31st 1798

JOHN ADAMS Esqr
President of the United States

SIR The Acts of Congress authorize the President to cause to be procured, from the Public Money appropriated for the purpose, and the public Spirit of the Citizens,

Six vessels not to exceed 18 Guns each
Twelve — not to exceed 24 Guns, &
Six — not less than 32 Guns —

Of the Six not to exceed 18 Guns, one I have directed to be purchased at Norfolk, from the very favorable representation of Capt McNeill of one he saw on the stocks — And two others, are building by the Merchants of Baltimore — The first I hope may be at sea, in five or six weeks — the other two, in three months — Of the 12 not to exceed 24 Guns, five have been procured by purchase — The *Herald* of Boston; — The *Ganges* & the *Delaware* of Philadelphia; and the *Baltimore* & the *Montezuma* of Baltimore. — The three first are at sea, unless the *Herald* should still remain at Boston, but at any rate, she must be now ready — One of the other two, at Baltimore, will be ready in a week, and the other in the month of August — And there have been contracted for, by the public, four Ships to carry 24 Guns — One at Portsmouth, one at New York, one at Newport, and one at Middleton, on Connecticut River — The three first will be launched within three months — I fear the other will be longer delayed. — The Merchants at Boston are building one 24 Gun Ship, the Merchants of Newbury another, and I have no doubt, another will be supplied by the Merchants of Richmond, Petersburg & Norfolk. —

Of the Six not to be less than 32 Guns, the Merchants of Philadelphia are building one to carry 44 Guns — The Merchants of New York, one to carry 36 Guns, and arrangements have been made for going on with the three Frigates so long ago begun, at Portsmouth, New York, and Norfolk. — There remains then, three ships not exceeding 18 Guns — one not exceeding 24 Guns, and one not less than 32 Guns to be provided — Of the three 18 Gun ships, I expect one will be obtained at Charleston, partly from Public — partly from private money, — One at Providence by the same means — and I hope the subscription at Salem, will at least furnish the other — The Merchants of Richmond, Petersburg and Norfolk, I rely will furnish the 24 Gun Ship; but I am at a loss at present to Judge, from whence the Ship of 32 Guns or upwards, will be obtained — Some steps must be speedily taken on the subject, and I will do myself the honor to advise you the moment, it is decided, how this ship is to be provided —

I do not expect that any of the Ships upwards of 32 Guns will be launched before next April, in that month I hope all will be launched, and no effort on my part shall be spared to have them launched sooner — all the other ships I hope will be at sea, long before that time

I have the honor to be Sir,

With the highest respect &c.

[NDA. GLB, Vol. 1.]

To Secretary of Treasury from Secretary of Navy

[PHILADELPHIA,]
Navy Departm^t 31st July 1798.

SEC^Y OF TREASURY

SIR, I have a Claim against the United States for my own Salary, as Sec^y of the Navy, & the Salary of Clerks employed in the Office up to the 30th June & including that day, to the Amount of 488 89/100 Dollars. —

It was no doubt intended by the Framers of the Law, establishing the department of the Navy, that the Clerks should receive such Compensation as the chief of the Departm^t thought their Services entitled them to receive and within the sum appropriated for the Payment of Clerks — but the Law is ambiguous and altho' the Congress made the Appropriation agreeably to my Estimate, allowing the Clerks higher Salaries than 500 Dollars each — yet the Law is construed & I believe according to the strict Letter of it, to admit of no higher Salaries to the Clerks than 500 Dollars. —

I have therefore the honor to request, that you will be pleased to direct an Advance to be made to Me of Four hundred and Eighty Eight Dollars & 89 Cents — to be applied to the Payment of my own Salary to the 30th June, & such Salaries of the Clerks up to that Time, as I think they merit. I must take upon Myself that Congress will alter the Law, and make it what was no doubt intended. —

I have the honor &^c

[NDA. Req. on US T, 1798–1803.]

[31 July 1798.]

Captain Truxtun's order concerning exercise of topmen

Mr Anderson in Exercising the top men in the use of loading, pointing down on a Ship's decks &^c, the Howitzers, will be very particular in explaining to the Midshipmen, and in fact every man Stationed in the tops in time of Action, every particular relating to the use of those important instruments of War, which if well managed, have often cleared the decks of an enemy, in a Short time — the lighting of one match by another, must be explained, for tho' topmen may be very usefull in time of Action, if they are not well initiated and made to understand in all respects what they are placed aloft for; they are of no Service Whatever, as I have seen in Several instances, as well as the reverse —

Mr Morgan will be particularly attentive to this order as Master Gunner, and explain it to Mr Anderson as his 1st Mate.

United States Ship *Constellation at* Sea July 31st 1798.

THOMAS TRUXTUN.

N. B. The Sea Lieu^ts will be pleased to take a Copyy of the above note to the Gunner, and cause it to be executed in the following manner viz. whenever the 1st Lieu^t brings 12 O'clock in the morning, the Gunners Mate aforesaid will exercise the fore top Men — When the 2nd Lieu^t brings 12 O'clock he will cause him to exercise the Main top men, and when the 3rd Lieu^t brings twelve O'Clock as aforesaid, the the said Gunners Mate will exercise the Mizen top men, So that the men of each top be exercised in Rotation each day. —

T. T.

[HS of Pa. NDA photostat. Truxtun's LB, 1798–9.]

Extract from journal of James Pity, U. S. Frigate *Constitution*, 31 July 1798, Tuesday

First part this 24 hours Fresh Breezes and Hazy W^r with a great Swell from the S. S. W. at ½ past 1 P. M. finish'd setting up the Rigging &^c at 10 P. M. T.K.D. Ship to the Northward & Eastw^d a 11 the W^r appearing dubious hauld down the M^n T. M. Stay Sail and Jibb. a 12 Sharp Lightning and heavy thunder attended with heavy Rain and Wind. Close Reeft Top Sails & haul'd up the Fore sail. Ship^t much Water Thro' the ports hauld in 6 Guns and Down ports at 12. Wore Ship again and let 1 Reef out Y^e top Sails at 10 Clear'd and Wash'd decks and birthed the Crew. Ends in clear W^r a Meridian. Tack'd Southward —

[Latitude observed 40°. 16^m N.]

[NDA.]

Extract from Captain Thomas Truxtun's journal, U. S. Frigate *Constellation*, 31 July 1798, Tuesday

Uncertain Weather, threatening heavy Squalls, and intermixed with fresh and light Airs, with some Calms, throughout the whole of this Day. No Vessels in Sight. Exercised the Cannon, and went through the Manuvres of Boarding. Employed at sundry necessary Jobs on the Rigging, and in the Carpenter's, and Gunner's Department, &c.

Made six large Fires below, under Care of the Carpenter, and his Crew, and I have directed in the most particular Manner, that the same be done on every Monday, Thursday, and Saturday; the other Days of the Week, the Appartments of the Crew, I have also repeated, according to former Orders, that they be washed with Vinegar, and Devil's burnt alternately.

At Noon the Depth of Water was twenty Fathoms, over a Bottom of fine black, and white Sands; Cape Roman at same Time bore North 10 Leagues, and Charleston Bar West B. North, 14 Leagues Distance.

Latitude observed 32° 34′ N^o

Longitude Account 79.52 W.

[HS of Pa. NDA photostat.]

To Secretary of War from Secretary of Navy

[PHILADELPHIA,]
Navy Department, 1st Augt 1798

SECY AT WAR

SIR, There are still to be provided, three Galleys or some small vessels, of the ten authorized by Law. I would wish to know, whether Galley's are essential to the defence of Rhode Island — and if they are, how many you think ought to be stationed there.

This Information I want immediately, as I wish to take immediate steps for procuring The Three Galleys, or other vessels to the Southward, if they are not deemed essential for The defence of Rhode Island. —

[NDA. Sec. War LB, 1798–1824.]

To Josiah Fox, naval constructor, from Secretary of Navy

[PHILADELPHIA,]
Navy Department 1st August 1798

Mr JOSIAH FOX *Navy Constructor*

SIR You are hereby appointed Navy Constructor, to superintend the building of the Frigate at Norfolk, for which service, a Salary will be allowed you, at the rate of Two Thousand Dollars per annum. — To commence from the first day of last month, July. — Your time having been since that time occupied in making Drafts & other matters relating to the Construction of Ships. —

You will prepare all necessary information, and send it to Mr Pennock, Navy Agent at Norfolk, that the materials may be provided; and when it becomes necessary for you to go to Norfolk, I will give you fuller Instructions. —

I am Sir &ca

[NDA. GLB, Vol. 1.]

Extract from the journal of Lieutenant John Mullowny, U. S. Frigate *United States*, 1 August 1798

Light breezes and pleasant. At 1 a sail in Sight bearing S. S. W. 5 or 6 leagues made sigl to the *Delaware* for strange sail being in Sight, at 3 made sigl to prepare for action all hands to Quarters, all Clear for action. At 4 P. M. dicovered the sail to be a Ship of War Capt Barry ordered the *Delaware* to keep under our lee. At 2 P. M. spoke the *Thetis* Capt Cochran of 44 Guns belonging to Great Britain.

Capt requested the honor of Capt Barry to come on board his ship & he would give him signal for the W India ships of war Capt Barry went on board in Capt C's Barge, when Capt B returned Capt C came on board with several of his officers at 9 they went to their ship when we steered our proper course.

[Latde Obsd 34.18]

[NA.]

[August 1, 1798.]

Extract from log book journal kept by Gilbert Howland, master of the Schooner *Betsey*, of Boston, passage from Curacao towards Boston

"Remarks on Bord Wensday August 1st 1798
first part of this 24 hours frish gails & havey Squales of Rain at 2 p. m. maid the Island of Saiona Baring N B W
Middle part — ditto
Latter part — ditto — at 8 a. m. maid Cape de F. Engono Baring N N W at 10 a. m. Carread away the Jaib Boom on account of a frinch Privateer in Chase of us — Capt Bowen still Capes Companay with us — So Ends all well on Bord
[noon Latitude July 31st 17° 40′ N.]

[Har. Coll. Lib.]

Extract from journal of James Pity, U. S. Frigate *Constitution*, 1 August 1798, Wednesday

First part this 24 hours clear and pleasant Weather. people employ'd Washing Decks. birth'd the people anew — at 8 P. M. Wore Ship to the Northd & Westd Middle part clear Wr all hands employ'd at Different Jobbs on Examing the Compasses I found they did not [agree] with any Two in the Ship by Reason of So much Iron Work Round the Binnacle had the Binnacles taken to pieces and took out of each 3½lb Nails and put them together again with copper Nails Since which they agree well. Latter part clear Weather Inclinable to Calm.

[Latitude observed 40.13]

[NDA.]

Extract from Captain Thomas Truxtun's journal, U. S. Frigate *Constellation*, 1 August 1798, Wednesday

Uncertain, squally, and very disagreeable, and unpleasant Weather all these 24 Hours; at 2 PM saw a Sail, made Sail, and gave Chace; at 4 Ditto spoke the *Issabella*,* which Vessel I examined two Days ago, she being a very dull sailing Schooner, and could make no Way close hawlled, against the southerly Wind, and Head Sea.

The Master informed me, that last Night in Sight of the Light House of Charleston, he spoke a Prize to a British Vessel, going in. I suppose rather it to have been some Vessel returning Home, that has been captured by Captain Cochran of the *Thetis*, and her Cargo taken out of Hallifax.

At 6 Ditto saw a Sail to the Southward, gave Chace, at half past 7, it being dark, lost Sight of her, shortened Sail, and stood to the Southward.

No observation of the ⊙ to Day, Charleston Bar at Noon bore West B. N. ¼ North, 9 Leagues Distance, Depth of Water 16 Fathoms.

Latitude Account 32°.35′ No
Longitude Account 80.7 W.

[* Also spelled *Essabella* in entry of 30 July, 1798.]
[HS of Pa., NDA photostat.]

To William Winder, Navy Department accountant, from Secretary of Navy

[PHILADELPHIA,]
Navy Department 2nd August 1798

Wm WINDER Esqr
E. Shore Maryland

SIR I am favoured with your letters of the 22nd & 28th Instant [July?] — I am very sorry that any circumstances should have prevented your coming to Philadelphia soon after the receipt of your Commission, which has been forwarded by the Secretary of State, and which you would no doubt receive soon after mine, informing you of your Appointment.

Real and great inconvenience results daily from the Office of Accountant, not being in operation, — Confusion I fear will be introduced, which it will be difficult to be extricated from.

Besides this — there are people frequently calling for settlement of accounts, which cannot be settled for want of the Accountant Office — It is impossible, that the commencement of this Office can be delayed 'till the 10th of September, and it will be injurious to delay it to the middle of this month —

I hope therefore your affairs can be so arranged as to permit your setting out in a day or two after the receipt of this —

After getting the office arranged and Clerks instructed in their duty, I presume it might not be inconvenient, that you might take time to return home for a fortnight to bring up your Family — which I would not advise you to do at present, on account of the danger of the Yellow Fever — of which however, there is at present no appearance. —

You will have two Clerks, @ 800 D each, and one at 600 Dollars. —

I am &c

(NDA. GLB, Vol. I.]

Extract from journal of Lieutenant John Mullowny, U. S. Frigate *United States*, 2 August 1798

Light airs

From 6 to 10 calm

A 11 a Light air from Sd

At 4 A.M. saw a sail gave chase and at M spoke her — a schooner from Boston bound to demarara

Trim'd ship, with the shifting ballast carried it forward, found her to sail faster.

[Latde Obsd 34.14]

[NA.]

Extract from journal of James Pity, U. S. Frigate *Constitution*, 2 August 1798, Thursday

First part this 24 hours Clear Wr all hands employ'd about Sundry Jobbs. at 3 P. M. Beat to Quarters and Exercized the Guns. a 6 P. M. Handed Main Sail & Sett the Spanker found our Compasses to agree exactly at 9 P. M. took in T. Gallt Sails at 11 P. M. wore Ship to the Northwd and Westd at ½ past 1 T. K. D. Ship to the

N. N. W. at ½ past 3 Sett Jibb at 4 Sett T. G. Sails at 6 Sett Royals and Main Sail a 9 Musterd the People.

Latter part Clear Weather.

[Latitude observed 40.17]

[NDA.]

Extract from Captain Thomas Truxtun's journal, U. S. Frigate *Constellation*, 2 August 1798, Thursday

Squally Weather with some Showers of Rain, Wind from South to South South West the first and middle, the latter it hawlled to the North North East.

At 10 AM saw a Sail in the South West, gave Chace, at ½ past 10, the Sail proving a Brig, and rigged Something like the Charleston Revenue armed Brig; I hoisted a United States Jack at the fore Top Gallant Mast Head, the Signal I gave the Pilots of Charleston to distinguish this Frigate by; but I soon after discovered, it was not that Vessel; at 11 however we spoke her, and she proved to be the *Eliza* from Savannah, bound to Boston out two Days, and had neither seen, or heard of any french Cruizers. People employed at Sundries.

Cape Roman at Noon bore N. W. eleven Leagues Distance. Depth of Water Twenty Fathoms, fine grey Sand.

Latitude observed 32°.41′ N°

Longitude Account 79.25 W.

[HS of Pa. NDA photostat.]

To Captain Mentges from Secretary of Navy

[PHILADELPHIA,]
Navy Department 3 August 1798

Capt MENTGES

On the subject of the remaining Prisoners at the Fort, taken in the *La Croyable*, French Schooner — It is desireable that they should be employed by the Farmers in the Country, or on the Works at the Fort, to save the expense of maintaining them — They are not Frenchmen and might become useful Citizens — But no compulsion must be used to induce them to work in the Country or on the Fort, and they must be suffered to make their own bargains as to Wages —

I have the honor to be &ca

[NDA. GLB, Vol. 1.]

To Gibbs & Channing, agents at Newport R, I., from Secretary of Navy

[PHILADELPHIA,]
Navy Department 3rd August 1798

Messrs GIBBS & CHANNING

GENTn Captain Nicholson in the Frigate *Constitution* will appear off Newport with the Swedish Flag hoisted on his main Top Mast head — permit me to solicit the favor of you to send the enclosed letter to him by a pilot Boat or other means — It is necessary he should receive it on his first appearance —

Pray favor me with your opinion as to the Duck, or Canvass made to the Eastward — It being a Home manufacture, it should be used in our Navy, if upon the whole it is not much inferior to the European — and if it is not much dearer — There is a prejudice against it here — but I wish to be able to Judge whether this prejudice be well, or ill founded —

I have the honor to be &c[a]

[NDA. GLB, Vol. 1.]

To William and Thomas Walter, merchants, Boston, from Secretary of State

DEPARTMENT OF STATE
Philadelphia Aug[t] 3. 1798.

WILLIAM and THO. WALTER Merchants, *Boston.*

GENTLEMEN, I have received your letter of the 28th ult. relative to a commission for the Ship *Merchant*, John Trail, commander, belonging to you, and which has sailed for London.

Expecting that a number of American vessels would wish to arm in England, I have sent to our Minister in London two or three parcels of Commissions, instructions and bonds, by as many different vessels; and I shall continue forwarding them, to increase the stock and multiply the chances of their arrival. I have desired M[r] King to make it known, thro' our consuls, in the different parts of England, that all who desire commissions may be furnished. I am gentlemen, Your obed[t] Servant,

TIMOTHY PICKERING

[SDA. Dom. L., Vol. 11.]

To President Adams from the Secretary of Navy

[PHILADELPHIA,]
Navy Department 3rd Aug 1798

JOHN ADAMS *Presid[t] U. S.*

SIR, The Reg[t] of Marines under the Command of Major Burrows, is to supply Detachments of Marines, to the Ships of War, as they shall be wanted.

A Detachment will be wanted in the Course of this Month, for the *Montezuma* at Baltimore, and in next Month, for the *Ganges* and for the *Norfolk*, a Brig of 18 Guns at Norfolk. It seems to be necessary then that a part of this Regiment should be raised without delay. I have the honor, therefore to enclose for your Consideration, a List of Names for officers in this Regiment, with the Names of the Persons by whom they have been recommended. There will be more officers, to appoint for the Marines, but the present Applicants do not appear to be so well divided among the States as they might be, & further Appointments may be delayed without injury.

The ship *Montezuma* at Baltimore, will be ready for sea in this Month and the French Schooner Prize, *La Croyable*, now called *Retaliation*, in twelve days — I have also enclosed List of Officers, with their Recommendations for these Vessels. This latter vessel was purchased for the Public a few days ago, at the sale — and may be considered as one of the Ten Gallies, or other small vessels, under the Act to "authorize the President of the United States, to cause to be purchased or built a Number of small Vessels to be equipped as Gallies or otherwise. —

I have the honor &^{c}

[NDA. Nom. Appts. LB, 1798–1820.]

Extract from journal of Lieutenant John Mullowny, U. S. Frigate *United States* 3 August 1798

Light airs, warm & clear

Saw a sail standing to the S^{d} & W^{d} so far to windward, no probability of overtaking her was we to chase — before it would be dark

Shortened sail the *Delaware* astern. A squall. — flashed pawder as a signal for the *Delaware*

[Lat^{de} Obs. 33.59]

[NA.]

Extract from journal of James Pity, U. S. Frigate *Constitution*, 3 August 1798, Friday

First part this 24 hours Pleasant Weather Saw a Sail bearing up before the Wind Call'd all hands hoisted in the Boats and made sail and gave chace to d^{o} at ½ past 4 P.M. TK Ship to West^{d} at 6 P. M. TK Ship Northw^{d} Furled T. Gall^{t} sails gave over chace at 12 A. M. hove too & Sounded & got ground in 40 fath^{ms} blue Clay intermixed with fine Sand.

at 12 A. M. Sounded got ground 38. fath^{ms} D^{o} Sounded at 4. 33 fm. fine Sand and made Sail at 5 AM Saw a Sail to the Northw^{d} at ½ past Seven Saw the Land of Long Island bear^{g} N. W. b. W. dist^{ce} 3 Leagues being West^{d} of Montok Point 8 Leagues TK Ship South^{d} & East^{d} at 9 Southampton N. W. b. W. 3 Leagues T.K.D. Ship so^{d} D^{o} bore W. N. W. b. W. Sounded 21 fath^{ms} grey sand with black Specks.

[Latitude observed 40.45]

[NDA.]

Extract from Captain Thomas Truxtun's journal, U. S. Frigate *Constellation*, 3 August 1798, Friday

Squally uncertain Weather throughout this Day, and a Swell from the Eastward. Stretched to the Eastward, and Westward, but saw no Vessel whatever. Employed the People at various little Repairings, and Fittings. Charleston Bar at Noon bore West B. North, Distance 15 Leagues, Depth of Water 17 Fathoms; Exercised Cannon, &c.

No observations of the ⊙.

Latitude Account 32° .33′ N^{o}

Longitude Account 79.47 W.

Vari^{n} per E Azimuth 5.16 East.

[HS of Pa. NDA photostat.]

CAPTAIN SAMUEL NICHOLSON, U. S. NAVY.

To Captain Richard Valentine Morris, U. S. Navy, from Secretary of Navy

[PHILADELPHIA,]
Navy Department 4. Augt 1798

R^d VALENTINE MORRIS *N York*

SIR, I beg the favor of you to get from the British Officers all the information you can on the subject of proper Guns for our Navy — & to furnish Me as quickly as possible, with all the Information you get, & your own Results.

It is of high importance that the Guns adopted in the Navy, be the best —

[NDA. GLB, Vol. 1.]

To Captain Samuel Nicholson, U. S. Navy, from Secretary of Navy

[PHILADELPHIA,]
Navy Department 4th August 1798

Capt SAM^l NICHOLSON

SIR, After receiving this Letter, you will please to stand off and on the Capes of Delaware, untill you hear from me, I mean so as that a Pilot boat may find you, in two or three days after leaving the Capes, and that a Pilot Boat may know in what direction to pursue you — I have to request that you will keep to the Southward of the Capes. —

I have the honor to be &c.

[NDA. OSW, Vol. 1.]

To Captain Richard Dale, U. S. Navy, from Secretary of Navy

[PHILADELPHIA,]
Navy Department 4th August 1798

Capt RICH^d DALE

SIR When you receive this by the hands of Capt Leonard, you will be pleased to return into Port with your Ship to be refitted properly for a Cruiser.

This City is at present not unhealthy, yet there is some little appearance of Fever about the Docks — not the Yellow Fever — But as that dreadful Calamity, if it prevails at all this year, would probably rage with most violence from the 20th August to the last of September, (the time you would be refitting), I think it most prudent that you should go to New York to have the necessary alterations in your Ship made there. —

You will please therefore go into the Port of New York, and have your Ship fitted there — Mr James Watson, the Naval Agent of that place, will give you all necessary assistance — I should wish to know as early after your arrival as possible, the alterations you deem necessary, to make the Ship as good a Sailor, & War Ship, as She is Capable of being made. —

I have the honor to be &c.

[NDA. OSW, Vol. 1.]

To Captain J. W. Leonard, Revenue Cutter *Governor Jay*, from Secretary of Navy

[PHILADELPHIA,]
Navy Department August 4th 1798

Capt J. W. LEONARD

SIR, In my Instructions of the 19th Ulto you were directed to fall in with the Ship *Ganges*, and to cruise with her under the orders of Capt Richard Dale — The Cutter *Genl Greene*, Capt Price was also to join you. She has been out some time, and I suppose has joined Capt Dale — I have now to direct that you will proceed as soon as you are ready, in search of Capt Dale, whose cruising Station is from Long-Island to Cape Henry — When he is joined by you and the Cutter *Genl Greene*, he will leave that Station, and come into port; of course the protection of that part of the Coast will devolve on Capt Price and yourself, untill an additional Force is provided, and I doubt not your united attention will be given to fulfil the object in view; Cruising from Long Island to Cape Henry, as formerly mentioned — You will not be left long without an additional Force, as I intend to order a Ship at Baltimore, now nearly ready to sail from Baltimore, to take the same station. — I have just received your Letter the 3rd Instant, and send you herewith the Marine Rules & Regulations — Also Rules for the Regulation of the Navy &c. &c. which last are in lieu of Articles of War. —

As it will be proper that I should have it in my power to communicate with you occasionally — I wish that once in every 10 or 12 days you would appear off Cape Henlopen, and remain for a day or two, in order that I may by means of a Pilot Boat, send you any additional Instructions that may be necessary. —

Captain Nicholson, in the Frigate *Constitution* will, I expect shortly be on the same Station with you — Keep a lookout for him, and deliver the enclosed Letter as soon as he appears.

I have the honor to be &c.

[NDA. OSW, Vol. 1.]

To James Watson, Navy Agent, New York, from Secretary of Navy

Navy Department 4. Augt 1798

JAMES WATTSON *New York*

SIR, I have directed Capt Dale in the *Ganges* to go into your Port to have alterations which may require a Month, made in his ship — & to put himself upon you — If I overburthen you, say so, that I may endeavour to find some other Gentleman, to take the trouble of smaller matters.

I am &c.

[NDA. GLB, Vol. 1.]

Extract from journal of James Pity, U. S. Frigate *Constitution*, 4 August 1798, Saturday

Pleasant Wr at Meridian extreme part of L. Island In sight bearg fm N. W. to N. E. b N. dist 4 Leagues at 2 P. M. T. K. Ship to Westd a 6 Do the Eastermost part Long Island bore N. E. dist 5 Leagues At ye Western part W. b N. 5 Leagues, at 7 ~~AK~~ Ship Eastd Southampton bore N. W. b N. 3 Leagues dist. Sounded 20 fathms grey sand black Specks a 12 $\overline{K}$ Ship Northw^{d} & West^{d} Sounded in 20 fath^{ms} as before.

Middle part clear Weather. Set Small Sails at 8 Wore Ship all hands employ'd setting up Rigging, Stays Etc. and prepar^{g} for bend^{g} Cables. West part long Island bore W. N. W. 4 Leagues dis^{t} East d^{o} N. E. b E. 4 Leagues dis^{t} a Current Sett^{g} West^{d} by the tide Rips which has not been allow^{d} I find myself short of Long^{d} 20 or 30 Miles in

Lati^{de} 40° 40^{m} N^{o}

[NDA.]

Extract from journal of Lieutenant John Mullowny, U. S. Frigate *United States*, 4 August 1798

Clear. —

Calm. — warm.

Made false fires, which was answered by the *Delaware*

At 4 A. M. saw a strange sail at 7 spoke her, she was from St Croix bound to Copenhagen, where she belongs, out 3 weeks. Spoke the *Delaware.*

[Long. Obs^{d} 11. 16]

[Lat^{de} Obs. 33.17]

[NA.]

Extract from Captain Thomas Truxtun's journal, U. S. Frigate *Constellation*, 4 August 1798, Saturday

Wind and Weather as before, without any very remarkable Circumstance occurring that is worth my Notice, except some Rum having been embezzled in the Hold of the Ship, for which I had just Cause to suppose Daniel Gorman, the Master's first Mate was privy. I accordingly suspended him from ever acting again in that Capacity under my Authority in this, or any other public Ship whatever, that I may command.

At 7 AM saw a Sail in the North North East, made Sail, but the Wind being light, and inclining to Calm; we had not neared her much from the Mast Head at Noon. Find a strong northerly Current.

Cape Roman at Noon bore North West 9 Leagues Distance, Depth of Water 14½ Fathoms.

Latitude observed 32°.47′N^{o}

Longitude Account 79.30 W.

[HS of Pa. NDA photostat.]

Extract from journal of James Pity, U. S. Frigate *Constitution*, 5 August 1798, Sunday

First part this 24 hours Moder^{te}W^{r}

Middle Squally with Lightening & Rain. Ship under close Reef^{t} Top Sails.

at 4 A. M. Wore Ship the land of Never Sink bore N° 7 Leagues dis^{t} out all Reefs. a Sail in Sight. gave chace Thick fogg coming on Lost Sight of her. Sett Steer^{g} Sails. Latter part thick foggy W^{r}

[No observations.]

[NDA.]

Extract from Captain Thomas Truxtun's journal, U. S. Frigate *Constellation*, 5 August 1798, Sunday

Light Winds throughout and variable, the first Part from the North Eastward, the Middle from the Southern Quarter, and the latter from the Westward.

At 6 AM saw a Sail, made Sail, and gave Chace, at 9 Ditto spoke the Chace, she proved to be an English Schooner called the *Thetis*, William Dunscomb, Master, from Charleston bound to Bermuda, left the Bar last Evening about 5 o'Clock. I examined his Papers, found them all clear, and suffered him to proceed, and then gave Chace to another Sail, that hove in Sight to the Northward. Shortly after a tremendous Water Spout rose up near to the Ship; kept away, and got ready to fire several Guns, but it soon after broke at a considerable Distance from us. Continued on the Chase at Noon within less than one League of her, fired a Shot athawt her Stern, when she immediately hoisted her Colours, and stood towards us. Cape Roman at Noon bore North North West, 15 Leagues, Depth of Water 55 Fathoms.

Latitude observed 32°.23′ N°
Longitude Account 79.30 W.

[HS of Pa. NDA photostat.]

To Secretary of State from U. S. Attorney David L. Barnes, Providence, R. I.

RHODE ISLAND DISTRICT
Providence 6. Aug. 1798 —

SIR I take the liberty to communicate the information I have received from Cap. Wilson Jacobs, who arrived here on the 3ᵈ Instant from Guadaloupe — He was taken on his passage from this port to Guadaloupe, about 5 miles from the harbour of Point Petre, by a small privateer manned & commanded by Blacks, carried in there, & vessel & Cargo. condemned. It was said the privateer belonged to Victor Hughe's Cook; but Cap. Jacobs is well satisfied She was principally owned by Hughes himself — In order to obtain as much favor as possible in purchasing his vessel, Jacobs professed a warm attachment to the French Republic, which was not inconsistant with his feelings at the time he left this place. — In consequence of this, he had frequent conversation with Hughes, and his associates. — He therefore states as within his Knowledge, that Hughes has a mercantile House by the firm of LeMaitre & C° at Guadaloupe, who carry on an extensive commerce. — That Champaigne of Baltimore and Dames of Guadalupe, by the firm of Champaigne & Dames carry on business between those places. — That Hughes, Dames, & others proposed to establish a house at Baltimore to insure vessels trading between the United States & Guadaloupe — and that all vessels which should be insured by them, if taken by privateers, should be acquitted by the Court. — That they intended also to purchase a number of fast sailing Schooners in the United States to be sent to the West Indies. — One of Victor Hughe's family & house of trade, by the name of Siemandy came passenger with Cap. Jacobs, and brought with him a large amount of Bills of Exchange on Baltimore, New York & Boston. — Cap. Jacobs says he has *no doubt* his object is to purchase vessels to send to the West Indies. — He went so far as to tell Jacobs, that if he would go to Baltimore he would give him "one superb long Schooner" to go in to Guadaloupe — Although I had no doubt of the hostile intentions of this man, I could not find any Law to authorize the detention of him. — Yesterday morning he left this place for New York. — He is about 35 or 40 years old of middling stature, round favored, rather light-complexioned, though very much sunburnt, He told Cap. Jacobs that he was acquainted at New York & Baltimore, & told a Frenchman here that he passed through this Town last winter.

I think it my duty to give this information that such use be made of it, as may be thought proper to prevent the execution of his designs.

With the most perfect respect
I am yr. m° obt Servt —

DAVID L BARNES
Attorney of the United States for Rhode Island District

Hone TIMOTHY PICKERING
Secretary of State

[SDA. Misc. L., Jan.–Aug. 1798, and RI Hist. Soc.]

To Captain John W. Leonard, Revenue Cutter *Governor Jay*, from Secretary of Navy

[PHILADELPHIA,]
Navy departmt August 6. 1798.

Capt J. W. LEONARD

SIR, Since my Letter of the 4th Instant was written, the Ship *Ganges*, Capt Dale, has arrived in our River, of course Capt Price and Yourself will have to cruise without him.

It is unnecessary for Me to add more, having already wrote you so fully. —

I am &c.

[NDA. OSW, Vol. 1.]

To Jeremiah Yellott, Navy Agent, Baltimore, from Secretary of Navy

[PHILADELPHIA,]
Navy Departmt Augt 6th 1798

J. YELLOTT

SIR, It is become important, that the Ship *Baltimore* should be got ready for Sea immediately, and I write by this Post urging Capt Phillips to use every possible Exertion, by Shipping the remainder of his Men & getting officers in lieu of such as have not come forward in consequence of their Appointments. I beg you will also urge Capt Phillips on this score, & that you will at once procure what may be necessary to the compleat Equipment of the ship, so that she may be ready to proceed to Sea, as soon as I forward my orders, which I shall do in the course of a few days.

I am &c.

[NDA. GLB, Vol. 1]

Extract from Captain Thomas Truxtun's journal, U. S. Frigate *Constellation*, 6 August 1798, Monday

At 2 PM spoke the Chace mentioned in the preceding Day at Noon; she was a Schooner called the *Harriot*, Samuel Campbell, Master, equipt as a Flag of Truce at Charleston to convey from thence to Portorica forty five french Passengers, that were in Distress. After examining the Papers of this Vessel, and being satisfied of their Correctness, I suffered the Master to proceed.

Very unsettled, and disagreeable Weather, with a Flood of Rain pouring down in Quantities, that equalled, and perhaps surpassed whatever before fell in the same Space of Time, in any Quarter of the Globe. In Fact our Scuppers could not carry it off the Decks as fast as it fell, the Consequence of which was, that it run over the Gunwales in immense Quantities. No Vessels in Sight.

At Noon the frying Pan Shoal off Cape Fear, bore West North West, sixteen Leagues Distance, and the Shoals off Cape Look out North East B. North, twenty Leagues Distance. Allowed for the Gulph Stream.

Latitude 33°. 20′ North
Longitude 77.20 W.

[HS of Pa. NDA photostat.]

Extract from journal of Lieutenant John Mullowny, U. S. Frigate *United States*, 6 August 1798

Disagreeably warm.

At 5 Calm

At 5 A. M. Capt Decatur made signal for strange sail, wore ship and gave chase

At 9 came up with a brig of & bound to Boston (Capt Bethon) the Capt came on board, and after some conversation with the Capt he returned.

[Latd Obsd 32.38.]

[NA.]

Extract from journal of James Pity, U. S. Frigate *Constitution*, 6 August 1798, Monday

First part this 24 hours fair Weather a 3 P. M. Saw a Sail bearg S. E. gave chace and hauld our Wind and fired a gun and Shortend sail. She provd a Schr from Boston bound to Phila Wm Hurd Comr a 7 P. M. the Eastern part Long Island bore N. E. dist 4 Leagues. a Eveng furld small sail & Reef'd Top Sails a 8 Sounded in 17. fathm Clew'd up the foresail.

a Midnight Sounded 25 fathm black pebbles with black Sand a 2 P. M. wore Ship & Stood Northwd a 5 Do saw Montick Point bearg N. E. 7. Leagues Dist at 2 the light house bore N. N. E. 3 Leagues dist Saw another Sail close in shore prov'd a Pilot boat. a Meridian Middle part block Island bearg No Distce 6 or 7 Miles the Eastern part N. N. E. Western Do N. W. b No clean'd out between decks and found several Hh'ds potatoes damagd

[Latitude observed 41° 00m]

[NDA.]

Presumably to Rufus King, United States Minister, London, from Consul Elias VanderHorst

BRISTOL *Aug*^t^ *7*^th^ *1798.*

DEAR SIR. I have rec^d^ both your favors of the 2^d^ & 6th Inst^a^ also the three Letters they enclosed for Mr Pickering, the *first* & the *Original* of the second (marked 1) I have enclosed in one of my own to that Gentleman & put them on board the American Ship *Roba & Betsey,* Capt Vimmo, a very fine Vessel mount^g^ 16 — 6 & 9 Pounders, with 30 Men, this Ship I expect will Sail this Even^g^ for Cork to Join Convoy, & then proceed to Virginia — the *Atlas,* for New York, Sailed yesterday for Cork also; to Join the Convoy: I have therefore enclosed your Letter (marked 2) in one of my own to the Secretary of State and delivered them to Capt Vimmo enjoining him to put them on board any *good* American Vessel he may meet with at Cork bound to Philadelphia or New York, with or without Convoy, and as I know I can depend on him you may be assured it will be done. I thank you for the information respect^g^ Genl Kosciuszko, and remain

Dear Sir,

Yours most Sincerely

ELIAS VANDERHORST

[SDA. Bristol, Vol. 1, 1791–1799.]

To Captain Samuel Nicholson, U. S. Navy, from Secretary of Navy

[PHILADELPHIA,]

Navy Departm^t^ *August 7*^th^ *1798*

Capt SAM^l^ NICHOLSON

SIR, This Letter is intended to be delivered to you, when you appear off Sandy Hook; and as I shall have further Instructions to give you, I request that you will hover off that place until you receive them which will be with as little delay as possible — after knowing that you are there.

I have the honor &c.

[NDA. OSW, Vol. 1.]

To John Brown, Providence, R. I., from Secretary of Navy

[PHILADELPHIA,]

Navy Department August 7th *1798*

Mr JOHN BROWN *Providence (R I)*

SIR The Secretary of the Treasury has handed to me, your Letter of the 14th June —

It would afford me the utmost pleasure to buy your Ship, because she is a fine one, and because She could go into immediate service — But the Acts of Congress will not permit this — The sum appropriated by Congress for the procurement &c^a^ of 6 Vessels not exceeding 18 Guns — 12 not exceeding 24 & 6 not less than 32 Guns is not sufficient to procure more than half the Number, and the public Spirit of the Country must be relied on for the rest — As far as the public Funds will authorize, I have already gone — Most of the Towns distinguished for Federalism, and public Spirit, are making efforts to furnish the vessels still wanted — The Town of Providence not less able, and not less patriotic, I am afraid has not yet taken up the Subject —

There are still wanted two vessels not exceeding 18 Guns, one not exceeding 24 — and one, not less than 32 Guns — If Providence would with, or without the aid of some public money, furnish one of these vessels, it would be very gratifying, and if you Sir, would use your Influence to bring it about, you would lay an additional obligation on your Country — The vessels intended for the public should be Copper Bolted, and sheathed, with Copper, and prepared to receive Guns by the Merchants, who undertake to furnish vessels, on the Terms of the Act of Congress, in Substance — *That they shall receive 6 per cent stock for their advances.* — But it is highly desireable that the vessels should be ready as early as possible.

I have presumed that Providence would furnish one of the 18 Gun Vessels, with, or without the aid of about 10,000 Dollars from the public. —

[NDA. GLB, Vol. 1.]

To James Barry, Batlimore, from Secretary of Navy

[PHILADELPHIA,]
Navy Departm^{t} 7th Augt 1798

JA^{s} BARRY *Baltimore,*

D^{r} SIR, I will take the first opportunity to provide the place of Midshipman for your Nephew. I am not certain, whether the two Ships at Baltimore are not more than provided with Midshipmen.

On the subject of the other part of your Letter — I have the pleasure to say, that the moment Capt Phillips, can join another Vessel at Cape Henry, the two will be ordered to Havanna to convey home our Vessels there. I have urged on this account the utmost diligence in getting out Phillips — I trust this to be used as your own discretion shall direct — I am greatly hurried & can only add, that

I am &^{c}

[NDA. GLB, Vol. 1.]

To James Watson, Navy Agent, New York, From Secretary of Navy

[PHILADELPHIA,]
Navy Department August 7th 1798

JA^{s} WATSON Esqr

SIR Should the Ship *Constitution,* Capt Saml Nicholson appear off Sandy Hook, as probably she may, I request you will cause the enclosed Letter to be delivered —

I have the honor to be &c^{a}

P. S. If Nicholson appears off that Hook please inform me of it immediately — He will wait there for orders —

[NDA. GLB, Vol. 1.]

To John Nevison and John Granbury, agents at Norfolk, Va., from Secretary of Navy

[PHILADELPHIA],
Navy Department August 7th 1798

JOHN NEVISON & JOHN GRANBERY Esqrs *Norfolk*

GENTn I have the pleasure to acknowledge the receipt of your favour of the 28th ult., and observe the Measures you had pursued for carrying into effect the patriotic Intentions of the Citizens of Petersburg, Richmond, Manchester & Norfolk — Your Idea that Celerity in bringing into operation the armed Force for the protection of our Commerce, is of primary Importance, coincides exactly with the views of Government, and it will be more agreeable, that a Force comparatively small, should speedily be in readiness — Than that one more considerable should be obtained, at the expense of delay — Either of the Brigs you mention will be acceptable, and as Captain Barron will be appointed to the Command, it may be adviseable, that he select out of the four, the one he most approves of — Copper & Nails shall speedily be sent on, and any other Articles that cannot be procured on the spot please to furnish a List of, and you will receive every aid that can possibly be given from this department, on an Occasion which reflects such high honor on the patriotism of your Citizens — The appearance, however of the Yellow Fever in this City may render supplies from hence very precarious — It will therefore be adviseable that you place as little dependence thereon as possible —

I have the honor &ca

[NDA. GLB, Vol. 1.]

Extract from Captain Thomas Truxtun's journal, U. S. Frigate *Constellation*, 7 August 1798, Tuesday

The Beginning fresh Gales from the West South West, and cloudy Weather. At 6 PM sounded in Twenty five Fathoms Water off Cape Look out; At half past 10 Ditto, a most violent Thunder Storm came on with a Torrent of Rain, which continued unabated untill half past AM, when we had a small Interval of Appearances of the Weather breaking, but at 2 AM it came on again very severe, and continued untill 4 Ditto, when it cleared away, and the Wind hawled to the Westward, and Northward, the Conductors being got up as soon as possible, after this Gust made it's Appearance, we sustained no Accident.

At noon saw a Sail to the Northward, gave Chace. Allowed for the Gulph Stream, which has run very strong. Cape Hatteras at Noon bore West North West, ten Leagues Distance.

Latitude observed 34°.55′ No
Longitude Account 75.10 W.

[HS of Pa. NDA photostat.]

Extract from journal of James Pity, U. S. Frigate *Constitution*, 7 August 1798, Tuesday

First part this 24 Hours fine and pleasant Weather. at Meridian a Pilot boat came from Block Island and put a pilot on board a 5

P. M. Spoke a Sloop from New London bound to New Port a D° fired a gun & tack'd Ship a 6 Spoke a Ship from New Port bound to Havanna Sam[l] Ellis Com[r] a 7 ⩞ Ship again and fired 3 Guns a 8 Sounded pumps & found 12 Inches Water in her. a ½ past the Pilot came on b[d] with fresh provisions for y[e] Officers &[c] a 2 P. M. wore Ship East[d] Light house bore N. b E. 11 Miles a 9. Musterd the Crew cleand out between Decks Sent up 2 Casks potatoes Damg[d] & 1 D° Indian Meal good.

[Latitude observed 41° 20[m] N°]

[NDA.]

Extract from journal of Lieutenant John Mullowny, U. S. Frigate *United States*, 7 August 1798

Clear.

In light sails appearance of a squall

Shifted Ballast forward found the ship was in trim, shifted it back again.

[Lat[de] Obs[d] 32.10]

[NA.]

To Samuel Hodgdon from Secretary of State

[PHILADELPHIA,]

To SAMUEL HODGDON Esq[r]

Be pleased to deliver to the order of the Secretary of the Navy, the eleven six pounders with their appurtenances which belonged to the Corvette *Le Cassius.*

TIMOTHY PICKERING

DEPARTMENT OF STATE
Aug[t] 8. 1798.

[SDA. Dom. L., Vol. 11.]

To Secretary of the Navy from Captain John Barry, U. S. Navy

Aug 8 1798

I do hereby Certify that Joseph Brussells has piloted the Frigate *United States*, from Philadelphia to Cape Henlopen, she drawing twenty two Feet 6 Inches Water & that he is entitled to be paid for twenty six lay days —

JOHN BARRY

The Hon[ble] BENJ[n] STODDERT Esq[r]
Sec[y] of the Navy.

[GAO. No. 9967.]

To Nehemiah Hubbard, agent, Middletown, Conn., from Secretary of Navy

[PHILADELPHIA,]
Navy departm[t] 8th Aug[t] 1798

NEHEMIAH HUBBARD *Middletown Connecticut*

SIR, I am honored with yours of the 6th Ins[t] — I have requested the Secretary of the Treasury to remit you 3000 dollars — Two parcils of copper Bolts have been forwarded to you, One Parcel by way of New Port Rhode Island — the other Parcel to the care of Mr Watson New York — Both Parcils will not make up the Quantity wanted — the residue shall be sent as soon as they can be prepared — Means have been adopted to get them in season, but the Effect has not been correspondent to the Means.

I wish you to pursue your own opinion & that of Judges with you, as to giving the ship more depth of hold. All knowledge of the subject of Ship building is not confined to Philadelphia. The ship should have Quarter Galleries. I know of no better Name for her than the *Connecticut* which please to call her — She ought to be provided with 100 rounds of shot — Two Thirds to be round Ball — the other third to be divided between Grape & double headed shot. The size of the ship being reduced, it is thought Nine Pounders will be heavy enough for her Gun Deck — & six pounders for the Quarter deck. I will, perhaps in a few days, send you the sizes of the Guns adopted in the Navy — but you must not wait, for this Information, so as to risk waiting for the Guns. Provisions shall be attended to in Time. —

[NDA. GLB, Vol. 1.]

To Lieutenant Henry Kenyon from Secretary of Navy

[PHILADELPHIA]
Navy departm^t^ August 8. 1798

Lieut^t^ HENRY KENYON

SIR, As you have been appointed a Lieutenant of the schooner *Retaliation*, now preparing for a Cruise, it is necessary that you should recruit with all possible expedition, the requisite Number of Men, say Thirty able Seamen and Twenty Landsmen and Boys. You will be careful not to enlist any but healthy sound People, and that no indirect or forcible Measures be used to induce them to enter into the service. No Negroes or Mulatoes are to be admitted, and as far as you can judge, you must be cautious to exclude all Persons whose Characters are suspicious — The Wages to be allowed to able Seamen is 17 dollars p. m^o^ & ordinary Seamen 10 doll^s^ and the Term of Enlistment must be One Year. By ordinary Seamen is usually meant Landsmen, but there is a Class of Men who tho' not equal to able Seamen are not very much inferior, Men who have perhaps been many voyages at Sea, and yet would not ship for able Seamen — Should you find it impracticable to procure the full Complement of able Seamen, you must substitute some of those, who you may allow 14 dollars p. Month. You will avoid any Advance of Money until you get them on board if possible, but should you find an Advance indispensable, you must in every Instance get Security to resort to in case of desertion, and will keep a regular Account of the Names and Places of Abode of each Person and a Description of their Persons, so that you may identify them if necessary. The present Appearance of the Yellow fever in this City, renders it important that you should compleat the Complement of Men with the utmost Expedition so as to remove them to get the schooner away before the contagion spreads — Your utmost Activity of Exertion will therefore be required, & I hope you will acquit yourself in such a Manner as to derive credit. It will be expected of every Man you ship, to take an Oath agreeably to a form which will be delivered to you with these

Instructions, and you will see that this is complied with in every Instance. You will also receive herewith a Shipping Paper wherein you will enter the Name Station Pay &c. of each Person on board, and this must be done with great Exactness, so that no Confusion may be. The Form of a Bond to be signed by the Persons, who are Sureties for the Seamen is likewise delivered to you, and you must be particular in ascertaining that they are Men of responsible good Character before you accept of their Security — It will be expected that the United States pay the Board & Wages from the Time of Shipment until the sailing of the vessel, and in this respect you will be required to make use of the strictest Economy in getting them supported on the most moderate Terms — A sum of six hundred dollars now advanced you, with which you will be charged and held accountable for, of course you will take regular Receipts for your Expenditures, so as to produce them & settlement — Without these Vouchers, your Accounts can not be admitted.

I am &c.

[NDA. OSW, Vol. 1.]

To Captain Robert Gill, storekeeper, from Secretary of Navy

[PHILADELPHIA,]
Navy Departm^t Augt 8th 1798

CAP^t ROB^t GILL

SIR, You will please to ship the following Articles for Norfolk as speedily as possible, to the address of William Pennock Esquire, for the Brig *Norfolk* Capt Williams

18 6 pound Cannon
1350 round shot for d^o
450 " Grape d^o
25 pair of Pistols
50 Muskets & Bayonets, complete
60 Cutlasses
6 Rheams of Musket Cartridge Paper
60 lb. of Match rope
27 Worms & Ladles
A Drum & Fife
18 tons of Iron Ballast
Flannel for 1000 Cartridges
Paper for 600 d^o

[NDA. GLB, Vol. 1.]

To Captain Robert Gill, storekeeper, from Secretary of Navy

[PHILADELPHIA,]
Navy Department 8th Augt 1798

CAP^t ROB^t GILL

SIR, You will please to furnish Mr Joshua Humphreys, with such Articles as he may require for the Schooner *Retaliation* now repairing by him & for the *Ganges*.

I am &c &c

[NDA. GLB, Vol. 1.]

Extract from journal of James Pity, U. S. Frigate *Constitution*, 8 August 1798, Wednesday

First part this 24 hours pleasant W[r] Kept Stan[d] off and on Newport harbour under easy Sail the harbour of Newport dis[t] 2 Leag[s] pilot boat in C[o] at Meridian TK to the Eastw[d] a 2 D[o] TK N.W. Y[e] Custom house boat came from Newport with 3 Gent[m] hove Ship too Light house bear[g] N. b W. 3 Leagues dis[t] At 3 P. M. Spoke a N. York packet from D[o] Several Gentlemen came on board from Newport Light house bear[g] N. b W. 4 Leagues Dis[t] Middle part of Block Island W. b. S[o] 5 Leagues dis[t] Nomans Land E. b S[o] 8 Leagues dis[t] a 6 pump Ship 13 Inches Water Sent dow[n] T Gall[t] Yards & Reeft Top Sails ever Since our mak[g] Block Island Kept a Sweedish Jack at M. T. G. Head. a 9 calld all hands & set up Rigging.

[Latitude 40°. 15[m] N[o]]

[NDA.]

Extract from Captain Thomas Truxtun's journal, U. S. Frigate *Constellation*, 8 August 1798, Wednesday

Moderate Breezes, and pleasant Weather. At half past 5 PM brought to after firing four Shot the Schooner *Nancy*, Worth Bates, Master, from Charleston, South Carolina, bound to Virginia, out three Days, and laden with Cotton, Sugar, &c., had seen no Cruizers, and had no News. At 9 AM exercised Great Guns &c.

At 10 AM saw a Sail to the North North East, made Sail, and gave Chace; find the Gulph Stream has run strong these Twenty four Hours, at the Rate of two Knots per Hour at least. Got the Sails up to air; employed at various Jobs, and fumigated below &c.

Cape Henry at Noon bore West North West half North, Twenty Leagues Distance.

Latitude observed 36°.30′ N[o]
Longitude Account 74.46 W.

[HS of Pa. NDA photostat.]

Extract from journal of Lieutenant John Mullowny, U. S. Frigate *United States*, 8 August 1798

Weather clear. —

All hands to quarters, exercised the crew at the great guns at small arms.

Saw a sail bearing E. by N.

At 6 A. M. the ship *Delaware* shew a signal for strange sail ans[d] her signal

Squally, in light sails.

[Lat[de] Obs[d] 30.50]

[NA.]

To William Pennock, Navy Agent, Norfolk, from Secretary of Navy

[PHILADELPHIA,]
Navy Department Aug[t] 9th 1798

WILLIAM PENNOCK Esq[r]

SIR I have just received your favour of the 3rd Instant with the enclosure from Capt[n] Truxton and I expect that he will shortly be in Hampton Roads, where I wish him to remain untill I forward Instructions, which I shall do, by next Mail, and you will please to inform him thereof

[NDA. GLB, Vol. 1.]

To Jeremiah Yellott, Navy Agent, Baltimore, from Secretary of Navy

[PHILADELPHIA,]
Navy Depart. Augt 9th 1798

JER^h YELLOTT Esqr

SIR, By the next Mail, orders will be transmitted for Capt Philips — and as you know the importance of dispatch, I pray you to urge his being ready to proceed the moment they arrive

[NDA. GLB, Vol. 1.]

To Nathaniel Fellows, merchant, Boston, from Secretary of State

DEPARTMENT OF STATE PHILADELPHIA *Augt 9, 1798.*

Mr NATHANIEL FELLOWS *Merchant Boston*

SIR, I inclose a bond to be signed by you and Mr Samuel Brown, who with Captain Malzar Joy, are owners of the private armed Ship *Nancy*, Melzar Joy, commander, for which a commission was yesterday issued from my office, on the application of your agents, Messrs Joseph Anthony and Son. To prevent any delay to your Ship, I concluded to issue the commission as soon as the bond should be signed by one of the owners who was here, and your agents and sureties. It is now transmitted for signature by you and Mr Brown, in presence of witnesses; after which you will be pleased to return it, to Sir &c

TIMOTHY PICKERING

[SDA. Dom. L., Vol. 11.]

To Captain Isaac Phillips, U. S. Navy, from Secretary of Navy

[PHILADELPHIA,]
Navy Department. Augt 9. 1798.

Capt ISAAC PHILLIPS.

SIR, Presuming that you Ship the *Baltimore*, must be now ready for sea, it is necessary that I should instruct you as to your future destination in the service of the United States. — Immediately upon the receipt of this Letter, or as soon after as possible you are to proceed with the Ship under your Command to Hampton Road where I expect you will meet with the Frigate *Constellation*, Capt Thomas Truxtun, in company with whom, and under whose Orders you are to cruise — Should you not find him at that Place, you are to proceed to sea in search of him, and there is little doubt but you will fall in with him between the Capes of Virginia and Charleston, on which Station he has been cruising some Time. —

It is hardly necessary to remind you of the Importance of discipline and good order on board of Ships of War, and in our Infant Navy particularly, early Attention should be given to introduce them to as high a degree as possible. Good Examples on the part of the Officers, will naturally lead to these Points with the Men.

You will receive herein an Act of Congress passed the Ninth day of July last, authorizing the Capture of the armed Vessels of the French Republic, also the President's Instructions founded on that Act. The Vessels of every other Nation are on no account to be molested, and I wish particularly to impress on your mind, that should you even see an American Vessel captured by the armed Ship of any Nation at War with whom We are at Peace, you can not Lawfully interfere to prevent the Capture, for it is to be taken for granted, that such Nation will compensate for such Capture, if it should prove to have been illegally made. —

It is highly proper that you should inculcate among your Officers and Crew a high respect for the Government to which they belong, & on no account permit them to follow the Example of some unprincipled Americans, who to the dishonor of the Name have not unfrequently indulged themselves in licentiously villifying their own Government and the best Characters in it. To command respect from Others, We must respect ourselves — It is Time We should establish a National Character, which ought to be a Love of our Country and Jealousy of it's honor, & amongst Seamen particularly a veneration for our Flag — When you join Capt Truxtun, it is intended that you both proceed without delay to the Havanna, there to take under Convoy a Number of American Vessels who are afraid to venture home unprotected and are waiting for your Arrival — Dispatch is necessary and should you not have compleated your full Complement of Men at Baltimore, I should suppose it might be as well to proceed to Hampton Road with what you have and obtain the rest at Norfolk. I sincerely wish you a successful Cruise, and by the Time you return on this Coast, arrangements will be taken for your further Employment. —

I have the honor &c.

[NDA. OSW, Vol. 1.]

[August 9 [?] 1798]

Affidavit of Anthony Atwood, of Little Egg Harbor, New Jersey

STATE OF NEW JERSEY }
County of Middlesex } *Ss.*

I Anthony Atwood of Little Egg Harbour in the County of Burlington and State of New Jersey do Solemnly Swear that on or about Thursday the ninth day of August Instant, I went with Hezekiah Brown and several other persons from the main land to the Beach near Little Egg Harbour Inlet. That there was there a Schooner lying off the Beach, which I took to be an Eastern built Schooner— That when I was on the Beach, a boat came to the shore from the said Schooner and landed a Frenchman, that in conversation with the said Frenchman he informed me that he had lately come from France in a Privateer, that he had cruised off Halifax and had captured two Vessels and had afterwards fell in with a British Ship which had taken him, and said that he would fit out another directly. He also said that the Americans were no better than Pirates in Arming their Vessels and going without Commissions — That the said Schooner on the same day came into the Inlet and laid there for three or four days or longer that during that time the Custom House Boat from Tuckertown went to the said Schooner, That on Tuesday the fourteenth day of August Instant The said Frenchman set out from Tuckertown for Philadelphia in the Stage. That I have heard from others of various expressions and delarations of the said Frenchman, which had induced me and other as I have been informed by them to believe that the said Frenchman is a dangerous person — The said Frenchman is rather above middle height, well set, rather swarthy, with dark coloured short hair, and has a scar over one of his Eyes. I did not hear his Name.

ANTHONY ATWOOD —

Subscribed and Sworn to at Perth Amboy in the said County of Middlesex, this 24th day of August 1798 — Before me

JOSEPH MARSH,
Justice of the peace for the County of Middlesex.

[Mass. HS. Pickering Papers, Vol. 42, p. 70.]

Extract from journal of James Pity, U. S. Frigate *Constitution*, 9 August 1798, Thursday

First part this 24 hours fine Weather with light winds all hands employ'd Setting up rigging Still in chace of a Vessell. a 1 P. M. Spoke a Brig fm New Bedford on a Whaling Voyage 38 Days out Thomas Whipple Comr who Inform'd us the Sail a head was a Ship fm N York bound to Dublin and that on ye 1st Augt She spoke The *Resolution* of 74 Guns and Ye *Topaz* Frigate belongg to the British Govt a 3 P. M. Saw a Sail Southwd a 7 finish'd shetg Riging & Wore Ship Northwd a 8 A. M. Saw two Sail a head fired a Gun at a Sloop to Windard but she wd not heave too' a 9 bore away fore a Brigt To Lewd a Meridian fir'd a Gun at her & bro't her two. She was from N. London bound to Martinico out 24 hours Chapman Master.

[Latitude observed 40.22]

[NDA.]

Extract from journal of Lieutenant John Mullowny, U. S. Frigate *United States*, 9 August 1798

Clear.

The crew called to Quarters to exercise at the stations. The *Delaware* hoisted a signal for strange sail, ansd

Cloudy.

[Latde Obsd 29.19]

[NA.]

Extract from Captain Thomas Truxtun's journal, U. S. Frigate *Constellation*, 9 August 1798, Thursday

Moderate Breezes and fine Weather. At 2 PM brought to with a Shot the Chace mentioned in Yesterday's Transactions at Noon; she was the Schooner *American Fabius**, Ebenezer Berry, Master, from

[* Might be the American Schooner *Fabius*.]

George Town, Maryland, bound to Trinadada. Came out last Evening, and saw no Vessels.

At 5 PM brought to by firing two Shot the Ship, *Suffolk* from Alexandria, bound to London, which Vessel came out in Company with the *Fabius*, saw no Cruizers.

At 7 ditto fired a Shot at a Schooner, it being dark we could not discern at first, what she was; she proved however a Pilot Boat, out of which I got a Pilot, and agreed to pay him one Dollar per Day, and four Pounds Pilotage in to Hampton Roads, and four Pounds out.

At 5 AM saw a Sail, gave Chace, and at 7 Ditto spoke the Brig *Maria* from Philadelphia bound to Charleston; informed me, the Frigate *United States* and *Delaware* Sloop of War were gone to Boston, and the *Ganges* had left the Coast, and gone up to Philadelphia. At 10 spoke a Dogger from Baltimore bound to Bremen, after having fired two Shot to bring her to. At 11 Ditto brought to by a Shot a Danish Ship from Norfolk bound to Hamburg; employed at Sundries.

Cape Henry at Noon bore West North West, ten Leagues Distance; Depth of Water sixteen Fathoms.

Latitude observed 36°.46′ N°
Longitude Account 75.16 W.

[HS of Pa. NDA photostat.]

To William Pennock, Navy Agent, Norfolk, Va., From Secretary of Navy

[PHILADELPHIA,]
Navy Department 10th August 1798

Wm PENNOCK Esqr *Norfolk*

SIR The enclosed Letter for Capt Truxton directs him to proceed to the Havanna, taking Capt Philips under his command — Duplicates are sent to Charleston, and by Capt Philips

Please to take the best means to get this Letter to Capt Truxton — If the last Letter I sent you for him, has been received — He will sometimes appear off the Light House. with a Swedish Flag hoisted on his main top Mast head — The Frigate *Constitution* will be on your Coast immediately — so that your Trade will have it's full share of protection.

I have the honor to be &c^a^

[NDA. GLB, Vol. 1.]

To James Simons, Charleston, from Secretary of Navy

[PHILADELPHIA,]
Navy Department 10th August 1798

JAMES SIMONS Esqr *Charleston*

SIR The enclosed Letter for Capt Truxton directs him to proceed to the Havanna, to convoy from thence the American Vessels I write also, by way of Norfolk — Be so good as to take the speediest means of getting this Letter to him — Capt Nicholson, in the Frigate *Constitution*, will proceed immediately to the southern Coast — so that your Trade will have its full share of the protection in the power of government to afford —

I have the honor to be &c^a^

[NDA. GLB, Vol. 1.]

[Enclosure]

To Captain Thomas Truxtun, U. S. Navy, from Secretary of Navy

Navy Departm^t^ 10 August. 1798

Capt TRUXTUN,

SIR, The enclosed Instructions were sent to Wm Pennock, to be forwarded to you, immediately after date. I am uncertain, whether you have yet received Them. —

Government have received Information to be relied on, that at least sixty American Vessels of considerable Value, are now at the Havanna, & will remain for Convoy, as without Convoy there is but little Chance of their escaping the French Cruisers in the same port, & prepared to follow them out.

Capt Phillips in the Ship *Baltimore* of 20 Guns, now at Baltimore will be ordered down to Hampton road, & to join you with all possible Expedition between that Place and Charleston, if he should not find you at Hampton road. You will endeavour to fall in with this Vessel as early as possible, and taking her under your Command, proceed without delay to the Havanna, where you will take under your Protection the American Vessels, in that Port, and convoy them to our Coasts, 'till you shall judge them to be out of danger. When you have performed this Service, You will repair to the Station pointed out in my Letter of 14 July, & so dispose of the force you will find on that Station, as you shall judge best for the Security of our Coast from Cape Henry to our Southern Extremities. This Force will consist of the *Baltimore*, and two or three Cutters.

It is not necessary to a Man of your understanding, to be particular on the subject of your expedition to the Havanna. You know the service to be performed, and you know the Importance of it. It is not doubted, that you will perform it well — avoiding to the Utmost, affording any cause of Irritation to the Spanish Government. We wish to keep Peace and preserve Friendship with all Nations who will permit us. We are at peace with Spain, Yet such is the influence of the French over Spain, that it may be prudent for you to keep out of the reach of the Guns of the —

Enclosed you will receive a Letter from the Secretary of State to the Governor of the Havanna.

Enclosed you have also a Copy of the Letter from the Secretary of State, to the Governor of the Havanna — It can not be presumed that the Governor will interpose to detain our Vessels — If he should, it will be contrary to Treaty & you will in that Case forcibly demand Them.

I have the honor &c.

To the same, 10 Aug^t^

Enclosed are Signals proposed by Admiral Vandeport to be observed between the American & British Ships of War — and which have been agreed to on our Part.

I have the honor &c.

[NDA. OSW, Vol. 1.]

To Jeremiah Yellott, Navy Agent, Baltimore, from Secretary of Navy

[PHILADELPHIA,]
Navy Department 10th August 1798

JERh YELLOTT Esqr *Baltimore*

SIR The *Baltimore* I hope is ready — orders for Capt Philips to proceed immediately to join Truxton at Cape Henry go with this — You know the importance of the service he is to perform, and I hope will suffer nothing to delay him —

I have the honor to be &ca

[NDA. GLB, Vol. 1.]

To Captain Isaac Phillips, U. S. Navy, from Secretary of Navy

[PHILADELPHIA,]
Navy Departmt Augt 10, 1798

Capt PHILLIPS

SIR, You will receive herein a List of Signals, furnished by Admiral Vandevert*, by which British and American Vessels may know each other at sea, and which have been agreed to on our Part —

SIR: This Letter will be handed to you by Mr Harrison Walker, a young Gentleman who has been particularly recommended to Capt Barry of the Frigate *United States* who destined him for one of his Midshipmen, but unfortunately he did not arrive from Virginia before Capt Barry's departure. I wish you, therefore, to receive him on board your ship the *Baltimore* in the Capacity of Midshipman, until an opportunity offers of his joining Capt Barry, which it is his intention to do.

I am &c.

[*Admiral Vandeput.]
[NDA. OSW, Vol. 1.]

To Thomas Lewis, marshal, from Secretary of Navy

[PHILADELPHIA,]
Navy Department 10 August 1798

THOs LEWIS Esqr *Marshall New Jersey*

SIR There will be delivered to you with this a few French Prisoners, who have been captured on board a privateer — I have the honor to request that you will have them received in some jail of New Jersey — The Jail at Burlington if convenient —

I am &ca

Colo Nicholls will arrange with you for their maintenance.

[NDA. GLB, Vol. 1.]

To Stephen Higginson, Navy Agent, Boston from Secretary of Navy

[PHILADELPHIA,]
Navy Department 10 August 1798

STEPn HIGGINSON Esqr

SIR I am honored with your Letter of the 4th Instant. I am gratified that you approve of the Enterprize under Barry — I am this day dispatching orders to Truxton in the Frigate *Constellation*, and a 20 Gun Ship at Baltimore, to proceed without delay to the Havanna, to convoy our Merchant Vessels — Truxton is on the southern Coast, but I expect my Letters will meet him at Norfolk — and that these Vessels will leave Cape Henry by the 20th Instant, perhaps sooner —

I requested the Secretary of the Treasury several days ago to remit you 20,000 Dolls

[NDA. GLB, Vol. 1.]

To Superintendent of the Mint from Secretary of Navy

[PHILADELPHIA,]
Navy Department. Augt 10th 1798

The SUPERINTENDENT OF THE MINT

SIR In addition to the Clippings of Cents already purchased for the Navy Department you will be so obliging as to pack up with all possible expedition — The Copper in small Bars, and that of a Black Cast which you was spoken to about this morning — The price to be what Mr Tench Francis has been in the Habit of paying for Copper of the same description —

As this Copper is intended to be shipped to another port, it will be of the utmost consequence that it be packed in strong casks well coopered —

When this is done — The superintendent will be good enough to deliver the whole to Capt Robert Gill, Storekeeper for this department, taking his receipt for the same —

[NDA. GLB, Vol. 1.]

[10 August, 1798]

Good Friends brings home crew of Ship *William Penn*

FROM THE LOG BOOK OF THE *Good Friends*

May 19, left the *Cordovan;* afterwards boarded by a British frigate (another in company) and after examination, politely dismissed. June 24, lat. 38, 24, long. 48, 50, spoke the brig *Nancy*, out 14 days from New York to Madeira, all well. July 12, spoke a Prussian brig, out 12 days from Baltimore to Oporto; 29th, spoke a British brig, 3 days out from New York to New-Foundland.

In the *Good Friends* came home, the crew of the ship *William Penn*, except the mate, who is detained as a prisoner of war, being an Englishman.

[LC, "Claypoole's American Daily Advertiser" (Phila.), 10 August 1798.]

[10 August 1798]

To Lieutenant Triplett, U. S. Marine Corps, from Captain Thomas Truxtun, U. S. Navy

SIR, It would only be regular, and proper, to have the Centinels for the Night always fixed in each Watch, before the Retreat is beat at Sun Down, as has always been my Practice, and as I have before mentioned and directed here. Last Evening, however, as I walked towards the Barricado, after 8 o'Clock, I heard a Noise, and high Altercations between the Marines, as to where they were to be placed, and stand Guard during the Night. — Being tired at finding Fault, I for the Moment resolved not to take Notice of this Impropriety untill to Day, and I now inform you, that a particular, and minute attention to this Order is expected, for the Conduct of those Marines would disgrace the most common and meanest of Privateers, if not checked.

I am Sir

Your most Obed^t humble Servant —

THOMAS TRUXTUN.

UNITED STATE'S SHIP, *Constellation*
at Sea 10th August 1798 —

Lieutenant TRIPLETT of Marines.

[HS of Pa. NDA photostat. Truxtun's LB, 1798–9.]

[10 August 1798]

Captain Thomas Truxtun's order respecting water

The Scuttle Casks may be filled; and kept filled with water, in future, provided the ordinary Seamen, and Others use it with Moderation, and not so, as to injure themselves, or risk the Introduction of a Dysentery among the Crew, which would probably prove fatal to many, and injurious to the Service.

THOMAS TRUXTUN.

UNITED STATE'S SHIP *Constellation*
at Sea, 10th August 1798. —

[HS of Pa. NDA photostat. Truxtun's LB, 1798–9.]

Extract from Captain Thomas Truxtun's journal, U. S. Frigate *Constellation*, 10 August 1798, Friday

Moderate Breezes and pleasant Weather. At 7 PM dispatched the Virginia * Revenue Cutter with a Letter for William Pennock Esquire, Naval Agent at Norfolk, requesting him to send me any Letters he may have from the Government for me. Stood off untill Day Light into seventeen Fathoms Water; then tacked, and stood in, and at 8 AM brought to with a Shot the Snow *Fair Columbia*, from Alexandria bound to Havannah, she left the Cape about 3 AM, and had seen, nor heard, of any Cruizers. Depth of Water ten Fathoms. Cape Henry North West, seven League Distance. At 11 ditto spoke a Pilot Boat, who informed me, a Coaster from North Carolina had seen a small french Privateer to the Southward; Schooner rigged but without Top Masts, not a very likely Circumstance; I therefore infer, it must have been some small Coaster lying to for a Pilot.

This day took off the Allowance of Water altogether, and filled the Scuttle Cask for the Use of the People.

Latitude observed 36°.42′ N°
Longitude Account 75.32 W.

[* This may be the name of the cutter, *Virginia*.]
[HS of Pa. NDA photostat.]

To Captain Francis Bright, Revenue Cutter *Virginia*, from Secretary of Navy

[PHILADELPHIA,]
Navy Department. 11th Augt 1798

Capt FRANCIS BRIGHT
of the Cutter *Virginia* at Norfolk.

SIR, The Secretary of the Treasury has delivered me your Letter of the 28th ulto addressed to him, it being arranged, that when the Cutters are ready for Sea, they are to be placed under the direction of this department —

I have read this Letter with attention, & am sensible of your merits, and they will not be overlooked, when an Opportunity offers of promoting your Views — At present however it is necessary that You should cruise in the Cutter *Virginia* now under your Command, and as your force is too small to promise much success if unsupported, you will as soon as possible join the Frigate *Constitution* Commanded by Capt Saml Nicholson, which vessel is to Cruise from Cape Henry to the Extremity of our Southern limits, and probably at the time you receive this, may be on that Station — You will therefore proceed to sea, and use all diligence to fall in with her, and when found you will act under the orders of Capt Nicholson — Should you from any unforeseen Circumstance not meet with him, You will then have to cruise alone, within the limits above mentioned — paying however most attention to the Chesapeake — as there is a 16 Gun Brig out of Charleston. —

You will find herein, an Act of Congress passed the 9th of July last, authorizing the Capture of all armed vessels belonging to the French Republic, and Instructions founded on that Act. —

You will no doubt take care to promote good Order & discipline on board your vessel, and you must be careful not to molest the Vessels of any other Nation than the French, You must not even attempt the Recapture of any American Vessel that may be captured by the Ships of any of the other Nations who may be at War, but who are at peace with us, because it is to be presumed if such captures prove illegal, Compensation will be made therefor — In the Course of your Cruize it may be of importance that I should have an opportunity of communicating with you by Letter, for which purpose it will be proper, that every 12 or 15 days you appear off Cape Henry, hoisting the Swedish Flag by which you will be known, and I will take measures for having Dispatches lodged with Mr Pennock of Norfolk to be forwarded to you if necessary — to facilitate which, you may Sail off & on for two or three days.

This precaution is taken in case you should not join Capt Nicholson, but if you should, he will of course received the Instructions, and you will, as beforementioned, act under his orders — Should you take any prizes, you are to send them to the nearest Port in the United States. —

It is desireable that I should hear from you, as often as opportunities offer — and it is probable you will frequently fall in with Vessels bound to our Ports. —

Wishing you success &c.

[NDA. OSW, Vol. 1.]

To President John Adams from Attorneys David L. Barnes, Providence, R. I.

PROVIDENCE *Augt 11. 1798*

SIR: The original, of which the inclosed* is a copy was sent by mail to the Secretary of State last Tuesday. — but hearing of your being at Quincy, I take the liberty to trouble you with this directly, in order that you may have the earliest information, of the arrival & object of Victory Hughes: partner and agent — To the inclosed I would add, that being at Newport this week, I found that the same Siemandy had been there twice or three times before — particularly last winter, he came there in a Snow from New York, bound to Guadaloupe. — he came down the Sound to avoid some British privateers said to be off the Hook. — a French emigrant at Newport from Guadaloupe, told me that Siemandy mentioned last winter his being particularly connected in business with Victor Hughes. — I mention these circumstances as they serve to corroborate the information received from Cap. Jacobs. —

With the most perfect Respect
I am Sir
Y^r M^o h^e Servt

(Signed) DAVID L. BARNES

JOHN ADAMS
President of the United States. —

[*NOTE.—For enclosure see letter of Aug. 6, 1798.]
[SDA. Misc. L. Jan.–Aug. 1798 and NDA.]

Extract from journal of James Pity, U. S. Frigate *Constitution*, 11 August 1798, Saturday

Thick foggy Weather a 1 P. M. Sounded in 18 fath^{ms} Water Grey Sand intermix^d wth pebbles and Shells @ 2 P. M. Sounded in 28 fath^{ms} a 6 Reef^t Top Sails.

At 11 A. M. Sounded in 25 fath^{ms} water

At 2 A. M. Sounded in 45 fath^{ms} white Sand with Shells.

At ½ past Sounded got ground 34 fath^{ms} fine black Sand Brown pebbles & White Shells.

Latter part foggy W^r

[No observations.]

[NDA.]

Extract from Captain Thomas Truxtun's journal, U. S. Frigate *Constellation*, 11 August 1798, Saturday

Fresh Breezes, and clear Weather; Stretched within three Leagues of Cape Henry, then stood off, and at 5 PM brought to with a Shot the Schooner *Sea Flower* of Philadelphia from Norfolk bound to Antigua, left the Capes two Hours ago.

At 8 AM fired a Shot, and brought to the Schooner *Marcia* of and from Norfolk bound to Charleston out fourteen Hours, and saw no Vessel.

At 11 ditto the Virginia Revenue Cutter returned, and brought me Dispatches from the Secretary of the Navy, to which I shall pay due attention.

Cape Henry at Noon bore West B. North half North, Distance nine Leagues, Depth of Water twelve Fathoms. Dispatched the Revenue Cutter with my Letters to the Secretary of the Navy, under Cover to Mr Pennock, Naval Agent, at Norfolk, with Directions to forward them to him without Loss of Time.

Latitude observed 36° .49′ No

Longitude Account 75.20 W.

[HS of Pa. NDA photostat.]

Extract from journal of Lieutenant John Mullowny, U. S. Frigate *United States*, 11 August 1798, Saturday

Clear weather.

Shewed false fires for the *Delaware*, not answer'd.

[Latd Obsd 27.23]

[NA.]

Extract from journal of James Pity, U. S. Frigate *Constitution*, 12 August 1798, Sunday

First part this 24 hours — Light Winds and Hazy —

a 11 oC A. M. call'd all hands aft to attend prayers. Doctr Blake stood Chaplain.

Middle part pleasant Number Porpoises in Sight Try'd catch some but could not —

Sounded white blk & yellow sand a 6 A. M. Set Main Sail K̄ Ship South & Eastwd Sounded 27 fathms —

Latter part Thick foggy Weather.

[Latitude observed 40° 47m No]

[NDA.]

Extract from Captain Thomas Truxtun's journal, U. S. Frigate *Constellation*, 12 August 1798, Sunday

Fresh Breezes and squally the first Part, the Middle moderate, and the latter light Winds, and clear Weather. At one PM discovered two Sail in Shore of us, gave Chace, and at two ditto fired a Shot, when one of them (a sloop from Boston bound to Charleston called the *Rangor*) shortened Sail, and stood towards us; the other was a Schooner, that I suspected from the Manuvres, was a French Privateer, particularly as he stood towards the Shore, and obliged me to chace him into six Fathoms Water, pretty near to the Beach, and then did not bring to untill I had fired five Shot over him. This Vessel however proved to be from Boston, and bound to Charleston also. Her Owner's Name Amory. Bearings at Noon Cape Henry North West B. West ¼ West, twenty Leagues Distance, Depth of Water 19½ Fathoms over a Bottom of fine whitish Sand, and some broken Shells. No other Vessels in Sight, or any other Circumstance worth recording.

Latitude observed 36°26′ No

Longitude Account 74.45 W.

[HS of Pa. NDA photostat.]

From Secretary of Navy to Lieutenant William Bainbridge, U. S. Navy

[PHILADELPHIA,]
Navy departm^t Augt 13. 1798.

The Commanding Officer, of the schooner *Retaliation*,
(Wm BAINBRIDGE.)

SIR, You will as early as possible, examine the Stores belonging to the Schooner *Retaliation* — and let Me know what will be wanted to fit her out for a Cruise of four Months — including every Article of Provision — Arms — Ammunition &^c

[NDA. OSW, Vol 1.]

To James Watson, Navy Agent, New York, from Secretary of Navy

[PHILADELPHIA,]
Navy Department Augt 13th 1798

JA^s WATTSON Esqr *New York*

SIR I am honoured with the receipt of your Letter of the 11th Instant, seven Tons of Copper have been purchased, and directions are given, to send it on to you with all possible dispatch — The Public offices are about to be removed this day to Trenton — from whence my next Letters will be dated, and to which place you will please to write me in future —

I shall leave orders to procure a further quantity of old Copper, but fear the prevailing Malady will render it difficult —

The enclosed Letter for Capt Nicholson of the Frigate *Constitution*, you will please to have delivered on board when she shall appear off Sandy Hook —

I have the honor to be &^a

[NDA. GLB, Vol. 1.]

To Colonel Ebenezer Stevens, New York, from Secretary of Navy

[PHILADELPHIA,]
Navy Department 13th August 1798

Col^o EB^r STEVENS, *New York*

SIR I am honoured with your letter of the 11th Instant — Being Just about to move to Trenton, on account of the Fever here, I have merely time to say, that of the Galleys authorized by Congress, only two remain to be procured — It is desireable to construct these two, so as to be most useful to New York & Rhode Island — Would you advise that these (there being only two) should be of the kind you recommend? Please to answer as soon as convenient, to Trenton

I have the honor to be &c^a

[NDA. GLB, Vol. 1.]

To Captain Samuel Nicholson, U. S. Navy, from Secretary of Navy

[PHILADELPHIA,]
Navy Department 13th Augt 1798

Capt SAM^l NICHOLSON

SIR Capt Truxton being ordered on a different service, you will proceed without delay to the Southward, and consider your Cruising

Ground to extend from Cape Henry to our Southern Extremity. —

You will find on this Station a Revenue Cutter of 14 Guns, Capt Bright, from Norfolk, and a vessel of the same size, Capt Cochran from Charleston, and it is probable that in two or three Weeks, two other Vessels of 10 & 14 Guns will join you — You will take this force under your Command, and so dispose it as best to protect our Commerce & to annoy the French Cruisers — It is not meant that you should be confined to a certain distance from the shores — Greater Latitude is allowed you for Enterprize — and it is imagined you may occasionally find French Cruisers in Latitude 34 & 33 & Longitude 72 to 60. —

On Capt Truxtons return from the Havanna it is probable other service may be found for you — In the mean time as it may be necessary that I should communicate with you — you will when convenient appear off Charleston, & the light House at Cape Henry from one or other of which places, I shall communicate with you. —

It will be agreeable to hear from you by all opportunities — Enclosed you will receive a List of Signals proposed by Admiral Vandeport [Vandiput], and agreee to, on our part, to be used between the American & British Ships of War.

Wishing you great success, &c.

[NDA. OSW, Vol. 1.]

To Captain Richard Dale, U. S. Navy, from Secretary of Navy

[PHILADELPHIA,]
Navy Department 13th Augt 1798

Capt Rd DALE

SIR, I am this day removing my office to Trenton, & shall be so distant from you, that I shall not be able to give you so much aid as I wish, in fitting Your Ship — The more must depend on yourself.

If you will give me as early as you can, an Account of all the Articles you will want for four Months I will have them provided in time if practicable.

I shall be glad to hear from you frequently at Trenton.

[NDA. OSW, Vol. 1.]

Extract from journal of James Pity, U. S. Frigate *Constitution*, 13 August 1798, Monday

First part this 24 hours clear Weather.

at 4 P. M. Sounded bottom 40 fms at 5 P. M. Do Bottom 35 fathms Dark Sand

at 8. K̅ Ship to S. E.

At Midnight Sounded got bottom 45 fathms fine blk Sand

at 4 A. M. Sounded got bottom 50 fathms hard Bottom at Ditto K̅ Ship to the N. W.

Latter part Thick foggy Weather.

[No observations.]

[NDA.]

Extract from Captain Thomas Truxtun's journal, U. S. Frigate *Constellation*, 13 August 1798, Monday

Moderate Breezes, and a Swell from the Southward. Set up the Rigging and employed the People pointing Ropes, grafting the Straps of Blocks, repairing Rigging and Sails, washing, scraping, and at a great Variety of other necessary Matters. At 6 PM saw a Sail in the South East (standing to the Northward) at a great Distance from the Mast Head, gave Chace and at 7 Ditto, it being dark, lost Sight of her, and in order to fall in with her again in the Morning, I observed the following Plan. Having previously observed her sailing, as we only altered her Bearing one Point of the Compass from the Time she was first [?] [discovered] to our losing Sight of her. As soon as it was dark, I kept the Ship away North East, untill I run seven Miles, then hawled up East North East, and run in that Direction four Miles, then hawled up East, and run four Miles, making on these three angles fifteen Miles; I then bore away North by Compass, and at four AM (it being Dawn of Day, after having run on that Course six Miles, she was discovered bearing about North B. West, one Quarter of a Mile Distance, at 5 ditto brought her to with a Shot. She was the Schooner *Polly* from Washington North Carolina, bound to New York, had seen no Cruizers.

Immediately after speaking this Vessel I gave Chace to another, and at 11 I spoke the *Betsey* from Boston bound to Wilmington North Carolina, had seen no Cruizers, saw a Brig to the Northward, to which we gave Chace. At Noon Cape Henry bore West, eleven Leagues Distance, Depth of Water seventeen Fathoms.

Latitude observed 36°.57′ N°
Longitude Account 75.10 W.

[HS of Pa. NDA photostat.]

Extract from journal of Lieutenant John Mullowny, U. S. Frigate *United States*, 13 August 1798

Clear weather
Calm
Capt Barry went on board to see Capt Decatur, returned at 4 P. M.
[Latitude Obs^d 27.7]

[NA.]

To Joshua Humphreys, Naval Constructor, from Secretary of Navy

[TRENTON]
*Navy Department 14th August 1798**

JOSHUA HUMPHREYS Esqr

SIR I have your Letter of the 12th Inst^t Col^o Pickering agrees that 6^lb Shot, or any thing wanting for the Cutters &c^a may be taken from the Algerine Vessels — pray so order it — And pray let Captain's Campbell & Brown wait for nothing — I want Brown to carry Arms &c^a to Carolina & Georgia — & Campbell to be at Norfolk by the 1st of October. —

[*NOTE.—This letter is located in the Letter Book among those dated 14th September 1798, and possibly 14th August is written in error.]
[NDA. GLB, Vol. I.]

Extract from Captain Thomas Truxtun's journal, U. S. Frigate *Constellation*, 14 August 1798, Tuesday

Fresh Breezes and cloudy, threatening a Gale, which terminated about 6 PM in a Squall only; the Night after was moderate, with some Intervals Calm, but the Morning brought us fine pleasant Weather, with smooth Water.

At 5 PM brought to, and spoke the Sloop *Drucilia*, of and from New Bedford, bound to Alexandria, out thirteen Days, and had seen no Cruisers.

At 7 PM a Pilot Boat came near us, and sent me some Norfolk News Papers; and at 11 AM another came along Side, when I endeavoured to negotiate with him to run up to Norfolk, and bring us off some Beans, Molasses, and other Supplies the Ship is now in Need of; but his Demands were so exorbitant, that I gave the Matter up. Exercised Great Guns &c: Bearings of Cape Henry at Noon West 3/4 North, eight Leagues Distance. Depth of Water twelve Fathoms.

Latitude observed 36°. 53′ N°
Longitude Account 75.21 W.

[HS of Pa. NDA photostat.]

Extract from Journal of James Pity, U. S. Frigate *Constitution*, 14 August 1798, Tuesday

First part this 24 hours foggy Wr & Calm. Swell fm S. b. W. at 2 P. M. Unbent the Courses and took all the points out of them and bent the New Royalls. people employ'd Variously. 1st Lieut employ'd taking the Discription of the people. a 1/2 past 7. furld Royalls a 9 furld F & Mizen T. G. Sails 1/2 past 6 Set F & Mizen T G Sails. Royalls & Stay sails a 8 Sounded got bottom 65 fms green & Oozy.

a 10 A. M. Set Spanker. a 11 Set foretop mast & Lower Steering Sails

a Swell fm N. W.

Latter part this 24 hours Thick foggy Wr

[No Observation.]

[NDA.]

To Lieutenant Cowper from Captain Thomas Truxtun, U. S. Navy

U. State's Ship *Constellation* 15th *August 1798*.

Sir, Agreeable to the eighth Article of my printed Instructions, it is ordered, "that at fair Day Light as well as at all other Times when necessary, the Sails are to be nicely trim'd, and the Ropes got up out of the Water" — So far from this being done, particularly in your Watch, that I have frequently, very frequently indeed, been on Deck, when I have been ashamed, after writing, printing, and speaking as I have done, to see the Lifts, and Trusses hanging slack, the Back Stays not set up, and not a Sail trimmed or Brace hawled properly in, and taught from one End of the Ship to the other, and often various Ropes, as well as the Weather main and fore Sheets, and the Lee, main, and fore Tacks towing in the Water. Sometimes I have of late even mentioned these Matters to you, at other Times again, *being almost exhausted*, I have passed them over, and directed the needful to be done myself.

Every Allowance has been made for your Want of seeing Regularity on Ship Board, and having Experience, but when the Duty is made so plain, as it is on Board of this Frigate; Surely with a little Attention it would be an easy Matter for you to perform, what has been assigned to you, and expected from you.

It is not to be expected, that in a Service so young as our's, where every Thing is to organize, and the most minute and trifling Matters to arrange that the Lieutenants of Ship are to remain idle, and indifferent Spectators of what is going on; but on the Contrary it is, and for Some Time to come, will be absolutely necessary, that they overlook the Duty of every Department on Board, and carry the Views of their Commander into Effect. A most minute Attention to Duty I have frequently observed, was highly and indispensibly necessary to the Making of a good Officer at Sea, and that to be such, great Circumspection in his Conduct, and Deportment, was necessary. Let me ask you, whether you have attended to this Part of my Observations, and say, if it is not beneath the Character of a Commissioned Officer, to converse with Seamen, and to suffer, and to see Pettee Officers box on Deck, independant of it's being positively forbid by the Articles of War; it is distressing for me to be obliged to address you on these Subjects, but the Salvation, the Existence of the Naval Service has called aloud for it, and I must do my Duty in every situation.

I have been told, that you say it would take an Attorney, to learn, and retain the Instructions in Print, I have only to observe, that when a School Boy at a Vacation, I have had three Times as much assigned me as a Task, and did not think it difficult.

It is unnecessary for me at present to add, I therefore shall expect in future the Orders of the Ship more attended to, and a Consistency more in Character observed.

You may rely, Sir, that it would give me at all Times, infinitely greater Pleasure to report favourably of my Officers, than to enter Complaints, but as it is of the greatest Consequence to the Public, to have good Officers in the Naval Service, I shall be obliged to state Things with Candor, and as I find them. I have frequently forbid the Setting on the Nettings, and Railing, still you practice it, tho' my Orders have been very pointed indeed.

If you have supposed, that Orders may be unattended to in our Naval Service, and that a democratic System is to govern on Board our Ships, I must inform you, that the Reverse is, and must be the Case.

I shall be extremely pleased to find the Good I have anticipated, arise from this Note, and that my Endeavors to put things right may have the desired Effect. I am, Sir,

Your Obedient humble Servant

THOMAS TRUXTUN

Lieutenant COWPER.

[HS of Pa. NDA photostat. Truxtun's LB, 1798–99.]

Extract from journal of James Pity, U. S. Frigate *Constitution*, 15 August 1798, Wednesday

First part this 24 hours Calm W^{r} all hands employ'd bend^{g} M. Top Sail and Main Stay Sail.

at 8 P. M. furld small Sails Sounded in 80 fath^{ms} fine dark Sand.

Middle part Calm. Sounded in 100 fath^{ms} Sand.

At Meridian Sounded in 97 fath^{ms} black Sand. Light breeze from Southward watch employ'd Sway^{g} up Main Yard and clearing between Decks Carpenters employ'd build^{g} a Boat

Latter part pleasant W^{r} Light breezes.

[Latitude observed 39° 58^{m} N°]

[NDA.]

Extract from Captain Thomas Truxtun's journal, U. S. Frigate *Constellation*, 15 August 1798, Wednesday

On examining the small Stores, and finding only two or three Days Allowance on Board, concluded on running into Hampton Roads in Order to get a Supply, and to make such Repairs as became indispensibly necessary, previous to the Autumnal Equinox.

At 4 PM we were abreast of the Light House on Cape Henry, and at 6 ditto, anchored at the upper Part of Lynn Haven Bay near to Willoughby's Spit. Old Point Comfort bearing West, Depth of Water five Fathoms.

At 8 AM Got under Way, and at Noon anchored in Hampton Roads in ten Fathoms Water, Sowel's Point bearing South South East, and Hampton Town North B. East. Employed putting the Ship in Order, and at the same Time the best Bower, and Sheet Anchors were ready to let go.

Hance Anderson, Gunner's first Mate, and Thomas Gummerson, a Quarter Gunner, having behaved exceeding ill to the Master's second Mate, Mr Smith, and in a mutinous Manner, I had them put in Irons and sent to Norfolk Jail.

[HS of Pa. NDA photostat.]

To Secretary of the Navy from Captain Thomas Truxtun, U. S. Navy

UNITED STATE'S SHIP *Constellation*
Hampton Roads 16th August 1798.

SIR, Having examined the Provisions, and finding only two or three Day's Allowance of small Stores remaining; I concluded on running into these Roads, In order to get a Supply, and to put the Ship in a State to meet any Weather previous to the approaching Equinox, which was highly necessary, as not only the Outside Work wanted Caulking, but the Decks were so open, that it has been with Difficulty, the various Stores could be preserved, and all this is owing to the Ship being caulked in the Winter Season, as I have before observed, without any Blame being imputable to any one.

Six Month's Beef and Pork being put on Board, previous to the Ship's Departure from this Bay, the Hold was so filled, that only two Months' Allowance of small Articles could conveniently be taken in, and as the Potatoes soon became rotten, and unfit for Men to eat, which was to be expected at this Season of the Year, I was obliged to substitute other Things in Lieu thereof, which is the Cause of the almost total Consumption of small Stores, and of my Return here sooner than I intended by several Days.

In Order to make Room in the Hold, I purpose throwing out some of the Shingle Ballast, and taking in Thirty Tons of Kentledge or Pig Iron, if the Agent at Norfolk can furnish either of those Articles; I have always been an Advocate for a Ship of War, carrying only one half of her Ballast at most, of Iron, on account of making her easy at Sea, and of obviating the Necessity of such heavy Rigging, as Vessels are often loaded with Aloft, which has a Tendency to make them Crank, strain their Spars by the Weight, and finally holds Wind, which obstructs their going (particularly by the Wind) makes them much more unhandy to work, and adds to their Cost in the first Instance, and of their being kept in Repair after.

The other half of the Ballast, should be clean Shingle, that is of small Stones, about the Size of Pease, and all stowed in the Cuntlings of the Water Casks, consequently it's being kept from the Bottom of the Vessel, and thus raised, has a Tendency to make a Ship roll, and pitch easy.

The *Constellation* being so uncommonly sharp, we have in proportion to that Sharpness, less Room in the Hold, than the Frigates of other Nations; so that I find it expedient to carry on Board of this Vessel ⅔ of the Ballast of Iron, and only ⅓ of Shingle. It is surprizing however, how little Ballast she takes, when compared with the English, and French Ships of 36 Guns, tho' her Size is so much greater, the whole Quantity of Kentledge &c (or Iron and Shingle Ballast) being only 135 Tons.

I have seen so much in the public Prints of the Sailing of Barry's Ship, and so much more bombastical Nonsense of that at Boston, that I am at a Loss to make a Report, with Respect to the Sailing of this Frigate on that Score, with any Degree of Satisfaction to myself. I shall therefore only say, that in no Instance of Chace during our Cruize, was half our Canvass necessary, to overhawll the fastest sailing Vessel we met, some of which were termed before Flyers.

Should we therefore meet the *United States*, and *Constitution*, you need not be surprized, if you hear, that in going by or large, she outsails them both, and she is in every Situation the easiest Ship I ever was in.

As there would have been too much Time lossed in waiting a Reply to my last of the 11th I shall set the Caulkers at Work immediately and as soon as they have done, and the Water and Stores replenished, the Ship will be ready (provided Mr. Pennock furnishes the Ballast) for any Expedition, and I expect this Business will all be completed before I can receive, in the usual Way, your Reply.

The Ventilators so often mentioned in my Letters, are much wanted, and would have saved double their Cost at least in Stores, had they been Sent round in May last.

For Want of these Apparatus, many Articles have been spoiled; but from the great Pains that have been taken to keep the Ship, and People clean, and sweet, the Crew perhaps at this Day surpass in Health, that of any other Ship in any Country, there being at this Day, only seven Men in the Surgeon's List with trifling Complaints) inclusive of one Man discharged on Account of Inability to do Duty from a Complaint of a dropsical Nature; and one other, sent to Norfolk, having met with an Accident in falling.

The Number of Men allowed this Ship are not sufficient; her Crew ought to consist of 330 at least, in Order to work her with Facility, & man the Guns well, and then a few out of this Number confined with Indisposition, or put on Board a Prize, would leave but a bare Sufficiency to sustain an Action with a Ship of equal Force. The Cannon of this Frigate are heavy, as also the Spars, there being only twenty seven feet in Length of a Difference between her Spars, and that of an English 64 Gun Ship, when the Length of every Mast and Yard &c: are added together, and a Comparison made between the two, as you will observe at the End of the Copy of my Journal. I enclose you herewith the following Papers to Vizt No. 1 Copy of my Journal. 2 Muster Roll, 3 Certificate of lost Anchor, 4 Copies of various Orders, 5 Charges against Hance Anderson, and Thomas Gummerson of Gunner's Crew. 6, 7. and 8 Charges against Mathew Talcott, a Midshipman; these Papers with this Letter will throw all the Light on the various Subjects. I have thought proper to communicate, that could be wished at present. The Dispatches forwarded me by Express Boat, has caused me to be rather more particular, perhaps, than I should otherwise have deemed necessary.

THOMAS TRUXTUN.

Honble BENJAMIN STODDERT
Secretary of Navy

[HS of PA. NDA photostat. Truxtun's LB, 1798–9.]

To Lieutenant William Cowper from Captain Thomas Truxtun, U. S. Navy

UNITED STATE'S SHIP *Constellation*
Hampton Roads August 16th 1798

Lieutenant Wm COWPER,

I have received your Note of last Evening in Answer to mine of same Date, An Attentive Zeal to promote the naval Service of the United States of America, with a becoming modest Deportment on Duty, and at the same Time Firmness, when necessary, will always be most agreeable to me, while acting as a Commander of any Ship in the Service.

I have spoken with Truth of the Want of Experience in Officers on several Occasions, for it has been pled as an Excuse to me, when I have had Occasion to mention repeated Neglects.

If Officers have not had Experience on Board Men of War, I do not consider that as a Crime; but when they have had the Foundation laid on Seamanship in Merchantmen, or other Vessels, they may soon become experienced, if attentive, and if a Man does not acquire in his Profession, that Knowledge, that is necessary, for the faithful and complete Discharge of his Duty (particularly in public Life) having Oppertunity, I consider him guilty of a heinous Crime indeed.

You and every Man sailing, or acting under my Orders, in any Situation, may rest assured, that I shall always be infinitely happier to promote their Views, if deserving, than to be compelled to observe a contrary Conduct towards them; I therefore receive your fair Promises with Pleasure.

The Infancy of the American Navy, holds out Prospects and Allurements to young, active, and expert Gentlemen of your Age, that ought to stimulate them to Exertions, that will cause their being noticed every where, as Men and Officers daily striving, and of Course daily gaining more & more Information in the wonderful and extensive Science of Naval Tactics, and naval Matters generally. In the organizing of a *Young Man of War*, and putting Things right from Time to Time, Matters by the Commander must be stated with Candor, and in such a Way, that no Mistakes, or Misconceptions happen.

Good Subordination must always be strictly kept up, among a Number of Men, but in being strict in Discipline, Justness must not be forgotten, or the Savage Character had Recourse to. Ordering of Punishment is to a Man possessing the Principles of a Gentleman, always painful, and however irritable he may become from vexatious Circumstances, frequently occurring; the more he reflects, and the less frequent his Punishments are, the better; In Fact they should only happen, when indispensibly necessary, and their Effect will be the greater.

I am, Sir,

Your very Obedient Servant,

THOMAS TRUXTUN.

[HS of Pa. NDA photostat. Truxtun's LB, 1798–9.]

Extract from journal of James Pity, U. S. Frigate *Constitution*, 16 August 1798, Thursday

First part this 24 hours pleasant W^r^

at 5 P.M. beat to Q^rs^ and Exerciz^d^ the great Guns & Small Arms.

At Meridian took in T. G. Sails and Sounded No bottom. TK Ship to Southw^d^ & Eastw^d^ at 4 P. M. TK Ship N. b. W. set Main sail & M. T. M. Stay Sail at ½ past 10 Made Sail got the Spanker Boom on Deck & Reduced it

all Hands Employ'd at Diff^t^ Jobbs.

[Latitude observed 40.36 —]

[NDA.]

Extract from Captain Thomas Truxtun's journal, U. S. Frigate *Constellation*, 16 August 1798, Thursday

All these Twenty four Hours, moderate Breezes, and pleasant Weather. This Day had a Copy of my Journal completed for the Secretary of the Navy, including the Transactions of Yesterday. Consequently in the next Copy, the Transactions of this Day must be included. The Carpenter employed searching for the Leak, and the People at getting up the Water Casks out of the Hold, and overhawlling them, repairing the Rigging, drying the Sails, and doing of various other necessary Jobs. Mr Garretson the Purser, dispatched with Anderson and Gummerson to Norfolk, and to procure Thirty Tons of Kentledge, or Pig Iron from the Agent, and fresh Provisions &c. for the Crew; returned a little after twelve o'Clock. Made up my Dispatches for the Secretary of the Navy (see Letter Book) which will be forwarded to Morrow the 17th Instant.

Many Vessels have arrived, since we anchored in these Roads, which inform that they have seen no Cruizers on the Coast.

[HS of Pa. NDA photostat.]

[16 August 1798.]

No 1 **Muster Roll of the Officers, Petty Officers, and Seamen, Ordinary Seamen, and Marines, on board the Frigate *Constellation* under the command of Captain Thomas Truxtun in the service of the United States, from the 16th day of August the time they were last mustered, to the 17th day of November 1798**

No.	Names	Rank	date of appointment or Entrance	for what time engaged	Advanced Pay by Mr Rodgers	Advanced Pay by Mr Cowper	Advanced Pay by Mr Triplett	Remarks and Alterations since last Muster
x 1.	Thomas Truxtun x	Comdr	Regt W. O.	[illegible]	"			Those marked with a Cross [x] to be sanctioned by the Government, as they are appointed by me. Signed. Thomas Truxtun.
x 2.	John Rodgers x	Lieut	do	"	"			
x 3.	Wm Cowper x	do	do	"	"			
x 4.	Andrew Sterett x	do	do	"	"			
x 5.	John Archer x	do	8th Novr	"	"			Sent Home in the Prize L'UNION 14 March 1799.
x 6.	Bartholw Clinch x	do Marine	15th do	"	"			
x 7.	George Balfour x	Surgeon	Regt W. O.	"	"			
x 8.	Isaac Henry x	do Mate	do	"	"			Turned over into L'INSURGENTE 15th Febry. 1799.
x 9.	Ambrose Shirly x	Master	do	"	"			
x 10.	Isaac Garretson x	Purser	do	"	"			
x 11.	John Allen x	Boatsn	12th Nov	"	Drs			Dischd St Kitts 14th January 1799.
x 12	James Morgan x	Gunner	9th May	"	40			
x 13.	James Yeomans x	Carptr	23rd March	"	40			
x 14.	James Webb x	Sail Mr	30th Apl	"	40			
x 15.	Henry Vandyke	Midshn	Regt W. O.	"				
x 16	John H. Dent	do	do	"				
x 17.	John M. Clogget	do	do	"				
x 18.	P. C. Wederstrant	do	do	"				
x 19.	James McDonough	do	do	"				Dischd 6th April 1799 Bassateer, St Kitts, having lost his Foot in Action of the 9th Febry 1799, & sent Home in the Prize Schooner UNION to the U. S.
x 20.	David Porter	do	16th Apl	"				Went in the Prize Schooner L'UNION 14 March 1799. Retd on Bd 1 June 1799.
x 21.	William Davis	do	24th June	"				Entered as an Ordinary Midshipman, & Lieutenant at Arms to receive full Seamans Pay 'till 1 Novr & full Mids Pay after and turned over into L'INSURGENTE 15 Febry. 1799.
x 22.	Joshua Herbert	do	13th Novr	"				
x 23.	Arthur Sinclair	do	15th do	"				Turned over into L'INSURGENTE 15. Febry 1799 returned
x 24.	Samuel Brooks	Mr Mate	14, May	"	34.			Made 4th Lieutenant 1st March 1799
x 25.	Daniel Gorman	do	26th March	"	40.			Dischd 30th May 1799
x 26.	Jos S. Smith	do	21st May	"	40.			Turned over into L'INSURGt 15 Febry 1799
x 27	John Pomery	Capt Clk	23rd May	"	20.			
x 28.	Thos McNamara	Bs Mate	3rd do	"	36.			
x 29	Jos Atkinson	do	14th June	"		34.		Turned over into L'INSURGENTE 5 March 1799
x 30	David Mulat	Coxen	7 May	"	34.			Dischd 30 May 1799

x 31.	Joshua Herbert	S. M. Mate	21. dº	"		20		Discharged 30th[?] May 1799
x 32.	James Pinkerton	Gunrs Mate	11 dº	"	34.			Dischd 27th May 1799.
x 33.	William Melvin	dº	11. dº	"	30.			Entered as Seaman 11th May, & remained so 'till 18th Augt from which Time he is to receive Gunner's Mate Pay. Dischd 27 May 1799.
x 34.	John Tilden	Gunrs Yeoman	11. dº	"	66.			Dischd 30th May 1799
x 35.	George McEzey	Carpt Mate	2 April	"	34.			Run 6th April 1799 Bassateer Road, St Christophors.
x 36.	James Butler	dº	5 May	"	30.			Dischd 30th May 1799.
x 37.	Joseph O. Bankson	Armor	1 dº	"	36.			dº 31 Dº 1799.
x 38.	John McHenry	Stewart	26th March	"	38.			dischd
x 39.	Thomas Kelly	Cooper	5th May	"	36.			Dischd 30th May 1799.
x 40	John Marshall	M. at Arms & fifer	11th dº	"	30.			Dischd 28th May 1799.
x 41.	Joseph Brown	Qr Gunner	21 Febry	"	20.			dº 27th dº 1799.
x 42.	John Lancaster	ditto	22d May	"		34.		Dº 26th Dº 1799.
x 43.	John Williams	ditto	21. ditto	"		34.		Entered as Seaman 21st May, & remained so, 'till 18 Augst from which Time he is to receive Qr Gunner's Pay. Dischd 28th May 1799.
x 44.	Alexander Mackey	ditto	3. dº	"	30.			Discharged at Bassaterre, St Christopher's 6th April 1799, being sick of the Flux, and sent Home to the U. S. in the Prize UNION, Schooner.
x 45.	Enoch Brown	ditto	24. dº	"	20.			Made Midshipman and turned over into L'INSURGENTE 1st March 1799.
x 46.	George Robinson	ditto	22. dº	"		34.		Dischd 26th May 1799.
x 47.	Charles Chase	ditto	30. dº	"		34.		Entered as Seaman 30 May, & remained so 'till 29th October, from which Time he is to receive Qr Gunner's Pay. Dischd 30 May 1799.
x 48.	Wm Wall	ditto	26. dº	"		34.		Discharged 27 May 1799.
x 49.	John Barnes	ditto	30. dº	"		34.		Dº 30 Dº 1799.
x 50.	Timothy Shields	Cook	30. April	"	20.			Dº 30 Dº 1799.
x 51.	Nathaniel Strong	Qr Master	26. May	"		34.		Dº 30 Dº 1799.
x 52.	Michl Clansy	ditto	11. dº	"	34.			Sent to the U. S. in the Prize Schooner L'UNION 15th March 1799.
x 53.	John Light	dito	1. June	"			29.	Turned over into the L'INSURGENTE 5th March 1799.
x 54.	John Ponsonby	ditto	28. May	"			$55. 72½	Dº into Dº 9 Dº 1799.
x 55.	John Wall	Loby Boy	1. June	"				Discharged 1 June 1799.
x 56.	Benjamin Deane	Seaman & Carp. Yeomn	24. April	"	34.			Sent to Sick Quarters at Norfolk the 22d May 1799.
x 57.	Richard Jackson	Seaman	11. May	"	34.			Dischd 26 May 1799.
x 58.	John Phillips	ditto	30. dº	"	34.			Turned over into the L'INSURGENTE 15. Febry 99.
x 59.	Thomas Bolam	ditto	25. dº	"			6	Dischd 26 May 99.
x 60.	Archibald Matthews	ditto	28. dº	"	34.			Dº 30 Dº 99.
x 61.	John Williams	dº	23. Augst	"				Dischd 29 Decr 98 sick Norfº
x 62.	Emanuel Causdell	dº	8. June	"		34.		Run St Piere's Martinica 28th April 1799.
x 63.	John Hutt	dº	30. May	"		34.		Dischd 30th May 99.
x 64.	John Robinson	dº	25. dº	"			20.	Dischd 26th May 99.
x 65.	John Welsh	dº	30. April	"	30.			Dº 26 May 99.
x 66.	John Lamp	dº	8. June	"		34.		Dº 9. June
x 67.	Joseph Livingston	dº	30. May	"		34.		Dischd 30th May 99.
x 68.	Thomas Green	dº	17. dº	"	10.			Dischd 27. May 99.
x 69.	Robt Townsend	dº	29. dº	"	34.			Dº 30 Dº 99.
x 70.	William Byron	Seaman	8th June	"		34.		Dischd 9th June
x 71.	William Brown	dº	22. May	"		34.		Discharged 26. May 99.

Nº 1 Muster roll of the Officers, Petty Officers, and Seamen, Ordinary Seamen, and Marines, on board the Frigate *Constellation* under the command of Captain Thomas Truxtun in the service of the United States, from the 16th day of August the time they were last mustered, to the 17th day of November 1798—Continued

No.	Names	Rank	date of appointment or Entrance	for what time engaged	Advanced Pay by Mr Rodgers	Advanced Pay by Mr Cowper	Advanced Pay by Mr Triplett	Remarks and Alterations since last Muster
x 72.	Samuel Thompson	Seaman	28. dº	"			5.	Sent to Sick Quarters at Norfolk 22d May 1799.
x 73.	Peter Peas	dº	29. dº	"	30.			Dischd 30. May 99.
x 74.	George White	dº	30. April	"	30.			Dischd 26 May 99.
x 75.	James Scott	dº	4. June	"	34.			Dº 5 June 99.
x 76.	John Koster	dº	17. May	"	30.			Dischd 26 May 99.
x 77.	Peter Sanonsan	dº	30. April	"	30.			Dº 26 Dº 99.
x 78.	George Appy	dº	25. May	"			$26. 33	Dº 26 Dº 99.
x 79.	Charles Carter	dº	2d June	"	34.			Dº 3 June 99.
x 80.	Samuel Sparks	dº	8. dº	"		34.		Dischd 9th June 1799.
x 81	William Harvey	dº	21. May	"		34.		Dischd 26 May 99.
x 82	Thomas Rounde	dº	30. dº	"		34.		Dº 30 Dº .
x 83.	James Morrison	dº	30. dº	"		34.		Dº 30 Dº .
x 84.	Daniel Phillips	dº	10. dº	"	20.			Run or drown 5th December 1798 in Newport Newse
x 85.	Owen Pritchard	dº	30. dº	"		20.		Dischd 30 May 99.
x 86.	Yergan Zebsance	dº	17. dº	"	30.			Dischd 26 May 1799.
x 87.	Thomas Hornsby	dº	29. dº	"	30.			Dº 30 Dº 99
x 88.	Thomas Walter	dº	1. June	"	34.			Dº 1 June 99
x 89.	Joseph Hart	dº	8. dº	"		34.		Dº 9 June 99
x 90.	Joseph Bradshaw	dº	25. May	"			7.	Dischd 26. May 99.
x 91.	Amos Loomoss	dº	4. June	"				Sent to Sick Quarters at Norfolk 22d May 1799.
x 92.	Ephrim Little	dº	30. May	"		34.		Dischd 30th May 99.
x 93.	Thos Wilson	dº	21. dº	"		34.		Died of wounds recd in Action 9th Febry 99, 10 Feby.
x 94.	Neal Harvey	dº	2d June	"	34.			Killed in Action 9th Dº
x 95.	John Brown	dº	22. dº	"		34.		26 June dischd '99
x 96.	Henry Varnam	dº	8. dº	"		34.		8 June dº '99
x 97.	Robert Purviants	dº	4. April	"				dischd
x 98.	Wm Bellam	dº	8. June	"		34.		Sent to Sick Quarters at Norfolk 22d May 1799.
x 99.	Nicholas Broughen	dº	8 dº	"		34.		Dischd 9 June 1799
x100.	John DeJust	dº	8 dº	"		34.		Dº 9 dº 99
101.	David Royalt	Seaman	8. June	[illegible]		34.		Discharged 9 June 1799.
102.	Anges McInnis	dº	8. dº	"		34.		Dischd 9 June 99.
103.	George Creighton	dº	4. June	"			$32. 66	Dº 5 Dº 99.
104.	John Jones	dº	28. May	"	34.			Turned over into L'INSURGENTE 3d March 1799
105.	James Thomas	dº	21. dº	"		34.		Dischd 27 May 99.
106.	Gideon Saul	dº	29. dº	"	34.			Dº 30 Dº 99.
107.	Abraham Lang	dº	26. dº	"		34.		Dischd 27 May 99.
108.	John Ballet	dº	29. dº	"	34.			Turned over into L'INSURG: 15th Feby 99.
109.	William Armstrong	dº	22. dº	"		34.		Dº Dº 15 Dº
110.	John Slater	dº	22. dº	"		34.		Dischd 27th May 99.

111.	Nathan Brown	dº	21. dº	"		34.		Turned over into L'INSURGENTE 15th Febry 99.
112.	George Mortimore	dº	2. dº	"	30.			Dischd 26 May 99.
113.	Thomas Jones	dº	22. dº	"		34.		Dischd 27 May 99.
114.	Peter Eddy	dº	26. dº	"		34.		Dº 27 Dº 99.
115.	Henry Jennings	dº	8. June	"		34.		Turned over into L'INSURGENTE 15th Febry 99.
116.	James Boos	dº	30. May	"		34.		Dischd 30th May 99.
117.	William Hacket	dº	30. dº	"		34.		Turned over into L'INSURGENTE 15th Febry 1799.
118.	Edward Phillips	dº	8. June	"		34.		Dischd 9 June 1799.
119.	Thomas Chisley	dº	30. May	"		34.		Turned over into L'INSURGENTE 15th Febry 99.
120.	Raymond Lee Kimble	dº	22. dº	"		34.		Discharged 27. May 99.
121.	John Clark	dº	29. dº	"	34.			Dº 30 Dº
122.	Wm Amon	dº	30. dº	"	34.			Run, the 21st April 1799 Bassateer; St Christopher's.
123.	Michael Neal	dº	28. dº	"	34.			Dischd 30th May 99.
124.	Thomas Lee	dº	21. dº	"		34.		Dischd 26 May 99.
125.	Joseph Hawkins	dº	29. dº	"	30.			Dº 30 Dº 99.
126.	John Torksey	dº	30. dº	"		34.		Dº 30 Dº 99.
127.	Charles Malone	dº	29. dº	"	34.			Turned over into L'INSURGENTE 15th Febry 99.
128.	John Oustend	dº	22. dº	"		34.		Dischd 26 May 99.
129.	Wm Young	dº	4. June	"	34.			Turned over into L'INSURGENTE 15th Febry 99.
130.	Ephrim Smith	dº	21. May	"		34.		Dischd 30 May 99.
131.	Gresham Flagg	dº	30. dº	"		34.		dº dº
132.	Wm Faner	dº	8. June	"		34.		Dischd 9. June 99.
133.	Isaac Martin	dº	30. April	"	30.			Dischd 26. May 99.
134.	Wm Chester	dº	29. May	"	30.			Dº 30 Dº
125.	Edmund Cowan	dº	30. dº	"	34.			Dº 30 Dº
136.	Alexander Addams	dº	26. dº	"		34.		Turned over into L'INSURGENTE 15th Febry 99.
137.	Francis Donel	dº	24. dº	"		34.		Dº Dº 5th March
138.	John Cooper	dº	24. dº	"		34.		Dischd 26 May 99.
139.	George Walters	dº	8. June	"		34.		Dischd 8 June 99.
140.	John Excel	dº	25. May	"			8.	Dischd 26 May 99.
141.	Wm Harrison	dº	29. dº	"	30.			Dº 30 Dº
142.	Robert Johnson	Seaman	12. June	"	34.			Turned over into L'INSURGENTE 15th Febry 99.
143.	Charles O'Neal	dº	8. dº	"		34.		Dischd 9th June 99.
144.	Philip Hunff	dº	8. dº	"		34.		Dº 9 Dº
145.	George Stoddart	dº	8. dº	"		34.		Dº 9 Dº
146.	Wm Dale	dº	19. dº	"		34.		Turn'd to In. —
147.	John Finlay	dº	22. dº	"		34.		Turned over into L'INSURGENTE 15th Febry 99.
148.	Henry Hobart	dº	22. dº	"				
149.	Joseph Gravell	dº	23. dº	"				
150.	Wm Balfour	Seaman	31. Augst	"				Dischd 17 June 99.
151.	James Row	dº	6. Novr	"				
152.	Thomas Yam	dº	6. dº	"				
153.	Matthew Rawlings	dº	6. dº	"				Turned over into L'INSURGENTE 15th Febry 99.
154.	John Smith	dº	6. dº	"				
155.	Wm Walker	dº	6. dº	"				Run from Bassateer Road St Christophers, 8th March 1799.
156.	Abraham Howard	dº	6. dº	"				
157.	Peter Sum	dº	6. dº	"				Sent to Sick Quarters at Norfolk 22d May 1799.
158.	Owen Perry	dº	6. dº	"				
159.	John Frazer	dº	6. dº	"				
160.	John Jones	dº	6. dº	"				
161.	Joseph Carter	dº	6. dº	"				
162.	Wm Wright	dº	6. dº	"				

No 1 Muster Roll of the Officers, Petty Officers, and Seamen, Ordinary Seamen, and Marines, on board the Frigate *Constellation* under the command of Captain Thomas Truxtun in the service of the United States, from the 16th day of August the time they were last mustered, to the 17th day of November 1798—Continued

No.	Names	Rank	date of appointment or Entrance	for what time engaged	Advanced Pay by Mr Rodgers	Advanced Pay by Mr Cowper	Advanced Pay by Mr Triplett	Remarks and Alterations since last Muster
163.	Stephen Kennelly	Seaman	8. Novr	"				Run, St Pieres, Martinica 28th April 1799.
164.	Robert Walden	do	8. do	"				
165.	Robert Cooper	do	8. do	"				
166.	Wm Rice	do	8. do	"				
167.	John Rush	do	9. do	"				
168.	Henry Allen	Ordy	22. May	"		20.		Turned over into L'INSURGENTE 15th Febry 99.
169.	Benjamin Cox	do	24. do	"		20.		Dischd 26 May 99.
170.	Richard Pry	do	18. do	"	20.			Do 26 Do
171.	James Barr	do	18. do	"	20.			Do 26 Do
172.	Wm Burnett	do	10. do	"	20.			Do 26 Do
173.	Wm Presson	do	22. do	"		20.		Do 30 Do
174.	Charles King	do	8. June	"		34.		Do 9 June 99.
175.	Spencer Grayson	do	22. May	"		20.		Turned over into L'INSURGENTE 15th Febry 1799.
176.	Francis Thompson	do	28. ditto	"			5.	Dischd 30th May 1799.
177.	John Walsburn	do	25. ditto	"			4.	Fell overboard and was drown on Wednesday the 5th Day of December 1798. in Newport Newse.
178.	John Mayberry	do	10. ditto	"	20.			Discharged 26 May 99.
179.	Hugh Courtney	do	23. do	"	20.			Dischd 26 May 99.
180.	Thomas Kelly	do	19. do	"				Discharged 26 May 99.
181.	John Brien	do	22. do	"	20.			Died, Bassaterre Road St Christophers, 3d May 1799 of a Fever.
182.	Samuel Brown	do	24. do	"		20.		Dischd 26. May 1799.
183.	Wm Jolly	do	22. do	"	20.			Dischd 27. May 99.
184.	Jacob Elsworth	do	28. do	"	20.			Turned over into L'INSURGENTE 15 Febry 99.
185.	Wm Taylor	do	21. do	"		20.		Turned over into L'INSURGENTE 15 Febry 99.
186.	Abraham Vermott	do	7. June	"	30.			Dischd 18 June 1799.
187.	Frederick Keener	do	21. May	"		20.		Dischd 26 May 99.
188.	Morris Dorsey	do	7. do	"	20.			Do 26 Do
189.	John Key	do	18. do	"	20.			Dischd 27 May 99.
190.	John Hodge	do	30. do	"			9.	Do 30 Do
191.	Richard B. Randolph	do	21. do	"		20.		Dischd 26 May 99.
192.	Daniel Wood	do	15. April	"				Do 26 May
193.	Wm Barry	do	11. May	"				Dischd 27 May 99.
194.	Simon Jones	do	14. do	"	20.			Do 27 May 99.
195.	Lewis Clarey	do	11. do	"	20.			Sent to Sick Quarters at Norfolk 22d May 1799—
196.	James Allen	do	30. do	"		20.		Do 30th May 99.
197.	Richd Reeves	do	28. do	"	20.			Do 30 Do
198.	Saml Woodcock	do	14. do	"	20.			Made Carpenter's 1st Mate 12th April 1799 from which time he is to receive C. Mate's pay Dischd 27 May 99.
199.	Wm Baker	do	8. June	"				Dischd 9 June 99.
200.	Willis Simmons	do	21. May	"		20.		Dischd 26 May 99.
201.	John Good	do	22. do	"	20.			Sent to Sick Quarters at Norfolk 24 May 1799—
202.	Patrick Kelly	do	19. do	"				Discharged 27 May 1799.

203.	Edward Fitzsgerrald	do	26. do	"			2.	Dischd 26 May 99.
204.	Michael Smith	do	8. June	"		34.		Do 9 June 99.
205.	Wm Dunn	do	8. May	"	20.			Dischd 27 May 99.
206.	Hiram Conan	do	21. do	"		20.		Dischd
207.	John Fullerton	do	30. April	"	20.			Dischd 26 May 99.
208.	Edward Allen	do	2. May	"	20.			Dischd 27 May 1799.
209.	James Doran	do	24. May	[illegible]		20.		Dischd 26 May 99.
210.	Wm McHatton	do	28. do	"	20.			Turned over into L'INS: 15 Feby 99. & made Mast 1st March 99.
211.	James Moore	do	15. do	"	30.			Dischd 30 May 99.
212.	Fairfax Ross	do	30. do	"		20.		Do 30 Do
213.	Conrad Baxter	do	2d do	"	20.			Turned over into L'INSURGENTE 15 Febry 99.
214.	John Rawlings	do	2. do	"	20.			Do Do 15 Do
215.	Robert Bell	do	8. June	"		34.		Dischd 9 June 99
216.	James Ash	do	22. May	"		20.		Turned over into L'INSURGENTE 15 Feby 99.
217.	John Andrews	do	30. do	"	34.			Sent to Bassateer Hospital, St Christophers, being wounded on the 14th Febry, & dischd 6th April 1799 at Bassateer, St[C.] & sent Home in the Prize Schooner UNION to the U. S.
218.	Anthony Demmervill	do	30th April	"	20.			Dischd 26 May 99.
219.	Wm Thompson	do	22. May	"		20.		Do 26 Do
220.	Wm Leonard	do	19. do	"	20.			do 26 Do
221.	Dennis Bryan	do	15. do	"	20.			Dischd 27 May 1799.
222.	Wm Denny	do	30. do	"		34.		Dischd 30 Do
223.	Samuel Burney	do	10. do	"	20.			Do 26 May 99.
224.	James O'Neale	do	30. April	"	20.			Do 26 Do
225.	Robert W. Boyd	do	1. May	"	20.			Do 26 Do
226.	Francis Gnunervil	do	26. do	"	15.			Do 26 Do
227.	Barnard Harley	do	16. do	"	20.			Dischd 27 May 99.
228.	Thomas Mahaffy	do	4. May	"	20.			Do 26 Do 99.
229.	John Cornelius	do	24. do	"		20.		Do 26 Do
230.	Joseph Henderson	do	30. do	"		20.		Do 30 Do
231.	Roger McBride	do	17. do	"				Discharged 26 May 99.
232.	Edward O'Gisburn	do	21. do	"		20.		Do 26 Do
233.	Richard Dailey	do	19. do	"	20.			Dischd 27 May 99.
234.	George Miller	do	28. do	"	20.			Do 1 June.
235.	Samuel Brown	do	25. do	"			$7. 44	Turned over into L'INSURGENTE 15 Feby 99.
236.	Peter Freeburne	do	19. do	"	20.			Dischd 27. May 99.
237.	Dennis Haley	do	19. do	"	10.			Do 26 Do 99.
238.	Daniel Pointer	do	26. do	"		12.		Do 30 Do
239.	Wm Smithers	do	31. do	"			$17. 50	Do 31 Do
240.	Edward Fitzsgerrald	do	17. do	"	30.			Dischd 27 May 99.
241.	Robert Woodward	do	26. do	"		12.		Do 30 Do
242.	Timothy Driscoll	do	21. do	"		20.		Dischd 26. May 99.
243.	John Joice	do	17. do	"	20.			Dischd 27. May 99.
244.	James Coyle	do	30. April	"	20.			Turned over into L'INSURGENTE 15 Febry 99.
245.	Thomas Brown	do	22. June	"				Discharged 29 June 1799.
246.	Thomas Dennis	do	13. Novr	"				Turned over into L'INSURGENTE 15 Febry 99.
247.	David Fitzsgibbons x	do	23. Augst					
248.	George Blueford x	do	23. do					
249.	John Hollensworth x	do	23. do					
250.	Joseph Vanderslice x	do	23. do					
251.	Matthew Poor x	do	27. do					
252.	James Wandrum	do	23. do					Dischd 1 June 99.
253.	Peter Turner x	do	1. Septr	"				

Nº 1 Muster Roll of the Officers, Petty Officers, and Seamen, Ordinary Seamen, and Marines, on board the Frigate *Constellation* under the command of Captain Thomas Truxtun in the service of the United States, from the 16th. day of August the time they were last mustered, to the 17th. day of November 1798—Continued

No.	Names	Rank	date of appointment or Entrance	for what time engaged	Advanced Pay by Mr Rodgers	Advanced Pay by Mr Cowper	Advanced Pay by Mr Triplett	Remarks and Alterations since last Muster
254.	George Hubert	Boy	26. May	“		12.		Discharged 27 May 99.
255.	Edward Frair	dº	8. June	“		12.		Fell from fore Top, and was killed 14 March 1799.
256.	Miles Welsh	dº	14. May	“	12.			Dischd 30. May 99.
257.	Eppes Prudeman	dº	11. dº	“	12.			Dº 30. Dº
258.	Samuel Wilson	dº	25. Dº	“			$21.33	Dischd 27 May 99.
259.	Allen Herst	dº	22. June	“		12.		Dischd 17 June
260.	John Carter	dº	22. dº	“		12.		Dischd 27. May 99.
261.	Richd Bossley	dº	31. May	“				Dº 31 Dº
262.	Joel Jackson	dº	22. dº	“		20.		Dischd 27 May 99.
263.	Gustavus Sines	dº	30. April	“				Do. 27 May 99.
264.	Peter Mosset	dº	6. Novr	“				
265.	Wm Jacobs	dº	13. June	“			$9.46	Dischd 13 June 99.
266.	Saml Hodges	dº	22. May	“		12.		Dischd 1 June 99.
267.	Benjamin West	dº	30. April	“	12.			Dischd 27 May 99.
268.	Joshua Lovett	dº	21. May	“		12.		Dº 27 Dº
269.	Thomas Diamond	dº	21. dº	“		12.		Dº 27 Dº
270.	Wm Howel	dº	30. dº	“		12.		Turned over into L'INSURGENTE 15th Febry 99.
271.	Thomas Collin	dº	30. dº	“		12.		Dischd 30 May 99.
272.	Thomas Benton	dº	21. dº	“		12.		Dischd 27. May 99.
273.	Robert Weir	dº	28. dº	“	12.			Dº 30 Dº 99.
274.	John Croger	do	22. dº	“		12.		Dischd 27. May 99.
275.	Wm Miller	dº	30. April	“	12.			Dº 27. Dº
276.	John Lawless	dº	14. May	“	12.			Dº 27. Dº
277.	Alexander Innis	1 S Marine	26. April	“			$6.85	Entered as 2d Corporal the 26 April, and remained so 'till 1st Novr from which Time he is to rec. Serjt Pay.
278.	Samuel Coleman	2d dº	5. May	“			9.	
279.	Edward Mercer	1 Corporal	7. April				6.60	
280.	James Hague	2 dº	27. dº	“			5.20	Entered as Private the 27th April, & remained so 'till 1st Novr from which Time he is to rec. Corpors Pay
281.	Thos H. Dunn	Private	14. dº	“			3.20	
282.	Isaac Gardner	dº	16. dº	“			2.80	
283.	Hezekiah Owens	dº	16. dº	“			2.80	
284.	John Dinin	dº	20. dº	“			4.	Dischd 31st May 99.
285.	Stephen Collins	dº	24. dº	“			3.20	
286.	George Herbert	dº	13. dº	“			12.80	
287.	Wm Justice	dº	13. dº	“			9.40	
288.	Richd Price	dº	19. dº	“			5.20	
289.	Barthow Duffy	dº	1. May	“			7.50	
290.	Michl McEntire	dº	3. dº	“				
291.	James Robb	dº	8. dº	“				
292.	Thomas Murry	dº	8. dº	“			4.50	Died 18th May 1799 of the Fleux, at Sea
293.	Wm Hook	dº	11. dº	“			1.50	

294.	James Hambleton	do	11. do	"			7.	
295.	Daniel McCarty	do	11. do	"				
296.	Michael Reynolds	do	16. do	"			2.	
297.	James O'Carroll	do	17. do	"			2.	
298.	George Simpson	do	21. do	"			2.	
299.	Oliver Arnold	do	21. Do	"			2.	
300.	Daniel Smith	do	22. do	"			3.	
301.	David Griffiths	do	22. do	"			10.	
302.	Edward Kenen	do	9th do	"			1.	
303.	Wm Williamson	do	25. do	"			3.	Dischd 31st May 1799
304.	Wm Rawlings	do	25. do	"			$2. 33	
305.	Benjamin Brown	do	25. do	"			3. 75	
306.	Christopher McCormick	do	28. do	"			2.	
307.	James Fitzsmorris	do	26. do	"	20.			
308.	Wm Nighton	do	25. do	"			4.	
309.	James Coughlan	do	2. June	"			4.	
310.	Joseph Butler	do	26. May	"			4.	
311.	John Shirley	do	29. do	"			8.	
312.	John Hunt	do	29. do	"			5. 33	
313.	James Mahoney	Private	26th May	"				
314.	Timothy Flaherty	do	2d June	"			3.	
315.	Aquilla Norris	do	30. May	"			5.	Dischd 31st May 1799
316.	Thomas Hardman	do	31. do	"			5.	
317.	Thomas Hall	do	25. do	"			10.	
318.	Hiram Chapin	do	28. do	"			7. 75	
319.	W. Robinson	Midshipn	6th Decr	"				Made Midsn & turned over into L. INSURGENTE 9th March 99.
320.	John Evans	Ordinary	25. ditto	"				
321.	David Cook	Seaman	16. ditto	"				
322.	James Linch	Boy	19. ditto	"				
323.	Elisha Dick	Ordinary	6th ditto	"				
324.	John Morrisson	Boy	18. Febry	"				
325.	xJohn Ankles	Ordinary	25. do	"				
326.	xIsaac Williams	Seaman	25. do	"				Sent Home in Prize Schooner L UNION 14th March 99 —
327.	xJohn Richards	do	25. do	"				
328.	xJohn Dorman	do	1st March	"				Run St Pieres, Martinica, 28th April 1799.
329.	xIssac Nye	[illegible] Mate	3. ditto	"				

The following Men accounted for, that were formerly entered, registered, and returned to Navy Office (per Muster Roll) to Vizt

Matthew Falcott	Midship						Dischd 16th Augst at Norfolk, as per Advice to Secty of Navy.
Samuel R. D. Henry	ditto						Dischd on Acct of his Health at his own Request 28th Augst.
Hance Anderson	Gs Mate			36.			Committed to Norf. Jail 16 Augst as per Advice to Sy of Navy.
Thos Gummerson	Qr Gunner			34.			Do do Do 16 Augst as per Advice to Do
Joseph Bull	ditto			30.			Discharged 29. October having an old Rupture.
Thomas Howard	Seaman				34.		Do 7. November.
John Anderson	ditto				34.		Missed at Sea 27. June, supposed to be drown.
Thomas Green	Boatswn			40.			Dischd 12th Novr as per Advice to Secretary of Navy.
John Cole	Seaman			30.			Drown at Sea 11th September.

The following Men accounted for, that were formerly entered, registered, and returned to Navy Office (per Muster Roll) to Vizt—Cont.

No.	Names	Rank	date of appointment or Entrance	for what time engaged	Advanced Pay by Mr Rodgers	Advanced Pay by Mr Cowper	Advanced Pay by Mr Triplett	Remarks and Alterations since last Muster
	Laban Whitehurst							Dischd at his own Request by sending John Brown on Board, a Seaman in his Room.
	Seth Hulbert	ditto				34.		Run, or drown 29. August.
	Thomas Sweet	ditto			34.			Dischd at his own Request 31. Augst being sick.
	Hugh Williams	ditto			30.			Acknowledged himself to be one of the Mutineers on Board the B. Frigate HERMOINE, delvd to the B. Consul, Norfolk 20th Augst 1798.
	Thomas Gilfoyle	ditto					$23.33	Dischd having a Dropsy 17. Augst Norfolk.
	Anthony Smith							Ditto at his own Request by sending on Board John Finlay a Seamen in his Room.
	Thomas Foss	Seaman					17.46	Dischd 29. Octr and sent to Norfolk, sick.
	Thomas Anderson	Ordy				20.		Do at his own Request by sending on Board James Row, Seaman, in his Room.
	Jeremiah Cowan	ditto						Dischd at his own Request by sending on Bd Peter Sum, Seaman, in his Room.
	William Street	Boy						Discharged at his own Request by sending Peter Mosset, another Boy, in his Room.
	Peter Walter	Ordy				20.		Dischd 29th October sick sent to Norfolk.
	Patrick Leonard	ditto			20.			Died at Sea 23d July.
	George Shore	ditto				20.		Dischd at hs own Request, and sent to Norfolk sick 31 August.
	John Hilsberry	ditto				20.		Dischd deranged by a Fall, sent to Nork 31st August.
	John Best	ditto			20.			Dischd 23d June.
	John Doyle	Seaman						Do 31st August, sent to Norfolk sick.
	James Renton	Ordy			20.			Do 31. Do sent to Do sick.
	George Alexander	ditto			20.			Do 29 Octr Norfolk, having an old Rupture.
	John Whelan	ditto			20.			Do 17 Augst sick at Norfolk.
	Job Swain	Marine					3.60	Do at his own Request 30th Augst and sent to Norfolk.
	William Loughborough	Ordy			20.			Discharged 17. November 1798 unfit for Service —
330.	Draper Nourthen	Seaman	5 March 99.					
331.	William Lawrance	ditto	5 ditto					
332.	Christian Sampson	ditto	5 ditto					
333.	George Bass	ditto	5 ditto					
334.	Frederick Elder	ditto	5 ditto	From the U. S. Brig NORFOLK				Run Bassateer St Kitts 18th March 1799.
335.	Wm Conner	ditto	5 ditto					
336.	John Wilson	Boatswain	5 ditto					
337.	John Morgan	Seaman	5 ditto					
338.	Edward Abbot	ditto	4 ditto					Run Bassateer St Kitts 21st April 1799.
339.	Fanna Aquetan	Ordinary	4 ditto	From L'INSURGENTE				Run St Pieres, Martinica, 28th April 1799.
340.	George Alexander	ditto	7 ditto					
341.	John Durant	Qr Master	7 ditto					Run St Kitt's, 4th May 1799.
342.	David Carnes	ditto	7 ditto					
343.	Wm Humphreys	Seaman	7 ditto					Run St Piere's, Martinica, 28th April 1799.

344.	John Maescale	Qr Master	7	ditto		
345.	Thomas Scott	Ordinary	1	ditto		
346.	John Lewis	Seaman	16	ditto		
347.	George Waters	ditto	16	ditto		Dischd 1 June 1799 having a Rupture.
348.	Patrick Martin	ditto	19	ditto		Run, St Pieres, Martinica 29th April 1799.
349.	Benjamin Bradford	ditto	19	ditto		
350.	Adam Sanit	ditto	20	ditto		Run St Pieres Martinica 28th April 1799.
351.	James Scott	ditto	20	ditto		
352.	Antonio Joseph	Ordinary	3	ditto		Run St Pieres, Martinicia 28th April 1799.
353.	Marno Blanco	ditto	3	ditto	From LA'INSURGENTE	
354.	Joseph Antonio	ditto	4	ditto		
355.	Francisco Antonio	ditto	4	ditto	or Francisco Pierre [?] to distinguish	
356.	Lewis Petein	ditto	4	ditto		
357.	George Hobdy	ditto	16	ditto		Dischd 31. May 1799
358.	John Oldman	ditto	16	ditto		
359.	Francis Corsay	ditto	16	ditto		Run, St Pieres, Martinica 28 April 1799.
360.	Thomas Marshall	Seamen	10	ditto		Died Staten Island 16 July 99.
361.	John Price	ditto	6	May		
362.	John Prim	ditto	6	do		
363.	Philip Smith	Boy	6	do		
364.	John Baptist	ditto	6	March		
365.	Mr John T. Fisher	Sailing Mastr	28	April		Dischd 2d June 1799.
366.	James Thomas	Ordinary	31	May		
367.	Benjamin Kingsman	Do	31.	Do		
368.	John Lin	Seaman	31.	Do		
369.	Owen Owens	Do	31.	Do		
370.	Fleet Potts	Ordy	30.	Do		
371.	Felix Branigan	Do	30.	Do		
372.	John Hogan	Do	30.	Do		
373.	Wm Potts	Do	30.	Do		
374.	Wm Lovett	Do	30.	Do		
375.	James Camby	Boy	30.	Do		
376.	Tenison Booker	Do	30.	Do		
377.	James Hill	Do	30.	Do		
378.	Benjamin Allen	Do	30.	Do		
379.	James Godfray	Do	30.	Do		
380.	George Clemon	Ordy	1.	June		
381.	Robert Blakely	Cooper	1.	Do		
382.	John Bressie	Ordy	1.	Do		
383.	Wm Taniss	Do	1.	Do		
384.	Wm Powell	Do	1.	Do		
385.	George Matthews	Do	1.	Do		
386.	John Robinson	Ordy	1.	June		
387.	William Allman	Boy	1.	Do		
388.	Charles White	Do	1.	Do		
389.	Dempsey Powell	Ordy	2.	Do		
390.	Thomas Moore	Carpts Mate	3.	Do		
391.	James Coile	Ordinary	3.	Do		
392.	John Baker	Do	3.	Do		
393.	Jonathan Bell	M. Mate	5.	Do		
394.	Thos Derbyshire	Ordy	5.	Do		
395.	John Innes	Do	5.	Do		

The following Men accounted for, that were formerly entered, registered, and returned to Navy Office (per Muster Roll) to Vizt—Con.

No.	Names	Rank	date of appointment or Entrance	for what time engaged	Advanced Pay by Mr Rodgers	Advanced Pay by Mr Cowper	Advanced Pay by Mr Triplett	Remarks and Alterations since last Muster
396.	John Theveatt	Ordy	5. June					
397.	James Nash	Coxswn	5. Do					
398.	George Davis	Boy	5. Do					
399.	Danl Pointer	Ordy	5. Do					
400.	John Fullerton	Do	6. Do					
401.	Frederick Graves	Boy	7. Do					
402.	James Davis	Seaman B	7. Do					
403.	William Sutton	Do B	7. Do					Run 19th June 1799. Brought on Bd 22d Do
404.	Thomas Sulvy	Do B	7. Do					
405.	John Gilphin	Do B	7. Do					
406.	James Bidgood	Ordy	7. Do					
407.	Edward Card	Do	7. Do					
408.	Edward Vaughan	Seaman	7. Do					
409.	John Dobbin	Do	9. Do					
410.	John Smith	Do	9. Do					
411.	Robt Howes	Lt	9. Do					
412.	John Reed	Ordy	9. Do					
413.	Wm Howell	Do	9. Do					
414.	John Wades	Boy	9. Do					
415.	Thomas Diamond	Do	9. Do					
416.	Wm Anderson	Masts Mate	11. June	Ran				
417.	Thomas Longwith	Seaman	11. Do					
418.	John Telfea	Do	11. Do					
419.	John Jones	Ordy	11. Do					
420.	Wm Jones	Do	11. Do					
421.	Thos Stanfield	Do	11. Do					
422.	Wm Owens	Do	11. Do					
423.	Joseph Farley	Do	11. Do					
424.	Hugh Baker	M. at Arms	13 June					
425.	Benjamin Brown	Ordinary	13 Do					
426.	William Taylor	Do	13 Do					
427.	Edward Compton (L:In:)	Do	13 Do					
428.	Thomas Wood (L:In:)	S. Steward	13 Do					
429.	John Highland	G. Mate	15. June B.					
430.	Newton Bose [or Rose]	Seaman	15 Do do					
431.	John Cook	Do	15 Do do					
432.	Emanuel Deist	Do	15 Do do					
433.	Josiah Elwell	Do	15 Do do					
434.	John Baker	Do	15 Do do					
435.	Edward Keener	Ordy	15 Do do					
436.	John Munroe	Do	15 Do do					

437.	Revil Shipham	Dº	15	Dº	dº					
438.	John Study	Dº	15	Dº	dº					
439.	George Brown	Dº	15	Dº	dº					
440.	George Watts	Dº	15	Dº	dº					Fell Overboard in the Jolly Boat, in Consequence of the Tackle giving Way the 23d June 1799. Hampton Roads, and was drown.
441.	John Trader	Dº	15	Dº	dº					
442.	Matthew Delany	Dº	15	Dº	dº					
443.	Asoie East	Dº	15	Dº	dº					
444.	Thos Fitzsgerrald	Dº	15	Dº	dº					
445.	Archibd Maffats	Dº	15	Dº	dº					
446.	George Johnson	Dº	15	Dº	dº					
447.	Thos Stephenson	Dº	15	Dº	dº					
448.	Joshua Commings	Dº	15	Dº	dº					
449.	Chas Savage	Dº	15	Dº	dº					
450.	Thos Saucer	Dº	15	Dº	dº					Dischz 28 June 1799.
451.	Wm Thomas	Dº	15	Dº	dº					
452.	Michl Nealen	Dº	15	Dº	dº					
453.	Thomas Ennis	Dº	15	Dº	dº					
454.	Risden Walston	Boy	15	Dº	dº					
455.	Henry Richardson	Seaman	15	Dº						
456.	Charles Walker	Dº	15	Dº						
457.	Alexander Hutchinson	Dº	15	Dº						
458.	Gersham Flag	Dº	15	Dº						Drown in coming from Norfolk
459.	John Hodge	Ordinary	15	Dº						
460.	Michl Smith	Cook	15	Dº						
461.	John Swinson	Boy	15	Dº						
462.	Charles Bently	Dº	15	Dº						
463.	Michl McIntire	Ordy	17	Dº						
464.	Stephen White	Dº	17	Dº						
465.	Eliga Moseley	Boy	17	Dº						
466.	John Emory	Seaman	17	Dº						
467.	John Joseph	Dº	17	Dº						
468.	Joshua Hewbert	S.M.	17	Dº						
469.	John Livingston	Qr Master	19	Dº						
470.	Matthew Rawlings	Seaman	19	June B						
471.	John Mayberry	Seaman	19	Dº						
472.	Robt Jacques	Dº	19	Dº						
473.	Alexander McCarter	Dº	19	Dº						
474.	John Mahoney	Dº	19	Dº						
475.	James Davinson	Dº	19	Dº						
476.	Benjamin Phillips	Ordy	19	Dº						
477.	William Parson	Dº	19	Dº						
478.	Aquilla Norris	Dº	19	Dº						
479.	Serjeant Rodgers	Marine	19	Dº						
480.	Corporal Crissmon	Dº	19	Dº						
481.	Robt Anderson	Private	19	Dº						
482.	Robt Hutson	Dº	19	Dº						
483.	Christopher Mc Cormick	Dº	19	Dº						
484.	Willis Nelms	Dº	19	Dº						
485.	Josiah Nelms	Dº	19	Dº						
486.	Wm Nighton	Dº	19	Dº						
487.	John Dinin	Dº	19	Dº						

The following Men accounted for, that were formerly entered, registered, and returned to Navy Office (per Muster Roll) to Vizt—Con.

	Names	Rank	Date of Appointmt or Entrance	for what time engaged	Advanced Pay by Mr Rodgers	Advanced Pay by Mr Cowper	Advanced Pay by Mr Triplett	Remarks and Alterations since last Muster
488.	John Hible	Do	19 Do					
489.	Elija Simpson	Do	19 Do					
490.	James Ware	Ordy	19 Do					
491.	Philip Collins	Seaman	20 Do					
492.	John Hays	Do	20 Do					
493.	William Smith	Do	20 Do					
494,	Thomas Martin	Qr Gunr	20 Do					
495.	John Hatfield	Qr Gunr	20 Do					
496.	Thomas Steward	Ordy	20 Do					
497.	William Oatis	Do	20 Do					
498.	Joseph Dill	Cs Mate	22 Do					
499.	William Clark	Seaman	22 Do					
500.	George Frazer	Do	22 Do					
501.	John Evans	Do	25 Do					
502.	George Snell	Do	25 Do					
503.	John Holden	Do	26 Do					
504.	John Weaver	Do	26 Do					
505.	Thomas Carroll	Do	26 Do					
506.	Walter Commisio [?]	Marine	26 Do					
507.	John Marshall	Seaman	28 Do					
	William Mc Causland [?]	Gunner's Yeoman	13 June					
	Wm Miller	Seaman	11 June					
	James Graves	Do	16 June					Recd on Board 5th July 1799, entd 16 June.
	Charles Lewis	Boy	10 June					[or 1t June]

[HS of Pa. NDA photostat.]

[16 August 1798]

Sale of the Revenue Cutter *Scammel*

Amount Sales of the Old Revenue Cutter *Scammel*, Hopley Jeaton late Commander, on the 16″ of August 1798 by Jack Walden Auctioneer for Account of the United States — Viz.

By Clement Jackson being the highest Bidder for-- 565 Doll^r
Charges Viz'^t

None, all expence on Said Schooner having been Carryed in to the Quarterly Accounts, and the Amount remains for future Instruction —

District of Portsmouth N Hampshire April 23rd 1799

THOS MARTIN
Agent for the Old Cutter Scammel.

I Certify that the above–mentioned Cutter, was sold by direction of the Secretary of the Treasury.

EDWARD JONES.

[GAO. No. 10, 588.]

To Tench Francis, Purveyor, from Secretary of Navy

[TRENTON,]
Navy Department 17th Augt 1798

TENCH FRANCIS Esqr

SIR The Bearer Garrett Hulschecamp has an account against the United States for services in carrying dispatches to our Ships of War — He has been employed 15 days & he charges 165 Dollars.

Having no money here, Mr Cottringer not having arrived — I request the favor of you to pay Mr Hulschecamp, his acc^t if he does not charge too much per day, of which you are a better Judge than I am —

I have the honor to be &c^a

[NDA. Req. on US T, 1798–1803.]

To Joshua Humphreys, Naval Constructor, from Secretary of Navy

[TRENTON,]
Navy Department 17th Augt 1798

JOSHUA HUMPHREYS Esqr

SIR I fear the French Cruisers will be on our Coasts before we are prepared for them — I hope you can get as many Carpenters as you can employ to advantage on the *Ganges*, and the more you can employ without being in each others way, The sooner the Ship will be prepared — The schooner *Retaliation* I presume will be down at Marcus Hook as soon as you receive this Letter — Pray do not let her be detained a moment longer than necessary — The getting her off in a few days—she may be able to join a Cutter which will sail from New York in a week, and together they will be able to meet French Privateers said to be on the Coast — Be pleased to let me know frequently how you go on, that I may endeavour to have every thing depending on me, ready as soon as Needful —

I have the honor &c^a

[NDA. GLB, Vol. 1.]

To Rufus King, United States Minister, London, from United States Consul Elias VanderHorst

BRISTOL *Augt 17th 1798.*

DEAR SIR. Your three Letters, which were enclosed in Mr Munro's to me of the 14th Inst^a have all been safely delivered to Cap^n Bliss, of the *Philadelphia*, which Vessel is now in King-Road waiting only for a fair Wind to proceed on her Voyage to that Port. — She is armed with 12 — 4 & 6 Pounders, with Men &c proportionate, and is in every respect a very complete Ship. — The *Roba & Betsey*, Capt Vimmo, Sailed hence the 14th Inst. for the Cove of Cork, in expectation of being in time to Join the Convoy there. I remain with great truth. Dear Sir.

Yours very sincerely

ELIAS VANDERHORST

RUFUS KING Esqr
London

[SDA. Bristol, Vol. 1, 1791–1799.]

To Captain Richard Dale, U. S. Navy, from Secretary of Navy

[TRENTON,]
Navy Department August 17th 1798

Capt RICHd DALE

SIR I have written to Mr Humpreys [Humphreys] to employ as many Clerks as can work to advantage on the *Ganges* — And the situation of Phila I presume will enable him to get as many as he pleases, so that I hope the Carpenters Work of the Ship will go on with great expedition

Will you be pleased to furnish me as early as you can with an account of every thing the Ship will want for six months — Including every kind of Stores, that I may make Arrangements in time for having them procured —

If your present Guns will answer it will be fortunate — But I think you said some of them wanted boreing — not being quite large enough for a Nine pound Ball — In this Case, such guns had better be sent to Mr Foxall near Philadelphia, & on the Schuylkill, soon, that he may have them bored in time — I think the French will not fight our Ships of equal force at a distance — But will depend much on boarding and that we ought to be provided with every Instrument necessary to repel such attempts — you are a better judge than I am —

I should be glad to hear from you frequently how you progress that I may endeavour to be prepared in time with every thing depending on me. —

[NDA. OSW, Vol. 1.]

[17 Aug. 1798]

To Mr. Yeomans, master carpenter, from Captain Thomas Truxtun, U. S. Navy

Mr YEOMANS

SIR, As the Master Carpenter of the Frigate, *Constellation*, under my Command, you will consider this as your Order, to search for the Leak, and to have the same well stopt, by ripping off such Copper, as may be necessary above Light Water Mark, and to caulk the Seams well underneath the same, and then to put the Copper on again. You will also overhawl the Bends, and other Works outside, and caulk where necessary, this being done; the Gun, and lower Deck is to be well caulked; this is the best Season for this Sort of

Work, and as a faithful Officer, you are to have it done with all possible Expedition, as we shall go to Sea, as soon after as possible, a twenty foot Mark must be put on forehead. A Gang of Caulkers to assist your Crew will come off from Norfolk. I am Sir

Your Obedient humble Servant

THOMAS TRUXTUN.

UNITED STATES SHIP, *Constellation*
Hampton Roads 17th Augst 1798.

[HS of Pa. NDA photostat. Truxtun's LB, 1798–9.]

Extract from journal of Lieutenant John Mullowny, U. S. Frigate *United States*, 17 August 1798

Clear and pleasant.
Here the trade wind struck us
Squally, in all the light sails.
Fresh breezes.

[Latd Obsd 21.27]

[NA.]

Extract from journal of James Pity, U. S. Frigate *Constitution*, 17 August 1798, Friday

First part this 24 hours Steady breezes and clear Weather. at 4 P. M. Saw Block Island bearg N. W. ½ N. dist 4 Leags at Do Saw a Small Sail boat Standg towds us. Hauld up the Courses and Soundd in 7 fathms hard Gravell wth black Shells. at 6 P. M. reefd the Top Sails a Do Spoke a Sloop from N. London a 2 A. M. K Ship to the N. W. a 4 Saw a Sail to Lewd gave chace provd a Schr from N. London bound to Cape Nichola Mole Jno Griffin Comr a 5 A. M. Saw block Island Light N. N. W. 5 Leagues dist a 9 Pilot boat came along Side took a pilot and Dischd the former. people employd Sundry Jobbs.

[Latitude observed 40°.41m. No]

[NDA.]

From President John Adams to Secretary Benjamin Stoddert

QUINCY *August 18. 1798*

SIR, Mr William Gray of Salem, a capital merchant of that place called on me to request a Convoy, for an hundred Sail of American vessels now at the Havanna, watched by twenty or thirty French Privateers. I desired him to write to you and to pray you to afford them a Convoy, if possible. Mr Simmons of Charleston S C on a visit to me yesterday informed me, that Dispatches & Petitions to Government had been forwarded, from the Havanna by the way of Charleston, requesting a Convoy. —

If it is possible for you to afford them the Protection they want, I wish you to give the necessary orders for that Purpose. I am, —

Sir, Yr mo obt Servant

JOHN ADAMS

Mr STODDERT
Secretary of the Navy. —

[NDA photostat.]

To Major Commandant Burrows, U. S. M. C., from Secretary of Navy

[Trenton,]
N. Department 18th Augt 1798

Major Burrows
Commanding the Corps of Marines

Sir You will be pleased to order a detachment of fifteen Marines with the proper officers, on board the schooner *Retaliation* — for a cruise — The men should be clothed properly — They will probably be out 3 or 4 months —

[NDA. GLB, Vol. 1.]

To Lieutenant William Bainbridge, U. S. Navy, from Secretary of Navy

[Trenton,]
Navy Department 18th Augt 1798

Lieutt & Commander Bainbridge

Sir You will be allowed the following Officers & Men for the Schooner *Retaliation*

1 Lieutenant
1 Midshipman — If he also acts as Clerk his pay must be 25 Dollars p. month
1 Surgeon's Mate
1 Gunners Mate
1 Boatswains Mate
1 Masters first Mate
1 ditto second do
1 Steward to act as Steward & Purser at 25 Dollars per month
1 Cook —
45 Seamen, ordinary Seamen & Boys
The Pay of able Seamen 17 dollars p. month
Boys & ordinary Seamen from 5 to 14 dollars per month according to merit.—

There is a Lieutenant & a Midshipman already appointed, and I will get a Surgeons Mate — You will select proper characters to fill the other Appointments, who will be approved of, and proceed to engage your men as soon as may be — Lieutenant Kenyon has already engaged some — I refer you to the Instructions given to him, and which you will receive from him, and be governed by them. —

You will receive from Mr Francis through the hands of Capt Robert Gill, every thing you will require for a cruise of four months. —

You will please to let me hear from you by all opportunities your progress. —

[NDA. OSW, Vol. 1.]

To Tench Francis, Purveyor, from Secretary of Navy

[Trenton,]
Navy Departt 18th Augt 1798

Tench Francis Esqr

Sir Altho it may not be strictly in the line of your duty — yet knowing that you had rather do more than duty requires, than less, and not Knowing how else to get the business done, I have the honor to request that you will provide every article of Provision, Arms and

Military Stores, Wanted by Lieutenant Commandant Bainbridge of the Schooner *Retaliation*, to fit that vessel out for a four months cruise — The Commander thinks that but few of the present Guns will answer and that the Schooner will carry 14 Guns to advantage — 4 of 6 pounders, and the rest four pounders — I could get the 4 pounders at once at New York, but that would be attended with delay, and I trust to your management to procure both these and the Six pounders at once.

Cannot some of those Cast for the Revenue Cutters be borrowed? Whatever you furnish (and you will please to furnish everything Mr Bainbridge requires, you will put into the hands of Capt Robt Gill, who will deliver them for the Schooner — — I understand there is Russia Hemp arrived at the Eastward. Be pleased to make arrangements to procure one hundred Tons —

[NDA. Req. on US T, 1798–1803.]

To Captain Alexander Murray, U. S. Navy, from Secretary of Navy

[Trenton,]
Navy Department 18th August 1798

Capt Alexr Murry

Sir I have the pleasure to enclose your Commission as Captain in the Navy of the United States — You are to command the Ship *Montezuma* at Baltimore, now fitting under the direction of Jeremiah Yellott Esqr and it is desireable that you proceed to that place as soon as convenient, and make the necessary arrangements for procuring a Crew in time, and to see that your Ship be fitted & armed to your mind. —

I will by the stage which leaves this on Tuesday next, write to you at Baltimore and send recruiting Instructions — & money, In order that you may put the recruiting Business in motion before you leave Baltimore. — The following Officers are appointed to the *Montezuma*, —

M. Simmons Bunbury of Balto Lieutt
John Shaw of do do
Surgeon's Mate Hanson Catlett Maryld
Purser — Joseph Richardson Balto
Midshipmen
Richd B. Brandt, Chs Coty Maryld
Richard Thomas } E. Shore of do
Horace Smith }

You will please to look out for proper characters to fill the other appointments? —

[NDA. OSW, Vol. 1.]

[August 18, 1798]

Extract from letter to President Adams from Secretary of State

* * * * * * *

The Toulon fleet, consisting of 400 transports, convoyed by 13 sail of the line and as many frigates departed from Toulon the 19th of May: Lord St Vincents was then off Cadiz with 25 sail of the line: Secret orders had been dispatched to Sir Roger Curtis to quit the

Irish Station and join Lord St Vincent with 10 sail of the line. This reinforcement probably joined Lord St Vincent by the 22^{d} of May. And immediately after the junction Lord St Vincents, leaving a sufficient force to block up Cadiz and watch the Gut of Gibraltar, was to enter the Mediterranean, to look for and fight the Toulon fleet which had Buonaparte on board.

It appears that Russia is endeavouring to form a new coalition against France: but difficulties are to be overcome, and particularly to bring together Austria and Prussia. Russia has recently promised to aid England as far as possible; and 10 Ships of the line and frigates were soon to appear in the North Seas. The authenticity of the proclamation which has lately appeared in the name of the Emperor Paul, relative to a fleet to oppose the French on account of their unjust proceedings against neutral commerce, seems to be doubted.

* * * * * * *

[SDA. Dom. L. Vol. 11.]

Extract from journal of James Pity, U. S. Frigate *Constitution*, 18 August 1798, Saturday

First Part this 24 hours fair & Pleasant Weather. At 4 P. M. Tack'd Ship to the Southward & Eastward.

At ½ past 5 T.K. Ship Northw^{d} & West^{d}

At 7 P. M. furld T. G^{t} Sail TK Ship South^{d} & Eastw^{d} The Light on Montick point, Long Island bear^{g} N. N. E. dist. 3 Leagues. a D^{o} Reeft Top Sails —

Sultry Weather —

At 2 A. M. Tack'd Ship to the Northw^{d} & Made Sail at 5 A. M. Saw the Land N. W. dist 5 Leagues. Unbent F. T. Sails & bent a new one.

[Latitude observed 40°.46^{m}. N^{o}]

[NDA.]

Extract from journal of James Pity, U. S. Frigate *Constitution*, 19 August 1798, Sunday

First part this 24 hours pleasant W^{r} Bent M. S. Sails. Coiled away Sheet Cable & Stream D^{o} clear^{d} the lower and upper Decks.

Armourers employ fitting Slings for yard & cross Jack Yard. Sail Makers Employ'd variously a Mer^{n} in Small Sails TK Ship N. W. a 9 TK Ship to the Southw^{d} Sounded in 25 fathoms white sand & black Specks. Spoke a N. York Pilot boat She G^{e} Capt her News papers on B^{d} made Sail in Com^{y} with her and beat her. a M^{n} high land Never Sink bear^{g} N. W. 4 Leagues dist.

[Latitude observed 40°.34^{m}.N^{o}]

[NDA.]

To Tench Francis, Purveyor, from Secretary of Navy

[Trenton,]
Navy Department 20th August 1798

Tench Francis Esqr

Sir Blunderbusses are hightly essential for our vessels to prevent their being boarded. — Be pleased to make enquiry and find out the size and kind most useful, and have 100 of such made or purchased, as early as possible — and delivered over to Capt Gill. —

[NDA. Req. on US T, 1798–1803.]

To Captain Hugh George Campbell, Revenue Cutter *Eagle*, from Secretary of Navy

[TRENTON,]
Navy Department 20th Augt 1798

Captn HUGH GEORGE CAMPBELL *Cutter Eagle*

SIR The Brig *Eagle*, Revenue Cutter, under your command being nearly ready to receive her Guns; you will take the speediest means in your power, to get all your Stores on board, and provisions for three, or, if you can find room, four months, — Mr Humphreys as heretofore, will pay for the different Articles you want — I have written to Mr Fitzsimons to make enquiry about proper characters for your Mates, and I expect in a few days they will be appointed —

In the mean time, you will endeavour to enlist not exceeding 40 able Seamen, at the rate of 17 Dollars p. Month, out of whom you will make your Carpenter, Boatswain & Gunner, on an addition of 3 Dollars per month, and a Cook on an addition of one dollar p. month. — You will also enlist 16 Boys, & ordinary Seamen, at such pay as their qualifications deserve, Between 5 Dollars and 14 Dollars p. month. —

When you are ready to receive them, there will be ordered on board from Major Burrow's Marine Corps, a Serjeant, Corporal & 12 Men for your Vessel. — Mr Humphreys will furnish money to recruit the men — You may, if necessary advance them two Months pay; taking care to get such Security as will enable you to recover the money if the men desert after receiving the advance. —

Enlist none but healthy, white men, and give a preference to Natives if they are to be had. —

[NDA. OSW, Vol. 1.]

To Rufus King, United States Minister, London, from United States Consul Elias VanderHorst

BRISTOL *Augt 20th 1798* —

DEAR SIR. I yesterday recd a Letter from Mr Munro dated the 18th Insta enclosing one from you to Mr Pickering, but I am sorry to inform you that it came too late for the *Philadelphia*, which Ship sailed on Saturday morng last for Cork in hopes of Joining the Convoy there, and which it is probable she will effect, as the wind has ever since been favorable; thus circumstanced your Letter will be forwarded by the *Ranger*, which Vessel is not only armed with 16 Guns but is a remarkable swift Sailer, and it is intended shall be ready for Sea by the first of next month. — If you can inform me what are the Rates of Salvage on recaptured American Vessels the favor of it would particularly oblige.

Dear Sir.

Yours very sincerely. —

ELIAS VANDERHORST

RUFUS KING Esqr
London.

[SDA. Bristol, Vol. 1, 1791–1799.]

To Joshua Humphreys, naval constructor, from Secretary of Navy

[TRENTON,]
Navy Department August 20th 1798

JOSHUA HUMPHREYS Esqr

SIR By an arrangement with the Secretary of the Treasury, he was to have the Cutters prepared for Sea; and when ready to sail to turn them over to me — But the pressure of his other business, has induced him to request me to take the direction of them, in their present state — To which I have consented, and have accordingly given Capt Campbell of the *Eagle* Cutter, orders to get on board his military and other kinds of Stores for four months; and to recruit his men as quickly as possible — The money for the Stores &ca, and to be advanced for the recruiting service to Capt Campbell, must still, as heretofore, go through your hands — You are still to consider yourself as agent for this Vessel; and will still get your supplies of Cash as before arranged with Mr Wolcott — I have desired the Captain to provide himself with every thing necessary to keep the French from boarding — The most material thing to be guarded against in all our Vessels —

Pray suffer as little delay as possible in getting out both this Vessel, and the Schooner *Retaliation* — These Vessels are on different Establishments — Nothing in the store kept by Capt Gill, must be taken for the *Eagle* —

I have written to Mr Francis to have 100 Blunderbusses made; but fear they cannot be prepared in time, for either of these Vessels. —

[NDA. GLB, Vol. 1.]

Extract from journal of James Pity, U. S. Frigate *Constitution*, 20 August 1798, Monday

First part this 24 hours fair & pleasant. the high land Never Sink in Sight dist 6 Leagues. a 2 P. M. Light house Sandy hook bore N. W. b. N. dist 5 Leagues a Do ⩞ Ship to the S. E. a 3 do Shortend Sail a 6 P. M. North Part Long Island bore N. E. b. N. 6 Leagues dist. ⩞ to S. & Eastwd at Extreme Long Island fm N. E. to N. b. W 5 Leagues.

Middle part Sultry Wear Sounded every hour fm 25 to 27 fathms white & black Sand with Shells.

At 7 P. M. furl'd Small Sails and Reeft. F. T. Sail wet lower deck with Vinegar. all hands employ'd differently.

[Latitude observed 39° 56m No]

[NDA.]

Extract from Journal of Lieutenant John Mullowny, U. S. Frigate *United States*, 20 August 1798

Pleasant weather

Bore away to speak the *Delaware* Capt Barry directed Capt Decatur to keep at a Distance in the morning as far as signals was Discoverable

Squally and rain

Set Studding sails

In royals & studding sails, joined the *Delaware*.

[Latd Obsd 13.]

[NA.]

Extract from journal of Lieutenant John Mullowny, U. S. Frigate *United States*, 21 August 1798

Made signal to speak the *Delaware*
Spoke the *Delaware*
Cloudy, rain, & lightning
Wore Ship to the N^{d}
Wore ship to the S^{d} clear & pleasant.

Spoke the *Delaware*, at 11 A. M. the *Delaware* shew'd signal, that they saw land. At M. Saw the East end of Barbadoes bearing W by N. dist 6 Leagues.

[Lat^{de} Obs^{d} 13.8]

[NA.]

Extract from journal of James Pity, U. S. Frigate *Constitution*, 21 August 1798, Tuesday

First part this 24 hours Light Airs.

At 3 P. M. Saw a Strange sail to Wind^{d} hauld our wind & gave chace at ½ past d^{o} fired a gun at the chace & Shortend Sail prov^{d} a Sch^{r} from New Bedford bound to Phila^{a} beat to Quarters and exercized the great guns a 7 Spoke a Sloop fm N. London bound to Phila^{a} Shortned Sail Sounded Sail from 8 to 12 depth f^{m} 23 to 26 fath^{ms} black & white Sand with hakes Teeth & Shells. Saw Long Island bear^{g} N. E. 3 Leagues dist. made Sail Steer^{g} Sails Set a 8 Saw Montock Light N. E. b. E dist. 5 Leag^{s} Latter part pleas^{t} Block Island Meet^{g} house N. N. W. 5 miles.

[Latitude observed 41°. 5^{m}. N^{o}]

Land In Sight Still.

at 1 P. M. Shortend Sail for a Pilot Boat from Block Island a 3 Made Sail and past the Island clear^{d} our Anchors and Cables got a Range of &^{c} a 4 P.M. Anchor'd in 10 fath^{ms} water. — the Town Newport bear^{g} E. S. E. 1 Mile distance Lighthouse S. W. b. W. Ross [or Rose] Island N. N. W. ¾ of a Mile fired a Salute of 15 Guns which was Answerd Gun for Gun from fort Wollcott. at Midnight Squally with Sharp Lightning cleard our Cables.

[NDA.]

To Captain Alexander Murray, U. S. Navy, from Secretary of Navy

[TRENTON,]
Navy Department 22nd August 1798

ALEX^{r} MURRAY Esqr

SIR It is necessary that you should make arrangements to commence recruiting the Crew of the Ship *Montezuma*, now under your command, that the Complement may be completed by the time the ship is ready for a cruise.

The Acts of Congress authorize the President, to regulate the number of Men, and the kind to be employed; but the Arrangements on this head, I conceive to be extremely incomplete, and very susceptible of Improvement. I have much confidence in your Judgment, you will therefore be pleased to take the subject under your consideration, and determine for yourself, and I shall be glad to learn the principles of your determination as soon as you can make it convenient to give me the Information — I hope some general arrangements will soon be adopted on this Subject, and your opinion will have its due weight in forming them. —

The Wages allowed to able seamen, are 17 Dollars p. month — and ordinary seamen 10 D.

It is certainly important and indispensibly necessary, that you should have a sufficient Number of able seamen; but it is good policy to creat seamen, and attention must be paid to the convenience of the Marchant-service — It is therefore desirable that no more than the requisite number of able seamen, should be taken and that your Crew be composed of as great a proportion of ordinary seamen & boys, as will consist with the good of the service. These you may allow from 5, to 14 dollars p. Month, according to merit.

You will see by a paper enclosed the number of Men heretofore allowed to ships of 20 Guns — I send this paper for your Information — not your Government. —

You will take a general view of this subject. — Employ as many, and such a proportion of each Class of Men, as you shall determine to be proper, and communicate your decision, at large, and as early as your convenience will permit. —

Marines will be sent you from Philadelphia, by the time you are ready to receive them. —

You will Instruct your recruiting officers to be careful, not to enlist any, but sound and healthy Persons; and that no indirect, or forcible measures be used, to induce them to enter into the Service. — No Negroes or Mulattoes are to be admitted, and as far as you can Judge, you will exclude, all persons of a suspicious Character. —

Avoid any advance of money if possible untill the men are got on board, but should it be impracticable to procure them on this Condition; Care in every case should be taken to obtain sufficient security, to resort to in the event of desertion. — And a regular Account must be kept of their Names, and places of abode of each individual, together with a description of his person, so that he may be Identifyed at any future period — Every man shipped must take an Oath agreeably to the Form you will receive herewith —

Enclosed is the form of a Shipping Paper Wherein the name, Station, Pay &c. of each person on board must be entered. — It will be necessary, to avoid Confusion, that this business be executed with the utmost exactness. —

The Form of a Bond to be signed by the sureties for the seamen &c[a] you will likewise receive, and particular care must be taken in ascertaining that the sureties are persons of good & responsible character, before they are accepted.

Lewis Bayly, son of Gen[l] Bayly of Fred[k] Town, is appointed Midshipman — You will have no occasion therefore to appoint one. —

I have the honor to be &c[a]

[NDA. OSW, Vol. 1.]

Extract from journal of James Pity, U. S. Frigate *Constitution*, 22 August 1798, Wednesday

Wind at N. E. and clear. Wash'd Decks and Ships Sides hoisted out our Pinnace & 1 Spare Lower Yard & 1 Spare Steer[g] Sail Booms.

Rec^d p^r Lighter 21 Hhd. Water 46½ bush^ls Potatoes the Packet came along Side with a Number Gen^t & Ladys stay'd the fore mast fore T. Mast & Set up the Rig^g Rec^d 600 lbs. Beef (fresh) for Ships Use. Mr Dogget the pilot went a Shore

[NDA.]

Extract from journal of U. S. Ship *Herald*, Captain James Sever, 22 August 1798

This 24 hours first Moderate gales and heazy Weather at 2 P M Spoak a British 64 gun Ship the *St Albin* Capt Pinder Comand had in Company a Brig from Bourdaux Bound To New York the Brig Belloning George Townd on hur Way To Halifax At 8 P M Tact Ship To the S S E Duble Reef^t Topsails

Midle Part at 11 am Spoak a Ship from Jamaica Bound Kenebeck. Saw another Ship To the Leward Spoak hur She was from Portland Bound to the Westindies Capt Skinner Comander

This is a mistake Speaking with the *St Albans* in this Days work----
----

Latter part pleasant Breezes and foggy Weather at Mrdn Brought Ship Tue under Short Sail

Latt^d Obrs 42„ 26 North

[NDA. Journal kept by Joseph Strout, 1798.]

Extract from journal of Lieutenant John Mullowny, U. S. Frigate *United States*, 22 August 1798

At 1/2 1 P. M. spoke the *Delaware*, wore ship to the south^d the S. E. point of Barbadoes bearing S. W. by S. dist 4 Leagues. At 3 P. M. saw a small sail, found her to be a fishing boat from barbadoes, at 5 P. M. stood in for Carlile Bay, an officer came on board from the Fort. Haled an American Ship and requested they would send a boat on board, which was complied with. the American Capt came on board, wore ship and stood off 2 American ship saluted us with 15 Guns each we ans^d the Salute with 3 Guns.

At 8 P. M. the S. W. point of Barbadoes bore E by N dist 4 Leagues. A 6 A. M. saw the E. end of Martinico bearing W. N. W. dist 5 leagues. At 10 saw a strange sail shewed a signal to the *Delaware* accordingly, set all sail & gave chace.

At M. the chace a head 8 Miles, West point of Martinico bearing S. W. by W. dist. about 4 Leagues Dominica bearing N W by N 6 leagues. At 1/2 P. M. the Chace bore away, with all sail set. out all studding sails royals &, spanker.

[NA.]

To First Lieutenant S. W. Geddes, U. S. M. C., from Commandant, U. S. Marine Corps

PHILA^d *August 23^d 1798*

Lieut. S W GEDDES

SIR You are to repair to Marcus Hook to relieve Lieut Carmick and place yourself under the orders of the Captain or Commanding Officer of the Ship —

As all orders will immediately come from the Captain to you it is expected you will pay implicit obedience to your superior officers as by your Example your soldiers will be taught to respect you and cheerfully obey you —

The Marines in all foreign services are excused from going aloft so that you must attend particularly to this regulation and by no means allow them to be ordered aloft, but if they wish to go — you may permit but not force them

You must notice all Deserters to me under Cover to the secretary of the Navy and advertize them immediately at the nearest town

Your Ob'd Ser

W W B [William Ward Burrows]
M C
M C

[MCA. LS, 1798–1799.]

To Lieutenant William Bainbridge, U. S. Navy, from Secretary of Navy

[Trenton,]
Navy Department 23 August 1798

Lieut^t Wm Bainbridge

Sir I have your Letter of the 21st Instant. You say it is best to have all your Guns four pounders — Agreed — but you have not told me how many of your present Guns will do, as four pounders; I suppose some of them will answer; and no more Guns should be bought than necessary.

You will leave all the Guns which will not answer, in the hands of Capt Gill, and let me know how many of them you take, and how many new ones you want, that I may write to New York to have them purchased

Have you got Shott enough? that, I believe cannot be procured at New York. It will I believe be best for you to go to New York and take in the Guns there. —

[NDA. OSW, Vol. 1.]

To Secretary of the Navy from Stephen Higginson, Navy Agent, Boston

Boston *Augt 23. 1798.*

Benjn Stoddert Esqr

Sir I remain without any Letters from you since my last. yesterday the *Herald* & *Pickering* sailed on their Cruise, after waiting several days for a wind with several other Vessels. Capt Sever has left with me the pay Roll, Muster Roll, watch list & quarter Bill, & a number of persons Oaths &c, which I shall forward to you, if they are to be in your Office, as I suppose. —

I mentioned in my last Capt Severs not having all his Marines, & sent you a copy of my note to him, to remove his doubts about going to Sea without them, which had its effect. Sever will be an excellent Naval Commander, he is a cool, firm, discreet gentleman like Man, who feels & conducts with the dignity & zeal proper to his Station. he is remarkable for discipline & regularity, his principal defect, if it may be called one, is a great attention to method

U. S. REVENUE CUTTER PICKERING.

& order; & his first Lt is a fine fellow, possessing every quality requisite to excel in the Naval line. You may be assured that Ship is well appointed, & will not be given away to any Vessel near her force. —

The Cutter also is well appointed, with good Officers & a good Crew. Capt Chapman is not inferior to any man in the Navy, many think him to excel, & his Officers are very good.

As Capt Sever was appointed and attended upon the frigate at Portsmh till she was suspended, he expects again to be called to attend upon her, no doubt, & at his return from this Cruise will be ready to do it; & Capt Chapman will be the man most agreeable to the Subscribers & the Committee for building the Ship in this Town, & would himself like to have her.

I will suggest to you an Arrangement which I think will be very agreeable to the people of influence and discernment here, & will be promotive of the public interest. if Capts Sever & Chapman shall be appointed to the Ships mentioned, they will prefer leaving their present commands, & attending to the building their new Ships, as they will wish to oversee & direct in many matters of interior construction, to conform to their own taste. Mr Hutchins, now first Lt of the *Herald*, can then take the *Herald* which he merits fully. & Mr Hillar first Lt of the *Pickering*, can be rewarded by the command of her. These two men are very efficient, & have great talents for the Navy, Hutchins is an uncommon man; & both are capable of greater energies than common men, & both have great spirit & ambition tempered with discretion. — This will leave the Ship building by Colo Hacket at Portsmh for Daniel McNeil, who I find has his Eye upon, & wishes to be appointed to her. I take the liberty of suggesting this arrangement, as one which will meet the desires of the Officers, the public Opinion & the good of the Service; & if it does not interfere with any other which you may have in view, I think I might venture to be responsible for the result. the only part I have any doubt is that of McNeil; but as he is to be provided for, & has a Commission, he had better have that Ship than one here.

I thought the 20M Dollars remitted last would have been sufficient for all demands this month; but I find the *Heralds* Bills amount to more than I expected, & more is called for from Portsmouth, so that another 20 M reme will be wanted. the Accounts for the *Herald* will be all in & ready next week to forward to you. will you have all the original Bills sent on, duplicates have been taken of most & may be forwarded if you wish them.

I am with respect your hum Servt

STEPHEN HIGGINSON

[*Note on back of letter.*] Boston Augt 23.1798 — Stephen Higginson recommending Capts Chapman & Sever — Lieuts Hutchings & McNeil requiring a remittance &c &c. — Informs — the *Herald*, and *Pickering* sailed yesterday; requires a remittance of 20,000 Dollars — mentions an arrangemt as to Capt Sever, Capt Chapman, Capt McNeil, — Lieutt Hutchings &c. &c.

[NDA. Area 7, Augt 23, 1798.]

To William Crafts, Charleston, S. C., from Secretary of Navy

[TRENTON,]
Navy Department 23rd August 1798

Wm CRAFTS Esquire
Chairman of the Committee at Charleston, S. Carolina

SIR I am honoured with your Letter of the 3rd Inst^t^ as chairman of the Committee &c^a^ and am happy to find that Charleston has lost none of its ancient Spirit.

The Act of Congress, alluded to by you, authorized the President, to accept of a certain number of Vessels armed and equipped, and to cause payment to be made for the same, in Six per cent Stock of the United States. — The Act also authorizes the President to accept of any number of Vessels Voluntarily given, beyond the number for which 6 per cent Stock may be paid. —

Your Letter seems to leave it in the option of the President, to accept of the Vessel so liberally offered, on either of the Conditions of the Law.

As the whole number of Vessels to be paid for in Stock, have not yet been engaged, The President cannot think of taking greater advantage than necessary, of the generous Spirit of the Citizens of Charleston. — He will therefore accept of the Vessel on the condition of making payment for the same, in 6 per cent Stock. —

There remains one Ship not less than 20, nor more than 24 Guns, and one not less than 32 Guns, still to be obtained. — I fear the reasons you assign, are conclusive against your undertaking the largest sized ship. Besides the state of our affairs may, in all reasonable probability make a smaller Ship, ready for service in the Spring, of more value to us, than a larger one at a more distant period. —

I have the honor therefore to enclose dimensions and draft of a Ship measuring about 538 Tons, calculated to carry 24 — 12 pound Cannon, on the Gun Deck, — Upon the Quarter Deck of which, 4 or 6 Cannon of smaller size may be mounted; & still she would be called a ship of 24 Guns. —

A Ship of this Model will not, I understand, require large Timber, nor crooked Timber; difficult to be procured. —

Such a ship has been lately built at Portsmouth, in New Hampshire, and met the approbation of the best Judges — It will be highly gratifying to the President to receive such a Ship from the Citizens of Charleston.

I need not urge the importance of having her ready for service as early as practicable

I should be glad to know your opinion, how soon she may be prepared for Sea — I will have provided in due time the Cannon & Military Stores —

It may be found useful, that the Captain, should pay some attention to the building of the Ship — I shall hope to receive from the subscribers for the Ship, the name of the Gentleman, they would wish to command her

It is the custom here, to use copper or Composition bolts & Spikes — and no Iron below the Wales — The Copper sheathing corrodes the Iron — I presume this is the custom with you also — Copper sheathing cannot be had from Boston to Norfolk for less than 50 cents per pound — Indeed I fear there is not enough in the Country to supply the public demand for the next three months. —

[NDA. GLB, Vol. 1.]

Extract from journal of Lieutenant John Mullowny, U. S. Frigate *United States*, 23 August 1798

Between Martinico & Domini.

All sail set in chace. A 8 P. M. fired a bow-gun at the Schoo[r] at ½ 8 fired another which brought the chace too. She proved to be the *Sans Pariel* of Guadaloupe, Cap[t] Touin Eighty seven men 10 Guns 6 of which were thrown overboard.

At 9 made a false fire for the *Delaware*. At 1 A. M. rec[d] all the prisoners on board & hoisted in the boat.

At 11 P. M. the *Delaware* came up. At 3 squally with rain Dominica in sight bearing E N E. 8 lea. distance, at 8 A. M. Tacked to the N[d]

[NA.]

Extract from journal of James Pity, U. S. Frigate *Constitution*, 23 August 1798, Thursday

Wind N E at day Light fired a Gun at 5 call'd all hands wash'd decks, hoisted out the pinnace and Yawl at ½ past 8 a Lighter came along Side with 96 Hds. Water of 100 Gall[s] each & Bushels potatoes Unbent the fore Sail to Reduce it loosed the Top Sails to dry at Even[g] bent d[o] & furled Sails Sent on Shore 25 Gang Casks and 1 Puncheon to be fill'd with water. took in 20 Tons Ballast stowed it in Midships of the Vessell.

[Near Block Island]

[NDA.]

[Aug. 23, 1798]

The following was sent to the Secretary of the Treasury, at his request, on the day of its date —

ABSTRACT of the permits issued by the President of the United States to the Collectors of the Customs to clear out Vessels for foreign ports, to aid the departure of French Persons with their goods and effects, in conformity with the 5th Section of the "Act to Suspend the commercial intercourse between the United States and France & c." —

Date of permit	Names of Vessels	Masters	Where Cleared	Vessels destination	Owners Names	Their residence
14. July 1798	Brigs LIBERTY	Thos Lillibridge	Philadelphia	Bordeaux	Stephen Girard	Philadelphia
do " do	Sloop LARK	Thos Adams	do	Cape Francois	Edwd Burrowes	do
do " do	Schr HARRIETT	Robt Cleaves	do	do do	David Lummis	do
16. " do	Schr WILLIAM	Capt Burr	New York	City of Santo Domingo	—	—
18. " do	Brigs AMIABLE ADELE	John Brown	Philadelphia	Port au Prince	Benjamin Nones	Philadelphia
19. " do	Schr COMMERCE	John Denabre	do	St Marks & Port au Prince	Lewis Crousillat	do
25. " do	Brigs MERMAID	Wm Canby	Norfolk	Cape Francois	James Maurice	Norfolk
do " do	Schr SWALLOW	Mattw Logan	do	do do	George Lynham	do
31. " do	Schr RANGER	—	Boston	Guadeloupe St Thomas & Gonaives	Joseph Howard	Boston
1. Augt do	Schr GENL GREENE	Wm Moodie	Philadelphia	Jacmel & the City of Santo Domingo	William Moodie	Philadelphia
3. " do	Brigs LIBERTY	Jesse Fearson	Baltimore	Cape Francois, St Marks & Port au Prince	Jesse Fearson	Baltimore
7. " do	Ship ADRASTUS	John Ricard	Philadelphia	Bourdeaux	Augs & Jno Bousquet	Philadelphia
8. " do	Schr DORADE	John Ennis	do	Cayenne	Jno E. Caldwell	do
13. " do	Brigs RAMBLER	Capt Woodbridge	do	For a French Port or Ports in St Domingo	James Yard	do
13. " do	Schooner FAME	—	Norfolk	St Thomas & St Domingo	Dallest & Carlier	Norfolk

August. 23, 1798

T. PICKERING

[SDA. Dom. L., Vol 11, 1798–1799.]

To Jeremiah Yellott, Navy Agent, Baltimore, from Secretary of Navy

[TRENTON,]
Navy Department 24th August 1798

JERh YELLOTT Esqr *Baltimore*

SIR Captt Alexr Murray, who I hope will be agreeable to you, and to the City of Baltimore in general, is to command the *Montezuma* — I suppose he is now with you — Will you be so good as to furnish him with some money, for recruiting men? — I will have money sent him in a few days, and he can then return it. —

The Officers recommended by you, have generally been appointed — I will attend to the Gentn mentioned as Surgeon. —

It is desireable to get out the *Montezuma* as early as possible — She can be usefully employed; and Captt Murray is an active Officer — When do you think she can be ready? — I hope as many of Mr Hughes's Cannon will prove good, as will answer for her. —

As to a convoy to Europe this Fall — I was much disposed the Merchants should dictate on that subject — The Merchants in Phila had it under consideration — They wrote to Baltimore & New York; and I was informed, the general opinion was against a convoy — I then gave up the Idea, and have made arrangements for the Vessels, without taking into consideration a convoy to Europe.

I have the honor to be &ca

P. S. Mr Ridgely's Price for cannon ball is too extravagant; and I hope you will obtain the quantity wanted from Mr Dunlap in time; as it will probably be three weeks before they will be required; and then not the whole. However, the sooner they can be got, the better — Mr Ridgely must not be gratified in his demands. —

[NDA. GLB, Vol. 1.]

To John Norris, Salem, from Secretary of State

DEPARTMENT OF STATE *Trenton Aug. 24. 1798.*

JOHN NORRIS Esqr *Salem*

SIR, I duly received your letter of the 11th giving an account of the capture & condemnation of your schooner *Trial* at Guadaloupe. I fear no benefit will ever result to you; but it is very well for the Government to possess abundant proofs of the piracies of the most profligate & corrupt government & nation upon earth.

I am with great regard &c

TIMOTHY PICKERING.

[Mass. HS. Pickering Papers, Vol. 37, p. 324.]

To Secretary of the Navy from Captain Thomas Truxtun, U. S. Navy

NORFOLK *24th August 1798* —

SIR/, I have received by the Hands of the Commander of the *Baltimore* Sloop of War, Copy of the several Letters &c. forwarded to Mr Pennock which arrived last Post, and was handed me. The other Copy sent to Charleston may not reach me; it would perhaps be well to have it returned to you.

The *Baltimore* arrived in Hampton Roads last Evening the Captain tells me, he wants about Thirty five Seamen to complete his Crew, tho' a less Number may be made to answer for the present; he also informs me, that all his Water has proved so extremely bad, that there is no bearing even the Smell of it; he is now about sending down some Craft to take in his Water Casks and as soon as his Water is changed, and he is ready for Sea, I shall proceed as you have directed. New Water Casks ought always to be well soaked, and when finally filled for stowing away, a little Lime put therein, as well as when the same are rinced, and soaked.

I am sorry to find from Capn Phillips's Account, that he has not a Dozen Seamen on Board, tho' his Numbers in other Respects are nearly complete.

I shall keep you regularly advised of the State of Things, untill my Departure, which shall be expedited as much as in my Power. I have the Honor to be, Sir, with great Respect

Your very Obedt humble Servant —

THOMAS TRUXTUN.

To BENJAMIN STODDERT Esqre

Secretary of the Navy

[HS of Pa. NDA photostat. Truxtun's LB, 1798–9.]

To John Harris, storekeeper, from Secretaries of War and Navy

[24 August 1798.]

[Duplicate]

[TRENTON,]

War Department 13 August 1798

SIR Be pleased to deliver to the order of the Secretary of the Navy Seven hundred of the worst of the old Muskets now in Store — to be valued by Mr Nicholson, and charged to Tench Francis — Purveyor —

(Signed) JAMES McHENRY

Navy Department

24th August 1798

Mr. JOHN HARRIS,

The order of which the above is a copy, was given before the Secy at War left Phila Why then is there any difficulty about delivering the Guns to Mr Francis?

(Signed) BEN STODDERT

[NDA. Req. on US T, 1798–1803.]

Extract from journal of Lieutenant John Mullowny, U. S. Frigate *United States*, 24 August 1798

Pleasant weather. at 5 P. M. Capt Barry informed Capt Decatur he intended to cruise 4 or 5 days to windward of Guadaloupe and appointed St Bartholomews as a place of Rendezvous

At 12 Tacked to the Sd At 4 Tacked to Nd At 10 A. M. saw Guadaloupe bearing N E distance 10 leagues.

[NA.]

Extract from journal of James Pity, U. S. Frigate *Constitution*, 24 August 1798, Friday

Wind S. W. with fresh Breezes at 5 call'd all hands out boats & Wash'd decks run out a Small anchor to warp round to keep Ships hause clear. coil'd away Stream Cable and Sheet d° Stowed Spare gun carriages Set up Mizen Rigging & Top Mast Ditto. Latter part wind increasing Let down our Cables fore and aft and overhauld a Range of ditto and cleard the Anchor.

Thomas Dennis came as Pilot from Rhode Island. So ends this 24 hours.

[Near Block Island]

[NDA.]

To Joseph Sterett from Captain Thomas Truxtun, U. S. Navy

UNITED STATES SHIP *Constellation*
Hampton Roads 25th August 1798

DEAR SIR, Several Masters of Vessels have called on me, and informed, that they have been ordered by their Owners to repair to Hampton Roads to join a Convoy for the Havannah. I am directed by the Secretary of the Navy, to take the *Baltimore* under my Orders, and to proceed with the *Constellation* and that Ship on an Expedition (which is described) without Delay — Orders so pointed, will not admit of Deviation.

I shall always be pleased at having it in my Power, to accommodate the Merchants of every Port of the United States, and to render the Trade as secure, as the Force I have in Command will warrant any reasonable Expectation from them. But it appears to me somewhat extraordinary, that Gentlemen would incur the Expence, and Delay of assembling their Vessels for Convoy to any particular Place without some previous Intimation from the Head of the Navy Department, or the Commander of a Squadron, or other Force as the Case may be. I am therefore not a little afraid, that something is wrong, and that Information flows from a dangerous Source, and as much Evil may result to the Service, if an Enquiry is not immediately made, I shall write the Secretary of the Navy on the Subject immediately. We have no Doubt, many bad People in this extensive Country, and if the Destination of Ships are known Weeks before their Departure; pilot Boats may be dispatched with Information to the Enemy, who will no Doubt take Benefit thereby.

I am, Dear Sir,
Your Obedt Servant

THOMAS TRUXTUN

N. B. As some People may be disappointed in a Convoy, let this Letter be made known.

To Mr JOSEPH STERETT

[HS of Pa. NDA photostat. Truxtun's LB, 1798–9.]

To President John Adams from Secretary Benjamin Stoddert

[TRENTON,]
Navy Department August 25, 1798.

SIR Not having the Honor to hear from you on the subject of my Letter of the 30th ultimo, I have presumed that you did not disapprove of the Arrangement therein proposed of our Vessels, and having good Information that about 80 American vessels with Cargoes to the amount of two millions of Dollars were blocked up at the Havana by a few French Privateers, and had little chance of escaping without Aid from their Government, I have ventured to order Captn Truxtun in the Frigate *Constellation*, and Captn Phillips in the Ship *Baltimore*, to proceed immediately to the Havana to convoy them to our Shores. — I hope Sir, this measure will meet your approbation. —

From information which cannot be doubted, the French have from 60 to 80 Privateers out of the little Island of Guadaloupe. — That Island is plentifully supplied with Provisions by means of the Captures they make — It seems in vain to guard our Merchants vessels on our own Coasts, if we suffer them to be taken about the Islands, and tho' our means may not entirely prevent this, it seems certainly in our power to lessen the Evil, and to inflict some degree of Punishment in our turn. — I know not how the British employ the immense force they have in the Islands — certainly not to afford much Protection to our Trade, nor to annoy much the Cruisers from any Island but that of St Domingo, where they have views of Conquest. — They some times indeed convoy a few of our vessels; I hope not merely that it may be talked about; yet I suspect we have ourselves alone to depend upon for the effectual Protection of our Commerce. — The French Privateers are but badly prepared for action. — they are seldom well armed, and they afford no Shelter to their Men — they cannot meet except to board vessels of equal force in Guns, fitted as ours are, and I cannot understand that they have any vessels equal to our 20 Gun Ships. —

The *Montezuma* of 20 Guns, Captn Murray, will be soon ready for Sea — She is a very fast Sailor and the Captain I beleive is a man of Bravery & Conduct. —

The Schooner *Retaliation* is a fast sailing vessel, mounting 12, 4 Pounders, and the *Eagle* Cutter of 14, 6 Pounders is thought to be a very fine vessel — I have directed the Captains to prepare the vessels well against being boarded, and Notwithstanding Barry and Decatur will not have returned from the West Indies, nor Truxtun and Phillips from the Havana, so soon as these vessels may proceed; I beg leave to propose that as soon as they are ready, if no change of Circumstances should forbid the Enterprize, they should proceed under the Command of Murray to the Island of Guadaloupe and with discretion to the Captain to cruize about that Island for one two three or four weeks according to circumstances. — There may be danger of one or more of the vessels being taken, but the chance I think greatly in favor of their taking a number of the French Privateers and retaking many of the American Vessels — At any rate a Spirit of Enterprize and Emulation should be excited in our Seamen. —

I have the honor to be with the highest respect & esteem, Sir Yr most obedt Servt

BEN STODDERT

[NDA photostat.]

Presumably to Secretary of the Navy from Joshua Humphreys, Naval Constructor

MARCUS HOOK *Augt 25th 1798*

SIR I was honor'd with your favor from Trenton & shall pay particular attention to it— last Tuesday I visited the City to meet Capt Bainbridge & to forward the Brig & Schoon but was not fortunate enough to see him — My last letter informed you all the Guns for the two revenue Vessels were ready but find I was mistaken — Capt Bainbridge informed me last informed me last [sic] Sunday it was your orders to have the Schooner fitted with four Guns more than you at first intended which has also causd much delay which will be difficult at present to procure — The *Retaliation* arrived at this place this morning without any Guns on board — From the number of Reports of Guns I heard the day before Yesterday at my house, I suppose the Capt of the Brig and Schooner, has proved the Guns, the result of which has not come to my knowledge — the Brig will soon be ready, I have advanced Capt Campbell One thousand Dollars to ship his men

In opening the Ship *Ganges*, I find many of her Timbers & Plank decayed especially the Beams, most of which are good for nothing. They are of White Oak — this Ship was launched in the Spring of 1795 which is little better than three Years; This shews the necessity of having Ships' beams of more durable Wood than White Oak, or of making use of some method of preserving them from decay — As there are several Vessels now building for the Naval Service would it not be advisable to have the ends bored the length of the Knees in each end of each beams within one inch of the Upper Side with 2½ inch Augre & then to be slit from one hole to the other with a saw, through the middle of the beam, that slit set open about one inch, a board nailed underneath & filled with salt, the holes at each end ramed full & bunged up; this will prevent the timber from healin & decaying — Pitch Pine beam was at first intended for all the Frigates, but my friend Truxtun frustrated that good plan & prevailed on the Secretary at War to substitute white Oak in their room except to the *United States.* in my opinion to the great injury of the Frigates Letters on this subject was addressed to the Secretary and experiment on the strength of pitch pine to that of white oak — The fact now before us will have its deserved weight — The Gun Deck Beams are preparing now at this place & will be put on board on Monday— the Carpenters will proceed to kneeing them— I have engaged the Gun carriages but cannot proceed with them until your orders are received about the Guns — I have only to repeat that nothing shall be wanting on my part to expedite the whole of the business without the limits of the City & Suburbs where I must confess I am afraid to enter

I am most Respect^{y}

[HS of Pa. NDA photostat.]

To Secretary of the Navy from Captain Thomas Truxtun, U. S. Navy

UNITED STATES SHIP, *Constellation,*
Hampton Roads, August 25th 1798 —

SIR, I hope, ere this you have received the Muster Roll, Copy of my Journal, and the other Papers enclosed in Packet, I forwarded by a Schooner bound to Philadelphia. I shall be obliged by your Information of their being at Hand, or not, in Order that I forward Copies on my Return, should they have miscarried, which, I hope, is not the Case. I must confess, I am much embarrassed, by the daily Assemblage of Ships in these Roads, to benefit by our Convoy to Havannah. Several from Baltimore, Alexandria, and one from the Delaware, are now at Omaha here, and more hourly expected.

I must beg leave to refer you to the within Copy of a Letter, I have written in Consequence of the probable Disappointment, that several Merchants may experience, as well as to justify my own Conduct, and that you may see I am suspicious, that Information has been improperly given, from some Quarter, or other. I questioned last Evening Captain Phillips on this Subject, and he informed me, that previous to his leaving Baltimore, our Destination was well known, at the Insurance Offices and other Places there. I cannot presume, that if it was intended the outward Trade to Havannah should be convoyed, that you would have been so silent on the Subject, or have omitted adding in your Letter of the 10th Current, after the Words "proceed without Delay" taking such Vessels under your Charge, as may be ready, and bound to that Port.

I shall however reflect seriously on the Subject, and act for the Best; Our young, and too little experienced Commanders in the Ways of the World, and of Business, should be very cautious, and not communicate their Instructions even to their most confidential Officers, tho' least Accident should happen to them, their Lieutenants should know where the public Papers are placed.

If this Precaution is not impressed upon their Minds; Mischief, Tho' perhaps innocently, may arise from loose volatile Habits.

I shall be ready on Tuesday for Sea, and if Phillips is successful in getting Men will proceed immediately, but he tells me he is miserably off for Seamen.

I have the Honor to be, Sir, with great Respect
You most Obedient humble Servant —

THOMAS TRUXTUN.

N. B. I sent you by last Post Copy of a Receipt of the Master (Matthew Doggett) of the Schooner *Betsey and Jenny*, by whom I forwarded the Packet mentioned above.

BENJAMIN STODDERT Esquire
Secretary of the Navy

[HS of Pa. NDA photostat. Truxtun's LB, 1798–9.]

To Tench Francis, Purveyor, from Secretary of Navy

[TRENTON,]
Navy Department 25th August 1798

TENCH FRANCIS Esqr

SIR It will be right to buy the whole of the 130 — or 140′ Tons of Hemp on board the *Voltaire* — and all the duck you can get from the owner, on Terms you think reasonable. —

Pray do not let Mr Hodgden, in times like the present, Stand upon Trifles & punctilio.

The Secretary at War has sent several orders for the delivery of all the Musketts wanted for the Navy — a vessel has gone to Norfolk with almost every other article Wanted, but musketts. — We shall be obliged to send another vessell with 25 Musketts — all this trouble & Expense for What? To shew that men overdo their duty —.

As for Capt. Bainbridge; I want him well equipped & armed, but not extravagantly — His danger will arrive from boarding — Everything necessary to prevent that, should be furnished. —

[NDA. Req. on US T, 1798–1803.]

To Messrs. George Crowninshield & Sons, merchants, Salem, from Secretary of Navy

Navy Department
August 25th 1798

Messrs. Geo. Crowninshield & Sons *Salem*

Gentn. I am honored with the receipt of your Letter of the 17th Instant, describing your two Ships *America* & *Bellisarius*; and offering to dispose of them for the service of the United States; but it is not in my power to purchase them; for by the Acts of Congress, The President can only procure by purchase, or accept on the Condition of paying in 6 per cent Stock Vessels now building or to be built. —

Of the Number of Vessels thus authorized; there remains now to be provided, only one not exceeding 18 Guns, and one not less than 32 Guns — I hope that the Town of Salem, no less important, and whose Citizens are considered to possess as much patriotism as those of other Towns, who have taken the lead of them in this respect, will supply one of the two Vessels yet to be obtained, on the condition of receiving payment in 6 per cent Stock; and if you Gentlemen will endeavour to bring this about, you will render essential service to your Country, at a time when it requires the aid of all virtuous men. —

The Ships preparing for the public are generally Copper bolted, & sheathed with Copper; and it is generally understood, that the Hull, Rigging & Sails are to be completed by the Citizens furnishing them; and that when delivered to the public they be ready to receive their Guns

It is desireable, that the 18 Gun Vessel still wanted, should be able to carry 18 nine pound Cannon on the Gun deck; for this purpose she should measure between 300 & 400 Tons —

[NDA. GLB, Vol. 1.]

Extract from journal of James Pity, U. S. Frigate *Constitution*, 25 August 1798, Saturday

Wind at S. W. a 5 Call'd all hands out boats a 8 a Lighter came along Side with 8 Large Casks and 25 Gang Casks of Water & 5 Coils Rigging & 2 Casks Vinegar 20 Do. Water 100 Galls each ½ bbl. Tallow. a 4 P. M. call'd all hands to unmoor Ship got a Spring on our Starboard Cable clear'd hause and hove Short on Ditto Run out our Stream anchor and Cable hove Taught on the Stream.

weigh'd both Anchors in order to proceed to Sea found it impossible a 8 Rec^d Orders to Moor Ship with the best Bower and Stream Cable to the N. E. Veer's the Service on the Cables out in wake of the Hawse holes and Stem. Secured our Stoppers and Set the Watch.

[Near Block Island]

NDA.]

Extract from journal of U. S. Ship *Herald*, Captain James Sever, 25 August 1798

This 24 hours first part moderate gales and heazey Weather Saw a Schooner Standing To the N N W at 3 P M Tact Ship To the Westward Sett all Sail at 4 pm saw a Brig To Leward gave Chace at 5 Spoak hur found hur to Bee the Brig *Neptune* Ezekiah Purkins master 62 Days from Liverpool Bound to New London in Latt^d 42. 00 N Longt^d of 36 West was Borded By the Brig *Tyger* from Cronea 16 guns 6 & 9 pounders at 10 pm Sett all Sail To the westward at 12 am Close Reeft Topsails at same Time Sounded in 55 fat^h weather thick. Rainey through out the Night at 8 Sounded in 40 fathoms gray sand with Shells at 10 am sett all Sail.

Latter part Raney and thick weather the Brig *Pickring* in Company

Latt^d Obrs 41„ 42 North

[NDA. Journal kept by Joseph Strout, 1798.]

Extract from journal of Lieutenant John Mullowny, U. S. Frigate *United States*, 25 August 1798

Light breezes and fair weather. At 4 P. M. wore ship to the S^d At ½ 11 P. M. Tacked ship to the N^d —

At 5 A. M. saw Dominica bearing E by N distance 10 leagues At 6 P. M. saw 2 sail & supposed to be our consorts, at 7 saw Montserat bearing W ½ N distance about 12 leagues.

[NA.]

August 26, 1798]

From New Hampshire Gazette, Portsmouth, N. H., Nov. 21, 1798

Extract of a letter from Thomas Snell, Commander of the private armed Schooner *Amphitrite*, to T. Stagg, Jun. at New-York.

GRENADA, *Sept. 27, 1798*

"* * * On 26th [August] in lat. 29, long. 53, fell in with a ship and schooner, being to windward of them, I bore down to speak the Ship, and getting so close as to take the trumpet to speak her, at that moment we received a whole broadside from the ship, but fortunately did no damage, my people being all at their quarters I returned him the compliment: — an action commenced which lasted two hours and twenty minutes; Six of my guns being dismounted and my ammunition expending fast, I thought it most prudent to quit her ***"

[LC newspapers.]

To Jeremiah Yellott, Navy Agent, Baltimore, from Captain Thomas Truxtun, U. S. Navy

UNITED STATES SHIP *Constellation*
Hampton Roads 26th August 1798.

SIR, I have received your Letter by Captain Richardson of your Schooner, *Art* [or *Arb*]. I hope you are not so little acquainted with me, as to suppose I would not willingly, and with Pleasure comply with your Request, was it consistent with the Duty assigned to me by the Government. Some Mistake, or Error has been committed, when or how it has happened, would be hard in me to conjecture, but so it is.

I have written a Letter to Mr Joseph Sterett, in Consequence of the Embarrassments I was under, in this particular Business, and annexed, you have a Copy of a Circular, given to the Masters of the different Vessels here, I hope these will be sufficient to satisfy Gentlemen unacquainted with me, of my Disposition to do all, that lays in my Power, to promote their Views by protecting an honorable and fair Commerce To those, who are acquainted with me, I trust little need be said on the Subject. I am, Sir,

Your most Obedt humble Servant —

THOMAS TRUXTUN.

To JEREMIAH YELLOTT Esqr *Baltimore.*

[HS of Pa. NDA photostat. Truxtun's LB, 1798–9.]

To Masters of Ships desiring convoy from Captain Thomas Truxtun, U. S. Navy

[Circular]

UNITED STATES SHIP *Constellation*
Hampton Roads 26th Augst 1798—

SIR, I have written, and forwarded a Letter to Mr Sterett at Baltimore, — which I have desired him to show the Owners of Vessels assembled in these Roads, for the Purpose of taking Benefit of Convoy for Havannah, in Order that they may be convinced, I have it not in my Power to make the Delay, a Fleet would naturally occasion.

Being thus circumstanced, and feeling a deep Regret for it, I can only recommend to such Masters of Vessels, as may be bound to the Southward from Cape Henry, to sail in Company with me; and if any, or all of them can keep up with the *Baltimore,* which is also put under my Command (and I presume sails much slower than the *Constellation*) I will give them every Protection in my Power against the french Cruizers, that may be met in the Route, I shall take.

There must have been some Mistake in this Business, that I cannot account for, as the Secretary of the Navy would otherwise in his very late Communications, have mentioned Something to me on the Subject of Outward Convoy, particularly as he is a very attentive Man. Where an Officer has a Charte Blanche, he exercises his own Judgement, but when he receives possitive Orders, there can be no Deviation I therefore cannot make Delay for any Vessel. Wishing you safe to your consigned Port, and that you may meet a good Market, and quick Dispatch.

I remain, Your Obedt humble Servant

To Master of the ————

[HS of Pa. NDA photostat. Truxtun's LB, 1798–9.]

Extract from journal of Lieutenant John Mullowny, U. S. Frigate *United States*, 26 August 1798

Light winds, At 6 the south point of Guadaloupe bore E S E and the N° point N E by N. At 7 A. M. saw Antigua bearing N by E. A sail in sight at 8 Tack'd ship and spoke a schooner Sloop belonging to St Bartholomews from Guadaloupe, wore ship and stood to the N^d^ —

[NA.]

Extract from journal of James Pity, U. S. Frigate *Constitution*, 26 August 1798, Sunday

Wind S. W. with Strong breezes all hands employ'd preparing for Sea at 9 o'clock weigh'd the Kedge. Veer'd out the best bower and moored Ship again. Sent on Shore empty Casks for Water compleat^d^ stow^g^ Provisions & Cleand between decks. Carpenters employ'd fitting a Martingail. Armourers and Gunners on their different duty. Latter part Squally let down our Cables this Day Mr Dogget our former pilot came on Board.

[Near Block Island]

[NDA.]

To Captain Thomas Truxtun, U. S. Navy, from Secretary of Navy

[TRENTON,]
Navy Department August 27th 1798

Capt^t^ THO^s^ TRUXTON

SIR Your Letter of 16th enclosing Muster Roll and sundry papers, only reached me yesterday —

I cannot Account for its delay; Nor have I time to attend to all the particulars — Indeed the service upon which you are ordered is so important, that I hope this Letter may not reach you at Norfolk. — I will only therefore say for the present, that you are at liberty to take the number of men you deem necessary, and that you must take Saml Reddick first Lieutenant of Marines, or Josiah Reddick 2nd Lieutenant — both at Norfolk — to command the Marines, in the room of Triplett. — If more time was allowed, I would send down a more experienced Officer than either of these Gentlemen. —

But the Nature of the Service you are to perform, will not admit of delay — And I again add my Wishes, that you may have left Norfolk before this Letter reaches that place — Should it be otherwise, regulate whatever is necessary, with respect to the officers Yourself —

I have the honor to be &c^a^

[NDA. OSW, Vol. 1.]

To President Adams from the Secretary of Navy

[TRENTON,]
Navy Department 27th August 1798

JOHN ADAMS Esqr
President of the
United States

Sir I am honored with your two Letters of the 18th Ins^t^ and am happy that your wishes on the subject of a convoy for the vessels at the Havanna, had been anticipated. —

The enclosed copy of a Letter from the Captn of a British Sloop of War to the British Consul at Charleston, affords no very honorable Testimony of the Courage of Capt Cochran, Commander of the Revenue Cutter— I am glad he was not on the Navy Establishment— I cannot learn the size of the British Sloop of War, the sight of which, produced such dreadful apprehensions; but I think a brave man would have retained, what Capt Cochran seems to have lost — his powers of discrimination, had she been a ship of the Line — This conduct of Capt Cochran, leaves captain Cross, the Gentleman so strongly recommended by the Merchants of Charleston, through Mr Rutledge, without a competitor, for the Command of the Ship, they are building at that place. —

If therefore Sir, you approve of Capt Cross to be a captain in the Navy; He shall be commissioned and measures taken to give him immediate employment.—

I have the honor to be, with
the highest respect & Esteem &c

[NDA. Nom. Appts. LB, 1798–1820.]

Extract from journal of Lieutenant John Mullowny, U. S. Frigate *United States*, 27 August 1798

At M saw Antigua, N. N. E. St Christophers West. St Eustatius W by N. and St Bartholomews N W b N. at ½ 7 P. M. wore ship to the southd At Midnight wore to the Nd fresh Gales and cloudy weather. At 3 wore to the Sd and at 4 to the Nd and stood for St Bartholomews. at 7 stood in for the Harbour saw several small vessels there. at 8 wore to the Sd & stood off at ½ 10 Tkd to the Nd

[NA.]

Extract from journal of James Pity, U. S. Frigate *Constitution*, 27 August 1798, Monday

Wind West ½ past 4 call'd all hands. Sent up T.G. yds. wind Veering North wighd the Kedge and unmoord a 7. ½ pt 7 hove Short on the best bower fired a Gun Signal for getting under way a Do weigh'd and made Sail Stood out of the Harbour of New Port a 8 came abreast of the Light house. at 10 hove too and discharged our Pilot Thos Dennis from R. Island hoist'd in our boats and made Sail Wind W. N. W. Course Steerd S. W.

[NDA.]

To Captain Isaac Phillips, U. S. Navy, of the *Baltimore*, from Captain Thomas Truxtun, U. S. Navy

No 1

United States Ship, *Constellation*—
Hampton Roads, 28th Augst 1798.

Sir, The Copy of the Signals you have received from the Secretary of the Navy; and that which I have on Board do not agree, owing to some Error of a Mr Fox, a Clerk in the War Office, or of the Printer.

The Signal Book I have therefore, in a great Measure, for the present set aside, and have issued, and enclosed you only such, as will answer our Purpose, untill the Book can be put right.

In the Organization of your Ship, or in any other Way, that I can be of Service to you, be pleased to call on me without Hesitation, and I will give you all the Aid in my Power. To have your Ship always prepared for Action, or to perform any Service immediately, on a Signal being made is what will be expected from you, and of Course will require your particular Attention.

The Merchantmen assembled here I cannot take so completely under my Charge as I could have wished, being ordered to proceed without Delay on the Business; you are acquainted with, and which is but too generally known. I have however given them Signals, and delivered each a Copy of the enclosed Circular.

In Case of parting you will proceed off the Havannah, but give no Information, where you left me, or the Fleet. In this Event of parting at Sea, and you arrive off the Havannah before me, you will follow the Instructions contained in No. 2, which I shall prepare as soon as I am a little at Leisure, and deliver it to you with the Compass Signals, before we go out of the Capes, or about that Time.

I am with great Respect

Your Obedient humble Servant

THOMAS TRUXTUN.

Captain PHILLIPS of the *Baltimore*

N° 2.

SIR, On your Arrival off the Havannah, should we be so unfortunate as to part at Sea, You will be pleased to cruize off and on for Eight Days (out of Gun Shot of the Morea) and if I do not heave in Sight in that Time. You will make yourself acquainted with the french Naval Force at that Place, and govern yourself accordingly to Viz[t]. If it is inferior to that of your Ship, make Application to the Governor to permit the American Vessels now lying in the Havannah to sail, and you will in that Case take them under your Charge, and convoy them to the Coast of the United States, untill you think they are out of Danger; but if the french Force should be so superior on undoubted Information, that you cannot venture to make the Application, for the Sailing of the Vessels, proceed immediately for Hampton Roads, and give Information to the Government accordingly.

I hope however there is no Danger of our parting, but that we shall be successful in completing the Business of our Mission in a short Time.

I am, Sir, &c.

THOMAS TRUXTUN.

[Enclosure]

Compass Signals to be observed by Captain Phillips to Viz[t]

Nº 131 North
132 N. B. E.
133 N. N. E.
134 N. E. B. N.
135 N. E.
136 N. E. B. E.
137 E. N. E
138 E. B. N.
139 East
140 E. B. S.
141 E. S. E.
142 S. E. B. E.
143 S. E.
144 S. E. B. S.
145 SSE
146 SBE
147.South
148 SBW
149 SSW
150 SWBS
151 SW
152 SWBW
153 WSW
154 WBS
155 West
156 WBN
157 WNW
158 NWBW
159 N. W.
160.N. W. B. N.
161.N. NW.
162 NBW

N. B. Captain Phillips will answer the Merchantmen's Signals, to which he is to attend also, with a Flag of three blue & three white Stripes, and the printed Signals, with the Flag ordered.

THOMAS TRUXTUN.

[HS of Pa. NDA photostat. Truxtun's LB, 1798–9.]

[Enclosure]

[About 28 August 1798]

Captain Phillips of the *Baltimore* will attend also to the aforegoing Signals, with the following in Addition, and to speak with me every Evening at, or about Sun Setting, without Signal being made, unless under Orders to the Contrary.

Nº —15. [?] Prepare for Battle
—16. Exercise great Guns, and small Arms
—17. To give Chace
—18. To quit Chace
—19. The Chase is a Friend
—20. The Chase is an Enemy
—21. To engage the smallest Vessel, if two are in Sight
—22. To come close, and rake a Ship of Force, while the *Constellation* is engaging her otherwise.
—23. To speak the *Baltimore*, and Vica Verca
—24. For Captain Phillips to come on Board
—25. For Captain Phillips to send an Officer on Board
—26. In Distress
—27. Keep your Station.
—28. Make the best of your Way, and use every Effort for your Safety.
—29. I gain on the Chace
—30. I cannot gain on the Chace
—31. Keep ahead, and carry a Light at Night
—32. I am in Soundings
—33. I see the Land
—34. I am in Danger
—35. I am a Ground
—36. The Chace is superior to me
—37. The Chace is superior to the Fleet
—38. To return from any Service
—39. Not to go on Shore, or send any Boat without Leave
—40. Be sure to keep a good Look out by Night and Day, and inform me, of what you discover, worth Communicating

Captain Phillips answering Flag is three blue, and three white Stripes.

T. T[RUXTUN]

[HS of Pa. NDA photostat. Truxtun's LB, 1798–9.]

[Enclosure]

[About 28 August 1798]

Night Signals

Nº — 1. To anchor, and if at Anchor, the same is the Signal to weigh
— 2. On seeing a strange Sail to Windward
— 3. On seeing a strange Sail to Leeward
— 4. Wanting to speak Commodore
— 5. To tack, or to ware
— 6. To hawl the Wind to Starboard
— 7. To hawl the Wind to Port
— 8. To bring to, and lie by Starboard Tack
— 9. To bring to, and lie by Larboard Tack
—10. To make Sail
—11. To shorten Sail
—12. On seeing Land
—13. On seeing Danger
—14. Danger to Northward
—15. Danger to Southward
—16. Danger to N. E.
—17. Danger to East
—18. Danger to S. E.
—19. Danger to S. W.
—20. Danger to West
—21. Danger to N. W.
—22. Avoid any Danger as soon as possible.
—23. Attack the Strange Sail if an Enemy; but if a friend order him along Side of me
—24. Disperse
—25. A superior Force
—26. An inferior Force
—27. Follow me
—28. Strange Ships approach us
—29. Strange Ships avoid us
—30. Go under easy Sail.

Nº — 1 is one Light—
— 2 is two Lights—
— 3 is three Lights
— 4 is four Lights
— 5 is five Lights
— 6 is six Lights
— 7 is seven Lights
— 8 is eight Lights
— 9 is nine Lights
—10 is one Gun

As for Instance, suppose I want to signal 27, I shall fire two Guns, and throw out seven Lights, wherever they can be best seen in a Range, at about one Fathom asunder.

T.[HOMAS] T.[RUXTUN]

[HS of Pa. NDA photostat. Truxtun's LB, 1798–9.]

[Enclosure]

[About 28 August 1798]

Fog Signals at Sea

N. B. The Guns to be fired from one Side, & the Time to be marked by the Second Hand of a Watch.

Guns	Signification.	How answered.
One Gun every ¾ of an Hour	xGoing at the same Rate Starboard Tack	Drums Starboard Tack.
One Gun every Hour	xLarboard Tack Ditto	Bells Larboard Tack
Two Guns xxxxx	To anchor, if at Anchor to weigh	
Three Guns	xTo tack, or ware	
Four Guns	To make Sail	
Five Guns	To shorten Sail	
Six Guns	xTo keep within hearing of Signals	
Seven Guns	Discovering of Danger, and avoiding it	

T. T.[RUXTUN]

[HS of Pa. NDA photostat. Truxtun's LB, 1798–9.]

Enclosure]

[About 28 August 1798]

Signals by Day for Merchantmen.

In Case of parting and meeting again, hoist your Ensign at the Main, and your Pendnant forehead; the *Constellation* will be known by a long Pendnant at the fore top Gallant Mast Head, and a broad Pendnant at the Main Top Gallant Mast Head.

The following Signals will be all that is necessary for you, under the Circumstances, I have stated in my Letter; those, who can keep up with me ~~Ships of War~~, will not spread much, but sail as compactly as the Weather will permit from Time to Time, particularly at Night. ~~If I had it in my Power to take regular Charge of your Vessels, as I shall those returning with me, I would issue further Signals, and Instructions~~ [obliterated]

The Fleet will get underway, Leewardmost Vessels first	Blue Pendnant with white Tail, with a red and white Colour underneath.
The Fleet will make more Sail	Red Pendnant
The Fleet will shorten Sail	White Pendnant
On seeing a strange Sail to Windward, Merchantmen to hoist	their Jack at the Fore
On seeing a strange Sail to Leeward, Merchantmen to hoist	their Jack at the Main
To tack or ware	Blue Pendnant with white Tail, and a white Colour underneath.
To make best of your Way	Red & white Colour, and a red Pendnant with white Tail underneath.
The Fleet to run into Port, and anchor	Blue Colour with a white Pendnant, and red Tail underneath.
The Fleet will observe the Motions of the Commodore, and follow the same; this Signal must be particularly attended to by Night, on Account of the Course, as no Compass Signals are given	Red and white Colour, with colour underneath.

To lay to on Starboard Tack	Red and white Colour, with blue and white Pendnant
To lay to on Larboard Tack	Red and white Colour, with red Colour underneath.
Any Master of a Merchantman wishing to speak with the Commodore, will stand towards him	and hoist his Ensign
To hawl the Wind the Starboard Tack	A blue Colour, with a white Colour underneath
To hawl the Wind the Larboard Tack	A blue Colour, with a blue Pendnant, with white Tail underneath.
On seeing Land, or Danger, speak one of Ships of War, who will make the Signal to the other &c	

T. T[RUXTUN]

[HS of Pa. NDA photostat. Truxtun's LB, 1798–9.]

To Captain James Sever, U. S. Navy, from Secretary of Navy

[TRENTON,]
Navy Department 28th August 1798

Capt. JAMES SEVER

SIR I am mortified that any circumstances should have intervened to prevent your sailing soon after the receipt of your cruising orders of the 30th July. — Calculating that you would certainly be out in a little time after, I have sent by different conveyances, to Captain Nicholson, to leave to you the protection of the Eastern Coast; and to proceed himself to the Southward. —

Before this day, he must have some one of my Letters, and if you are still in Port, the Eastern Coast must be without protection. — I understand from a Letter from Boston of the 16th you were waiting for a few Marines; and a Letter from Captn Chapman of the 20th leads me to conclude, that he expected to receive my answer while he remained at Boston.

Under the circumstance I have mentioned, of the Eastern Coast being without a guard, it would not be Justifiable in me to acquiesce in your remaining in Port for your full complement of men; and from Mr Higginson's Information, you must nearly have your full complement, You will therefore, immediately on receipt of this, proceed with Capt. Chapman to sea, and govern yourself by your Instructions of the 30th July. — In addition to the Ports, off which in the said Instructions you were directed to appear, to receive dispatches &ca, Gloucester on Cape Ann, you will likewise occasionally call at; by which means our communications may be facilitated.

[NDA. OSW, Vol. 1.]

To Captain Jonathan Chapman, Revenue Cutter *Pickering*, from Secretary of Navy

[TRENTON,]
Navy Department 28th August 1798

Capt. JONATHAN CHAPMAN

SIR I have this day received your Letter of the 20th dated Boston. — I am mortified that you should have been at Boston instead of being at sea, as I hoped and expected on the 20th or before and still more mortified that you expect an answer at Boston; because it implies an opinion that you would not sail on the Cruise ordered the 30th July, before September —

I wrote Mr Higginson, and I now repeat to you; that Justice shall be done to your own merits, and the merits of your officers in the arrangement shortly to be made of Navy officers. — No appointments have been made, since I have been in office, but for the vessels ready for service — a general arrangement has been delayed, for better Information — It will soon take place; and you will be appointed to the Command of one of the Ships. — Equal Justice will be done yr officers.

I have the honor &ca

[NDA. OSW, Vol. 1.]

To Stephen Higginson, Navy Agent, Boston, from Secretary of Navy

[TRENTON,]
Navy Department 28th August 1798

STEPHEN HIGGINSON Esqr

SIR, Altho' I do not reply to all the particulars, contained in your Letters of the 10th 13 & 16th Instant, yet they do not escape my attention. — I have no authority (proper as the measure would be) to lay in a Stock of Timber. — Such things must be attended to in future. —

I will attend to your suggestion as to Guard Ships. — Your letter to Capt Sever was certainly a very proper one, and such as shou'd have caused him to proceed to sea, without more delay; Yet I fear from a Letter I have received from Capt Chapman (the answer to which is enclosed) he is still in Port. —

I will not indulge a suspicion, that Capt Sever wants, zeal, activity or any other essential quality of an Officer — But without any reference to him, I have always entertained an opinion that men who suffer trifling difficulties to interpose between them and their duty; are unfit for public service — It shall be my endeavour to rid our Navy of such men — If our Officers cannot be inspired with the true kind of Zeal & Spirit, which will enable us to make up for the want of great Force, by great Activity, we had better burn our Ships, and commence a Navy at some future time when our Citizens have more Spirit. —

I enclose a Letter for Capt Sever, if he should still be in Port. Has he not delayed too long on a most frivolous pretence? does he deserve the high character given of him?

[NDA. GLB, Vol. I.]

Extract from journal of James Pity, U. S. Frigate *Constitution*, 28 August 1798, Tuesday

First part this 24 hours light Winds with a head beat Sea S. S. E. a 2 P. M. S. E. part block Island bore W. S. W. 3 Leags dist employ'd Stowg Anchors found Ship too much by the head Shifted 2 fore castle guns aft on the Quarter deck and 4 Casks Water Shifted the Sheet anchor abaft the fore Chains on the Starboard Side a 6

Middle part block Island bore N. W. b. W. 4 Leagues from which I take my dep^{re} In Latt^d 41° 10 Long^d 71.23. Middle part dark with Sharp Light^s ℞ Ship West^d Sounded in 40 fath^{ms} green ozy bottom. Saw 4 Sail diff^t directions. Wore Ship a M. These 24 hours ends fresh breezes & hazy W^r

[Latitude observed, 40°. 46^m. N^o]

[NDA.]

Extract from journal of Lieutenant John Mullowny, U. S. Frigate *United States*, 28 August 1798

Stiff gales and cloudy A 2 P. M. Tacked to the S^d at 3 saw a sail made sail for her, spoke her, she proved to be a schooner from St Vincents bound to St Bartholomews, gave chace to a Schooner, which we found to be a privateer from Antigua called the *Experiment* at 8 P. M. Tkd ship to the S^d lowered Topsails down set up the Rigging and fited a New Fore Top Mast stay.

[NA.]

Extract from journal of U. S. Ship *Herald*, Captain James Sever, commander, 28 August 1798

This 24 hours first Part moderate gales and thick fogg at 5 p m Duble Reeft Topsails at 12 am Calm flatening held up fore Sail Down Jibb thick fogg at 2 P m Sounded in 48 fathoms Watter Sandy Bottom at 6 am heavy thunder with heavy Rain at 9 am Clear

Midle Part fine weather Sett all Sail By the wind Lusd Stearing sails To Try all hans Employd in Spining Spun yarn and Sundry other Jobbs at mrdn Saw three Sail to S/W

Latter Part Moderate gales and heazey weather under all Sail By the wind the Brig *Pickring* Still in Companey

Latt^d Obbrs 40..42 North

[NDA. Journal kept by Joseph Strout, 1798.]

To Captain Silas Talbot, U. S. Navy, from Secretary of Navy

[TRENTON,]
Navy Department August 29th 1798

Capt SILAS TALBOT *New York*

SIR Mr John Brown of Providence, Rhode Island, offers for Sale to the public, his Ship the *George Washington*; which he describes as a ship built of Cedar and live Oak, coppered, two suits of Sails, completely rigged, and fitted in all respects for a Ship of War; and that she can be sent on a cruise with very little expense, and without delay. — He represents her as one of the best Sailers in America, and capable of carrying 24 Twelve pound Cannon, — or 32 Guns, 9 & 6 pounders. —

For the sake of adding one more to the number of the ships capable of immediate service, I have determined to buy this of Mr Brown's; if on examination, She proves to be a sound, strong, fast sailing vessel, and well qualified to make a serviceable cruiser; — and capable of carrying 24 Twelve pound Cannon, or 32 — 9 & 6 pound Guns. For this examination, and to enable me to Judge, whether I ought, or ought not to purchase her for the public service, I must rely entirely upon you. —

Permit me therefore, to request, that you will, as early as possible, proceed to Providence, and examine strictly, and critically this ship belonging to Mr Brown, & furnish me as early as you can, Your full opinion of her construction and fitness for a Vessel of War; The probability of her being a fine sailer; her soundness, Strength, and the number of Guns She is capable of mounting; The quality & Sufficiency of her sails, Rigging, Cables, and Anchors; and in Short, of every particular relating to her, which you shall judge necessary to enable me to determine, whether I should, or should not purchase her. —

I would wish also to have the dimensions of the Ship; (which Mr Brown has never given) and your Opinion of the Alterations (if any) which ought to be made in her, previous to the receipt of her Guns; and of the time it would require to make the alterations, and the probable expense.

I shall, as before observed, be governed intirely by your Opinion as to this Ship. —

I understand Mr Brown is a Gentn of very great Influence in Providence. — Judge whether you will want a Carpenter to assist in the examination; and whether you can depend upon getting the assistance of one in Providence, who will not be under the influence of Mr Brown. — And if you think it proper take a Carpenter with you from New York. —

Any expense you are at in this business will chearfully be paid by the public — And I hope you will without reluctance undertake this, perhaps important service — The first Cost is but a trifle, compared with the consequences of putting a Commander & Crew on board of a good, or a bad Ship. —

I am &ca

[NDA. GLB, Vol. 1.]

Letter from Captain John Morrison, Master of the Armed Ship *Eliza*, of Charleston, S. C., relating to convoy

[Charleston, S. C.]
Ship Eliza, off the Bar, 28th August, 1798.

Messieurs Freneau & Paine,

You will please take notice, that on Sunday morning, the 19th inst. I sailed from the Havanna, with a convoy of sixty-five sail of Americans, bound for different ports of the Continent, under my direction. Nothing happened worth noticing 'till Sunday, the 26th; then, in Latitude of 20° 11′ N., I saw a strange sail to windward, coming down for the convoy; I immediately hauled the wind for her, and found, on coming near, that she was a man of war. I made the signal for a friend, by firing a gun to leeward, and hoisting my colors, which she answered by repeating the same, with British colors. At three P. M. she came within hail and, after the usual mode desired me to collect my convoy, that he wanted to board the Danes.

I instantly made the signal for the convoy to close with me, which I kept up 'till dark, going under easy sail, the convoy much in confusion, and a great many paying no attention to the signal, but the fastest sailors getting off as fast as they could. Kept on all night under an easy sail, with the heavy sailing vessels. At day light I found the man of war had kept company all night, and at sunrise boarded the Danes in the convoy and stood on with them to the Southward and Eastward.

Many of our convoy made off in the night. I kept on with the remainder 'till Latitude 32° 0′ N., when I hauled in for the land, with the vessels bound for this port. The rest of the convoy kept on with the other armed vessels. I am immediately to make sail after them. The man of war's name is the *Prevoyante*.

I am, Gentlemen,
With respect,
Your most obedient servant,

JOHN MORRISON

[LC, "City Gazette & Daily Advertiser" (Charleston), Wednesday, August 29, 1798.]

To Messrs. Brown and Ives, Providence R. I., from Secretary Pickering

DEPARTMENT OF STATE TRENTON, NEW JERSEY,
29 Augt 1798.

Messrs BROWN and IVES *Providence Rhode Island.*

GENTLEMEN, I have this day sent Mr Joseph Anthony a Commission for the private Armed Ship *Ann and Hope*, belonging to you; and now enclose to you a blank bond to be executed by yourselves and two Sufficient Sureties, which being done, you will be pleased to return the same to me. The act of Congress requiring the description of the vessel, for which a Commisssion is requested, to be signed by the applicant, and this being omitted in the one transmitted to me by Mr Anthony, I inclose it to you, that the deficiency may be corrected.

I am, Gentlemen, &c

TIMOTHY PICKERING.

[SDA. Dom. L., Vol. 11.]

To Captain Alexander Murray, U. S. Navy, of the *Montezuma*, from Secretary of Navy

[TRENTON,]
Navy Depart 29th Augt 1798

Capt ALEXr MURRAY

Sir I am honored with your Letters of the 24th & 26th Instant — Baltimore it is true has furnished an over-proportion of seamen; yet I fear you must depend upon Baltimore and Alexandria (perhaps Norfolk may afford aid) for your Crew — The fever in Phila & New York will make it difficult and dangerous to get men from either of these places — And the Eastern seamen will only go in ships fitted to the Eastward —

I think you must therefore try to procure a Crew at Baltimore & Southward —

It is but right you should give to the Midshipmen you find deserving, the encouragement you suggest — I shall always be glad to receive your observations on every thing respecting the Navy — I entered upon Office, ignorant of all my duties; but with the disposition to learn them by all the means in my power.

The Captains of the Navy must afford me a great deal of Instruction — especially those who are experienced. —

I am projecting (but this you will keep to yourself) an enterprize for you, and two smaller, but well fitted vessels, under your Command, — and am the more anxious that your Ship should be ready as early as possible, that the time for its execution may not elapse —

I am &c[a]

[NDA. OSW, Vol. 1.]

To Captain Thomas Truxtun, U. S. Navy, from Captain Isaac Phillips, U. S. Navy

[Copy]

Ship *Baltimore* 29th *August 1798* —

Sir, I have now on Board for my nine Pound Cannon, the following Quantity of Shot — 509 Round
357 double head
121 Cannister

Also for the four Pound Cannon as follows —
298 Round
100 Cannister

I wish you to oblige me with your Opinion, whether that Quantity is sufficient, however it is all I have.

With Respect your most
humble Servant

Isaac Phillips.

N. B. Should you order the Pilot Boat to Baltimore, I should be glad to send a Letter.

Commodore Truxtun
Hampton Roads.

[HS of Pa. NDA photostat. Truxtun's LB, 1798–9.]

Extract from journal of Lieutenant John Mullowny, U. S. Frigate *United States*, 29 August 1798

Cloudy weather. At 1 P. M. a sail in sight bearing S. W. at 5 P. M. spoke her, she was the Brig *Kitty* Capt McBride from Martinico bound to Liverpoole, at 5 A. M. two sail in sight found them to be the *Kitty* and *Experiment*, Brig and schooner before spoke with. at 10 A. M. hove too off St Bartholomews and sent Lt Barron on shore he returned in 4 hours.

[NA.]

Extract from journal of James Pity, U. S. Frigate *Constitution*, 29 August 1798, Wednesday

First part this 24 hours Steady breezes with a head Sea from the Southward. Ship in Chace Spoke Do proved the Brigt *Mercury*

Wm Miller Comr from Rotterdam bound to Philada 11 Weeks out Short of provisions (own'd by Mr Foster of Said port) Supply'd them with 1C pork 1C Bread and one Qr Cask Water @ 5 p. m. made Sail got up our Lightning rods.

Middle part Squally with rain at 1½ past 10. Winds Variable. Saw a Schr to Windard Standg Northwd at Midnight Took in Sail it being Squally with heavy Showers rain at 6 made Sail Saw a Sail Standg S. W. Spoke her prov'd the Brigt WM of N York Jno Johnson Comr bound to Greenock. Musterd the Crew & Regulated the Watch.

[Latitude observed 39° 50m No]

[NDA.]

Extract from journal of U. S. Ship *Herald*, Captain James Sever, U. S. Navy, commander, 29 August 1798

This 24 hours first part moderate gales and hazey weather at 2 p m Spoak a Brittish 64 gun Ship the *St Albins* Capt Pender had in Companey a Brig from Bourdaux Bound To New York the Brig Beloning To George Townd on there way to Halifax at 8 pm Tact Ship S S E Dubble Reef the Topsails

Midle Part Calm flattening weather With Rain at 6 am had a Squall from the W S W thunder attended with heavy Rain saw a Ship To the E S E hove out Signal the Brig *Pickring* To give Chace at 10 am Spoak hur found hur to Bee the Ship *Carlonia* of Portland Bound to Philadelphia from Liverpool 50 days out

Latter part moderate gales and Cloudy weather with Drizeley Rain

No Obrs To Day

[NDA. Journal kept by Joseph Strout, 1798.]

To Major Commandant Burrows, U. S. M. C., from Thomas Pinckney, Charleston, S. C.

CHARLESTON *30th Aug: 1798*

MY DEAR SIR: Give me leave to congratulate you on the appointment to the Command of the Corps of Marines & at the same time to convey to you Mrs. Pinckney & my affectionate respects to Mrs. Burrows & yourself — Pursuant to the desire of the Secretary of the Navy I (after making the necessary enquiries) appointed Mr. John Maine of this city to the 2nd Lieutenancy of Marines — Mr. Maine bears a very good character in general, is a very active intelligent militia officer & his friends are only surprised at his accepting so low a grade in the Army.

I procured for him & Mr. Hall the money desired but I have doubts of them raising the number of men you expect — The Artillery Officers recruiting here offer 10 or 12$ bounty which I apprehend will give them the preference.

We have raised 114,000$ here to build & equip a vessel of war to be loaned to the Government & we have built three gun boats & have nearly finished a small fort on Sullivan's Island & laid out considerable sums in other defensive preparations so that I trust South Carolina will not be among the most backward in support of our Government & Independence.

I remain with much respect & esteem — My Dear Sir —

Truly yours

THOMAS PINCKNEY.

[Original Letter not in MCA.]
[Recruiters' Bulletin, October 1916, p. 15.]

To Stephen Higginson, Navy Agent, Boston, from Secretary of Navy

[TRENTON,]
Navy Department August 30th 1798

STEPHEN HIGGINSON Esqr *Boston*

SIR I am honored with your Letter of the 23 Instant — I have requested the Secretary of the Treasury to remit you 20,000 Dollars —

I am very happy that the *Herald* and Cutter have sailed — and that your opinion of Capt Sever is so favorable — I began to think unjustly of his Zeal & Activity, as you will perceive by my Letter to him, enclosed in my last to you — I am always glad in such cases, to find myself mistaken —

I see no objection to the arrangement you suggest as to Capts Sever & Chapman. and their Officers, and will endeavor to effect it — Perhaps Capt McNeill may be provided for at Providence, (R. I.) where I am in Treaty for the purchase of a Ship, tho not strictly within the Law — It would be desireable that New Hampshire should furnish one Captain, — if they have a fit man —

Please to forward the pay Roll, Muster Roll &ca left by Captain Sever — The accountt of the Navy Department is just commencing his duty. —

The powder and arms wanted for the Ship at Portsmouth, shall be forwarded in time, as also Iron Ballast — She must be called the *Portsmouth* — please to direct the head according to your own Judgment — Heads are not useful, and I believe injure a ship — If we must preserve an useless ornament (& I suppose we must) — they ought not to be expensive. —

I wish it was in my power to contract for Timber for future Ships — however proper it is, Congress have made no appropriation for this purpose — They must look better forward, in future. —

The sickness in the different Towns, disappoints the revenue — and the utmost Occonomy must be attended to in the different departments — My view heretofore has been, to have the Crew enlisted by the time the Vessel was ready to receive them — so as not to have men waiting for a ship, nor a ship for men —

However proper it might be, to procure such ships as you suggest, for the purpose of recruiting and training our men, I doubt whether it would not encrease the expense — I will however, better understand this subject —

P. S. to the foregoing Letter to S. Higginson Esqr

I presume the Portsmouth Ship might sail in one fortnight after launching, — if every proper previous arrangement be made. — When do you suppose she will be launched?

[NDA. GLB, Vol. 1.]

To Captain Richard Dale, U. S. Navy, from Secretary of Navy

[TRENTON,]
Navy Department 30th August 1798

Capt RICHARD DALE

SIR I am honoured with your Letters of the 22 & 28th Instant — I am very sorry you hold out the Idea of quitting the service —

It is likely our Country will want the aid of brave men. — I have not understood that you were to lose your rank, because the Frigate intended for you, was discontinued; but my Idea has been the contrary. — I can not however be certain how this point is to be determined; — but if this is the only objection to your continuing in the service, you should not determine to quit it, until this point is determined against you. — I should be glad to hear from you on this subject. — If at all events, you mean to quit the service, it will be necessary that I should know it. —

I am very sorry the Ship proves so defective — The Guns must be regulated according to your own Judgment — Get as many new ones as you think proper — Mr Foxall will cast them according to your directions — Judge whether he can get them done in time; and the sooner he is set about them, the better — I have written him to prepare such Guns as you require, and will direct the proper Hearth or Camboose from New York — Mr Francis will have the Bower Cable such as you direct, made out of Hemp he has lately purchased.

I should be glad to know your opinion of the number of men, the Crew of the *Ganges* should consist — she must mount only 24 Guns, I believe to comply with the Law. —

It is doubted by the Purser whether the Beef will answer for another cruise — Should it not be overhauled and repacked? — by this means the greater part may be saved. —

[NDA. OSW, Vol. 1.]

To Joshua Humphreys, naval constructor, from Secretary of Navy

Navy Department
Trenton August 30th 1798

Mr JOSHUA HUMPHREYS

SIR Captain Dale writes to me on the subject of the Guns for the *Ganges;* and I write this day to Mr Francis, that he must procure from Foxalls Foundery, such as Captain Dale shall direct. — They will of course be nine pounders, and you can give orders about the carriages accordingly — I have also written to Mr Francis to procure sundry Stores, ordered by Capt Dale; supposing that he will be able to collect them with more facility, than it may be in your power to do. —

I remain sir &ca

[NDA. GLB, Vol. 1.]

To Captain John Brown, Revenue Cutter *Diligence*, from Secretary of Navy

[TRENTON,]
Navy Department August 30th 1798

Capt JOHN BROWN
Cutter *Diligence*

SIR: The Schooner *Diligence* Revenue Cutter under your Command, being now nearly ready to receive her Guns & Stores; you will proceed without delay to get them on board. —

Mr Joshua Humphreys will supply the Money for the several articles you may require — and also two months provisions. —

There will be ordered on board from the Marine Corps a Serjeant and 8 Marines, and you will immediately take measures for enlisting fifteen able seamen, & seven Boys for twelve months; which with the Marines will be a sufficient Crew for your Schooner. — If necessary you must advance each man, two months pay; but in this case, you should get Security that those you pay it to, do not run away — The Wages to able seamen are 17 Dollars p. Month — The boys you will give from 5 to 14 Dolls p. month, according to merit. —

Mr Humphreys will also furnish you with money for this service, and you will be careful to enlist none, but healthy, sober people; prefering Americans, if to be had —

Out of the 15 seamen allowed, you will appoint your Boatswain, Carpenter & Gunner allowing each of them 3 Dolls p. Month, more than seamen's Wages —

When you are ready to receive them, Major Burrows will be directed to send on board your vessel; a Serjeant and eight Marines, which will complete your Crew. — These men will be sent with arms — The Muskets you have, will supply your seamen.

[NDA. OSW, Vol. 1.]

Extract from journal of U. S. Ship *Herald*, Captain James Sever, U. S. Navy, commander, 30 August 1798

This 24 hours Begins pleasant gales and heazey Weather at 12 pm Saw a Brig Standing to the S S E gave Chase at 4 pm Spoak hur Was from New port Bound to Hamburg 48 hours out at 8 pm Sounded in 40 fathoms

Midle part pleasant and Light wind from the westward and at 6 am Lett out all Reeffs and Lusd all Sails To Dry at 10 out Jolly Boat to Scrub the Sides all hans Employd in Ships Duty

Latter Part allmost Calm Sounded in 38 fathoms Watter Sandy Bottom The Brig *Pickering* Still in Compan[y]

Latt Obrs 40..40 N.

[NDA. Journal kept by Joseph Strout, 1798.]

Extract from journal of Lieutenant John Mullowny, U. S. Frigate *United States*, 30 August 1798

At 4 Saw 4 Sail to the Sd & Ed two proved to be Capt Decatur and the prize Schooner, the others Sweedish small schooners Appearance of very bad weather, squally, Thunder, lightning and very heavy rain

At 7 A. M. saw the *Delaware*, shortened sail for her, at 10 A. M. hoisted out the Cutter and sent for Capt Decatur to come on board.

[NA.]

Extract from journal of James Pity, U. S. Frigate *Constitution*, 30 August 1798, Thursday

First part this 24 hours Light Winds & pleasant @ 1 P. M. Set the Spanker and Stay Sails. Two Sail in Sight @ 6 P. M. Sounded with 90 fathms Line No Bottom @ 6 pumped Ship 10 Inches Water.

Middle part Light Airs from N. E. and Clear Wr a Do hauld down Jibb & Stay Sails.

At Day Light Hoisted out our Yaul 3 Sail in Sight.

@ 11. A. M. Set the Stay Sails 3 Sail still in Sight.

Latter part Moderate & Clear.

[Latitude observed 39°.11m.No]

[NDA.]

To William Pennock, Navy Agent, Norfolk, from Secretary of Navy

Navy Department,
Trenton 31st August 1798

Wm Pennock Esqr *Norfolk*

I have received your three Letters of the 18, — 21st & 23 Current. — I had hoped that Captain Truxton would have been on his way to the Havanna before this. — I shall request the Secretary of the Treasury to transmit you, six Thousand Dollars. — Instead of drawing on me, furnish me with Estimates of the money you will require in every month, and I will cause it to be remitted to you. — I have this day written to James Watson Esqr of New York, and requested him to ship from thence to your address, — Two Cambooses intended for the two Brigs. It gives me pleasure to learn that the Schooner from Philadelphia has arrived — You have consequently received the eighteen six pounders. — I beg you will inform me, what prospect you have, of procuring the Six Guns, yet remaining to be purchased for the two Brigs. — My object is to bring into operation, as early as possible, all our Naval strength, and I flatter myself that my views will be furthered by your Activity and exertions. —

[NDA. GLB, Vol. 1.]

To Messrs. Gibbs & Channing, agents, Newport, R. I., from Secretary of Navy

Navy Department Trenton Augt 31. 1798

Messrs Gibbs & Channing

I am honored with the receipt of your several Favors dated the 7th 9th & 14th Instant which would have been sooner acknowledged but for the derangement attending the removal of the Offices to this place.

You will find enclosed a List of the Stores considered as necessary for a Ship of 24 Guns, also a List of Colours. — The Signal Colours shall be supplied from hence. —

The Ship may be called the *General Green*; and altho' I believe Heads rather injure Ships, yet I suppose our Ships must have them; please therefore have such a Head made, as in your Judgment will be proper; avoiding much expence.

Of the Articles mentioned in the enclosed List the Powder, Muskets, & Bayonets are in Store, and shall be sent in season the Drums & Fifes also.

Let me know early which of the other Articles you can not procure.

[NDA. GLB, Vol. 1.]

To Major Commandant Burrows, U. S. M. C., from Secretary of Navy

[TRENTON,]
Navy Department 31st Augt 1798

Major BURROWS

SIR Marines will be wanted shortly at the following places —

at Portsmouth New Hampshire	25
at Newbury Port	25
at Newport Rhode Island	25
at Boston	25

I request you will cause the men to be enlisted at places the most convenient — If those wanted for Portsmouth & Newbury Port are engaged at Boston, where there is a contractor, who must supply Rations, they can easily be sent to the places where wanted. —

Arms will be sent to Boston from Springfield, for the men, and will be directed to Stephen Higginson Esqr to whom I will write to procure them clothing. —

Fifty Marines will also be wanted at Norfolk. — You will please have these also enlisted. — They will be supplied with Rations by the Contractor there — & Cloathing and Arms, & Accoutrements, must be sent for them from Phila .—

I have requested the Secretary of the Treasury to advance you fifteen hundred dollars, for the recruiting service, and such proper advances to the officers, as can safely be made, and are indispensible —

Please to direct that Natives be preferred Indeed if they can be obtained, none others ought to be enlisted. —

[NDA. GLB, Vol. 1.]

To Chevalier de Yrujo, Minister Plenipotentiary of His Catholic Majesty, from Secretary Pickering

DEPARTMENT OF STATE
Trenton Augt 31. 1798.

SIR, I have received your letter of the 27th stating that "by letters which you had just received from the Commandant General of Luisiana, you were informed, that in the District of Natches there is assembling a small American Army, whose force already amounts to some thousand men with a great deal of Artillery, and it is added, that still more hoops and cannon are expected." And you mention your own knowledge "that two of the armed boats built at Pittsburgh have already descended the Ohio with the same destination, and that others will follow them so soon as they are finished."

How you should "know" the "destination" not only of the gun-boats already built, which have descended the Ohio, but of those which are building, I cannot tell; it *conjecture* that these boats were destined to contribute to the maintenance of the Posts and the rights of the United States on the Mississippi would have been natural; seeing Spain maintains a number of gun-boats on the same river, for the like purpose on her part.

With regard to the Statement that "a small Army already amounting to some thousand men, is assembling at the Natchez," the Commandant General of Luisiana knows that it is not true: it is therefore not necessary to enquire into the destination of an army which has no existence. But it is not diffiuclt to conjecture the object of the Commandant General: After evading for more than a year, the evacuating of the Posts and the running of the boundary line, he would probably interrupt the latter, if he could find any new pretense. Hence the insinuations of hostile views on the part of the United States; and hence his attempt to alarm Mr Ellicot and induce him to quit the business by formally announcing to him the dissatisfaction of the Indians, and their intention, "to surprise the Commissioners for running the boundary line, and to treat the *Americans* in an outrageous manner." If sir, such interruption and outrage should take place, we shall be at no loss for its origin: the Indians will not be inclined to outrage and hostilities, unless excited by the secret Agents of the Commandant General. It is time, sir, after patiently bearing so many vexatious delays, to speak plain: the warm professions and solemn assurances of the Commandant General, have ceased to inspire confidence. So repugnant, indeed, has been his conduct to his professions, that fresh assurances serve rather to excite fresh suspicions. At the same time the interests of the two Nations are so obviously concerned in maintaining a fair and good understanding with each other, you may rely that when the acts of the Officers of his Catholic Majesty shall bear the evident marks of sincere amity, they will be cordially reciprocated on the part of the United States.

I am, Sir,

Your most obedt servt

(Signed) TIMOTHY PICKERING.

CHEVALIER DE YRUJO

Minister Plenipotentiary of His Catholic Majesty

[SDA. Dom. L., Vol. 11.]

To Rufus King, United States Minister, London, from United States Consul Rob W. Fox

[from] R. W. Fox —

FALMOUTH *31 August 1798*

RUFUS KING Esq:

ESTEEMED FRIEND, I have to trouble thee on the following occasion. Peter Vignon Passenger on board the Brig *Hope* Capt: Wheelwright, under American Colours was captur'd on the Voyage from Bordeaux to New York and sent into this Port. Part of the Cargo is his property, & he being a Citizen of the United States of America I gave him a Certificate thereof, & the Mayor granted him a Licence for a Month to reside here, which is now nearly expired, & the Collector tells him he must in future obtain it from the Duke of Portland, which I know no way of obtaining but through thee. He has given me Copies of his Certificates of Citizenship which I enclose thee as well as his letter to me. He staid about 9 Months in France; in the first place he was stopp'd as an Emigrant, & afterwards a suitable opportunity did not present for his return for some Months. I conclude he is fully entitled to thy Protection.

I am with much respect

Thy assured Friend

ROB W FOX.

[SDA. Falmouth, C. L., Vol. 1, 1790–1802.]

To Lieutenant Saunders, U. S. M. C., from Captain Thomas Truxtun, U. S. Navy

UNITED STATES SHIP *Constellation*
Hampton 31st August 1798.

SIR, I send you herewith a printed Copy of my private Instructions for your Government. In the Organization of our Infant Navy, it is highly necessary, that great Attention be paid to every Order, and Regulation. And as the Articles of War, the President's Instructions, and my private Orders are the basis from which all Duty and Etiquette is to be performed, you will be pleased to particularly attend to the same. We have a national Character to support, and it is my anxious Desire that we appear when in Company with the Ships of our own, and other Nations as well disciplined, and regular as any of them. From your Character I have every Reason to suppose, that I may calculate on your steady Attention to the Rules, and Regulations laid down, and of the keeping the Marines neat clean, and in good Order, which from the Inattention of their late Officer, I am sorry to say they have been shamefully neglected, particularly in Port, and since I first went on Shore at Norfolk. Daily Orders are generally given in a Book, whenever any Part thereof relates to your Department, the Officer of the Watch will inform you. I am, Sir, with great Respect —

Your Obedient humble Servant

THOMAS TRUXTUN.

Lieut SAUNDERS. —

[HS of Pa. NDA photostat. Truxtun's LB, 1798–9.]

To William Pennock, Navy Agent, Norfolk, from Captain Thomas Truxtun, U. S. Navy

UNITED STATES SHIP *Constellation*
Hampton Roads 31 August 1798 —

DEAR SIR At the Request of the five following Persons (Job Swain, Thos Sweet, George Shore, John Doyle, James Renton, & John Hilsbury) praying that they might be Landed on accot of their Health, I have directed that they be put on Shore at Norfolk, on condition of their discharge being accepted; but I have promised that you shall furnish quarters for them, untill they can Shift for themselves, or hear from the Secy of the Navy on the Subject. —

The Publick must not be put to any expence, that can be avoided for not a man who I have granted a discharge to, from the Commencement of fitting this Ship to the present Time has ever earned his Victuals. —

I am Sir Your Obt Servt

THOMAS TRUXTUN.

Wm PENNOCK Esqr
N. A.

[HS of Pa. NDA photostat. Truxtun's LB, 1798–9.]

[31 August 1798]

Complement of U. S. Ship *Baltimore*

Officers of every Description on Board the United States Ship *Baltimore, Isaac Phillips Esqr Commander* .... No 46

Able Seamen	"	–30–
Half ditto	"	– 3–
Active Boys	"	– 8–
Ordinary Seamen	"	–19–
Landsmen	"	–16–
Marines	"	–24–
Total Number of every Description		–146

Hampton Roads 31st August 1798.

Signed — ISAAC PHILLIPS.

Commodore TRUXTUN.
Hampton Roads.

[HS of Pa. NDA photostat. Truxtun's LB, 1798–9.]

Extract from journal of Lieutenant John Mullowny, U. S. Frigate *United States*, 31 August 1798

At M. saw a sail off the E. end of Saba Set all sail in chace, came up with and spoke the Schooner *Gilblass* Capt Ponsonby, who is an impertinent man, belonging to Tortola 4 Guns. At 8 P. M. Saba bore N E b. N Dist 8 miles. At 4 hove to spoke the *Delaware* bore away for St Croix at 7 A. M. saw St Croix W S W. Dist 8 leagues, — at 10 Saw a sail to Leward.

[NA.]

Extract from journal of James Pity, U. S. Frigate *Constitution*, 31 August 1798, Friday

First part this 24 hours Steady Breezes ½ past Mern Saw a Sail ahead @ 5 Shortend Sail and fired a gun @ Ye Chace prov'd an English Ship from St. Johns N Brunswick bound to Baltimore 18 Days out Wm Proctor Comr Wore Ship Southward at 7 P. M. Ҡ Ship to the Northd & Westd at Midnight Ҡ Ship to the S. E. @ 6 A. M. Set T. Gallt Sails at 8 A. M. Saw a Schr Standg N. W. abt 2 miles to Windward fired a Gun but she not bearg downward Seeing a Large Sail a head gave her Chace at 9 A. M. Unbent the Main Sail and reduced it by cutting of 2 feet in the wake of the 2d Reef thereby havg the Reef out entirely.

[Latitude observed 39. 32.]

[NDA.]

[About 31 August 1798]

Presumably list of Captain Truxtun's convoy from Hampton Roads

Vessels Names & what rigged	Master's Names	Owner's Names	Owner's Residence	Lading	Where bound	Tonage
Ship ABIGAL	Robert Kean	John Hollins	Baltimore	Dry Goods	Havannah	173 Ton.
Schooner HANNAH	Nathl Ogder	McFadon & Co.	ditto	Flour	ditto	
Brig LOUISA	Thomas Davis	Robt Gilmore & Co	ditto	Flour	ditto.	180
Snow MICHAEL	Wm Weeks	James Barry	ditto	Flour	ditto.	216
Schooner PARK	Wm Creighton	John Hollins	ditto	Flour, Dry Goods &c	ditto.	78.
Schooner CITIZEN	Anthy Daniels	David Stewart & Co	ditto	Flour &c	ditto.	109.
Schooner HOPE	James Benson	Roger & Ownens	ditto	Flour	ditto.	86.
Schooner ARB[?]	Wm Richardson	J. Yellott	ditto	Flour	ditto.	
Schooner MARY	Alexr Huis	Ard Stewart	ditto	Flour	ditto.	99.
Brig SWIFT	Peter Savensen	D. Steward & Sons	ditto	Flour	ditto.	137.
Schooner DISPATCH	M Sawberion	Peter D. Goveots	ditto	Flour dry Goods &c	ditto.	85.
Schooner GREY HOUND	J. Deshields	Gittings & Smith	ditto	Flour	ditto.	78.
Schooner EAGLE	John Davis	Moses Myers	ditto	Flour	ditto.	40.
Schooner DAPHNEL	Joseph Ripley	Jos Donah	Phila	Flour	ditto.	84.
Schooner SYREN	Jarad Arnold	Jno McFadon & Co	Baltimore	"	ditto.	113.

[HS of Pa. NDA photostat. Truxtun's LB. 1798–9.]

To Captain Thomas Truxtun, U. S. Navy, from Secretary of Navy

[TRENTON,]
Navy Department 31st August 1798

Capt Thos TRUXTUN

SIR I am honored with yours of the 24th Instant. It is unfortunate that Capt Philips is so badly prepared for the Expedition. — I hope your Activity & Management, will remove all difficulties.

I will attend to your observations. — I am informed, that the Merchants of Baltimore, particularly James Barry, as well as those at other places, have a good deal of Money at the Havanna, which they are desirous you should receive on board your Frigate, for greater safety. — I have no doubt you will be disposed to do them all the service you can, in this and every other particular, — which will be complying with the wishes of the Government .—

[NDA. OSW, Vol. 1.]

Extract from Captain Thomas Truxtun's journal, U. S. Frigate *Constellation*, at Hampton Roads, 31 August 1798, Friday

Since the 16th Instant up to this Day, we have been employed stopping Leakes; caulking the Ship inside and out; taking in Iron Ballast, and stowing the same; receiving Water, and Provisions; repairing Rigging and Sails, tarring, painting, and putting the Ship in the best possible Order; and now having accomplished all these Objects, and got our Stores on Board, and every Thing ready for Sea . . . . I shall embrace the first Opportunity, when the Wind (which is light, and ahead) comes favourable for getting under way, and proceeding on the Expedition directed by the Secretary of the Navy, taking the *Baltimore* of 24 Guns under my Command, and several Merchantmen (to whom I have issued Signals) provided they can keep up with the Ships of War. John Watson a principal Mutineer on Board of his Britannick Majesty's late Ship *Armoine*, and who entered and went by the Name of Hugh Williams, on Board the *Constellation* being Yesterday discovered, I immediately ordered him in Irons, and dispatched Lieutenant Sterett with him in Charge to Norfolk, there to be delivered to the British Consul, which was done agreeable to Mr Hambleton's Letter to me, in Answer to mine of the above Date.

[HS of Pa. NDA photostat.]

To Nicholas Johnson, Newbury Port, from Secretary of Navy

[TRENTON]
Navy Department 1st Septr 1798

Mr NICHOLAS JOHNSON
Newbury Port

SIR It being necessary that a person of character & Judgment Should be appointed, to act as the agent of the public, in Superintending the Equipment of the Ship building at Newbury Port, by the Patriotic Subscriptions of your Citizens, and as you have already had an agency, as I am informed, with respect to her, and are mentioned in favorable Terms by Mr Bartlett; I request that you will also undertake to Act for the Public. —

I enclose for your Government a List of the Articles, considered as necessary for a Ship of that Force, and it will be desireable, that the whole of them Should be procured by you, except the Powder & Muskets, which will be Supplied from hence. — If however you Should find that there are any other of the articles, contained in the enclosed List, that you cannot furnish, please to Send me an Exact List of them, that they may be Sent to you in time. —

The customary Commission allowed to the Navy Agents in other ports, is two Pr Cent on the amount of Expenditures; and you will charge the same. — With which I hope you will be content; as you will also possess the gratification of rendering Service to your Country at this important period. — — —

It is the more desireable that you Should furnish the whole of the Supplies, as the Situation of Phila & New York, in consequence of the prevailing Fever, will render very uncertain, the obtaining them from either of those places — In order that you may commence your purchases, I have directed a remittance of two thousand Dollars to be Sent to you; and Whenever you require further Sums, you will please to advise me, and they Shall be forwarded. —

[NDA. GLB 1.]

To Colonel Pickering, Secretary of State, from B. Goodhue, Salem

SALEM *1st Septr 1798*

DEAR SIR When I first got home I found there had been a while before a subscription for building a Ship handed about but the amount subscribed being but 15,000$ a sum so inadequate that the matter has been asleep ever since — on enquiring of some Gentlemen how the sum came to be so small, I was told that it was first handed to Mr Derby who put down only $5000 and he being considerd the richest deter'd others from puting down sums which they otherwise would have done, This morning I received yours of 25 Ulto, and have shewn it to Mr Derby and Mr Gray and will shew it to others, the former said he calculated on the cost of a 20 Gun Ship to be $50,000 and estimating his commercial capital to 1/10 of the Town he had subscribed in that proportion — his sons being present observ'd that he was 2/10th of the trade and his subscription ought to have been in that ratio, and from what pass'd I am inclined to beleive he will still come forward at that rate, Mr Gray told me he was deter'd from subscribing more than what he did on account of Mr Derbys not being more but that a Ship we must have and should have and if others did not subscribe a sufficient sum he would, thus the matter is at present I suppose a meeting will be called in a day or two, when I shall be able to give you further information — I have very little doubt from the spirited conversation of Mr Gray who could build such a Ship and not feel it, that a Ship of 20 Nine pounders will be built, in such a case it would be gratifying to the Merchants to have the nomination of the Officers and the public probably be as well or better served and the Crew by that means be much sooner got in this Neighbourhood. — I will write you in a few days more fully after the Gentlemen have had their meeting —

Gerry is worse then even I thought him by his staying in Paris after receiving the instructions of the 23^d of March — and he is yet to learn from Talleyrand the *Ultimate views of France towards this Country.* — I perceive he is to be an infinite vexation to us, for he will come here with some insidious project of Talleyrand mingled with expressions of their diabolical fraternity in order to palsey the measures of our Gov^t and strengthen their party here and he Gerry will be such a dupe or something worse as to favour the project and probably write a Book as many of our worthless public characters have already done — I hope the President will learn a little discretion in future from the very severe mortification he must have from his appointment — the Yellow fever is in Boston and Portsmouth, in the latter worse than the former, and in the lower part of this Town four or five persons have died lately of a fever pretty similar to it — your Friends are well

in haste —

Your affectionate

B. GOODHUE.

Col. PICKERING

[Mass. HS. Pickering Papers, Vol. 23.]

To President John Adams from the Secretary of Navy

[TRENTON,]
Navy Department 1st September 1798

JOHN ADAMS Esqr
President of the United States

SIR The paper N° 1, will exhibit a view of the Ships already in service, and those which are building in different parts of the United States and their Commanders. —

Of the ships building, to which Commanders have not been appointed, those at Newbury Port, Middleton, & Norfolk, are in the greatest forwardness — and are in a situation to require the attention of their Captains — But as Captain Tingey is represented by a great many Gentlemen of Reputation, to be highly qualified for a command in the Navy, and has the appearance of being so, and as Capt Chapman, Commander of the Revenue Cutter from Boston, from the representation of Stephen Higginson Esquire, is a very meritorious man, and well qualified to rank high in the Navy, It appears proper, that these Gentlemen should now be appointed, tho Ships are not immediately ready for them, that they may take Rank of the Captains for Newbury Port, Middleton, & Norfolk, who may be equally meritorious but are not so well known. Capt Sever it is presumed will be called upon to attend the Frigate at Portsmouth, when his present Cruise is over, and Chapman can then take the Command of the *Herald*; and Dale will not go out again in the *Ganges*; but if he continues in service, which I fear is doubtful, will superintend one of the Frigates, which will make a vacancy in the *Ganges* for Tingey —

I have therefore the honor to submit the Gentlemen named in the paper Nº 2, as officers in the Navy; and have enclosed Commissions to be signed, if they meet your approbation — I have added the names of inferior officers, who are immediately wanted for the vessels, to which they are named.

[NDA. Nom. Appts., LB, 1798–1820.]

[Enclosure with letter of 1 September 1798 to President Adams from Secretary of the Navy]

[No. 1.]

SHIPS OF 32 GUNS & UPWARDS IN SERVICE & BUILDING

In Service	Building	by whom building	Commanders
1 UNITED STATES, Frigate	— —	— —	John Barry
1 CONSTITUTION do	— —	— —	Saml Nicholson
1 CONSTELLATION do	— —	— —	Thos Truxton
1 — — —	at Portsmouth	Public	
1 — — —	at New York	Public	Silas Talbot
1 — — —	at Ditto	Citizens	
1 — — —	at Philada	Ditto	
1 — — —	at Norfolk	Public	
8			
1 Wanting —			

SHIPS OF 20 & 24 GUNS, IN SERVICE & BUILDING

In Service	Building	by whom building	Commanders
1 GANGES	— —	— —	Richard Dale
1 DELAWARE	— —	— —	Stephen Decatur
1 MONTEZUMA	— —	— —	Alexr Murray
1 BALTIMORE	— —	— —	Isaac Philips
1 PORTSMOUTH	at Portsmouth	Public	Daniel McNeill
1 — —	at Boston	Citizens	— —
1 MERRIMACK	at Newbury Port	Ditto	Moses Brown
1 GENERAL GREENE	at Newport	Public	Christo Raymd Perry
1 CONNECTICUT	at Middleton	Ditto	Moses Tryon
1 ADAMS	at New York	"	Richd V Morris
1 — —	at Charleston	Citizens	— —
11			
1 Wanting, Measures are taken to get it at Providence —			

SHIPS OF 18 GUNS IN SERVICE & BUILDING

In Service	Building	by whom buildg	Commanders
1 Ship HERALD	— —	— —	James Sever
1 — —	at Baltimore	Citizens	— —
1 — —	at Ditto	Ditto	— —
1 Brig NORFOLK	at Norfolk	Public	Thos Williams
1 " RICHMOND	at Ditto	Citizens	— —
5			
1 Wanting. —			

[NDA. Nom. Appts. LB, 1798–1820.]

Engraved by R.W. Dodson from a drawing by J.B. Longacre, after a Portrait by J. Wood in Peale's Museum New-York.
RICHARD DALE.
U.S.N.

CAPTAIN RICHARD DALE, U. S. NAVY.

Extract from journal of Lieutenant John Mullowny, U. S. Frigate *United States*, 1 September 1798

Light Breezes and clear weather, at 1 Discovered the sail to leeward to be a ship of war, all hands to Quarters, & the ship clear'd for action, at 4 P. M. came up with the chace which proved to be his Bratanic Majesty's Ship *L'Perdrix,* another sail which was to leeward Capt Foye of *L'Perdrix* informed us she was the *L'Scourge* belonging to Great Britain both Sloops of War. on a cruise Capt sent me on board Capt Decatur and from her to go to Tortola in the Prize to see what American vessels and sailors I could collect there.

[NA.]

To Captain Richard Dale, U. S. Navy, from Secretary of Navy

[TRENTON]

Capt RICHd DALE *Navy Department 1st September 1798*

SIR I had the pleasure to write you on the 30th Ultimo; acknowledging the receipt of yours of the 22nd & 28th, since when, yours of the 30th has also been received; Whereby I find that the defect in the main mast of the *Ganges* is so great, as to require its being replaced by a new one; and this being the case, you were right, in directing Mr Humphreys to procure it. — As it will probably be more convenient to Mr Francis to supply the several articles mentioned in your List, than for Mr Humphreys to do it, I have sent him a Copy thereof, and I have no doubt he will procure them as soon as possible.—

I did not direct him to procure the provisions, because it will be time enough, after the other Articles are provided. — You have enclosed, a List of the Monthly pay, to be allowed the Petty officers —

I have written to New York for a Camboose of the dimensions you gave. —

[NDA. OSW, Vol. 1.]

To President John Adams from George Crowninshield and Sons, Salem.

SALEM *1st Septembr 1798*

SIR We had the honor to tender the offer of two very fine, fast sailing Ships to the Secretary of the Navy, on loan, as you will be satisfied by our letter of the 16th August, a Copy of which, with his answer we beg leave to enclose to you, as we fear the Secrety has not rightly understood our meaning. — We had no idea of offering the two Ships for Sale, our intention was, *and still is,* to present them to Government *as a loan,* if they should be deemed worthy the acceptance, the obvious inference is, that we should, in this case, expect to receive "6 pr Cent Stock" in payment. —

We shall be always happy to render every service in our power to our Country, and will not be the last to join in bringing about any measures calculated for its assistance, but Sir it must strike you, as natural enough, that in respect to procuring vessels of force. We as a family, can do no more than we have now offered, and should they not be accepted we as Citizens of the town of Salem, attatched to its honor and general good charecter, shall always regret, that we can not be gratified with the idea of having contributed our mite to the scale of patriotic donations. —

We hope Sir you will pardon the liberty we have taken in this informal application, and as we shall immediately employ the Ships on East India voyages, if they are not accepted, may we still intrude in the request to be indulged with your determination respecting them as soon as you can conveniently. —

We have the honor to be with very great respect
Your Excellency's
Most Obed^{t} & most humble Servt
GEORGE CROWNINSHIELD AND SONS —

To His Excellency JOHN ADAMS
President of the United States

P. S. The bearer Captn Benjn Crowninshield will consider himself honored in answering any questions the President may be pleased to put to him respecting the vessels. —

[NDA photostat.]

Extract from journal of James Pity, U. S. Frigate *Constitution*, 1 September 1798, Saturday

First part this 24 hours Light Winds and Variable all Sails Set in Chace in Chace of a Ship bear^{g} N^{o} & West^{d} appear^{g} to be an Arm'd Vessel. at 2 P. M. call'd all Hands to clear Ship @ 5 Beat to Quarters and Stow'd our hammocks in the Nettings and in the Tops and fill'd our Lockers with Shot. at 3 P. M. Punish'd 3 Men Viz^{t} Dennis Carney, Jno Brown & Richard Sullivan (all Irish) with one Dozen each on the Bare Back for making use of Mutinious Expressions and fighting with the Master at Arms. fired two Guns at a Sch^{r} & Brot her too. She was from Savannah bound to Boston (at 2 P. M.)

[Latitude observed 38°. 35^{m} N^{o}]
Bear^{g} Cape Henery L. 56 W. dist^{ce} 174 Miles.

[NDA.]

Extract from Captain Thomas Truxtun's journal, U. S. Frigate *Constellation*, 1 September 1798, Saturday

At 6 AM made the Signal for the Fleet to get underway, and hove short the Wind being at North North West, but it soon after came to the North Eastward, and light with a strong Tide of Flood, hawlled down the Signal for weighing, and put Service on the Cable in the Hawse. The People employed at scraping, washing, and cleaning the Ship out Side, and in. Several Vessels have arrived from the Leeward Islands, &c. but no News.

[HS of Pa: NDA photostat.]

Extract from journal of James Pity, U. S. Frigate *Constitution*, 2 September 1798, Sunday

First part this 24 hours fresh Breezes. @ 3 P. M. Saw a Sail bear^{g} S. W. gave chace @ 4 A. M. fired a Gun Prov^{d} a Dutch Dogger from St Ubes bound to Baltimore informed us She spoke an English Privateer the day before Several Sail in Sight.

Middle part Fresh Breezes @ 1/2 4 Made Sail wind veer^{g} N. E. haul'd in the W^{r} Brace & sett Light Sails call'd all hands to Prayers @ 11. Saw 2 Sail to Wind^{d} gave Chace to Nearest prov^{d} a Sloop from Savannah bound to Norfolk. Spoke a Brig^{t} from D^{o} place under Danish Col^{rs} bound to Boston.

[Latitude observed 35°. 36^{m} N^{o}]

[NDA.]

Extract from Captain Thomas Truxtun's journal, U. S. Frigate *Constellation*, 2 September 1798, Sunday

Fresh Gales from the East North East, and every Appearance of bad Weather, several Arrivals from various Quarters, but no News, the Pilot Boat passing, and repassing frequently to Norfolk, for the Purpose of keeping our Water filled up. The People employed at various Jobs necessary to keep in Repair the Hull, and Furniture of the Ship.

[HS of Pa. NDA photostat.]

Extract from journal of John Mullowny, U. S. Frigate *United States*, 2 September 1798

Clear. At 1 hove to, off the Harbour of St Thomas — and sent a boat on shore to enquire if any Americans wanted convoy. At 6 the boat returned, some Americans toak passage, lay off and on. At 3 A. M. spoke the Ship *La Perdrix* Capt Fahie mounting 24 Guns belonging to His Britanic Majesty, at 7 A. M. returned to the Ship with Capt Decatur 3 American Seamen came with me from Tortola. Sent the Pinnace to the Shore.

[NA.]

Extract from journal of U. S. Ship *Herald*, Captain James Sever, U. S. Navy, commander, 2 September 1798

This 24 hours Begins modarate gales and heazey Weather under all Saill Before the Wind at 8 p m Saw a Schoner gave Chase found hur to Bee from Boston Bound To Sevannah Left gay Head this morning

Middle part Steady gales and Clear Weather at 12 a m Sounded in 35 fath at 2 p m Sounded in 30 fathoms at 4 in 25 fathoms at 5 a m made a Learge Island Bearing from N W To N n E 6 Leagues Distns hald in N W at 8 am Tact Ship to S E

Latter part Strong gales Saw Ship Standing S W at Mmdn 2 Reeff in Each Top sail

Latt obrs 40..28 N

[NDA. Journal kept by Joseph Strout, 1798.]

To H. W. Desaussure, agent for galleys, Charleston, from Secretary of Navy

[TRENTON,]
Navy Department Septr 3rd 1798

H. W. DESAUSSURE, Esqr
Charleston, S. C.

SIR I am honored with your Letter of the 14th Ult^o, and will in future correspond with Mr Crafts on the Subject of the Galleys and any other business relating to the Navy

The removal of the Public Offices from Philadelphia, and the absence of the President, has occasioned more delay than I had calculated on, in forwarding Commissions for the two Gentlemen So well recommended to command the Gallies — They will assuredly get their Commissions in a few days. —

I take the liberty to enclose the copy of a Letter from the Captain of the *Musquito* British Sloop of War — I have had no communication on the Subject it refers to, from Captn Cochran, or any Gentleman in Charleston — It is a delicate question — but I hope you will answer it, in perfect confidence, that your name Shall never be mentioned, in relation to this business — Is the Statement made by the British Captain tolerably correct? —

I have the honor &c^a

[NDA. OSW, Vol. 2, 1799.]

To Jeremiah Yellott, Navy Agent, Baltimore, from Secretary of Navy

[TRENTON,]
Navy Department 3 Septr 1798.

JER^h YELLOTT Esqr
Baltimore

SIR I am favored with yours of the 29th Ult^o — It was meant in mine of the 27th that the Grape Shot to be Sent to Norfolk, Should be 450 Cannisters; — but if Iron bottoms & Pins can be cast, they will answer as well as Tin Cannisters. — Indeed better; And will come cheaper; and are therefore to be preferred. — Tin Cannisters have been used at Philad^a, because Iron bottoms & Pins could not be had. —

If they can be had with you, it will hardly be necessary to have the Shot put up; as the Gunners can do it on board. —

Pray inform me, whether you can have Hangers, Such as Marines & Sailors will require, made with expedition in Baltimore; and on what terms. — Also Pistols, Proper for Ships; and the price p^r pair. — I give no description of these Articles, because I really am not a Judge; and can find no person here, whose Judgment I would So Soon rely on as yours. — If you can have 200 Hangers (I believe they need not have Scabbards) and one hundred Pairs of Pistols, with proper moulds for Bullets, made expeditiously or purchased, and on terms you Judge reasonable, be So good as to have it done. — I mean over and above those wanted for the *Montezuma*.

I have the honor &c^a.

[NDA. GLB No. 1.]

Extract from journal of Lieutenant John Mullowny, U. S. Frigate *United States*, 3 September 1798

Pleasant weather. at 1 P. M. the Pinnace returned, hoisted her in, bore away and stood through the Sail Rock passage, spoke a shooner from Baltimore. At 7 P. M. the east end of Portorico bore S. W. by W. 6 leagues Dist. — At 6 A. M. Saw the land to the south, found we had fell to Leeward of St Johns hauled our wind & beat up.

[NA.]

Extract from journal of James Pity, U. S. Frigate *Constitution*, 3 September 1798, Monday

First part this 24 Hours fresh Breezes and Hazy weather at Merid^n^ saw 3 Sail a head one of which shew British Col^rs^ Took in Light Sails Stood to Sou^d^ @ ½ p^t^ 2 P. M. came on Squally 2 Reefs in Top Sails. Sent down T. G. Yards. Several Sail in Sight belon^g^ to Havannah Convoy bro^t^ too a Sch^r^ belong^g^ to the fleet bound for N York, call'd the *Return* who inform'd us She Sail'd in C^o^ with 65 Sail under the Convoy of the *Eliza* of Salem and a 16 Gun Ship belon^g^ to Charleston. @ D^o^ wore Ship Spoke a Sch^r^ Saml Gardner Master bound to Phila^a^ Came under D^o^ Convoy @ ½ 5 made Sail after a Ship Leward spoke her call'd the *Hope* of N York She saw but one Cruizer which was British. Latter part light winds with a heavy Sea from E. N. E.

[Latitude observed 34°. 44^m^. N^o^]

[NDA.]

Extract from Captain Thomas Truxtun's journal, U. S. Frigate *Constellation*, 3 September 1798, Monday

Wind and Weather &c. &c. &c. as before. Several Vessels arrived, give an Account of speaking the Havannah Fleet consisting of Seventy five Sail, and that thirteen of them had been taken by British Privateers, and sent to New Providence shortly after coming out, on Suspicion of having Spanish Property on Board.

The Wind being directly in from the Sea, and the Ship drawing Twenty two Feet and a half of Water, the Pilot declares it impracticable to beat out; and unpleasant as it is laying here, I must, under the present Circumstance, wait a Change with as much Patience, as possible.

[HS of Pa. NDA photostat.]

[4 September 1798]

To Secretary Benjamin Stoddert from Captain Thomas Truxtun, U. S. Navy

Sir, I have little to say at present further than to inform you, I have this Moment discharged the Pilot, and shall proceed, as you have directed with the *Baltimore* in Company. Several Days past the Wind has been blowing fresh Easterly, which prevented my Sailing, and now it is so light, that the Ship has hardly Steerage Way.

I am disappointed in not hearing from you, in Reply to my several Letters forwarded, since my Arrival in Hampton Roads.

The Ship has had as good an Overhawl, as the Time, and Circumstances of our Situation would permit, and I hope she will now prove sufficiently tight. I have the Honor to be, Sir, with great Respect,

Your very Obedient Servant

THOMAS TRUXTUN.

UNITED STATES SHIP, *Constellation*
at Sea 4th September 1798 —

Honorable BENJAMIN STODDERT
Secretary of Navy —

N. B. After writing the above I agreed to keep the pilot on board.

T. T.

[HS of Pa. NDA photostat. Truxtun's LB, 1798–9.]

To Captain Isaac Phillips, U. S. Navy, from Captain Thomas Truxtun, U. S. Navy

UNITED STATES SHIP *Constellation*
4th Septr 1798.

SIR, After correcting the Copies of Signals received from the Navy Office, which I delivered you, I now forward those for the Merchantment, annexing the Compass Signals with an Alteration in the Numbers. You will therefore please to return the first Copy delivered you by Mr Sterett. I am, Sir,

Your very Obedient humble Servt

THOMAS TRUXTUN.

ISAAC PHILLIPS Esqr
Commander of the *Baltimore*.

[NS of Pa. NDA photostat. Truxtun's LB, 1798–9.]

Extract from journal of James Pity, U. S. Frigate *Constitution*, 4 September 1798, Tuesday

First part this 24 hours fine Wr a Swell from the Eastward. Saw 2 Sail one a Schooner the other a Ship who appeard Suspicious crowded all sail after them. @ 4 P. M. beat to Quarters ½ past Do came up with the chace fired a Gun but they not heavg too fired another when they brot' too hoisted out our Pinnace and brot' both Captains with Several other Capts that had been taken by the French and their Vessels condemn'd. on examination the Schr provd to be an English Privateer of 10 Guns and 31 Men Jno Newton, Comr from Antigua. The Ship *American* Jno De Sheild Master from St Bart's bound to Baltimore @ 9 P. M. wore Ship Northwd hoisted in the pinnace.

Middle part dark wth Rain.

Latter part Squally. Reeft Top Sails.

[Latitude observed 34°. 32m. No]

[NDA.]

Extract from Captain Thomas Truxtun's journal, U. S. Frigate *Constellation*, 4 September 1798, Tuesday

The Wind shifting to the Westward in the Night, at Day Light I made the Signal for getting underway which was answered by the *Baltimore*, and soon complied with by all the Fleet; at Noon we were abreast of Cape Henry, when the Wind fell so light, the Ship had scarsely Steerage Way, and the Tide of Flood running in strong, we made no Progress in getting out of Pilot Ground.

Several Vessels arrived from the West Indies, and different Ports in the United States, by none of which could I learn any Intelligence of any Importance.

[HS of Pa. NDA photostat.]

Extract from journal of Lieutenant John Mullowny, U. S. Frigate *United States*, 4 September 1798

Moderate & Pleasant Breezes, discoverd three sail standing in for St Johns harbour, lay off and on all night. At 6 A. M. spoke the *Delaware*, sent our boat on board Capt Decatur, saw a sail in the offing, made sail, & spoke a schooner from St Thomas bound to Port Dauphin. At 11 A. M. saw another sail gave chase, all sail set, left the *Sans Periel* with the *Delaware*

[NA.]

To Lieutenant William Bainbridge, U. S. Navy, from Secretary of Navy

[TRENTON,]
Navy Department September 5th 1798

Lieut^t^ Command^t^ Wm BAINBRIDGE

SIR The enclosed is the copy of a Letter I wrote you the 31st ult^o^ —

Mr Fauxhall can supply your Guns this Week; You will take them then, as your carriages are ready. —

Your first cruise will be from Sandy Hook, to Cape Henry, but probably for not more than 30 days — And for such a cruise, I suppose, 60 men will be sufficient in your small vessel. — Indeed from Capt Dale's opinion you cannot find room for more. —

I shall send you orders for your cruise, on Monday next, directed to Philadelphia — I imagine that will be as soon as you are ready. —

Mr Humphreys will advance you some money, to make up the men necessary. —

I am Sir &c^a^

[NDA. OSW, Vol. 1.]

To Major Commandant Burrows, U. S. M. C., from Simon W. Geddes, Marcus Hook

MARCUS HOOK *Septemb^r^ 5th 1798*

DEAR SIR It is with much regret I have to inform you of the death of Searg^t^ Wooley; who had a Severe attack of the yellow fever. I conceived it my duty (tho very much indisposed) to attend upon him; and was present when he expired. I had his Coffin made immediately and I applied to have him interred in the Church burying ground but was refused; upon which I took a detachment and dug his grave in a Gentlemans orchard & procured a prayer Book and read the Customary prayer over him. The Day after I was attacked with the same dreadful disorder — took it in time Dr Rush immediately bled me and gave me mercurial Pills every two hours & the succeeding day fever powders every two hours which effectually conquered the infernal disorder five persons were taken about the same time and was attended by the town Physician — who treated them in a different manner & every one of them died — I feel quite clear of fever; but my mouth, tongue, and throat excessively sore from the salivation occasioned by the Mercury & a general debility— there has been 15 or 20 cases in and about the Neighbourhood & they have all been fatal Doctr Rush thinks he could have saved the Sergt if he had been here. — Be kind enough to detach a Sergt as it is absolutely essential one should be here immediately, as the Corporal is as raw and as unsteady as any of the recruits & I shall not be able to do any kind of duty this three weeks for I shall think myself very fortunate if I recover my strength in that time Sergt Scroub would do very well as he could teach them their duty & would prevent desertion by having a good Non Commissioned in the barracks with them I could return him to you when the Ship Sails if you wished it the *Ganges* will not be ready to sail before November — I feel myself so weak that I must conclude

I am Dear Sir

Your friend & Obedt Servt

SIMON W. GEDDES

I have not touched any kind of Sustenance this four day's but a little barley soup. —

Please to send by the Seargt the articles of War the Size & description Roll of this Detachment for without it any desertion should take place I should not be able to advertize them in the Neighbouring papers —

WILLIAM WARD BURROWS Esqr

Philadelphia.

[MCA. LR, 1798.]

To Major Commandant Burrows, U. S. Marine Corps, from Secretary of Navy

[TRENTON,]

Navy Department 5th September 1798

Major BURROWS of the Marine Corps

SIR I mentioned to you in conversation, the propriety of enlisting only Natives, or the greater proportion of Natives, for the Marine Corps —

It becomes more apparent every day, that but few Foreigners Should be admitted into this Service, if it be possible to obtain Natives —

I must request therefore, that you instruct your recruiting Officers, to take none but Natives or at any rate, not more of Foreigners (I mean the Natives of other Countries, tho naturalized) than in the proportion of one, for every three Natives — It may be impossible to get Natives, but at least we must make the Trial. —

I have the honor to be &c^{a}

[NDA. GLB No. 1.]

Extract from journal of Lieutenant John Mullowny, U. S. Frigate *United States*, 5 September 1798

Pleasant, all sail set in chase of a sloop, at 4 P. M. fired a shot to bring the chase to, fired several in the course of the afternoon and evening at 11 She bro't to all standing. She is a sloop from Guadaloupe, on a cruise commanded by Citoyen Joseph Renne, called the *Jealous* of 8 Guns had thrown 6 overboard a few days, previous to our falling in with her, she was then chased by a british frigate. She took a Sloop belonging to New London with Cattle, bound to Cape Nicola Mole Mr Banning took charge as prize Master. — hauled our wind to beat up. to St John Harbour.

[NA.]

Extract from journal of James Pity, U. S. Frigate *Constitution*, 5 September 1798, Wednesday

First part this 24 hours fresh Breezes and clear @ 4 P. M. Saw the Land of N. Carolina nearest part call'd Ockvikok N. Inlet bear^{g} N. W. b. N. dist. 6 Leagues distance Sounded in 19 fath^{ms} white Sand with brown Shells @ ½ 5 TK Ship Southw^{d} Sounded in 18 fath^{ms} black Specks and white Sand @ 6 Cape Hatteras bore N. W. Dist. 4 Leagues a Current Setting N. E. for which I allow 2 Miles p^{r} hour.

[Latitude observed 34°. 12^{m}. N^{o}]

[NDA.]

Extract from Captain Thomas Truxtun's journal, U. S. Frigate *Constellation*, 5 September 1798, Wednesday

At a little before one PM it being calm, and the Flood Tide with a heavy Swell from the Eastward, set the Ship so fast on towards Cape Henry, that we were obliged to anchor in about 13 Fathoms Water, the Light House bearing South West, Distance near one League; Between 3 & 4 a Breeze having sprung up from the Southward, and the Flood being well spent, got underway, and worked out clear of the middle Ground. At 7 PM the Light on Cape Henry bore West, three Leagues Distance from which I take my Departure. Carried a Light in the Poop Lanthorn.

At three AM reefed Top Sails, and shortened Sail for the *Baltimore* to come up, she being considerably aStern, and the Wind blowing fresh.

At 6 Ditto employed unbending the Cables, and stowing the Anchors; clearing the Ship &c. &c. &c; Eleven Sail (out of 15) of the Merchantmen that came out with us in Sight.

The Latitude of Cape Henry is 36°.57′ North, and Longitude 75°.51′ West from Greenwich in GB.

Latitude observed 35°.50′ N.

Longitude Account 75.13 West

[HS of Pa. NDA photostat.]

Extract from journal of James Pity, U S. Frigate *Constitution*, 6 September 1798, Thursday

First part this 24 hours Clear weather @ 5 P. M. Saw the Shoals of Cape Lookout bearg from N. W. b. N. to West b. N. Distance the Lewardmost part 4 Miles, the Windwardmost Do 5½ Miles. TK'D Ship to the Eastward and Sounded in 15 fms brown Sand with black Specks & Shells. @ 11 P. M. Squally reef'd Top Sails @ Midnight heavy Gales, attended with Thunder Lightning & Rain handed all our Sails except the F. Top Mast Stay Sail and Scud her before it. @ 6 A. M. Set the Jibb and fore Sail @ 9 Saw a Sail out Reef gave chace fired a Gun and bro't her too prov'd the *Nonpariel* fm Wilmington bound to N York

Latter Part Squally Wr

[Latitude observed 34°. 8m. No]

[NDA.]

Extract from Captain Thomas Truxtun's journal, U. S. Frigate *Constellation*, 6 September 1798, Thursday

Fresh Southerly Gales and cloudy Weather with some hard Squalls of Wind, Hail, and Rain; and an Abundance of Lightning, Tho' but little Thunder. Carried a constant Light in the Poop Lanthorn; the *Baltimore* showed a top Light at Times; four of the Fleet still in Company. Set up the Rigging, and repaired several of the Sails, that got a little injured. The Weather still having a threatening Appearance.

Shifted five Tons of Kentledge from out of the Spirit Room, and placed the same in the Fore hold, near the Afterpart of Fore Orlop, the Ship being too much by the Stern.

Latitude Account 36° .00′ North

Longitude Account 73 .09 West

[HS of Pa. NDA photostat.]

Extract from journal of U. S. Ship *Herald*, Captain James Sever, U. S. Navy, commander, 6 September 1798

This 24 hours first Part Clear Weather and pleasant all Sail Sett at 6 p m Montock Pint Bore By Compass North 3 Leagues Distns took in Stearing Sails and Reeft the Topsails hald up the Courses and hald off at 8 pm Sounded in 13 fathoms Light W N W Distns 2 Leagues

Midle Part moderate and Smoth Sea the Light still Bore South allmost Calm

Latter Part Light Breezes and Smoth Sett all Sail By the wind at 11 wore Ship to the Northward

The Brig *Pickering* Still in Company Block Island Bore South 2 Leagues

Latt Obbr 41″ 24 N

[NDA. Journal kept by Joseph Strout, 1798.]

Extract from journal of Lieutenant John Mullowny, U. S. Frigate *United States*, 6 September 1798

Moderate Breezes, the Prize in tow, beating up for St Johns.

[NA.]

To Captain J. W. Leonard, Revenue Cutter *Governor Jay*, from Secretary of the Navy

[TRENTON,]
Navy Department Septr 7th 1798

Capt J. W. LEONARD

SIR I have received your Letter of the 6th Instant and have nominated for surgeon's Mate of your Vessel Doctr Peter Faugues of New York, who is well recommended, and who will, I expect, hold himself in readiness to join you, as soon as he is informed of his nomination.—

In the course of a few days the schooner *Retaliation*, Commanded by Capt Wm Bainbridge will sail, and it is intended, that you shall cruise in Company with this Vessel, which carries 14 Guns. — I shall give the Captain directions accordingly, and you will, I hope meet with one, or both of the privateers you mention — and render a good account of them. —

As the supplying of Vessels with stores, provisions &ca will in future be under the direction of this department, you will of course draw such as you may from time to time require, from the Navy Agents at the different Ports where you may be — At New York James Watson Esqr is the Agent, and will furnish you with the articles that you may stand in need of *there*. —

Capt Bainbridge will sail from the Capes of Delaware, and be directed to seek you off Sandy Hook.

[NDA, OSW, Vol. 1.]

To Lieutenant William Bainbridge, U. S. Navy, from Secretary of the Navy

[TRENTON,]
Navy Department, 7th Septr 1798

Lieutt Commandt
Wm BAINBRIDGE

SIR I have in my late Letters, left it with yourself to determine, whether to go to New York for your remaining Guns, or to take them from Mr Foxall's Works. — If they can now be furnished from the latter, I presume it will occasion less delay to take them from thence, as the Fever prevails in New York, nearly as bad, as in Philadelphia. I mentioned too, Capt Dale's opinion, that you could not find room for 70 men.

I hope you have men enough to justify your proceeding to sea; And under that impression, I now enclose your Instructions. — Also the private signals as directed by Captain Barry, and the private signals to be observed between our Vessels of War, and those of the British Nation. —

Capt Leonard, of the Revenue Cutter *Governor Jay* of 14 Guns, is now, and will be for several days, cruising off Sandy Hook. —

You will proceed as soon as you can to sea, & endeavour to fall in with this vessel, and cruize in Company with her, until early in October. —

On the Tenth day of that Month, you will go with your vessel to the harbour of Norfolk, in Chesapeake Bay, and apply to Wm Pennock at Norfolk, with whom a Letter will be lodged for your future Government. —

In the mean time you will consider your cruising ground to extend from Long Island to Cape Henry, and give to this Extent of Coast, and to our Merchants Vessels, all the protection in your power against the French Cruisers.

You are to keep in mind, that we are at War only with French Vessels, and that the Vessels of all other Nations, are entitled to our civility & Friendship. —

Wishing you Sucess

&c° &c°

[NDA. OSW, Vol. 1.]

To Captain Alexander Murray, U. S. Navy, from Secretary of the Navy

[Trenton,]
Navy Department 7th September 1798

Capt Alexr Murray

Sir I have the honor to acknowledge the rect of yours of the 4th Instant. —

Your requisition of Spy Glasses & Surgical Instruments — I have ordered to be sent from Phila but there are no Blunderbusses to be had. —

The Fever in Phila & New York renders it impossible to get any thing made at either place. —

I enclose you commissions for the following officers

Jno Shaw for the 1st Lieutenant
M Simons Bunbury 2nd — ditto —
Hanson Catlett, Surgeon's Mate
Joseph Richardson — Purser
Richard Thomas } Midshipmen
Rd B. Brent — [Brandt] } Midshipmen

You will find oaths enclosed with the several Commissions, which the officers will take previously to your delivering them their Commissions; and you will be pleased to have all their oaths returned to this office, that they may be regularly filed. —

You are at liberty to engage a Seaman — as Midshipman, whose appointment will be confirmed — I approve of your appointment of Mark Game as Carpenter — The Marines are ordered for Balt° from Phila — Respecting a Clerk you may manage as you please — The only Articles of War, you will find in a pamphlet herewith, entitled "Rules & Regulations for the Navy" —

Will you take a full view of all circumstances, and say when you think the *Montezuma* will be ready to sail from Baltimore on a cruise — I wish this information, that I may make other arrangements respecting the subject of a former Letter. —

[NDA. OSW, Vol. 1.]

Extract from journal of Lieutenant John Mullowny, U. S. Frigate *United States*, 7 September 1798

These 24 hours as the preceeding. A 8 A. M. Capt Decatur came on board. At 11 A. M. bore away St Johns bore S by E ½ E Dist 15 leagues.

[NA.]

Extract from journal of James Pity, U. S. Frigate *Constitution*, 7 September 1798, Friday

First part this 24 hours Steady Breezes Ship in Chace @ 1 P. M. fired at Do @ ½ past 1 Spoke Do prov'd a Schr from Havanna bound to Baltimore out 9 Days. Saw one British Ship hauld our Wind again & Stood Soud

Middle part Light winds. Inclinable to Calm with Lightning. a 2 A. M. Made Sail at 8 K Ship Westwd @ ½ past Do K Ship to Southwd the Master Purser & Lieut examind the Hold & found all in Good Order furld Main Sail & T. Gt Sails in all Light Sails. Sent down Top Gallt Yards. Ends Squally.

No observation.

[NDA.]

Extract from Captain Thomas Truxtun's journal, U. S. Frigate *Constellation*, 7 September 1798, Friday

Cloudy unpleasant Weather. Under an easy Sail regulated to keep Company with the *Baltimore*. Employed repairing of Sails, and Rigging; washing, and cleaning below; exercising Great Guns, and Marines.

Three of the Fleet in Company, that sailed with us; besides the *Baltimore*.

Latitude observed 35°. 21′ North
Longitude Account 72 . 11 West

[HS of Pa. NDA photostat.]

To Captain Thomas Williams, U. S. Navy, in command of Brig *Norfolk*, from Secretary of the Navy

[TRENTON],
Navy Department. 8th Septr 1798.

Capt THOS WILLIAMS

SIR I have delayed forwarding your Instructions for recruiting your Crew; because I wished to send on at the same time, appointments for your officers. —

These I cannot yet send, but expect to do it in two or three days. — A Lieutenant & 20 Marines will be put on board of the Brig *Norfolk* —

Besides these, your Crew must consist of two Lieutenants, two Midshipmen, a Surgeon, Purser, Sailing Master, a Sailing Master's Mate, a Boatswain, Gunner, Carpenter & Cook. — and not exceeding 96 Seamen, ordinary Seamen, & Boys. — In order to create Seamen, as well as because so many will be found useful, you ought to have as many Boys as Guns, if they are to be obtained. — You will proceed then, without delay, to recruit not exceeding 96 Seamen, ordinary Seamen, & Boys. — For the former you may allow 17 Dollars per month; — to the ordinary Seamen 14 Dollars, and boys from 5 to 14 D^s^ per month. —

I say not exceeding 96 Men &c^a^, because I leave it to your own Judgment, to get as good a Crew within that Limitation as may be in your power; at the same time that I consider that number as more than sufficient. — You will find herein the Form of a Shipping Paper, & of a Bond to be signed by the persons who become Sureties for the Money to be advanced; for I take it for granted you will not get men, without two Months advance. — In which case, they must be gratified. — But you will be careful that the persons that persons whom they offer as Sureties, are men of responsibility, and equal to the repayment of the advance, In case the men should run away. — You must be careful to enlist none but healthy people, of good character, — Natives must in every Instance be preferred; and on no account whatever, must Force, or indirect means be used to procure them. —

I inclose you a List of the wages to be allowed to the Petty officers &c^a^ &c^a^ —

All but the Lieutenants, Surgeon, Midshipmen, & Master & Master's Mate, you will appoint, and let me know their names early, that Warrants may be sent them. — I hope you will get your Crew, and have every thing ready by the 5th of October for a Cruise. —

You will apply to Mr William Pennock for one thousand Dollars to begin with —

Lieut^t^ McRea of Alexandria, will I expect, be one of your Lieutenants. —

[NDA. OSW, Vol. 1.]

To Secretary of Treasury from Secretary of Navy

[Trenton,]
Navy Department 8th September 1798

Secret^y^ of the Treasury

Sir In answer to your reference of the Letter from Lane & Salter, I have the honor to inform you that Foxall's Works engaged in casting Cannon for the Navy, will furnish them as fast as they will be wanted for the Navy — I mean as fast as they will be wanted from Pennsylvania.

In most places where Ships are preparing, the Cannon will be obtained in the neighborhood of such places. — Advances have been made to both Foxall, & Lane & Co — I will keep Foxall employed — let the Sec^y^ at War then, who wants more cannon, employ Lane & Co

I am thus particular, that this matter may be perfectly understood.

I have the honor &c^a^

[NDA. Req. on US T, 1798–1803.]

To Josiah Parker from Secretary of Navy

[TRENTON,]
Navy Department 8th September 1798

JOSIAH PARKER Esqr

SIR Mr McRea of Alexandria, has been nominated to the President as Lieutenant in our Navy, to be employed on board the Brig *Norfolk*, Capt Williams — There will be another Lieutenant wanted for that Vessel, Two Midshipmen, a purser, a Sailing Master, and a Sailing Master's Mate — Will you permit me to request the favor of you, to Select proper Characters for these appointments, and to Send me their names without delay? — They ought to be persons who can at once enter upon their duties — It will be desireable that the Captain Should be consulted, as to the appointment of the Sailing Master & Mate — You mentioned in your Letter to the Secy at War, Messrs M. Wright, & W. Davis, in Strong terms for Midshipmen — and thought Mr Wright qualified for an higher appointment —

I presume, but do not know, that a Brig has been bought at Norfolk by the Citizens for the public, to be commanded by Capt Barron — Officers will be wanted for this Vessel also; and I Should be glad to hear from you on the Subject. —

[NDA. GLB 1.]

Extract from journal of James Pity, U. S. Frigate *Constitution*, 8 September 1798, Saturday

First part this 24 Hours fresh Breezes and Squally. Set our Top Sails and Let out one Reef.

Middle part Light Winds with Lightning @ 7 A. M. Saw a Ship a head Looking like a Cruizer Crowded all Sail and beat to Quarters clear'd our Guns fore and aft for Action @ ½ past 11 hoisted our Colrs and fired a Gun to bring her too She hauld up her Courses and hoisted English Colrs She answd with a Gun to Lewd but wd not heave too being within pistol shot the Capt Haild her telling him if he made any Resistance he wd give him no Quarter.

[Latitude 33°. 10m. No]

[NDA.]

Extract from Captain Thomas Truxtun's journal, U. S. Frigate *Constellation*, 8 September 1798, Saturday

Light variable Winds with a Swell from the South East all these Twenty four Hours. Saw several Vessels to the Westward, which I take to be a Part of the Fleet, that came out with us, as they are evidently Merchantmen of their Appearance, and are standing our Course; People employed as before. The same Vessels with us, as mentioned in Yesterday's Transactions. All the light Sails set.

Latitude observed 34° .41′ North
Longitude Account 71.38 West

[HS of Pa. NDA photostat.]

Extract from journal of U. S. Ship *Herald*, Captain James Sever, U. S. Navy, commander, 8 September 1798

This 24 hours first part fresh gales and thick weather at 3 p m Road Island Light House Bore N W B N 2 miles Distns Lying off an on watting for a Boat from Shore at 4 p m the gale Came on Strong from the Eastward Con[c]luded to goo in and anchor at 7 p m Came Tue with Small Bower in 9 fathom Watter paid out 50 fathoms Cable at the Same Time the Brig *Pickring* anchor'd and Road in Company goat Island Bearing East half a mile Rowers Island N N E half mile Distns Brintons Pint S S E one mile Distns at 10 a m Strong gales attended with Sharp Litning and Showers of Rain at 4 a m Calm Latter part fresh gales from S W Clear pleasant Weather all hans Employd in Ships Duty

[NDA. Journal kept by Joseph Strout, 1798.]

Extract from journal of Lieutenant John Mullowny, U. S. Frigate *United States*, 8 September 1798

Pleasant Breezes the *Delaware* and prize a stern, the Sloop prize in tow.

Gave chace to a sail in the N E. she proved to be a Brig of & from Halifax bound to Jamaica

Exercised the crew at the Guns & small arms.

[Long. Obs^{d} 66.51
Lat. Obs^{d} 21″ 48]

[NA.]

To Secretary of the Navy from William Pennock, Navy Agent, Norfolk

NORF^{o} *Septr 9th 1798*

BENJ. STODDERT Esqr

SIR The two last Posts brought me Letters for Capt Truxtun under Blank Covers I should have wrote by last Post but was unwell but am now pretty well recovered — Capt Truxtuns Letter will advise his geting to Sea on Monday where he would have been several days sooner but for Adverse Winds — The *Norfolk* is stowing her Water but she has not an Officer on board but the Captain she ought now to have the whole as nothing will prevent her being ready to drop down on Sunday Week but the want of them & until she gets into Hampton Roads it is of no use ship^{g} Men as they cannot be kept on board. Capt Williams has shewn me yours of 27th Ulto saying that Leiutenants would be appointed but he is at a Loss to know wheather the person he recommended is the Man for his other Officers as * * * he is to Nominate them it will be best sending blank Appointments or Commissions as the whole may not be fill'd up but a few days before she Sails — I am requested by Capt Barron to recommend Capt James Boush of this place as his first Lieutenant & in it I join knowing him to be a Man worthy of trust.

I am yours respectfully

Wm PENNOCK
Naval Agent

[NDA. Area 7, September 9, 1798.]

Extract from journal of U. S. Ship *Herald*, Captain James Sever, U, S. Navy, commander, 9 September 1798

This 24 hours first part fresh gales from the S W and Clear weath[er Lying to anchor in New port harbour all hans Employed in Sundry Jobbs Ships Duty

Midle part fresh gales from S W and Clear Weather five vessells arived here from the hevanah at 6 am Pilot Came on Bord hove Short and Came To Sail and Beat out of the Harbour in Companey with The Brig *Pickring* and 6 other Vessells at 9 am Road Island Light Bore N W B N 1½ mile Distns Discharged the Pilot Lett out all Reefs

Latter Part Clear weather and Smoth Sea all Sail Sett Lattd obrs 41″

[NDA. Journal kept by Joseph Strout, 1798.]

Extract from journal of Lieutenant John Mullowny, U. S. Frigate *United States*, 9 September 1798

A seaman name Cole fell overboard the life buoy was let go by which means he was saved —

Made false fires as signals for the *Delaware* & prize —

[Long. Obs^d^ 67.43
Lat. Obs^d^ 23.46]

[NA.]

Extract from journal of James Pity, U. S. Frigate *Constitution*, 9 September 1798, Sunday

First part this 24 hours fine W^r^

Obliged the Chace to hoist out 2 Boats upon examining her papers had reason to Suspect her being a french Cruizer. Sent Mr Beale, 3^d^ Lieu^t^ on b^d^ & took possession of her She was call'd the *Niger* and Mounted 24 Guns and carried 70 Men a 2 P. M. Remov^d^ the Officers & Crew on B^d^ the frigate and confind the Crew.

Middle part fair prize in Comp^y^ @ 9 A. M. hove too & order'd the prize to hoist out her Boat & send her on B^d^ ye Frigate wth the Command^g^ Officer upon Examining Martin de Rose Seaman on b^d^ the Frigate *Constitution* he made affadavit that the Boatswain of *L'Niger* had taken him in the *Masy* of Portsmouth N. H. plundered him of every thing and carried him into Gaudaloupe.

The Officers & Crew behaving very Improperly observed their Conduct Strictly

Latter part Clear & pleasant.

[Latitude observed 34. 11]

[NDA.]

Extract from Captain Thomas Truxtun's journal, U. S. Frigate *Constellation*, 9 September 1798, Sunday

Light Breezes from West South West, to East North East, and a Swell from the Eastward. Saw a strange Sail at 10 A M in the South East; gave Chace, and at Noon spoke the Brig *Industry* from Jacquemel bound to Portland, out sixteen Days, had seen no french Cruizers, but met several English in the Bight of Leogane. No News.

Bore away after speaking the above Brig, to the Southward, and soon after the *Baltimore* made the Signal for a strange Sail, which we had previously seen, and by her Manuvres found she must be a friendly Merchantman bound Home. Continued on our Course. All the light Sails set, and all the Vessels in Company as before.

Latitude observed 33°.32′ North
Longitude account 71.30 W.

[HS of Pa. NDA photostat.]

To Captain Robert Cochran, Charleston, S. C., from Secretary of Navy

[TRENTON,]
Navy Department 10th Septr 1798.

Capt ROB. COCHRAN *Charleston, S. C.*

SIR I have received your favour of 23rd Ultimo — with its enclosure. — The President being absent, it is not immediately in my power to lay before him your request for a board of enquiry into your conduct, in relation to the affair with the British Sloop of War *Musquito* — This however Shall be done as Soon as circumstances will permit. — But as it would be improper that you Should take the command of an Armed Vessel belonging to the United States, while Suspicions exist against your character, I have desired Capt Cross (lately appointed a Captain in the Navy of the United States) to take the Command of the Brig preparing for public Service at Charleston, & which was intended for you. — — —

[NDA. GLB, No. 1.]

To Lieutenant Saunders of Marines from Captain Thomas Truxtun, U. S. Navy

UNITED STATES SHIP, *Constellation*
10th Septr 1798 —

SIR, It is at all Times very unpleasant to flog Men, if it can in any Way be avoided, and in an infant, and totally unorganized Navy, Ways and Means more mild, should be devised to correct Inattention, Neglect, and other Faults.

I have duly considered the Complaint made against the two Marines under Confinement, and of every Circumstance, that can in any Way tend to promote the Good of the American Navy; but our pecular Situation must be taken into View, and altho' the Crime of sleeping upon Duty, is a very heinous one, we will once more pardon the Offence, and release from Confinement the two Men in Question, on their Promise of not doing the like again; but at the same Time they will receive a Reprimand from you, & be informed that half their Allowance of Rum is to be stopped, untill the first Day of October next ensuing.

I am Sir,
Your Obedient humble Servt —

THOMAS TRUXTUN.

Lieutenant Saunders of Marines —

[HS of Pa. NDA photostat. Truxtun's LB, 1798–9.]

To Captain George Cross, U. S. Navy, from Secretary of the Navy

[TRENTON,]
Navy Department, September 10th 1798

Capt GEORGE CROSS *S. Carolina*

SIR I have the honour to enclose your Commission as Captain in the Navy of the United States; also the form of an Oath, which you will take & return, with your acceptance of the Commission to this Office. —

Captain Cochran has requested that an enquiry might be instituted in relation to his conduct in his affair with the British Sloop of War *Musquito*. —

Whether the President shall determine to gratify his Wishes, or otherwise, it seems improper that while suspicions exist against his character, that he shou'd command an armed vessel of the United States. —

You will therefore please immidiately to take the Command of the Brig fitting out at Charleston for the public service. — I have written Capt Cochran, that you would do so; and presuming that the Brig will be quickly ready for a Cruise; I shall in a day or two send your Instructions accordingly. —

[NDA. OSW, Vol. 1.]

Extract from Captain Thomas Truxtun's journal, U. S. Frigate *Constellation*, 10 September 1798, Monday

Moderate Breezes and fine Weather with some few Squalls of Rain last Evening; took in the Royals before Night, and set them again at Day Light. At 7 AM brought to with a Shot the Brig *Harmony Hall* from North Carolina, bound to Jamaica, out seven Days, and had seen no Cruizers of any Sort.

Employed at Sundries, unbent the old fore Sail, and bent the new One; the three Vessels before mentioned, with the *Baltimore* in Company.

Latitude observed 31°.10′ North
Longitude Account 71.30 W.

[HS of Pa. NDA photostat.]

Extract from journal of U. S. Ship *Herald*, Captain James Sever, U. S. Navy, commander, 10 September 1798

This 24 hours first Part Strong gales and Clear weather at mrdn Nomans Land Bore E B N 1 League Distance from which I take my Departure allowing it to Bee in the Lattd of 41″ 15 North Longitude of 70″ 25 West at 5 p m Saw Two Briggs gave Chace at 7 P m Spoak With them one from New York Bound To hamburg the other from baltimore Bound to New port at 8 P m handed all Light Sails Duble Reeft Topsails Sounded in 35 fathoms watter Blue mud at 10 P m Sounded in 43 Bottom the Same at 10 Sounded in 43 and at 12 a m Sounded in 42 at 2 a m Sounded in 43 on Bent [unbent] Topsails and Bent old Topsails Sounded Severall other times Latter part the Brig *Pickring* in Company

Lattd Obrs 40″ 45 North

[NDA. Journal kept by Joseph Strout, 1798.]

Extract from journal of James Pity, U. S. Frigate *Constitution*, 10 September 1798, Monday

First part this 24 hours fine W^r and Clear @ 3 P. M. Mr Beals went on board the prize & hoisted in the Boat & made Sail. @ 5 P. M. beat to Quarters @ 6 Shortend Sail @ 2 A. M. Shew'd Two Lights and fired a gun Signal for Tacking Ship @ 6 P. M. Saw Cape Hatteras bear^g from West to N. W. Sounded in 45 fath^ms black and White Sand @ ½ past D^o Search'd the Prisoners and found considerable Gold & Silver Money and other articles of value about them @ 10 haild the Prize and Ordered her to Send Mr Parisa a Lieu^t on B^d which was done. Ends Clear.

[Latitude observed 35.16. N^o]

[NDA.]

Extract from journal of Lieutenant John Mullowny, U. S. Navy, U. S. Frigate *United States*, 10 September 1798

Pleasant Breezes
Squally with rain
Clear — & fair —
The *Delaware* in chace to the Eastward
Shifted the Ballast aft — to trim ship. —
[Long. Obs^d 68.25
Lat^d Obs^d 25.22]

[NA.]

Recruiting instructions from the Secretary of the Navy

[TRENTON,]
Navy Depart^t 11th Septr 1798

Recruiting Instructions To Commanders of Gallies Viz^t

LAURENCE A. DORSEY Esqr, WILLIAM M^cKERALL Esqr — *Wilmington North Carolina*
JAMES PAYNE Esqr, SAM^l HEYWARD Esqr — *Charleston South Carolina*
JOHN F. RANDOLPH Esqr, JOHN BRADDOCK Esqr — *Savannah Georgia*

As your name has been transmitted with your recommendations to the President of the United States, I expect you will shortly receive your appointment to the Command of one of the Gallies at ———— and therefore it is necessary that you should begin to recruit a sufficient number of men for your Crew, to consist of 1 Lieutenant, 1 Boatswain, & 25 privates — The men to be enlisted to serve one year.

It being important that those who enlist should feel an Inclination for the service — no indirect means are to be used in inveigle them, and therefore no Individual must be enlisted while in a state of intoxication, nor must he be sworn until 24 hours after signing the enlistment — no Individual is to be enlisted who is not five feet six Inches high without shoes, & above eighteen, & under 40 years of age — He must be healthy, robust & sound, in his Limbs & body — Any recruiting officer enlisting a vagrant, transient person who shall desert, shall reimburse out of his pay, the loss sustained by such desertion. —

The oath shall be as follows;

"I . . . . do solemnly swear to bear true allegiance to the United States of America, and to serve them faithfully against all their Enemies, or opposers whomsoever, and to obey the orders of the President of the United States of America and the orders of the Officers appointed over me according to the Articles of the Navy." —

You will keep a recruiting Book, in which you will record,

1st The name, Trade & description of the Recruit. —

2ndly A Copy of the Oath (original of which to be sent on to this office) taken before the Magistrate — Signed by the Magistrate & recruit. —

3. The money paid to every recruit

You will appoint a Boatswain, informing me his name, that a Warrant may be sent for him.

And out of the 25 men, you will select one for a Drummer, and another for Cook. —

The Pay established for the Gallies is

40	Dolls per mo	& 3 Rations per day to the			Commander
30	do	——	2 — do	————	Lieutenant
20	do	——	2 — do	————	Boatswain
6	do	——	1 — do	————	Seamen

One Dollar per month Extra may be allowed to the Cook, and the same to the Drummer. —

You will give to each man duly enlisted & attested, after being attested, a Bounty of two Dollars.

And you will be allowed, one dollar besides your Pay & Ration, for each man enlisted & attested; — to reimburse the Cost of attesting, & all other expenses. —

[NDA. OSW, Vol. 1.]

Circular from Secretary of the Navy

[TRENTON,]
Navy Department 11th Septr 1798

Circular to Saml Hayward Esqr Charleston (S. C.)
Jas Payne Esqr Ditto—
Jno F. Randolph Esqr
Jno Braddock Esqr Savannah Georgia
In the Letters sent to Jas Payne & Saml Hayward Esqr The first Blank was filled up with the word "Charleston" — & the second Blank with "Charleston Harbour,"

Your name having been mentioned to the President, as Master & Commander of one of the Gallies built at ; and not doubting that you will be so commissioned, I have the honor to request, that you will appoint, to act until the Presidents approbation shall be known, Suitable persons to be your Lieutenant, and Boatswain; & proceed to recruit 25 Privates, one of whom to act as Drummer, one as Cook. —

At foot you have the pay established for the officers & men of the Gallies, which are to be employed for the defence of and you will so employ the one under Your Command; and consider this Letter your Commission for so doing until further orders. —

The third Blank with "William Crafts Esq[r]" The fourth blank with "one hundred D[s]" & The fifth blank with "M[r] Crafts" In the Letters sent to Jn[o] F. Randolph & Jn[o] Braddock Esq[r] The first blank was filled up with the words "In Georgia" The 2nd blank with "the Inlets & Rivers of Georgia" The 3rd blank with "Ebenezer Jackson Esq." The 4th blank with "one hundred" & The 5th blank with "M[r] Jackson"

You will receive herewith recruiting Instructions, which you will please to observe. —

will furnish you with

Dollars for the recruiting service. — He will also take measures for contracting to supply Rations for your Crew. — These will be issued by the Contractor on your return, or in your absence. —

The Return of the Lieutenant, which signed by the person appointed to receive the Provisions, will be the Contractors voucher for settling his accounts. —

You will therefore be very particular, in making your provision — Returns, that the number of Rations required, be stated in writing; — not in figures.

You will see by the Act providing a Naval Armament the rations allowed. —

The privates besides their pay, are to be allowed annually, one complete suit of Clothes; consisting of the following Articles. —

1 Hat, 2 p[r] Woolen overalls, 2 p[r] Linen do.
1 Coat, 1 Vest, 1 Stock of black Leather & Clasp
4 Shirts, 4 p[r] Shoes, and 1 Blankett. —

I have requested, to provide 25 Suits, and to deliver them over to you, for your men, to be given out by you, as they want them. — It will be necessary that you keep an account, of Cloathing so distributed, against each man, and you should exercise your discretion as to the time of distribution, so as to make the Cloathing last the year out. —

You will be charged with the Clothing delivered to you, and credited by your delivery of them to the men, and will be held accountable for any deficiency — For this service you will be allowed five Dollars per month, in addition to your pay as Commander. — You will receive enclosed, Rules & Regulations of the Navy for your Government in all cases where they will apply. —

[NDA. OSW, Vol. 1.]

To Major Commandant Burrows, U. S. M. C., from Secretary of Navy

[Trenton]
Navy Department 11th Sept[r] 1798.

Major Burrows

Sir, The Ship *Montezuma*, Cap[t] Murray at Baltimore, will want quickly, a Lieutenant, and 25 Marines, including non commissioned Officers — and the Brig *Norfolk*, Cap[t] Williams at Norfolk will want 20 under the Command of a Lieutenant, with the proper number of non commissioned Officers. — You will please to Send off these two detachments as early as possible — It will be best to Send the detachment for Norfolk by Land to Baltimore — from whence, a water conveyance can be had, through the means of Jeremiah Yellott Esquire. — And I presume it will be necessary to hire a Waggon to carry their Baggage to Baltimore. They Should draw provisions to last them to that place and the Commanding Officers Should halt their men, a Mile out of Baltimore Town, and call themselves, on Capt Yellott for instructions where to March their men. —

I have the honor &ca

[NDA. GLB No. 1.]

To William Crafts, Navy Agent, Charleston, from Secretary of Navy

[Trenton]

Navy Department 11th September 1798.

Wm Crafts Esqr
Charleston
So: Carolina

Sir I am honored with the receipt of your favors of the 17th & 24th Ultimo. — In my last of the 3rd Instant, I enclosed you a list of the Articles which had been ordered from Philadelphia for the Gallies; and I hope they are arrived. —

I perceive by the estimate you enclose, that the Cost of these Gallies, exceeds the amount of Mr Humphrey's Estimate. — But I hope this additional Cost will be compensated for, in their Strength & Service. —

Four thousand Dollars have been remitted to Mr Desaussure; and I shall direct a further remittance to be made to you of 2808 Dollars, being the Balance of your Estimate — And twelve hundred Dollars for the purposes hereafter mentioned. —

You were right in taking two of the Twelve 24 Pounders for the Gallies — Two of them were also intended to be Sent to Mr Amaziah Jocelin of Wilmington North Carolina — and two, to Ebenezer Jackson Esqr of Savannah in Georgia; for the Gallies building in those places. — You will be pleased to have them Shipped to the address of these Gentlemen as speedily as possible, together with one Cask of Small Grain, & three of large grain powder to each, out of the quantity purchased by Mr Desaussure — It is not in my power to Send on the Commissions for Captains Heyward & Payne — But I have notwithstanding, Sent them Instructions to appoint officers, and recruit men. And as those Gallies will be employed at, and near Charleston, I have to request, that you will contract with Some qualified person, to furnish rations by the day, Week or Month, as the Service they may be employed in, Shall require. —

The price received by the Contractor for the Troops Stationed at Charleston, will be a guide for you. — I mention by the week or month, that as the Gallies may Sometimes be absent from Charleston, the Contractor Shall, not withstanding, Supply them with provisions; by putting enough on board to last until their return, or by furnishing it wherever they are.

The Captain's Provision-Return, or in his absence the return of the Lieutenant, and a receipt upon it, by the person appointed to receive the Rations, to be the voucher for Settling for the rations delivered with the Contractor —

Too much attention cannot be paid, to guard against abuse, in this particular — You will settle with the Contractor monthly, and forward to me, every quarter, ending 30th September, 30th December, 30th March & 30th June, the Accounts and Vouchers. — I shall hereafter write you on the subject of paying the Officers & Men — In the mean time, you will please advance to each of the Captains, one hundred dollars to recruit their Men — The Crew is to consist of —

1 Master & Commander	@ 40 D^s p^r m^o	& 3 Rations p/day		
1 Lieutenant	@ 30	Do.	2	—
1 Boatswain	20		2	Do.
25 privates, out of whom are to be made a Drummer & a Cook @ 1 D. each Extra	6 D^s & 1 Ration			

The privates are to be allowed one Complete suit of Clothes p^r annum; to consist of —

1 Hat, 1 Coat, 1 Vest — 2 p^r Woolen Overalls — 2 p^r Linen do. 4 Shirts 4 p^r Shoes, 1 Stock of black Leather & Clasp — & 1 Blanket } Estimated at about 25 Dollars a suit —

You will please to have 50 Suits provided, and delivered over, 25 Suits to each of the Captains who will deliver them out to the men, as they stand in need of them. —

I enclose you the Act providing a Naval Armament, by which you will see the Rations allowed in the Navy, to which, you will please to conform as nearly as you can, — using however, your own discretion, by Substituting in lieu of such Articles as cannot be procured, others, which your Country will afford; and with which the Officers & Men will be satisfied. —

The Treasury arrangements make it necessary that you should render Separate Accounts — On this subject I must refer you to a Letter which will be written you shortly by William Winder Esqr Accountant of the Navy Department. — — —

I have the honor to be &C^a

[NDA. GLB No. 1.]

Extract from journal of U. S. Ship *Herald*, Captain James Sever, U. S. Navy, commander, 11 September 1798

This 24 hours first part modarate gales Clear weather at 2 p m hald Tue N N W at 3 p m Saw two Ships & 1 Brigg to the Eastward gave Chace at 6 P m spoak the Ship *Newport* from Boston Bound Norfolk the other Ship from Newbury port the Brigg from Salem at 6 p m wore Ship To the N N W handed all our Light Sails Sounded in 38 fathoms watter Sandy Bottom at 11 a m Sounded in 65 Saw a Sail Standing To the S S E at 12. Sounded in 65 fathoms at 4 a m Sounded in 85 fathoms at 6 a m Sett all Sail at 9 a m Sounded in 90 fathoms Soft Blew Clay at 10 a m fresh gales

Latter part Strong gales with flying Clouds under Duble Reef Topsails the Brig *Pickring* in Companey

Latt Obrs 41″ 48 North

[NDA. Journal kept by Joseph Strout, 1798.]

Extract from the journal of Lieutenant James Mullowny, U. S. Frigate United States, 11 September 1798

Light winds & variable, the *Delaware* still in chace The *Delaware* in sight from the mast head bearing East. — Made false fires which was answered by the Sloop. — Lost sight of the *Delaware* and Schooner, prize. — people employed in setting up the rigging.

[Long. Obs^d 68″36]
[Lat^d Obs^d 26″1]

[NA.]

Extract from journal of James Pity, U. S. Frigate, *Constitution*, 11 September 1798, Tuesday

First part this 24 hours fresh breezes & Clear @ 1 sounded 60 fath^{ms} no bottom @ ½ past 3 got ground in 35 fath^{ms} Saw the land bear^{g} S. b. W. Same time Saw 4 Sail to Wind^{d} Middle part sultry with lightning @ 5 Light airs from N. N. W. @ ½ past 9 'K Ship to the No^{d} & West^{d}
employ'd bend^{g} cables & painting the boats.
Latter part moderate & Clear. Ends clear.
[Latitude observed 35°. 53^{m}. N^{o}]

[NDA.]

Extract from Captain Thomas Truxtun's journal, U. S. Frigate *Constellation*, 11 September 1798, Tuesday

The Beginning of this Day a fresh pleasant Breeze. The Middle moderate, and the latter light and squally; took in and set small Sails according to the Weather. The *Baltimore*, and the three other Vessels in their Stations. The People employed as usual, and Nothing further remarkable; or worth Notice in a private Journal.
Latitude observed 29°.21′ North
Longitude Account 71.30 W.

[HS of Pa. NDA photostat.]

To Secretary Benjamin Stoddert from Captain Samuel Nicholson, U. S. Navy

Constitution Hampton Road
Sep^{t} 12th 1798

The Honble Secretary of the Navy

Sir I have the pleasure to inform you that I arrived here Yesterday Even^{g} I have been much retarded in my passage to our Southern boundary, which I was endeavouring to effect agreable to your orders. by contrary winds, Calms, & the chasing, and speaking the great number of vessells; I fell in with at Sea. The Havanna fleet and many others, mostly Americans, when on the 8th Ins^{t} at 6 AM in Latt^{d} 33:10 N^{o} & Long^{d} 74:00 West from London a Man from our Mast Head made a sail steering to the Northw^{d} Westw^{d} We made all sail and gave him chace he then tack'd and stood by the Wind to the S^{o} East we soon perceived him to be a Ship of War. he kept his Ship close by the Wind. ab^{t} 10 AM he tack'd and Stood to the Northw^{d} & Westw^{d} he found we came down on him fast. he then tho't to try us two Points from the Wind, he was still no match for our Ship. he was much decieved in our Ships size. I came close on his beam, *End on* within half gun shot, when I fired a shot over him and hoisted my Collours he then the first time shew me an English Ensign and fired one Gun to Leward, he then kept by the Wind all sail set and endeavour'd to get the wind of us untill we came close on board of him when he haul'd up his Courses and back'd his main top Sail, all hand to Quarters in a very minute and complete manner, as we were also, I had from his manouvering every reason to expect a broad side from him every moment untill my 3^{d} Lieu^{t} Mr Beal was actualy on board of him &

order'd & drove his Men from their Quarters. who were constantly trailing and pointing their Guns into us, as we alter'd our posisions. we were then within pistol shot of each other, and if he had caught me one Instant off our guard I am convinced he would have fired his broadside into us. I hail'd them and was answer'd very Impertinently in broken English by their Boatswain, who seem'd the Commanding person on board. the Capt afterwards appollogised to me on that account, that it was his Boatswain. I order'd them to hoist out their boats and for their Captain to come on board the *Constitution* with his papers, they at first refused I repeated my Request and told them if they offer'd to make Sail or give me any further trouble by attempting to get away I would absolutely fire into them, sink them and give them no Quarters. I was convinced they were pirates. they then sent a small boat with the 2d Capt, a frenchman on board with four men, the Remainder still at their Quarters trailing their Guns. I kept them and sent the boat back with my own people, with orders to send their first Capt and a Boat full of those people, as my officer was not safe in the hands of such a Set, for they had absolutely laid a train of Gun Powder to their Magazine in order to blow up the Ship, their boat and first Capt now came on board, each had the french National Uniform on, they said they were french — Royalists and bound from Jamaica to Philadelphia & had a Commission from the English Government, and a Register and Clearance from Jamaica, all which I believe to be Counterfeits, they have no articles, Shipping paper or Logg book &c. they have I suppose 30 Hhds Sugars & 12 or 15 Hhds Rum on board, the Crew is made up of 7 french officers — Frenchmen — Spaniards 3 English — Portuguese — Italians 1 American — Dutch & — Negroes in all about 75 Men. a British officer and an American Gentleman belonging to Baltimore Passengers. The Ship is called the *Niger* built by the Spanish Government taken by the British and sold at Jamaica 2 or 3 Years since has Quarter Galleries and a scroll head, mounts twenty four nine & twelve pounders built of Cedar and copperd and as completely sound as any Ship of War whatever. they have a great deal of Money on board, & I am Informd a large sum under the Magazine the Crew have their pocketts full. there was a Disburbance amonghst them a few Nights agoe fighting with Knives &c on which I orderd them to be search'd & Deprived of their Knives, Money, Watches &c every one of those People have one or two Trunks American made full of good Cloaths &c which I have no Doubt have been plundered from the Americans. The French Capt was very solicitous on his first coming on board to have his french Boatswain excused being put in Irons, with the Rest of his People but one of my Men named Martin Rose swears that seven months ago he was on board a Schooner from Portsmouth, N. H. bound to the West Indies and was taken by a french Schooner of which this same man was boatswain Stripped Start Naked; and by him carried to Gaudaloupe, we are really put on our guard by these people for of all beings I ever beheld in human Shape I declare I never saw so Impudent and darring a Set of Rascalls, and I have had a great many to take care of in my time. it is my real opinion if they could get an opportunity they would blow our Ship up by way of Revenge. They are fit for and capable of any thing be it ever so Desperate. I have come in with them myself I was really afraid to trust her alone with so many Prisoniers on board knowing the Men, their great Rage and Disappointment notwithstanding every officer is a very active and Dilligent Man. I have no Doubt she will be condemn'd to us Should that be the Case I would Recommend her to the President of the United States as a very fast Sailing Ship mounting completely 24 Guns ready for immediate use and 400 Tons burthen. They have Treated their Passengers in such a brutish manner that they are exasperated with them and are happy in the change, and in my possession. The English Officer is Quarter Master, & pay Master to the 58th Regt on his passage to America with his Lady & 2 Children for their health, whom they have turned out of their Cabin previous to which this officer tells me they had attempted to poison him by giving him Druggs in his Wine. This Ship was certainly cruizing (and is not consigned to any person in Philadelphia) and capturing our American homeward bound East and West India Men. I have no Doubt but different Sets of Papers and various Methods will be made use of when ever any of those people fall into our hands to decieve us they will no doubt endeavour to cover themselves all in their power this we must expect It is certain they cleared from Jamaica and Said they were bound to Philadelphia, but that they ever meant to go there with that Crew, before they had disposed of the greater part of them in Prizes I cannot concieve, or believe at any rate I had a Duty to do wch I tho't oblig'd me to see this Ship into port. She was they say bound to Philadelphia & I have taken care of her and brot' her into Virginia I shall deliver the Prisoniers into the Hands of the Marshall and make no doubt but the District Judge with my Agent under your orders will take the necessary steps to have her Condemn'd to us. I have taken a french Royalist I don't know them. and as I have no orders Respectg such a Nation *or People* I was at no difficulty in my own Mind at taking possession and sending them into port for the examination & decision of our Government on this head, and what those people are to shew for Collours. they had English & National Collrs both bent, when my officer boarded them, it appears to us they sailed from port Royal, to port Antonio, with a few hands on board, and in the Night they saild from port Antonio, on this Voyage or Cruize. This mixed unprincipaled, Set of People came, on board I suppose by assistance, in breaking Goal, and to go off in this Ship. the English Sailors are deserters from Men of War, this appears to me evident as they had neither Articles, Logg Book, or any thing else, as other Nations at Sea are by Law accustomed too. they could not stay at Jamaica, on acct of the Inclos'd Proclamation of that Govt I am Informed that the Revenue Cutter, is gone to Sea from this place with your Dispatches for me. In that case I shall wait here, till I receive your orders, as it is uncertain when the Cutter will return. in the mean time I will fill up my Water, and prepare for Sea, at the shortest Notice.

I have the Honor to be Sir
Your Obedient Servant

(signed) SAM. NICHOLSON

P. S. We have but two people that are unwell on board and they are Recovering fast I have taken them quite unawares here as they have not any place to Receive the Prisioners but they will be landed in the fort in Two or three Days when the Commandg officer will Reciept for them as prisioners of War. and they are now making preparations to Recieve them. We are put to great difficulty & expence here on account of the public officers that will have to libel and arrange the business for the Condemnation of Prizes, in the admiralty Courts residing at a great distance

Norfolk Sept 14. 1798 Capt Bright in the Revenue Schooner from this place is this Moment come into the House from the Sea, where he spoke a Pilot Boat, that Informed him the *Constitution* was gone for Norfolk, he has no Letter for me, and has shewn me his Orders. we shall now fill our Water up as fast as possible, and proceed to Sea agreeable to former Orders, recd at Newport.

This letter will now go by the common mail

I have the Honor to be with Respect

Your obedt Hbe Servt

(signed) Sam. Nicholson

[NDA photostat.]

To Ameziah Jocelin, agent, Wilmington, N. C., from Secretary of Navy

[Trenton,]
Navy Department September 12th 1798

Ameziah Jocelin Esqr
Wilmington N. Carolina

Sir I have received from the Secretary of the Treasury of the 28th June, 12th July and 20th August, by which I am informed of the progress that has been made in the building of the Gallies. —

The Secretary at War, sent some 24 pound Cannon for Charleston, in May last; and I have requested William Crafts Esqr of that place, to forward two of them on to you, if not before done; and I have ordered to be sent from Philadelphia the articles mentioned at foot; — Howitzers are not to be had; and the situation of the principal Towns in this Quarter, renders it impossible to have them made; so that you must manage as well as you can with the Articles sent you. —

It would have been agreeable, if you had mentioned in your Letters, proper Characters to command these Gallies — I have named to the President, Capt William McKerall – & Lawrence A. Dorsey, whom I have no doubt will be appointed, and I have written them to recruit men, & to make temporary Appointments of a Lieutenant & Boatswain; each, to act until the President shall determine to Commission them, or to appoint others =

I request that you will write to me fully & freely, the characters of these Gentlemen and of the Officers they select; — and that you will as freely mention others, better qualified for Commissions, under the fullest confidence that your name will never be used, to subject you to any inconvenience. —

I have now to request that you will contract with some qualified person to furnish rations for the Crews of the Gallies by the day, week or month, as the service they may be employed in shall require, —

The Terms allowed to the Contractors for supplying the Troops at your place may be some guide to you — I mention by the week or month, that as the Gallies may sometimes be absent from Wilmington, the Contractors shall notwithstanding, supply them with Provisions, by putting enough on board to last, until their return, or by furnishing it wherever they are — The Captain's provision-return or in his absence, the return of the Lieutenant and a receipt upon it, by the person appointed to receive the rations, to be the Voucher for settling for the Rations delivered with the Contractor. —

Too much attention cannot be paid to guard against abuse in this particular — You will settle with the Contractor monthly and forward to me every quarter, ending 30th September, 30th December, 30th March & 30th June the Accounts & Vouchers.

I enclose you the Act establishing a Naval Armament, by which you will see the rations allowed in the Navy, to which you will please conform as nearly as you can; using however your own discretion by substituting in lieu of such Articles as cannot be procured, others which your Country will afford, and with which the officers & men will be satisfied — — —

I Shall hereafter write you on the Subject of paying the officers & Men In the mean time, you will please advance to each of the Captains, one hundred Dollars to recruit their Men. — —

The Crew is to consist of—

1 Master & Commander at	40 D^s p/m^o	& 3 rations p^r	day.
1 Lieutenant	30 "	& 2	do
1 Boatswain	20 "	& 2	do
25 privates—out of whom are to be made a drummer @ a Dollar each Extra p^r mo	6	& 1	do

The privates are to be allowed, one compleat Suit of Clothes, p^r annum, to consist of,

1 Hatt, 1 Coat, 1 Vest 2 p^r woolen Overalls 2 p^r Linen Ditto — 4 Shirts, 4 p. Shoes — 1 Stock of Black Leather & Clasp — & 1 Blanket	Estimated to cost about 25 Dollars

You will please to have 50 Suits provided, & delivered over — 25 Suits to each Captain, who will deliver them out to the men, as they Stand in need of them. The Treasury arrangements make it necessary that you Should render Seperate Accounts — On this Subject I must refer you to a Letter which will be written you Shortly by Wm Winder Esqr Accountant of the Navy Department. — I have requested the Sec^{ry} of the Treasury to remit you $3,000.

[NDA. GLB No. 1.]

To Ebenezer Jackson, Navy Agent, Savannah, from Secretary of Navy

[TRENTON,]
Navy Department September 12th 1798

EBENEZER JACKSON Esqr
Savannah

SIR I had the honor to write you yesterday, and have now to request that you will contract with some qualified person to furnish rations for the Crews of the Gallies, by the day, week, or Month, as the service they may be employed in shall require. — I mention by the Week or Month that as the Gallies may sometimes be absent from Savannah, the Contractors shall notwithstanding Supply them with provisions, by putting enough on board to last until their return, or by furnishing it wherever they are. — The Captain's provision-Return, or in his absence the return of the Lieutenant, and a receipt upon it by the person appointed to receive the Rations, to be the Voucher for settling for the Rations delivered with the Contractor. — Too much attention cannot be paid to guard against abuse in this particular —

You will settle with the Contractor Monthly and forward to me every quarter, ending 30th Septr 30th December, 30th March, & 30th June, the accounts & Vouchers. — I enclose you the act establishing a Naval Armament; by which you will see the rations allowed in the Navy, to which you will please conform as nearly as you can, using however your own discretion, by substituting in lieu of such Articles as cannot be procured. — others which your Country will afford, and with which the Officers & Men will be satisfied. — I shall hereafter write you on the subject of paying the officers & men — In the mean time you will please advance to each of the Captains one hundred Dollars to recruit their men. — The Crew is to consist of,

1 Master & Commander at 40 Dolls pr Mo. & 3 Rations
1 Lieutenant — @ 30 do — & 2 Ditto
1 Boatswain — @ 20 do — & 2 Ditto
25 Privates (out of whom are to be made a drummer & Cook at a Dollar extra Each} 6 Drs pr mo & 1 Ration

The Privates are to be allowed, one complete suit of Clothes per annum to consist of

1 Coat, 1 Hat, 1 Vest, 2 pr Woolen overalls, 2 pr Linen do, 4 Shirts, 4 Pr Shoes — 1 stock of black Leather & Clasp — 1 Blankett} Estimated to Cost about 25 Dollars —

You will please to have 50 Suits provided and delivered over, 25 Suits to each of the Captains who will deliver them out to the men, as they stand in need of them. — The Treasury arrangements make it necessary that you should render separate accounts — On this subject I refer you to a Letter which will be written to you shortly, by William Winder Esquire, Accountant of the Navy Department. —

Instead of the Two thousand, five hundred Dollars mentioned in my Letter of yesterday, I have requested the Secretary of the Treasury to remit you four thousand Dollars. —

I observe by your Letters to the Secretary of the Treasury, that this Agency for the Gallies, is not an agreeable business to you; but I know not who else to call upon to execute the duties required in this Letter; and I hope you will continue to Act, at least untill you name some person to me who may be confided in. —

You will please to procure one such boat as you recommend for each Galley, to row with 10 or 12 Oars, and a 4 or 6 pound Gun to be fixed in the Bow — The Guns you must also procure —

When the Boats are obtained, I presume it will be necessary to increase the number of men —

I have the honor &c

[NDA. GLB, No. 1.]

To Captain Alexander Murray, U. S. Navy, from Secretary of the Navy

[TRENTON,]
Navy Department 12th September 1798

Capt ALEXr MURRAY

SIR Agreeably to your request, I send you herewith a List of the monthly pay of Petty Officers, Seamen &ca — Since the date of the list sent Capt Truxton, (which is prior to the one sent you) a considerable alteration in the Pay was conceived to be expedient, & consequently adopted. — The two Lists therefore *should* disagree.

The one sent you however, is the latest, & you will govern yourself accordingly. — Your signal Flag must be a green Flag. —

I approve of the men whom you have nominated to the appointment of Sailing Master — Boatswain, & Carpenter, to Wit; Robert Wells for Sailing Master — John Frazier for Boatswain, and Mark Game for Carpenter — You will receive them on board in the Stations to which you have respectively recommended them. — I will nominate them to the President; and have no doubt but they will be confirmed in their respective offices. — Mr Calder is intended for a Midshipman on board the *Montezuma* — You will therefore receive him in that capacity. —

You may also receive Mr Michael Carroll as a Midshipman on board of your Vessel — The former is already appointed — The Latter I will nominate to the President for his approbation. —

Mr Geoffrey Dillon Shanly is nominated to the President as Surgeon of the *Montezuma*. — I have not yet received your nomination to the appointment of Sail Maker and Gunner. — Be pleased to select proper characters, and mention them to me as early as you can. —

A list of Private Signals &ca shall be sent in due time. —

Pay & Subsistence of Officers, Petty Officers &ca — . —

Commander	75	Dolls per mo	& 6	Rations
Lieutenants	40	" do	& 3	Ditto
Surgeons	50	" do	2	Ditto
Surgeon's Mate	30	Dolls per mo	& 2	Rations
Pursers	40	" do	& 2	Ditto
Sailing Master	40	do	2	Ditto
Masters Mates	20	do	1	Ditto
Captain's Clerk	25	do	1	Ditto
Midshipmen	19	do	1	Ditto
Boatswain	20	do	1	Ditto
Gunner	20	do	1	Ditto
Carpenter	20	do	1	Ditto
Cook	18	do	1	Ditto
Sail Maker	20	do	2	Ditto
Steward	18	do	1	Ditto
Cooper	18	do	1	Ditto
Boatswain's Mate	18	do	1	Ditto
Gunners Mates	18	do	1	Ditto
Carpenters Mates	18	do	1	Ditto
Master at Arms	18	do	1	Ditto
Quarter Gunners	17	do	1	Ditto
Armourer	18	do	1	Ditto
Able Seamen	17	do	1	Ditto

[NDA. OSW, Vol. 1.]

[12 September, 1798]

Captain Gay's account of the capture of the Schooner *Liberty*

Norfolk, Nov. 3.

Capt. Gay arrived here on Wednesday from Antigua, has handed us the following account of his capture by the French.

I sailed from Norfolk on the 29th July last, as captain of the schooner *Liberty*, bound to Barbadoes. On the 12th Sept. in lat. 13, 3, long.

58, was captured by a French schooner privateer of 12 guns, and sent into Guadaloupe; vessel and cargo condemned, and all hands thrown into prison, where I should also have got a birth, were it not for the humanity of an inhabitant who concealed me in his house until I got an opportunity of making my escape, which I did on the 17th of the same month, destitute of every article of cloathing, &c. in company with a captain Daymond, belonging to Portsmouth, N. E. and got to the island of Antigua on the 20th, where I luckily met with a friend, mr. John Taylor, of said island, who rendered me every assistance, and supplied me with cloaths and money.

From every information capt. Gay could obtain, he says. there were a great many American captains and supercargoes prisoners in Guadaloupe, among whom was capt. Crandon, of Wiscasset, N. E. Who formerly commanded the United States brig, which brought captain O'Brien from his captivity in Algiers.

The Americans carried into Guadaloupe are put in irons and thrown into prison, as Victor Hugue's looks upon this country to be in actual war with the "great nation," France.

[LC, "Claypoole's American Daily Advertiser" (Phila.), 13 November 1798.]

Extract from journal of James Pity, U. S. Frigate *Constitution*, 12 September 1798, Wednesday

First part this 24 hours Light Airs and pleasant @ 6 P. M. hoisted a Sweedish Jack @ M. T. head & cleard Ship for action @ 8 in Light Sails & back M. T. sail try'd for Sound^{gs} all Night no bottom @ 2 A. M. Saw a Sail on the lee bow. @ 5 Saw a Sail to ye Eastw^{d} & one to the Westw^{d} Spoke a pilot from patomack Sounded in 37 fath^{ms}. @ 9 D^{o} in 25 fathm^{s} @ 10 in Light Sails Double Reeft Top Sails Weather very Squally. ½ past 10 pilot boat came a Long Side and put a pilot on Board of us.

Latter part fresh Breezes.

Ends in Clear Weather.

[Latitude observed 37°. 01^{m}. N^{o}]

Remarks. Sep^{t} 12. Continued

Fresh breezes and fair Weather, prize in Company. @ 3 P.M. bent thick cable Set Steer^{g} Sails & got Ready for Anchor^{g} @ 5 P. M. Anchor'd with the Small bower veerd away the Short Service. Willougby's point bear^{g} E. ½N. old point Comfort N. E. ½ N. Sewals point S. b. E. distant from the Southern point 4 Miles @ ½ past 6 Sent down T. G^{t} yards & prepar'd for Mooring Ship @ 8 Set the Watch weather Moderate Ship at Single Anchor.

[NDA.]

Extract from Captain Thomas Truxtun's journal, U. S. Frigate *Constellation*, 12 September 1798, Wednesday

Moderate Breezes, and very squally disagreeable weather all these 24 Hours. At 5 A M saw two Sail in the North East, gave Chase, and at 10 A M spoke the British Brig *Harliquin*, Benjamin Stiles, Master, mounting 10 Guns, and carrying 26 Men, loaded with Rum and Sugar, from Barbadoes, bound to Baltimore, in Company with the Ship *General Smallwood*, (American) from the same Place, bound to Alexandria, Johnson, Master. The *Marliquin* informed, that the

Frigate *United States*, and *Delaware* were in Barbadoes. Vessels in Company as before. Fell overboard and was drown, John Cole, a Seaman. Nothing further remarkable.

Latitude observed 28°.26′ North.
Longitude Account 71°.42 W.

[HS of Pa. NDA photostat.]

Extract from journal of Lieutenant John Mullowny, U. S. Frigate *United States*, 12 September 1798

Light winds. —
A sail in sight bearing N W distance 5 or 6 leagues
Squally, with heavy rain, lighting and thunder. —
The Sloop's tow rope parted —

[Long. Obs^{d} 69.15]
[Lat^{d} Obs^{d} 27.13]

[NA.]

To Thomas Pinckney, Charleston, S. C., from Secretary of Navy

[TRENTON,]
Navy Department 13th September 1798

THO^{s} PINCKNEY Esqr *Charleston S. C.*

SIR, I have the honour to enclose the Copy of a Letter from the Captain of the British Sloop of War, *Musquito*, in relation to the disgraceful affair between him, & Captain Cochran. — A publication of Capt Cochran's Officers, cut out of a Charleston paper, and enclosed to me, by him, does not place the transaction in a light more honorable for Capt Cochran; nor does the late mutiny of his men, of which I have received information from himself only, tend to raise his Character. —

Under such Impressions, I have felt it my duty to direct that Capt Cross lately appointed a Captain in the Navy, should take Command of the Brig preparing for Capt Cochran — — — But it would give me pain to injure a man of Merit — and of Capt Cochran I know nothing, except the Circumstances alluded to, nor is it possible to get information here, of his true Character. — — Will you then Sir, permit me the Liberty of Soliciting his Character from you? — It will be my duty to consider as entirely confidential, any information on this subject, with which you may be so good as to favor me. — — —

[NDA. GLB No. 1.]

To Messrs. Thomas Morris, Henry Laurens, William Crafts, and A. Tunno, Charleston, S. C., from Secretary of Navy

[TRENTON,]
Navy Department 13 September 1798.

THO^{s} MORRIS
HENRY LAURENS
WILLIAM CRAFTS
A TUNNO
} Esq^{r}s. Charleston S. Carolina

GENTLEMEN: I am honoured with your Letter of the 21st Ult^{o} — Having in my Letter of the 23rd Augt anticipated most of the information required in your letter now before me, I have only at present to say, that the President will accept with pleasure, of the Vessel proposed to be built under your direction of the burthen of 550 Tons, or thereabouts, and constructed to carry 20—22, or 24 Guns on one Deck, the same to be accepted in a state suitable to be armed and without the necessary War equipments, and on the Terms of the Act of Congress of the 30th June 1798 — The subscribers for building the said ship to be paid in stock of the United States, bearing an Interest of 6 pr Cent.

Referring to my Letter of the 23rd Ultimo to William Crafts Esquire for other particulars —

I have the honor to be &ca

[NDA. GLB No. 1.]

To Secretary of War from Secretary of Navy

[TRENTON,]
Navy Department September 13th 1798

SECY of WAR

SIR, Mr. Humphreys represents to me that two of the Cutters cannot proceed to Sea, for want of some Cutlasses, Pistols, Flints & Powder; tho wanting nothing else, and that in the present calamitous situation of Philadelphia, there is no probability of getting these articles, except from the military Store. —

I have the honor therefore to request that you will be pleased to send me an order on Mr. Hodgdon, or Mr. Harris, to furnish on the return of Mr. Humphreys any quantity of the above mentioned articles he may require to fit out the *Eagle & Diligence*, Two Revenue Cutters — It is not probably Mr. Humphreys will call for more of these articles than necessary and it is not possible for me to ascertain the quantity wanted. —

I have the honor to be
&c &c &ca

[NDA. Sec War LB, 1798–1824.]

Extract from journal of U. S. Ship *Herald*, Captain James Sever, U. S. Navy, commander, 13 September 1798

This 24 hours first part allmost Calm & flatening weather gott up Cables on Deck To Dry at 2 p m Saw a Brig in the N W all hans to quarters all hans Employd in Sundry Jobbs Ships Duty at 7 p m Litens from the S W ward

Midle part modrate and pleasant under Two Reef Topsails

Latter part modarate gales and fair weather Nothing Remarkable the Brig *Pickring* Still in Companey

Lattd Obbrs 42″ 33 North

[NDA. Journal kept by Joseph Strout, 1798.]

Extract from journal of James Pity, U. S. Frigate *Constitution*, 13 September 1798, Thursday

Light airs & fair Weather fired the Morng Gun @ 6 Weighed the Small bower & let go the best bower Anchor & moor'd Ship @ 8

A. M. hoisted out the pinnace Answer'd a Salute from an Arm'd Schooner. Capt Nicholson & 2 Officer went on board the prize & from thence to Norfolk. Capt Abrams came on boad for the Surgeon to visit one of his crew that was hurt by a fall. Fired the Eveng Gun & Set the Watch.

[NDA.]

Extract from journal of Lieutenant John Mullowny, U. S. Frigate *United States*, 13 September 1798

Light winds
Took the sloop in tow. —
Exercised the crew at the great Guns and small arms
[Long. Obsd 69.42
Latd Obsd 28.13]

[NA.]

Extract from Captain Thomas Truxtun's journal, U. S. Frigate *Constellation*, 13 September 1798, Thursday

Light Winds, and variable all these Twenty four Hours with a Swell from the South East. Made and shortened Sail according to the Weather, and sailing of the *Baltimore*, for which Ship we lossed much Way.

Employed repairing Rigging and Sails; making Spun Yarn, Sennet &c. &c. &c.

Latitude observed 27°.40′ North
Longitude Account 72.00 W.

[HS of Pa. NDA photostat.]

Presumably to Rufus King, United States Minister, London, from United States Consul Elias VanderHorst

BRISTOL *Sepr 14th 1798.*

DEAR SIR. Since my last of the 5 Inst. I have not had the pleasure of hearing from you. —

The American Ship *Foxwell*, Capt Stephens, Mounting 20 Guns (4 & 6 pounders) with 30 Men will, the Capt assures me, be ready to Sail hence for Boston, at farthest, by the 25th of this Month — the Only Vessel besides now here, bound to that quarter is the Brig *Pallas*, Capt Collins, which I expect will be ready to Sail for Charleston in about 3 or 4 Weeks from this time — She is a small Vessel and the Capt tells me will be armed.

The American Ship *Hannah*, Capt Morland, arrived here yesterday from Virginia† with Tobacco. I cannot learn that she brings any thing Interestg

I have procured some News Papers from the Capt up to the 31st of July which I shall forward to you by the Mail Coach today. I remain with great truth

Dear Sir,
Yours very Sincerely

ELIAS VANDERHORST

† In 35 Days.

[SDA, Bristol, Vol. 1, 1791–1799.]

To Lieutenant William Bainbridge, U. S. Navy, from Secretary of the Navy

[TRENTON,]
Navy Department September 14th 1798

Lieut Commandt
Wm BAINBRIDGE
Marcus Hook

SIR Instead of pursuing strictly my former Instructions, you will please convoy off the Coast, the Ship *Pigon*, now ready for Sea

And then endeavour to fall in with Capt Leonard, and govern yourself by my former Instructions. —

P. S. If the Ship is not ready, your are not to wait for her. —

I am &ca

[NDA. OSW, Vol. 1.]

To William Pennock, Navy Agent, Norfolk, from Secretary of Navy

[TRENTON,]
Navy Department September 14th 1798

Wm PENNOCK Esqr
Norfolk

In the present situation of Philadelphia, it is impossible to get any thing shipped from thence; I therefore request that you will cause to be procured 25 suits of Marine Cloathing for the use of the Marines to be raised for the Brigantine *Norfolk* — —

The suit will consist of,

1 Coat, 1 Hat, 1 Vest —
2 pr Woolen Overalls
2 pair Shoes —
1 Black leather stock & Clasp
} Supposed in the Estimates to Congress to Cost about 20 Ds
1 Blanket —

The Coat to be short blue Cloth, with a red Belt, edged with red, and turned up with the same, with common small naval Buttons — The overalls Blue, edged with red — & red Vests — These articles you will please deliver to Lieut Wm Cammock; who will give you a receipt for them, which will by your Voucher on the settlement of your Account. — — — I write to him by this conveyance. — —

P. S. Lieutenant Cammock can if necessary be Supplied with Arms out of those formerly sent you. —

[NDA. GLB, No. 1.]

To Secretary of the Navy from Major Commandant Marine Corps

MARINE CAMP, *14th Sept. 1798*

SIR The Detachment for Baltimore will march tomorrow at 12 O'Clock —

The Officers who have been order'd upon these different Detachments have express'd uneasiness at going to Sea without a Commission. I wish Commissions could be sent for all Officers that are appointed. I shall send out this day a recruiting party to German Town in hopes to reinforce my Camp, for tomorrow I shall be left with about five Men — I have the honor to be

Your ob[t] &c

W. W. B. [William Ward Burrows]

Benj[n] Stoddert Esq[r]
Secret[y] of the Navy.

[MCA. LS, 1798–1799.]

To Captain Thomas Williams, U. S. Navy, of the Brig *Norfolk*, from Secretary of the Navy

[Trenton,]
Navy Departm[t] 14 Sep[t] 1798.

Cap[t] Tho[s] Williams.
Norfolk

Sir, I have named M[r] M[c]Rea of Alex[a] to the President, to be your first Lieut[t], and have written to M[r] M[c]Rea to repair to Norfolk, & put himself under your command. With His Assistance, I hope you will soon get your Men.

I have already written to you, to select fit Persons for certain Stations on board your Brig. I had before written to another Gentleman on the subject of your higher officers — but it is probable I may not hear from him in Time. — I request then that you will look out for proper Characters to fill these Appointments; if Col[o] Parker should be in Norfolk, consult him on the subject — shew him this Letter — and if he agrees in opinion with you, as to the characters, you may receive them on board — to act until the President's Pleasure be known — which cannot be, before you sail on a cruise, as he is at a distance from hence — There can be no doubt — that he will approve — and that the Gentlemen will be commissioned — and they must act in the first Instance on my Appointment. They will be entitled to all the Emoluments &[c] as if they had Commissions. The officers about whom I have written to another Gentleman, are

1. Lieutenant
2. Midshipmen
1. Purser
1. Sailing Master
1 Sailing Masters Mate; also
A Surgeon, must be fixed on for the first Cruise.

I shall make arrangements for the Brig, on the Presumption that she will be ready to proceed on a cruise by the 5th of Oct[r]. It will be important that I should not be disappointed in this. —

[NDA. OSW, Vol. 1.]

To Joshua Humphreys, Naval Constructor, from Secretary of Navy

[Trenton,]
Navy Department 14th August 1798

Joshua Humphreys Esq[r]

Sir I have your Letter of the 12th Ins[t] Col[o] Pickering agrees that 6# Shot, or any thing wanting for the Cutters &C[a] may be taken from the Algerine Vessels — pray so order it. — And pray let Captain's Campbell & Brown wait for nothing — I want Brown to carry Arms &C[a] to Carolina & Georgia — & Campbell to be at Norfolk by the 1st of October. — — —

[NDA. GLB No. 1.]

To Secretary of War from Secretary of Navy

[TRENTON,]
Navy Department 14th September 1798

The SEC[y] AT WAR

SIR Sick sailors have been left at Newport Rhode Island, and at Norfolk — and will in future, probably be left at New York, Boston & Philadelphia. —

In the instances which have occurred they have been boarded, & Doctors have been employed to attend them. — This is attended with considerable expense; nor does it seem to promise, any certainty, that the man on recovery, will not be lost to the Service. —

Can you assist me with any arrangements through the means of your Troops & Surgeons Stationed at any of these places? —

[NDA. Sec War LB, 1798–1824.]

Extract from journal of Lieutenant John Mullowny, U. S. Frigate *United States*, 14 September 1798

Light Breezes & Clear weather. 2 sail in sight — bearing S S W.
Squally with rain —
Fresh gales parted with the Sloop — at 3 lost sight of the Sloop
Stiff gales with rain. —
Split the jib.
[Long. Obs[d] 70.47]
[Lat. Obs[d] 30.10]

[NA.]

Extract from journal of James Pity, U. S. Frigate *Constitution*, 14 September 1798, Friday

Begins pleasant & calm. fired the Morn[g] Gun wash'd decks & loos'd Sails to Dry @ 5 the Revenue Cutter came too in the Road @ 6 The Ship *Delight* from Cedar Point Sent her boad Requested a Coffin to be made for the Cap[t] Dec[d] examined the Prisoners found several had got their Irons off. Secured them all. got a New Messenger fitted it the old one being too small. Several Vessels pass[d] bound to different ports.

[NDA.]

Extract from Captain Thomas Truxtun's journal, U. S. Frigate *Constellation*, 14 September 1798, Friday

The first and latter Part of this Day, the Weather was moderate, and pleasant, and smooth Water throughout.

But between 6 P M and 2 A M it was very uncertain. Tremendous black Clouds commenced rising to the Eastward in the Evening, which went over and settled to the Northward and Westward, having but little Wind in them, and only moderate Showers of Rain. At 11 P M those Clouds rose up again to the N. N. W., and produced an Abundance of Rain, and a smart Tornado. Took in every Rag of Canvass, except the fore top Mast Stay Sail, under which we scudded before the Wind; housed the Guns; put in the Dead Lights, and secured every Thing in the best Manner, expecting a Hurricane, as it is the Season for them. At Day Dawn Appearances being more favourable, made Sail again, as did all the Fleet, which as to Numbers, are as before mentioned.

All Hands employed at doing the necessary Duty of the Ship. Saw a loaded Merchant Brig at Noon, standing to the Northward; suppose her to be one of our own Homeward bound Vessels.

Latitude observed 26°.38′ N°
Longitude Account 72.00 W.

[HS of Pa. NDA photostat.]

To Lieutenant John McRea, U. S. Navy, from Secretary of the Navy

[Trenton,]
Navy Department 15th September 1798

Mr John McRea *Norfolk*

Sir I enclose you your Commission, as a Lieutenant in the Navy of the United States. —

You will communicate to me, your acceptance of this appointment, and return the enclosed Oath. —

You will immediately enter on board of the *Norfolk*, Capt Williams, and place yourself under his command, and conform yourself to the rules & regulations of the Marine Service. —

I am Sir &ca

[NDA. OSW, Vol. 1.]

To Captain Alexander Murray, U. S. Navy, from Secretary of the Navy

[Trenton,]
Navy Department September 15th 1798

Capt Alexr Murray
Baltimore

Sir The President has reserved to himself the power of settling hereafter, the relative rank of the Captains in our Navy — Until he exercises this power, the dates of Commissions must of course be the rule of Precedency. —

In my projected enterprize for you, I contemplate that the Brig at Norfolk, Capt Williams, should go under your Command, yet his commission bears an earlier date than yours — Please to send me your Commission —

I mean to insert in it, that you are to rank from a day, to give you the Command of Williams, unless the President, to whom I have written, should forbid it — You will see the propriety of keeping the contents of this Letter to yourself.

I have the honor &ca

[NDA. OSW, Vol. 1.]

To Captain Thomas Tingey, U. S. Navy, from Secretary of the Navy

[TRENTON,]
Navy Department 15th September 1798

Captn THOMAS TINGEY

SIR I have the pleasure to enclose you a Commission as Captain in the Navy of the United States, which I hope you will accept.

The President reserves to himself, the right of settling hereafter, the relative rank of the Captains in our Navy; but it is possible, difficulties may occur to prevent the exercise of this right, and the rule of precedency, may be the dates of Commissions. —

At the same time that he appointed you, four other Gentlemen were appointed, and it was his desire that your Commission should bear the earliest date, which is so arranged. —

Should he take up the subject of the relative rank of the Captains, hereafter, it is not probable you will be injured thereby. —

It is intended that you should take the Command of the *Ganges*. — Captn Dale is desirous of attending to his private affairs, as soon as he can be relieved from his attendance on that vessel. — The sooner therefore you can take charge of her, and make your arrangements for a cruise, the more agreeable it will be. —

I have the honor &ca

[NDA. OSW, Vol. 1.]

To Secretary of State Pickering from Secretary of Navy

[TRENTON]
Navy Department September 15th 1798

Colo PICKERING,

SIR The Cutters *Eagle* & *Diligence* at Marcus Hook want Six pound Shot, which in the present situation of Philadelphia can be had only from the Vessels Setting out for the Algerines. — Mr. Foxal was to have made the Shot, but has not done it. — If you will be So good as to give an order to Captain Campbell for the Six pound Shot he wants — I will have it replaced by the time it will be wanted for the Algerine Vessels.

I have the honor to be &ca

[NDA. Sec State LB, 1798–1824.]

To Joshua Humphreys, Naval Constructor, from Secretary Pickering

DEPARTMENT OF STATE *Trenton Sepr 15. 1798.*

Mr JOSHUA HUMPHREYS *Marcus Hook.*

SIR, The Navy Department being destitute of six pound round and double headed shot, I have this day given an order to Capt Maley and the captains of the other two armed vessels destined for Algiers to supply the Quantity wanted for the *Eagle* Cutter — viz. 500 round and 200 — double headed shot. It is not improbable that the *Diligence* Cutter, which it seems carries four pounders, may want shot also: if she does, I pray you to cause her to be furnished in the like manner out of the Algerine vessels, without suffering any time to be lost. The Sec.y of the Navy will replace them in due season. I am &c

TIMOTHY PICKERING

[SDA. Dom. L., Vol. 11.]

Extract from journal of James Pity, U. S. Frigate *Constitution*, 15 September 1798, Saturday

Begins with clear Weather @ 8 A. M. Sent up T. G[t] Yards. @ 10 a Sch[r] came for empty casks @ ½ past one Spoke Ship *Newport* from Boston 6 days out, who Spoke U. S. Sloop *Herald & Pickering* Brig[t] Carpenters employ'd Shifting the Main Shrouds forward Set up the Rigging & Squared the Ratlines. —

[NDA.]

Extract from Captain Thomas Truxtun's journal, U. S. Frigate *Constellation*, 15 September 1798, Saturday

Light variable Winds, and very squally uncertain Weather with much Thunder and Lightning accompanied with an Abundance of Rain; Several Land Birds were caught and seen such as Doves, Yellow Birds &c. The *Baltimore* and a Schooner of the Fleet astern at Noon, the two Brigs near us.

These twenty four Hours, I have lost much way waiting for the *Baltimore*, tho' the Winds have been very light. At 11 A M saw a Sail to the Eastward at a great Distance, most likely one of the Fleet that parted with us. The Crew employed as usual in keeping in Repair the Rigging and Sails &c. &c.

Watland's Island at Noon bore South West ½ South forty five Leagues Distance.

Latitude Account 25°.46′ North
Longitude Account 73.00 W.

[HS of Pa. NDA photostat.]

To George Washington from Secretary Benjamin Stoddert

TRENTON, *16 Sept[r] 1798*

BENJAMIN STODDERT to GEORGE WASHINGTON.

SIR, You will, I know, pardon me for trespassing on your time, my object being the public good.

If we are to create such a navy as will make our commerce respected, and this, I cannot doubt, will be the policy of our country, one navy-yard at least must be established for building ships. This subject will probably engage the attention of Congress at the ensuing session, and it will be my duty to lay before them the best information in my power to obtain.

The place marked out on the plan of the city of Washington, for the Marine Hospital, has always appeared to me to be among the most eligible situations in the United States for a navy-yard. The result of all the enquiries I have been able to make, since I have been in office, serves but to confirm me more strongly in this opinion. No place farther south will admit of the same degree of security against an enemy. No place to the northward or eastward will afford timber so good, so cheap, or in such abundance. I might add all other materials for building and arming of ships. The springs in the neighbourhood, at least, forty feet higher than the surface of the river water; on Goose creek or Rock creek, any of them would afford water to fill locks, to prevent the difficult, and sometimes dangerous, operation of launching; and ships, by means of such locks, could be repaired without the tedious operations of discharging and heaving down. It is perhaps desireable that the principle navy-yard should be under the eye of Government. It is certainly just that it should be in the centre of the union, if it can be so placed with equal advantages to the whole community.

Nothing of consequence to the welfare of the country escapes your penetration. Will you, Sir, permit me the liberty of soliciting your opinion on this very important subject? The depth of water in every part of the channel of the river is a consideration of great magnitude. It has been suggested, that, about Maryland point, the water is too shallow to admit the passage of ships of the line, drawing, fully armed and provisioned, 24 feet.

Joining in the universal prayer for the preservation of a life of inestimable value to the Country, I have the honor to be &c[a] &c[a]

BENJAMIN STODDART.

[Harvard College Library.]

To President John Adams from Staats Morris

FORT M[c]HENRY SUNDAY
16th Sept[r] 1798

SIR By a vessel this moment arrived in a quick passage up the bay, I have certain information of the capture a French privateer mounting 20 Guns & 200 men by the United States Frigate *Constituion.* — She was directly from france with orders to cruise on our Coast, & was anchored in Hampton Roads on Wednesday last. Conceiving this information to be of some importance I have taken the liberty of communicating it, & I beg leave to add that if it should be thought proper to direct the prisoners to this port, by reducing my Centinals I can furnish a sufficient Guard from my Command to march them wherever the Government may direct.

I have the honor
to be (in haste)
Sir
Your obed[t] Serv[t]

STAATS MORRIS

[NDA photostat.]

Extract from Captain Thomas Truxtun's journal, U. S. Frigate *Constellation*, 16 September 1798, Sunday

All these Twenty four Hours clear and pleasant Weather, Except the first Hour or two when we had some Rain. The Middle the Wind was light, and variable. The latter a steady Breeze at about South East, which may be considered as the Commencement of the Trade Wind. The Vessels as before in Company.

Watland's Island at Noon bore South South West, half West, sixteen Leagues Distance.

Latitude observed 24°.43′ N°.
Longitude Account 73.34 W.

[HS of Pa. NDA photostat.]

Extract from journal of Lieutenant John Mullowny, U. S. Frigate *United States*, 16 September 1798

Stiff gales and cloudy.
Spoke Brig *Charlotte* from Barbadoes bound to Alexandria
Sounded — no bottom —
[Long. Obs^d^ 74.34
Lat^d^ Obs^d^ 36″53]

[NA.]

Extract from journal of James Pity, U. S. Frigate *Constitution*, 16 September 1798, Sunday

Begins with clear Weather Wind N. N. W. @ 8 the Revenue Cutter came along Side and tooke the prisoners 75 in Number belonging to the *Niger* on b^d^ under a guard of our Marines and Order'd them for Norfolk. got the Sheet Anchor of the gun Wale @ 4 P. M. Mr Jno Welsh pilot was discharged & Mr George Latimer took charge of the Ship as Pilot, in his Room.

[NDA.]

To William Smith, United States Consul, Lisbon, from Richard O'Brien, United States Consul, Algiers

Copy

ALGIERS *17th of Septr 1798*

WILL^m^ SMITH Esqr *Lisbon*

SIR, I received on the 3^d^ your favour of the 22^d^ of June &14th of July, & its inclosed to Monsr Famin; the inclosed are a Copy of a Letter to Capt Ingraham in Tripoli, a letter addressed to the Secretary of State, which I wish you to take a Copy of such parts as you think proper, & forward to him, you will also receive a Note of the Regala, to the Ministry, the account current between the U. S. & the House of Joseph Coen Barri, & a note of the Regala, customary to be given to the Regency on a new Deys coming to the Throne, which is a Copy of what has been forwarded to you before, but I have no information that you rec^d^ it. I think you will see the situation of our affairs so stated in those dispatches as to give you full information.

I have of late received several very pressing Letters from our Agents at Tunis & Tripoli — where general discontent seems likely soon to take place, the Algerines at present are something content, but I fear the storm is gathering, that if not checked, will burst forth with such fury as to bear down all remonstrance & reason, but I hope the speedy arrival of the Vessels will prevent those disagreeable consiquences.

I wish you to be a little particular, in acknowledging the Letters you may receive from me, for I am a little suspicious that a number of Letters, I have wrote by the way of Alicante have miscarried, as you do not acknowledge many I have wrote. —

These dispatches are by a Gibralter Privateer, directed to Mr Gavino American Agent at Gibralter, which I think is a tolerable safe conveyance. —

I hope Sir you will be so good, as to give me every information in your power, relative to those Corsairs, their detention gives me much pain & care, as I am continually under the necessity of fabricating some story or other to satisfy the impatiance of the Regency

Sir you may rest assured of my greatest exertions, to keep up harmony & good will between this Regency & the U. States as well as the other Barbary States.

I Am with the greatest respect & esteem Your most

Ob^{t} Hb^{l} Servt

P. S. We are informed, that the French have taken Alexandria by force of Arms, they not wishing the French to enter their dominions, we have this from good authority.

The Algerines this season are strong in Cruisers, 11 sail went out a few days past, & there are four more remaining in Port, stronger than they have been known to be for a number of years.

You will observe Sir that all letters I send to you, for the Secretary of State, that are unsealed are first for your perusal, now it often happens that I have an opportunity to write to you the same information as to the Secretary of State & so that I know you receive it, it is sufficient for what is requisite you will write him.

N B I am affraid that we shall finde great difficulty in unshiping Monsr Famin.

Your Most Ob^{t} Servt Rich^{d} OBrien

[SDA. Algiers, Vol. 3, 1798.)

To Captain Alexander Murray, U. S. Navy, from Secretary of the Navy

[TRENTON,]
Navy Department September 17th 1798

Capt ALEX^{r} MURRAY

SIR Be pleased to receive Mr John Barry Nephew of James Barry Esquire, on board of Your Ship as one of your Midshipmen. —

If you already [have] Midshipmen enough, Mr Barry can be put on board of another vessel hereafter. —

[NDA. OSW, Vol. 1.]

To Captain John Adams from Secretary of the Navy

[TRENTON,]
Navy Department September 17th 1798

Capt JOHN ADAMS

SIR The Cutter *Scammel* under your Command being launched you will proceed to enlist (so as to have them ready as soon as your vessel is ready) Your crew, to consist of 30 men & Boys; fifteen to be able seamen at 17 Dollars per month.* They must be enlisted for 12 months; and if necessary, you may advance each of them two months pay; — taking security that they do not run away after enlistment — for this purpose I enclose you the form of a Shipping Paper, and another of a Bond, which the sureties must sign, as well as the men. — John Martin Esquire will furnish you with the money necessary, and you must be careful to enlist none but healthy, sober, capable people; prefering Americans to Foreigners. —

* Eight ordinary Seamen and 7 Boys from 5 to 14 Doll^{s} per month

Out of the 15 Seamen allowed, you may appoint your Boatswain, Carpenter & drummer — to each of whom may be allowed three dollars per month, beyond Seamen's Wages. — I write to Mr Martin also, to furnish every thing necessary to equip your Vessel for a Cruise of 3 Months, and you will assist him by your attention & Exertions.

I cannot discover whether you have any Mates — If your have not, Mr Martin will assist in procuring three, at 35, 30 & 25 Dollars per month. — Their names must be early communicated to me, that I may lay them before the President. —

You will write me fully as to your Situation, & prospects of getting to Sea. —

I am &c^a

[NDA. OSW, Vol. 1.]

To John Chaplin, Jr., and others, Beaufort, S. C., from Secretary of Navy

[TRENTON,]
Navy Department September 17th 1798

Jno CHAPLIN J^r
& others—*Beaufort*
So: Carolina

I am honored with your Letter of the 27th Ult^o In mine of the 28th July, I did not mean to confine you in the Cost of the Galley authorized to be built for the public, to the estimated Sum. — On that Subject I had no doubt of your doing as well for the public, as you could for yourselves. — —

It is extremely difficult to procure any thing to be done in Philadelphia, or New York, in the present calamitous situation of these places — Unfortunately they have been looked to by all parts of the Union, for particular Articles — Copper bolts, Spikes & Nails, can be procured in none of the Towns Eastward. And I do not believe it would be possible for me, to send you Copper bolts, Spikes & Nails, even for one Galley, so as to reach you sooner than three months. — I shall not therefore, attempt it, but shall trust they can be furnished in Charleston; But I will direct that a sufficient quantity of Sheathing Copper (an Article also very Scarce) Shall be forwarded to William Crafts Esquire of Charleston, for your Galley.— And this you may calculate on receiving in full time. —

Altho the present laws will not permit the President to accept the Sloop of War you have in contemplation, on the terms you mean to offer her, there can be no doubt, that Congress will, at their next Sitting, enable him to accede to Conditions so reasonable, and so patriotic. — —

I have the honor to be &C^a

[NDA. GLB no. 1.]

To James Barry, Baltimore, from Secretary of Navy

[TRENTON,]
Navy Department September 17th 1798

JAs BARRY Esqr
Baltimore

SIR I have been so much engaged, that I could not attend earlier to your favour of the 7th. Instant

On the subject of Convoys, our force is yet too small, I am afraid to afford them to Europe. — Perhaps on receiving timely notice, I could generally provide a force to convoy vessels as far as the Islands. — Perhaps, until they were out of danger from the cruisers belonging to the Islands. The Calamitous situation of most of the large Towns, will prevent our force from encreasing so fast as it would have done.

I have written to Captain Murray to receive your Nephew on board the *Montezuma* in quality of Midshipman —

I am &Ca

[NDA. GLB No. 1.]

[Sept. 17, 1798.]

[Translation of statement of master of the *Niger*]

Account of the capture or detention of the English Ship *Niger* by the American Frigate *Constitution*, Captain Nicholson

On the 8th of September, at 7 in the morning, sailing close to the wind, heading W. N. W., I perceived a vessel to windward; I took her bearings N. ¼ N. E. The weather was very black and stormy in the north, which caused her to be hidden from me for some time. At 9:30 I again saw this vessel; her course was set to cross mine. I did not change my Course, always steering close to the wind. For a few moments I was uncertain as to what this vessel was, but shortly thereafter I made her out to be a warship and judged her to be American. Having approached me within a canon-shot, she hoisted the American colors, and fired a shot. Whereupon I hoisted the English colors and fired a shot to leeward. I then had my lower sails brailed and my mizen-topsail at the mast. Having come within hailing distance, they shouted to me from the vessel to send an officer on board with the ship's papers. I sent my First Lieutenant with my register and my two war commissions, one against France, and the other against Spain. Hardly had my boat come alongside when they called out to me to strike all my sails, to lower another boat and to come myself. I immediately went on board, accompanied by Mr. Jackson, a passenger on my ship and an Englishman by nationality: I had hardly climbed to the forecastle of the frigate, when I was surrounded by great numbers of men armed with sabers and pistols. The Captain asked me whence I came — from Kingston, I told him — when did you leave — the 11th of August and since then I touched at Port Antonio in order to take these two English vessels, *Pushy Park*, Captain Lawrey, and *Favourite*, Captain Wm. Spark, which I had recaptured from a French privateer — Very well, where are your papers — You have them: here is my general clearance which I forgot to send you — I do not want these papers; I want your French commission — I have none, I have been in the service of the English for five years: I command English ships, I have been in command of this vessel for three years. She belongs to a merchant of Jamaica — Let me have your dagger — no, sir, I am English and a friend of your nation: I should not be disarmed — Give it to me, or I shall have it taken from you; I shall tell you why afterwards — Then I gave it to him. — After this short dialogue he told me to go down to his room where I found my First Lieutenant (Mr. Dubouitier) seated on a chair, with a soldier standing guard over him and holding a bayonet pointed at his chest. He asked me if I had other passengers than Mr. Jackson. I said yes, even one of his compatriots, Mr. Garts of Baltimore. He gave orders to have them brought, sending back Mr. Jackson, who told him that he had his wife and two children aboard. The crew of my two boats was guarded and put in irons on board the frigate; and he put an officer and some of his sailors in my boat.

I do not know what the Officer did when he boarded my ship, I was not there.

Presently they fetched Mr. Belmont and Mr. Demanes, both commissioned officers in the service of His Britannic Majesty who showed him their commissions: he asked by what chance they were to be found on my ship, since I and my lieutenant were wearing French uniforms: they answered him that we had no uniforms and that these were the clothes we always wore: he ordered them to remain on board, and then permitted Mr. Demanes to return to the ship in order to get some shirts and other linen for our use. In a little while the boat returned with a part of my crew, which was immediately put in irons; subsequently all were transported and put in irons; they left me my servant to wait on me; and four Americans who belonged to my crew were not put in irons until the next day. That day I dined with the Captain, who told me that I was to have his cabin and the entire quarter-deck as a prison: I told him again that my ship was English; that a part of my cargo belonged to Philadelphia merchants; that since I fell under his suspicion, nothing was simpler than to detain me and to convoy my ship to the nearest port; but I begged to him to leave on board one of my officers with ten of my crew in order to look after the cargo and the various things belonging to me, to my passengers and to my crew, and in order to relieve him of any responsibility connected therewith. He answered me, that I was not to teach him his trade and that he did not need my advice. Thus everybody was transferred to the frigate, with the exception of three negroes, my servants, one a cook, the other a baker, and another, who was in charge of my provisions, five sick sailors and Mr. Chappelain, a commissioned officer in the service of His Britannic Majesty, a passenger on my ship who was also ill.

In the evening Lieutenant Bills who had been named Prize Captain took with him Mr. Paris, my second Lieutenant on the *Niger*. At about 6 o'clock in the evening the two ships set sail. I went down to the Captain's cabin — what are you going to do here — drink a glass of water — do not set foot in this room again; Let this man be shown where he is to stay. They lodged me with the frigate's officers, who never ceased to overwhelm me and all my passengers with attentions during the entire period of our detention.

Captain Nicholson took possession of all my papers, such as my Log Book of this voyage and preceding voyages, my register, (The Register is in the name of Mr. John Richards, merchant at Kingston.) my two war commissions, my general clearance, all my bills of lading, my charter party issued by the government for chartering my vessel, all the orders of various Santo Domingo Generals, all my private papers, such as letters and accounts relative to my dealings with the various merchants of Jamaica, and more than one hundred letters, which were entrusted to me at Kingston to be delivered to various merchants in Philadelphia.

On the 9th we hove to, and Mr. Bills was told to come aboard the frigate with Mr. Jackson, an English passenger: I do not know what he said to the Captain of the frigate, he said nothing to me, and I was not present during their interview: they returned at about 11 o'clock.

In the afternoon the boat came back again to the frigate: I noticed that Mr. Bills was sitting on my English colors: I went to him and told him that he could take a red, blue or yellow flag, but not the colors of His Britannic Majesty, which were not made to be sat on by any one whoever he might be; that especially in the position in which I found myself it was particularly insulting; therefore I prayed him to remove it: — English flag, French flag, it is all the same to me; I pay no attention to it; the officer replied to me: — I pray you to do so, and I withdrew. When this officer returned aboard the *Niger*, I stood on the ladder to see if my colors had been removed: I saw him who sat down on them: since this officer speaks French very well, I begged him again to remove my flag: — it is mine, he answered; it belongs to me, and I do what I please. Considering this as an insult to the British flag, I then told him in English to remove this flag, that it was not made to be insulted by any one; he pushed off without replying to me. I was exasperated; I immediately went to the captain; I laid my complaint before him, and told him that it was my duty to make representations to him: it was then that I was insulted; he treated me like a pirate; he told me that he would have me hanged, and used a hundred thousand still more insulting epithets, such as rascal, abominable wretch etc. which he also applied to my unfortunate passengers. Bring me, I said to him, before a court of justice; if I am a pirate, I will be hanged; you are not my judge, and your position obliges you to treat me well, and to respect the flag under which it pleases you to arrest me. On the morrow of this horrible scene, they took my servant away from me, and quartered us aft, with seven paces walking space and a sentinel, who followed us wherever our needs obliged us to go; at night we had two sentinels at the door of our cabins.

On the 10th the boat came alongside, we were permitted to send for linen aboard the *Niger*. Mr. Paris was sent aboard the frigate. In the afternoon at three o'clock, Mr. de Belmont was taken below, and his pockets were searched. Mr. Garts, an American merchant, one of my passengers, came on board; he told us that it was absolutely a mystery to him why we were detained, that he had assured the Captain of the frigate, that I had been in the service of H. B. M. for a long time. I asked for logbooks: Mr. Bills said he would ask the Captain, who probably refused, since we have not had any. On the 11th the boat did not come; a vessel had been sighted; I hoped that she might be English and would serve to identify us; we were made to go below before she was within hailing distance. On the 12th the pilot came on board and we entered Chesapeak Bay. I saw the *Niger* hoist an American flag and a French flag under it: I shall not venture upon any reflections; let those who shall read my account judge for themselves.

On the 13th as Captain Nicholson was preparing to land, I asked his permission to go ashore with him, in order to go to the English Consul; he refused; a moment later my passengers and I got orders to go below; I was detained until the 16th when I was transferred to the fort; I was not allowed to communicate with the shore, the letters which were written to me from ashore were intercepted and were not given to me until the moment of my departure.

When I left the frigate I obtained permission to send Mr. Paris, my second Lieutenant aboard the *Niger* in order to get a bag of silver coin, which he had in his trunk, which included some foreign pieces; arriving on board, he found his trunks open, in spite of the fact that he had the keys in his pocket, all his belongings scattered about the room, and his bag empty.

When I arrived at the fort, I was treated by Mr. Clayborn with honor and consideration: this officer did everything in his power to lighten my captivity and that of my unfortunate passengers; my crew also shared in his kindness: I cannot praise enough this officer as well as Mr. Wilkins, his second in command: let me herewith express to the officers of the frigate *Constitution* my gratitude and that of all my passengers, who will never forget their kindness.

(Signed) GEORGE DU PETIT-THOUARS
master of the Ship
DU BOUETIER,
English commissioned officer, first mate on the Niger
Paris, 2d Lieut

FORT NORFOLK *17 Sepbre 1798.*

Witnesses C. DEMANES,
English commissioned Officer, passenger
I. [?] BELMONT,
English Commissioned Officer.
JEAN PEYRANNE
Officer in the English service

A true copy from the original — JACOB WAGNER

Representation of the Captain, officers and Passengers of the British Letter of Marque Ship *Niger*, relative to the circumstances of her capture by the United States' Frigate *Constitution*, Capt. Nicholson. — 17 Sep. 1798.

[SDA. Misc. L., Sept.–Dec. 1798.]

To Secretary of the Navy from Captain Thomas Tingey, U. S. Navy,

KINGSTON (NEW JERSEY) *17th Septr 1798*

SIR I have the honor to acknowledge receipt of Yours of 15th instant, enclosing me a Commission of Captain in the Navy of the United States; which call to the service of my country I readily accept, and shall with celerity obey.

I request your acceptance of my thanks for the polite and friendly manner in which your communication is couch'd — and when announcing to the President my acceptance, may I beg of you to inform him how highly I appreciate the precedence he was pleas'd to confer on me in the appointment, and that I consider it as a mark of his attention, which I shall constantly emulate to deserve.

The President having reserved to himself the right of taking up the relative seniority of rank, in the Captains appointed to the *late establishment*, I have hope that no difficulty will occur to prevent his exercise of that right whenever he shall see fit, after the appointments are complete. In respect to myself, I am not so sanguine in expectation, but that I shall readily concede precedence to any individual, who may hereafter be appointed on *this establishment*, who shall have superior claim to me, on the same ground that I found mine, with respect to some of those previously appointed.

I shall ever strenuously advocate the most strict observance of orders, and that no Officer whatever be permitted to hesitate, but promptly to obey those he receives from the head of the Department. Nevertheless I have reasons cogent in the extreme, for wishing to decline acceptance of the command of the *Ganges:* the particulars of which I reserve for verbal communication. — were it indispensibly necessary for the good of the service, and she fitting as an additional ship, *no private consideration* should deter me, but, as this apparently is in no wise the case, I have hope You will approbate my views for this indulgence

I have the honor to be

Sir &c. &c. &c.

The Hon[ble] B. Stoddert
Sec[y] of the Navy Trenton

P. S. I shall have the honor to wait on you in person on Wednesday, when, if the reasons I have to prefer, for not joining the *Ganges*, should not appear of sufficient force to you, I shall make arrangements for a prompt observance of your orders.

[NDA, Tingey LB, 1798–1800.]

Extract from journal of James Pity, U. S. Frigate *Constitution*, 17 September 1798, Monday

Begins with Cloudy W[r] Unmoord Ship & Came to Sail under Top Sails & Stay Sails 2 Miles Nearer Norfolk, and came too in 5-½ fath[ms] Water. @ 5 P. M. Moor'd Ship Wind E. N. E. Rec[d] a Quantity of fresh Beef on board. also Water fired the Morn[g] & Even[g] Guns as usual.

[NDA.]

Extract from Captain Thomas Truxtun's journal, U. S. Frigate *Constellation*, 17 September 1798, Monday

Moderate Breezes all these Twenty four Hours. Run all Night under an easy Sail, so as not to come up with the Keys before Day Light. At 5 AM it being Day Light made Sail, and a little after 7 Ditto made Otwood's Keys bearing South South East five Leagues

Distance, and at 10 Ditto made Crooked Island the Body bearing South. Bent the Larboard Bower Cable, and sailed along the Island to the Westward, so as to hawl round the Bird Rock, and go through that Passage. The *Baltimore* and the other Vessels a little astern. I observed with Astonishment the Number of Houses, and Settlements made on this Island since I passed it last in the Year 1775, when there was no such Thing as a House, or human Being settled on it, in Fact it now appears to have a Number of well cultivated Plantations, very many Houses, and at a Distance two good looking Forts, on one of which I observed an English Flag flying.

By the Lunar Observation I made at about 3 PM the Longitude of this Island (say the Bird Rock) is very accurately fixt at 74°.26′ W. from Greenwich, and by the Observation at Noon to Day, the Latitude of that Rock is 22°.49′ North.

Latitude observed 22°.59′ North
Longitude observed 74.10 W.

[HS of Pa. NDA photostat.]

Extract from journal of Lieutenant John Mullowny, U. S. Frigate *United States*, 17 September 1798

Spoke sloop *Minerva* from Havanna bound to Rhode Island, bent the Cables. —

Sounded in 20 fathoms
Sounded 23 D°
Sound every hour from 18 to 23 fathoms — —
Exercised the crew at the Guns at small arms —

[Long. Obs^d 74″41
Lat^d Obs^d 38.4]

[NA.]

To the Secretary of State, from David Humphreys, United States Minister to Spain

(No. 163)

MADRID *Septr 18th 1798*

SIR, My last letter to you was dated the 14th ins^t, and was forwarded by way of Lisbon under cover to Mr Smith. A Copy of the Arrête of the French Directory for taking off the Embargo from American Vessels in the ports of France was enclosed in it. I thought any remarks on the extraordinary phraseology of that Paper superfluous, as you would of course make your own observations on it.

This is to go by way of Malaga, from whence six armed American Merchantmen are to sail together in a few days for New York. One of them was purchased & armed by a Citizen of the U. S. in Malaga. — The French Privateers have as yet kept at a respectful distance from our armed merchant vessels in the Mediterranean; but it is reported to me that French Privateers of a larger size are about being fitted out to attack them.

Lord St Vincent has within a short time past permitted several loaded vessels from the U. S. to enter the port of Cadiz.

To my great astonishment, the Supreme Council of War has confirmed the Sentence of Condemnation in the case of the Brig belonging to Mr Nissen of New York. A re-hearing will be demanded.

M. de Saavedra is gaining health much faster since he was at the Escurial than was expected. He is still very feeble. — His recovery becomes every day more requisite for the public Service; and particularly for the continuance of the friendly relations between this Country & the U. S. — If you see the French News Papers, you must see a strange quantity of falsehoods respecting Spain.

By the tenor of the last Notes which have passed between the French & Imperial Ministers at Radstadt, it seems that the negociations must positively result in peace or war, in a very short period.

With sentiments of great regard & esteem

I have the honour to be,

Sir

Your M^o ob. & M^o H^ble Servt

D. [AVID] HUMPHREYS.

The SECRETARY OF STATE
&c &c &c

[SDA. Disp. Spain, Bk. 4, Humphreys.]

To Captain John Brown, Revenue Cutter *Diligence*, from Secretary of the Navy

[TRENTON,]
Navy Department, September 18th 1798

Capt. JOHN BROWN
Cutter Diligence

SIR Your Letter of the 15th Instant I have recd —

Mr Francis & Capt Gill having both been written to, for the purpose of providing all the Articles necessary for your vessel, will furnish a few Medicine's agreeably to your desire, upon your shewing them this Letter. — After receiving on board, the Articles for Wilmington, North Carolina, & Savannah in Georgia, mentioned in my Letter of the 15th, you are to proceed to these respective Ports, and deliver them agreeably to the receipts signed by you —

You have already been furnished with the regulations of the Navy, which are to supply the place of Articles of War, and I now enclose you, an act of Congress passed the last session, with Instructions founded upon that act, authorizing Captures of French Armed Vessels; you will observe however that you are not to attempt a recapture of any American Vessel, which may have been taken by the Cruisers of any other Nation than the French; because it is presumable that if such captures prove illegal, the Government of such Nation will make compensation. — You will be attentive to introduce and keep up a due discipline on board your vessel and promote a proper respect for the American flag.

When you have delivered the Articles as above mentioned, you are to consider your cruising ground to extend from Cape Fear, to Cape Hatteras, paying particular attention to the former, and you will sometimes look into Core Sound and Ocrocoek [Ocracoke] Inlet — In order that the Inhabitants may see that they are attended to; And finally I request that you will do every thing in your power to afford as ample protection to the Commerce of North Carolina as your force will admit of. — When I wish to make any Communications to you, it shall be done through Major Jnº G. McRea at Wilmington in North Carolina, who will act as the Agent for your vessel —

I wish you success — & shall be glad to hear from you when any occurrences takes place, which you deem worthy of Notice. —

P. S. You have enclosed the private signals Established in the Navy, and also a List of Signals by which our Vessels and the British may know each other.

[NDA. OSW, Vol. 1.]

To Captain Patrick Fletcher, U. S. Navy, from Secretary of the Navy

[TRENTON]
Navy Department September 18th 1798

Capt PATRICK FLETCHER

SIR The President has appointed you a Captain in the Navy of the United States. —

You will signify your acceptance or nonacceptance of this appointment — In case you accept; you will take the oath of allegiance, which is enclosed, and forward it to this Office with your acceptance. —

N. B. It is probable that your services will be required in the course of 8 or 10 days; you will therefore hold yourself in readiness to Act immediately when called upon. —

I am &ca

[NDA. OSW, Vol. 1.]

To President John Adams from Daniel Davis, Portland

PORTLAND *Sept. 18th 1798*

SIR — The inclosed letter came to hand by this Evening's Mail. It contains all the information I possess upon the subject, excepting that I have been informed, the Bristol schooner mentioned in the letter, was captured by a French privateer; that the crew remained on board, and a few days after the capture, rose upon the four Frenchmen who were put on board to carry her into port, and retook her, and arrived safe in the port of Damarascota with the French prisoners.

Mr Tinkham, the writer of the letter, is a deputy-marshall who lives at Wiscassett. I have taken the liberty to inform him as the best opinion I could form upon a case intirely new to me, that if money must be advanced for the immediate necessary support of the Prisoners, it should be done by the Collector of the Port of Waldoborough, within whose District the schooner first arrived; and that I had no doubt the Collector would have it allowed him in his quarterly accounts —

I have thought it my duty to transmit to you this information, in order that your "pleasure may be known" concerning the Prisoners; the law of Congress of the 25th of June last, having authorised the President to determine what shall be done with them —

I have the honour to be
with the highest respect
Your Hble Servt

DAN'L DAVIS
D. Atty Maine

[NDA photostat.]

[Enclosure]

To Daniel Davis, District Attorney, from Joseph Tinkham, Wiscasset

WISCASSET *17 Sept 1798* —

DEAR SIR Major McKenn [?] has just arrived with the 4 French Prisioners retaken in the Bristol schooner Capt Dickey, he took them upon "an Act further to protect the Commerce of the United States" which Act is Published in the Centinel of the 8th Augt — the 8th Sec of which says they shall be reported to the Collecter of the port in which they shall first Arrive — & be delivered to the Custody of the Marshall &c &c who shall take charge for their safe keeping & support at the expense of the United States — Collector Cook as they did not first arrive in his District don't choose [?] to have any thing to do with them, and there being no Majistrate in this place at this time I think the Law authorises & makes it my duty to commit them to Goal which I shall do immediately —

I must request you to write me by return of Post — directing me how to proceed with them — likewise to send me an order where I am to draw for Mony for their dailey Subsistence. Fay [or Fry] the Jailor's circumstances is such that he can't advance for them & I am sure mine is *such* that I cant — Mr Cook I suppose is the proper person — pray don't fail answering this by next post —

the Names of the Prisioners are —

Etienne Richard Prize Master
Francois Maurlin [?] } Seamen
Pierre Severe [?] Petit } Seamen
Pierre Casmagnale — [?] } Seamen

They belong'd to the French Privateer Schooner *La Fleur de la Mer*.

I remain with Esteem
Your most obedt Servt

JOSEPH TINKHAM *D. Marshall*

DANIEL DAVIS Esq.
District Atty

[NDA photostat.]

To Secretary of the Navy from Major Commandant Burrows, U. S. M. C.

MARINE CAMP *Sept. 18. 1798.*

SIR, I just now received your Commands to send a Detachment to the *Eagle* cutter, but it will not be possible to compleat the order immediately, I have at present but five men fit having yesterday sent the Detachment to Baltimore. I have an Officer recruiting at Germantown, and expect he will meet with Success. My recruiting Officer at N. York says he has about 1 dozen men. I have ordered him to send them on immediately, and as soon as they arrive they shall be accoutred and sent to the *Eagle* Cutter.

I have the Honour to be
Y. Ob. Ser.

W. W. B. [WILLIAM WARD BURROWS]
M. C.
M. C.

To the SECy OF THE NAVY

[MCA. LS, 1798–1799.]

To John Brown, Providence, R. I., from Secretary of Navy

[Trenton,]
Navy Department September 18th 1798

John Brown Esqr
Providence

Sir I have only received Capt Talbot's report of your Ship the *George Washington* this day. —

That you may not be kept in suspense, I just write to inform you that I will take her for the public on your Terms, 40,000 Dolls 10,000 in Cash, and the balance in 6 pr Ct Stock. — It is not worth disputing about Trifles, and if you insist on it, I must add the 400 Dollars for the expense since your offer; tho' I really think you ought not to ask it. — —

My chief object in buying this Ship, is to have an additional vessel of her Force in immediate Service. — In this I hope there will be no disappointment. — —

Tomorrow I will make the necessary arrangements, and will write you again. —

The Guns, I mean the 9 pounders, will be wanted —

I have the honor
&C &ca

[NDA. GLB No. 1.]

Extract from journal of James Pity, U. S. Frigate *Constitution*, 18 September 1798, Tuesday

Foggy Weather with Rain @ 5 A. M. calld all hands, and wash'd Decks. @ 7 put the Empty Water Casks on Bd the Pilot boat @ 9 a Sloop came along Side with water and Tar. Unbent the best Bower & bent it to the larboard Cable. Carpenters altering the fore Channels for the better Security of the Masts. all hands employd variously.

[NDA.]

Extract from Captain Thomas Truxtun's journal, U. S. Frigate *Constellation*, 18 September 1798, Tuesday

Moderate Breezes all these Twenty four Hours, and fine Weather. At 4 PM discovered an English Sloop of War in the Crooked Island Passage, standing to the Northward close in with the Land. We gave her Chase and she first hoisted American Colours, but after firing several Shot at her to bring her to, she hawlled them down, and hoisted the English red Ensign, and fired a Gun to Leeward.

Having to go through a narrow and intricate Channel, I hoisted the Signal for the *Baltimore* to quit the Chace, and stood on our Course to pass Cape Verde.

At 5 AM found we were on the Edge of the Bahama Bank, hawlled off to the Southward, and kept about it's Edge, untill we passed Key Verde, which was at 9 AM, and then steered West South West by Compass.

I find all the Charts to be very erroneous as to the placing of Key Verde, which is certainly seven Leagues further to the Southward, than it is placed. I make Key Verde to be in Latitude 21° .47′ North; and it is undoubtedly on the Edge of the Bahama Bank. The *Baltimore*, and other Vessels in Company as usual.

Latitude observed 21° .38′ N°
Longitude Account 76 .17 W.

[HS of Pa. NDA photostat.]

Extract from journal of Lieutenant John Mullowny, U. S. Frigate *United States*, 18 September 1798

Light Winds, foggy. —

Sounded, 14 fathoms, fine grey sand, sounded 10 fathoms Saw the land bearing N. W. by W. distance 8 leagues —

Kept the lead going every half hour in the night.

Saw a pilot-boat bearing N W. made a Signal for a pilot. at 8 A. M. he came on board

At M the light house on Cape Henlopen bore N W by W.

Got the Anchors all clear for letting go. — — —

[NA.]

To Joshua Humphreys, Naval Constructor, from Captain John Barry, U. S. Navy

FRIGATE U. S. [*United States*] OFF BOMBAY HOOK
Septem^r^ 19th 1798

D^r^ SIR Agreeably to your request, I now transmit you an account of the qualities of the Frigate, *United States*, and such remarks as I have made since I left the Delaware. No ship ever went to sea steers & works better, and in point of sailing, I have every reason to believe, she is equal, if not superior to any ship I ever saw. I have seen nothing that I could not with the greatest ease, outsail, and on a sea, an easier vessel perhaps never spread canvas; if there was a press of canvas carried on her, it might probably bury her more than it ought, but I do not think that could be ascribed to the form of the bottom, but perhaps to the Fore Mast being too far forward; but in this I would make no alterations untill I had more trial. I think if her masts raked a little more it would help her pressing so much, and I have reason to believe she would sail faster — respecting the Masts, I can say nothing more, untill I have a better trial —

At present we have but one hundred Tons of Iron Ballast, but if I possibly can, I'll get twenty or twenty five tons more, or shot in proportion, this I think will help her, as she is at present somewhat tender, — on our arrival at Boston, I made James Morris take the heights of the Midship ports, his report was that the lower sail was seven feet 6 Inches above the water — I am of opinion, if it would not have made her labour in a Sea, that she would have been a better ship with a little more beam, say twelve or eighteen inches — with a tender of my best respects to Mrs Humphreys & Family

I am Dear Sir
Your esteemed Friend
& very Humble Servt

JOHN BARRY

Mr JOSHUA HUMPHREYS
*Philadel^a^*

[HS of Pa. NDA photostat.]

To Captain Samuel Barron, U. S. Navy, from Secretary of the Navy

[TRENTON,]
Navy Department September 19th 1798

Capt SAML BARRON *Norfolk.*

SIR Your Letter of the 8th Instant, communicating the information, that the Merchants had bought Mr Myer's Brigantine [*Richmond*] has been received. —

Besides a Lieutenant of Marines & 20 Privates which will be provided by the Major of the Marine Corps, You will be allowed,

Two Lieutenants
Two Midshipmen
One Surgeon
One Purser
One Sailing Master
One Sailing Master's Mate
One Boatswain
One Gunner
One Carpenter
One Cook — and not exceeding 90 Privates, to consist of able Seamen Ordinary Seamen & Boys. —

No general arrangements having been made respecting the proportion of the different descriptions of men — It is certainly however, our soundest policy to create Seamen — It is therefore adviseable, that the ordinary number of able Seamen be lessened, and a larger proportion of ordinary Seamen and Boys be employed, than have heretofore been in the Navy Service — I am persuaded that our Vessels have been crowded with more men & Guns, than is necessary — Experience proves, that Boys are very serviceable — probably one Boy to each Gun may not be too many — I wish you however, to give this Subject your full consideration and communicate your opinion at large —

It is only by the collective wisdom of experienced Men, that a Judicious arrangement can be made —

You will nominate suitable characters for your Officers — If Colo Josiah Parker, is in Norfolk, consult with him on the subject.

It is all important that men of Experienced Courage and Integrity be employed to fill the several stations. —

I will give you Instructions to recruit your Crew, as soon as your Brige is ready to receive them. —

I have the honor to be &ca

[NDA OSW, Vol. 1.]

To John Caldwell, Hartford, Conn., from Secretary of Navy

[TRENTON,]
Navy Department September 19th 1798

JOHN CALDWELL Esqr
Hartford, Connectt

SIR Mr Wolcott has referred to me, that part of your letter, of the 22nd Ultimo which relates to a Convoy. — —

Our Force is yet too small to admit of convoying our Trade; and it has been thought, it would be rendered the most effectual Security to it, in our power to render, to find employment for the French Cruisers, about their own Islands, by attacking them there — If however, you will let me know the number of Vessels to leave Connecticut about the 1st of November, I will endeavour so to arrange a part of our force, as to give them some protection if practicable. — —

I have the honor to be &c

[NDA. GLB No. 1.]

To William Pennock, Navy Agent, Norfolk, from Secretary of Navy

[TRENTON,]
Navy Department September 19th 1798

Wm PENNOCK Esqr *Norfolk*

SIR In one of your Letters you mention some sick Seamen, who had been sent on shore by Capt Truxton — and on this subject I can only request that you will continue to have them carefully attended, with as much frugality as their situation will admit of, — until some general arrangement can be made, and in the Interim if they have recovered, they should immediately repair on board of any of the Ships of War that may be in Port. —

With respect to those who are in confinement for Mutiny, you will direct that care be taken to prevent their escape, until they can be brought to a Court Martial — —

P. S. The Pork, Beef, & Bread I mentioned in another Letter, may be soon wanted — Have the bread set about, and let me know the Price at which you engage it — It should not be Pilot Bread — But such as the British use for Seamen. — —

I have the honor

&c &c

[NDA. GLB No. 1.]

Extract from journal of Lieutenant John Mullowny, U. S. Frigate *United States*, 19 September 1798

Entered the bay of Delaware at 7 P. M. came to off Bombay hook.

[NA.]

Extract from Captain Thomas Truxtun's journal, U. S. Frigate *Constellation*, 19 September 1798, Wednesday

Pleasant Breezes, and fine Weather. At 7 P M made the Signal for the Fleet to hawl the Wind on the Larboard Tack, as I thought it imprudent running in this Part of the Strait at Night, having found the Charts very erroneous, and Current setting strong to the N. E.

At A M made the Signal for the Fleet to ware and hawl the Wind on the Starboard Tack, and at 5 A M it being Day Light, made Sail, the low Land of Cuba forming innumerable Islands, and Reefs on it's Coast bearing from South East to West South West, and those abreast of us at the Distance of 5 Leagues. Employed at Sundries.

Latitude observed 22°.1' North
Longitude Account 77.50 W

[HS of Pa. NDA photostat.]

Extract from journal of James Pity, U. S. Frigate *Constitution*, 19 September 1798, Wednesday

Winds at S. W. with light Airs @1/2 past 5 A. M. a Lighter came along Side with fresh Beef, corn, & Water. @ 6 A. M. loos'd all Sails to dry. Fleeted[?] the Main Shrouds & set up the Rigging. All hands employ'd variously.

[at Hampton Roads]

[NDA.]

To Mr. Sagué, merchant, New York, from Jacob Wagner

DEPARTMENT OF STATE, *Sepr 20, 1798.*

Mr SAGUÉ Merchant *New York.*

SIR, The Secretary of State has received your letter of the 17th current, requesting a prolongation of time allowed in the Act of Congress for the entry of vessels from French ports, so far as respects the vessel you are about to dispatch for St Domingo: and he directs me to inform you, that any vessel clearing out from the United States under the President's permission and bona fide employed in aiding the departure of French persons, will be permitted of course to return, altho' she should not arrive until after the 1st of December next. In such case no new act of the President will be necessary to admit her to an entry: but the permission to clear will be of itself a sufficient document for that purpose: and to prevent embarrassment it will be adviseable for the vessel to return to the port of her clearance, as the permission to clear will be filed with the Collector of that Port.

I am, Sir, very respectfully, &c.

JACOB WAGNER.

[SDA. Dom. L., Vol. 11.]

To President John Adams from the Secretary of Navy

[TRENTON,]
Navy Department September 20th 1798

JOHN ADAMS Esqr
President of
the U. States

SIR I have not yet received Official accounts of the Capture of the French 20 Gun Ship by Nicholson — but the account comes so well authenticated from different quarters, that the fact is not to be doubted — I hope this ship will prove a useful addition to our Navy —

I have the honor to be &c^a

[NDA. Nom. Appts. LB, 1798–1820.]

To Captain Silas Talbot, U. S. Navy, from Secretary of Navy

[TRENTON,]
Navy Department September 20th 1798

Capt SILAS TALBOT

SIR As I have concluded to buy the Ship *George Washington*, belonging to John Brown Esquire of Providence; I have the honor to request, that you will proceed to that place as soon as your Affairs will permit, and I hope this will be immediately, and take upon yourself the direction of fitting and preparing her for Service. —

It is greatly to be desired that She be fitted with all practicable expedition, and that at all events she be ready to proceed on a cruise some time in the month of December, if not in the beginning of that month. — —

I will remit to you by the time you reach Providence 2500 Dollars, and will supply when wanted, any further sum necessary. — —

The ship must be delivered to you with the Articles contained in the Inventory, which you have enclosed. — —

You will judge whether the whole of these articles are necessary for the Ship as a Vessel of War; and should any of them be unnecessary, Sell them for public Account, giving Credit in your account for the amount of the Sale. — —

It is a fortunate Circumstance that no alteration of the Decks will be necessary — A spar deck you think may be added with advantage — please to have this done; as well as every other thing which shall in your Judgment be essential to make her a complete War Ship. — —

I observe there are 47 Water Casks, in the Inventory. — If the Ship can Stow them, with provisions enough for Six months, She ought to have as many Water Casks as will contain 25,000 Gs You will judge, and have the number of Casks Wanted, made immediately; that they may have sometime to soak — New Casks should be well soaked & rinced, and when filled, should have some Lime put therein. — Please to attend to this. Inconveniences have arisen from the Water turning sour & Smelling, in New Casks. — —

Mr John Brown will furnish 24 nine pound Cannon, and 8 Six pounders. — — It will be well to get these early, prove them, and have the carriages made, and have a sufficient quantity of Ball, Grape & round headed shot cast in time. — These Mr Brown can also furnish.

The price of Bal is £.25 pr Ton in Pensylvania. — Mr Brown, who Seems to be a complete Master of the Art of bargain making, will probably ask more. — You must do the best you can with him, and let the public be Screwed as little as possible. — I will send you soon, a List of other Articles to be got in Rhode Island. —

Please to take notice, that besides the sails contained in the Inventory, Mr Brown is to furnish a new main Sail, a new lower Studding Sail, and a new top Gallant Studding sail. — Any other sails you deem necessary to make two Suits of tolerably good sails for the ship, you will have procured — Also a Sufficient quantity of Spare rigging, Anchors & Cables. — —

I cannot tell at this moment who will Command this Ship. I think a Captain from Massachusetts. — All the other officers I wish to get from Rhode Island, and must rely greatly on your opinion.

Be pleased therefore, as early as you can, after getting to Providence furnish me with a List of names you would recommend for the different stations. — — If you think Jacobs will make as good a Lieutenant as can be had, you may employ him in assisting about the Ship, and I will name him to the President. — —

You know the Importance of good men to the service. If Rhode Island cannot furnish such, they must be got elsewhere — —

The officers should be appointed, and the men recruited so as to procure a Crew by the time the Ship will be ready to receive them. — I shall get this business on foot, as soon as I hear from you, when it will be proper to begin. —

You may employ a Clerk, at such reasonable Compensation as you shall Judge proper. — His Expenses & yours will be paid; and your other compensation for this Service will be at least equal to your Pay & Emoluments as Captain in the Navy. — —

I have the honor

&c &c

[NDA. GLB, No. 1.]

Extract from journal of James Pity, U. S. Frigate *Constitution*, 20 September 1798, Thursday

Winds Variable @ 7 A. M. a boat came along side with fresh Beef for the Ships use at 8 A. M. Mr Ward acting Masters Mate was broke for abusing the Ships Steward @ 3 P. M. Capt Nicholson went on boad the *Virginia* Cutter to proceed to Williamsburg. Recd 30 Gang casks Water.

[NDA.]

Extract from Captain Thomas Truxtun's journal, U. S. Frigate *Constellation*, 20 September 1798, Thursday

Throughout these Twenty four Hours, very fresh Breezes. At 2 P M it began to get squally; at 4 Ditto the Weather became uncertain; took in the light Sails, handed the Mizen top Sail, close reefed the fore, and double reefed the Main Top Sails, and furled the Main Sail; at Dark hawlled up the fore Sail, and run under the Main, and fore Top Sails reefed as aforesaid, with the fore Top Mast Stay Sail. The Fleet keeping stationary, thro' the Night, untill about half past Eleven, or thereabouts, was as tremendous and awful, as any Thing I had ever seen in either Quarter of the Globe. The Lightning, and Claps of Thunder in Fact surpassed any Description that could be given, and the Squalls of Wind, and Rain were heavy, but of short Duration. Add to this, we were in the most narrow Part of the Straits, when this dreadful Night came on, I however had the Ship steered a steady Course, and passed through, leading the Fleet without any Accident whatever.

At 2 A M it cleared away finely and at half past 3 Ditto, the *Baltimore* having made a Signal previously of seeing a strange Sail, I was fearful some Cruizer would capture, and take off one of the Merchantmen, I hove out the Signal for bringing to on the Starboard Tack, and at Day Light Nothing being in Sight made all Sail, and stood down towards the Western Part of the Straits.

At Noon Key Sal Islands bore West B. North 3/4 North, fourteen Leagues Distance. The Fleet in Company astern.
Latitude observed 23°.22′ N°
Longitude Account 79.21 W.

[HS of Pa. NDA photostat.]

Extract from journal of Lieutenant John Mullowny, U. S. Frigate *United States*, 20 September 1798

After leaving Bombay hook came to off New Castle.

[NA.]

To President John Adams from the Secretary of Navy

[TRENTON,]
Navy Department Sept. 21st 1798

JOHN ADAMS Esqr
President of the U. States

SIR I have a Letter dated the 13th from Pennock, the Naval Agent at Norfolk, saying that Nicholson had brought into Hampton Road, a Ship of 20 or 24 Guns, [*Niger*], full of men, who refused to give any Account of themselves, and who are supposed to be Pirates — I hope by the Mail of this evening to receive more certain Intelligence. —

Capt Barry to my surprize made his appearance here at 1 oClock — His ship with about 100 Frenchmen & negroes aboard he left at Chester. Decatur with 30 or 40 more, was following him in, with two prizes, a Sloop & a Schooner taken in the West Indies. —

Barry returned too soon — His reason, apprehensions from the Hurricanes in the West Indies at this Season. —

Upon the whole it is better than to have kept the Ships sleeping on our own shores. — Tho' the result of the enterprize falls very far short of my hopes.

Murray, to whom I am sending orders this day, to proceed to the West Indies with the *Montezuma*, the Brig *Norfolk*, the Cutter *Eagle*, & the *Retaliation*, will return with more Brilliancy. —

I have no time to add more, than that I have the honor to be &ca

[NDA. Nom. Appts. LB, 1798–1820.]

To William Pennock, Navy Agent, Norfolk, from Secretary of Navy

[TRENTON,]
Navy Department September 21st 1798

Wm PENNOCK Esqr
Norfolk.

SIR I have your Letter of the 13th Instant — The Newspapers also mention the Capture of the vessel by Nicholson. — But I am still at a loss as to her situation, — Whether she be a French Privateer, or a pirate. — If she be a French Privateer, she must be immediately sent to Baltimore under the Command of Capt Barron, who, without interfering with Capt Williams' enlistment, must hire seamen to navigate her to Baltimore, with her Crew on board, from whence I will take measures to have them secured. —

If the vessel be a Pirate, and the Crew can be secured in Goals; (in your & the nieghbouring County Goals) this must be done. — and you must get them furnished with provisions by contract on the best terms in your power; contracting that they be supplied with 1 lb of Coarse Bread, ½# of Meat — & 1# Potatoes turnips, or any other kind of vegetables, pr day. — — — —

But if they cannot be secured in the Neighbouring Goals, they must be sent in the Ship to Baltimore, altho they be Pirates. — If you contract for their Supplies of food, let me know the Terms, which ought to be as reasonable as possible. — If the Crew goes to Baltimore in the Vessel, then the Commanding Officer of the Fort, must be applied to for a guard, to keep the Prisoners secured to Balto, Where they must be delivered over to the Commanding Officer of the Fort at Whetstone Point — Enclosed is an order from the secretary at War to the Commanding Officer of the Fort, for this purpose — — I hope I shall receive Intelligence this Evening by the mail. —

Capt Nicholson must have a Midshipman and another Inferior Officer to give Evidence on the Trial of the Ship; without which, she cannot be condemned. — —

I am &Ca

[NDA. GLB, No. 1.]

To Mr. Barry or Mr. Palyart from Captain Thomas Truxtun, U. S. Navy

United States Ship *Constellation*
off the Morro 21st September 1798.—

Sir I enclose you several Letters which please to deliver. Several Vessels, that I have convoyed hither will give you the Public Prints, which however contain Nothing very interesting at present.

A Supply of a few Barrels of Limes, and Orranges, some Pines, and a little other Fruit, with about Twenty Boxes of the very best Segars, is all I have occasion for at present. On your sending them off, I will give a Bill for the Amount.

On the 27th Instant I purpose leaving this Station for the Coast of the United States. Be pleased to give public Notice of my Determination. I am Sir,

Your Obedient Servant

Thomas Truxtun.

To Mr Barry or Mr Palyart.

Public Notice

To the Merchants and Masters of American Vessels at Havannah

Gentlemen: Having just arrived off the Morro Castle, I take the most early Opportunity to inform you, that I shall stand off and on, waiting for such Vessels as can be got ready to sail (and joins me on this Station) by the 27th Instant; on which Day, I purpose to return to the Coast of the United States.

The great Fleet of our Vessels having sailed, which was the Object of my Expedition here, I think proper to inform you, that I can not exceed the above Time.

Such as can benefit by the Convoy now offered, will please to call on Board for Signals &c. as soon as they get out of the Harbour. I am, Gentlemen,

Your Obedient Servant

THOMAS TRUXTUN.

UNITED STATES SHIP *Constellation*
off the Morro Castle 21st Sept. 1798

[HS of Pa. NDA photostat. Truxtun's LB, 1798–9.]

[21 September 1798]

To Lieutenant of Marines Saunders from Captain Thomas Truxtun, U. S. Navy

Official

Commodore TRUXTUN to Lieutenant SAUNDERS

SIR, On your being landed at the Havannah, you will wait upon the Governor, and deliver the Packet addressed for him without Delay.

I also request you will be pleased to deliver as soon after as possible the other Letters herewith handed you.

It is my Wish, that you return on Board on Monday, if possible. You will be pleased to inform those, who it may concern, that I certainly leave this Station on the 27th Instant for the Coasts of the United States. Great Prudence is necessary to be observed towards the Government Laws &c. &c &c. The public Paper enclosed you will paste up, wherever the Change or Coffee House may be —

I hope to see you speedily, and am, Dr Sir

Your Obedient Servant

THOMAS TRUXTUN.

[HS of Pa. NDA photostat. Truxtun's LB, 1798–9.]

To His Excellency the Governor of Havanna from Captain Thomas Truxtun, U. S. Navy

UNITED STATES SHIP *Constellation*
off the Morro Castle 21st September 1798. —

SIR, I have the Honor to inclose your Excellency, under Cover with this Note, a Letter from the Secretary of State; and hasten to dispatch Lieutenant Saunders with Directions to wait upon your Excellency, and deliver the same without Delay.

The numerous Captures, and unprovoked, and unparralled Depredations committed on our lawful Commerce, by the armed Vessels of France, and her Colonies, for which, Redress has hitherto not been attainable, and a number of these depredations being made in this Quarter has induced the President of the United States who is sensible of the Reciprocity and Convenience to both Nations, that so valuable a Branch of our Trade, as that to the Havannah, should not go wholly unprotected, to Cause two Frigates to be dispatched, under my Command, for the Purpose of convoying Home, such of our Merchant Vessels, as may be ready to return from your Port, and it is not doubted but your Excellency will accord with his Views, by granting permission (agreeable to the 7th Article of the Treaty of Friendship, Limits, and Navigation between his Catholic Majesty, and the United States) for the Vessels of my Nation now ready to sail from the

Havannah to depart without Delay, and take the Benefit of my Convoy. I shall accordingly with your Excellency's Permission stand off and on, before the Morro, for a few Days, untill they come out.

The Government of the United States ever desirous of giving new Proofs to Spain, of its real Friendship and unremitting Solicitude, that a perfect Harmony should always subsist between the two Nations, and that the Benefits to be derived from a lawful Commerce, be encouraged, have directed me to manifest this Disposition on our Part to the Spaniards, whenever and wherever I meet them, and I can assure your Excellency, that I shall always feel infinite Pleasure in obeying the Order.

I have the Honor to be with the highest Respect,

Your Excellency's most Obedt & very humble Servt

THOMAS TRUXTUN.

N. B. Lieutenant Saunders will receive your Communications

His Excellency The GOVERNOR of HAVANNAH.

[HS of Pa. NDA photostat. Truxtun's LB, 1798–9.]

To Captain Alexander Murray, U. S. Navy, from Secretary of the Navy

[TRENTON,]
Navy Department September 21st 1798

Capt ALEXr MURRAY

SIR Enclosed are Instructions authorizing the Capture of French Armed Vessels on the high Seas. — I expect the Brig *Norfolk*, Capt Williams at Norfolk, of 18 — 6 pound Cannon, will be ready for a cruise between the 5th & 10th of October; And I have ordered the Brig *Eagle* of 14 Guns, Capt Campbell, & the Schooner *Retaliation*, Lieut Commandant Bainbridge, of 14 — 4 pounders to rendezvous at that place about the 5th of that Month. —

You will take these three Vessels under your Command, & proceed to the West Indies for the purpose of seizing or destroying French Armed Vessels, and giving protection to our Commerce. Attacking French cruisers on their own grounds, will perhaps, be the most effectual mode of protecting our Vessels on our own Coasts' from their depredations. —

It will be necessary that you examine at Norfolk, the State of the provisions, Water, and Military Stores of all the Vessels; and that they receive such supplies there, as will enable them to keep the sea for at least three months. —

The *Eagle* & *Retaliation* will not carry more than two months water. — But you should be careful to have as much water & provisions on board all the Vessels. — The *Montezuma*, the *Norfolk*, the *Eagle*, and the *Retaliation* as will be sufficient for all, for three months. —

Wm Pennock Naval Agent at Norfolk, will supply whatever may be wanted. —

It is presumed that the British will attend sufficiently to the Island of St Domingo. — Guadaloupe, St Martins, Porto Rico; and other places where French Privateers are fitted out, or harbored, any or all of them, as circumstances in your own Judgment shall direct, you will attend to. I say as circumstances in your own Judgment shall direct, because I mean not to confine your exertions by any particular Instructions — The object of your cruise as already observed, is to take and destroy French Armed Vessels. — You will Judge from the Information you can obtain, how you can best effect this object, and so direct your operations.

But in attending to this object, you will also give all the aid & protection to our own Vessels in your power. — It is not necessary for me, to a man so sensible of the necessity of order & Discipline as you are, to recommend the strictest attention to it, on board of your own, and the Vessels under your Command. Too much attention cannot be paid, nor too much pains taken to impress on the Minds of the Officers & Men, a high respect for the honor of our Flag. — I will write you, to reach you at Norfolk. —

Wishing you success & honor,

I remain &c^{a}

P. S. I send you herewith, private signals for the Ships of War of the United States, also private signals to be used between his Britannick Majesty's Ships of War, and the Ships of the United States. —

NB You will see the propriety of keeping these Instructions profoundly a secret. —

[NDA. OSW, Vol. 1.]

To Captain Hugh G. Campbell, Revenue Cutter *Eagle*, from Secretary of the Navy

[TRENTON,]
Navy Department September 21st 1798

Capt HUGH G. CAMPBELL

SIR Enclosed you will receive an Act of Congress of the 19th July last, authorizing the Capture of French armed Vessels, together with Instructions founded on that Act, by which you are to be governed. — Also Private signals, and signals which have been fixed upon to enable the British & American Cruisers to know each other when they meet. —

I likewise enclose the Rules & Regulations adopted by Congress for the Government of the Navy, and Marine Regulations which you will observe yourself, and cause to be observed by those under your command. — You will introduce regular discipline among your Crew, and teach them to entertain a proper respect for the American Flag.

Presuming that you are ready, you will immediately proceed to sea, cruising from the Capes of Delaware, to the Capes of Virginia until the 5th day of October, on which day, or if that be impracticable, as soon after as possible, you must be at Norfolk, where you will find Capt Alex^{r} Murray of the Ship of War *Montezuma*, under whose orders you are to act. —

I have the honor &c^{a}

[NDA. OSW, Vol. 1.]

To Captain Alexander Murray, U. S. Navy, from Secretary of the Navy

[TRENTON,]
Navy Department September 21st 1798

Capt ALEXr MURRAY *Baltimore*

SIR I return your Commission altered as I proposed; I have not had an opportunity of receiving the President's concurrence. — I have no doubt of it; Yet if I should be mistaken, You must be content to take your old Commission again, I mean without the words "To take rank from the 1st July 1798." —

Your sentiments on this subject are so truly patriotic & virtuous, and your character stands so Justly, so high, that I am sure the President will lament as much as I shall, if unconquerable difficulties, in the arrangement of our officers should occur, to prevent your retaining at least the rank now given. —

I have the honor to be
&ca &ca —

[NDA. OSW, Vol. 1.]

To Benjamin Lincoln, Collector, Boston, from Secretary Pickering

DEPARTMENT OF STATE TRENTON *Sept 21. 1798.*

BENJAMIN LINCOLN Esqr Collector, *Boston.*

SIR, I have received a letter dated the 15th inst at Boston, signed Lasmartres, requesting the President's passport for the schooner *Eagle*, burthen seventy-five tons, to carry sixty French persons from Boston to Cape François and Port au Prince or Pettitguave. I now inclose the passport to you, with a blank for the names of the Master and owner, which names, when known, I beg you to communicate to me.

Mr Lasmartres also desires permission to receive his dues from the French Government, and vest the same in a cargo to be brought back in the Schooner: but no special permit is given, or necessary in such case, provided she returns to some port in the United States by or before the first day of December next, agreeably to the 3d Section of the Act for putting an end to the intercourse between the U. States and the French Dominions. I am respectfully &c.

TIMOTHY PICKERING.

[SDA. Dom. L., Vol. 11.]

Extract from Captain Thomas Truxtun's journal, U. S. Frigate *Constellation*, 21 September 1798, Friday

Fresh Breezes, and squally Weather. At 4 P M passed Key Sal, and thus considered myself clear of the old Straits of Bahama.

At 2 A M a strange Sail was discovered ahead, called all Hands, cleared Ship, and got to Quarters; soon after Day Light, spoke the Schooner *Hope* from Baltimore bound to Havannah, one of the small Vessels that sailed in Company with us, and crossed the Bahama Bank.

At 11 A M being nearly abreast of the Morro Castle, dispatched Lieutenant Saunders with my Dispatches &c for the Governor of the Havannah, and put him on Board the Brig *Louisa* one of our Fleet, all of which that kept with us stood in to Havannah, and anchored safe.

It being probable, or at least not unlikely, that the French may after capturing our Vessels oblige the Prisoners to answer as they may direct. I am determined to board, and examine all Vessels bound into the Havannah, unless well convinced of it's being unnecessary.

At Noon the Morro bore South, three Miles Distance, the *Baltimore* only in Company.

Latitude observed 23°.15′ N°
Longitude Account 82.18 W.

[HS of Pa. NDA photostat.]

Extract from journal of James Pity, U. S. Frigate *Constitution*, 21 September 1798, Friday

Begins calm & Clear fresh Breezes & Clear. all hands employ'd shifting the spare Anchors further aft. Recd Some Water. all hands employ'd Variously. Doctr Read and Mr Nicholson taken very sick.

[NDA.]

To Benjamin Lincoln, Collector, Boston, from Secretary Pickering

DEPARTMENT OF STATE TRENTON *Sept. 22. 1798.*

BENJAMIN LINCOLN Esqr Collector, *Port of Boston.*

SIR, Yesterday I sent you the President's permit to clear out the Schooner *Eagle*, for Mr Lasmartres, to carry French persons, to St Domingo. In the first instance of issuing a permit for clearing out a vessel from your office, I dropped a caution to prevent any collusion as to the *goods* and *effects* of the passengers, in contravention of the Act of Congress. A recent application from Norfolk, and information of such a fact elsewhere, induces a suspicion that in some instances, the persons sending out these *cartels*, as some call them chuse fast sailing vessels on purpose to be sold to the French for privateers. Besides the mischief to be apprehended from this source, it seems a direct evasion of the act, whose object was *to put an end to all commercial intercourse with the French*, and consequently a commerce in the selling and buying of vessels — and above all of vessels adapted to war. I have therefore submitted to the President this point — Whether the applicants for permits, or the owners of the vessels employed to carry away French persons, should not be required to give bond with sureties, that such vessel should not be sold, but return to the port whence they sailed, or some other port of the U. States; — and whether also the permits should not be restricted to vessels ascertained by the Collector to be *not adapted* for vessels of war. As you are near the President, I beg you to take his opinion and direction, before you act on the permit transmitted on the application of Mr Lasmartres. I am &c.

TIMOTHY PICKERING.

[SDA. Dom. L., Vol. 11.]

To Governor James Jackson, of Georgia, from Secretary Pickering

DEPARTMENT OF STATE TRENTON, *Sept. 22. 1798.*

[To] His Excellency JAMES JACKSON Esqr
Governor of the State of Georgia

SIR, On the 13th instant I received from the President of the U. S. who is at his seat near Boston, your letter of the 8th Augt describing the exposed situation of the State of Georgia and the defensive measures you deem necessary for its security in the impending war with the French; and agreeably to his directions have conversed with the Secretary of War, to whom you had before made a similar communication. The latter has shown me the answer he has lately written to you; and informs me, he shall very soon write you again on the same subject.

He says also, that he shall order the Fort near St. Mary's to be manned and defended with the troops and guns now at that place: and by Mr Seagrove's letter of the 11th July to your Excellency, it seems that in his opinion those troops are competent for the garrison. By the same letter it appears that the militia, tho' good, are destitute of arms and amunition. But Thomas King Esqr, in his letter of July 10th to your Excellency, says that the militia is *unorganized.* This is a defect which, depending on the government of Georgia to remedy, will certainly have engaged the requisite attention on your part to effect the same.

The Secretary further informs me, that Major Freeman, who is daily expected at the Northward, from whence he will immediately return to Georgia, will be specially instructed on the subject of the defence of the seacoast of that State.

The business pertaining to another department, I will only take the liberty to add a few remarks. Your representation points to so many places as necessary to be fortified, as apparently to surpass the means at the disposal of the Executive of the United States to accomplish. You mention four works (and one of them a strong one) as necessary for the security of Savannah alone: and it would seem, that unless all can be raised, any one would be of little or no use; except perhaps one which should immediately defend the town of Savannah from armed vessel, that might pass up the River to lay the town under contribution; and gallies probably would be a preferable and more certain defence from such an attack, seeing no heavy vessels can approach the town.

But admitting that forts were to be erected at all the places you have mentioned; how are they to be manned? Northern troops would soon be buried there: and the unhealthiness of the situations in general is so well known, that it would be difficult to draw even your own citizens from the back country to constitute the garrisons. My enquiries also lead me to think, that an enemy of force to attempt an invasion, would easily find landing places and evade all the fortifications which have been proposed. Upon the whole therefore it would seem, that gallies manned with negroes for working them, and with white men to serve the guns, would form a better and cheaper defence.

On the subject of the small Spanish Schooner burnt at Savannah, the prompt steps taken by your Excellency to discover the perpetrators of that outrage, and to communicate a correct statement of the affair to the Governor of East Florida, meet the President's entire approbation. I shall address a letter to the District Attorney for Georgia to add his endeavours to those of your Excellency to bring the offenders to justice. I have &c

TIMOTHY PICKERING.

[SDA. Dom. L., Vol. 11.]

To Tench Francis, Purveyor, from Secretary of Navy

[TRENTON,]
Navy Department September 22nd 1798

TENCH FRANCIS ESQR.

SIR, I return the Letter of S. Walker — His articles are Such, as will be wanted only by the public.

There is no danger of their being purchased by Individuals — It will be best therefore, not to embarrass ourselves with Contracts, which circumstances may render it inconvenient to comply with. —If such of the articles as the public want in Mr Walkers list, Should be imported by others, before Mr Walker's arrives, we Should leave ourselves at liberty to buy them. —

Enclosed you will receive the copy of a Letter from the Purser of Barry's Ship. — How comes it that the Bread & Fish turn out So bad? Ought not the man who Sold the Bread, no doubt for very fine, to take back what remains on hand? I think he ought, and that you insist upon his doing So — or that if he will not, he Should be sued for fraud on the public. — The fish too — That Subject requires attention. The Idea that it is no harm to cheat the public cannot be too Soon exploded. —

I want Barry to Sail from New Castle in ten days from this date — Before he goes, he must have bread — Pray take instant and decisive measures to Supply him with 2400Wt. of good Sound Ship Bread fit for Seamen — and let it be delivered to Captt Gill, to be forwarded by him to New-Castle — If Phila cannot supply it, you can have it Supplied from Towns below. —

I am &ca

[NDA. Req. on US T, 1798–1803.]

To Robert Hamilton, Marshal of Delaware, from Secretary of Navy

[TRENTON,]
Navy Department September 22nd 1798

ROBt HAMILTON Esqr *Marshal of Delaware Wilmington,*

SIR The Acts of Congress direct, that French Prisoners, Captured on board of French Armed Vessels shall be reported to the Collector of the Port where they shall first arrive, and shall be delivered to the Custody of the Marshal, or of some civil or Military Officer of the United States, who shall take charge for their safe keeping, and support at the expense of the United States, — —

Capt Barry has lodged a number of French Prisoners in the Goal of Newcastle, where it is apprehended they are not in sufficient security.

I have the honor to request, that you will take charge of these Prisoners, & any that may hereafter arrive in your district, and distribute them in the different Goals, if one can not be found large enough for the whole. — —

And that you will be pleased to make contracts, for supplying them with rations on the best terms in your power. — — The Ration to consist of, 1# of bread, half a pound, sometimes Fresh, sometimes Salt meat, and one pound of Potatoes, or Cabbage, Turnips, or other Wholsome Vegetables equivalent to 1# of Potatoes. — It is meant, that the Prisoners should have enough of wholsome, but cheap food. — I will not limit you as to the price of the Ration. — You will of course consult the public Interest in your Contracts

The payments to be made monthly to the Contractor, through your hands, and the money shall be furnished to you for the purpose. —

Be pleased to let me know how the Prisoners are disposed of, and the Terms of your Contracts for their Supply —

I presume there will be no difficulty in getting a Militia Guard to take the Prisoners to the Goals Selected by you, for their Safe keeping.

If not too distant, the Marines of the Ship might be employed on that service, on your application to Capt Barry. — —

Should Guards be necessary at the Goals, it will be desireable to get them into one Goal, that one Guard may suffice

I have the honor to be

&ca

[NDA. GLB No. 1.]

To William Winder, Accountant for the Navy Department, from Secretary of Navy

[TRENTON,]
Navy Department, September 22nd 1798

Wm WINDER Esqr
Accott of the Navy

SIR Captn Truxton's order for Six months pay & Rations must be paid — The difficulty I understand, arises from the circumstance of a Balance remaining against Capt Truxtun, on the Books of the Accountant of the War Department, because account of his for expenses in superintending the building of the Frigate, (which the secretary at War thinks reasonable & Just & that it ought to be paid, has not been admitted by the Accountant. — —

Without undertaking to decide between the secretary at War, and the Accountant, we must not give our Captains just cause of complaint — — If the account of Capt Truxton for his Expenses should not be admitted he is able to refund the money to the United States — The present order is part of the provision he has relied on, for his Family, while absent himself on the public service. —

You will please to ascertain the amount of the order, and I will give a Warrant —

I have the honor

&Ca

[NDA. GLB No. 1.]

To Messrs. L. Hollingsworth & Sons, Philadelphia, from Secretary of Navy

[TRENTON,]
Navy Department September 22nd 1798

Messrs L. HOLLINGSWORTH
& SONS *Phila* ————

GENTn The Frigate *United States*, Capt Barry, at New Castle, is in want of 20 Tons of Iron Ballast — Either Kentledge, or Pig Iron will do — I know not where to get it so quickly as the ship ought to have it — she ought to be out in 8 days, or 10 at most from this time. — Perhaps there may be Iron at the head of Elk — you know where it is to be had; permit me then, to depend on you, to have 20 Tons of Iron Ballast, sent to the ship immediately — Please to have the account sent to me including all expences, and your Commission, and it shall be paid at sight — But recollect that depending on you I make no other arrangement for the Iron.—

I am &ca

[NDA. GLB No. 1.]

To Otway Byrd, Collector, Norfolk, from Secretary Pickering

DEPARTMENT OF STATE TRENTON *Sept. 22, 1798.*

[To] OTWAY BYRD Esqr *Collector Port of Norfolk*

SIR, I have received from your deputy, Mr Reuben Long, a letter dated the 3d instant, stating, That "Dallert and Cartier finding that the vessel, to which a permit was granted some time ago, insufficient for the accommodation of all passengers who wish to leave this country, have solicited permission for the Schooner *South-Packet* to take passengers for Jacmel and Aux Cayes;" and that "*this is a new vessel now on the stocks.*" The latter circumstance naturally suggested the idea, that she was calculated for a fast-Sailor, and was really destined, after landing her cargo of passengers, to be sold to the French for a privateer. I have since heard of an instance of the kind, which confirms my suspicions. I do not therefore think it proper to issue a permit. I shall lay the matter before the President, who I believe will not in future grant his permit to any vessel without bonds, without competent sureties, being previously given to the Collector, that she shall not be sold, but return into the port whence she sailed, or some other port in the United States. As soon as I receive the President's direction on this subject I will again write you. In the mean time I remain &c.

TIMOTHY PICKERING

[SDA. Dom. L., Vol. 11.]

Extract from Captain Thomas Truxtun's journal, U. S. Frigate *Constellation*, 22 September 1798, Saturday

A fresh Trade Wind, and some few smart Squalls of Rain. Stood off and on the Morro all the Twenty four Hours. At 4 P M an American Brig by her Colours went into the Havannah keeping under the Guns along Shore, and in Fact otherwise too near the Rocks for me to venture in with a Ship drawing Twenty two Feet Water, particularly as there was no object in running a Risk, which in Case of a Calm with a Sea, and Current setting in, would have proved fatal to the Vessel. At 6 P M brought to and spoke the Schooner *Jane* of and from Boston bound to Havannah, out 25 Days, the Master informed me, that he had been overhawlled on Sunday last by two English Cruizers, and suffered to proceed, but saw no French Cruizers of any Sort.

At 10 A M spoke the Ship *Hope* of Providence, Rhode Island, from Turk's Islands, bound to the Havannah; sent the *Baltimore's* Boat on Board her to examine her Papers, and afterwards run down, and saw her safe within the Morro, which at Noon bore South, 3 Miles Distance. Exercised Great Guns, and Marines, and bent the new Main, and fore top Sails, the Others being much worn, and wanting repair.

[HS of Pa. NDA photostat.]

Extract from journal of James Pity, U. S. Frigate *Constitution*, 22 September 1798, Saturday

Begins clear with fresh breezes a Sloop came along Side with 30 Puncheons & 23 gang casks, water. Spoke a Ship from Liverpool out 79 Days. Jn° M°Bride master Several of our officers on Shore at Norfolk return'd on Board.

[NDA.]

Extract from journal of U. S. Ship *Herald*, Captain James Sever, commanding, 22 September 1798

This 24 hours first part modarate gales and fair pleasant weather at 2 p m Cald all hans To quarters To Exercise the guns fore and aft at 8 p m Squaley Dubble Reeft the Topsails at 9 handed them Dark Squaley weather attended with heavy Rain midle part Squaley weather and heavey Rain at 3 a m Saw three Sail Sett Topsails out all Reefs and Sett all Sail fore and aft and gave Chace at 4 a m Spoak with them The British frigate *Hind* a Brig in Companey and an american with them a prise from the westw[d] at ½ past 6 a m Squaley handed T g sail Duble Reeft Topsails Sounded in 40 fathoms watter soft owesey Bottom Latter part fresh gales Brig *Pickring* in Company

Lattd Obbrs 40..24 North

[NDA. Journal kept by Joseph Strout, 1798.]

Extract from Captain Thomas Truxtun's journal, U. S. Frigate *Constellation*, 23 September 1798, Sunday

Moderate Breezes, and pleasant Weather, standing off and on the Morro Castle, waiting for our Homeward Fleet of Merchantmen to come out. Gave Chase to several Vessels, but they stood close in with the Rocks of the Shore, of Course we could not overhawl them.

At 10 A M the American Consul one of the young Orleans, and M[r] Palyart with a Number of other Gentlemen came off, and visited me, bringing with them various Fruits, &c:

The Consul informed me, three french Frigates were daily expected from Cape Francois, and that all our Vessels would be out on Saturday.

[HS of Pa. NDA photostat.]

Extract from journal of Lieutenant John Mullowny, U. S. Frigate *United States*, 23 September 1798

the *Delaware* and prize *Sans Pareil* arrived — [Off Newcastle]

[NA.]

Extract from journal of James Pity, U. S. Frigate *Constitution*, 23 September 1798, Sunday

Moderate & Clear. Spoke a Schr from N York. 5 days out Inform'd us the *United States* & *Delaware* had taken 2 french Cruizers @ 1 P. M. Doctr Read of Norfolk came on Bd to attend our Surgeon & Mr Nicholson Jr who continue very Ill.

[NDA.]

[24 Sept. 1798]

To Major Commandant Burrows, U. S. M. C., from Lieutenant James James, U. S. M. C.

Major W. W. Burrows

Capt Dale has given permission that in case I should not be fortunate in the recruiting service for the Marine Corps that four of those belonging to the *Ganges*, may be removed on board the *Diligence* Cutter, as it may be the case; it, would be necessary that the Cloathing necessary and belonging to the Detachment should be forwarded to them; the Sickness here, is to say not in favour.

The names of those intended for the Cutter are James Brown, Edward W. Burton Wm. Frazier & Cornelius Mullen: Capt Brown informs me that from the Camp you are to furnish 8 Marines & 1 Sergt or Corpl the 4 here included your further command shall be duly attended to, Capt Brown informs me he will be ready for Sea on Thursday next.

A coppy of the pay & Cloathing role would be of much service for those attach'd to the *Ganges*

I am Sir Yr Obt Sert

James James
1 Lt Marines Sloop of War
Ganges Marcus Hook
Septr 24th 1798

[Major W. Burrows Esqr
Marine Camp near Philadelphia]

[MCA. LR, 1798.]

To Captain Hugh G. Campbell, Revenue Cutter *Eagle*, from Secretary of the Navy

[Trenton,]
Navy Department September 24th 1798

Capt Hugh G. Campbell

Sir I have received, three days after its date your Letter of the 19th I am sorry you have met with so much difficulty & delay; but it is essential that you should follow my Instructions of the 21st Instant, and be at Norfolk the 5th of October at all events, whether you are completely fitted or otherwise — If you should not be, you can be completed at Norfolk

You will please to govern yourself accordingly and let nothing but unforseen calamity, at sea, prevent your being at Norfolk by the time appointed. —

I am &ca

[NDA. OSW, Vol. 1.]

To Captain Thomas Williams, U. S. Navy, from Secretary of the Navy

[Trenton,]
Navy Department September 24th 1798

Capt Thos Williams *Norfolk*

Sir In my Letter to you, of the 21st I requested you to appoint suitable persons to fill the several stations vacant, on board of your Vessel; since then I received yours of the 13th nominating

Thomas Calvert as a Lieutenant
John K. Read------ Surgeon
John Muse--------- Purser
Robert Warren----- Midshipman

Mr John McRea being appointed your first Lieutenant, Mr Calvert must be contented to take Rank as second Lieutenant, in which capacity you are at Liberty to receive him on board of your Vessel. — Mr Thomas Reynolds has been appointed surgeon, but if he does not appear by the time you are ready, you may take John K. Read as your surgeon — You may receive Mr John Muse as your Purser & Robt Warren as midshipman. — You will inform all the Gentlemen whom you appoint, that they will be entitled to the same Emoluments acting under your appointment as if regularly commissioned — And that they will be nominated to the President, and receive their Commissions on their return — The President is in Massachusetts at present — of course 'tis impossible to have them regularly commissioned before you sail. —

I am &ca

[NDA. OSW, Vol. 1.]

To Captain Thomas Williams, U. S. Navy, from Secretary of the Navy

[Trenton,]
Navy Department September 24th 1798

Capt Thos Williams *Norfolk*

Sir Presuming that you have acted upon my Letter of the 21st Instant, directing you to take measures without delay for providing the Officers &ca of the Vessel under your Command, and having her in all respects, prepared to sail on a cruise by the 5th of October

I send you herewith, Instructions, authorizing the Capture of French Armed Vessels, whereever found on the high seas. — Also the recapture of any American Vessels which may have been captured by the French. — You are however to remember, that we are at Peace with all Nations, but the French — should you therefore even see an American Vessel captured by the armed Ship of War, of any Nation at War, with whom we are at peace, you cannot lawfully interfere to prevent such Capture. — It must be presumed, until the contrary be proved, that the Courts of that Nation will render Justice; nor must you recapture any American Vessels taken by the Ships of any such Nation. —

You will place yourself under the command of Captn Alexr Murray, of the Ship of War, the *Montezuma*, who I expect will be at Norfolk about the 5th of October. —

I enclose you the rules & regulations adopted by Congress for the Government of the Navy, and Marine regulations, which you will observe yourself, and cause to be observed by those under your command — Using every means in your power to introduce order & discipline, and to inculcate on the minds of your Officers & Men, a high sense of the importance of maintaining at every hazard, the honor of the American Flag. —

You have also enclosed, the private signals to be used between the Ships of War of the United States, — and the private signals between our Ships & those of his Britannic Majesty — also your Commission, as Captain in the Navy of the United States — all of which you will acknowledge Receipt of. —

Wishing you all possible success & honor

I remain yr &ca

[NDA. OSW, Vol. 1.]

From Secretary Pickering to the Chevalier de Yrujo

DEPARTMENT OF STATE TRENTON, *Sept. 24, 1798.*

[To] The CHEVALIER DE YRUJO *Minister plenipotentiary &c. &c. &c. of His Catholic Majesty.* ————

SIR, The governor of Georgia has transmitted to the Executive of the United States, information of an outrage committed at Savannah, in the burning of a small Spanish Schooner, of twelve tons, from St Augustine.

It seems that this Schooner, not long before, had been a privateer from St Augustine, and had captured two vessels going from Savannah to the West Indies, and carried them into St Augustine; where after a thorough examination, they were honourably released by Governor White. It seems also that two persons of her crew, on her arrival at Savannah, had been officers on board her when she was armed, and captured by two vessels above mentioned. These two men as well as the Schooner, were recollected, and the resentment of some of the Sufferers by the captors, probably excited a mob, who in the night went on board the Schooner and burnt her. This outrage, in itself unjustifiable, and after the very honourable conduct of the Governor of East Florida, wholly inexcusable, drew the attention of the magistrates; and the Governor of Georgia, besides explaining the matter fully to Governor White, issued his proclamation, offering a reward of four hundred dollars, to be paid on the discovery and conviction of the Offenders. The immediate flight of the four Spaniards who composed the Schooners crew, deprived the magistrate of the benefit of their information and testimony.

I have now written to the District Attorney of Georgia, to use his endeavours also to bring the offenders to justice. I am, Sir, your ob^t^ Servt

TIMOTHY PICKERING.

[SDA. Dom. L., Vol. 11.]

To Mr. Hawly, United States Consul, Havanna, from Captain Thomas Truxtun, U. S. Navy

UNITED STATES SHIP *Constellation*
off the Morro Castle 24th September 1798 —

DEAR SIR, I send you enclosed a Sett of Signals for the Merchantmen You will deliver a Copy to each of the American Masters, on their Departure from the Harbour; as I must leave this Station on Saturday I shall expect all the Vessels bound to the United States out agreeable to your Promise.

Accept my best Wishes for your Health, and Prosperity, and be assured I am with great Respect

Your very Obedient Humble Servant

THOMAS TRUXTUN.

To Mr HAWLY *Consul Havannah*

N. B. Mr Hawley will be kind enough to be particular in furnishing an exact Copy of the enclosed Circular, as well as the Day, and Night Signals, to each Master of a Vessel; and to have the Flags of the Day Signals painted, which can very soon be done; and by all Means to have the Fleet out by Saturday Morning next without Fail. As the Signals are agreeable to a System I have prepared, he will place my Signature at the Foot of each Copy.

THOMAS TRUXTUN.

[HS of Pa. NDA photostat. Truxtun's LB, 1798–9.]

(Circular)

[Enclosure]

Constellation OFF THE MORRO
24th Sept. 1798.

SIR, A few Signals are all that is necessary for the Fleet of Merchantmen about to sail from Havannah under Convoy of the United States Ships of War, *Constellation* and *Baltimore,* especially as I shall consider them out of all Danger of french Cruizers, when well through the Gulph of Floriday, say as far to the Northward as the Southern Extremes of the United States. I am, Sir, wishing you safe Home

Your Obedient humble Servant

THOMAS TRUXTUN.

To Captain [ ]
of the American Ship, or Vessel
Called the ———— of ————

[Enclosure]

[24 Sept. 1798]

Signals by Day

Nº 99. The Fleet will make more Sail ----- —×—

100. The Fleet will shorten Sail --------- —×—

155. To sail in close Order ------------- —×—

160. To sail in open Order ------------- —×—

246. To follow the Motions of Commodore —×—

120. To tack ------------------------ —×—

121. To ware ------------------------ —×—

137. To lay to on Starboard Tack ------ —×—

138. To lay to on Larboard Tack ------- —×—

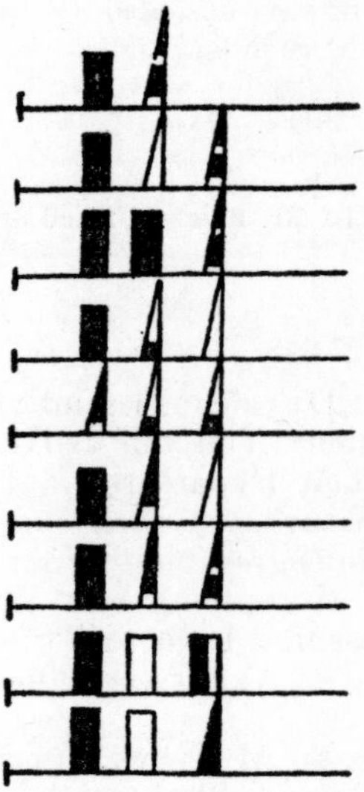

A strange Sail to Windward —×— Merchantmen to hoist their Colours at fore top Mast or top Gallant Mast Head.

A strange Sail to Leeward —×— Merchantmen to hoist their Colours at Main

125. To make best of your Way —×—

× 139. On seeing Danger of any Sort, or Land a Merchantman to speak the *Constellation*, or *Baltimore* whichever is nearest, who will make the Signal to the Other, as painted ----------- — —

× A Merchantman wanting to speak the Commodore will hoist his Colours, and stand towards him — —

6. In Distress ---------------------- —×—

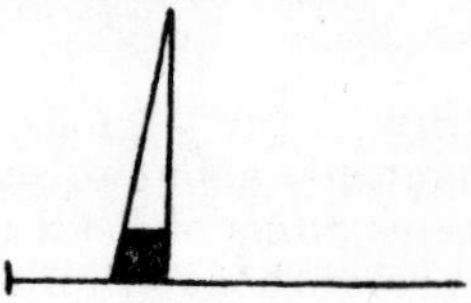

N. B. In Case of parting and meeting again, the Ships of War, forming this Convoy, will be known by a red Pendnant at the Main top Gallant Mast Head, a blue Pendnant at the fore, and a white Pendnant at the Mizen Top Gallant Mast Head, to be answered by the Merchantmen by their hoisting their Ensign, or Jack at the Main Top Mast, or top Gallant Mast Head, and a Pendnant at the fore top Mast, or top Gallant Mast Head; or if a Sloop a Pendnant over the Ensign at her top Mast Head.

THOMAS TRUXTUN.

N. B. Merchantmen not having a Pendnant with a white Tail, which is the Signal of Distress, will hoist their Colours in the Shrouds, Union down. —

Nº 1 is a blue Colour
–2 is a white Pendnant with red Tail.
–3 is a white Colour.
–4 is a blue Pendnant with white Tail.
–5 is a red Colour
–6 is a red Pendnant with white Tail.
–7 is a red, and white Colour
–8 is a red Pendnant
–9 is a white, and blue Colour.
–0 is a white Pendnant

The Duplicate Pendnant is white, red, blue, white, blue, and red, it is used where there are not two Pendnants of the same

THOMAS TRUXTUN.

Signals by Night

On seeing a strange Sail to Windward, Merchantmen will hoist two Lights, and speak one of the Ships of War.
On seeing a strange Sail to Leeward, Merchantmen will hoist one Light, and speak one of the Ships of War.
To tack, or ware Commodore will hoist five Lights.
To hawl the Wind to Starboard, six Lights.
To hawl the Wind to Port, seven Lights,
To heave to on Starboard Tack eight Lights.
To heave to on Larboard Tack, nine Lights.
To make Sail, one Gun.
To shorten Sail, two Guns.
On seeing Land, or Danger, two Lights, and one Gun.
Avoid the Danger, three Lights, and two Guns.
Disperse, four Lights, and three Guns.
The Fleet to follow the Commodore, five Lights, and four Guns.
To go under an easy Sail, three Lights.

N. B. All Lights will be hoisted in a Range, and the *Constellation* will carry a Poop, and top Light every Night, and the *Baltimore* a top Light only. The *Baltimore,* will keep the Rare, and answer Signals in the Day by a Flag of three Blue, and three white Stripes; and by Night immediately hoisting two Lights, which will be hawlled down, as well as the Signal, as soon as the Commodore sees them.

The Fleet will sail as compactly as possible keeping at a proper Distance in Calms, and bad Weather.

Fog Signals at this Season of the Year, are not necessary to give the Merchantmen in the Tract of Sea we are to pass through; Captain Phillips, however, having those Signals, as well as the general Day, and Night Signals, will attend to them, whenever necessary to be made.

THOMAS TRUXTUN.

[HS of Pa. NDA photostat. Truxtun's LB, 1798–9.]

To William Pennock, Navy Agent, Norfolk, from Secretary of Navy

[TRENTON]
Navy Department September 24th 1798

Wm PENNOCK Esqr *Norfolk*

SIR Your Letters to the 15th came regularly to hand; but I did not receive Capt Nicholson's 'till the last mail. — —

From the Account given by Capt Nicholson, it is impossible for me to form any Accurate Judgment of the real character of the ship *Niger*, brought into Hampton by him —

That She is not a Ship commissioned under the Authority of the French Republic, Seems more than probable, I think too it is more than probable that She is a Ship belonging to or hired by French Loyalists, who unable to find refuge in any other Quarter of the Globe; meant to make the United States an asylum for their persons & property — — The Train of Gun Powder, of which Capt Nicholson Speaks, might have been intended to prevent their falling into the hands of French National Ships, or Privateers. — The Crew being a mixture of all Nations, and an abandoned set of wretches, may be accounted for, from the circumstance of the owners (not allowed to take British sailors from British Islands) being under the necessity of taking such men as they could pick up. — Capt Nicholson indeed Strongly reports, that this Ship was certainly cruising, & Capturing our East & West India homeward bound vessels — If this be fact, there will be no difficulty in the business; but he does not state, that he has any evidence of this Fact; and he omits to say a word about the Account given by the Passengers, on this, or any other material point. — a most material omission! Upon the whole, I am almost as much at a Loss as to the Character of the Ship, as I was, before the receipt of his Letter. — There is no doubt he did his duty in bringing her into Port — And She must now be left to the decision of our Courts. But believing it most probable, that the Owners, and perhaps the Officers of the Ship are oppressed men, coming to our Country for refuge It becomes the American Character to treat them with Justice & humanity. — If they are in confinement, they should be liberated on Parole, and assured that Justice will be done them; and if innocent; that they have nothing to apprehend —

I think too it would be but right to advise them to able & honorable Counsel — While due care is taken of the claim of the United States, and Capt Nicholson and his Crew — We must not forget that the American Government & people want no more than Justice — As to the Prisoners, I mean the Common Sailors & Petty Officers; as they are already secured in the Fort, I suppose they may as well remain there until, the fate of the Vessel be determined, instead of sending them to the Country Goals, as mentioned in my last — But in future when Prisoners arrive at your port, you will please to have them delivered over to the Marshal, who, will, as the Law directs, take order for their safe keeping. — The Ration to be allowed them must Consist of one pound of Bread, — half a pound of Meat, and one Pound of Potatoes, or other Wholesome Vegetable, equal in value & nutriment to one pound of Potatoes — and must be Supplied by Contract, as mentioned in my last. —

The secretary of State, I expect will write to the district attorney, on the Subject of the Ship —

I have the honor to be

&ca &ca

P. S. The utmost care, and attention should be paid to the safety of the Money & Goods of this Ship — If She be restored to the Captain or owners, every thing taken from her, or her Crew should be restored with her. — —

[NDA. GLB No. 1.]

To President John Adams from the Secretary of Navy

[TRENTON,]
Navy Department Sepr 24th 1798

JOHN ADAMS *Presidt U. States*

I recd only on Saturday Evening, the Letter from Capt Nicholson, of which the enclosed is a Copy.

It is I think highly probable, that the Ship brought into Hampton by Nicholson, belongs to, or has been hired by that unfortunate class of Frenchmen, who call themselves Loyalists, & who adhering to the British till a place of Refuge is denied them in the West Indies come to America as the only assylum for their persons & property. The train of Gun powder mentioned by Nicholson might have been intended to prevent the greater calamity of falling into the hands of their Countrymen; The number of the Crew does not appear to be larger than necessary to defend the Ship against the French Privateers they might expect to meet with — and the Crew being made up all Nations, & of the abandoned of all Nations, may be accounted for on the ground of their not being allowed in a British Island, to take British Sailors. If indeed it be true, as Nicholson so strongly asserts, that "the Ship was cruising & capturing our homeward bound East & West India Men" the business will be easily settled — But it is remarkable that he says nothing about any evidence he has of this all important fact — and it is also remarkable, that tho' there were reputable passengers on board & passengers too, irritated by the ill treatment they had received He does not attempt to detail any information received from them — nor to depend upon the evidence in their power to give. I fear the real truth has not been so much the object of his enquiries, as might have been wished in an Officer of his high Rank in the American Navy. I will not however Sir trouble you with further comments on this extraordinary *Official* Letter. I have written to the Navy Agent at Norfolk, to liberate on Parole, the Officers & owners if they are confined, unless there are stronger reasons than I am informed of, to suspect them of Piracy, & to tell them, they have nothing to apprehend, if innocent — and I have desired him to recommend them to able & honorable Counsel, which I have no doubt wlll meet with your approbation.

[NDA. Nom. Appts. LB, 1798–1820.]

Extract from journal of James Pity, U. S. Frigate *Constitution*, 24 September 1798, Monday

Begins with clear Weather @ 10 Capt Nicholson came on Boad from Williamsburg clean'd between Decks & Sprinkled them with Vinegar Spoke a Schr from N York & Ship from Europe. Doctr Galt came on Board from Hampton to attend the Sick. Ends in Clear Wr

[NDA.]

Extract from Captain Thomas Truxtun's journal, U. S. Frigate *Constellation*, 24 September 1798, Monday

Moderate Breezes, and pleasant. At 3 P M gave Chace to two Sails, that were discovered to Leeward, soon after I saw they were Frigates. At half past 4 Ditto being under my three top Sails, and prepared for Action, they hawlled their Wind to the Northward, and made Sail; and soon after bore down upon us, seeming determined to exchange a Broad Side, & run for the Morro, had we proved an Enemy; at five they passed me under a Crowd of Sail standing in for the Morro; we hailled each Other, and being satisfied they were two superb Spanish 44s I could only be surprised at their Conduct. After speaking us in running . . . . . . immediately into the Havannah, without further ceremony, I stood on my Tacks all Night.

At Noon the Morro Castle bore South East half a Mile Distance, the *Baltimore*, that I ordered to chase a small Sail to Leeward at 9 A M not returned, tho' at the Distance of only two Leagues under the Lee.

[HS of Pa. NDA photostat.]

To Captain George Cross, U. S. Navy, from Secretary of the Navy

[Trenton,]
Navy Department September 25th 1798. —

Capt Geo: Cross
Charleston (S. C.)

Sir In my Letter of the 10th Instant; I enclosed your commission as Captain in the Navy of the United States; and requested that you would immediately take the Command of the Vessel before commanded by Capt Cochran. —

I know not precisely whether the Brig *Unanimity* still remains in the public service, or whether her Stores &ca have been transferred to the new Vessel contracted for, by the Collector — Whatever vessel is in the public service it is intended you shall take the command of her. —

I know not the number of men engaged as Seamen. You ought to have 70 besides Commissioned Officers. — These should consist of a Serjeant, Corporal, & 12 Marines, to be furnished by the commanding officer of Marines at Charleston. — And any number you think right, not exceeding 40 able seamen at 17 Dolls per month, the residue of Boys & ordinary seamen from 5 to 14 Dolls per mo according to merit. — The Collector will as usual furnish the Supplies, and money for recruiting, & pay of the Crew — The vessel you are to command — in the present Instance, being still considered on the Revenue Cutter Establishment. — If the Crew now belonging to the Vessel be not such as is described, & engaged for 12 months, on these conditions, you should as fast as the times of Service of the present Crew expire, engage a new Crew on these conditions. —

If you have a Boy for every Gun, there will not be too many boys. — The situation and prospects of our Country, require that we should create seamen. — If you think proper, you may take two spritely young men of good character as midshipmen @ 19 Dollars per month. —

I enclose you the form of a Shipping Paper, & of a Bond to be signed by the persons who become Sureties for the money to be advanced.— For I take it for granted, that you will not get men without two months advance. — In which case they must be gratified — — You will be careful that the sureties are men of responsibility before you receive them, and equal to the repayment of any advance in case of desertion. —

I have the honor to be &c[a]

[NDA. OSW, Vol. 1.]

To Captain George Cross, U. S. Navy, from Secretary of the Navy

[TRENTON,]
Navy Department September 25th 1798

Capt GEO: CROSS —

SIR Enclosed you will receive Private Signals — & those between the United States Ship of War & those of Great Britain — also rules & regulations for the Navy and Marine regulations for the Government of yourself & Crew; and which you will cause to be observed so far as they will apply — You have also enclosed, Instructions founded on the Acts of Congress, authorizing you to Capture French armed Vessels where ever found on the high seas, or in our harbours, Rivers or Inlets. — And to recapture Vessels Captured by the French. — You will proceed to sea as early as possible — Your Cruising Ground to extend from Cape Fear to our Southern Extremity; — but you will consider the Port & Harbour of Charleston, the Harbour of Beaufort, and the Georgia Coast, as demanding your most particular attention. —

Commanding for the present, a Revenue Cutter, you will pay attention to the Instructions of the Treasury Department On the Subject of our own commercial Vessels, & others bound into our Ports. —

It will be necessary that you appear off the Harbour of Charleston every twelve or 15 Days to receive any communications, which may be sent you from hence. —

Capt Nicholson of the Frigate *Constitution*, & Capt Bright of the Brig *Virginia*, are cruising from Cape Henry to our southern Extremity. — And it is probable you will fall in with these Vessels. —

You cannot be too attentive to the Introduction of order & discipline among your Crew, and you should be assiduous in endeavours to inspire your officers & men with a high sense of the honor of the American Flag, which must be maintained at every hazard. —

But you must not forget that we are at War, only with Frence Armed Vessels, and the men found on board of them. — The Vessels of other Nations are entitled to, and must receive from us, civility & Friendship. — You are not, even to recapture a Vessel of our own, taken by the Vessels of any of the Nations at War, but the French — We are at peace, and wish to remain so, with all other Nations, and we must presume their Courts will render Justice. —

You will let me hear from you, as often as opportunity offers — giving me information of every material Occurrence —

Wishing you Success & honor

I have the honor to be &c^a

[NDA. OSW, Vol. 1.]

To Captain Patrick Fletcher, U. S. Navy, from Secretary of the Navy

[TRENTON,]
Navy Department September 25th 1798

Capt PATRICK FLETCHER *Boston*

SIR Presuming that agreeably to my notification of the 18th Instant you have made preparation to enter upon the duties of your appointment as Capt in the Navy of the United States. — I have now to request, that you will immediately repair to Providence, and there take the Command of the Ship *George Washington* lately purchased by the public —

I wish to have this Vessel in readiness for a cruize as early as possible; — Capt Silas Talbot acts as Agent for the Public at Providence, so that no inconvenience or detention will arise from inattention. — I shall expect on your part every attention to the Equipment and Manning of this Vessel — The officers must be appointed from Rhode Island.

You will write me immediately on the receipt of this Letter, and say whether you can repair immediately to Providence or not; And if you can, what time you will be there. — That I may forward the necessary Instructions by the time you arrive; If you should find it inconvenient to repair there immediately, I shall be under the necessity of providing another Commander for the *George Washington.*

I am Sir &ca

[NDA. OSW, Vol. 1.]

To Captain Isaac Phillips, U. S. Navy, from Captain Truxtun, U. S. Navy

UNITED STATES' SHIP *Constellation*
off the Morro Castle 25th September 1798 —

SIR, I do myself the Pleasure to send you by Lieutenant Sterett a Sett of Signals for the Fleet to be placed under our Convoy, from the Havannah, Home.

As these Signals are merely to enable the Merchantmen to keep Company with us, there are but few of them Compass Signals at Night, or to follow the Commodore in the Day, you have in the printed Signals. The Merchantmen must attend to the Motions of the Ships of War in all Cases, where to them no Signal is made. You will carry a top Light every Night, and after speaking with me about Sun Set, bring up, and sail in the Rear of the Fleet.

The former Signals you will please to send me back in Return, and attend to the printed Signals from the Department of the Navy as well as those accompanying this Note.

I shall have the Pleasure to show you on our Return to Hampton Roads, a Sett of Signals, (of which the inclosed are a Part of the Numbers) that I am now completing, intended for a Fleet of any Number of Ships of the Line in all Cases as well as Merchantmen Transports under Convoy.*

I am, Sir, Wishing us better Luck with great Respect
Your very Obedient hble Servant

THOMAS TRUXTUN.

Captain PHILLIPS
U. S. Ship, Baltimore

* In the Signals I now send you for the present Convoy, there are only four Numbers [word mutilated] Vizt. N° N° N° N°
99 120 125 6 which can interfere with the printed Signals, and to obviate any Difficulty, or Mistake on that Score, I shall never hoist them to you (while in Company with the present Fleet) to be understood as a Part of the Printed Signals without being accompanied by a United States' Jack being displayed near the same Place immediately, [word mutilated] about the same Time. Should we unfortunately by any unforeseen Circumstance be separated during our Passage Home, you will in that Case take a Range along the Southern Coast [from] St. Mary's towards Savannah, Charleston and North Carolina, and then return to Hampton Roads; In this Range you will examine all foreign Vessels, and such of our own, as are in any way suspicious, at the same Time interrupt the Trade as little as possible by unnecessary Detention.

[HS of Pa. NDA photostat.]

Extract from Captain Thomas Truxtun's journal, U. S. Frigate *Constellation*, 25 September 1798, Tuesday

Pleaseant Breezes, and but little, if any Current; if any it must run to Leeward.

The Schooner I ordered the *Baltimore* to chase Yesterday proved to be an American from Havannah bound to New Orleans.

At Day Dawn this Morning heard several Guns fired in the Harbour, or at the Morro, and at fair Day Light discovered a Fleet of four Men of War, and a Number of Merchantment coming out. This Fleet was that bound to La Vera Cruz, which I was informed a few Days ago was ready for Sea.

Shortly after I ascertained this Fleet, I observed a Number of American Vessels coming out, which I understood from our Consul would sail to Day; they are under Convoy of two Ships belonging to Philadelphia of Eighteen Guns each, a Force sufficient to repel the Attack of any french Privateers in these Seas, as I am well informed the heaviest french Privateer that has been off here this War only mounted 16 Guns, six Pounders, and was rigged a Schooner; all the

Others were two, four, and six Gun Vessels. At Noon the Morro bore South East, 2 Leagues Distance, the *Baltimore* a little Astern.

[HS of Pa. NDA photostat.]

Extract from journal of U. S. Ship *Herald*, Captain James Sever, commanding, 25 September 1798

This 24 hours first part Calm flattening weather out Cutter and Scrubd the Bottom at 3 p m Sett Stearing Sails Loo and Loft and gave Chase to Sail in western quarter at 10 p m Spoak hur a Schooner from Turks Island Bound To New port

Middle part Strong gales from the North Close Reeft Topsails Send Down Top g yards at 9 a m housd T G mast handed Mizen T Sail

Latter part hard gales and heavy Sea under Close Reef main T sail and F Sail Brig *Pickring* in Companey

Lattd Obbsr 40..12 N

[NDA. Journal kept by Joseph Strout, 1798.]

Extract from journal of James Pity, U. S. Frigate *Constitution*, 25 September 1798, Tuesday

Strong Breezes from the N. W. W. & Clear W^r^ @1/2 past 9 A. M. Mr Samuel Nicholson Midshipman on Board the Frigate *Constitution* & Eldest Son of Saml Nicholson Esq^e^ (Com^r^ of Said Ship) departed this Life aged 16 Years, of the prevailing epedemic fever after an Illness of 4 days. The Coll^rs^ of ye Frigate Cutter *Virginia* & *Niger* were hoisted half Mast. got a Coffin made & prepar'd to bury him @ 10 Capt Bright of the Cutter *Virginia* came on B^d^ to attend the funeral. Made Signal for a Boat @ 1/2 past 11 a Sch^r^ came along side and took on Board the Corps of Nicholson which was carried to Hampton attended by Several officers & Men. At 1/2 past 7 the boat Return'd from Hampton having buried Mr Nicholson in the Church yard by the Side of Commodore Mowat. @ 8 sent Doct^r^ Read on Shore being Ill of the same fever.

[NDA.]

To Captain Alexander Murray, U. S. Navy, commanding *Montezuma*, from Secretary of the Navy

[TRENTON,]
Navy Department September 26th 1798

Capt ALEX^r^ MURRAY

SIR, Referring to my Letter of Instructions of the 21 Instant; you will perceive that I have been very general in my directions; my intention then being to leave you much at large, to act upon the information you may obtain in the West Indies, or in going thither as your own Judgment shall direct you, will best promote the object of your Enterprize. —

You must not forget that you are at War with French Armed Vessels, and the persons found on board of them only. We are at peace, and wish to keep at peace with all other Nations; should you therefore meet with American Vessels that have been captured by the Vessels of other Nations at War. Should you even see them in the Act of making the Capture, you must not interfere, but must presume that the Courts of Such Nations will render Justice. —

The length of time consumed in your Expedition will depend on Events. — You will probably return at a season, when it would be hazardous for the Vessels under your Command to go to Philadelphia or Baltimore; You will therefore return to Norfolk, or if you cannot readily enter the Chesapeake, to New York; with the Vessels under your Command; giving me instant notice of your arrival. —

If you fall in with Vessels bound to New York, on your return, it will be proper for you to Write by such opportunities, that I may have a chance of hearing of your being on the Coast before your arrival. —

I hope you will not be delayed many days for the Brig *Norfolk;* and I have been so positive; in my Instructions to Capt Campbell & Lieutenant Bainbridge, that I cannot doubt of their being at Norfolk by the 5th of October. — Whatever these Vessels want, Mr Pennock must instantly Supply. — Should you return by way of the Havanna, in that case Capt Campbell of the Brig *Eagle* may be ordered to Savannah in Georgia, & where, (deeming such an event possible) I shall have Instructions lodged for him. —

Should you find your Squadron encumbered with French Prisoners in the W Indies, altho' there is no express Law authorizing it, you are at Liberty to exchange such prisoners for American Seamen Captured by the French. — If you cannot do this, you may deliver them to any British Officer who will give a receipt for them. — I mean this in the event of your having too many prisoners. —

I am &ca

[NDA. OSW, Vol. 1.]

To Secretary Benjamin Stoddert from George Washington

MOUNT VERNON, *Septr 26th 1798.* —

SIR, It will afford me pleasure to give you any information in my power, and any opinion, so far as I am able to form one, on the subject of your letter of the 16th instant; which did not come to my hands till the 24th.

I cannot entertain a doubt, but it will be the policy of this Country to create such a Navy as will protect our commerce from the insults and depredations to which it has been subjected of late, and to make it duly respected. — To effect this, there must be, as you observe, at least one Navy Yard established for building Ships. — That this should be under the Eye of the Government, and as near the centre of the United States as it can be fixed, with equal advantages to the whole of the Community, I think no one will deny. —

Whether or not the States to the northward of the Potomac are able to supply timber for Ship-building in such quantities — of such quality, and upon such terms as may be desireable, is more than I can tell. — But I will venture to say, that no place, either north or south of this, can be more effectually secured against the attack of an Enemy and that the Banks and vicinity of this River, both above and below tide water, abound with the best of Ship timber, is well known. — Whenever the Navigation above tide water shall be completed (which

I trust will be at no very distant period) there will be opened, not only an inexhaustible store of timber for building; but an abundant supply of the largest and best white pine trees for masts of any dimensions, as there are extensive forests of them about the head of the Potomac. — Besides which, no part of the United States affords better Cedar & Locust than the Lands about this River. — You know that Iron of the best quality can be furnished from the works on the River, and as cheap as from any part of the United States; and the establishment of a public foundry and Armory at the junction of the Potomac and Shanandoah, will afford no small advantage in arming the Ships. —

The articles of Tar, Pitch, Live-Oak &c, can be brought here *at least* upon as good terms as to any place north of this: And if hemp, cordage &c are to be imported, they can certainly come here as readily as to any other part of the United States. — But, should hemp be furnished from our own lands, (which is very desireable) this River is the Market to which it would be most likely to be brought in the greatest abundance; for, to say nothing of the rich bottoms on this River and its branches, which are exceedingly well calculated for raising hemp, it is so valuable an article that it will bear transportation across the Allegany from the rich lands of the Ohio, where it can, and undoubtedly will be produced in large quantities.

With respect to security against the attacks of an Enemy, no place can have advantages superior to the Federal City and Alexandria. — Should proper works be erected on Diggs' point (which you well know) at the junction of the Potomac and Piscatiqua Creek, it would not be in the power of all the Navies in Europe to pass that place, and be afterwards in a situation to do mischief above; for every Vessel, in passing up the River, must, from the course of the channel, (and the channel is so narrow as to admit but of one vessel's going abreast) present her bows to that point long before she comes within gun-shot of it, and continue in that direction until she comes directly under the point, from whence shot may be thrown upon her deck almost in a perpendicular direction.

Should she be so fortunate as to pass the works, she must expose her stern to the fire from them, as far as a shot can reach. — Thus exposed to be raked fore and aft, for such a distance, without once being able to bring her broadside to bear upon the Fort, you can readily see how almost impossible it will be for a vessel to pass this place; provided it be properly fortified and well supplied. — And what makes it the more important, is, that it cannot be attacked by land with any prospect of success; for it has the River on one side — Piscataqua Creek on another side (each nearly a mile wide) and the opposite Banks very low — a very deep Ravine (level with the Creek) on the third side — from whence the height is almost, if not altogether, inaccessable — and a very narrow approach on the fourth side. — In a word, the works might be insulated — and one range of batteries over another constructed sufficient for an hundred or more pieces of Cannon. —

Another advantage which this River affords is, that altho' the distance, in the course of the River, from its mouth to the Federal City, is between 150 and 200 miles; yet, from the heights about Cedar point (say Laidler's Ferry) no vessel can enter the River undiscovered —

and by means of Signals established on the prominent Eminencies, between that place and the site just mentioned, and the Federal City, notice thereof, and of the number & description of the Vessels, may be conveyed to those places in a few minutes. — Besides, there are not many winds, I believe, that will serve Vessels the whole distance. —

How far the place marked out in the plan of the Federal City, for a Marine Hospital, may be eligible for a Navy Yard, either from its situation or extent, I am unable to say. From your knowledge and information on this subject you are better able to judge than I am. — But that Locks or dry Docks, for building or repairing Ships, are essential to a Navy Yard, is certain; and there is no doubt but abundance of Water, to supply such, may be had from the Streams which you mention. And I think it is by no means chimerical to say, that the water of the Potomac may, and will be brought from above the Great Falls into the Federal City, which would, in future, afford an ample supply for this Object. —

But, after enumerating all the superior advantages which this River offers for the establishment of a Navy-Yard, every thing will depend upon the depth of water; and this is so important a point, that an accurate examination of it should be made, and no reliance placed on vague information. —

Should it not be found sufficient for Ships of the Line fully armed & provisioned, might not some measures be taken to deepen the channel over the bar at Maryland point, the only place, I am told, that requires it? — Or, might not a Naval Arsenal, or a depot for provisions, be established, with security, below the shallow parts of the River, where the Ships might Arm or take in their provisions? — These, however, are mere suggestions, which may, or may not be worth attending to. —

I thank you, Sir, for the good wishes you express for my health, which I most sincerely reciprocate, — and beg you to be assured that I am, with great respect &
esteem,
Your most Obedient Servant

G. WASHINGTON

BENJAMIN STODDERT Esqr
Secretary of the Navy

[Conn. Hist. Soc. Mss. No. 42.]

To Captain Stephen Decatur (senior), U. S. Navy, from Secretary of the Navy

[TRENTON,]
Navy Department September 26th 1798

Capt STEPHEN DECATUR

SIR As this is the season when our vessels may be expected from Europe; and as it is probable attempts may be made by the French Cruisers, to intercept them on, or near our own Coasts, you will please to proceed to sea, as soon as your ship is Watered, and you get on board the few Supplies you want. — Your object must be to protect the Trade from New York to the Chesapeake and doubting neither your discretion, Bravery, nor Enterprize, I leave it to yourself to Judge, in what manner you can best effect this object. — I will only observe, that Capt Barry will cruize from the Delaware Eastward. — It will be proper then, for you to pay most attention southward — There will, I imagine, be but little danger of Enemy Vessels on our Coasts, by the 15th November, you will therefore (no circumstances arising which in your Judgement shall make a longer cruize necessary) come into the Delaware, and up to Philadelphia about that time. —

Before you sail, be pleased to write me, what your Ship will want on your return, for another cruize of three months —

I have the honor &ca.

[NDA. OSW, Vol. 1.]

To the Marshal of Delaware from Secretary of Navy

[TRENTON,]
Navy Department September 26th 1798

To the Marshal of Delaware or whoever has the Custody of the French Prisoners, brought in by Capains Barry & Decatur.

SIR It appearing from Capt Decatur's information, that John Buffington, an american Native Citizen, taken in the Prize Sloop brought in by you, was forced into the Service of the French Cruisers, and continued in it against his will. — You will please to release the Said Buffington to Capt Decatur and for So doing, this will be your Authority —

I am Sir &ca

[NDA. GLB, No. 1.]

To William Nicholls, Marshal of Pennsylvania, from Secretary of Navy

[TRENTON,]
Navy Department 26th Septr 1798

Wm NICHOLLS Esqr
Philada

SIR, General Hand of Lancaster, has taken some trouble respecting the French Prisoners at that place, and has incurred expense by employing a Guard of Militia to assist the Sheriff in keeping them Secured — This expense, I have informed him, you will repay, as well as any further expense that may be necessary for their safe keeping, and for Supplying them with rations. — I request therefore that you will be pleased to attend particularly to this object as soon as possible — You will have them Supplied by Contract, on the best Terms in your power, with 1# of Coarse Bread, ½# of Meat, and 1# of Potatoes, Turnips, or any other kind of vegetables pr day. — This you will consider the rule, in all future cases, and you will have the Accounts rendered & Settled monthly —

I have no doubt you will get this Service performed with Occonomy. —

P. S. Genl Hand has probably not paid the Guard, and may not wish to be troubled on the Subject, you had better therefore prevent this, by paying the Guard Yourself. —

I have the honor &ca

[NDA. GLB No. 1.]

CAPTAIN STEPHEN DECATUR (SENIOR), U. S. NAVY.

To General Hand, Lancaster, from Secretary of Navy

[TRENTON,]
Navy Department 26th September 1798.

GENERAL HAND
Lancaster

SIR The Secretary at War has referred to me, your Letter to him, of the 31st Ult°

The Acts of Congress direct, that French prisoners shall be delivered to the Marshal of the District where they arrive, or some Civil, or Military officer of the United States, or of any State, who shall take order for their safe keeping at the expense of the United States; So that I have really no proper Authority to interfere in the business — But as Congress have appropriated no Money for the Maintenance of prisoners, or guarding them; As they must be maintained and guarded; and as those taken by our Armed Vessels, are supposed to come under my direction, in cases where the Law has not made proper provision; — I advanced money out of the Navy appropriations to Major Nicholls the Marshall for feeding the Prisoners — I will write to him, to pay the Guard also. — — And any Guard in future found necessary, as well as for their rations; of the Strength of which, I have the honor to request, you will still be so good as to Judge — —

I have the honor &ca

[NDA. GLB No. 1.]

Extract from journal of James Pity, U. S. Frigate *Constitution*, 26 September 1798, Wednesday

Light Breezes from the N. N. W. @ 10 A. M. Discover'd our Main Top mast Trussel Trees to be broke Sent down T. Gt Yds & T. Gallt Mast on Deck. stripped the Topmast Carpenters fitted a New pair of Tressel Trees. rigged the Top Mast anew & sent up T. Gallt Yards. @ 3 A. M. a Boat came along side from Norfolk with Mr Russell our fst Lieut & Several other officers from the Interment of Doctr Read who died this Morning he was buried with Military Honors.

[NDA.]

Extract from Captain Thomas Truxtun's journal, U. S. Frigate *Constellation*, 26 September 1798, Wednesday

Standing off and on the Morro as before with the *Baltimore* in Company. Brought to with Shot several small Vessels close in Shore that had the Appearance of french Privateers, but they proved to be Spanish Coasters, and other friendly Vessels. At Noon the Morro bore South West about one Mile Distance. A Boat from our Consul came off with a Letter, by which I forwarded a second Copy of my Signals for the Fleet, having previously sent him a Copy by the *Sisters of Norfolk*, Anderson, Master, which Vessel I brought to this Morning, and saw safe in the Harbour, she was from Teneriff.

[HS of Pa. NDA photostat.]

To Secretary Stoddert from Major Commandant W. W. Burrows, U. S. M. C.

MARINE CAMP, *Sept. 27, 1798.*

SIR, I expect this day to send off to Charleston, some articles for the Marine Soldiers expected to be raised there: and have desired Lieut Hall to supply Capt. Cross, with the necessary Compliment of men, when required. I have a Letter from Major Pinkney informing me that he has appointed John Maine, 2d Lieut of Marines. I have to request leave to be allowed to appoint a Contractor for the Marine Corps. The Vagabond, Matthew Spillard who has been appointed for the Army, from growing rich, grows insolent. I have never had any personal Insult from himself, but he insults my Officers and men, sends impertinent messages to Camp, orders us to draw 4, 5 days provisions as suits him, when he knows that meat will not keep sound 2 days, and yesterday I wrote him an Order to come to me this morning, and he has sent me a verbal message, that I may come to him if I want him, that if I am not satisfied with him I may get another Contractor, and that he will not supply me after this month. From the situation of the times, I cannot get at any knowledge how to proceed against him; but at any Rate I ought to have a Contractor that will obey orders or I cannot execute those I receive. This fellow puts every impediment in my way. He detained the detachment going to Baltimore one day, and if I want a Cart or Waggon, I am obliged to look after it myself, for he sends words he won't — This matter must be remedied, and I know of no better way than to appoint some one, that will obey orders from you and those under you

I have the Honor to be
Yo: Ob: Ser:

W. W. B[URROWS]
M[*ajor*] C[*ommandant*]
M[arine] C[orps]

Since writing the above, my Capt., presented me with the enclosed elegant Composition, which I submit to your perusal, and ask if it be possible to exist with such a mass of Ignorance and Insolence

B. STODDERT Esq:
Secy of the Navy.

[MCA. LS, 1798.]

To President John Adams, from the Secretary of Navy

[TRENTON,]
Navy Department September 27th 1798

JOHN ADAMS Esqr
President U. S.

SIR Having left behind me, when I came into Public Service, a wife & seven Children, whom I am anxious to see, and to remove to Philadelphia as soon as prudence will permit, I have the honor to solicit permission to transfer the duties of my office to Colo Pickering, about the 15th or between the 15th & 20th of October — for about three weeks — possibly some necessary attention to my private affairs will require an absence of four — but this I do not expect will be the case. —

I mention Col° Pickering, because the duties of the Secretary at War will require all his attention, particularly during the time I shall be absent — and Mr Wolcott proposes to go to Connecticut for Mrs Wolcott —

I shall endeavour to leave my business in such a Train, that it may be perfectly understood without requiring too much of the attention of Col° Pickering. —

Decatur is ordered to cruise from Delaware to Cape Henry, 'till the 15th November, when he is to return into Port — I shall to morrow send orders to Barry to cruise for the same time from Delaware Eastward. — Truxton with Philips may be expected before the 15th November from the Havanna and I shall before I leave Trenton make arrangements to have as much Force as possible in readiness in the month of December to proceed to the West Indies, or wherever ordered — I should suppose that the three frigates and Six or Seven 20 to 24 Gun Ships, and some vessels of smaller size, which will be prepared by that time, might be employed to advantage in the West Indies during the Winter months, when there will be little danger of enemy vessels on our Coasts; & when of course, our own vessels cannot be employed on our Coasts to much advantage. —

[NDA. Nom. Appts. LB, 1798–1820.]

Extract from Captain Thomas Truxtun's journal, U. S. Frigate *Constellation*, 27 September 1798, Thursday

Light variable Winds this first Part. At 6 P M it began to look very threatening, dark Clouds rising to the Westward, with Lightning and Thunder. Got up the Conductors as usual on the Appearance of squally, or bad Weather, took in all the light Sails, close reefed the top Sails, and handed the fore, and main Courses.

At 11 P M saw a Sail in Shore of us, gave her Chase, and at A M fired two Shot, and brought her to. She was a Schooner from Havannah bound to Tonica, a little to Windward. At 9 Ditto made Sail, gave Chase, brought to, and spoke another Schooner from Havannah bound to same Place.

Saw several Coasters in Shore, and at Noon passed a Raft of fine Timber with a Mast standing on the Same.

The Morro Castle at Noon bore S. W. B. W. three Leagues Distance.

[HS of Pa. NDA photostat.]

Extract from journal of U. S. Ship *Herald*, Captain James Sever, commanding, 27 September 1798

This 24 hours first part Strong gales and heavy Sea with flying Clouds at 2 p m gott F g y[?] thought at 5 p m Lett out all Reefs out Topsails up T g yards and Sett F g Sails mad Long Island Bearing N n E at 10P M Montock pint Light Bore By Compass North 2 Leagues at 12 a m the middle of Block Island Bore E n E at 2 a m Saw Road Island Light Bearing N N E at 4 a m hove Tue Waiting for Boat at 6 a m fired Signal gun and hoisted Signall Flagg at 10 Strong gales

and Squaley Latter part Continues Strong gales Still Lying By waiting for a Boat Brig *Pickring* in Companey from Newport
Lattd Obbrs 41..26 North

[NDA. Journal kept by Joseph Strout, 1798.]

Extract from journal of James Pity, U. S. Frigate *Constitution*, 27 September 1798, Thursday

Cloudy W^r^ Wind S. b. W. @ 11 A. M. Sent Mr Dorant 1st Masters Mate on Shore on Acc^t^ his being Sick of a fever @ 1/2 past 4 haild a Sch^r^ from Norfolk made her heave too and Sent a Boat on B^d^ wth Capt letters @ 1/2 past 9 spoke the Sch^r^ *Boston* from Cape Nichola Mole Inform'd us the English had evacuated that place the day before he saild Mr Tarbell Midshipman Return'd from Hampton Left Mr Dorant getting better.

[NDA.]

To Captain Alexander Murray, U. S. Navy, from Secretary of the Navy

[TRENTON,]
Navy Department September 28th 1798

Capt ALEX^r^ MURRAY

SIR I am honored with your Letter of the 25th Your detention in Baltimore is not to be regretted, as you will be at Norfolk quite as soon as the other Vessels will be prepared to receive you. I hope the Glasses and Instruments will be received before this. Should the Fever prevail at Norfolk, (and you seem to be positive on that point) it will indeed be very unfortunate. — If this Letter reaches you at Baltimore — please to recruit if you can readily obtain them, 20, 30, or even 40 men, more than your complement, to be put on board the other Vessels, if they should be wanted, which in all probability will be the case. —

The Brig *Eagle*, Campbell still in the Delaware, still wants men. I have given the most positive orders for her to sail to Norfolk in her present State. Should you carry in all the Vessels, rather more men than necessary, they will be useful in manning Prizes.

I do not mean that my Instructions, (those you have received, or those additional ones already sent to Norfolk, where you will receive them) should be considered as compulsory on you, to proceed instantly after the 5th of October to sea. — And if you find it impossible to get in any reasonable time, the whole of the Vessels under your Command in readiness, you are at Liberty to leave one behind: Tho' I shou'd wish the one so left, not to be the Brig *Norfolk*, as she is a strong Vessel. —

Barry & Decatur have returned, as you will have seen by the papers. Barry was instructed to give any assistance conveniently in his power to the Ship *New Jersey*, belonging to Nicklin & Griffith, now in Portorico. She was captured by the French & condemned. Nicklin & Griffith have bought her in; but cannot get her away from Portorico. I am not acquainted with all the circumstances — They will write you on the subject at Norfolk — And as her duties in this Country would amount to 10,000 D^s^; And as it is right to give all the assistance we can to our Merchant Vessels, any service you can render to this Vessel will be grateful to the Government. — Not only in assisting her out of the Port, (however, without offence to the Spanish Government) but affording her convoy, till you consider her out of danger from the French Privateers. —

I am &c

[NDA. OSW, Vol. 1.]

From Secretary Pickering To Charles Lee, U. S. Attorney General

DEPARTMENT OF STATE TRENTON *Sept. 28, 1798.*

[To] CHARLES LEE Esqr *Attorney General of the United States.*

SIR, I duly received your letters of Septr 18th and 22^d relative to the armed vessel *Niger* captured by the frigate *Constitution*, Capt Nicholson, and carried into Norfolk. The circumstances detailed even by Captain Nicholson himself, in his letter to the Secretary of the Navy, furnished no satisfactory ground to suppose the *Niger* either a French or a piratical vessel; and I have written to Mr Nelson, the district Attorney of Virginia, expressing this idea; and have urged this consideration as a new motive for expediting the trial: for a trial there must be, as well to satisfy Captain Nicholson, as to ascertain by testimony the facts requisite to vindicate the Government and fix the blame of the capture, and its consequences, where they ought to attach. — Under these circumstances it is not necessary at this moment to take up the question you have proposed for consideration; altho' its importance in respect to future captures which may implicate Americans in French armed vessels, renders it expedient to have it decided as early as may be.

* * * * * * *

I am very respectfully, Sir, &c.

TIMOTHY PICKERING.

[SDA. Dom. L., Vol. 11.]

To Captain Christopher R. Perry, U. S. Navy, Ship *General Greene*, from Secretary of the Navy

[TRENTON,]
Navy Department September 28th 1798

Capt CHRISTOPHER R. PERRY

SIR Your Letter of the 17th Instant I have received — Your observations respecting Mr Coggeshall shall be attended to — I wish you would select, and nominate to me, suitable characters for your officers — It is of every importance, that men of courage, abilities & patriotism, & such men only, shou'd be employed in our infant Navy. —

I expect to leave the duties of my office about the 15th October, to be executed by Col^o Pickering for three weeks — I should therefore be glad to hear from you immediately — Remember that your Ship must be got out in December, if it be possible, and say what I can do before I leave this, to promote that object. —

[NDA. OSW, Vol. 1.]

To Captain Richard Dale, U. S. Navy, from Captain Thomas Tingey, U. S. Navy

KINGSTON (N. J.) *28th Septr 1798*

I had the pleasure to write you from Trenton on monday last — I visited that place again yesterday, and inform'd the Secretary of the Navy that I had made up my mind to receive the command of the *Ganges*, which for your satisfaction should have been instantly communicated, but really for want of time. I have learned one thing since I accepted the Commission, which had I known timely 'tis probable would have deter'd me — I mean your idea of quitting the service; not but that I approve of your intention to support your claim to your rank as per first establishment — yet I think, that will be understood, and settled without difficulty.

I shall hasten my concerns so as to relieve you as soon as possible, but I doubt whether I can effectuate all I am under urgent necessity personally to attend to, in much less than four weeks. I will however endeavor to visit the Hook perhaps in all next week, if I hear from you timely.

It will I think be eligible that you instantly inform all the Officers and men, now belonging to the Ship — of this arrangement, that I may receive possitive information if any mean to quit her, of their names and quality, without delay, that proper and timely means may be used to supply the places so vacated.

It is also desireable that you send me a complete account of the Officers and Crew, who mean to proceed on the next destin'd cruise. I shall advocate and approve every one holding their former situation who has your sanction. The gentleman who acted as your clerk, will doubtless be an acquisition, as he must now have gain'd much information, in the nature of the service.

I have seen and approbate your list of the Crew for the intended cruise, except that I think the number of boys, may be more than doubled, it will prove of future use to the service. Let me hear from you without loss of time, as I shall make no arrangement for visiting the Ship, till I receive your reply. Inform me your actual opinion, as to the time it will take to compleat her, and whether a Captains presence is indispensibly necessary.

I am — my friend &c. &c.

RICHd DALE Esqr
Commandr of the U. S. Ship Ganges
at Marcus Hook

[NDA. Tingey LB, 1798–1800.]

To Messrs. Nicklin & Griffith, owners of Ship *New Jersey*, from Secretary of Navy

[TRENTON,]
Navy Department September 28th 1798

Messrs NICKLIN & GRIFFITH

GENTn I lament that the New Jersey recd no aid from Barry. — Capt Alexr Murray, whom I believe you know, will sail from Norfolk for the West Indies, from the 8th to the 15th October — possibly about the 10th — He will have three or four Vessels under his Command. —

I have written him to give any aid in his power to the *New Jersey,* in getting her out of Port Torico, and in convoying her out of danger from French Cruisers — But have referred him to you for the circumstances attending the Vessel. — — If you think he can be of service, please direct to him at Norfolk, to the care of Wm Pennock — I would advise that your Letters reach Norfolk by the 8th or 10th of October — —

I have the honor &c^{a}

[NDA, GLB No. 1.]

To the Secretary of State, from D. Humphreys, United States Minister to Spain

(N° 164)

MADRID *September 28, 1798.*

SIR, Altho' I would not trespass on your time by communicating the great variety of contradictory reports which have lately prevailed respecting the English and French fleets in the Mediterranean; yet I think it may be so interesting for you to receive, at as early a period as possible, the authentic account of the defeat or rather destruction of the latter, that I hasten to forward it by several different conveyances. I understand from good authority that such details have been received at the Secretary of State's office from the Spanish Ambassador at Paris, as leave no room to doubt that most of the French ships of the line and transports have been entirely destroyed. It is said fourteen ships of war were blown up or sunk. I enclose an extract from the Clef du Cabinet, which, in endeavouring to soften the severity of the blow, tends to confirm the truth of the fact. And I have seen another Gazette of Paris dated the 16th of Septr in which it is said "It was in the bay of Alexandria that our fleet was attacked and perished". A day or two previous to the publication of this news in Paris, the Directory had sent a Message to the council of Five Hundred, announcing the object of the expedition to be against Egypt; and that Buonaparte had landed and taken possession of Alexandria and Cairo.

Eight American vessels, richly laden with cocoa, sugar, coffee, tobacco, rice, flour, staves, &c. have lately arrived at Cadiz. The brig *Amelia,* captain Logan, belonging to Messrs William Craig and Henry Sadler of New York, having been taken by a French privateer, three of the crew endeavoured unsuccessfully to retake the vessel, and were put to death .... the captain, who was not at first privy to their design, on discovering it attempted to succour them, and was wounded.

We have nothing new of importance at this Court. The health of Mr de Saavedra continues to improve.

With sentiments of great regard and esteem

I have the honour to be,

Sir,

Your most obed^{t} and most humble Servant

D. HUMPHREYS

The SECRETARY OF STATE &c &c &c

(SDA. Disp. Spain, Bk 4, Humphreys.]

[28 September, 1798.]

Remarks made on board the Ship *America*, at Havana, regarding several ships and Americans on Ship *Julia*

An obliging correspondent has favoured us with the following remarks made on board the ship America, at the Havanna.

Sept. 28, sailed from Havanna; same day at noon fell in with a French privateer schr. which we fired several shot at, she taking the advantage of a light breeze rowed away. Same day spoke the frigate *Constitution*, in company with the ship *Baltimore*, waiting for the fleet to come out; crews of both ships all well, there had not been a sick person on board.

Sept. 29, the fleet sailed and joined the convoy, consisting of 43 sail, among which were the brigs *Molly*, Kilby; *George* Harden; *Florida*, Hase: *Polly*, Howard; *Susan*, Smiley; sloop *Friends*, Moore: schooner *Brothers*, White, of Baltimore; ship *Sally*, Smith, of do. *Patty Washington*, Stocker, do. the schooner *Experiment*, Knap, had sailed for a port to leeward.

Oct. 1st, parted company with the fleet off the Florida Shore, in lat. 24, 28, N.

Oct. 2, fell in with the armed ship *Zenobia*, from Jamaica, bound to Providence, in company with a brig and a schooner.

Oct. 12, off Cape Hatteras spoke the schr. *Friendship*, which had been re-taken by the mate and one man; she was from Jamaica bound to Boston.

The *America* left at the Havanna the ship *Citizen*, of New York; *Olive*, of do. brig *Maria*, of Philadelphia, schooner *Daphney*, of do. schooner *Minerva*, of do. six sail of the line, five frigates, and 5 sloops of war.

American produce very low, their produce high.

A French privateer belonging to Guadaloupe, has been sunk in the W. Indies, by the British frigate *Concord*. What renders this circumstance melancholy is, that the privateer had several Americans on board; particularly the crew of the sloop *Julia*, captain Green of East Haddam, which she had taken a few days before.

[LC, "Independent Chronicle" (Mass.), Nov. 1–5, 1798, p. 146.]

Extract from journal of U. S. Ship *Herald*, Captain James Sever, U. S. Navy, commanding, 28 September 1798

This 24 hours first part Strong gales and Squaley at 2 p m a Boat Came on Bord from New Port with Letters for Capt Sever at p m the gale Encrest thought it most prudent To Run in and anchor at 4 p m Came To anchor in 9½ fathoms watter goat Island Bearing East ¾ of mile Rowes Island Bearing N N W and Brintins point Bearing S B E one mile Distance at 10 p m Strong gales attended with heavy Rain Sent Down T G yards and Bent the Best Bower at 4 a m the gale abated the wind hald To the westward at 6 a m Sent up Top Gallant Yards

Latter part mordarate and flatning with Drizely Rain at 10 a m Sent the Cutter on Shore for watter all hans Employd in Ships Duty

[NDA. Journal kept by Joseph Strout, 1798.]

Extract from journal of James Pity, U. S. Frigate *Constitution*, 28 September 1798, Friday

Fresh Breezes from N. N. W. @ 2 P. M. call'd all hands aft to Muster and read the Articles of War. Rec^{d} from the *Niger* 27 Men. Set Q^{r} Watches as usual.

[NDA.]

Extract from Captain Thomas Truxtun's journal, U. S. Frigate *Constellation*, 28 September 1798, Friday

Light Breezes with some black Squalls of Rain and very uncertain Weather, throughout these Twenty four Hours. Made, and took in Sail according to the Weather, in Order to keep my Station off the Morro as near as possible, untill the Fleet are out, but the Current running strong to the Eastward, at Day Light was at least four Leagues above the Dragon, a little Fort to Windward of the Morro, which may be easily known, by it's standing on an apparently low Rock at the Water's Edge, having at each Corner a Pillar with a round Ball on the same. At Day Light discovered a small Schooner in shore, which I took for a Privateer, gave Chase, and made the Signal for the *Baltimore* to do the same, but the Wind being light, and this Vessel having a Number of Sweeps out, and at the same Time keeping in the Counter Current, which runs near the Verge of the Breakers, we could not come up with her, in Fact we chased so near in that it was necessary as the Wind fell very light, to get the Boat out and tow. Several Vessels came out, but we were too far to Windward at Noon to discover who they were. At Noon the Morro bore South West, between three and four Leagues Distance.

[HS of Pa. NDA photostat.]

To Secretary Pickering from W. Vans Murray, United States Minister to The Netherlands

29. Sep. 1798.

Private —— COLONEL PICKERING.

DEAR SIR, On the 19th I had the honour to write a few lines to inform you that the Fleet which convey'd Buonaparte's army to Egypt was defeated by Nelson about the first of last month — Since, particular accounts have reached us of that fact — and information very circumstantial of the defeat of his army in July.

The Porte may be considered in a State of War with France — I seize an opportunity to Hamburgh and have but a moment.

I am with the greatest respect & Sincere esteem

Dear Sir, Y^{rs}, &^{ca}

W. V. MURRAY.

Col. PICKERING

[Mass. HS. Pickering Papers, Vol. 23.]

Extract from Captain Thomas Truxtun's journal, U. S. Frigate *Constellation*, 29 September 1798, Saturday

At One P M a Squall of Wind preceded by Rain came up. Stood along the Coast towards the Morro, shortly after the little Privateer of one Gun, that we chased into the Verge of the Breakers as mentioned in Yesterday's Transactions, came out from under the Land, and stood so near the *America* (a Merchant armed Ship of 18 Guns, belonging to Philadelphia, and one that came out of Havannah this morning) that Captain Cunningham fired into him, and as we have been informed, killed two of his Men, and wounded three more. She sheered off, and run in Shore immediately, where it is impossible to get at them with a heavy Ship, which shows that the best Protection for our Trade to Havannah, would be to send two fast sailing Schooners of twelve or fourteen Guns, and Seventy five Men to cruize between Key Sal, and Havannah as far Northward as the said Key Sal.

Standing off and on the Morro, waiting for the Fleet to come out, at Noon I counted forty Sail without the Harbour. Several of the Masters complained, that the Consul had not handed them the Signals I had sent him for the Fleet. I however furnished Others.

[HS of Pa. NDA photostat.]

Extract from journal of James Pity, U. S. Frigate *Constitution*, 29 September 1798, Saturday

@ 5 A. M. Call'd all hands to Veer away cable — The Starboard cable & hove Short hoisted an American Jack at Main Top Mast head Signal for a boat. @ 7 Man'd our Boat & sent on B^d^ y^e^ *Niger* for the Rem^t^ of our people hoisted Signal for Sailing @ 2 P. M. Doct^r^ Galt came on B^d^ a Surgeon for the cruize. Rec^d^ on b^d^ 1 Pipe & 11 bbls. Vinegar & one drip Stone Sarved the cable in the wake of ye hawse holes.

[NDA.]

To Secretary Pickering from President Adams

QUINCY *Septr 30 1798*

DEAR SIR I have received your favour of the 24th and have read carefully over all the Inclosures. Such as ought to remain in your office I return inclosed in this.

There is nothing that requires any Remarks from me; because I think all is well considered and well done. It may not however be amis to observe to Mr. Adams, that he need not be Solicitous about his success in making Treaties with Prussia and Sweeden at present. That I am fully convinced as he is, that both will affect to refuse any Treaty upon the Terms in his Instructions. This will not alarm me at all — and if both Powers finally refuse to agree to any stipulations, without the Articles in contemplation, We shall not be very uneasy. Our Commerce is of more consequence to them than their's to us: and with or without treaties we shall have all we want.

But we should be very improvident at the moment of being forced into a war, to bind ourselves to permit France & her Colenies to be supplied with every Thing even our own Produce in Prussian & Sweedish or Danish Ships.

I am, Sir your most ob^t^ &

JOHN ADAMS

The *Constitutions* Prize, must be tried and fairly determined by Law. I hope and believe that care will be taken, that no suspicions of plundering any thing may arise.

TIMOTHY PICKERING Esqr

Secretary of State.

[SDA. Misc. L., Sept.–Dec. 1798.]

[30 September, 1798.]

Letters regarding conduct of Captain Leonard, of *Governor Jay*, with reference to the *Factor-Hazard* incident, and controversy between Captain Leonard and Henry M. Rutledge

PORT OF NEW-YORK, ON BOARD THE
U. STATES CUTTER *Governor Jay,*
October 29th, 1798.

To the EDITOR OF THE COMMERCIAL ADVERTISER.

SIR, Upon our arrival here on Wednesday last, we found, to our great astonishment, certain scandalous representations in circulation, respecting the conduct of John W. Leonard, Esq. commander of the United States cutter *Governor Jay*, with regard to the ship *Factor*, Captain Kemp, whom we fell in with at sea, on the 30th ult. lat 39, 20, N.

As we have the honour of holding commissions under Capt. Leonard, on board said cutter, we conceive it a duty we owe him as our commander, our country in whose service we are engaged, and ourselves, to declare that the abovementioned reports are false, and scandalous fictions, which must have proceeded from some imprudent or malicious persons, with an intention of derogating from Capt. Leonard's conduct, courage and character, as an officer, and to throw the infant navy of our country into contempt and disrepute. We trust, however, that the malicious intention of these malicious reports will be baffled, and the authors and propagators of them treated by every true friend to government with the contempt and resentment which actuates ourselves. To those who know Capt. Leonard it is needless to say any thing; they must be convinced from that circumstance alone, that any reports of the above nature are false and without foundation; to those who are unacquainted with his zeal for the service of his country, his genuine attachment to the federal government, and detestation of French principles and French philosophy, his prudence and skill as a naval commander, and above all that true fortitude and dauntless firmness which mark the character of the man of true courage, and which captain Leonard has upon all occasions evinced — to those, the candid relation of facts which are about to be laid before you, may not be unnecessary.

On the 29th September last, cruizing in company with the United States schooner *Retaliation*, commanded by Lieutenant W. Benbridge, we discovered and gave chace to a schooner; we came up with her in a short time, and she proved to be the *Hazard*, Capt. Kelly, of and for New York from L'Anceveaux; but the wind blowing exceedingly fresh we were unable to board her. Some time afterwards one of the officers of the *Retaliation* informed us that she was owned by French merchants in the West Indies. Upon this information Captain Leonard determined at all events to board her in the morning. Soon after we discovered a ship to leeward, we accordingly gave chace in company, and came up with her before night, near enough to discover she was armed, but night coming on we deferred speaking her till morning, and stood under easy sail to the westward, the same way the ship was steering; at 5 o'clock in the morning discovered the ship much in the same position, with regard to us, as we left her in the preceding evening, and the schooner *Hazard* some distance ahead. The ship shewed her colours, but we were unable to distinguish what they were. It was then determined to stand after the *Hazard*, as she was steering the same course with the ship, and satisfy our doubts with respect to her being French property, and then to speak the ship. We accordingly made sail and gave the signal for chasing in company with the *Retaliation*. At 10 A. M. the *Retaliation* bore away for the ship, which Captain Leonard thought rather extraordinary, as we were by agreement the signal vessel: he however concluded that Captain Bembridge meant to reconnoitre, while we boarded the *Hazard*, which we were afterwards convinced of, as he made the private signals for the American frigates and cruizers. We soon after came up with and boarded the *Hazard*, and being satisfied as to her being American property, wore and stood for the *Retaliation*, intending to go down to the ship and find out what she was. We came up with Captain Bembridge, and to our astonishment he informed us he had spoken the ship. We further declare, that it was never contemplated by Captain Leonard to leave the ship without boarding her. This ship was the *Factor*.

This, Sir, is a fair exposition of facts, which cannot be denied or contradicted with any regard to truth. Consider, then, Sir, how great was our surprize, when, on our arrival, we heard the conduct of our brave commander impeached, and his name branded with cowardice, by false and malicious representations; and what our feelings when we heard it reported from a gentleman of respectability who came passenger in the *Factor*, that he was called up to prepare for action with two schooners, who were supposed to be French privateers; that one of them, which he afterwards understood to be the *Governor Jay* (taking the *Factor* for a French armed vessel) hauled her wind, and basely and cowardly went off, and infamously deserted her consort; that the private signals made by the *Retaliation* were for the *Governor Jay* to bear away for the ship, and that the officers of the *Retaliation* who boarded the *Factor* informed him that Capt. Bembridge was surprized at the conduct of the Captain of the *Governor Jay*.

Now, Sir, this is absolutely untrue, we were upon a wind when we first discovered the *Factor*, in the morning, consequently we could not haul our wind. The *Hazard* being directly ahead of the *Factor*, all steering the same course, and we directly to windward, we consequently could have betrayed no disposition to run off. That Captain Bembridge made no other signal but that abovementioned, consequently he did not expect us to accompany him. We had not the smallest supposition of the *Factor's* being a French vessel. And we declare upon the very best authority, that this gentleman never spoke to the officers of the *Retaliation*, but that all his information was collected from the boat's crew of the *Retaliation* — five boys!

Can it be justifiable in *any person* to circulate reports of this nature upon so slender a foundation?

When we afterwards spoke Capt. Bembridge, he expressed neither then nor at any subsequent period, the least surprize that we did not go down with him to the ship, but immediately made enquiries concerning the *Hazard;* said that he had taken the ship in question for one of the American cruizers, but that she had proved to be the *Factor* from London, and mentioned several articles of political intelligence he had obtained from her.

For a person unskilled in maritime affairs, whatever his opinion may be, to express it publickly upon so delicate a point as the manoeuvring of an armed vessel, when it is generally the intention of the commander to conceal his motive; when that commander is just coming forward in an infant navy, and not present at the time to demand redress, is at least uncandid, ungenerous, and unjust, if not highly criminal.

The vile misrepresentations in question may, perhaps, have originated from the *imprudence* of this gentleman, perhaps to add a little to his consequence, or to retaliate upon a person then absent, any fears that he himself might have betrayed upon the occasion.

Capt. Kemp, we are informed, has given Captain Leonard the most polite and candid explanation upon the subject, and we are convinced, that the latter will never let the affair rest, until he has obtained full and ample satisfaction.

But to conclude — as Capt. Leonard never executed any manoeuvre, however minute and trifling, without consulting his officers, we consider ourselves injured in the nicest point, and if we cannot obtain that satisfaction which we have a right to expect from the *drawer* of this falsehood, we shall individually claim our right to redress from any of the *endorsers.*

JOHN SQUIRE, *jun. 1st Lt.*
NATH. HARRIOTT, *2d do.*
W. A. DUER, } *Midshipmen.*
J. E. FISHE, }

[LC, "Claypoole's American Daily Advertiser" (Phila.), 2 Nov. 1798.]

NEW YORK, *November 9, 1798.*

To the Editor of the Commercial Advertiser.

SIR, However painful it may be to the feelings of every man of delicacy, to become the object of public attention, there are cases, in which it does not depend upon himself to be introduced to their notice. I find myself reduced to this situation by a publication which appeared in your paper of the 30th ultimo, signed by Messrs Squire and Harriot, 1st and 2d lieuts. and by Messrs. Fisher and Duer, Midshipmen, on board the *Governor Jay*, United States Revenue Cutter.

The purport of the piece, is to induce a belief, that a passenger on board the *Factor*, had misrepresented the conduct of the commander of the *Governor Jay*, on the 30th of September, the day on which he fell in with this ship, and at the same time, to give the public notice, that satisfaction was intended to be demanded, for the injury which they alledge, has been done to their feelings, — it is pretty generally understood that the passenger in question, is myself, and altho' they have not named me in the publication, I consider it as addressed to me. I therefore think it necessary to lay before the public, an account, of what has been my conduct relative to this affair, that I may avoid what I much dread, the censure of a respectable community. I therefore beg leave to state as follows — viz. On the 26th ultimo, on returning home to prepare for a journey to the Country, I found the following letter addressed to me from Capt. Leonard.

"PORT OF NEW YORK, ON BOARD THE UNITED STATES CUTTER,
Gov. Jay, Oct. 26, 1798.

"SIR, On my arrival from a late cruize, I was informed by a number of gentlemen of respectability, that certain reports had been made, respecting my conduct on the 30th day of September last, the day I fell in with the ship *Factor*, on board of which I am informed you were then a passenger.

"Sir, as all these reports have a direct tendency to create an unfavorable opinion in the public mind, I presume you will freely indulge me with a particular statement, of what you have been pleased to advance on the subject, that an explanation may be had; this Sir, I consider, indispensible from the duty I owe the service in which I have the honor to be employed, and that which every man owes to himself.

Sir,

Your humble servant,

(Signed) JOHN W. LEONARD,
Commander of the U. S. Cutter Governor Jay."

This letter requires no remark. Captain Leonard had a right to know what I had related respecting the affair in question, and I complied without hesitation with his desire, by returning the following answer:

"NEW YORK, *Oct. 26th, 1798.*

"SIR, I received your letter of this morning, a few moments ago, and as I am to leave town in an hour or two, I have not leisure to give you as detailed an answer, as may be expected. I was a passenger on board the *Factor*, and on the 30th Sept. was called up at daylight, together with the rest of the passengers, and people, to prepare for action, with two Schooners which appeared to windward and which were imagined to be French privateers. After being on deck some little time, we saw one of the schooners, approach the other, and as we conceived, speak with her. As we had little doubt of the plan being formed, to attack us, captain Kemp immediately ordered to be hoisted, the French National colors; to the best of my recollection, a few moments afterwards, the vessel which had approached the other, hauled close upon a wind and went off. The other, after some manoeuvring, came down, prepared for action, and proved to be the *Retaliation* of Philadelphia. She sent on board of the *Factor*, an officer whom I understood to be a Lieut. He then informed us that Captain Bembridge who commanded the *Retaliation*, had not known what to make of us (to use his own phrase) and had made signals to the vessel in company, to bear down with him, and discover whether or no we were an enemy's ship, and in the event of our proving such to join in the attack. This vessel he informed us was the *Governor Jay*, and he added that Capt. Bembridge had expressed his surprize, at the conduct of the commander of the *Jay*.

"This, Sir, is as correct a statement as I can with brevity give you. This is the substance of what I have mentioned since my arrival at New York, nor am I, I believe, singular in mentioning it. The Captain of the *Factor* and the other passengers on board of her, will give you the same account. As I had the honor to observe to you in the commencement of this letter, I am just quiting town on business, and am therefore too much hurried to add any thing else, than that I expect to return in the course of a week, when I shall with pleasure await your commands if you have any other for me."

I have the honor to be Sir,

Your most obt. servt.

(Signed) HENRY M. RUTLEDGE.

Capt. LEONARD, of the *Gov. Jay* Cutter."

I accordingly left New York with the full persuasion that if any further steps were to be taken on the subject of capt. Leonard's letter, they would at least be deferred, until the moment of my return. My surprise may be easily conceived, when I saw at Trenton, on the 1st of November, your paper of the day before, containing the publication signed by his officers. Not a little indignant at the scurrility with which it was marked, and at the public manner in which they threaten that capt. Leonard should demand satisfaction of the person alluded to throughout the whole of the publication. Imaginning that these gentlemen had nothing more impatiently at heart, than to put into practice their threats, I immediately sat out from Trenton, and arrived at New York the afternoon following. On the morning of the succeeding day (3d November,) I sent on board of the cutter, by a friend, a letter, in which I announced to capt. Leonard, my having returned within the time prescribed, and after making a few remarks on the publication in question, I concluded with acquainting him, that I was ready to give him the satisfaction which was threatened to be demanded. The third and fourth passed without hearing from him, and on this morning the 5th November, capt. Leonard called upon me, and in the presence of several gentlemen declared to me, that the publication on the part of his officers was without his privity, as to its contents, that he had only, at their request, consented, that they should publish an extract of what was entered on his log book, on the day that he fell in with the *Factor*, and that he utterly disclaimed the personalities contained in the piece. I persisted in the statement that I had furnished him in my first letter, and which he mentioned to have shewn to his officers, and he, on his part, had nothing to require of me. With respect to that statement, which is taxed with being a misrepresentation, I have to add, that since my return to town, I have called on the only passengers in the *Factor*, who remain upon the spot, and they have with cheerfulness certified the truth and exactness of a copy which I communicated to them, in the following terms, viz. "We certify the above, to be a true and exact statement of what happened on the morning of the 30th Sept.

Signed F. MENIER. TH. BUTLIN.
T. FEDON. J. WADDINGTON."

I have thus endeavoured to present to the public, as brief a statement as possible, of the affair, which has been without my consent, intruded on their notice. I have only now to add a few remarks on the publication of which it has been the subject. With respect to the merits of this production, I have no inclination to discuss them in a newspaper, nor would the public probably have leisure to attend to the dispute. I am satisfied to rest their opinion of the propriety of my conduct, on the relation of facts which I submitted to their view. But before I take my leave of them, I will request one favor, viz that they will turn their eyes to the bullying threats, with which the publication in question is concluded, and then to form their opinions of the authors of it, when they shall be informed that they suffered the object of their wrath to remain for three days in New York, after he had announced his arrival, without having taken any notice of that communication. It is not consistent with my usual mode of proceeding, to proclaim it to the world, either when I intend to demand or when I purpose to give satisfaction; but we are sometimes under the necessity of meeting men on the ground which they have taken; I must therefore declare to these gentlemen, that the drawer, as they are pleased to term him, will remain for some days longer on the spot, and will give to each of them, the satisfaction he may be disposed to require, proceeding agreeably to their respective grades. He will soon leave New York for a distant part of the continent; he will have nothing more to say to them thro' the medium of the newspaper, and he subscribes himself

HENRY M. RUTLEDGE.

[LC, "Claypoole's American Daily Advertiser" (Phila.), 9 Nov. 1798.]

Thursday morning, Henry M. Rutledge, Esq. and capt. Leonard, of the *Governor Jay* cutter, met within a mile of Powles hook, accompaned by their seconds, (pursuant to a message from the latter to the former) for the purpose of terminating a dispute already known to the public. Two cases of pistols were discharged — Captain Leonard's first fire passed through Mr. Rutledge's cloathes and grazed him slightly, when capt. L. declared himself "perfectly satisfied," — there the matter ended.

The foregoing is a correct statement of the circumstances which we both witnessed.

JOHN E. FISHER.
JOHN HENRY.

[LC, "Claypoole's American Daily Advertiser" (Phila.), 13 Nov. 1798.]

Extract from journal of James Pity, U. S. Frigate *Constitution*, 30 September 1798, Sunday

Wind @ N. N. W. @ 5 A. M. calld all hands & hove Short. @ 7 Weigh'd & Proceeded out of the Roads falling calm came to anchor of Willoughbys point @ 4 spoke Brig^t *George* of Portland Waite Master. Weigh'd our anchor and came too in hampton Roads again. Wind @ E. b. S.

[NDA.]

Extract from Captain Thomas Truxtun's journal, U. S. Frigate *Constellation*, 30 September 1798, Sunday

At 3 P M all the Fleet being out consisting of 43 Sail of Merchant Vessels belonging to various Parts of the United States, I hoisted the Signal for forming into close Order which Signal was answered by the *Baltimore*. We then proceeded on keeping by the Wind on the Starboard Tack, carrying Poop, and Top Lights at Dark, and the Battle Lanthorns all lighted. At 8 Ditto tacked, and stood to the Southward, at 10 Ditto tacked and stood by the Wind as per Column, all Hands at Quarters, Guns ready to fire at a moment's Warning.

At Day Light discovered a Schooner on the Weather Bow, which I took for a french Privateer, gave Chase, and brought her to after firing two Shot. She proved to be a Spaniard from Havannah bound to Charleston, South Carolina, and laden with Sugar, and Fruit, carrying no Guns, and only eight Men. The Master requested my Protection, but this was inadmissible, as we are at Peace with Great Britain.

At Noon the Bay of Matanzas under the Pan bore South, South East, ten Leagues Distance, from which I take my Departure. All the Fleet that came out with us in Sight and well.

Latitude observed at Noon, when the above Bearings were taken 23°.42 North. Received by the *Belvidera*, that came out of the Havannah Yesterday, and is one of the Fleet, an Answer from the Governor General of the Island of Cuba, to my Letter of the 21st Instant, on the Subject of the Departure of the Fleet, now under my Convoy Home. The Signal almost constantly flying to keep the Fleet in close Order, notwithstanding which the Masters would scatter, without paying any Attention to it.

Longitude at Noon calculated from the Pan of Matanzas 81°.28′W.

[HS of Pa. NDA photostat.]

[October, 1798]

Information furnished by Captain West regarding the Schooner *Amphitrite*, Thomas Snell, master, and prisoners taken by the French Privateer *Fleur de la Mer*, commanded by Pierre d'Pine

Yesterday arrived here, the schooner *Rover*, captain P. West, in 24 days from Curracoa. The following persons came passengers in the *Rover*. Captain Garret Berry of the snow *Fanny*, of this port, and his mate, taken when bound for Laguira; James Duncan, mate of the brig *Philip*, Captain Gorsuch and three of his men; one of captain Roxborough's, of the snow *Maryland*; and the sailing master and two men of the armed schooner *Amphitrite*.

Captain West has politely favored us with the following information:

The schooner *Amphitrite*, armed with 10 guns, and 22 men, Thomas Snell, master, sailed from New York on the 12th of August last. on a voyage to Demarara, from thence to Grenada, where she arrived on the 20th of September. Left the last mentioned port on the 4th of October, bound for Curracoa, but on the 6th of the same month was stranded on the isle of Aves, a barren, uninhabited place, where they got safe on shore, and saved some of the materials belonging to the schooner. After they had been six days on the island they purchased a boat, which the captain and four men was to get to Curracoa in, and endeavour to procure some small vessel for the purpose of taking them off: on the 13th, the brig *Philip*, of this port, Captain Gorsuch, made her appearance; the men on shore made signals of distress, which Captain Gorsuch took notice of, and went to their assistance. Took from the island three of the schooner's crew, and then departed for Curracoa; when within three miles of her port of destination, they were boarded by a French privateer, one Dupang commander, who had on board three Americans, viz. John Mathers, native of this port, late mate of the snow *Maryland*, John Roxborough; Solomon Geer, formerly master and late mate of the schooner *Lucinda* John Murry Cambbell, master; one Laycock, late gunner of the ship *Stag*, of Norfolk; when the officer of the privateers was on board of the *Philip*, they enquired of Captain Gorsuch whether all these men belonged to the brig? the captain answered no — where did you get them? I took them from an American schooner stranded on the isle of Aves. They then took the whole crew of the *Philip* on board the privateer, except Captain Gorsuch one man and a boy, put people on board, and dispatched her for St. Domingo, as he said; and made the best of his way for the island of Bonair. where he landed all he had on board: left that place and made the best of his way for the wreck — when arrived there he anchored his schooner and went on shore. When first on shore told James Connor, sailing master of the distressed, that he had received orders from the Governor of Curracoa to come and take them with all they had saved, and carry them for Curracoa, but after a short time they were convinced to the contrary, being ordered on board the privateer in a very rude manner, and a strong guard put over what was saved from the schooner; our John Mathers being one of the guard. After James Connor had been a short time on board, and very strictly examined by Dupang, they both went on shore, and Dupang told Conner, that if he should find any goods whatever concealed, he might expect to be severely handled. Dupang landed, and searched above and under ground, until he was weary, but found nothing more than what was mentioned; they took what they pleased and put on board, and then burnt the remainder; left Connor on shore under guard with the rest during the night; before morning John Mathers struck James Connor with his naked cutlass three times, and made him lay on his face the remainder of the night, in the sand. The day following Captain Snell arrived with a small schooner he had got at the aforesaid place, but to his great astonishment found Dupang there, and his people in a far worse condition than when he left them; being robbed of what little they had got on shore. Capt. Snell came to with his schooner some small distance from Dupang; they got the privateer under way and run close to Captain Snell and ordered him to hoist out his boat and come on board, which Snell immediately did; when on board was most shamefully abused; Dupang threatened to put him on a small sand-key destitute of every necessary of life; took from Snell his boat, put all his people on board and discharged him for the place from whence he came, and staid by the wreck for more plunder, if possible to be had. He had before their departure got the foremast, cables, anchors, sails, ropes, main boom, and main mast, from the wreck. so that poor Snell had the schooner to pay for without reaping the benefit of what was saved from the wreck. Captain Snell arrived at Curracoa on the 20th of October, with a double misfortune: first stranded, and then robbed.

I Peleg West, have had the opportunity of bringing the undersigned to the port of Baltimore, belonging to the *Amphitrite*, who are here ready to attest the same.

JAMES CONNOR, *Sailing Master*.
LEVI BARDIN, *First Mate*.

[LC, "Claypoole's American Daily Advertiser" (Phila.), 7 Dec. 1798.]

[From the New-York Daily Advertiser]

FRENCH ATROCITY

The following detail will be read by every American with feelings of mingled horror and detestation. The conduct of the French in this instance has been so abominable, so fiend-like, that we want words to express our boiling indignation. Our only consolation is, that the spirit of our countrymen is awakened and that similar outrages will seldom occur in future. Our young navy is growing a pace, and spreading its protecting wings over our wide spreading commerce; and ere long, will be able to repel injuries and avenge insults from whatever quarter they may come.

[COPY.]

CURRACOA

By this public instrument and protest, be it known and made manifest unto all whom it doth or may concern, That on this 15th day of October, 1798, before me B. H. Philips, consul of the United States of America at Curracoa, personally came and appeared Thomas Snell, late master of the schooner *Amphitrite*, of New-York, who being duly sworn on the Holy Evangelists of Almighty God, DEPOSETH, that he sailed in the said schooner from New-York, on the 12th day of August last, loaded with provisions, bound to the West-Indies, and on the 20th of September arrived at Grenada, where he sold part of her cargo; and on the 4th inst. left Grenada with the remaining part of her cargo, bound to Curracoa. That on the 6th inst. at meridian, he saw the island called Roca, it bore by his compass S. E. by E. distant about six leagues, when the schooner was hauled to the south and westward, in order to pass between the above-named island and the isles of Avis, supposing that there was a current setting strong to windward, from the small progress the vessel made. That on the 7th inst. at half past twelve A. M. he saw the breakers under the lee bow, when the helm was immediately put down to bring the vessel round; but before she came to and the sails trimmed, she struck on the reef on the north side the isles of Avis, and there she stuck fast. That the guns were immediately thrown overboard to ease the vessel, and at day break the boat was put out, and sent with the first mate and six people on shore with some provisions. That the 8th and 9th inst. were occupied in getting provisions on shore for the crew to subsist on; the said island not being inhabited. That on the 11th inst. the weather being moderate, a stage was made, and by its help got on shore the main sail, fore sail, and some light sails; but finding that there was no possibility of saving the vessel and cargo without more assistance, the boat was prepared and fitted in the best manner that circumstances would allow; and on the 13th inst. the deponent, with four of the crew, sailed from the isles of Avis for Curracoa, where they arrived the 14th inst. That immediately on their arrival at Curracoa, he, this deponent, waited on his Excellency the Governor, and told him his situation, who with great complaisance and apparent friendship, offered him any assistance in his power, and afterwards on the said consul, to advise with him, who joined in opinion that a vessel should be procured with the utmost dispatch, to bring away the people of the said schooner, and what could be saved from the wreck for the benefit of whoever it might concern; and agreeable thereto he paid a Spanish schooner (the only vessel at that time to be got) called *Santa Antonio Abad*, Manuel Corson, master, to proceed to the wreck, and there to wait eight days, and then proceed to Curracoa, for which he agreed to pay him 320 dollars, and to insure his vessel, valued at 1050 dollars, at the rate of five per cent.

That he sailed from Curracoa in the said vessel so hired, for the Isles of Avis, on the 16th inst. taking on her deck the boat in which he and his four people arrived at Curracoa, and that they arrived at the Isles of Avis on the 18th instant. And on the 20th instant, came James Conner, sailing-master; Levi Bordine, first mate, and Lifter Asguith, second mate, all late of the said schooner *Amphitrite.* who having been also severally duly sworn, did confirm the foregoing, so far as relates to the sailing from New-York, and until said Snell left the Isles of Rois.

Afterwards, that is to say, on the 22d inst. came said Thomas Snell and Frederick Bareth. Said Bareth having been duly sworn, deposeth that he went with said Thomas Snell to the Isles of Avis, and there acted as interpreter on the following occasion: that on their arrival at the Isles of Avis, they found a privateer under French colours (but owned as they are informed in Curracoa) called "*Fleur de la Mer*," commanded by Pierre d'Pine, lying at anchor.

That the day before their arrival at the Isles of Avis, the said Pierre d'Pine had made prisoners of all the people of the *Amphitrite*, who remained there and had taken possession of all they had got on shore from the wreck, with the vessel's log book, journal, &c. and that by order of one of the privateer's prize masters, a hut where some of the people lived, was burned with all their clothes.

That the privateer being then under way, said Pierre d'Pine ordered the deponents to come on board the privateer, and bring all the *Amphitrite's* papers with them. The privateer soon after came to anchor, when the deponents, along with Capt. Corson, went on board, when the said d'Pine demanded the papers. A letter from the Governor of Curracoa, and a certificate from the said consul, were handed him, both of which he treated with great contempt, and told them that he was Governor of the Isles of Avis, and that he would take from the wreck of the schooner *Amphitrite* what he thought proper, and every thing from the shore that he might want which had been saved from the wreck — he had already taken possession of the *Amphitrite's* boat, and ordered the people to go on board the

Spanish schooner with what clothes they had on; he gave them two barrels of beef, part of four barrels of flour, and half a barrel of bread. He then demanded to know what was become of all the arms, powder, &c. Captain Snell told him that he did not know, that he believed he had in his possession already all that had been saved from the wreck; to which he replied he had not, and said that the people had hid them under ground, and that if he did not tell him where every article was, he would put him and his people on a sand-key, without bread or water, or would carry them to St. Domingo and put them in prison. Capt. Snell replied that he was in his power, and that he might do as he thought proper, that he could not tell him what he did not know; afterwards he told said Snell he might go on board the Spanish schooner if he pleased, which he did, and staid with the people of the *Amphitrite*.

That on the morning of the 19th inst. a signal was hoisted by the Spanish schooner for the privateer to send a boat on board (they having none of their own) which they did, and the deponents went on board the privateer. That previous to their leaving the privateer, they saw the *Amphitrite's* boat, with a number of the privateer's people, rowing for the wreck; and about sun-down, they saw return loaded with rigging, gun-powder, butter, &c. That thus finding the determination of the said Pierre d'Pine was to take every thing from the wreck, they asked his permission to sail for Curracoa, which he granted, and ordered his boat hauled up to put them on board the Spanish schooner: mean time, and while the boat was getting ready, he told them that the Americans were *a pack of villains without humanity; and rather than they should save a single thing from the wreck, he would set fire to her, and burn her up.* That soon after they were put on board the Spanish schooner, 7 o'clock P. M. of the 19th instant, they got under way, and the next day, at three P. M. they arrived at Curracoa.

These deponents thereupon, for the reason above written, do protest, and I the said consul at their request, do solemnly protest against the said current, which drove the schooner out of her course, which caused her to stick on the aforesaid reef, to stick fast and to be wrecked — Against the said French privateer, called *Fleur de la Mer*, officers and crew, for having deprived them of the property saved from the wreck of the *Amphitrite*, and of the wreck also; and against that government which has given her a commission to rob and plunder American persons and property; these acts having been done in a time of peace between America and France, and on the Spanish ground — For all losses, costs, hurts, delays, detriments and damages suffered, or to be suffered or sustained by reason of the premises, reserving to the said deponents, and to myself as consul on the part of the United States of America, the right to enter all further protests and proceeds as may at any time hereafter be needful in respect to the premises.

In testimony of the truth whereof, the said deponents have hereunto subscribed their names.

(Signed) THOMAS SNELL,
JAMES CONNER,
LEVI BORDINE,
LISTER ASGUITH,
FREDERICK BARRET.

And in faith of the truth whereof, and in testimony, I have hereunto set my hand & seal of office, at Curracoa, this 29th day of October, 1798, and in the 23d year of the Independence of the United States of America.

B. H. PHILIPS, (L. S.)

[LC, "Claypoole's American Daily Advertiser" (Phila.), 21 December 1798.]

To Captain Isaac Phillips, U. S. Navy, from Captain Thomas Truxtun, U. S. Navy

[1 October 1798.]

SIR, You have done well, by detaining the little British Privateer, for my further Examination; with Respect to the Seamen she has on Board, you have my Consent to take them out, provided you can ascertain beyond all Doubt, that they are Citizens of the United States, & that they are willing to enter with you, but not otherwise; our Government wishes to be on good Terms with Great Britain, and we must not counteract, what it desires.

The Privateer may be dismissed, on Condition of his going immediately out of Sight of the Fleet to Leeward.

I am, Dear Sir, with great Respect,

Your Obedient humble Servant,

THOMAS TRUXTUN.

UNITED STATES SHIP *Constellation*
1st October 1798 — — —
Captain PHILLIPS.

[HS of Pa. NDA photostat. Truxtun's LB, 1798–9.]

To the Secretary of State from D. Humphreys, United States Minister to Spain

(No. 165)

MADRID *Octr 1st 1798*
10 O'Clock at Night

SIR, By a private gentleman who goes Post to Lisbon & will arrive before the mail, I have just time to confirm the News communicated in my last of the destruction of the French fleet in a bay near Alexandria. The substance of the details as rec'd by a Courier from Naples are; that Admiral Nelson with 11 Ships of the line attacked the French fleet of the same number (I think on or about the 4th of Augst) that the action continued for three days; that the English took seven Ships of the line (whose names are all mentioned in the relation) two others blew up, and two more (the *Guilliame Tell & Genereux*) escaped to Corfu; that two French frigates were likewise sunk; that the English had upwards of 800 men killed & wounded (one Captn in the number of the first, & Admiral Nelson in that of the last) that the French had lost upwards of 21000, with a great many wounded . . . There is no particular account of the number of transports destroyed, . . those which were not destroyed but had sought for shelter near the shore, were said to have been repulsed by the Inhabitants. Bonaparte was also reported to have met with considerable resistance. Admiral Nelson was sending the prizes to

Gibraltar, & proposed to remain before Alexandria with such of his ships as were best able to keep the Sea.

With sentiments of great regard & esteem,

I have the honour to be,

Sir,

Your m° ob^t & m° h^ble Servt

D. HUMPHREYS

The SECRETARY OF STATE

&c &c &c

[SDA. Disp. Spain, Bk. 4, Humphreys.]

To Captain H. G. Campbell, Revenue Cutter *Eagle*, from Secretary of the Navy

[TRENTON,]

Navy Department October 1st 1798

Capt H. G. CAMPBELL

Cutter *Eagle*

SIR I have your Letter of this day. — I was in hopes my last orders would have been considered so positive, that you would have obeyed them. — I have now to request, that you will lose no time at Philadelphia, but proceed without the least delay, to Norfolk; where your Gun-Carriages may be altered if necessary, and where you may get the Articles, if any Still Wanted; — Please to write to me, the day you sail. — —

I am Sir

&c^a

[NDA. OSW, Vol. 1.]

To Captain John Barry, U. S. Navy, from Secretary of the Navy

[TRENTON,]

Navy Department October 1st 1798

Capt JOHN BARRY

SIR I presume you are by this time supplied with your requisition of Cordage, Cheese & Bread. —

As this is the season when our vessels may be expected from Europe; And as it is probable attempts may be made by the French Cruisers to interrupt them on or near our own Coasts, it becomes necessary that you proceed to sea as soon as your Ship is watered. The Bread Cordage & Cheese, I hope you have received. — —

Your Object must be to protect the Trade from Delaware to New Hampshire, and doubting neither your discretion, Bravery, nor Enterprize, I leave it to yourself to judge in what manner you can best effect this object. — Captain Decatur will cruise from New York to the Chesapeake. —

There will be, I imagine, but little danger of Enemy Vessels on our Coasts by the 15th November — You will therefore, (no circumstance arising, which in your Judgment shall make a longer cruise necessary) go into Newport, Rhode Island about that time. —

Before you sail be pleased to write me, what your ship will want on your return, for another cruise of four months. —

If there should be occasion to communicate with you, it will be most conveniently done from Rhode Island; — You will please therefore, every twleve or fifteen days appear off the Harbour of Newport — with the French Flag hoisted on your main-top-mast-head, — and hover off & on, long enough to be seen from Newport and to receive a boat; should it be necessary to send one to you — —

I am &c^a

[NDA. OSW, Vol. 1.]

To Captain Thomas Tingey, U. S. Navy, from Captain Richard Dale, U. S. Navy

MARCUS HOOK [1] *Octr 1798*

Your favor of 28th Ult^o I received yesterday — I am happy to hear that you have accepted of the appointment to the *Ganges* But I am sorry it will take you some time (on account of your business) before you can join the Ship. It is highly necessary that you should come down to the Ship, as soon as possible, for a day or two: I will then inform you of every thing that lays in my power, respecting the Ship, Officers & Men. I long to see you & shall look for you in 5 days.

I am — your friend &c. &c.

Signed R^d DALE

To Captn TINGEY (*Kingston*)

[NDA. Tingey LB, 1798–1800.]

Extract from Captain Thomas Truxtun's journal, U. S. Frigate *Constellation*, 1 October 1798, Monday

Light Breezes Easterly, and a Squall from that Quarter, all the Fleet in Sight.

At 10 P M a small Privateer from New Providence, called the *Nancy*, commanded by one George Broadwater, from the Eastern Shore of Virginia, got along Side of the *Baltimore*, and was preparing to board her, but discovering her Mistake Captain Phillips detained her untill 10 A M, and sent her Master to me. I ordered her discharged, and directed that she immediately proceed to Leeward of the Fleet.

At Noon the Key Largo on the Florida Shore, discovered at 11 A M from the top Mast Head bore North, seven Leagues Distance. The Signal almost constantly flying to keep the Fleet in close Order, notwithstanding which, the Masters would scatter without paying any Attention to it.

Latitude observed 24°.30′ N°.
Longitude Account 81°.12′ W.

[HS of Pa. NDA photostat.]

Extract from journal of James Pity, U. S. Frigate *Constitution*, 1 October 1798, Monday

Begins with light airs Inclinable to calm. Saw a Ship in ye Road at Anchor with American Coll^rs Union down. Sent our Yaul with Lieutenant Hull to enquire the Reason who was Inform'd the people Refused to do their duty was directed to put 4 Men in Irons. @ 7 our boat went on B^{d} with Lieu^{t} Hull & Master at Arms, who Confind the According to Orders. @ 5 P. M. a Boat came with 3 Head of Neat Cattle @ 6 Let go our Anchor & veer'd away the Short Service hoisted in our Yaul.

[NDA.]

To Captain Alexander Murray, U. S. Navy, commanding *Montezuma*, from Secretary of the Navy

[Trenton,]
Navy Department October 2nd 1798

Capt Alex^{r} Murray

Sir Since my last Instructions, I have received a Letter from Messrs Nicklin & Griffith who will write to you particularly on the subject of the *New Jersey.* — It seems a part of the money to be paid by them remains at St Thomas's, & must be delivered at St Domingo. If you can, without interfering with the general object of your Enterprize, affording assistance in convoying this Money will be agreeable to Government. But this is a point on which you must yourself Judge.

Notwithstanding my most positive orders, Capt Campbell of the *Eagle* Cutter, still remains in Delaware. She has been delayed by the Fever, and I suspect a little by other causes. — I have repeated my Instructions to him, to sail instantly for Norfolk. If he obeys, I fear on his arrival he will want both men & military Stores. Have these wants Supplied, if you can, from Norfolk. Perhaps you may have them to spare. If however you find it impossible to take this Vessel with you, and the Brig *Virginia*, Capt Bright should be in Port, have her prepared with as much Expedition as possible, & take her: leaving in this case Campbell, to whom I shall send orders to be observed in the Event of his not going with you. —

Please to be attentive to the conduct of this Gentleman, indeed of all the officers, that you may enable me on your return to understand confidentially their characters. —

I have the honor &c^{a}

[NDA. OSW, Vol. 1.]

To Captain Alexander Murray, U. S. Navy, from Secretary of the Navy

[Trenton,]
Navy Department October 2nd 1798

Capt Alex^{r} Murray

Sir Enclosed is a Letter to Capt Bright, which you will use, or not, as circumstances may require. — . —

[NDA. OSW, Vol. 1.]

To Captain Francis Bright, commanding U. S. Brig *Virginia*, from Secretary of the Navy

[Enclosure to letter of 2 Oct. 1798 to Captain Murray]

NAVY DEPARTMENT
October 2nd 1798

Capt FRANCIS BRIGHT

SIR If this Letter should find you at Norfolk, you will put yourself Vessel, & Crew, under the Command of Capt Alexr Murray.

Any Supplies you may want, or money to enlist men, must as usual, be furnished by the Collector, — who will continue to act as Agent for the Brig *Virginia* — She being on the Revenue Cutter Establishment —

I have the honor &ca

[NDA. OSW, Vol. 1.]

To the Secretary of State, from D. Humphreys, United States Minister to Spain

(No 166)

MADRID *October 2nd 1798.*

SIR, In confirmation of what I wrote to you last night, respecting the issue of the engagement between the English and French fleets near Alexandria, I now enclose a Paper containing the names of the ships taken by Admiral Nelson, together with some other circumstances which I was not then able to communicate. A combat of so decisive a nature, in which the English have gained the complete command of the Mediterranean, can scarcely fail to open the Mediterranean again for the commerce of that nation. But the Dutch, who had formerly so lucrative a share of the carrying trade in that sea, cannot now, if ever, expect to recover it. The Swedes and Danes are wisely endeavouring to give countenance to their Merchant vessels by constantly keeping some armed vessels in the Mediterranean. Considering the enterprising character of our Citizens, it appears to me that the United States might profit extremely of the actual circumstances by encreasing their trade to the ports which they have been accustomed to frequent, and extending it much farther, if Government could send one frigate and three or four strong sloops of war to protect our Merchant vessels against French Privateers. It is true our armed Merchant vessels will be of sufficient force to repulse the greater part of the French Privateers, especially such as have hitherto been at sea. But since the owners of them have seen our armed Merchant vessels put their Privateers at defiance, and arrive safe with valuable cargoes, they are fitting out larger ones, and some which are even to carry a few twenty four pounders. Lord St Vincents now permits all American loaded vessels to enter Cadiz, but no other Neutrals. At that port several cargoes belonging to our Citizens have lately sold at 150 per cent profit at least. It appears to me it would be wise on our part to encourage so rich a commerce, if possible, by detaching an armed force from the United States, particularly during the winter season, when it could not cruize on the coast of America. This measure, if practicable, seems the more strongly recommended by two considerations. In the first place, this armed force would give our flag an unequivocal superiority over all the French Privateers which are now fitting out, and which will otherwise almost certainly still do considerable damage to our commerce. In the second place, the appearance of these armed vessels in the Mediterranean would very probably prevent any of the Barbary Powers from commencing hostilities against us — a conduct to which they will possibly be instigated — in such sort, that if precautions are not taken to avoid it, I should not be surprized to receive the news of it at any moment.

The Commander of a Swedish armed vessel at Malaga, having lately declined to take American vessels under his convoy in going out of the Streight of Gibraltar, because he had no Instructions for the purpose, the Swedish Minister here has written to his Government (at my instance) to suggest the expediency of having such Instructions given for the future.

The Court is to remove this day from St Ildefonso to the Escurial—where Mr de Saavedra continues still incapable of attending to business.

With sentiments of perfect consideration
I have the honour to be,
Sir,
Your most obt and most hbe Servant
D. HUMPHREYS

The SECRETARY OF STATE &c. &c. &c.

[SDA. Disp. Spain. Bk. 4, Humphreys.]

[2 OCTOBER 1798]

To Captain Henry Geddes from Clement Humphreys, bearer of dispatches to France

To Capt HENRY GEDDES Commander of the Brig *Sophia*, belonging to the United States of America.

SIR, The President of the United States, has directed me, to request, that you will proceed immediately with the *Sophia*, to New Castle, Delaware, and on your arrival there inform the Secretary of State, who is now at Trenton, New Jersey.

Wishing you a pleasant voyage,
I remain Sir, with much
respect,
Your obet St
C[LEMENT] HUMPHREYS

CAMBRIDGE *Octr 2d 1798.* —
(Copy)

[HS of Pa. NDA photostat.]

To Secretary Pickering from W. Vans Murray, United States Minister to The Netherlands

Private THE HAGUE *2. Octr 1798.*

Col. PICKERING

DEAR SIR, The French official accounts differ so widely from the Constantinople letters that it is impossible to say whether Buonaparte is even at Cairo or Damietta — The French here admit that he has received a severe check from 20,000 horse between Alexandria & Cairo. The loss of the Fleet, two ships excepted is certain — This great event, so critically occurring, is not that I know of, the source of any new idea or plan on the Continent.

*　　*　　*　　*　　*　　*　　*

Six or Seven Frigates left Brest about three weeks since & with a few other Ships have 3000 men on board — destination unknown — Supposed to be for Ireland — They may be for the W. Indies.

I am with respectfuly esteem

Dear Sir

Yr mo. ob. Svt &c &c

W. V. MURRAY.

Col. PICKERING

[Mass. HS. Pickering Papers, Vol. 23.]

Extract from journal of U. S. Ship *Herald*, Captain James Sever, U. S. Navy, commanding, 2 October 1798

This 24 hours first part modarate gales and Clear pleasant weather at mrdn Block Island Bore west 5 Leagues Distns from which we Teake Our Departure allowing it to Bee in the Latt of 41. .15 N Longetud of 71. .37 west at 5 p m Saw a Schooner Standing to the N N E at 8 p m handed T G Sails one Reef in Each F Sail

Midle part modarate gales and Clear pleasant weather at 8 a m Sounded in 40 fathoms Watter Soft Bottom

Latter part modarate and fair pleasant weather the Brig *Pickring* in Companey

Lattd Obbrs 40. .26 North

[NDA. Journal kept by Joseph Strout, 1798.]

Extract from journal of Lieutenant John Mullowny, U. S. Frigate *United States*, 2 October 1798

Sent the sloop and schooner (prizes) to Mud-fort under charge of Mr Caldwell Midshipman. —

[NA.]

Extract from Captain Thomas Truxtun's journal, U. S. Frigate *Constellation*, 2 October 1798, Tuesday

The Beginning of this Day clear with the Wind light, & variable. The Middle and latter a fresh Trade, and cloudy Weather. Thirty six of the Convoy in Sight.

No perceptible Current such as is usual in the Gulph of Florida, has been yet felt, and although but little of any is discernable at present that little has been westerly.

At Noon spoke the Schooner *Sally* from Havannah bound to Beaufort, North Carolina, this Vessel came out one Day after the Fleet to join the Convoy, seven of which have left us, I suppose, on Account of the bad Sailing of many of the Vessels, and the Negligence, and Inattention of their Masters. The *America*, and *Belvidera*, two armed Ships, mounting each 18 Guns, and well manned are among the Number left us. The Signal almost constantly flying to keep the Fleet in close Order, notwithstanding which, the Masters would scatter without paying any Attention to it.

At Noon the Florida shore bore from N. B. E. to N. W. B. N, five or six Leagues Distance.

Latitude observed 24°.34′ North
Longitude Account 81.12 W.

[HS of Pa. NDA photostat.]

Extract from journal of James Pity, U. S. Frigate *Constitution*, 2 October 1798, Tuesday

Begins with fresh Breezes call'd all hands washed Decks &c unbent main & Mizn Top Sails & bent others in their Room Two boats came from Shore on Bd on[e] Mr James Coline Glazier to mend cabin Windows all hands employ'd variously unbent Sprit Sail & put it below Furl'd Top Sails and clear'd Decks Hoisted in Boats.

[NDA.]

To Stephen Higginson, Navy Agent, Boston, from Secretary of Navy

[TRENTON,]
Navy Department October 3rd 1798.

S. HIGGINSON Esqr *Boston*

SIR, I have too long delayed acknowledging receipt of your Letter of the 10th Ulto — I have now before me also yours of the 25th — I had contemplated Capt McNeill's taking the Command of the ship at Providence — But I afterwards found, or at least believed he would not be so agreeable to the people there as I expected — and it seemed too, that the President understood he was to command the Ship at Portsmouth, and I gave up the Idea of sending him to providence. This I intended, but omitted to inform you —

The President has appointed Capt Fletcher, a Captain in the Navy. — I hope he merits the distinction. — I have written him to go to Providence — I find by a Letter from him, that he is Selected by the Merchants to superintend their Ship. — I wait however his Answer to my Letter directing him to Providence. — If he declines, it is not unlikely that Capt Chapman may be sent to Providence, and Sever's first Lieut appointed to command the *Herald*, or Chapman's Vessel. — There is great Anxiety in Providence to furnish the Captain. — If they should not be gratified sending a man already a Captain, will be less offensive, than making one to send there — But if Fletcher should not go, it is not improbable they may be gratified — At any rate I shall not forget your suggestions on the subject of the Officers in Chapman & Sever's Vessels. — —

Fearing that Portsmouth will not get clear of the Fever, which every wher from Philadelphia Eastward, has greatly retarded the preparations for the Navy, I do not expect the ship at that place can be got to sea before January. — I hope she may by that time be ready, with a view to the Employment suggested in your Letter of the 10th It was with this view too, that I purchased the Ship at Providence. — I wrote to McNeill, that his Officers must be got in New Hampshire, thinking that state could and would at least expect to furnish the Subalterns if they did not the Captain. — Enclosed is his Answer — I mean to leave Trenton about the 15th Instant; and perhaps for four Weeks — certainly for three. — I wish to make such arrangements as shall prevent the *Portsmouth* ship being retarded by my absence. With this view I have written the enclosed Letter for him, which please to have sent to him after you possessed yourself of the contents. — Col° Pickering, I expect will attend to the business of the Navy in my absence, and will cause to be remitted you any Money you shall find necessary. —

On the subject of the Ballast for the *Portsmouth* Ship, I requested Mr Watson of New York to send you 50 Tons of Kentledge and a Hearth. — I also requested him to send sheathing Copper &Ca to Newbury Port. — His Letter in answer I enclosed to you — Never having directed Kentledge, or a Hearth for Newbury, I never doubted that these Articles were for you — — I have this day written him to send you 25 Ton Pig Iron, (Kentledge tho long ago contracted for, not being to be had instantly) provided the Kentledge already sent was destined for you — But if that was sent for Newbury, in consequence of a requisition directly to him, from that place. — Then I have requested him to contract for, & send you in three weeks 50 Tons of Kentledge. — I presume it will be in time, to be shipped three weeks hence. — To save you the trouble of havg a Copy made of my Letter to McNeill, I enclose a Copy of that. — And a List of Provisions deemed necessary for the Ship at Portsmouth for six Months. — —

I have the honor &Ca

[NDA. GLB No. 1.]

Extract from journal of James Pity, U. S. Frigate *Constitution*, 3 October 1798, Wednesday

Begins with light winds from East @ 5 Call'd all hands & Wash'd decks and Sprinkled them with Vinegar Recd two new Boomkins from Hampton In hoisting them in Thos Webb a Boy was dangerously hurt. Lieu't Beale & several Gentn came on Board with Letters for Capt Nicholson Ship lying at Single anchor. [Hampton Roads.]

[NDA.]

Extract from Captain Thomas Truxtun's journal, U. S. Frigate *Constellation*, 3 October 1798, Wednesday

Fresh Gales from the North Eastward, and squally Weather from Sun down to Sun Rise, with a heavy Sea running, which indicated a strong Windward Current, which in some Measure has been experienced under double reefed Top Sails only, Courses handed.

Thirty of the Fleet in Sight, several of the Vessels having left the Fleet since Yesterday of their own accord, as from the easy Sail we carried, and our Lights being constantly kept up by Night, they might have stayed round the Ships of War at short Distance with great Ease.

At 10 A M made the Florida Shore bearing North North West about seven Leagues Distance.

Tacked.

Latitude observed 24°.52′ North
Longitude Account 80.41 W.

[HS of Pa. NDA photostat.]

[4 October 1798]

To Captain Preble of the Ship *Dolphin* from Captain Thomas Truxtun, U. S. Navy

DEAR SIR I am extreemly Sorry for Your Misfortune and will render you any Service I have in My power, by furnishing Cordage, Sail Cloth, Spars, or Such other Articles as You are in Need of. —

As I do not think it proper, to detain the fleet any longer than is Absolutely Necessary, I request you will let me know your wants as Soon as possible, in order that I proceed. —

As soon as You was Near enough to let us know, what was the Cause of your Making the Signal of distress, I hoisted Out my boat and dispatched Lieutenant Sterett, with directions to offer My Services in any respect, which I have no doubt of his doing, and as the pump tacks [?] was the only article he informed me, You immediately wanted I Sent them — I directed Captn Phillips also to Send you a boat, which he informed Me he had done — I Should Suppose Your best Way would be, to proceed to Savannah or Charlston, Where you may Arrive in a few days

I am &c.

Captn PREBLE
Ship Dolphin
UNITED STATES SHIP *Constellation*
in the Gulph of Florida
4th OCTOBER 1798. —

[HS of Pa. NDA photostat. Truxtun's LB, 1798–9.]

To Captain Samuel Barron, U. S. Navy, of the *Richmond*, from Secretary of the Navy

[TRENTON,]
Navy Department, 4. October, 1798.

Capt SAML BARRON

SIR: Presuming that your Brig will shortly be ready to receive her Crew, I have now to direct that you proceed to commence recruiting, not exceeding Ninety Hands, to consist of Able-Seamen — Ordinary Seamen, & Boys —

I informed you in my Letter of the 19th Ultimo, that no general Arrangement had yet been made respecting the proportion of the different kinds of Men, to be employed in the Navy of the United States, — To that Letter I refer you for other Observations on this subject — And I leave it to your own Judgment to decide, respecting the proportion of the different Descriptions of Men, to be employed by you. —

You will not enlist any but sound &c (See Instructions to Capt Brown Page (232). this Letter was exactly similar. —

Messrs John Nevison & John Granbury will advance the Money necessary for recruiting the Men &c &c See Instructions to Capt Brown Page 232. —

I enclose you your Commission —

I am &c

[NOTE: Page 232 contains letter to Capt. Brown, dated October 4th, 1798.]
[NDA. OSW, Vol. 1.]

To the Secretary of State from the Secretary of War

[TRENTON,]
War Department 4th October 1798

SIR, I enclose an Engagement, on the behalf of th United State's of America, under my hand, and the seal of the War Office, in conformity with the stipulations, proposed through Mr. Liston, his Britannic Majesty's Envoy Extraordinary, and Minister Plenepotentiary to the United States, by his Royal Highness Prince Edward, relative to a Loan of twenty four pieces of cannon, French twentyfour pounders, now at Halifax, Nova Scotia, formerly belonging to the *Foudroyant*, with about eighteen hundred shot, for the same —

I am Sir
with the greatest respect
your obedt hble. servant

JAMES MCHENRY

The SECRETARY for the Department of State —

[SDA. Miscl., Sept.–Dec. 1798.]

To Captain Moses Brown, U. S. Navy, from Secretary of the Navy

[TRENTON,]
Navy Department Octr 4th 1798

Capt MOSES BROWN
of the *Merrimack* Newbury Port

SIR You will make immediate Arrangements to commence recruiting the Crew of the *Merrimack*, now under your Command, that the complement may be completed by the time the Ship is ready for a cruise. Your Crew must be enlisted for one year. —

You are allowed (besides a Lieutenant of Marines, and 21 privates, which will be supplied you by the Major of the Marine Corps) for your vessel, not exceeding 105 Men. You will therefore enlist, not exceeding Sixty five able seamen: The residue of your Crew to consist of ordinary Seamen & Boys. — I leave it to your own Judgement to get as good a Crew within this limitation as may be in your power. — It is our best policy to create Seamen — Therefore you will take as large a proportion of Boys, as can be found useful on board. You will allow able Seamen 17 Dollars per month — Ordinary Seamen & Boys from 5 to 14 Dollars, according to Merit.— You will be careful not to enlist any but sound and healthy persons. — And that no indirect, or forcible means be used, to induce them to enter into the Service. No Negroes, or Mulattoes are to be admitted, and as far as you can judge, you will exclude all of a suspicious character. — Avoid any advance of money if possible, until the men are got on board. But should you find it impracticable to procure them on these terms, you may gratify them. — In this case you will take care to obtain Sufficient security to resort to, in the event of desertion — And you will allow two months advance — You will have a regular account kept, of the Name & Station of each recruit, together with a description of his person, and his usual place of residence, so that they may be identified at any future period. —

Every man shipped must take an oath agreeably to the Form you will receive herewith. —

Enclosed is the Form of a shipping paper, wherein the name, Station & pay of each person on board must be entered. It will be necesaary, to avoid confusion, that this business be executed with the utmost exactness. — The Form of a Bond to be signed by the sureties for the Seamen &c^a^ you will also receive; And particular care must be taken, that the sureties must be persons of good & responsible characters, before they are accepted. —

Mr Nicholas Johnson will advance the money necessary for enlisting your Crew. — And you must advance to the recruiting Officers, who must Settle their Accounts with you. — They will be allowed besides their pay & Rations, Two dollars for each recruit in full for every expense of attesting; Ribbon, Punch &c^a^ In short, every expense, but that of provisioning the men enlisted at a distant Port, — And in such cases, the unavoidable expense for their Conveyance to the Ship. But they must observe the utmost Occonomy; for extravagant charges for those expenditures will not be allowed. And no charge will be allowed, without a proper voucher to support it. —

Mr Bartlett has nominated; Michael Fitcomb J^r^ 1st Lieutenant — Saml Chase 2nd Lieut^t^ Jonathan Fitcomb J^r^ Sailing Master, Nathaniel Broadstreet Surgeon, Joseph Hooper, Purser; Joseph Brown, Midshipman; Nathan Fletcher, ditto; Francis Salter, Gunner; James Couch, Carpenter; — These officers I shall immediately nominate to the President; and there is no doubt, but they will be appointed; — But should you find their services, or the services of any or either of them necessary, before they receive their appointments, which unavoidably be some time first (the President being in Massachusetts) you are at liberty to receive them in the Capacities to which they have been nominated by Mr Bartlett.

I enclose your Commission as Captain in the Navy of the United States —

I have the honor &c^a^

[NDA. OSW, Vol. 1.]

To Captain Daniel McNeill, U. S. Navy, commanding the *Portsmouth*, from Secretary of the Navy

[TRENTON,]
Navy Departm^t^ 4 Octr 1798

Capt DAN^l^ M^c^NEILL

SIR, You will in concert with Stephen Higginson, Esqr, make such arrangements for recruiting a Crew for the *Portsmouth*, now under your Command, as to have her Complement completed by the Time she is ready for a Cruise. Your Crew must be entered for one Year.

You are allowed (besides a Lieut^t^ of Marines & 21 Privates, w^c^ will be supplied you by the Major of the Marine Corps) not exceeding 115 hands, to consist of able Seamen, Ordinary Seamen & Boys. You will therefore enlist not exceeding 70 Able Seamen: The residue to be ordinary Seamen & Boys. &^c^ &^c^ &^c^ See

(Instructions to Capt Moses Brown) Page (232)

Stephen Higginson Esqr will supply you, with Money, necessary for enlisting your Crew — ; & you must advance to your recruiting officers, who must settle their acc^ts^ with you. &^c^ &^c^ See Page (232) —

I enclose a List of Commissioned & Petty Officers, the latter of which you will appoint —

[NOTE.—Page 232 contains letter to Capt. Moses Brown, dated October 4th, 1798.]

[NDA. OSW, Vol. 1.]

Extract from Captain Thomas Truxtun's journal, U. S. Frigate *Constellation*, 4 October 1798, Thursday

Moderate Breezes with a few flying Clouds producing light Squalls of Wind. At 7 P M the *Dolphin* of Boston, one of the Fleet, made the Signal of Distress, and soon after spoke, and informed us, the Ship *Harmony* of Charleston, had run on Board her, did her much Damage, and that they were sinking.

I hoisted out a Boat, and sent to her Assistance, and directed Captain Phillips of the *Baltimore* to do the same.

Made the Signal for the Fleet to stand on the Larboard Tack, and determined to keep by her, untill Day Light.

At 6 A M sent some Rigging, Plank, Spikes, and Nails &c. on Board the *Dolphin*, which did not leak as bad as was represented, tho' otherwise much injured; the Master informed me after, that he was in Want of Nothing else. I made the Signal for the Fleet to make Sail, and stood on to the Northward.

Latitude observed 25°.40′ N°
Longitude Account 80.25 W.

[HS of Pa. NDA photostat.]

Extract from journal of U. S. Ship *Herald*, Captain James Sever, U. S. Navy, commanding, 4 October, 1798

This 24 hours first part Light wind and Clear pleasant weather Saw a Dead whale Bearing South hoisted out Cutter and went and Examined it at 5 p m Sprung up a Small Breeze from the Eastward Tact Ship To the Southward out Reefs out Topsails Sett T G Sails Sounded in 31 fathoms at 12 a m Sounded in 42 fathoms Sandy Bottom at 4 a m Sounded in the Same Saw a Brig hove out Cutter and Borded hur found itt T[o] Bee the Brig *Charlotte* Capt Stubbs from Lisbon Bound To Providence 45 Days out at 10 a m one Reef in Each Topsail

Latter part Strong gales and flying Clouds at mrdn Stod Jibb braild up mizen Brig *Pickering* Still in Company

Lattd Obbrs 40 . . 08 North

[NDA. Journal kept by Joseph Strout, 1798.]

Extract from journal of James Pity, U. S. Frigate *Constitution*, 4 October 1798, Thursday

Light airs from N. E. and clear Weather hove up our Best Bower (it being foul) & Clear'd it let go Small bower and veer'd away to the Short Service. Cutter *Virginia* Boat came on Board a Schr came in Dismasted in Longd 68 West on 25 Sept in a hard Gale Wind boarded Brig bound to Boston Saml Allen Master Carpenters employ'd fitting New Boomkins.

[NDA.]

To Captain Samuel Nicholson, U. S. Navy, from Secretary of the Navy

[TRENTON,]
Navy Department October 5th 1798

Capt SAM^{l} NICHOLSON

SIR I wrote the 1st October, deeming it barely possible that my letter might find you at Hampton. — Your Letter of the 26th with a P. S. of the 27th Ult^{o} makes it too probable that you are still there. —

It was most unfortunate, that, if it was absolutely necessary for you to conduct with your Frigate, the *Niger* into Port, that you did not immediately proceed again to sea, in pursuance to my Instructions of the 13th August. — This, you must have judged was the more essential, as you knew that Capt Truxton, having gone to the Havanna, there remained no adequate Force on the Southern Coasts, to protect our Commerce in that Quarter. — Should the Fever, which has attacked your Crew, continue its ravages, I request that you will instantly concert with Mr Pennock, means for having such as are infected removed to the most airy & healthy situation in the neighbourhood of Norfolk. I hope Mr Pennock can procure Tents, or provide a house, and I write to him, to employ, Skilful, medical assistance, and to procure all necessaries for the sick — With the healthy part of your Crew, you will proceed immediately to Sea; And if your men continue healthy, You will remain on the Southern Coasts, & govern yourself by my Instructions of the 13th August, until the 15th November, when I presume you may return to Hampton without danger of the Fever, and take on board such of your Crew left at Norfolk, as shall have survived the Fever, and without remaining at Norfolk, longer than necessary to take on board these men, you will then immediately proceed to the Port of Boston, & conduct yourself, as directed in my Letter of the 1st Ins^{t}

But if after getting to Sea, in the first Instance, from Hampton Road, you should discover any symptoms of the Fever among your Crew; you will in that case, instead of remaining on the Southern Coast, proceed with all expedition to Newport, Rhode Island — and leaving just men enough on board the Frigate to secure her in Harbour, you will remove all the rest of your Crew to some high & healthy part of the Country, which will be provided by Messrs Gibbs & Channing, to whom I shall write on the Subject. — This you will do, without any further communication with the Town of Newport, than absolutely necessary to obtain supplies —

I have the honor to be &c^{a}

This Letter was not delivered to Captn Nicholson, but returned by Mr Pennock at the desire of the Sec^{y} of the Navy
GC

[NDA. OSW, Vol. 1.]

To William Pennock, Navy Agent, Norfolk, from Secretary of Navy

[TRENTON,]
Navy Department October 5th 1798

Wm PENNOCK Esqr
Norfolk

SIR By a letter from Capt Nicholson of the 26th & 27th September, I am mortified to find that he Still remained at Hampton. — Where he ought not to have remained for two days — and to add to the Calamity, his Crew is seized with the prevailing Malady. — —

I have directed him to concert with you instantly, measures for getting all his sick Men, landed and removed to a high and airy place in the Neighbourhood of Norfolk — Pray without delay Select such a place, provide Tents, or an airy and large house — Employ able medical assistance, and have the best possible care taken of the men — Let this be done instantly if you please — and give Nicholson no more advice to remain in Port — for that injudicious part of his conduct, he mentions your advice. — He will proceed to Sea, if he has healthy men enough to Navigate his vessel; and will be governed by the health of his Crew, whether to return to the Eastward, or to remain on the Southern Coast. — If he wants a doctor on board, and a good one can be obtained at Norfolk, he shall have the appointment promised him, to obtain his services at this time.—

[NDA. GLB No. 1.]

To Tench Francis, Purveyor, from Secretary Pickering

TRENTON *Oct. 5. 1798.*

[To] TENCH FRANCIS Esqr *Purveyor.*

SIR, I received your letter of the 3d and delayed an answer because I was at a loss to determine what ought to be done. However, I had concluded to detain Mr Murrays ship, loading for Algiers, until the three armed vessels bound thither were ready to convoy her. Since I had come to this clonclusion, this morning, Mr Murray fortunately called upon me. I observed to him, that I originally expected his ship would have been ready to take in her loading long before she came round to Philadelphia; and in that case the three armed vessels would have been also got ready and sailed before the yellow fever deranged all business; that this delay of his Ship induced me to order the armed vessels to receive no more men than were requisite to keep them in port; and that now it was impracticable to man them: that probably in two weeks such a change as to the fever might take place as would enable us to proceed; and then as much dispatch as possible should be given.

Mr Murray acquiesces willingly; and will give orders to delay manning his ship: he is equally anxious with us that she should go under convoy. He is going to Mr Warder's (at Peele Hall) where perhaps you may see him, and converse about the ships bringing back the crews of the armed vessels.

I am respectfully yours

TIMOTHY PICKERING.

P. S. It will be important to arm Mr Murray's Ship: I suppose the public could loan some guns. Mr Murray engaging for their value if lost. Please to confer on this point with him. —

[SDA. Dom. L., Vol. 11.]

To President John Adams from the Secretary of Navy

[TRENTON,]
Navy Department October 5th 1798

JOHN ADAMS Esqr
President of the United States

SIR I have the honor to enclose a Letter from Capt Nicholson of the 26 & 27 September; which I had the mortification to receive last evening. There seems to be no calculating the Evils of his first false step.

His Letter of the 12th exhibited a very strong disposition to remain in Port, to secure at all events his prize. — But the return into port of the vessel, which he Idly supposed had been sent out with orders for him, depriving him of all pretence, he promised to proceed with all expedition to sea, after filling his Water. — He had watered little more than a fortnight before in Rhode Island. — His present Letter will shew his proceedings since, and the consequences. —

I know of nothing better to be done, in his present Situation, than to order him to Land instantly at Norfolk, all his infected men; and to proceed instantly to sea, if symptoms of the disorder prevail on board, to make for Rhode Island — And there to leave enough of his Crew on board to take care of the vessel and to March the rest, into a high and healthy part of the Country, — without communicating with Newport farther than necessary to procure Supplies. —

By this Arrangement there will be a chance of his meeting with Frost, a fortnight earlier than in the South — and a chance of preserving the lives of a Number of his Crew. —

I have the honor to enclose a copy of my Letter to him. — I fear this Gentleman will fulfil all the predictions of Boston concerning him.

I have the honor to be

&ca

[NDA. Nom. Appts. LB, 1798–1820.]

To Secretary Stoddert from Josiah Parker, chairman of committee, House of Representatives

NORFOLK 5th *October 1798*

SIR, Having recovered from a severe and dangerous indisposition I have found it convenient to Visit the Brigg *Norfolk*. Capt Williams and the Brigg Capn Barron. the first is nearly manned and lays at Sewels point, she is a fine looking Vessell and will sail fast, has nearly all her Stores on board & may be got ready for Sea in a few days but I fear her Marines will be wanted. Lt J. Reddick is recruiting at Suffolk and ready to obey his orders but at present I understand he is to hold himself in readiness for the *Constellation*, my being unwell in the Country has given Williams an opportunity of gratifying himself in respect to his Officers — except as to Lt McRae, I will furnish you with a list of them by next post with my remarks — Upon examining the Rigging of the *Norfolk* I am sorry to say the greater part of the running Rigging is worse than ought to be in any Vessell for Sea, this I have mentioned to Williams who tells me it was the best that could be got.

I do myself the honor to enclose a list of officers for Captⁿ Saml Barron, they are not only his choice, but the choice of Messrs Nevison & Granberry as well as my own, they will in my opinion do credit to their appointments — the Brigg will soon be ready & I will be much deceived if in all respects she is not what ought to be expected from you — the Agents having more money than will fitt her, appear desirous of the honor of compleating her with provisions, Stores Men &c that they may have the entire merit or discredit of her, but from the Agents and the Captain & his officers I flatter myself that all they may have done will be as it should be —

Officers for the Brigg at present called the *Augusta*, Saml Barron esqr Commander, to be loaned to the U. S. by the Merchts of Norfolk &c. —

James Boush first Lt
John Ballard Second do
John Cowper Sailing Master
Wm Cowper do Mate
Richard Henry Lee Lawson, first Midshipmen
Roe Lattimer - - - - - - - - - - - - - - - - 2d ditto
Buller Cocke Purser

Dr Reynolds I am told has been appointed to the *Norfolk*, but not being ready to go on board Dr J. K. Reade is on board the *Norfolk* as Surgeon and I think he is worthy the appointment. Reynolds will be ready for Barron.

With much respect & esteem
I have the honor to be
Your most obedient Servant

J. PARKER

BENJⁿ STODDERT

[NDA. Area 7, October 5, 1798.]

Remarks extracted from the log book of the Schooner *Clara*, Captain F. Hill

The following remarks are extracted from the log book of the schooner *Clara*, captain F. Hill, from Grenada to New York.

October 4, saw two schooners ahead, which proved to be armed vessels from Martinico, bound to New York. Capt. Thomas of the privateer schooner, sent his boat for me and my papers, examined them very strictly, broke open some letters, otherwise behaved very polite and dismissed me.

October 5, at 4 P. M. the before mentioned armed schooners brought too and made a prize of a small schooner under Danish colours. At 9 do. the weather very dark, fell on board one of the schooners, carried away our jib boom and moved the bowsprit in. — Now fairly tired of being convoyed, made sail for the passage. At 9 A. m. was spoke by a British 20 gun ship, but did not stop us.

October 6, two schooners in sight, one to the east, the other to the south; employed securing the bowsprit. At 4 P. M. the bowsprit fast, made all sail, the schooner astern in chase of us. At 9 P. M. the weather very threatening took in all light sails, and brought too under main sail and jib. At half past do. two shot was fired at us — one of which fell very near: at same time saw a light astern, showed a light immediately and was hailed by the three masted schooner *Wanspite*, capt. Mollineaux, who threatened to fire a twelve pounder into us immediately, if we did not send our boat on board: I told him we had but two men and the mate that could stand the deck, and the weather was so bad it was impossible for us to get her out; but he was inflexible, and fired a musket over us, threatening to fire a broadside if the boat was not hoisted out directly: I promised to do my best, at same time very ill, my wound* not being well. After threatening in this manner near an hour, and our bot not yet out, he sent his boat with four armed men — I was obliged to go on board his schooner, where I was treated very politely, and soon dismissed; it appeared my setting so much sail was my only crime, and having so few hands, one of the privateer'smen, in my absence, threatened to murder one of my sick men because he was a Dane.

October 6, spoke the schooner *Rover*, Capt. West, of Norfolk, from Baltimore, bound to Curracoa, out 14 days all well.

* This wound Capt. Hill received on board of an English ship, at Grenada while assisting to quell a mutiny. The contents of a pistol, (discharged by accident) went through his thigh.

[LC "Claypoole's American Daily Advertiser" (Phila.), 13 November 1798.]

Extract from journal of James Pity, U. S. Frigate *Constitution*, 5 October 1798, Friday

Wind at N° hazy W^{r} @ ½ past 7 A. M. came to Sail Cutter *Virginia* in Company found we could not get out of the Roads Let go our Anchor in 9 fath^{ms} Hampton Inlet bore N. b. E. ½ E. Willoughby Point E. b. N° Old Point Comfort N. E. b. E. Cutter also put back with several other Vessells. at ½ past 11 a Brig^{t} Anchor'd with her main Mast gone.

[NDA.]

Extract from Captain Thomas Truxtun's journal, U. S. Frigate *Constellation*, 5 October 1798, Friday

Moderate Breezes, and fine clear Weather all these Twenty four Hours. At half past 5 P M made the Florida shore bearing N. W. B. W at the Distance of six Leagues, and at 8 Ditto tacked, and stood to the Eastward. At A M tacked, and stood to the North Westward, at 4 Ditto tacked, and stood to the Eastward, and at 9 Ditto, tacked to the North Westward. Twenty four Sail of the Convoy with us, besides the *Baltimore*.

At Noon we were Midway between the black Rock off the River Saint Lucia, on the Coast of Florida, which is a short Distance to the Northward of Greenville Inlet, and that noted Rock, or Key, on the Edge of the Bahama Bank, called Memory Rock, Distance from each twenty five Miles.

Latitude observed 27°.00′ N°
Longitude Account 80.13 W.

[HS of Pa. NDA photostat.]

To Joshua Sands, Collector, New York, from Secretary Pickering

DEPARTMENT OF STATE,
Trenton New Jersey Octr 6. 1798

[To] JOSHUA SANDS Esqr
Collector of the Customs New York

SIR There being reason to apprehend, that some of the vessels to which the President's permission to clear for French ports may be issued, may after landing their passengers be sold to the French, it became necessary to devise expedients in order to prevent a traffic so contrary to the meaning of the Act of Congress, and which if they are sold for vessels of war, which is the most likely case, may prove so detrimental to our commerce. It is therefore the command of the President, that before you issue his permission in future cases, you take a bond with sufficient sureties, conditioned that the vessel return to the United States forthwith after the performing of her voyage and be entered with some Collector: I enclose the form of the condition of the bond, the penalty whereof is to be the amount of the value of the vessel as nearly as you can estimate the same. But as by a collusion between the owner of the vessel and the French Officers in the port or ports of her destination, she may be sold under the mask of a pretended seizure, it is also the President's direction that, before issuing his permission to clear any vessel for a French Port, you cause it to be ascertained, that she is not a fast sailing vessel or calculated to be converted into a privateer: if she be of that description the permission is to be withheld. I am &c.

TIMOTHY PICKERING

P. S. I enclose permissions to clear the Brig *Sally* for St Thomas' and St Domingo, and the Sch^r *Fanny* for Cape Francois.

[SDA. Dom. L. Vol. 11.]

[Enclosure]

PERMISSION TO CLEAR SHIPS

Whereas the President of the United States, in pursuance of an Act of the Congress of the United States, passed on the 13th day of June 1798, entitled "An Act to suspend the commercial intercourse between the United States and France and the dependencies thereof," hath on the day of the date hereof, issued to the said Charles Pond, as owner of the Brigantine called the *Sally*, whereof Anthony Stow is at present Master, a permission authorizing the Collector of the Customs for the port of New York to clear the said Brigantine for the Island of St Thomas' and St Domingo, to aid the departure of French persons, who have been resident within the United States with their goods and effects:

Now the condition of the above obligation is such, that if the said Brigantine shall forthwith after the accomplishment of her said voyage proceed for and arrive within some port in the United States and shall be duly reported and entered with the Collector thereof, all unforeseen and inevitable restraints and accidents being excepted, then the above obligation to be void otherwise to be and remain in full force and virtue.

[SDA. Dom. L., Vol. 11, 1798–1799.]

From Jacob Wagner to John Marrauld, Philadelphia

DEPARTMENT OF STATE
Trenton, New Jersey Oct 6, 1798

[To] Mr JOHN MARRAULD *Philadelphia*

SIR, By the direction of the Secretary of State I am to inform you, that he has just sent to the Collector of Norfolk a permission to clear the Schooner *Little John* for the Islands of St. Thomas and St Domingo, to whom you will therefore direct the owner Mr Marresst to apply for the same. The Collector will make known to him the terms on which it will be granted to him. I am, Sir, &c.

JACOB WAGNER.

SDA. Dom. L., Vol. 11.]

From Secretary Pickering to Secrectary of the Navy

DEPARTMENT OF STATE,
Trenton Oct. 6. 1798.

[To] BENJAMIN STODDERT Esqr
Secretary of the Navy.

SIR, There are at Halifax, Nova Scotia, twenty four cannon, French 24 pounders, and about eighteen hundred shot belonging to them. The cannon were taken in the French Ship *Foudroyant*, and given by King George the Second to the province of South Carolina. When Charleston surrendered to the British Army, in the American War, these guns fell of course to the Victors, who on the evacuation of that city afterwards, took the cannon and shot with them. Upon an application to the British Minister, Mr Liston, to procure a restoration of them, for the immediate defence of Charleston, he wrote to Prince Edward, who commanded the British troops in Nova Scotia, and to Sir John Wentworth the Governor of that province; and the Prince agreed that the cannon and shot should be delivered *on loan* to the United States, as he had no authority to *give* them. The condition of the loan was, that they should be relanded, when required, and without expence, in any part of His Britannic Majesty's American Dominions which should be designated.

The cannon probably may weigh each 3 tons	72
The 1800 shot at 27½ lbs English each, about	22
	94

The total weight may be supposed about ninety or ninetyfour tons. As the guns have been lain by, unused, probably they are without carriages or implements: if however there are both or either, they will doubtless be delivered with the cannon, to which they are exclusively adapted: and it will be well to direct your officer charged with the transportation, to make the enquiry. I will hint these articles to Mr Liston, that he may mention them in his letters.

Mr Liston has informed me, that if the terms of the loan should be approved by the President, and the Secretary of War should consequently come under an engagement for the purpose, "and a vessel should be sent properly authorized and protected, to convey the guns and shot to Charleston, he would give the Commander such letters, addressed to Prince Edward and Sir John Wentworth, as would procure their delivery to him." — Yesterday I sent to Mr Liston the Engagement of the Secretary of War, and will furnish you with a copy of it, duly attested, to be sent to your officer, if I can obtain it in time. I desired Mr Liston to write to Halifax immediately, that the requisite orders might be issued, to prevent any delay when your vessel or vessels should arrive there. I will write him again to day, and desire him to send duplicate letters, to the care of Gibbs and Channing in Newport, to be by them delivered to Captain Sever or other officer having orders on this subject.

I am very respectfully &c.

TIMOTHY PICKERING

[SDA. Dom. L., Vol. 11.]

To Captain James Sever, U. S. Navy, of the *Herald*, from Secretary of the Navy

[TRENTON,]
Navy Department October 6th 1798

Capt JAMES SEVER,

SIR You will perceive by the enclosed Copy of a Letter from the Secretary of State to me, that there is a parcel of Cannon & Shot at Halifax, which are to be transported from thence to Charleston, South Carolina, under Convoy. —

If your Ship and Capt Chapman's, can take these Guns & Shot on board, without being too deeply laden for defence, or offence, in that case you will proceed with these Vessels under your Command to Halifax, and take on board the Guns & Shot, and carry them to Charleston. — But if you judge that this cannot be done — then Messrs Gibbs & Channing of Newport will hire a proper vessel, to proceed under the Convoy of your two vessels to Halifax, and from thence with the Guns & Shot on board to Charleston, South Carolina, where they are to be delivered to William Crafts Esquire — Agent for the War Department. — After performing this service you will return with both the Vessels under your Command, to the Eastward, and about the 20th of November, go into the Harbour of Boston, where you will wait for further orders. —

Should you arrive at Charleston in the Month of October, which is hardly to be expected, you will in that case, cruise on the Southern Coast, just long enough to admit of your return to Boston, about the 20th November. —

Messrs Gibbs & Channing will furnish you with 400 Dollars Specie, for the Expenses of getting the Guns on board at Halifax. — Should you deem it necessary that money should be furnished for the Officers & men of either of your Vessels, Messrs Gibbs & Channing will advance that also; And will furnish any Supplies of provisions & Stores, you may require. —

I expect Mr Liston will enclose to Messrs Gibbs & Channing, such Letters for you to take to Halifax, as will render unnecessary the enclosed engagement, on the part of the Secretary at War; — But if such Letters should not be received, then this Engagement of the Secretary at War, will shew the Commanding Officer at Halifax, that the Terms required on the part of the British for the delivery of the Guns &c^a^, have been complied with. —

P. S. Capt Barry will be on the Eastern Coast —
I have the honor &c^a^

[NDA. OSW, Vol. 1.]

To Captain Patrick Fletcher, U. S. Navy, from Secretary of the Navy

[TRENTON,]
Navy Department 6 October, 1798. —

Capt PATRICK FLETCHER.

SIR, You will make Arrangements to commence recruiting a Crew for the *George Washington*, now under your Command, that her Complement may be completed by the Time she is ready for a cruise.

You are allowed not exceeding 120 Hands, to consist of able-Seaman — Ordinary Seamen, & Boys — You will therefore enlist not exceeding 70 Able Seamen; the residue to consist of Ordinary Seamen & Boys — &^c^ &^c^ See Page 232.

You will not enlist any but sound & healthy Persons, &^c^ &^c^ &^c^ See Page 232.

Capt Silas Talbot will supply you with the Money necessary &^c^ &^c^ See Page 232 —

The Petty officers you will appoint yourself. —

See Instructions to Capt Brown Page 232. —

You will be allowed Officers of Marines & 30 Privates exclusive of the 120 Hands.

[NOTE: Page 232 contains letter to Capt. Moses Brown, dated October 4th, 1798.]
[NDA. OSW, Vol. 1.]

To Captain Jonathan Chapman, U. S. Navy, from Secretary of the Navy

[TRENTON,]
Navy Department October 6th 1798

Capt JONATHAN CHAPMAN

SIR, My Instructions of the 12th & 30th of July last placing you in the first Instance under the command of Capt Barry, and in the Second Instance under Capt Sever, were not particular on the subject of the Armed Vessels of other Nations than the French; because having given them respectively to the Captains under whose command you were instructed to cruise, I presumed you would have received the necessary information from them. —

As we are only at War with French Armed Vessels, and the persons found on board of them, you are not authorized to Recapture any American Vessels, which may have been captured by the Armed Vessels of any other Nation at War than the French.

Should you even see one of those Vessels about to Capture an American Vessel, you cannot lawfully interfere to prevent such capture. — It must be presumed until the contrary be proved, that the Courts of such Nation will render Justice. —

[NDA. OSW, Vol. 1.]

To Captain Chapman, U. S. Navy, commanding Revenue Cutter *Pickering*, from Secretary of the Navy

[TRENTON,]
Navy Department 6th October 1798

Capt CHAPMAN

SIR Enclosed is your Commission as Captain in the Navy. — Your Officers will be attended to — After performing the present service, I hope a better vessel will be given to you. —

I know not for what time your men have been engaged — should their time of Service expire before the 20th November, I hope you can engage them to continue till that time. — The Fever in Boston, makes it dangerous to return to that place, 'till after severe Frost. — I have the honor &ca

[NDA. OSW, Vol. 1.]

Extract from Captain Thomas Truxtun's journal, U. S. Frigate *Constellation*, 6 October 1798, Saturday

Fresh Breezes and squally at Times, but generally clear Weather, with a Swell from the N. E. running very high. Tacked occasionally and at Noon sounded in Fifty two Fathoms Water off Cape Caneveral Shoals, over a Bottom of darkish Sand, mixed with Mud; set up the Rigging, &c.

Twenty seven Sail of the Convoy in Sight, many of which pay but little Attention to Signals or to our Lights at Night; and this is a Complaint always made of the Americans, by the Captains of British Men of War, having them under Convoy. The Owners of Ships, and Underwriters ought most undoubtedly to pay some Attention to this Subject, as it is of serious Moment to them.

The Brig *Fair Eliza* of Bristol, Rhode Island, Oliver P. Earle Master, hoisted the Signal of Distress, and bore down on us. I ordered the Boat hoisted out, and sent some Lead, Nails &c. with the Carpenter on Board her, who soon returned, the Leak having been stopped by our Carpenter.

Latitude observed 28°.10′ No
Longitude Account 80.13 W.

[HS of Pa. NDA photostat.]

Extract from journal of James Pity, U. S. Frigate *Constitution*, 6 October 1798, Saturday

Wind at N. b. E. fresh Breezes & Cloudy Wr call'd all hands out pinnace @ 5 the dismasted Brig pass'd us bound to Norfolk Crew employ'd at Sundries.

[NDA.]

Extract from journal of James Pity, U. S. Frigate *Constitution*, 7 October 1798, Sunday

Fresh Breezes & Clear Wr a 4 A. M. call'd all hands up Anchor and came to Sail Cutter *Virginia* in Co @ 6 came abreast of old point Comfort @ 1/2 7 shortened Sail for the *Virginia*. Saw a

Ship at Anchor South of Cape Henery With the head of her main mast gone. I take my Departure from Cape Henery Light Latt^d 36.57 N° Long^d 76.04 West. dist. 3 Leagues Course S. E. Steer'd by Compass for 1 hour 7 Knots, unbent Two Cables & Stow'd the Anchors. Light house bore S° 2 Miles distant.

[Latitude observed 36°. 50^m N°]

[NDA.]

Extract from Captain Thomas Truxtun's journal, U. S. Frigate *Constellation*, 7 October 1798, Sunday

Moderate Breezes variable, but chiefly from North, to North North East, accompanied with a great Swell from the North East Quarter. Stood on the most favourable Tack, to take Advantage of the Gulf Stream, without meeting any Thing remarkable. Twenty seven Sail of the Convoy in Sight. Many of the Masters shamefully neglectful of their Duty.

Latitude observed 29°.9′ N°
Longitude Account 80.00 W.

HS of Pa. NDA photostat.]

To Captain Alexander Murray, U. S. Navy, from Secretary of the Navy

[TRENTON,]
Navy Department 8th Octr 1798

Capt ALEX^r MURRAY

SIR, This Letter I expect will find you at Norfolk; Your own vessel, William's & Bainbrdige's ready for Sea. The Brig *Eagle* Campbell, of 14 Six pounders, I fear may not be at Norfolk so soon. She will, by my acc^t leave Marcus Hook to morrow. I have taken great pains to get her off before, and know not whether to attribute the delay entirely to the Fever, or to divide it between the Captain and the Fever. — Bainbridge I have no doubt will answer the high expectations formed of him; Williams I don't know; & Campbell I am afraid wants Energy. — I shall hope to receive on your return your free and candid opinion of these and other Officers under your Command. It is the duty & the Interest of every brave man in the Navy to assist in ridding it of those of a different character. —

I have not fettered you by Instructions, but have left you at large to act from the dictates of your own Judgement. I need not prompt you to enterprize, and you will not forget, that it is the duty of a commanding officer to be prudent, as well as brave.

If you return by the Havanna, perhaps you will at least have an opportunity of Convoying to our Coasts, some American Vessels. Still I wish you to understand that you are to Judge for yourself in returning in that or any other direction. Wishing you as much success & honor as possible

I am &c^a

P. S. I have said in a former Letter you are at Liberty to proceed with three, instead of the four Vessels; should you find that waiting for one would occassion long detention; — but perhaps you had better wait a day or two after the receipt of this, for Campbell. —

[NDA. OSW, Vol. 1]

To Captain Samuel Nicholson, U. S. Navy, commanding the *Constitution*, from Secretary of the Navy

[TRENTON,]
Navy Department Octr 8th 1798

Capt SAM^{l} NICHOLSON

SIR I am honored with your Letter of the 26th & 27th September. — I am very glad to find, by a Letter of the 29th from Mr Pennock, that the Alarm of the Fever had subsided on board your Frigate, — and that you would on that day proceed to Sea.

As the Southern Coast was without protection, I could not help being mortified at your long detention at Hampton. — Having watered so lately at Rhode Island, I did not suppose it was necessary that you should water again at Norfolk so early. —

This Letter I presume, will get to your hands towards the last of this month; as you suggest in yours, that you should put into Hampton about that time. —

I hope no circumstance will arise, to make it necessary for you to continue at Hampton two days. — You will please to proceed to Sea, with as little delay as possible. — And as far as our Southern Extremity, & in a Course more likely to fall in with French Cruisers. — You will then proceed Eastward, pursuing a course with the same View, and endeavour to arrive at Boston Harbour, nothing intervening to make a longer cruise essential in your Judgment, about the 20th Nov^{r}

Immediately on getting to Boston, you will cause proper surveys to be made of your provisions & Stores; and make immediate returns to the Navy Agent at that Port, of the Supplies you will want for a Cruise of Six Months. —

I have the honor &c^{a}

[NDA. OSW, Vol. 1.]

To Captain Samuel Barron, U. S. Navy, commanding the *Richmond*, from Secretary of the Navy

[TRENTON,]
Navy Department 8 October 1798

Capt SAM^{l} BARRON *Norfolk*

SIR In my Letter of the 19th Sep^{t} I requested you to select and nominate your officers. I have not heard from you in answer. — I expect to leave this for three weeks, on the 15th Instant, and before that time I hope to hear from you. —

But to prevent delay in getting your Crew, be pleased to understand that the Officers you select, and recommend, shall be nominated to the President; — And there is no doubt, will be appointed by him — You will therefore call such Gentlemen into service as soon as their services are wanted — And if you can get four, instead of two respectable young men for midshipmen, it will be agreeable. —

Should you be ready for Sea, before the Officers get their Commissions, they must be under your appointment; but this I do not expect will be the Case. —

Messrs Nivison & Granbury mention in their Letter to me, that they expect the Brig will be ready to receive the men by the 20th of this month

Perhaps you had better not begin to recruit till she is ready — Should you get your Crew, & every thing prepared to sail by the 1st of December, it will be as soon as I expect — But I much wish that you should not be delayed beyond that time, because by that time, there will be another Vessel ready to cooperate with you — You will please to write at least twice a week how you go on, in fitting & arming your Vessel —

Remember that you will have to contend with an Enemy, who will depend much upon boarding —

I have the honour &a

[NDA. OSW, Vol. 1.]

To Rufus King, United States Minister, London, from James Maury, United States Consul, Liverpool

LIVERPOOL *8. Oct 1798*

DEAR SIR, I will have the pleasure to communicate to our Captains the Information You have been pleased to give me in your Letter of the 6th Instant.

The Original of your Dispatch is in the *Warren*, Fawn the Copy in the *Caledonia*, Melloby both armed & to sail this week for New York. I annex a List of the Vessells to sail in the Course of eight or ten days.

I am very much obliged by your good offices in Favor of the *Adolphe*.

I have the Honor to be with perfect Respect
Your Excellency's
Most obt Servant

JAMES MAURY

His Excellency RUFUS KING
Minister Plenipy to the U. S. America
London

[Enclosure]

Sally	Boston	unarm'd
Accepted Mason	"	unarm'd
Liberty	Phila	armd
Alliance	New York	"

[SDA, Liverpool. Vol. 1, C. L., 1790–1800.]

Extract from journal of James Pity, U. S. Frigate *Constitution*, 8 October 1798, Monday

First part this 24 hours Fresh Breezes & Cloudy Wr all hands employ'd Stowing Anchors &c. Saw a Sail bearg West with her Masts gone. Haild the *Virginia* and orderd her to shew a Light.

Middle part Pleasant & Clear. Saw a Schr to lewd Steer'g for some port to the Northward. Saw another Sail to Windward appearg Large haul'd our Wind close & Stood after her. Made Signal for the Cutter to give chace which she Answered @ Merdn the Schooner was hull down Ends clear & Pleasant Ship in chace upon a Wind.

[Latitude 34.50.No]

[NDA.

Extract from journal of Lieutenant John Mullowny, U. S. Frigate *United States*, 8 October 1798

[New Castle, Del.]

Unmoored to proceed to sea

[NA.]

Extract from Captain Thomas Truxtun's journal, U. S. Frigate *Constellation*, 8 October 1798, Monday

Moderate Breezes all these twenty four Hours, intermixed with some Calms, and Nothing very remarkable. Twenty seven Sail of the Convoy in Sight.

People employed, with the Sail Maker, repairing the Sails, and at sundry necessary Jobs.

Latitude observed 30°.32′ N°.
Longitude Account 80.00 W.

[HS of Pa. NDA photostat.]

Extract from journal of U. S. Ship *Herald*, Captain James Sever, U. S. Navy, commanding, 8 October 1798.

This 24 hours first part the wind Hald To the S S W a havy Swell from East at 8 p m Strong gales Close Reeft Topsails

Middle part Clear weather and Strong Gales Tryd for Sounding No Bottom at 6 a m out one Reef out East T Sail Lusd all Light Sails To Dry at 7 am Saw a Schooner to N n E out Sett T G Sails gave Chase at 7 Spoak the Chase from St Croix Bound Kenebunk. Saw a Brig To the N W gave Chase at Mrdn Spoak hur from St Johns New Brunswick Bound To philadelphia 3 days out Latter part strong gales and heavy Swell from Eastward Brig *Pickring* in Companey

Lattd Obbrs 40. .40 N°.

[NDA. Journal kept by Joseph Strout, 1798.]

To Captain Isaac Phillips, U. S. Navy, from Captain Thomas Truxtun, U. S. Navy

UNITED STATES SHIP, *Constellation 9th. Oct. 1789.*

To Captn. PHILLIPS

After the receipt of this, you will proceed to the Westward, untill you are out of Sight of the *Constellation* (so that it may not be known, where you are going) and then make the best of your Way off Charlston Bar, examining all strange Vessels. On your Arrival off the Bar, cruize there four Days, and then return to Hampton Roads, continuing from the Time you leave the Fleet to examine as aforesaid all Vessels you meet. On your Arrival in the Roads, you will make Report, to me, what you have meet &c. I wish you Success —

[HS of Pa. NDA photostat. Truxtun's LB, 1798–9.]

To the Secretary of State from D. Humphreys, United States Minister to Spain

(Nº 167)

MADRID *Octr 9th 1798*

SIR As I am persuaded you will receive from all quarters the particulars of the victory obtained by Admiral Nelson over the French fleet near Alexandria (as mentioned in my late letters) I forbear enclosing other Papers on the Subject. But I cannot dispense with repeating the suggestion contained in my last of the expediency of our having a frigate & a few sloops of war, if possible, in the Mediterranean — The necessity of this measure has been always felt & urged by all who have had any knowledge of our relations with the Barbary States. And it would certainly be more requisite now than at any former period, for the sake of giving a compleat defense to our merchant vessels against the large French Privateers which are preparing in the Ports of Spain; & of affording our Merchants an opportunity of gaining a full share in the Mediterranean trade before the English shall return to carry it on thro' the ancient channels. I think it proper to add my opinion, that a small public armed force, in addition to that of our private armed vessels, would be adequate for these purposes. — That the crews of French Privateers love plundering better than fighting has been demonstrated on several late occasions. — One Privateer has lately returned to St Sebastian, with the Captn first L^t^ & seven Men killed, & in a very shattered condition; while the American armed Merchant vessel which had been attacked by the Privateer pursued her voyage. On the 30th of Sep^t^ ten American vessels sailed together from Malaga, while the French privateers in that Port did not dare to molest them.

We can procure no business of any consequence to be done at this Court. — where some changes still continue to take place. The Confessor of the Queen (who was lately supposed to be in high credit) has been dismissed; & yesterday the Governor of the Council of Castille was changed. — M. de Saavedra gains health slowly. —

We have had a report that war was declared by the Emperor against France; but it is not confirmed by this day's Courier.

It appears that the Grand Signor has been much alarmed by the Invasion of Egypt & that hostilitys between him & the Directory may probably be the result.

In the last French Gazettes, the Editors have scarcely deigned to make mention of the U. S. — Some of them have however inserted the English official Acc^t^ of the Capture of the French Corps which had landed in Ireland, & many details of the loss of their fleet at Alexandria.

I have this day rec'd letters from Captn OBrien at Algiers, in date to the 26th of Sep^r^, copies of which I shall enclose in my next.

With Sentiments of great regard & esteem, I am

Sir

Your mo. ob. & mo. h^ble^ Ser^nt^

D. HUMPHREYS

The SECRETARY OF STATE

&c. &c. &c.

[SDA. Disp. Spain, Bk. 4, Humphreys.]

To Secretary Benjamin Stoddert from Captain Thomas Truxtun, U. S. Navy

UNITED STATES SHIP *Constellation,*
off the coast of Georgia October 9th 1798.

SIR, Having sailed from the Chesapeake Bay the 5th Ultimo on the Expedition directed, I proceeded without Delay, taking Care of such Merchantmen, as could keep pretty well up with the Ships of War; and on the 21st I arrived off the Morro Castle, where I immediately dispatched Lieutenant Saunders, with a Letter to his Excellency, the Governor of the Island of Cuba &c, Copy of which, and Governor's Answer are here enclosed, as also Copy of a public Notice given the Merchants and Masters of Vessels, as to the Time I had fixed for Sailing, with the Signals sent the Consul to be delivered to each Vessel, on their being under Sail.

Two Days after I forwarded these Papers, I received a Visit from Mr Hawley our Consul, who earnestly solicited me to extend my Departure, from six or seven days, the Time I had given for the Vessels to get ready, and join the Ships of War without the Harbour, a couple of Days longer, otherwise a Number of Vessels would be left behind to the great Injury of their Owners &c as it was not probable, another Convoy would offer for Some Time to come, under such Circumstances I determined to acquiesce with the Consul's Request, and on the 29th forty four Sail of our Vessels sailed, with which I proceeded to Windward and steered for the Gulph; but the Wind soon proving adverse, with a Lee Current between Cuba, and Florida, many dull sailing Vessels, and great Inattention in several of the Masters; some of the fast Sailors, and the two armed Ships belonging to Philadelphia, the *America,* and *Belvidere,* proceeded on, but not before they were, as I conceived, clear of all Danger from french Privateers; for this Description of our Enemies in that Quarter being weak (and by no Means so numerous, as we have been led to suppose) they seldom go any Distance from Cuba, especially as the New Providence Cruizers are much stronger, and many more of them in Number.

After passing through the Gulph of Florida and reaching the 31st of North Latitude on our own Coast which is to the Northward of the Southern Limits of the United States, and being fully convinced there was no further Risk to be apprehended from the French in the passage of the Convoy Home, I made the Signal for the Fleet to make the best of their way, & each one of Course steered according as he was bound, and I have no Doubt but they will all reach their respective Ports of Destination in a very few Days, unless prevented by some Cause other than french Cruizers.

Every Occurrence during the Expedition, that appeared of sufficient Magnitude to Journalize, you will find in a Copy of my Records, which I shall forward immediately on my Arrival in Hampton Roads.

In the Course of this Voyage, I have only seen one french Privateer Schooner Rigged Boat, mounting as I was informed one Gun, and that Vessel I chased almost into the very verge of the Breakers on the Coast of Cuba, a few Leagues to Windward of Havannah, but it falling calm, she got off with the Help of her Sweeps, and was afterwards fired into by the *America* belonging to Philadelphia, which Ship she attempted to approach.

We have brought to, and examined many Merchantmen of various Sorts, but none under Circumstances, that would warrant the smallest Detention. A New Providence Privateer (called the *Nancy*) got among the Fleet off the Coast of Florida, the Master of which (George Broadwater) who is an American from the Eastern Shore of Virginia, behaved very improperly, I ordered him out of the Fleet, and desired him on his Peril not to attempt to hover about it again, he went off and I saw no more of him, but not without attempting to speak one of the Vessels, as he steered away.

During my Cruize off the Havannah, some Arrivals from Cape Francois announced, that three french Frigates, that were laying there was ready, and waiting only an Oppertunity of slipping out, and passing the British Ships of War on that Station, and that their Destination, was certainly and beyond all Doubt, to the Havannah, for in Fact they could no where else get a Supply of Provision, either for a Cruize, or to carry them to France. It may therefore be considered a fortunate Circumstance, that the Convoy got away so early, otherwise it might have been detained for some Time, waiting for an Oppertunity, that would justify the Sailing of so valuable an Assemblage of Vessels.

The only Ships of War I have seen, since I left the Chesapeake Bay, were two Spanish 44 Gun Frigates that I bore down on with the *Baltimore* in Company, and spoke on the Coast of Cuba. If I may except half a Dozen Others that came out of Havannah, while I was on that Station, with two Convoys, one for Spain, and Porterica, & the Other for La Vera Cruze.

I am perfectly well satisfied with the Conduct and Attention of Captain Phillips of the *Baltimore*, to every part of his Duty, and I beg Leave to recommend him to your particular Notice, and shall be obliged by your mentioning him to the President in my Name. I have the Honor to be, Sir, with great Respect,

Your very Obedient & humble Servant.

Honble BENJAMIN STODDERT

Secretary of the Navy.

[HS of Pa. NDA photostat. Truxtun's LB, 1798–9.]

To Joshua Humphreys, Naval Constructor, from Secretary Pickering

DEPARTMENT OF STATE TRENTON *Oct. 9. 1798*

[To] Mr JOSHUA HUMPHREYS

SIR, I have informed you of the arrival of the *Sophia* at Boston: your Son [Clement] I expect will come on by land without delay.

You informed me that the masts of one of the Algerine vessels were to be shortened; and that the other two were to be tried, and their masts also shortened, if found needful. It is desirable that these alterations should be made immediately, and the vessels got ready for sea. The ship destined for Algiers with a cargo of stores is loaded; and waits only for the further abatement of the fever in Philadelphia, or rather for the manning and victualling the three armed vessels which the sickness has hitherto delayed. Mr Murray, the owner of the transport ship has agreed to let her wait a fortnight. I must beg you to write me immediately when the three armed vessels may be got ready for their voyage.

I am with much esteem &c.

TIMOTHY PICKERING

[SDA. Dom. L. Vol. 11.]

To Captain Richard Dale, U. S. Navy, from Secretary of the Navy

[TRENTON,]
Navy Department October 9th 1798

Capt Rd DALE.

SIR I intend to leave this place for Maryland about the 15th and mean to return with my Family to Philadelphia about the 10th or 12th of Novr

I have made a representation to the President, on the subject of the rank of the first six Captains appointed in the Navy — And I anxiously hope, that that matter may be settled to your satisfaction, and without losing the services of either yourself, Talbot, or Truxton. I do not expect however, it will be finally arranged before the 1st day of December —

And I must entreat that you will not think of a resignation of your Commission before that time — If you should do it afterwards; which I hope however will not be the Case. — For I am firmly persuaded that our Navy is to be an useless Expense, & a disgrace to the Country; or its best, and most honorable Defence — As Indifferent, or meritorious men are at the head of it — And thus thinking, I cannot contemplate with patience, any circumstance, which should occasion the Loss of yourself, Talbot, or Truxton to the Navy. —

I have the honor to be

&ca &ca

[NDA. OSW, Vol. 1.]

To Benjamin Goodhue, Salem, from Secretary of Navy

[TRENTON],
Navy Department October 9th 1798

BENJn GOODHUE Esqr
Salem.

SIR, I am honored with your Letter of the 3rd Instant; and am highly gratified by the Information it contains —

The Gentlemen who Subscribe to the loan for the purpose of Building a Ship for Government, are so much better Judges than I am, of the best mode to be pursued, to get the Ship well, and expeditiously built, that I shall not pretend to interfere as to the mode proper for them to adopt.

If they appoint an Agent to conduct the Business, paying him a Salary or Commission, no doubt such expense must be considered as part of the Cost of the Ship, and paid for by Government, in Certificates bearing an Interest of 6 per Cent, as well as every other expense relating to the Ship — In short, the subscribers to the loan, will divise such plan as they deem best, in disposing of the Money Subscribed in building a Ship, and all the expense incurred in carrying such measure into execution, must be considered as the Cost of the Ship, and must be paid for by Government. —

It will be well for the subscribers, a Committee of the Subscribers, or the Agent, to determine as early as can be done, how far the money subscribed will go in Rigging, & equipping the Ship as a Vessel of War; & to mark distinctly to me what they will do, and what will remain for the Public to do; that arrangements may be made by me in time for such things as the public must supply, to prevent any delay in getting the Ship to Sea, after the subscribers turn her over to the Public —

It will be expected that the Subscribers will build and rigg the Ship. They will determine whether their money will hold out to furnish her with two Suits of Sails. — If not, one Suit must be furnished by the Public. — Should they however, be able to do this, they will then determine how far they will go in providing, first, Water Casks, next, Iron Ballast, then Guns, & so on to the complete equipment of a Vessel of War. — But unless Ship-Building be much cheaper at Salem, than in any other part of the United States, — or the Citizens of that place exceed all others in Liberality & Public Spirit, I suspect the private Contributions must Stop, with the Completion of the Ship to receive her Guns — and probably with one suit of Sails —

The model & dimensions of the Ship must be left with the Subscribers to determine; — I should be glad however, to be furnished with a Draft of her, that if she should turn out a fine Sailer, we may profit by it hereafter. —

The persons the Subscribers appoint to be their Agent, or any other person they recommend, shall be the Agent on the part of the Public to procure Such Articles as the public must Supply. —

The Ship should be Copper Bolted & sheathed — If Copper, or Composition Bolts can not be had to the Eastward — Messrs James & Ebenezer Watson of New York, will be able to supply them. —

I have said nothing about the size of the Ship, that being a point to be determined by the amount of the Subscription — But if she could be made a Frigate to carry 32 Guns, every thing authorized by the Acts of Congress in relation to Ships would be obtained. —

The President being in Massachusetts, I cannot at this moment obtain his consent, that the Captain to Command the ship, and all the Officers shall be appointed by the Gentlemen who contribute to the Expense. But this is a measure so obviously right, and affords so infinitely the best chance of having the Ship well officered, that I am sure I risk nothing in undertaking for his chearful and hearty concurrence in it. The Gentlemen on their part, I am sure will consider the importance of brave, & active men, to the honor of our Navy. —

I expect to leave this for Maryland before I can have the pleasure of hearing from you in reply — and shall return with my Family to the seat of Goverment about the 10th of November. —

P. S. Should the services of the Captain be wanted at the commencement of the Ship, the Gentlemen will please to call into service the person they select. — His Pay &c^a^ will go on from that time. —

I have the honor

&c.

[NDA. GLB No. 1.]

To Messrs. Gibbs & Channing, agents, Newport, R. I., and others, from Secretary of Navy

[TRENTON,]
Navy Department, October 9th 1798

Messrs GIBBS & CHANNING
Newport R. Island,

A Letter of the same Tenor & date was sent Capt Silas Talbot Agent for the Ship *George Washington* at Providence, R. I. Also to Stephen Higginson Esqr Agent for the Ship *Portsmouth* at Portsmouth

GENT^n I have directed Major Burrows Commandant of the Marine Corps, to give you a discription of the Uniform, and I must request you to have the Clothing made in Conformity for the Marines that will be sent on board the Ship *Genl Greene*, consisting of a Corporal serjeant, Drummer, Fifer, & 30 Privates. — Each must have a complete suit, consisting of the following Articles,

1 Wool Hat, 1 Coat, 1 Vest, 2 p^r Woolen overalls, 2 p^r Linen Ditto, 4 shirts, 4 p^r Shoes, 4 p^r Socks, 1 Stock & Clasp, & 1 Blankett. —

You will please to have the whole delivered to the Lieutenant appointed to Command; taking his receipt for them, which you will remit to the Accountant of this department. —

The Regulations of Congress, permit Slops to be provided for the Sailors. — They are to be delivered over to the Purser, who sells them at the Price fixed on, to the Sailors, to be deducted out of their Pay. — This is meant as a humane Regulation, to prevent the sailors from suffering, & to prevent Imposition on the part of the Pursers — Please therefore have provided, to be delivered over to the Purser, such a Number of each of the following articles, not exceeding the number of Sailors to compose the Crew of the *Genl Greene*, and excluding the Marines, as you shall on consultation with the Captain & Purser Judge necessary for six Months — Shirts, Frocks, Outer Jackets, Under Jackets, Flannel Drawers, shoes, Wool Hats, Blankets — & Mattrasses, a few of which I suppose will answer. — These Articles should be delivered to the Purser, with an Invoice of the Prices — They should be bought by wholesale; and ten per Cent should be added to the Price, in the invoice delivered to the Purser to make up for Losses. — It not being intended that the United States are to lose any thing by this provision, Nor that they should gain at the Expense of the Sailors. — You will forward a Duplicate of the Invoice given the Purser, to Wm Winder, Esqr Accountant of the Navy Department, that he may make his charge against the Purser. — In addition to these articles you will please to provide 15 Watch Coats, to be delivered also to the Purser, but to be supplied to the sailors on Watch in Cold Weather, at the discretion of the Captain. — —

I have the honor to be
Sir
&c^a

[NDA. GLB No. 1.]

To Stephen Higginson, Navy Agent, Boston, from Secretary of Navy

[Trenton,]
Navy Department, October 9th 1798

Stephen Higginson Esqr *Boston* —

Sir There has been a great many difficulties & mistakes about Ballast for the *Portsmouth* — The 25 Tons directed for you have got to Newbury Port — I have directed 50 Tons Pig Iron to be sent to you from New York — (Kentledge is not now to be had — should you have made provision for Ballast, this may be kept at Boston for the Merchants Ship

I have the honor &ca

P. S. I have Letters from Norfolk, saying that Nicholson's Crew had not the Yellow Fever, and that he would go to Sea on the 29th Septr

[NDA. GLB No.1.]

To Major Commandant Burrows, U. S. M. C., from Secretary of Navy

[Trenton,]
Navy Department 9th October 1798

Major Burrows,

Sir, David Stickney of Newbury Port, is recommended by the Merchants building a Ship for Government at that place, to Command the Marines. — I have therefore named him to the President, and no doubt he will be appointed a first Lieutenant. — This Ship, the *Merrimack*, will require a Lieutenant, Serjeant, Corporal, Music, & 21 Privates. — Be pleased therefore without delay, to send on Instructions to this Office to recruit the men. — Guns will be sent from Philadelphia — Clothes for the Marines will be provided by Nicholas Johnson Esqr at Newburyport; to whom pleased to give a description of the Uniform. — I sent you 1500 Ds instead of the 1000 you asked, that you might have money to send to this, & other Officers. — You had better enclose your Letter for Stickney, to Mr Johnson. —

There will also be immediately wanted on board the Ship *George Washington*, Capt Fletcher, at Providence, Rhode Island, 30 Privates, and Officers to command them. . Please to have these immediately sent on board that ship — you have, I presume Officers & Marines enlisted in the Eastern States, In pursuance of my Letter of the 31st August. — —

There will be wanted in a month from this time, the same number of Marines, as for the *George Washington*, for the Ship *Portsmouth*, Capt McNeill, at Portsmouth, New Hampshire. — and a like number for the Ship *Genl Greene* at Newport Rhode Island, — These two last detachments will be wanted in a month, — The other Detachments immediately. — —

I have written to Stephen Higginson Esqr of Boston, to procure the clothing for the Marines for the *Portsmouth* Ship. — To Messrs Gibbs & Channing of Newport, to procure the Clothing for the

Marines for the *Genl Greene* — And to Capt Silas Talbot at Providence, to procure the Clothing for the Marines for the *George Washington* — you will please to give each of these Gentlemen, as well as Mr Johnson, a description of the Uniform. — Guns & accoutrements for the whole must be sent from Philadelphia.

I have the honor &ca

[NDA. GLB No. 1.]

To President John Adams from the Secretary of Navy

[Trenton,]
Navy Department October 9th 1798

John Adams Esqr
President of the U. States

Sir Colo Pickering thinking that cases might occur, to make it necessary to shew that it was your pleasure he should execute the duties of my Office, in the absence, which you have done me the favor & honor to permit; I have taken the Liberty to enclose a paper to that effect. He does not think it necessary that I should remain here until he receives this paper. —

Mr Pennock the Navy agent at Norfolk, writes me the 29th of September, that Nicholson & his Crew, had got over their apprehensions of contagious Fever. And would proceed to Sea that day in pursuance of his Instructions, received at Newport, to guard the Southern Coast; which from his unnecessary & improper detention at Norfolk, has been too long without adequate protection.

I have the honor to be

&ca

[NDA. Nom. Appts. LB, 1798–1820.]

Extract from Captain Thomas Truxtun's journal, U. S. Frigate *Constellation*, 9 October 1798, Tuesday

Light and variable Winds, with a Swell from the Eastward. At 8 A M being about four or five Leagues to the Southward of the Light House on the Enterance of the Tybee leading to Savannah, and about Twenty Leagues to the Eastward of it, and judging that the Convoy (Twenty seven in Sight) was perfectly safe as to any Danger from french Privateers between this, and the various Ports of their Destination, I made the Signal for them to proceed, and make the best of their Way Home; and at the same Time I gave Captain Phillips a Letter of Instructions to proceed off Charleston Bar, and cruize four Days, so that in that Time the several Vessels bound to Charleston will in all Probability arrive. At the Expiration of Captain Phillips's four Day's Cruize above mentioned, I have directed him to return to Hampton Roads, and there report to me, what he may meet &c. Exercised Great Guns, Marines &c; at Noon the Wind being light, all the Convoy were still in Sight, and Charleston Bar bearing N. W. ½ N. Twenty three Leagues Distance.

At 8 A M when I made the Signal for the Fleet to make the best of their Way, and the *Baltimore* to proceed, we sounded with 90

Fathoms of Line up and down, and got no Ground; at the same Time we wore along Side of the *Baltimore*, at least at a very short Distance from her.

Latitude observed 31°.47′ N°
Longitude Account 79 .48 W.

[HS of Pa. NDA photostat.]

Extract from journal of James Pity, U. S. Frigate *Constitution*, 9 October 1798, Tuesday

First part this 24 hours clear Weather & Steady Breezes Ship in Chace @ ½ past one in T. G^{t} Sails & Spanker. hoisted our Coll^{rs} and fired a Gun at the Chace which made her come within hail she prov'd the Brig^{t} *Betsey* f^{m} Edenton N. Carolina bound to Antigua @ 5 loos'd T. Gall^{t} Sails & Set Main Stay Sail.

Ends Clear W^{r}

[Latitude observed 34° 11^{m} N°]

[NDA.]

To the Secretary of State from H. R. Saabye, United States Consul, Copenhagen

Copenhagen y^{e} *10th Octob^{r} 1798*

Sir: I had the honour to inclose in my last letter, a list of those American Ships, which arrived in our Seas in the fall of the last Year. This I hope came to hand, and I transmit now a similar one of the Ships, which appeared since the beginning of the Year until the End of the month of June. Their number exceeds my Expectations, for the depredations of the french occassioned the well grounded apprehension, that Americas navigation to the northern Seas, might be much deminish'd I rejoice that my fear has been thus annihilated, and I add with much satisfaction, that not a single American Ship, bound to the Baltic, has become a victim to the Greediness of the french Privateers. Englands superiority on the Ocean, and the care which she has taken, not only to block up many French harbours, but likewise to keep a considerable number of Cruisers on their coast, compell'd them to remain in port, lest they might be captured by the watchful English. It is to be hoped that the much wish'd for peace, may be restored to Europe, by Englands steady and manly resistance, to the new fangled french system of conquest and oppression, and by her success in annihilating, as it were, nearly the whole of the french Marine

The French themselves however, by provoking all Nations, seem themselves to accelerate the approach of this event, which is so absolutely necessary to the world.

The danish trade, being as much as possible every where protected by armed Ships, has suffer'd much less than might have been reasonably apprehended. American Trade to these Northern Ports, during the course of this Year, will prove as considerable as advantageous. In consequence of the surprizing changes which this War produced, this place and Hamburg, have next to England, become the most important Marts for East and West India Produce The prices obtain'd for these articles, exceed by far those of former times, which appears from the Price Current, which I ask leave to Send you inclosed

I have the honour to remain with great respect

Sir

Your m° obed hb[le] Serv[t]

H. R. SAABYE.

[SDA. Copenhagen, Vol. 1, 1792–1811.]

Circular to the Collectors of the Revenue from Secretary of Navy

[TRENTON]

Navy Office 10th October 1798

Circular
To the Collectors
of the Revenue

I have the honor to enclose a copy of the Instructions, which at the request of the Secretary, I have given to the Captain of the Cutter of your State, and for which you act as Agent. — At the request of the Secretary of the Treasury too, this Cutter will cruise under my orders; which will always be given with a view to the service for which she was originally destined, unless particular circumstances should for a short space, require a different arrangement. —

All other regulations will be made by the Secretary of the Treasury as heretofore, — But I would beg leave to suggest the propriety of frequent settlements with the Captain, as well in relation to the pay of the Crew, as the provisions consumed

You know the Rations allowed to seamen, & should judge whether due care be taken of the Provisions, which without great attention on the part of the Captain, (which will be best insured by great attention on the part of the Agent) will be found a most expensive Article. —

In former Letters to the Captains of the Cutters, I have directed them to apply to the Agents for the proper supplies of Arms & Military Stores, without well knowing what these Supplies ought to be. —

In general it will be right that they should always have about 40 Rounds of Ammunition for each Gun, and about two months provision on board.

N. B. The above Instructions were Sent to the following: Viz[t]

Names	Collector of	Agent for
Benjamin Lincoln	Boston	PICKERING, Cutter 14 Guns.
Joshua Sands	New York	JAY " 14 Guns.
George Lattimer	Philadelphia	GEN[l] GREENE " 10 Guns.
Otway Bird	Norfolk	VIRGINIA " 10 Guns.
Griffith J[no] M[c]Rea	Wilmington	DILIGENCE " 10 Guns.
John Habersham	Savannah	EAGLE " 14 Guns.
Thomas Martin	New Hampshire Portsmouth.	SCAMMEL " 10 Guns.

[NDA. GLB No. 1.]

Circular to Commanders of Revenue Cutters from Secretary of the Navy

[TRENTON]
Navy Department October 10th 1798.

Circular To the Commanders of the Revenue Cutters

The Crew of your Cutter may consist of ———— Men & Boys, if you Judge so many necessary; Of this Number you may recruit not exceeding —— Able Seamen — The residue to be ordinary Seamen, Landsmen & Boys

It is our best policy to create Seamen; It may therefore be proper to lessen this proportion of able Seamen, and encrease the number of ordinary Seamen, Landsmen & Boys. I conceive too, that our Vessels have been hitherto too much crouded with men; and it might be for the good of the Service, if you were to lessen the whole number of your Crew. — I leave this Arrangement however, to be determined by your own Judgment: But the proportion of able Seamen must not exceed ———— And the whole number of your Crew must not exceed ————.

Able Seamen you will allow 17 Dolls per month; ordinary Seamen, Landsmen & Boys from 5 to 14 Dollars per month according to merit. All to be recruited to serve for 12 months.

If the number already on board be less than these limitations, you may, should you find more necessary, take the first opportunity of encreasing it. And if you have on board more than these limitations admit, you will discharge the men as their terms of service Expire, until the number be reduced to —— You must recruit none but sound and healthy men; — No Negroes or Mulattoes are to be admitted; and as far as you can Judge, you will exclude all of a suspicious character.

You may, if necessary, advance your Recruits, Two Months pay; — But in this case you must take care to obtain sufficient security, to resort to, in the event of desertion.

The Collector of the Customs will make the necessary Advances of Money to you, for the purposes of recruiting; — And you must settle your Accounts with him, and lodge in his hands as often as you go into Port, a correct List of your Crew, with their monthly Pay annexed to their names.

List of the Captains, to whom the above Circular was sent; and of the Number of Men they were severally instructed to recruit. &c.

Captains Names	Commanding the Cutter	Aggregate Number of Men & Boys, not to exceed	The proportion of able-seamen, not to exceed
Jonathan Chapman	PICKERING of Massa. District	Seventy	Thirty five
John W. Leonard	[GOV.] JAY. of N. York	ditto	ditto
Hugh G. Campbell	EAGLE. of Georgia	ditto	ditto
George Price	GENl GREENE, of Pennsa	Thirty	Fifteen
Francis Bright	VIRGINIA of Virga	ditto	ditto
John Brown	DILIGENCE of N. C.	ditto	ditto
John Adams	SCAMMEL of New Hampshire	ditto	ditto

N.B. The Circular to John Adams, was dated the 19th all the rest the 10th Octr 1798.

[NDA. OSW, Vol. 1.]

Extract from journal of James Pity, U. S. Frigate *Constitution*, 10 October 1798, Wednesday

First part this 24 hours Moderate and clear carpenters employ'd rigging New Royal Masts @ 4 P. M. beat to Quarters to exercize the Men at their Guns. @ 6 P. M. Shorten'd Sail.

Middle part Light Airs attended with rain lost Sight of the Cutter. Reef'd Top Sails at 12 Saw her again of the lee Quarter bore down towards her and Spoke her Let Reefs out of Top Sails Wind coming N° Squared the Yards.

Latter part Light airs & Clear Weather Ends Clear

[Latitude Observed 34° 22m N°]

[NDA.]

Extract from Captain Thomas Truxtun's journal, U. S. Frigate *Constellation*, 10 October 1798, Wednesday

Light Airs of Wind the most Part of this Day, and Night, and fine Weather. Let at least five Tons of Water into the Ship to sweeten her, as the Bilge was becoming offensive. Thirteen of the Convoy still in Sight. Bent the Cables &c. &c. &c.

Latitude observed 32°.26′ N°
Longitude Account 79.05 W.

[HS of Pa. NDA photostat.]

To Benjamin Lincoln, Collector, Boston, from Secretary Oliver Wolcott

TRENTON *October 11th 1798.*

BENJAMIN LINCOLN Esq.
Collector Boston, Massachusetts.

SIR, With a view of producing a concert in the direction of the naval forces of the United States it has been decided that the armed Revenue Cutters Shall be placed at the disposition of the Secretary of the Navy. I have therefore to request that you will comply with all such instructions as you may receive from the Secretary of the Navy in relation to the equipping arming manning provisioning and paying of the crew of the Cutter belonging to your district. The accounts however are to be discharged and settled by you in the mode heretofore practised.

I am with consideration Sir,
Your Mo. Obedt. Servt.

OLIVER WOLCOTT.

[TDA. Coast Guard, Out. Letters, No. 0, 1790–1833; also TDA, Sec. Files, Let to Coll., Boston, Vol. 2, 1797–1808.]

To Rufus King, United States Minister, London, from Elias VanderHorst, United States Cousul, Bristol, England

BRISTOL *Octr 11th 1798.*

DEAR SIR. Since my last of the 9th Inst. I have not had the pleasure of hearing from you. — the American Ship *Hannah*, Capt Morland, & the American Brig *Pallas*, Capt Collins, the former with 18 Guns & the Latter with 14, the first for Boston the 2d for Charleston, I expect will be ready for Sea at this Port on or about the 20th Inst. and intend to Sail in concert as far as the course of their different Voyages will permit. — I beg leave to observe that Mr Falconer, who was lately my Agent at Milford, kept the Post-Office there, as his Death must occasion a vacancy in it, if it should not already be disposed of, it might probably prove acceptable to Mr Folger. I take the Liberty to mention this for your consideration, and am very truly.

Dear Sir

Yours most sincerely

ELIAS VANDERHORST

RUFUS KING Esqr
&c &c:
London.

[SDA. Bristol, Vol. 1, 1791–1799.]

Extract from journal of James Pity, U. S. Frigate *Constitution*, 11 October 1798, Thursday

First part this 24 hours light Airs & pleasant Weather at 3 P. M Set Main Top Gallt Royal at 5 P. M. hauld up S. W. b. S. Spoke the *Virginia* Cutter & Inform'd her the Course to be Steer'd by Compass. at ½ past 6 Sent down Royals & took in T. Gt Sails @ 6 A. M. Sent down Fore Top Gt Yard & Mast @ 7 got up a New T. Gt Mast and a New Stept Royal Mast. got up the Yards & Set the Sails Carpenters employ'd fitting New Main T. Gt Mast and New Royal Mast. Sailmakers Middle Stiching the Top Sails.

[Latitude Observed 33° 54m No]

[NDA.]

Extract from Captain Thomas Truxtun's journal, U. S. Frigate *Constellation*, 11 October 1798, Thursday

Uncertain Weather all these twenty four Hours, with light Winds, and smooth Water. Employed repairing the Sails, and Rigging, hawlling the Limber Ropes, and at such other Matters as required Attention; ten Sail of the Convoy in Sight of us in Shore.

Sounded at Noon in twenty Fathoms water Reddish Sand, the frying Pan Shoals bearing North, sixteen Leagues Distance.

Latitude observed 32°.50′ No

Longitude Account 79.00 W.

[HS of Pa. NDA photostat.]

Extract from journal of U. S. Ship *Herald*, Captain James Sever, commander, 11 October 1798

This 24 hours first part modarate gales and Clear weather In Chase of sail in the N E at 6 p m Spoak the Ship *Nancy* from Cork Bound To Boston Capt Orn at 8 p m Trid for Sounding found None

Midle part modrate gales and Clear at 5 a m Saw Two Sail To the westward wore Ship Sett all Sail and gave Chace at 9 a m Spoak the Ship *Hope* from Baltimore Bound To St Johns Bay fundy Capt Stokston

Latter part modarate gales and Clear Weather in Chase of a Sail in the S W Brig *Pickring* in Companey

Lattd Obbrs 42..37 No

[NDA. Journal kept by Joseph Strout, 1798.]

To Secretary of State from Richard O'Brien, United States Consul in Algiers

ALGIERS *October the 12th 1798.*

To the SECRETARY OF STATE.

SIR I have to inform you that on the 5th Inst was Sent into this port by an Algerine Corsaire of 16 Guns the Brig *Mary,* belonging to Philadelphia Joseph Isreal master, with a valuable Cargo of wines which Cost. in St Lucar. in Spain 18 thousand dollars. Consigned To James Yard Esqr of Philadelphia. Said Brig had an American Register &c Sea letter, and unfortunately no Medditeranian passport.

Richard O Brien 12 Octr 1798
By Mr Carr

"This Vessel haveing no Medditeranian pass. by the Algerine marine Laws and the Custom of this government. with all nations the[y] are at peace with, is that, it is by the medditeranian pass & the Colours that Said Vessel is Known by the Barbary States to be A nation the[y] are at peace with. The fatal Consequence of haveing no Medditeranian pass — is that the master and Crew is liable to be made Slaves of, and the Vessel and Cargo, declared a legal prize

"The latter part of the 4th article of the treatie of the United States with Algiers, runs thus, That Eighteen months Shall be the term allowd for furnishing the Ships of the United States with passports. As this Vessel Came in Sight I was Very Suspicious, by her appearance, that Said Vessel was an American, and therefore I went to the Marine, and had prepared the Minds of the necessary persons, in Case I should want theire assistance, and when The Captain of the port returned on Shore after Visiting the Brig & brought on Shore a letter from the prize master, written by the Captain of the *Corsaire,* giveing an account of the manner of his taking Said Vessel and his Motives for Sending her in. This acct or Circumstance was Mentioned in My presence. I told the general of the Marine that before I could Judge relative to this Vessel I must first See her papers, and as the Capt aport must go and make the Report to the Dey, I tryed to Bias him to make it as favourable on my part as possible, as the news Spread &c Seemed that the general Cry was a good prize. — On this I requested that the papers of Said Vessel would be brought on Shore. The general Sent Of. for Said papers, and I then found her Register & Sea letter to be American and no Medditeranian pass. The Register being indorsed & haveing allso a Bill of Sale of Said Brig. with a button Seal. The property transfered by Mr Pintard to Capt Isreal and Robt Stevenson: of Philadelphia.

I declared that the bill of Sale was: A Pass. avant and Consular Certificate. This I seen the necessity of to Save the Crew. The Capt aport returned to the marine and told the general it was the deys orders that Said Crew of Said Brig Should be Sent to the Slave prison, but I declaring that the Pass avant or Consular Certificate was given on account of this Vessel haveing been taken and plundered both by the french and British, and papers deranged, and her detention in Europe — that Said Vessel was proceeding to America to Obtain A Meditteranian pass. and aided in this report by the General, the Capt aport was Sent to the dey at my request and with this Statement &c requested that the Crew Should not be Sent to the Slave prison. The dey permited she Should remain in my Custody untill that. The board of admiralty Should determine on Sd Crew — The master Crew and passengers was permited to go to the American house, and the Brig *Mary* left and kept in the posesion of the Algerines. I was fully employed with the Bocries, whose assistance depend has been very great to me on this affaire, as well as on all Occasions relative to the affairs of the U States.

"On the morning of the 6th of October I went to the Marine The general of Marine and the board of Admiralty being met with the general as the president. The[y] Contended that this Vessel haveing no Meditteranian pass, that Vessel and Cargo was a legal prize, that it was Customary for Algiers to act so with all nations, but I declareing sd Vessel to have been taken and her papers plundered & her Pass avant or Consular Certificate and my promises of 2500 Dollars to be divided in the usual way. The[y] declared that this altered the Case and made this report of the pass avant to the Dey, and that the[y] hoped & that it was theire request that the Dey would for once pardon this vessel the American peace being new &c we as yet not fully acquainted with the nature & Consequence of not haveing a good Meditteranian pass — The Capt aport went to the dey and made no favourable report. The Dey desired the admiralty to take Care that the[y] were not Bribed. That this vessel haveing no Meditteranian pass. was a good prize, and that, he Should take a few days to Consider fully on this business. The Capt aport with the owners of the *Corsaire* was of One party against Clearing the Vessel. I, immediatly with those of more powerfull influence dureing this interval I immediatly Commenced my plans against the next decision, and made out a strong Consular Certificate which would back & Strengthen any thing I had Said or Could Say, relative to a pass. avant, this I seen the necessity of

In order at all events to Save the Crew and passengers, the[re] being 21 — &c Knowing them to be worth at least 42 thousand dollars, if Condemned The U. S. would have to redeem them & the invoice of the Cargo. I made out anew in the room of Eighteen Thousd I reduced it to 8, and by Miciah Bocries Calculation to the dey it was reduced to 3 Thousd dlrs On the Morning of the 9th of October, the board of admiralty met again when all the papers was examined into, and other persons Called to read & explain theire Contents, now, when the pass avant and Consular Certificate was read, the[y] declared I had told them the truth and examined theire books to 150 years back, and in Sd Book of Marine laws and Customs on the like Occasions. One leafe Condemns & the other Clears — & the[y] determined the 2d time as the[y] did at first and finally the dey declared Said Vessel a Legal prize, but that, for my acct and his good Opinion of the U S. he Cleared Said Vessel and Cargo, declareing that he favoured me on this Occasion but Could never again &c —

that any Vessel without a pass. would be Condemned, and that no Consular Certificates Should with him or his people be Sufficient to Save either Vessel Or Cargo — and for me to give this information to the United States

I have examined fully our passports, and find them defective in Consequence. I Send you with these dispatches a Spanish Mediterranian pass. which I think much Superior done than. Those of the U S — our passes is too long & broad the great Breadth the more liable to Error, and therefore, the Cut or top which the barbary Corsairs has does not agree with that nicety that is requisite and with the pass. which the Merch^t Vessels of the United States has in Consequence it is the Custom here, and all nations at peace with those people has Submited to it. That when the top does not exactly agree with the bottom that the Cargo is Condemnd — and in Consequence of these very visable defects in the present American passports many of our Vessels will be met with and unavoidably theire Cargoes Condemned. This requires remidying immediatly and I Should propose Something Similar to the Spanish pass. on better paper, or on Such parchment as would be thick not liable to Shrink or extend, One part being damp the other part perhaps folded & dry, would Occasion the top not agreeing with the bottom, and in Consequence a due Cargo. government gives both top & bottom & if the[y] do not agree & in Consequence the Merchants Suffer will the[y] not blame theire government, which gave them the pass will the[y] not Sue &^c recover damages from the government.

I inclose you an american pass & 2 tops or Cuts to Shew you the defect and I point out the necessity of remedying it. The N° 1 on top and bottom of the American pass being kept Close or on the line. The top is longer then the bottom by 1/10th of an inch and this defect will be the means of Confiscateing many A Cargo if not remedied —

As the french Spanish and British has taken and Condemned & Sold So Many American Vessels the[y] haveing of Course with them theire Mediterranian pass. Of Course many of those Vessels has been resold to other nations & of Course the[y] have many of our passports. Under this pretence we Claim it as a right to Change our passports on this plan which I presume to Suggest to you Sir, takeing 18 Months for all American Vessels to have the new pass. given out, and the Same time, for the Old pass. to be good untill the Vessels has procured the new and as the[y] have the new the[y] need not Carry the Old, the tops of the news passes to Send to Algiers Tunis & Tripolia So that we might furnish the new passes. and with them the old untill that all American Vessels has got the new passes. which I think the[y] Can have in the run of 18 Months or 2 years, and from what I State and Sugest I hope that I Shall Shortly have youre Ans^r on these great affairs — which I think will draw youre most Serious attention and prevent many Valuable american Cargoes from being Condemned on account of a deficiency in the pass. many instances of this nature I have known during my Captivity of 10 y^rs & 41 days.

I would propose a Ship under Sail with her American Ensign aft to her top G^lt mast heads. The American Flag — the top to Cut by the 1st reefe in the main top Sail and to the 3^d or Close reefe in the fore topsail and by the Close reefe of the Mizen topsail, with a Star on the Close reefed fore topsail a half Moon on the 1st reefe of the Main topsail and a Star on the head of the Mizen top Sail. all this to be done, very elegantly, well engraved and Cut with the greatest exactness.

Those Meditteranian passes when Once on this plan we might then expect Safety and those passes Should not be doubled, but rolled up and a tin Canister made to keep it in

this Meditteranian pass.	on Each of these
Sea letter on good paper.	documents Should
Register on parchment.	be Stampt the arms
Role De Equipage —	of the United States
& Each Sailor his protection	None of yr buton Seals
and Real American Colours.	Now. The public Seal
Crews 2/3ds Americans	or its Stamp Should
No fancy flags, enforce the Laws &	be to all those documents

I shall Observe that the Dey was not Satisfyed that this Brig *Mary* was an American Vessel untill that I compared & Shewn the Public Seal of my Consular Commision which I Convinced the Ministry was the Same, and exactly alike unto the Public Seal on the Brig *Marys* Sea letter and a Mr Abraham K. Bracher had a Lieuts Commision in the New York Militia and the Seal of New York thereto, Signed under the Seal John Jay — This I knew & with persuasion I Could make the Algerines know why because the[y] Could not read English & the Seal had not the Stars or Eagle on it — for if those people Cannot read the Christian print or writeing if the[y] See the Seal of the United States, or the arms thereof the[y] know it, but the[y] Cannot read the writeings, but the Seal is expressive. I presume if I have not fully described, that you very easily perceive what I would wish to explain and point out, and Shall Observe that all persons that Grants Certificates to any person going to Europe Should have the Seal of the United States, or its arms on the Seal — Supose the port of Norfolk, Collectors Seal, the arms of the U. S. & the requisite writeings on the Seal, I hope that those that might frequent the Meditteranian will have the real American Colours — if the[y] have those State flags, the[y] will not do, with even a good pass. The Algerines will not belive or know them to be Americans. Why because the[y] have not American Colours & the[y] know nothing about yr State Colours — The[y] will declare the[y] made a peace with one nation & one flag, not with 16 nations &c 16 flags — look out. O'Brien will give you true Soundings

[SDA. Algiers, Vol. 3, 1798.]

To Henry William Desaussure, agent for galleys, from Secretary of Navy

[TRENTON,]
Navy Department October 12th 1798.

HENRY WM DESAUSSURE, ESQr

SIR I am honored with your Letter of the 20th Ulto and thank you sincerely for your candid reply to my enquiry. —

You know before this, that Capt Cross has been directed to take the Command of the vessel destined for Capt Cochran. — It could not be otherwise —

Capt Cochran being in the Revenue Cutter, and not the Navy Service, cannot I believe, be indulged in his wishes for a Court of enquiry — How could such a Court be constituted? To be very plain, whatever might be the report of a Court of Enquiry, It never could in my opinion be right to trust a second time, an Armed Vessel & with it the honor of the Country in the hands of a man, who had fled under Such circumstances, from a Vessel of Force inferior to his own. — When he left the Harbour of Charleston, he knew he had no Commission, and the defect of his Vessel; These Circumstances Should have operated to have prevented his Sailing, or not at all — Unless our Navy Officers are taught early to know, that they must do their duty in the Face of an Enemy, we had better at once give up the Idea of Naval Defence. —

Had Capt Cochran been commissioned in the Navy Service, I should have felt it my duty to have brought him to a Court Martial — I rejoice on account of his good Intentions, good private character, and the Interest you feel for him, that this was not the Case. —

I am sure I may rely on your candor, & good sense to forgive the freedom of observation, dictated by my earnestness for the honor & usefulness of the cheapest & best defence of the Country — at least of the Southern part of the Country —

I have the honor
to be with Esteem
&c.

[NDA. GLB No. 1.]

To W. J. Bigar, merchant, Philadelphia, from Jacob Wagner

DEPARTMENT OF STATE
Trenton New Jersey Oct. 12. 1798.

[To] W. J. BIGAR *Merchant Philadelphia.*

SIR, The Secretary of State has received your letter of yesterday's date, soliciting a special permission for your vessel to proceed as a Cartel to Porto Rico and St Thomas'; and he directs me to inform you that the laws place no restriction to the going to either of those places, and therefore, if the vessel is not destined for a French port also in the course of her voyage, no special permission is necessary. I am Sir, respectfully &c.

JACOB WAGNER.

[SDA. Dom. L., Vol. 11.]

To Captain Christopher R. Perry, U. S. Navy, from Secretary of the Navy

[TRENTON,]
Navy Department October 12th 1798

Capt CHRISTr R. PERRY
of the Genl Greene

SIR: You will make such Arrangements To commence recruiting a Crew for the *Genl Greene* now under your Command, as to have her complement completed by the Time she is ready for a Cruise.

You are allowed (besides officers of Marines & 30 Privates, which will be supplied you by the Major of the Marine Corps; and your

Commissioned & Petty Officers, the latter of which you will appoint) not exceeding one hundred & fifteen men & Boys.

Of this Number you will recruit not exceeding 70 Able Seamen: the residue to consist of Ordinary Seamen & Boys.

It is our best policy &c &c &c See Instructions to Captain Moses Brown page 232.

Messrs Gibbs & Channing, will advance the monies necessary for the purposes of recruiting &c &c See page 233.

[NOTE.—Pages 232 and 233 contain letter to Capt. Brown, dated October 4th, 1798.]
[NDA. OSW, Vol. 1.]

Purchase of Ship *George Washington*

[12 OCTOBER 1798]

JOHN BROWN *Providence*
Receipt for 10,400 dols
Part of the Purchase money for Ship *George Washington*
Warrant N° 15

Providence OCTOBER *12th 1798.*

Receiv'd of Benjamin Stoddert Esquire, Commisioner of the Navy, Ten thousand four hundred Dollars, on Account of the Ship *George Washington*, sold him by contract, in a draught on the Providence Bank, for which I have given a duplicate hereof. — the Warrant was N° 15 —$10,400

JOHN BROWN

[NDA. Area 7, October 12, 1798.]

[12 October, 1798]

Launching of the *Merrimack*, and description of her figurehead

NEWBURYPORT, *Oct. 12.*

THE LAUNCH

This day, at 15 minutes past one, our beautiful patriotic ship, majestically descended from her native land, to the embrace of the watery God, without the least accident. She is called the *Merrimack*, will mount 20 nines and 8 sixes, is finely coppered, and the best judges say, she would not suffer by a comparison with the finest vessel of her size ever built. Captain William Hacket, the constructor and superintendant, and Major Cross, the contractor, are entitled to all the merit which can be attached to their profession.

Her head is a group composed of an Eagle perched upon the Globe, supported on one side by an elegant figure representing COMMERCE, and on the other by a beautiful female, strikingly emblematical of JUSTICE, in front is borne the arms of the U States. The design is excellent; and the execution does honor to the artist, Mr. Dearing, of Portsmouth.

A vast concourse of people attended, to be witnesses of the interesting scene. A federal salute from the artillery pieces, announced to distant friends, the happy issue of the launch. As she went, joy advanced upon the anxiety which at first was depicted upon almost every countenance, and ended in acclamations which made the air resound on the joyful occasion.

The keel of this ship was laid on the 9th of July, since which there have been 74 working days; and we dare presume to say, that from the spirit which has attended the business, she will be ready for sea in 14 days, as numbers of the hardy sons of Neptune stand ready to enlist under her worthy commander, and who have been so long waiting for an opportunity to manifest their zeal and ability, in defence of their injured country and sea-faring brethren.

[LC, "Claypoole's American Daily Advertiser" (Phila.), 22 Oct. 1798.]

Extract from Captain Thomas Truxtun's journal, U. S. Frigate *Constellation*, 12 October 1798, Friday

Very squally, dirty and uncommonly disagreeable Weather with some Rain, and heavy Clouds continually rising all these twenty four Hours, with the Wind variable; in Fact constantly flying about in the Squalls from N. N. E. to S. S. E. Spoke the *Caroline* and *Felicity*, two of the Convoy, both belonging to Baltimore; at Noon sounded in 70 Fathoms Water; Cape Look out bearing N. E. b. N. 33 Leagues Distance.

Latitude observed 32°.54′ N°
Longitude Account 78.9 W.

[HS of Pa. NDA photostat.]

Extract from journal of James Pity, U. S. Frigate *Constitution*, 12 October 1798, Friday

First part this 24 hours Steady Breezes & pleasant
@ 3 P. M. furl'd Sprit Sail Top Sail
@ 8 P. M. Took in T. G^t Sails & Spoke the Cutter *Virginia*
@ 10 P. M. Braild up the Mizen & furl'd M. T. Stay sail
@ 11 P. M. Weather look^g squally Reef'd Top Sails. Spoke the Cutter Inform'd her the course to be Steer'd after Midnight S. W. b. W. @ ½ past 3 Set M. Top Mast Stay Sail
@ 6 A. M. out Reefs & Set T. G^t Sails at 8 A. M. Settled down T. G^t Sails & Set ye Jibb @ 9 lowered Down M^n Top Sail & Sent down M. T. G^t Y^ds & Mast. @ ½ past 10 fidded M. T. G^t Mast & Sent it aloft. @ ½ past 11 Sent up M. T. G^t Yard.

[Latitude observed 32°. 42^m]

[NDA.]

To William Crafts, Navy Agent, Charleston, S. C., from Secretary of Navy

[TRENTON,]
Navy Department October 13th 1798

Wm CRAFTS Esqr
Charleston S. C.

SIR, Should Capt Truxton appear off Charleston, be pleased to send him the enclosed Letter.

I have the honor &c^a

[NDA. GLB No. 1.]

To Captain Thomas Tingey, U. S. Navy, commanding the *Ganges*, from Secretary of the Navy

[TRENTON,]
Navy Departm^{t} 13th Octr 1798.

Capt THO^{s} TINGEY

SIR, You will make such Arrangements to commence recruiting a Crew for the *Ganges*, now under your Command, as to have her Complement completed by the Time she is ready for a Cruise.

You are allowed, besides Officers of Marines & 21 Privates, & your commissioned & petty officers, the latter of which you will appoint, not exceeding "One hundred Men and Boys —

Of this Number you will recruit not exceeding 66 able Seamen: the residue to consist of ordinary Seamen & Boys.

It is our best Policy &^{c} &^{c} See page 232.

Monies will be advanced you from this department, and you will be held accountable for each Expenditure. You will advance to your recruiting officers, who will Settle their accounts with you: &^{c} &^{c} See page 232.

[NOTE: Page 232 contains letter to Capt. Moses Brown, dated October 4th, 1798.]

[NDA. OSW, Vol. 1.]

To Major Commandant W. W. Burrows, U. S. M. C., from Secretary of Navy

[TRENTON,]
Navy Department Octr 13th 1798.

Major W. W. BURROWS

SIR, A guard to consist of a Lieutenant, Serjeant, Corporal, & 18 Privates are Wanted at New Castle for the Safe keeping of the Prisoners landed from on board the Frigate *United States*, and Ship of War *Delaware* at that place, You will please to Send off this guard as soon as possible, letting them draw Rations sufficient to last them until they get there — After which they will be supplied under a Contract, which I have directed, the Marshall, Robt Hamilton Esqr to make for the purpose. — The Lieutenant will apply to this Gentleman on his arrival — and they will concert the best mode of accomplishing the object in view. —

I have the honor &C^{a}

[NDA. GLB No. 1.]

To William Pennock, Navy Agent, Norfolk, from Secretary of Navy

[TRENTON,]
Navy Department October 13th 1798

Wm PENNOCK Esqr *Norfolk*

SIR You will be pleased to send the enclosed Letter to Capt Truxton, should he return to Hampton, or be near your Coast — There is also enclosed a Letter for Capt Campbell of the Brig *Eagle*, who will be at Norfolk, probably before this —

I have the honor &C^{a}

[NDA. GLB No. 1.]

To Captain Thomas Truxtun, U. S. Navy, from Secretary of the Navy

[Trenton,]
Navy Department 13th October 1798

Capt Thos Truxton

Sir Presuming you may receive this, either at Charleston or Hampton, on your return from the Havanna, I have the honor to request, that after obtaining the necessary refreshment for your Crew, you will continue on the Southern Coast agreeably to my orders of the 14th July, till the 10th of November, when if no circumstance should turn up, to render, in your opinion, a longer cruise necessary, you will steer Eastward, and if in your power, to safely pass the Barr, about thirty miles from New York, of which there are doubts, put into the Harbour of New York — Otherwise into that of Newport, Rhode Island. —

Messrs James & Ebenezer Watson are the Navy Agents at New York, Messrs Gibbs & Channing at Newport. — You will as quickly after Arrival as possible, make a return to me, of every thing wanting to fit your Frigate for a Six Months Cruise — And give a copy for the Agents. —

Capt Philips of the *Baltimore*, you will direct to proceed to Baltimore at the same time, with similar Instructions, as to the Wants of his Ship — provided his Ship does not draw too much Water to get to Baltimore — In this case he must put into Norfolk. — If you remain at Hampton long enough, take in a full supply of Bread for six months — It is not only better, but cheaper, than New York can Supply — If you want Masts too, it would be proper to get them at Norfolk, if to be done without too much delay. —

I have the honor to be &ca

[NDA. OSW, Vol. 1.]

To Captain Hugh G. Campbell, U. S. Navy, from Secretary of the Navy

[Trenton,]
Navy Departmt October 13th 1798

Capt Hugh G. Campbell

Sir, If Capt Murray should have left Norfolk before your Arrival, a circumstance which ought not to have taken place, and for which you will account in a manner more satisfactory than I can at present imagine. You will in that case proceed to Savanna in Georgia, and let it be known to John Habersham Esqr that you have arrived. — Without wasting time in Port, you will immediately put to sea again, and try to fall in with Enemy Vessels. —

You will consider your cruising ground to extend from St Mary's River to Charleston, and you are to use your best endeavours to protect this extent of Coast from the depredations of French Cruisers, as well as to give all the protection in your power to the Commerce of the Country. —

You are not confined to any certain distance from the Coast, but are allowed to indulge a Spirit of Enterprize; if you should hear of Enemy Vessels further North or South, than your Limits — But are more particularly to pay attention to St Mary's River & the Coasts of Georgia. —

You will promote discipline & order among your Crew — and inculcate a high Sense of the Honor of the American Flag, which is to be maintained at every hazard. —

You will remember, that we are at War only with the French Armed Vessels. — The Vessels of all other Nations are entitled to, & must receive from you civility & good offices. — Should you even meet an American Vessel captured by the Vessels of any of the Nations at War, Except the French, you cannot go to recapture such Vessel, It must be presumed that the Coasts [Courts] of such Nation, will render Justice. —

You will by every opportunity write me the events of your Cruize, & never omit to do this, when you go into any Port. —

Having the Command of a Revenue Cutter you are to [obey] the Orders you will receive from the proper Authority on the Subject of the Revenue. —

I remain &c^a

[NDA. OSW, Vol. 1.]

To Stephen Higginson, Navy Agent, Boston, from Secretary of Navy

[Trenton,]
Navy Department October 13th 1798.

Stephen Higginson Esqr *Boston*

Sir I shall leave this place in a few days not to return till the 10th or 12th of November —

I believe I have anticipated every thing respecting the ship at Portsmouth, Capt McNeill — If I have not, Col^o Pickering will attend to the duties of my Office in my absence. —

The *Constitution* will return to Boston, about the 15th or 20th November. — So will the *Herald* and the *Pickering*. — It will be desireable to get these Vessels out again in two or three weeks. You will, I presume, have some Beef & Pork on hand, or in your power under former orders. — It will be necessary that Bread should be provided, to make up with what they have on hand of the old stock, a sufficiency for a Cruise of 6 months. — also Fish, & in short every Article composing the Ships Provisions authorized by the Acts of Congress — For your Information, and lest you should not have the Acts of Congress by you, I have at foot, added an extract from the Law. — Will you be pleased to have laid in, a supply for these Ships, for about four months. — I suppose they may have on hand for two months, of former Supplies — On the Arrival of the Vessels, the Captains will make returns to you, of what will be wanted for Six months — And you can then make up any deficiency — and you will be pleased to do this — Not only as it respects provisions, but every thing wanted, which the Laws authorize. —

I enclose Letters to the Commanding Officers, to be delivered on their Arrival. Col^o Pickering will on your requisition cause money to be remitted to you. —

Not knowing what has been advanced to the Officers & Crew of the *Constitution*, I know not what to say on the subject of pay, but this will be attended to in time. —

Besides these Vessels — The two other Frigates, Six Ships of 20 Guns & upwards, four or five Brigs of 14 & 18 Guns, and some of the

Revenue Cutters — Perhaps the Ship at Portsmouth and one at Newport, will be ready to proceed wherever directed, early in December. — Will you be so good as to give me your Opinion, to reach me the 12th or 15th Nov. at Phila, how this Force should be employed this Winter — I have already your Ideas on this subject; but wish to have it again.

I have the honor

&ca

(NDA. GLB No. 1.]

Circular to J. & E. Watson, Navy Agents, and others, from Secretary of Navy

[Trenton]

Navy Department October 13th 1798.

Circular to
J. & E. Watson — *New York*
S. Higginson — *Boston*
Wm Pennock — *Norfolk*
Wm Crafts — *Charleston*
Jerh Yellott — *Baltimore*—
Gibbs & Channing — *Newport*
Jacob Sheaffe — *Portsmouth*
Ameziah Jocelin — *Wilmington, N. C.*
Ebenezer Jackson — *Savannah Georgia*

Should French Prisoners be sent into your Ports, by the Frigates or Ships of War of the United States, you will please, as soon after their arrival as possible, cause them to be delivered to the Marshal of the district, who will as the Law directs, take measures for their safe keeping. —

It will be best for the Marshal to supply them by Contract, with rations to consist of one pound of coarse bread, half a pound of meat, & one pound of Potatoes, or other wholesome Vegetables, equal in Nutriment to a pound of Potatoes, the accounts for which, to be rendered & settled monthly — The money will be supplied by this Department. —

I have the honor &ca

[NDA. GLB No. 1.]

To Robert Hamilton, Marshal, Delaware, from Secretary of Navy

[Trenton,]

Navy Department 13th October 1798

Robt Hamilton Esqr
Marshal Delaware.

Sir, I have received your Letter of the 10th Instant, and shall immy direct a guard consistg of a Lieutt, Serjeant, Corporal, & 18 Marines from the neighbourhood of Philadelphia, to aid you in the safe keeping of the French Prisoners. — You will be so good as to Contract for Rations, for this guard on the best Terms possible, and render your Accounts in the like manner as is directed in the Case of the Prisoners.

At foot you have the ration in Philadelphia. It is furnished at 18⅚ Cents. — Please to inform me whether with this guard, they can be kept perfectly secure at New Castle, because if they cannot, measures will be taken to remove them elsewhere. —

There is no regulation, which will warrant supplying them with Clothing — But Humanity dictates that they ought not to suffer. — The Secy of State has written to Mr Le Tombe former French Consul, on this subject; but if he does not in the course of 10 or 12 days supply their Wants, you will please to purchase a Blanket, for each Wanting one and a sufficient Quantity of Straw. — This is all that can consistently be done for them under present circumstances, and more than would probably be done by their Government for our Citizens under Similar Circumstances. —

Please to inform me the Exact Number of Prisoners. —

Rations agreeably to Law

1¼# Beef or ¾# Pork

18 oz. Bread or Flour

A Gill of Rum, Brandy or Whiskey

And at the rate of 2 q^{ts} Salt, 2 quarts Vinigar, 4# Soap, & 1½# Candles to every hundred Rations. — —

[NDA. GLB No. 1.]

Extract from journal of James Pity, U. S. Frigate *Constitution*, 13 October 1798, Saturday

First part this 24 hours Strong Breezes. @ ½ past $Merd^n$ $Reef^d$ Top Sails and Sent down Top $Gall^t$ yards. @ ½ past 6 hauld up the foresail Close Reeft Top Sails @ ½ 7. furl'd M. Top Sails Spoke our Consort & Inform'd her if we should get Soundings we Should wear & Stand $Northw^d$ Weather very Squally with Rain $Short^{nd}$ Sail for the *Virginia* it $blow^g$ Very hard. @ 8 Wind $veer^g$ $West^d$ Saw 2 Sail $bear^g$ W. S. W. made Signal for Chace which was $answ^d$ by the *Virginia* @ $Merd^n$ Spoke the Nearest proved a $Brig^t$ from Havanna bound to N York who Informed us the other was a Ship from D^o bound to D^o

Ends Cloudy Weather.

No. observation —

[NDA.]

Extract from Captain Thomas Truxtun's journal, U. S. Frigate *Constellation*, 13 October 1798, Saturday

Violent Squalls of Wind, and Rain with some Lightning, and a few Claps of Thunder. The Wind very variable all the 24 Hours; in Fact it has been round the Compass; stood on the most favourable Tack from Time to Time, as per Column, and sounded frequently, having at no Time less than 70 Fathoms Water, and at Noon 85, a Sort of ouze and green Sand.

At 6 P M spoke the Sloop [space] from Georgia bound to New York, out 6 Days; had neither seen, or heard of any french Cruizers on the Coast.

Made and took in Sail according to the Weather, which I always make a Point of doing, when not in Chase, so as to preserve the Spars, Rigging, and Sails, and favour the Hull of the Ship as much as possible.

Cape Look out Shoals at Noon bore N. N. E. ½ E. 33 Leagues Distance, and those of the Frying Pan N. N. W. 16 Leagues.

Latitude Account 32°.45′ N.

Longitude Account 78.00 W.

[HS of Pa. NDA photostat.]

Extract from journal of James Pity, U. S. Frigate *Constitution*, 14 October 1798, Sunday

Beginning with fresh breezes Cloudy & Squally Several sail in Sight @ 1 P. M. Spoke the Ship *Mary* from Havanna bound to N York Saild In C° with 45 Sail American Merchant[n] under Convoy of U. S. Frigate *Constellation* & *Baltimore* Slp. [of] War. At 2 P. M. Saw a Sch[r] who look'd Rogueish by her crowd[d] Sail from us. called all hands & made Sail for chace @ 3 fir'd a gun & bro't her too She was an English Arm'd Sch[r] from Charlestown bound to Martinico ordered her to hoist out her boat & bring her papers on B[d] of us. examined her and Suffer'd her to proceed. She was call'd the *Hibernia* (Bates) Com[r] @ 6 P. M. Spoke a Sch[r] from Jamaica bound to Portsmouth (Virginia) Robert Cooley Master. at Midnight sounded & got ground coarse dark Sand @ 1 P. M. Sounded in 44 fath[ms] dark Sand Intermixed with Yellow Specks gravel & small shells. at 6 A. M. Sounded in 35 fath[ms] at 10 A. M. Sounded in 25 fath[ms]

Ends with heavy gales and Squally W[r]

[Latitude observed 31.48 N°]

[NDA.]

Extract from Captain Thomas Truxtun's journal, U. S. Frigate *Constellation*, 14 October 1798, Sunday

Very uncertain Weather with a Swell from the Eastward. Unbent the old, and bent the new Main Sail, and employed the People at Sundries.

Saw two Sail of the Convoy. Frying Pan Shoals at Noon bore N. B. W. ½ W. twenty six Leagues Distance.

Latitude observed 32°.17′ N°

Longitude Account 78.00 W

[HS of Pa. NDA photostat.]

Correspondence between Secretary Benjamin Stoddert and Secretary Oliver Wolcott

Oct[r] 15. 1798.

Sir, Enclosed is the copy of a letter written by me to Gen[l] Washington — & his answer.*

Now that I have given you space to recover your astonishment at my selfish partiality, for the District of Columbia — let me throw you into still greater astonishment at my folly, by telling you that it is my sincere opinion that a long & a vigorous Naval war, could not be carried on by this Country without the resources of the Chesapeake, but more particularly of the Potomak. There is not a single article — Pork, beef, cheese, live oak & Fish excepted, necessary to be used in the construction fitting & equipment of Ships of War, which cannot be afforded in great abundance & on cheaper terms, on Potomak than in any other part of the U States. It would take too much time to enter into the proof of this assertion but nothing is more true. Independent of this consideration, nothing strikes my

[*See letter Stoddert to Washington, of 16 Sept. 1798; also Washington to Stoddert, of 26 Sept. 1798.]

mind with more irresistable force, than the necessity of paying so much attention to the follies & prejudices if you please, but I must add, the Interest of the Southern States, as to place one of the Navy yards for building ships, so far South, as the Centre of the United States — perhaps it is fortunate, that one cannot with propriety be placed nearer to them. One other Navy yard, to gratify the pride the prejudices & the Interest of the E States ought to be with them — but not so far East as N Hampshire — where the timber tho abundant, is too bad — where they have no keels[?] — no locust — no Iron — it should be in Connecticut R. Island or Massachusetts — I think R Island, if a safe & proper place can be found — but I know nothing — or comparatively nothing of the E States, & if the Idea of Established Navy Yard be adopted — I shall need all your present information, & all you can get to give me.

I say to gratify the pride &ca — because the real truth is, that there ought I believe to be but one Navy Yard for building, and that ought to be on Potomak.

Humphreys tells me there can be no Navy Yard on Delaware — a Frigate can pass up the North River, in spite of West point — I need not say more as to N York.

But be the Navy Yard where it may to the Eastward of Chesapeake, it must be conducted with greater disadvantages to the Public, than one on Potomak — where the timber is good & so plenty that it can almost be had for Cutting — & where Iron of the best kind abounds, where hemp can be had, the growth of the Country to supply more than the Public demand, where the Coal is not to be exhausted — In short where nothing is wanted — Except indeed that noble animal Man, to enjoy the bounty given by Providence, to that best part of the American Empire.

I believe the efforts of the present year will exhaust the whole seasoned timber of the Country — that be it ever so essential, no more can be done in the ensuing year, than to complete the Vessels on the stocks — & make preparations for another year.

This is a situation to which we shall always be exposed, if places are not established for the reception & care of timber — And it is a situation which we should not be in, if to be avoided — hence the necessity of Navy Yards.

I wish you to consider the whole of this subject seriously, & to give me your candid opinion, without the least respect to my prejudices or follies — when I have the pleasure of seeing you in Phila — I submit the thing to you, that you may convince my reason, if I am wrong — if right, as I believe most seriously I am, assist me in it. Indeed, I am so far gone in error, if in error, that if I had the power, I would this very winter fortify Digges' point; that our Ships might have a safe place to retire behind, if a superior naval force should come on our Coast. I know not where else, our Ships could find protection against such a force. The Depth of water at Maryd point, is 21 feet low, 25 feet high tide — it may be more, but I know it is this.

I am with great esteem
D Sir Yr most obed. serv

BEN STODDERT

[TO OLIVER WOLCOTT]

The enclosed papers, exhibit the waters & woods above the Town of Cumberland on Potomak — & a sketch of the River & Streams emptying into Potomak, between   & Cumberland. will observe that there are two maps, in Different scales. This was done by F Dickins, & is entirely accurate & shews better than any thing else, the connexion between the Eastern & Western Waters.

[Conn. HS. Mss. 42, Oliver Wolcott Papers.]

To General George Barnwell, Beaufort, S. C., from Secretary of Navy

[TRENTON,]
Navy Department Octr 15th 1798.

Genl GEORGE BARNWELL
Beaufort, So. Carolina

SIR, It may be of the utmost Importance, that our Ships of War should have a Harbour on the Southern Coast. — There is no place south of Chesapeake that will answer, unless Port Royal will. — Knowing your Character, I make no apology for the Liberty I take, in requesting the favor of you to take the trouble to have the depth of Water over the Bar ascertained accurately — And to prevail on one or two persons of good Character, I mean among the Pilots, to qualify themselves for taking into that Harbour, Ships drawing 23 feet Water. —

Be so good as to favor me with y^r opinion whether Fortifications can be erected, to protect our Ships in that Harbour against a superior Naval Force. —

For the expense of ascertaining the depth of Water — and for getting one or two Pilots to qualify themselves for taking Ships into the Harbour, be pleased to draw on me, as Sec^y of the Navy. —

[NDA. GLB No. 1.]

To Thomas Pinckney, Charleston, S. C., from Secretary of Navy

[TRENTON,]
Navy Depart^t Octr 15th 1798

THO^s PINCKNEY Esqr
Charleston, S. C.

SIR I have for some time been honored with your Letter of the 31st August, and lately with that of the 25th September. —

I have to thank you for the trouble you have taken with respect to the Marine officers. — Your order for 500 D^s has appeared, and been paid. —

The persons you mention as Officers in the Navy shall be attended to. — On this subject, I should be glad to receive through you, a List of proper characters to Officer the ship building at Charleston. Mr Smith, Nephew of Bishop Smith, is set down to be Junior Lieutenant; But if he should be appointed before another, he will be senior Lieutenant. —

The usefulness & honor of the Navy depend upon the men selected as Officers — We had better burn the Ships, than put on board of them Officers without energy. —

I have written to Gen! Barnwell, to take measures, at the public Expense, to ascertain the depth of Water over the Bar at Port Royal, and to have pilots qualified, to conduct into that Harbour our Ships. — If the place will admit of Fortifications to protect our Ships against a superior Naval Force, such fortifications should be erected — But this is not within my department.

I am very sorry that the Southern Coast has not, for the last four or five Weeks, had the protection I calculated on — Truxton was not ordered to proceed to Savannah 'till full time for Nicholson to get on that Coast —

Nicholson, unfortunately, fell in with a Ship Officered by Frenchmen early in September which he conducted as a prize into Norfolk — where he remained the 6th of October; & where he should not have remained one day

I have the honor to be

&ca

[NDA. GLB No. 1.]

To Josiah Parker, Norfolk, from Secretary of Navy

[Trenton,]
Navy Department October 15th 1798.

Josiah Parker Esqr
Norfolk

Sir, I am honored with your Letter of the 27th Ultimo. — I am greatly obliged by your attention to the Navy Business at Norfolk. I lament that your Indisposition prevented your aid in the Selection of Williams's Officers. We had better have no Navy than have it commanded by indifferent men; and it Shall be my Study to rid the service of such men, as fast as possible. The Officers for Barron in your List will have Commissions sent them in about 15 days — It will take so long to send them to and get them from the President. —

I have sent some days past, recruiting Instructions to Barron, and have written to Messrs Nivison & Granbury to supply every thing —

There can be no occasion for Pennock's Interference, further than to supply any thing belonging to the public, which these Gentlemen cannot get elsewhere. —

Nicholson, to my Mortification & Astonishment has been at Hampton from about the 11th Septr to the 6th October — perhaps longer; Tho' under positive orders to guard the Southern Coast from Cape Henry. — For the last 8 or 10 days, there has been no excuse for the intolerable delay, but want of a Wind to carry him out. — Can it be possible that he could have been kept at Hampton from 29th September to the 6th October (& god knows how much longer) for want of Wind? Pray be so good as to answer this question in Confidence. —

I expect to set out for George Town in two days, not to return, till I can move my Family to Philadelphia, which I do not expect will be Sooner than the 15th November. — Please to direct for me at George Town. — I have made arrangements to prevent any delay of Capt Barron's, or any other Vessels by my absence. — Doct^r Reynolds has been directed to go on board of Barron —

I have the honor &c.

[NDA. GLB No. 1.]

To Robert Oliver, Baltimore, from Secretary of Navy

[TRENTON,]
Navy Department October 15th 1798

ROBt OLIVER Esqr
Baltimore.

SIR The Bearer Capt Spotswood, son of Genl Spotswood of Virginia, has been recommended as a Captain in the Navy by Genl Washington, Genl Lee & other respectable men of Virginia. When the Citizens furnish Vessels for the public, it is the wish of the President to consult them — Indeed to pay very great respect to their recommendation, in the choice of Officers. — If Capt Spotswood be appointed, a Captain, it would be desireable to give him the Command of a Vessel from Virginia or Maryland. — In Virginia there is no Vessel, which is not already provided with a Commander —

If you and the Committee directing the building of the two Baltimore Vessels, have not fixed upon two Captains to recommend, Capt Spotswood I dare say Would do honor to your recommendation, to the Command of one of them — Tho a young man, he is an experienced seaman.

I have the honor to be
&Ca

[NDA. GLB No. 1.]

To Messrs. Joseph Anthony & Co. from Gibbs & Channing, agents, Newport, R. I.

NEWPORT *October 15 1798.*

Messrs JOSEPH ANTHONY & Co

DEAR SIRS We wrote you ye 10th in reply to your favor — We have now to ask the favor of you to engage your most skilfull Carver, to carve a man figure head for a Ship of War we are building for Government, of about 600 Tons — to carry 24 Guns — the Ship is called the *General Greene*, and as we are informed your best Carver can cut good likenesses we wish him to endeavour to carve it to the likeness of the late General Greene — We learn there is a portrait of him at Peales Museum — from which we suppose a likeness could be taken — The length of the figure to be nine feet, to be made light, a due regard however being paid to proportion — The trail board & brackets we should also wish carved — As the ship we expect will be launched in all next month, we wish to have the head immediately done & that you would forward it by first oppty [opportunity]. — Having understood a preference is given to the carved work done in your city, we are under the necessity of troubling you with our present request. —

[Newport HS. N. War C, Gibbs & Channing LB.]

Extract from journal of James Pity, U. S. Frigate *Constitution*, 15 October 1798, Monday

First part this 24 hours Strong Breezes & hazey Weather at Merdn sounded 20 fathms Dark Shells. Spoke the *Virginia* & Inform'd her what Course we meant to steer for St. Marys as soon as we got of S^{d} Port we should K Ship & Stand to Northw^{d} @ 4 P. M. Sounded in 20 fath^{ms} at 6 in 27 f^{ms} black Sand @ 7 P. M. Single reef'd Top Sails hauld up the fore Sail — sounded in 30 f^{ms} Wore Ship & Stood for the *Virginia* fired one Gun & hoisted Two lights in the Starboard Main Shrouds as signal to our Consort Spoke D^{o} and understood She Was leakey Shortend Sail & Sounded in 30 f^{ms} — @ ½ p^{t} 8 she Spoke with us & Inform'd us that her beams work'd so that She was In danger of being Swampt. Saw a Strange Sail to S. E. Up T. G^{t} Yards.

Spoke the Sch^{r} *Virginia* during the Night and on Acc^{t} of his Vessell Labouring so much Capt Nicholsons Orders were that If he could not with Safety keep Company he had better make the best of his way for Virginia.

[Latitude observed 31° 0^{m}. N^{o}]

[NDA.]

Extract from Captain Thomas Truxtun's journal, U. S. Frigate *Constellation*, 15 October 1798, Monday

Very uncertain squally Weather, as before, with a high Sea running, occasioned in a great Measure, by the Gulph Stream, spoke one of the Convoy, and saw another.

Nothing further worth remarking, except that the Winds we have had since leaving our Station off the Havannah, have been very much against the Convoy, and of the making a Passage, and by the present Appearances, there is not much Likelihood of a speedy change tho' the ◑ quartering to Morrow may bring it about.

At Noon Cape Look out Shoales bore N. B. E. twenty three Leagues Distance, and those of Cape Hatteras N. E. B. N. forty five Leagues Distance.

Latitude observed 33°. 2′ N^{o}
Longitude Account 77.13 W.

[HS of Pa. NDA photostat.]

To James F. Goelet, Sailing Master, from Captain Thomas Tingey, U. S. Navy

16th Octr 1798

Sir Having obtain'd for you the appointment of Sailing-Master of the United States Ship of War *Ganges*, you will please to proceed with all possible expedition to Marcus Hook in the Delaware, where the ship now lies; and on your arrival deliver the letter herewith to Captain Dale, who will make you acquainted with the other officers, & put you in possession of your station.

You will soon perceive from the state of the Ship, how necessary the utmost exertions of every Officer will be to facilitate her dispatch: and I shall rely on your vigilance being unremitted. You will immediately on joining the Ship, affix your name to the articled list — which however is only temporary till I also join her, which I intend in the ensuing week. — You will also take immediate superintendance of the Log-book, and cause to be clearly particularized all daily occurences

I am Sir &c.

Mr Ja^s^ F. GOELET.
appointed Sailing Master
of the United States Ship of War Ganges

[NDA. Tingey LB, 1798–1800.]

To Secretary Pickering from Secretary of Navy

[TRENTON,]
[Rec^d^ *October 16, 1798*]

The following vessels in service, will probably require little or none of the attention of Col^l^ Pickering.

The *United States* — Frigate — Barry, has orders to cruise from Delaware Eastward, & to put into the port of New port, about the 15. Nov.

The *Constitution* — Nicholson — has orders to cruise from Cape Henry, Southward, & to go to Boston Harbour, about the 20' Nov.

The *Constellation* — Truxton — sailed for the Havanna, the beginning of September & may be now expected back. orders have been sent to Norfolk — & Charleston — to continue on the Southern Coast, till the middle of Nov. — & to go to New York about the 20th — or if the Bar should be an impediment to Newport, R Island.

The *Delaware* — Decatur — is cruising from Delaware, to Cape Henry, to return to Phil^a^ about the 15 Nov^r^

The *Baltimore*, 22 guns — Phillips is with Truxton — & is ordered to return to Balt about the 20 Nov^r^ — or if there should not be depth of Water sufficient, to stop at Norfolk.

The *Montezuma* 20 Guns — Murray — is ordered on an expedition to the West Indies — taking under command — the Brig *Norfolk* of 18 Guns — Williams — the Schooner *Retaliation* 14 guns, Bainbridge — & the *Eagle* Cutter Brig, Campbell of 14 Guns. It is probable from the shameful delay of Campbell in the Delaware he may have arrived at Norfolk too late to join Murray — in which case, he is to proceed to Georgia where the Cutter belongs, & guard that coast.

The *Herald*, 20 Guns — Sever

The *Pickering* — 14 or 16 guns — Chapman — are ordered on the service to Hallifax, with which Col. Pickering is acquainted. & are to return to Boston by the 20 Nov^r^

The other Vessels in Service, consist of Cutters — the most important of which are the [*Governor*] *Jay*, Leonard of New York — cruising from New York, South —

The *Virginia* — Bright, cruising from Norfolk South. —

There are three other Cutters, of 20 Guns belonging as follows

The *Scamnel* — Adams, N Hampshire
Genl Green — Price — Penn^a^
Diligence — [John] Brown — N Caro^a^

The *Scammel* is in port — has rec^d^ cruising & sailing orders — The *Genl Green* is fitting at Chester, & has sailing orders. *Diligence* is gone to North Carolina — under cruising orders. As to the Revenue

Cutters, the system established, will probably preclude all occasion of trouble to Col Pickering.

It will be observed by Col Pickering that all the Vessels will be in port, about the 15 to 20th Nov — that is a tempestuous Season, when there will be but little danger of Enemy Vessels on our Coasts — and in three or four weeks — at any rate, before the Rivers Freeze —, it may be desirable, that the whole should be sent into service in a warmer climate — with a view to which, orders have been given to

Mr. Higginson — Boston.
Gibbs & Channing — New port.
W Pennock — Norfolk.
J & E Wattson — New York —

naval agents — to make preparations as to provisions &ca

The Vessels not in Service — but which will certainly be ready to sail in Decbr are the *George Washington* — 32 guns — Flectcher — at Providence, where Capt Talbot acts as agent.

The *Ganges* — 26 guns — Tingey — Humphreys Agent. The *Merrimack*, Newbury — [Moses] Brown. 22 Guns.

The Brig (The Merchants are to name her) Capt Barron at Norfolk — 18 Guns — Nevison & Granbury appointed by the Merchts [to] act as agents.

I think I have made every necessary arrangement as to these vessels, so as to leave little to be done here — except perhaps, to remit some money to Talbot —

The Vessels which by great exertion on the part of the agents & Captains might be got into service in Decbr & I presume will be in Service in Jany are

The *Portsmouth* — McNeil — Portsmouth — 24 Guns — Higginson Agent.

The *Genl Green* — Perry — New port, of 24 Guns — Gibbs & Channing Agents.

The *Adams* — Morris, of 24 Guns — New York — J & E Wattson — agent.

As to these, I hope the arrangements made will prevent much trouble, to Col Pickering. The following vessels may probably, some of them get into service late in the winter — the Frigates, not till late next summer.

2 Brigs, building by the Merchts of Balto of 18 Guns each —
1 Ship 24 Guns, — building by the merchants of Charleston.
1 Ship 24 Guns — by the merchants of Boston.

And it is to be expected that Salem will undertake one Ship of 32 Guns.

1 Frigate building by the Merchts of Phila
1 by the Merchts of New York —
1 Public Frigate building at the same place Jas & E Wattson Agents.
1 Public Frigate building at Portsmouth, — J. Sheaffe Agent.
1 Public Frigate — building at Norfolk, Wm Pennock Agent.

With some of these Col Pickering may have some trouble — Mr Pennock, will not I believe want money 'til my return — nor J & E Wattson — J Sheaffe may.

The different agents have been written to on the subject of French Prisoners — Should any arrive, perhaps the arrangements made may, be found sufficient.

On anything that may occur requiring Col Pickering's attention, Mr Cottringer will examine what has been recd & written on such subject — & inform Col Pickering of the result.

On points relating to Commissions or appointments of officers, Mr. Goldsborough, having that branch of the business, in his charge, can give information.

Sincerely hoping that Col Pickering will find but little trouble in the business which he is so good to undertake, I have the honor to remain with the most perfect respect & esteem

His obliged & obed. Servt

BEN STODDERT.

Capt Talbott is to send on a list of officers for the *George Washington,* which list is to be presented to the President. In the meantime Talbot may call into Service, such as he finds necessary, under the assurance they will be appointed. The same thing respecting the Newbury port Committee.

[SDA. Misc. L., Sept.–Dec. 1798.]

To Surgeon Thomas Reynolds from Charles W. Goldsborough for Secretary Stoddert

[TRENTON,]
Navy Department October 16th 1798

Doctr THOMAS REYNOLDS

SIR, As you did not receive my Letter of the 15th in time to repair on board of the *Norfolk,* I have now to direct, that without delay you repair to Norfolk, and enter on board of the Vessel commanded by Capt Samuel Barron as Surgeon, and conform yourself to the Rules & Regulations of the Marine Service, and the Commands of your Superior Officers when you arrive at Norfolk, you will inform me of it. —

Messrs Nivison & Granbury will supply you with money to procure a chest of Medicine & Surgical Instruments —

I enclose you your Commission, as Surgeon in the Navy of the United States.

I am Sir &ca

CHS W. GOLDSBOROUGH
for BEN STODDERT —

[NDA. OSW, Vol. 1.]

To Purser Isaac Garretson from Captain Thomas, Truxtun U. S. Navy

[16 October 1798]

Whereas the Master of the United States Ship, *Constellation,* under my Command, has represented to me, that a Puncheon of Rum stowed in the Hold, has leaked out; I do hereby direct, that one of the Sea Lieutenants, with the said Master, and either the Boatswain or Carpenter, or both, hold a Survey on the said Puncheon, and issue Certificate, as shall be just, and honorable, setting forth how, and in what Manner, or from what Cause the said Puncheon of Rum has leaked out.

Given from under my Hand on Board the said Ship the 16th Day of October 1798.

To Mr ISAAC GARRETSON
Purser of the U. S. Ship Constellation.

[HS of Pa. NDA photostat. Truxtun's LB 1798–9.]

Extract from journal of U. S. Ship *Herald*, Captain James Sever, commander, 16 October 1798

This 24 hours first part modarate gales and Clear weather a Long Swell heaving from E n E under Duble Reef Topsails at 9 p m Boarded the Brig *Patty* from Baltimore 8 Days out Samuel Allen master Bound To Boston

Midle part modarate and Clear at 8 a m Lusd Light Sails To Dry

Latter part modarate and Clear under Duble Reef Topsails the Brig *Pickering* in Companey

Lattd Obbrs 39..45 North

[NDA. Journal kept by Joseph Strout, 1798.]

Extract from journal of James Pity, U. S. Frigate *Constitution*, 16 October 1798, Tuesday

First part this 24 hours fresh Breezes & Hazey Wr @ 2 P. M. ꝁ Ship Northwd & Sounded in 60 fms Sent down T. Gt Yards & Spoke our Consort. @ 8 Sounded in 32 fms @ 10 Sounded in 30 fms @ 12 Do sounded in 26 fathms colour'd Soundings. Spoke the *Virginia* & inform'd her the depth of Water let one Reef out of each Top Sail & set the Jibb & Main Sail @ 6 Saw a Ship Standg to the Southwd @ 7 up T. Gt Yards & set T. Gt Sails and gave chace. ꝁ Ship in Order to gain the Wind @ ½ past 7 the Chace hoisted a Red flagg at the Mizen T. Gt Mast head. finding her to be a friend Answd the Signal by a Checker'd flagg at Mizen T. Gt Mast head likewise our own private Signal at the Maine Do & Clear'd Ship for Action @ ½ past 8 in Small Sails the Chace having haul'd up our Courses. @ ½ past 9 Spoke the chace. She proved the U. S. Sloop of War *Baltimore* (Isaac Phillips Commander) of 18 Guns. Captain Nicholson ordered him to hoist out his boat and come on Board with Capt Phillips Spoke the *Virginia* and orderd the Capt of her to come on bd @ 10 A. M. the *Baltimores* boat Returnd and we Sail again both Vessels in Compy

[Latitude observed 31°. 45m No]

Ends in Pleasant Breezes and fair Weather.

[NDA.]

Extract from Captain Thomas Truxtun's journal, U. S. Frigate *Constellation*, 16 October 1798, Tuesday

Fresh Breezes, and Squally the first and Middle, the latter moderate, and fair: spoke one of the Convoy. At 7 A M sounded and found 130 Fathoms Water, fine dark and light Sand intermixed, this is the deepest Water I have any where found on Soundings Southward of Long Island, and believe it has not often been met with, as it must be a narrow Spit, running out between the Shoals of Cape Hatteras, and Cape Look out. Employed repairing the Rigging and Sails &c. &c. &c.

At Noon the South Shoal of Cape Hatteras bore N. N. E. ½ E. Twenty five Leagues Distance.

Latitude observed	33° .38′ Nº
Longitude observed	
⊙ West of ☽	76 .30 W.

[HS of Pa. NDA photostat.]

To President John Adams from the Secretary of Navy

[TRENTON,]
Navy Department October 17th 1798

JOHN ADAMS Esqr
President of the United States

SIR The Arrangement of the Rank of the Captains in the Navy, is a Subject which will soon demand attention. —

It will I believe be of great consequence to the character of our Navy, that the last four of the first Six Captains appointed, should be retained in the Service. They seem to be men who would do honor to any service. The paper enclosed Nº 1, details particularly, the circumstances connected with the pretensions of these Gentlemen. —

Talbot & Dale contend for the Rank given them by the first appointment in 1794: And without obtaining it, I fear neither will continue in the Service. If they do obtain it, I fear Truxton, a man of equal merit will not. — They served last War, — Truxton did not — In 1794 they were appointed to rank above Truxton; and have by no act of their own forfeited their right to such Rank. — On the other hand Truxton is in possession — his Commission, I understand is Nº three.

He may urge in his favor the Act of Congress, directing the building of three Frigates & discontinuing the other three; And the Act of the Executive in making a second nomination of Talbot, Dale & Sever; on the principle no doubt that their former appointments ceased to exist, when the building of the Frigates destined for them was abandoned.

It is probable an opportunity will offer in December of getting these three men together, — And some mode may be devised to give satisfaction to them all — In the mean time I have written to Talbot & Dale, that the subject will then be taken up, and have urged to retain their Commissions at least till that time. —

The relative rank of the Captains who have been lately appointed, seems to require more immediate consideration — Almost any arrangement of these officers can be made now, and without producing resignation, at least without producing Resignations of those most desireable to be retained in the Service.

It is however strictly right to exercise the power of giving them (I mean those who have been appointed since I have been in Office, beginning with Philips) the relative rank to which their respective merits entitle them: For they have generally been appointed, not because the person appointed was to be preferred to others at the time on the List of Candidates, — (The Rule which governs in all other cases) but merely because a vessel was in greater forwardness at the place where he happened to reside, than at other places. And it was conceived to be proper to make appointments only as employment could be found for the Captains appointed, and to make them from the places furnishing the vessels, & where the Crews were to be obtained. Thus Philips of Baltimore was appointed the 3rd July because the ship at that place required the attention of a Captain — And the Merchants there, knew of no person to recommend in Preference. — Thus too Williams of Norfolk was appointed the 17th July, because a Brig at Norfolk was expected to be soon in Service. —

The paper No 2 Exhibits the names of all the Captains with the order of their appointments, placing some of the least experienced, if not the least meritorious Captains too high in Rank — and others of greater Experience, and I believe greater merit too low. —

I therefore take the Liberty to propose; — To place McNeill, Murray, Tingey, Fletcher & Chapman, and in the order they are named, between Morris & Philips.

The arrangement of Captains not noticing the first six, would then Stand — Decatur of Pensylva Perry of Rhode Island; Morris of New York, McNeill of Massachusetts, Murray of Pennsylvania; Tingey of New Jersey, Fletcher of Massachusetts, Chapman of Massachusetts, Philips of Maryland, Williams of Virginia, Cross of S. Carolina, Barron of Virginia, Tryon of Connecticut; Brown of Massachusetts. —

Williams, under Murray's Command on the Expedition to the West Indies, had a Commission older than Murray's — But having confidence in Murray, and not knowing Williams's true character, indeed being afraid to trust him with a Command of so much importance to the honor of the Navy, I was reduced to the necessity of losing the service of Williams's Brig of 18 Guns, or giving the Command to Murray, by inserting words in his Commission, to give him rank before the date of Williams's Commission, but under the express condition that the Words so inserted should be erased on his return from the Expedition, and that he should not on that account quit the service.

Should the Idea I have suggested, placing him & others, higher on the List of Captains, than their present standing, be approved, it can easily be done without altering the dates, by inserting in their Commissions the words "To take rank from any particular period." —

I am confident no Injury can result to the service, from the proposed arrangement. And if it be not made, it will frequently occur that the services of a vessel must be lost because the Commander cannot be trusted with the command of more vessels than his own; as would have been the case in the late instance of Murray & Williams, had it not been for the Expedient I ventured to adopt.

I have the honor to be &ca

[NDA. Nom. Appts. LB 1798–1820.]

To Secretary of State from James Yard

BRUNSWICK *Octr 17. 1798.*

SIR. Having resolved, by the advice of my friends, to Suspend any publication respecting the Report, lately circulated on my Subject,

I think it incumbent on me to transmit to you Copies of the Documents on which it has been founded, in order that you may be able to form a proper Estimate of its Merits

I am with Sentiments of Respect

Sir

Your mo h^ble^ Servt

JAMES YARD

TIMOTHY PICKERING Esqr

Secretary of State.

[Mass. HS. Pickering Papers, Vol. 23.]

[Enclosure No. 1]

STATEMENT OF GEORGE GILLASPY

Mr Yard was Supposed by Persons in the West Indies, to be an Agent of V. Hughes, for the following Reasons, that his Vessels traded there without any Danger of being Captured by french privateers — That not long Since one of his Vessels was captured but on her being carried in She was immediately cleared by Victor Hughes and the Prize Master put in Irons and sent to France, for treating the Captain of the said Vessel ill, a Merchant of St Bartholomews, whose name is Joseph Crathorn & another Gentleman mentioned those Circumstances on the Frigates Quarter Deck in the Hearing of Several Gentlemen, when I immediately made a memorandum of it —

(Signed) GEO. GILLASPY.

[Mass. HS. Pickering Papers, Vol. 23.]

[Enclosure No. 2]

JOINT STATEMENT OF THOMAS FITZSIMONS AND PHILIP NICKLIN

We were present at a Meeting between Mr Yard & Capt Barry at Richardets Tavern, when the former asked the latter upon what authority he had reported his (Mr Yard's) being Concerned in Privateers under French Colours— Capt Barry replied that it had been mentioned to him by a Mr Mullowny one of his Officers, who had been on Shore at Tortola, where it was told to him by a Dr Bartlett, that a Letter from Mr Yard to a Mr Reeve of St Croix, or from Mr Reeve to Mr Yard had been intercepted, and that Mullowny had in his possession a Memorandum written, but as he believed not Signed by the Said Bartlett to that Effect— and that when Mr Mullowny first told him (Capt Barry) of the Declaration he replied that he did not believe it & Supposed the author was Some worthless privateersman & an Enemy of Mr Yards — That Since his arrival he had mentioned the Circumstance in the hearing of a person who he Supposed had repeated it; He always impressed his Disbelief of the Truth of it which indeed was his Reason for mentioning it, because he Supposed others would Speak of it without that Qualification — He added that he understood Bartlett's Character was notorious as a rapacious privateer owner; upon which Mr Yard Said there was a Bartlett who formerly commanded a Privateer, when Capt Barry remarked that he did not know whether it was him or not, but believed the Man in Question was called Dr Bartlett — The

Conversation then turning upon the Writing in Mr Mullowny's possession. Capt Said that Mr Yard Should have a Copy of it if he required it; on which Mr Yard told him he should be obliged to him for it — This being the Substance of what passed at the Meeting we have committed it to Writing while fresh in our Memories to be referred to by either party if they Should deem it necessary —

Signed Thos Fitzsimons
Philip Nicklin

September 29th 1798.

[Mass. HS. Pickering Papers, Vol. 23.]

[Enclosure No. 3]

To Thomas Fitzsimons from Captain John Barry, U. S. Navy

Frigate *United States Oct. 1, 1798.*

Dear Sir The Within Memorandum alluded to in yours of the 28 Ulto cannot at present be found, however, to obviate that I have requested Mr Mullowny to give a minute Detail of the Conversation that took place between him & Mr Bartlett in such a Manner as to be able if called upon to prove it & in order to give you every Satisfaction respecting that Business I have likewise inclosed a Copy of a Conversation that took place between Dr Gillespie & a Gentleman from St Bartholomews a few days previous to Mr Mullowny's been sent to Tortola —

I am with Esteem
Dear Sir
Your most Humble Servt

(Sigd) John Barry —

Thomas Fitzsimons Esqr —

[Mass. HS. Pickering Papers, Vol. 23.]

[Enclosure No. 4]

To Captain John Barry, U. S. Navy, from Lieutenant John Mullowny, U. S. Navy

Frigate *United States*
Off New Castle — Oct. 1, 1798.

John Barry Esqr

Sir According to your orders I proceeded to Tortola, after Landing, I met two Gentlemen, who said they were Americans, I was in their Company a few Minutes at the Tavern, when a Gentleman (whose name was Bartlett) came to me & said as I was an American officer he would feel himself honoured, if I would go to his House, I told him as it was the Nation he respected, I would accept the Invitation and accompanied him to his House, he procured me a Horse & went with me to the President of the Island, it was in the Course of Conversation he informed me, any property of Mr Thomas Reeves of St Croix was condemnable in St Croix Tortola as being concerned in French privateers, and that it was Supposed Mr James Yard Merchant of Philadelphia was concerned with him, this I took in writing & gave it to you when I returned to the Ship in the Presence of Capt Decatur.

Doctor Bartlett appears to be a Man of Confidence with the president of the Island, and to all appearance a Man [of] Respectability, as the Memorandum is mislaid, that I gave you, the following is near the same taken from Dr Gillaspy's Book of Notes —

"An intercepted Letter from Mr Reeve (with whom Mr Yard is Supposed to be concerned) to a french Man is on Record at Tortola Extract" My dear friend The owners of Small picaroons make rapidly large fortunes & I think we with our large Capitol ought to do it much sooner — The Impression this Information made on my mind was Strongly against Mr Yard as I had heard a corroborating Report at St Bartholomews, Tho' I was willing to disbelieve it, as I mentioned to some of my fellow officers, that I was sorry to hear it, as I always esteemed Mr Yard as a friend of mine & at the Same Time mentioned an Instance of a friendly offer he had made to serve me, the above I believe is the substance of the Information obtained at Tortola and all I can Say against Mr Yard or his Character —

I am Sir

Your Hum. Servt

(Signed) Jno Mullowny.

[Mass. HS. Pickering Papers, Vol. 23.]

Extract from journal of Lieutenant John Mullowny, U. S. Frigate *United States*, 17 October 1798

A 10 A. M. Cape Henlopen bore W. by N. Distance 3 leagues.

[NA.]

Extract from journal of James Pity, U. S. Frigate *Constitution*, 17 October 1798, Wednesday

First part this 24 hours fresh breezes and clear Weather. Saw a Strange Sail a head made all sail and gave chace @ ½ past 2 Saw the land bearg W. N. W. 6 Leagues dist. at 3 took in Light Sails and K Ship & Stood to the Southwd Sounded in 10 fathms @ 4 Spoke the *Virginia* Capt Bright Comr who Inform'd us that he Spoke a Brig from Newby Port bound to Charleston S. Carolina Said he Saw the Light of Do on the 16th Inst bearg N. b. W. @ 6 P. M. Sounded in 12 fms at [space] the *Baltimores* boat came on bd for Orders. @ 10 P. M. Sounded in 18 fms In T. Gt Sails. at Midnight Steady breezes @ 6 A. M. K Ship N. W. & Westd at 10 call'd all hands to Muster at the Same time Capt Nicholson Declar'd Phillip Jarvis to be actg Lieut & Major of the Signals.

[Latitude observed 31°. 23m No]

[NDA.]

Extract from Captain Thomas Truxtun's journal, U. S. Frigate *Constellation*, 17 October 1798, Wednesday

A strong Northerly Gale with a very cross and high Head Sea, under close Reefed Top Sails and Courses most of the Time, keeping on the most favourable Tack, to take Advantage of the Current; and place Ourselves in an eligible Situation, for a natural Change.

Employed all Hands at making sundry Repairs in the Rigging &c; occasioned by the Gale, and great Agitation of the Ship, owing to the Sea, and Gulph Stream. Saw two of the Convoy plying to Windward; I suppose, most of them are a Head, as I have endeavoured to keep without them.

The South Shoal of Cape Hateras at Noon bore N. N. E. Eleven Leagues Distance.

Latitude observed 34°.15′ Nº
Longitude Account 75.36 W.

[HS of Pa. NDA photostat.]

To Tench Francis, Purveyor, from Secretary of State

TRENTON *Oct. 18. 1798.*

TENCH FRANCIS Esqr *Purveyor.*

SIR, A letter rec^d last evening from Clement Humphreys informed me of the Arrival of the *Sophia*, Captain Geddes, at New Castle, and that she was coming up to Marcus Hook. You suggested the idea of her being employed to bring home the crews of the armed vessels. Mr Joshua Humphreys (to whom I proposed the question) answered that she could be armed as a vessel of war in three weeks. I wish you could consult with him — make a calculation of the expence — and of the expence also of sending her to Algiers for the sole purpose of bringing home those crews. Altho' she should be fully armed, her crew should be moderate, to make room for the others in returning.

It is time to see what is wanting to send the three Algerine vessels to sea, and have the whole put on board. I have answered the Messrs Murray's that I shall not employ their ship for the return of our seamen. — The season wastes apace — no time is now to be lost.

I am &c.

T. PICKERING

[SDA. Dom. L., Vol. 11.]

To the First Secretary of State (Spain) from D. Humphreys, United States Minister to Spain

MADRID *October 18th 1798*

(Nº 171)

To the first SECRETARY OF STATE

SIR, Notwithstanding several of my letters to your Excellency on important subjects have remained for so long a time unanswered; I cannot avoid bringing the following new cases to your knowledge. A short time ago, Captain Henry Prince of the Ship *Astrea* and Captain Henry Bool of the Ship *Joseph* (belonging to Citizens of the U. S. of America) asked and obtained permission of the Governor of Cadiz to put some cannon on board, for their self defense, in their passage home to America. After they had been at a very considerable expence in consequence of the said permission, the aforesaid Governor sent for them, took from them the *written Licenses*, and informed them that they could not depart from that port, without first landing their guns, or until he should receive farther orders from his Court. I have, therefore, to request that the competent instructions for authorizing the departure of the vessels in question, with their Guns &c. (in conformity to the original Licences) may be expedited as early as possible to the aforesaid Governor; and that a similar authority may be extended to cases of farther applications — without which, it appears an obvious truth, that the commerce between the ports of the U. S. and those of Spain (so interesting to both countries) will incur the danger of being entirely annihilated. In confirmation of the good policy of this measure, particularly for Spain, I beg leave to mention it has recently been practical with such success at Malaga, that ten vessels (belonging to Citizens of the U. S.) sailed from thence together, loaded with Spanish produce, which would not otherwise have been exported.

With sentiments of perfect respect

I have the honour to be, &c

D. HUMPHREYS

[SDA. Disp. Spain, Bk 4, Humphreys.]

From Mariano Luis de Urquijo, Madrid, to D. Humphreys, United States Minister to Spain

[Translation]

[14 November 1798]

I am in possession of Your Excellency's note of the 18th of last month in which you advise me that after the Governor of Cadiz had given permission to Henry Prince and Henry Bool, masters of the vessels *Astrea* and *Josef*, owned by citizens of the United States of America, to provide the said vessels with cannon for defence in their return passage to America, he informed them that they could not depart from that port without landing the said cannon, or until he had instructions from the Court in the matter, and Your Excellency begs me to give as promptly as possible the necessary orders to the said Governor for permitting the said vessels to sail without delay with their guns, asking at the same time that this authority be extended to similar cases of further application.

In reply I have to inform Your Excellency that the King my Master has ordered that none of the said vessels be permitted to carry guns.

May God preserve Your Excellency for many years.

Sn. LORENZO.

14 Nov. 98.

I kiss your hand and am your very obedient servant

Acting for Dn. Franco. de Saavedra prevented by illness

MARIANO LUIS DE URQUIJO

Extract from journal of U. S. Ship *Herald*, Captain James Sever, U. S. Navy, commander, 18 October 1798

This 24 hours first part modarate gales and Cloudy weather under Duble Reef Topsails at 6 p m Sounded in 21 fathoms Course red Sand at Sounded in same at 10.20 fathoms

Midle part modarate gales and Clear weather at 12 Sounded in 20 Sounded Every hour at 5 a m 17 fathoms wore Ship To

Eastward Saw a Ship in the N E out Reef Sett Top G Sails and gave Chase the Ship *Favourate* from New York Bound To Jamaica 24 hours out

Latter part fresh gales and thick Dark Cloudy weather Brig *Pickring* in Company

No Obbrs To Day

[NDA. Journal kept by Joseph Strout, 1798.]

Extract from journal of James Pity, U. S. Frigate *Constitution*, 18 October 1798, Thursday

First part this 24 Fresh breezes and clear Weather. @ 2 P. M. K to the Northward @ 4 D^{o} Shorten'd Sail for the *Baltimore* She being to Leward five Miles tried for Sound^{gs} 100 f^{ms} No Bottom @1/2 past 7 Spoke the *Baltimore* Inform'd her that at 8 P. M. we should hoist 3 Lights at the Mizen Peake and K Ship wch was done Accordingly and Stood to the N^{o} & Eastw^{d} @ 4 A. M. Sounded in 40 f^{ms} @ 7 Saw a Strange sail ahead made more Sail at the Same time a Man f^{m} Mast head made the Land a head @ 1/2 p^{t} 10 the *Baltimore* made ye Signal for Land @ 1/2 past 11 Bore away. Kept the Lead going in both chains depth of Water 7 f^{ms} Ships Crew empl^{yd} differently.

[Latitude Observed 32.46. N^{o}]

[NDA.]

Extract from Captain Thomas Truxtun's journal, U. S. Frigate *Constellation*, 18 October 1798, Thursday

Fresh Gales, and cloudy Weather with a high Sea running from the North East, under close Reefed Top Sails, and fore Sail most of the Time. Several of the Convoy in Sight beating to Windward. Employed repairing, and keeping in Order the Rigging and Sails &c. &c. &c. Sounded at 5 P M, and found 25 fathoms Water; at Meridian sounded again, and got no Ground.

Cape Hatteras at Noon bore W. 3/4 N 16 Leagues Distance.

Latitude observed 35°.00′ N^{o}

Longitude Account 74.48 W.

[HS of Pa. NDA photostat.]

To Secretary of State from Samuel Hodgdon

PHILADELPHIA *19th Octo. 1798.*

DEAR SIR — I know not to whom it officially appertains to put the Algerine Fleet to Sea — but as it appears to me that something is wrong in the business as it now stands, I have thought it will not be amiss, to state to you that needless expense is accumulating — The Ship is ready for Sea, and has fallen down to the Cove to wait her orders for sailing — the Captain expects demurrage to commence immediately — this I conclude is understood by the Charter Party, of which he may have no knowledge — Captain Mayley says he is ready to sail at an hours notice, but does not know who to look to for orders — the other Vessels are *not* ready — Cap^{n} Smith is at this late hour looking for *ballast* — the Season is far advanced, and unless the death of the Dey may have caused a pause, I see not why they may not proceed — I am myself at a loss to determine, whether the getting them away falls under your notice or that of the Secretary of the Navy — but I do know that the business is at a stand, and all immediately concerned are desireous to receive orders to govern them in the present State of things — I conclude you are enjoying the Company of the Worthy Pinckney — will not his Country delight to honor him too — I trust they will — but Gerry — poor Gerry is in the back ground I hope he will also come forward, and prove that he is entitled to the Aye — well done good and faithful Servant — Present our respects to Mrs Pickering — Many Deaths this morning — We all remain well — adeiu —

Affectionately yours

SAMUEL HODGDON.

Colonel TIMOTHY PICKERING —

[Mass. HS. Pickering Papers, Vol. 42, p. 98.]

Extract from journal of U. S. Ship *Herald*, Captain James Sever, U. S. Navy, commander, 19 October 1798

This 24 hours first part Strong gales and Cloudy weather at 3 p m Saw 3 Sail at 5 p m the one Standing To the S S E past us hoisted English Coulors Shoing a Teer of guns wore Ship and gave Chace Sett all Sail at 6 gave over Chace halld Tue By the wind at 7 Close Reeft Topsails at 10 Reeft Foresail handed Fore & mizen Topsail

Midle part Strong gales and thick weather at 12 a m wore Ship Sent Down F G Yards hausd T G mast at 3 a m a Learg Ship under Short Sail Run foul of us Cared away our figger Head and Jibb Boome and Spritsail yard all By the Board and Sprung our Bowsprit house all aback and Dropt Clear of hur Latter part hard gales and Cloudy weather under Reef Foresail and Close Reef main Topsail

No obbrsvation To Day

[NDA. Journal kept by Joseph Strout, 1798.]

Extract from journal of James Pity, U. S. Frigate *Constitution*, 19 October 1798, Friday

First part this 24 hours fresh Breezes & Clear Weather @ 1 P. M. a Pilot came along Side in wch Capt Nicholson sent his letters @ 2 Charlestown light bore W. b. S. dist. 3 Leagues Sound^gs^ from 6 to 8 f^ms^ @ 3 P. M. haild the *Baltimore* and told him we Intended to stand off and on all Night and run in for the Light house in the Morn^g^ haild the *Virginia* and told him to stand off and on with the *Baltimore* Shortend Sail @ 8 made Sail again.

Middle part Cloudy. at 6 A. M. Saw the Land on the lee bow. @ 7 fired a Gun & hoisted our Colo^rs^ a Signal for a Pilot boat a head @ 8 She came along Side Capt Phillips of the *Baltimore* came on b^d^ Charlestown light W. N. W. 4 Leagues dist.

[Latt^d^ p^r^ Md^n^ Altitude 32° 50^m^ N^o^.]

[NDA.]

Extract from journal of Lieutenant John Mullowny, U. S. Frigate *United States*, 19 October 1798

Stiff gales, and rain
Set up Larboard Top-mast rigging
At 3 P. M. down royal masts
At 4 wore ship to set up S^{d} Topmast rigging. Strong Gales —
Very hard Gales — handed the Fore Top-sail
A heavy sea from the N. E.
Ship pitching very much the sea running very high
[Long. Obs^{d} 73.47
Lat^{d} p^{r} acc^{t} 37.50.]

[NA.]

Extract from Captain Thomas Truxtun's journal, U. S. Frigate *Constellation*, 19 October 1798, Friday

Sounded at 2 P M and found Seventy five Fathoms Water, Cape Hatteras at that Time bearing West ½ North, about 13 Leagues Distance.

A heavy Gale of Wind from the Northward and a high sea running accompanied with hazy Squalls of small Rain, and heavy Clouds; Launched Top Gallant Masts, and got in Jib of Jib Boom, unbent the Spritsail and got up Runners, and Tackles, as an additional Security to the lower Masts &c.

Under the close Reefed Main top Sail, and double reefed fore Sail, Mizen, Mizen and fore top Mast Stay Sail.

Latitude Account 35°.21′ N.
Longitude Account 74.12 W.

[HS of Pa. NDA photostat.]

Extract from journal of James Pity, U. S. Frigate *Constitution*, 20 October 1798, Saturday

First part this 24 hours hazy Weather fired a gun & hoisted our Coll^{rs} @ ½ past 1 the pilot boat came along Side with Mr Henery Long for our Pilot.

Middle part fresh Breezes & Clear @ ½ past 1 A. M. Saw a Sail on our weather bow bear^{g} down on us. haild him but Rec^{d} no Answer. find^{g} he was likely to Run foul of us put our helm up in order to avoid him @ 7 Sent down Mizen T. G. T. Mast & got up a New fidded Royal mast

Ship Stand^{g} off and on Charleston Light house Ships Company employ'd variously Capt Nicholson put the people on allowance of 5 pints water p^{r} day.

[NDA.]

Extract from journal of Lieutenant John Mullowny, U. S. Frigate *United States*, 20 October 1798

Very hard gales —
A violent squall, Split the Fore Sail — handed the weather side & lay to under goose wing
A very heavy head sea at ½ 4 P. M. spring the Bowsprit, kept the ship before the Wind, to secure the Fore Mast & Bowsprit —
At midnight, more moderate

All hands employed in repairing the damage done during the Gale
☞ those remarks ought to be 35.10 for the following day and them for this.

[Long. p^{r} Acc^{t} 73..19]
[Lat^{d} Obs^{d} 35.18]

[NA.]

Extract from Captain Thomas Truxtun's journal, U. S. Frigate *Constellation*, 20 October 1798, Saturday

Hard Gales, and a high Sea running. The Ship under the same Canvass as Yesterday. The Guns housed on both Sides, and Ports lashed in. Spoke one of the Convoy, the Schooner *Venus* bound to New York, and saw several Others.

Latitude observed 35°.40′ N^{o}
Longitude Account 74.12 W.

[HS of Pa. NDA photostat.]

To Joseph Hiller, Collector, Salem, from Secretary of State

DEPARTMENT OF STATE
Trenton New Jersey Oct. 21. 1798

JOSEPH HILLER Esqr *Collector of the Customs Salem.*

SIR, — I have before me a letter of the 10th inst. from George Crowningshield and Sons to the Comptroller of the Treasury, which mentions that you have doubts of the propriety of granting a commission under the "Act further to protect the commerce of the United States," for the Ship *America*.

Though the *America* appears not to be entitled to a Register or Mediterranean passport, yet as she is American property and entitled to protection as such, and as the policy of the act above cited is entirely different from those by which the privileges of American built vessels are defined and secured under the laws of Revenue, I am of opinion, that a commission may be properly granted. The Secretary of the Treasury entirely concurs with me in this opinion.

I am, Sir, respectfully &c.

TIMOTHY PICKERING.

[SDA. Dom. L. Vol. 11.]

Extract from journal of Lieutenant John Mullowny, U. S. Frigate *United States*, 21 October 1798

Hard Gales — reefed fore sail & Mizen Stay sail —
The Shifting Ballast broke loose & Killed a Mirine Name James Jackson & injured another very much
Burried the Mirine —
In Mizen Topsail gale increasing, washed away some part of the Carved work of the head —

[Long. p^{r} acc^{t} 71.42
Lat^{d} Obs^{d} 35.10]

[NA.]

Extract from journal of James Pity, U. S. Frigate *Constitution*, 21 October 1798, Sunday

First part this 24 hours fresh Breezes & Clear Weather. @ ½ past one a Boat came from Charleston and Several Gentlemen came on Board. @ ½ past 5 the Light house bore west dist. 7 Leagues. Ship Stand^{g} off & on under easy Sail. Light airs from the N^{o} & Westw^{d} Middle part calm. @ 1 A. M. a Light breeze Sprin^{g} up wore Ship to the westw^{d} @ 3 Wore Ship to the Eastward @ 6 A. M. wore Ship to the Westw^{d} again Got our Anchor up & Buoy Rope Ready for com^{g} too off Charleston Barr @ 10 A. M. Anchor'd with our Starboard Anchor in 7 fath^{ms} water hard Bottom Light house bear^{g} W. N. W. Dis^{t} 7½ miles Rec^{d} on B^{d} from a Pilot Boat a quantity Ships Stores.

[NDA.]

Extract from Captain Thomas Truxtun's journal, U. S. Frigate *Constellation*, 21 October 1798, Sunday

Throughout the whole of these Twenty four Hours, we have had a hard and violent Gale of Wind from the Northward, with a heavy and cross Sea running; two Schooners of the Convoy in sight. Laying to most of the Time, under a double reefed fore Sail. At 9 A M discovered the Head of the Rudder to be split; Shipt the spare Tiller in the Cabbin, and steered with it, intending to examine the Head of the Rudder below the Cabbin Deck, as soon as it is moderate, and we can get at it.

Latitude observed 35°.56′ N.
Longitude Account 73.29 W.

[HS of Pa. NDA photostat.]

To Captain John Adams, Revenue Cutter *Scammel*, from Timothy Pickering, for Secretary of Navy

[TRENTON,]
Navy Department 22nd October 1798

Capt JOHN ADAMS
of the Cutter Scammel

SIR Presuming that your Vessel is prepared in all respects for a Cruise, I have now to direct, that you proceed to sea, and consider your Cruising ground to extend from Portsmouth Eastward as far as Machias, & Southward, as far as Cape Cod & Nantucket. —

You are to use your best endeavours to protect this extent of Coast from the depredations of French Cruisers, as well as to give all the protection in your power to the Commerce of the Country. —

You are not confined to any distance from the Coast, but are allowed to indulge a spirit of Enterprize; And if you should hear of Enemy Vessels further North or South, than your Limits, you will consider that you are not confined to Limits. —

You will promote discipline and order among your Crew, and inculcate a high sense of the honor of the American Flag, which is to be maintained at every hazard. — They should be exercised daily at your Guns. —

You will remember, that we are at War only with the French Armed Vessels, and persons found on board of them. — All other Nations are entitled to, and must receive from you, Civility & good offices

Should you meet any American Vessels, Captured by the Armed Vessel of any other Nation at War except the French, you must not attempt a Recapture. — And should you see the armed Vessel of any other Nation than the French in the Act of Capturing any American Vessel, you cannot lawfully interfere to prevent such Capture. — It must be presumed that the Courts of such Nation will render Justice. —

You will by every opportunity write me the events of your Cruise, and never omit doing it when you go into any Port. —

Having the Command of a Revenue Cutter, you are to obey the orders you will receive from the proper authority; on the subject of the Revenue. —

I enclose Instructions authorizing the Capture of French Armed Vessels &c[a] —

I have the honor to be, &c[a]

TIMOTHY PICKERING
for the Sec[y] of the Navy.

[NDA. OSW, Vol. 1.]

To Joshua Humphreys, Naval Constructor, from Secretary of State

DEPARTMENT OF STATE
Trenton Oct. 22. 1798.

M[r] JOSHUA HUMPHREYS.

SIR, I have concluded to send the *Sophia* to Algiers to bring home the officers and crews of the three armed vessels destined thither. Capt. Geddes informs me that the *Sophia* is not calculated to be mounted with the complement of cannon proportioned to her tonnage on account of the height of her deck: but that she could take on board a few carriage guns. Carronades would be best, if we could get them. I beg you immediately to consult with Capt. Geddes and arm her in such manner as you and he shall think best.

I understand that Captain Maley is ready for sea, or can be ready in two days. I have concluded that he should sail with the large Store Ship, and convoy her to Algiers. The ship being a dull sailer, by having the start of the other vessel by a fortnight, or ten days, she may arrive about as soon as the other two armed vessels and the *Sophia*. Captain Geddes says the *Sopia* wants a mainmast and perhaps some spars, and a pump. I shall rely on your providing these things expeditiously.

Whatever is wanting to complete the armed brigantine and the other Schooner I must desire you to have provided without delay. For whatever depends on M[r] Francis you will write to him.

If any difficulties present, inform me without delay. I am with great regard &c.

TIMOTHY PICKERING.

[SDA. Dom. L., Vol. 11.]

To Thomas Nelson, U. S. Attorney, Virginia District, from Secretary of State

DEPARTMENT OF STATE
Trenton Oct. 22. 1798.

THOMAS NELSON Esq[r]
Att[y] U. States, Virg[a] District.

SIR, On Saturday evening, the 20th instant, I received your letter of the 10th relative to the ship *Niger*, captured by Captain Nicholson in the *Constitution* frigate.

The case appeared to me, and I believe to the Secretary of the Navy, to warrant an immediate discharge of the *Niger:* but Captain Nicholson's letters to him manifested his conviction that she was a good prize. I saw the letters and I recollect in one he said he had engaged Mr. Wickham in the prosecution and that it was M[r] Wickham's opinion that the *Niger* was a good prize. Indeed the eagerness of Captain Nicholson to procure a condemnation savoured of rapacity. And in the very letter in which he informed of the death of his son (the consequence of this unfortunate capture) his thoughts seemed wholly engrossed with his prize and the means of ensuring, if possible, a condemnation. The captain and other officers of the *Niger* complain bitterly of the rough, ungentlemanly treatment they experienced from Captain Nicholson, while they speak in handsome and grateful terms of his officers and of the Artillery officers at Norfolk to whose care they were committed. Upon the whole view of the case, I am inclined to think that there is not another captain in the American Navy who with the evidence of the Ship's papers and the information of the passengers (one of them an American citizen) would have imagined the *Niger* a subject of capture. But it would seem that Captain Nicholson made no enquiry whatever of the passengers; for in his letters to the Secretary of the Navy he does not let drop a word of information from them; altho', as above mentioned, one was an American Gentleman, and the other an English Officer with his Lady and Children. Such characters were peculiarly qualified, and, one would suppose, inclined to give correct information. I expect it will appear on the trial that the capture was wholly unwarrantable; and consequently that damages must be decreed to the captured. Nevertheless, I have thought it expedient that the trial should be had, in order not only to prevent any complaint on the part of Captain Nicholson and ship's company, that a good prize was improperly given up, of which they would have been entitled to one half, — but by clearly ascertaining the facts, to enable the President to form a correct opinion of Captain Nicholson's conduct. This conduct I am persuaded will excite some resentment in the breast of every man concerned for the honour of his country: yet I wish not that resentment should in the Statement aggravate a fault; but pity, on the other hand, should nothing extenuate.

The British Minister has written to me concerning the *Niger*, declaring her to be a British vessel, and desiring she may be immediately restored. A copy of his letter is inclosed. M[r] Bond the British Consul at Philadelphia, had before written to me on the same subject: but I answered him that it was judged adviseable to let a trial take place. I have now only to express my hopes that the trial will be had and finished at the time appointed by the Judge for the sitting of the Court — the last Tuesday of the present month. Any further delay will swell the bill of damages and costs; and perhaps be peculiarly injurious to the officers and owners of the *Niger* in regard to a depending voyage. And the case being a clear one, any adjournment of the cause will appear to the owners and officers very vexatious.

I am very respectfully, Sir, your most obt servant

TIMOTHY PICKERING

[SDA. Dom. L., Vol. 11.]

To John Murray and Son, New York, from Secretary of State

DEPARTMENT OF STATE
Trenton Oct. 22. 1798

Messrs JOHN MURRAY AND SON *New York.*

GENTLEMEN: Since I last wrote you, I have concluded to order one of the armed vessels destined for Algiers (a Schooner, Captain Maley) to be dispatched immediately, and to take the store ship *Hero* under her convoy, if the latter should not sail too soon. I understand Captain Maley might be got to sea in two or three days. I have sent orders accordingly. The *Hero* and Captain Maley by having the start of the other armed vessels, by ten days or a fortnight, may reach Algiers as soon as the latter.

The Secretary of the Treasury has put into my hands your letter to him of the 16th instant, making a tender of about 10,000 lbs of good powder and about 13 tons of copper in blocks. The powder he thinks we do not want: the copper may be convenient in the naval department, for which, in the absence of Mr Stoddert, I am acting. I therefore take the liberty to refer you to James Watson Esqr Naval Agent at New York; who may want the copper to make bolts for the ships building at New York. You may also, if you please, inform me of the price of your powder, noting whether it is cannon or musket powder, and if both, the proportion of each.

I am &c.

TIMOTHY PICKERING.

[SDA. Dom. L., Vol. 11.]

Extract from journal of James Pity, U. S. Frigate *Constitution*, 22 October 1898, Monday

First part this 24 hours light airs Inclining to calm. Several Gentn came on Bd from Charleston to View the Ship @ 5 P. M. the Company departed man'd the yard & gave them 3 Cheers.

Middle part Light Breezes & clear Weather @ 5 A. M. call'd all hands & Wash'd Decks.

Latter part clear Weather Stay'd the fore mast & Set up the Rigging Fleeted the main Stay & Set it up with the Rigging Sail makers making Hammock Cloths & Waist Cloths. Ship Laying at Single Anchor.

[NDA.]

Extract from Captain Thomas Truxtun's journal, U. S. Frigate *Constellation*, 22 October 1798, Monday

The first Part fresh Breezes, the Middle and Latter moderate, and fair Weather with a very high and cross Sea running. Employed drying various Stores and Materials, repairing little Rubbings, occasioned by the Gale &c.

Three Vessels in Sight, which I take to be Part of the Convoy.
Latitude observed 36°.6′ N°.
Longitude Account 73.46 W.

[HS of Pa. NDA photostat.]

To Captain Moses Brown, U. S. Navy, from Secretary of Navy

[TRENTON,]
Navy Department October 23rd 1798

Capt MOSES BROWN
of the Merrimack

SIR I have received your Letter of the 17th Instt informing of the Launching of the Ship *Merrimack.* —

You will find enclosed a List of the Pay allowed to the Petty Officers in the Navy —

I have the honor &ca

G. C.[GARRETT COTTRINGER]
for the Secy. of the Navy

[NDA. OSW, Vol. 1.]

To John Habersham, Collector, Savannah, from Secretary of State

DEPARTMENT OF STATE
Trenton Octr 23, 1798.

JOHN HABERSHAM Esq.
Collector — Savannah

SIR, The Secretary of the Treasury has handed me your letter to him of the 1st of this month. I have already forwarded to you a permission to clear Mr Anciaue's vessel wherein there was a blank left for the master's name. You now request on the owner's behalf that permission may be granted to him to import on her return a cargo of coffee from the French West Indies. The Act of Congress suspending commercial intercourse with the French possessions authorizes the President to grant Special exemptions from its operation only for two purposes, that of aiding the departure of Frenchmen from the United States and also of national and political intercourse: it is plain therefore that he can give no authority to individuals to import or export merchandize by way of trade and commerce. But as some of the merchants have debts owing them in the French possessions, which were contracted previous to the passing of the Act, its spirit is considered as not prohibiting vessels sailing under the President's permission from bringing back the amount of such debts either in cash or merchandize: this indulgence will accordingly be allowed to them but to prevent fraud, probably a circular instruction to the Collectors, respecting the entry of these vessels on their return, will be framed and transmitted.

I am, Sir, &c.

TIMOTHY PICKERING.

[SDA. Dom. L., Vol. 11.]

From Lieutenant Anthony Gale, U. S. M. C., to Major Commandant Burrows, U. S. M. C.

NEW CASTLE *Octr 23, 1798*

SIR Excuse my not writing before as the Marshall (Mr. Hamilton) was out of Town at a Vendue for three days when he returned he informed me the prisoners were to remain here if in his opinion they can be kept with safty; he has given his opinion to the Secretary of the Navy that they can be kept with perfect safty. The men are very well situated and a very good Barrack and every thing very comfortable I got the last check changed this day by the contractor, there are nine men and a corporal obliged to mount guard every day which keeps them to their duty very strict

Am your most
Obt Servt

ANTHONY GALE *Lt M.[arines]*

W. W. BURROWS
Majr Commandant of the Marine Corps

[MCA. LR, 1798.]

Extract from journal of James Pity, U. S. Frigate *Constitution*, 23 October 1798, Tuesday

First part this 24 hours pleasant Weather. @ 8 P. M. Wind blowing Fresh with dark Flying Clouds. got the Messenger Round the Capstan & Shipped the Barrs in order for heaving up the Anchor.

Middle part fresh Breezes & cloudy Weather Wind at S. S. W. @ 2 A. M. the Pilot Boat run under our Stern & Inform'd us that she had Spoke two Arm'd Ships from Liverpool bound to Charleston. @ 4 P. M. Michael Salvers a Boy fell down & broke his thigh. Mr Deblois with the Navy agent came on b^d from Charleston @ 11 A. M. the *Virginia* cutter of 12 Guns Anchor'd under our Stern.

[NDA.]

Extract from Captain Thomas Truxtun's journal, U. S. Frigate *Constellation*, 23 October 1798, Tuesday

Fresh Breezes all these twenty four Hours, a head Sea, and very uncertain Weather; the first Part clear; the Middle and latter Cloudy with some Rain, Several Vessels standing in for the Land, which I take for a Part of the Convoy: Regulated our Sail according to the Weather. At Noon under close reefed top Sails, and double reefed fore Sail. At 2 A M sounded in fifty Fathoms Water; at which Time I judged myself nine Miles to the Southward of Cape

Henry, and 90′ to the Eastward of the said Cape, which Cape at Noon bore W. 1/4 S. twenty three Leagues Distance. I find the Current of the Gulph Stream on getting Soundings, has been very strong for several Days. By the Soundings however, I regulate the Longitude to Day.

Latitude observed 37°.00′ N°
Longitude Account 74.25 W.

[HS of Pa. NDA photostat.]

Extract from Captain Thomas Truxtun's journal, U. S. Frigate *Constellation*, 24 October 1798, Wednesday

Fresh Gales, and clear Weather. At 5 P M brought to with a Shot the United States' Brig *Eagle*, Captain Hugh Campbell from Philadelphia on a Cruize, two Days out.

At 7 A M made the Land, and at 10 Ditto the Light House on Cape Henry was seen bearing W. N. W. A little after we made the Light House, a Brig came out of the Chesapeake Bay, which passed us to Windward, and stood on to the Eastward, but as she was steering in a Direction for the *Eagle*, I let her pass as the *Eagle* would of Course visit her which she did. At Noon spoke a Pilot Boat, No News, the Light House at same Time bore N. W. six Leagues Distance, Depth of Water, Eleven Fathoms, fine white Sand with some black Specks.

Latitude observed 36°.48′N°
Longitude Account 75.35 W.

[HS of Pa. NDA photostat.]

Extract from journal of James Pity, U. S. Frigate *Constitution*, 24 October 1798, Wednesday

First part this 24 hours Light breezes & Clear Weather. All hands employ'd dischar^{g} a Sloop loaded with water for Ships Use. @ 4 P. M. fired a Salute of 15 guns and @ 1/2 past D° Rec^{d} a Salute of 15 Guns from an English Ship answerd D° with 3 Guns.

Middle part fresh breezes & Clear W^{r} call'd all hands & up Anchor. @ [space] an Officer of the *Baltimore* came on b^{d} & Capt Bright to Receive Orders. at D° the Gen^{tn} & pilot left the Ship Made Signal for the fleet to make Sail in C° with *Baltimore*. and 11 Sail of Merchant Men bound for the Havanna at 8 A. M. Charleston Light House bore N. W. b. W. dist^{ce} 6 Leag^{s} from wch I take my Dep^{re} being in Latt^{d} 32.42 & Long^{d} 80.10 West.

[NDA.]

Extract from journal of U. S. Ship *Herald*, Captain James Sever, U. S. Navy, commander, 24 October 1798

This 24 hours first part Cloudy weather at 1 p m made montock Light Bearing N E B N 3 Leagues Distns at 2 p m Sett Stearing Sails & Royals at 7 p m Squal from N W in all Light Sails Close Reeft Topsails sent Down Top g yard at 10 past Block Island at

12 Saw Road Island Light Bearing N N E 3 Leagues Distns at 3 a m Came to anchor in New port harbour goat Island Bearing E B N Rowes Island Bearing N N W Brintens point Bearing S b E Brig *Pickring* in Companey

Latter part Squaley weather all hans Employd in Ships Duty

[NDA. Journal kept by Joseph Strout, 1798.]

Extract from journal of Lieutenant John Mullowny, U. S. Frigate *United States*, 24 October 1798

Taut gales, split the Main Top sail, unbent reefed the Foresail & handed the Main sail —

Squally with rain —

At 2 P. M. sent down M & Mizen Top Gallant Masts —

Heavy squalls with Thunder and Lightning

At 6 bent a New Main Top sail & set him close reefed —

Strong breezes and clear weather

Sail Maker & crew employed Mending Fore Sail & Main Topsail.

[Lattd 36.10]

[NA.]

To Mr. Létombe, late French Consul General, from Secretary of State

DEPARTMENT OF STATE
Trenton Oct. 25. 1798.

Mr LÉTOMBE
late Consul General of the French Republic.

SIR, This evening I received your letter marked with the date of *to-morrow, the 26th*, covering an arret of the Executive Directory of France, of the 14th of last May, ordaining, "That vessels bearing the *American flag* should no more be admitted, under any pretext, into the military ports of Brest, l'Orient, Rochefort, Toulon and Dunkirk."

You express your regret that a dispatch of such importance, sent to you by M. Talleyrand, Minister of foreign affairs under date of June 9th should have been so long in coming to you: But there was no cause for this regret; the Congress of the United States, four days after the date of M. Talleyrand's letter, having forbidden all commercial intercourse of the vessels of the United States with any *French ports whatever*, without discrimination.

I thank you for the trouble you took to furnish me with a copy of the Decree of the French Convention of the 1st of October 1793, referred to in the arret of the Directory of the 31st of July last. But as this arret is perfectly illusory, seeing it leaves all the other arrets of the Directory and decrees of the Convention, and the interpretations of the minister of Justice, Merlin, in consequence of which such abominable depredations have been committed on the commerce of the United States, in full force — so the Decree of the Convention of Oct. 1. 1793, to which your privateers are *especially* required to conform, will not produce the smallest change in their conduct towards neutral Nations; its object being merely to effect the speedy condemnation of prizes, and to regulate the distribution of the prize money among the captors.

I am with much regard &c.

TIMOTHY PICKERING

(N. B. This letter having been mislaid, a fair transcript was not sent to Mr Letombe till November 5.)

[SDA. Dom. L., Vol. 11.]

To William Pennock, Navy Agent, Norfolk, from Captain Thomas Truxtun, U. S. Navy

Constellation OFF CAPE HENRY
25th Octr 1798 — 10 A M.

DEAR SIR, I arrived Yesterday off this Cape, and have just this Moment anchored a little within it. We sailed from the Havannah the 30th Ultimo, with 44 Sail of Vessels under Convoy, all of which we saw into the Gulph of Florida without missing any one. After we reached that far, several of the Armed and fast Sailing Vessels, took their Leave of the Fleet, and proceeded on. I however kept with the principal part of the Fleet, and the slowest Sailing Vessels, untill we reached the Coast of Georgia (Lat. 31° 47′ No.) I then made the Signal for each to make the best of his Way; since which we have had a succession of Easterly and Northerly Winds, Gale after Gale, in Fact we have not had one Hour of fair Wind, since leaving our Station off the Morro Castle. Send me what Letters you have —

I am &c.

THOMAS TRUXTUN.

WILLIAM PENNOCK Esqr
Naval Agent, Norfolk.

[HS of Pa. NDA photostat. Truxtun's LB, 1798–9.]

To John Caldwell, Hartford, Conn., from Secretary Timothy Pickering, acting for Secretary Stoddert

Navy Department
Trenton October 25th 1798

JOHN CALDWELL Esqr
Harford Connecticut

SIR, Being in the absence of Mr Stoddert charged with the Current business of this department, I acknowledge the receipt of your Letter of the 15th Instant, requesting to be informed whether a convoy can be furnished for a fleet of Connecticut vessels destined for the W. Indies, and to sail about the 1st of November. —

Upon examining the orders given by the Secretary of the Navy to the several armed Vessels prepared for service, and which are now cruising, it does not appear practicable to furnish the convoy you request.— The other Armed vessels now in port will not, any of them, be ready to go to sea 'till late in November, or the beginning of December. —

I am sorry that the actual disposition made of the Armed Vessels of the United States, is such, that the wishes of yourself & fellow Citizens for a Convoy cannot be gratified. —

I am &c[a]

T PICKERING

[NDA. GLB No. 1.]

Extract from journal of James Pity, U. S. Frigate *Constitution*, 25 October 1798, Thursday

First part this 24 hours Light Winds & vble [variable] Convoy in Company.

At 6 A. M. Shortend Sail for the fleet to come up.

Middle part Light Airs and pleasant Weather. at 7 A. M. out all Reefs. at 9 A. M. Double Reef'd top Sails find[g] we Sail'd too fast for the Convoy. @ 10 Made Signal for the Fleet to make Sail

At Merd[n] Made Signal for the *Baltimore* to fall in the rear of the fleet

[Latitude observed 31. 54. N[o]]

[NDA.]

Extract from journal of Lieutenant John Mullowny, U. S. Frigate *United States*, 25 October 1798

A heavy sea from the Northward

A man fell overboard, was saved by the life Buoy being thrown to him the sea being high, lost the Buoy. —

Pleasant weather

Carpenters employed repairing the Head rails, and gratings.

(Latt[d] 36.46]

[NA.]

Extract from Captain Thomas Truxtun's journal, U. S. Frigate *Constellation*, 25 October 1798, Thursday

Moderate Breezes all these twenty four Hours, and fair Weather. Brought to with a Shot, and spoke the Ship *Union* of Baltimore bound to Hamburgh, the Brig *Eagle* of and from the same Place, bound to Falmouth, and several Pilot Boats. Continued working to Windward untill half past eleven P M, then anchored with small Bower in seven Fathoms Water, the Light on Cape Henry bearing West B. North two Leagues Distance. Gave the Ship the short Service, and handed the Sails.

At 7 A M got under Way with a light Breeze, and the first of the Tide of Flood, and stood to Windward between Cape Henry and the Middle on our Tacks, and at 11 Ditto the Wind falling light, anchored in the Tail of the Shoe in ten Fathoms Water, the Light House on Cape Henry bearing N. B. E. 1/2 E. two Thirds of a League Distant. Dispatched the Jolly Boat on Shore with Lieutenant Saunders having Charge of my Letters for the Naval Agent, Norfolk.

Latitude Account 37°.00′ N[o]

Longitude Account 75.52 W.

[HS of Pa. NDA photostat.]

To Jeremiah Yellott, Navy Agent, Baltimore, from Captain Thomas Truxtun, U. S. Navy

UNITED STATES SHIP *Constellation*
Hampton Roads 26th October 1798 —

JEREMIAH YELLOTT Esqr
Naval Agent, Baltimore.

DEAR SIR, I should have answered your Letter of the 27th August last earlier, but when it came to Hand, I was on the Point of sailing for to convoy Home the Havannah Trade, and in Fact my Hands have been full, and my Mind much engaged in other Respects, as was to be expected from the Infancy of our Navy, and Officers.

As you have commenced the Building the two Sloops of War at Baltimore, I shall say Nothing, of their Construction below the Whales, but as you request my Opinion in the Business must advise by all Means, a light Spar Deck being put on them, otherwise you will be much crowded, when a full Compliment of Men are on Board.

Most Commanders more from Ambition and Pride perhaps, than any other Consideration, urge the putting too many Cannon on Vessels of War, and should you be induced by Persuasion (which I trust cannot be the Case) to make this Mistake, it will probably much injure the Sailing of these sharp built Vessels, and as their Swiftness will be of the greatest Consequence in the West Indies, or on our Coast, I cannot recommend you to mount more than Twenty four Guns on either of the Ships in question to Vizt —

Twenty Cannon on the Main Deck carrying six Pound Ball, and to weigh each about thirteen hundred Weight Gross, and four Cannon of like Calibre on upper Deck, and to weigh each about nine hundred Weight Gross. —

The Upper Deck Guns may have their Breechings to go with Hooks and Thimbles, so that at any Time, they can be shifted from Place to Place, as Occasion may require.

I have long since remarked the great Folly of mounting too many Guns on Ships of every Description with all the Consequences attending it, to Vizt —

The making them laboursome and crank; encreasing the Compliment of Men, and the Quantity of Water and Provisions; having the Crew too much crowded, which breeds Disease, and causes Sickness. Putting the Vessel too deep in the Water, which not only injures their Sailing, but makes them wet, uncomfortable, and difficult to fight, and keep dry the Contents of Guns; and after all these Disadvantages, it has been often proved, that much greater Execution is done by a few Pieces of Artillery well served, than by many where the Want of good Room renders their being well worked impracticable.

With Twenty-four Guns of the above Weight, each Ship will have occasion for One Hundred, and twenty-five Men, including Officers of every Description, and Marines, and to take Men as we generally find them, I should consider that Number fully sufficient; at any Rate I would not put more than One Hundred, and thirty on Board; the British Ships of War carry a less Number of Men, than the Ships of other Nations, and yet they do their Business better.

I annex Dimensions of Masts and Spars according to my Ideas, as also Weights of Anchors, and Size of Cables for your Sloops of War; Variations, however, may properly be made, if the Ships are either built more full, or on a sharper Construction than mentioned in your Letter to me; But after having approved Masts, and Spars, the next nice Object is to hit the Placing of the Masts in the Body of a Vessel, and of the raking them properly, and this Part of the Business requires great Judgment and Attention, and if we succeed completely, we ought never to forget to give Mr *Chance* his proportion of Credit for it, as it is a well known Fact, that some Ships have been known to sail the fastest, when their Masts have been shifted in the Body, contrary to every Rule, and all Modes of good reasoning on the Subject. I would give you the Place for each Mast in the Body of the Vessel according to my System published some Time ago in Philadelphia, but I understand your Decks are framed, Partners fixed, and Mast Holes cut out; all of which I suppose is done according to your own Judgment, founded on the Construction of the Vessels, and I hope will succeed to your most sanguine Expectations or Wishes. I have the Honor to be, Dear Sir,

Your very Obedt humble Servant

T. T[RUXTUN]

N. B. This Letter was begun agreeable to the Date &c. but not concluded untill the the 8th January 1799.

Dimensions of Masts and Spars. Weight of Anchors, and Size of Cables for a Ship of 87 Feet Keel strait Rabbit, and 29 feet Beam &c. building at Baltimore for the Service of the United States of America.—

3 Cables not to exceed 14½ Inches, and to be 120 Fathoms long.
3 Anchors of 24 Cwt. Gross each.
1 Stream Cable of 8 Inches, and 120 fathoms long.
1 Ditto Anchor of 7 Cwt. Gross.
1 Tow-Line not to exceed 5 Inches, & to be 120 Fathoms long.
1 Kedge Anchor of 2½ Cwt Gross.

Masts and Spars to Vizt —

Main Mast the whole Length	68 Feet	Head	10	Feet
Main top Mast____ditto	41 do	do	6	ditto
Main top Gallant Mast	36 ditto	ditto	12	ditto
Main Yard	62 ditto	ditto	3½	ditto
Main top Sail Yard	43 ditto	ditto	3½	ditto
Main top Gallant Yard	31 ditto	ditto	2	ditto
Fore Mast the whole	64 ditto	ditto	10	ditto
Fore top Mast	39 ditto	ditto	6	ditto
Fore top Gallant Mast	33 ditto	ditto	11	ditto
Fore Yard	57 ditto	Arms	3½	ditto
Fore top Sail Yard	40 ditto	ditto	3½	ditto
Fore top Gallant Yard	30 ditto	ditto	2	ditto
Mizen Mast the whole Length	64 ditto	Head	8½	ditto
Mizen top Mast	30 ditto	ditto	4½	ditto
Mizen top Gallant Mast	27 ditto	ditto	9	ditto
Cross Jack Yard	45 ditto	Arms	3½	ditto
Mizen top Sail Yard	33 ditto	ditto	2	ditto
Mizen top Gallant Yard	24 ditto	ditto	1½	ditto

Bowsprit the whole Length	43 Ft.
Jib Boom____ditto	33 do
Gaff Do	32 do
Spanker Boom	42 ditto

Main Top 16 feet wide Fore top 15 feet Wide. Mizzen top 12 feet wide.

T. T[RUXTUN]

[HS of Pa. NDA photostat. Truxtun's LB, 1798–9.]

Extract from Captain Thomas Truxtun's journal, U. S. Frigate *Constellation*, 26 October 1798, Friday

About 1 P M got underway, and stood towards Hampton Roads, and at 8 Ditto anchored abreast the Town of Hampton in 15 Fathoms Water; Shortly after the Jolly Boat returned from landing Lieutenant Saunders in Lynn Haven Bay.

At 7 A M got Underway again, and dropt the Ship a little higher up in the Roads, then anchored, and moored in ten Fathoms Water; Old Point Comfort, when moored bearing N. E. and Sowel's Point S. S. E. Got down the top Gallant Yards, and top Gallant Masts. Commenced overhawlling the Rigging, clearing the Hold, and repairing the Rudder &c. &c. &c. At same Time I was preparing my Letters for Secretary of Navy, and Clerk copying the Journal including this Day's Transactions.

[HS of Pa. NDA photostat.]

Extract from journal of James Pity, U. S. Frigate *Constitution*, 26 October 1798, Friday

First part this 24 hours Moderate & Clear W^r Sloop of War *Baltimore* T. K. D. Ship and Sent her Boat on Board with a Midship^n & a Letter for Capt Nicholson @ ½ past 1 P. M. the Boat Return'd with a Letter for Capt Phillips @ D^o fill'd M. T. Sail all the fleet in Sight the fleet making more Sail. @ 11 A. M. fired a gun to give Notice that a Signal was to be made by the *Constitution* by hoisting 3 Lights abreast at the Mizen Peak for the fleet to tack to the Northw^d and Eastward. @ 11 D^o Saw a Strange Sail to the Southw^d fired a gun & hoisted a Signal at the Mizen Peak & Shew^d a false fire @ ½ past D^o fired another Gun. The Strange Sail prov'd a Brig from Havanna bound to Corunna Ordered her to Stay by us till Daylight At 6 A. M. Let out one Reef out of the Top Sails

[Latitude observed 32° 11^m N^o]

Several Captains came on Board belonging to the Convoy & at Merd^n. Return^d on b^d their Respective Vessells.

The Strange Sail Spoke with was a Brig belon^g to Benjn Homes of Boston, Wm Brown Master.

[NDA.]

To Lewis Crousillat, Philadelphia, from Jacob Wagner, for Secretary of State

DEPARTMENT OF STATE,
Trenton Oct. 27, 1798.

Mr LEWIS CROUSILLAT *Philadelphia.*

SIR: In consequence of your letter of the 8th of this month, requesting a special permission to clear out the Schooner *Minerva*, with passengers, for Port au Prince, I am directed by the Secretary of State to inform you, that he has this day written to the Collector of the Customs Mr Latimer, who on your complying with the terms prescribed by the government, will grant the clearance you desire on application to him.

I am, &c.

JACOB WAGNER.

[SDA. Dom. L., Vol. 11.]

To Rufus King, United States Minister, London, from James Maury, United States Consul, Liverpool

LIVERPOOL *27th Oct 1798*

SIR: I have the honor to annex the names of the vessels about to depart for the U. S. A. besides which there, probably, will be others, which I cannot ascertain to day

By desire of Mr Gore, I pray you will be so good as inform him that I had the pleasure to deliver his letter to Mr Thornton with the charge he directed. This gentleman sailed a few days ago in the *Caledonia* for New York.

I have the honor to be with
Perfect Respect
Your Excellencys
Most Obet Sert

JAMES MAURY

[SDA. Liverpool, Vol. 1, C. L., 1790–1800.]

[Enclosure]

	Liberty, Brae, arm'd	Phila
unarm'd	*Eliza*, McConnell	Virginia
unarm'd	*Accepted Mason*, Delano	Massachusetts
unarm'd	*America*, Chadwick	Massachusetts
unarm'd	*Merchant*, Fitzgerald,	do
unarm'd	*Joseph*, Stone,	Baltimore

Since writing the above I find the *America* is armd.

J. M.

James Maury
27 Oct: 98

His Excellency
RUFUS KING
Minisr pleny to the U. S. of America
London

[SDA. Liverpool, Vol. 1, C. L., 1790–1800.]

To Secretary of the Navy from Captain Thomas Truxtun, U. S. Navy

UNITED STATES SHIP, *Constellation*
Hampton Roads, 27th *October 1798*—

SIR, I enclose you herewith, Copy of my Letter of the 9th Current, fowarded by the Schooner, *Arb* belonging to J. Yellott of Baltimore, which Vessel, I am in Hopes, has arrived before this. By the *Arb* I also sent you Copy of my Letter to the Governor of Havannah, and the Answer he returned me &c &c &c and I now enclose you another Copy of my said Letter, with Copy of my Journal from the Time it was last forwarded up to my Arrival here Yesterday. On leaving the Fleet, I directed Cap^tn Phillips to proceed off the Bar of Charleston to reconnoitre that Coast, and after Cruizing four Days, which would give the Charlston Ships (which were the only Vessels in the Fleet belonging to the Southward of Cape Hatteras) an Oppertunity to get in to proceed here, and join me in these Roads for further Orders (enclosed is a Copy of my Instructions to him) on his Arrival here, I shall direct him to proceed as you have ordered.

Since the 9th Instant untill Yesterday that we arrived, and moored in these Roads, we have experienced the most unseasonable Weather I ever met on the Coast of America, Nothing but a continual Succession of light Winds, Calms, and heavy Gales, and altho' I kept in the Offing of the Northern Part of the Fleet, after separating from them, leaving them in Shore of me, as we coasted it along, and going most of the Time under very low Canvass in Order to give them all an Opportunity to arrive before me, I find several bound into this Bay have not yet appeared; am therefore fearful they have either foundered, or got dismasted, tho' by their being in Shore of me, and out of the Gulph Stream, they may not have experienced the Weather so severe, as I did in the Gulph. The Number of Vessels however arrived dismasted at Norfolk, and at other Ports Northward of that Place, added to the miserable Condition of several Vessels in the Fleet, that I assisted from sinking by sending my Carpenters &c. on Board, and supplying them with Necessaries, has excited my Fears for their Safety.

On the 21st Instant in a violent Gale of Wind, and a Cross hollow Sea Running the Neck of our Rudder, which was almost as strong, and well secured, as Wood and Iron could make it, complained very much; but by shipping a Tiller in the Head, and steering in the Cabbin, and unshipping the Iron Tiller in the Gun Room, we managed to get into these Roads without further Accident, but I can assure you our Rigging has stretched astonishingly, and our Sails are all very thin (owing to the Badness of the Canvas in the first Instance) in Fact they are so much so, that for an Eastern, or Northern Expedition or Cruize, a new Suit would be indispensable. But for the West Indies they may answer. I am repairing the Rudder, which will be complete in a Day or two.

With Respect to French Privateers being on the Coasts of the United States, it is a Folly to suppose it; besides the innumerable Angles I have made, the Number of Vessels I have spoke (without one single Exception) report, that they have neither seen or heard of any french Cruizers, they are therefore all to the Southward (what there is of them) you may depend.

The French Privateers off the Havannah and the Matanzas have never exceded three, or four, the largest of which was a Schooner of 14 Guns, and she has for some Time past as the Consul informed me, disappeared. The Others are one, and two Gun Vessels, that keep close in Shore; so that if they take a Prize they in Fact if the Wind is light, tow her to her Moorings in a very short Time. But I am convinced, the Government of that Island discountenances that French Banditti of Sea Robbers as much as they can consistent with their

Situation with France. If you send a Schooner of the Force of the *Retaliation* well armed, and manned, with Sweeps, and boarding Nettings, and a smart Brig equipt in like Manner, to cruize from the Pan of Matanzas to Havannah, it will knock up the Privateering System altogether, unless the Spaniards should be brought to declare against us, which they will avoid, if possible. These Vessels can run, or with Sweeps pull into Shoal Water, and with the light winds common in the Mornings among the Islands (which is the Time those Piccaroons are off a few Leagues from the Land watching to take Hold of Vessels, that have stretched pretty well in, so as to enter their Port at Day Light) they will have ten Times the Chance of a Frigate, or any other large Ship in making Captures; add to which, they can see safe into Port every American Vessel bound in, that they meet to Windward of the Morro, and whenever a few are ready to sail, Convoy them as far as the Gulph, and then return to their Stations.

Altho' the Government of Cuba may not be fond of our Vessels of War expressly stationed on their Coast coming in generally for Refreshments; I am fully of Opinion, they will take no Notice of any Capture being made near the Coast, unless under their Forts. For in the Case of the *America* of Philadelphia fireing into the little Privateer as mentioned in my Letter of the 9th the Captain landed, and complained at being fired at near the Morro; the Governor replied he had no Business near that Vessel; the Frenchman said, he only went to look at her, when the Governor observed, that if he could have taken the American Ship in that Situation, he certainly would as he had Others, and the Master of the *America* knowing that Circumstance, had undoubtedly a Right to take Care of himself, or Words to this Effect.

You mention six Months' Provisions to be put on Board this Ship, none of our Frigates can carry it, this is one of the Mistakes that I foresaw in the Plan, before the Keel of any one of them was laid. I shall proceed, however, without Delay, to put the Ship in the best possible State, and take in as much as can with Propriety be stowed away. About the beginning of next Month, Shall be enabled to write you on the Subject of the Outfits, and Repairs here more fully.

Our Ship is very healthy, scarsely a Man under any Sort of Complaint, Cleanliness, and the great Attention of our Surgeon to every Complaint, be it ever so small, is the Cause of this.

I have the Honor to be, Sir, with great Respect

Your very Obedient Servant,

THOMAS TRUXTUN.

Honble BENJAMIN STODDERT

Secretary of the Navy.

[HS of Pa. NDA photostat. Truxtun's LB, 1798–9.]

Etract from journal of James Pity, U. S. Frigate *Constitution*, 27 October 1798, Saturday

First part this 24 hours Light Winds & Clear Wr Convoy in Company @ ½ past 4 hoisted a Signal for the fleet to close @ Do Reeft Top Sails at Ditto beat to Quarters & Exercized the great guns @ 5 P. M. Shortend Sail for the fleet to come up 12 Sail in Sight.

Middle part Light Airs Inclinable to Calm. Made & Shorten'd Sail as occasion Required @ 6 A. M. all the fleet in Sight Saw 2 Strange Sail to the N. E. Made all Sail & gave chace prov^d a Ship from St Petersburg bound to Charleston S. C. Jno Ingraham Master 59 days out Saw a British Frigate dismasted in the Line gale.

Latter part fresh Breezes. Ends clear.

[Latitude observed 33° 07^m N^o]

[*Baltimore* in chace of a Strange Sail]

[NDA.]

To Lieutenant Archibald McElroy from Captain Thomas Tingey, U. S. Navy

PHILAD^a *28th Octr 1798*

SIR Since you left the Ship yesterday, I have receiv'd so bad an account of the fever in the City, that I am apprehensive, although your success in recruiting might be equal to our wishes — yet the men you engage may most probably be in a latent unhealthy state from the infection; of course improper to be sent on board — till the contagion has to a degree of certainty entirely subsided. On these considerations — The unprepared state of the Ship to receive the Crew — and the Danger of taking the sickness yourself, which you will necessarily incur. I have therefore determin'd to postpone opening the rendezvous till to morrow week.

If this meets You directly, I would wish to see you, and my servant will shew you the way to me — if he does not find you, order Lewis Albertus to speak to a number of good men — and inform them you will be up to open rendezvous on Monday next the 5th November — Men being plenty and should 8 or 10 *real good seamen* in full health be obtainable, take them down with you to morrow — but do not exceed the last number, nor on any account delay in the City for the purpose

I am Sir

&c &c

T.[HOMAS] T.[INGEY]

To Lieut^t ARCH^d M^{c}ELROY.

[NDA. Tingey LB, 1798–1800.]

Extract from journal of James Pity, U. S. Frigate *Constitution*, 28 October 1798, Sunday

Beginning with fresh breezes and clear W^r at ½ past 11 A. M. hoisted a Signal for the *Baltimore* to give over chace. @ 2 P. M. hove the Main & Mizen Top Sails to the Mast for the Rear of the fleet to come up. The *Baltimores* boat came along Side for additional Signals double Reeft Top Sails @ 5 P. M. Spoke the *Baltimore* and order'd Capt Phillips to Speak the Brig^{ts} *Norfolk* & *Friendship* and inform them that they have been very Remiss in their not making use of every effort to keep up with the fleet. Capt Nicholsons Orders are that if they do not be more Industrious he will leave them and Inform the Underwriters of it.

Middle part clear.

At 1/2 past 6 A. M. Sprung our Bowsprit Calld all hands in order to Secure it Got up our runners and Two foremast Shrouds to the Cat Heads in Order to prevent the Foremast going over board Sent down our Royal masts & Top Gallants Masts & Yards, on Deck unbent the Jibb & Fore top Mast Stay sail and got our Top Mast Stays thro' the hawse holes the better to secure the Bowsprit. Made Signal for the *Baltimore* to take Charge of the Fleet & proceed to the Havanna. Capt Nicholson call'd his Officers and consulted wth them what was best to be done They gave it as their Opinion that for the Safety of the Ship he had better make the Best of his way into Port. (The fish of the fore mast was also Sprung.) and taking all Circumstances into view this was the determination The Straps of the Bob Stay's giving way was Supposed to be the cause of this Accident. All hands employ'd fishing the Bowsprit. Ends Squally.

No observation.

[NDA.]

[29 October, 1798.]

Letter from Captain John M'Dougall, of the Ship *Two Friends*, to his owner in Philadelphia, regarding capture by French privateer *Good Fortune*

Ship *Two Friends*, Margate Road

DEAR Sir, I have the pleasure to inform you of the safe arrival of your ship *Two Friends*, after being taken by the French privateer *Good Fortune* of Bourdeaux, mounting 18 guns, in lat. 28, and in long. 28, who took out my two mates and nine of my hands, and sent me for Spain, with a prize master and seventeen men. I was in their possession for twelve days, when with three men and myself, I retook the ship with very little trouble. — Two of the French are badly cut in the head, and another in five different places. I am now so far on my way for London. We were almost killed, for we were under the necessity of keeping the decks six days and six nights.

I am dear sir, yours truly,

JOHN M'DOUGALL.

[LC, "Claypoole's American Daily Advertiser" (Phila.), 29 Oct. 1798.]

Extract from journal of James Pity, U. S. Frigate *Constitution*, 29 October 1798, Monday

First part this 24 Hours fresh Breezes & Squally W^r all hands employ'd fishing the bowsprit &c. @ 5 P. M. Let one Reef out the fore top sail and set fore top mast Stay sail Let one reef out the Mizen Top Sail. @ 6 A. M. Set the Main Sail & Let one Reef out the Mizen Top Sail and got up fore top Gall^t Mast. @ 11 Set T. G^t Sail but found that the Bowsprit worked so much that for the Safety of Fore Mast & Bowsprit we got them down on Deck. @ Merd^n in Light Sails & Reef the Top Sails.

Carpenters employ'd making a New fish for the foremast

[Latitude observed 35°.01^m N^o]

[NDA.]

Extract from journal of Lieutenant John Mullowny, U. S. Frigate *United States*, 29 October 1798

Fresh breezes, hazy. — Passed by a ships mast. Tacked at 2 to the Sd

Saw two sail one in the N. E. the other in the S. W. Spoke the ship *Mary* from the Havanna, for New York, she sail'd in Company with a fleet under convoy of Capt Truxton, Frigate *Constilation*

A 6 P. M. Tacked to the Nd At 8 Sounded in 43 fathom.

Tacked to the Sd

Sounded 32 fathom.

" 27 Do

" 26 Do

Tacked to the Nd

[Lattd 38.50]

[NA.]

To Garrett Cottringer from Captain Thomas Tingey, U. S. Navy

Ganges, Marcus Hook *30th Octr 1798*

Dear Sir As the Ship progresses in preparation to receive her stores &c. &c. — the lateness of the season renders it highly incumbent, that every article should be in readiness for delivery immediately to my order.

You will therefore be so obliging as inform me to whom the several indents have been forwarded, that I may know where to apply, in order to facilitate my dispatch, and with as little delay as possible — It will be necessary that the code of signals, be immediately prepar'd for me at the Office, as those Captn Dale has, are very deficient — there appears to have been no form established when he sail'd on the former voyage.

I am

Dr Sir

&c. &c.

T. T. [Thomas Tingey]

To Garrett Cottringer, Esqr

Naval Office — Trenton

[NDA. Tingey LB, 1798–1800.]

To Captain J. W. Leonard, Revenue Cutter *Governor Jay*, from Garrett Cottringer for Secretary of the Navy

Revenue Cutter *Governor Jay*,

[Trenton,]

Navy Department, October 30th 1798.

Capt J. W. Leonard

Sir, I have in the absence of the Secretary of the Navy received your Letter of the 29th Instant, informing of your arrival at New York. — On the subject of accounts you must arrange with the Collectors of the Customs as already advised. —

I am Sir &ca

G[arrett] C[ottringer] &ca

[NDA. OSW, Vol. 1.]

To Lieutenant Cowper from Captain Thomas Truxtun, U. S. Navy

United States Ship *Constellation 30th Octr 1798.*

Sir, You will proceed to Norfolk, and enter sixteen Seamen, as soon as possible, at the Rate of seventeen Dollars per Month, and call on Mr Garretson for Money, to advance them two Months' Pay; they must sign the Articles, take the Oath, and give Security as before, when you will send them on Board immediately after.

Let me here once more call your Attention to the great Necessity of making Exertions, and to execute speedily, and with Spirit, every Order issued to you, as an Officer. In Naval Life, no Man can look forward to become conspicuous, by rapid Promotion or otherwise, unless by his unremitting Attention to Duty, and from a regular Deportment, he can signalize himself from the Slothfull, and inactive. It is an artful Imposition, often attempted to be practiced by Delinquents, in performing the Functions annexed their Office, which are assigned to them, to talk of Hardships, that do not exist; by Way of Extenuation of their Faults, or their Neglects, and like a Distemper similar to a contagious Fever, it spreads by their working Others into a Belief, that they are really aggrieved, but the Fact is this.

Every Officer that performs his Duty well, will be respected, those who neglects his Duty, must at least expect a Rebuke. In European Navies, it is different for there, an Officer, who neglects his Duty, is arrested, and broke, our Officers all came on Board young and alike inexperienced. I have endeavoured by various Ways and Means to bring them to a proper Sense of Naval Discipline, and I am in Hopes still to succeed. Every Citizen in private Life is his own Master, but when he enters into the Navy, or Army, he is no longer so, for he must submit to strict Subordination. With Respect to myself, my Superiors will always testify, how far I put in Practice those Doctrines; when I am possitively Ordered to do any particular Service, I never demur, or offer an Opinion. When I am asked an Opinion, I give it with Candor; and when I have a Charte Blanche, I do my Utmost to promote the Interest and Good of the United States, considering well, the Intention and Wish of the Executive Government.

As to Sacrifices, no Man in the Service has sacrificed what I have done, and no Man certainly is half so great a Slave as I am, and have been, in attending to all the various Duties, connected with it.

In the Organization of our Infant Navy, much more is to be done, *by every Officer*, than in an established Navy, where every subordinate Officer is well acquainted with his Duty; hence arises the Necessity of very great Attention to place every Thing on a proper Establishment besides the Officers generally in our Navy, tho' young and inexperienced, have this Advantage over those in European Navies, by having been brought up as hardy Seamen, without much Indulgence, consequently it ought not to be expected, that all at Once, before they are initiated themselves, that they should wish at the Expense, and real Injury of the Service, to meet all that Sort of Indulgence, given to Gentlemen in Navies well organized &c. There is a Time for all Things, and when we have every Thing, as well fixed, and regulated as they have in Europe, then may we indulge, as they do, but untill then, let every Officer say, I prefer the Attention I owe the Infant

Marine of my Country, to every Indulgence, and Pleasure. To such the Government will reward, and to such I shall never be unmindful.

I wish, Sir, the above hasty Observations may have a Tendency, whenever made to any Gentlemen to open their Eyes, and stimulate them to hasten, themselves into the Esteem of their most Obedient and very humble Servant

THOMAS TRUXTUN.

Lieutenant COWPER.

[HS of Pa. NDA photostat. Truxton's LB, 1798-9.]

To William Crafts, Charleston, S. C., from Timothy Pickering, acting for Secretary of Navy

[TRENTON,]
Navy Department October 30th 1798

Wm CRAFTS Esqr
Charleston

SIR, I am honored with the receipt of your Letters of the 5th & 9th Instant, addressed to the Secretary of the Navy who is now absent, and for whom I have undertaken to attend to the Current business of the department until his return. — With respect to the pay stipulated for the Crew of the Gallies, it has been considered that six dollars a month, & 1 ration pr day, was a sufficient compensation for the Class of men contemplated to be employed. — Able seamen I presume, are not necessary for this service, and ordinary seamen, or landsmen ought not to expect more. However on this subject you will hear more pointedly in a few days. —

Observing it to be the wish of the Committee, that Capt Cross should remain to superintend the building of the Frigate, I write him by this Conveyance to act accordingly; and to deliver possession of the Brigantine *Pinckney* to Capt Samuel Heyward, who is so well recommended. — In consequence of this arrangement a person will be wanted to command the Galley intended for Heyward, and I request that you will select a character suitable therefor, and advise me his name, that he may be nominated to the President. In the interim he may act as if appointed, and his Commission in due time will be transmitted to him. Captain Heywards Commission as Capt of a Galley may be altered by Mr Simons & yourself, by the Erasure of the Word "Galley" and substituting "Revenue Cutter"; And I will thank you to take the trouble of seeing this done. —

I have the honor &C

T[IMOTHY] PICKERING.

[NDA. G.L.B. No. 1.]

Extract from journal of James Pity, U. S. Frigate *Constitution*, 30 October 1798, Tuesday

First part this 24 hours fresh Breezes a Swell from the N. W. Employ'd preparing fishes for the foremast.

Middle part Strong Breezes & Cloudy Wr Reeft Top Sails.

@ 6 A. M. Weather dark and squally with Rain furl'd Mizen Top Sail & Close Reef'd M^n^ & Fore Top Sails Sent down Top G^t^ Yards. & Masts. @ 10 Wore Ship

Carpenters employ'd Raizing the Coomings of the Hatches.

[Latitude by dead Reckoning 35.50 by an Indifferent observation 36°.16^m^ N°]

[NDA.]

Extract from journal of Lieutenant John Mullowny, U. S. Frigate *United States*, 30 October 1798

Tacked to the S^d^ at 1/2 past 3 saw a sail in the west standing to the N^d^

At 5 spoke a Pilot Boat — Hove to and got a Pilot —

Sounded frequently in 14 fathom to 20.

Sounded in 14 fathom saw the Land bearing West. A M saw the Light House on Cape Henlopen bearing N. W. Dist 5 leagues, got the cables bent & anchors clear —

[NA.]

To William Bartlett, Newburyport, from Charles W. Goldsborough, for Secretary Stoddert

[TRENTON,]
Navy Department October 31st 1798

Wm BARTLETT Esqr
Newburyport

SIR The Gentlemen mentioned in your List for Appointments on board the Ship *Merrimack* vizt

Michael Fitcomb J^r^	1st Lieutenant
Saml Chase	2nd ditto
Jon^a^ Fitcomb J^r^	Sailing Master
David Stickney	Lieut^t^ of Marines
Nathl Broadstreet	Surgeon
Joseph Hooper	Purser
Joseph Brum	Midshipman
Nathan Fletcher	ditto
Francis Salter	Gunner
John Coust	Carpenter,

have all been confirmed in their appointments by the President of the United States. —

I have the honor to request, that you will be so obliging as to notify those Gentlemen respectively of their appointments; and that you will desire them to communicate their acceptances in writing, and to take the enclosed oaths respectively, and forward them to this office — Upon doing this, they shall all receive their Commissions & Warrants. —

I have the honor &C^a^

CH. W. GOLDSBOROUGH
for B[ENJAMIN] STODDERT,
Sec^y^ of the Navy.

[NDA. GLB No. 1]

To Thomas Morris, Charleston, S. C., from Timothy Pickering, for Secretary of Navy

[TRENTON,]
Navy Depart^t October 31st 1798

THO^s MORRIS Esqr
Charleston, S C

SIR, In the absence of the Secretary of the Navy, being charged with the Current business of this department, I have received your Letter of the 9th Instant, by which I perceive that the appointment of Capt Cross to the Command of the Cutter *Pinckney*, you consider as likely to prove detrimental to the building of the Frigate commenced by the Merchants at Charleston; And as this I am Sure could not have been in the Contemplation of Mr Stoddert, when that arrangement was made, I chearfully do, what I know will be agreeable to him, and meet the views of the Committee, by consenting that Capt Cross Shall remain to Superintend the Frigate; and that the Command of the *Pinckney* shall be given to Captn Heyward to whom I write by this Conveyance. —

I must request you Sir, in conjunction with Mr Crafts to fix on a proper character to take the place of Capt Heyward as Commander of the Galley, and inform me his name, in order that he may be nominated to the President —

I am Sir &C^a

T. PICKERING
for the Sec^y of the Navy.

[NDA. GLB No. 1.]

To Captain George Cross, Revenue Cutter *Pinckney*, from Timothy Pickering, for Secretary of the Navy

[TRENTON,]
Navy Departm^t Octr 31st 1798.

Capt GEO: CROSS
Ch: ton S. C. [*Charleston*].

SIR Your Letter of the 9th Instant I received in the absence of the Secretary of the Navy: and observing the Fears entertained by the Committee, that your appointment to the Command of the *Pinckney* Cutter will be detrimental to the progress of the Ship building by the Merchants; I write them by this conveyance, giving my consent to your removing on shore to superintend that Vessel. — Inconsequence of this arrangement, another Capt must be appointed for the *Pinckney*, and Capt Samuel Heyward being highly spoken of, I agree that he shall take the Command — You will please therefore to give him possession of the Vessel, and communicate to him the several instructions you have received from this department, respecting your intended cruise. — It would have been more agreeable, could you have continued in the Command of the *Pinckney* until the Frigate was well advanced; but as the committee seem anxious on the subject, I could not avoid a compliance with their request. —

I am Sir &c^a
Y^r m^o ob. Ser^t

T. PICKERING

[NDA. OSW, Vol. 1.]

To James Simons, Charleston, S. C., from Timothy Pickering, for Secretary of Navy

[TRENTON,]
Navy Department Octr 31st 1798.

JA^s SIMONS Esqr
Charleston, S. C.

It having been considered expedient, that Captn George Cross, who at present commands the Brigantine *Pinckney* should resign the Command of that Vessel, to attend to the building of the Merchants Frigate at Charleston, Capt Saml Heyward has been recommended to succeed him. — This Gentleman now holds a Commission as Captain of a Galley, and as there is not time to procure the Signature of the President to a new one, it will answer the purpose to erase the word "Galley", and Substitute "Revenue Cutter" which I request you will be pleas'd to See done, and deliver the Same to Capt Heyward, who with Wm Crafts Esqr will wait on you for the purpose. —

I have the honor &C^a

T[IMOTHY] PICKERING.

[NDA. GLB No. 1.]

To Secretary of the Navy from Captain Jonathan Chapman, U. S. Navy

NEWPORT *Oct^o 31st 1798*

SIR I have the pleasure to inform you that on the 24th ins^t I arrived here with the United States Brig *Pickering* under my command and all well. This Cruise has been very unpleasant attended with much Stormy weather, in which the *Pickering* has sustained some damage. — On the 20th a Sea struck on the Starboard Bow, carried away one of the fore shrouds with the bob-stay, and right arm of the figure. —

We met with nothing remarkable until the 19th ins^t when a Ship with nine or ten ports of a Side and full of Men, came up and passed us under English colours. from her appearance and manoeuvers, I am very suspicious this was a French Privateer —

I was duly honoured with your favours of the 15th Sept and 6th Oct^o enclosing the Oath, and a Commission appointing me a Captain in the Navy. — With a strong inclination to serve my Country together with a view of an early appointment in the Navy, I was induced to take command of the *Pickering;* and Mr Higginson (the agent) assured me that the motives that induced you to send me a Commission as Master of a Revenue Cutter should be no obstacle to my ranking in the Navy from that date (30th June) and this was what I fully expected, otherwise I should not have taken charge under the Revenue. — I accept, Sir, of this honourable appointment, presuming that on a reviewal of this business, you will place me in that rank unto which (I presume) I have an additional claim for thus early engaging in Actual service. — I am not disposed Sir, to ask any thing improper, but must request you will write me fully on this subject. I conversed with Mr Higginson before I left Boston about a better Ship. he supposed I should be appointed to the one now building in Portsmouth, but as that Ship has a Commander I shall consider myself very much honoured in being appointed to command the Ship now building in Boston. —

I herewith enclose you a Schedule of the State and Condition of the *Pickering* with a list of the Crew and their times of entry. Should their times expire before this business is compleated, you may be assured Sir, I shall have influence enough to continue them to the end of this service. — I also enclose you the Oath unto which I have subscribed and sworn, and remain with much respect

Your Obed^t^ Servant

JONA^n^ CHAPMAN

Honble BENJAMIN STODDER Esqr
Secretary of the Navy

N. B. I beg leave to recommend to you Benjamin Hillar for my 1st Lieut. and John Hills who is now Sailing-Master for 2nd Lieut. I have discharged James Atwood who was my 2nd Lieut. — being sick and unfit for the service and have promoted John Hills to act as 2^d^ Lieut Pro. tem. and David Bruce now Master's Mate, to act as Sailing-Master. —

JONA^n^ CHAPMAN

[NDA. Area 7, October 31, 1798.]

To Secretary of War from Secretary of Navy, pro tempore

[TRENTON,]
Navy Department October 31st 1798

SEC^y^ AT WAR

SIR, I am honored with your Letter of the 27th Instant, enclosing a referrence of the 26th arising out of an act of the Legislature of New York, directing a sum not exceeding 150,000 Dollars to be laid out in fortifications, for the defence of the City of New York, in confidence that such expenditure would be indemnified and allowed by the United States; — Govr Jay's Letter to the President on the subject of the said act — The Presidents reply — and also his Letter to General Hamilton. —

The acts of Congress of the last session, not being to be had at this place, I cannot have reference to them. If I understand your detail of the acts, on this particular subject, there is one condition required by them, before credit can be admitted in favour of Debtor States, for sums laid out by such States in fortifications. The condition I mean is this; — That the fortifications so erected, with their privileges & appurtenances shall be, and shall be declared & established as the property of the United States, while maintained by them. —

But perhaps this matter ought to be then understood; — That tho' the president may properly authorize the expenditure of money on Fortifications by a debtor State; yet such expenditure is not to be admitted to the credit of the State, until the fortification so erected be declared and established as the property of the United States, while maintained by them. In this view of the subject, which, under all other circumstances, and the propriety of erecting without delay, fortifications for the defence of New York, I deem the proper one, I am of opinion that the act of the President ought to be confirmed officially by the Secretary at War, that the Instruction as proposed by the Secretary at War should be given to General Hamilton. —

1st That the Act of the President ought to be confirmed officially by the Secretary at War.

2ndly That the Instructions as proposed by the Secretary at War be given to Genl Hamilton.

3rdly That the Governor of New York be informed of the premises, and that the sums expended under the superintendence of General Hamilton or with his approbation, not exceeding 150,000 Dollars, will be considered as coming within the meaning of the 2nd Section of the act of the 3d of May 1798, and be passed to the Credit of the State of New York, on account of the balance found, and reported against the said State, by the Commissioners for settling the accounts between the United States & the Individual States whenever the fortifications &ca shall be declared and established as the property of the United States, while maintained by them. —

I have the honor &ca

[NDA. Sec War LB, 1798–1824.]

To Captain Samuel Heyward from Timothy Pickering, Secretary of the Navy, pro tempore

[TRENTON,]
Navy Department October 31st 1798

Capt Saml HEYWARD
Charleston S. C.

SIR It having been determined that Capt George Cross, lately appointed to command the Briga *Pinckney* should remain to superintend the Frigate building by the Merchants of Charleston, and your recommendations being respectable, I have in the absence of the Secretary of the Navy, though proper to give you the Command of the said Cutter, & you will please to consider yourself in that capacity. — The Commission lately sent you may be altered, so as to apply to the change, and I write to the Collector James Simons Esqr & Wm Crafts Esqr on the subject. Capt Cross will deliver to you the Instructions which he received from this department, by which you will be Strictly governed, and I flatter myself your conduct will be such, as to merit the confidence reposed in you.

I am Sir
Your obt &ca

T. PICKERING —
Secy of the Navy pro tempore

[NDA. OSW, Vol. 1.]

To Joshua Humphreys, naval constructor, from Secretary of State

DEPARTMENT OF STATE
Trenton Oct. 31, 1798.

Mr JOSHUA HUMPHREYS
Chester or Marcus Hook

SIR, Captain Robinson master of the Ship *Hero*, laden for Algiers has just called on me. He is now on his way to his ship, which is ready for Sea. I wrote you lately, desiring that Capt. Maley's schooner might sail with him as a convoy: and that the *Sophia* should be prepared to go with the other two armed vessels to Algiers, to bring back all their crews. I have not since heard from you.

Captain Robinson expressed a desire to have two or four of Maley's guns, with amunition, put on board his ship; informing at the same time that his owners refused to make any kind of provision for arming him.

I see but one objection to his request — that his ship is a dull sailer, and might be taken, when Maley's Schooner might escape from a superior force; whereby so many guns, adapted to the Schooner might be lost. I would therefore prefer putting two, or even four other guns on board the *Hero*, which might be taken out at Algiers, and put into the hold of the *Sophia* for ballast.

I will thank you for an immediate answer concerning the vessels destined for Algiers. In the mean time, I remain &c.

TIMOTHY PICKERING.

[SDA. Dom. L., Vol. 11.]

To Major Commandant Burrows, U. S. M. C., from Lieutenant Anthony Gale, U. S. M. C.

NEW CASTLE *October 31, 1798*

SIR I rec^d your letter dated the 27 instant — as to a guard for the Prisoners I dont know of any except the Troops under the Command of Capt Miller — as long as the men remain here they shall be well exercised, as I take care to drill them every evening, for two Hours; you would be surprised to see how much they have improved since my arrival here and I have the pleasure to inform you of their being talk'd of as being sober well behaved men and keeping themselves cleaner than any men they seen this long time. I have listed two men and wish to know will they get clothing here or at Marcus Hook.

One of the Prisoners a Duch man wants to list, he was taken by the French on his passage to this Country and made to serve on board of the Privateer; I would not list him until I acquainted you on the subject. The men are in a bad way for want of Socks, and watch coats, as the weather is very cold here, if you think proper to send either of the above mentioned articles the N. Castle Stage Boats go to Philad^a in which you can send them.

The men are very desirous to get Baynet Scabbards; there is a man here that will make them, for three shillings each or less, they are satisfied to pay what they cost above what Goverment allows for them if you think proper. Sergt Dongan wants to go to Sea in *Ganges* as he wishes to be out of the way of some of his friends, and wishes if you think proper to be appointed Sergt on board of s^d Ship; he has behaved with the greatest propriety and deserves my greatest praise

I have the Honor to be

Sir

Your most Obt & Hmbl Servt

ANTHONY GALE,
Lieut Marines

N. B. Pope has neglected to get a pair of woolen overalls you will please to send them and one Privates Vest for Warner as there was none when he came away, the overalls are charged to Pope but did not get them

A. G.

W. W. Burrows
Maj^r Commandant of the Marine Corps

[MCA. LR, 1798.]

To William Eaton, United States Consul, Tunis, from Secretary Pickering

Trenton *Oct. 31. 1798.*

William Eaton Esqr

Sir, The season requires that the vessels destined for Algiers should depart in a few days. By the time you can reach Philadelphia I presume they will be ready for sea.

I have paid your draught for five hundred dollars of which you wrote to me some time since.

I am with esteem &c.

Timothy Pickering.

[SDA. Dom. L., Vol. 11.]

Extract from journal of James Pity, U. S. Frigate *Constitution*, 31 October 1798, Wednesday

First part this 24 hours cloudy W^r at ½ past 12. Wore Ship to the Northward @ 1 P. M. Let a Reef out of the Top Sails at 3 P. M. reef'd the Top Sails again. @ 5 P. M. made more Sail the W^r more Moderate.

Middle part Squally Winds Variable with Rain

@ 6 P. M. Winds Varible wth some Thunder @ 8 A. M. a sudden Gale came on from the W. N. W. Reeft & furld the Top Sails Wind Increasing haul'd up the fore Sail & furld him. Split the fore & main Stay Sails hous'd the Guns fore and aft & made all Secure. Reeft the Mizen Stay Sail & Ballance reef'd the Mizen got a New fore Stay Sail up & bent him.

[Latitude by Account 37°. 29^m N^o]

[NDA.]

Extract from journal of Lieutenant John Mullowny, U. S. Frigate *United States*, 31 October 1798

At 6 P. M. came to an anchor in 8 fathoms water Cape Henlopen Light bearing S ½ E. distance 16 miles, the Buoy of the Brandywine shoal N ½ W 1½ mile, Blows hard, so much so as to prevent our getting under way —

Snow. very thick. at ½ past 11 passed by the Buoy of the Ledge, at ½ past M. run ashore on the upper end of the Ledge, got the Boats out, the stream anchor in the Lanch, at ¼ past one she got off without any Damage, more clear saw the Buoy of the Middle, bearing N. W. by W. ½ mile. at ½ past 6 came to an anchor near the upper end of reedy Island strong breezes with rain —

[NA.]

INDEX

INDEX

Page

Abbot, Edward, seaman, Constellation ... 472
Abbott, John, ordinary seaman, Constellation ... 328
Abbreviations, index to sources ... xx
Abernethy, Mr., passenger on ship Alexander Hamilton ... 478
Abigail, schooner of Boston, Capt. James Atwood, captured ... 25, 35, 41
Abigail, ship, Robert Knox, in Baltimore-Lisbon convoy ... 304
Abrams, Captain, went aboard Constellation ... 408
Accepted Marsh, Delano, master, sailed from Liverpool ... 304, 305
Accountant, Office of. See Office of Accountant.
Accountant for Navy Department. See Winder, William.
Accounting Office, General, acknowledgement to ... vi
Act, American schooner, condemned and sold ... 22
Active, brig, Captain Hawkins, captured, sent to St. Martins ... 106
Active, revenue cutter, sale of ... 32
Active, schooner, captured by French privateer Flying Fish ... 23, 24
Adams, captain of sloop Lark ... 231
Adams, Mr., concerning treaties with Prussia and Sweden ... 488
Adams & Loring, owners of brig Sally ... 56
Adams, Charles Francis, acknowledgement to ... vi
Adams, Henry, acknowledgement to ... vi
Adams, John, Capt. U.S. R.C. Scammel. See Scammel.
Adams, John, President of the United States:
Barnes, David L., Attorney, correspondence with ... 204
Crowninshield, George and Benj. offer two sailing vessels ... 380, 381
Davis, Daniel, reports re capture of Adams schooner ... 124, 125
Decision of, requested regarding bond for vessel carrying French passengers ... 429
Empowered to acquire additional ships ... 77
Instructions to commanders of armed vessels ... 86, 137
Knox, H., regarding preparation for war ... 120, 121
Létombe, Mr., permitted to continue removing French citizens ... 318
Liberty, brigantine, may sail with French passengers ... 308
Morris, Staats, concerning guard for prisoners from Constellation ... 459
Navy, Secretary of:
Convoy for vessels at Havana ... 310, 349
Disposition of United States naval forces ... 255, 256, 336
Leave of absence requested ... 405
Nouvelon, Captain, delay of, at Hampton Roads ... 473
Niger, opinion of capture ... 149
Operations of naval forces ... 530
Paper enclosed, order and sailing abstract ... 314
Relative rank of officers ... 442, 443
Ship captured by Captain Nicholson ... 457, 460
Vessels authorized, status of ... 262, 263, 287, 288
Nominations for officers of Marine Corps ... 289
Permits to ... for clearances of vessels ... 422
Powers of present emergency, debatable ... 46, 73
Prohibits clearances of ships calculated for privateers ... 498
State, Secretary of:
Affairs between England and France ... 321, 322
Report of depredations on our commerce, submitted to Congress ... 5, 6
Treaties with Prussia and Sweden ... 488
Adams, Thomas, master, sloop Lark ... 232
Adams, U.S. ship, Capt. R. V. Morris:
Building at New York, by ... 282
Dimensions forwarded to James Watson for ... 136
Officers warranted for ... 190
Will be ready for service in December or January ... 569

INDEX

Page

Abbot, Edward, seaman, *Constellation* 312
Abbott, John, ordinary seaman, *Constitution* 225
Abbreviations, index to sources x
Abernethy, Mr., passenger on ship *Alexander Hamilton* 178
Abigail, schooner of Boston, Capt. James Atwood, captured 26, 35, 81
Abigal, ship, Robert Kean, in Hampton Roads convoy 364
Abrams, Captain, went aboard *Constitution* 403
Accepted Mason, Delano, master, sailing from Liverpool 505, 566
Accountant, Office of. See *Office of Accountant.*
Accountant for Navy Department. See *Winder, William.*
Accounting Office, General, acknowldgement to vii
Act, American schooner, condemned and sold 22
Active, brig, Captain Simkins, captured, sent to St. Martins 106
Active, revenue cutter, sale of 59
Active, schooner, captured by French privateer *Flying Fish* 28, 29
Adams, captain of sloop *Lark* 251
Adams, Mr., concerning treaties with Prussia and Sweden 468
Adams & Loring, owners of brig *Sally* 35
Adams, Charles Francis, acknowldgment to vii
Adams, Henry, acknowledgment to vii
Adams, John, Capt., U. S. R. C. *Scammel.* See *Scammel.*
Adams, John, President of the United States:
- Barnes, David L., Attorney, correspondence with 293
- Crowninshield, George and Sons, offer two sailing vessels 369, 370
- Davis, Daniel, reports recapture of Bristol schooner 421, 422
- Decision of, requested regarding bond for vessels carrying French passengers 436
- Empowered to acquire additional ships vi
- Instructions to commanders of armed vessels 88, 187
- Knox, H., regarding preparation for war 139–141
- Létombe, Mr., permitted to continue removing French citizens 218
- *Liberty*, brigantine, may sail with French passengers 206
- Morris, Staats, concerning guard for prisoners from *Constitution* 410
- Navy, Secretary of:
  - Convoy for vessels at Havana 319, 342
  - Disposition of United States naval forces 255, 256, 336
  - Leave of absence requested 460
  - Nicholson, Captain, delay of, at Hampton Roads 495
  - *Niger*, opinion of capture 449
  - Operations of naval forces 430
  - Paper enclosed by for use during absence 514
  - Relative rank of officers 542, 543
  - Ship captured by Captain Nicholson 427, 430
  - Vessels authorized, status of 262, 263, 367, 368
- Nominations for officers of Marine Corps 269
- Permits to collectors for clearance of vessels 332
- Powers in present emergency, debatable 75, 76
- Prohibits clearances of ships calculated for privateers 498
- State, Secretary of:
  - Affairs between England and France 321, 322
  - Report of depredations on our commerce, submitted to Congress 5, 6
  - Treaties with Prussia and Sweden 468

Adams, Thomas, master, sloop *Lark* 332
Adams, U. S. ship, Capt. R. V. Morris:
- Building at New York, by public 368
- Dimensions forwarded to James Watson for 195
- Officers warranted for 186
- Will be ready for service in December or January 539

Page

Addams, Alexander, seaman, *Constellation* 307
Adolphe, reference to 505
Adrastus, ship, John Ricard, permit for clearance of 332
Adriana, barque, Captain Dale ordered to convoy 91
Adriana, ship:
    Description of 62
    Materials and equipment for 103, 128
    Name changed to *Baltimore* 153
    Officers and men for 128
    Purchase of 62, 63
    Status of 123
Aix, Tribunal of:
    Flora, returned to Captain Calder by 97
    Vessels, American, condemned by, list of 79, 81
Alaise, ———, captain of French privateer *La Courageuse* 81
Albertus, Lewis, reference to 569
Aldbro, John, ordinary seaman, *Constitution* 226
Alden, C. S., Prof., U. S. N., acknowldgment to VII
Alexander Brown, ship, captured by French privateer 177
Alexander, George, ordinary seaman, *Constellation* 312
Alexander Hamilton, ship, Captain Wyse, captured by French privateer *La Croyable* 175–179
Alexandria, Egypt, French operations against 412, 465, 480, 485, 507
Alexandria, Va., recruiting for *Constellation* at 77, 78, 114, 115
Alfred, ship, Captain Asquith, taken into Cadiz 27
Algers, Oliver, seaman, *Constitution* 225
Algiers:
    Dey, reference to death of 550
    Mary, brig, captured and taken to 520–523
    Mediterranean passports required by 520–523
    Recognizes only United States seal 523
    Somewhat content at present 411
    Strength of marine force 40, 412
    Vessels for:
        Preparation and departure of 6, 10, 111, 202, 212, 213, 509, 547, 549, 550, 556, 580
        Shot, etc., from, for cutters 297, 405, 406, 408
        Sophia to bring back crews of 554, 578, 579
        To convoy Mr. Murray's ship 494
Alicante, captures of American vessels at 26, 35, 36
Allen, Benjamin, boy, *Constellation* 313
Allen, Edward, ordinary seaman, *Constellation* 309
Allen, Gardner, W. acknowledgment to VII
Allen, Henry, ordinary seaman, *Constellation* 308
Allen, James, ordinary seaman, *Constellation* 308
Allen, John, boatswain, *Constellation* 304
Allen, John, seaman, taken from brig *Friendship* 24
Allen, Samuel, master of brig boarded by *Constitution* 492
Allen, Samuel, captain of brig *Patty* 541
Alliance, frigate, sale of in 1785, left seaborne commerce unprotected v
Alliance, sailing from Liverpool 505
Allman, William, boy, *Constellation* 313
Allotments of pay, instructions to Captain Sever 160, 161
Almy, Pardon, master of brigantine *Electa* 31
Amelia, brig, Captain Logan, captured by French privateer 465
Amelia, brig, Samual Williams, captured at St. Jago, Cuba 34
America, armed ship, Captain Cunningham, operations of 466, 468, 486, 508, 568
America, armed ship, Chadwich, master, sailing from Liverpool 566
America, ship, commission may be granted 552
America, ship of Crowninshield & Sons cannot be bought 339
America, ship, letter, regarding purchase of 57
American, ship, brought to by *Constitution* 374
American Fabius. See *Fabius*.
American Hero, brought into Nantes by privateer 23
American Navy should be employed in destroying the French while they have little force in the West Indies 256

Page

American Philosophical Society, Philadelphia, acknowledgment to — VII
American Universal Magazine, picture of U. S. frigate *United States* taken from — IX
American vessels. See *Vessels, American.*
Amiable Adele, brigantine, John Brown, permit for clearance — 332
Amon, William, seaman, *Constellation* — 307
Amory, vessel of, brought to by *Constellation* — 294
Amphitrite, armed schooner, Capt. Thomas Snell:
- Engagement with unnamed ship — 340
- Wrecked and plundered by French privateer — 475–480

Anciaue, Mr., may not bring coffee from French West Indies — 557, 558
Anderson, master of *Sisters of Norfolk* — 459
Anderson, Hance, gunner's mate, *Constellation* — 263, 264, 300–303, 311
Anderson, John, seaman, *Constellation* — 311
Anderson, Robert, private, *Constellation* — 315
Anderson, Samuel, to report on *Delaware* as surgeon's mate — 160
Anderson, Thomas, ordinary seaman, *Constellation* — 312
Anderson, William, master's mate, *Constellation* — 314
Andrew, schooner, brought to by *Constellation* — 151
Andrews, E. F., artist, painting of Secretary Stoddert — IX
Andrews, John, ordinary seaman, *Constellation* — 309
Ankles, John, ordinary seaman, *Constellation* — 311
Ann, ship, Capt. David Black, convoyed by *Constellation* — 135
Ann and Hope, private armed ship, commission for — 353
Ann and Mary, ship, captured by privateer *Vulture* — 36
Ann and Susan, American ship, sold previous to condemnation — 22
Antelope, condemned at L'Orient — 26
Anthony, Captain, reference to — 229, 236
Anthony, Joseph:
- Commission for *Ann and Hope* — 353
- Construction of ship by merchants of Providence — 220, 221

Anthony, Joseph & Co., figurehead for *General Greene* — 536
Anthony, Joseph & Son, agents for ship *Nancy* — 284
Anthony Wallis, schooner, Capt. Isaac Luke, convoyed by *Constellation* — 135
Antonio, Francisco, ordinary seaman, *Constellation* — 313
Antonio, Joseph, ordinary seaman, *Constellation* — 313
Antonio, Sigue, one of prize crew of *Planter* — 248
Appleton, Thomas, regarding uniforms for consuls — 39
Appy, George, seaman, *Constellation* — 306
April, Thomas, ordinary seaman, *Constitution* — 226
Aquetan, Fanna, ordinary seaman, *Constellation* — 312
Aquilon, H. M. S., American ship recaptured by — 200
Aranjuez (Spain), Royal Cedula issued at — 20
Arb, schooner, belonging to Jeremiah Yellott — 341, 364, 566
Archer, John, Lt., *Constellation* — 304
Argus, or Greenleaf's Daily Advertiser, New York, extracts from — 149
Armament, naval:
- Acts providing for — 7–9, 58, 127, 128
- Money appropriated for — 46, 58, 211

Armoine, H. B. M. S., reference to — 365
Armstrong, David, seaman, *Constitution* — 226
Armstrong, William, ordinary seaman, *Constitution* — 223
Armstrong, William, seaman, *Constellation* — 306
Arnold, Jarad, master of schooner *Syren* — 364
Arnold, Oliver, private, *Constellation* — 311
Art, schooner. See *Arb*, schooner.
Articles of War, extracts from, published by Captain Truxtun — 156, 157
Ash, James, ordinary seaman, *Constellation* — 309
Ashly, Warren, one of charterers of *Lovely Lass* — 31
Asquith, Captain of ship *Alfred* — 27
Asquith, Lister, mate of schooner *Amphitrite* — 478, 479
Assistance, H. B. M. S., Captain Hardy, spoken by *United States* — 215
Astrea, ship, awaiting permission to sail from Cadiz — 547, 548
Atalanta, brig, Capt. Elnathan Minor, captured by French privateer — 81
Atkins, Ambrose, master of schooner *Orrington* — 27, 28, 81
Atkins, Nathanial, master of schooner *Active* — 28

Page
Atkinson, Joseph, boatswain's mate, *Constellation* 304
Atlantic, ship, captured by *Missicipian* 34
Atlantic, Western North and Carribean Sea map of Facing page 34
Atlas, sailed from Bristol 277
Atwood, Anthony, concerning fitting out of privateers 285, 286
Atwood, James, captain of *Abigail* 26, 35, 81
Atwood, James, second lieutenant, cutter *Pickering* 577
Augusta, brig, officers recommended for 495, 496
Aurora, brig, Capt. J. Frankfort, captured by *Pauline* 34
Avery, Thatcher, part owner of schooner *Orrington* 28
Babcock, Adam, reference to importation of saltpeter 129
Bacchus, ship, captured by French privateer 23, 35
Bailey, Samuel, cook, *Constitution* 226
Bainard, Roger, ordinary seaman, *Constitution* 223
Bainbridge, William, Lt., U. S. schooner *Retaliation:*
  Factor-Hazard incident 469–472
  Orders and instructions to 295, 320, 328, 375, 379, 380, 404
  See *Retaliation.*
Baker, Hugh, master at arms, *Constellation* 314
Baker, John, seaman, *Constellation* 313, 314
Baker, Joseph, quartermaster, *Constitution* 223
Baker Library, Harvard University, acknowledgment to vii
Baker, William, ordinary seaman, *Constellation* 308
Baldwin, William, captain of schooner, *Hope* 135
Balfour, George, surgeon, U. S. frigate *Constellation* 42, 125, 155, 304
Balfour, William, seaman, *Constellation* 307
Ballard, John, recommended as second lieutenant, brig *Augusta,* 496
Ballet, John, seaman, *Constellation* 306
Baltimore, Md.:
  Baltimore (formerly *Adriana*), purchased at 62, 262
  Collector permitted to clear *Liberty* 196
  Constellation, completion and fitting out of 9, 17, 18, 42–44, 49
  Guns for Algerine frigate desired from 10
  Guns for ships preparing at 124, 243
  Marines will be sent to 404
  Materials and equipment for ships at 103, 145, 173, 239
  Merchants of:
    Desire money brought from Havana on Captain Truxtun's frigate 365
    Ships building by 143, 145, 146, 170, 173, 220, 242, 243, 262, 368, 539
  Montezuma, purchase and outfitting of 143, 262, 321
  Ship of 20 guns to proceed with *Constellation* to Havana 290
  Spotswood, Captain, recommended for command of ship at 536
  Trade with Guadeloupe by firm of 274
  Two ships from, ready soon 166
  Vessels for sale at, to be examined 116
Baltimore, U. S. ship, Capt. Isaac Philips:
  Materials and equipment for 126, 234, 235, 239, 240, 257, 334, 354, 528
  Movements of 238, 256, 275, 278, 334, 341, 373–375, 377, 378, 381, 386, 387, 393, 409, 419, 423, 424, 429, 436, 445, 450, 459, 461, 466, 467, 475, 480, 482, 489, 492, 497, 509, 515, 541, 546, 549, 550, 559, 562, 565, 569, 570.
  Name changed from *Adriana* 153
  Officers and men 153, 173, 179, 193, 260, 285, 289, 334, 363
  Orders and instructions 275, 284, 285, 287–289, 335, 336, 344, 506, 514, 528, 538, 567
  References to 262, 333, 368, 403, 565
  Signals for use of 289, 343, 345–349, 374, 452, 453
Banks & Co., loaders of cargo of *Rainbow* 22
Bankson, Joseph O., armorer, *Constellation* 70, 71, 305
Banning, Mr., put on sloop *Jealous* as prize master 377
Baptist, John, boy, *Constellation* 313
Barbary Powers:
  Interfered with our commerce v
  Vessels needed in Mediterranean for use against 485, 507
Bardin, Levi, first mate, schooner *Amphitrite* 477, 478, 479
Bareth (or Barret) Frederick, schooner *Amphitrite* 478

Page
Barnes, Mr., pilot, dispatched to *Constellation* with letters ---- 245
Barnes, David L., United States Attorney, Providence, R. I ---- 274, 275, 293
Barnes, John, quarter gunner, *Constellation* ---- 305
Barnewall, George, et al. See *Murray, John, Merchants' Committee of New York.*
Barney's squadron shut in Cape Francois by French ---- 200
Barns, Henry, seaman, *Constitution* ---- 225
Barnwell, George, Gen., regarding to use of Port Royal harbor by ships of war ---- 534, 535
Barr, James, ordinary seaman, *Constellation* ---- 308
Barre, captain of French privateer *L'Espeigle* ---- 30
Barri, Joseph Coen ---- 411
Barron, Mr ---- 233
Barron, James, Lt., U. S. frigate *United States* ---- 354
Barron, Samuel, Capt., U. S. N ---- 279, 383, 430, 543
Officers for ship of ---- 384, 425, 504, 505, 535
Orders and instructions to ---- 425, 489, 504, 505
See *Richmond.*
Barry, Mr., pilot, water for *Constellation* ---- 139
Barry, Mr., regarding stores for *Constellation* ---- 431
Barry, Mrs ---- 56
Barry, James, Baltimore, Md ---- 278, 365, 412, 414
Barry, James, owner of snow *Michael* ---- 364
Barry, John, Capt., U. S. frigate *United States*:
Bearer of letter to governor of Puerto Rico ---- 192, 203
Fitzsimons, Thomas; James Yard connection with French privateers ---- 544, 545
Orders and instructions ---- 16, 37, 55, 56, 69, 78, 161, 162, 174, 189–192, 199, 278, 414, 481, 482
Picture of ---- Facing page 114
Porter, David, asks for a command ---- 55
References to ---- vi, 70, 163, 172, 240, 265, 289, 297, 301, 336, 368, 380, 462
Report of ---- 232
See *United States*, U. S. frigate.
Barry, John, midshipman ---- 412
Barry, William, ordinary seaman, *Constellation* ---- 308
Bartlett, Dr., regarding case of James Yard ---- 544–546
Bartlett, William, equipment and officers for *Merrimack* ---- 214, 366, 491, 574
Barton, Seth, of Baltimore:
Adriana purchased from ---- 62, 63
Has a ship for sale ---- 116
Bass, George, seaman, *Constellation* ---- 312
Bates, Commander, English schooner *Hibernia* ---- 532
Bates, James, ordinary seaman, *Constitution* ---- 226
Bates, Worth, master of schooner *Nancy* ---- 283
Baudot, P. T., and Rabainne, Boston. See *Rabainne and P. T. Baudot.*
Bayard, William. See *Murray, John, et al.*
Bayly, Lewis, midshipman for *Montezuma* ---- 326
Baxter, Conrad, ordinary seaman, *Constellation* ---- 309
Beale, Richard C., Lt., U. S. frigate *Constitution* ---- 109, 111, 385, 388, 393, 415, 416, 488
Beaufort, S. C., construction of galley at ---- 246, 247, 413
Beaver, brig, of Philadelphia, spoken by *Constellation* ---- 184
Becker, Francis, owner of brigantine *Harmony* ---- 30
Bell, brig, captured by *Favourite* ---- 34
Bell, Jonathan, M., mate, *Constellation* ---- 313
Bell, Robert, ordinary seaman, *Constellation* ---- 309
Bellam, William, seaman, *Constellation* ---- 306
Belleville, French consul, Genoa; American sloop *Prudence* released by ---- 80, 98
Bellisarius, ship of Crowninshield & Sons cannot be bought ---- 339
Belmont, Mr., passenger on *Niger* ---- 415, 417
Belvidera (Belvidere) in convoy from Havana ---- 475, 486, 508
Bembridge (or Benbridge), Lieutenant. See *Bainbridge, Wm.*
Benjamin Franklin, ship, transportation of French citizens ---- 100
Benoist, Mr., regarding evacuation of Spanish posts ---- 39
Benson, captain of armed vessel *Eliza* ---- 184

Page

Benson, James, master of schooner *Hope* 364
Bently, Charles, boy, *Constellation* 315
Benton, Thomas, boy, *Constellation* 310
Berril, Captain, of *Venus* 23
Berry, Mr., account of, for pilotage of *Constellation* 141
Berry, Ebenezer, master of schooner *American Fabius* 286
Berry, Garret, captain of snow *Fanny* 475
Best, John, ordinary seaman, *Constellation* 312
Bethon, captain of brig chased by *United States* 276
Betsey, brig, Capt. James Freeman 78, 79
Betsey, brigantine from Edenton, N. C., spoken of *Constitution* 515
Betsey, from Boston, spoken by *Constellation* 297
Betsey, schooner, of Boston, extract from journal of 266
Betsey and Jenny, schooner, Master Matthew Doggett 338
Betsy, of Boston, Captain Snow, taken by French privateer 27
Betsy, schooner, of Philadelphia, captured by *Revenge* 34
Bickerton, Mr., reference to 167
Biddle, Charles, letter to, from Captain Truxtun 118, 119
Bidgood, James, ordinary seaman, *Constellation* 314
Bijar, W. J., vessel of, allowed to sail 524
Bills, Lieutenant, prize captain on *Niger*. See *Beale, Richard C.*
Birch, Hugh, ordinary seaman, *Constitution* 225
Bird, Otway, collector, Norfolk, *See* Byrd, Otway 516
Bittinger, Charles, acknowledgment to VII
Black, David, captain of ship *Ann* 135
Blake, Charles, surgeon's mate, U. S. frigate *Constitution* 107, 169, 294
Blake, Richard C., Lt., U. S. frigate *Constitution* 169
Blakely, Robert, cooper, *Constellation* 313
Blanco, Marno, ordinary seaman, *Constellation* 313
Blanden, Rufus, ordinary seaman, *Constitution* 226
Blaw, Richard, seaman, *Constitution* 224
Bliss, captain of armed ship *Philadelphia* 317, 318
Blueford, George, ordinary seaman, *Constellation* 309
Bocries, Miciah, assisted in negotiating release of *Mary* and crew 521
Bolam, Thomas, seaman, *Constellation* 305
Bold & Rhodes, loaders of cargo of *Rainbow* 22
Bonaparte, reports concerning 465, 480
Bond, Mr., British consul, declares *Niger* British vessel 555
Bonds:
  Vessels, armed merchant, required to furnish 136, 181, 182
  Vessels with French persons to insure return to United States 498
Booker, Tenison, boy, *Constellation* 313
Bool, Henry, captain of armed ship *Joseph* 547, 548
Boos, James, seaman, *Constellation* 307
Booth, Constant, master of schooner *Dorchester* 34
Bordine, Levi. See *Bardin, Levi.*
Bose (or Rose), Newton, seaman, *Constellation* 314
Bossley, Richard, boy, *Constellation* 310
Boston Atheneaum, acknowledgment to VII
Boston Gazette, Boston, Mass., extracts from 83
Boston, Mass.:
  Cannon for defense of 92
  Fever prevalent at 502
  Fire engines for *Constitution* 10
  Herald, purchased at 262
  Marines wanted at 360
  Ship construction by merchants 56, 137, 143, 145, 146, 168, 170, 173, 262, 329, 368, 539
  Timber from, for Portsmouth frigate 214, 215
Boston Navy Yard, picture of Capt. Samuel Nicholson published by courtesy of IX
Boston Public Library, acknowledgment to VII
Boston, schooner, spoken by *Constitution* 462
Bostonian Society, acknowledgment to VII
Botsford, William, seaman, *Constitution* 223
Boush, James, recommended as first lieutenant 384, 496

Page
Bousquet, Augustine and John, owners, ship *Adrastus* 332
Bowen, Captain, in company with schooner *Betsey* 266
Bowen, Jabez, Jr., midshipman, *Constellation* 42
Boyd, Robert W., ordinary seaman, *Constellation* 309
Boyle, Thomas, captain of brig *Mary* 24
Boys in U. S. Navy 127, 131, 173
Bracher, Abraham K., formerly in New York militia 523
Braddock, John, Capt., Savannah galley, instructions to 388–390
Bradford, Benjamin, seaman, *Constellation* 313
Bradford, Gershom, acknowledgment to VII
Bradshaw, Joseph, seaman, *Constellation* 306
Bradshaw, William, captain of *Polly* 27, 32, 81
Brae, master of armed ship *Liberty* 566
Brandt, Richard B., midshipman on *Montezuma* 321, 380
Branigan, Felix, ordinary seaman, *Constellation* 313
Bras, captain of French privateer *Foundling* 30, 32
Breath, James, captain of *Briseis* 23
Brent, Richard C. See *Brandt, Richard C.*
Bressie, John, ordinary seaman, *Constellation* 313
Breuil, Francis, owner, ship *Benjamin Franklin* 100
Brien, John, ordinary seaman, *Constellation* 308
Bright, Francis, Capt., U. S. R. C. *Virginia* 292, 296, 396, 454, 483, 484, 559
See *Virginia, U. S. R. C.*
Briseis, brought to Nantes by French privateer 23
Bristol, England:
Arrivals and departures of American ships 277, 403, 518
Schooner from, recaptured from French prize crew 421, 422
British. See *Great Britain.*
Broaders, Mrs., house of, in Boston used as rendezvous 73
Broadstreet (Bradstreet), Nathaniel, surgeon, U. S. ship *Merrimack* 491, 574
Broadwater, George, captain of English privateer *Nancy* 482, 509
Brooks, Samuel, mate, *Constellation* 304
Brooks, William, seaman, *Constitution* 223
Brothers, Captain Sumner, captured by French cruiser 26
Brothers, schooner, Captain White, joined Havana convoy 466
Broughen, Nicholas, seaman, *Constellation* 306
Brown & Ives, bond for ship *Ann and Hope* 353
Brown and Tracey, owners of ship *Charles* 135
Brown, captain of ship *Friendship* of Boston 251
Brown, Alexander, ship. See *Alexander Brown.*
Brown, Benjamin, ordinary seaman, *Constellation* 311, 314
Brown, Enoch, quarter gunner, *Constellation* 305
Brown, George, ordinary seaman, *Constellation* 315
Brown, George, seaman, *Constitution* 225
Brown, Henry, seaman, *Constitution* 226
Brown, Hezekiah 285
Brown, James, marine for cutter *Diligence* 442
Brown, John and J. Campbell, owners of *Bacchus* 23
Brown, John, Capt., U. S. R. C. *Diligence* 297, 358, 406, 420
See *Diligence*, U. S. R. C.
Brown, John, master, brigantine *Amiable Adele* 332
Brown, John, one of charterers of *Lovely Lass* 31
Brown, John, ordinary seaman, *Constitution* 226
Brown, John, owner of *Mary* 23
Brown, John, Providence, R. I.:
George Washington, purchase and equipment 351, 352, 423, 428, 429, 525
Ship desired from citizens of Providence 278
Ship of, cannot be purchased 277, 278
Brown, John, punished on *Constitution* 370
Brown, John, seaman, *Constellation* 306
Brown, Joseph, master of ship *Fame* 32
Brown, Joseph, nominated as midshipman for *Merrimack* 491
Brown, Joseph, quarter gunner, *Constellation* 305
Brown, Moses, acknowledgment to VIII
Brown, Moses, Capt., U. S. ship *Merrimack* 368, 489–492, 543, 557
See *Merrimack*, U. S. ship.

Page
Brown, Nathan, seaman, *Constellation* 307
Brown, Philip, captain of brig *Dispatch* 81
Brown, Samuel, ordinary seaman, *Constellation* 308, 309
Brown, Samuel, part owner of armed ship *Nancy* 284
Brown, Thomas, ordinary seaman, *Constellation* 309
Brown, Wm., master of brig of Benjamin Holmes 565
Brown, William, seaman, *Constellation* 305
Brown, William and Abra., builders of U. S. R. C. *Eagle* 114
Bruce, David, master's mate, cutter *Pickering* 577
Brum, Joseph, appointed midshipman, *Merrimack* 574
Brum, Philip, captain of brig *Dispatch* 27
Brush, J., charterer of Danish brig *Uricke Kock* 29
Brussells, Joseph, bill for pilotage of *United States* 240, 280
Bryan, Dennis, ordinary seaman, *Constellation* 309
Bryant, John, master and owner of *Royal Captain* 25
Buchanan & Young, owners of *Isabella and Hope* 28
Buchard, Peter, master of English schooner *Concord* 228
Buffington, John, release from prison requested 458
Bull, Joseph, qr. gunner, *Constellation* 311
Bumford, Thomas, seaman, *Constitution* 224
Bunbury, M. Simons, second lieutenant, U. S. ship *Montezuma* 321, 380
Buonaparte, defeat of, reported 467, 485
Buonaparte, Lucien, owner of French privateer *Patroit* 98
Buonoparte, French privateer, captured *Virginia Packet* 26
Burchard, Moses, seaman, *Constitution* 224
Burkley, James J., owner of *Oneida* 23
Burlington, N. J., jail at, suggested for French prisoners 289
Burnett, Henry, seaman, *Constitution* 224
Burnett, William, ordinary seaman, *Constellation* 308
Burney, Samuel, ordinary seaman, *Constellation* 309
Burns, Hugh, ordinary seaman, *Constitution* 225
Burns, Robert, capture of *Ann and Mary* by privateer *Vulture* 36, 37
Burr, captain of schooner *William* 229, 332
Burr, Colonel, reference to 70
Burrowes, Edward, owner of sloop *Lark* 206, 332
Burrows, Mrs 355
Burrows, Wm. W., Major Commandant, U. S. M. C.:
Contractor needed for Marine Corps 460
Geddes, lieutenant, ordered to relieve Lieutenant Carmick 327
Guard for prisoners at Newcastle 527, 558, 579, 580
Marines for ships 269, 320, 358, 390, 391, 422, 442, 513, 514
Marines to be sent to Baltimore 404
Recruiting instructions to 360, 376
References to 323, 512
Burton, Edward W., marine, for *Diligence* 442
Butler, Benjamin, ordinary seaman, *Constitution* 225
Butler, James, carpenter's mate, *Constellation* 305
Butler, Joseph, private, *Constellation* 311
Byrd, Otway, collector, Norfolk:
Agent for U. S. R. C. *Virginia* 516
Southern Packet, refused clearance 440
Two flags of truce, stopped by 237
Byron, William, seaman, *Constellation* 305
Cables, anchor, suggestions by Captain Truxtun 563, 564
Cadiz, Spain:
American ships brought to, by French privateers 27
American vessel detained at 20, 547, 548
American vessels permitted to enter 419, 484
American vessels recently arrived at 465
Blockaded by Admiral Jarvis' fleet 32
French consul at, wishes to condemn American vessels 3
Governor of, revoked licenses for American vessels to sail 547, 548
St. Vincents, Lord, with 25 ships, cruising off 321
Calais, ship *William* of Portland, sent to 35
Calais, tribunal of, condemns cutter *Dark* 25
Calbraith, W. Hector, owner of *Mercury* 23

Page
Calder, George, midshipman, U. S. ship *Montezuma* 153, 199
Calder, Samuel, Capt., ship *Flora*, of Gloucester:
American Consul Leghorn, requests assistance to 98
Captured by French privateer *Patroit*, near Leghorn 79, 97
Tribunal of Commerce orders ship returned to 97
Caldwell (James R.), midshipman, commands prizes sent to Mud-fort 486
Caldwell, John, chief clerk, War Department, shot for vessels for Algiers 212, 213
Caldwell, John, Hartford, Conn., regarding naval convoy 425, 426, 561, 562
Caldwell, John E., owner schooner *Dorade* 332
Caledonia, Mr. Thornton sailed in 566
Caledonia, Melloby, master, bears despatch from Rufus King 505
Callender, Benjamin, owner of French privateer *Eagle* 35
Calvert, Thomas, named lieutenant of *Norfolk* 443
Cambbell, John Murry, master of schooner *Lucinda* 476
Cambooses 145, 257, 357, 359, 369
Camby, James, boy, frigate *Constellation* 313
Cammack, Lieutenant, U. S. M. C., equipment for marines on *Norfolk* 404
Campbell, captain of *Sally* 184
Campbell & Yates, auctioneers, cutter *Active* 59
Campbell, Archibald, ships building by merchants at Baltimore 220
Campbell, Colin, captain of ship *William* 35
Campbell, Hugh, Capt., U. S. R. C. *Eagle* 323, 434, 442, 443, 481, 527–529
See *Eagle*, U. S. R. C.
Campbell, J., and John Brown, owners of *Bacchus* 23
Campbel', James, vessel built by citizens of Petersburg and Richmond 261
Campbell, Samuel, master, schooner *Harriot*, flag-of-truce 276
Canby, William, master, brigantine *Mermaid* 332
Cannon:
Foxhall (Foxall) will furnish for Navy 382
George Washington, ship 428
Loan of 24 at Halifax to United States 499–501
Montezuma by Mr. Hughes 333
Proving of 82, 92, 233, 234
Sent to Charleston for galleys 396
Sophia 554
Cannon and spars of *Constellation*, too heavy 302
Cannonades for *Constitution*, to be cast 57
Canoneir, French privateer, captured brig *Woolwich* 34
Cape Francois:
Barney's squadron shut in 200
Consul at, furnishes register of French Commission 21
French forces blocked in, by English 189, 255, 509
French passengers sent to, in *Harriet* and *Lark* 206
Liberty captured and sent to 187
Vessels condemned at 24, 28–30, 32
Cape Henry:
Bright, Captain, cutter *Virginia*, to appear off 292
Constellation and *Baltimore* departure for Havana 290
Philips, Captain, to join Truxtun at 289
Truxtun, Captain, to appear at, periodically 208
Cape Nickola Mole, *Industry* captured and ordered to 30
Captains of condemned American ships, arrival at Paris 24
Captains, U. S. Navy, relative rank of 407, 408, 542, 543
Capture of American vessels by France, abstract of 28–33
Captures by belligerent powers 20, 21
Captures by Spanish, data filed in State Department 22
Captures by U. S. vessels, condemnation procedure 182
Card, Edward, ordinary seaman, *Constellation* 314
Caribbean Sea area, map of facing page 34
Carlier and Dallest, owners, schooner *Fame* 332
Carlile Bay, frigate *United States* approaches 327
Carlonia, ship; spoken by *Herald* and *Pickering* 355

Page

Carmick, Daniel, lieutenant of Marines:
Appointed to *Ganges* 66
Equipment for Marines on *Ganges* 76
Geddes, S. W., lieutenant, ordered to relieve 327
Marines for *Ganges* to be recruited 66
Carneau, Captain, in command of *Catherine* 23
Carnes, David, quartermaster, *Constellation* 312
Carnes, Samuel, warrant as sailing master 174
Carney, Dennis, seaman, *Constitution* 223, 370
Carolina, brig, Captain Morton, condemned at Bayonne 23
Caroline, brig, captured by *Triumphant* 34
Caroline, Captain Motley, will sail from Liverpool 138
Caroline, spoken by *Constellation* 526
Carondelet, Baron de, Governor of Louisiana, regarding evacuation of posts 39
Carpender, Benjamin, warranted a midshipman 186
Carr, Mr 520
Carroll, Michael, midshipman on *Montezuma* 399
Carroll, Thomas, seaman, *Constellation* 316
Carter, Charles, seaman, *Constellation* 306
Carter, James, seaman, *Constitution* 223
Carter, John, boy, *Constellation* 310
Carter, Joseph, seaman, *Constellation* 307
Carthagena, American vessels condemned at 26, 35
Cartier and Dallert. See *Dallert and Cartier.*
Cartridges for frigate *United States* 38
Caruth, John, seaman, *Constitution* 224
Cary, James, seaman, *Constitution* 225
Casmagnale, Pierre, prisoner from *La Fleur de la Mer* 422
Cassation, tribunal of, to try *Hope* and *Antelope* 26
Castle Island, Boston Harbor, cannon at, for frigate *Constitution* 92, 96
Cathalan, Stephen, United States agent at Marseilles:
Distressed seamen sent home 78, 79
Reports captures of American vessels 78–80, 97, 98
Sends list of captured and condemned vessels 81
Cathcart, James L., reports cruisers fitting out for Algiers 202
Catherine, brought into Nantes by French privateer 23
Catherine, schooner, taken into St. Domingo 24
Catholic Majesty of Spain, Royal Cedula protecting American vessels 20
Catlett, Hanson, surgeon's mate on *Montezuma* 321, 380
Caton, Charles, seaman, *Constitution* 226
Causdell, Emanuel, seaman, *Constellation* 305
Caverly, Joseph, master builder of *Adriana* 62
Cavilier, Samuel, seaman, *Constitution* 224
Cayenne, Danish brig *Uricke Rock*, taken at 29
Ceres, British frigate, captured schooner *Industry* 30
Ceres, captured by French privateer *Hydra* 35
Ceuta, ship *Polly* carried to, by Spanish privateer 32
Chadwick, master of *America* 566
Champaigne & Dames, firm trading from Baltimore 274
Champlin, George, Newport, R. I.:
Shipbuilding at Warren 146
Shipbuilding by Gibbs & Channing, purchase of 147
Channing & Gibbs. See *Gibbs & Channing.*
Chapin, Hiram, private, *Constellation* 311
Chaplin, John, Jr., Beaufort, S. C.:
Construction of galleys 246, 247, 413
Sloop of war cannot be accepted 413
Chapman, master of brig spoken by *Constitution* 286
Chapman, Jonathan, Capt. U. S. R. C. *Pickering* 96, 107, 109, 112, 158, 159, 197, 256, 257, 329, 349, 350, 356, 367, 487, 501, 502, 543, 576, 577
See *Pickering*, U. S. R. C.
Chappelain, Mr., passenger on British ship *Niger* 415
Charles, ship, Capt. Joseph Perkins, convoyed by *Constellation* 135

Charleston, S. C.: Page
Baltimore to cruise off 514
Cannon received to be sent to Wilmington 396
Captured cannon taken to Halifax 499–501
Copper bolts, etc., for Beaufort, S. C., galley 413
Cross, Captain, to command brig at 387, 450, 451
Cross, Captain, to command merchants' ship at 343, 573, 575, 576
Encounter between *Unaniminity* and *Musketo* 252
Galleys at—
Construction and equipment 246, 249, 391, 392
Officers and men for 247, 389–391
Letters for Captain Truxtun 243
Merchants of, request convoy of vessels from Havana 250
Vessel building at, by citizens 230, 247, 249, 262, 330, 355, 368, 401, 402, 539
Vessel of Wm. Pritchard should be purchased 249
Charleston, brig, Captain Reed, taken by French privateer 35
Charlotte, Captain Lindsay, brought into Nantes by privateer 22
Charlotte, Captain Vincent, brought into Dunkirk and condemned 25
Charlotte, brig, Capt. John Mallory, Capt. Robert Burns as passenger 36
Charlotte, brig, Captain Stubbs, brought to by *Herald* 492
Charlotte, brig, spoken by frigate *United States* 411
Chase, Charles, quarter gunner, *Constellation* 305
Chase, Josiah, seaman, *Constitution* 224
Chase, Samuel, second lieutenant, U. S. ship *Merrimack* 491, 574
Chesapeake Bay:
Constellation lying in 18
Instructions for entering 148
Virginia, cutter, ordered to patrol 292
Chester, Pa., Barry, captain, left his ship at 430
Chester, William, seaman, *Constellation* 307
Chisley, Thomas, seaman, *Constellation* 307
Choates, captain of ship *Mary* 35
Christie, Mr., of London, lanterns purchased from 132
Churn, Robt., master of schooner *Sally* 34
Cincinnatus, Captain Martin, sent to L'orient 26
Circulars:
Navy, Secretary of, to—
Collectors of revenue 516
Commanders of armed vessels 187
Commanders of galleys 388–390
Commanders of revenue cutters 517
Navy agents 530
Treasury, Secretary of, to Collectors of Customs 4, 5
Truxtun, Thomas, Capt. to ships desiring convoy 341
Citizen, schooner, Anthony Daniels, in Hampton Roads convoy 364
Citizen, ship, of New York, at Havana 466
City Gazette and Daily Advertiser, Charleston, S. C., extract from 353
Clagett, John M., midshipman, *Constellation* 42, 155, 304
Claghorne, George, [naval constructor], to delay launching *Constitution* 17
Clansy, Michael, quartermaster, *Constellation* 305
Clapp, Samuel, master of brigantine *Harmony* 30
Clara, schooner, Capt. F. Hill:
Brought to by privateer schooner, Captain Thomas 496, 497
Brought to by schooner *Wanspite,* Captain Mollineaux 496, 497
Extract from log of 496, 497
Rover, schooner, spoken by 497
Clarey, Lewis, ordinary seaman, *Constellation* 308
Clark, master of brig *Neutrality* 34
Clark, John, owner of ship *Louisa* 32
Clark, John, seaman, *Constellation* 307
Clark, Wm., master of *Rebecca,* captured by *Sans Pareil* 34
Clark, William, seaman, *Constellation* 316
Clarke, T., Philadelphia, engraver, of picture of U. S. frigate *United States* IX
Clarkhill, Samuel, captain of ship *Outram* 81
Clason, J. C. See *Murray, John,* et al.

Page

Clay, captain of ship *New Jersey* 190
Clayborn, Mr 417
Claypoole's American Daily Advertiser, extracts from 36, 37, 53, 55, 106, 168, 187, 200, 231, 235, 241, 290, 400, 469–473, 477, 496, 497, 525, 526, 570
Clazen, Mr., owner of *Hare* 25
Cleaves, Robert, master, schooner *Harriett* 332
Clemon, George, ordinary seaman, *Constellation* 313
Clerk (Clark), Lemuel, Lt., U. S. M. C. 67, 74, 169
Clerks, Secretary of Navy, authorized to appoint 60
Clerks in the Navy Department, salaries of 263
Clinch, Bartholomew, Lt., U. S. M. C., *Constellation* 155, 304
Clogget, John M., midshipman, *Constellation*. See *Clagett, John M.*
Cloney, Mr., recruiting for *Constellation* 49, 50
Clothing, enlisted personnel 41, 390, 392, 398, 404, 512
Coast Guard, acknowledgment to vii
Cochran, Captain, H. M. S. *Thetis;* visits frigate *United States* 265, 266
Cochran, Robt., Capt., U. S. R. C., *Unanimity* 230, 343, 386, 387, 401, 450, 523, 524
Musketo incident 252, 372, 386, 387
See *Unanimity.*
Cocke, Buller, recommended for purser, brig. *Augusta* 496
Cockle, John, loader of cargo of *Charlotte* 22
Coffee, transportation of, from French West Indies 557, 558
Coffin, Will, quartermaster, *Constitution* 226
Coggeshall, Mr., reference to 463
Coile, James, ordinary seaman, *Constellation* 313
Cole, John, seaman, *Constellation* 311, 401
Cole, Thomas, Capt., superintendent of Baltimore Navy Yard 103
Cole, Thomas, seaman, *Constitution* 224
Coleman, Samuel, marine, *Constellation* 310
Colhoun, Gustavus, and H., Philadelphia, reference to 105
Coline, James, glazier, employed on board *Constitution* 487
Collectors of Customs 4, 5, 114, 250, 261, 332, 438, 516, 517
Collin, Thomas, boy, *Constellation* 310
Collins, captain, brig *Pallas* 403, 518
Collins, Henry, seaman, *Constitution* 224
Collins, Philip, seaman, *Constellation* 316
Collins, Richard, ordinary seaman, *Constitution* 224
Collins, Stephen, private, *Constellation* 310
Collins, William, seaman, *Constitution* 226
Columbian Centinel, Boston, extracts from 60, 73, 74, 175, 176, 259
Commerce, brig, brought to, by *Constellation* 242
Commerce, brig, Capt. Dan'l Green, captured by *Serpausonet* 34
Commerce, brig, Captain Thurston, plundered by privateer *La Revenge* 54, 55
Commerce, schooner, John Denabre, master, clearance of, with French persons 332
Commerce, ship, Captain Wood, captured by privateer *L'Espeigle* 30
Commerce in Mediterranean in a disagreeable state 108
Commerce of the United States:
Dale, Richard, instructed to protect 77
Depredations committed on 1–6
Protection off Havana 468
Commings, Joshua, ordinary seaman, *Constellation* 315
Commisio [?], Walter, marine, *Constellation* 316
Committees, Congressional. See *Congress.*
Compensation for revenue cutters extended to mariners and marines 9
Compensation to agent for building ship at Middleton 185
Complaints against France by United States citizens 1, 2, 5
Compton, Edward, ordinary seaman, *Constellation* 314
Comptroller of the Treasury. See *Treasury, Comptroller of.*
Conan, Hiram, ordinary seaman, *Constellation* 309
Conchlin, master, ship *Maria* 260
Concord, British frigate, sinks privateer in West Indies 466
Concord, English schooner, Peter Buchard, spoken by *Constellation* 228

Page

Condemnation of prizes taken by United States 182
Confederacy, Capt. Scott Jenks, brought into Nantes by privateers 23
Congas, captain of unarmed vessel *Trio* 184
Congress:
Acts of v, VIII, 7–9, 46, 58, 59, 60, 64, 87, 88, 127, 128, 135–137, 181–183, 188, 211
Captures by belligerent powers furnished to 20, 21
Estimate to equip and man three frigates 19
Expected to adjourn without declaration of war 204, 207
Measures to protect commerce and defend territory 52, 53
Report from President Adams, respecting depredations on commerce 5, 6
Connecticut Historical Society:
Acknowledgment to VII
Records published by courtesy of 163, 457, 534
Connecticut State Library, acknowledgment to VII
Connecticut, U. S. ship, building at Middleton by public 281, 368
Connell, James, boatswain, *Constitution* 225
Conner, William, seaman, *Constellation* 312
Connor, James, sailing master of schooner *Amphitrite* 476–479
Constellation, U. S. frigate, Capt. Thomas Truxtun:
Baltimore in company with 284, 285, 287, 288, 290, 335, 336, 365, 373–375, 377, 378, 386, 387, 393, 409, 419, 423, 424, 436, 450, 459, 475, 480, 482, 497, 549, 559, 562, 565.
Basis of conduct for an officer by Captain Truxtun 12–15, 572, 573
Berry, Mr., account for pilotage 141
Communications to and from 148, 159, 208, 245, 250, 287, 333, 526, 527
Complement, recruiting, etc 40–42, 49–51, 67, 71, 77, 78, 96, 104, 114–116, 118, 119, 135, 212, 302, 572, 573
Completion and equipment 7, 9, 17, 18, 42–44, 46
Convoy duty 133, 135, 250, 335, 338, 341, 364, 431, 432, 445, 486, 488, 489, 492, 502, 503, 506, 508, 509, 561, 566–568
Dianen, John, flogged 160
Draught of 132
Equipment and supplies 9, 10, 17, 18, 45, 54, 56, 93–95, 102, 104, 105, 122, 125, 132–135, 143, 209, 301, 303, 431, 528, 540
Extracts from journal of Captain Truxtun 134, 135, 139, 143, 148, 151, 153–155, 159, 160, 163, 164, 169, 172, 180, 184, 187, 195, 196, 201, 205, 210, 211, 215, 218, 219, 222, 228, 231, 232, 235, 240, 242, 243, 245, 250, 251, 253, 259, 260, 264, 266, 268, 270, 273, 274, 276, 279, 283, 286, 291, 293, 294, 297, 298, 300, 303, 365, 370, 371, 373, 375, 377, 378, 381, 383, 385–387, 393, 400, 403, 406, 407, 409, 410, 418, 419, 423, 426, 429, 435, 436, 440, 441, 450, 453, 454, 459, 461, 467, 468, 475, 482, 486, 488, 492, 497, 502, 503, 506, 514, 515, 518, 519, 526, 531, 532, 537, 541, 542, 546, 547, 549, 551–553, 557–559, 562, 565.
Gorman, Daniel, mate, suspended 273
Guns and tonnage 160
Hawley, Mr., U. S. Consul, Havana, came on board 441, 508
Leonard, Patrick, ordinary seaman, death of 235
Letter from Secretary of State for Governor of Havana 288, 432
Movements of 54, 104, 110, 114, 115, 118, 122, 133–135, 139, 143, 152, 159, 166, 212, 300, 301, 365, 368, 370, 431, 432, 461, 468, 493, 508, 514, 561, 571
Muster roll of 304–316
Officers of 42, 56, 82, 104, 155, 342, 495
Orders and instructions 82, 92, 93, 110, 118, 142, 206, 207, 284, 287, 288, 290, 335, 336, 342, 528, 538
Organization and management, internal 12–16, 61, 70, 71, 98–100, 102, 103, 108, 109, 124–126, 130, 131, 138, 144, 152, 156–158, 168, 200, 201, 232, 233, 253, 254, 263, 264, 290, 291, 298, 299, 302, 303, 362.
Philips, Captain:
Cruising instructions to 344, 506, 514
Signals furnished to 343–349, 374, 452, 453
Quarters for disabled men at Norfolk requested 362

Constellation, U. S. frigate, Capt. Thomas Truxtun—Continued. Page
Records forwarded from 133, 211, 243, 302, 303
Repairs to 318, 319, 374
Sailing qualities of 133, 212, 301, 302
See *Truxtun, Thomas.*
Sick seamen sent on shore 426
Signals, convoy 134, 445, 452, 453
Signals for use between American and British ships 288
Swedish flag to be hoisted by 207, 208
Transportation of money from Havana desired 365
Vessels spoken by 151, 152, 163, 184, 195, 215, 222, 223, 228, 242–245, 251, 253, 254, 259, 260, 266, 268, 274, 276, 283, 286, 287, 291, 293, 294, 297, 298, 385, 387, 400, 435, 441, 467, 475, 509, 526, 552, 559, 562.
Virginia, cutter, communications with 291, 293, 294
Watson, John, mutineer on H. B. M. S. *Armoine*, found on board 365
Constitution, U. S. frigate, Capt. Samuel Nicholson:
Completion and preparation for sea vi, 7, 17, 46, 65, 97, 111, 166, 171, 172
Crew of, data regarding 65, 66, 73, 74, 111, 159, 172, 223–226, 370, 494, 495, 513, 514, 529, 551, 558
Dennis, Thomas, came on board, as pilot 335
Dogget, pilot, came aboard 342
Dogget, pilot, went ashore 327
Equipment and supplies for 10, 38, 39, 53, 54, 56, 57, 92, 95–97, 280, 529
Extracts from journal of James Pity 236, 240, 241, 243, 245, 250, 253, 259, 264, 266, 267, 270, 272, 273, 276, 279, 283, 286, 293, 294, 296, 298, 300, 303, 319, 322, 324, 325, 326, 327, 331, 335, 339, 340, 342, 343, 350, 351, 354, 355, 359, 363, 370, 371, 373, 374, 377, 378, 381, 383, 385, 388, 393, 400, 402, 403, 406, 409, 411, 418, 423, 427, 429, 436, 441, 442, 450, 454, 459, 462, 467, 468, 474, 482, 483, 487, 488, 492, 497, 502, 503, 505, 515, 518, 519, 526, 531, 532, 536, 537, 541, 546, 549, 550, 551, 553, 556, 558, 559, 562, 565, 568, 569, 570, 573, 574, 580.
Fever on board has subsided 504
Letters to and from 198, 268, 272, 287, 550
Niger, regarding capture and detention of 385, 393, 396, 410, 411, 414–417, 427, 430, 448, 449, 463, 467–469, 535, 555, 556
Officers of, data regarding 40, 57, 65, 67, 97, 106, 107, 111, 112, 169, 171, 172, 186, 205, 233, 436, 442, 468, 494, 529, 546
Operations of 272, 287, 292, 368, 396, 451, 494, 495, 529, 568, 569
Orders and instructions for 65, 66, 172, 179, 197–199, 256, 257, 271, 277, 295, 296, 493, 504, 538
References to 159, 301
See *Nicholson, Samuel, Capt.*
Signals proposed by Admiral Vandiput, sent to 296
Vessels sighted or spoken by 243, 253, 354, 355, 370, 371, 373, 374, 378, 383, 409, 462, 466, 474, 492, 515, 532, 550
Virginia in company with 492, 497, 502, 505, 519, 526, 531, 536, 537, 541, 546, 550, 558
Visits to 327, 541, 550, 553, 556, 558, 559, 565
Consul, American, visited, frigate *Constellation*, off Morro Castle 441
Consular letters, extracts from, respecting captures by French 22–36
Consuls and vice consuls, uniform of Navy may be worn by 39
Convoys:
Connecticut vessels, regarding 425, 426, 561, 562
Havana to United States 288, 290, 319, 336, 344, 352, 353, 373, 431–433, 452, 453, 466, 486, 488, 508, 514, 561, 567, 568
Two left Havana with Spanish frigates 509
United States to Europe 333, 414
United States to Havana 288, 334, 335, 338, 341, 364
Cook, Collector, will not subsist French prisoners 422
Cook, David, seaman, *Constellation* 311
Cook, John, seaman, *Constellation* 314
Cooley, Robert, master, schooner from Jamaica, spoken by *Constitution* 532
Coolidge, J., & Sons, subscribed money for building ship for United States 168
Coolidge, William, ordinary seaman, *Constitution* 224

Page
Cooper, John, seaman, *Constellation* 307
Cooper, Robert, seaman, *Constellation* 308
Cooper, William, third lieutenant, *Constellation* 42
Copeland, John, boatswain's mate, *Constitution* 224
Copeland, Joseph, seaman, *Constitution* 226
Copper, spikes, nails, etc., for ships 145, 185, 217, 227, 243, 290
Corbett, Robert, seaman, *Constitution* 225
Cordis, John B., Lt., *Constitution* 107, 169, 171, 205, 223–226
Cornelius, John, ordinary seaman, *Constellation* 309
Corsairs, information of, requested by United States Consul O'Brien at Algiers 411, 412
Corsay, Francis, ordinary seaman, *Constellation* 313
Corson, Manuel, master of Spanish schooner *Santa Antonio Abad* 478
Corunna, Spain, captain of *Ann & Mary* turned ashore at 36
Cosgrave, Michael, ordinary seaman, *Constitution* 225
Coster, John, and Joseph, owners of *Lovely Lass* 31
Coster Brothers, loaders of cargo of *American Hero* 23
Cotton, Elihu, master of brig *Caroline* 34
Cottringer, Garrett, acting for Secretary of Navy 317, 540, 557, 571
Couch, James, nominated as carpenter for *Merrimack* 491
Coughlan, James, private, *Constellation* 311
Court of Claims, acknowledgment to VII
Courtney, Hugh, ordinary seaman, *Constellation* 308
Coust [Coush], John, appointed carpenter, ship *Merrimack* 574
Cowan, Edmund, seaman, *Constellation* 307
Cowan, Jeremiah, ordinary seaman, *Constellation* 312
Cowper, John, recommended as sailing master, brig *Augusta* 496
Cowper, William, Lt., U. S. frigate *Constellation:*
Instructions from Captain Truxtun 298, 299, 302, 303, 572, 573
Invitation to dine with Captain Truxtun 155
Name on muster roll 304
Recommended as sailing master's mate, brig *Augusta* 496
Recruiting for the *Constellation* 104
Cox, Captain, may serve as midshipman on *Baltimore* 260
Cox, Benjamin, ordinary seaman, *Constellation* 308
Cox, John S. K., warranted midshipman on *Herald* 174
Cox, William, ordinary seaman, *Constitution* 225
Coyle, James, ordinary seaman, *Constellation* 309
Craft, John, captain of *Pomona* 26, 35
Crafts, William, Navy agent, Charleston, S. C.:
Cannon from Halifax to be delivered to 500
Cannon to be forwarded to Wilmington by 396
Copper for Beaufort, S. C., galley to be forwarded through 413
Cross, Captain, is to superintend building of frigate 573
Galleys, construction and preparation for sea 248, 372, 391, 392, 573, 575
Letter for Captain Truxtun, to be delivered by 526
Prisoners, instructions regarding 530
Reference to 578
See *Morris, Thomas, et al.*
Shipbuilding by citizens, instructions regarding 330
Craig, William, and Henry Sadler, owners of brig *Amelia* 465
Crandon, Captain, of Wiscasset, prisoner in Guadaloupe 400
Crathorn, Joseph, merchant of St. Bartholomews 544
Craufurd, James, to report on suitability of *Ganges* 58, 59
Crawdhill, James, captain of *Sally* 26
Crawford, James, owner of schooner *Active* 28
Creighton, George, seaman, *Constellation* 306
Creighton, William, master of schooner *Park* 134
Crescent, frigate, built for Dey of Algiers 6, 61, 108, 162
Crissmon, Corporal, marine, *Constellation* 315
Croger, John, boy, *Constellation* 310
Crooker, Nathan, seaman, *Constitution* 223
Crosby, Peter, master's mate, *Constitution* 225
Cross, Major, contractor for *Merrimack* 525

Page

Cross, George, Capt.:
- Brig (revenue), command of — 386, 387, 401, 450–452, 523
- *Fox*, brig, regarding claim — 105
- Frigate building at Charleston to be superintended by — 343, 573, 575, 576, 578
- Marines to be furnished by Lieutenant Hall — 460
- May fall in with *Constitution* and *Virginia* — 451
- Offers himself for command of an armed vessel — 105, 106
- Relative rank of — 543

Crousillat, Lewis:
- Clearance for schooner *Minerva* — 565
- Owner of schooner *Commerce* — 332

Crowninshield, Benjamin, Capt. — 370

Crowninshield, George, & Sons, Salem, Mass.:
- Commission for ship *America* — 552
- Loan of two vessels offered — 369, 370
- Ship of, cannot be purchased — 339

Cruft, John, Capt., *Sally*, brig., captured by *La Decade* — 259

Cruising grounds:
- Atlantic coast, changes in — 256
- *Baltimore*, Captain Phillips — 461
- *Constellation*, Captain Truxtun — 93, 110, 159, 207, 461
- *Constitution*, Captain Nicholson — 197, 199, 292, 295, 296
- *Delaware*, Captain Decatur — 457, 458, 461
- *Diligence*, cutter, Captain Brown — 420
- *Eagle*, cutter, Captain Campbell — 528
- *Ganges*, Captain Dale — 77, 93, 197, 204, 221, 222
- *Herald*, Captain Sever — 254
- *Pinckney*, cutter, Captain Cross — 451, 452
- *Retaliation*, Lieutenant Bainbridge — 375, 380
- *Scammel*, Captain Adams — 553
- *United States*, Captain Barry — 161, 162, 458, 461

Cuba, *Sophia* to bring back destitute seamen from — 113

Culnam, John, consul at Teneriffe, capture of *Virginia Packet* — 26

Cunningham, captain of armed ship *America* — 468

Curacao:
- American vessels brought into port of — 22, 32, 241
- Burghers of, owners of privateer *La Raquir National* — 241

Curtis, Roger, Sir, to join Lord St. Vincent — 321, 322

Curtis, Thomas, Capt., in command of *Mary* — 23

Cushman, Clark, ordinary seaman, *Constitution* — 225

Customs, Bureau of, acknowledgment to — VII

Customs, Collectors of. See *Collectors of Customs.*

Cutter, Mitchell, master of brig *Honey* or *Aloney* — 34

Cutters. See *Revenue Cutters.*

Cutts, Joseph, seaman, *Constitution* — 225

D., of New York, Capt. Andrew Foster, condemned — 25, 26

Da Costa, Francis, to examine guns and howitzers — 75, 82

Dade, John, master's mate, *Constitution* — 226

Dailey, Richard, ordinary seaman, *Constellation* — 309

Dale, Edward C.:
- Acknowledgment to — VII
- Picture of Capt. Richard Dale reproduced through courtesy of — IX

Dale, Richard, Capt., U. S. ship *Ganges:*
- Command of *Ganges* — 51, 65, 72
- Frigate, new, will be offered to — 367
- *Ganges* commanded by, when purchased — 63
- Officers for *Ganges* to be named by — 72
- Orders and instructions to — 51, 72, 73, 77, 89, 110, 128, 145, 204, 205, 221, 222, 238, 271, 296, 318, 357, 369, 464, 510
- Picture of — Facing page 368
- References to — 93, 141, 256, 368, 375, 379, 408
- Relative rank — 357, 510, 542
- See *Ganges*, U. S. ship.
- Will not go out again in *Ganges* — 367

Dale, William, seaman, *Constellation* — 307

Dallert and Cartier, request clearance for *Southern Packet* — 440

Page

Dallest and Carlier, owners, schooner *Fame* 332
Dames and Champaigne. See *Champaigne* and *Dames*.
Daniels, Anthony, master of schooner *Citizen* 364
Daphnel, schooner, Joseph Ripley, in convoy from Hampton Roads 364
Daphney, schooner, at Havana 466
Darby, James, mate, taken from brig *Friendship* 24
Dark, cutter, Captain Davison, condemned at *Calais* 25
Darnel, William, master of sloop *Olinda* 30
Davenport, Anthony and Moses, owners of *Catherine* 23
David, owner of schooner *Anthony Wallis* 135
Davinson, James, seaman, *Constellation* 315
Davis, Benjamin, seamen, *Constitution* 224
Davis, Daniel, district attorney, Portland, Maine 421, 422
Davis, Daniel, ordinary seaman, *Constitution* 223
Davis, Edward, *Herald* purchased from 120, 121
Davis, Ezekiel, ordinary seaman, *Constitution* 223, 225
Davis, George, boy, *Constellation* 314
Davis, James, seaman B., *Constellation* 314
Davis, John, master of schooner *Eagle* 364
Davis, Thomas, master of brig *Louisa* 354
Davis, Timothy, captain of *Sally* 25
Davis, W., recommended as midshipman on *Norfolk* 383
Davis, William, Lt., *Constellation* 155, 200, 201, 304
Davison, captain of cutter *Dark* 25
Dawson, Philemon, master of *Adriana* when purchased 62
Dawson, William, seaman, forcibly taken from brig *Friendship* 24
Daymond, Captain, reference to 400
Deane, Benjamin, seaman and carpenter yeoman, *Constellation* 305
Dearing, Mr., artist who executed figurehead of *Merrimack* 525
Deaths 164, 235, 308, 310, 454, 459, 552
Deblois, James L., purser, U. S. frigate *Constitution* 107, 169, 172, 558
Debon, captain of French privateer *L'Espiegle* 29
Decatur, Stephen, Mr.:
  Acknowledgment to VII
  Picture of Capt. Stephen Decatur published by courtesy of IX
Decatur, Stephen, Capt., U. S. ship *Delaware*:
  Orders and instructions to 116–118, 141, 142, 149, 150, 174, 175, 192, 193, 457, 458
  Picture of Facing page 458
  References to 142, 151, 199, 203, 204, 256, 334, 336, 359, 368, 371, 381, 543, 545
  Report from 176, 177
  See *Delaware*, U. S. ship.
Decius, French privateer, captured brig *Philanthropist* 29
Decrees, French, references to 1–4, 32, 560
Deforest, Isaac, part owner of cargo of brig *Nabby* 29
Deist, Emanuel, seaman, *Constellation* 314
De Just, John, seaman, *Constellation* 306
Delano, master of *Accepted Mason* 566
Delany, Mr., pilot, reported on *Constellation* 243
Delany, Matthew, ordinary seaman, *Constellation* 315
Delany, Sharp, collector of customs at Philadelphia 63, 68, 114
Delaware, Marshal of, to release John Buffington from prison 458
Delaware, U. S. ship, Capt. Stephen Decatur:
  Crew of 110, 117, 119, 127
  Decatur, Stephen, Sr., to take command 116
  Formerly *Hamburgh Packet*, which see.
  French prisoners captured by 183, 203, 527
  La Croyable, captured French privateer 175, 176, 183, 231, 258
  Letters for 151, 175
  Material and equipment 82, 92, 101, 118, 120
  Officers for 116, 117, 151, 160
  Operations of VI, 145, 149, 158, 169, 203, 209, 211, 215, 220, 222, 250, 253, 255, 265, 270, 273, 276, 283, 286, 287, 294, 324, 325, 327, 331, 359, 363, 375, 384, 385, 388, 392, 401, 430, 442, 462
  Orders and instructions for 116–118, 128, 141, 142, 149, 150, 162, 174, 175, 192, 198, 199, 324, 457, 461, 538
  References to 190, 193, 254, 258, 297, 368, 442, 481

Page
Delight, ship, sent to *Constitution* for coffin 406
De Lozier, Daniel, surveyor of district of Baltimore 62
Demanes, C., passenger on British ship *Niger* 415, 417
Demmervill, Anthony, ordinary seaman, *Constellation* 309
Denabre, John, master, schooner *Commerce* 332
Denmark, trade of, protected everywhere by armed ships 484, 515
Dennis, Richard, owner of brigantine *Maria* 30
Dennis, Thomas, ordinary seaman *Constellation* 309
Dennis, Thomas, pilot, *Constitution* 335, 343
Denny, William, ordinary seaman, *Constellation* 309
Dent, John H., midshipman, *Constellation* 42, 155, 304
Depredations on our commerce, report of Secretary Pickering sent to Congress 5, 6
Deputy Collector, Lewistown, Del., to deliver instructions to *Ganges* 89
Derby, Mr., subscriber for ship to be built at Salem 366
Derbyshire, Thomas, ordinary seaman, *Constellation* 313
Desausure, Henry Wm., Charleston, S. C.:
Cochran. Captain. will not be tried by navy court 523, 524
Construction of ships and galleys 248, 249, 372, 391
Desertion, rules concerning 41, 42, 43, 49, 66, 73
Desforgues, M., French Minister for foreign affairs 3
De Shield, John, master of *American* 374
Deshields, J., master of schooner *Grey Hound* 364
Design and construction of ships to be dealt with in later volume VI
Desmoliers, captain of French privateer *Hydra* 35
Dey of Algiers. See *Algiers.*
Diamond, Thomas, boy, *Constellation* 310, 314
Diana, American ship, Captain Williams, bearer of letters 167
Dianen, John. See *Dinin, John.*
Dick, Elisha, ordinary seaman, *Constellation* 311
Dickason, Thomas, Jr., subscribed money for building ship for United States 168
Dickey, captain of Bristol schooner 422
Dickins, F., reference to 534
Diligence, U. S. R. C., Capt. John Brown:
Crew of 358, 442, 517
Equipment for 402, 408, 421
Griffith, John McRea, agent for 516
Operations of 442, 538
Orders and instructions 358, 420, 421
To carry arms, etc., to Carolina and Georgia 297, 406, 420
Dill, Joseph, captain's mate, *Constellation* 316
Dillaway, Henry, steward, *Constitution* 223
Dinin, John, private, *Constellation* 160, 310, 315
Disability, provisions for officers, marines and seamen 8, 189
Dispatch, brig, Captain Brown captured by French privateer 27, 81
Dispatch, schooner, M. Sawberion, in Hampton Roads convoy 364
Dixon, Henry, one of charters of *Lovely Lass* 31
Dobbin, John, seaman, *Constellation* 314
Dobree, P. F., consul at Nantz, American prizes captured 22, 23, 27, 28
Dodge, Levi, seaman, *Constitution* 224
Dodson, R. W., engraver of picture of Capt. Richard Dale IX
Dogget, Mr., pilot, *Constitution* 327, 342
Doggett, Matthew, master of schooner *Betsey and Jenny* 338
Dolphin, ship, Captain Preble, in collision with *Harmony* 489, 492
Donah, Joseph, owner of schooner *Daphnel* 364
Donaldson, John, cannon for *United States* purchased from 122, 123
Donaldson, John, to examine *Ganges* 58, 59
Donaldson, Joseph, owner of cargo of *Uricke Kock* 29
Donaldson, Thomas, notary public, Baltimore County 179
Donel, Francis, seaman, *Constellation* 307
Dongan, sergeant of Marines 579
Donolly, John, ordinary seaman, *Constitution* 225
Dorade, schooner, John Ennis, clearance permitted 332
Doran, James, ordinary seaman, *Constellation* 309
Dorant, master's mate, *Constitution*, sent ashore, ill 462

Page

Dorchester, schooner, captured by *Francis Zerby* 34
Dorman, John, seaman, *Constellation* 311
Dorsey, Lawrence A., in command of Wilmington galley 388, 396
Dorsey, Morris, ordinary seaman, *Constellation* 308
Douglass & Lawrence, loaders of cargo of *American Hero* 23
Dove, John, captain of ship *Governor Mifflin* 26, 81
Doyle, John, seaman, *Constellation* 312, 362
Doyle, John, seaman, *Constitution* 224
Driscoll, Timothy, ordinary seaman, *Constellation* 309
Driver, captain of armed ship *Planter* 132
Driver, sloop, Alexander McGivan, spoken by *Constellation* 260
Dronne, James, ordinary seaman, *Constitution* 226
Drucilia, sloop, spoken by *Constellation* 298
Drunkenness, Captain Truxtun's attitude toward 15
Dubouitier, (Du Bouetier) officer of *Niger* 415, 417
Duel between Capt. John W. Leonard, and Henry M. Rutledge 474
Duer, W. A., midshipman, U. S. R. C., *Governor Jay* 471
Duffy, Bartholomew, private, *Constellation* 310
Duncan, James, mate of brig *Philip* 475
Dunkirk, American vessels not admitted to 560
Dunlap, Mr., cannon ball may be obtained from 333
Dunn, Thomas H., private, *Constellation* 310
Dunn, William, ordinary seaman, *Constellation* 309
Dunscomb, William, master of English schooner *Thetis* 274
Dupayn (Dupang or d'Pine), captain of French privateer *Flower of the Sea* 200, 475–480
du Petit-Thouars, George, master of British ship *Niger*, account of capture by *Constitution* 414–417
Durant, John, quartermaster, *Constellation* 312
Durnant, Edward, master's mate, *Constitution* 226
Dynoff, William Tilton, customhouse, Philadelphia 63
Dyson Lieutenant, to furnish recruits to *Constellation* 93, 96
Eagle, brig, brought to by *Constellation* 559, 562
Eagle, French privateer, captured *Raven* 35
Eagle, schooner, John Davis, in Hampton Roads convoy 364
Eagle, schooner, permitted to clear, with French passengers 435, 436
Eagle, ship, Capt. Stephen Sweet, captured 79, 98
Eagle, U. S. R. C., Capt. Hugh Campbell:
- Brown, W. and A., builders of, paid on account 114
- Crew for 323, 324, 337, 422, 517
- Habersham, John, collector at Savannah, agent for 516
- Material and equipment 324, 402, 408, 434, 481
- Orders and instructions 323, 434, 442, 443, 481, 528, 529, 538
- Pennock, William to deliver letter to 527
- References to 336, 406, 430, 433, 455, 462, 483, 503

Earle, Johiel, ordinary seaman, *Constitution* 225
Earle, Oliver P., master of brig *Fair Eliza* 502
East, Asoie, ordinary seaman *Constellation* 315
Eaton, William, U. S. consul, Tunis, regarding vessels for Algiers 580
Eddy Peter, seaman, *Constellation* 307
Edward, Prince, agreed to loan cannon to United States 499, 500
Edwards, Philip, lieutenant of Marines, *Constellation* 42
Edwin, engraver of picture of Captain Barry IX
Elder, Frederick, seaman, *Constellation* 312
Eldridge, Daniel, master, U. S. frigate *Constellation* 126
Electra, brigantine plundered by French privateer 31
Eliot, Samuel, subscribed money for building ship for United States 168
Eliza, McConnell, master, sailing from Liverpool 566
Eliza, armed ship, Captain Benson, sailing from Liverpool 184
Eliza, armed ship, John Morrison, master 352, 353, 373
Eliza, brig, brought to by *Constellation* 223, 268
Eliza, brig, Capt. Alex. McConnel, convoyed by *Constellation* 135
Eliza, brig of Salem, Captain Mugford, captured 26, 35
Eliza, ship, Capt. Neal MacNeal captured by French privateer 164, 165, 245
Ellicot, Mr. reference to 361
Ellis, Samuel, commander of ship spoken by *Constitution* 280

Page
Elsworth, Jacob, ordinary seaman, *Constellation* 308
Elwell, Josiah, seaman, *Constellation* 314
Emory, John, seaman, *Constellation* 315
Engagements:
America, ship, with French privateer near Havana 466
Amphitrite with unnamed ship 340
Eliza, ship, with French privateer *L'Huereux Decidé* 164, 165
Unanimity, revenue brig, and H. M. S. sloop *Musketo* 252
Ennis, John, master, schooner *Dorade* 332
Ennis, Thomas, ordinary seaman, *Constellation* 315
Essabella (Issabella), schooner, spoken by the *Constellation* 260
Essenburgh, John, seaman, *Constitution* 224
Essex Institute, acknowledgment to vii
Esther and Eliza, American schooner, condemned by French 22
Evans, John, seaman, *Constellation* 311, 316
Evens, Thomas, ordinary seaman, *Constitution* 223
Excel, John, seaman, *Constellation* 307
Experiment, schooner, Captain Knap 466
Experiment, schooner, spoken by *United States* 351, 354
Fabius, schooner, Ebenezer Berry, master, spoken by *Constellation* 286
Factor, ship, Captain Kemp, spoken by *Retaliation* 470
Factor-Hazard incident, alleged conduct of Captain Leonard in 469–473
Fahie, captain of British sloop *La Perdrix* 371
Fair American, ship, Capt. O. P. Finley, convoyed by *Constellation* 135
Fair Columbia, snow, brought to by *Constellation* 291
Fair Eliza, brig, Oliver P. Earle, hoisted distress signal in convoy 502
Falconer, Mr 519
Falcott, Matthew, midshipman, *Constellation* 311
Fame, schooner, clearance of, with French persons 332
Fame, ship, Capt. J. Brown, captured and sold 22, 32
Fame, ship, of Philadelphia, exchanged salutes with *United States* 169
Famin, Monsieur, reference to 411, 412
Faner, William, seaman, *Constellation* 307
Fanning, captain of ship *Nonpareil* 83
Fanny, schooner, permitted to clear 498
Fanny, snow, Capt. Garrett Berry, captured 475
Farley, Joseph, ordinary seaman, *Constellation* 314
Farmer, brig, Capt. Jacob Whittimore, captured and sent into Bordeaux 55
Faugues, Peter, nominated as surgeon's mate on *Governor Jay* 379
Favourate, ship, from New York, spoken by *Herald* 549
Favourite, British ship, recaptured from French privateer by *Niger* 414
Favourite, French privateer, captured *Sally*, *Industry*, and *Bell* 34
Fawn, master of *Warren* 505
Fay (or Fry), jailor at Wiscasset 422
Fearson, Jesse, owner of brigantine *Liberty*, clearance permitted 196, 332
Featherstone, James, master's mate, *Constitution* 226
Felichy, Philip, American consul, Leghorn, assistance to Captain Calder 98
Felicity, spoken by *Constellation* 526
Fellows, Nathaniel, bond for private armed ship *Nancy* 284
Fells Point, Baltimore, rendezvous to be opened at 49
Felt, William, sailmaker, *Constitution* 224
Fenno, Mr 168
Fenwich, Mr 36
Fenwicke, J., consul at Bordeaux, reports captures of American vessels 23
Ferrall, auditor's office, sale of revenue cutter *Active* 59
Fever, prevalence of 271, 295, 366, 367, 375, 376, 493, 494, 502
Figurehead of Herald, carried away by gale 550
Figurehead of Merrimack, description of 525
Finlay, John, seaman, *Constellation* 307
Finley, O. P., captain of ship *Fair American* 135
Fire engines for Constitution by Thayer of Boston 10
Fisher, (Fishe), J. E., midshipman, U. S. R. C. *Governor Jay* 471, 474
Fisher, John F., sailing master, *Constellation* 313
Fisher, Samuel, express rider 90
Fisher, Thomas, witness to bill of sale of *Adriana* 63
Fitcomb, Jonathan, Jr., sailing master *Merrimack* 491, 574

Page

Fitcomb, Michael, Jr., first lieutenant, *Merrimack* 491, 574
Fitsgerrald, Edward, ordinary seaman, *Constellation* 309
Fitzgerald, master of *Merchant* 566
Fitzgerald, John, collector, Alexandria, money for recruiting *Constellation* 114–116
Fitzsgerrald, Thomas, ordinary seaman, *Constellation* 315
Fitzsgibbons, David, ordinary seaman, *Constellation* 309
Fitzsimons, Mr., written to about mates for cutter *Eagle* 323
Fitzsimons, Thomas, Philadelphia, Pa.:
- Agreement for timber for *Philadelphia* 215, 216
- Merchants of Philadelphia asked to build a frigate 143
- Statement relative to James Yard 544, 545

Fitzsmorris, James, private, *Constellation* 311
Flag:
- French to be used as signal 482
- Swedish to be flown by U. S. ships 207, 208, 255, 283, 292
- United States Jack, hoisted as signal on *Constellation* 243

Flag, Gersham, seaman, *Constellation* 307, 315
Flags of truce:
- French citizens may continue to depart 218
- Rozier, M., to clear for St. Domingo 213
- Two stopped at Norfolk by collector 237

Flaherty, Timothy, private, *Constellation* 311
Fletcher, Nathan, midshipman, U. S. ship *Merrimack* 491, 574
Fletcher, Patrick, Capt., U. S. Navy 186, 233, 421, 452, 487, 501, 543
- See *George Washington*, U. S. ship.

Fleur de la Mer, French privateer, Captain d'Pine (Dupang), depredations by 475–480
Flinn, Edmund, ordinary seaman, *Constitution* 225
Flogging on Constellation 157, 160, 386
Flora, ship, Capt. S. Calder, captured by privateer *Patroit* 79, 97
Florida, brig, Captain Hase, joined Havana convoy 466
Floridas, British should take possession of 118
Flower of the Sea, French privateer, Captain Dupayn, captures by 200
- See also *Fleur de la Mer*.

Flunewell, Richard, part owner of schooner *Orrington* 28
Flying Fish, French privateer, captured schooner *Active* 29
Flying Fish, of Philadelphia, Garrett Holsteincamp, pilot, in command 90
Fogues, French privateer, captured brig *John* 34
Folger, Mr 519
Forbes, Allen, acknowledgment to VIII
Forbes, John and R. B., part owners of money from brig *Commerce* 55
Forrest, George, loader of cargo of *Charlotte* 22
Fort, Joseph, seaman, *Constitution* 224
Fort Mifflin:
- French prisoners guarded at 203
- Guard to be returned to 16
- *La Croyable*, brought to, by *Delaware* 175
- Mutiny threatened by Negroes in Delaware River 149, 150
- Permission sought to land goods and prisoners from French prize 183, 184

Fort Wolcott, salutes exchanged with *Constitution* 325
Fortifications for city of New York 577, 578
Fortune, ship, Captain Smith 79
Foss, Thomas, seaman, *Constellation* 312
Foster, Mr., member of Congress 112
Foster, Mr., owner of brigantine *Mercury* 355
Foster, Andrew, captain of *D.* of New York 25, 26
Foster, Job, seaman, *Constitution* 225
Foudroyant, French ship, cannon formerly in, to be loaned to United States 490, 499, 500
Foundling, French privateer, Captain Bras:
- Captured ship *Louisa* 32
- Recaptured schooner *Industry* 30

Fox, brig, capture and condemnation of, reference to 105

Fox, Josiah: Page
Appointed navy constructor for frigate at Norfolk 265
Crescent, notice of launching 6
Letter to Captain Truxtun 10
Materials for frigate building at Norfolk 265
References to 233, 343
Fox, Rob W., U. S. Consul, Falmouth, correspondence with Rufus King 121, 122, 361, 362
Foxhall, Mr.:
Cannon to be furnished by, for Navy 382
Guns for *Ganges* 318, 357
Guns for Lieutenant Bainbridge 375, 379
Shot for *Eagle* and *Diligence* 408
Foxwell, American ship, Captain Stephens, sailing from Bristol 403
Frair, Edward, boy, *Constellation* 310
France:
Alexandria, Egypt, taken by 412
American vessels condemned by, in Spanish ports 20
Armed vessels of—
Congressional authority to capture 87, 88, 135–137, 181–183
Instructions to officers regarding capture of 77, 192, 194, 197, 204, 207, 433, 434
Attacks on cruisers of, on own ground, best protection to American trade 425, 426, 433
British seek engagement with Toulon fleet 321, 322
Cruising radius of privateers of 36
Decrees of, references to 1–4, 32, 560
Depredations of, along Spanish coast 26, 27
Flags of truce—
Permitted to clear with French citizens 100, 196, 206, 229
Stopped at Norfolk 237
Fleet of—
Defeated by Admiral Nelson 465, 480, 481, 485, 507
Departed from Toulon, Buonaparte on board 321, 322
Forces in West Indies—
Blocked up by English at Cape Francois 189, 255, 441, 509
Depend upon captures of bread and salt meat 255
Passengers on *Melpomene* permitted to land 162, 163
Porte in a state of war with 467
Privateers of:
Act authorizing capture of 87, 88, 135–137, 181–183
Activity of, seems to increase 35
America, shots exchanged with 466, 468
American vessels bound to Baltic not captured by 515
American vessels captured by 20, 22–36, 76, 79–81, 83, 145, 164, 165, 175–177, 187, 245, 251, 259, 399, 400, 421, 422, 465, 570
Amphitrite plundered by 475–480
Badly prepared for action 336
Barry, Captain, to lead squadron against 190
Betsey, brig, visited by 79
Betsey, schooner, chased by 266
Buonoparte, captured *Virginia Packet* 26
Constellation encountered only one during cruise 508
Dale, Captain, in search of 101
Destitute seamen in West Indies enter on 113
Equipped to operate against our commerce to be arrested by collectors of customs 5
Fear armed ships 419, 507
Hughes, Victor, operations of 274
If without commission, to be tried as pirate 77
La Croyable captured by *Delaware* 175
La Croyable, sale of 231, 258
Larger size to be fitted out 419, 484
L'Heureux Decidé captured ship *Eliza* 164, 165, 245
Men put on vessel bound for Alexandria, Va., by 78
Operations in West Indies 190, 319, 336, 508, 567
Prepared in Spain 507

France—Continued.
Privateers—Continued. Page
Prevent American vessels sailing from Malaga 20
Pushy Park and *Favourite* recaptured from, by *Niger* 414
Sans Pareil arrived at Newcastle 442
Sans Pareil captured by *United States* 331
Sunk by British frigate *Concord* 466
U. S. coast free of 166, 567
Very, Captain, ship of, boarded by 60
Yard, James, interested in operation of 544, 545
Quasi-war with:
Causes of v
1798–1801, selected as date to start publication v
Russia endeavoring to form new coalition against 322
Seven frigates left Brest recently 486
Ship of war at Lattimers wharf, information regarding 208, 209
Ship of war said to be on U. S. coast 110
Vessels, armed of. See *Armed vessels of France.*
Francis, Tench, purveyor:
Algiers, stores for 111, 494
Baltimore, spy glasses for 240
Blunderbusses for ships of war 322–324
Bread for Captain Barry's ship 438
Constellation, anchor for 17
Duck and hemp to be procured 321, 338
Ganges to be supplied by 76, 357, 369
Hulsecamp, Garrett, to be paid by 317
Muskets wanted for Norfolk 339
References to 10, 16, 39, 54, 104, 290, 334, 357, 420, 554
Retaliation to be supplied by 320, 321
Rope for Captain Barry's ship 163
Sophia to return crews of Algerine vessels 547
Francis, Messrs. Willings &. See *Willings & Francis.*
Francis, Thomas Willing, et al., *Ganges*, purchased from 63, 64
Francisco, Anthonio, seaman, *Constitution* 226
Francis Zerby, French privateer, captured schooner *Dorchester* 34
Francois, Jean, one of prize crew of brig *Planter* 248
Frankford, John, master of brig *Aurora*, captured by *Pauline* 34
Franklin, Benjamin, ship. See *Benjamin Franklin.*
Franklin, brig, Capt. Augustus Peck, taken into St. Domingo 24
Frazer, George, seaman, *Constellation* 316
Frazer, John, seaman, *Constellation* 307
Frazier, John, boatswain, *Montezuma* 399
Frazier, N., subscribed money for building ship 168
Frazier, William, marine for cutter *Diligence* 442
Frenau & Paine, letter to, from Captain Morrison of *Eliza* 352, 353
Freeburne, Peter, ordinary seaman, *Constellation* 309
Freeman, Major 437
Freeman, James, captain of brig *Betsey*, of Boston 78, 98
Free Mason, brig, Capt. John Wier, taken into St. Domingo 24
Fricon, Pon, prize master of brig *Planter* 248
Friends, sloop, Captain Moore, joined Havana convoy 466
Friendship, brigantine, of Salem, Captain Hodges, capture of 24, 25, 28
Friendship, brigantine urged to keep up with convoy 569
Friendship, schooner, spoken by *America* 466
Friendship, ship, of Boston, Captain Brown, capture of 251, 252
Friendship, ship, of Providence, Captain Proud, captured and condemned 26, 81
Frigates, U. S. See *Vessels, ships of war.*
Frothingham, Capt. Thomas G., O. R. C., acknowledgment to VII
Fry, Captain 70
Fry, David, ordinary seaman, *Constitution* 225
Fulkes, William, seaman, *Constitution* 224
Fullerton, John, ordinary seaman, *Constellation* 309, 314
Fullman, Holder, master of ship *Louisa* 32
Fund, special, for printing naval manuscripts, requested by President Roosevelt III

Page
Furman, Gabriel, alderman, New York 251, 252
Furnace, Wm., master of ship *Providence* 22
Gabot, captain of French privateer *Decius* 29
Gale, Anthony, lieutenant, U. S. M. C., guarding prisoners at New Castle 558, 579, 580
Gale, Moses, part owner of brig *Nathaniel* 29
Galleys:
Acquisition of, authorized 64
Construction and equipment, instructions regarding 246, 248, 249, 391, 392
Construction of, for Ohio and Mississippi Rivers 19
Materials and equipment 246, 249, 391, 392, 396–398, 413
Officers and men 64, 247, 249, 372, 388–392, 396–398, 573
Preferable for defense of Georgia 437
Rhode Island, number of, necessary for defense of 265
Yet to be procured 265, 295
Galt, Doctor 450, 468
Game, Mark, carpenter on *Montezuma* 380, 399
Ganges, U. S. ship, Capt. Richard Dale:
Barry, Captain, to go on board 78
Description of 63
Despatches for 89, 90, 112, 151, 175, 203, 238
Inventory of stores to be made 73
Listed as in service 368
Marines for 72, 269, 442
Material and equipment for 65, 69, 71, 73, 74, 76, 238, 282, 318, 337, 357, 369, 571
Officers of 65, 66, 72, 367, 408, 417, 418, 464, 482, 537, 538
Operations of vi, 101, 141, 145, 151, 162, 197, 204, 221, 256, 272, 275, 287, 376, 539
Orders and instructions 72, 74, 77, 91, 110, 204, 205, 221, 222, 238, 257, 271, 272
Preparation for sea 65, 317, 318
Purchase of vi, 51, 63, 64, 262
Recruiting for 72, 73, 527, 569
See *Dale, Richard C.*
Signals of, are deficient 571
Suitability for war to be ascertained 58, 59
Tingey, Captain, to relieve Captain Dale 408
Gardiner, Sharp, cook, *Constitution* 226
Gardner, Isaac, private, *Constellation* 310
Gardner, Samuel, master of schooner spoken by *Constitution* 373
Garretson, Isaac, purser, *Constellation* 42' 49, 125, 132, 155, 209, 303, 304, 540, 572
Garriscan, captain of French privateer *Pandor* 22
Garrison, captain of French privateer *Le Pandour* 32
Garts, Mr., passenger on British ship *Niger* 415, 416
Gates, Thomas E., commander of brigantine spoken by *Constitution* 236
Gavino, John, United States consul, Gibraltar 228, 229, 236, 411
Gay, captain of schooner *Liberty* 400
Gay, John, seaman, *Constitution* 224
Gazette, Portsmouth, N. H., extract from 340
Gazette of the United States, extract from 168
Geddes, Henry, master, brigantine *Sophia* 46–48, 485, 547, 554
Geddes, Simon W., lieutenant, U. S. M. C 327, 375, 376
Geer, Solomon, on board *Fleur de la Mer* 476
Gendall, John, ordinary seaman *Constitution* 224
General Accounting Office, *See Accounting Office, General.*
General Greene, schooner, William Moodie, permitted to clear 332
General Greene, U. S. R. C., Capt. George Price:
Collector at Philadelphia, agent for 516
Cruising instructions 221
Number of men allowed for 517
Operations 257, 272, 275, 538
Ready for sea when manned 210

Page

General Greene, U. S. ship, Capt. C. R. Perry:
Materials and equipment 359, 360, 512, 513, 536
Officers and men for 463, 513, 524, 525
State of preparation for sea 463, 538, 539
General Smallwood, ship, Captain Johnson, in company with *Harliquin* 400
General Tousaint, French privateer, captured brig *Sea Nymph* 34
Genereux, French warship, escaped to Corfu 480
Genoa, Italy, *Prudence*, sloop, carried into, by Corsican privateer 80, 98
George, brig, Captain Harden, joined Havana convoy 466
George, brig, Captain Rust, captured by French cruiser 27
George, brigantine, of Portland, Captain Waite, spoken by *Constitution* 474
George, sloop, Capt. John Grant, captured by French privateer 32
George, Richard, captain of *Bacchus* 23
George the Second, King of England, cannon presented to South Carolina 499
George Washington, U. S. ship, Capt. Patrick Fletcher:
Material and equipment 423, 428, 512, 514
Officers and men for 429, 452, 501, 513, 540
Purchase of 351, 352, 423, 428, 525
Talbot, Silas, instructed to outfit 428, 429
Will be ready to sail in December 539
Georgia:
Defensive measures for protection of 437, 438
Galleys, building in 246
Timber for frigate at New York, to be secured in 217
Georgia, Governor of, burning of Spanish schooner 437, 438, 444, 445
German, John, master, ship *South Carolina* 196
Gerry (Elbridge), Minister to France 46, 79, 109, 367, 550
Geyer, John, owner of *Rainbow* 22
Gibbs and Channing, Newport, R. I.:
Agents for the *General Greene* 539
Authorized to transport guns from Halifax 500, 501
French prisoners, disposition to be made of 530
Opinion of canvas asked 269
To deliver letter to Captain Nicholson 268
Vessel fitting out by 217, 227, 359, 360, 512–514, 525, 528, 536
Vessel of, at Warren, considered for purchase 146–148
Will assist in caring for sick of *Constitution* 493
Gibbs, Caleb 170, 215
Gibraltar:
Commissions for armed ships *Washington* and *Mercury* forwarded 228, 229, 236
Prizes sent to, by Admiral Nelson 480
Gibson, John, loader of cargo of *Catherine* 23
Gideon, American schooner, condemned and sold by French 22
Gilblass, schooner, Captain Ponsonby, spoken by *United States* 363
Gilbouin, ——, captain of French privateer *La Revanche* 81
Gilfoyle, Thomas, seaman, *Constellation* 312
Gill, Robert, Capt., storekeeper:
Articles, stores, etc., for ships 234, 235, 240, 282, 320–324, 328, 420, 438
Copper to be delivered to by Superintendent of Mint 290
Gillaspy, George, surgeon, U. S. Navy 16, 74, 544
Gilmore, Robert, & Co., owners of brig *Louisa* 364
Gilphin, John, seaman, *Constellation* 314
Girard, Stephen, owner of brigantine *Liberty* 206, 332
Gittings & Smith, owners of schooner *Grey Hound* 364
Glasses, spy and night, to be procured for *Baltimore* 240
Gnunervil, Francis, ordinary seaman, *Constellation* 309
Godfray, James, boy, *Constellation* 313
Goelet, James F., sailing master, *Ganges*, instructions to 537, 538
Goldsborough, Ch. W., for Secretary of the Navy:
Appointments of officers for *Merrimack*, approved 574
Can give information relative to commissions, etc 540
Commission as surgeon sent to Dr. Thomas Reynolds 540
Gonaives, vessels taken to, by privateers 24, 31
Good, John, ordinary seaman, *Constellation* 308
Good Fortune, French privateer, captured ship *Two Friends* 570

Good Friends: Page
Boarded by a British frigate 290
Extract from log of 290
Nancy, brig, spoken by 290
William Penn, crew of, brought home by 290
Goodhue, Benjamin, regarding ship built by Salem merchants 366, 367, 510, 511
Gore, Mr 566
Gorman, Daniel, mate, *Constellation* 273, 304
Gorsuch, captain, brig *Philip* 475, 476
Gosport, Va., vessel of N. Harbut, purchase and fitting out 207, 208
Goveots, Peter D., owner of schooner *Dispatch* 364
Governmental agencies, archives accessible in preparation of this work VII
Governor General of Bengal in Council 129
Governor General of Louisiana 39
Governor Jay, U. S. R. C., Capt. John W. Leonard:
Accounts of, must be arranged with Collector of Customs 571
Factor-Hazard incident 469–474
Faugues, Peter, nominated as surgeon's mate 379
Fitting out 222, 239, 244, 379, 517
Operations 221, 222, 257, 272, 275, 379, 380, 404, 538
Sands, Joshua, collector at New York, agent for 516
Governor Mifflin, ship, Capt. John Dove, captured by *La Zenadore* 26, 81
Governor of Havana. *See Havana, Governor of.*
Governors Island, N. Y., cannon for *United States* 70
Govett, Wm., witness to bill of sale of *Ganges* 64
Graaft, Peter, loader of cargo of *Charlotte* 22
Grafts, John, captain of ship *Pomona* 81
Graham, captain of brigantine *Washington* 23
Grallet, captain of French privateer *La Revenge* 55
Granberry and Nevison. See *Nevison and Granberry.*
Grand Signor of Egypt, alarmed at invasion 507
Grant, John, master of sloop *George* 32
Grant, Wm., master of schooner *Needham* 34
Grant, William, ordinary seaman, *Constitution* 224
Gravell, Joseph, seaman, *Constellation* 307
Graves, Frederick, boy, *Constellation* 314
Graves, James, seaman, *Constellation* 316
Gray, Mr., subscriber for ship to be built at Salem 366
Gray, W. W., charterer of ship *Sally* 23
Gray, William, of Salem, requested convoy for vessels at Havana 319
Grayson, Spencer, ordinary seaman, *Constellation* 308
Great Britain:
American trade not afforded much protection by 336
Brigantine of, captured by French privateer *La Croyable* 175, 176
Captures by 21, 22
Convoy furnished to American trade from 129, 130
Court of Vice Admiralty organized at Mole of St. Nicholas 21
Custom of, not to cruise in West Indies during hurricane season 255, 258
Failed in attack on Porto Rico 118
Fleet of to join for an attack on Toulon fleet 321, 322
French fleet in Mediterranean destroyed by 465
French frigates at Cape Francois blocked up by 255
Frigate of, boarded *Good Friends* but dismissed her 290
Frigates, measurements of, as compared with U. S. frigates 160
Frigates protecting 13 American vessels sailing from Malaga 27
Impressment of American seamen from *Lark* by *Hannibal* 251
Information to be secured from officers of, relative to guns 271
Minister of, declared *Niger* to be British 555
Nancy detained by U. S. Ship *Baltimore* 480, 482
Navy of, prevents invasion of Southern States from West Indies 140
Port au Prince vacated by 118
Privateer of, brought to by *Constitution* 374
Privateer of, held up Havana convoy 352, 353, 373
Property of consul at Baltimore taken from *Alexander Hamilton* 178

Great Britain—Continued. Page
Roman Emperor, rescued schooner *John* ... 31
Russia has promised to aid ... 322
St. Domingo, island of, will be attended to by ... 433
Sloop of war of, chased by *Constellation* and *Baltimore* ... 423
Watson, John, mutineer, delivered to consul at Norfolk ... 365
Green, captain of sloop *Julia*, captured ... 466
Green, Daniel, master of brig *Commerce*, captured by *Serpausonet* ... 34
Green, John, ordinary seaman, *Constitution* ... 225
Green, Thomas, boatswain, *Constellation* ... 209, 311
Green, Thomas, seaman, *Constellation* ... 305
Greene, General, figurehead for cutter to be likeness of ... 536
Grey Hound, schooner, J. Deshields, in Hampton Roads convoy ... 364
Griffin, John, commander of schooner from New London ... 319
Griffith and Nicklin. See *Nicklin and Griffith.*
Griffith, John McRea, collector, Wilmington, agent for *Diligence* ... 516
Griffith, Robert E., part owner of *Hamburgh Packet* ... 67, 68
Griffiths, David, private, *Constellation* ... 311
Grimes, William, seaman, *Constitution* ... 224
Grog, allowance of, to crew of the *Constellation* ... 152
Gross, Simon, first lieutenant, *Constellation*, instructions to ... 12–16
Guadeloupe:
French have 60 to 80 privateers out of ... 336
Montezuma, *Retaliation*, and *Eagle* to cruise around ... 336, 433, 434
Sophia to bring back seamen from ... 113
Trade with Baltimore by firm of Champaigne & Dames ... 274
Vessels taken to and condemned ... 29, 31, 333, 400
Guilliame Tell, French ship-of-the-line, escaped to Corfu ... 480
Gummerson, Thomas, quarter gunner, U. S. frigate *Constellation* ... 302, 303, 311
Guns:
For ships ... 82, 122–124, 195, 199, 227, 257, 318, 321, 328, 337, 357, 359, 379, 494
Morris, Richard V., to secure information from British officers ... 271
Truxtun, Captain, suggestions for mounting, etc ... 563, 564
Guns, etc., of captured vessels must not be disposed of in foreign ports ... 136
Habersham, John, collector, Savannah ... 516, 528, 557, 558
Hacker, Captain, recommended for appointment in Navy ... 102
Hacket, William, Captain, constructor of *Merrimack* ... 525
Hackett, James, Portsmouth, N. H.:
Engaged to build a ship at Portsmouth ... 130, 214
Frigate *Crescent* for Dey of Algiers, built by ... 6
McNeill, Daniel, may be appointed to ship building by ... 329
Hackett, William, captain of brig *Leonard*, of Newburyport ... 25
Hackett, William, seaman, *Constellation* ... 307
Hague, James, second corporal, *Constellation* ... 310
Hale, Henry, mate, ship *Alexander Hamilton* ... 178, 179
Haley, Dennis, ordinary seaman, *Constellation* ... 309
Haley, John, seaman, *Constitution* ... 225
Halifax, N. S.:
Cannon at, loan of to U. S ... 490, 499, 500, 501
Cargo of brig *South Carolina* landed at ... 251
Recaptured ship *Liberty* sent to, by H. M. S. *Lynx* ... 187
Hall, Captain, H. M. S. *Lynx*, *Liberty*, ship recaptured by ... 187
Hall, Mr., money procured for, for recruiting marines ... 355
Hall, Elijah, part owner of ship *Fame* ... 32
Hall, (John), Lieutenant, to supply Captain Cross with marines ... 460
Hall, John, master of schooner *Rebecca* ... 31
Hall, Thomas, ordinary seaman, *Constitution* ... 224
Hall, Thomas, private, *Constellation* ... 311
Hall, William, ordinary seaman, *Constitution* ... 226
Halley, Captain of *Hare* ... 25
Hambleton, Mr ... 365
Hambleton, James, private, *Constellation* ... 311
Hambleton, Robert, of Alexandria, owner of ship, *Ann* ... 135

Hamburgh Packet, ship: Page
Description of 68
Medicine chest of, to be inspected by Dr. Gillaspy 74
Purchase of, from Nicklin & Griffith 67, 68
See *Delaware*, U. S. ship.
Hamilton, Alexander, ship. See *Alexander Hamilton.*
Hamilton, Alexander 74–76, 102
Hamilton, Beth, *Constitution* 225
Hamilton, Colonel, and others, owners of ship *Providence* 22
Hamilton, General 220, 578
Hamilton, Robert, Marshal of Delaware, care of French prisoners 527, 530, 531, 558
Hamilton, William, seaman, *Constitution* 225
Hampton, Va., Samuel, Nicholson, Jr., buried at 454
Hampton Roads, Va.:
Constellation arrived at 122
Constellation ran into, for repairs and provisions 300
Convoy assembling for Havana 288, 334, 335, 338, 341, 364
Instructions for Captain Truxtun will be sent to 283, 284
Privateer captured and carried into, by *Constitution* 410, 430
Stores for *Constellation* shipped to 105
Hancock, John, seaman, *Constitution* 224
Hand, General, will be reimbursed for expense of French prisoners 458, 459
Hand, Major General 220
Hanna, ship, Captain Morland, to sail from Bristol 518
Hannah, American ship, Captain Morland, arrived at Bristol 403
Hannah, schooner, Nathaniel Ogder, in Hampton Roads convoy 364
Hannibal, British frigate, Captain Smith, impressment of eight seamen from *Lark* 251
Hansford, Edward, captain of schooner *Zephir*, arrived in Paris 24
Hansford, Edward, sailing master, *Constellation* 42
Harbut, N., vessel of, at Gosport, suitable for public service 207, 208
Harden, captain of brig *George* 466
Hardman, Thomas, private, *Constellation* 311
Hardy, captain of British 50 gun ship *Assistance* 215
Hardy, John, seaman, *Constitution* 224
Hare, Halley, Captain, taken into Dieppe and libeled 25
Harley, Barnard, ordinary seaman, *Constellation* 309
Harliquin, British brig, Capt. Benjamin Stiles, spoken by *Constellation* 400
Harmon, John, captain of brig *Venus* 24
Harmony, brigantine, captured by French privateers 30
Harmony, ship of Charleston, collided with *Dolphin* 492
Harmony Hall, brig, brought to by *Constellation* 387
Harper, Robert G., Capt. George Cross desires command of an armed vessel 105
Harriett, schooner, Robert Cleaves, permission to clear 206, 332
Harrington, Artemas, seaman, *Constitution* 226
Harriot, brig, spoken by *Constellation* 243
Harriot, flag of truce, Samuel Campbell, stopped by *Constellation* 276
Harriott, Nath., second lieutenant, U. S. R. C. *Governor Jay* 471
Harris, John, storekeeper, articles, etc., for ships 37, 38, 45, 56, 69, 71, 76, 82–87, 92, 95, 96, 101, 120, 334, 402
Harrison, William, seaman, *Constellation* 307
Hart, Joseph, seaman, *Constellation* 306
Harvard College Library:
Acknowledgment to VII
Records published by courtesy of 266, 410
Harvard University, Baker Library, acknowledgment to VII
Harvey, Dr 155
Harvey, Neal, seaman, *Constellation* 306
Harvey, Samuel, ordinary seaman, *Constitution* 224
Harvey, William, seaman, *Constellation* 306
Harwood, (Richard), lieutenant of Marines, ordered to recruit for *Baltimore* 193
Hase, captain of brig *Florida* 466
Hassan Bashaw, brig, fitting out by United States for Dey of Algiers 202
Hastin, George, master of brig *Sea Nymph* 34

Page

Hatfield, John, quarter gunner, *Constellation* 316
Havana, Cuba:
Arrival of Captain Truxtun at Norfolk from, reported 561
Best protection for trade to, would be two fast sailing schooners 468
Convoy bound for 335, 338, 364
Convoy from, by *Constellation* and *Baltimore* 288, 290, 319, 336, 344, 373, 431, 432, 433, 466, 486, 488, 508, 514, 515, 561, 565–568
Convoy from, under armed ship *Eliza* 352, 353
Maria, condemned and sold at 30
Merchants of Charleston, S. C., request convoy of vessels from 250
Merchants request money be brought from, by Captain Truxtun 365
Signals for use of vessels convoyed from 445–447, 514
Havana, Governor of:
Dispatches conveyed to, from Captain Truxtun 288, 432, 433, 436, 508
Letter from, on board schooner *Arb* 566
Permission requested of, for American merchant vessels to depart 432, 433
Havre de Grace, France:
Juliana, from Norfolk, sent into 26
Sophia, brig, bearing dispatches for envoys in France 46, 47, 78
Haverford College Library, acknowledgment to VII
Hawkins, Joseph, seaman, *Constellation* 307
Hawly, Mr., U. S. consul, Havana 445, 508
Hayman, William, seaman, ship *Alexander Hamilton* 178, 179
Hays, Mr 229, 236
Hays, John, seaman, *Constellation* 316
Hayward, captain of the *Juliana*, from Norfolk 26
[**Haywood**] **Heyward, Samuel**, capt., U. S. N.:
Pinckney, cutter, to be commanded by 573, 575, 576, 578
To recruit men 391
Hazard, schooner, Capt. William Montgomery, convoyed by *Constellation* 135
Hazard, schooner, of New York, Captain Kelly, boarded by *Governor Jay* 469, 470
Hazard, Stanton, to be appointed midshipman 260
Hazer, Benjamin, seaman, *Constitution* 225
Hazlehurst, Robert, & Co., Charleston, S. C 250
Head for General Greene will be procured 360
Heads for ships, useless ornaments, should not be expensive 356
Health, order for preservation of, on the *Constellation* 122
Hebe, Captain Lindegreen, brought into Nantes by French privateer 22
Hellen, brig, from Charleston, spoken by *Constellation* 228
Helm, James, captain of scow *Isabella* 28
Hemmingway, Joseph, ordinary seaman, *Constitution* 225
Hemp, Russia, Tench Francis, to procure 100 tons 321
Hempstead, Joseph, master of brigantine *Patty* of Weathersfield 4
Henderson, Alexander, loader of cargo of *Catherine* 23
Henderson, Joseph, ordinary seaman, *Constellation* 309
Hendrickin, John, ordinary seaman, *Constitution* 224
Henlopen, Cape, *Governor Jay*, to appear off, for communications 272
Henrietta, unarmed vessel, Captain Stevenson, sailing from Liverpool 183, 184
Henry, Isaac, surgeon's mate, *Constellation* 42, 304
Henry, John, witnessed duel between Captain Leonard and Henry M. Rutledge 474
Henry, Samuel R. D., midshipman, *Constellation* 311
Henry, Thomas, Jr., Dr., bearer of letter to Governor of Porto Rico 199
Herald, U. S. ship, Capt. James Sever:
Accounts for, will be forwarded by Stephen Higginson 329
Armament of 210
Complement of 171, 173, 210
Description of 121
Extracts from journal of Joseph Strout 327, 340, 351, 355, 358, 371, 378, 383, 384, 387, 392, 402, 441, 454, 461, 462, 466, 486, 492, 506, 519, 541, 548, 549, 550, 559, 560.
Figurehead carried away by gale 550
Listed as in service 368
Marines for 173, 328
Money for outfitting and recruiting 166, 167, 171
Officers for 107, 109, 111, 112, 166, 171, 329, 367, 487

Herald, U. S. ship, Capt. James Sever—Continued. Page
Operations of — 159, 166, 167, 171, 190, 193, 194, 198, 199, 254–258, 328, 349, 355, 500, 501, 529, 541
Pay and muster rolls, etc., left with Stephen Higginson — 328
Pickering sailing in company with — 340, 351, 356, 358, 379, 384, 385, 387, 392, 402, 441, 454, 462, 486, 492, 506, 519, 541, 549, 560
Purchase of, by United States — 120, 121, 262
Recruiting instructions for — 170, 171, 173
Supplies, etc., for — 529
Vessels spoken by — 327, 340, 355, 392, 441, 492, 519, 549
Herbert, George, private, *Constellation* — 310
Herbert, Joshua:
Invited to dine with Captain Truxtun — 155
Midshipman on rolls of *Constellation* — 304
Sailing master's mate on rolls of *Constellation* — 305
Herman, Wm., distressed seaman, left brig *Independent* — 78
Hermoine, British frigate, Hugh Williams, mutineer on — 312
Hero, ship, Captain Robinson, loaded with supplies for Algiers — 578, 579
Hero, storeship, to be convoyed to Algiers — 556
Herst, Allen, boy, *Constellation* — 310
Hetty Jane, ship, condemnation of, at Basseterre — 235
Hewbert, Joshua, S. M., *Constellation* — 315
Heyward, Samuel, See *Haywood, Samuel.*
Hibernia, English schooner. Bates, Commander, examined by *Constitution* — 532
Hible, John, private, *Constellation* — 316
Hickey, Valentine, ordinary seaman, *Constitution* — 226
Higginson, Stephen, Navy agent, Boston:
Agent for U. S. ship *Portsmouth* — 539
Articles for fitting out ships — 166, 194, 210, 512, 513, 529
Barry to sail without *Pickering* if she is not ready — 199, 200
Cutters fitted out by Treasury, turned over to Navy — 166
Equipment of the new revenue cutter may be assigned to — 159
French prisoners, disposition of — 530
Hackett, Mr., engaged to build a ship at Portsmouth — 130
Herald, ship, purchased by, for United States — 120, 121
Marines of *Portsmouth*, clothing for — 360, 512, 513
Naval affairs, discussions of — 166, 167, 194, 198, 199, 210, 258, 289, 328, 329, 350, 356, 487, 488, 513, 529, 530
Officers, selection of, comments on — 106, 107, 109, 111, 112, 159, 167, 487, 488
Orders to make preparations to send vessels to warmer climate — 539
References to — 255, 349, 576
Remittances to, made, or ordered — 171, 258, 290, 329, 529
Subscribed money for building a ship for United States — 168
To deliver letter to Captain Barry, for Governor of Porto Rico — 203
Will supply money for recruiting for *Portsmouth* — 491
Higginson, Stephen, Jr., subscribed money for building a ship for United States — 168
Highland, John, G. mate, *Constellation* — 314
Hill, F., Capt., schooner *Clara*, extract from log of — 496, 497
Hill, James, boy, *Constellation* — 313
Hill, Samuel, captain of ship, carried into Carthagena — 26
Hillar (Benjamin), Lt., U. S. R. C. *Pickering* — 329, 577
Hiller, Joseph, collector, Salem, commission to ship *America* — 552
Hills, John, recommended for second lieutenant, cutter *Pickering* — 577
Hilman, Robert, ordinary seaman, *Constitution* — 226
Hilsberry, John, ordinary seaman, *Constellation* — 312, 362
Hincks, James, ordinary seaman, *Constitution* — 225
Hind, British frigate, spoken by U. S. ship *Herald* — 441
Historical Society of Old Newbury, acknowledgment to — VII
Hobart, Henry, seaman, *Constellation* — 307
Hobdy, George, ordinary seaman, *Constellation* — 313
Hodgden, Mr., agent for Quartermaster General — 90
Hodgden, Samuel, to Secretary of State, delay of Algerine vessels — 549, 550
Hodgdon, captain of brig *Philanthropist* — 29
Hodgdon, Samuel, storekeeper, stores etc., for ships — 45, 53, 54, 95, 96, 280, 338, 402

Page
Hodge, Charles, ordinary seaman, *Constitution* 225
Hodge, John, ordinary seaman, *Constellation* 308, 315
Hodge, Michael, surveyor of Newburyport 121
Hodges, Benjamin, part owner of brigantine *Friendship* 28
Hodges, George, master of brigantine *Friendship* 28
Hodges, Samuel, boy, *Constellation* 310
Hodgson, M., owner of *Sally* of Alexandria 26
Hoff, John, captain of *Light Horse* 23
Hogan, John, ordinary seaman, *Constellation* 313
Hogg, Caleb, acting midshipman, *Constitution* 226
Holden, John, seaman, *Constellation* 316
Holland, William, seaman, *Constitution* 226
Hollensworth, John, ordinary seaman, *Constellation* 309
Hollingsworth, L. & Sons, requested to furnish ballast for *United States* 440
Hollingsworth, Zebulon, at Elkton, to receive guns for *United States* 123
Hollins, John, owner of schooner *Park* 364
Hollins, John, owner of ship *Abigal* 364
Hollins, John, owner, ship *Alexander Hamilton,* plundered by *La Croyable* 177
Holmes, Benjamin, Boston, Mass., brig of, spoken by *Constitution* 565
Holmes, Robert, Capt., in command of *Mary* 23
Holsteincamp, Garrett, pilot, bearer of dispatches 83, 90, 151, 175, 203, 317
Holston, John, seaman, *Constitution* 223
Honey or Aloney, brig, captured by *Pauline* 34
Hook, William, private, *Constellation* 310
Hooper, Joseph, purser, ship *Merrimack* 491, 574
Hooton (or Hoston), Isaac, ordinary seaman, *Constitution* 223
Hope, brig, Captain Wheelwright, captured and sent into Falmouth 361
Hope, schooner, Capt. Wm. Baldwin, convoyed by *Constellation* 135
Hope, schooner, from Baltimore, spoken by *Constellation* 435
Hope, schooner, James Benson, in convoy from Hampton Roads 364
Hope, ship, Capt. John Rogers, captured by French privateer *O'Hardy* 26, 28
Hope, ship, from Baltimore, Captain Stokston, spoken by *Herald* 519
Hope, ship, of Providence, R. I., spoken by *Constellation* 441
Hope, ship, spoken by *Constitution* 373
Hopkins, captain of ship *Sarah* 108
Horn, George, seaman, *Constitution* 225
Hornsby, Thomas, seaman, *Constellation* 306
Hospital in Paris, distressed condition of our seamen in 25
Hospital stores, U. S. frigate *Constellation* 93, 125
Hoston (or Hooton), Isaac, ordinary seaman, *Constitution* 223
Howard Abraham, seaman, *Constellation* 307
Howard, captain of brig *Polly* 466
Howard, Cornelius, ordinary seaman, *Constitution* 224
Howard, Joseph, owner, schooner *Ranger* 332
Howard, Thomas, seaman, *Constellation* 311
Howel, William, boy, *Constellation* 310
Howell, Governor of New Jersey, disposition of French prisoners 203
Howell, William, ordinary seaman, *Constellation* 314
Howes, Robert, lieutenant, *Constellation* 314
Howland, Gilbert, captain of brig *Two Friends* 81
Howland, Gilbert, master schooner *Betsey,* extract from journal of 266
Howland, John, captain of schooner *Rainbow* 24
Hoyt, James, seaman, *Constitution* 223
Hubbard, Nehemiah, agent, Middleton, Conn., shipbuilding 185, 218, 219, 227, 280, 281
Hubert, George, boy, *Constellation* 310
Huchings, William V., Lt., U. S. ship *Herald* 174
Hughes, Samuel, cannon for ships 10, 195, 234, 333
Hughes, Victor:
  Activities of, brought to attention of President Adams 293
  Privateer owned by, captured vessel of Capt. Wilson Jacobs 274
  Yard, James, supposed to be an agent of 544
Hugues, Victor, French agent in the West Indies 4, 400
Huis, Alexander, master of schooner *Mary* 364
Hulbert, Seth, seaman, *Constellation* 312
Hull, Isaac, Lt., U. S. N 169, 483

Hulsecamp, Garrett, pilot. See *Holsteincamp, Garrett.* Page
Humphreys, Mrs., reference to 232, 424
Humphreys, Clement, bearer of dispatches to France 46–48, 78, 485, 509, 547
Humphreys, David, United States Minister to Spain:
American vessels may not sail from Cadiz carrying guns 547, 548
Defeat of French fleet by Admiral Nelson 465, 480, 481, 507
Eliza, crew of, marched as prisoners into France 245, 246
French operations about Spain discussed 419, 420
Mediterranean, possibilities of trade in, discussed 484, 485
Urges the expediency of having armed ships in the Mediterranean 507
Humphreys, Joshua, naval constructor:
Agent for ship *Ganges* 539
Algerine vessels to furnish shot, etc., for cutters 297, 405, 406, 408
Barry, Captain, reports on sailing qualities of *United States* 232, 233, 424
Brown, William and Abra, paid on account for building *Eagle* 114
Campbell and Brown, Captains, to wait for nothing 405, 406
Constellation, report of launching of, by Captain Truxtun 17
Constitution, state of, requested from Captain Nicholson 171
Cost of galleys 248, 249, 391
Eagle and *Retaliation* to be put to sea 324
Fitting out and repairs to ships 82, 92, 282, 318, 323, 337, 357, 369, 402, 547
French schooner captured by Captain Decatur, to be prepared for sea 184
French warship at Lattimers wharf, information concerning 208, 209
Ganges and *Retaliation* to be prepared for sea 317
Instructions relative to preparation of Algerine vessels 509, 510, 578, 579
La Croyable, prize schooner, to be bid for at sale 258
Money to be furnished by 323, 358, 375
Morris, James, reports on sailing qualities of *United States* 233
Ordered to Baltimore relative to launching of *Constellation* 9
Ships for sale in Baltimore to be examined by 116
Sophia has arrived at Boston 509
Sophia to bring back American crews from Algiers 554
Superior, ship, at wharf in Philadelphia, to be bought by 129
Table giving dimensions of ships of war, prepared by 154
Two Friends, to examine and report on fitness of 57
United States launched in yard of 5
United States to be examined and repaired by 45
Humphreys, William, seaman, *Constellation* 312
Hunff, Philip, seaman, *Constellation* 307
Hunt, Gideon, seaman, *Constitution* 225
Hunt, John, private, *Constellation* 311
Hunt, John, ordinary seaman, *Constitution* 223
Hurd, William, commander of schooner spoken by *Constitution* 276
Hurricanes in West Indies, S. Higginson asked for opinion 258
Hurricanes keep British cruisers out of West Indies 255, 256, 258
Hutchins, Lieutenant, command of *Herald* suggested for 329
Hutchins, William, seaman, *Constitution* 226
Hutchinson, Alexander, seaman, *Constellation* 315
Hutson, Robert, private, *Constellation* 315
Hutt, John, seaman, *Constellation* 305
Hydra, French privateer, captured ships *Ceres*, *Sally*, and *Bacchus* 35
Hydrographic Office, Navy Department, acknowledgment to VII
Illustrations, list of IX
Imprisonment of American seamen by British frigate *Hannibal* from sloop *Lark* 251
Independent, American brig, at Alicante 78
Independent Chronicle, Boston, Mass., extracts from 252, 466
Indians, not to be enlisted in Marine Corps 41
Individuals cooperating in preparation of this work VII, VIII
Industry, brig, spoken by *Constellation* 385
Industry, schooner, Captain Misroon, captured by *Favourite* 34
Industry, schooner, captured by British frigate *Ceres* 30
Industry, ship, sighted by *Constitution* 253
Infantry, U. S. Army, marines to be recruited from 110

Page

Ingraham, Captain, in Tripoli, reference to ... 411
Ingraham, John, master of ship, brought to by *Constitution* ... 569
Ingraham, Nathaniel and Comfort Sands, owners of *Light Horse* ... 23
Injuries to United States commerce from French, enumeration of ... 1, 2
Innes, John, ordinary seaman, *Constellation* ... 313
Innis, Alexander, Marine, *Constellation* ... 310
Instructions to commanders of armed vessels ... 88
Isabella, snow, Capt. James Helm, condemned by French ... 22, 28
Island belonging to Isaac Pollock, purchase of considered ... 137
Israel, Joseph, master of brig *Mary* ... 520
Issabella (Essabella) schooner, spoken by *Constellation* ... 266
Ives and Brown. See *Brown & Ives.*
Jackson, Mr., passenger on British ship *Niger* ... 414, 415
Jackson, Clement, highest bidder for old U. S. R. C. *Scammel* ... 317
Jackson, Ebenezer, navy agent, Savannah, Ga.:
  Galleys, fitting out of ... 391, 397, 398
  Prisoners, disposition of ... 530
Jackson, Henry, Gen., navy agent, Boston ... 10, 38, 39, 96, 108, 179
Jackson, James, Governor of Georgia, protection of the State ... 437
Jackson, James, marine on *United States*, killed by shifting ballast ... 552
Jackson, James, ordinary seaman, *Constitution* ... 226
Jackson, Joel, boy, *Constellation* ... 310
Jackson, Richard, seaman, *Constellation* ... 305
Jacobs, may be used in fitting out *George Washington* ... 429
Jacobs, Captain, information of operations of Victor Hughes ... 293
Jacobs, William, boy, *Constellation* ... 310
Jacobs, Wilson, Capt., vessel of, captured by privateer ... 274
Jacques, Robert, seaman, *Constellation* ... 315
James, James, lieutenant of Marines ... 442
Jane, schooner, of Boston, overhauled by two English cruisers ... 441
Jarvis, Admiral, Cadiz, port of, blockaded by ... 32
Jarvis, Philip, acting lieutenant, *Constitution* ... 205, 546
Jay, John, Governor of New York:
  Cannon, loan of ... 44, 55, 70
  Fortifications for New York City ... 577
  Reference to ... 523
Jealous, sloop, Capt. Joseph Renne, captured by *United States* ... 377
Jean Rabel, vessels taken to ... 30, 32
Jeanet, French agent at Cayenne ... 29
Jeaton, Hopley, late commander of Old U. S. R. C. *Scammel* ... 317
Jefferson, John, seaman, forcibly taken from brig *Friendship* ... 24
Jeffrey & Russell subscribed money for building ship for United States ... 168
Jeffries, Joseph, seaman, *Constitution* ... 225
Jenkins, George, seaman, *Constitution* ... 224
Jenks, Scott, Capt., in command of *Confederacy* ... 23
Jennings, Henry, seaman, *Constellation* ... 307
Jeremie, neutral vessels bound to, to be captured ... 4
Jet, William, owner of schooner *Hope* ... 135
Jocelin, Ameziah, naval agent, Wilmington, N. C.:
  Galleys, fitting out of ... 391, 396, 397
  Prisoners, disposition of ... 530
John & James, condemned by French in Spanish port ... 28
John, Capt. James Scott, condemned at Morlaix ... 25, 26
John, Capt. John Tucker, captured by French privateer *Fogues* ... 34
John, schooner, plundered by French ... 31
John, ship, *United States* fired at wreck of ... 201
Johnson, captain of *John & James* ... 28
Johnson, George, ordinary seaman, *Constellation* ... 315
Johnson, Henry, on *Constitution* ... 226
Johnson, John, commander of brigantine *William* ... 355
Johnson, Nicholas, agent, Newburyport, Mass ... 365, 366, 491, 513
Johnson, Robert, seaman, *Constellation* ... 307
Joice, John, ordinary seaman, *Constellation* ... 309
Jolly, William, ordinary seaman, *Constellation* ... 308
Jones, Mr., Treasury Department, information requested of ... 123
Jones, Edward, certifies to sale of Old U. S. R. C. *Scammel* ... 317

Page
Jones, John, seaman, *Constellation* 306, 307, 314
Jones, John Coffin, owner of *Mercury* and *Washington* 228, 229, 236, 239
Jones, Lloyd, master, ship *Benjamin Franklin* 100
Jones Simon, ordinary seaman, *Constellation* 308
Jones, Thomas, seaman, *Constellation* 307
Jones, William, seaman, *Constitution* 223, 314
Jose, Michael, master of ship *Atlantic* 34
Joseph, Antonio, ordinary seaman, *Constellation* 313
Joseph, armed ship, Capt. Henry Bool, detained at Cadiz 547, 548
Joseph, John, seaman, *Constellation* 315
Joseph, Stone, master, sailing from Liverpool 566
Josephus, Anthony, ordinary seaman, *Constitution* 223
Joy, Malzar, captain, private armed ship *Nancy* 284
Julia, sloop, Captain Green, loss of crew of 466
Juliana, Captain Hayward, captured and sent into Havre 26
Juna, Captain Walter, brought into Nantes by French privateer 22
Juno, brig, Capt. W. H. Nickols, captured by *Reserve* 34
Jurisdiction of United States on our coast, extent of, defined 77
Justice, William, private, *Constellation* 310
Kean, Robert, master of ship *Abigal* 364
Kearney, captain of British vessel *Roman Emperor* 31
Keener, Edward, ordinary seaman, *Constellation* 314
Keener, Frederick, ordinary seaman, *Constellation* 308
Kelly, captain of schooner *Hazard* 469
Kelly, Patrick, ordinary seaman, *Constellation* 308
Kelly, Thomas, cooper, *Constellation* 305
Kelly, Thomas, ordinary seaman, *Constellation* 308
Kemble, Robert, ordinary seaman, *Constitution* 223
Kemp, captain of ship *Factor* 469, 471, 472
Kenen, Edward, private, *Constellation* 311
Kennedy, Mr., of Baltimore, vessel of, left convoy 148
Kennelly, Stephen, seaman, *Constellation* 308
Kenyon, Henry, Lt., U. S. schooner *Retaliation* 281, 282, 320
Kerling, Christopher, seaman, *Constitution* 225
Kerry, Mr., French consul, Leghorn 98
Kerumhappuch, brig, taken into St. Domingo 24
Key, John, ordinary seaman, *Constellation* 308
Kilby, captain of brig *Molly* 466
Kimble, Raymond Lee, seaman, *Constellation* 307
King, Charles, ordinary seaman, *Constellation* 308
King, Rufus, United States Minister in London 121, 122, 132, 138, 167, 175, 183, 237, 269, 277, 317, 318, 323, 361, 362, 403, 505, 518, 519, 566
King, Thomas, reference to 437
Kingsman, Benjamin, ordinary seaman, *Constellation* 313
Kirby, captain of ship *Polly* of Baltimore 33
Kirby, Nicholas, master of ship captured at St. Jago, Cuba 34
Kirk, Henry, seaman, *Constitution* 223
Kitchin, Mr., reference to 176
Kitty, brig, Captain McBride, spoken by *United States* 354
Kitty, schooner, Capt. J. Singleton, captured by *Trois Soeurs* 34
Knap, captain of schooner *Experiment* 466
Knox, General, referred to 220
Knox, Dudley W., Capt., U. S. N. (retired) Preface, v–viii
Knox, H., Boston, letter to President 139–141
Knox, Henry J., midshipman, U. S. N 169
Knox, Mrs. D. W., acknowledgment to viii
Knitmyer, David, seaman, *Constitution* 223
Kosciuszko, General, reference to 277
Koster, John, seaman, *Constellation* 306
Lacassas, French privateer, captured brig *Nathaniel* 29
La Cassius, corvette, guns belonging to 280
La Courageuse, French privateer, Captain Alaise, captured ship *Outram* 81

Page

La Croyable, French privateer:
Capture of, by *Delaware* 175–179
Picture of Frontispiece
Prisoners from, to be allowed to work for wages 268
Sale of 231, 258, 261
Vessels captured by 175–179
La Decade, French frigate, *Sally*, brig, Captain Cruft, captured by 259
La Fleur de la Mer, French privateer, prisoners from 422
La Fortune, French privateer, captured ship *Friendship* 81
La Furet, French privateer, captured ship *Plato* 81
Lamberton, N. J., prison at, suitable for French prisoners 203
L'Amiable Louise, French privateer, captured brigantine *Harmony* 30
Lamp, John, seaman, *Constellation* 305
Lamson, John, captain's clerk, *Constitution* 226
Lancaster, John, quarter gunner, *Constellation* 305
Lancaster, Pa., French prisoners at 242, 458, 459
Landen, John, seaman, *Constitution* 225
Lane & Salter, Secretary of War may employ them 382
Lang, Abraham, seaman, *Constellation* 306
La Pearl, French privateer, captured brigantine *Maria* 30
La Perdrix, H. M. S., spoken by *United States* 371
La Raquir National, French privateer, captured schooner *Lemmon* 241
L'Archaye, neutral vessels bound to, to be captured 4
Larcom, Amos, ordinary seaman, *Constitution* 226
Large, J. H., & Co., owners of *Charlotte* 22
Lark, sloop, owner Edward Burrowes, granted free clearance 206
Lark, sloop, prisoners from *Friendship* put on board, 251
Lark, sloop, Thomas Adams, permit issued for clearance 332
La Revanche, French privateer, Captain Gibouin 81
La Revenge, French privateer, Captain Grallet; plundered brig *Commerce* 54, 55
La Rochelle, tribunal of, cleared American ship *Roxana* 25
Lasmartres, Mr., passport to clear schooner *Eagle* 435, 436
Las Pasages, Spain, landing at, of American prisoners from *Eliza* 164
Lattimer, George, collector of revenue, Philadelphia 206, 411, 516, 565
Lattimer, Roe, recommended as midshipman, brig *Augusta* 496
Laurens, American ship, captured by French privateers 3
Laurens, Henry. See *Morris, Thomas, et al.*
La Vengeance, French frigate, reference to VI
Lawless, John, boy, *Constellation* 310
Lawrance William, seaman, *Constellation* 312
Lawrence, Andrew, captain of ship *Plato* 81
Lawrence, John, master of brig *Nabby* 29
Lawrey, captain of British ship *Pushy Park* 414
Lawson, Richard H. L., recommended as midshipman, brig *Augusta* 496
Laycock, late gunner of ship *Stag* 476
La Zenodore, French privateer, Captain Poule, captures of 81
La Ziza, French privateer, Capt. Clement Roux, captures of 81
Leader, Henry, captain of sloop *Peggy* of Bristol 81
Leander, schooner, captured by French privateer 177
Lebas, ———, French agent to Windward Islands 4
Leblanc, French agent to Leeward Islands 3
Le Brun, M., French minister for foreign affairs 2, 3
Le Chasseur, French privateer, captures by 28, 33
Le Chauffeur, French privateer, capture of schooner *Orrington* 81
Lee, General, recommends Captain Spotswood 536
Lee, Major General, referred to 220
Lee, Charles, United States Attorney General, *Niger* controversy 463
Lee, Stephen, sailing master, warranted for duty on *Adams* 186
Lee, Thomas, seaman, *Constellation* 307
Leeward Islands 3, 4, 21
Leffingwell & Pierpont, owners of *Confederacy* 23
Leghorn, French consul at, *Flora*, capture of 79
Lella Aisha, schooner, fitting out for Dey of Algiers 202
Le Maitre & Co., mercantile house of Victor Hughes 274
Lemmon, schooner, Thomas Smith, captured 241
Le Neuf Thermidor, French privateer, capture of *Orrington* 28
Le Neuf Thermidor, French privateer, capture of ship *Polly* 33

Page

Leonard, brig, taken into Dieppe 25
Leonard, John W., Capt., U. S. R. C. *Governor Jay*:
 Bearer of letter to Captain Dale 271
 Factor-Hazard incident, duel with Henry M. Rutledge 474
 Letter regarding conduct of, by officers of *Governor Jay* 469–471
 Orders and instructions to 222, 239, 272, 275, 379, 571
 See *Governor Jay, U. S. R. C.*
Leonard, Patrick, ordinary seaman, *Constellation* 235, 312
Leonard, William, ordinary seaman, *Constellation* 309
Leoradie, French privateer, captured brigantine *Six Brothers* 29
Le Pandour, French privateer, captured ship *Fame* 32
L'Espeigle, French privateer, captures by 29, 30
Les Thermidor, French privateer; captures by 81
Le'tombe, Mr., Consul General of French Republic:
 American vessels no longer admitted into French ports 560, 561
 Clothing for French prisoners 530, 531
 Granted permission to remove French citizens 218
 Two flags of truce stopped at Norfolk 237
Le Triumphant, French privateer, captured *Friendship* 28
La Vengence, French privateer, capture of *Harmony* 30
Lewis, Charles, boy, *Constellation* 316
Lewis, Charley, one of prize crew of brig *Planter* 248
Lewis, Daniel, commander, ship *Louisa* 259
Lewis, John, impressed on British frigate *Hannibal* 251
Lewis, John, seaman, *Constitution* 223, 225
Lewis, John, seaman, *Constellation* 313
Lewis, Thomas, marshal, New Jersey; custody of French prisoners 289
Lewis, Thomas, and Son, owners of ship *Industry* 253
L'Heureux, Decidé, French privateer, captured *Eliza* 164, 165
L'Hirondelle, French privateer, captured sloop *George* 32
Libby, Jacob, carpenter, *Constitution* 224
Liberty, armed ship, Brae, commander, sailing from Liverpool 566
Liberty, armed ship, sailing from Liverpool 505
Liberty, brigantine, Jesse Fearson, master, clearance given 196, 332
Liberty, brigantine, owner Stephen Girard, clearance permitted 206
Liberty, brigantine, Thomas Lillibridge, master, clearance given 332
Liberty, schooner, Captain Gay, account of capture of 399, 400
Liberty, ship, Captain Verdenberg, captured by *La Croyable* 175, 176, 177
Liberty, ship, captured by French privateer 187
Library of Congress, Manuscript Division and Rare Book Room, acknowledgment to VII
Light Horse, brought into Nantes by privateer 23
Light, John, quartermaster, *Constellation* 305
Lillibridge, captain of brig *Kerumhappuch*, arrived in Paris 24
Lillibridge, Gardner, master of ship captured at St. Jago, Cuba 34
Lillibridge, Thomas, master, brigantine *Liberty* 332
Lin, John, seaman, *Constellation* 313
Linch, James, boy, *Constellation* 311
Lincoln, Benjamin, collector, Boston:
 Commissions, etc., for armed ships 186, 236, 250
 Cutter, construction and fitting out 56, 516, 518
 Officers for cutter 158, 159
 Passport to clear schooner *Eagle* with French passengers 435, 436
 Reference to 229
Lindegreen, Captain, in command of *Hebe* 22
Lindsay, Captain, in command of *Charlotte* 22
L'Insurgent, French privateer VI, 304–314
Liston, Robert, British Minister to United States:
 Cannon at Halifax, loan of to United States 490, 499, 500
 French passengers on *Melpomene* permitted to land 162, 163
 Saltpeter, importation of, from Calcutta 129, 130
 Signals received from Admiral Vandeput 227, 235
Little Egg Harbor, N. J., Frenchman landed at 285
Little, Ephrim, seaman, *Constellation* 306

Little John, schooner: Page
Assistance to distressed seamen at St. Jago, Cuba 33
Collector at Norfolk authorized to clear 499
Little William, ship, Capt. James Wilkerson, convoyed by *Constellation* 135
Lively, brig of Philadelphia, Captain Stewart 251
Lively, schooner, of Portland, captured, at St. Jago, Cuba 34
Liverpool, England, vessels sailing 132, 138, 167, 183, 184, 566
Livingston, John, quartermaster, *Constellation* 315
Livingston, Joseph, seaman, *Constellation* 305
L'Niger, British 24-gun ship. See *Niger*.
Lobo (Sobo), Anthony, in command of French privateer *Triumphant* 24, 28
Lockey, George, loader of cargo of *Rainbow* 22
Logan, captain of brig *Amelia* 465
Logan, Matthew, master, schooner *Swallow* 332
Logistics, to be dealt with in later volume VI
Lombard, captain of French privateer *Voltaguere* 22
Long, Abraham, boatswain, *Constellation* 98, 99
Long, Henry, pilot for *Constitution* 551
Long, Reuben, suggests restricting permits for clearance of vessels 440
Longacre, J. B., drawing by, of Capt. Richard Dale IX
Longwith, Thomas, seaman, *Constellation* 314
Loomoos, Amos, seaman, *Constellation* 306
Loran, captain of French privateer *La Raquir National* 241
Lorenzo, Sn., American armed vessels may not sail from Cadiz 548
L'Orient:
American vessels no longer admitted to 560
American vessels taken to or condemned at 26, 28, 35
Loring and Adams, owners of brig *Sally* 35
Lorman, Mr. of Baltimore, has a ship for sale 116
Loughborough, William, ordinary seaman, *Constellation* 312
Louisa, brig, Thomas Davis, master, in Hampton Roads convoy 364, 436
Louisa, ship, Capt. Holder Fullman, captured by *Foundling* 32
Louisa, ship, Daniel Lewis, chased by *Constitution* 259
Louisiana, Commandant General of 360
Louisiana, Governor General of 39
Lovell, James, attester to sale of ship *Herald* 121
Lovely Lass, Capt. Wm. Moore, captured by two barges 31
Lovett, Joshua, boy, *Constellation* 310
Lovett, William, ordinary seaman, *Constellation* 313
Low, Mr., packet for, on board *Henrietta* 183
Low, Rufus, master of schooner *Industry* 30
Low, William, seaman, forcibly taken from brig *Friendship* 24
L'Perdrix, H. B. M. S., brought to by *United States* 369
L'Scourge, H. B. M. S., brought to by *United States* 369
Lucinda, schooner, John Murry Cambbell, master 476
Luke, Isaac, captain of schooner *Anthony Wallis* 135
Lummis, David, owner, schooner *Harriett* 332
L'Union, French prize, seamen from *Constellation* sent home in 304, 305, 309, 311
Lyman, Theodore, subscribed money for building a ship for United States 168
Lynham, George, owner, schooner *Swallow* 332
Lynx, H. M. S., Captain Hall, recaptures American ship *Liberty* 187
Macbeth & Ross, loaders of cargo of *Charlotte* 22
McBride, captain of brig *Kitty* 354
McBride, John, master, ship spoken by *Constitution* 441
McBride, Roger, ordinary seaman, *Constellation* 309
McCabe, Alexander, ordinary seaman, *Constitution* 225
McCandless, Byron, Captain U. S. N., acknowledgment to VII
McCarter, Alexander, seaman, *Constellation* 315
McCarty, Daniel, private, *Constellation* 311
McCausland [?], William, gunner's yeoman, *Constellation* 316
McCauslin, Marcus, brig of, spoken by *Constellation* 152
McClellan, E. N., Colonel, U. S. M. C., acknowledgment to VII
McClintock, John, part owner of ship *Fame* 32
McConnel, Alex., captain of brig *Eliza* 135
McConnell, master of *Eliza* 566
McCormick, Christopher, private, *Constellation* 311, 315
McCullock, William, seaman, *Constitution* 224

Page
McCutchin, T., master of brig *Woolwich* 34
McDonald, John, seaman, *Constitution* 226
McDonald, William, & Co., guns for *United States* 123
McDonough, James (J. M.), midshipman, U. S. N. 65, 155, 304
McDougall, Alexander, Capt., *American Hero* 23
McDougall, Archibald, quartermaster, *Constitution* 225
McDougall, John, captain of ship *Two Friends* 570
McElroy, Archibald, Lt., U. S. ship *Ganges* 569
McEntire, Michael, private, *Constellation* 310
McEzey, George, Carpenter's mate, *Constellation* 305
McFadon & Co., owners of schooner *Hannah* 364
McFadon, John, & Co., owners of schooner *Syren* 364
McGivan, Alexander, Master, sloop *Driver* 260
McHatton, William, ordinary seaman, *Constellation* 309
McHenry, James. See *War, Secretary of.*
McHenry, John, steward, *Constellation* 305
McInnis, Anges, seaman, *Constellation* 306
McIntire, Michael, ordinary seaman, *Constellation* 315
Mack, John P., midshipman, *Constitution* 223
McKenn, Major, arrived at Wiscasset with French prisoners 422
McKerall, William, to command galley at Wilmington 388, 396
Mackey Alexander, quarter gunner, *Constellation* 305
McKinsey, Francis, ordinary seaman, *Constitution* 225
McKnight, James, Lt., U. S. M. C 119, 120
McLaughlin, James, ordinary seaman, *Constitution* 225
McLean, Archibald, seaman, taken from brig *Friendship* 24
McMacklin, William, cooper, *Constitution* 226
McNamara, Thomas, boatswain mate, *Constellation* 304
MacNeal, Neil, captain of ship *Eliza* 164, 165, 245
McNeill, Daniel, Capt., U. S. N., 207, 227, 262, 329, 356, 368, 487, 488, 491, 492, 513, 529, 543
See *Portsmouth*, U. S. ship.
MacPherson, W., reference to 68
McRea, Lieutenant, frigate *United States* 16, 37
McRea, John, Lt., U. S. brig *Norfolk* 382, 383, 405, 407, 443, 495
McRea, John G., Maj., Wilmington, N. C 421
Maescale, John, quartermaster, *Constellation* 313
Maffats, Archibald, ordinary seaman, *Constellation* 315
Magill, Arthur, of Middleton, owns well-seasoned timber 185
Mahaffy, Thomas, ordinary seaman, *Constellation* 309
Mahany, John, seaman, *Constitution* 226
Mahany, William, seaman, *Constitution* 225
Mahoney, John, seaman, *Constellation* 311, 315
Maine Historical Society, acknowledgment to VII
Maine, John, second lieutenant of Marines 355, 460
Maisden, John, seaman, *Constitution* 226
Major, Charles, seaman, *Constitution* 224
Malaga, Spain:
American vessels, blockaded at 20, 27
American vessels captured near 28, 32, 33
American vessels sailing from 419, 507, 548
Malcolm, Mr., commissions etc., for President's signature 169, 174, 186
Maley, captain of schooner for Algiers:
Instructed to supply *Eagle* with shot 408
Ready to sail 549
To sail with storeship *Hero* under convoy 554, 556, 578, 579
Malone, Charles, seaman, *Constellation* 307
Manchester, Petersburg, Richmond and Norfolk. See *Petersburg*, etc.
Marcia, schooner, of Norfolk, brought to by *Constellation* 293
Maria, brig, of Philadelphia, at Havana 466
Maria, brig, spoken by *Constellation* 287
Maria, brigantine, Capt. John Morgan, captured by *La Pearl* 30
Maria, ship, Conchlin, master, brought to by *Constellation* 260
Mariegalante, master of snow *Isabella* carried to 28
Marine Corps. See *Marines, U. S.*
Marine Corps, act of July 11, 1798, for establishment 188, 189

Page

Marine Corps Historical Section, acknowledgment to ... VI
Marine Hospital, site for, considered for navy yard ... 409, 410, 457
Mariner, Mr., may be employed as coasting pilot ... 128
Marines, U. S.:
  Arms, accouterments and clothing for ... 37, 76, 107, 120, 131, 360, 404, 512, 513, 514
  Commissions should be sent to all officers ... 404
  Duties of ... 130, 131, 138, 290, 291, 328
  For vessels ... 7, 40, 66, 67, 110, 269, 320, 323, 326, 328, 358, 380, 381, 390, 422, 425, 442, 460, 490, 491, 495, 501, 513, 524, 525, 527
  For stations ... 360
  Guard for prisoners at New Castle ... 439, 579, 580
  Names on muster roll of *Constellation* ... 304–316
  Names sent to President for officers ... 269
  Pay of ... 7, 41, 44, 65, 66, 69, 110, 188
  Recruiting of ... 40–42, 65, 72–74, 117, 119, 173, 355, 360
  Rules and regulations ... 8, 40–42, 58, 66, 67, 188, 189, 376, 377
  Uniform of, described ... 404
Marliquin. See *Harliquin*, British brig.
Marrasett, Mr., owner of schooner *Little John* ... 499
Marrauld, John, Philadelphia, Pa., clearance for schooner *Little John* ... 499
Marseilles, Commercial Agent at, reports captures ... 78–80, 97, 98
Marsh, Joseph, justice of peace, Middlesex County, N. J ... 285, 286
Marshal of Delaware, release of John Buffington ... 458
Marshall, Mr., and other Envoys to France, instructions to ... 46
Marshall, Mr., at Nantes about to sail for Alexandria ... 109
Marshall, James B., owner of *Mary* ... 23
Marshall, John, seaman, *Constellation* ... 316
Marshall, John, ordinary seaman, *Constitution* ... 224
Marshall, John, master at arms and fifer, *Constellation* ... 103, 305
Marshall, John, warrant as gunner ready for President's signature ... 174
Marshall, Thomas, seaman, *Constellation* ... 313
Martha, ship, to bring saltpeter from Calcutta ... 129, 130
Martin, captain of *Cincinnatus* ... 26
Martin, Isaac, seaman, *Constellation* ... 307
Martin, John, to assist Captain Adams ... 412, 413
Martin, Patrick, seaman, *Constellation* ... 313
Martin, Thomas, agent for sale of *Scammel* ... 317, 516
Martin, Thomas, quarter gunner, *Constellation* ... 316
Mary, Captain Choates, brought into Nantz ... 35
Mary, Capt. Robert Holmes, brought into Nantes ... 23
Mary, Capt. Thomas Curtis, brought into Nantes ... 23
Mary, brig, Capt. Thomas Boyle, taken into St. Domingo ... 24
Mary, brig, Joseph Israel, captured by Algerine corsair ... 520–523
Mary, brigantine, Capt. J. Southworth, detained at Island of Rhe ... 35, 36
Mary, schooner, Alexander Huis, in Hampton Roads convoy ... 364
Mary, ship, spoken by frigate *Constitution* ... 532
Mary, ship, spoken by *United States* ... 571
Maryland Historical Society, acknowledgment to ... VII
Maryland, snow, Capt. John Roxborough ... 475, 476
Masquerade, John, seaman, *Constitution* ... 225
Massachusetts, Governor of, cannon, loan of ... 92, 96
Massachusetts Historical Society:
  Acknowledgment to ... VII
  Illustration published by courtesy of ... IX
  Records published by courtesy of ... 39, 97, 107, 109, 112, 141, 286, 333, 367, 467, 486, 544, 545, 546, 550
Massachusetts Institute of Technology, acknowledgment to ... VII
Master at Arms on Constellation, duties of ... 103
Masters of captured American vessels at St. Jago, Cuba, statement by ... 33, 34
Masts and Spars, dimensions of, by Captain Truxtun ... 563, 564
Masy, of Portsmouth, captured by *L'Niger* ... 385
Mathers, John, late mate of snow *Maryland* ... 476
Matthews, Archibald, seaman, *Constellation* ... 305

Page
Matthews, George, ordinary seaman, *Constellation* 313
Maurice, James, owner, brigantine *Mermaid* 332
Maurlin, Francois, prisoner from privateer *La Fleur de la Mer* 422
Maury, James, U. S. Consul, Liverpool 132, 138, 167, 183, 505, 566
May, John, captain of brig *Nancy* 24
Mayberry, John, seaman, *Constellation* 308, 315
Mayer, Jacob, Consul at Cape Francois 21, 24
Mayflower, sloop, shot, etc., for *Constellation* 104, 105, 122
Medicine chest and instruments for Constitution 57
Medicine chests and instruments of Ganges and Hamburgh Packet 74
Mediterranean:
- Armed force should be sent to, by United States 484
- Depredations to our commerce, severe v
- Frigate and sloops recommended for, by D. Humphreys 507
- Swedes and Danes keep armed forces in 484

Mellings, Andrew, seaman, *Constitution* 223
Melloby, master of *Caledonia* 505
Mellory, John, captain of brig *Charlotte* 36
Melony, brig, spoken by *Constellation* 251
Melpomene, French passengers will be permitted to land 162, 163
Melvin, William, gunner's mate, *Constellation* 305
Mentges, Captain, to allow prisoners from *La Croyable* to work 268
Mentges, Colonel, to muster marines 37
Mercer, Edward, first corporal, *Constellation* 310
Merchant, Fitzgerald, master, sailing from Liverpool 566
Merchant, ship, Capt. John Trail, commission for 249, 250, 269
Merchantmen, *Constellation* to convoy from Hampton Roads 365
Merchants building vessels for public to receive 6% stock 278
Merchants Coffee House, Philadelphia, Pa 258
Merchant vessels. See *Vessels, merchant.*
Mercury, armed ship, commission forwarded to Gibraltar 228, 229
Mercury, brigantine, Capt. William Miller, spoken by *Constitution* 354, 355
Mercury, Capt. Thomas Vicoun, brought into Nantes by privateer 23
Mercury, schooner, captured at St. Jago, Cuba 34
Merlin, Minister of Justice, reference to 560
Mermaid, brigantine, William Canby permit issued for clearance of 332
Merrimack, U. S. ship, Capt. Moses Brown:
- Building at Newburyport by citizens 368
- Complement allowed 490, 491
- Figurehead, description of 525
- Launched 525, 526, 557
- Marines for 513
- Officers for 214, 513, 574
- Recruiting orders for 490, 491
- Will be ready to sail in December 539

Michael, snow, William Weeks, in Hampton Roads convoy 364
Michel, captain of French privateer *Buonoparte* 26
Middleton, Conn., shipbuilding at 185, 186, 218, 219, 227, 262, 280, 281, 367, 368
Military stores for ships 53, 54, 71, 84, 101
Militia of Georgia, state of 437
Miller, Captain, guard for prisoners at New Castle 579
Miller, Asher, evacuation of Spanish posts in Louisiana 39
Miller, Edward, Capt., U. S. Army, to recruit marines 110
Miller, George, ordinary seaman, *Constellation* 309
Miller, William, boy, *Constellation* 310
Miller, William, commander of brigantine *Mercury* 355
Miller, William, seaman, *Constellation* 316
Minerva, schooner, at Havana 466
Minerva, schooner, clearance of, will be given 565
Minerva, sloop, spoken by *United States* 419
Minor, Elnathan, captain of brig *Atalanta* 81
Mint, superintendent of, directed to prepare copper for shipment 290
Misroon, master of schooner *Industry* 34
Missicipian, French privateer, captured ship *Atlantic* 34
Mole of St. Nicholas, British court of Vice Admiralty 21
Mollineaux, captain of schooner *Wanspite* 497

Page
Molly, brig, Captain Kilby, joined Havana convoy 466
Molly, Captain Stumper, taken into Bilbao by privateer 23
Money advanced for building ships, to be returned in 6% stock 147
Money desired brought from Havana on Captain Truxtun's frigate 365
Money, prize, derived from sale of *La Croyable* 258
Monroe, Mr., Minister to France 2–4
Montezuma, U. S. ship, Capt. Alexander Murray:
Bright, Captain, to be under command of 484
Campbell, Captain, to join 434, 528
Instructions and orders for 321, 325, 326, 353, 354, 380, 381, 430, 433, 434, 454, 455, 462, 463, 483, 503, 538
Listed in service 368
Material, stores, equipment 124, 128, 195, 234, 235, 239, 333, 372, 380, 433
Marines for 269, 326, 380, 390
Officers for 153, 260, 269, 321, 326, 333, 380, 399, 412, 414
Purchase of 123, 124, 128, 143, 262
Signals for 399, 434
State of readiness 256, 269, 333, 336
Williams, Captain, to place himself under 407, 444
Montgomery, Robert, consul at Alicante 26, 35, 36
Montgomery, Wm., captain of schooner *Hazard* 135
Moodie, William, master and owner, schooner *General Greene* 332
Moody, Thomas, ordinary seaman, *Constitution* 226
Moore and Cloney, recruiting by 51
Moore, captain of sloop *Friends* 466
Moore, Captain, recruiting by 50, 77, 78, 115
Moore, James, seaman, *Constitution* 224
Moore, James, ordinary seaman, *Constellation* 309
Moore, Thomas, carpenter's mate, *Constellation* 313
Moore, William, master of *Lovely Lass* 31
Morgan, captain of armed ship *Sally* 183, 184
Morgan, James, gunner, *Constellation* 99, 100, 102, 124, 264, 304
Morgan, John, master of brigantine *Maria* 30
Morgan, John, seaman, *Constellation* 312
Morgan, John T., agreement for furnishing timber 215, 216
Moriarty, G. A., acknowledgment to VII
Morlaix, vessels taken to by privateers 26, 35
Morland, captain of ship *Hanna* 403, 518
Morphy, Michael, American consul, reports French depredations 26, 27
Morris, Mr., packet for, in armed ship *Sally* 183
Morris, James, carpenter, *United States* 233, 424
Morris, Richard V., captain, U. S. N 151, 271, 368, 543
See *Adams*, U. S. ship.
Morris, Staats, captain commanding fort at Whetstone Point 9, 51, 410
Morris, Thomas, Charleston, S. C 573, 575
Morris, Thomas, Henry Laurens, William Crafts, and A. Tunno 401, 402
Morris, William, seaman, *Constitution* 224
Morrison, James, seaman, *Constellation* 306
Morrison, John, captain *Eliza* informs H. B. M. S. *Prevoyante* detained convoy 352, 353
Morrisson, John, boy, *Constellation* 311
Mortimore, George, seaman, *Constellation* 307
Morton, captain of brig *Carolina* 23
Morton, Mr., will bring water for *Constitution* 171
Moseley, Eliga, boy, *Constellation* 315
Mosset, Peter, boy, *Constellation* 310
Motley, captain of the *Caroline* 138
Mountflorence, Major, Chancellor to Consul General Skipwith 48, 79
Mowat, Commodore, reference to 454
Mozard, M., Consul of French Republic, passport for 237, 238
Mud-Island, French prisoners detained at 203
Mugford, William, captain of *Eliza* 26, 35
Mulat, David, coxen, *Constellation* 304
Mullen, Cornelius, marine from *Ganges* for cutter *Diligence* 442

Mullowny, John, Lt.: Page
Extract from journal of frigate *United States* 163, 169, 174, 201, 203, 209, 211, 215, 220, 222, 250, 253, 260, 265, 267, 270, 273, 276, 280, 283, 286, 294, 297, 319, 324, 325, 327, 331, 334, 340, 342, 343, 351, 354, 358, 359, 363, 369, 371, 373, 375, 377, 379, 381, 384, 385, 388, 392, 401, 403, 406, 411, 419, 424, 426, 430, 442, 486, 506, 546, 551, 552, 560, 562, 571, 574, 580
Military stores to be delivered to 38
Sent aboard Captain Decatur's ship, *Delaware* 369
Sent to Tortola in prize to collect American vessels 369
Statement by, relative to James Yard 544, 546
Mumford and Murray, owners of ship *Commerce* 30, 55
Mumford, J. P. See *Murray, John, et al.*
Munro, Mr., reference to 317, 323
Munroe, John, ordinary seaman, *Constellation* 314
Murray, Messrs., owners of vessel loading with stores for Algiers 494, 509, 547
Murray & Mumford, owners of ship *Commerce* 30, 55
Murray, Alexander, Capt., U. S. ship *Montezuma* 333, 336, 368, 543
Orders and instructions to 321, 325, 326, 353, 354, 380, 381, 398, 399, 407, 408, 412, 433, 434, 435, 454, 455, 462, 463, 483, 503
See *Montezuma*, U. S. ship.
Murray, John, and Son, New York 556
Murray, John, Merchants' Committee of New York 146, 153
Murray, W. Vans, United States Minister to the Netherlands 467, 485, 486
Murrey, George, seaman, *Constitution* 225
Murry, Thomas, private, *Constellation* 310
Muse, John, named to act as purser for the *Norfolk* 443
Musketo. See *Musquito.*
Musquito, British sloop of war, Captain Whyte:
Cochran, Captain, conduct of, to be investigated 386
Encounter of, with *Unanimity* referred to 372, 387, 401
Encounter with *Unanimity*, Captain Cochran 252
Extract from log book of 252
Muster Roll, U. S. frigate *Constellation* 304–316
Mutiny, threatened by Negroes on board vessels in quarantine 149, 150
Mutiny, threats of on board *Constellation* 156–158
Myers, Mr., brigantine [*Richmond*] purchased from by merchants 425
Myers, M., owner of ship *Fair American* 135
Myers, Moses, owner of schooner *Eagle* 364
Nabby, brig, captured by French privateer *L'Espiegle* 29
Nancy, brig, Capt. John May, taken into St. Domingo 24
Nancy, brig, from New York, spoken by *Good Friends* 290
Nancy, Capt. Wm. Perry, captured by French privateer *Pandor* 22
Nancy, English privateer, Capt. George Broadwater 482, 509
Nancy, private armed ship, Capt. Melzar Joy, bond for 284
Nancy, schooner, Benjamin West, brought to by *Constellation* 154
Nancy, schooner, Capt. Worth Bates, brought to by *Constellation* 283
Nancy, ship, Captain Orn, spoken by *Herald* 519
Nantes, American ships taken to by privateers 22, 23, 27, 28, 35
Nash, James, coxswain, *Constellation* 314
Natches, Miss., rumor American Army is assembling at 360, 361
Nathaniel, brigantine, captured by French privateer *Lacassas* 29
National character defined by Secretary of Navy 205, 207, 285
National Convention, French, decrees of, reference to 1–3
Naval Academy, United States, acknowledgment to VII
Naval affairs, summary of and location of ships 538–540
Naval forces of the United States:
Proposed distribution of 256
Ready for operation in one month 166
Naval Historical Foundation, acknowledgment to VII
Naval Historical Society Collection, New York Historical Society, records published by courtesy of 119
Naval History Society, acknowledgment to VII
Naval Records, Office of, adequately housed III
Naval Records and Library, Office of, authority to print VIII
Naval War College, U. S., acknowledgment to VII

Page

Navvy, George Washington's idea of — 455
Navy, Secretary of, Benjamin Stoddert:
Arrival of, in Philadelphia, expected — 110
Correspondence with—
Adams, John, Capt., U. S. R. C. *Scammel* — 412, 413, 553, 554
Adams, John, President, United States — 255, 256, 262, 263, 269, 270, 319, 336, 342, 343, 367, 368, 427, 430, 449, 460, 461, 495, 514, 542, 543.
Anderson, Samuel, Dr — 160
Anthony, Joseph — 220, 221
Bainbridge, William, Lt., U. S. N — 295, 320, 328, 375, 379, 380, 404
Barnwell, George, Gen — 146, 153, 154, 534, 535
Barron, Samuel, Capt., U. S. N — 425, 489, 504, 505
Barry, James, Baltimore, Md — 278, 414
Barry, John, captain, U. S. frigate *United States* — 161, 162, 174, 189–192, 199, 200, 280, 481
Bartlett, William, Newburyport, Mass — 214, 574
Bayard, Wm., New York — 146
Bright, Francis, Capt., U. S. R. C. *Virginia* — 292, 484
Brown, John, Capt., U. S. R. C. *Diligence* — 358, 420, 421
Brown, John, Providence, R. I — 277, 278, 423, 525
Brown, Moses, Capt., U. S. S. *Merrimack* — 490, 491, 557
Burrows, W. W., Major Commandant, U. S. M. C — 320, 360, 376, 390, 391, 404, 422, 460, 513, 514, 527
Caldwell, John, Hartford, Conn — 425, 426, 561
Campbell, Archibald, Baltimore, Md — 220
Campbell, Hugh G., Capt., U. S. R. C. *Eagle* — 323, 434, 442, 443, 481, 528, 529
Campbell, James, Petersburg, Va — 261
Champlin, George, Newport, R. I — 146
Chaplin, John, Beaufort, S. C — 246, 247, 413
Chapman, Jonathan, Capt., U. S. R. C. *Pickering* — 197, 257, 349, 350, 501, 502, 576, 577
Clason, J. C., New York — 146, 147
Cochran, Rob., Capt., Charleston, S. C — 386
Collectors of revenue, circular — 516
Commanders of armed U. S. vessels, instructions to — 187
Commanders of galleys, circular — 388, 389, 390
Commanders of revenue cutters, circular — 517
Crafts, William, Charleston, S. C — 330, 391, 392, 401, 526, 530, 573
Cross, George, Capt., U. S. N — 387, 450–452, 575
Crowninshield, George, & Son, Salem — 339
Dale, Richard, Capt., U. S. S. *Ganges* — 110, 145, 204, 221, 222, 238, 271, 296, 318, 357, 369, 510, 511
Decatur, Stephen, Capt., U. S. S. *Delaware* — 127, 128, 141, 149, 150, 174, 192, 457
Desaussure, H. W., Charleston, S. C — 248, 249, 372, 523, 524
Fitzsimmons, Thomas, Philadelphia, Pa — 143
Fletcher, Patrick, Capt., U. S. N — 233, 421, 452, 501
Fox, Josiah, Navy constructor — 265
Francis, Tench, purveyor, Philadelphia, Pa — 163, 240, 317, 320–323, 338, 339, 438
Gibbs and Channing, agents, Newport, R. I — 147, 148, 217, 268, 359, 360, 512, 530
Gill, Robert, Capt., storekeeper, Philadelphia, Pa — 282
Goodhue, Benjamin, Salem, Mass — 510, 511
Hamilton, Robert, Marshal of Wilmington — 438, 530, 531
Hand, General, Lancaster — 459
Harris, John, storekeeper — 334
Harwood, Richard, Lt., U. S. M. C — 193
Heyward (Haywood), Samuel, Capt., U. S. R. C. *Pinckney* — 578
Higginson, Stephen, navy agent, Boston, Mass — 166, 167, 194, 198, 199, 200, 203, 210, 258, 289, 328, 329, 350, 356, 487, 488, 513, 529, 530

Navy, Secretary of, Benjamin Stoddert—Continued.
Correspondence with—Continued. Page
Hollingsworth, L. & Sons, Philadelphia, Pa 440
Hubbard, Nehemiah, agent, Middletown, Conn. 185, 218, 219, 280, 281
Hulsecamp, Garrett, pilot, Philadelphia, Pa 175, 203
Humphreys, Joshua, Navy constructor 129, 208, 209, 258, 297, 317, 324, 337, 357, 405, 406
Jackson, Ebenezer, navy agent, Savannah, Ga 197, 397, 398, 530
Jackson, Henry, Gen 179
Jocelin, Ameziah, agent, Wilmington, N. C 396, 397, 530
Johnson, Nicholas, Newburyport, Mass 365, 366
Jones, Mr., Treasury Department 123
Kenyon, Henry, Lt., U. S. S. *Retaliation* 281, 282
Laurens, Henry, Charleston, S. C 401, 402
Leonard, John W., Capt., U. S. R. C. *Governor Jay* 222, 239, 272, 275, 379, 571
Lewis, Thomas, Marshal, New Jersey 289
Lincoln, Benj., collector, Boston 518
McRea, John, Lt., U. S. S. *Norfolk* 407
Malcolm, Mr 169, 174, 186
Marshal of Delaware 458
McNeill, Daniel, Capt., U. S. S. *Portsmouth* 491, 492
Mentges, Captain 268
Mint, Superintendent of 290
Morris, Richard V., New York 271
Morris, Thomas, Charleston, S. C 401, 402, 575
Mumford, J. P., New York 146, 147
Murray, Alexander, Capt., U. S. S. *Montezuma* 321, 325, 326, 353, 354, 380, 381, 398, 399, 407, 412, 433, 434, 435, 454, 455, 462, 463, 483, 503.
Murray, John, New York 146, 153, 154
Nevison, John, and John Granbery, Norfolk, Va 279, 535
Nicholls, William, Marshal of Pennsylvania 458, 459
Nicholson, Samuel, Capt., U. S. frigate *Constitution* 172, 197, 198, 205, 256, 257, 271, 277, 295, 296, 393–396, 493, 504
Nicklin and Griffith, Philadelphia, Pa 151, 464, 465
Oliver, Robert, Baltimore, Md 242, 243, 536
Parker, Josiah, Norfolk, Va 383, 495, 496, 535
Pennock, William, navy agent, Norfolk, Va 159, 207, 208 283, 284, 287, 359, 384, 404, 426, 430, 431, 448, 449, 494, 527, 530
Perry, C. R., Capt., U. S. S. *General Greene* 463, 524, 525
Phillips, Isaac, Capt., U. S. S. *Baltimore* 179, 260, 261, 284, 289
Pinckney, Thomas, Charleston, S. C 247, 401, 534
Pollock, Isaac, Washington, D. C 137
Price, George, Capt., U. S. R. C. *General Greene* 221
Reynolds, Thomas, surgeon, U. S. N 540
Sears, David, Boston, Mass 170
Sever, James, Capt., U. S. S. *Herald* 160, 161, 166, 170–173, 193, 194, 254, 255, 349, 350, 500, 501
Sewall, Samuel, in Congress 131, 160
Sheafe, Jacob, agent, Portsmouth, N. H 214, 215, 530
Simons, James, Charleston, S. C 230, 287, 576
Speake, Josias, M., Lt., Alexandria 180
State, Secretary of 78, 91, 227, 235, 408, 499, 500, 538–540
Stevens, Ebenezer, Col., New York 295
Stewart, David, Baltimore, Md 170
Talbot, Silas, Capt., U. S. N 351, 352, 428, 429
Tingey, Thomas, Capt., U. S. S. *Ganges* 408, 417, 418, 527
Treasury, Secretary of 123, 126, 130, 167, 210, 240, 244, 261, 262, 263, 382, 532, 533
Truxtun, Thomas, Capt., U. S. frigate *Constellation* 142, 158, 206, 207, 288, 300–302, 333, 334, 335, 337, 338, 342, 365, 373, 374, 508, 509, 528, 566–568.
Tunno, A., Charleston, S. C 401, 402
Wadsworth, Charles, purser, U. S. frigate *United States* 131
War, Secretary of 183, 184, 234, 235, 247, 265, 402, 406, 499, 577, 578
Washington, George 409, 410, 455–457

Navy, Secretary of, Benjamin Stoddert—Continued.
Correspondence with—Continued. Page
Watson, James, navy agent, New York 150, 165, 195, 217, 227, 238, 272, 278, 295, 530
Wharton, Robert, Capt., U. S. A. 242
Williams, Thomas, Capt., U. S. S. *Norfolk* 381, 382, 405, 443, 444
Winder, William, Navy Department accountant 267, 439
Yellott, Jeremiah, navy agent, Baltimore 122, 123, 124, 128, 145, 153, 173, 195, 233, 234, 239, 257, 275, 284, 289, 333, 372, 530
Duty of 59, 60
Expects to go to Maryland for his family 510, 511
Expects to leave for Georgetown 535
Goldsborough, Charles W., signs for 540
Instructions to commanders of armed vessels 187
Naval affairs will soon be put in train by 107
Oath of office to be taken June 19, 1798 123
Pay of 60
Records, etc., in War Department, authorized to take possession of 60
Revenue cutters placed at disposition of 518
Revenue cutters, policy relative to 166
State, Secretary of, to assume duties during absence 460, 461, 463
Stoddert, Benjamin, commissioned 78
Vacancy in office of, principal clerk to take charge 60
Navy, U. S., serviceability of vessels of 538, 539
Navy Department:
Act establishing 59, 60
Moved to Trenton, N. J., Aug. 13, 1798 296
Navy played notable part in development of national spirit III
Navy Yard, Washington, site for 455–457, 533
Neal, Michael, seaman, *Constellation* 307
Neale, Henry, deputy collector, Lewis Town 89
Neale, James, seaman, *Constitution* 225
Nealen, Michael, ordinary seaman, *Constellation* 315
Needham, Isaac and **John**, owners of brigantine *Six Brothers* 29
Needham, schooner, Capt. Wm. Grant, captured by *Trois Soeurs* 34
Negroes, manning sloop-of-war, attempt to incite mutiny 149
Negroes, mutinous, to be prevented from landing by *Delaware* 150
Negroes, not to be enlisted in Marine Corps 41
Nelms, Josiah, private, *Constellation* 315
Nelms, Willis, private, *Constellation* 315
Nelson, Admiral:
American vessels given protection by 20
French fleet defeated by 467, 480, 481, 484, 507
Nelson, Thomas, seaman, *Constitution* 226
Nelson, Thomas, District Attorney of Virginia, *Niger*, trial of 463, 555, 556
Neptune, brig, Master Ezekiah Purkins, boarded by brig *Tyger* 340
Neutrality, brig, Captain Clark, captured by *Pauline* 34
Nevison and Granbury, agents, Norfolk, Va. 279, 489, 496, 504, 535, 539, 540
Newbern, N. C., crew of *Planter* lodged in jail at 248
Newbury, Old, Historical Society of, acknowledgment to VII
Newburyport, Mass.:
Brown, Moses, Capt., recommended to command ship at 214
Inhabitants of, complimented for patriotic exertions 214
Johnson, Nicholas, agent for citizen's vessel 365, 366
Marines wanted at 360
Material for ships at 214, 366, 488, 513
Officers for ship at 540, 574
Vessels, building at 96, 120, 158, 159, 166, 167, 262, 367, 368
Newburyport Public Library, acknowledgment to VII
New Castle, Del.:
French prisoners lodged at 438, 439, 558
Guns for *United States* to be delivered at 122
Marine guard for French prisoners at 527, 558, 579, 580
Pilot boat ordered to 83
New England, protection of, left to its militia 140
New Hampshire, desirable that a captain be furnished by 356
New Hampshire Gazette, Portsmouth, N. H., extract from 340

Page

New Haven Colony Historical Society, acknowledgment to ---------- VII
New Jersey, Governor of, disposition of French prisoners ---------- 203
New Jersey, Marshal of, French prisoners, custody of ---------- 289
New Jersey, ship of Nicklin and Griffith ------ 190, 191, 199, 462, 464, 465, 483
Newman, James, commander of British frigate *Ceres* ---------- 30
Newman, Timothy, Capt., Algerine frigate *Crescent* -------- 61, 108, 112, 113
Newport Historical Society:
Acknowledgment to ---------- VII
Records published by courtesy of ---------- 536
Newport, R. I.:
Herald to touch at, for communications ---------- 254, 255
Marines wanted at ---------- 360
Material for ships building at ---------- 217, 536
Sick sailors left at ---------- 406
Vessels building at ---------- 217, 227, 246, 262, 368
Newport, ship, spoken by *Constitution* ---------- 409
Newport, ship, spoken by *Herald* ---------- 392
New Providence, ships sent to, by British privateers ---------- 373
Newton, John, commander of British privateer brought to, by *Constitution* ---------- 374
New York Daily Advertiser, extract from ---------- 477–480
New York Historical Society:
Acknowledgment to ---------- VII
Picture of *United States*, reproduced by courtesy of ---------- IX
Records published by courtesy of ---------- 119
New York, N. Y.:
Articles for ships to be obtained at - 145, 216, 217, 257, 321, 328, 357, 369, 513
Defense of harbor of ---------- 70, 102, 577, 578
Ganges ordered to, for repairs ---------- 271
Governor Jay, U. S. R. C., fitting for sea at ---------- 239
Navy Yard at, appropriation for ---------- 46
Sick sailors will probably be left at ---------- 406
Troops should be assigned to protect ---------- 140
Vessels building at ---------- 130, 143, 145–147, 150, 153, 154, 165, 170, 173, 195, 204, 217, 244, 256, 262, 295, 368, 539
New York Public Library:
Acknowledgment to ---------- VII
Records published by courtesy of ---------- 114
Nicholas, John, one of prize crew of brig *Planter* ---------- 248
Nicholls, Ichabod, part owner of brigantine *Friendship* ---------- 28
Nicholls, William, Marshal of Pennsylvania:
Expenses of French prisoners ---------- 289, 458, 459
La Croyable advertised for sale by ---------- 231
La Croyable, prize, amount paid to ---------- 261
Nichols, Wm. H., master of brig *Juno* ---------- 34
Nicholson, Mr., to value muskets ---------- 334
Nicholson, Samuel, Capt., U. S. frigate *Constitution* ---------- 106, 107, 111, 112, 161, 169, 171, 255, 268, 278, 295, 368, 403, 429, 431, 450, 488, 494, 535, 565
Niger, British ship, capture of. See *Niger.*
Orders and instructions issued by ---------- 569
Orders and instructions to ---------- 40, 57, 65, 66, 96, 172, 197, 198, 205, 256, 257, 271, 277, 295, 296, 493, 504
Picture of ---------- facing page 270
Report by ---------- 393–396
See *Constitution*, U. S. frigate.
Nicholson, Samuel, Jr., midshipman, *Constitution*:
Death and burial of ---------- 454
Ill on *Constitution* ---------- 436, 442
Nickells, Richard, seaman, *Constitution* ---------- 224
Nicklin and Griffith, Philadelphia, Pa.:
Hamburgh Packet purchased from ---------- 67, 68
New Jersey, ship of, given assistance ---------- 190, 199, 462, 464, 465, 483
Requested to deliver dispatches to Captain Decatur ---------- 151
Nicklin, Philip, et al. See *Fitzsimmons, Thomas.*

Page

Niger, British armed schooner:
Account of capture of 385, 393–396, 414–417
Accounts of Captain Nicholson vague 448, 449, 463
Beale, Lieutenant, sent on board, from *Constitution* 385
Brought into Hampton Roads, by Captain Nicholson 430, 493
Disposition to be made of 430, 431
Flag, half mast, due to death of Midshipman Nicholson 454
Men belonging to *Constitution* returned from 467, 468
Money and goods of, must be restored 449
Opinion of Secretary of State 555, 556
Prisoners, disposition of 385, 395, 411, 415, 431, 448
Trial is necessary to fix blame 463, 469
Nighton, William, private, *Constellation* 311, 315
Nissen, Mr., sentence of condemnation of vessel of, confirmed 419
Noble, Philemon, ordinary seaman, *Constitution* 224
Nones, Benjamin, owner brigantine *Amiable Adele* 332
Nonpareil, ship, Captain Fanning, captured by French privateer 83
Nonpariel from Wilmington, spoken by *Constitution* 378
Norfolk, Petersburg, Richmond, and Manchester. See *Petersburg.*
Norfolk, U. S. brig, Capt. Thomas Williams:
Articles for 282, 404, 495
Building at Norfolk by public 368
Crew, composition of 382
Marines for 269, 381, 390, 495
McRea, John, Lt., ordered to report on board 407
Officers, selection of 381–384, 405, 443
Orders and instructions for 381, 382, 430, 433, 443, 444, 455, 462, 538, 569
Reynolds, Dr., did not receive orders in time to report 540
Seamen from, transferred to *Constellation* 312
Signals sent to 444
State of preparation for sea 433, 443, 495, 503
Norfolk, Va.:
Baltimore to recruit at 285
Eagle, Captain Campbell, to hasten to 297, 443, 481, 483
Flags of truce stopped at 237, 440
Marines wanted at 360
Navy yard at, appropriation for 46
Norfolk, brig, to join *Montezuma* at 444
Prisoners from British ship *Niger*, landed at 417
Saunders, Lieutenant, sent to, with letters from Captain Truxtun 562
Shot to be sent to, by Jeremiah Yellott 372
Sick, care of 362, 363, 406, 494, 495
Vessels, building, fitting out 137, 207, 208, 220, 242, 262, 265, 367, 368, 383, 539
Norris Aquilla, ordinary seaman, *Constellation* 311, 315
Norris, James, seaman, *Constitution* 224
Norris, John, Esq., owner of captured schooner *Trial* 333
Norris, John, owner of ship *Polly* 32
Norris, Joseph, ordinary seaman, *Constitution* 226
Norton Rufus, ordinary seaman, *Constitution* 225
Nourse, Joseph, Register of Treasury 63, 68, 120
Nourthen, Draper, seaman, *Constellation* 312
Nutt, Adam, seaman, *Constitution* 224
Nye, Isaac, mate, *Constellation* 311
Oakes, Samuel, carpenter's mate, *Constitution* 223
Oath, requirement of 41, 42, 50, 189, 389
Oatis, William, ordinary seaman, *Constellation* 316
O'Brien, Richard, United States consul, Algiers 40, 61, 400, 411, 412, 507, 520–523
O'Carroll, James, private, *Constellation* 311
Office of Accountant, Navy Department:
Accountant is commencing duty 356
Clerks, number allowed, and salaries 267
Delay in opening causes great inconvenience 267
See *Winder, William.*

Officers: Page
Appointments, selections, etc 6–8, 42, 57, 58, 69, 72, 106, 107, 128, 145, 153, 169, 171, 172, 205, 269, 320, 321, 329, 350, 366, 367, 380, 405, 425, 443, 491, 496, 504, 505, 511, 540, 574
Disabled, provision for 8
Duties of, at sea in suppressing mutiny 156
Higginson, Stephen, comments concerning 106, 107, 111, 112
Invited to dine with Captain Truxtun 155
Marine Corps. See *Marine, U. S.*
Names on muster roll of *Constellation* 304–316
Pay, etc 7, 44, 69, 127, 160, 161, 389, 399
Rank of 510, 542, 543
Revolutionary War bad school to educate 111
To be governed by rules of Congress of 1775 8
Ogder, Nathaniel, master of schooner *Hannah* 364
O'Gisburn, Edward, ordinary seaman, *Constellation* 309
O'Hardy, French privateer captured ship *Hope* 28
Ohio River, boats built for use on 361
Ohio, ship from New York, captured at Alicant 35
Oldman, John, ordinary seaman, *Constellation* 313
Old Tom spoken by *United States* 260
Olinda, sloop, captured by French privateer *L'Espiegle* 30
Olive, ship, of New York, at Havana 466
Oliver, Robert, Baltimore, Md., ships building 146, 242, 243, 536
O'Meara, captain of schooner *Sophia* 26
O'Neal, Charles, seaman, *Constellation* 307
O'Neale, James, ordinary seaman, *Constellation* 309
Oneida, Captain Sherry, brought to Nantes by French privateer 23
Operations of ships and naval units, only, included in first volume VI
Orange, American brig, condemned and sold by French 22
Ordinance, French, cited in case of schooner *Rebecca* 32
Organizations and individuals cooperating in preparation of this work VII, VIII
Orn, captain of ship *Nancy* 519
Orrington, schooner, captured by French privateers 27, 28, 81
Osborn, Robert, seaman, forcibly taken from brig *Friendship* 24
Osborn, William, ordinary seaman, *Constitution* 223
Osmant, John, ordinary seaman, *Constitution* 226
Otis, Mr., mentioned by Stephen Higginson 107
Oustend, John, seaman, *Constellation* 307
Outram, ship, captured by French privateer *La Courageuse* 81
Outten, Abraham, deposition of, relative to capture of *Planter* 247, 248
Overton, Seth, Chatham, material for ships 185, 218, 219
Ownens and Roger, owners of schooner *Hope* 364
Owens, Hezekiah, private, *Constellation* 310
Owens, Owen, seaman, *Constellation* 313
Owens, William, ordinary seaman, *Constellation* 314
Paine & Freneau. See *Freneau & Paine.*
Pallas, brig, Captain Collins, will soon sail from Bristol 403, 518
Palyart, Mr 431, 441
Pandor, French privateer, captures *Nancy* 22
Park, schooner, William Creighton, in Hampton Roads, convoy 364
Parker, I., subscriptions for vessel in Boston 168
Parker, Josiah, in Congress:
Destitute seamen, return of, to United States 113
Ship construction at Norfolk 383, 405, 425, 495, 496, 535
Parkman, Samuel, subscribed money for building ship for United States 168
Paris (Parisa), Lieutenant, on British ship *Niger* 388, 415–417
Parson, William, ordinary seaman, *Constellation* 315
Parsons, Eben, subscribed money for building ship for United States 168
Parsons, Williams, subscribed money for building ship for United States 168
Passport, changes recommended in, by Richard O'Brien 522, 523
Patersons, James, seaman, *Constitution* 223
Patroit, French privateer, Capt. Felix Potestat, captured ship *Flora* 97, 98
Patty, American brigantine, master, Joseph Hempstead 4
Patty, brig, Capt. Samuel Allen, boarded by *Herald* 541
Patty Washington, ship, Captain Stocker, joined Havana convoy 466

Page

Paul, Emperor — 322
Pauline, French privateer, captures by — 34
Pay:
- Allotments of, to wives and children — 160, 161
- Boys in the Navy — 127
- Crews of galleys — 389, 397, 398, 573
- Enlisted men of U. S. Navy — 7, 43, 44, 49, 58, 65, 66, 69, 71, 72, 117, 128, 281, 326, 382, 389, 399, 412, 490, 517
- Marines — 7, 41, 43, 44, 65, 66, 69, 110, 188
- Officers — 7, 44, 58, 64, 69, 127, 128, 179, 389, 397, 398, 399
- Secretary of Navy and clerks — 60

Payne, James, to secure personnel for his galley — 388–391
Peabody Museum, acknowledgment to — VII
Peale's Museum, New York — IX
Peale's Museum, portrait of General Greene in — 536
Pearce, John, ordinary seaman, *Constitution* — 224
Pearce, William, ordinary seaman, *Constitution* — 225
Pearsall, John, mariner, capture of *Friendship* — 251, 252
Pearsoll & Pell, loaders of cargo of *Briseis* — 23
Peas, Peter, seaman, *Constellation* — 306
Pease, captain of schooner *Little John* — 33
Pease, Marshall, master of ship captured at St. Jago, Cuba — 34
Peck, August, captain of brig *Franklin* — 24
Peggy, schooner. spoken by *Constellation* — 215
Peggy, ship of New York, captured by privateer *Vulture* — 36
Peggy, sloop, Captain Leader, captured by *Les Thermidor* — 81
Penchen, captain of privateer *Vulture* — 36
Pender, captain of British ship of war *St. Albins* — 355
Pennock, William, navy agent, Norfolk — 382, 504, 514, 539
- Bearer of messages to officers — 159, 206, 208, 245, 283, 284, 287, 288, 291, 292, 294, 333, 380, 465, 527
- Equipment stores, etc., for ships — 104, 132, 134, 265, 282, 301, 359, 404, 426, 433, 535
- Money, remittance of, by direction of Secretary of Navy — 359
- *Niger*, disposition of, etc — 430, 431, 448, 449
- Officers for ships — 384
- Owner of ship *Little William* — 135
- Preparations to send vessels to warmer climate — 539
- Prisoners, French, disposition of — 530
- Purchase and fitting out of vessel of N. Harbut — 207, 208
- Seamen, care of sick; and mutinous — 362, 426, 493, 494
- Truxtun, Captain, informs of his arrival from Havana — 561

Pennsylvania, Governor of — 149
Pennsylvania Historical Society, acknowledgment to — VII
Pennsylvania Historical Society, records published by courtesy of — 17, 51, 56, 61, 71, 78, 99, 100, 101, 102, 103, 104, 109, 122, 125, 126, 131, 133, 134, 135, 138, 139, 141, 143, 144, 152, 153, 154, 155, 158, 160, 163, 164, 168, 169, 172, 180, 184, 188, 196, 201, 205, 209, 210, 211, 212, 215, 218, 219, 223, 228, 231, 232, 233, 236, 240, 242, 244, 245, 251, 253, 254, 260, 264, 266, 268, 270, 273, 274, 276, 279, 283, 287, 291, 294, 297, 298, 299, 300, 302, 303, 319, 334, 335, 337, 338, 341, 345, 346, 347, 348, 349, 354, 362, 363, 364, 365, 370, 371, 373, 374, 375, 378, 381, 383, 386, 387, 393, 401, 403, 407, 409, 410, 419, 424, 426, 430, 432, 433, 436, 441, 445, 447, 450, 453, 454, 459, 461, 467, 468, 475, 480, 482, 485, 487, 488, 489, 492, 497, 502, 503, 506, 509, 515, 518, 519, 526, 531, 532, 537, 542, 547, 549, 551, 552, 553, 557, 559, 561, 562, 564, 565, 568, 573.
Pennsylvania, laws of, do not permit landing of prisoners — 183
Pennsylvania, University of, Library, acknowledgment to — VII
Perkins, Colo., to deliver shot to *Constitution* for proving — 171
Perkins, James & T. H., subscribed money for building ship for United States — 168
Perkins, James, sailmaker's mate, *Constitution* — 226
Perkins, Joseph, captain of ship *Charles* — 135
Perkins, Samuel G., subscribed money for building ship for United States — 168
"Permission to clear ships", form used — 498

Page
Pero, Peter, ordinary seaman, *Constitution* 223
Perry, Christopher R., Capt., U. S. ship *General Greene* 146, 147, 368, 463, 524, 525, 543
See *General Greene*, U. S. ship.
Perry, Owen, seaman, *Constellation* 307
Perry, Wm., master of ship *Nancy* 22
Petein, Lewis, ordinary seaman, *Constellation* 313
Petersburg, Richmond, Manchester, and Norfolk, shipbuilding by 261, 262, 279
Petit, Pierre Severe, prisoner from privateer *La Fleur de la Mer* 422
Peyranne, Jean, witness to statement by master of *Niger* 417
Phelps, Henry, ordinary seaman, *Constitution* 225
Phelps, Jacob, ordinary seaman, *Constitution* 225
Philadelphia, Pa.:
Citizens of, complaints for losses from French 1, 2
Delaware purchased at 262
Fever, reported at 17
Ganges, purchased at 63, 64, 262
Hamburgh Packet (*Delaware*), purchase of 67, 68
La Croyable advertised for sale 231
Liberty, *Lark*, and *Harriet* allowed to clear from 206
Marines will be sent from, for *Montezuma* 326
Materials, etc., for ships 104, 137, 215–217, 360
Prison at, too crowded to admit French prisoners 203
Sick sailors will probably be left at 406
United States, frigate, launched at 5
Vessels, building and fitting out 143, 145–147, 166, 170, 173, 210, 246, 262, 368, 539
Philadelphia, ship, Captain Bliss, bearer of letters 318, 323
Philadelphia, U. S. frigate, contract for timber for 215, 216
Philanthropist, brigantine captured by French privateer, *Decius*, 29
Philbrook, John, carpenter's mate, *Constitution* 225
Philip, brig, Captain Gorsuch, captured by French privateer 476
Philips, Henry, owner of ship *America* 57
Philips, William, Esq., subscribed money for building ship for United States 168
Phillips, B. H., U. S. Consul, reports captures at Curacoa 22, 477
Phillips, Benjamin, ordinary seaman, *Constellation* 315
Phillips, Daniel, seaman, *Constellation* 306
Phillips, Edward, seaman, *Constellation* 307
Phillips, Isaac, Capt., U. S. ship *Baltimore:*
Orders and instructions to 179, 284, 285, 289, 452, 453, 480
References to 153, 173, 180, 275, 278, 287, 336, 338, 365, 368, 509, 528, 541–543, 550, 565
See Baltimore, U. S. ship.
Phillips, John, seaman, *Constellation* 305
Phillips, Samuel, seaman, *Constitution* 226
Philosophical Society, American of Philadelphia, acknowledgment to. VII
Pickering, Mrs., reference to 550
Pickering, Timothy, Secretary of State:
Acting for Secretary of Navy during his absence 460, 461, 463, 488, 529, 561, 562, 573, 575
Acting for Secretary of War during his absence 114–116
Reference to 538, 539, 540
See *State, Secretary of.*
Pickering, U. S. R. C., Capt. Jonathan Chapman:
Cutter building at Newburyport to be named *Pickering* 96
Equipment and supplies 159, 199, 529
Lincoln, Benj., collector, agent for 516
Officers and men 96, 107, 159, 329, 517, 577
Operations 199, 200, 328, 340, 350, 351, 355, 358, 379, 384, 385, 387, 392, 402, 409, 441, 454, 462, 486, 492, 500, 506, 519, 529, 541, 549, 560, 576, 577
Orders and instructions 197, 257, 501, 538
Picture of Facing page 328
To be placed under Secretary of Navy 197

Page

Pierpont & Leffingwell, owners of *Confederacy* 23
Pierpont Morgan Library, acknowledgment to VII
Pigon, ship, to be convoyed by Lieutenant Bainbridge 404
Pilot, coasting, Captain Decatur authorized to employ 128
Pilot boats, used to communicate with 89, 90, 91, 198, 354
Pinckney, Mrs., reference to 355
Pinckney, Charles C., General, Minister to France 4, 35, 36, 46, 79, 109, 220, 550
Pinckney, Thomas, Charleston, S. C., officers for ships 247, 355, 401, 460, 534
Pinckney, U. S. R. C., Capt. Samuel Haywood:
- Commander for 573, 575, 576, 578
- Recruiting instructions 388–390, 391

Pinder, Captain of British ship *St. Albin* (*Albans*) 327
Pinkerton, James, gunner's mate, *Constellation* 305
Pitman, John, Capt., extract of letter concerning Captain Very's ship 60
Pitts, Thomas, ordinary seaman, *Constitution* 225
Pittsburgh, Pa.:
- Boats built at, for use on the Ohio 360, 361
- Galleys to be built near 19

Pity, James, extracts from journal of U. S. frigate *Constitution* kept by 236, 240, 241, 243, 245, 250, 253, 259, 264, 266, 267, 270, 272, 273, 276, 279, 283, 286, 293, 294, 296, 298, 300, 303, 319, 322,324, 325, 326, 327, 331, 335, 339, 340, 342, 343, 350, 351, 354, 355, 359, 363, 370, 371, 373, 374, 377, 378, 381, 383, 385, 388, 393, 400, 402, 403,406, 409, 411, 418, 423, 427, 429, 436, 441, 442, 450, 454, 459, 462, 467, 468, 474, 482, 483, 487, 488, 492, 497, 502, 503, 505, 515, 518, 519, 526, 531, 532, 536, 537, 541, 546, 549, 550, 551, 553, 556, 558, 559, 562, 565, 568, 569, 570, 573, 574, 580.
Planter, armed ship, Captain Driver, to sail from Liverpool 132
Planter, brig, Abraham Outten, account of recapture of 247, 248
Plato, ship, Capt. Andrew Lawrence, captured by La Furet 81
Plummer, Wm. S., captain of *Telemachus* 26, 35, 81
Pointer, Daniel, ordinary seaman, *Constellation* 309, 314
Polacre, with stores for Algiers, captured by Spanish cruiser 20
Poland, Joseph (or Voland), armourers mate, *Constitution* 224
Pollard, Captain of *Roxana* 25
Pollock, Isaac, purchase of island of, considered 137
Polly & Maria, schooner, captured, at St. Jago, Cuba 34
Polly, brig, Captain Howard, joined Havana convoy 466
Polly, Captain Kirby, aided distressed men at St. Jago, Cuba 33
Polly, schooner, spoken by *Constellation* 297
Polly, ship, Capt. Wm. Bradshaw, captured by French privateers 27, 32, 33, 81
Polly, ship, spoken by *Constellation* 243
Polly, sloop, Capt. W. D. Wilson, captured by *Trois Soeurs* 34
Polly, sloop, captured at St. Jago, Cuba 34
Pomeroy, Ralph, part owner of brig *Nabby* 29
Pomery, John, captain's clerk, *Constellation* 304
Pomona, ship, Capt. John Craft (Grafts), captured 26, 35, 81
Pond, Charles, owner of brig *Sally* 498
Ponsonby, Captain of schooner *Gilblass* 363
Ponsonby, John, quartermaster, *Constellation* 305
Poor, Matthew, ordinary seaman, *Constellation* 309
Pope, marine, wants overalls 579, 580
Port au Prince:
- British have left 118
- *Lovely Lass* captured near 31
- Neutral vessels bound to, to be captured 4

Port de Paix, ships captured and taken to 29, 30, 32
Porte in state of war with France 467
Porter, David, Capt., sale of revenue cutter *Active* 59
Porter, David, midshipman, *Constellation* 56, 155, 304
Porter, David, Sr., to Captain Barry wants a command 55
Porto Rico:
- Barry, Captain, to deliver letter to Governor of 203
- Barry, Captain, to secure release of seamen 190, 192
- British failed in their attack on 118

Page

Porto Rico—Continued.
Governor of, requested to protect Dr. Henry ---- 199
Governor of, return of American seamen requested from ---- 190–192
Sophia sent to, to aid destitute American seamen ---- 113
Port Royal, S. C ---- 534, 535
Portsmouth, N. H.:
Articles for ships at ---- 10, 17, 18, 137, 166, 214, 215, 488
Crescent, frigate built by James Hackett, launched ---- 6
Hackett, Mr., engaged to build ship at ---- 130
Marines wanted at ---- 360
McNeill, Captain, intended for command of ship at ---- 487
Navy yard at, appropriation for ---- 46
Sever, Captain, superintended work on frigate ---- 329
Vessels building at ---- 214, 215, 262, 356, 368, 539
Portsmouth, U. S. ship, Capt. Daniel McNeill:
Building at Portsmouth, by public ---- 356, 368, 539
Complement allowed ---- 491
Marines will be wanted for ---- 513
Materials for ---- 512, 513
Officers for, from New Hampshire ---- 487
Recruiting instructions to Captain McNeill ---- 491
Potestat, Felix, captain of French privateer *Patroit* ---- 97
Potts, Fleet, ordinary seaman, *Constellation* ---- 313
Potts, William, ordinary seaman, *Constellation* ---- 313
Poule, ———, captain of French privateer *La Zenodore* ---- 26, 81
Powell, Demsey, ordinary seaman, *Constellation* ---- 313
Powell, William, ordinary seaman, *Constellation* ---- 313
Preble, captain of ship *Dolphin* ---- 489
Preble, Edward, First Lt., *Constitution* ---- 107, 109, 111, 233
Preeble, Mr. See *Preble, Edward*.
Presson, William, ordinary seaman, *Constellation* ---- 308
Prevoyante, British man-of-war, held up convoy from Havana ---- 352, 353
Price, George, Capt. U. S. R. C. *General Greene* ---- 221
See *General Greene, U. S. R. C.*
Price, John, seaman, *Constellation* ---- 313
Price, Richard, private *Constellation* ---- 310
Prim, John, seaman, *Constellation* ---- 313
Prince, Henry, captain of armed ship *Astrea* ---- 547, 548
Printing of naval records, act authorizing ---- VIII
Prisoners:
American—
Captured in *Friendship* and put on *Lark* ---- 251
Captured in *Mary* by Algerine corsair ---- 520, 523
Eliza, crew of ---- 164, 165, 245
Mate of *William Penn* taken by British ---- 290
British, captured in *Niger* ---- 395, 411, 417, 431, 448, 449
French—
Arrival of, to be reported to collector of port ---- 438
Captured by *Delaware*, disposition of ---- 183, 203, 289, 438, 439, 530, 558
Clothing for ---- 530, 531
Fort Mifflin, permission to land at, requested ---- 183
Guard for ---- 242, 439, 527, 579, 580
Lamberton prison suggested for ---- 203
Marshal of Port shall have custody ---- 438, 530
Murray, Captain, authorized to exchange for American prisoners ---- 455
New Castle, confined at ---- 438, 439, 530, 558
Nicholls, William, to repay expense of, at Lancaster ---- 458, 459
Philadelphia prison too crowded to receive ---- 203
Prize crew of Bristol schooner, Capt. Dickey ---- 421, 422
Prize crew of brig *Planter* lodged in Newbern jail ---- 248
Rations for ---- 439, 458, 530, 531
Subsistence should be provided by collector of Waldoborough ---- 421
Taken in *La Croyable* to be allowed to work ---- 268
Pritchard, Owen, seaman, *Constellation* ---- 306
Pritchard, Paul, vessel building by ---- 249
Pritchard, Wm., vessel of recommended for purchase ---- 230, 249
Privateer, Corsican, captures by ---- 79, 98

Privateers, British. See *Great Britain.*
Privateers, French, operations of. See *France.*
Prize money. See *Money prize.* Page
Prizes, captures and disposition of 175, 176, 182–184, 198, 255, 292, 442
Proctor, William, commander of ship brought to by *Constitution* 363
Providence, Capt. William Furnace, captured by *Voltaguere* 22
Providence, R. I.:
Cannon will be ordered from, for defense of Boston Harbor 92
George Washington, purchase and outfitting of 351, 352, 358, 423, 428
Vessel, building at 220, 221, 262, 278, 368, 487
Proud, John, captain of brig *Friendship* 26, 81
Prudeman, Eppes, boy, *Constellation* 310
Prudence, sloop, Capt. Eliha Russell, captured by Corsican privateer 80, 98
Prussia, no need to be solicitous about making treaty with 468
Pry, Richard, ordinary seaman, *Constellation* 308
Publication of early naval documents, act authorizing VIII
Puerto, Rico, ship *Commerce*, captured and sent to 30
Punishment on Constellation 14, 156–158, 370
Purkins, Ezekiah, master of brig *Neptune* 340
Purviance, Robert, Collector, of Baltimore 59, 306
Purviants, Robert, seaman, *Constellation* 306
Pushy Park, British vessel, Captain Lawrey 414
Quasi-War with France, 1798–1801, selected as starting date of publication V
Queen, H. M. S 177
Quincy, Mass., President Adams addressed at 293
Rabaine and P. T. Baudot, permit for clearance of schooner *Ranger* 261
Rachel, ship, of Charleston, spoken by *Constellation* 184
Raimond, French agent for Leeward Islands 3
Rainbow, Captain Smith, brought into Nantes by privateer 22
Rainbow, schooner, Capt. John Howland, taken into St. Domingo 24
Rambler, brigantine, Captain Woodbridge, permit for clearance 332
Randolph, John F., Capt., instructions to, for outfitting galley 388–390
Randolph, Richard B., ordinary seaman, *Constellation* 308
Ranger, armed ship, to sail from Bristol 323
Ranger, schooner, clearance with French persons 261, 332
Rangor, sloop, from Boston, spoken by *Constellation* 294
Rank, relative, of captains in the Navy 542, 543
Rations 7, 8, 37, 42, 107, 188, 391, 392, 396–398
Rations for prisoners 431, 439, 448, 458, 530, 531
Raven, captured by *Eagle*, released at L'Orient 35
Rawlings, John, ordinary seaman, *Constellation* 309
Rawlings, Matthew, seaman, *Constellation* 307, 315
Rawlings, William, private, *Constellation* 311
Ray, William, seaman, *Constitution* 224
Raynal's Atlas, map taken from IX
Read, Dr. J. K 442, 443
Read, William, surgeon, U. S. N 107, 169, 436, 454, 459
Rebecca, schooner, Capt. John Hall, captured by privateers 31, 32
Rebecca, sloop, Capt. Wm. Clark, captured by *Sans Pareil* 34
Recapture of American vessels not authorized 182, 191, 204, 207, 292
Records and Library, Office of. See *Naval Records and Library, Office* of.
Records, naval, in War Department 60
Recruiting advertisement by Captain Nicholson 73, 74
Recruiting, marines 40, 42, 513
Recruiting, naval 40–42, 43, 49–51, 65, 66, 72, 179, 281, 388, 389, 495
Recruiting, revenue cutters 323, 517
Recruiting Officer, accounts 41, 42
Recruits on Constitution, cash advanced to 223–226
Reddick, Josiah, second lieutenant of Marines 342, 495
Reddick, Samuel, lieutenant of Marines 342
Reed, captain of brig *Charleston* 35
Reed, John, ordinary seaman, *Constellation* 314
Reed, Patrick, ordinary seaman, *Constitution* 225
Reeve, Mr., of St. Croix 544, 545, 546
Reeves, Richard, ordinary seaman, *Constellation* 308

Regulations: Page
Officers and men to be governed by 8
Uniform. See *Uniform regulations.*
Reilly, captain of ship *Raven* 35
Renne, Joseph, commander of sloop *Jealous* 377
Renton, James, ordinary seaman, *Constellation* 312, 362
Republican, schooner, spoken by *Constellation* 159, 160, 244
Reserve, French privateer, captured brig *Juno* 34
Resolution, British 74-gun ship 223, 286
Retaliation, U. S. schooner, Lt. William Bainbridge:
Factor-Hazard incident 469–472
Fitting out 269, 281, 282, 295, 320, 321, 328, 337, 339, 375, 379, 380
Formerly French prize schooner *La Croyable* 269
Operations 317, 324, 336, 375, 379, 380, 404, 430, 433, 455, 503, 538, 568
Purchased for public 269
Return, schooner, brought to by *Constitution* 373
Revenge, French privateer, captured schooner *Betsy* 34
Revenue cutter Active, sale of 59
Revenue Cutters:
Equipment of 56, 408, 516
Operations of 8, 159, 166, 167, 190, 193, 194, 204, 210, 255, 258, 517
Personnel affairs 9, 127, 159, 244, 516, 517
Policies respecting vi, 8, 127, 166, 292, 324, 516, 517, 518
Revere, Mr., cannonades for *Constitution*, to be prepared by 57
Reynolds, Michael, private, *Constellation* 311
Reynolds, Thomas, surgeon 443, 496, 535, 540
Rhé, Island of, *Mary*, detained at 36
Rhee, Island of, *Sally*, brig, and *Bacchus*, ship, sent to 35
Rhode Island:
Constitution to make for, if fever continues 495
Galleys for defense of 265, 295
Troops should be assigned to protect 140
Rhode Island Historical Society, acknowledgment to vii
Rhode Island State Library, acknowledgment to vii
Ricard, John, master, ship *Adrastus* 332
Rice, William, seaman, *Constellation* 308
Richard, Etienne, prisoner from *La Fleur de la Mer* 422
Richards, John, merchant of Kingston 416
Richards, John, seaman, *Constellation* 311
Richardson, Captain 341
Richardson, Henry, seaman, *Constellation* 315
Richardson, Joseph, purser on *Montezuma* 321, 380
Richardson, William, master of schooner *Arb*[?] 364
Richmond, American schooner, condemned by French 22
Richmond, U. S. Brigantine, Capt. Samuel Barron:
Building at Norfolk, by citizens 368
Personnel of 425, 489, 495, 496, 504, 505, 535, 540
Purchased from Mr. Myer by merchants 425
Will be ready to sail in December 539
Richmond and Petersburg, citizens of, to furnish ship 261
Richmond, Petersburg, Manchester, and Norfolk. See *Petersburg, etc.*
Ridgely, Mr., price for cannon ball too high 333
Ripley, Joseph, master of schooner *Daphnel* 364
Roath, Roswell, captain of ship *Ceres* 35
Roba and Betsey, ship, Captain Vimmo:
Boarded by French privateer 145
Sailed from Bristol for Cork 318
Sailing from Bristol 277
Robb, Andrew, ordinary seaman, *Constitution* 224
Robb, James, private, *Constellation* 310
Robinson, captain ship *Hero*, guns wanted 578, 579
Robinson, George, quarter gunner, *Constellation* 305
Robinson, John, seaman, *Constitution* 223
Robinson, John, seaman, *Constellation* 305, 313
Robinson, Thomas J., to dine with Captain Truxtun 155
Robinson, W., midshipman, *Constellation* 311
Robson, John, seaman, *Constitution* 224

Page

Rochefort, American vessels not admitted to 560
Rochelle, ship *Ceres* captured and sent to 35
Rodgers, Sergeant, Marine, *Constellation* 315
Rodgers, John, Lt., *Constellation* 42, 49, 71, 78, 104, 122, 155, 209, 304
Rodney, Daniel, deputy collector, Lewis Town 89
Roger & Ownens, owners of schooner *Hope* 364
Rogers, John, master of ship *Hope* 28
Rôle d' équipage, required of American vessels 20, 21
Roll, muster, U. S. frigate *Constellation* 304–316
Rolls, muster, instructions regarding 43, 66, 73, 356
Roman Emperor, British vessel, rescued schooner *John* 31
Roosevelt, Franklin D.:
- Acknowledgment to VII
- Congressional authorization for publication of early documentary naval material obtained at instance of III, V
- Foreword by III

Rose, Martin, in crew of *Constitution* 385, 393
Rose (or **Bose**), **Newton**, seaman, *Constellation* 314
Ross, captain of ship, taken by privateer of Bayonne 23
Ross, David, Lt., reports arrival of supplies for *United States* 114
Ross, Fairfax, ordinary seaman, *Constellation* 309
Rounde, Thomas, seaman, *Constellation* 306
Roux, Clement, captain of French privateer *La Ziza* 81
Rover, schooner, Capt. P. West:
- Information furnished by 475–477
- Spoken by schooner *Clara* 497

Row, James, seaman, *Constellation* 307
Rowland, Thomas, recommended for surgeon 234
Roxborough, John, captain of snow *Maryland* 475,476
Royal Captain, condemned by tribunal of Bologne 25
Royal Cedula, of His Catholic Majesty of Spain 20, 22
Royalt, David, seaman, *Constellation* 306
Rozier, M., French vice consul at New York 213
Rum, investigation of leakage on *Constellation* 540, 541
Rush, Dr., treated Lieutenant Geddes for yellow fever 376
Rush, John, seaman, *Constellation* 308
Russell, ———, first lieutenant, U. S. frigate *Constitution* 459
Russell, Benjamin, captain of *Sally* 23
Russell, Elisha, captain, sloop *Prudence*, taken to Genoa by privateer 80, 98
Russia, coalition against France 322
Rust, captain of brig *George* of Salem 27
Rutgers, Seaman & Ogdin, owners of *Briseis* 23
Rutledge, Mr., recommends Captain Cross for command 343
Rutledge, Henry M., controversy about *Factor-Hazard* incident 469–473
Saabye, H. R., U. S. consul, Copenhagen, commerce 515, 516
Saavedra, Dn Franco de, reference to 420, 465, 485, 507, 548
Sadler and Craig. See *Craig and Sadler.*
St. Albins, British 64-gun ship, spoken by *Herald* 327, 355
St. Bartholomews, *United States*, sent Lieutenant Barron ashore at 354
St. Jago, Cuba:
- American vessels, captured, at, list of 34
- Condition of American crews at 21
- Masters of captured ships, statement of conditions 33, 34
- United States agent suggested for 33, 34

St. Johns, P. R., vessels taken to 190
St. Juan, P. R., vessels carried into 29, 30
Saint Lucia, neutral vessels bound to, to be captured 4
Saint Marc, neutral vessels bound to, to be captured 4
St. Martins, vessels carried into 31, 32, 106
St. Mary's, Georgia fort near, to be manned 437
St. Memin, reference to IX
St. Nicholas, Mole of, American property condemned 21
St. Nickola, schooner *John* acquitted at 31
St. Omer, civil tribunal of, confirms condemnation of *Royal Captain* 25

Page

St. Sebastian:
French privateer returned to, with killed and wounded 507
Prisoners, American, detained at 165
St. Thomas, Americans wanting convoy from 371
St. Vincents, Lord:
American vessels permitted to enter Cadiz 419, 484
Sir Roger Curtis to quit Irish station and join 321, 322
With 25 sail of the line, off Cadiz 321, 322
Salem, Mass.:
Collector authorized grant commission to *America* 552
Shipbuilding at 262, 339, 366, 367, 510, 511, 539
Salem, Sip (black man), forcibly taken from brig *Friendship* 24
Salisbury, Samuel, subscribed for building ship for United States 168
Salisbury, William, seaman, *Constitution* 223
Sally, American sloop, condemned and sold by French 22
Sally, armed ship, Captain Morgan, sailing from Liverpool 183, 184
Sally, brig, Capt. Eden Wadsworth, captured by *Hydra* 35
Sally, brig, Capt. John Cruft, captured by *La Decade* 259
Sally, brig, permitted to clear 498
Sally, Capt. Benjamin Russell, brought into Nantes 23
Sally, Captain Campbell, sailing from Liverpool 184
Sally, Capt. Js. Crawdhill, condemned at Morlaix 26
Sally, Capt. Timothy Davis, carried into Dieppe 25
Sally, sailing from Liverpool 505
Sally, schooner Capt. Robert Churn, captured by *Favourite* 34
Sally, schooner from Charleston, spoken by *Constellation* 259
Sally, schooner from Havana, joined convoy under *Constellation* 486
Sally, ship, Captain Smith, joined Havana convoy 466
Salter Francis, gunner, ship *Merrimack* 491, 574
Salvage must be paid by owners of recaptured vessels 136, 182
Salvers, Michael, boy on board *Constitution* 558
Sampson, Christian, seaman, *Constellation* 312
Sancree, Peter, ordinary seaman, *Constitution* 226
Sand, Charles, seaman, *Constitution* 225
Sanford, Thomas, part owner of brig *Nabby* 29
Sands and Ingraham, owners of *Light Horse* 23
Sands, Joshua, collector, New York:
Agent for U. S. R. C. *Governor Jay* 516
Authorized to clear *Sally* and *Fanny* 498
Commercial relations with St. Domingo 213
French persons, deported, to carry out "goods and effects" only 229, 230
Vessels clearing for French ports must furnish bond 498
Sandy Hook, *Constitution* expected to appear off 277, 295
Sanit, Adam, seaman, *Constellation* 313
Sanonsan, Peter, seaman, *Constellation* 306
Sans Pareil, French schooner, Captain Touin:
Captured by frigate *United States* 331
Captured sloop *Rebecca* 34
Delaware arrived off Newcastle with 442
Delaware left in charge of 375
Santa Antonio Abad, Spanish schooner 478
Santhonax, French agent to Leeward Islands 3
Santo Domingo:
American vessels condemned at 22, 24
Commercial relations discussed 213
Sophia to bring back destitute American seamen 113
Trade around, protected by British 336, 433
Santo Domingo Agents of French Executive Directory, order of, Facing page 218
Sagué, Mr., New York, flags of truce 427
Sarah, Capt. Timothy Newman, passenger from Algiers on 108
Saucer, Thomas, ordinary seaman, *Constellation* 315
Saul, Gideon, seaman, *Constellation* 306

Saunders, Lieutenant, U. S. M. C., U. S. frigate *Constellation*: Page
Bearer of dispatches for Governor of Havana 432, 433, 436, 508
Dispatches for naval agent at Norfolk 562, 565
Informed marines asleep on duty will not be flogged 386
Instructions from Captain Truxtun 362
Saunders, Major, brig of, brought to by *Constellation* 154
Savage, Charles, ordinary seaman, *Constellation* 315
Savannah, Ga.:
Spanish schooner burned at, by mob 437, 438, 444, 445
Vessels building and outfitting 389, 390, 391, 397, 398, 420
Savensen, Peter, master of brig *Swift* 364
Sawberion, M., master of schooner *Dispatch* 364
Sawyer, John, quartermaster, *Constitution* 223
Sawyer, Jonathan, acknowledgment to vii
Scammel, Old, U. S. R. C., Capt. Hopley Jeaton, sale of 317
Scammel, U. S. R. C., Capt. John Adams:
Cruising ground of 553
Martin, Thomas, collector, Portsmouth, N. H., agent for 516
Orders and instructions for 538, 553, 554
Personnel for 412, 413, 517
To be equipped for 3 months' cruise 413
Schofield, William, seaman, *Constitution* 225
Scott, James, captain of *John* of Boston 25, 26
Scott, James, seaman, *Constellation* 306, 313
Scott, Thomas, ordinary seaman, *Constellation* 313
Scroub, Sergeant, U. S. M. C., desired for duty on *Ganges* 376
Sea Flower, brought to by *Constellation* 293
Seagrove, Mr 228, 437
Sea lieutenants and masters of Constellation, orders to 152
Seal of United States, preferable on documents 523
Seamen:
Assistance to, in French ports 47, 48
Confined at Norfolk for mutiny 426
Constellation, muster roll of 304–316
Destitute—
Brought home from Porto Rico 113
Enter on board French privateers in West Indies 113
Governor of Porto Rico requested to release 192
Placed in French hospital 25
Sophia sent to return them to United States 47, 48, 78, 79, 113
Forcibly taken from brig *Friendship* by French privateer *Triumphant* 24
Impressment of, by British frigate *Hannibal* 251
Number allowed vessels 43, 65, 127, 171, 425, 450, 490, 491, 501, 517, 525, 527
Pay allowances to families of 160, 161
Pay of 43, 44, 49, 65, 66, 69, 72, 117, 128, 223, 226, 281, 323, 326, 382, 389, 399, 412, 450, 490, 517.
Provision made for disabled 8
Rescued from St. Thomas and Tortola 371
Term of enlistment 8, 16, 43, 49, 58, 281
Sea Nymph, brig, captured by *General Tousaint* 34
Sears, David, et al., Boston, Mass.:
Order for timber 170
Subscribed money for building ship for United States 168
Seber, Captain of French privateer *L'Hirondelle* 32
Sedition, order of Captain Truxtun to suppress 156–158
See Blhum, Bremen vessel, captured by frigate *Triton* 122
Senate Library, U. S., acknowledgment to VII
Serpausonet, French privateer, captured brig *Commerce* 34
Sever, James, Capt., U. S. ship *Herald* 112, 121, 174, 197, 258, 328, 329, 350, 356, 367, 368, 466, 487, 542
Orders and instructions to 160, 161, 170–173. 193, 194, 254, 255, 349, 500, 501
See, *Herald*, U. S. ship.

Page

Sewall, Samuel, in Congress:
- Advised *United States* requires more men than authorized 131
- Captures by belligerent powers, information to 20, 21
- Estimates for frigates forwarded to 160
- Provisional measures for protection of our commerce, etc., sent to 51–53

Shanly, Geoffrey Dillon, nominated for surgeon on *Montezuma* 399

Sharkey, Robert, ordinary seaman, *Constitution* 226

Shaw, John, appointed lieutenant on *Montezuma* 321, 380

Shaw, William, on *Constitution* 226

Sheafe, James, owner of *Juna* 22

Sheaffe, Jacob, navy agent, Portsmouth, N. H.:
- Agent for frigate building at Portsmouth 539
- Anchor for *Constellation* 18
- French prisoners, instructions relative to 530
- Frigates at Portsmouth, New York, and Norfolk to be finished 214, 215

Shepherd, John, seaman, *Constitution* 224

Sherry, Captain, in command of *Oneida* 23

Shields, Timothy, cook, *Constellation* 305

Shipham, Revil, ordinary seaman, *Constellation* 315

Ships. See *Vessels.*

Shirley, Ambrose, master, U. S. frigate *Constellation*:
- Duties outlined by Captain Truxtun 126
- Invitation to dine with Captain Truxtun 155
- On muster roll 304
- Potatoes on *Constellation* surveyed by 209

Shirley, John, private, *Constellation* 311

Shore, George, seaman, *Constellation* 312, 362

Sidons, Edward, ordinary seaman, *Constitution* 223

Siemandy, Mr., activities of, with Victor Hughes 274, 293

Signals:
- *Constellation* and *Baltimore* do not agree 343
- Convoy, by Captain Truxtun 134, 343–349, 374, 445–447, 452, 453
- Vessels furnished with 379, 380, 399, 421, 434, 444, 451
- Vandeput, British Admiral, furnishes 227, 288, 289, 296

Simkins, captain of brig *Active* 106

Simmons, Willis, ordinary seaman, *Constellation* 308

Simons, James, collector, Charleston, S. C.:
- Instructions to 287, 576
- Reference to 319, 578
- Vessel to be constructed by citizens 230, 247, 249

Simpson, Elija, private, *Constellation* 316

Simpson, George, private, *Constellation* 311

Sinclair, Arthur, midshipman, U. S. frigate *Constellation* 153, 155, 304

Sines, Gustavus, boy, *Constellation* 310

Singleton, Jacob, master of schooner *Kitty* 34

Sisters of Norfolk, Anderson, master 459

Six Brothers, captured by French privateer *Leoradie* 29

Skinner, captain of ship spoken by *Herald* 327

Skipwith, Fulwar, consul at Paris:
- Captures of American ships by privateers 25
- Humphreys, Clement, to be assisted by 48
- Progress in adjustment of claims 4
- Provisional appointment of consul for Paris 2
- Report of complaints against French Government made by 2, 3

Skjoldebrand, schooner, fitting out for Dey of Algiers 202

Slater, John, seaman, *Constellation* 306

Smiley, captain of brig *Susan* 466

Smith and Ridgway, Messrs., permission to clear sloop *Lark* 206

Smith, Captain, command of *Rainbow* 22

Smith, captain of British frigate *Hannibal* 251

Smith, captain of one of Algerine vessels 549

Smith, captain of ship *Fortune* 79

Smith, captain of ship *Sally* 466

Smith, Mr., Lisbon, commissions, etc., for private armed vessels 237

Smith, Mr., master's second mate, *Constellation* 300

Smith, Mr., suggested for appointment as lieutenant 534

Smith, Anthony, *Constellation* 312

Page

Smith, Bishop ---- 534
Smith, Daniel, private, *Constellation* ---- 311
Smith, Ephrim, seaman, *Constellation* ---- 307
Smith, Horace, appointed midshipman on *Montezuma* ---- 321
Smith, John, seaman, *Constellation* ---- 307, 314
Smith, John, seaman, *Constitution* ---- 224
Smith, John N., seaman, *Constitution* ---- 226
Smith, Joseph S., mate, *Constellation* ---- 304
Smith, Lindal, captain of ship *Three Brothers* ---- 27, 81
Smith, Michael, cook, *Constellation* ---- 315
Smith, Michael, ordinary seaman, *Constellation* ---- 309
Smith, Philip, boy, *Constellation* ---- 313
Smith, Sam, witness to sale of *Ganges*, and *Hamburgh Packet* ---- 64, 68
Smith, Thomas, master of schooner *Lemmon*, captured ---- 241
Smith, Thomas, master of ship captured at St. Jago, Cuba ---- 34
Smith, Thomas, seaman, *Constitution* ---- 225
Smith, Thomas, witness to sale of ship *Herald* ---- 121
Smith, William, ordinary seaman, *Constitution* ---- 223
Smith, William, seaman, *Constellation* ---- 309, 316
Smith, William, United States Consul, Lisbon, Barbary affairs discussed 411, 412
Smith & Gittings, owners of schooner *Grey Hound* ---- 364
Snell, George, seaman, *Constellation* ---- 316
Snell, Thomas, master, *Amphitrite*, wreck of ---- 340, 475–480
Snow, Gideon, master of *Betsy of Boston* ---- 27
Sobo (Lobo), Anthony, in command of French privateer *Triumphant* ---- 24, 28
Solomon, Philip, ordinary seaman, *Constitution* ---- 226
Sophia, brig, Capt. Henry Geddes:
- Bearer of letters for envoys in France ---- 46–48
- Cannon for ---- 554
- Mainmast wanted for ---- 554
- Movements of ---- 78, 509, 547
- Orders to ---- 485
- Rescue seamen in France ---- 47, 48
- Rescue sufferers in West Indies ---- 21, 113
- Return crews of Algerine vessels ---- 547, 554, 579

Sophia, schooner, Captain O'Meara, released after capture ---- 26
South Carolina:
- Cannon by King George the Second ---- 499
- Truxtun and Decatur to protect ---- 142

South Carolina, brig, taken by English frigate, *Thetis* ---- 251
South Carolina, ship, John German, master ---- 195, 196
Southern Coast, Captain Truxtun to defend ---- 82, 142
Southern States, invasion of, by French, prevented by British Navy ---- 140
South-Packet, schooner, refused permit to clear ---- 440
Southworth, Jedediah, captain of brigantine *Mary* ---- 35
Spain:
- American vessels captured by ---- 20, 22, 32
- Cadiz. See *Cadiz, Spain.*
- Frigates of, left Havana with two convoys ---- 509
- Interfered with our commerce ---- v
- Protest by Minister of ---- 360, 361
- Relations with, discussed ---- 213, 245, 246, 507
- United States desirous of maintining friendship of ---- 288, 433
- Vessel of burned, by mob at Savannah ---- 437, 444

Spanish. See *Spain.*
Spark, William, captain of British ship *Favourite* ---- 414
Sparks, Samuel, seaman, *Constellation* ---- 306
Speake, Josias M., Lt., U. S. Navy:
- Appointment for *Adriana*, recommended ---- 128
- Nominated by President for appointment as lieutenant ---- 153
- Recruiting instructions to ---- 179, 180

Spellings, punctuations, etc., reproduced as found in archives ---- VII
Spells, Thomas, seaman, *Constitution* ---- 226
Spillard, Matthew, contractor for supplies for Army ---- 460

Page
Spotswood, Captain, recommended for command of ship ... 536
Spotswood, General, of Virginia ... 536
Spriggs, Daniel, ordinary seaman, *Constitution* ... 224
Springfield, arms and powder from ... 95, 360
Squire, John, Jr., first lieutenant, U. S. R. C. *Governor Jay* ... 471
Stag, ship, of Norfolk ... 476
Stagg, T., Jr., New York, reference to ... 340
Stanfield, Thomas, ordinary seaman, *Constellation* ... 314
Stansbury, Tobias E., master of ship captured at St. Jago, Cuba ... 34
State Department, Archives Division, acknowledgment to ... VII
State, Secretary of, Timothy Pickering:
  Acting for Secretary of Navy ... 460, 461, 463, 488, 529, 561, 562, 573, 575
  Acting for Secretary of War ... 114–116
  Benjamin Franklin, clearance of ... 100
  Correspondence with—
    Adams, John, President, U. S ... 321, 322, 468
    Appleton, Thomas ... 39
    Barnes, David L., Providence ... 274, 275
    Brown & Ives, Providence ... 353
    Byrd, Otway, collector, Norfolk ... 440
    Caldwell, John, Hartford, Conn ... 561, 562
    Cathlan, Stephen, agent, Marseilles ... 78–80, 97, 98
    Coffin, John, Boston ... 229
    Congress ... 1–4, 5, 6, 20–36
    Crafts, Wm., Charleston ... 573
    Cross, George, Capt ... 575
    Crousillat, Lewis, Philadelphia ... 565
    Decatur, Stephen, Capt ... 176
    Eaton, William, consul, Tunis ... 580
    Fellows, Nathaniel, Boston ... 284
    Fitzgerald, John, collector, Alexandria ... 114, 115
    Francis, Tench ... 111, 467, 485, 486, 494, 547
    Gavino, John, U. S. Consul, Gibraltar ... 228
    Geddes, Henry, Capt ... 46, 47
    Goodhue, B., Salem ... 366, 367
    Habersham, John ... 557, 558
    Hiller, Joseph, collector, Salem ... 552
    Hodgdon, Samuel ... 280, 549, 550
    Hollis, John ... 177
    Howell, Mr., Governor of New Jersey ... 203
    Humphreys, Clement ... 47, 48
    Humphreys, David, Minister to Spain ... 419, 420, 465, 480, 481, 484, 485, 507
    Humphreys, Joshua ... 408, 509, 510, 554, 578, 579
    Jackson, James, Governor of Georgia ... 437, 438
    King, Rufus ... 175
    Latimer, George, collector, Philadelphia ... 206
    Lee, Charles, U. S. Attorney General ... 463
    Le'tombe, Mr., French Consul General ... 218, 237, 238, 560, 561
    Lincoln, General, collector, Boston ... 186, 236, 237, 435, 436
    Liston, Robert, British Ambassador to United States ... 129, 162, 163
    Masters of captured ships at St. Jago, Cuba ... 33, 34
    Murray, John, and Son, New York ... 556
    Murray, W. Vans, United States Minister to Netherlands ... 467, 485
    Navy, Secretary of ... 78, 91, 227, 235, 408, 499, 500, 538–540
    Nelson, Thomas, United States Attorney, Virginia District ... 555, 556
    Newman, Timothy, Capt ... 108, 112, 113
    Norris, John, Salem ... 333
    O'Brien, Richard, consul, Algiers ... 520–523
    Parker, Josiah ... 113
    Porto Rico, Governor of ... 199
    Purviance, Robt., collector, Baltimore ... 196
    Rabaine and Boudot, Boston ... 261
    Saabye, H. R., consul, Copenhagen ... 515, 516
    Sands, Joshua, collector, New York ... 213, 229, 230, 498
    Sewall, Samuel ... 20, 21

State, Secretary of, Timothy Pickering—Continued.
Correspondence with—Continued. Page
Simons, James, Charleston 576
Thompson, Col. Thomas 61
Treasury Department, Comptroller of 196
Triplett, James, lieutenant of Marines 115
Truxtun, Thomas, Capt 115
Vanderhorst, Elias, Bristol 144
Walter, Wm. and Thomas, Boston 249, 250, 269
War Department 212, 213, 490
Williams, T 96, 97
Yard, James, Brunswick 543–546
Yrujo, Chevalier de, Minister, Spain 360, 361, 444, 445
Liberty, brigantine, granted free clearance 206
Louisiana, evacuation of Spanish forts in, statement of 39
References to 138, 183, 277, 297, 323, 405, 406
Stationery, U. S. frigate *Constellation* 94
Stationery for ships, to be furnished by pursers 108
Stay [?], **Daniel,** captain of schooner *Catherine* 24
Steel, Mr., information from concerning ship *Superior* 129
Steel, Isaac, warrant as sailmaker on *Herald* 174
Stephens, captain American ship *Foxwell* 403
Stephens, Earl, impressed on British frigate *Hannibal* 251
Stephenson, Thomas, ordinary seaman, *Constellation* 315
Sterett, Mr., to aid Lieutenant Rodgers in recruiting 50
Sterling, armed ship, of Boston, spoken by *Constellation* 163
Sterrett, Andrew, Lt., U. S. frigate *Constellation*:
Dispatched to Norfolk with John Watson as prisoner 365
Invitation to dine with Captain Truxtun 155
Reference to 304
Signals for delivery to Captain Phillips 374, 452, 453
To assist *Dolphin* 489
Sterrett, Samuel and Joseph, navy agents, Baltimore:
Constellation, Mr. Berry's account for pilotage of, sent to 141
Owners of vessels are expecting convoy to Havana 335, 341
Reference to 132, 148
Supplies and equipment for ships 50, 51
To prepare estimates for three frigates 19
Stevens, Ebenezer, Colo., New York:
Galleys, opinion requested as to construction of two 295
Observations on fortifications for New York harbor 70
Stevens, Isaac, ordinary seaman, *Constitution* 225
Stevenson, captain of unarmed vessel *Henrietta* 183, 184
Steward, D., & Sons, owners of brig *Swift* 364
Steward, Thomas, ordinary seaman, *Constellation* 316
Stewart, captain of brig *Lively* of Philadelphia 251
Stewart, Mr., guns for *United States* to be sent by 122
Stewart, Archibald, owner of schooner *Mary* 364
Stewart, David & Co., owners of schooner *Citizen* 364
Stewart, David, of Baltimore, shipbuilding by citizens 170
Stewart, L. S., Comdr., U. S. N., acknowledgment to VII
Stewart, Walter, surveyor of District of Philadelphia 63, 68
Stickney, David, appointed lieutenant of Marines, ship *Merrimack* 513, 574
Stiles, Benjamin, master of British brig *Harliquin* 400
Stocker, captain of ship *Patty Washington* 466
Stoddart, George, seaman, *Constellation* 307
Stodder, David, naval constructor, *Constellation*, completion and launching 9, 17, 18
Stoddert, Benjamin, Secretary of the Navy:
Absent from office 556, 561
Appointment acknowledged and accepted to Secretary of State 91
Commission as Secretary of the Navy, sent to 78
Picture of facing page 78
Request for leave 460
See *Navy, Secretary of.*
Stokston, captain of ship *Hope* 519
Stone, master of ship *Joseph* 566

Page

Stores and provisions, quantity to be allowed ships 166
Stow, Anthony, master of brig *Sally* 498
Street, William, boy, *Constellation* 312
Strong, Nathaniel, quartermaster, *Constellation* 305
Strout, Joseph, Lt:
 Commission as lieutenant, ready for President's signature 174
 Extracts from journal of Herald, kept by 351, 355, 358, 371, 378, 383, 384, 387, 392, 402, 441, 454, 461, 462, 466, 486, 492, 506, 519, 541, 548–550, 559, 560.
Stuart, Gilbert, artist of painting of Capt. John Barry IX
Stubbs, captain of brig *Charlotte* 492
Study, John, ordinary seaman, *Constellation* 315
Stumper, captain of *Molly* 23
Suffolk, ship, brought to by *Constellation* 287
Sullivan, Richard, punished on board *Constitution* 370
Sullivans Island, S. C., fort built on, by citizens of Charleston 355
Sulvy, Thomas, seaman B., *Constellation* 314
Sum, Peter, seaman, *Constellation* 307
Summis, David, owner of schooner *Harriet* 206
Sumner, James, captain of *Brothers* 26
Superintendent of Documents, authorized to sell publications VIII
Superior, ship, purchase of 129
Surgeon for Constitution may be obtained at Norfolk 494
Surgeon for Montezuma, appointment of 333
Susan, brig, Captain Smiley, joined Havana convoy 466
Sutton, Philip, seaman, *Constitution* 226
Sutton, William, seaman B., *Constellation* 314
Swain, Job, marine, *Constellation* 312, 362
Swain, John, seaman, *Constitution* 225
Swain, Silas, master of *Hamburgh Packet* when purchased 68
Swallow, schooner, Matthew Logan, permit for clearance of 332
Swan, Peter, seaman, *Constitution* 224
Swarbuck, E., owner of *Hebe* 22
Sweden:
 Armed force kept in Mediterranean to encourage commerce 484
 Commander of vessel of, refused to convoy American vessels 485
 No need to be solicitous about making treaty with 468
 Vessels of, share same fate as American 106
Swedish flag used by United States ships of war 207, 208, 255, 283, 292
Sweet, Stephen, captain of ship *Eagle,* captured 79, 98
Sweet, Thomas, seaman, *Constellation* 312, 362
Swift, brig, Peter Savensen, in Hampton Roads convoy 364
Swift Packet, ship, spoken by *Constellation* 253
Swinney, John, quartermaster, *Constitution* 226
Swins, John, seaman, *Constitution* 224
Swinson, John, boy, *Constellation* 315
Syren, schooner, Jarad Arnold, in Hampton Roads convoy 364

Talbot, Colonel, son of 113
Talbot, Silas, Capt., U. S. Navy:
 Command of shipbuilding at New York 368
 George Washington, fitting out of 351, 352, 428, 429, 501, 539
 Relative rank of 510, 542
Talcott, Matthew, midshipman, *Constellation* 302
Talleyrand, M., Minister of Foreign Affairs 367, 560
Taniss, William, ordinary seaman, *Constellation* 313
Tarbell (Joseph), midshipman, *Constitution,* returned to ship 462
Taylor, Charles H.:
 Acknowledgment to VII
 Picture of cutter *Pickering,* published by courtesy of IX
Taylor, John, of Antigua, assisted Captain Gay 400
Taylor, William, Baltimore, *Montezuma,* ship, purchased from 123, 143
Taylor, William, ordinary seaman, *Constellation* 308, 314
Taylor, William, seaman, *Constitution* 224
Telemachus, brig, captured by French privateers 26, 35, 81

Page

Telfea, John, seaman, *Constellation* 314
Territorial limits of the United States defined 77
Texel, port of, American ships take risk to enter 121, 122
Tew, Captain, vessel of, available for loading stores for Algiers 111
Thayer, Mr., fire engines for *Constitution* 10
Thetis, British frigate, Captain Cochran:
  Reference to 266
  South Carolina, brig, taken by 251
  Spoken by *United States* 265
Thetis, English schooner, stopped by *Constellation* 274
Theveatt, John, ordinary seaman, *Constellation* 314
Thomas, Captain, of armed schooner from Martinico 496
Thomas, James, seaman, *Constellation* 306, 313
Thomas, Richard, midshipman, U. S. ship *Montezuma* 321, 380
Thomas, William, ordinary seaman, *Constellation* 315
Thompson, Captain, to pay portage bill of Captain Newman 112
Thompson, Mr., deputy collector, Lewis Town 89
Thompson, Archibald, seaman, *Constitution* 224
Thompson, Francis, ordinary seaman, *Constellation* 308
Thompson, John, seaman, *Constitution* 225
Thompson, Samuel, seaman, *Constellation* 306
Thompson, Thomas, Capt., to examine ships offered for sale 57, 116
Thompson, Thomas, Col., to settle accounts of crew of *Crescent* 61
Thompson, William, ordinary seaman, *Constellation* 309
Thorndike, Larkin, commission as surgeon, ship *Herald* 174
Thornton, Mr 566
Three Brothers, ship, captured by *La Ziza* 27, 81
Thurston, John B., Capt., of brig *Commerce* 54, 55
Tilden, Mr., son of owner of brigantine *Mary* 35
Tilden, John, gunner's yeoman, *Constellation* 305
Timber for ship construction 137, 214–216,, 242, 350
Tingey, Thomas, captain, U. S. Navy 367, 408, 464, 482, 543
  Orders and instructions to 408, 482, 527
  Reports from 417, 418, 571
  See *Ganges,* U. S. ship.
Tinkham, Joseph, deputy marshal, Wiscasset, Maine, French prisoners 421,422
Tobago, neutral vessels bound to, to be captured 4
Topaz, British frigate, reference to 286
Torksey, John, seaman, *Constellation* 307
Torrey, Joseph, gunner, *Constitution* 224
Tortola, Lieutenant Mullowny to collect American vessels at 369
Touin, captain of French schooner *Sans Pareil* 331
Toulon, American vessels no longer admitted to 560
Toussard, Lewis, Maj., Fort Milflin, regarding sloop manned by Negroes 149
Townsend, Robert, seaman, *Constellation* 305
Tracey and Brown, of Newberry, owners of ship *Charles* 135
Trader, John, ordinary seaman, *Constellation* 315
Traill, John, commander of ship *Merchant* 249, 250, 260
Treasury, Comptroller of:
  Advised *Liberty* has been granted clearance 196
  To suggest draft of letter to collectors 196
Treasury, Secretary of, Oliver Wolcott:
  Circular to collectors of customs 4, 5
  Correspondence with—
    Lincoln, Benjamin, collector, Baltimore 56, 158, 159, 518
    Navy, Secretary of 123, 126, 130, 167, 210, 240, 244, 261, 262, 263, 382, 532, 533.
  References to 10, 103, 109, 111, 112, 123, 124, 129, 146, 166, 197, 222, 227, 230, 234, 239, 248, 290, 292, 317, 324, 356, 359, 360, 397, 398, 461, 516
Treaty between United States and France, violation of 1, 2
Trenton, N. J., navy department, removal to 295, 296
Trial, schooner, of John Norris, captured and condemned 333
Tribunal of Aix, American vessels condemned by 79, 81
Trio, Captain Congas, sailing from Liverpool 184

Page

Triplett, James, Lt., U. S. Artillery, on *Constellation:*
Admonished by Captain Truxton for neglect of duty____ 253, 254, 290, 291
Did not come down with Rogers to join *Constellation*____________ 122
Duties outlined by Captain Truxtun______________________ 130, 131, 138
Invitation to dine with Captain Truxtun____________________ 155
Recruiting expenses incurred by_________________________ 114–116
Recruiting instructions to, from Captain Truxtun________________ 77, 78
Reference to____ 104, 342
To report to Captain Truxtun for orders____________________ 93
Tripoli, general discontent likely to take place in, soon_____________ 411
Triton, frigate, captured Bremen vessel *See Blhum*_______________ 122
Triumphant, French privateer, captured brig *Caroline*______________ 24, 34
Trois Soeurs, French privateer, captured *Kitty, Needham,* and *Polly*____ 34
Truman, Barnard, *Constitution*_____________________________ 226
Truxtun, Harry, son of Captain Truxtun________________________ 119
Truxtun, Thomas, Capt., U. S. frigate *Constellation:*
Bearer of letter for Governor of Havana___________________________ 288
Biddle, Charles, discussion of public and private affairs____________ 118, 119
Extracts from journal, U. S. frigate *Constellation*________________ 134, 135, 139, 143, 148, 151, 153, 154, 155, 159, 160, 163, 164, 169, 172, 180, 184, 187, 195, 196, 201, 205, 210, 211, 215, 218, 219, 222, 228, 231, 232, 235, 240, 242, 243, 245, 250, 251, 253, 259, 260, 264, 266, 268, 270, 273, 274, 276, 279, 283, 286, 291, 293, 294, 297, 298, 300, 303, 365, 370, 371, 373, 375, 377, 378, 381, 383, 385, 386, 387, 393, 400, 403, 406, 407, 409, 410, 418, 419, 423, 426, 429, 435, 436, 440, 441, 450, 453, 454, 459, 461, 467, 468, 475, 482, 486, 488, 492, 497, 502, 503, 506, 514, 515, 518, 519, 526, 531, 532, 537, 541, 542, 546, 547, 549, 551, 552, 553, 557, 558, 559, 562, 565.
Instructions, etc., issued by_______________________________ 12–17, 49–51, 61, 70, 71, 77, 78, 98–100, 102–104, 108, 109, 124–127, 130, 131, 138, 141, 144, 152, 156–158, 168, 200, 201, 232, 253, 254, 263, 264, 290, 291, 298, 299, 302, 303, 341, 343–349, 362, 386, 431, 432, 445–447, 506, 540, 541, 572, 573.
Officers invited to dine with______________________________ 155
Orders and instructions to_____________________________ 6, 10, 42, 82, 92–95, 104, 105, 115, 142, 158, 206, 207, 288, 342, 365, 528
References to____________________208, 295, 296, 336, 359, 368, 384, 527, 535
Relative rank of_____________________________________ 510, 542
Reports from_______________________________________ 122, 132–134, 171, 172, 211, 212, 300–302, 333–335, 337, 338, 362, 363, 373, 374, 508, 509, 566–568.
See *Constellation*, U. S. frigate.
Yellott, Jer., suggestions to, for construction, etc., of ships________ 563, 564
Tryon, Moses, Capt.:
In command of *Connecticut*, building at Middleton_______________ 368
Relative rank of_____________________________________ 543
Tucker, John, master of brig *John*____________________________ 34
Tunis, general discontent likely to take place in soon______________ 411
Tunno & Cox, loaders of cargo of *Juna*_______________________ 22
Tunno, A. See *Morris, Thomas, et al.*
Turner, Peter, ordinary seaman, *Constellation*____________________ 309
Two Friends, brig, captured by *Les Thermidar*____________________ 81
Two Friends, ship:
J. Humphreys and T. Thompson to examine_______________________ 57
Recaptured from prize crew of *Good Fortune*______________________ 570
Two Sisters, brig, captured at St. Jago, Cuba_____________________ 34
Tyger, brig, boarded brig *Neptune*_____________________________ 340
Unanimity, U. S. R. C., Capt. Robt. Cochran:
Articles from may be used for Mr. Pritchard's vessel________________ 230
Cannot be made a proper cruiser_______________________________ 230
Musketo, encounter with___________________ 252, 372, 386, 387, 401
Nicholson, Captain, to take under his command___________________ 296
Reference to status of____ 450

Page

Uniform:
Consuls and vice consuls may wear that of Navy 39
Marine Corps, description of 404
Regulations of August 24, 1797 10–12
Union, ship of Baltimore, brought to by *Constellation* 562
United States, U. S. frigate, Capt. John Barry:
Accounts of 240, 280
Appropriation for 46
Capture of two French cruisers by, reference to 442
Chapman, Captain, to be under command of 197, 501
Decatur, Captain, of *Delaware* came aboard 203, 204, 358, 359, 381
Defects of, to be repaired 45
Extracts from journal of Lt. John Mullowny 163, 169, 174, 201, 203, 209, 211, 215, 220, 222, 250, 253, 260, 265, 267, 270, 273, 276, 280, 283, 286, 294, 297, 319, 324, 325, 327, 331, 334, 340, 342, 343, 351, 354, 358, 359, 363, 369, 371, 373, 375, 377, 379, 381, 384, 385, 388, 392, 403, 406, 411, 419, 424, 426, 430, 442, 486, 506, 546, 551, 552, 560, 562, 571, 574, 580
French flag to be hoisted on 482
Herald failed to join on cruise 254
Herald ordered to join 193, 194
Hulsecamp, Garrett, to deliver letters to 175
Jealous, sloop, from Guadaloupe, captured by 377
Joint force of, sufficient for West Indies enterprise 258
Launching 5, 16
Listed as in service 368
Manning of 7, 69, 131
Materials and equipment, etc 37, 38, 51, 56, 83–87, 114, 122, 123, 163, 337, 438, 440
Operations v, vi, 145, 151, 158, 166, 169, 193, 194, 201, 211, 215, 220, 222, 250, 253, 255, 256, 260, 265, 267, 270, 273, 287, 294, 324, 325, 327, 351, 354, 363, 369, 371, 373, 381, 384, 385, 388, 396, 401, 411, 419, 430, 442, 464, 486, 501, 571, 580.
Orders and instructions 16, 44, 49, 69, 70, 141, 161, 162, 174, 189–192, 198–200, 334, 438, 458, 461, 462, 481, 482, 538
Picture of Facing page 162
Prisoners and guard for 430, 438, 439, 527
Ross, Lt. David, reports readiness of 114
Sailing qualities of 232, 233, 301, 424
Sans Pareil, French schooner, captured 331
Uricke Kock, Danish brig, taken by armed force at Cayenne 29
Urquijo, Mariano Luis de, Madrid, American vessels may not sail from Cadiz carrying guns 548
Valck & Co., owners of schooner *Rebecca* 31
Valeria, brig, captured, at St. Jago, Cuba 34
Vandeport, Admiral, signals for British and American ships 227, 235, 288, 289, 296
Vander Horst, Elias, United States consul, Bristol:
Arrivals and departures of American ships 277, 403, 518, 519
Instructions from Secretary of State will be attended to 144
Letters from Rufus King to be forwarded 317, 318, 323
Vanderslice, Joseph, ordinary seaman, *Constellation* 309
Van Dyke, Henry, midshipman, U. S. frigate *Constellation* 42, 155, 304
Varnam, Henry, seaman, *Constellation* 306
Vassure, Francis, ordinary seaman, *Constitution* 225
Vaughan, Edward, seaman, *Constellation* 314
Venus, American brig, condemned at Cape Francois 24
Venus, schooner, spoken by *Constellation* 552
Venus, taken into Bordeaux by privateer 23
Verdenberg, captain of ship *Liberty* of Philadelphia 175–177
Vermott, Abraham, ordinary seaman, *Constellation* 308
Very, Captain of Salem 60
Vessels, Algerine. See *Algiers*.

Vessels:
American merchant— Page
Act authorizing seizure of French armed vessels by 87, 88
Act for further protection of commerce 181–183
Act to authorize defense of, against French depredations 135–137
Arming of, circular relative to 4, 5
Assembled at Hampton Roads for convoy to Havana 288, 334, 335, 338, 341, 364
Assembled for convoy from Havana 288, 290, 319, 336, 344, 373, 431, 432, 466, 486, 488, 508, 514, 515, 561, 565–568
Blockaded at Malaga 20, 27
Blocked up at Havana by French privateers 336
Bond required of when armed 136, 181, 182
Building at Gosport, Va., by N. Harbut 207, 208
Captured and condemned at Aix, list of 79, 81
Captured by any but French vessels, cannot be captured 191, 198, 204, 207, 285, 292, 420, 444, 455, 501, 529, 554
Captured by belligerents 20, 21
Captures by French, extracts from consular letters, etc 22–36
Captures of French armed ships by, act authorizing 135–137, 182
Citizens with whom we are at peace must be respected 192, 194, 204, 207
Claims for detention of, by French, remain undetermined 3
Commanders and crews of armed, instructions for 88, 137, 187
Commissions and bonds for when armed 136, 181, 182, 237, 269
Commissions, etc., for arming, sent to collector, Boston 186
Commissions issued to, reference VI
Condemned by French commission 25
Condemned in Spanish ports by France 27, 28
Convoyed by *Constellation* 135
Convoyed by *Constellation* and *Baltimore* 475
Convoy refused by Swedish commanders 485
Convoy requested for, from Havana 319
Decree for capture of, by French privateers 3
Desiring convoy from Havana to ask for signals, etc 432
Fail to heed convoy signals 502, 503
For sale at Baltimore 116
Instructed to grant free passage to brigantine *Liberty* 206
Lawful to arm, against East India pirates 5
License for armed vessels to depart from Cadiz 547, 548
Mullowny, Lieutenant, sent to Tortola to collect for convoy 369
Must furnish description with application for commission 181
None has been captured bound to the Baltic 515
Not allowed to sail from Cadiz with guns 548
Notice to, of intended departure of *Constellation*, from Havana 431, 432
Permission requested from Governor of Havana for departure of 432, 433
Prizes taken by, act providing disposition of 181–183
Protected most effectually by attacking French cruisers on own grounds 433
Recaptured, disposition of 182
Recently arrived at Cadiz 465
Risk incurred in entering Port of Texel 121, 122
Sailing from Bristol 277, 403, 518
Sailing from Liverpool 132, 138, 505, 566
Sale of, for foreign privateers 195
Salvage on, when recaptured 136, 323
Signals furnished, for convoy from Havana 344–349, 445–447
To sail from Malaga in a few days 419
Unlawful to arm, when bound to Europe and West Indies 5
Arming by strangers to capture American ships 5
Bound into Havana to be boarded by Captain Truxtun 436
Danish and Swedish share same fate as Americans 106
Flags of truce, clearing with French persons:
Permitted to return to United States 427
To furnish bond to insure return to United States 436, 498
French. See *France, vessels of*.

Page

Vessels:
Neutral—Complaints regarding capture of 1–5
Of every nationality condemned by French 79
Revenue cutters. See *Revenue Cutters.*
Ships of war:
Act for construction of six frigates, reference to v
All will be in port about 15th of November 539
Authorized by acts of Congress 58, 165, 243, 262, 277
Bill passed for completing and manning, reference to 6
Building at Baltimore 170, 242, 243, 262, 539, 563
Building at Boston 170, 262, 539
Building at Charleston, S. C 330, 402, 539
Building at Middleton, Conn 185, 218, 219
Building at Newburyport 262
Building at New York 150, 151, 153, 154, 165, 195, 262
Building at Philadelphia 262
Building at Salem, Mass 366, 510, 511
Building at Warren, by Gibbs and Channing 147, 148
Building by merchants of various cities 262
Complement allowed to a frigate 7
Construction and equipment of, cheaper on Potomac than elsewhere 532
Essential qualities of, required by United States 165
Frigate and sloops recommended for Mediterranean by D. Humphreys 484, 485, 507
Frigates, three, to be completed v, 7, 19, 46, 262
Furnished by Richmond and other Virginia cities 261, 262
Furniture for, list of 38
Government owned, grew to, 54 vi
Money appropriated for pay, etc., of three frigates 46
Money apropriated only sufficient for half the number authorized 277
Not sufficient to furnish convoy for Connecticut vessels 561, 562
Now in service, duty of 538, 539
Number that might be employed in West Indies during winter 461
Of not less than 32 guns 211, 230, 262, 278, 339
Of or not to exceed 18 guns 220, 230, 249, 262, 277, 278, 339, 368, 539
Of or not to exceed 24 guns 150, 151, 185, 219, 230, 243, 261, 262, 277, 278, 330, 368, 402, 539
Of or not to exceed 32 guns 249, 330, 539
Of 20 guns or more 239, 243, 330, 368
Of 32 guns and upward 173, 368
Of 36, 38, and 44 guns, dimensions of 153, 154
President empowered to acquire additional vi
Purchase of, authorized by act of Congress 262
Ready for operation in 1 month 166
Retaliation with a brig could break up privateering off Havana 568
Sailing dates, probable 529, 530, 539
Should be kept in Mediterranean 484, 485, 507
Signals, received from Admiral Vandeport, will be sent to 227
Smaller ones to be furnished by smaller towns 146, 173
Three, already built, larger than those in Europe 143
Timber, etc., for construction of 137, 211, 533
To proceed to West Indies, under Captain Barry 198, 199
United States, Delaware, Herald, and revenue cutter to join for cruise 193, 194

Vessels, Spanish. See *Spain, vessels of.*
Veterans' Administration, acknowledgment to VII
Vicoun, Thomas, Capt., in command of *Mercury* 23
Vignon, Peter, passenger on brig *Hope*, detained at Falmouth 361, 362
Vincent, John, captain of *Charlotte* 25
Vimmo, captain of ship *Roba and Betsey* 145, 318
Virginia, body of troops should be assigned to protect 140

Page

Virginia, U. S. R. C., Capt. Francis Bright:
- Collector at Norfolk, agent for — 484, 516
- Complement of — 517
- Operations of — 291, 293, 294, 492, 497, 502, 519, 526, 531, 541, 546, 550, 558
- Orders and instructions for — 292, 296, 483, 484, 505, 536, 537
- References to — 429, 451, 454, 538

Virginia Packet, sent into Teneriffe by privateer *Buonoparte* — 26
Voland, (or Poland), Joseph armourer's mate, *Constitution* — 224
Voltaguere, French privateer, captured ship *Providence* — 22
Voltaire, all hemp on board, to be purchased — 338
Vulture, French privateer, captured *Ann and Mary* and other vessels — 36, 37
Wades, John, boy, *Constellation* — 314
Wadsworth, Charles, purser, informed price of a ration is 28¢ — 131
Wadsworth, Eden, captain of brig *Sally* — 35
Wagner, Jacob, State Department:
- Certifies to statement of master of *Niger* — 417
- Correspondence with—
  - Bigar, W. J — 524
  - Crousillat, Louis — 565
  - Marrauld, John — 499
  - Sagué, Mr — 427

Waite, master of brigantine *George* — 474
Wake, Matthew, ordinary seaman, *Constitution* — 224
Walden, Jack, auctioneer who sold Old U. S. R. C. *Scammel* — 317
Walden, Robert, seaman, *Constellation* — 308
Waldoborough, collector at, to furnish subsistence for prisoners — 421
Walker, Charles, seaman, *Constellation* — 315
Walker, Harrison, recommended as midshipman on *Baltimore* — 289
Walker, S., contract with, not to be made — 438
Walker, William, seaman, *Constellation* — 307
Wall, James, seaman, *Constitution* — 223
Wall, John, lobby boy, *Constellation* — 305
Wall, William, quarter gunner, *Constellation* — 305
Walsburn, John, ordinary seaman, *Constellation* — 308
Walston, Risden, boy, *Constellation* — 315
Walter, Captain, in command of *Juna* — 22
Walter, James, seaman, *Constitution* — 226
Walter, Peter, ordinary seaman, *Constellation* — 312
Walter, Richard, seaman, *Constitution* — 223
Walter, Thomas, seaman, *Constellation* — 306
Walter, Wm. and Thomas, Boston, commission for ship *Merchant* — 249, 250, 269
Walters, George, seaman, *Constellation* — 307
Wandrum, James, ordinary seaman, *Constellation* — 309
Wanspite, schooner, Captain Mollineaux, brought to *Clara* — 496, 497
War College, U. S. Naval, acknowledgment to — VII
War Department, Old Records Division, acknowledgment to — VII
War, Secretary of, James McHenry:
- Correspondence with—
  - Barry, John, Capt — 16, 37, 49, 55, 69, 78
  - Carmick, Daniel, lieutenant of Marines — 66
  - Claghorn, George — 17
  - Clerk, Lemuel, lieutenant of Marines — 67
  - Cole, Thomas, Capt., Nary Yard, Baltimore — 103
  - Crawfurd and Donaldson — 58, 59
  - Da Costa, Francis — 75, 82
  - Dale, Richard, Capt — 51, 65, 72, 77, 91, 110
  - Deblois, James S., purser — 107, 108
  - Decatur, Stephen, Capt — 116–118
  - Dyson, Lieutenant — 96
  - Fisher, Samuel — 90
  - Francis, Tench — 17
  - Gillaspy, Dr — 74
  - Governor of Massachusetts — 92
  - Hamilton, Alexander — 74–76, 102
  - Harris, John — 37, 38, 45, 56, 69, 71, 76, 82, 83, 92, 101, 120, 334
  - Higginson, Stephen — 106, 107, 109, 111, 112
  - Hodgdon, Samuel — 53, 54, 95

War, Secretary of, James McHenry—Continued.
Page
Correspondence with—Continued.
Holsteincamp, Garrett 83, 90
Humphreys, Joshua 9, 45, 57, 116
Jackson, Henry, Gen., agent, Boston 10, 38, 39
Jackson, James, Governor of Georgia 437
Jay, John, Governor of New York 44, 70
Lieutenant of Marines, *Constellation* 40–42
McDonough, James, midshipman 65
McKnight, James, lieutenant of Marines 119
Miller, Edward, Capt 110
Morris, Staats 9
Navy, Secretary of 183, 184, 234, 235, 247, 265, 402, 406, 499, 577, 578
Nicholson, Samuel, Capt 40, 57, 65, 66, 96
Phillips, Henry 57
Pilot at Lewis Town 89
Rodgers, John, Lt 71
Rodney, Neal and Thompson, collectors, Lewis Town 89
Sewall, Samuel 51–53
Sheafe, Jacob, navy agent, Portsmouth 18
State, Secretary of 490
Sterrett, Samuel and Joseph 19, 51
Stodder, David 18
Thompson, Thomas, Capt 57, 116
Toussard, Louis, Maj 149
Truxtun, Capt. Thomas 6, 42–44, 82, 92, 93, 104, 105, 115, 122, 132–134, 211
Wilkins, J 19
Willings and Francis, agents, Philadelphia 65, 112
Pickering, Timothy, Secretary of State acting for 114–116
Recruiting instructions to lieutenant of Marines, *Constellation* 40–42
References 249, 339, 501
Uniform regulations issued by 10–12
United States, launching of, memorandum 5
Ward, Mr., acting master's mate, *Constitution* 429
Warder, Mr., reference to 494
Ware, James, ordinary seaman, *Constellation* 316
Warner, a marine, wants a vest 579
Warren, Fawn, master; bearer of dispatch from Rufus King 505
Warren, Robert, midshipman for *Norfolk* 443
Warren, shipbuilding at, by Gibbs & Channing 146, 147, 148
Washington, armed ship, commission and bond for 228, 229
Washington, brigantine, taken into Bordeaux by privateer 23
Washington, D. C., navy yard site at, discussed 409, 410, 455–457
Washington, George:
Navy yard site in Washington 409, 410, 455–457
Reference to v, 140, 455, 532
Spotswood, Captain, recommended by, for command 536
Watches on Constellation, order of Captain Truxtun 108, 109, 290, 291
Water, allowance of, on *Constellation* 152, 153, 232, 291
Water, allowance to men on board ship 157
Waters, George, seaman, *Constellation* 313
Waters, J., Jr., witness to sale of ship *Herald* 121
Watson, James, seaman, *Constitution* 226
Watson, J. and E., navy agents, New York:
Agents for vessels building at New York 539
Commission allowed for services 151
Equipment and materials for ships 151, 195, 227, 238, 271, 272, 281, 295, 359, 379, 488, 511, 556
Dimensions, for ship for Captain Morris 195
Instructions for construction of 24-gun ship 150, 151
Letters to be delivered by 238, 278, 295
Reference to 528, 530, 539
To finish New York frigate 217
Treasury, Secretary of, to remit money to 227
Vessel building by Silas Webb to be purchased 165
Watson, John (alias Hugh Williams), mutineer, *Armoine* 365

Page
Watts, George, ordinary seaman, *Constellation* 315
Watts, W. C., Rear Admiral, U. S. N., acknowledgment to VII, VIII
Weaver, John, seaman, *Constellation* 316
Webb, James, sailmaker, *Constellation* 304
Webb, Silas, purchase of vessel of, considered 165
Webb, Silas S., supercargo of *Nonpareil* 83
Webb, Thomas, boy, *Constitution* 225, 488
Wederstrandt, P. C., midshipman, U. S. frigate *Constellation* 42, 155, 304
Wederstrandt, R., witness to bill of sale of *Adriana* 63
Weeks, William, master of snow *Michael* 364
Weir, Robert, boy, *Constellation* 310
Welde, Benjamin, attester to sale of ship *Herald* 121
Wells, ——, Doctor, recommended as surgeon's mate of *Baltimore* 153
Wells, Mr 171
Wells, A., Sr., subscribed money for building ship for United States 168
Wells, Robert, captain of *Virginia Packet* 26
Wells, Robert, named sailing master on *Montezuma* 399
Welsh, John, pilot, *Constitution*, discharged 411
Welsh, John, seaman, *Constellation* 305
Welsh, Miles, boy, *Constellation* 310
Welsh, Thomas, seaman, *Constitution* 226
Wendale, Isaac, ordinary seaman, *Constitution* 224
Wentworth, John, Governor of Canada, loan of cannon to United States 499, 500
Wessen, A. J., acknowledgment to VIII
West, Benjamin, boy, *Constellation* 310
West, Benjamin, master of schooner *Nancy* 154
West, Edward, seaman, *Constitution* 224
West Indies:
Hurricanes, effect of, on operations of ships 255, 256, 258
Map of Facing page 546
Neutral vessels bound to, to be captured 4
Privateers, French, operations of 21, 336
References to VI, 1, 3, 140
Sophia to bring back destitute seamen from 113
United States, *Delaware*, and revenue cutter sent to 190, 191, 255
Vessels to be employed in, during winter 461
West, John, Lt., U. S. ship *Baltimore* 153, 179
West, Peleg, Capt., *Rover*, statement of *Amphitrite* 475, 477
Wharton, Robert, Capt., guard to escort French prisoners 242
Wheelwright, captain of brig *Hope* 361
Whelan, John, ordinary seaman, *Constellation* 312
Whetstone Point, guns at, for *Constellation* and *United States* 9, 51
Whipple, Thomas, commander of brig spoken by *Constitution* 286
White, captain of schooner *Brothers* 466
White, Charles, boy, *Constellation* 313
White, George, seaman, *Constellation* 306
White, Governor of Florida, release of American vessels 444
White, Joseph, Jr., master of ship captured at St. Jago, Cuba 34
White, Stephen, ordinary seaman, *Constellation* 315
Whitehurst, Laban, *Constellation* 312
Whittimore, Jacob, captain of brig *Farmer* 55
Whittle, Conway, owner of brig *Eliza* 135
Whyte, captain of H. M. sloop *Musketo* 252
Wickham, Mr., prosecutor in *Constitution-Niger* case 555, 556
Wier, John, captain of brig *Free Mason* 24
Wilkens, J., galleys for Ohio and Mississippi Rivers 19
Wilkerson, James, captain of ship *Little William* 135
Wilkins, Mr 417
William, brigantine, spoken by *Constitution* 355
William, captured by French privateer 35
William, schooner, Captain Burr, permitted to clear 229, 332
William Penn, ship, crew of, brought home by *Good Friends* 290
Williams, captain of armed American ship *Diana* 167
Williams, Hugh (John Watson), mutineer on H. B. M. S. *Armoine* 312, 365
Williams, Isaac, seaman, *Constellation* 311
Williams, John, seaman, *Constellation* 305

Page
Williams, John, quarter gunner, *Constellation* 305
W(illiams), J(ohn) F(oster), not considered suitable for *Pickering* 96
Williams, Michale, commander of French privateer *La Pearl* 30
Williams, Richard, seaman, *Constitution* 224
Williams, Sam, master of brig *Amelia* 34
Williams, Samuel; consulship and agency in London accepted by 97
Williams, Seth, Col., U. S. M. C., acknowledgment to VIII
Williams, T., discusses selection of officer for *Pickering* 96
Williams, Thomas, Capt., U. S. brig *Norfolk* 159, 207, 208, 368, 383, 407, 430, 543
 Orders and instructions to 381, 382, 405, 443, 444
 See *Norfolk*, U. S. brig.
Williams, Thomas, impressed on British frigate *Hannibal* 251
Williams, Thomas, seaman, *Constitution* 224
Williamson, William, private, *Constellation* 311
Willick, Thomas, owner of schooner *Hazard* 135
Willing, John, seaman, *Constitution* 225
Willing, Thomas Mayne, etal., *Ganges*, ship, purchased from 63, 64
Willings & Francis, agents, Philadelphia, Pa.:
 Agency offered for *Ganges* 65
 Dale, Captain, informs them he is at sea 101
 To deliver letter to Captain Dale 112
Wilmington, N. C.:
 Galleys, outfitting and manning of 391, 396, 397, 420
 Nonpareil brought into, by prize master 83
Wilmington, schooner, captured, at St. Jago, Cuba 34
Wilson, John, boatswain, *Constellation* 312
Wilson, John, seaman, *Constitution* 225
Wilson, Samuel, boy, *Constellation* 226, 310
Wilson, Thomas, seaman, *Constellation* 306
Wilson, Wm. Deane, master of sloop *Polly* 34
Winder, William, Navy Department accountant:
 Commission has been forwarded to 267
 Invoice, to be delivered to 512
 Reference to 392, 397, 398
 Truxtun, Captain, pay and rations of, must be paid 439
 Urged to report for duty without delay 267
Windward Islands:
 Commission at, condemns brig *Nabby* 29
 Decrees of French agents at, reference to 4, 32
 Neutral vessels bound to, to be captured 4
Wise & Grant, owners of sloop *George* 32
Wise (Wyse), William, Capt., ship *Alexander Hamilton* 177, 178
Wolcott, Mrs., reference to 130
Wolcott, Oliver, Secretary of Treasury. See *Treasury, Secretary of.*
Wood, Daniel, ordinary seaman, *Constellation* 308
Wood, Godfrey, master of ship *Commerce* 30
Wood, J., portrait by, of Capt. Richard Dale IX
Wood, Thomas, S. steward, *Constellation* 314
Woodbridge, captain of brigantine *Rambler* 332
Woodcock, Samuel, ordinary seaman, *Constellation* 308
Woodend, James, master of brig *Bell* 34
Woodman, Tom, seaman, *Constitution* 226
Woodward, Robert, ordinary seaman, *Constellation* 309
Wooley, Sergeant, U. S. M. C., death and burial of 375, 376
Woolwich, brig, Capt. T. McCutchin, captured by *Canoneir* 34
Worth, Wm., master of brig *Two Sisters* 34
Wright, M., recommended as midshipman on *Norfolk* 383
Wright, William, seaman, *Constellation* 307
Wyman, Simeon, steward, *Constitution* 224
Yard, James, Philadelphia, Pa.:
 Cargo of brig *Mary* consigned to 520
 Documents for Secretary of State 543–546
 Owner, brigantine *Rambler* 332
 Suspected as agent of Victor Hughes 544
Yam, Thomas, seaman, *Constellation* 307

Page

Yates & Campbell, auctioneers, sale of revenue cutter *Active* — 59
Yeaton, Hopley, Capt., revenue service. See *Jeaton, Hopley.*
Yellott, Jeremiah, navy agent, Baltimore:
- *Arb*, schooner of — 341, 364, 566
- *Baltimore*, preparation of — 126, 257, 275
- Equipment and materials for ships — 122, 126, 128, 145, 173, 195, 234, 239, 372
- Instructions for proving cannon — 233, 234
- *Montezuma*, preparation of, for sea — 123, 124, 128, 143, 239, 321
- Murray, Captain, to be furnished money for recruiting — 333
- Officers recommended by — 145, 153, 333
- Orders for Captain Phillips, will be sent to — 284, 289
- References to — 530
- Remittance made to — 257
- Ship construction at Baltimore discussed — 170, 173
- Transportation for marines — 390, 391
- Truxtun, Captain, suggestions from, for construction, etc — 563, 564

Yeomans, James, master carpenter, *Constellation* — 61, 209, 304, 318, 319
Yonge, Philip, witness to bill of sale of *Hamburgh Packet* — 68
Young & Buchanan:
- Owners of ship *Hope* — 28
- Owners of snow *Isabella* — 28

Young, David, master of brig *Nathaniel* — 29
Young, Moses, consul, Madrid, deposition of Neil MacNeil — 164, 165
Young, William, seaman, *Constellation* — 307
Yrujo, Chavalier de, Minister of Spain:
- Assembling of American forces at Natches, Miss., rumors of — 360, 361
- Informed of burning of Spanish schooner at Savannah — 444, 445

Yznardi, Joseph, consul, Cadiz, reports capture of brig *George* — 27
Zebsance, Yergan, seaman, *Constellation* — 306
Zenadore, French privateer, captures *Governor Mifflin* — 26
Zenobia, armed ship, fell in with *America* — 466
Zephir, schooner, brought into St. Domingo by privateer — 24

O